LONGMAN

HANDY LEARNER'S DICTIONARY OF AMERICAN ENGLISH

Longman

Longman Group UK Limited,
*Longman House, Burnt Mill, Harlow,
Essex CM20 2JE, England
and Associated Companies throughout
the world.*

First published 1983
ISBN 0 582 09483 6
Second impression 1994

British Library Cataloguing-in-Publication
Data.
A catalogue record for this book is avail-
able from the British Library

Set in 6 on 61/2 point Nimrod

Printed in Hong Kong
NPC/02

Publisher
Lizzie Warren

Lexicographers
Coleen Degnan-Veness
Orin Hargraves

Editor
Alison Steadman

Pronunciation Editor
Dinah Jackson

Design
Ken Brooks
Paul Price-Smith
Peter White OTS (Typesetting) Ltd

Cover
Jamie Mason

Production
Clive McKeough

*The publishers also gratefully acknowledge
the original contribution of the lexicographers and editors of the Longman Handy
Learner's Dictionary, upon which this
edition is based.*

Contents

Guide to the dictionary

Spelling
different spelling

> **age·is·m**, **agism** /ˈeˠdʒɪzəm/ n [U] the making of unfair differences between people because of their age, esp. treating young people more favorably than old people **ageist**, **agist** adj, n

irregular plurals

> **ap·pen·dix** /əˈpɛndɪks/ n **–dixes** or **–dices** /-dəsiˠz/ **1** small organ leading off the bowel **2** something added at the end of a book

irregular verbs

> **a·rise** /əˈraɪz/ vi **arose** /əˈroʷz/, **arisen** /əˈrɪzən/ happen; appear

Pronunciation/stress
Pronunciations are shown using symbols from the International Phonetic Alphabet – see inside front cover.

> **ba·by** /ˈbeˠbiˠ/ n **1** very young child: (fig.) the baby of the class (= the youngest) **2** very young animal or bird: a baby monkey **3** infml person, esp. a girl or woman **4** infml one's special responsibility **~ish** adj like a baby

Stressed syllables are clearly marked.

> **bal·loon** /bəˈluʷn/ n **1** bag filled with gas or air so that it can float **2** small rubber bag that can be blown up and used as a toy **3** line around words thought or spoken by a CAR·TOON character ♦ vi swell up like a balloon

Meaning
Clear and simple explanations using a defining vocabulary of 2000 words

> **beam**[1] /biˠm/ n long heavy piece of wood, esp. used to support a building

words with the same spelling but different use or meaning

> **an·tique** /ænˈtiˠk/ adj old and therefore valuable ♦ n valuable old object

more than one meaning

> **be·come** /bɪˈkʌm/ v **became**, **become 1** begin to be: become king | become warmer **2** vt be suitable for: Such behavior hardly becomes someone in your position. **becoming** adj **1** attractive **2** suitable

Words that you may know are written LIKE THIS. You can find all these words in the dictionary.

> **be·drag·gled** /bɪˈdrægəld/ adj wet, LIMP, and muddy

Common idioms and phrases are shown in **bold** type.

> **bee** /biˠ/ n **1** stinging insect that makes HONEY **2 a bee in one's bonnet** fixed idea; OBSESSION **3 the bee's knees** infml the best person or thing

phrasal verbs (= verbs which have a special meaning when they are used with a particular adverb or preposition)

boil¹ /bɔɪl/ *vi/t* **1** bring or come to the temperature at which a liquid changes to gas: *212°F is the boiling point of water.* **2** cook at this temperature: *to boil eggs* **3 boil down** boil till almost no water remains ♦ *n* [S]: *Bring the soup to a boil.*

boil away *phr vi* disappear by boiling

examples showing how to use the word or phrase

boil down to *phr vt* be no more than: *It all boils down to a question of money.*

labels showing style, region, etc.

close call /ˌkloʷs ˈkɔl/ *n infml* situation in which something dangerous or very unpleasant is only just avoided

Grammar

parts of speech

bone-dry /ˌ· ˈ·◂/ *adj* perfectly dry

bon-fire /ˈbɑnfaɪər/ *n* large outdoor fire

countable and uncountable nouns

choc-o-late /ˈtʃɔkəlɪt, ˈtʃɑ-/ *n* **1** [U] solid brown substance eaten as candy **2** [C] small candy covered with this **3** [U] hot drink made from this ♦ *adj* dark brown

transitive and intransitive verbs

co-in-cide /ˌkoʷɪnˈsaɪd/ *vi* **1** happen at the same time **2** (of opinions, etc.) agree

com-pli-ment² /ˈkɑmpləˌment/ *vt* express admiration of **~ary** /ˌkɑmpləˈmentəriʸ◂/ *adj* **1** expressing admiration **2** given free: *complimentary tickets*

Words which are part of the same word family and which have different parts of speech are often shown at the end of an entry. Sometimes they have a definition, but if their meaning is clear they do not.
The following symbols are used to show exactly how these words are formed:

shows that a related word is exactly the same as the headword

an-ger /ˈæŋgər/ *n* [U] fierce displeasure and annoyance ♦ *vt* make angry

shows that a related word is formed by adding an ending directly to the headword

an-nounce /əˈnaʊns/ *vt* state loudly or publicly: *He announced the winner of the competition.* **~ment** *n* public statement

shows that the form of the headword changes slightly before the new ending can be added

a-nom-a-ly /əˈnɑməliʸ/ *n fml* something different from the usual type: *A cat with no tail is an anomaly.* **-lous** *adj*

ap-pro-pri-ate² /əˈproʷpriʸˌeʸt/ *vt* **1** set aside (money) for a purpose **2** take for oneself **-ation** /əˌproʷpriʸ-ˈeʸʃən/ *n* [C;U]

A

A, a /eʸ/ the 1st letter of the English alphabet

a /ə; *strong* eʸ/ also (*before a vowel sound*) **an** — *indefinite article, determiner* **1** one: *a pencil* | *a doctor* | *a thousand dollars* **2** (*before some words of quantity*): *a few weeks* | *a little water* **3** for each: *6 times a day* | *$2 a dozen*

a·back /əˈbæk/ *adv* **be taken aback** be suddenly shocked

ab·a·cus /ˈæbəkəs/ *n* frame with sliding balls on wires, used for counting

a·ban·don /əˈbændən/ *vt* **1** leave completely **2** give up: *to abandon our search* **3** give (oneself) up completely to a feeling: *He abandoned himself to grief.* ~**ment** *n* [U]

a·base /əˈbeʸs/ *vt fml* make (esp. oneself) lose respect for oneself

a·bashed /əˈbæʃt/ *adj* uncomfortable and ashamed

a·bate /əˈbeʸt/ *vi fml* (of wind, pain, etc.) become less fierce ~**ment** *n* [U]

ab·bey /ˈæbiʸ/ *n* house of religious men or women; MONASTERY or CONVENT

ab·bot /ˈæbət/ *n* man who is the head of a MONASTERY

ab·bre·vi·ate /əˈbriʸviʸˌeʸt/ *vt* make shorter –**ation** /əˌbriʸviʸˈeʸʃən/ *n* short form of a word

ab·di·cate /ˈæbdɪˌkeʸt/ *vi/t* give up (a position or right) officially –**cation** /ˌæbdɪˈkeʸʃən/ *n* [U]

ab·do·men /ˈæbdəmən, æbˈdoʷ-/ *n* part of the body containing the stomach **abdominal** /æbˈdɑmənəl/ *adj*

ab·duct /æbˈdʌkt, əb-/ *vt* take (a person) away illegally; KIDNAP ~**ion** /-ˈdʌkʃən/ *n* [U]

ab·er·ra·tion /ˌæbəˈreʸʃən/ *n* [C;U] change away from usual behavior

a·bet /əˈbɛt/ *vt* –**tt**– aid and abet *law* give help to (a crime or criminal) ~**tor** *n*

a·bey·ance /əˈbeʸəns/ *n* [U] *fml* **held in abeyance** kept from acting

ab·hor /əbˈhɔr, æb-/ *vt fml* hate very much ~**rent** /əbˈhɔrənt, -ˈhɑr-, æb-/ *adj* deeply disliked ~**rence** /-/ *n* [U]

a·bide /əˈbaɪd/ *vt* **abided** or **abode** /əˈboʷd/, **abode** bear; TOLERATE: *I can't abide rudeness.*

abide *by* *phr v(t)* obey (laws, etc.)

a·bid·ing /əˈbaɪdɪŋ/ *adj* without end: *an abiding love*

a·bil·i·ty /əˈbɪləṭiʸ/ *n* [C;U] power; skill

ab·ject /ˈæbdʒɛkt, æbˈdʒɛkt/ *adj fml* **1** deserving great pity: *abject poverty* **2** without respect for oneself; HUMBLE: *an abject apology* ~**ly** *adv*

a·blaze /əˈbleʸz/ *adj* **1** on fire; burning **2** shining brightly

a·ble /ˈeʸbəl/ *adj* **1** having the power, time, etc., to do something: *Will you be able to come?* **2** clever; skilled

a·blu·tions /əˈbluʷʃənz/ *n* [P] *fml* washing oneself

a·bly /ˈeʸbliʸ/ *adv* skilfully

ab·nor·mal /æbˈnɔrməl/ *adj* not ordinary; unusual ~**ly** *adv* ~**ity** /ˌæbnɔrˈmæləṭiʸ, -nər-/ *n* [C;U]

a·board /əˈbɔrd, əˈboʷrd/ *adv, prep* on or onto (a ship, plane, etc.)

a·bode /əˈboʷd/ *v past t. and p. of* ABIDE

a·bol·ish /əˈbɑlɪʃ/ *vt* bring to an end by law –**ition** /ˌæbəˈlɪʃən/ *n* [U]

a·bom·i·na·ble /əˈbɑmənəbəl/ *adj* hateful; very bad –**bly** *adv*

ab·o·rig·i·nal /ˌæbəˈrɪdʒənəl◂/ *adj* (of people and living things) having lived in a place from the earliest times **aboriginal** *n*

ab·o·rig·i·ne /ˌæbəˈrɪdʒəniʸ/ *n* an aboriginal, esp. in Australia

a·bort /əˈbɔrt/ *v* **1** *vt* cause (a child) to be born too soon for it to live **2** *vi/t* end before the expected time: *abort the space flight* ~**ive** *adj* unsuccessful; coming to nothing ~**ion** /əˈbɔrʃən/ *n* [C;U] medical operation to abort a child

a·bound /əˈbaʊnd/ *vi* [(**in, with**)] exist or have in large numbers or great quantity

a·bout¹ /əˈbaʊt/ *prep* **1** on the subject of: *a book about cats* **2** near; close to: *He's about my height.* **3** concerning: *She told us all about the stars.* **4** on every side of; around: *about the town* **5** what/how about: a (making a suggestion): *How about a drink?* **6** what news or plans do you have concerning: *What about Jack?*

about² *adv* **1** a little more or less than: *about 5 miles* **2** nearly; almost: *He's about ready.* **3** somewhere near: *Is there anyone about?* **4** in all directions or places; around: *papers lying about on the floor* **5** so as to face the other way **6** on every side; in every direction: *Look about and see if it's here.* **7** be about to be going to: *We're about to leave.*

about-face /ˌ·ˈ·, ˈ·, ·ˈ·/ *n* change to the opposite position or opinion

a·bove¹ /əˈbʌv/ *prep* **1** higher than; over: *fly above the clouds* **2** more than **3** too good, honest, etc. for: *He's* *not above stealing.* **4 above all** most important of all

above² *adv* **1** higher: *the clouds above* **2** more: *aged 20 and above* **3** earlier in a book: *the facts mentioned above* | *the* **above-mentioned** *facts*

a·bove·board /ə'bʌv₁bɔrd, -₁boʷrd/ *adj* without any trick or attempt to deceive

a·bra·sive /ə'breʸsɪv, -zɪv/ *adj* **1** causing the rubbing away of a surface **2** rough and annoying: *an abrasive personality*

a·breast /ə'brest/ *adv* **1** side by side **2 keep/be abreast of** know the most recent facts about

a·bridge /ə'brɪdʒ/ *vt* make (a book, etc.) shorter

a·bridg·ment /ə'brɪdʒmənt/ *n* something abridged: *an abridgment of the play for radio*

a·broad /ə'brɔd/ *adv* to or in another country

ab·ro·gate /'æbrə₁geʸt/ *vt fml* put an end to (a law, etc.)

a·brupt /ə'brʌpt/ *adj* **1** sudden and unexpected: *an abrupt stop* **2** (of behavior, etc.) rough and impolite ~**ly** *adv* ~**ness** *n* [U]

ab·scess /'æbses/ *n* swelling on or in the body, containing PUS

ab·scond /æb'skand, əb-/ *vi fml* go away suddenly because one has done something wrong

ab·sence /'æbsəns/ *n* **1** [C;U] (period of) being away: *absence from work* **2** [U] lack: *the absence of information about the crime*

ab·sent¹ /'æbsənt/ *adj* **1** not present **2** showing lack of attention: *an absent look on his face*

ab·sent² /əb'sent, æb-/ *vt* keep (oneself) away

ab·sen·tee /₁æbsən'tiʸ◂/ *n* person who is absent from a place

absent-mind·ed /₁···'··◂/ *adj* so concerned with one's thoughts as not to notice what is happening, what one is doing, etc.

ab·so·lute /'æbsə₁luʷt, ₁æbsə'luʷt/ *adj* **1** complete; undoubted: *absolute nonsense* **2** having unlimited power: *an absolute ruler* **3** not measured by comparison with other things; not RELATIVE ~**ly** /₁æbsə'luʷtliʸ◂/ *adv* **1** completely **2** certainly: *'Do you think so?' 'Absolutely'*

ab·solve /əb'zalv, -'salv/ *vt* free (someone) from fulfilling a promise, or from punishment

ab·sorb /əb'sɔrb, -'zɔrb/ *vt* **1** take in (liquids, heat, etc.) **2** fill the attention of: *I was absorbed in a book.* | *an absorbing task* ~**ent** able to ABSORB (1) **absorption** /-ɔrpʃən/ *n* [U]

ab·stain /əb'steʸn/ *vi* keep oneself from drinking, voting, etc. ~**er** *n*

ab·ste·mi·ous /əb'stiʸmiʸəs/ *adj* not allowing oneself much food, etc.

ab·sten·tion /əb'stenʃən, -tʃən/ *n* [C;U] act of abstaining, esp. from voting

ab·sti·nence /'æbstənəns/ *n* [U] abstaining, esp. from alcoholic drink

ab·stract /'æbstrækt/ *adj* **1** existing as a quality or CONCEPT rather than as something real or solid: *Beauty is abstract but a house is not.* | *The word 'hunger' is an* **abstract noun.** **2** general rather than particular: *an abstract discussion of crime, without reference to actual cases* **3** (in art) showing things as a camera would see them ♦ *n* **1** abstract work of art **2** short form of a statement, speech, etc.

ab·struse /əb'struʷs, æb-/ *adj fml* difficult to understand

ab·surd /əb'sɜrd, -'zɜrd/ *adj* unreasonable; (funny because) false or foolish ~**ly** *adv* ~**ity** /əb'sɜrdəţiʸ, -'zɜr-/ *n* [C;U]

a·bun·dant /ə'bʌndənt/ *adj* more than enough ~**ly** *adv* –**dance** *n* [S;U]

a·buse¹ /ə'byuʷz/ *vt* **1** say bad things to or about **2** use badly: *abuse one's power*

a·buse² /ə'byuʷs/ *n* **1** [U] cruel or rude words **2** [C;U] wrong use: *the abuse of drugs* **abusive** *adj* using cruel or rude words

a·bys·mal /ə'bɪzməl/ *adj* very bad

a·byss /ə'bɪs/ *n* great hole that seems to have no bottom

AC /₁eʸ 'siʸ/ *n* [U] AIR-CONDITIONING

ac·a·dem·ic /₁ækə'demɪk◂/ *adj* **1** about schools and education **2** not related to practical questions; theoretical (THEORY): *a purely academic question* ♦ *n* **1** university teacher **2** someone who values skills of the mind more than practical skills ~**ally** /-kliʸ/ *adv*

a·cad·e·my /ə'kædəmiʸ/ *n* **1** society of people interested in the advancement of art, science, or literature **2** school for training in a special skill: *a military academy*

ac·cede /æk'siʸd, ək-/ *vi fml* **1** agree to a demand, etc. **2** come to a high position

ac·cel·e·rate /ək'selə₁reʸt/ *vi/t* (cause to) move faster –**ration** /ək₁selə'reʸʃən/ *n* [U]

ac·cel·e·ra·tor /ək'selə₁reʸţər/ *n* instrument in a car, etc., that is used to increase its speed

ac·cent¹ /'æksent/ *n* **1** particular way of speaking, usu. connected with a place or a nationality **2** mark written over or under a letter, such as that on the 'e' of 'café' **3** importance given to a word or part of a word by saying it with more force

ac·cent² /ˈæksɛnt/ vt pronounce with added force

ac·cen·tu·ate /əkˈsɛntʃuˌeɪt, æk-/ vt direct attention to; give importance to

ac·cept /əkˈsɛpt/ v 1 vi/t receive (something offered), esp. willingly 2 vt believe or agree to: Did she accept your reasons for being late? ~**able** adj good enough; worth accepting: an acceptable gift ~**ance** n [C;U]

ac·cess¹ /ˈæksɛs/ n [U] 1 way in; entrance 2 means of using or getting something: Students need access to books. ~**ible** /əkˈsɛsəbəl/ adj easy to get or get to ~**ibility** /əkˌsɛsəˈbɪlətiʸ/ n [U]

access² vt obtain (stored information) from a computer's memory

ac·ces·sion /əkˈsɛʃən/ n 1 thing added 2 [U] increase by addition

ac·ces·so·ry /əkˈsɛsəriʸ/ n 1 thing that is added but is not a necessary part: car accessories such as a radio | a black dress with matching accessories (= hat, bag, shoes, etc.) 2 law person who is not present at a crime but who helps in doing it

access time /ˈ·· ˌ·/ n [U] time taken by a computer to find and use a piece of information in its memory

ac·ci·dent /ˈæksədənt, -ˌdɛnt/ n something, usu. unpleasant, that happens unexpectedly: serious accidents on the freeway | I met her **by accident.** ~**al** /ˌæksəˈdɛntəl◄/ adj ~**ally** adv

ac·claim /əˈkleɪm/ vt greet with public approval **acclaim** n [U]

ac·cli·mate /ˈækləˌmeɪt, əˈklaɪmɪt/ vi/t make or get used to the weather in a new place **acclimation** /ˌækləˈmeɪʃən/ n [U]

ac·co·lade /ˈækəˌleɪd/ n strong praise

ac·com·mo·date /əˈkɑməˌdeɪt/ vt fml 1 provide with a place to live in 2 help by making changes: to accommodate your wishes –**dating** adj helpful –**dations** /əˌkɑməˈdeɪʃənz/ n [P] room and food

ac·com·pa·ni·ment /əˈkʌmpəniʸmənt/ n 1 something which is used or provided with something else 2 music played at the same time as singing or another instrument

ac·com·pa·nist /əˈkʌmpənɪst/ n player of a musical accompaniment

ac·com·pa·ny /əˈkʌmpəniʸ/ vt 1 go with, as on a journey 2 happen at the same time as: Lightning usually accompanies thunder. 3 play a musical accompaniment to

ac·com·plice /əˈkɑmplɪs/ n person who helps someone to do wrong

ac·com·plish /əˈkɑmplɪʃ/ vt succeed in doing ~**ed** adj skilled ~**ment** n

1 [C] something one is skilled at 2 [U] act of accomplishing something

ac·cord /əˈkɔrd/ n [U] 1 **in accord (with)** in agreement (with) 2 of one's own accord without being asked; willingly

ac·cord·ance /əˈkɔrdns/ n **in accordance with** in a way that agrees with

ac·cord·ing·ly /əˈkɔrdɪŋliʸ/ adv because of what has happened; therefore

according to /·ˈ·· ˌ·/ prep 1 from what is said or written: According to my watch, it's 4 o'clock. 2 in a way that agrees with: paid according to the amount of work done

ac·cor·di·on /əˈkɔrdiʸən/ n musical instrument played by pressing the middle part together to force air through holes controlled by KEYS¹ (3) worked by the fingers

ac·cost /əˈkɔst, əˈkɑst/ vt go up and speak to (esp. a stranger), often threateningly

ac·count¹ /əˈkaʊnt/ n 1 report; description: give an account of what happened | **By all accounts,** (= according to what everyone says) she's a good player. 2 record of money received and paid out 3 money kept in a bank or other institution where one saves money 4 arrangement that lets one buy goods and pay for them later 5 customer: one of our biggest accounts 6 **bring/call someone to account** cause (someone) to give an explanation 7 **on account of** because of 8 **on no account/not on any account** not for any reason 9 **take into account/take account of** give thought to; consider

account² v **account for** phr vt 1 give or be an explanation for 2 give a statement showing how money has been spent

ac·count·a·ble /əˈkaʊntəbəl/ adj responsible –**bility** /əˌkaʊntəˈbɪlətiʸ/ n [U]

ac·count·ant /əˈkaʊntənt/ n person who controls and examines money accounts

ac·cred·it·ed /əˈkrɛdɪtɪd/ adj 1 officially recognized as reaching a certain standard or quality: an accredited college 2 officially representing one's government in a foreign country 3 having the power to act for an organization

ac·crue /əˈkruʷ/ vi fml come as an increase or advantage

ac·cu·mu·late /əˈkyuʷmyəˌleɪt/ vi/t make or become greater; collect into a mass –**lation** /əˌkyuʷmyəˈleɪʃən/ n [C;U]

ac·cu·ra·cy /ˈækyərəsiʸ/ n [U] being accurate; exactness

ac·cu·rate /ˈækyərɪt/ *adj* exactly correct ~**ly** *adv*

ac·cu·sa·tion /ˌækyəˈzeʸʃən/ *n* [C;U] (statement) accusing someone of something

ac·cuse /əˈkyuʷz/ *vt* charge (someone) with doing wrong: *He was accused of murder.* | *The accused (men) were found guilty.* **accuser** *n* **accusingly** *adv*

ac·cus·tom /əˈkʌstəm/ *vt* be accustomed to be in the habit of; be used to

AC/DC /ˌeʸ siʸ ˈdiʸ siʸ/ *adj sl for* BISEXUAL

ace /eʸs/ *n* **1** playing card with one mark or spot on it **2** person of the highest skill **3** (in tennis) very fast and strong SERVE that the opponent cannot hit back ♦ *adj infml* very good or very skilled

a·cer·bic /əˈsɜrbɪk/ *adj* (of a person or manner) clever in a rather cruel way

ache /eʸk/ *vi* have a continuous dull pain: *My head aches.* | (fig.) *I'm aching to go to the party.* **ache** *n: a headache*

a·chieve /əˈtʃiʸv/ *vt* **1** finish successfully **2** get by effort: *achieve results* ~**ment** *n* **1** [U] successful finishing of something **2** [C] something achieved

A·chil·les' heel /əˌkɪliʸz ˈhiʸl/ *n* small but important weakness

ac·id /ˈæsɪd/ *adj* sour; bitter **acid** *n* **1** [C;U] chemical substance containing HYDROGEN **2** [U] *sl* the drug LSD

acid rain /ˌ·· ˈ·/ *n* [U] rain containing harmful quantities of acid as a result of industrial pollution (POLLUTE)

acid test /ˌ·· ˈ·/ *n* test of the value of something

ac·knowl·edge /əkˈnɑlɪdʒ/ *vt* **1** admit; recognize as a fact: *to acknowledge defeat* | *an acknowledged expert* **2** show one is grateful for **3** state that one has received: *acknowledge a letter* **4** show that one recognizes (someone) as by smiling, etc. ~**edgment**, ~**edgement** *n* [C;U]

ac·ne /ˈækniʸ/ *n* [U] skin disorder common among young people, in which spots appear on the face and neck

a·corn /ˈeʸkɔrn, ˈeʸkərn/ *n* nut of the OAK tree

a·cous·tics /əˈkuʷstɪks/ *n* **1** [U] scientific study of sound **2** [P] qualities that make a place good or bad for hearing in **acoustic** *adj*

ac·quaint /əˈkweʸnt/ *vt fml* **1** **acquaint someone with** tell; make known to **2** **be acquainted (with)** have met socially; know ~**ance** *n* **1** [C] person whom one knows slightly

2 [S;U (with)] knowledge gained through experience

ac·qui·esce /ˌækwiʸˈɛs/ *vi* agree, often unwillingly –**escent** *adj*

ac·quire /əˈkwaɪər/ *vt* gain; come to possess

ac·qui·si·tion /ˌækwəˈzɪʃən/ *n* **1** [U] act of acquiring **2** [C] something acquired –**tive** /əˈkwɪzətɪv/ *adj* in the habit of acquiring things

ac·quit /əˈkwɪt/ *vt* –**tt**– decide that (someone) is not guilty: *The jury acquitted him (of murder).* ~**tal** *n* [C;U]

a·cre /ˈeʸkər/ *n* a measure of land equal to 4,840 square yards

a·cre·age /ˈeʸkərɪdʒ/ *n* [S;U] area measured in acres

ac·rid /ˈækrɪd/ *adj* (of taste or smell) bitter; stinging

ac·ri·mo·ny /ˈækrəˌmoʷniʸ/ *n* [U] bitterness of manner or language –**nious** /ˌækrəˈmoʷniʸəs◂/ *adj*

ac·ro·bat /ˈækrəˌbæt/ *n* person skilled in walking on ropes, etc., esp. at a CIRCUS ~**ic** /ˌækrəˈbætɪk◂/ *adj* ~**ics** *n* [P;U]

ac·ro·nym /ˈækrənɪm/ *n* word made from the first letters of a name, such as NATO

a·cross /əˈkrɔs/ *adv, prep* from one side to the other; on or to the other side (of): *a bridge across the river* | *Can you swim across?*

a·cross-the-board /ˌ·,· · ˈ·/ *adj* influencing or having effects on people or things of all types or at every level **across-the-board** *adv*

act¹ /ækt/ *vi* **1** do something: *She acted on my suggestion.* | *The doctor acted correctly.* **2** *vi/t* perform in a play or film **3** *vi* produce an effect: *Does the drug take long to act?*

act up *phr vi* behave badly

act² *n* **1** something that one has done; an action of a particular kind: *an act of terrorism* | *a kind act* **2** law made by congress, etc. **3** main division of a stage play **4** short event in a stage or CIRCUS performance **5** example of insincere behavior used for effect: *She was just putting on an act.* – see also ACT OF GOD

act·ing /ˈæktɪŋ/ *adj* appointed to do the duties of a position for a short time

ac·tion /ˈækʃən/ *n* **1** [U] process of doing something: *We must take action quickly.* **2** [C] something done; ACT: *Her prompt action saved his life.* **3** [C;U] way something works **4** [U] effect: *the action of light on photographic film* **5** [C;U] military fighting or a fight **6** [U] main events in a book, play, etc.: *The action takes place in Italy.* **7** [C;U] *law* legal charge of guilt: *bring an action against him* **8** **in/into action**

in/into operation **9 out of action** not working **10 take action** begin to act – see also JOB ACTION

ac·ti·vate /ˈæktəˌveɪt/ vt make active –**ation** /ˌæktəˈveɪʃən/ n [U]

ac·tive /ˈæktɪv/ adj doing things; able to take action ~**ly** adv

ac·tiv·ist /ˈæktəvɪst/ n person taking an active part in politics

ac·tiv·i·ty /ækˈtɪvətiʲ/ n **1** [U] movement or action: political activity **2** [C] something done, esp. for interest or pleasure: leisure activities

act of God /ˌ··ˈ·/ n major event that can't be controlled, like a flood or EARTHQUAKE

ac·tor /ˈæktər/ **actress** /ˈæktrɪs/ fem. — n person who acts in a play, film, etc.

ac·tu·al /ˈæktʃuʷəl, ˈækʃuʷəl/ adj existing as a fact; real ~**ly** /ˈæktʃuʷəliʲ, -tʃəliʲ, ˈækʃuʷəliʲ/ adv **1** in fact; really **2** (showing surprise): He actually offered me a drink!

ac·u·men /əˈkyuʷmən, ˈækyəmən/ n [U] fml ability to judge quickly

ac·u·punc·ture /ˈækyəˌpʌŋktʃər/ n [U] method of curing diseases by putting special needles into certain parts of the body

a·cute /əˈkyuʷt/ adj **1** severe; very great: acute shortage of water **2** (of the mind or senses) working very well **3** (of an angle) less than 90° **4** (of a mark) put above a letter, e.g. é, to show pronunciation ~**ly** adv ~**ness** n [U]

ad /æd/ n infml advertisement

AD /ˌeɪˈdiʲ/ (in the year) since the birth of Christ: in 1492 AD

ad·age /ˈædɪdʒ/ n old wise phrase; PROVERB

ad·a·mant /ˈædəmənt/ adj fml refusing to change one's mind

Ad·am's ap·ple /ˌædəmz ˈæpəl/ n lump at the front of the throat that moves when one talks or swallows

a·dapt /əˈdæpt/ vt make suitable for new conditions ~**able** adj able to change –**ability** /əˌdæptəˈbɪlətiʲ/ n [U] –**ation** /ˌædəpˈteɪʃən, ˌædæp-/ n [C;U] act of adapting: an adaptation of the play for television

a·dapt·er, -or /əˈdæptər/ n **1** person who adapts **2** electrical PLUG allowing more than one piece of equipment to run from the same SOCKET

add /æd/ v **1** vt put with something else: add a name to the list **2** vi/t join (numbers) together **3** vt say also

add to phr vt increase: His absence added to our difficulties.

add up phr vi make sense; seem likely: The facts just don't add up.

ad·der /ˈædər/ n small poisonous snake

ad·dict /ˈædɪkt/ n person who

cannot stop a harmful habit ~**ion** /əˈdɪkʃən/ n [C;U] ~**ive** /əˈdɪktɪv/ adj habit forming

ad·dict·ed /əˈdɪktɪd/ adj dependent on something, esp. a drug

ad·di·tion /əˈdɪʃən/ n **1** [U] act of adding **2** [C] something added **3 in addition (to)** as well (as) ~ **al** adj as well; added ~**ally** adv also

ad·di·tive /ˈædətɪv/ n substance, esp. a chemical one, added to something else

ad·dle-brained /ˈædl breɪnd/ adj infml having become confused

add-on /ˈ· ·/ n piece of equipment that can be connected to a computer that increases its usefulness

ad·dress /əˈdres, ˈædres/ n **1** number, town, etc., where someone lives **2** speech made to a group of people ♦ vt **1** write a name and ADDRESS (1) on **2** direct a speech to: She addressed the crowd.

ad·ept /əˈdept/ adj highly skilled **adept** /ˈædept/ n person who is adept at something

ad·e·quate /ˈædəkwɪt/ adj enough; good enough ~**ly** adv –**quacy** n [U]

ad·here /ədˈhɪər/ vi stick firmly, as with glue **adherence** n [U] **adherent** n loyal supporter of something

adhere to phr vt remain loyal to (an idea, plan, etc.)

ad·he·sive /ədˈhiʲsɪv, -zɪv/ n, adj (a substance such as glue) that can stick –**sion** /ədˈhiʲʒən/ n [U]

ad hoc /ˌæd ˈhɑk, -ˈhoʷk/ adj made for a particular purpose

ad·ja·cent /əˈdʒeɪsənt/ adj fml very close; (almost) touching

ad·jec·tive /ˈædʒɪktɪv/ n word which describes a noun, such as black in a black hat –**tival** /ˌædʒɪkˈtaɪvəl/ adj

ad·join /əˈdʒɔɪn/ vi/t fml be next to (one another)

ad·journ /əˈdʒɜrn/ vi/t stop (a meeting, etc.) for a while ~**ment** n [C;U]

ad·ju·di·cate /əˈdʒuʷdɪˌkeɪt/ vi/t fml act as a judge; decide about –**cator** n –**cation** /əˌdʒuʷdɪˈkeɪʃən/ n [U]

ad·junct /ˈædʒʌŋkt/ n something added without being a necessary part

ad·just /əˈdʒʌst/ vi/t change slightly so as to make right ~**able** adj ~**ment** n [C;U]

ad lib /ˌæd ˈlɪb/ adv spoken, played, performed, etc., without preparation **ad-lib** vi –**bb-** invent and say without preparation **ad-lib** adj

ad·min·is·ter /ədˈmɪnəstər/ vt fml **1** manage (business affairs, etc.) **2** (to) give: administer medicine/punishment

ad·min·is·tra·tion /ədˌmɪnəˈstreɪʃən/ n 1 [U] management or direction of the affairs of a business, government, etc. 2 [C] national government: *the Bush Administration* 3 [U] act of administering **–trative** /ədˈmɪnəˌstreɪ̯tɪv/ *adj* **–trator** /-ˌstreɪ̯t̬ər/ *n*

ad·mi·ra·ble /ˈædmərəbəl/ *adj* very good **–bly** *adv*

ad·mi·ral /ˈædmərəl/ *n* naval officer of high rank

ad·mire /ədˈmaɪ̯ər/ *vt* regard with pleasure; have a good opinion of **admiring** *adj* **admirer** *n* **admiration** /ˌædməˈreɪ̯ʃən/ *n* [U] feeling of pleasure and respect

ad·mis·si·ble /ədˈmɪsəbəl/ *adj* that can be accepted or considered

ad·mis·sion /ədˈmɪʃən/ *n* 1 [U] being allowed to enter a building, join a club, etc. 2 [U] cost of entrance: *Admission $1* 3 [C] statement admitting something; confession (CONFESS)

ad·mit /ədˈmɪt/ *vt* **-tt-** 1 allow to enter; let in 2 agree to the truth of (something bad) **~tance** *n* [U] right to enter **~tedly** *adv* it must be agreed that

ad·mon·ish /ədˈmɑnɪʃ/ *vt fml* scold gently; warn **-ition** /ˌædməˈnɪʃən/ *n* [C;U]

ad nau·se·am /ˌæd ˈnɔziʸəm/ *adv* repeatedly and to an annoying degree

a·do /əˈduʷ/ *n* without more ado with no further delay

ad·o·les·cent /ˌædlˈesənt◂/ *adj, n* (of) a boy or girl who is growing up **–cence** *n* [S;U]

a·dopt /əˈdɑpt/ *vt* 1 take (someone else's child) into one's family forever 2 take and use (a method, suggestion, etc.) **~ive** *adj* having adopted a child **~ion** /əˈdɑpʃən/ *n* [C;U]

a·dore /əˈdɔr, əˈdoʷr/ *vt* 1 love and respect deeply; worship 2 like very much **adorable** *adj* very lovable **adoring** *adj* loving **adoration** /ˌædəˈreɪ̯ʃən/ *n* [U]

a·dorn /əˈdɔrn/ *vt* add beauty to; decorate **~ment** *n* [U]

a·dren·a·lin /əˈdrenl-ɪn/ *n* [U] chemical made by the body during anger, etc., causing quick or violent action

a·drift /əˈdrɪft/ *adv, adj* (of boats) floating loose; not fastened

a·droit /əˈdrɔɪt/ *adj* quick and skilful **~ly** *adv*

ad·u·la·tion /ˌædʒəˈleɪ̯ʃən/ *n* [U] *fml* praise or admiration that is more than is necessary or deserved

ad·ult /əˈdʌlt, ˈædʌlt/ *adj, n* (of) a fully grown person or animal

a·dul·ter·ate /əˈdʌltəˌreɪ̯t/ *vt* make impure by adding something of lower quality

a·dul·ter·y /əˈdʌltəriʸ/ *n* [U] sexual relations between a married person and someone outside the marriage **adulterer, adulteress** /-trɪs/ *fem.* *n* **–terous** *adj*

ad·vance¹ /ədˈvæns/ *vi/t* go or bring forward in position, development, etc. **advanced** *adj* **1** far on in development **2** modern

advance² *n* **1** forward movement or development **2** money provided before the proper time **3** in advance before in time ♦ *adj* coming before the usual time

advanced de·gree /·ˈ··ˌ·/ *n* degree higher than a BACHELOR'S

ad·vanc·es /ədˈvænsɪz/ *n* [P] efforts to become friends or lovers with someone

ad·van·tage /ədˈvæntɪdʒ/ *n* **1** [C] something that may help one to be successful **2** [U] profit; gain **3** take advantage of: a make use of somebody, as by deceiving them b make use of; profit from **~ous** /ˌædvænˈteɪ̯dʒəs, -vən-/ *adj*

ad·vent /ˈædvɛnt/ *n* the advent of the coming of (an important event, etc.)

ad·ven·ture /ədˈvɛntʃər/ *n* **1** [C] exciting and perhaps dangerous experience **2** [U] excitement; risk **–turer** *n* **1** person who has or looks for adventures **2** person who hopes to make a profit by taking risks with his/her money **–turous** *adj* **1** also **adventuresome** /ədˈvɛntʃərsəm/ fond of adventure **2** exciting

ad·verb /ˈædvɜrb/ *n* word which adds to the meaning of a verb, an adjective, another adverb, or a sentence, for example *slowly, tomorrow,* and *here* **~ial** /ədˈvɜrbiʸəl/ *n, adj*

ad·ver·sa·ry /ˈædvərˌseriʸ/ *n fml* opponent; enemy **–sarial** /ˌædvərˈseəriʸəl/ *adj*

ad·verse /ədˈvɜrs, æd-, ˈædvɜrs/ *adj fml* unfavorable: *adverse comments* **~ly** *adv* **–sity** /ədˈvɜrsəṭiʸ, æd-/ *n* [C;U] bad luck; trouble

ad·ver·tise /ˈædvərˌtaɪz/ *vi/t* make (something for sale) known to people, e.g. in a newspaper **–tiser** *n* **–tising** *n* [U] business of doing this **~ment** /ˌædvərˈtaɪzmənt, ədˈvɜrtɪz-, -ədˈvɜrtɪs-/ also **ad** *infml* — *n* notice of something for sale or wanted

ad·vice /ədˈvaɪs/ *n* [U] opinion given to someone about what to do

advice col·um·nist /·ˈ·ˌ···/ *n* person who gives advice in the part of a newspaper or magazine that contains letters from readers about their personal problems

ad·vise /ədˈvaɪz/ *vt* 1 give advice to 2 [(of)] *fml* inform: *Please advise me of the cost.* 3 **well-advised/ill-**

advised wise/unwise **advisory** giving advice **adviser** also **advisor** n **advisable** adj sensible; wise

ad·vo·cate /'ædvəkɪt, -ˌkeɪt/ n person who speaks in defense of another person or of an idea; supporter **advocate** /-ˌkeɪt/ vt

ae·gis /'iːdʒɪs/ n **under the aegis of** with the protection or support of

aeon, eon /'iːən, -ɑn/ n indefinitely long period of time

aer·i·al¹ /'eəriəl/ n wire, rod, etc., that receives radio or television signals

aerial² adj in or from the air: *aerial photography*

aer·o·bat·ics /ˌeərəˈbætɪks/ n [U] ACROBATIC tricks done in an aircraft **aerobatic** adj

aer·o·bics /eəˈrowbɪks/ n [U] active physical exercise done to strengthen the heart and lungs

aer·o·dy·nam·ics /ˌeərowdaɪˈnæmɪks/ n [U] science of movement through the air **aerodynamic** adj **1** concerning aerodynamics **2** using the principles of aerodynamics

aer·o·nau·tics /ˌeərəˈnɔtɪks/ n [U] science of the flight of aircraft

aer·o·sol /'eərəˌsɔl, -ˌsɑl/ n container from which liquid is forced out in a fine mist

aer·o·space /'eərowˌspeɪs/ n [U] the air around the Earth and space beyond it

aes·thet·ics also **es-** /ɛsˈθɛtɪks, ɪs-/ n [U] science of beauty, esp. in art **aesthetic** adj **–ically** /-kliy/ adv

af·fa·ble /'æfəbəl/ adj friendly and pleasant **–bly** adv

af·fair /əˈfeər/ n **1** event; set of events **2** something to be done; business **3** sexual relationship outside marriage – see also FOREIGN AFFAIRS

af·fect /əˈfɛkt/ vt cause a change in; influence: *Smoking affects your health.* **~ed** adj not natural; pretended **~ation** /ˌæfɛkˈteɪʃən/ n [U] unnatural behavior

af·fec·tion /əˈfɛkʃən/ n [U] gentle, lasting fondness **~ate** adj **~ately** adv

af·fi·da·vit /ˌæfəˈdeɪvɪt/ n law written statement for use as proof

af·fil·i·ate /əˈfɪliˌeɪt/ vi/t (esp. of a group) join to a larger group **–ation** /əˌfɪliˈeɪʃən/ n [C;U]

af·fin·i·ty /əˈfɪnətiy/ n [C;U] close connection or liking

af·firm /əˈfɜrm/ vt fml declare; state **~ative** n, adj (statement) meaning 'yes' **~ation** /ˌæfərˈmeɪʃən/ n [C;U]

af·firm·a·tive ac·tion /əˌfɜrmətɪv ˈækʃən/ n [U] action to provide equal job possibilities for everyone regardless of race, religion, sex, etc.

af·fix¹ /əˈfɪks/ vt fml fix; fasten

af·fix² /'æfɪks/ n group of letters added to the beginning or end of a word to change its meaning or use (as in 'untie', 'kindness')

af·flict /əˈflɪkt/ vt cause to suffer; trouble **~ion** /əˈflɪkʃən/ n [C;U] fml

af·flu·ent /'æfluwənt/ adj wealthy; rich **–ence** n [U]

af·ford /əˈfɔrd, əˈfowrd/ vt **1** be able to pay for **2** be able to risk: *I can't afford to neglect my health.*

af·front /əˈfrʌnt/ vt be rude to; offend **affront** n

a·fi·cio·na·do /əˌfɪʃəˈnɑdow/ n **–dos** someone who is keenly interested in a particular activity or subject

a·field /əˈfiːld/ adv **far afield** far away

AFL-CIO /ˌeɪ ɛf ˌɛl ˌsiy aɪ ˈow/ n [the] American Federation of Labor and Congress of Industrial Organizations; an association of American labor unions

a·float /əˈflowt/ adv, adj **1** floating **2** on a ship **3** out of debt

a·foot /əˈfʊt/ adv, adj being prepared; happening

a·fore·said /əˈforsɛd/ adj said or named before

a·fraid /əˈfreɪd/ adj **1** frightened: *afraid of the dark* **2** sorry for something that has happened or is likely to happen: *'Are we late?' 'I'm afraid so.'*

a·fresh /əˈfrɛʃ/ adv fml again

Af·ro /'æfrow/ n bushy hair

af·ter /'æftər/ prep, conj **1** later than: *after breakfast | after you leave* **2** following: *Your name comes after mine in the list. | It rained day after day.* **3** because of: *After all that did I don't want to see him.* **4** in spite of: *After I packed it so carefully, the clock arrived broken.* **5** looking for: *The police are after him.* **6** fml in the style of: *a painting after Rembrandt* **7 after all** in spite of everything ♦ adv later; afterwards

af·ter·ef·fect /'æftərɪˌfɛkt/ n effect (usu. unpleasant) that follows some time after the cause

af·ter·math /'æftərˌmæθ/ n period following a bad event: *the aftermath of the war*

af·ter·noon /ˌæftərˈnuwn◂/ n [C;U] time between noon and sunset

af·ter·thought /'æftərˌθɔt/ n idea that comes later; something added later

af·ter·wards /'æftərwərdz/ adv later; after that

a·gain /əˈgɛn/ adv **1** once more; another time: *Say it again.* **2** back to the original place or condition: *He's home again now.* **3** besides; further: *I could eat as much* (= the same amount) *again.* **4 again and again** very often

a·gainst /ə'genst/ prep **1** in the direction of and meeting or touching: *The rain beat against the windows.* **2** in opposition to: *Stealing is* **against the law. 3** as a protection from: *They were vaccinated against cholera.* **4** having as a background: *The picture looks good against that red wall.*

age /eʸdʒ/ n **1** [C;U] length of time someone has lived or something has existed: *What are the children's ages?* **2** [U] one of the periods of human life: *to look after her in her old age* **3** [C] period of history: *This is the nuclear age.* **4** [C] long time: *We haven't met for ages.* **5 of age** old enough (usu. at 18 or 21) to be responsible in law for one's own actions **6 under/over age** too young/too old to be legally allowed to do something ♦ vi/t make or become old **aged** adj **1** /eʸdʒd/ of the stated number of years: *a boy aged 10* **2** /'eʸdʒɪd/ very old: *an aged man*

age·ism, agism /'eʸdʒɪzəm/ n [U] the making of unfair differences between people because of their age, esp. treating young people more favorably than old people **ageist, agist** adj, n

a·gen·cy /'eʸdʒənsiʸ/ n work or business of an agent: *an employment agency*

a·gen·da /ə'dʒendə/ n **-das** list of things to be talked about at a meeting

a·gent /'eʸdʒənt/ n **1** person who does business for other people: *A travel agent arranges travel.* **2** person or thing that produces a result: *Soap is a cleansing agent.*

ag·gran·dize·ment, -disement /ə-'grændɪzmənt/ n [U] increase in size, power, or rank

ag·gra·vate /'ægrə,veʸt/ vt **1** make worse **2** annoy: *an aggravating delay* **-vation** /,ægrə'veʸʃən/ n [C;U]

ag·gre·gate /'ægrəgɪt/ n [C;U] total

ag·gres·sion /ə'greʃən/ n [U] starting a quarrel or war without just cause **-sor** /ə'gresər/ n person or country that does this

ag·gres·sive /ə'gresɪv/ adj **1** always ready to attack **2** brave and determined

ag·grieved /ə'griʸvd/ adj fml showing hurt feelings

a·ghast /ə'gæst/ adj surprised and shocked

ag·ile /'ædʒəl, 'ædʒaɪl/ adj able to move quickly **agility** /ə'dʒɪləṭiʸ/ n [U]

ag·i·tate /'ædʒə,teʸt/ v **1** vt shake (a liquid) **2** vt make anxious; worry **3** vi (**for**) argue strongly in public **-tator** n person who agitates for

political or social change **-tation** /,ædʒə'teʸʃən/ n [U]

a·glow /ə'gloʷ/ adj bright with color or excitement

ag·nos·tic /æg'nastɪk, əg-/ n, adj (person) believing that nothing can be known about God **~ism** /-tɪ,sɪzəm/ n [U]

a·go /ə'goʷ/ adj, adv back in time from now: *a week ago*

a·gog /ə'gag/ adj excited and eager

ag·o·nize /'ægənaɪz/ vi infml make a long and anxious effort when trying to make a decision, etc. **-nized** adj expressing great pain **-nizing** adj causing great pain

ag·o·ny /'ægəniʸ/ n [C;U] great suffering

ag·o·ra·pho·bi·a /,ægərə'foʷbiʸə/ n [U] fear of open spaces

a·grar·i·an /ə'greəriʸən/ adj fml of land, esp. farm land

a·gree /ə'griʸ/ v **1** vi/t share the same opinion; say 'yes': *I agree with you.* | *We agreed to go home.* | *They met at the agreed place.* **2** vi (of statements, etc.) be the same; match **~able** adj pleasant **~ably** adv **~ment** n **1** [U] state of agreeing: *The 2 sides cannot reach agreement.* **2** [C] arrangement between people or groups; CONTRACT: *to break an agreement*

agree with phr vt **1** suit the health of **2** be in accordance with

ag·ri·cul·ture /'ægrɪ,kʌltʃər/ n [U] growing crops; farming **-tural** /,ægrɪ'kʌltʃərəl◂/ adj

ag·ron·o·my /ə'granəmiʸ/ n [U] science of managing soil and growing crops

a·ground /ə'graʊnd/ adv, adj (of a ship) on or onto the shore or bottom of a sea, lake, etc.

a·head /ə'hed/ adv, adj **1** in front **2** into the future: *to plan ahead* **3** (**of**) in advance; succeeding better: *to get ahead of our rivals*

AI /,eʸ 'aɪ/ n [U] ARTIFICIAL INTELLIGENCE

aid /eʸd/ n **1** [U] help: *She came to my aid at once.* | *to collect $1,000 in aid of medical research* **2** [C] person or thing that helps: *an aid in learning a language* – see also FIRST AID ♦ vt fml help

aide /eʸd/ n person who helps

AIDS, Aids /eʸdz/ n [U] Acquired Immune Deficiency Syndrome; very serious disease caused by a VIRUS which breaks down the body's natural defenses against infection

ail /eʸl/ vi be ill: *an ailing child* **~ment** n illness

aim /eʸm/ v **1** vi/t point (a weapon, etc.) towards **2** vi direct one's efforts; intend: *I aim to be a writer.* ♦

n **1** act of directing a shot **2** desired result; purpose: *What is your aim in life?* **– less** *adj* without purpose

ain't /eɪnt/ *nonstandard*: am not, is not, are not, has not, *or* have not

air¹ /eər/ *n* **1** [U] mixture of gases that we breathe **2** [U] space above the ground: *travel* **by air 3** [C] general character of a person or place: *an air of excitement at the meeting* **4** clear the air get rid of misunderstanding, etc., by stating the facts clearly **5 in the air: a** (of stories, talk, etc.) being passed on from one person to another **b** uncertain **6 on/off the air** broadcasting/not broadcasting – see also HOT AIR, THIN AIR **airs** *n* [P] unnatural behavior to make one seem important

air² *v* **1** *vi/t* make or become fresh by letting in air: *to air the room* **2** *vt* let people know: *He's always airing his opinions.* **3** *vt* broadcast **airing** *n* [C;U]

   air out *phr v* air² (1)

air·borne /ˈeərbɔrn, -boʷrn/ *adj* **1** carried by the air **2** (of aircraft) flying

air-con·di·tion·ing /ˈ· ·,···/ also **AC** *n* [U] system using machines (**air-conditioners**) to control the indoor air temperature **–tioned** *adj*

air·craft /ˈeərkræft/ *n* **-craft** flying machine

aircraft car·ri·er /ˈ·· ,···/ *n* military ship that carries aircraft

air·field /ˈeərfiʷld/ *n* place where aircraft can land

air·force /ˈeərfɔrs/ *n* branch of a country's military forces that fights in the air

air·i·ly /ˈeərəliʸ/ *adv* in a light AIRY (2,3) manner

air·lift /ˈeər,lɪft/ *n* carrying of large numbers of people or amounts of supplies by aircraft, esp. to or from a place that is difficult to get to **airlift** *vt*

air·line /ˈeərlaɪn/ *n* business that carries passengers and goods by air

air·lin·er /ˈeər,laɪnər/ *n* large passenger aircraft

air·lock /ˈeərlɑk/ *n* **1** BUBBLE in a tube, etc., that prevents the flow of liquid **2** enclosed space or room into which or from which air cannot accidentally pass

air·mail /ˈeərmeʸl/ *n* [U] system of sending letters, etc., by air

air·plane /ˈeərpleʸn/ *n* flying vehicle with wings and one or more engines

air·port /ˈeərpɔrt, -poʷrt/ *n* place where aircraft regularly land, with buildings for waiting passengers, etc.

air raid /ˈ· ·/ *n* attack by military aircraft

air·ship /ˈeər,ʃɪp/ *n* aircraft which is lighter than air with an engine but no wings

air·space /ˈeərspeʸs/ *n* [U] sky above a country, regarded as that country's property

air·strip /ˈeər,strɪp/ *n* piece of ground where aircraft can land if necessary

air·tight /ˈeərtaɪt/ *adj* not letting air in or out

air-to-air /ˌ·· ˈ·◂/ *adj* to be fired from one aircraft to another

air·way /ˈeərweʸ/ *n* AIRLINE

air·wor·thy /ˈeər,wɜrðiʸ/ *adj* (of an aircraft) in safe working condition **–thiness** *n* [U]

air·y /ˈeəriʸ/ *adj* **1** open to the fresh air **2** not practical: *airy notions* **3** cheerful and careless

aisle /aɪl/ *n* passage between seats in a church, theater, etc.

a·jar /əˈdʒɑr/ *adv, adj* (of a door) slightly open

aka *abbrev. for:* also known as

a·kim·bo /əˈkɪmboʷ/ *adj, adv* (of the arms) bent at the elbows and with the hand on the HIPS

a·kin /əˈkɪn/ *adj* ((to)) like; similar

a·lac·ri·ty /əˈlækrətiʸ/ *n* [U] *fml* quick and willing readiness

a·larm /əˈlɑrm/ *n* **1** [C] warning of danger **2** [U] sudden fear **3** [C] apparatus that gives a warning: *a burglar alarm* **4** [C] clock that can be set to make a noise at any time to wake people: *set the alarm (clock) for 6:30* ♦ *vt* frighten: *alarming news* **~ ist** *n* person who always expects danger, often without good reason, and says so to others **~ ist** *adj*

a·las /əˈlæs/ *interj lit* (cry expressing sorrow)

al·beit /ɔlˈbiʸɪt, æl-/ *conj fml* even though: *an important, albeit small, mistake*

al·bi·no /ælˈbaɪnoʷ/ *n* person or animal with white skin, very light hair, and pink eyes

al·bum /ˈælbəm/ *n* **1** book for sticking photographs, etc., into **2** longplaying record

al·che·my /ˈælkəmiʸ/ *n* [U] former science concerned with turning metals into gold **–mist** *n*

al·co·hol /ˈælkə,hɔl, -,hɑl/ *n* [U] (drinks containing) the liquid that makes one drunk **~ism** *n* [U] diseased condition caused by the continued drinking of too much alcohol **~ ic** /ˌælkəˈhɔlɪk◂, -ˈhɑ-/ *adj* /person unable to stop drinking alcohol

al·cove /ˈælkoʷv/ *n* small partly enclosed space in a room for a bed, etc.

ale /eʸl/ *n* [U] kind of beer

a·lert /əˈlɜrt/ *adj* quick to see and

ask; watchful ♦ *n* **1** warning of danger **2 on the alert** ready to deal with danger ♦ *vt* warn

al·fal·fa sprout /æl'fælfə‚spraʊt/ *n* small green SALAD plant

al·fres·co /æl'freskⁿ/ *adj, adv* in the open air

al·gae /'ældʒiʸ/ *n* [P] very small plants that live in or near water

al·ge·bra /'ældʒəbrə/ *n* [U] branch of MATHEMATICS using letters to represent values

a·li·as /'eʸliʸəs/ *n* **-ases** false name used esp. by a criminal ♦ *adv* also called: *Edward Ball, alias John Smith*

al·i·bi /'ælə‚baɪ/ *n* proof that a person charged with a crime was somewhere else when it happened

a·li·en /'eʸliʸən/ *n* **1** foreigner who has not become a citizen of the country where he or she lives **2** (in films and stories) a creature from another world ♦ *adj* **1** foreign **2** different and strange

a·li·en·ate /'eʸliʸə‚neʸt, 'eʸlyə-/ *vt* make unfriendly –**ation** /‚eʸliʸə-'neʸʃən, ‚eʸlyə-/ *n* [U]

a·light /ə'laɪt/ *vi* **alighted** *or* **alit** /ə'lɪt/ *fml* get down; come down: *to alight from a train*

a·lign /ə'laɪn/ *vi/t* **1** come or put into a line **2 align oneself with** come into agreement with: *They aligned themselves with the army.* ~**ment** *n* [C;U]

a·like /ə'laɪk/ *adj, adv* like one another; the same

al·i·men·ta·ry /‚ælə'mentəriʸ/ *adj* concerning food and the way it is treated: *the alimentary canal (= tube-like passage leading from the mouth else to the stomach)*

al·i·mo·ny /'ælə‚moʷniʸ/ *n* [U] money that one must pay regularly to a former wife or husband

a·live /ə'laɪv/ *adj* **1** living; in existence: (fig.) *The argument was kept alive by the politicians.* **2** full of life; active **3 alive to** AWARE of **4 alive with** covered with (insects, etc.)

al·ka·li /'ælkə‚laɪ/ *n* **-lis** *or* **-lies** [C;U] substance that forms a chemical salt when combined with an acid –**line** *adj*

all¹ /ɔl/ *determiner* the whole of; every one of: *all the bread | all these questions | He ate it all.*

all² *adv* **1** completely: *It's all dirty. | He's all alone.* **2** for each side: *The score was 3 all.* **3 all along** from the beginning **4 all at once** suddenly **5 all out** using all possible strength and effort **6 all over** everywhere **7 all right: a** safe or satisfactory **b** I agree; yes **8 all the** by so much: *If you help, we'll finish all the sooner.* **9 all there** having a good quick mind **10 all the same** even so; in any case **11 all the same to** making no difference to: *It's all the same to me what you do.* **12 all told** all together **13 all up** at an end; ruined **14 not all that** *infml* not very

all³ *pron* **1** everyone or everything: *This is all I have. | I brought all of them.* **2 all in all** considering everything **3 (not) at all** (not) in any way: *I don't agree at all.* **4 in all** counting everyone or everything **5 once and for all** for the last time

Al·lah /'ælə, 'alə/ *n* (the Muslim name for) God

al·lay /ə'leʸ/ *vt fml* make (fear, etc.) less

all clear /‚· '·/ *n* [*the*+S] **1** signal that danger is past **2** GO-AHEAD

al·lege /ə'ledʒ/ *vt fml* declare without proof: *an alleged thief* **allegedly** /ə'ledʒɪdliʸ/ *adv* **allegation** /‚ælɪ'geʸʃən/ *n fml* unproved statement

al·le·giance /ə'liʸdʒəns/ *n* [U] loyalty to a leader, country, etc.

al·le·go·ry /'ælə‚goriʸ, -‚goʷriʸ/ *n* [C;U] (style of) story, poem, etc., in which the characters represent ideas and qualities

al·ler·gy /'ælərdʒiʸ/ *n* condition of being made ill by a particular food, drug, etc. –**gic** /ə'lɜrdʒɪk/ *adj*

al·le·vi·ate /ə'liʸviʸ‚eʸt/ *vt* make (pain, etc.) less –**ation** /ə‚liʸviʸ-'eʸʃən/ *n* [U]

al·ley /'æliʸ/ *n* **1** narrow street or path between larger streets **2** track along which balls are rolled in BOWLING **up/down one's alley** suitable

al·li·ance /ə'laɪəns/ *n* **1** [C] close agreement or connection made between countries, etc., for a shared purpose **2** [U] act of forming an alliance or state of being in an alliance

al·li·ga·tor /'ælə‚geʸtər/ *n* animal like a CROCODILE

all-night /'· ·/ *adj* open all night: *an all-night pharmacy*

al·lo·cate /'ælə‚keʸt/ *vt* give as a share –**cation** /‚ælə'keʸʃən/ *n* [C;U]

al·lot /ə'lɑt/ *vt* **-tt-** allocate

al·lot·ment /ə'lɑtmənt/ *n* [C;U] allocation

al·low /ə'laʊ/ *vt* **1** let (someone) do something without opposing them; let (something) be done; permit: *They allowed him to come.* **2** provide (esp. money or time) ~**able** *adj* ~**ance** *n* **1** money provided regularly **2 make allowances** take something into consideration

  allow for *phr vt* take into consideration: *We must allow for the train being late.*

al·loy /'ælɔɪ/ *n* mixture of metals

all right /ˌ·ˈ·/ adj, adv **1** safe, unharmed, or healthy **2** acceptable **3** I/we agree **4** infml beyond doubt **5** That's/It's all right (used as a reply when someone thanks you or says they are sorry for something they have done)

all-round /ˌ·ˈ·◄/ adj having ability in many things, esp. in various sports ~ er /ˌ·ˈ·◄/ n

al·lude /əˈluːd/ v **allude to** phr vt fml speak about indirectly **allusion** /əˈluːʒən/ n [C;U]

al·lure /əˈlʊər/ vt attract or charm by the offer of something pleasant: an alluring smile

al·ly /ˈælaɪ, əˈlaɪ/ n person, country, etc., that helps one or agrees to help ♦ /əˈlaɪ, ˈælaɪ/ vt **1** unite by agreement, marriage, etc. **2** allied (to) related or connected (to)

al·ma ma·ter /ˌælmə ˈmɑːtər, ˌæl-/ n school, college, etc., which one attended

al·ma·nac /ˈɔːlmənæk/ n book giving general information

al·might·y /ɔːlˈmaɪti/ adj very great

al·mond /ˈɑːmənd, ˈæm-/ n kind of nut

al·most /ˈɔːlmoʊst, ɔːlˈmoʊst/ adv very nearly: almost everyone | almost finished

alms /ɑːmz/ n [P] money, food, clothes, etc., given to poor people

a·loft /əˈlɒft/ adv fml high up

a·lone /əˈloʊn/ adv, adj **1** without others: He lives alone. **2** only: You alone can do it. **3** leave/let alone **a** leave untouched or unchanged **b** allow to be by oneself

a·long /əˈlɒŋ/ adv **1** forward; on: Come along! **2** with others: Bring your sister along (with you). ♦ prep **1** from end to end of: walk along the road **2** somewhere on the length of

a·long·side /əˌlɒŋˈsaɪd/ adv, prep close to the side (of)

a·loof /əˈluːf/ adj, adv distant in feeling; not friendly ~ ness n [U]

a·loud /əˈlaʊd/ adv in a voice that can be heard: to read aloud

al·pha·bet /ˈælfəbet/ letters used in writing ~ ical /ˌælfəˈbetɪkəl◄/ adj in the order of the alphabet

al·read·y /ɔːlˈrediy/ adv **1** by or before an expected time: Are you leaving already? **2** before now: I've seen the film twice already.

al·right /ɔːlˈraɪt/ adj, adv ALL RIGHT

al·so /ˈɔːlsoʊ/ adv **1** as well; besides **2** not only ... but also ... both ... and ...

also-ran /ˈ··ˌ·/ n person who has failed to win at a sport or in an election

al·tar /ˈɔːltər/ n table used in a religious ceremony

al·ter /ˈɔːltər/ vi/t make or become different ~ ation /ˌɔːltəˈreɪʃən/ n [C;U]

al·ter·ca·tion /ˌɔːltərˈkeɪʃən/ n [C;U] noisy argument or quarrel

al·ter e·go /ˌɔːltər ˈiːgoʊ/ n alter egos **1** very close and trusted friend **2** part of one's personality which people do not usually see

al·ter·nate¹ /ˈɔːltərnɪt/ adj (of two things) happening in turns; first one and then the other: He works on alternate days. ~ ly adv

al·ter·nate² /ˈɔːltərneɪt/ vi/t happen or follow by turns –nation /ˌɔːltərˈneɪʃən/ n [C;U]

al·ter·na·tive /ɔːlˈtɜːrnətɪv/ adj **1** to be done or used instead; other **2** different from what is usual or traditional (TRADITION): alternative medicine **3** not based on or not accepting the established standards of ordinary society: alternative theater ♦ n [(to)] something that can be used or done instead ~ ly adv

al·though /ɔːlˈðoʊ/ conj though

al·ti·tude /ˈæltɪtuːd, -ˌtjuːd/ n height above sea level

al·to /ˈæltoʊ/ n –tos (person with) a singing voice between SOPRANO and TENOR

al·to·geth·er¹ /ˌɔːltəˈgeðər◄/ adv **1** completely; altogether different **2** considering everything together: Altogether, it was a good trip.

altogether² n in the altogether NUDE

al·tru·is·m /ˈæltruːˌɪzəm/ n [U] unselfishness –ist n –istic /ˌæltruːˈɪstɪk◄/ adj

a·lu·min·um /əˈluːmɪnəm/ n [U] light silver-white metal

aluminum foil /·ˌ···ˈ·/ n [U] very thin bendable sheet of shiny metal

al·ways /ˈɔːlweɪz, -wiːz, -wɪz/ adv **1** at all times: The sun always rises in the east. **2** for ever: I'll always love you. **3** very often and annoyingly: He's always complaining.

am /m, əm; strong æm/ v 1st person sing. present tense of BE

am, AM /ˌeɪ ˈem/ abbrev. for **1** ante meridiem = (Latin) before noon (used after numbers expressing time) **2** amplitude modulation, the part of the radio band used by most stations: We broadcast on 670 AM and 98.2 FM.

a·mal·gam /əˈmælgəm/ n mixture or combination

a·mal·gam·ate /əˈmælgəˌmeɪt/ vi/t (of businesses, etc.) unite; combine –ation /əˌmælgəˈmeɪʃən/ n [C;U]

a·mass /əˈmæs/ vt gather or collect in great amounts

am·a·teur /ˈæmətʃər, -ˌtʃʊər, -tɜːr/ n person who does something for enjoyment and without being paid: *amateur actors* | *amateur sport* ~ **ish** *adj* lacking skill

a·maze /ə'meʸz/ *vt* fill with great surprise: *I was amazed to hear the news.* | *An amazing film* ~ **ment** [U] **amazingly** *adv*

am·a·zon /'æməzən, -zən/ *n* tall, strong woman

am·bas·sa·dor /æm'bæsədər/ *n* official of high rank representing his/her own country in another country

am·bas·sa·dress /æm'bæsədrɪs/ *n* 1 female ambassador 2 wife of an ambassador

am·ber /'æmbər/ *n* [U] (yellow color of) a hard substance used for jewels

am·bi·dex·trous /ˌæmbɪ'dekstrəs◄/ *adj* able to use both hands equally well

am·bi·ence /'æmbiʸəns, ˌæmbiʸ-'ɑns/ *n* feeling of a place; ATMOS-PHERE (3)

am·big·u·ous /æm'bɪgyuʷəs/ *adj* having more than one meaning; not clear **-uity** /ˌæmbə'gyuʷəţiʸ/ *n* [C;U]

am·bi·tion /æm'bɪʃən/ *n* 1 [U] strong desire for success 2 [C] whatever is desired in this way: *to achieve one's ambitions* **-tious** *adj* **-tiously** *adv*

am·biv·a·lent /æm'bɪvələnt/ *adj* having opposing feelings about something **-lence** / əns/ *n*

am·ble /'æmbəl/ *vi* walk at an easy gentle rate

am·bu·lance /'æmbyələns/ *n* motor vehicle for carrying sick people

am·bush /'æmbʊʃ/ *n* [C;U] surprise attack from a place of hiding **ambush** *vt*

a·me·lio·rate /ə'miʸlyəˌreʸt/ *vt fml* improve **-ration** /əˌmiʸlyə'reʸʃən/ *n* [U]

a·men /eʸ'men, ˌɑ-/ *interj* (at the end of a prayer) may this be true

a·me·na·ble /ə'miʸnəbəl, ə'me-/ *adj* willing to be influenced

a·mend /ə'mend/ *vt* change and improve

a·mend·ment /ə'mendmənt/ *n* agreed change to an existing law, esp. the US Constitution

a·mends /ə'mendz/ *n* [P] **make amends** pay for harm or damage done

a·me·ni·ty /ə'menəţiʸ, ə'miʸ-/ *n* something (e.g. a park or swimming pool) that makes life pleasant

am·e·thyst /'æməθɪst/ *n* [C;U] (purple color of) a stone used in jewelry

a·mi·a·ble /'eʸmiʸəbəl/ *adj* good tempered; friendly **-bly** *adv*

am·i·ca·ble /'æmɪkəbəl/ *adj* done in

a friendly way: *reach an amicable agreement* **-bly** *adv*

a·mid /ə'mɪd/ also **amidst** /ə'mɪdst/ — *prep fml* among

a·miss /ə'mɪs/ *adj, adv fml* 1 wrong(ly) or imperfect(ly) 2 **take something amiss** be offended

am·i·ty /'æməţiʸ/ *n* [U] *fml* friendship

am·mo·ni·a /ə'moʷnyə/ *n* [U] 1 gas with a strong smell, used in explosives and chemicals 2 liquid used in house cleaning

am·mu·ni·tion /ˌæmyə'nɪʃən/ *n* [U] bullets, bombs, etc.

am·ne·si·a /æm'niʸʒə/ *n* [U] loss of memory

am·nes·ty /'æmnəstiʸ/ *n* general act of forgiveness, esp. by a state to people guilty of political offences

a·moe·ba, ameba /ə'miʸbə/ *n* **-bas** or **-bae** /-biʸ/ living creature that consists of only one cell **-bic** *adj*

a·mok /ə'mʌk, ə'mɑk/ also **amuck** — *adv* **run amok** run wildly about trying to kill people

a·mong /ə'mʌŋ/ also **amongst** /ə'mʌŋst/ — *prep* 1 in the middle of: *a house among the trees* 2 in the group of; one of: *He's among the best of our students.* | *They talked about it among themselves.* (= together) 3 to each of (more than 2): *Divide it among the 5 of you.*

a·mor·al /eʸ'mɔrəl, eʸ'mɑrəl, æ-/ *adj* having no understanding of right or wrong

am·o·rous /'æmərəs/ *adj* feeling or expressing love, esp. sexual love ~ **ly** *adv*

a·mor·phous /ə'mɔrfəs/ *adj* having no fixed form or shape

a·mount¹ /ə'maʊnt/ *n* quantity; total: *large amounts of money*

amount² *v* **amount to** *phr vt* be equal to

amp /æmp/ also **ampere** /'æmpɪər/ — *n* standard measure of the quantity of electricity

am·phet·a·mine /æm'feţəˌmiʸn, -mɪn/ *n* [C;U] drug used esp. illegally, by people wanting excitement

am·phib·i·an /æm'fɪbiʸən/ *n* animal, such as a FROG, that can live both on land and in water **-ious** *adj*

am·phi·the·a·ter /'æmfəˌθiʸəţər/ *n* open building with rows of seats round a central space

am·ple /'æmpəl/ *adj* enough; plenty **amply** *adv*

am·pli·fy /'æmpləˌfaɪ/ *vi/t fml* 1 explain in more detail 2 make (esp. sound) stronger **-fier** *n* instrument for making sound louder **-fication** /ˌæmpləfə'keʸʃən/ *n* [U]

am·pu·tate /'æmpyəˌteʸt/ *vi/t* cut off (part of the body) for medical reasons –**tation** /ˌæmpyəˈteʸʃən/ n [C;U]

a·muck /əˈmʌk/ adv AMOK

am·u·let /ˈæmyələt/ n object worn to protect one against evil, bad luck, etc.

a·muse /əˈmyuʷz/ vt **1** cause to laugh: an amusing story **2** cause to spend time pleasantly ~**ment** n **1** [U] state of being amused **2** [C] something that passes the time pleasantly

amusement park /·ˈ··· ˌ·/ n park with amusements and machines to ride on

an /ən; strong æn/ indefinite article, determiner (used before a vowel sound) a: an elephant

a·nach·ro·nis·m /əˈnækrəˌnizəm/ n person, thing, or idea placed in the wrong period of time: To say 'Julius Caesar looked at his watch' is an anachronism. –**nistic** /əˌnækrəˈnɪstɪk◄/ adj

an·a·con·da /ˌænəˈkɑndə/ n large S American snake

an·a·gram /ˈænəˌgræm/ n word made by changing the order of the letters in another word: 'Silent' is an anagram of 'listen'.

a·nal /ˈeʸnl/ adj of, concerning the ANUS

an·al·ge·sic /ˌænlˈdʒiʸzɪk, -sɪk/ n, adj (substance) which makes one unable to feel pain

a·nal·o·gy /əˈnælədʒiʸ/ n **1** [C] degree of likeness **2** [U] explaining one thing by comparing it to something else –**gous** /-gəs/ adj like or alike in some ways

a·nal·y·sis /əˈnæləsɪs/ n **1** [C;U] examination of something; analyzing **2** [U] PSYCHOANALYSIS **analyst** /ˈænl-ɪst/ n **analytic** /ˌænlˈɪtɪk◄/ adj

an·a·lyze /ˈænlˌaɪz/ vt examine carefully, often by dividing something into parts

an·ar·chy /ˈænərkiʸ/ n [U] **1** absence of government **2** social disorder –**chism** n [U] –**chist** n person who wishes for this –**chic** /æˈnɑrkɪk/ adj

a·nath·e·ma /əˈnæθəmə/ n something hated

a·nat·o·my /əˈnætəmiʸ/ n **1** [U] scientific study of living bodies **2** [C] way a living thing works: (fig.) the anatomy of modern society –**mical** /ˌænəˈtɑmɪkəl◄/ adj

an·ces·tor /ˈænˌsestər/ n person from whom one is descended –**tral** /ænˈsestrəl/ adj

an·ces·try /ˈænˌsestriʸ/ n [C;U] all one's ancestors

an·chor /ˈæŋkər/ n **1** piece of heavy metal for lowering into the water to stop a ship from moving **2** some-

thing that makes one feel safe ♦ v **1** vi lower the anchor **2** vt fix firmly in position ~**age** n place where ships may anchor **3** anchorperson

an·chor·per·son /ˈæŋkərˌpɜrsən/ also –**man** /-ˌmæn/ masc., –**woman** /-ˌwʊmən/ fem. —n broadcaster usu. on television, in charge of a news broadcast, to connect one part of the broadcast with the next

an·cho·vy /ˈænˌtʃoʷviʸ, -tʃə-, ænˈtʃoʷviʸ/ n –**vies** or –**vy** small fish with a strong taste

an·cient /ˈeʸnʃənt, ˈeʸntʃənt/ adj **1** of times long ago: ancient Rome **2** very old

an·cil·la·ry /ˈænsəˌleriʸ/ adj providing additional help

and /ənd, ən; strong ænd/ ænd/ conj **1** (joining 2 things) as well as: John and Sally | We're cold and hungry. **2** then; therefore: Water the seeds and they will grow. **3** (showing that something continues without stopping): We ran and ran. **4** (used instead of to after come, go, try): Try and open it.

an·droid /ˈændrɔɪd/ n (in stories) ROBOT in human form

an·ec·dote /ˈænɪkˌdoʷt/ n short interesting story that is true –**dotal** /ˌænɪkˈdoʷtl/ adj containing or telling anecdotes

a·ne·mi·a /əˈniʸmiʸə/ n [U] also anaemia lack of enough red blood cells –**mic** adj

an·es·the·sia, anae- /ˌænəsˈθiʸʒə/ n [U] state of being unable to feel pain, etc.

an·es·thet·ic /ˌænəsˈθetɪk/ n [C;U] substance that stops one from feeling pain, either in a part of the body (**a local anesthetic**) or in the whole body, making one unconscious (**a general anesthetic**) –**thetist** /əˈnesˌθɪtɪst/ n –**thetize** vt

a·new /əˈnuʷ, əˈnyuʷ/ adv again

an·gel /ˈeʸndʒəl/ n **1** messenger of God **2** very kind and beautiful person ~**ic** /ænˈdʒelɪk/ adj

an·ger /ˈæŋgər/ n [U] fierce displeasure and annoyance ♦ vt make angry

an·gle[1] /ˈæŋgəl/ n **1** space between 2 lines that meet, measured in degrees **2** corner **3** point of view **4** **at an angle** not upright or straight ♦ vt **1** turn or move at an angle **2** represent (something) from a particular point of view

angle[2] vi catch fish with a hook and line **angler** n someone who fishes for enjoyment

angle for phr vt try to get, by tricks or indirect questions: to angle for an invitation

an·gli·cize /ˈæŋgləˌsaɪz/ vt make English

an·gry /ˈæŋgriʸ/ adj 1 full of anger 2 (of the sky or clouds) stormy **angrily** adv

angst /æŋst/ n [U] anxiety and anguish caused esp. by considering the sad state of the world

an·guish /ˈæŋgwɪʃ/ n [U] great suffering, esp. of the mind ~**ed** adj

an·gu·lar /ˈæŋgyələr/ adj 1 having sharp corners 2 (of a person) thin

an·i·mal /ˈænəməl/ n 1 living creature that is not a plant 2 all these except human beings 3 MAMMAL 4 person considered as lacking a mind and behaving like a wild nonhuman creature ♦ adj 1 of animals 2 of the body

an·i·mate¹ /ˈænəmɪt/ adj alive

an·i·mate² /ˈænəˌmeʸt/ vt give life or excitement to —**mated** adj cheerful and excited: an animated discussion —**mation** /ˌænəˈmeʸʃən/ n [U] 1 cheerful excitement 2 process of making CARTOONs

an·i·mis·m /ˈænəmɪzəm/ n [U] religion according to which animals, plants, etc., are believed to have souls

an·i·mos·i·ty /ˌænəˈmɒsətiʸ/ n [C;U] powerful hatred

an·kle /ˈæŋkəl/ n thin part of the leg, above the foot

an·nals /ˈænlz/ n [P] history or record of events, etc., produced every year: It will go down in the annals (= history) of modern science.

an·nex /ˈæneks, ˈænɪks/ n building added to a larger one ♦ **annex** /əˈneks, ˈæneks/ vt take control of (land, etc.) ~**ation** /ˌænekˈseʸʃən/ n [C;U]

an·ni·hi·late /əˈnaɪəˌleʸt/ vt destroy completely —**lation** /əˌnaɪəˈleʸʃən/ n [U]

an·ni·ver·sa·ry /ˌænəˈvɜrsəriʸ/ n day that is an exact number of years after something happened

an·no·tate /ˈænəˌteʸt, ˈænoʷ-/ vt fml add notes to (a book) —**tation** /ˌænəˈteʸʃən/ n

an·nounce /əˈnaʊns/ vt state loudly or publicly: He announced the winner of the competition. ~**ment** n public statement

an·nounc·er /əˈnaʊnsər/ n person who reads the news, etc., on radio or television

an·noy /əˈnɔɪ/ vt make a little angry; cause trouble to: an annoying delay ~**ance** n [C;U]

an·nu·al¹ /ˈænyuʷəl/ adj 1 happening once every year 2 for one year: my annual salary ~**ly** adv

annual² n 1 plant that lives for one year 2 book produced each year with the same name but new contents

an·nu·i·ty /əˈnuʷətiʸ, əˈnyuʷ-/ n fixed sum of money paid each year to someone

an·nul /əˈnʌl/ vt -ll- cause (a marriage, etc.) to stop existing ~**ment** n [C;U]

an·ode /ˈænoʷd/ n part of an electrical instrument which collects ELECTRONs

an·o·dyne /ˈænəˌdaɪn/ adj unlikely to offend or annoy anyone

a·noint /əˈnɔɪnt/ vt put oil on, esp. in a ceremony

a·nom·a·ly /əˈnɒməliʸ/ n fml something different from the usual type: A cat with no tail is an anomaly. -**lous** adj

a·non¹ /əˈnɒn/ adv lit soon

anon² abbrev. for ANONYMOUS

a·non·y·mous /əˈnɒnəməs/ adj without a name; not giving the name: an anonymous letter —**mity** /ˌænəˈnɪmətiʸ/ n [U]

an·o·rex·i·a /ˌænəˈreksiʸə/ n [U] dangerous condition in which there is a loss of desire to eat -**ic** adj

an·oth·er /əˈnʌðər/ determiner, pron 1 one more: Have another drink. 2 a different one: I'll do it another time. 3 more; in addition: It'll cost you another $20. 4 **one another** each other

an·swer¹ /ˈænsər/ n 1 what is said or written when someone asks a question or sends a letter; reply 2 something expected by thinking: I'm getting fat — the answer is to eat less.

answer² v 1 vi/t give an answer (to): She answered with a smile. 2 vi/t attend or act in reply to (the telephone ringing, a knock at the door, etc.): Answer the phone, will you! | The dog answers to the name of Fred. 3 vi/t be as described in: He answers to the description you gave. 4 vt be satisfactory for ~**able** adj 1 able to be answered 2 responsible: The school is answerable to your parents for your safety.

answer back phr vi/t reply rudely (to)

answer for phr vt 1 be responsible for 2 pay or suffer for

ant /ænt/ n insect living on the ground and famous for hard work

an·tag·o·nize /ænˈtægəˌnaɪz/ vt make into an enemy —**nism** n [U] hatred; opposition -**nist** n opponent

Ant·arc·tic /æntˈɑrktɪk, -ˈɑrtɪk/ adj, n (of or concerning) the very cold most southern part of the world

an·te·bel·lum /ˌæntiʸˈbeləm/ adj before the American CIVIL WAR

an·te·ced·ents /ˌæntəˈsiʸdənts/ n [P] fml past family or past history

an·te·cham·ber /ˈæntiˌtʃeʸmbər/

also **anteroom** — n small room leading to a larger one

an·te·di·lu·vian /ˌæntɪdəˈluᵛviʸən/ adj very old-fashioned

an·te·lope /ˈæntəˌloᵘp/ n -lopes or -lope graceful animal like a deer

an·ten·na /ænˈtenə/ n 1 pl. -nae /-niʸ/ insect's FEELER 2 AERIAL¹

an·them /ˈænθəm/ n religious or national song of praise

an·thol·o·gy /ænˈθaɪədʒiʸ/ n collection of poems or other writings

an·thro·poid /ˈænθrəˌpɔɪd/ adj like a person

an·thro·pol·o·gy /ˌænθrəˈpaɪədʒiʸ/ n scientific study of the human race –gist /n

an·thro·po·mor·phic /ˌænθrəpə-ˈmɔrfɪk/ adj regarding a god, animal, etc., as having human qualities

an·ti·bi·ot·ic /ˌæntɪbaɪˈaɪtɪk, ˌæntaɪ-/ n medical substance, such as PENICILLIN, that can kill harmful bacteria in the body

an·ti·bod·y /ˈæntɪˌbadiʸ/ n substance produced in the body which fights disease

an·tic·i·pate /ænˈtɪsəˌpeʸt/ vt 1 expect: We anticipate trouble. 2 do something before (someone else) 3 guess (what will happen) and act as necessary –pation /ænˌtɪsəˈpeʸʃən/ n [U]

an·ti·cli·max /ˌæntɪˈklaɪmæks/ n unexciting end to something exciting

an·tics /ˈæntɪks/ n [P] strange, amusing movements or behavior

an·ti·dote /ˈæntɪˌdoᵘt/ n something that prevents the effects of a poison or disease

an·ti·freeze /ˈæntɪˌfriʸz/ n [U] chemical put in water to stop it freezing, esp. in car engines

an·ti·nu·cle·ar /ˌæntɪʸˈnuᵘkliʸər, -ˈnyuᵘ-, ˌæntaɪ-/ adj opposing the use of NUCLEAR power or weapons: an antinuclear demonstration

an·tip·a·thy /ænˈtɪpəθiʸ/ n [C;U] fixed strong dislike; hatred

an·ti·quat·ed /ˈæntɪˌkweʸtɪd/ adj old-fashioned

an·tique /ænˈtiʸk/ adj old and therefore valuable ♦ n valuable old object

an·tiq·ui·ty /ænˈtɪkwəṭiʸ/ n 1 [U] great age 2 [U] ancient times 3 [C] something remaining from ancient times

an·ti·Sem·i·tism /ˌæntiʸ ˈsemə-ˌtɪzəm, ˌæntaɪ-/ n hatred of Jews –Semitic /-səˈmɪtɪk◂, ˌæntaɪ-/ adj

an·ti·sep·tic /ˌæntəˈsɛptɪk◂/ n, adj (chemical substance) preventing disease by killing bacteria

an·ti·sla·ve·ry /ˌæntiʸˈsleʸvəriʸ, ˌæntaɪ-/ n opposition to slavery

an·ti·so·cial /ˌæntiʸˈsoᵘʃəl◂, ˌæntaɪ-/ adj 1 harmful to society 2 not liking to mix with people

an·tith·e·sis /ænˈtɪθəsɪs/ n -ses /-siʸz/ fml direct opposite

an·ti·trust /ˌæntɪˈtrʌst, ˌæntaɪ-/ adj (of laws) opposing practices that limit competition

ant·ler /ˈæntlər/ n horn of a deer

an·to·nym /ˈæntəˌnɪm/ n word opposite in meaning to another word

ant·sy /ˈæntsiʸ/ adj infml nervous

a·nus /ˈeʸnəs/ n hole through which solid waste leaves the bowels

an·vil /ˈænvɪl/ n iron block on which metals are hammered to the shape wanted

anx·i·e·ty /æŋˈzaɪəṭiʸ/ n 1 [C;U] fear and worry 2 [U] strong wish: anxiety to please him

anx·ious /ˈæŋkʃəs, ˈænʃəs/ adj 1 worried and frightened 2 causing worry 3 wishing strongly: anxious to please them ~ly adv

an·y /ˈɛniʸ/ determiner, pron 1 no matter which: Take any you like. 2 some; even the smallest number or amount: Are there any letters for me? 3 in any case also at any rate — a whatever this means b besides ♦ adv at all: I can't stay any longer.

an·y·bod·y /ˈɛniʸˌbadiʸ, -ˌbʌdiʸ, -badiʸ/ pron anyone

an·y·how /ˈɛniʸˌhaᵘ/ adv 1 carelessly 2 in spite of everything

an·y·one /ˈɛniʸˌwʌn, -wən/ pron 1 all people; no matter who: Anyone can cook. 2 even one person: Is anyone listening?

an·y·place /ˈɛniʸˌpleʸs/ adv infml for ANYWHERE

an·y·thing /ˈɛniʸˌθɪŋ/ pron 1 any object, act, event, etc.; no matter what: He'll do anything for a quiet life. 2 even one thing: Can you see anything? 3 anything but not at all 4 anything like at all like 5 as easy as anything very easy

an·y·way /ˈɛniʸˌweʸ/ adv in spite of everything; anyhow

an·y·where /ˈɛniʸˌhwɛər, -ˌwɛər/ adv 1 at or to any place 2 anywhere near at all near or nearly

a·or·ta /eʸˈɔrtə/ n largest ARTERY in the body

a·pace /əˈpeʸs/ adv quickly

a·part /əˈpɑrt/ adv 1 distant; separated: towns 3 miles apart 2 into parts: to take a clock apart 3 apart from: a except for b as well as 4 tell/know apart be able to see the difference between

a·part·heid /əˈpɑrtaɪt, -teʸt, -taɪd/ n [U] (in South Africa) the system established by government of keeping different races separate

a·part·ment /əˈpɑrtmənt/ n room or

set of rooms on one floor of a building

apartment house /·'·· ,·/ n building containing a number of apartments

ap·a·thy /'æpəθi/ n [U] lack of interest in things **–thetic** /,æpə'θet-ɪk◄/ adj

ape /eɪp/ n large monkey with no tail ♦ vt copy (behavior) stupidly

a·per·i·tif /ə,perə'tiɪf, a–/ n alcoholic drink before a meal

ap·er·ture /'æpərtʃər, –ˌtʃʊər/ n hole; opening

a·pex /'eɪpeks/ n **–es** /'eɪpəsiɪz/ highest point: the apex of a triangle

aph·o·rism /'æfə,rɪzəm/ n short wise saying

aph·ro·dis·i·ac /,æfrə'dɪziɪ,æk/ n, adj (drug, etc.) causing sexual excitement

a·piece /ə'piɪs/ adv each: They cost 10c apiece.

a·plomb /ə'plam/ n [U] calm self-control

a·poc·a·lypse /ə'pakəlɪps/ n [U] (writing about) the end of the world **–lyptic** /ə,pakə'lɪptɪk◄/ adj telling of great future misfortunes

a·poc·ry·phal /ə'pakrəfəl/ adj (of a story) probably untrue

a·pol·o·get·ic /ə,palə'dʒetɪk◄/ adj making an apology **–ally** /–kliɪ/ adv

ap·o·lo·gi·a /,æpə'loʊdʒiɪə, –dʒə/ n formal defense or explanation

a·pol·o·gist /ə'palə,dʒɪst/ n person who strongly supports a particular belief and can give arguments in defense of it

a·pol·o·gize /ə'palə,dʒaɪz/ vi say one is sorry for a fault **–gy** n statement of sorrow for a fault, for causing trouble, etc.

ap·o·plex·y /'æpə,pleksiɪ/ n [U] sudden loss of ability to move, feel, think etc.; STROKE[1] (5) **–plectic** /,æpə'plektɪk◄/ adj **1** of or concerning apoplexy **2** violently excited and angry

a·pos·tle /ə'pasəl/ n **1** one of the 12 first followers of Christ **2** leader of a new faith

a·pos·tro·phe /ə'pastrəfiɪ/ n the sign ('), as in I'm

a·poth·e·o·sis /ə,paθiɪ'oʊsɪs, ,æpə-'θiɪəsɪs/ n **–ses** /–siɪz/ **1** highest possible honor and glory **2** perfect example

ap·pall /ə'pɔl/ vt shock deeply: We were appalled to hear the news. **~ing** adj **1** shocking **2** of very bad quality **~ingly** adv: an appallingly bad driver

ap·pa·ra·tus /,æpə'rætəs, –'reɪtəs/ n [C;U] set of instruments, tools, etc. needed for a purpose

ap·par·el /ə'pærəl/ n [U] fml clothes

ap·par·ent /ə'pærənt, ə'peər–/ adj **1** easily seen: The reason became apparent. **2** not necessarily real; seeming: her apparent lack of concern **~ly** adv it seems that

ap·pa·ri·tion /,æpə'rɪʃən/ n GHOST

ap·peal /ə'piɪl/ n **1** [C;U] strong request for something: an appeal for forgiveness **2** [U] attraction; interest: He doesn't have much sex appeal. **3** [C;U] formal request (in law, sports) for a new decision ♦ vi **1** make a strong request: to appeal for money **2** please; attract: Does the job appeal to you? **3** ask for a new decision **~ing** adj attractive

ap·pear /ə'pɪər/ vi **1** come into sight: Spots appeared on my skin. | They finally appeared (= arrived) at 9:00. **2** come in view of the public: Her new book appears next month. | He's appearing (= performing) at Caesar's Palace. **3** seem: He appears to be angry. **4** be present officially, as in a court of law **~ance** n [C;U] **1** (an example of) the act of appearing **2** way a person or thing looks: He changed his appearance by growing a beard. **3** put in/make an appearance (at) attend (a meeting, party, etc.), esp. for a short time only

ap·pease /ə'piɪz/ vt satisfy, esp. by agreeing to demands **~ment** n [C;U]

ap·pel·la·tion /,æpə'leɪʃən/ n fml name; title

ap·pend /ə'pend/ vt fml add (esp. something written onto the end of a letter) **~age** n something added to, or hanging from, something else

ap·pen·di·ci·tis /ə,pendə'saɪtɪs/ n [U] disease of the appendix (1)

ap·pen·dix /ə'pendɪks/ n **–dixes** or **–dices** /–dəsiɪz/ **1** small organ leading off the bowel **2** something added at the end of a book

ap·per·tain /,æpər'teɪn/ v **appertain to** phr vt fml belong to

ap·pe·tite /'æpə,taɪt/ n [C;U] desire, esp. for food

ap·pe·tiz·er /'æpə,taɪzər/ n something eaten to increase the appetite **–tizing** adj causing appetite: appetizing smells

ap·plaud /ə'plɔd/ vi/t **1** praise by striking one's hands together; CLAP **2** approve strongly **applause** /ə'plɔz/ n [U] loud praise

ap·ple /'æpəl/ n kind of hard round juicy fruit – see also ADAM'S APPLE

ap·pli·ance /ə'plaɪəns/ n apparatus; machine

ap·pli·ca·ble /'æplɪkəbəl, ə'plɪkə-bəl/ adj having an effect; related: The rule is applicable only to US citizens.

ap·pli·cant /'æplɪkənt/ n person who applies for a job, etc.

ap·pli·ca·tion /ˌæplɪˈkeɪʃən/ n 1 [C;U] request: *to write applications for jobs* 2 [U] act of putting something to use 3 [C] particular practical use: *the industrial applications of this discovery* 4 [C;U] putting something on a surface 5 [U] careful effort

ap·ply /əˈplaɪ/ v 1 vt request officially: *apply for a job* 2 vt use for a purpose: *apply the brakes* 3 vt put onto a surface: *apply ointment to your skin* 4 vi/t give or have an effect: *Does the rule apply to me?* 5 vt cause to work hard: *apply oneself to the task* **applied** adj practical: *applied physics*

ap·point /əˈpɔɪnt/ vt 1 choose for a job 2 fml fix; decide: *the appointed time* **~ment** n [C;U] (arrangement for) a meeting

ap·por·tion /əˈpɔrʃən, əˈpoʷr-/ vt divide and share out

ap·po·site /ˈæpəzɪt/ adj fml exactly suitable

ap·praise /əˈpreɪz/ vt fml judge the value of **appraisal** n

ap·pre·cia·ble /əˈpriːʃəbəl, -ʃiʲə-/ adj noticeable: *an appreciable difference* **~bly** adv

ap·pre·ci·ate /əˈpriːʃiʲˌeɪt/ v 1 vt be thankful for 2 vt understand and enjoy the good qualities of: *She appreciates good wine.* 3 vt understand fully: *I appreciate your difficulties.* 4 vi (of property) increase in value **~ciative** /-ʃətɪv, -ʃiʲə-/ adj: *an appreciative audience* **~ciation** /əˌpriːʃiʲˈeɪʃən/ n [C;U]

ap·pre·hend /ˌæprɪˈhend/ vt fml ARREST

ap·pre·hen·sion /ˌæprɪˈhenʃən, -tʃən/ n [U] anxiety; fear **~sive** /-sɪv/ adj worried

ap·pren·tice /əˈprentɪs/ n person learning a skilled trade ♦ vt [(to)] send as an apprentice: *apprenticed to an electrician* **~ship** n [C;U]

ap·prise /əˈpraɪz/ vt fml tell or inform

ap·proach[1] /əˈproʷtʃ/ v 1 vi/t come near 2 vt make an offer or request to: *approach him about borrowing the money* 3 vt begin to consider or deal with

approach[2] n 1 act of approaching: *the approach of winter* 2 way of getting in 3 method of doing something 4 speaking to someone for the first time **~able** adj easy to speak to or deal with

ap·pro·pri·ate[1] /əˈproʷpriʲɪt/ adj correct; suitable **~ly** adv

ap·pro·pri·ate[2] /əˈproʷpriʲˌeɪt/ vt 1 set aside (money) for a purpose 2 take for oneself **~ation** /əˌproʷpriʲˈeɪʃən/ n [C;U]

ap·prov·al /əˈpruʷvəl/ n [U] 1 favorable opinion 2 official permission 3 **on approval** (of goods from a store) to be returned without payment if unsatisfactory

ap·prove /əˈpruʷv/ v 1 vt [(of)] have a favorable opinion: *I don't approve of smoking.* 2 vt agree officially to **approvingly** adv

ap·prox·i·mate /əˈprɑksəmɪt/ adj nearly correct but not exact **~ly** adv: *approximately 300* ♦ /-ˌmeɪt/ vi come near **—mation** /əˌprɑksəˈmeɪ- ʃən/ n [C;U]

a·pri·cot /ˈæprɪˌkɑt, ˈeɪ-/ n 1 [C] round orange or yellow fruit with a pit 2 [U] color of this fruit

A·pril /ˈeɪprəl/ n 1 the 4th month of the year 2 **April fool** /ˌ·· ˈ·/ n (person who has been deceived or made fun of by) a trick played on April 1st

a·pron /ˈeɪprən, ˈeɪprɪn/ n garment worn to protect the front of one's clothes

apt /æpt/ adj 1 likely: *apt to slip* 2 exactly suitable: *an apt remark* 3 quick to learn **~ly** adv **~ness** n [U]

ap·ti·tude /ˈæptəˌtuʷd, -ˌtyuʷd/ n [C;U] natural ability

aq·ua·lung /ˈækwəˌlʌŋ/ n apparatus for breathing under water

aq·ua·ma·rine /ˌækwəməˈriʷn◂/ n 1 [C] glass-like stone used for jewelry 2 [U] its blue-green color

a·quar·i·um /əˈkweəriʲəm/ n **—iums** or **—ia** /-iʲə/ glass container for live fish

a·quat·ic /əˈkwætɪk, əˈkwɑtɪk/ adj living or happening in water

aq·ue·duct /ˈækwəˌdʌkt/ n bridge that carries water across a valley

Ar·a·bic /ˈærəbɪk/ n main language of North Africa and the Middle East ♦ adj: *The signs 1, 2, 3, etc., are* **Arabic numerals.**

ar·a·ble /ˈærəbəl/ adj (of land) used for growing crops

ar·bi·ter /ˈɑrbətər/ n someone who is in a position to make influential judgments or to settle an argument

ar·bi·trage /ˈɑrbəˌtrɑʒ/ n [U] process of buying something (esp. a CUR- RENCY or COMMODITY) in one place and selling it at another place at the same time in order to profit from differences in price between the two places

ar·bi·tra·ry /ˈɑrbəˌtreriʲ/ adj 1 based on chance rather than reason 2 typical of uncontrolled power **—rily** /ˌɑrbəˈtreriliʲ/ adv **—riness** /ˈɑrbəˌtreriʲnɪs/ n [U]

ar·bi·trate /ˈɑrbəˌtreɪt/ vi/t act as judge in an argument **—trator** n **—tration** /ˌɑrbəˈtreɪʃən/ n [U] settlement of an argument by the decision of a person or group chosen by both sides: *go to arbitration*

arc /ɑrk/ *n* part of the curve of a circle

ar·cade /ɑrˈkeʸd/ *n* passage or building covered by an arch or arches, esp. one containing amusements

ar·cane /ɑrˈkeʸn/ *adj* mysterious and secret

arch /ɑrtʃ/ *n* curved part over a doorway or under a bridge ♦ *vi/t* make an arch: *The cat arched her back.*

ar·chae·ol·o·gy /ˌɑrkiʸˈɑlədʒiʸ/ *n* [U] study of ancient remains **–gist** *n* **–gical** /ˌɑrkiʸəˈlɑdʒɪkəl/ *adj*

ar·cha·ic /ɑrˈkeʸɪk/ *adj* no longer used; old

arch·bish·op /ˌɑrtʃˈbɪʃəp◂/ *n* chief BISHOP

ar·cher /ˈɑrtʃər/ *n* person who shoots with a BOW² (1) **~y** *n* [U]

ar·che·type /ˈɑrkɪˌtaɪp/ *n* **1** original of which others are copies **2** perfect example **–typal, –typical** /ˌɑrkɪˈtɪpɪkəl◂/ *adj*

ar·chi·pel·a·go /ˌɑrkəˈpɛləˌgoʷ/ *n* area with many small islands

ar·chi·tect /ˈɑrkəˌtɛkt/ *n* person who plans buildings **~ure** /-ˌtɛktʃər/ *n* [U] art of building; way of building

ar·chives /ˈɑrkaɪvz/ *n* [P] **1** historical records **2** place where these are kept

Arc·tic /ˈɑrktɪk, ˈɑrṭɪk/ *n, adj* **1** (*cap.*) (of or concerning) the very cold most northern part of the world **2** very cold

ar·dent /ˈɑrdnt/ *adj* very eager **~ly** *adv*

ar·dor /ˈɑrdər/ *n* [C;U] *fml* strong excitement

ar·du·ous /ˈɑrdʒuʷəs/ *adj fml* needing effort; difficult **~ly** *adv*

are /ər; *strong* ɑr/ *v present tense pl. of* BE

ar·e·a /ˈɛəriʸə/ *n* **1** [C;U] size of a surface **2** [C] part of the world's surface: *a parking area behind the restaurant* **3** [C] subject of activity: *the area of language teaching*

a·re·na /əˈriʸnə/ *n* **1** enclosed space used for sports **2** place of competition: *the political arena*

aren't /ˈɑrənt/ *v short for*: **1** are not **2** (in questions) am not

ar·got /ˈɑrgət, -goʷ/ *n* [C;U] speech spoken and understood by only a small group of people

ar·gue /ˈɑrgyuʷ/ *v* **1** *vi* express disagreement; quarrel **2** *vi/t* give reasons for or against something **arguable** *adj* perhaps true, but not certain **arguably** *adv*: *Arguably, the criminal is a necessary member of society.*

ar·gu·ment /ˈɑrgyəmənt/ *n* **1** [C] quarrel **2** [C;U] reason given for or against; use of reason **~ative** /ˌɑrgyəˈmɛnṭəṭɪv/ *adj* quarrelsome

ar·id /ˈærɪd/ *adj* **1** (of land) very dry **2** uninteresting; dull

a·rise /əˈraɪz/ *vi* **arose** /əˈroʷz/, **arisen** /əˈrɪzən/ happen; appear

ar·is·toc·ra·cy /ˌærəˈstɑkrəsiʸ/ *n* government by people of the highest social class **–rat** /əˈrɪstəkræt/ *n* person of high birth **–ratic** /əˌrɪstəˈkræṭɪk◂/ *adj*

a·rith·me·tic /əˈrɪθməˌtɪk/ *n* calculation by numbers **~al** /ˌærɪθˈmɛṭɪkəl/ *adj*

ark /ɑrk/ *n* large ship, esp. the one described in the Bible

arm¹ /ɑrm/ *n* **1** upper limb **2** something shaped like this: *the arm of a chair* **3** part of a garment that covers the arm **4** part or division of the armed forces **5 arm and a leg** high price **6 arm in arm** (of 2 people) with arms joined **7 keep someone at arm's length** avoid being friendly with someone **8 with open arms** gladly and eagerly – see also ARMS

arm² *vi/t* supply with weapons: *the* **armed forces**

ar·ma·da /ɑrˈmɑdə, -ˈmeʸ-/ *n* collection of armed ships

Ar·ma·ged·don /ˌɑrməˈgɛdn/ *n* (esp. in the Bible) great battle or war causing terrible destruction and bringing the end of the world

ar·ma·ment /ˈɑrməmənt/ *n* **1** [C] weapons or other fighting equipment of an army, etc. **2** [U] act of preparing for war

arm·chair /ˈɑrmtʃɛər/ *n* chair with supports for the arms ♦ *adj* ready to give advice or pass judgment, but not taking an active part

armed forc·es /ˌ· ˈ··/ *n* [P] see FORCES

ar·mi·stice /ˈɑrməstɪs/ *n* agreement to stop fighting for a time

ar·mor /ˈɑrmər/ *n* [U] **1** protective covering for the body in battle **2** protective metal covering on military vehicles: *an* **armored car** **~y** *n* place where weapons are stored

arm·pit /ˈɑrmˌpɪt/ *n* hollow place under one's arm

arms /ɑrmz/ *n* [P] **1** weapons **2 lay down one's arms** stop fighting and yield **3 take up arms** get ready to fight with weapons **4 up in arms** very angry and ready to argue: *They're up in arms over/about the low pay.* – see also SMALL ARMS

ar·my /ˈɑrmiʸ/ *n* **1** military forces that fight on land **2** large group: *an army of ants*

a·ro·ma /əˈroʷmə/ *n* pleasant smell **~tic** /ˌærəˈmæṭɪk◂/ *adj*

a·rose /əˈroʷz/ *past t. of* ARISE

a·round /əˈraʊnd/ adv, prep **1 a** in various places: *I'll show you around (the house).* **b** somewhere near: *Is there anyone around?* **2** a little more or less than; about: *around 10 o'clock* **3 a** moving in a circle; measured in a circle: *turn around and around* | *3 yards around* **b** on all sides: *The children gathered around.*

a·rouse /əˈraʊz/ vt **1** fml cause to wake **2** make active; excite: *arouse suspicion*

ar·range /əˈreɪndʒ/ v **1** vt put in order: *arrange flowers* **2** vi/t plan: *arrange to meet her* **3** vt set out (music) for different instruments, etc. ~**ment** n **1** [C;U] (act of making) an agreement or plan: *make arrangements for the wedding* | *I have an arrangement with the bank.* [C] something that has been put in order: *a beautiful flower arrangement* **3** [C] (example of) the setting out of a piece of music in a certain way

ar·ray /əˈreɪ/ n fine show, collection, or ordered group

ar·rears /əˈrɪəz/ n [P] money owed from the past: *He was two weeks in arrears with the rent.* (= he owed rent for two weeks)

ar·rest /əˈrest/ vt **1** seize by the power of the law **2** stop (a process) **3** attract (attention) ♦ n [C;U] act of arresting

ar·riv·al /əˈraɪvəl/ n **1** [U] act of arriving **2** [C] person or thing that has arrived: *to welcome the new arrivals*

ar·rive /əˈraɪv/ vi **1** reach a place: *arrive home* **2** happen; come: *The day arrived.* **3** win success

arrive at phr vt reach; come to: *arrive at a decision*

ar·ro·gant /ˈærəgənt/ adj proud in a rude way ~**ly** adv **–gance** n [U]

ar·row /ˈærəʊ/ n **1** pointed stick to be shot from a BOW² (1) **2** sign (→) used to show direction

ar·se·nal /ˈɑːsənəl/ n place where weapons are stored

ar·se·nic /ˈɑːsənɪk/ n [U] very poisonous substance

ar·son /ˈɑːsən/ n [U] crime of setting fire to property ~**ist** n

art /ɑːt/ n **1** [U] the making or expression of what is beautiful, as in music, literature, or esp. painting **2** [U] things produced by art, esp. paintings: *an art gallery* **3** [C;U] skill in doing anything: *the art of conversation* **arts** n [P] subjects of study that are not part of science – see also FINE ARTS

ar·te·fact /ˈɑːtɪfækt/ n ARTIFACT

ar·te·ry /ˈɑːtəriʲ/ n **1** tube that carries blood from the heart **2** main road, passage, etc.

art·ful /ˈɑːtfəl/ adj **1** cleverly deceitful **2** skilfully put together ~**ly** adv

ar·thri·tis /ɑːˈθraɪtɪs/ n [U] painful disease of the joints **–tic** /ɑːˈθrɪtɪk/ adj

ar·ti·choke /ˈɑːtɪˌtʃəʊk/ n [C;U] **1** also **globe artichoke** — plant whose leafy flower is eaten **2** also **Jerusalem artichoke** — plant whose potato-like root is eaten

ar·ti·cle /ˈɑːtɪkəl/ n **1** thing; object: *an article of clothing* **2** piece of writing in a newspaper **3** complete or separate part in a written law agreement **4** word used with nouns, such as *a*, *an*, and *the* in English

ar·tic·u·late¹ /ɑːˈtɪkjəlɪt/ adj **1** (of people) able to express thoughts and feelings clearly in words **2** (of speech) having clear separate sounds and words ~**ly** adv

ar·tic·u·late² /ɑːˈtɪkjəleɪt/ v vi/t speak or say clearly **–lation** /ɑːˌtɪkjəˈleɪʃən/ n [U]

ar·ti·fact, arte- /ˈɑːtɪˌfækt/ n something made by people

ar·ti·fice /ˈɑːtɪfɪs/ n **1** [C] clever trick **2** [U] CUNNING

ar·ti·fi·cial /ˌɑːtɪˈfɪʃəl◂/ adj **1** made by people; not natural **2** not sincere ~**ly** adv ~**ity** /ˌɑːtɪfɪʃiˈælətiʲ/ n [C;U]

artificial in·tel·li·gence /ˌ··· ·ˈ····/ n [U] branch of computer science which aims to understand, make machines that can understand, make judgments, etc., in the way humans do

artificial res·pi·ra·tion /ˌ····· ··ˈ···, ···ˌ·· ··ˈ···/ n [U] making someone breathe again by pressing the chest, blowing into the mouth, etc.

ar·til·le·ry /ɑːˈtɪləriʲ/ n [U] (part of the army that uses) large guns

ar·ti·san /ˈɑːtəzən, -sən/ n CRAFTSMAN

art·ist /ˈɑːtɪst/ n **1** person who works in one of the arts, esp. painting **2** inventive and skilled worker **3** professional singer, dancer, etc., who performs in a show ~**ry** n [U] inventive imagination and ability ~**ic** /ɑːˈtɪstɪk/ adj **1** of art or artists **2** showing skill in art ~**ically** /-kliʲ/ adv

art·less /ˈɑːtlɪs/ adj simple and natural; almost foolish ~**ly** adv

as¹ /əz; strong æz/ adv, prep **1** (used in comparisons and examples) equally; like: *He's as old as me.* | *small animals such as cats and dogs* | *She escaped dressed as a man.* **2** when considered as being: *As a writer, she's wonderful.* **3 as far as** to the degree that

as² conj **1** (used in comparisons): *He's as old as I am.* **2** in the way that: *Do as I say!* | *Leave it as it is.* **3** because: *As I have no car, I can't go.* **4** when; while: *He saw her as she was* getting off the bus. **5** though: *Tired as I was, I tried to help.* **6 as for** when we speak of; concerning **7 as if/though** in a way that seems **8 as it is** in reality **9 as it were** one might say **10 as of** starting from (a time) **11 as yet** *fml* up until now

asap /ˌeʸ es eʸ ˈpiʸ, ˈeʸsæp/ *abbrev. for*: as soon as possible

as·bes·tos /æsˈbestəs, æz-, əs-, əz-/ n [U] soft gray material that protects against fire or heat

as·cend /əˈsend/ *vi/t fml* **1** go up **2 ascend the throne** become king or queen ~**ancy**, ~**ency** n [U] controlling influence; power ~**ant**, ~**ent** n **in the ascendant** having or nearly having a controlling power or influence

as·cent /əˈsent/ n **1** [C;U] act or process of **2** [C] ascending; way up

as·cer·tain /ˌæsərˈteʸn/ *vt fml* discover; make certain ~**able** adj

as·cet·ic /əˈset̬ɪk/ n, adj (a person) avoiding physical pleasures and comforts, esp. for religious reasons ~**ism** /əˈset̬əsɪzəm/ n [U]

ASCII /ˈæskiʸ/ n [U] American Standard Code for Information Interchange; a set of 128 letters, numbers, etc., used for easy exchange of information between a computer and other data processing (DATA) machinery

as·cribe /əˈskraɪb/ v **ascribe to** phr vt believe to be the work of: *He ascribes his success to luck.*

a·sep·tic /eʸˈseptɪk, ə-/ adj without bacteria; clean

a·sex·u·al /eʸˈsekʃuʷəl/ adj **1** without sex **2** not interested in sex

ash /æʃ/ n [U] also **ashes** pl. — powder left when something has been burned ~**en** adj pale gray **ashes** [P] remains of a dead body after burning

a·shamed /əˈʃeʸmd/ adj feeling shame

a·shore /əˈʃɔr, əˈʃoʷr/ adv on or to the shore

ash·tray /ˈæʃtreʸ/ n dish for tobacco ash

a·side /əˈsaɪd/ adv to the side: *She stepped aside to let them pass.* ♦ n remark not intended to be heard by everyone present

ask /æsk/ v **1** vi/t say a question: *'Where is it?' she asked.* | *Ask him where to go.* **2** vi/t make a request for: *She asked him to wake her at 6:00.* **3** vt invite: *Ask them for dinner.* **4 ask for trouble/it** behave so as to cause (something bad): *If you park there, you're really asking for trouble!*

ask after phr vt ask for news of

a·skance /əˈskæns/ adv **look askance** without liking or pleasure

a·skew /əˈskyuʷ/ adv not properly straight

a·sleep /əˈsliʸp/ adj **1** sleeping **2** (of an arm or leg) unable to feel

asp /æsp/ n small poisonous snake

as·par·a·gus /əˈspærəgəs/ n [U] plant whose stems are eaten as a vegetable

as·pect /ˈæspekt/ n **1** particular side of a plan, problem, etc. **2** direction in which a room, building, etc., faces

as·per·sion /əˈspərʒən, -ʃən/ n fml unkind or harmful remark: *They cast aspersions on my new book.*

as·phalt /ˈæsfɔlt/ n [U] black material used for road surfaces

as·phyx·i·ate /æsˈfɪksiʸˌeʸt, əs-/ vt kill by lack of air —**ation** /æsˌfɪksiʸˈeʸʃən, əs-/ n [U]

as·pire /əˈspaɪər/ vi direct one's hopes and efforts **aspiration** /ˌæspəˈreʸʃən/ n [C;U] strong desire

as·pi·rin /ˈæspərɪn/ n –**rin** or –**rins** [C;U] (TABLET of) medicine that lessens pain and fever

ass /æs/ n **1** taboo sl BOTTOM (2) **2** DONKEY **3** foolish person

as·sail /əˈseʸl/ vt fml attack ~**ant** n fml attacker

as·sas·sin /əˈsæsən/ n person who assassinates

as·sas·sin·ate /əˈsæsəˌneʸt/ vt murder a ruler, politician, etc. –**ation** /əˌsæsəˈneʸʃən/ n [C;U]

as·sault /əˈsɔlt/ n [C;U] sudden violent attack **assault** vt

as·sem·ble /əˈsembəl/ vi/t gather or put together: *to assemble radios* | *A crowd assembled.*

as·sem·bly /əˈsembliʸ/ n **1** [C] group of people gathered together for a purpose **2** [U] assembling of machine parts

assembly line /·ˈ··· ·/ n arrangement of workers and machines in which each person has a particular job, the work being passed from one worker to the next until the product is complete

as·sent /əˈsent/ vi fml agree ♦ n agreement

as·sert /əˈsɜrt/ vt **1** declare forcefully **2** make a strong claim to: *He asserted his authority.* **3 assert oneself** act in a way that shows one's power ~**ive** adj forceful; showing CONFIDENCE ~**ion** /əˈsɜrʃən/ n forceful statement or claim

as·sess /əˈses/ vt judge the value or amount of ~**ment** n [C;U]

as·set /ˈæset/ n **1** property that has value and may be sold **2** valuable quality or skill

asset-strip·ping /ˈ··· ˌ··/ n practice of buying a company cheaply, selling all its assets to make a profit, and closing it down

ass·hole /ˈæshoʷl/ *n taboo* **a** the ANUS **b** stupid annoying person

as·sid·u·ous /əˈsɪdʒuʷəs/ *adj* with careful attention **~ly** *adv*

as·sign /əˈsaɪn/ *vt* **1** give as a share or duty **2** decide on; name: *assign a day for the meeting* **~ment** *n* **1** [C] duty or piece of work **2** [U] act of assigning

as·sig·na·tion /ˌæsɪgˈneʸʃən/ *n* (secret) meeting, usu. for sex

as·sim·i·late /əˈsɪməˌleʸt/ *vi/t* take in and accept (food, ideas, foreign people) **–lation** /əˌsɪməˈleʸʃən/ *n* [U]

as·sist /əˈsɪst/ *vi/t fml* help **~ance** *n fml* **–ant** *n* person who helps

as·so·ci·ate /əˈsoʷʃiʸˌeʸt/ *v* **1** *vi/t* join as friends or partners **2** *vt* connect in the mind **associate** /əˈsoʷʃiʸɪt, -siʸɪt/ *n*: *He's a business associate.*

as·so·ci·a·tion /əˌsoʷsiʸˈeʸʃən, -ʃiʸˈeʸ-/ *n* **1** [C] society of people joined together **2** [U] act of joining together **3** [C;U] connecting things in the mind

as·sort·ed /əˈsɔrtɪd/ *adj* of various types; mixed

as·sort·ment /əˈsɔrtmənt/ *n* mixture

as·suage /əˈsweʸdʒ/ *vt fml* reduce (suffering)

as·sume /əˈsuʷm, əˈsyuʷm/ *vt* **1** believe without proof: *Let's assume he isn't coming.* **2** begin to use or perform: *to assume control* **3** pretend to have: *to adopt an assumed name*

as·sump·tion /əˈsʌmpʃən/ *n* **1** [C] something believed without proof **2** [U] act of assuming

as·sure /əˈʃʊər/ *vt* **1** tell firmly; promise **2** make (oneself) sure or certain **assurance** *n* **1** [U] belief in one's own powers **2** [C] firm promise **assured** *adj* certain, esp. of one's own powers

as·te·risk /ˈæstərɪsk/ *n* star-like mark *

a·stern /əˈstɜrn/ *adv* in or at the back part of a ship

as·te·roid /ˈæstəˌrɔɪd/ *n* very small PLANET

asth·ma /ˈæzmə/ *n* [U] disease that causes difficulty in breathing **~tic** /æzˈmætɪk/ *adj*

as·ton·ish /əˈstɑnɪʃ/ *vt* surprise greatly: *His rudeness astonished me.* **~ment** *n* [U]

as·tound /əˈstaʊnd/ *vt* shock with surprise

a·stray /əˈstreʸ/ *adj, adv* off the right path

a·stride /əˈstraɪd/ *adv, prep* with a leg on each side (of)

as·trin·gent /əˈstrɪndʒənt/ *adj* **1** able to tighten the skin and stop bleeding **2** bitter; severe

as·trol·o·gy /əˈstralədʒiʸ/ *n* [U] study of the supposed influence of the stars on events and character **–ger** *n* **–gical** /ˌæstrəˈlɑdʒɪkəl◂/ *adj*

as·tro·naut /ˈæstrəˌnɔt/ *n* traveler in a spacecraft

as·tron·o·my /əˈstranəmiʸ/ *n* [U] scientific study of the sun, stars, etc. **–mer** *n* **–mical** /ˌæstrəˈnɑmɪkəl/ *adj* **1** of astronomy **2** very large: *astronomical sums of money*

as·tro·phys·ics /ˌæstroʷˈfɪzɪks, ˌæstrə-/ *n* [U] science of the nature of the stars and the forces that influence them **–ical** *adj*

as·tute /əˈstuʷt, əˈstyuʷt/ *adj* able to see quickly something that is to one's advantage **~ly** *adv* **~ness** *n* [U]

a·sy·lum /əˈsaɪləm/ *n* **1** [U] protection and shelter **2** [C] MENTAL hospital

a·sym·met·ric /ˌeʸsəˈmɛtrɪk, ˌæ-/ also **–rical** /-kəl/ *adj* having sides that are not alike

at /ət; *strong* æt/ *prep* **1** (showing where): *at the airport* **2** (showing when): *at Christmas* **3** towards: *Look at me.* **4** by: *surprised at the news* **5** (showing how someone does something): *good at games* **6** (showing a state or continued activity): *at school | at war* **7** (showing price, level, age, etc.): *sold at 10 cents each | to stop work at 60* **8** at a/an in only one: *He went up the stairs 2 at a time.*

ate /eʸt/ *past t.* of EAT

a·the·ism /ˈeʸθiʸˌɪzəm/ *n* [U] belief that there is no God **–ist** *n*

ath·lete /ˈæθliʸt/ *n* person who practices athletics

ath·let·ics /æθˈlɛtɪks/ *n* [U] physical exercises such as running and jumping **athletic** *adj* **1** of athletics **2** physically strong and active

at·las /ˈætləs/ *n* book of maps

at·mo·sphere /ˈætməsˌfɪər/ *n* **1** gases surrounding a heavenly body, esp. the Earth **2** air **3** general feeling of a place **–spheric** /ˌætməsˈfɛrɪk◂/ *adj* **1** of or concerning the Earth's atmosphere **2** mysteriously beautiful and strange: *atmospheric music*

at·oll /ˈætɔl, ˈætəl, ˈætoʷl/ *n* ring-shaped CORAL island

at·om /ˈætəm/ *n* smallest unit of an ELEMENT **–ic** /əˈtɑmɪk/ *adj* **1** of atoms **2** using the power that comes from splitting atoms

atom bomb /ˌ·· ˈ·/ also **atomic bomb** /·ˌ·· ˈ·/ — *n* bomb that uses the explosive NUCLEAR power produced by splitting atoms

a·tone /əˈtoʷn/ *vi* make repayment (for a crime, etc.) **~ment** *n* [U]

a·tro·cious /əˈtroʷʃəs/ *adj* very cruel or bad **~ly** *adv*

a·troc·i·ty /ə'trɒsəṭiʸ/ n 1 very cruel act 2 something very ugly

at·ro·phy /'ætrəfiʸ/ vi/t (cause to) lose flesh and muscle; weaken **atrophy** n [U]

at·tach /ə'tætʃ/ vt 1 fasten 2 cause to join: *He attached himself to another group of tourists.* 3 regard as having (special meaning or importance) 4 **be attached to** be fond of ~**ment** n [C;U]

at·tach·é /ˌæṭə'ʃeʸ/ n person who helps an AMBASSADOR

attaché case /·ˌ··'·/ n thin hard case with a handle, for carrying papers

at·tack /ə'tæk/ n 1 [C;U] (act of) violence 2 [C] words intended to hurt 3 [C] sudden illness ♦ vt 1 make an attack 2 begin (something) with eagerness and interest ~**er** n

at·tain /ə'teʸn/ vt fml succeed in; reach ~**able** adj ~**ment** n 1 [U] act of attaining 2 [C] a skill

at·tempt /ə'tempt/ vt try: *I attempted to leave.* ♦ n 1 effort made to do something 2 **attempt on someone's life** effort to murder someone

at·tend /ə'tend/ v 1 vt be present at: *attend the meeting* 2 vi give attention 3 vi look after ~**ance** n 1 [C;U] act of being present 2 [C] number of people present: *a large attendance* ~**ant** n person who looks after a place or people

at·ten·tion /ə'tenʃən, -tʃən/ n [U] 1 careful thought: *pay attention to the teacher* 2 particular care or consideration: *Old cars need lots of attention.* 3 **at attention** (of a soldier) standing straight and still

at·ten·tive /ə'tentɪv/ adj 1 listening carefully 2 politely helpful ♦ **ly** adv ~**ness** n [U]

at·ten·u·ate /ə'tenyuʷˌeʸt/ vi/t (cause to) become thin, weak, less valuable, etc.

at·test /ə'test/ vt fml 1 declare to be true 2 be proof of: *His success attests (to) his ability.*

at·tic /'æṭɪk/ n room below the roof of a house

at·tire /ə'taɪər/ n fml clothes ♦ vt put on clothes

at·ti·tude /'æṭəˌtuʷd, -ˌtyuʷd/ n 1 way of feeling and behaving 2 fml position of the body

at·tor·ney /ə'tɜrniʸ/ n person whose profession is the LAW (2)

attorney gen·er·al /·ˌ·· '···/ n chief attorney of a state or country who represents the government

at·tract /ə'trækt/ vt 1 excite the admiration or interest of: *He was attracted by her smile.* 2 draw towards: *Flowers attract bees.* ~**ive** adj interesting, pleasing ~**ively** adv ~**iveness** n [U] state of being

attractive ~**ion** /ə'trækʃən/ n 1 [U] power of attracting 2 [C] something attractive

at·tri·bute¹ /'ætrəˌbyuʷt/ n 1 quality that belongs to a person or thing 2 something regarded as a sign of a person or position

at·tri·bute² /ə'trɪbyət/ v **attribute to** phr vt 1 believe to be the result of: *He attributes his success to hard work.* 2 ASCRIBE to

at·tri·tion /ə'trɪʃən/ n [U] process of tiring, weakening, or destroying by continual worry, hardship, or repeated attacks: *a war of attrition*

at·tune /ə'tuʷn, ə'tyuʷn/ v **attune to** phr vt make used to or ready for

a·typ·i·cal /eʸ'tɪpɪkəl/ adj not typical ~**ly** /-kliʸ/ adv

au·burn /'ɔbərn/ adj, n [U] (esp. of hair) reddish brown

auc·tion /'ɔkʃən/ n public meeting to sell goods to whoever offers the most money ♦ vt sell by auction

auc·tio·neer /ˌɔkʃə'nɪər/ n person in charge of an auction, who calls out the prices

au·da·cious /ɔ'deʸʃəs/ adj 1 (foolishly) daring 2 disrespectful ~**ly** adv ~**city** /ɔ'dæsəṭiʸ/ n [U]

au·di·ble /'ɔdəbəl/ adj able to be heard ~**bly** adv

au·di·ence /'ɔdiʸəns/ n 1 people listening to or watching a performance 2 formal meeting with someone important: *have an audience with the Pope*

au·di·o /'ɔdiʸˌoʷ/ adj of sound radio signals

audio-vis·u·al /ˌ··· '····◂/ adj of both sight and hearing

au·dit /'ɔdɪt/ vt examine (business accounts) officially **audit** n ~**or** n

au·di·tion /ɔ'dɪʃən/ n test performance given by a singer, actor, etc. **audition** vi

au·di·to·ri·um /ˌɔdə'tɔriʸəm, -'toʷr-/ n space where an AUDIENCE (1) sits

aug·ment /ɔg'ment/ vi/t fml increase

au·gur /'ɔgər/ vi **augur well/ill (for)** be a sign of good/bad things in the future (for): *This rain augurs well for farmers.*

au·gust /ɔ'gʌst/ adj noble and grand

Au·gust /'ɔgəst/ n the 8th month of the year

aunt /ænt, ɑnt/ n sister of one's father or mother, or wife of one's uncle

au pair /ˌoʷ 'peʸər/ n young foreigner who lives with a family and helps with work in their home

au·ra /'ɔrə/ n effect or feeling produced by a person or place

au·ral /'ɔrəl/ adj of or related to the sense of hearing

aus·pic·es /ˈɔspəsɪz, -ˌsiˠz/ n [P] *fml* **under the auspices of** helped by

aus·pi·cious /ɔˈspɪʃəs/ *adj fml* showing signs of future success ~**ly** *adv*

aus·tere /ɔˈstɪər/ *adj* **1** without comfort; hard: *an austere life* **2** without decoration; plain ~**ly** *adv* **-terity** /ɔˈsterəti/ n [C;U]

au·then·tic /ɔˈθentɪk/ *adj* known to be real; GENUINE ~**ally** /-kliˠ/ *adv* ~**ate** *vt* prove to be authentic ~**ation** /ɔˌθentɪˈkeˠʃən/ n [U] ~**ity** /ˌɔθenˈtɪsətiˠ, ˌɔθən-/ n [U] quality of being authentic

au·thor /ˈɔθər/ **authoress** /ˈɔθərɪs/ *fem.* — n **1** writer **2** person who thinks of an idea or plan ~**ship** n [U]

au·thor·i·tar·i·an /ɔˌθɔrəˈteəriˠən, əˌθɑr-/ n, *adj* (person) demanding total obedience to rules ~**ism** n [U]

au·thor·i·ta·tive /əˈθɔrəˌteˠtɪv, əˈθɑr-/ *adj* deserving respect; able to be trusted ~**ly** *adv*

au·thor·i·ty /əˈθɔrətiˠ, əˈθɑr-/ n **1** [U] power to command: *Who is in authority here?* **2** [C] person or group with this power **3** [C] authoritative person, book, etc.: *He's an authority on plants.*

au·thor·ize /ˈɔθəˌraɪz/ *vt* give formal permission for **-ization** /ˌɔθərəˈzeˠʃən/ n [U]

au·to·bi·og·ra·phy /ˌɔtəbaɪˈɑgrəfiˠ/ n written account of one's own life **-phical** /ˌɔtəˌbaɪəˈgræfɪkəl/ *adj*

au·to·crat /ˈɔtəˌkræt/ n **1** ruler with unlimited power **2** person who behaves like that ~**ic** /ˌɔtəˈkrætɪk◂/ *adj*

au·to·graph /ˈɔtəˌgræf/ n SIGNATURE of someone famous ♦ *vt* sign one's name on

au·to·mate /ˈɔtəˌmeˠt/ *vt* change (a process, etc.) to automation

auto·mat·ic /ˌɔtəˈmætɪk◂/ *adj* **1** (esp. of a machine) able to work by itself **2** done without thought **3** certain to happen ♦ n (automatic) gun ~**ally** /-kliˠ/ *adv*

au·to·ma·tion /ˌɔtəˈmeˠʃən/ n [U] use of machines that need no human control

au·tom·a·ton /ɔːˈtɑmətn/ n **-ta** /-tə/ *or* **-tons 1** thing or machine that works by itself **2** person who acts without thought or feeling

au·to·mo·bile /ˌɔtəməˈbiˠl, ˈɔtəməˌbiˠl/ n *fml for* car

au·ton·o·mous /ɔˈtɑnəməs/ *adj* governing itself

au·ton·o·my /ɔˈtɑnəmiˠ/ n [U] government or control (esp. of a country) by the people who live there

au·top·sy /ˈɔˌtɑpsiˠ/ n POSTMORTEM

au·tumn /ˈɔtəm/ n [C;U] season between summer and winter ~**al** /ɔˈtʌmnəl/ *adj* – see FALL²

aux·il·i·a·ry /ɔgˈzɪlyəriˠ, -ˈzɪləriˠ/ *adj* helping; adding support **auxiliary** n **1** helper **2** foreign soldier in the service of a country at war **3** an auxiliary verb

a·vail /əˈveˠl/ *vi* **avail oneself of** *fml* make use of ♦ n [U] **of/to no avail** of no use; without success

a·vai·la·ble /əˈveˠləbəl/ *adj* able to be gotten, used, etc.: *Those shoes are not available in your size.* **-bility** /əˌveˠləˈbɪlətiˠ/ n [U]

av·a·lanche /ˈævəˌlæntʃ/ n mass of snow crashing down a mountain: (fig.) *an avalanche of letters*

av·ant-garde /ˌɑvɑntˈgɑrd, ˌæ-◂/ *adj*, n [U] (of) people who produce the newest ideas, esp. in the arts

av·a·rice /ˈævərɪs◂/ n GREED for wealth **avaricious** /ˌævəˈrɪʃəs◂/ *adj*

a·venge /əˈvendʒ/ *vt* punish for harm done; REVENGE: *to avenge his death*

av·e·nue /ˈævəˌnyuˠ, -ˌnuˠ/ *also* **Ave.** *written abbrev.* — n **1** wide road, esp. between 2 rows of trees **2** way to a result

a·ver /əˈvɜr/ *vt* **-rr-** state forcefully

av·e·rage /ˈævərɪdʒ/ n **1** [C] amount found by adding quantities together and then dividing by the number of quantities **2** [C;U] level regarded as usual ♦ *adj*: *the average rainfall* | *girls of average intelligence* ♦ *vt* **1** calculate the average of **2** be or do as an average: *I average 8 hours' work a day.*

a·verse /əˈvɜrs/ *adj* not liking

a·ver·sion /əˈvɜrʒən, -ʃən/ n **1** [S;U] strong dislike **2** [C] hated person or thing

a·vert /əˈvɜrt/ *vt* **1** prevent from happening: *avert accidents* **2** *fml* turn away (one's eyes)

a·vi·a·ry /ˈeˠviˠˌeriˠ/ n cage for keeping birds in

a·vi·a·tion /ˌeˠviˠˈeˠʃən/ n [U] flying in aircraft **-tor** /ˈeˠviˠˌeˠtər/ n

av·id /ˈævɪd/ *adj* extremely enthusiastic ~**ly** *adv*

av·o·ca·do /ˌævəˈkɑdoˠ, ˌɑ-/ n **-dos** *or* **-does** green tropical fruit

a·void /əˈvɔɪd/ *vt* keep away from, esp. on purpose ~**able** *adj* ~**ance** n [U]

av·oir·du·pois /ˌævərdəˈpɔɪz/ n, *adj* [U] system of weights in which the standard measures are the OUNCE, POUND, and TON

a·vowed /əˈvaʊd/ *adj* openly admitted: *his avowed supporters*

a·vun·cu·lar /əˈvʌŋkyələr/ *adj* of or like an uncle

a·wait /ə'weʸt/ vt fml wait for

a·wake¹ /ə'weʸk/ adj not asleep

a·wake² also **awaken** /ə'weʸkən/ – vi/t awoke /ə'woʷk/ or **awakened**, **awoken** /ə'woʷkən/ or **awaked** wake: (fig.) *People must be awakened to the dangers of nuclear weapons.*

a·wak·en·ing /ə'weʸkənɪŋ/ n **1** act of waking from sleep: (fig.) *her awakening to social injustice* **2 rude awakening** sudden consciousness of an unpleasant state of affairs

a·ward /ə'wɔrd/ vt give officially: *award prizes* ♦ n something awarded

a·ware /ə'wɛər/ adj having knowledge or understanding: *politically aware* ~**ness** n [U]

a·way¹ /ə'weʸ/ adv **1** to or at another place: *Go away!* | *She lives 3 miles away.* **2** so as to be gone: *The sounds died away.* **3** continuously: *He's hammering away.*

away² adj (of a sports match) played at the place, sports field, etc., of one's opponent

awe /ɔ/ n [U] respect mixed with fear

awe·in·spir·ing /'···ˌ··/ adj causing feelings of awe

awe·some /'ɔsəm/ adj **1** causing feelings of awe **2** sl surprisingly good

aw·ful /'ɔfəl/ adj **1** very bad: *awful weather* **2 very great:** *an awful lot of work* ~**ly** adv very

a·while /ə'hwaɪl, ə'waɪl/ adv short period of time: *wait awhile*

awk·ward /'ɔkwərd/ adj **1** not moving skillfully: CLUMSY **2** difficult to handle **3** inconvenient: *They came at an awkward time.* **4** EMBARRASSING: *an awkward silence* ~**ly** adv ~**ness** n [U]

aw·ning /'ɔnɪŋ/ n movable cloth roof put up as a protection against sun or rain

a·woke /ə'woʷk/ past t. of AWAKE

a·wok·en /ə'woʷkən/ past p. of AWAKE

AWOL /'eʸˌwɔl, 'eʸˌwɑl, ˌeʸ ˌdʌbəlyuʷ ˌoʷ 'ɛl/ adj, adv absent without leave: *AWOL soldiers/He went AWOL.*

a·wry /ə'raɪ/ adj, adv **1** not in the planned way **2** twisted or bent

ax /æks/ n axes /'æksɪz/ **1** tool for cutting down trees **2 have an ax to grind** have a selfish reason for one's actions ♦ vt put a sudden end to (jobs, plans, etc.)

ax·i·om /'æksiʸəm/ n principle accepted as true ~**atic** /ˌæksiʸə 'mætɪk◂/ adj not needing proof

ax·is /'æksɪs/ n axes /'æksiʸz/ **1** line around which something spins: *the Earth's axis* **2** fixed line against which positions are measured on a GRAPH

ax·le /'æksəl/ n bar on which a wheel turns

a·ya·tol·lah /ˌaɪə'tɑlə/ n Shiite Muslim religious leader

aye /aɪ/ n, adv (person who votes) yes

az·ure /'æʒər/ adj, n [U] bright blue

B

B, b /biʸ/ the 2nd letter of the English alphabet

b *abbrev. for*: born

baa /ba/, *bæ*/ *vi, n* (make) the sound a sheep makes

bab·ble /ˈbæbəl/ *vi/t* talk quickly and foolishly **babble** *n* [S]

babe /beʸb/ *n lit* **1** baby **2** *sl* woman

ba·boon /bæˈbuʷn/ *n* kind of large monkey

ba·by /ˈbeʸbiʸ/ *n* **1** very young child: (fig.) *the baby of the class* (= the youngest) **2** very young animal or bird: *a baby monkey* **3** *infml* person, esp. a girl or woman **4** *infml* one's special responsibility **~ish** *adj* like a baby

baby-sit·ter /ˈ·· ˌ··/ *n* person who looks after children while their parents are out **baby-sit** *vi* **–sat**; *pres. p.* **–sitting**

bach·e·lor /ˈbætʃələr/ *n* unmarried man

bachelor's de·gree /ˈ··· ·ˌ·/ *n* degree given after four years' college or university study

back¹ /bæk/ *n* **1** the part of one's body opposite the chest, from the neck to the bottom of the SPINE (1) **2** the part furthest from the direction that something moves in or faces: *the back of the aircraft/of the house* | *the back wheel of a bicycle* **3** the less important side of something **4** the part of a chair that one leans against **5** the end of a book or newspaper **6 back to back** with the backs facing each other **7 be glad to see the back of someone** be glad when someone goes away **8 behind someone's back** without their knowledge **9 be flat on one's back** be helpless because of illness etc. **10 get off someone's back** stop annoying someone **11 have/with one's back to the wall** (be) in the greatest difficulties **12 turn one's back on someone** leave someone (esp. when one should stay) **~less** *adj*: *a backless dress*

back² *adv* **1** in or into an earlier place: *Put the book back on the shelf.* **2** towards the back: *Lean back.* **3** away from the speaker: *Stand back!* **4** in reply: *Phone me back.* **5** in an earlier time: *back in 1983* **6 back and forth** in one direction, then in the opposite direction

back³ *v* **1** *vi/t* more backwards: *back the car down the road* **2** *vt* support and encourage **3** *vt* risk money

on (the result of a horse race, etc.) **4** *vt* be or make the back of: *curtains backed with satin* **– er** *n* **1** someone who supports a plan with money **2** someone who risks money on a horse, etc.

back down also **back off** *phr vi* give up an argument

back onto *phr vt* (of a place) have at the back: *a house backing onto the river*

back out *phr vi* not fulfil a promise

back up *phr vt* **1** support in an argument, etc. **2** move a vehicle backwards **3** copy a computer FILE

back·ache /ˈbæk͵eʸk/ *n* [C;U] pain in the back

back·bit·ing /ˈbæk͵baɪtɪŋ/ *n* [U] unkind talk about someone who is absent

back·bone /ˈbækboʷn/ *n* **1** [C] SPINE (1): (fig.) *She's the backbone* (= main support) *of the parents' committee.* **2** [U] strength of character

back·break·ing /ˈbæk͵breʸkɪŋ/ *adj* (of work) very hard

back burn·er /͵· ˈ··/ *n* condition where no action will be taken: *a project on the back burner*

back·date /͵bækˈdeʸt/ *vt* make effective from an earlier date

back·drop /ˈbækdrɑp/ *n* background

back·fire /ˈbækfaɪər/ *vi* **1** (of a car, etc.) make a noise because the gas explodes too soon **2** have the opposite effect to that intended

back·ground /ˈbækgraʊnd/ *n* **1** scenery behind the main object **2** (information about) conditions existing when something happens or happened **3** person's family, experience, education, etc.

back·hand /ˈbækhænd/ *n* stroke (in tennis, etc.) with the back of the hand turned in the direction of movement [U] writing that leans to the left **~ed** *adj* **1** using or made with a backhand **2** indirect, esp. sarcastic (SARCASM) **~er** *n* backhand

back·ing /ˈbækɪŋ/ *n* **1** help; support **2** something that makes the back of an object

back is·sue /͵· ˈ··/ *n* newspaper, etc., earlier than the most recent one

back·lash /ˈbæklæʃ/ *n* sudden violent movement, esp. against a political or social movement

back·log /ˈbæklɒg, -lɑg/ *n* things (esp. work) remaining to be done

back·pack /ˈbækpæk/ *n* a large bag carried on the back; esp. by walkers, etc. **~er** *n* **~ing** *n* [U]: *to go backpacking in the mountains* ♦ *vi* walk distances with a backpack

back·ped·al /'bækˌpedl/ vi 1 PEDAL backwards 2 take back a statement; change an earlier opinion

back·road /'bækroʷd/ n road away from the main roads in the country

back seat /ˌ·ˈ·◄/ n 1 [C] seat at the back of a car 2 [S] less important position

back·side /'bæksaɪd/ n one's BOTTOM[1] (2)

back·slap·ping /'bækslæpɪŋ/ adj (of behavior) too friendly and noisy

back·slide /'bækslaɪd/ vi go back to a worse condition **–slider** n

back·stage /ˌbækˈsteʲdʒ◄/ adv, adj 1 behind a theater stage 2 in private

back·stroke /'bækstroʷk/ n way of swimming on one's back

back·track /'bæktræk/ vi 1 go back over the same path 2 BACKPEDAL (2)

back·up /'bækʌp/ n [C;U] 1 thing or person ready to be used in place of or to help another 2 line of traffic stretching back from where its flow has been halted (HALT)

back·ward /'bækwərd/ adj 1 towards the back 2 late in development: a backward child **~ness** n [U]

back·wards /'bækwərdz/ adv 1 towards the back, the beginning, or the past: say the alphabet backwards 2 with the back part in front: put one's hat on backwards 3 **know something backwards** know something perfectly

back·wa·ter /'bækˌwɔtər, -ˌwɑtər/ n 1 part of a river outside the current 2 place not influenced by outside events

back·woods /'bækwʊdz/ adj thought to lack good manners because of not living in the city

back·yard /ˌbækˈyard◄/ n 1 yard behind a house 2 area under one's personal control

ba·con /'beʲkən/ n [U] pig meat, smoked or preserved in salt

bac·te·ri·a /bækˈtɪriʲə/ n sing. **–rium** /-riʲəm/ [P] very small living creatures that may cause disease

bad /bæd/ adj worse /wɜrs/, worst /wɜrst/ 1 unpleasant: bad news 2 morally wrong 3 unhealthy: Smoking is bad for you. 4 not of acceptable quality 5 severe: a bad cold 6 ROTTEN: The apples went bad. 7 disobedient: a bad boy 8 **feel bad about** be sorry or ashamed about 9 **have/get a bad name** lose or have lost people's respect 10 **in a bad way** very ill or in trouble 11 **not bad/not so bad** good **~ly** adv 1 in a bad way: We played badly. 2 seriously: We were badly beaten. 3 a great deal: He needs help badly.

bad blood /ˌ·ˈ·/ n [U] angry or bitter feeling

bad debt /ˌ·ˈ·/ n debt that is unlikely to be paid

bad·dy /'bædiʲ/ n infml bad person

bade /bæd, beʲd/ past t. and p. of BID[2]

badge /bædʒ/ n something worn to show one's rank, membership, etc.

bad·ger /'bædʒər/ n black and white night animal that lives in holes in the ground

badger[2] vt ask again and again

bad·lands /'bædˌlændz/ n rocky uneven land

badly-off /ˌ·· ˈ·◄/ adj 1 poor 2 lacking

bad·min·ton /'bædˌmɪntən/ n [U] game similar to tennis, played with a SHUTTLECOCK over a high net

bad-mouth /ˈ· ·/ vt sl speak badly of

baf·fle /'bæfəl/ vt be too difficult for (someone): a baffling question

bag[1] /bæg/ n 1 soft container that opens at the top: a shopping bag 2 **in the bag** certain to be won, gained, etc.

bag[2] v **-gg-** 1 vt put into a bag 2 vt kill (animals or birds) 3 vt take possession of 4 vi be baggy

ba·gel /'beʲgəl/ n hard round bread with a hole in the centre

bag·gage /'bægɪdʒ/ n [U] LUGGAGE

bag·gy /'bægiʲ/ adj hanging in loose folds: baggy jeans

bag·pipes /'bægpaɪps/ n [P] musical instrument with pipes and a bag of air

bail[1] /beʲl/ n [U] 1 money paid so that a prisoner may be set free until tried (TRY (3)) 2 **go/stand bail** pay this money

bail[2] v **bail out** phr v 1 vt pay bail for someone 2 vt help someone with money 3 vi/t remove water from a boat 4 vi escape from an aircraft

bai·liff /'beʲlɪf/ n 1 law officer in a court 2 farm manager

bait /beʲt/ n [S;U] food used to attract fish, etc., to be caught ♦ vt 1 put bait on (a hook, etc.) 2 make (an animal or a person) angry intentionally

bake /beʲk/ 1 vi/t (cause to) cook in an OVEN 2 vi/t (cause to) become hard by heating 3 vi become hot: I'm baking! **baker** n person who bakes bread for sale **bakery** place where bread is baked (and sold)

bak·ing pow·der /ˈ·· ˌ··/ n [U] powder used to make bread and cakes light

baking so·da /ˈ·· ˌ··/ n powder used to make cakes etc. rise

bal·ance[1] /'bæləns/ n 1 [S;U] state in which weight is evenly spread: It was difficult to keep my balance on the icy path. 2 [C] instrument for weighing 3 [C] amount remaining somewhere: *my bank balance* **4 in the balance** uncertain(ly) **5 on balance** considering everything

balance² *v* **1** *vi/t* keep steady **2** *vi* (of 2 things, esp. debts) be equal **3** *vt* compare (2 things): *balance the advantages against the disadvantages*

balance of pay·ments /ˌ··· ˈ·ˌ·/ *n* [(the) S] the difference between the amount of money coming into a country and the amount going out, including trade in insurance, between banks, etc.

balance of trade /ˌ··· ˈ·/ *n* [(the) S] the difference in value between a country's IMPORTS and EXPORTS

bal·co·ny /ˈbælkəniʸ/ *n* **1** piece of floor that sticks out from an upstairs wall **2** upstairs seats in a theater

bald /bɔld/ *adj* **1** with no hair on the head **2** plain: *a bald statement* **~ing** *adj* becoming bald **~ness** *n* [U]

bal·der·dash /ˈbɔldərˌdæʃ/ *n* [U] *infml* nonsense

bale¹ /beʸl/ *n* large tightly tied mass of esp. soft material: *a bale of cotton*

bale² *v* **bale out** *phr vi/t* remove water from a boat

balk /bɔk/ *vi* be unwilling to agree: *I balked at the price.*

ball¹ /bɔl/ *n* **1** round object used in games **2** round mass: *a ball of string/clay* **3** round part of the body: *eyeballs* **4 on the ball** showing up-to-date knowledge and readiness to act **5 play ball** COOPERATE **6 start/keep the ball rolling** begin/continue something **balls** [P] *taboo sl* TESTICLES

ball² *n* **1** formal occasion for dancing **2 have a ball** have a very good time

bal·lad /ˈbæləd/ *n* **1** poem that tells a story **2** popular love song

bal·last /ˈbæləst/ *n* [U] heavy material carried to keep a ship steady, or to be thrown from a BALLOON (1) to make it rise higher ♦ *vt* fill or supply with ballast

ball·cock /ˈbɔlkɑk/ *n* hollow floating ball that opens and closes a hole through which water flows

bal·le·ri·na /ˌbæləˈriʸnə/ *n* female ballet dancer

bal·let /ˈbæleʸ, ˈbæleʸ/ *n* **1** [C] dance with music in which a story is told **2** [C] music for such a dance **3** [S;U] art of doing such a dance **4** [C] group of ballet dancers

ball game /ˈ· ·/ *n infml* state of affairs

bal·lis·tic mis·sile /bəˌlɪstɪk ˈmɪsəl/ *n* MISSILE that is guided as it rises into the air but then falls freely

bal·lis·tics /bəˈlɪstɪks/ *n* [U] science

of the movement of objects, such as bullets fired from a gun **ballistic** *adj*

ball of wax /ˌ· · ˈ·/ *n infml* matter, affair, thing

bal·loon /bəˈluʷn/ *n* **1** bag filled with gas or air so that it can float **2** small rubber bag that can be blown up and used as a toy **3** line around words thought or spoken by a CARTOON character ♦ *vi* swell up like a balloon

bal·lot /ˈbælət/ *n* **1** [S;U] (paper used in a) secret vote **2** [C] number of votes recorded ♦ **1** *vi* vote or decide by secret ballot **2** *vt* find out the views (of a group) by holding a vote

ballot box /ˈ··· ·/ *n* box in which voters put their BALLOTs (1)

ball park /ˈ· ·/ *n* **1** park where BASEBALL is played **2** [S] *infml* range of numbers, prices, etc., within which the correct figure is likely to be

ball·point /ˈbɔlpɔɪnt/ *n* pen with a ball at the end that rolls thick ink onto the paper

ball·room /ˈbɔlruʷm, -rʊm/ *n* large room suitable for a BALL² (1)

bal·ly·hoo /ˈbæliʸˌhuʷ/ *n* [U] noise, advertising, etc., done to gain public attention

balm /bɑm/ *n* [C;U] oily liquid used to lessen pain

balm·y /ˈbɑmiʸ/ *adj* **1** (of air) soft and warm **2** *sl* foolish; crazy

ba·lo·ney /bəˈloʷniʸ/ *n, interj* [U] nonsense

bal·sa /ˈbɔlsə/ *n* [C;U] (light wood of) a tropical tree

bal·us·trade /ˈbæləˌstreʸd/ *n* upright posts with a bar along the top, guarding an edge where people might fall

bam·boo /ˌbæmˈbuʷ◄/ *n* **-boos** [C;U] (hollow jointed stems of) a tropical plant of the grass family

bam·boo·zle /bæmˈbuʷzəl/ *vt sl* deceive

ban /bæn/ *vt* **-nn-** forbid ♦ *n* order forbidding something

ba·nal /bəˈnæl, bəˈnɑl, ˈbeʸnl/ *adj* uninteresting because ordinary **~ity** /bəˈnælətiʸ/ *n* [C;U]

ba·na·na /bəˈnænə/ *n* long yellow tropical fruit

banana split /·ˌ··· ˈ·/ *n* ICE CREAM served between banana halves topped with whipped cream

band¹ /bænd/ *n* **1** narrow piece of material for fastening, or putting round something: *a rubber band* **2** STRIPE (1) **3** broadcasting range over which radio stations can be received: *fm band*

band² *n* group of people, esp. musicians playing popular music – see also ONE-MAN BAND; STEEL BAND

band³ v **band together** phr vi unite for a purpose

ban·dage /ˈbændɪdʒ/ n narrow piece of cloth for tying around a wound ♦ vt tie up with a bandage

Band-Aid /ˈbænd eɪd/ n tdmk (a thin band of) material that can be stuck to the skin to protect small wounds

b and b /ˌbiʸ ən ˈbiʸ/ abbrev. for: (small hotel providing) bed and breakfast

ban·dit /ˈbændɪt/ n armed robber

band·stand /ˈbændstænd/ n raised place open to the air, for a band to play on

band·wa·gon /ˈbændˌwægən/ n **jump on a bandwagon** join something that is popular, for personal gain

ban·dy /ˈbændiʸ/ vt **bandy words** quarrel

bane /beɪn/ n cause of trouble ~**ful** adj harmful

bang¹ /bæŋ/ vi/t hit violently and noisily: I banged my head against the ceiling. **bang** n

bang² adv exactly: bang in the middle

ban·gle /ˈbæŋgəl/ n band worn as decoration on the wrist

bangs /bæŋz/ n [P] hair hanging over the forehead

ban·ish /ˈbænɪʃ/ vt **1** send away as a punishment **2** stop thinking about ~**ment** n [U]

ban·is·ter /ˈbænəstər/ n also **banisters** — upright posts with a bar along the top, beside a flight of stairs

ban·jo /ˈbændʒoʷ/ n **-jos** or **-joes** stringed instrument used esp. to play popular music

bank¹ /bæŋk/ n **1** land beside a river or lake **2** raised heap of earth, etc. **3** mass of snow, clouds, etc.

bank² n **1** place where money is kept and paid out on demand **2** place where something is kept for use: a blood bank ~**er** n person who owns, works in, or controls a BANK² (1)

bank³ vi/t keep (money) in a bank **bank on** phr vt depend on

bank⁴ vi (of an aircraft, etc.) raise one side while turning

bank·ing /ˈbæŋkɪŋ/ n [U] business of a BANK² (1)

bank note /ˈ· ·/ n piece of paper money

bank·roll /ˈbæŋkroʷl/ n supply of money ♦ vt infml supply money for or pay the cost of (a business, plan, etc.)

bank·rupt /ˈbæŋkrʌpt/ adj unable to pay one's debts: (fig.) morally bankrupt (=completely without morals) ♦ n person who is bankrupt

♦ vt make bankrupt or very poor ~**cy** n [C;U] state of being bankrupt

ban·ner /ˈbænər/ n **1** lit flag **2** piece of cloth with a political message on it, carried by marchers

ban·quet /ˈbæŋkwɪt/ n formal dinner **banquet** vi

ban·ter /ˈbæntər/ n [U] light joking talk **banter** vi

bap·tis·m /ˈbæptɪzəm/ n **1** [C;U] Christian religious ceremony of touching or covering a person with water **2 baptism by fire:** a soldier's first experience of war **b** any unpleasant first experience ~**tize** /bæpˈtaɪz/ vt perform baptism on

bar /bɑr/ n **1** long narrow piece of solid material: a bar of soap | (fig.) bars of sunlight **2** length of wood or metal across a window, etc. **3** group of musical notes **4** place where drinks, etc., are served **5** bank of sand or stones under water **6** BARRIER **7** (cap.) the legal profession: She was called to the Bar. (= became a lawyer) **8 behind bars** in prison ♦ vt **-rr-** **1** close with a bar: They barred themselves in. | (fig.) to bar the way to success **2** forbid; prevent: He was barred from playing football. ♦ prep **1** except **2** bar none with no exception

barb /bɑrb/ n sharp point of a fish hook, etc., with a curved shape ~**ed** adj **1** with short sharp points: barbed wire **2** (of speech) sharply unkind

bar·bar·i·an /bɑrˈbeəriʸən/ n wild uncivilized person

bar·bar·ic /bɑrˈbærɪk/ adj **1** very cruel **2** like a barbarian –**barism** /ˈbɑrbərɪzəm/ n [U] condition of being a barbarian –**barous** adj –**ity** /bɑrˈbærəṭiʸ/ n [C;U] great cruelty

bar·be·cue /ˈbɑrbɪkjuʷ/ n **1** party where meat etc. is cooked outdoors **2** metal frame on which this is done ♦ vt cook on a barbecue

bar·ber /ˈbɑrbər/ n person who cuts men's hair

bar·bi·tu·rate /bɑrˈbɪtʃərɪt, -ˌreʸt/ [C;U] drug that makes people sleep

bard /bɑrd/ n **1** poet **2 the Bard** Shakespeare

bare /beər/ adj **1** without clothes or covering **2** with nothing added: the bare facts **3** empty: a room bare of furniture ♦ vt bring to view; EXPOSE ~**ly** adv hardly

bare·back /ˈbeərbæk/ adj, adv riding, esp. a horse, without a SADDLE (1)

bare bones /ˌ· ˈ·/ n [P] simplest but most important parts or facts

bare·faced /ˈbeərfeʸst/ adj shameless

bare·foot /ˈbeərfʊt/ adv without shoes

bar·gain¹ /ˈbɑrgɪn/ n **1** agreement to do something in return for something else **2** something sold cheap **3 into the bargain** besides everything else

bargain² vi talk about the conditions of a sale, etc.

bargain for/on phr vt take into account; expect

barge¹ /bɑrdʒ/ n boat with a flat bottom

barge² vi move heavily and rudely

barge in phr vi rush in rudely; interrupt

bar hop /ˈ· ·/ n sl visit to several bars

bar·i·tone /ˈbærəˌtoʷn/ n (man with) a singing voice between TENOR and BASS

bark¹ /bɑrk/ v **1** vi make the noise dogs make **2** vt say in a fierce voice **3 bark up the wrong tree** infml have a mistaken idea ♦ **bark** n **1** sharp loud noise made by a dog **2 his bark is worse than his bite** infml he is not as bad-tempered, unfriendly, etc., as he appears

bark² n [U] outer covering of a tree

bar·ley /ˈbɑrliʸ/ n [U] grasslike grain plant grown as a food crop

barn /bɑrn/ n farm building for storing things in

bar·na·cle /ˈbɑrnəkəl/ n small SHELLFISH that collects on rocks, ships, etc.

ba·rom·e·ter /bəˈrɑmətər/ n instrument for measuring air pressure so as to judge what weather is coming: (fig.) a barometer of public opinion

bar·on /ˈbærən/ n powerful man in business

ba·roque /bəˈroʷk, bəˈrɑk/ adj **1** in a decorated style fashionable in 17th-century Europe **2** (too) greatly ornamented

bar·racks /ˈbærɪks/ n building where soldiers live

bar·rage¹ /bəˈrɑʒ/ n heavy gunfire: (fig.) a barrage of questions

bar·rage² /ˈbɑrɪdʒ/ n bank of earth, etc., built across a river

bar·rel /ˈbærəl/ n **1** round wooden container: a beer barrel **2** long part of a gun, etc. that is shaped like a tube **3 over a barrel** in a difficult position

barrel or·gan /ˈ·· ˌ··/ n musical instrument on wheels, played by turning a handle

bar·ren /ˈbærən/ adj **1** unable to produce children, fruit, crops, etc. **2** useless; empty: a barren discussion ~ness n [U]

bar·ri·cade /ˈbærəˌkeʸd, ˌbærəˈkeʸd/ n something quickly built to block a street, etc. ♦ vt close or defend with a barricade

bar·ri·er /ˈbæriʸər/ n something placed in the way to prevent movement: (fig.) a barrier to success | the sound barrier

bar·ring /ˈbɑrɪŋ/ prep except for

bar·row /ˈbæroʷ/ n **1** small cart to be pushed **2** WHEELBARROW

bar·tend·er /ˈbɑrˌtendər/ n person who serves drinks in a BAR (4)

bar·ter /ˈbɑrtər/ vi/t exchange goods for other goods **barter** n [U]

base¹ /beʸs/ n **1** part of a thing on which a thing stands **2** origin from which something develops or is made **3** center from which something is controlled, plans made, etc. **4** center for military operations, stores, etc. **5** main part or substance of a mixture: a vegetable base **6** point which a player must touch in BASEBALL while running **7 not get to first base (with)** not even begin to succeed (with) **8 off base** wrong or unacceptable ♦ vt provide with a center: a company based in Paris ~less adj without good reason

base on/upon phr vt form by using something else as a starting point: a film based on a novel

base² adj **1** esp. lit (of people or behavior) dishonorable **2** (of metal) not regarded as precious ~ly adv ~ness n [U]

base·ball /ˈbeʸsbɔl/ n **1** [U] outdoor ball game played by 2 teams of 9 players each **2** [C] ball used in this game

base·board /ˈbeʸsbɔrd, -boʷrd/ n board fixed along the base of an inside wall

base·ment /ˈbeʸsmənt/ n room in a house below ground level

bas·es /ˈbeʸsiʸz/ n pl. of BASIS

bash /bæʃ/ vt hit hard ♦ n **1** hard blow **2** party

bash·ful /ˈbæʃfəl/ adj SHY ~ly adv

ba·sic /ˈbeʸsɪk/ adj most necessary; FUNDAMENTAL: basic principles ~ally /-kliʸ/ adv in spite of surface behavior or details; in reality

basics n [P] basic parts or principles

ba·sin /ˈbeʸsən/ n **1** round container for liquids; bowl **2** SINK² **3** hollow place where water collects **4** large valley

ba·sis /ˈbeʸsɪs/ n bases /ˈbeʸsiʸz/ **1** the facts, principles, etc., from which something is formed, started, or developed: the basis of an opinion **2** the stated way of carrying out an action, process, etc.: working on a part-time basis

bask /bæsk/ vi lie in enjoyable warmth: (fig.) She basked in (= enjoyed) her employer's approval.

bas·ket /ˈbæskɪt/ n light woven container: a shopping basket

bas·ket·ball /ˈbæskɪtˌbɔl/ n 1 [U] game in which players try to throw a ball into a basket 2 [C] large ball used in this game

basket case /ˈ·· ˌ·/ n person who can't deal with a situation

bass¹ /beɪs/ n 1 (man with) the lowest human singing voice 2 instrument with the same range of notes as this: *a bass guitar* 3 DOUBLE BASS

bass² /bæs/ n kind of fish that can be eaten

bass fid·dle /ˌbeɪs ˈfɪdl/ n DOUBLE BASS

bas·soon /bəˈsuːn, bæ-/ n large WOODWIND musical instrument

bas·tard /ˈbæstərd/ n 1 child of unmarried parents 2 sl unpleasant person 3 sl man of the stated kind: *You lucky bastard!*

baste /beɪst/ vt 1 pour fat over (meat) during cooking 2 sew loosely

bas·ti·on /ˈbæstʃən/ n 1 part of a castle wall that sticks out 2 place where a principle is defended: *a bastion of freedom*

bat¹ /bæt/ n stick for hitting the ball in BASEBALL, etc.

bat² vi/t 1 strike or hit (as if) with a bat 2 vt **not bat an eyelid** show no sign of shock

bat³ n 1 mouselike animal that flies at night 2 **as blind as a bat** not able to see well

batch /bætʃ/ n group; set

bat·ed /ˈbeɪtɪd/ adj **with bated breath** too frightened or excited to breathe

bath /bæθ/ n **baths** /bæðz, bæθs/ 1 act of washing one's whole body at one time 2 liquid in a container used for some special purpose: *an eyebath* 3 BATHTUB 4 place with baths for public use

bathe /beɪð/ v 1 vi have a BATH (2) 2 vt put in liquid: *bathe your eyes* ♦ **bather** n swimmer

ba·thos /ˈbeɪθɒs/ n [U] sudden change from beautiful ideas to ordinary foolish ones

bath·robe /ˈbæθroʊb/ n DRESSING GOWN worn before or after bathing

bath·room /ˈbæθruːm, -rʊm/ n room with a bath and a TOILET (1)

bath·tub /ˈbæθtʌb/ n container in which one sits to wash the whole body

bat·on /bəˈtɑn, bæ-/ n short stick used by the leader of an ORCHESTRA, or as a weapon by a policeman, etc.

bat·tal·ion /bəˈtælyən/ n army unit of 500-1,000 soldiers

bat·ten /ˈbætn/ v **batten down** phr vt fasten with boards

bat·ter¹ /ˈbætər/ vi/t 1 beat hard and repeatedly 2 cause to lose shape by continual use

batter² n [U] mixture of flour, eggs, and milk for making PANCAKES, etc.

batter³ n player in BASEBALL who tries to hit the ball with a BAT¹ (1)

bat·ter·ing ram /ˈ··· ˌ·/ n (in former times) heavy log used for breaking down castle doors

bat·ter·y /ˈbætəriʲ/ n 1 apparatus for producing electricity 2 army unit of big guns 3 set of things used together: *a battery of tests*

bat·tle /ˈbætl/ n short fight between enemies or opposing groups ♦ vi fight; struggle

bat·tle·ax /ˈbætl-æks/ n **axes** 1 heavy ax for fighting 2 fierce woman

bat·tle·field /ˈbætlˌfiʲld/ n place where a battle is fought

bat·tle·ments /ˈbætlmənts/ n [P] wall around a castle roof, with spaces to shoot through

bat·tle·ship /ˈbætlˌʃɪp/ n large ship with big guns, used in war

bat·ty /ˈbætiʲ/ adj sl slightly crazy

bau·ble /ˈbɔbəl/ n cheap jewel

bawd·y /ˈbɔdiʲ/ adj about sex in a rude, funny way **–ily** adv **–iness** n [U]

bawl /bɔl/ vi/t 1 shout loudly 2 CRY¹(1)

bay¹ /beɪ/ n 1 wide opening along a coast 2 division of a large room or building, separated by shelves, etc.

bay² vi make the deep cry of a large hunting dog

bay³ n **hold/keep at bay** keep (an enemy, etc.) away

bay·o·net /ˈbeɪʲənɪt, -ˌnɛt, ˌbeɪʲəˈnɛt/ n knife on the end of a RIFLE ♦ vt drive a bayonet into

bay win·dow /ˌ·· ˈ··/ n window with three sides sticking out from a wall

ba·zaar /bəˈzɑr/ n 1 sale to get money for some good purpose 2 market in an Eastern town

ba·zoo·ka /bəˈzuːwkə/ n long gun that rests on the shoulder and fires ROCKETS

BC /ˌbiʲ ˈsiʲ/ abbrev. for: before (the birth of) Christ

be¹ /bi; strong biʲ/ v aux pres. t. sing. **I am**, you **are**, he/she/it **is**; pres. t. pl. we/you/they **are**; past t. sing. **I was**, you **were**, he/she/it **was**; past t. pl. we/you/they **were**; past p. **been**; pres. p. **being** 1 (forms continuous tenses with **–ing**): *I am/was reading.* 2 (forms passives with **–ed**): *We are/were invited.* 3 (used with **to**) a must: *You are not to smoke.* b (shows future plans): *They are to be married soon.*

be² v 1 (shows that something is the same as the subject): *Today is*

Tuesday. **2** (shows where or when): *He's upstairs.* **3** (shows a group or quality): *She's a doctor.* | *I'm cold.* | *Be careful!* **4** (shows that something exists): *There's a hole in your sock.*

beach /biʸtʃ/ *n* sandy or stony shore ♦ *vt* move (a boat) onto a beach

beach ball /ˈ· ·/ *n* large light ball to play with on the beach

beach bug·gy /ˈ· ˌ··/ *n* motor vehicle for use on sandy beaches

beach·comb·er /ˈbiʸtʃˌkoʷmər/ *n* **1** person who lives on a beach **2** person who searches a beach for useful things to sell

beach·head /ˈbiʸtʃhɛd/ *n* area on an enemy's shore that has been won by an opposing force

beach·wear /ˈbiʸtʃwɛər/ *n* [U] clothing for the BEACH

bea·con /ˈbiʸkən/ *n* fire or flashing light that gives warning

bead /biʸd/ *n* **1** small ball with a hole through it, for putting on string **2** drop of liquid: *beads of sweat* ~**ed** *adj*

bead·y /ˈbiʸdiʸ/ *adj* (of eyes) small and bright

bea·gle /ˈbiʸgəl/ *n* hunting dog with short legs

beak /biʸk/ *n* bird's hard horny mouth

bea·ker /ˈbiʸkər/ *n* glass cup used in chemistry

beam¹ /biʸm/ *n* long heavy piece of wood, esp. used to support a building

beam² *n* **1** line of light from some bright object **2** radio waves sent out to guide aircraft, etc. **3** bright look or smile ♦ *v* **1** *vi* (of the sun, etc.) send out light (and heat) **2** *vt* send out (esp. radio or television signals) in a certain direction **3** *vi* smile brightly

bean /biʸn/ *n* **1** seed or POD of any of various plants, esp. used as food: *baked beans* | *coffee beans* **2** full of beans a full of life and energy b consisting of nonsense **3** spill the beans tell a secret

bear¹ /bɛər/ *n* large, heavy furry animal that eats meat, fruit, and insects

bear² *v* bore /bɔr, boʷr/ borne /bɔrn, boʷrn/ **1** *vt* carry **2** *vt* support (a weight) **3** *vt* have; show: *The letter bore no signature.* | *to bear a famous name* **4** *vt* suffer or accept (something unpleasant) without complaining **5** *vt fml* give birth to **6** *vi/t* produce (a crop or fruit) **7** *vi* move in the stated direction: *Cross the field, bear left, and you'll see the house.* **8** *vt* be suitable for: *His words don't bear repeating.* **9** *vt fml* keep (a feeling toward someone) in one's

mind: *I don't bear him a grudge.* **10** bear in mind remember to consider **11** bring something to bear (on) direct something, e.g. force or persuasion on: EXERT ~**able** *adj* tolerable (TOLERATE) ~**ably** *adv*

bear down *phr v* **1** *vt fml* defeat **2** *vi* use all one's strength and energy

bear down on/upon *phr vt* come towards forcefully and threateningly, esp. at high speed

bear on/upon *phr vt* relate to

bear out *phr vt* support the truth of

bear up *phr vi* show courage or strength in spite of difficulties

bear with *phr vt* show patience towards

beard /bɪərd/ *n* hair on the face below the mouth ~**ed** *adj*

bear·er /ˈbɛərər/ *n* **1** person who brings or carries something, e.g. the body at a funeral **2** person to whom a check is to be paid

bear·ing /ˈbɛərɪŋ/ *n* **1** [S;U] way of behaving **2** [S;U] connection; relevance (RELEVANT): *This has no bearing on the subject.* **3** [C] direction shown by a compass **4** understanding of one's position: *get/lose one's bearings*

beast /biʸst/ *n* **1** animal with four feet **2** person or thing one does not like ~**ly** *adj* bad; nasty

beat¹ /biʸt/ *v* beat, beaten /ˈbiʸtn/ or beat **1** *vt* hit again and again, esp. with a stick: *beat a drum* | *the rain beating against the windows* **2** *vt* mix with a fork, etc.: *beat the eggs* **3** *vi* move regularly: *I could hear his heart beating.* **4** *vt* defeat: *I beat him at tennis.* **5** beat about the bush talk indirectly about something **6** Beat it! *infml* Go away! **7** beat one's brains out try very hard to think or remember **8** beat the rap avoid punishment **9** beat time make regular movements to measure the speed of music ~**er** *n* tool for beating things ~**ing** ♦ *n* **1** act of giving repeated blows, usu. as punishment **2** defeat

beat² *n* **1** single stroke or blow: *the beat of the drum* **2** regular STRESS (4) in music or poetry **3** usual path followed by someone on duty

be·a·tif·ic /ˌbiʸəˈtɪfɪk◂/ *adj* showing joy and peace: *a beatific smile*

beau·ti·cian /byuʷˈtɪʃən/ *n* person who cuts women's hair and gives beauty treatments

beau·ti·ful /ˈbyuʷtəfəl/ *adj* giving pleasure to the mind or senses ~**ly** *adv* –**tify** *vt* make beautiful

beau·ty /ˈbyuʷtiʸ/ *n* **1** [U] quality of being beautiful **2** [C] someone or something beautiful

beauty par·lor /ˈ·· ˌ··/ *n* place

where women get beauty treatments for face, hair, etc.

bea·ver /ˈbiˀvər/ n animal like a big rat that builds walls of sticks etc. across streams

be·calmed /bɪˈkɑmd/ adj (of a sailing ship) unable to move because there is no wind

be·came /bɪˈkeˀm/ past t. of BECOME

be·cause /bɪˈkɔz, -ˈkʌz/ conj 1 for the reason that: *I do it because I like it.* 2 **because of** as a result of: *I came back because of the rain.*

beck /bɛk/ n **at one's beck and call** always ready to do what one asks

beck·on /ˈbɛkən/ vi/t call with a movement of the finger

be·come /bɪˈkʌm/ v became, become 1 begin to be: *become king | become warmer* 2 vt be suitable for: *Such behavior hardly becomes someone in your position.* **becoming** adj 1 attractive 2 suitable

bed¹ /bɛd/ n 1 [C] piece of furniture to sleep on 2 bottom or base: *bed of a river* 3 [C] piece of ground for plants 4 [U] making love; sex

bed² vt -dd- 1 put in or on a bed: *a machine bedded in cement* 2 plant 3 have sex with

bed down phr v 1 vt make (a person or animal) comfortable for the night 2 vi make oneself comfortable for the night

bed·clothes /ˈbɛdkloˀz, -kloˀðz/ n [P] sheets, etc., on a bed

bed·ding /ˈbɛdɪŋ/ n [U] materials for a person or animal to sleep on

be·dev·il /bɪˈdɛvəl/ vt -l- cause continual trouble for

bed·fel·low /ˈbɛdˌfɛloˀ/ n 1 person who shares a bed 2 close companion; partner

bed·lam /ˈbɛdləm/ n [S;U] place of wild noisy activity

bed of ros·es /ˌ· · ˈ··/ n [S] happy comfortable state

bed·pan /ˈbɛdpæn/ n container for a sick person's body waste

be·drag·gled /bɪˈdrægəld/ adj wet, LIMP, and muddy

bed·rid·den /ˈbɛdˌrɪdn/ adj too ill or old to get out of bed

bed·room /ˈbɛdruˀm, -rʊm/ n room for sleeping in

bed·side /ˈbɛdsaɪd/ n 1 side of a bed: *bedside lamp* 2 **bedside manner** way in which a doctor behaves when visiting a sick person

bed·sore /ˈbɛdsɔr/ n sore place on the skin, caused by lying too long in bed

bed·spread /ˈbɛdsprɛd/ n decorative cover for a bed

bed·stead /ˈbɛdstɛd/ n main framework of a bed

bed·time /ˈbɛdtaɪm/ n time for going to bed

bee /biˀ/ n 1 stinging insect that makes HONEY 2 **a bee in one's bonnet** fixed idea; OBSESSION 3 **the bee's knees** infml the best person or thing

beech /biˀtʃ/ n large forest tree with green or shiny brown leaves

beef¹ /biˀf/ n [U] meat of farm cattle ♦ ~y adj (of a person) big and strong

beef² vi complain

beef up /ˌ· ˈ·/ phr vt make stronger or more complete

bee·hive /ˈbiˀhaɪv/ n HIVE

bee·line /ˈbiˀlaɪn/ n **make a beeline for** go straight towards

been /bɪn/ n 1 past participle of BE 2 gone and come back: *Have you ever been to England?*

beep /biˀp/ vi/t 1 sound a car horn 2 attract attention using a small electronic machine (**beeper**) ♦ n 1 sound of a horn or beeper 2 short high sounding note, esp. as given on the radio to show the exact time

beer /bɪər/ n [U] alcoholic drink made from MALT ~y adj: *beery breath*

beet /biˀt/ n 1 root from which sugar is made 2 large red root vegetable

bee·tle /ˈbiˀtl/ n insect with hard wing coverings

be·fall /bɪˈfɔl/ vi/t befell /-ˈfɛl/, be-fallen /-ˈfɔlən/ fml happen (to)

be·fit /bɪˈfɪt/ vt -tt- fml be suitable for: *befitting behavior*

be·fore /bɪˈfɔr, -ˈfoˀr/ prep 1 earlier than 2 ahead of; in front of ♦ adv already; formerly: *I've seen you before.* ♦ conj 1 before the time when 2 rather than

be·fore·hand /bɪˈfɔrˌhænd, -ˈfoˀr-/ adv before something else happens

be·friend /bɪˈfrɛnd/ vt fml be a friend to

beg /bɛg/ v -gg- 1 vi/t ask for (food, money, etc.) 2 vt fml request politely: *I beg to differ.* 3 **beg the question** to take as true something that is not yet proved

be·get /bɪˈgɛt/ v begot /bɪˈgɑt/, be-gotten /bɪˈgɑtn/ lit become the father of; produce

beg·gar /ˈbɛgər/ n person who lives by begging ~ly adj much too little

be·gin /bɪˈgɪn/ vi/t began /bɪˈgæn/, begun /bɪˈgʌn/ 1 start; make the first step 2 **to begin with** as the first reason ~ner n person starting to learn ~ning n [C;U] starting point

be·grudge /bɪˈgrʌdʒ/ vt to GRUDGE

be·guile /bɪˈgaɪl/ vt fml 1 charm 2 deceive; cheat

be·half /bɪˈhæf/ n **on behalf of** for;

in the interests of: *I'm speaking on John's behalf.*

be·have /bɪˈheɪv/ *vi* **1** (of people or things) act in a particular way **2** show good manners

be·hav·ior /bɪˈheɪvyər/ *n* [U] way of behaving

be·head /bɪˈhed/ *vt* cut off the head of

be·hest /bɪˈhest/ *n fml* **at someone's behest** by someone's command

be·hind /bɪˈhaɪnd/ *prep* **1** at or to the back of: *hide behind the door* **2** less good than: *He's behind the others in mathematics.* **3** in support of ◆ *adv* **1** behind something **2** where something was before: *I've left the key behind!* **3** late; slow: *We're behind with the rent.* ◆ *n infml* BUTTOCKS

be·hold /bɪˈhoʊld/ *vt* beheld /bɪˈheld/ *lit* see

be·hold·en /bɪˈhoʊldn/ *adj* **be beholden to** owing something to

beige /beʒ/ *adj, n* pale brown

be·ing¹ /ˈbiːɪŋ/ *n* **1** [U] existence: *When did the club come into being?* **2** [C] living thing, esp. a person

being² *v present participle of* BE

be·lat·ed /bɪˈleɪtɪd/ *adj* delayed; too late ~**ly** *adv*

belch /beltʃ/ *v* **1** *vi* pass gas up from the stomach **2** *vt* send out (large amounts of smoke, etc.) **belch** *n*

be·lea·guer /bɪˈliːɡər/ *vt fml* **1** surround with an army **2** worry continuously

bel·fry /ˈbelfriː/ *n* tower for bells

be·lie /bɪˈlaɪ/ *vt fml* give a false idea of

be·lief /bəˈliːf/ *n* **1** [S;U] feeling that something is true, or can be trusted **2** [C] idea that is believed: *religious beliefs*

be·lieve /bəˈliːv/ *v* **1** *vt* consider to be true **2** *vi* have religious faith **believable** *adj* that can be believed **believer** *n*

believe in *phr vt* **1** think that (something exists): *believe in fairies* **2** feel sure of the value of: *believe in lots of exercise*

be·lit·tle /bɪˈlɪtl/ *vt fml* **cause to seem unimportant**: *Don't belittle your efforts.*

bell /bel/ *n* **1** metal object that makes a ringing sound: *church bells* | *a bicycle bell* **2** object shaped like a cup: *the bell of a flower* **3** **ring a bell** remind one of something

bell-bot·toms /ˈ· ˌ··/ *n* [P] trousers with legs that are wider at the bottom

bel·lig·er·ent /bəˈlɪdʒərənt/ *n, adj* **1** (country that is) at war **2** (person who is) ready to fight

bel·low /ˈbeloʊ/ *vi/t* shout in a deep voice

bel·lows /ˈbeloʊz/ *n* [P] –**lows** instrument for blowing air into a fire, etc.

bel·ly /ˈbeliː/ *n* **1** *infml* the part of the human body between the chest and legs **2** curved surface like this: *the belly of a plane* ~**ful** /-fʊl/ *n infml* too much

bel·ly·ache /ˈbeliːˌeɪk/ *vi* complain repeatedly

belly but·ton /ˈ·· ˌ··/ *n infml* NAVEL

be·long /bɪˈlɔŋ/ *vi* be in the right place: *This chair belongs upstairs.* ~**ings** *n* [P] one's property

belong to *phr vt* **1** be the property of **2** be a member of

be·lov·ed /bɪˈlʌvd, bɪˈlʌvɪd/ *n, adj* (person who is) dearly loved

be·low /bɪˈloʊ/ *adv, prep* in a lower place (than); under: *He saw the valley below.* | *below the knee* | *see page 85 below*

belt¹ /belt/ *n* **1** band worn round the waist **2** circular piece of material that drives a machine **3** area with a particular quality, crop, etc. **4** BELTWAY **5** **below the belt** *infml* unfair or unfairly – see also BLACK BELT

belt² *v* **1** *vt* fasten with a belt **2** *vt infml* hit hard

belt out *phr vt infml* sing loudly

belt·way /ˈbeltweɪ/ *n* road that goes around a town

be·moan /bɪˈmoʊn/ *vt fml* express sorrow for

be·mused /bɪˈmyuːzd/ *adj* unable to think clearly

bench /bentʃ/ *n* **1** [C] long seat **2** [C] long table for working on: *a carpenter's bench* **3** **a** [*the*+S] place where a judge sits in court **b** judges as a group

bend /bend/ *vi/t* bent /bent/ (cause to) move into a curve or move away from an upright position: *bend the wire* | *bend down to kiss the child* ◆ *n* **1** curve: *a bend in the road* **2** **round the bend** *infml* crazy **bends** [P] pain suffered by divers (DIVE) who come to the surface too quickly

be·neath /bɪˈniːθ/ *adv, prep fml* **1** below; under **2** not worthy of: *beneath contempt*

ben·e·dic·tion /ˌbenəˈdɪkʃən/ *n* religious blessing

ben·e·fac·tor /ˈbenəˌfæktər/ **benefactress** /-trɪs/ *fem.* — *n* person who gives money, etc. –**tion** /ˌbenəˈfækʃən/ *n* **1** [U] giving of money **2** [C] money given

ben·e·fi·cial /ˌbenəˈfɪʃəl◂/ *adj* (of things) helpful; useful

ben·e·fi·cia·ry /ˌbenəˈfɪʃiːˌeriː, -ˈfɪʃəriː/ *n* receiver of a benefit

ben·e·fit /ˈbɛnɪfɪt/ n 1 [U] advantage; profit: *She's had the benefit of a very good education.* 2 [C] money paid by an insurance agreement: *widow's benefit* 3 [C] event to raise money for some person or special purpose 4 **the benefit of the doubt** favorable consideration given because there is no proof of guilt or wrongness ♦ v 1 vt be helpful to 2 vi gain advantage

be·nev·o·lent /bəˈnɛvələnt/ adj wishing to do good; kind –**lence** n [U]

be·nign /bɪˈnaɪn/ adj kind and harmless

bent¹ /bɛnt/ v 1 past t. and p. of BEND 2 **bent on** determined on: *She's bent on winning.*

bent² n special natural skill: *a natural bent for languages*

be·queath /bɪˈkwiːð, bɪˈkwiːθ/ vt fml give to others after death

be·quest /bɪˈkwɛst/ n fml something bequeathed

be·rate /bɪˈreɪt/ vt fml speak angrily to

be·reaved /bəˈriːvd/ adj fml having lost someone by death: *a bereaved mother* **bereavement** n [C;U]

be·reft /bəˈrɛft/ adj completely without: *bereft of hope*

be·ret /bəˈreɪ/ n round soft flat cap

ber·ry /ˈbɛriː/ n small soft fruit with seeds

ber·serk /bərˈsɜrk, -ˈzɜrk/ adj violently angry

berth /bɜrθ/ n 1 sleeping place in a ship or train 2 place where a ship can be tied up in harbor 3 **give someone a wide berth** avoid someone ♦ vi/t tie up (a ship)

be·seech /bɪˈsiːtʃ/ vt besought /bɪˈsɔt/ or **beseeched** fml ask eagerly

be·set /bɪˈsɛt/ vt beset, present participle **besetting** attack continuously: *beset by doubts*

be·side /bɪˈsaɪd/ prep 1 at the side of 2 in comparison with 3 **beside oneself** almost crazy (with joy, etc.) 4 **beside the point** having nothing to do with the main question

be·sides /bɪˈsaɪdz/ adv also ♦ prep in addition to

be·siege /bɪˈsiːdʒ/ vt surround (a place) with armed forces: (fig.) *They besieged her with questions.*

be·sot·ted /bɪˈsɑtɪd/ adj made foolish or unable to behave sensibly

best¹ /bɛst/ adj (superlative of GOOD) the highest in quality or skill: *the best tennis player in America* **The best part of** most of – see also SECOND BEST

best² adv (superlative of WELL) 1 in

the best way: *She did best.* 2 to the greatest degree; most: *He thinks he knows best.*

best³ n [S] 1 the greatest degree of good: *She wants the best for her children.* 2 one's best effort: *I did my best.* 3 **All the best!** (used when saying goodbye) I wish you success! 4 **at its/one's best** in as good a state as possible 5 **at (the) best** if the best happens 6 **make the best of** do as well as one can with (something unsatisfactory)

bes·ti·al /ˈbɛstʃəl, ˈbiːs-/ adj (of human behavior) very cruel ~**ity** /ˌbɛstʃiˈæləˌtiˌ, ˌbiːs-/ n [U]

best man /ˌ· ˈ·/ n man attending the BRIDEGROOM at a wedding

be·stow /bɪˈstoʊ/ vt fml give

best·sel·ler /ˌbɛstˈsɛlər/ n book, etc., that sells in very large numbers

bet /bɛt/ n 1 agreement to risk money on a future event 2 sum of money risked in this way ♦ vi/t bet or betted; pres. p. **betting** 1 risk (money) on a race, etc. 2 be sure: *I bet he's angry!*

be·tide /bɪˈtaɪd/ vt lit **woe betide you, him, etc.** you, he, etc., will be in trouble

be·tray /bɪˈtreɪ/ vt 1 be unfaithful to 2 make known (a secret): (fig.) *Her face betrayed (= showed) her nervousness.* ~**er** n ~**al** n [C;U]

be·trothed /bɪˈtroʊðd/ adj lit having promised to marry

bet·ter /ˈbɛtər/ adj 1 higher in quality; more good: *a better way to do it* 2 well again after illness ♦ adv 1 in a better way: *It works better now.* 2 **go one better (than)** do better (than) 3 **had better** ought to; should: *I'd better not tell him.* 4 **know better (than)** be sensible enough not to ♦ n **get the better of** defeat ♦ vi/t 1 improve 2 **better oneself: a** earn more **b** educate oneself ~**ment** improvement **betters** n [P] people better than oneself

better off /ˌ·· ˈ·/ adj 1 having more money 2 improved

be·tween /bɪˈtwiːn/ prep 1 in the space or time that separates: *Stand between Sue and Brian.* | *Don't eat between meals.* 2 (shows connection): *an air service between Boston and Houston* 3 (shows division or sharing): *The difference between spaghetti and noodles.* | *Between us, we collected $17.* ♦ adv 1 in the space or time between things 2 **few and far between** very rare

bev·el /ˈbɛvəl/ vt -l- make a sloping edge on **bevel** n

bev·er·age /ˈbɛvərɪdʒ/ n fml liquid for drinking, esp. one that is not water or medicine

bev·y /ˈbɛviː/ n large group

be·wail /bɪ'weɪl/ vt fml express sorrow for

be·ware /bɪ'weər/ vi/t (used in giving orders) Be careful!: *Beware of the dog.*

be·wil·der /bɪ'wɪldər/ vt confuse: *a bewildering mass of detail*

be·witch /bɪ'wɪtʃ/ vt **1** use magic on **2** charm: *a bewitching smile*

be·yond /bɪ'yɑnd/ prep **1** on the further side of: *beyond the mountains* **2** outside the limits of; more than: *beyond belief* **3 beyond me** too hard for me to understand ♦ adv further: *fly to Cairo and beyond*

bi·as /'baɪəs/ n [C;U] fixed unfair opinion; PREJUDICE ♦ vt **-s-** cause to form fixed opinions: *a biased judgment*

bib /bɪb/ n **1** piece of cloth or plastic tied under a child's chin **2** top part of an APRON

Bi·ble /'baɪbəl/ n holy book of the Christians and Jews: (fig.) *This dictionary is my bible.* **biblical** /'bɪbl‚kəl/ adj

bib·li·og·ra·phy /‚bɪbli'ɑgrəfiy/ n list of writings on a subject **-pher** person who writes such a list

bi·car·bon·ate of so·da /baɪ‚kɑrbənɪt əv 'sowdə, -neyt-/ n [U] chemical used in baking and as a medicine; BAKING SODA

bi·cen·ten·ni·al /‚baɪsen'teniyəl/ n 200th ANNIVERSARY **bicentennial** adj

bi·ceps /'baɪseps/ n **biceps** muscle of the upper arm

bick·er /'bɪkər/ vi quarrel about small matters

bi·cy·cle /'baɪsɪkəl/ n vehicle with two wheels ridden by pushing its PEDALs **bicycle** vi

bid¹ /bɪd/ vi/t **1** offer (a price) at a sale **2** (in card games) declare what one intends to win ♦ n **1** amount that is bid **2** attempt: *a rescue bid* ~**der** n

bid² vt **bade** /bæd, beyd/ or **bid, bidden** /'bɪdn/ or **bid;** pres. p. **bidding** lit order: *She bade him come.* ~**ding** n [U]

bide /baɪd/ vt **bide one's time** wait till the right moment

bi·en·ni·al /baɪ'eniyəl/ adj happening once every 2 years n plant that makes flowers in its second year, then dies

bier /bɪər/ n movable table for a COFFIN

bi·fo·cals /'baɪ‚fowkəlz, baɪ'fowkəlz/ n [P] glasses made in 2 parts, suitable both for looking at distant objects and for reading **bifocal** adj

big /bɪg/ adj **-gg-** **1** of more than average size, importance, etc.: *big ears | a big decision* **2** generous: *big hearted* **3** infml very popular

big·a·my /'bɪgəmiy/ n [U] being married to 2 people at the same time **-mist** n **-mous** adj

big game /‚· '·/ n [U] lions, elephants, etc., hunted for sport

big·head·ed /'bɪg‚hed'ɪd◄/ adj infml CONCEITed

big·ot /'bɪgət/ n person who will not change an unreasonable opinion ~**ry** n [U] behavior typical of a bigot

big shot /‚· '·/ also **big noise** — n person of great importance or influence

big·wig /'bɪgwɪg/ n infml important person

bi·jou /'biyʒuw/ adj (esp. of a building) small and pretty

bike /baɪk/ n , vi BICYCLE

bi·ki·ni /bɪ'kiyniy/ n clothing worn by a woman for swimming, consisting of two separate pieces

bi·lat·er·al /baɪ'lætərəl/ adj with 2 sides or 2 groups: *a bilateral agreement*

bile /baɪl/ n [U] **1** liquid formed in the LIVER **2** bad temper

bilge /bɪldʒ/ n [U] **1** ship's bottom, with dirty water in it **2** infml foolish talk

bi·lin·gual /baɪ'lɪŋgwəl/ adj using 2 languages

bil·ious /'bɪlyəs/ adj sick because food is not DIGESTed properly

bill¹ /bɪl/ n **1** list of things that must be paid for **2** plan for a future law **3** piece of paper money **4** printed notice **5 fill the bill** be suitable **6 foot the bill** pay and take responsibility (for) ♦ vt **1** send a bill to **2** advertise in printed notices **3** arrange a performance

bill² n bird's beak

bill·board /'bɪlbɔrd, -bowrd/ n large board usu. outdoors on which advertisements are put

bil·let /'bɪlɪt/ n private home where soldiers are put to live ♦ vt put in billets

bill·fold /'bɪlfowld/ n WALLET

bil·liards /'bɪlyərdz/ n [U] game played on a table, with balls and long sticks

bil·lion /'bɪlyən/ determiner, n **billion** or **billions** one thousand million ~**th** determiner, n, adv

bil·low /'bɪlow/ n rolling mass of smoke, etc., like a large wave **billow** vi

bil·ly club /'bɪliy ‚klʌb/ n short thick stick used as a weapon by a policeman

billy goat /'bɪliy ‚gowt/ n male goat

bin /bɪn/ n large container for storing things, or for waste

bi·na·ry /'baɪnariy/ adj **1** double **2** using only 0 and 1 as a base: *the binary scale*

bind /baɪnd/ v **bound** /baʊnd/ **1** vt tie up: bind the prisoner's arms | bind up a wound | (fig.) bound together by friendship **2** vt fasten (a book) into its cover **3** vi/t (cause) to stick together in a mass **4** vt cause to obey, esp. by a law or a promise: a binding agreement | He felt bound to tell her. ~**er** n **1** person or thing that binds books **2** removable cover for holding sheets of papers, etc. ~**ing** n book cover

binge /bɪndʒ/ n infml period of drinking and wild behavior

bin·go /ˈbɪŋgoʷ/ n [U] **1** game played for money, by covering numbered squares on a card **2** infml (an expression of pleasure)

bi·noc·u·lars /bɪˈnɑkyəlɚz, baɪ-/ n [P] pair of glasses like short TELESCOPES for both eyes

bi·o·chem·is·try /ˌbaɪoʷˈkemɪstriʸ/ n [U] chemistry of living things

bi·o·de·gra·da·ble /ˌbaɪoʷdɪˈgreʸdəbəl/ adj able to be made harmless by the chemical action of bacteria, etc.

bi·og·ra·phy /baɪˈɑgrəfiʸ/ n written account of someone's life –**pher** a person who writes this –**phical** /ˌbaɪəˈgræfɪkəl◂/ adj

bi·ol·o·gy /baɪˈɑlədʒiʸ/ n [U] scientific study of living things –**gist** n –**gical** /ˌbaɪəˈlɑdʒɪkəl◂/ adj

bi·on·ic /baɪˈɑnɪk/ adj having more than human strength, speed, etc.

bi·o·pic /ˈbaɪoʷˌpɪk/ n biographical film

bi·op·sy /ˈbaɪˌɑpsiʸ/ n removal of material from a living body to test it for possible disease

bi·o·tech·nol·o·gy /ˌbaɪoʷtekˈnɑlədʒiʸ/ n [U] use of living cells, bacteria, etc., in industry

bi·ped /ˈbaɪpɛd/ n creature with two feet

bi·plane /ˈbaɪpleʸn/ n aircraft with 2 pairs of wings

birch /bɜrtʃ/ n **1** tree with smooth wood and thin branches **2** rod made from this wood, used for punishing

bird /bɜrd/ n **1** [C] creature with wings and feathers that can fly **2 birds of a feather** people of the same kind – see also EARLY BIRD

bird's-eye view /ˌ·ˈ· ˌ·/ n view seen from above, like a map

birth /bɜrθ/ n **1** [C;U] act, time, or process of being born: She gave birth to a fine baby. **2** [U] family origin: French by birth

birth con·trol /ˈ· ·ˌ·/ n [U] CONTRACEPTION

birth·day /ˈbɜrθdeʸ/ n ANNIVERSARY of the day one was born

birth·mark /ˈbɜrθmɑrk/ n mark on the skin at birth

birth·rate /ˈbɜrθreʸt/ n number of births during a particular time

birth·right /ˈbɜrθraɪt/ n something that belongs to someone because of the family or nation they were born into

bis·cuit /ˈbɪskɪt/ n small round bread-like cake often eaten with GRAVY

bi·sect /ˈbaɪsɛkt, baɪˈsɛkt/ vt divide into 2

bi·sex·u·al /baɪˈsɛkʃuʷəl/ adj sexually attracted to people of both sexes

bish·op /ˈbɪʃəp/ n **1** Christian priest of high rank **2** piece in CHESS ~**ric** /ˈbɪʃəprɪk/ n DIOCESE

bi·son /ˈbaɪsən, -zən/ n bisons or bison **1** large wild hairy cowlike animal **2** BUFFALO

bis·tro /ˈbiʸstroʷ, ˈbɪ-/ n small BAR (4) or restaurant

bit¹ /bɪt/ v past t. of BITE

bit² n **1** small piece: bits of paper/of news **2** a short time: We walked around for a bit. **3 a bit** rather: I'm a bit tired. **4 every bit as** quite as; no less: She's every bit as good as you are. **5 not a bit** not at all

bit³ n single unit of computer information

bit⁴ n part of a BRIDLE that goes inside the horse's mouth

bitch /bɪtʃ/ n **1** female dog **2** derog unpleasant woman ♦ vi sl **1** complain continually **2** make nasty or unpleasant remarks about others ~**y** adj making nasty remarks about people

bite /baɪt/ v bit /bɪt/, **bitten** /ˈbɪtn/ **1** vi/t cut with the teeth **2** vi/t (of snakes and insects) sting **3** vi (of fish) accept food on a hook **4** vi take firm hold: This clamp won't bite the wood. **5** accept an offer esp. one that is meant to deceive: When they offered, I bit. **6 bite off more than one can chew** attempt too much **7 bite the bullet** suffer bravely **bite the dust** infml be killed or defeated ♦ n **1** [C] piece removed by biting **2** [C;U] wound made by biting **3** [S] something to eat **4** [U;S] sharpness; bitterness **biting** adj painful: biting wind/remarks

bit·ter /ˈbɪtɚr/ adj **1** not sweet; tasting like beer or black coffee **2** very cold: a bitter wind **3** causing grief: bitter disappointment **4** full of hate: bitter enemies **5 to the bitter end** to the end in spite of all unpleasant difficulties ~**ly** adv ~**ness** n [U]

bit·ter·sweet /ˈbɪtɚrˈswiʸt◂/ adj pleasant, but mixed with sadness

bi·tu·men /bɪˈtuʷmən, -ˈtyuʷ-, baɪ-/ n [U] sticky black substance used esp. in making roads

biv·ou·ac /ˈbɪvuʷˌæk, ˈbɪvwæk/

camp without tents ♦ *vi* **-ck-** spend the night in a bivouac

bi·zarre /bɪˈzɑr/ *adj* very strange ~**ly** *adv*

blab /blæb/ *vi* **-bb-** *sl* tell a secret

black /blæk/ *adj* **1** of the color of night: (fig.) *Your hands are black.* (= very dirty) **2** of a race of people with dark skin, esp. of the Negro race **3** (of coffee) without milk **4** very bad; hopeless **5** very angry: *a black look* **6** (of humor) funny about unpleasant or dangerous people or events: *black humor* ♦ *n* **1** [U] black color **2** [C] black person ♦ *vt* make black ~**ly** *adv* **1** angrily **2** sadly ~**ness** *n* [U]

black·ball /ˈblækbɔl/ *vt* vote against (someone who wants to join a club)

black belt /ˌ· ˈ·/ *n* (person who holds) a high rank in JUDO, KARATE, etc.

black·board /ˈblækbɔrd, -boʷrd/ *n* board used in schools for writing on

black box /ˌ· ˈ·/ *n* apparatus fitted to an aircraft to record information about an accident

black cher·ry /ˌ· ˈ··/ *n* very dark red fruit with a pit

black·en /ˈblækən/ *vi/t* make or become black: (fig.) *They blackened his character by spreading lies.*

black eye /ˌ· ˈ·/ *n* dark skin round the eye, from being hit

black·guard /ˈblægɑrd, -ɑrd/ *n* SCOUNDREL

black·head /ˈblækhed/ *n* spot on the skin with a black top

black hole /ˌ· ˈ·/ *n* area in outer space into which everything is pulled, even light itself

black·jack /ˈblækdʒæk/ *n* **1** [C] type of fighting weapon carried in the hand **2** [U] type of POKER game

black·list /ˈblækˌlɪst/ *n* list of people to be avoided or punished **blacklist** *vt*

black mag·ic /ˌ· ˈ··/ *n* magic used for evil purposes

black·mail /ˈblækmeʸl/ *n* [U] **1** getting money by threatening to make known unpleasant facts **2** influencing of someone's actions by threats, causing anxiety, etc.: *He accused his mother of using emotional blackmail to stop him leaving home.* ♦ **blackmail** *vt* ~**er** *n*

black mar·ket /ˌ· ˈ···/ *n* [S] unlawful buying and selling of goods, etc.: *We bought our dollars on the black market.* ~**eer** /ˌ· ··ˈ·/ *n*

black·out /ˈblækaʊt/ *n* **1** darkness, caused by electrical failure **2** short loss of consciousness **3** intentional prevention of reporting: *a news blackout* **black out** *vi/t*

black pow·er /ˌ· ˈ··/ *n* [S] movement

for the political and economic power of black people

black sheep /ˌ· ˈ·/ *n* family member who brings shame on it

black·smith /ˈblækˌsmɪθ/ *n* person who works metal and makes iron things

blad·der /ˈblædər/ *n* **1** skin bag inside the body, where waste liquid collects **2** any bag that can be filled with air or liquid

blade /bleʸd/ *n* **1** sharp cutting part of a knife, etc. **2** flat part of an OAR, PROPELLER, or BAT[1] (1) **3** long narrow leaf: *blades of grass*

blame /bleʸm/ *vt* **1** consider responsible for something bad **2 be to blame** be guilty ♦ *n* [U] responsibility for something bad ~**less** *adj* free from guilt ~**worthy** *adj* guilty

blanch /blæntʃ/ *vi/t* **1** make or become white **2** cook a short time in boiling water

bland /blænd/ *adj* **1** (of food) without much taste **2** (of people or their behavior) showing no strong feelings or opinions, esp. so as to avoid giving offense ~**ly** *adv* ~**ness** *n* [U]

blan·dish·ments /ˈblændɪʃmənts/ *n* [P] FLATTERY

blank[1] /blæŋk/ *adj* **1** without writing **2** empty or expressionless: *My mind went blank.* ~**ly** *adv*: *He looked at me blankly.* ~**ness** *n* [U]

blank[2] *n* **1** empty space **2** CARTRIDGE with no bullet in it **3 draw a blank** be unsuccessful

blank check /ˌ· ˈ·/ *n* **1** check that is signed, but with the amount left blank **2** complete freedom to do what one wants

blan·ket /ˈblæŋkɪt/ *n* thick bed covering: (fig.) *A blanket of snow covered the hills.* – see also WET BLANKET ♦ *vt* cover as with a blanket ♦ *adj* including all cases: *a blanket rule*

blank verse /ˌ· ˈ·/ *n* [U] poetry that does not RHYME

blare /bleɑr/ *vi/t* make the loud noise of a horn **blare** *n* [S]

bla·sé /blɑˈzeʸ/ *adj* seeming not to be concerned or excited about something, or about things in general

blas·phe·my /ˈblæsfəmi/ *n* [C;U] bad language about God and holy things –**mous** *adj* blaspheme /blæsˈfiʸm, ˈblæsfiʸm/ *vi*

blast[1] /blæst/ *n* **1** strong air movement **2** rush of air from an explosion **3** sound of a brass wind instrument **4 at full blast** as hard as possible

blast[2] *v* **1** *vi/t* break up (rock, etc.) with explosives **2** *vt* DAMN

blast off *phr vi* (of a spacecraft) leave the ground **blast-off** /ˈ· ·/ *n* [U]

blast fur·nace /ˈ· ͵··/ n FURNACE for separating iron from the rock in which it is found

bla·tant /ˈbleʸtnt/ adj too noticeable; shameless ~**ly** adv **–tancy** n [U]

blaze /bleʸz/ n 1 [S] bright flame: (fig.) a sudden blaze of anger 2 [C] big dangerous fire ♦ vi 1 burn or shine brightly 2 spread news about: The news was blazed across the front page. 3 **blaze a trail** lead the way

blaz·er /ˈbleʸzər/ n JACKET which fits loosely, sometimes with the sign of a school, etc., on it

bleach /bliʸtʃ/ vi/t make or become white or pale ♦ n [U] chemical used for bleaching cloth

bleach·ers /ˈbliʸtʃərz/ n [the-P] cheap seats, open to the air, for watching a game

bleak /bliʸk/ adj cold and cheerless: bleak weather | (fig.) bleak prospects ~**ly** adv **–ness** n [U]

blear·y /ˈbliʸəriʸ/ adj (of eyes) red and tired **–ily** adv **–iness** n [U]

bleat /bliʸt/ vi , n (make) the sound of a sheep or goat

bleed /bliʸd/ v **bled** /bled/ 1 vi lose blood 2 vt draw blood from, as doctors once did 3 vt draw off liquid or air from 4 **bleed for someone** feel pity

bleep /bliʸp/ n repeated high sound made by a machine to attract attention ♦ vi/t make this sound

blem·ish /ˈblemɪʃ/ n mark, etc., that spoils perfection **blemish** vt

blend /blend/ vi/t mix together ♦ n mixture ~**er** kitchen mixing machine

blend in phr vi go together well

bless /bles/ vt **blessed** or **blest** /blest/ 1 ask God's favor for 2 make holy 3 **be blessed with** be lucky enough to have ~**ed** /ˈblesɪd/ adj 1 holy 2 desirable 3 infml (used to give force to expressions of annoyance)

bless·ing /ˈblesɪŋ/ n 1 [C] God's favor 2 [C] something one is glad of 3 [U] approval

blew /bluʷ/ past t. of BLOW¹

blight /blaɪt/ n 1 [U] disease of plants 2 [C] something that spoils 3 [U] condition of ugliness, disorder, and decay **blight** vt: (fig.) blighted hopes

blind¹ /blaɪnd/ adj 1 unable to see 2 unwilling to recognize: blind to her faults 3 without reason or purpose: blind panic 4 drunk 5 **turn a blind eye (to)** pretend not to see or notice (something, esp. something illegal) ♦ vt 1 make unable to see or understand 2 **blind with science** confuse or fill with admiration by a show of detailed or specialist knowledge ~**ly** adv ~**ness** n [U]

blind² n place where one may watch animals, birds etc. without being seen

blind al·ley /͵· ˈ··/ n narrow street with no way out

blind drunk /͵· ˈ·/ adj extremely drunk

blind·ers /ˈblaɪndərz/ n [P] leather pieces fixed to prevent a horse from seeing sideways

blind·fold /ˈblaɪndfoʷld/ vt cover (the eyes) with a piece of cloth ♦ n piece of material to cover the eyes ♦ adv with the eyes covered: I could do it blindfold.

blind spot /ˈ· ·/ 1 part of an area that cannot easily be seen 2 something one is never able to understand

blink /blɪŋk/ vi/t shut and open (the eyes) quickly: (fig.) The lights blinked in the distance. **blink** n 1 act of blinking 2 **on the blink** not working properly

blink·ers /ˈblɪŋkərz/ n [P] 1 leather pieces fixed to prevent a horse from seeing sideways 2 flashing lights on a car showing which way it will turn 3 inability to see or understand **blinkered** adj

bliss /blɪs/ n [U] complete happiness ~**ful** adj ~**fully** adv

blis·ter /ˈblɪstər/ n 1 watery swelling under the skin 2 swelling like this on a rubber tire, painted wood, etc. ♦ vi/t form blisters ~**ing** adj 1 very hot 2 very angry and intended to hurt: a blistering attack

blithe /blaɪð, blaɪθ/ adj free from care ~**ly** adv

blitz /blɪts/ n 1 sudden violent attack, esp. from the air 2 period of great activity for some special purpose: an advertising blitz

bliz·zard /ˈblɪzərd/ n severe snowstorm

bloat·ed /ˈbloʷtɪd/ adj unpleasantly swollen

blob /blɑb/ n drop of liquid or small round mass

bloc /blɑk/ n group of people, nations, etc., acting as a unit – see also EN BLOC

block /blɑk/ n 1 solid piece of material: a block of wood/ice 2 sl head: I'll knock your block off. 3 distance between one street and the next: The store is 4 blocks away. 4 group of things considered together: a block of theater seats 5 blockage ♦ vt 1 prevent movement through 2 shut off from view 3 prevent the success of: to block legislation

block·ade /blɑˈkeʸd/ n surrounding of a place, by ships or soldiers, to stop people or goods from going in or out: to raise/lift (= end) a blockade ♦ vt surround in this way

block·age /'blɑkɪdʒ/ n something that stops movement; OBSTRUCTION: *a blockage in the pipe*

block·bust·er /'blɑk‚bʌstər/ n something very big, effective, or successful

blond /blɑnd/ adj 1 (of hair) light in color; yellow 2 (**blonde** *fem.*) having blond hair **blonde** /blɑnd/ n blonde woman

blood /blʌd/ n 1 [U] red liquid that flows through the body: *blood donors* 2 [U] family relationship: *people of noble blood* 3 **in cold blood** cruelly and on purpose 4 **make someone's blood boil** make someone very angry 5 **make someone's blood run cold** frighten someone ~**less** adj without fighting ~**y** adj bleeding ~**ily** adv

blood·bath /'blʌdbæθ/ n merciless killing; MASSACRE

blood broth·er /‚· '··/ n one of two or more men who have promised complete loyalty to one another

blood·cur·dling /'blʌd‚kɜrdlɪŋ/ adj very frightening

blood group /'· ·/ n class of human blood

blood·hound /'blʌdhaʊnd/ n large dog that tracks people and animals

blood poi·son·ing /'· ‚···/ n [U] condition in which an infection spreads from a part of the body through the BLOODSTREAM

blood pres·sure /'· ‚··/ n [C;U] measurable force with which blood flows through the BLOODSTREAM

blood·shed /'blʌdʃed/ n [U] killing, usu. in fighting

blood·shot /'blʌdʃɑt/ adj (of the eyes) red

blood·stain /'blʌdsteʸn/ n spot of blood ~**ed** adj

blood·stream /'blʌdstriʸm/ n flow of blood through the body

blood·suck·er /'blʌd‚sʌkər/ n 1 creature that bites and then sucks blood from the wound 2 person who tries to get as much money as possible from other people

blood·thirst·y /'blʌd‚θɜrstiʸ/ adj eager to kill; too interested in violence

blood·y mur·der /‚·· '··/ n **scream/ shout bloody murder** *infml* complain very loudly

bloom /bluʷm/ n 1 flower 2 **in the bloom of** at the best time of/for ♦ vi 1 produce flowers 2 show as healthy color 3 BLOSSOM (2)

bloom·ers /'bluʷmərz/ n [P] women's short loose trousers gathered at the knee

blos·som /'blɑsəm/ n 1 flower of a tree or bush 2 **in blossom** bearing flowers ♦ vi 1 produce blossoms 2 develop favorably

blot¹ /blɑt/ n 1 spot, esp. of ink 2 shameful fault: *a blot on her character* 3 something ugly: *a blot on the landscape*

blot² vt –tt– 1 make blots on 2 dry up (ink)

blot out phr vt cover; hide: *Clouds blotted out the sun.*

blotch /blɑtʃ/ n large spot or mark ~**y** adj

blot·ter /'blɑtər/ n large piece of BLOTTING PAPER

blotting pa·per /'·· ‚··/ n [U] thick soft paper used to dry wet ink after writing

blot·to /'blɑtoʷ/ adj drunk

blouse /blaʊs, blaʊz/ n woman's shirt

blow¹ /bloʷ/ v blew /bluʷ/, blown /bloʷn/ 1 vi/t send out air; move by the force of air: *The wind blew the tree down.* | *He blew the candle out.* 2 vi/t sound made by blowing: *to blow a trumpet* 3 vt clean (one's nose) by blowing through it 4 vi/t melt (an electrical FUSE) 5 vt sl lose (a favorable chance) as the result of foolishness 6 vt *infml* spend (money) freely 7 vi sl leave quickly 8 **blow hot and cold (about)** be favorable (to) at one moment and unfavorable (to) at the next 9 **blow one's own trumpet** *infml* praise oneself 10 **blow one's top/ stack** sl explode with anger 11 **blow someone a kiss** kiss one's hand, then wave or blow over it towards someone 12 **blow someone's brains out** *infml* kill someone by a shot through the head 13 **blow someone's mind** sl fill someone with wonder 14 **blow the whistle on** sl cause something undesirable to stop, by bringing it to the attention of esp. the public

blow over phr vi (of a storm) stop blowing: (fig.) *The scandal will soon blow over.*

blow up phr v 1 vi/t explode 2 vt fill with air: *blow up the tires* 3 make (a photograph) larger: (fig.) *The affair was blown up by the newspapers.* 4 get angry suddenly 5 (of bad weather) start blowing: *There's a storm blowing up.*

blow² n act of blowing: *Give your nose a good blow.*

blow³ n 1 hard stroke with the hand or a weapon 2 sudden misfortune 3 **come to blows** start to fight – see also BODY BLOW

blow-by-blow /‚·· '··◂/ adj with full details, given in the order in which they happened

blow·er /'bloʷər/ n apparatus for producing a current of air or gas

blown /bloʷn/ past p. of BLOW¹

blow·out /'bloʷaʊt/ n 1 very big

meal **2** bursting of a container (esp. a tire)

blow·torch /ˈbloʷtɔrtʃ/ n lamp that blows a flame (e.g. for burning off paint)

BLT /ˌbiʸ ɛl ˈtiʸ/ n bacon, lettuce and tomato sandwich

blub·ber¹ /ˈblʌbər/ n [U] fat of sea creatures, esp. WHALES

blubber² vi weep noisily

blud·geon /ˈblʌdʒən/ vt **1** hit with something heavy **2** force to do something, by threats

blue /bluʷ/ adj **1** of the color of the clear sky **2** sad; DEPRESSed **3** concerned with sex; improper: blue films ♦ n [U] **1** blue color **2** out of the blue unexpectedly **blues** n **1** [S;U] slow sad song or music from the South **2** [U] sadness

blue·ber·ry /ˈbluʷˌbɛriʸ, -bəriʸ/ n garden bush with small blue berries

blue·blood·ed /ˌ·ˈ·◂/ adj of noble birth

blue book /ˈ· ·/ n **1** book listing names of well known and important people **2** book of empty pages with a blue cover for writing college examinations

blue chip /ˌ·ˈ·/ n, adj (an industrial stock) that is expensive and in which people have confidence

blue-col·lar /ˌ·ˈ·◂/ adj of or concerning workers who do hard or dirty work with their hands

blue jay /ˈ· ·/ n bright blue bird from eastern North America

blue laws /ˈ· ˌ·/ n laws forbidding drinking, dancing etc.

blue moon /ˌ· ˈ·/ n [S] **once in a blue moon** infml almost never

blue·print /ˈbluʷˌprɪnt/ n copy of a plan for making or building something: (fig.) a blueprint for the reforms

blue-sky /ˌ·ˈ·◂/ adj done in order to test ideas, rather than for any particular practical purpose

blue·stock·ing /ˈbluʷˌstakɪŋ/ n woman thought to be too highly educated

blue tail fly /ˌ·· ˈ·/ n large bluegreen fly

bluff¹ /blʌf/ vi **1** deceive someone by pretending to be stronger or cleverer than one is: They say they'll blow up the place, but they're only bluffing. **2** bluff it out escape trouble by continuing a deception **bluff** n [S;U] **1** action of bluffing **2** call someone's bluff tell someone to do what they threaten to do

bluff² adj (of a person) rough and cheerful

blun·der /ˈblʌndər/ n stupid mistake ♦ vi **1** make a blunder **2** move awkwardly ~**er** n

blunt /blʌnt/ adj **1** not sharp: a blunt pencil **2** not trying to be polite ♦ vt make less sharp ~**ly** adv roughly and plainly ~**ness** n [U]

blur /blɜr/ n [S] something whose shape is not clearly seen ♦ vt –rr– make hard to see: (fig.) to blur a distinction

blurb /blɜrb/ n short description of the contents of a book

blurt /blɜrt/ v

blurt out phr vt say suddenly without thinking

blush /blʌʃ/ vi become red in the face, from shame **blush** n ~**ingly** adv

blus·ter /ˈblʌstər/ vi **1** speak roughly and noisily **2** (of wind) blow roughly **bluster** n [U] ~**y** adj windy

B-mov·ie /ˈbiʸ ˌmuʷviʸ/ n cheaply made film not considered to be of very good quality

BO /ˌbiʸ ˈoʷ/ n [U] body odour; unpleasant smell from a person's body

boar /bɔr, boʷr/ n wild pig

board /bɔrd, boʷrd/ n **1** [C] flat piece of wood, etc.: floorboards | a notice board | a chessboard **2** BLACKBOARD **3** (cost of) meals: room and board **4** committee of people controlling something **5** above board completely open and honest **6** across the board including all groups or members, as in an industry: a raise of $10 a week across the board **7** go by the board (of plans) come to no result **8** on board on a ship or public vehicle ♦ v **1** vt cover with boards **2** vt go on board a ship, etc. **3** vi/t get or supply meals and a room for payment: to board with a friend ~**er** n person who pays to live and receive meals somewhere

board game /ˈ· ·/ n game played by moving pieces on a marked board

board·ing·house /ˈbɔrdɪŋˌhaʊs, ˈboʷr-/ n private lodging house that supplies meals

boarding pass /ˈ··· ·/ n official card to be given up when one enters an aircraft

boarding school /ˈ··· ˌ·/ n [C;U] school at which children live instead of going there daily from home

board·walk /ˈbɔrdwɔk, ˈboʷrd-/ n wide path along the coast in a tourist town

boast /boʷst/ v **1** vi talk too proudly **2** vt have (a cause for pride): This computer boasts many ingenious features. ♦ n **1** act of boasting **2** cause for pride ~**ful** adj full of praise for oneself

boat /boʷt/ n water vehicle, esp. smaller than a ship – see also **in the same boat** (SAME¹) ♦ vi go in a boat, esp. for pleasure

boat·er /ˈboʷtər/ n stiff hat made of STRAW

boat·swain /ˈboʷsən/ n chief seaman on a ship

boat·train /ˈ· ·/ n train that takes people to or from ships in port

bob¹ /bab/ vi **-bb-** move quickly up and down: *a boat bobbing on the water*

bob² vt cut (a woman's hair) to the shoulder or shorter ♦ n a bobbed haircut

bob·bin /ˈbabɪn/ n small roller for thread

bob·ble /ˈbabəl/ vt to drop a BASEBALL vi to BOB¹

bobby pin /ˈbabiʸ ˌpɪn/ n flat pin for holding hair

bobby socks, bobby sox /ˈbabiʸ ˌsaks/ n [P] girl's socks reaching above the ankle

bob·sled /ˈbabsled/ vi, n (ride in) a small vehicle that runs on metal blades, used for sliding down snowy slopes

bode /boʷd/ vi bode well/ill be a good/bad sign for the future

bod·ice /ˈbadɪs/ n top part of a woman's dress

bod·i·ly /ˈbadl-iʸ/ adj of the human body; PHYSICAL ♦ adv taking hold of the whole body

bod·y /ˈbadiʸ/ n **1** person or animal's whole physical structure, alive or dead **2** this without the head or limbs **3** main part of something: *The important news comes in the body of the letter.* **4** group of people: *an elected body* **5** object; piece of matter: *The sun is a heavenly body.* **6** large amount of: *a body of water such as a lake* **7** keep body and soul together** remain alive (by getting money for food)

body blow /ˈ·· ·/ n **1** (in boxing (BOX²)) blow that falls below the breast and above the waist **2** a serious SETBACK

bod·y·guard /ˈbadiʸˌgard/ n man or group of men guarding someone important

bod·y·work /ˈbadiʸˌwɜrk/ n [U] outside parts of a motor vehicle

bog¹ /bag, bɔg/ n [C;U] area of soft wet ground ~gy adj

bog² v bog down phr vi/t **-gg-** sink into a bog: (fig.) *to get bogged down in one's work*

bog·gle /ˈbagəl/ vi pause in shocked surprise

bo·gus /ˈboʷgəs/ adj pretended; false

bo·gy /ˈboʷgiʸ/ n imaginary evil spirit

bo·he·mi·an /boʷˈhiʸmiʸən/ adj not following accepted social customs

boil¹ /bɔɪl/ vi/t **1** bring or come to the temperature at which a liquid changes to gas: *212°F is the boiling point of water.* **2** cook at this temperature: *to boil eggs* **3** boil down till almost no water remains ♦ n [S]: *Bring the soup to a boil.*

boil away phr vi disappear by boiling

boil down to phr vt be no more than: *It all boils down to a question of money.*

boil over phr vi **1** (of a boiling liquid) flow over the sides of the container **2** get out of control (and develop into): *The conflict boiled over into war.*

boil up phr v **1** vt make hot and cook **2** vi reach a dangerous level

boil² n painful infected swelling under the skin

boil·er /ˈbɔɪlər/ n large container for boiling water, e.g. to provide heating in a house

bois·ter·ous /ˈbɔɪstərəs/ adj noisily cheerful ~ly adv

bold /boʷld/ adj **1** daring; courageous **2** without respect or shame **3** clearly marked: *a bold drawing* ~ly adv ~ness n [U]

bol·lard /ˈbalərd/ n short thick post for tying boats to

bol·ster¹ /ˈboʷlstər/ n long PILLOW

bolster² v bolster up phr vt encourage; support

bolt¹ /boʷlt/ n **1** bar that fastens a door or window **2** screw used with a NUT (2) to hold things together **3** THUNDERBOLT **4** a bolt from the blue something unexpected and unpleasant – see also NUTS AND BOLTS

bolt² v **1** vt fasten with a BOLT¹ (1) **2** vi run away suddenly **3** vt swallow (food) hastily ♦ n [S] **1** act of running away **2** make a bolt for it run away ♦ adv bolt upright straight and stiff

bomb /bam/ n **1** [C] container filled with explosive **2** [the+S] the NUCLEAR bomb **3** bad film **4** bombs away!** let's go! ♦ v **1** vt attack with bombs **2** vi infml move quickly **3** vi infml fail ~er n aircraft that drops bombs **2** person who throws bombs

bom·bard /bamˈbard/ vt attack heavily with gunfire: (fig.) *He was bombarded with questions.* ~ment n [C;U]

bom·bas·tic /bamˈbæstɪk/ adj using impressive but meaningless words ~ically /-kliʸ/ adj

bomb·shell /ˈbamʃɛl/ n great shock

bo·na fi·de /ˈboʷnə ˌfaɪd, ˈbanə-, ˌboʷnə ˈfaɪdiʸ/ adj real

bo·nan·za /bəˈnænzə, boʷ-/ n something very profitable

bond /band/ n **1** something that unites: *a bond of friendship* **2**

written promise, esp. to pay back money with interest **3** state of being stuck together ♦ *vt* unite; stick **bonds** *n* [P] chains or ropes for tying someone up

bond·age /'bɒndɪdʒ/ *n* [U] *lit* slavery

bone /boʊn/ *n* [C;U] **1** any of the various hard parts of the body which are surrounded by flesh and skin **2 cut to the bone** reduce as much as possible **3 feel in one's bones** believe strongly though without proof **4 have a bone to pick with someone** have something to complain about **5 make no bones about** feel no doubt or shame about – see also BARE BONES, FUNNY BONE ♦ *vt* take bones out of (fish, etc.) ~**less** *adj* **bony** *adj* **1** very thin, showing the bones **2** (of food) full of bones

bone-dry /ˌ· '·◄/ *adj* perfectly dry

bone·yard /'boʊnyard/ *n infml* CEMETERY

bon·fire /'bɒnfaɪər/ *n* large outdoor fire

bonkers /'bɒŋkərz/ *adj* crazy

bon·net /'bɒnɪt/ *n* round hat tied under the chin worn esp. by babies

bon·ny /'bɒniʲ/ *adj* pretty and healthy

bo·nus /'boʊnəs/ *n* **1** additional payment beyond what is usual **2** anything pleasant in addition to what is expected

boo /buʷ/ *interj, n* **boos** shout of disapproval ♦ *vi/t* shout 'boo'

boo·by /'buʷbiʲ/ *n* fool

booby prize /'·· ˌ·/ *n* prize given for the worst performance in a competition

booby trap /'·· ˌ·/ *n* thing which looks harmless, used for surprising people unpleasantly, such as a hidden bomb ♦ **booby-trap** *vt* –**pp**-

book[1] /bʊk/ *n* **1** set of sheets of paper fastened together, to be read or written in: *books on trains | a bookseller | bookshelves | a bookstore* **2** collection of matches, tickets, etc., fastened like a book **3** main division of the Bible or of a long poem **4 a closed book** subject about which one knows very little **5** by the book according to the rules **6** in one's book in one's opinion **7** throw the book at (esp. of the police) make all possible charges against **books** *n* [P] business accounts

book[2] *vt* write down a legal charge against: *booked for speeding* ~**able** *adj*

book·case /'bʊk-keʲs/ *n* piece of furniture to hold books

book club /'· ·/ *n* club that offers books cheaply to its members

book·end /'bʊkend/ *n* support for a row of books

book·ing /'bʊkɪŋ/ *n* planned performance of a professional entertainer

book·keep·ing /'bʊkˌkiʲpɪŋ/ *n* [U] keeping business accounts –**er** *n*

book·let /'bʊklɪt/ *n* small thin book

book·mak·er /'bʊkˌmeʲkər/ *also* **bookie** /'bʊkiʲ/ *infml* – *n* person who takes BETs (2) on races

book·mark /'bʊkmark/ *n* something put in a book to keep one's place

book·mo·bile /'bʊkmoʷˌbiʲl/ *n* library kept in a motor vehicle that travels from town to town

book·worm /'bʊkwɜrm/ *n* person who loves reading

boom[1] /buʷm/ *vi* **1** make a deep hollow sound **2** grow rapidly: *Business is booming.* **boom** *n*: *a boom in exports*

boom[2] *n* **1** long pole to which a sail is fastened **2** heavy chain across a river to stop logs floating down or to prevent ships sailing up **3** long pole on the end of which a camera or MICROPHONE can be moved about

boo·mer·ang /'buʷməˌræŋ/ *n* curved stick which makes a circle and comes back when thrown ♦ *vi* have the opposite effect to that intended

boon /buʷn/ *n fml* comfort; help

boon·docks /'buʷndɑks/ *n* [*the*+P] *infml* rough country area where few people live

boor /bʊər/ *n* rude person ~**ish** *adj* ~**ishly** *adv*

boost /buʷst/ *vt* raise; increase **boost** *n* ~**er** **1** something that boosts **2** additional amount of a drug

boot[1] /buʷt/ *n* **1** heavy shoe that comes up over the ankle **2 give/get the boot** *infml* dismiss/be dismissed from a job **3 lick someone's boots** work very hard to gain someone's favour **4 put the boot in** *sl* kick someone **5 too big for one's boots** too proud

boot[2] *vt infml* kick

boot out *phr vt infml* send away rudely and sometimes with force

boot[3] *n* **to boot** in addition

booth /buʷθ/ *n* **1** tent, hut, etc., where goods are sold **2** small enclosed space: *a telephone/voting booth*

boot·leg /'buʷtleg/ *vi/t* –**gg**– make, carry or sell (alcoholic drink) illegally ~**ger** *n*

booze /buʷz/ *vi sl* drink alcohol ♦ *n* [U] *sl* alcoholic drink **boozer** *sl* person who boozes

bor·der[1] /'bɔrdər/ *n* **1** edge **2** line between 2 countries

border[2] *vt* put or be a border to

border on *phr vt* be very much like: *Your remarks border on rudeness!*

bor·der·line /ˈbɔrdərˌlaɪn/ *adj* that may or may not be something: *Anne will pass the exam, but Sue is a borderline case.* (= may pass or fail) ♦ *n* (line marking) a border

bore[1] /bɔr, boʷr/ *v past t. of* BEAR[2]

bore[2] *n* dull person or activity ♦ *vt* make (someone) tired or uninterested: *a boring job* ~**dom** *n* [U] state of being bored

bore[3] *vi/t* make a round hole (in) ♦ *n* 1 hole made by boring 2 measurement of the hole inside a gun, pipe, etc.

born /bɔrn/ *adj* 1 **be born** come into existence by birth 2 being something by nature: *a born leader* 3 **born and bred** having grown up from birth in the stated place 4 **born of** owing existence to

born-a·gain /ˈ· ˈ··/ *adj* having accepted a particular religion, esp. EVANGELICAL Christianity, esp. through a deep experience of the spirit: *a born-again Christian* | (fig.) *a born-again jogger*

borne /bɔrn, boʷrn/ *v past p. of* BEAR[2]

bo·rough /ˈbɜroʷ, ˈbʌroʷ/ *n* town, or division of a large town, esp. New York

bor·row /ˈbɑroʷ, ˈbɔroʷ/ *v* 1 *vi/t* receive something that is lent, and will be returned 2 *vt* copy (ideas, words, etc.) ~**er** *n*

bos·om /ˈbʊzəm, ˈbuʷ-/ *n lit* 1 the front of the human chest, esp. the female breasts 2 place where one feels love, sorrow, etc. 3 **a bosom buddy** a very close friend 4 **in the bosom of** in a close relationship with

boss /bɔs/ *n infml* person who controls others; employer, etc. ♦ *vt* give orders to ~**y** *adj* too fond of giving orders

bot·a·ny /ˈbɑtn-iʸ/ *n* [U] scientific study of plants -**nist** *n* -**nical** /bəˈtænɪkəl/ *adj*

botch /bɑtʃ/ *vt* do a repair (of something) badly

both /boʷθ/ *determiner, pron* this one and that one: *both of us* | *both New York and London*

both·er /ˈbɑðər/ *v* 1 *vt* cause inconvenience to; annoy in little ways: *Does the noise bother you?* 2 *vi* trouble oneself: *Don't bother to lock the door.* ♦ *n* [C;U] trouble; inconvenience ~**some** *adj* causing bother

bot·tle /ˈbɑtl/ *n* 1 container with a narrow neck for liquids 2 container for holding a baby's milk 3 **the bottle** alcoholic drink, esp. when drunk too much: *He's on/hitting the bottle again.* ♦ *vt* put into bottles

bottle up *phr vt* control (feelings) in an unhealthy way

bot·tle·neck /ˈbɑtlˌnɛk/ *n* narrow part of a road which slows down traffic: (fig.) *a bottleneck in production*

bot·tom[1] /ˈbɑtəm/ *n* 1 [C] base; lowest part or level: *the bottom of the stairs* | *He was the bottom of the class.* 2 [C] part of the body that one sits on 3 [S] ground under the sea, a lake, etc. 4 last half of an INNING in baseball 5 [S] cause: *get to the bottom of the trouble* 6 **at bottom** really 7 **from the bottom of one's heart** truly 8 **knock the bottom out of** take away the necessary support on which something rests ~**less** *adj* very deep

bottom[2] *v* **bottom out** *phr vi* reach the lowest point before rising again

bottom line /ˌ·· ˈ·/ *n* [*the*+S] 1 the amount of money shown (as profit or loss) at the bottom of a set of accounts 2 the most important result in the end, esp. with regard to money

bot·u·lis·m /ˈbɑtʃəˌlɪzəm/ *n* [U] form of food poisoning

bou·doir /ˈbuʷdwɑr/ *n lit* woman's private room

bough /baʊ/ *n* large branch of a tree

bought /bɔt/ *v past t. and p. of* BUY

boul·der /ˈboʷldər/ *n* large rock

bounce /baʊns/ *v* 1 *vi* (of a ball) spring back again: *The ball bounced against the wall.* 2 *vi/t* move up and down quickly: *She bounced into the room.* 3 *vi* (of a check) be returned by the bank as worthless ♦ *n* 1 [C;U] act of bouncing 2 [U] behavior which is full of life **bouncer** *n* strong person employed (esp. at a club) to throw out unwelcome visitors **bouncing** *adj* (esp of babies) strong and healthy

bound[1] /baʊnd/ *v past t. and p. of* BIND

bound[2] *adj* **bound to** sure to: *It's bound to rain.* **bound up in** busy with

bound[3] *vi* jump; LEAP **bound** *n* – see also BOUNDS

bound[4] *adj* going to (a place): *bound for home*

bound·a·ry /ˈbaʊndəriʸ/ *n* outer limit; border

bound·less /ˈbaʊndlɪs/ *adj* unlimited

bounds /baʊndz/ *n* [P] 1 furthest limits 2 **out of bounds** a forbidden to be visited **b** (of a ball in sports) outside the playing area

boun·ty /ˈbaʊntiʸ/ *n* 1 [C] something given out of kindness, or offered as a reward 2 [U] *fml* generosity -**tiful** *adj fml* generous

bou·quet¹ /boʷˈkeʸ, buʷ-/ n bunch of flowers

bouquet² /buˈkeʸ/ n smell of a wine

bour·geois /bʊərˈʒwa, ˈbʊərʒwa/ n, adj 1 (person) of the MIDDLE CLASS 2 (person) too interested in material possessions ~**ie** /ˌbʊərʒwaˈziʸ/ n [U] the MIDDLE CLASS

bout /baʊt/ n short period of activity or illness

bou·tique /buʷˈtiʸk/ n small fashionable shop, esp. for clothes

bou·ton·niere /ˌbuʷtnˈɪər/ n flower worn on a man's coat

bo·vine /ˈboʷvaɪn/ adj slow and dull, like a cow

bow¹ /baʊ/ vi/t bend forward, to show respect **bow** n

bow out phr vi give up a position or stop taking part in something

bow to phr vt obey; accept: I bow to your judgment.

bow² /boʷ/ n 1 piece of curved wood with a string, for shooting arrows 2 similar piece of wood for playing stringed musical instruments 3 knot formed by doubling a string into two curved pieces ♦ vi/t 1 bend; curve 2 play (music) with a bow

bow³ /baʊ/ n front of a ship

bowd·ler·ize /ˈbaʊdləraɪz/ vt remove unacceptable parts from (a book)

bow·els /ˈbaʊəlz/ n [P] 1 pipe that carries waste matter from the stomach 2 inside part: the bowels of the Earth

bowl¹ /boʷl/ n 1 deep round container for liquids, etc. 2 anything in the shape of a bowl

bowl² v 1 vi/t throw or roll (a ball) in a sport 2 vi play LAWN BOWLS or BOWLING

bowl over phr vt surprise greatly

bow·leg·ged /ˈboʷˌlɛgɪd, -ˌlɛgd/ adj having legs curving outwards at the knees

bowl·er /ˈboʷlər/ n person who bowls

bowl·ing /ˈboʷlɪŋ/ n [U] indoor game in which a big ball is rolled along a track (a **bowling alley**)

bow tie /ˌboʷ ˈtaɪ/ n TIE¹ (1) fastened at the front with a BOW² (3)

bow win·dow /ˌboʷ ˈwɪndoʷ/ n curved window

box¹ /bɑks/ n 1 [C] stiff container for solids: a box of chocolates 2 [C] small enclosed space: a box at the theater – see also BLACK BOX, PANDORA'S BOX ♦ vt put in boxes

box in phr vt enclose in a small space

box² /bɑks/ vi/t fight with the FISTS, for sport: a boxing match ~**er** n ~**ing** n [U]

box num·ber /ˈ· ˌ··/ n number used as a mailing address, esp. in replying to newspaper advertisements

box of·fice /ˈ· ˌ··/ n place where tickets are sold in a cinema, etc.: The show was a box-office success. (= made a large profit)

boy /bɔɪ/ n young male person ~**hood** n time of being a boy ~**ish** adj like a boy

boy·cott /ˈbɔɪkɑt/ vt refuse to trade with or take part in **boycott** n

boy·friend /ˈbɔɪfrɛnd/ n woman's male companion

bo·zo /ˈboʷzoʷ/ n sl stupid person

bra /brɑ/ n woman's undergarment supporting the breasts

brace¹ /breʸs/ n something that stiffens or supports **braces** n [P] wire worn to straighten the teeth

brace² vt 1 support 2 prepare (oneself) **bracing** adj (of weather) cold but usu. healthy

brace·let /ˈbreʸslɪt/ n decoration for the wrist

brack·en /ˈbrækən/ n [U] FERN which grows in forests

brack·et /ˈbrækɪt/ n 1 support for a shelf, etc. 2 either of various pairs of signs used for enclosing a piece of information, for example [ ] 3 group of people: the 16–25 age bracket ♦ vt put in brackets

brack·ish /ˈbrækɪʃ/ adj (of water) not pure; a little salty ~**ness** n [U]

brag /bræg/ vi -**gg**- talk too proudly; BOAST

braid /breʸd/ n 1, vt twisted length of hair 2 n [U] threads of silk, gold, etc., twisted together to decorate the edges of material: gold braid

braille /breʸl/ n [U] type of raised printing that blind people can read

brain /breʸn/ n 1 the organ in the head that controls thought 2 mind; INTELLIGENCE 3 infml clever person 4 have something on the brain think about something continually, or too much ♦ vt infml hit on the head ~**less** adj stupid ~**y** adj clever **brains** n [U] 1 material of which the brain consists 2 ability to think

brain·child /ˈbreʸntʃaɪld/ n [S] someone's successful idea

brain drain /ˈ· ·/ n movement of skilled people to other countries

brain·pow·er /ˈbreʸnˌpaʊər/ n [U] ability to reason

brain·storm /ˈbreʸnstɔrm/ n sudden clever idea ~**ing** n [U] rapid exchange of ideas among a group to find answers to problems ♦ vi practice brainstorming

brain·wash /ˈbreʸnwɑʃ, -wɔʃ/ vt force someone to change their beliefs ~**ing** n [U]

braise /breɪz/ vt cook (meat or vegetables) slowly in a covered dish

brake /breɪk/ n apparatus for slowing or stopping a vehicle **brake** vi/t

bram·ble /ˈbræmbəl/ n common wild prickly bush

bran /bræn/ n [U] crushed skin of grain

branch[1] /brɑːntʃ/ n 1 stem growing from the trunk of a tree 2 division; part: *branch of a bank/of a family*

branch[2] vi form branches

   branch out phr vi add to one's range

brand /brænd/ 1 product of a particular producer: *my favorite brand of soup* | (fig.) *his own brand* (= special kind) *of humor* 2 mark made, esp. by burning, to show ownership ♦ vt 1 give a lasting bad name to: *He was branded as a liar.* 2 mark with a BRAND (2): (fig.) *The experience branded her for life.*

bran·dish /ˈbrændɪʃ/ vt wave (e.g. a weapon) about

brand-new /ˌbræn ˈnuː◂, -ˈnjuː◂, ˌbrænd-/ adj just bought or made

bran·dy /ˈbrændiː/ n [C;U] strong alcoholic drink made from wine

brash /bræʃ/ adj bold and disrespectful ~**ly** adv ~**ness** n [U]

brass /bræs/ n [U] 1 bright yellow metal 2 musical instruments made of this: *a brass band* – see also TOP BRASS

bras·siere /brəˈzɪər/ n fml BRA

brat /bræt/ n derog child, esp. one with bad manners

bra·va·do /brəˈvɑːdoʊ/ n [U] unnecessary show of boldness

brave /breɪv/ adj ready to meet pain or danger; fearless ♦ vt meet (danger, etc.) without showing fear ~**ly** adv ~**ry** /ˈbreɪvəriː/ n [U]

bra·vo /ˈbrɑːvoʊ, brɑːˈvoʊ/ interj, n –**vos** (shout of) well done!

brawl /brɔːl/ n noisy quarrel **brawl** vi

brawn /brɔːn/ n [U] human muscle –**y** adj strong

bray /breɪ/ vi make the sound a DONKEY makes **bray** n

bra·zen /ˈbreɪzən/ adj without shame

bra·zier /ˈbreɪʒər/ n container for burning coals

breach /briːtʃ/ n 1 [C;U] act of breaking a law, promise, etc.: *breach of contract* 2 [C] hole (in a wall, etc.) 3 breach of the peace *law* fighting in public ♦ vt break through

bread /bred/ n [U] 1 food made of baked flour 2 food as a means of staying alive: *earn one's daily bread* 3 sl money 4 bread and butter one's way of earning money to live

on 5 know which side one's bread is buttered know who or what will be of most gain to oneself

bread·crumb /ˈbredkrʌm/ n very small bit of bread

bread-line /ˈbredlaɪn/ n on the breadline very poor

breadth /bredθ, bretθ/ n [U] 1 width 2 broad range; SCOPE

bread·win·ner /ˈbredˌwɪnər/ n person whose wages support a family

break[1] /breɪk/ v **broke** /broʊk/, **broken** /ˈbroʊkən/ 1 vi/t separate suddenly into parts: *to break a window* | *The rope broke.* 2 vi/t make or become by breaking: *The box broke open.* 3 vi/t make or become useless as a result of damage: *a broken watch* 4 vt disobey; not keep: *break a promise/an appointment* 5 vi/t interrupt; stop: *break the silence* 6 vi/t (cause to) fail or be destroyed: *The scandal could break him politically.* 7 vi/t bring or come into notice: *The news broke.* 8 vt do better than (a record) 9 vi (of a voice) change suddenly 10 vt discover the secret of (a CODE) 11 break new/fresh ground do something new and different 12 break one's back make every possible effort 13 break the back of finish the main or worst part of 14 break the ice begin to be friendly with people one did not know before 15 break wind let out gases from the bowels

   break away phr vi escape: (fig.) *break away from old traditions*

   break down phr v 1 vi/t destroy; to be reduced to pieces: (fig.) *They broke down her resistance.* 2 vi (of machinery) stop working 3 vi fail: *The peace talks have broken down.* 4 vi (of a person) lose control of one's feelings 5 vi/t separate into kinds; divide: *break the figures down into several lists*

   break even phr vi make neither a loss nor a profit

   break in phr v 1 vi enter a building by force 2 vi interrupt 3 vt make (a person or animal) accustomed to something new

   break into phr vt 1 enter by force 2 begin suddenly: *to break into song* 3 interrupt 4 use part of, esp. unwillingly: *We'll have to break into our savings.*

   break of phr vt cure (someone) of (a bad habit)

   break off phr vi/t 1 stop; end 2 separate from the main part: *A branch broke off.*

   break out phr vi 1 (of something bad) start suddenly: *War broke out.* 2 show or express something suddenly: *He broke out in a rash.* 3 escape

break through phr vi/t **1** force a way through **2** make a new advance

break up phr vi/t **1** vi/t divide into small pieces; separate **2** vi/t bring or come to an end: Their marriage broke up. **3** vi/t (cause to) suffer greatly **4** vi (of a crowd) cease to be together **5** vi amuse greatly

break with phr vt end one's connection with

break² n **1** act of breaking or a condition produced (as if) by breaking: a break in the clouds **2** pause for rest: a coffee break **3** change from the usual pattern or custom: a break from the past | a break in the weather **4** infml chance (esp. to make things better); piece of good luck **5** break of day DAWN **6** make a break for it try to escape

break·able /ˈbreʸkəbəl/ n, adj (something) easily broken

break·age /ˈbreʸkɪdʒ/ n [C;U] **1** example of breaking **2** something broken

break·a·way /ˈbreʸkə‚weʸ/ n person or thing that escapes: a breakaway group

break·down /ˈbreʸkdaʊn/ n **1** sudden failure in operation: a breakdown in the peace talks **2** sudden weakness or loss of power in body or mind: a mental breakdown **3** division into kinds; detailed explanation (of figures, etc.) – see also NERVOUS BREAKDOWN

break·er /ˈbreʸkər/ n **1** large wave rolling onto the shore **2** person or thing that breaks something: an ice-breaker

break·fast /ˈbrɛkfəst/ n [C;U] first meal of the day – see also CONTINENTAL BREAKFAST, ENGLISH BREAKFAST breakfast vi

break-in /ˈ‚·‚·/ n entering of a building illegally and by force

break·out /ˈbreʸkaʊt/ n violent or forceful escape from an enclosed space or a difficult situation, esp. an escape from prison

break·through /ˈbreʸkθru/ n important advance or discovery

break·up /ˈbreʸkʌp/ n **1** coming to an end **2** division into parts

breast /brɛst/ n **1** part of a woman's body which produces milk: a breast-fed baby **2** upper front part of the body: his breast pocket | a bird with a red breast **3** make a clean breast of tell the whole truth about ♦ vt push aside with one's chest: (fig.) The ship breasted the waves.

breath /brɛθ/ n **1** [U] air taken into and breathed out of the lungs **2** [C] single act of breathing air in and out once **3** sign or slight movement (of something): There's a breath of spring in the air. | There wasn't a breath of wind. **4** moment: In one breath he said he loved me, in the next that he didn't. **5** get one's breath (back) also catch one's breath — return to one's usual rate of breathing **6** hold one's breath stop breathing for a time **7** out of breath breathing very fast, as after running **8** take one's breath away surprise one greatly **9** under one's breath in a whisper **10** waste one's breath talk uselessly ~less adj ~lessly adv

breathe /briʸð/ v **1** vi/t take (air, etc.) into the lungs and send it out again **2** vt say softly; whisper **3** vt send out (a smell, feeling, etc.) **4** breathe again feel calm after feeling anxious **5** breathe down someone's neck infml keep too close a watch on someone **6** breathe one's last fml die ~er n short rest

breath·tak·ing /ˈbrɛθ‚teʸkɪŋ/ adj very exciting or unusual

breech·es /ˈbrɪtʃɪz/ n [P] short trousers fastened at or below the knee

breed /briʸd/ v bred /brɛd/ **1** vi (of animals) produce young **2** vt keep (animals, etc.) for the purpose of producing young ones **3** vt produce; cause: Flies breed disease. ♦ n kind of animal or plant: a new breed of rose ~er n person who breeds animals or plants ~ing n [U] **1** business of breeding animals, etc. **2** polite manners

breed·ing-ground /ˈ‚·· ·/ n **1** place where the young, esp. of wild creatures, are produced **2** place or point of origin: a breeding-ground for disease

breeze /briʸz/ n **1** light gentle wind **2** sl something easily done ♦ vi come and go quickly and without ceremony **breezy** adj **1** rather windy **2** cheerful in manner

breth·ren /ˈbrɛðrən/ n [P] (used in church, etc.) brothers

brev·i·ty /ˈbrɛvətiʸ/ n [U] shortness

brew /bru/ vi/t prepare (beer, tea, coffee): (fig.) Trouble is brewing. ♦ n result of brewing: a strong brew ~er n person who makes beer ~ery n place where beer is made

bribe /braɪb/ vt influence unfairly by gifts ♦ n something offered in this way: judges who take bribes ~ry /ˈbraɪbəriʸ/ n [U] giving or taking bribes

bric-a-brac /ˈbrɪk ə ‚bræk/ n [U] small decorations in a house

brick /brɪk/ n **1** [C;U] (piece of) baked clay for building: brick walls **2** something shaped like a brick **3** bang/beat one's head against a brick wall waste one's efforts by trying to do something impossible

♦ *v* **brick in/up** *phr vt* fill or enclose with bricks

brick·bat /'brɪkbæt/ *n* **1** broken piece of brick **2** an attack using words

brick·lay·er /'brɪkˌleɪ⁹ər/ *n* workman who puts bricks in place –**ing** *n* [U]

brid·al /'braɪdl/ *adj* of a bride or wedding

bride /braɪd/ *n* woman about to be married, or just married

bride·groom /'braɪdgruːᵐ, -grʊm/ *n* man about to be married, or just married

brides·maid /'braɪdzmeɪᵈd/ *n* girl attending the bride at a wedding

bridge¹ /brɪdʒ/ *n* **1** structure carrying a road or railroad over a river, etc. **2** raised part of a ship where the captain and officers stand **3** upper part of the nose **4** part of a musical instrument over which the strings are stretched **5** piece of metal that keeps false teeth in place ♦ *vt* build a bridge across

bridge² *n* [U] card game for 4 players

bridge·head /'brɪdʒhed/ *n* position far forward in enemy land

bri·dle /'braɪdl/ *n* leather bands around a horse's head to control its movements ♦ *v* **1** *vt* put a bridle on **2** *vi* show displeasure

brief¹ /briːf/ *adj* **1** short: *a brief visit* **2 in brief** in as few words as possible –**ly** *adv*

brief² *n* short statement of facts or instructions – see also BRIEFS ♦ *vt* give necessary instructions or information

brief·case /'briːfkeɪˢs/ *n* flat leather case for papers

briefs /briːfs/ *n* [P] short UNDER-PANTS

bri·gade /brɪˈgeɪᵈd/ *n* **1** army unit of about 5,000 soldiers **2** organization with certain duties

brig·a·dier /ˌbrɪgəˈdɪər◂/ also **brigadier general** *n* officer with rank just above a COLONEL and below a MAJOR GENERAL

bright /braɪt/ *adj* **1** giving out light; shining **2** (of a color) strong: *bright red* **3** cheerful; happy **4** clever **5** showing hope or signs of future success: *a bright future* —**en** *vi/t* make or become bright –**ly** *adv* –**ness** *n* [U]

bril·liant /'brɪlyənt/ *adj* **1** very bright: *brilliant blue* **2** very clever: *a brilliant idea* **3** very hopeful; successful: *a brilliant career* –**ly** *adv* –**liance**, –**liancy** *n* [U]

brim /brɪm/ *n* **1** edge of a cup, etc. **2** bottom part of a hat ♦ **brimming** *adj*

brine /braɪn/ *n* salty water

bring /brɪŋ/ *vt* **brought** /brɔt/ **1** carry or lead towards someone: *Bring him to the party.* **2** cause to come: *His letter brought many offers of help.* **3** be sold for **4** *law* make (a charge) officially **5 bring home** make very clear **6 bring to bear** use **7 bring to light** REVEAL **8 bring to mind** cause to remember

bring about *phr vt* cause

bring around *phr vt* persuade into a change of opinion

bring back *phr vt* **1** return or cause to return: *That song brings back memories.* **2** obtain and return with

bring down *phr vt* **1** cause to fall or come down: *bring down prices* **2** reduce or lower: *to bring someone down to your own level* **3** DEPRESS

bring down on *phr vt* cause (something bad) to happen: *bring trouble down on the family*

bring forward *phr vt* **1** introduce; suggest: *bring forward a plan* **2** bring something in the future nearer to the present

bring in *phr vt* **1** cause to come; introduce **2** produce as profit; earn

bring off *phr vt* succeed in doing

bring on *phr vt* **1** cause to happen: *bring on a fever* **2** help to develop; improve

bring out *phr vt* **1** produce; cause to appear: *Responsibility brings out the best in her.* **2** encourage, esp. to talk

bring round/to *phr vt* cause to regain consciousness

bring through *phr vt* cause to come successfully through (illness, etc.)

bring together *phr vt* cause (esp. a man and a woman) to meet

bring up *phr vt* **1** educate and care for (children) **2** mention a subject **3** VOMIT (food)

brink /brɪŋk/ *n* edge; VERGE: *on the brink of disaster*

brink·man·ship /'brɪŋkmənʃɪp/ *n* [U] *infml* art of trying to gain an advantage by going to the limit of safety, esp. in international politics, before stopping

brisk /brɪsk/ *adj* quick and active: *a brisk walk* –**ly** *adv* –**ness** *n* [U]

bris·tle /'brɪsəl/ *n* [C;U] short stiff hair on a brush, etc. ♦ *vi* (of hair) stand up stiffly: (fig.) *bristling with anger* –**tly** /'brɪsliʸ/ *adj*

bristle with *phr vt* have plenty of: *streets bristling with armed guards*

brit·tle /'brɪtl/ *adj* **1** hard but easily broken **2** lacking WARMTH or depth of feeling

broach /broʷtʃ/ vt introduce (a subject) for conversation

broad /brɔd/ adj **1** large when measured from side to side; wide **2** not limited; respecting the ideas of others: broad opinions | a **broad-minded** person **3** not detailed: in broad outline **4** full; clear: in broad daylight **5** (of speech) showing clearly where the speaker comes from: a broad Southern accent **6** not acceptable in polite society: broad humor ~**en** vi/t make or become broader: Travel broadens the mind. ~**ly** adv more or less; mostly ~**ness** n [U]

broad·cast /ˈbrɔdkæst/ n radio or television program ♦ v broadcast **1** vi/t send out (broadcasts) **2** vt make widely known: He broadcast the news to his friends. ~**er** n ~**ing** n [U]

broad jump /ˈ· ·/ n [S] sport of jumping as far as possible along the ground

broad·side /ˈbrɔdsaɪd/ n **1** large advertisement on a wall **2** firing of all the guns on one side of a ship

Broad·way /ˈbrɔdweʸ/ n part of New York City where theaters are

bro·cade /broʷˈkeʸd/ n [U] decorative cloth with a raised pattern

broc·co·li /ˈbrɑkəliʸ/ n green vegetable similar to a CAULIFLOWER

bro·chure /broʷˈʃʊər/ n small book of instructions, or giving details of a service offered

brogue[1] /broʷg/ n strong thick shoe

brogue[2] n Irish ACCENT (1)

broil /brɔɪl/ vi/t cook over or under direct heat: (fig.) broiling hot weather

broke[1] /broʷk/ v past t. of BREAK[1]

broke[2] adj completely without money

bro·ken[1] /ˈbroʷkən/ v past p. of BREAK[1]

broken[2] adj **1** violently separated; damaged: a broken window | (fig.) broken dreams | (fig.) a broken man **2** not kept to; destroyed: a broken promise | a broken home (= where a child's parents do not live together) **3** imperfectly spoken or written: broken English

broken·heart·ed /ˌbroʷkənˈhɑrtɪd/ adj filled with grief

bro·ker /ˈbroʷkər/ n person who buys and sells stock, etc., for others

bro·ker·age /ˈbroʷkərɪdʒ/ n [U] **1** (place of) business of a broker **2** amount of money charged by a broker

bron·chi·al /ˈbrɑŋkiʸəl/ adj of the tubes of the WINDPIPE

bron·chi·tis /brɑŋˈkaɪtɪs/ n [U] illness of the bronchial tubes

bronze /brɑnz/ n [U] **1** (the red-brown color of) a metal that is a mixture of copper and tin **2** MEDAL made of bronze ♦ vt give this color to: bronzed by the sun

brooch /broʷtʃ, bruʷtʃ/ n decoration pinned to a dress

brood /bruʷd/ n family of birds, etc. ~**y** adj **1** (of a hen) wanting to sit on eggs **2** sad and silent ~**ily** adv ~**iness** n [U] ♦ vi think long and sadly about something

brook /brʊk/ n small stream

broom /bruʷm, brʊm/ n sweeping brush with a long handle

broth /brɔθ/ n [U] thin soup

broth·el /ˈbrɑθəl, -ðəl, ˈbrɔ-/ n house of PROSTITUTES

broth·er /ˈbrʌðər/ n **1** male relative with the same parents **2** male member of the same profession, religious group, etc. ~**hood** n **1** [U] condition or feeling of friendliness and companionship **2** [C] all the people in a profession, etc. ~**ly** adj **1** like a brother **2** friendly

brother-in-law /ˈ· · ·ˌ·/ n brothers-in-law brother of one's husband or wife; one's sister's husband

brought /brɔt/ v past t. and p. of BRING

brow /braʊ/ n **1** EYEBROW **2** FOREHEAD **3** top of a hill

brow·beat /ˈbraʊbiʸt/ vt -beat, -beaten /-biʸtn/ frighten into doing something

brown /braʊn/ adj, n (of) the color of earth or coffee ♦ vi/t make or become brown

brown·ie /ˈbraʊniʸ/ n cake-like COOKIE made with chocolate

Brownie point /ˈ· · ˌ·/ n [usu. pl.] mark of notice and approval for something good that one has done

brown-nose /ˈ· ·/ vi sl try to win approval dishonestly, esp. from a teacher

browse /braʊz/ vi **1** read without clear purpose **2** feed on young plants, grass, etc. **browse** n [S]

bruise /bruʷz/ n discolored place where the skin has been hurt ♦ v **1** vt cause a bruise on **2** vi show a bruise

brunch /brʌntʃ/ n [C;U] late morning meal that is both breakfast and LUNCH

bru·nette /bruʷˈnɛt/ n person of a race with fair skin and dark hair

brunt /brʌnt/ n bear the brunt of suffer the heaviest part of (an attack)

brush[1] /brʌʃ/ n **1** [C] instrument for sweeping, painting, etc., made of hair, nylon, etc.: a toothbrush | a clothes brush **2** [C] act of brushing **3** [C] short unpleasant meeting: a *brush with the police* **4** [U] (land covered by) small rough trees and bushes **5** [C] bushy tail

brush² v **1** vt clean with a brush **2** vi/t touch or move lightly

brush aside/away phr vt refuse to pay attention to

brush off phr vt refuse to listen to or have a relationship with (someone) **brush-off** /'··/ n [the+S] clear refusal to be friendly: *She gave me the brush-off.*

brush up phr vt improve one's knowledge of (something known but partly forgotten) by study: *I must brush up (on) my French.*

brusque /brʌsk/ adj quick and rather impolite ~ **ly** adv ~ **ness** n [U]

brus·sels sprout /ˌbrʌsəlz 'spraʊt, ˌbrʌsəl-/ n vegetable like a very small CABBAGE

bru·tal /'bruᵗtl/ adj without tender feeling; cruel ~ **ly** adv ~ **ity** /bruˈtæləᵗi/ n [C;U]

brute /bruᵗt/ n **1** rough cruel person **2** animal ♦ like (that of) an animal in being cruel or very strong: *brute force* **brutish** adj like animals rather than people

bub·ble /'bʌbəl/ n hollow ball of liquid containing air or gas ♦ vi **1** form, produce, or rise as bubbles: *She was bubbling (over) with happiness.* **2** make the sound of bubbles rising in liquid **bubbly** adj **1** full of bubbles **2** showing happy feelings freely

bubble gum /'·· ˌ·/ n [U] CHEWING GUM that can make bubbles

buck¹ /bʌk/ n **1** [C] male of certain animals, esp. the deer, cat, and rabbit **2** [C] dollar **3** [the+S] responsibility: *to pass the buck*

buck² v **1** vi (of a horse) jump up with all 4 feet off the ground **2** vt throw off (a rider) by doing this

buck·et /'bʌkᵻt/ n **1** (contents of) an open container with a handle, for liquids **2** large quantity: *The rain came down in buckets.* ~ **ful** /-fʊl/ n contents of a bucket

bucket shop /'·· ·/ n dishonest BROKERAGE house

buck·le¹ /'bʌkəl/ n metal fastener for a belt, etc.

buckle² vi/t **1** fasten with a buckle **2** bend; twist: *a buckled wheel* **3** begin to yield: *Her knees buckled.*

buckle down phr vi begin to work seriously

bud /bʌd/ n **1** flower or leaf before it opens **2** nip something in the bud do harm to (something), esp. so as to keep from succeeding – see also TASTE BUD ♦ vi -**dd**- produce buds ~ **ding** adj beginning to develop

Bud·dhis·m /'buᵂdɪzəm, 'bʊ-/ n [U] eastern religion based on Buddha's teachings **Buddhist** n, adj

bud·dy /'bʌdiᵞ/ n **1** infml companion; friend **2** sl man (used as a form of address)

budge /bʌdʒ/ vi/t move a little

bud·get /'bʌdʒɪt/ n **1** plan of how to spend money, esp. public money taken in by taxation **2** amount of money stated in this ♦ vi plan one's spending ♦ adj cheap: *budget rentals*

buff¹ /bʌf/ n, adj [U] (of) a faded yellow color

buff² vt polish (metal) with something soft

buff³ n person interested in a subject: *a film buff*

buf·fa·lo /'bʌfəloᵂ/ n large wild cow-like animal; BISON

buff·er /'bʌfər/ n spring on a railroad car that takes the shock when it hits anything

buffer zone /'·· ·/ n NEUTRAL area separating opposing forces or groups

buf·fet¹ /'bəfeᵞ, bʊ-/ n table, etc., where one can get food to be eaten nearby

buf·fet² /'bʌfɪt/ vt hit sharply: *buffeted by the wind*

buf·foon /bəˈfuᵂn/ n noisy fool

bug /bʌg/ n **1** any insect **2** GERM **3** apparatus for secret listening **4** eager interest in something: *the travel bug* **5** fault in a machine, esp. a computer ♦ vt -gg- **1** fit with a BUG (3) **2** trouble (someone) continually

bug·bear /'bʌgbeər/ n something feared

bug·ger /'bʌgər/ n friend or child: *a cute little bugger* ~ **y** n [U] SODOMY

bug·gy /'bʌgiᵞ/ n **1** light carriage **2** small chair on wheels for a child

bu·gle /'byuᵂgəl/ n brass musical instrument **bugler** n

build¹ /bɪld/ vi/t built /bɪlt/ make by putting pieces together: *build houses/ships* | (fig.)*Hard work builds character.* ~ **er** n ~ **ing** n **1** thing with a roof and walls; house, etc. **2** work of a builder

build on phr vt **1** base on **2** depend on

build up phr v **1** vt increase; develop: *build up a business* **2** vt praise (something or someone) so as to influence the opinion of others

build² n shape and size of one's body

bulb /bʌlb/ n **1** round root of certain plants **2** glass part of an electric lamp ~ **ous** adj fat and round

bulge /bʌldʒ/ n **1** swelling on a

surface **2** sudden increase ♦ *vi* swell

bulk /bʌlk/ *n* **1** [U] great size or quantity **2 in bulk** in large quantities **3 the bulk of** most of ~**y** *adj* large and fat

bulk·head /ˈbʌlkhɛd/ *n* wall which divides a ship, etc., into several parts

bull /bʊl/ *n* **1** male of cattle and some other large animals **2 bull in a china shop** person who is rough where care is needed **3 take the bull by the horns** face difficulties with courage

bull·doze /ˈbʊldoʷz/ *vt* move (earth, etc.) with a powerful machine (*a bull-dozer*): (fig.) *bulldoze a bill through the House*

bul·let /ˈbʊlɪt/ *n* piece of shot fired from a small gun: *a bullet-proof* ~ – see also **bite the bullet** (BITE)

bul·le·tin /ˈbʊlətn, ˈbʊlətɪn/ *n* short official report

bul·lion /ˈbʊlyən/ *n* [U] bars of gold or silver

bull·ish /ˈbʊlɪʃ/ *adj* marked by, tending to cause, or hopeful of rising prices (as in a STOCK EXCHANGE)

bull·ock /ˈbʊlək/ *n* BULL that cannot breed

bull's-eye /ˈ· ·/ *n* center of a TARGET

bull·shit /ˈbʊlˌʃɪt/ *n* [U] *sl* nonsense ♦ *vi/t* –tt– *sl* talk nonsense, esp. confidently in order to deceive, persuade, or get admiration

bul·ly /ˈbʊliʸ/ *n* person who hurts weaker people ♦ *vt* hurt in this way

bul·rush /ˈbʊlrʌʃ/ *n* tall grasslike waterside plant

bul·wark /ˈbʊlwərk, ˈbʌl-/ *n* wall built for defense

bum /bʌm/ *n sl* TRAMP (1) or lazy person ♦ *vt* –mm– *sl* ask for; beg

bum out *phr vt* DEPRESS

bump /bʌmp/ *v* **1** *vi/t* knock violently **2** *vi* move along in an uneven way ♦ *n* **1** (sound of) a sudden blow **2** swelling ~**y** *adj* uneven

bump into *phr vt* meet by chance

bump off *phr vt infml* kill

bump·er /ˈbʌmpər/ *n* protective bar on the front or back of a car ♦ *adj* very large: *a bumper harvest*

bun /bʌn/ *n* **1** small round sweet cake **2** bread in a particular shape: *hotdog bun* **3** hair twisted into a tight shape

bunch /bʌntʃ/ *n* **1** number of small things fastened together: *a bunch of girls* ♦ *vi/t* form into a bunch

bun·dle /ˈbʌndl/ *n* **1** number of articles fastened together: *a bundle of sticks/laundry* **2** a mass: *a bundle of nerves/laughs* ♦ *v* **1** *vi/t* hurry roughly **2** *vt* make into a bundle

bung /bʌŋ/ *n* round piece of material to close the hole in a container

bun·ga·low /ˈbʌŋgəˌloʷ/ *n* small house all on one level

bun·gle /ˈbʌŋgəl/ *vt* do (work) badly –gler *n*

bunk /bʌŋk/ *n* bed above or below another

bun·ker /ˈbʌŋkər/ *n* **1** place to store things **2** shelter for soldiers

bun·kum /ˈbʌŋkəm/ *n* insincere talk

bun·ny /ˈbʌniʸ/ *n* (child's word for) a rabbit

buns /bʌnz/ *n sl* BUTTOCKS

buoy¹ /ˈbuʷiʸ, bɔɪ/ *n* floating object fastened to the bed of the sea to show a danger, rocks, etc.

buoy² *v* **buoy up** *phr vt* **1** keep floating **2** keep high

buoy·an·cy /ˈbɔɪənsiʸ, ˈbuʷyənsiʸ/ *n* [U] **1** tendency to float **2** cheerfulness **3** ability, e.g. of prices or business activity, to remain or return quickly to a high level after a period of difficulty –ant *adj* showing buoyancy

bur·den /ˈbɜrdn/ *n fml* heavy load or duty ♦ *vt fml* load; trouble

bur·den·some /ˈbɜrdnsəm/ *adj* being a burden: *a burdensome task*

bu·reau /ˈbyʊəroʷ/ *n* **bureaus 1** CHEST OF DRAWERS **2** government department **3** business office

bu·reauc·ra·cy /byʊˈrɑkrəsiʸ/ *n* **1** [U] group of government officials who are appointed, not elected **2** [C;U] government by such a group, usually supposed to be ineffective and full of unnecessary rules –rat /ˈbyʊərəˌkræt/ *n* appointed official –ratic /ˌbyʊərəˈkrætɪk◂/ *adj* –ratically /-kliʸ/ *adv*

bur·geon /ˈbɜrdʒən/ *vi fml* grow; develop

bur·glar /ˈbɜrglər/ *n* thief who breaks into buildings ♦ –glarize /ˈbɜrgləˌraɪz/ — *vt* break into (a building) to steal ~**y** *n* [C;U] (example of) the crime of being a burglar

bur·i·al /ˈbɛriʸəl/ *n* [C;U] (ceremony of) burying

bur·ly /ˈbɜrliʸ/ *adj* (of a person) strong and heavy

burn¹ /bɜrn/ *v* **burnt** /bɜrnt/ *or* **burned 1** *vi* be on fire: *a burning match/house* **2** *vt* damage or destroy by fire or acid: *burn old letters* **3** *vt* use for heating or lighting: *a wood-burning stove* **4** *vi* be very hot: *burning sands* **5** *vi* feel or wish very strongly: *She's burning to tell you.* **6 burn one's bridges** destroy all means of going back, so that one must go forward **7 burn one's fingers** also **get one's fingers burnt** *infml* — suffer the unpleasant results of a foolish action

8 burn the candle at both ends *infml* use up all one's strength by doing too many different things **9 burn the midnight oil** work very late ~ **er** *n* part of a stove, etc. that produces flames ~ **ing** *adj* **1** on fire **2** very strong and urgent

burn away *phr vi* disappear by burning

burn down *phr vi* destroy (a building) by fire

burn out *phr v* **1** *vt* make (a building) hollow by fire **2** *vi* stop burning because there is nothing left to burn **3** *vi/t* stop working through damage caused by heat: (fig.) *He was burned out* (= no longer active) *at 38.*

burn up *phr vt* **1** destroy completely by fire or great heat **2** become angry

burn² *n* mark or hurt place made by burning

bur·nish /'bɜrnɪʃ/ *vt* polish by rubbing

burn·out /'bɜrnaʊt/ *n* [C;U] **1** moment when the engine of a ROCKET or JET uses up all its fuel and stops operating **2** state of not operating from overwork

burp /bɜrp/ *v, n* BELCH

bur·row /'bɜroʊ, 'bʌroʊ/ *n* hole where a rabbit, etc., lives ♦ *vi/t* make a hole; dig

bur·sar /'bɜrsər, -sɑr/ *n* person in a college who has charge of money, buildings, etc.

bur·sa·ry /'bɜrsəriʸ/ *n* where the bursar works

burst¹ /bɜrst/ *vi/t* **burst 1** break suddenly by pressure from inside: *a burst pipe* **2** (cause to) come into the stated condition suddenly, often with force: *They burst open the door.* **3** be filled to breaking point (with a substance or usu. pleasant feeling): *I'm bursting* (= very eager) *to tell someone the news.* | *The river burst its banks.*

burst in on *phr vt* interrupt noisily

burst into *phr vt* **1** enter quickly and suddenly **2** BREAK **into** (2)

burst out *phr v* **1** *vi* begin suddenly (to use the voice without speaking): *They burst out laughing/crying.* **2** say suddenly

burst² *n* sudden OUTBREAK or effort: *a burst of speed*

bur·y /'beriʸ/ *vt* **1** put into a grave **2** hide away: *buried treasure* | (fig.) *She buried her head in her hands.*

bus /bʌs/ *n* large motor vehicle for carrying passengers ♦ *vt* **-ss-, -s-** take by bus

bus·boy /'bʌsbɔɪ/ *n* person who clears restaurant tables

bush /bʊʃ/ *n* **1** [C] low woody plant: rose bush **2** [U] wild land in Australia **3** beat about the bush avoid coming to the main point ~ **y** *adj* (of hair) growing thickly

busi·ness /'bɪznɪs/ *n* **1** [U] trade; the getting of money **2** [C] activity which earns money; store, etc. **3** [C;U] one's employment; duty: *A teacher's business is to teach.* **4** [S] affair; matter **5 have no business to** have no right to **6 like nobody's business** very fast or well **7 Mind your own business!** Don't ask about things that don't concern you. ~ **like** *adj* doing things calmly and effectively

busi·ness·man /'bɪznɪsˌmæn/, **-woman** /-ˌwʊmən/ *fem.* — *n* **-men** /-mɛn/ person in a business firm

bus stop /'··/ *n* place where buses stop for passengers

bust¹ /bʌst/ *vt* **busted** or **bust** *infml* **1** break, esp. with force **2** *sl* (of the police) take to a police station **3** *sl* (of the police) enter without warning to look for something illegal **4** **-buster** *infml* person who destroys or breaks up the stated thing: *a crimebuster* ♦ *adj infml* **1** broken **2 go bust** (of a business) fail

bust² *n* **1** human head and shoulders as shown in a SCULPTURE **2** woman's breasts

bus·tle /'bʌsəl/ *vi* be busy, often noisily **bustle** *n* [S]

bus·y /'bɪziʸ/ *adj* **1** working; not free **2** full of work: *a busy morning* **3** (of telephones) in use ♦ *vt* keep (oneself) busy **busily** *adv*

but /bət; *strong* bʌt/ *conj* **1** rather; instead: *not one, but two* **2** yet at the same time; however: *I want to go, but I can't.* **3** (shows disagreement or surprise): *But I don't want to!* | *But that's wonderful!* ♦ *prep* **1** except: *nobody but me* **2** except for; without ♦ *adv lit* **1** only: *You can but try.* **2 all but** almost ♦ *n* unwanted argument: *No buts! No going!*

butch·er /'bʊtʃər/ *n* **1** person who kills animals for food, or sells meat **2** cruel killer ♦ *vt* kill and prepare for food **3** kill in a bloody way ~ **y** *n* [U] cruel needless killing

but·ler /'bʌtlər/ *n* chief male servant

butt¹ /bʌt/ *vi/t* push with the head or horns

butt in *phr vi* interrupt

butt² *n* **1** person that people make fun of **2** end of something: *cigarette butt* **3** BOTTOM¹ (2)

but·ter /'bʌtər/ *n* [U] yellow fat made from cream ♦ *vt* spread butter on

butter up *phr vt sl* praise too much; FLATTER

but·ter·cup /'bʌtərˌkʌp/ *n* yellow wild flower

but·ter·fin·gers /ˈbʌtərˌfɪŋgərz/ n person likely to drop things

but·ter·fly /ˈbʌtərˌflaɪ/ n 1 insect with large colored wings 2 person who spends all his/her time running after pleasure: a social butterfly 3 **have butterflies in one's stomach** feel very nervous before doing something

but·ter·scotch /ˈbʌtərˌskɑtʃ/ n sweet food made from sugar and butter boiled together

but·tocks /ˈbʌtəks/ n [P] the fleshy parts on which a person sits

but·ton /ˈbʌtn/ n 1 small round object passed through a hole to fasten a garment, etc. 2 button-like object pressed to start a machine ♦ vi/t fasten with a button

but·ton·hole /ˈbʌtnˌhoʷl/ n hole for a button ♦ vt stop and force to listen

but·tress /ˈbʌtrɪs/ n support for a wall ♦ vt support; strengthen

bux·om /ˈbʌksəm/ adj (of a woman) fat and healthy, esp. having large breasts

buy /baɪ/ vi/t **bought** /bɔt/ 1 obtain by paying money 2 accept; believe ♦ n something bought ~ **er** person who buys, esp. professionally for a firm

buy·out /ˈbaɪaʊt/ n situation in which a person or group gains control of a company by buying all or most of its stock

buzz /bʌz/ v 1 vi make the noise that bees make: (fig.) The room buzzed with excitement. 2 vi/t call someone with an electrical signaling apparatus (a **buzzer**) 3 fly low and fast over: Planes buzzed the crowd. ♦ n 1 [C] noise of buzzing 2 infml telephone call: Give me a buzz. 3 sl pleasant feeling as if from a drug

buzz off phr vi infml go away

buzz·word /ˈbʌzwɜrd/ n word or phrase, esp. related to a specialized subject, which is thought to express something important but is often hard to understand

by /baɪ/ prep, adv 1 beside; near: Sit by me. 2 through; using: enter by the door | travel by car | earn money by writing 3 past: He walked by (me) without speaking. 4 before: Do it by tomorrow. 5 (shows who or what does something): a play by Shakespeare | struck by lightning 6 (shows amounts and measurements): They overcharged me by $3. | a room 15 feet by 40 | pay by the hour 7 (shows how or with what): hold it by the handle 8 (in promises, etc.): By God, he's done it! 9 (shows the size of groups following each other): The animals went in two by two. 10 during: to sleep by day 11 **by and by** before long 12 **by and large** on the whole; usually

bye /baɪ/ also **bye-bye** /ˌ·ˈ·, ˈ·∨/ — interj infml goodbye

by·gone /ˈbaɪgɔn, -gɑn/ adj past: in bygone days ♦ n [P] **let bygones be bygones** forgive past quarrels

by·law /ˈbaɪlɔ/ n rule governing a company or organization

by·pass /ˈbaɪpæs/ n road that goes around a busy town, etc. ♦ vt avoid by going around

by·play /ˈbaɪpleʸ/ n [U] action of less importance going on at the same time as the main action

by·prod·uct /ˈ·ˌ··/ n something produced while making something else

by·stand·er /ˈbaɪˌstændər/ n person who watches without taking part

byte /baɪt/ n unit of computer information equal to eight BITs[3]

by·way /ˈbaɪˌweʸ/ n smaller road or path which is not much used or known

by·word /ˈbaɪwɜrd/ n (name of a) person, place, or thing thought to represent some quality: a byword for cruelty/hospitality

by·zan·tine /ˈbɪzənˌtiʸn, -taɪn/ adj secret, indirect, and difficult to understand

C

C, c /siʸ/ the 3rd letter of the English alphabet

c *written abbrev. for:* **1** cent(s) **2** CIRCA **3** CUBIC **4** centimetre(s) **5** COPYRIGHT

C *abbrev. for:* **1** CELSIUS **2** century

cab /kæb/ *n* **1** taxi **2** the part of a bus, train engine, etc., where the driver sits ◆ **–bbie** *n* cab driver

cab·a·ret /ˌkæbəˈreʸ/ *n* [C;U] performance of music and dancing in a restaurant, etc.

cab·bage /ˈkæbɪdʒ/ *n* [C;U] round vegetable with thick green leaves

cab·in /ˈkæbɪn/ *n* **1** small room on a ship **2** small roughly built house

cab·i·net /ˈkæbənɪt/ *n* **1** piece of furniture with shelves and drawers **2** chief officials of a government

ca·ble /ˈkeʸbəl/ *n* **1** [C;U] thick heavy rope used on ships etc.: *a cable trolley* **2** [C] wire carrying electricity, telephone messages, etc. **3** [C] TELEGRAM ◆ *vi/t* send or tell by TELEGRAM

cable car /ˈ·· ·/ *n* car driven by an underground cable, esp. in San Francisco

cable TV /ˌkeʸbəl tiʸ ˈviʸ/ *n* special system for providing more programs on television

ca·boose /kəˈbuʷs/ *n* last car on a train

cab·stand /ˈkæbstænd/ *n* place where taxis wait for passengers

cache /kæʃ/ *n* secret store of things

cack·le /ˈkækəl/ *vi* **1** make the noise a hen makes **2** laugh unpleasantly **cackle** *n*

ca·coph·o·ny /kəˈkɑfəniʸ/ *n* [C;U] unpleasant mixture of loud noises **–nous** *adj*

cac·tus /ˈkæktəs/ *n* **–tuses** *or* **–ti** /-taɪ/ fleshy desert plant with PRICKLES

ca·det /kəˈdɛt/ *n* young person training in the armed forces or police

cadge /kædʒ/ *vi/t derog* get or try to get by taking advantage of a person's friendship or generosity

ca·dre /ˈkædriʸ, ˈkɑdrə/ *n* (member of) an inner group of trained people

Cae·sar·e·an, Cesarian /sɪˈzɛəriʸən/ *n* operation to take a baby out by cutting, instead of by ordinary birth

caf·e /kæˈfeʸ, kə-/ *n* small restaurant serving light meals and drinks

caf·e·te·ri·a /ˌkæfəˈtɪəriʸə/ *n* restaurant where people collect their own food

cage /keʸdʒ/ *n* container with bars, for keeping birds or animals in ◆ *vt* put in a cage

cag·ey /ˈkeʸdʒiʸ/ *adj* secretive

ca·hoots /kəˈhuʷts/ *n* **in cahoots with** working secretly with, usu. to cause harm

Cain /keʸn/ see **raise Cain** (RAISE)

ca·jole /kəˈdʒoʷl/ *vt* persuade by praise or false promises

cake /keʸk/ *n* **1** [C;U] soft sweet food baked with flour, etc.: *a birthday cake* **2** [C] flat piece of something: *a cake of soap* **3** (sell) **like hot cakes** very quickly **4 have one's cake and eat it too** have the advantages of something without the disadvantages that go with it – see also PIECE OF CAKE ◆ *vt* cover thickly: *shoes caked with mud*

CAL /ˌkæl, ˌsiʸ eʸ ˈɛl/ *abbrev. for:* computer-assisted learning

Cal *written abbrev. for:* California (a state in the US)

ca·lam·i·ty /kəˈlæmətiʸ/ *n* terrible misfortune **–tous** *adj*

cal·ci·um /ˈkælsiʸəm/ *n* [U] metal substance found in bones and chalk

cal·cu·late /ˈkælkyəˌleʸt/ *vt* **1** find out by using numbers: *calculate the cost* **2** plan, intend: *take a calculated risk* **-lable** *adj* able to be measured **-lator** *n* small machine that calculates **-lation** /ˌkælkyəˈleʸʃən/ *n* [C;U]

cal·cu·lat·ing /ˈkælkyəˌleʸtɪŋ/ *adj* coldly SHREWD

cal·en·dar /ˈkæləndər/ *n* **1** list of the days and months of the year **2** system of naming and dividing the months, etc. **3** a daily record of events, meetings, etc. in one's life

calf¹ /kæf/ *n* **calves** /kævz/ [C] young of cattle and some other large animals **2** [U] its leather: **calfskin** *boots*

calf² *n* **calves** back of the human leg, between knee and ankle

cal·i·ber /ˈkæləbər/ *n* **1** [S;U] quality: *work of (a) high caliber* **2** inside size of a tube or gun; bullet size

cal·i·co /ˈkælɪˌkoʷ/ *n* printed cotton cloth ◆ *adj* (of a cat) with three colors

call¹ /kɔl/ *v* **1** *vi/t* speak or say loudly **2** *vt* name: *We'll call the baby Jean.* **3** *vt* tell to come: *Call a doctor!* **4** *vi/t* telephone **5** *vi fml* make a short visit: *Let's call at Bob's.* **6** *vt* say publicly that something is to happen: *call a meeting/an election/a strike* **7** *vt* consider to be: *She called me a coward.* **8** *vt* waken: *Please call me at 7.* **9 call it a day** quit **10 call the shots** be in control

call back *phr v* **1** *vt* cause (someone) to return **2** *vi/t* return a telephone call

call for *phr vt* **1** demand **2** need; deserve **3** collect

call in *phr vt* ask to come: *call the doctor in*

call off *phr vt* **1** decide not to have (a planned event) **2** tell to keep away

call on/upon *phr vt fml* **1** visit **2** ask to do something

call out *phr vt* **1** order officially to help: *Call out the army!* **2** order to STRIKE

call up *phr vt* **1** telephone **2** order to join the armed forces

call² *n* **1** shout; cry **2** telephone conversation **3** short visit **4** demand; need: *There's no call for rudeness.* **5** command to meet, come, or do something **6** **on call** ready to work if needed

call box /'· ·/ *n* outdoor telephone for calling the police

call·er /'kɔlər/ *n* person who visits or makes a telephone call

call girl /'· ·/ *n* woman PROSTITUTE who makes her arrangements by telephone

cal·lig·ra·phy /kə'lɪgrəfiʲ/ *n* (U) (art of) beautiful writing

call·ing /'kɔlɪŋ/ *n fml* profession; trade

cal·i·pers /'kæləpərz/ *n* [P] instrument for measuring distance between surfaces

cal·lous /'kæləs/ *adj* unkind; without sympathy ~**ness** *n* [U]

cal·low /'kæloʷ/ *adj* young and inexperienced

call num·ber /'· ˌ··/ *n* number on books in a library

cal·lus /'kæləs/ *n* an area of hard skin

calm /kɑm/ *adj* **1** not excited; quiet **2** (of weather) not windy **3** (of the sea) smooth **calm** *n* [S;U] **calm** *vi/t* make or become calm: *We tried to calm him down.* ~**ly** *adv* ~**ness** *n* [U]

cal·o·rie /'kæləriʲ/ *n* unit of heat, or of ENERGY produced by a food

calve /kæv/ *vi* give birth to a CALF

calves /kævz/ *n pl. of* CALF

ca·lyp·so /kə'lɪpsoʷ/ *n* kind of West Indian song

cam·ber /'kæmbər/ *n* upward curve in the middle of a road surface

came /keʲm/ *v past t. of* COME

cam·el /'kæməl/ *n* large animal with a long neck and one or two large HUMPs on its back

cam·e·o /'kæmiʲoʷ/ *n* –os **1** piece of jewelry consisting of a raised shape on a darker background **2** short piece of fine writing or acting which shows the character of a person, place or event

cam·e·ra /'kæmərə/ *n* **1** apparatus for taking photographs or moving

pictures **2** **in camera** in secret

cam·ou·flage /'kæmə‚flaʒ, -‚flɑdʒ/ *n* [C;U] use of color, shape, etc. to hide an object ♦ **camouflage** *vt*

camp¹ /kæmp/ *n* **1** [C;U] place where people live in tents or huts for a short time **2** [C] group of people with the same esp. political ideas **3** **break/strike camp** take up and put away tents ♦ *vi* set up or live in a camp: *We go camping every summer.*

camp² *adj infml* **1** (of a man) behaving or looking like a woman, esp. intentionally **2** so unreal, unnatural, etc., as to be amusing

camp·er /'kæmpər/ *n* [C] **1** person who camps **2** motor vehicle big enough to live in on vacation, usu. having cooking equipment and beds

cam·paign /kæm'peʲn/ *n* connected set of military, political, or business actions intended to obtain a particular result ♦ *vi* lead, take part in or go on a campaign

camp ground /'· ·/ *n* place for camping

cam·pus /'kæmpəs/ *n* [C;U] grounds of a university, college or school: *campus* (= university) *life*

can¹ /*strong* kæn; kən/ *v aux* **1** be able to: *Can you swim?* | *I can't hear you.* **2** be allowed to; may: *You can go home now.* **3** (shows what is possible): *He can be very annoying.* | *It can't be true.*

can² /kæn/ *n* **1** metal container for foods or liquids: *a can of beans* | *a gas can* **2** **can it!** be quiet! ♦ *vt* –**nn**- preserve (food) in a can

ca·nal /kə'næl/ *n* watercourse dug for boats to travel along or to bring water

ca·nar·y /kə'neəriʲ/ *n* small yellow bird which sings beautifully

can·cel /'kænsəl/ *vt* –l– also –ll- **1** decide not to have (a planned event): *cancel a trip* **2** destroy the value of (a check, etc.) by stamping it ~**lation** /‚kænsə'leʲʃən/ *n* [C;U]

cancel out *phr vi/t* balance; equal: *The 2 debts cancel each other out.*

can·cer /'kænsər/ *n* [C;U] diseased growth in the body ~**ous** *adj*

can·did /'kændɪd/ *adj* honest; sincere ~**ly** *adv*

can·di·date /'kændə‚deʲt, -dɪt/ *n* **1** person to be chosen or elected for a position **2** person taking an examination ~**dacy** *n* [U] being a candidate

can·died /'kændiʲd/ *adj* covered with shiny sugar

can·dle /'kændl/ *n* wax stick with string inside, which gives light when it burns: *We ate by candlelight.*

can·dle·stick /ˈkændlˌstɪk/ n holder for a candle

can·dor /ˈkændər/ n [U] being CANDID

can·dy /ˈkændiʸ/ n [C;U] sweets, chocolate, etc.

candy strip·er /ˈkændiʸ ˌstraɪpər/ n young woman who helps in a hospital without pay

cane /keʸn/ n stem of certain tall plants, used for making furniture, for punishing children, etc. ♦ vt hit with a cane

ca·nine /ˈkeʸnaɪn/ adj, n (of, for, typical of) a dog

can·is·ter /ˈkænəstər/ n metal box for holding a dry substance or a gas

can·ker /ˈkæŋkər/ n [C;U] disease of trees, and of animal and human flesh

can·na·bis /ˈkænəbɪs/ n [U] drug produced from HEMP, smoked in cigarettes

can·ner·y /ˈkænəriʸ/ n factory where food is put in cans

can·ni·bal /ˈkænəbəl/ n 1 person who eats human flesh 2 animal that eats its own kind ~**ism** n [U]

can·non /ˈkænən/ n cannons or cannon big gun, fixed to a carriage or used on military aircraft

cannon fod·der /ˈ·· ˌ··/ n [U] ordinary soldiers thought of as nothing but military material without regard for their lives

can·not /ˈkænɑt, kæˈnɑt, kə-/ v fml can not: We cannot accept.

can·ny /ˈkæniʸ/ adj clever; not easily deceived

ca·noe /kaˈnuʷ/ n light boat moved by a PADDLE

can·on /ˈkænən/ n 1 religious law 2 accepted standard of behavior or thought 3 kind of Christian priest ~**ize** vt declare to be a SAINT ~**ical** /kaˈnɑnɪkəl/ adj according to religious law

can o·pen·er /ˈ·· ˌ···/ n tool for opening cans

can·o·py /ˈkænəpiʸ/ n 1 cloth roof over a bed, etc.: (fig.) a canopy of leaves 2 cover over the front of a plane

cant /kænt/ n [U] insincere talk

can't /kænt/ v short for: can not: I can't come tonight.

can·tan·ker·ous /kænˈtæŋkərəs/ adj quarrelsome

can·teen /kænˈtiʸn/ n 1 small container used by soldiers for carrying water 2 place in a factory, office, etc., where food is served

can·ter /ˈkæntər/ n [S] horse's movement, slower than a GALLOP canter vi/t

can·ti·le·ver /ˈkæntlˌiʸvər, -ˌevər/ n armlike beam sticking out from an upright support, esp. for a bridge

can·vas /ˈkænvəs/ n 1 [U] strong cloth used for tents, etc. 2 [C] oil painting done on this

can·vass /ˈkænvəs/ vi/t go through (a place) or to (people) to ask for votes or find out opinions ~**er** n

can·yon /ˈkænyən/ n deep narrow valley

cap /kæp/ n 1 soft flat covering for the head, with no BRIM 2 protective top of a bottle, etc. 3 small quantity of explosive in paper for toy guns ♦ vt –**pp**– 1 cover the top of 2 do or say better than: He capped my joke with a funnier one.

ca·pa·ble /ˈkeʸpəbəl/ adj 1 clever: a very capable doctor 2 able to do or be: That remark is capable of being misunderstood. –**bly** adv –**bility** /ˌkeʸpəˈbɪlətiʸ/ n 1 [C;U] having skills and apparatus necessary for the stated type of war: nuclear capability 2 [P] undeveloped qualities and abilities

ca·pac·i·ty /kəˈpæsətiʸ/ n 1 [S;U] amount that something can hold: The seating capacity of this theater is 500. 2 [C;U] ability; power 3 [C] position: speaking in my capacity as mayor 4 filled to capacity completely full

cape¹ /keʸp/ n loose outer garment without SLEEVES

cape² n piece of land sticking out into the sea

ca·pil·la·ry /ˈkæpəˌlɛriʸ/ n very thin tube, esp. a blood vessel

cap·i·tal /ˈkæpətl/ n 1 [C] town where the center of government is 2 [S;U] wealth, esp. when used to produce more wealth or start a business 3 [C] letter in its large form; A, B, C, etc.: write in capitals/in **capital letters 4** make capital of use to one's advantage ♦ adj punishable by death: a capital offense

cap·i·tal·is·m /ˈkæpətlˌɪzəm/ n [U] system based on the private ownership of wealth –**ist** n person who owns capital

cap·i·tal·ize /ˈkæpətlˌaɪz/ vt 1 write with a capital letter 2 supply money to (a firm)

    capitalize on phr vt use to one's advantage

capital pun·ish·ment /ˌ··· ˈ···/ n [U] punishment by death according to law

Cap·i·tol /ˈkæpətl/ n [the] building in Washington D.C. where Congress meets

ca·pit·u·late /kəˈpɪtʃəˌleʸt/ vi accept defeat; stop opposing –**lation** /kəˌpɪtʃəˈleʸʃən/ n [C;U]

ca·price /kəˈpriʸs/ n [C;U] sudden foolish change of behavior

−pricious /kə'prɪʃəs/ adj changing; untrustworthy

cap·size /'kæpsaɪz, kæp'saɪz/ vi/t (cause a boat) to turn over

cap·stan /'kæpstən/ n round object turned to raise a ship's ANCHOR, etc.

cap·sule /'kæpsəl, -syuʷl/ n 1 very small container of medicine to be swallowed whole 2 part of a spacecraft where the pilots live

cap·tain /'kæptən/ n 1 leader of a team 2 person in command of a ship or aircraft 3 officer of middle rank in the armed forces ♦ vt be the captain of

cap·tion /'kæpʃən/ n words written above or below a picture or newspaper article

cap·ti·vate /'kæptə,veʸt/ vt charm; attract: her captivating beauty

cap·tive /'kæptɪv/ n prisoner, esp. taken in war ♦ adj: (fig.) a captive audience (= group not able or not allowed to stop watching or listening) −**tivity** /kæp'tɪvətiʸ/ n (U) state or condition of being a captive

cap·tor /'kæptər/ n person who captures someone

cap·ture /'kæptʃər/ vt 1 make a prisoner of; take control of by force 2 preserve on film, in words, etc. ♦ n 1 (U) capturing; being captured 2 (C) person or thing captured

car /kɑr/ n 1 vehicle with wheels and a motor, used for carrying people 2 vehicle that is pulled

car·a·mel /'kærəməl, -ˌmel, 'kɑrməl/ n 1 (U) cooked sugar 2 (C) candy made of boiled sugar

car·at /'kærət/ n unit expressing the purity of gold, or the weight of a jewel

car·a·van /'kærə,væn/ n group of people with vehicles or animals crossing a desert, etc.

car·a·way /'kærəweʸ/ n plant whose seeds have a strong taste and are used to give a special taste in food

car·bo·hy·drate /ˌkɑrboʷ'haɪdreʸt, -drɪt, -bə-/ n (C;U) food such as sugar which provides heat and ENERGY

car·bon /'kɑrbən/ n 1 (U) substance found in diamonds, coal, etc. 2 (C;U) a paper with a coat of ink used for making copies b copy made with this

car·bun·cle /'kɑrˌbʌŋkəl/ n large painful swelling

car·bu·re·tor /'kɑrbə,reʸtər,-byə-/ n apparatus that mixes the air and gas in a car engine

car·cass /'kɑrkəs/ n dead body, esp. of an animal

car·cin·o·gen·ic /ˌkɑrsɪnə'dʒenɪk◂/ adj causing CANCER

card /kɑrd/ n 1 a (C) one of 52 pieces of stiff paper used for various games b (P) games played with these 2 (C) piece of stiff paper with various uses: a membership card | a birthday card | a postcard 3 (U) cardboard 4 lay/put one's cards on the table say what one intends to do 5 on the cards probable: They say war's on the cards 6 play one's cards right act in the most effective manner to get what one wants

card·board /'kɑrdbɔrd, -boʷrd/ n (U) thick stiff paper: a cardboard box

car·di·ac /'kɑrdiʸ,æk/ adj of the heart

car·di·gan /'kɑrdəgən/ n short knitted (KNIT) coat with SLEEVES, usu. fastened at the front

car·di·nal /'kɑrdn-əl, 'kɑrd-nəl/ n 1 priest of the highest rank in the Roman Catholic church 2 red bird ♦ adj fml most important; main

cardinal num·ber /ˌ··· '··/ n 1, 2, 3, etc.

card·sharp /'kɑrdʃɑrp/ n someone who cheats (successfully) at playing cards

care¹ /keər/ n 1 (C;U) worry; anxiety: free from care | her many cares 2 (U) protection; charge: under a nurse's care 3 (U) serious attention: Take care not to drop it. 4 care of also in care of abbrev. c/o (used when addressing letters to mean) at the address of 5 take care of be responsible for ~**ful** adj attentive; CAUTIOUS ~**fully** adv ~**less** adj 1 not taking care; inattentive 2 free from care; not worried ~**lessly** adv ~**lessness** n (U)

care² vi 1 be worried; mind: I don't care where we go. 2 care to like to; want: Would you care to sit down?

care for phr vt 1 look after; nurse 2 like to have: Would you care for a drink?

ca·reen /kə'riʸn/ vi lean or move quickly to one side while in a vehicle

ca·reer /kə'rɪər/ n 1 profession 2 general course of a person's life

care·free /'keərfriʸ/ adj free from anxiety

ca·ress /kə'res/ n light loving touch ♦ vt give a caress to

care·tak·er /'keər,teʸkər/ n person employed to look after a building

car·go /'kɑrgoʷ/ n −**goes** or −**gos** (C;U) goods carried by a ship, plane, or vehicle

car·i·ca·ture /'kærəkə,tʃʊər, -tʃər/ n funny drawing (or written description) of someone to make them seem silly ♦ vt make a caricature of

car·nage /'kɑrnɪdʒ/ n (U) killing of many people

car·nal /'kɑrnl/ adj physical, of the flesh, or esp. sexual: carnal desires

car·na·tion /kɑrˈneʸʃən/ n white, pink or red flower with a sweet smell

car·ni·val /ˈkɑrnəvəl/ n [C;U] **1** period of public rejoicing **2** traveling amusement park

car·ni·vore /ˈkɑrnəˌvɔr, -ˌvoʷr/ n animal that eats flesh –**vorous** /kɑrˈnɪvərəs/ adj

car·ol /ˈkærəl/ n religious song of joy, esp. sung (SING)at Christmas

carp[1] /kɑrp/ n carp or carps large FRESHWATER fish

carp[2] vi complain unnecessarily

car·pen·ter /ˈkɑrpəntər/ n person who makes wooden objects –**try** n [U] work of a carpenter

car·pet /ˈkɑrpɪt/ n [C;U] cloth for covering floors – see also RED CARPET ♦ vt cover (as if) with a carpet

car pool /ˈ· ·/ n agreement made by people to take turns driving each other to work, etc. ♦ vt take part in a car pool

car·riage /ˈkærɪdʒ/ n **1** [C] vehicle, esp. one pulled by a horse **2** [U] (cost of) moving goods **3** [C] movable part of a machine: *the carriage of a typewriter* **4** [S;U] *fml* way of walking

car·ri·er /ˈkæriʸər/ n **1** person or business that carries goods **2** person or animal that passes diseases to others without catching them **3** military vehicle or ship that carries soldiers, etc.: *aircraft carrier*

car·ri·on /ˈkæriʸən/ n [U] dead or decaying flesh

car·rot /ˈkærət/ n long orange root vegetable

car·ry /ˈkæriʸ/ v **1** vt move while supporting; have with one: *carry a gun* | *carry a child on one's back* **2** vt take from one place to another: *Pipes carry oil across the desert.* | *Flies carry disease.* **3** vt bear the weight of: *This beam carries the whole roof.* **4** vt have as a usual or necessary result: *Such a crime carries a serious punishment.* **5** vt contain; have: *All the newspapers carried the story.* **6** vt win by voting: *The motion was carried.* **7** vi reach a distance: *Her voice doesn't carry very far.* **8 be carried away** get excited **9 carry a torch for** be in love with

carry off phr vt perform successfully

carry on phr vi **1** continue: *carry on talking* **2** behave in a foolish excited manner **carry-on** /ˈ··· ·/ n piece of light LUGGAGE

carry on with phr vt **1** have a love affair with (someone) **2 to carry/be carrying on with** for the present time

carry out phr vt fulfil; complete ♦ **carryout** n (meal from) a restaurant that sells food to eat elsewhere

carry through phr vt **1** help to continue: *Her courage carried her through.* **2** fulfil; complete: *carry a plan through*

car·ry·all /ˈkæriʸˌɔl/ n large basket, bag, etc.

carrying charge /ˈ··· ˌ·/ n money added to the price of things bought by INSTALLMENT PLAN

cart /kɑrt/ n **1** wheeled vehicle pulled by an animal, or pulled or pushed by hand: *shopping cart* **2 put the cart before the horse** do things in the wrong order ♦ vt **1** carry in a cart **2** carry; take: *carting these books around*

carte blanche /ˌkɑrt ˈblɑnʃ, -ˈblɑntʃ/ n [U] full freedom

car·tel /kɑrˈtɛl/ n combination of independent firms, to limit competition

cart·horse /ˈkɑrthɔrs/ n heavy powerful horse, used for heavy work

car·ti·lage /ˈkɑrtl̩-ɪdʒ/ n [C;U] elastic substance found around the joints in animals

car·ton /ˈkɑrtn̩/ n CARDBOARD box

car·toon /kɑrˈtuʷn/ n **1** humorous drawing of something interesting in the news **2** film made by photographing a set of drawings ~**ist** n

car·tridge /ˈkɑrtrɪdʒ/ n **1** tube containing explosive and a bullet for a gun **2** part of a record player that holds the needle **3** container of MAGNETIC TAPE or photographic film

cart·wheel /ˈkɑrt-hwiʸl, -wiʸl/ n circular movement in which a person turns over by putting their hands on the ground and moving their legs sideways in the air

carve /kɑrv/ v **1** vt make by cutting wood, stone, etc.: *carve one's name on a tree* | (fig.) *She carved herself (out) a good position in business.* **2** vi/t cut (cooked meat) into pieces **carver** n **1** person who carves **2** knife for carving meat –**ery** n restaurant specializing in meat **carving** n something carved from wood, etc.

cas·cade /kæˈskeʸd/ n waterfall ♦ vi pour like a waterfall

case[1] /keʸs/ n **1** [C] example; situation: *I'll make an exception in your case.* | *several cases of fever* | *police investigating a case of robbery* **2** [C] legal question to be decided; arguments supporting one side of a question: *to judge this case* | *the case for the defense* **3** [C;U] gram form of word showing the part it plays in a sentence **4** [C] person having medical treatment **5 in any case** whatever happens **6 in case of: a** because of anxiety about: *insure the house in case of fire* **b** if (something)

happens: *In case of fire, ring the bell.*
7 (just) in case so as to be safe (if): *Take your coat in case it rains.*

case² *n* large box or container: *a packing case* | *a suitcase*

case·ment /'keʸsmənt/ *n lit* window

cash /kæʃ/ *n* [U] **1** money in coins or notes **2** money in any form ♦ *vt* exchange (a check, etc.) for cash

   cash in on *phr vt* take advantage of

cash crop /'· ·/ *n* crop grown for sale

ca·shew /'kæʃuʷ, kæ'ʃuʷ, kə-/ *n* (tropical American tree with) a small curved nut

cash·ier¹ /kæ'ʃiər/ *n* person who receives and pays out money in a bank, store, etc.

cash·ier² /kæ'ʃiər, kə-/ *vt* dismiss with dishonor from service in the armed forces

cashier's check /·'· ·,·/ *n* check from a bank signed by a cashier of that bank

cash·mere /'kæʒmiər, 'kæʃ-/ *n* [U] fine soft wool

cash reg·is·ter /'· ,···/ *n* machine for recording the amount of sales

cas·ing /'keʸsɪŋ/ *n* protective covering, as on a tire

ca·si·no /kə'siʸnoʷ/ *n* **-nos** building where people play cards or other games for money

cask /kæsk/ *n* barrel for liquids

cas·ket /'kæskɪt/ *n* **1** COFFIN **2** box for jewels, letters, etc.

cas·se·role /'kæsəˌroʷl/ *n* deep dish for cooking and serving meat; food cooked in this

cas·sette /kə'set, kæ-/ *n* container of MAGNETIC TAPE, or of photographic film

cas·sock /'kæsək/ *n* priest's long garment

cast¹ /kæst/ *vt* **cast 1** *fml* throw: *cast a net* | *a snake casting off its skin* | *The sun casts long shadows.* **2** give (a vote) **3** make by pouring hot metal: *cast a statue* **4** choose as an actor; choose actors for (a play) **~ing** *n* thing made by pouring metal

   cast aside *phr* get rid of

   cast off *phr vi/t* unloose (a boat)

cast² *n* **1** actors in a play, film, etc. **2** act of throwing a fishing line, etc. **3** hard covering to protect a broken bone **4** object made by casting metal **5** general shape or quality: *an inquiring cast of mind* **6** slight SQUINT (1)

cas·ta·nets /ˌkæstə'nets/ *n* [P] musical instrument made of 2 hollow shells to be knocked together

cast·a·way /'kæstəˌweʸ/ *n* person

cast up on shore from a wrecked ship

caste /kæst/ *n* [C;U] Hindu social class

cast·er /'kæstər/ *n* small wheel on a chair, etc.

cas·ti·gate /'kæstəˌgeʸt/ *vt fml* punish severely; criticize (CRITIC)

cast·ing vote /ˌ·· '·/ *n* deciding vote when both sides have an equal number of votes

cast i·ron /ˌ· '··/ *n* hard but easily breakable type of iron **cast-iron** /ˌ· '··◄/ *adj* **1** made of cast iron **2** very strong; unbreakable: *a cast-iron stomach* | *a cast-iron excuse*

cas·tle /'kæsəl/ *n* large building that can be defended against attack

cast-off /'· ·/ *n, adj* (piece of clothing) thrown away by the original owner

cas·tor oil /ˌkæstər 'ɔɪl◄/ *n* [U] thick vegetable oil used as a LAXATIVE

cas·trate /'kæstreʸt/ *vt* remove the sex organs of (a male) **-tration** /kæ'streʸʃən/ *n* [C;U]

cas·u·al /'kæʒuʷəl/ *adj* **1** informal: *casual clothes* **2** resulting from chance: *casual meeting* **3** employed for a short time: *casual labor* **4** not serious or thorough: *the casual reader* **~ly** *adv*

cas·u·al·ty /'kæʒuʷəlti, 'kæʒəlti/ *n* person killed or hurt in an accident or battle

cat /kæt/ *n* **1** small furry animal often kept as a pet **2** animal related to this; lion, tiger, etc. **3** *sl* man **4 let the cat out of the bag** tell a secret (usu. unintentionally) **5 rain cats and dogs** rain very heavily

cat·a·clysm /'kætəˌklɪzəm/ *n fml* violent event, such as an EARTHQUAKE **-ic** /ˌkætə'klɪzmɪk◄/ *adj*

cat·a·comb /'kætəˌkoʷm/ *n* underground burial place with many rooms

cat·a·log, -logue /'kætlˌɔg, -ˌɑg/ *n* list of places, goods for sale, etc., in order ♦ *vt* make a list of

cat·a·lyst /'kætlˌɪst/ *n* something that quickens activity without itself changing

cat·a·pult /'kætəpʌlt, -ˌpʊlt/ *n* ancient military machine for throwing stones ♦ *vt* fire (as if) from a catapult: (fig.) *He was catapulted to fame.*

cat·a·ract /'kætəˌrækt/ *n* **1** large waterfall **2** eye disease causing blindness

ca·tarrh /kə'tɑr/ *n* [S;U] disease of the nose and throat, causing a flow of liquid

ca·tas·tro·phe /kə'tæstrəfiʸ/ *n* sudden terrible misfortune **-phic** /ˌkætə'strɑfɪk◄/ *adj*

cat bur·glar /'· ,··/ *n* thief who

enters buildings by climbing walls, pipes, etc.

cat·call /'kætkɔl/ v, n (make) a loud whistle or cry expressing disapproval, esp. at the theater, etc.

catch¹ /kætʃ/ v **caught** /kɔt/ **1** vt get hold of (a moving object) and stop it: *catch a ball* **2** vt make a prisoner; trap: *catch a fish/a thief* **3** vt discover doing something: *I caught him reading my diary.* **4** vt be in time for: *catch a train* **5** vt get (an illness) **6** vi/t get hooked or stuck: *My skirt caught in the door.* **7** vt hear; understand **8** vt to hit (a person or animal) **9 catch fire** start to burn **10 catch it** *infml* be in trouble for doing something wrong **11 catch one's breath** **a** stop breathing for a moment because of surprise or shock **b** rest for a short while after hard work **12 catch sight of** see for a moment **13 catch someone's eye** attract someone's attention by looking at them ~**ing** adj infectious

catch on phr vi **1** become popular **2** understand

catch up phr vi/t **1** come up from behind; draw level **2 caught up in** completely interested in or involved

catch² n **1** getting and holding a ball **2** (amount of) something caught: *big catch of fish* **3** hook, etc. for fastening something **4** hidden difficulty; SNAG ~**er** n position behind the BATTER in BASEBALL

catch-22 /ˌkætʃ twɛntiᵉ 'tuʷ/ n [U] situation from which one is prevented from escaping by something that is part of the situation itself: *I can't get a job unless I belong to the union, and I can't join the union until I have a job — it's a catch-22 situation!*

catch·phrase /'kætʃfreᵉz/ n fashionable phrase that everyone uses

catch·y /'kætʃiᵉ/ adj (of a tune, etc.) easy to remember

cat·e·gor·i·cal /ˌkætəˈgɔrɪkəl, -ˈgɑr-/ adj (of a statement) unconditional; made without doubt ~**ly** /-kliᵉ/ adv

cat·e·go·ry /'kætəˌgɔriᵉ, -ˌgoʷriᵉ/ n division in a system; class –**gorize** /-gəˌraɪz/ vt put in a category

ca·ter /'keᵉtər/ vi provide food and drinks at a party ~**er** n

cater for phr vt provide what is necessary: *magazines catering for all opinions*

cat·er·pil·lar /'kætərˌpɪlər, 'kætəˌpɪlər/ n **1** wormlike creature that eats leaves **2** (cap.) tdmk vehicle with endless chain of plates on the wheels

cat·fish /'kætˌfɪʃ/ n FRESHWATER fish used for food

cat·gut /'kætgʌt/ n [U] cord used for the strings of musical instruments

ca·thar·sis /kəˈθɑrsɪs/ n –**ses** /-siᵉz/ [C;U] getting rid of bad feelings by expressing them through art or by reliving them **cathartic** adj

ca·the·dral /kəˈθiᵉdrəl/ n chief church of a DIOCESE

cath·ode /'kæθoʷd/ n part of an electrical instrument from which ELECTRONS leave

cath·o·lic /'kæθəlɪk/ adj **1** fml general; broad: *catholic tastes* **2** (cap.) ROMAN CATHOLIC ♦ n (cap.) a ROMAN CATHOLIC

Cath·o·li·cism /kəˈθɑləˌsɪzəm/ n [U] teachings of the ROMAN CATHOLIC church

cat·nap /'kætnæp/ n short light sleep

cat·sup /'kɛtʃəp, 'kæ-, 'kætsəp/ n KETCHUP

cat·tle /'kætl/ n [P] cows and BULLS

cat·ty /'kætiᵉ/ adj indirectly SPITEful

cat·walk /'kætwɔk/ n narrow raised PLATFORM (2)

cau·cus /'kɔkəs/ n political meeting to decide future plans

caught /kɔt/ v past t. and p. of CATCH

caul·dron /'kɔldrən/ n lit large pot for boiling things

cau·li·flow·er /'kɔliˌflaʊər, 'kɑ-/ n [C;U] green vegetable with a large white head of flowers

cause /kɔz/ n **1** [C;U] thing that produces a result: *the cause of the accident* **2** [U] reason: *no cause for complaint* **3** [C] purpose strongly supported: *good causes such as famine relief* ♦ vt be the cause of: *to cause trouble*

cause·way /'kɔzweᵉ/ n raised road across water, etc.

caus·tic /'kɔstɪk/ adj **1** able to burn by chemical action **2** (of remarks) bitter; nasty

cau·tion /'kɔʃən/ n **1** [U] great care **2** [C] spoken warning by a policeman, etc. – see also **throw caution to the wind** (THROW) ♦ vt warn ~**ary** adj giving a warning

cau·tious /'kɔʃəs/ adj with caution; careful ~**ly** adv

cav·al·cade /ˌkævəlˈkeᵉd, ˌkævəlˈkeᵉd/ n procession of riders, vehicles, etc.

cav·a·lier /ˌkævəˈlɪərˌ/ adj thoughtless; OFFHAND

cav·al·ry /'kævəlriᵉ/ n [U] soldiers on horseback, or (now) with armored vehicles

cave¹ /keᵉv/ n underground hollow place

cave² v **cave in** phr vi **1** (of a roof) fall down **2** give up opposition; YIELD

ca·ve·at /ˈkæviˌæt, ˈkɑviˌɑt/ n law warning

cav·ern /ˈkævərn/ n large cave ~**ous** adj (of a hole) very large

cav·i·ar /ˈkæviˌɑr, ˌkæviˈɑr/ n [U] salty eggs (ROE) of a large fish

cav·il /ˈkævəl/ vi -l- also -ll- find fault unnecessarily

cav·i·ty /ˈkævəṭi/ n fml hole in a solid mass, such as a tooth

ca·vort /kəˈvɔrt/ vi infml (esp. of a person) jump or dance about noisily

CB /ˌsiˈbiʸ◂/ n [U] Citizens' Band; radio by which people can speak to each other privately

cc abbrev. for: CUBIC centimetre

CD /ˌsiˈdiʸ◂/ n COMPACT DISC

CD-ROM /ˌsiˌdiʸ ˈrɑm/ n COMPACT DISC on which very large quantities of information can be stored for use by a computer

cease /siʸs/ vi/t fml stop (an activity) ~**less** adj unending; continuous ~**lessly** adv

cease-fire /ˌ·ˈ·, ˈ·◂/ n agreement to stop fighting; TRUCE

ce·dar /ˈsiʸdər/ n C;U (wood of) a tall EVERGREEN tree

cede /siʸd/ vt fml give (esp. land, after losing a war)

ceil·ing /ˈsiʸlɪŋ/ n 1 upper surface of a room 2 official upper limit on prices, etc.

cel·e·brate /ˈsɛləˌbreʸt/ v 1 vt/i mark (an event) by enjoying oneself 2 vt praise; honor ~**brated** adj famous ~**bration** /ˌsɛləˈbreʸʃən/ n [C;U]

ce·leb·ri·ty /səˈlɛbrəṭi/ n 1 [C] famous person 2 [U] fame

cel·e·ry /ˈsɛləriʸ/ n [U] plant whose green-white stems are eaten as a vegetable

ce·les·tial /səˈlɛstʃəl/ adj fml of the sky or heaven

cel·i·bate /ˈsɛləbɪt/ n , adj (person who is) unmarried and not sexually active, esp. for religious reasons ~**bacy** n [U]

cell /sɛl/ n 1 small room: prison cell 2 small unit of living matter 3 apparatus for making electricity chemically 4 single group of people in a secret organization: Communist cells

cel·lar /ˈsɛlər/ n underground room for storing things: wine cellar

cel·lo /ˈtʃɛloʸ/ n -los kind of large VIOLIN held between the knees **cel·list** n person who plays a cello

cel·lu·lar /ˈsɛlyələr/ adj 1 having many holes; POROUS 2 consisting of cells (2)

cel·lu·loid /ˈsɛlyəˌlɔɪd/ n [U] tdmk 1 strong plastic formerly made for making photographic film 2 **on celluloid** on cinema film

Cel·si·us /ˈsɛlsiʸəs, -fəs/ adj , n (in) the temperature scale in which water freezes at 0° and boils at 100°

Cel·tic /ˈsɛltɪk, ˈkɛl-/ adj of the Celts, a European people who include the Welsh and Bretons

ce·ment /sɪˈmɛnt/ n [U] 1 grey powder that becomes hard like stone when mixed with water, and is used in building 2 any thick sticky glue used for filling holes or joining things ♦ vt join with cement: (fig.) to cement our friendship

cem·e·ter·y /ˈsɛməˌtɛriʸ/ n piece of ground used for burials

cen·o·taph /ˈsɛnəˌtæf/ n MONUMENT in memory of people killed in war

cen·sor /ˈsɛnsər/ n official who examines books, films, etc., to remove anything offensive ♦ vt examine or remove material as a censor: a censored book/film ~**ship** n [U] work of a censor; censoring

cen·so·ri·ous /sɛnˈsɔriʸəs, -ˈsoʸr-/ adj fml always looking for mistakes and faults; severely CRITICal

cen·sure /ˈsɛnfər/ n fml blame; disapproval ♦ vt express disapproval of

cen·sus /ˈsɛnsəs/ n official counting, esp. of a country's population

cent /sɛnt/ n (coin equal to) 0.01 of any of certain units of money, e.g. the dollar

cen·taur /ˈsɛntɔr/ n imaginary creature, half man and half horse

cen·ten·ni·al /sɛnˈtɛniʸəl/ n 100th ANNIVERSARY

cen·ter /ˈsɛntər/ n 1 [C] middle point 2 [C] place for a particular activity: a shopping center 3 [the+S] a middle position, in politics, not supporting EXTREME (2) ideas ♦ vi/t gather to a center: His interests are centered on/around his family.

cen·ti·grade /ˈsɛntəˌgreʸd/ adj, n CELSIUS

cen·ti·me·ter /ˈsɛntəˌmiʸṭər/ n (unit of length equal to) 1/100 of a meter

cen·ti·pede /ˈsɛntəˌpiʸd/ n wormlike creature with many legs

cen·tral /ˈsɛntrəl/ adj 1 at the center 2 most important; main ~**ly** adv ~**ize** vt bring under central control ~**ization** n [U] /ˌsɛntrələˈzeʸʃən/

central heat·ing /ˌ·· ˈ··/ n [U] heating buildings by pipes from a single point

central pro·ces·sing u·nit /ˌ·· ˈ·· ˌ··/ also CPU — the most important controlling part of a computer system

Central time /ˈ·· ˌ·/ n time used in the Midwest and S Central part of the country, one hour behind Eastern time

cen·ter·piece /ˈsɛntərˌpiʸs/ n thing

in the central or most important position

cen·tri·fu·gal /sen'trɪfyəgəl, -fə-/ *adj* tending to move out from the center

cen·trist /'sentrɪst/ *n, adj* (of) a person who supports the CENTER (3)

cen·tu·ry /'sentʃəriʸ/ *n* 1 100 years 2 period of 100 years counted forwards or backwards from Christ's birth

CEO /ˌsiʸ iʸ 'oʷ/ *n abbrev. for* CHIEF EXECUTIVE OFFICER

ce·ram·ics /sə'ræmɪks/ *n* [U;P] (making of) pots, bricks, etc. **ceramic** *adj*

ce·re·al /'sɪəriʸəl/ *n* 1 [C] food grain 2 [C;U] breakfast food such as CORNFLAKES

ce·re·bral /sə'riʸbrəl, 'serə-/ *adj* 1 of or connected with the brain 2 showing too much serious thinking

cer·e·mo·ni·al /ˌserə'moʷniʸəl◄/ *adj* for a ceremony: *ceremonial banquet* ♦ *n* [C;U] ceremony

cer·e·mo·ni·ous /ˌserə'moʷniʸəs◄/ *adj* formally polite

cer·e·mo·ny /'serəˌmoʷniʸ/ *n* 1 [C] set of solemn actions to mark an important event: *a wedding ceremony* 2 [U] formal behavior

cer·tain¹ /'sɜrtn/ *adj* 1 sure; without doubt: *I'm certain he saw me.* | *It's certain to rain.* 2 sure to happen: *facing certain death* 3 **make certain** do something to be sure: *Make certain he knows.* ~**ly** *adv* of course

certain² *determiner, pron* 1 some, not named: *There are certain reasons against it.* 2 some, not a lot: *a certain amount of profit*

cer·tain·ty /'sɜrtntiʸ/ *n* 1 [C] established fact 2 [U] freedom from doubt

cer·tif·i·cate /sər'tɪfəkɪt/ *n* official paper stating facts: *marriage certificate*

cer·ti·fied mail /ˌ···· '·/ *n* method of sending mail by which one gets official proof that it has been delivered

cer·ti·fy /'sɜrtəˌfaɪ/ *vt* declare officially that something is true: *to certify the prisoner insane* **–fiable** *adj*

cer·ti·tude /'sɜrtəˌtuʷd, -ˌtyuʷd/ *n* [U] *fml* state of being or feeling certain

cer·vi·cal /'sɜrvɪkəl/ *adj* of the narrow opening (**cervix**) of the WOMB

ce·sar·e·an /sɪ'zeəriʸən/ *n* CAESAREAN

ces·sa·tion /se'seʸʃən/ *n* [C;U] *fml* short pause or stop

cess·pool /'ses-puʷl/ *n* underground hole where a house's SEWAGE is gathered

cf *written abbrev. for*: compare

ch *written abbrev. for*: CHAPTER (1)

chafe /tʃeʸf/ *v* 1 *vt* rub; make sore by rubbing 2 *vi* become impatient: *chafe at the delay*

chaff /tʃæf/ *n* [U] outer covers of seeds, separated from the grain

chag·rin /ʃə'grɪn/ *n* [U] *fml* annoyance and disappointment

chain /tʃeʸn/ *n* 1 length of metal rings joined together 2 set of connected things: *chain of mountains/of events* ♦ *vt* fasten with a chain: *prisoners chained to the wall*

chain gang /'· ·/ *n* group of prisoners chained together while working

chain re·ac·tion /ˌ· ·ˌ···, ˌ· ·'···/ *n* set of events so related that each causes the next

chain-smoke /'· ·/ *vi/t* smoke (cigarettes) continually **–smoker** *n*

chain store /'· ·/ *n* group of stores under one ownership

chair /tʃeər/ *n* 1 movable seat for one person 2 position of a chairperson 3 position of a PROFESSOR ♦ *vt* be chairperson of

chair·man /'tʃeərmən/ **–woman** /-ˌwumən/ *fem. n* — **–men** /-mən/ person in charge of a meeting, or directing the work of a group

chair·per·son /'tʃeərˌpɜrsən/ *n* chairman or chairwoman

chal·et /ʃæ'leʸ, 'ʃæleʸ/ *n* 1 Swiss wooden house 2 small house or hut in mountains

chalk¹ /tʃɔk/ *n* 1 [U] kind of soft white rock 2 [C;U] this material used for writing or drawing **~y** *adj*

chalk² *vt* write with chalk

    chalk up *phr vt* 1 ATTRIBUTE 2 succeed in getting

chalk·board /'tʃɔkbɔrd, -boʷrd/ *n* board used in schools for writing on

chal·lenge /'tʃæləndʒ/ *vt* 1 invite to a fight, match, etc. 2 question the loyalty or rightness of ♦ *n* 1 invitation to compete 2 something exciting that needs a lot of effort **–lenging** *adj* difficult but exciting **–lenger** *n*

cham·ber /'tʃeʸmbər/ *n* 1 *lit* BEDROOM 2 a body that makes laws b room where it meets 3 enclosed space: *the 4 chambers of the heart*

cham·ber·maid /'tʃeʸmbərˌmeʸd/ *n* woman who cleans hotel BEDROOMS

chamber mu·sic /'·· ˌ··/ *n* [U] music for a small group (a **chamber orchestra**)

cha·me·le·on /kə'miʸlyən, -liʸən/ *n* small LIZARD that changes color to match its surroundings

champ¹ /tʃæmp/ *vi* 1 (of a horse) bite noisily 2 be impatient 3 **champ at the bit** be restless and difficult to control because of being impatient to do something

champ² *n infml abbrev. for* CHAMPION (1)

cham·pagne /ʃæmˈpeʸn/ n [U] expensive white wine with BUBBLES

cham·pi·on /ˈtʃæmpiʸən/ n 1 person or animal that wins a competition 2 person who defends a principle or another person: *champion of justice* ♦ vt defend; support ~**ship** n 1 competition to find the champion 2 position of being the champion 3 act of championing

chance /tʃæns/ n 1 [U] good or bad luck 2 [C;U] likelihood: *no chance of winning* | *The chances are* (= it is likely) *he already knows.* 3 [C] favorable occasion; OPPORTUNITY: *a chance to travel* 4 [C;U] risk 5 **by chance** by accident 6 **on the (off) chance** in view of the (unlikely) possibility ♦ v 1 vt take a risk 2 vi fml happen accidentally: *We chanced to meet.* ♦ adj accidental –y adj risky

chan·cel /ˈtʃænsəl/ n part of a church where the ALTAR is

chan·cel·lor /ˈtʃænsələr/ n (often cap.) university or legal official of high rank

chan·de·lier /ˌʃændəˈliʳər/ n branched hanging holder for lights

change /tʃeʸndʒ/ v 1 vi/t make or become different: *change the subject* | *water changed into ice* 2 vt give and receive in return: *change a library book* | *change pounds into dollars* 3 vi/t put different clothes on 4 vi/t leave and enter (different vehicles): *change (trains) at Chicago* 5 **change one's mind** form a new opinion ♦ n 1 changing; something new: *a change of clothes* | *Let's have fish for a change.* 2 a money returned when something bought costs less than the amount paid **b** coins or notes of low value – see also SEA CHANGE ~**able** adj often changing

change of life /ˌ··'·/ n MENOPAUSE

chan·nel /ˈtʃænl/ n 1 narrow sea passage 2 passage for liquids 3 television station 4 way along which information passes: *go through the official channels* vt –l also –ll– send through channels; direct: *channel my abilities into something useful*

chant /tʃænt/ vi/t sing (words) on one note ♦ **chant** n

cha·os /ˈkeʸɑs/ n [S;U] complete confusion –**otic** /keʸˈɑtɪk/ adj

chap /tʃæp/ vi/t –pp– (cause to) become sore, rough and cracked: *chapped lips*

chap·el /ˈtʃæpəl/ n small Christian church

chap·er·on, **-one** /ˈʃæpəroʷn/ n older person who goes with a younger person and is responsible for their behavior ♦ **chaperon**, **-one** vt

chap·lain /ˈtʃæplin/ n priest in the armed forces, a hospital, etc.

chaps /tʃæps/ n [P] strong leather covering to protect COWBOYS' legs

chap·ter /ˈtʃæptər/ n 1 main division of a book, usu. numbered 2 special period of history 3 local branch of a society, club, etc.

char /tʃɑr/ vi/t –rr– blacken by burning

char·ac·ter /ˈkærɪktər/ n 1 [C;U] qualities that make a person or thing different from others: *a man of good character* | *the character of the town* 2 [U] moral strength, honesty, etc. 3 [C] person in a book, etc. 4 [C] person, esp. an odd one 5 [C] written letter or sign: *Chinese characters* ~**less** adj ordinary; dull

char·ac·ter·is·tic /ˌkærɪktəˈrɪstɪk◂/ adj typical ♦ n special quality ~**ally** /-kliʸ/ adv

char·ac·ter·ize /ˈkærɪktəˌraɪz/ vt 1 be typical of 2 describe the character of

cha·rade /ʃəˈreʸd/ n 1 [C] foolish unnecessary action 2 [P] game in which words are acted by players until guessed by other players

char·broil /ˈtʃɑrˌbrɔɪl/ vt BARBECUE ~ed adj: *charbroiled steak*

char·coal /ˈtʃɑrkoʷl/ n burned wood, used for drawing with, cooking fires, etc.

charge /tʃɑrdʒ/ v 1 vt/i ask in payment 2 vt record (something) to someone's debt 3 vi/t rush as if to attack 4 vt ACCUSE of a crime: *charged with stealing* 5 vt fml command; give as a duty 6 vt/i (cause to) take in electricity: *charge a battery* | (fig.) *a highly charged political question* (= causing strong feelings or much argument) ♦ n 1 [C] price asked or paid 2 [U] control; responsibility: *I'll take charge of the money.* 3 [C] statement blaming a person for wrongdoing: *a charge of murder* 4 [C] rushing attack by soldiers, animals, etc. 5 [C;U] electricity put into a BATTERY 6 **in charge (of)** responsible (for)

charge account /'· ··,·/ n arrangement with a particular store that allows one to buy goods and pay for them later

charge card /'· ·/ n plastic card which allows one to obtain goods at a particular store and pay later

char·gé d'af·faires /ʃɑrˌʒeʸ dəˈfeɑr/ n official who represents his/her government where there is no AMBASSADOR

char·i·ot /ˈtʃæriʸət/ n ancient vehicle with 2 wheels, pulled by a horse

char·i·o·teer /ˌtʃæriʸəˈtɪər/ n driver of a chariot

cha·ris·ma /kəˈrɪzmə/ n [U] fml great charm; power to win public admiration ~**tic** /ˌkærɪzˈmætɪk◂/ adj: charismatic leader

char·i·ty /ˈtʃærəti̯/ n **1** [U] generosity and help to the poor, etc. **2** [U] kindness shown in judging others **3** [C] organization for helping people –**table** adj –**tably** adv

char·la·tan /ˈʃɑrlətən, -lətn/ n person who falsely claims a special skill

charm /tʃɑrm/ n **1** [C;U] power to delight people **2** [C] magic words; SPELL **3** [C] object worn to bring good luck **4 work like a charm** happen or take place with complete success ♦ vt **1** please; delight: charming manners **2** control by magic ~**er** n person who charms ~**ing** adj very pleasing

chart /tʃɑrt/ n **1** information in the form of a picture or GRAPH: a sales chart **2** map, esp. of the sea ♦ vt make a chart of

char·ter /ˈtʃɑrtər/ n **1** [C] official statement of rights and freedoms **2** [U] hiring of buses, planes, etc.: charter flights ♦ vt hire (a bus, etc.)

charter mem·ber /ˌ·· ˈ··/ n [C] original member of a society or organization

chase /tʃeɪs/ vi/t follow rapidly, in order to catch or drive away ♦ n **1** chasing something or someone **2 give chase** chase someone

chasm /ˈkæzəm/ n very deep crack in the earth

chas·sis /ˈʃæsi̯, ˈtʃæ-/ n **chassis** /-si̯z/ frame on which a vehicle is built

chaste /tʃeɪst/ adj avoiding wrong sexual activity

chas·ten /ˈtʃeɪsən/ vt improve by punishment or suffering

chas·tise /tʃæˈstaɪz, ˈtʃæstaɪz/ vt fml punish severely

chas·ti·ty /ˈtʃæstəti̯/ n [U] being chaste

chat /tʃæt/ vt -**tt**- talk informally **chat** n ~**ty** adj **1** fond of chatting **2** having the style of informal talk: chatty letter

châ·teau /ʃæˈtoʷ/ n -**teaus** or -**teaux** /ʃæˈtoʷz, -ˈtoʷ/ French castle

chat·ter /ˈtʃætər/ vi **1** talk rapidly about small things **2** (of the teeth) knock together from cold or fear ♦ n [U] **1** chattering talk **2** rapid speechlike sounds ~**er** n

chat·ter·box /ˈtʃætərˌbɑks/ n person who chatters

chauf·feur /ˈʃoʷfər, ʃoʷˈfɜr/ **chauffeuse** /ʃoʷˈfuz, -ˈfɜz/ fem. — n paid driver of a private car **chauffeur** vi/t

chau·vin·is·m /ˈʃoʷvəˌnɪzəm/ n proud belief that one's own country,

or one's own sex, is the best –**ist** n, adj – see also MALE CHAUVINIST

cheap /tʃiːp/ adj **1** low in price **2 a** of poor quality **b** offensively unpleasant **3** without serious feeling: cheap emotions **4** needing little effort: a cheap victory **5** infml STINGY **6 feel cheap** feel ashamed ♦ adv at a low price ~**en** vi/t make or become cheaper ~**ly** adv ~**ness** n [U]

cheap·skate /ˈtʃiːpskeʲt/ n person who is unwilling to spend money

cheat /tʃiːt/ vi/t **1** act dishonestly; treat someone deceitfully: cheating at cards | cheat her out of her money **2** avoid or escape as if by deception: to cheat death ♦ n person who cheats

check /tʃɛk/ n **1** [C] examination to make sure something is correct **2** [S;U] stop; control: keep the disease in check **3** [C;U] pattern of squares **4** [C] restaurant bill **5** [C] written order to a bank to pay money **6** [C] mark (✓) put against an answer to show that it is correct or next to a name to show the person is present (2) **7** [U] (in CHESS) position of the king when under direct attack ♦ v **1** vi/t examine; make sure: check a letter for spelling mistakes **2** vt hold back; control: check the increase in crime **3** vt put somewhere to be looked after: check one's coat at the theater **4** vt mark with a check (6) see also BLANK CHECK, TRAVELER'S CHECK

check in phr vi report one's arrival at an airport, etc. **check-in** /ˈ· ·/ n [C;U]

check out phr vi **1** leave a hotel after paying the bill **2 a** find out if something is true by making inquiries **b** be found to be true after inquiries have been made **3** have the removal of (an article) recorded

check up on phr vt inquire thoroughly about

check·book /ˈtʃɛkbʊk/ n book of checks

checking ac·count /ˈ·· ·ˌ·/ n person's main bank account which can be used for writing checks

check·ered /ˈtʃɛkərd/ adj partly bad and partly good: his checkered career

check·ers /ˈtʃɛkərz/ n [P] game played by two people on a board (**checkerboard**) with squares

check·list /ˈtʃɛkˌlɪst/ n complete list; INVENTORY

check·mate /ˈtʃɛkmeʲt/ n [C;U] **1** (in CHESS) position of a king when under direct attack so that escape is impossible **2** complete defeat ♦ vt **1** (in CHESS) win the game with a checkmate **2** stop; completely defeat

check·out /ˈtʃɛk-aʊt/ n pay desk in a SELF-SERVICE store

check·point /ˈtʃɛkpɔɪnt/ n place where a CHECK (1) is made on people, traffic, etc.

check·room /ˈtʃɛk-ruːm, -rʊm/ n [C] place in a station where one can leave one's bags

checks and ba·lanc·es /ˌ · · ˈ····/ n system of limiting the power of the three branches of the US government

check·up /ˈtʃɛk-ʌp/ n general medical examination

cheek /tʃiːk/ n 1 [C] either side of the face below the eye 2 [U] rude behavior ~**y** adj rude

cheer /tʃɪər/ n 1 [C] shout of praise or joy 2 [U] happiness; good spirits
♦ vi/t 1 make or become happy: cheering news | Cheer up! 2 shout in approval; encourage by shouting ~**ful** adj happy ~**fully** adv ~**less** adj lacking cheerful qualities ~**y** adj merry

cheer·lead·er /ˈtʃɪərˌliːdər/ n [C] person who calls for and directs cheering e.g. at a football game

cheese /tʃiːz/ n [C;U] solid food made from milk

cheese·cake /ˈtʃiːzkeɪk/ n 1 [C] cake in a sweet pastry case which contains soft cheese 2 [U] pictures of women with few clothes on

chee·tah /ˈtʃiːtə/ n spotted African animal of the cat family, able to run very fast

chef /ʃɛf/ n chief cook in a restaurant, etc.

chem·i·cal /ˈkɛmɪkəl/ adj of chemistry ♦ n chemical substance

chem·ist /ˈkɛmɪst/ n scientist specializing in chemistry

chem·is·try /ˈkɛməstriː/ n [U] science of natural substances and how they combine and behave

chem·o·ther·a·py /ˌkiːˈmoʊ·ˈθɛrəpiː, ˌkɛ-/ n [U] use of chemical substances to treat and control diseases

cher·ish /ˈtʃɛrɪʃ/ vt fml 1 care for; love 2 keep (hope, etc.) in one's mind: cherish a memory

cher·ry /ˈtʃɛriː/ n small round fruit with a pit

cher·ub /ˈtʃɛrəb/ n 1 pretty child, esp. one with wings in a painting 2 (pl. −ubim /-əbɪm, -yəbɪm/) kind of ANGEL ~**ic** /tʃəˈruːbɪk/ adj

chess /tʃɛs/ n [U] board game for 2 players

chest /tʃɛst/ n 1 upper front part of the body 2 large strong box 3 **get (something) out of one's chest** bring (a worry) out into the open by talking

chest·nut /ˈtʃɛsnʌt/ n 1 kind of smooth red-brown nut 2 joke or story so old and familiar that it is no longer funny or interesting ♦ adj red-brown

chest of drawers /ˌ · · ˈ·/ n piece of furniture with drawers

chew /tʃuː/ vi/t 1 crush (food, etc.) with the teeth 2 **bite off more than one can chew** attempt more than one can deal with or succeed in finishing

chew over phr vt infml think about (a question, problem, etc.)

chew out phr vt speak to (someone) angrily esp. because they have done (something) wrong

chewing gum /ˈ·· ˌ·/ n sweet sticky substance to be chewed but not swallowed

chic /ʃiːk/ adj, n [U] (with) good style

Chi·ca·no /tʃɪˈkɑnoʊ/ n [C] US citizen from Mexico, or whose family come from Mexico

chick /tʃɪk/ n baby bird

chick·en¹ /ˈtʃɪkən/ n 1 [C] common farmyard bird, esp. a young one 2 [U] its meat 3 **count one's chickens before they're hatched** make plans depending on something which has not yet happened ♦ adj sl cowardly

chicken² v **chicken out** phr vi sl decide not to do something because one is frightened

chicken pox /ˈtʃɪkən ˌpɑks/ n [U] infectious disease that causes spots

chic·o·ry /ˈtʃɪkəriː/ n [U] plant whose roots are made into powder and added to coffee

chide /tʃaɪd/ vi/t **chided** or **chid** /tʃɪd/, **chid** or **chidden** /ˈtʃɪdn/ fml or lit speak to (someone) angrily; REBUKE

chief /tʃiːf/ n leader; head of something: the chief of police ♦ adj 1 highest in rank 2 **main 3 -in-chief** of the highest rank: commander-in-chief ~**ly** adv mainly; specially

chief ex·ec·u·tive of·fi·cer /ˌ · · ·ˈ··· ˌ····/ also **CEO** — n top director of a company

chief·tain /ˈtʃiːftən/ n leader of a tribe, etc.

child /tʃaɪld/ n **children** /ˈtʃɪldrən/ 1 young human being 2 son or daughter 3 someone who behaves like a child ~**hood** n [C;U] time of being a child ~**ish** adj unsuitable for a grown person ~**less** adj having no children ~**like** adj simple; lovable

child sup·port /ˈ·· ˌ·/ n [U] money given to a woman for her children by their father who doesn't live with them

chill /tʃɪl/ vi/t 1 make or become cold 2 (cause to) have a feeling of cold as from fear: a chilling murder story ♦ n 1 [C] illness with coldness and shaking 2 [S] unpleasant cold

chill·y /'tʃɪliʸ/ adj **1** rather cold **2** unfriendly

chil·i /'tʃɪliʸ/ n [C;U] **1** (powder made from) the red seed case of a kind of pepper which tastes very hot **2** dish with meat, beans, and chili

chime /tʃaɪm/ n sound of a set of bells ♦ vi/t **1** make this sound **2** infml be in agreement

chim·ney /'tʃɪmniʸ/ n hollow passage to let out smoke from a fire

chim·pan·zee /ˌtʃɪmpæn'ziʸ, tʃɪm-'pænziʸ/ also **chimp** /tʃɪmp/ n kind of African APE

chin /tʃɪn/ n the part of the face below the mouth

chi·na /'tʃaɪnə/ n [U] **1** baked clay **2** plates, cups, etc., made from this

Chi·na·town /'tʃaɪnəˌtaʊn/ n [C;U] part of a city where there are Chinese restaurants, shops, etc.

chink[1] /tʃɪŋk/ n narrow crack

chink[2] n, v CLINK

chip[1] /tʃɪp/ n **1** small piece broken off **2** place from which this was broken **3** thin piece of food: *chocolate chip* **4** small piece of material on which an INTEGRATED CIRCUIT is formed **5** flat plastic object used for representing money in certain games **6** a chip off the old block a person very like their father in character **7** have a chip on one's shoulder be quarrelsome or easily offended, as a result of feeling badly treated **8** when the chips are down when a very important point is reached – see also BLUE CHIP ~**per** adj happy; cheerful; active

chip[2] vi/t -pp- (cause) to lose a small piece from the edge

 chip in phr vi/t infml add (one's) share of money)

chi·rop·o·dist /kə'rɑpədɪst, ʃə-/ n person who treats the human foot -**dy** n [U]

chirp /tʃɜrp/ vi make the short sharp sound of small birds **chirp** ♦ n ~**y** adj (of people) cheerful

chis·el /'tʃɪzəl/ n metal tool for shaping wood or stone ♦ vi/t -l- cut with a chisel

chiv·al·ry /'ʃɪvəlriʸ/ n [U] **1** beliefs and practices of KNIGHTS in the MIDDLE AGES **2** good manners shown by a man towards women – rous adj

chlo·rine /'klɔriʸn, 'klɔʷr-/ n [U] greenish yellow substance with a strong smell, used to DISINFECT places, esp. swimming pools

chlor·o·form /'klɔrəˌfɔrm, 'klɔʷr-/ n chemical used as an ANESTHETIC

chock-full /ˌtʃɑk 'fʊl◄/ adj infml completely full

choc·o·late /'tʃɔkəlɪt, 'tʃɑ-/ n **1** [U] solid brown substance eaten as candy **2** [C] small candy covered

with this **3** [U] hot drink made from this ♦ adj dark brown

choice /tʃɔɪs/ n **1** [C] act of choosing **2** [U] power of choosing: *have no choice but to obey* **3** [C] variety to choose from: *a big choice of stores* ♦ adj **1** of high quality **2** well chosen

choir /kwaɪər/ n **1** group of singers **2** part of a church where they sit

choke /tʃoʷk/ v **1** vt/i stop breathing because the breathing passage is blocked **2** vt fill (a passage) completely: *roads choked with traffic* ♦ n apparatus that controls air going into a gas engine

 choke back phr vt control (esp. violent or sad feelings) as if by holding in the throat: *He choked back his tears.*

chol·e·ra /'kɑlərə/ n [U] serious tropical disease of the stomach and bowels

cho·les·te·rol /kə'lɛstəˌrɑl, -ˌroʷl/ n [U] substance found in all cells of the body, which helps to carry fats

choose /tʃuʷz/ vi/i chose /tʃoʷz/, chosen /'tʃoʷzən/ **1** pick out from many: *choose a cake* **2** decide: *choose where to go*

chop[1] /tʃɑp/ vt -pp- cut with a heavy tool: *chop wood/onions*

chop[2] n **1** quick cutting blow **2** piece of lamb or PORK with a bone in it

chop·per /'tʃɑpər/ n **1** heavy tool for chopping **2** sl HELICOPTER

chop·py /'tʃɑpiʸ/ adj (of water) with short rough waves

chop·sticks /'tʃɑpstɪks/ n [P] pair of thin sticks used in East Asia for lifting food to the mouth

cho·ral /'kɔrəl, 'koʷrəl/ adj of a CHOIR

chord /kɔrd/ n **1** 2 musical notes sounded together **2** straight line joining 2 points on a curve – see also **strike a chord** (STRIKE[1])

chore /tʃɔr, tʃoʷr/ n piece of regular or dull work

chor·e·og·ra·phy /ˌkɔriʸ'ɑgrəfiʸ, ˌkoʷr-/ n arranging dances for the stage –**pher** n ♦ **choreograph** /'kɔriʸəˌgræf, 'koʷr-/ vt

chor·is·ter /'kɔrɪstər, 'koʷr-, 'kɑr-/ n singer in a CHOIR

chor·tle /'tʃɔrtl/ vi give several laughs of pleasure and satisfaction **chortle** n

cho·rus /'kɔrəs, 'koʷrəs/ n **1** [C] group of singers **2** [C] part of a song repeated after each VERSE **3** [S] something said by many people together: *a chorus of groans* ♦ vt sing or say together

chose /tʃoʷz/ v past t. of CHOOSE

cho·sen /'tʃoʷzən/ v past p. of CHOOSE

chow /tʃau/ n infml food

chow-der /ˈtʃaudər/ n soup that uses milk as its base

Christ /kraɪst/ n man on whose teaching Christianity is based; Jesus

chris-ten /ˈkrɪsən/ vt 1 make into a member of the Christian church by giving of a name at BAPTISM 2 name (esp. a ship) at an official ceremony 3 use for the first time ~ing n ceremony of BAPTISM

Chris-ten-dom /ˈkrɪsəndəm/ n [U] lit all Christian people or countries

Chris-tian /ˈkrɪstʃən/ n person who believes in the teachings of Christ ♦ adj 1 of Christianity 2 having qualities such as kindness, generosity, etc.

Chris-ti-an-i-ty /ˌkrɪstʃiˈænəti/ n [U] the religion based on the life and teachings of Christ

Christian name /ˈ·· ˌ·/ n (esp. in Christian countries) a person's FIRST NAME

Christ-mas /ˈkrɪsməs/ n 1 also **Christmas Day** /ˌ·· ˈ·/ — holy day in honor of Christ's birth; December 25th 2 period before and after this

chrome /kroʊm/ n [U] hard metal used esp. as a shiny covering on car parts, etc.

chro-mo-some /ˈkroʊməˌsoʊm/ n extremely small thread in every living cell that controls the nature of a young animal or plant

chron-ic /ˈkrɑnɪk/ adj (of a disease) lasting a long time

chron-i-cle /ˈkrɑnɪkəl/ n record of historical events ♦ vt make a chronicle of

chro-nol-o-gy /krəˈnɑlədʒi/ n 1 [U] science that gives dates to events 2 [C] list of events in order **-ogical** /ˌkrɑnəˈlɑdʒɪkəl◄/ adj arranged in order of time

chro-nom-e-ter /krəˈnɑmətər/ n very exact clock

chrys-a-lis /ˈkrɪsəlɪs/ n shell-like form of an insect that will become a MOTH or BUTTERFLY

chry-san-the-mum /krɪˈsænθəməm/ also **mum** — n garden plant with large flowers in bright colors

chub-by /ˈtʃʌbi/ adj pleasantly fat

chuck /tʃʌk/ vt infml 1 throw 2 sl give up; leave: chuck (in) his job 3 throw away

chuck-le /ˈtʃʌkəl/ vi laugh quietly **chuckle** n

chum /tʃʌm/ n friend ~**my** adj friendly

chump /tʃʌmp/ n sl fool

chunk /tʃʌŋk/ n thick lump ~**y** adj thick

church /tʃɜrtʃ/ n 1 [C] building for public Christian worship: a regular **churchgoer** 2 [S] profession of priests and ministers: enter the church 3 [C] (usu. cap.) branch of Christianity: the Catholic Church

church key /ˈ· ˌ·/ n infml bottle opener

church-yard /ˈtʃɜrtʃyard/ n church burial ground

churl-ish /ˈtʃɜrlɪʃ/ adj bad-tempered; rude **~ly** adv

churn¹ /tʃɜrn/ n container in which cream is shaken to make butter

churn² vi/t shake about violently **churn out** phr vt produce a large quantity of

chute /ʃuʷt/ n sloped passage for something to slide down

chut-ney /ˈtʃʌtni/ n [U] mixture of fruits which has a hot taste

chutz-pah /ˈhutspə, ˈxʊt-/ n very high confidence in oneself

CIA /ˌsiʸ aɪ ˈeʸ/ n Central Intelligence Agency; US government department that collects information, esp. secretly

ci-der /ˈsaɪdər/ n [U] drink made from apples, either sweet cider (non-alcoholic) or hard cider (alcoholic)

ci-gar /sɪˈgar/ n roll of tobacco leaves for smoking

cig-a-rette /ˌsɪgəˈret, ˈsɪgəˌret/ n paper tube of cut tobacco for smoking

cinch /sɪntʃ/ n [S] infml 1 (something) done easily: The exam was a cinch. 2 (something) certain to happen: It's a cinch that we'll win.

cin-der /ˈsɪndər/ n piece of burned coal, etc.

cin-der-block /ˈsɪndərˌblɑk/ n building block made from cement and cinders

cin-e-ma /ˈsɪnəmə/ n 1 [C] theater where films are shown also **movie theater** 2 [S] films as an art or industry

cin-na-mon /ˈsɪnəmən/ n [U] yellow-brown SPICE used in cooking

ci-pher /ˈsaɪfər/ n 1 system of secret writing 2 unimportant person

cir-ca /ˈsɜrkə/ prep fml (used with dates) about: circa 1000 AD

cir-cle /ˈsɜrkəl/ n 1 curved line on which every point is equally distant from the center 2 ring 3 group of people 4 upper floor in a theater ♦ vi/t 1 move around in a circle 2 draw a circle around

cir-cuit /ˈsɜrkɪt/ n 1 circular journey around an area 2 circular path of an electric current **~ous** /sərˈkyuʷətəs/ adj going a long way around: a circuitous route

cir-cu-lar /ˈsɜrkyələr/ adj 1 shaped like a circle 2 moving in a circle 3

cir·cu·late /ˈsɜːkjəˌleⁱt/ vi/t **1** move along a closed path **2** spread widely: *circulate rumors* **3** move about freely ~**lation** /ˌsɜːkjəˈleⁱʃən/ n **1** [U] flow around a closed system: *the circulation of the blood* **2** [U] passing of money among people: *the number of $5 bills in circulation* **3** [S] number of copies of a newspaper sold

cir·cum·cise /ˈsɜːkəmˌsaɪz/ vt cut off the skin at the end of the male sex organ or part of the sex organ (CLITORIS) of a woman ~**cision** /ˌsɜːkəmˈsɪʒən/ n [C;U]

cir·cum·fer·ence /sərˈkʌmfərəns/ n distance around: *the Earth's circumference*

cir·cum·nav·i·gate /ˌsɜːkəmˈnævəˌgeⁱt/ vt fml sail right around

cir·cum·scribe /ˈsɜːkəmˌskraɪb/ vt fml limit

cir·cum·spect /ˈsɜːkəmˌspɛkt/ adj fml careful

cir·cum·stance /ˈsɜːkəmˌstæns/ n **1** (usu. pl.) conditions that influence a person or event **2 in/under no circumstances** never **3 in/under the circumstances** because of the conditions

cir·cum·stan·tial /ˌsɜːkəmˈstænʃəl/ adj fml **1** (of a description) detailed **2 circumstantial evidence** information worth knowing but not directly important

cir·cum·vent /ˌsɜːkəmˈvɛnt, ˈsɜːkəmˌvɛnt/ vt avoid by cleverness: *circumvent the tax laws*

cir·cus /ˈsɜːkəs/ n performance of skill and daring by a group of people and animals

cir·rho·sis /səˈroʷsɪs/ n [U] serious LIVER disease

cis·tern /ˈsɪstərn/ n container for storing water

ci·ta·tion /saɪˈteⁱʃən/ n **1** notice to appear in court **2** traffic ticket

cite /saɪt/ vt **1** fml mention as an example **2** law call to appear in court

cit·i·zen /ˈsɪtəzən/ n **1** person living in a city or town **2** person with full membership of a country ~**ship** n [U]: *apply for French citizenship*

Cit·i·zens' Band /ˌ··· ˈ·/ n [U] CB

cit·ric ac·id /ˌsɪtrɪk ˈæsɪd/ n [U] weak acid from fruit juice

cit·rus /ˈsɪtrəs/ adj (of fruit) of the orange family

cit·y /ˈsɪti/ n **1** [C] large important town **2** [C] its citizens **3** [S] (cap.) the center for money matters in London — see also INNER CITY

city hall /ˌ··· ˈ·/ n often cap. (public building used for) a city's local government

civ·ic /ˈsɪvɪk/ adj of a city or its citizens

civ·il /ˈsɪvəl/ adj **1** not military or religious **2** polite ~**ly** adv politely ~**ity** /səˈvɪləti/ n [C;U]

civil en·gi·neer·ing /ˌ·· ··ˈ··/ n [U] building of public roads, bridges, etc.

ci·vil·ian /səˈvɪlyən/ n, adj (person) not of the armed forces

civ·i·li·za·tion /ˌsɪvələˈzeⁱʃən/ n **1** [U] high level of human development and social organization **2** [C] particular civilized society: *ancient civilizations*

civ·i·lize /ˈsɪvəˌlaɪz/ vt **1** bring to civilization: *civilized nations* **2** improve in manners

civil rights /ˌ·· ˈ·/ n [P] a citizen's rights to freedom and equality

civil ser·vant /ˌ·· ˈ··/ n person employed in the civil service

civil ser·vice /ˌ·· ˈ··/ n [the+S] **1** FEDERAL government departments, except the armed forces and law courts **2** people employed in this

civil war /ˌ·· ˈ·/ n war between people from the same country

clad /klæd/ adj lit clothed; covered

claim /kleⁱm/ v **1** vt/i demand (something) as one's right: *claim on the insurance* **2** vt declare to be true: *He claims to be rich.* ♦ n **1** demand for something as one's right; right to something **2** something claimed, esp. money under an insurance agreement **3** statement; declaration

clai·mant /ˈkleⁱmənt/ n fml person who claims something

clair·voy·ant /klɛərˈvɔɪənt/ adj, n (of a) person who can see what will happen in the future ~**ance** n [U]

clam[1] /klæm/ n large SHELLFISH

clam[2] v **clam up** phr vi become silent

clam·bake /ˈklæmbeⁱk/ n informal party by the sea, esp. where clams are cooked and eaten

clam·ber /ˈklæmbər/ vi climb with effort

clam·my /ˈklæmi/ adj unpleasantly wet and sticky

clam·or /ˈklæmər/ n [S;U] loud confused noise, esp. of complaint ♦ vi demand noisily: *a baby clamoring to be fed*

clamp[1] /klæmp/ n apparatus with a screw, for fastening things together

clamp[2] vt fasten with a clamp

clamp down on phr vt limit; prevent: *clamp down on drunk driving*

clampdown /ˈklæmpdaʊn/ n

clan /klæn/ n Scottish family group

clan·des·tine /klænˈdɛstɪn/ adj secret ~**ly** adv

clang /klæŋ/ vi/t make a loud ringing sound **clang** n [S]

clank /klæŋk/ vi/t make a sound like a heavy metal chain **clank** n [S]

clap /klæp/ v –pp– **1** vi/t strike (one's hands) together: *The audience clapped loudly.* **2** vt strike lightly with the open hand: *clap him on the back* **3** vt infml put quickly: *clapped her in jail* ♦ n **1** [C] loud explosive noise, esp. of thunder **2** [S] clapping: *Give him a clap!* **3** [S] sl GONORRHEA

clap·board /'klæp͜ˌbɔrd, -͜ˌbɔʳrd/ n board covering the outer walls of a house

clap·trap /'klæptræp/ n [U] nonsense

clar·et /'klærət/ n [U] red wine from Bordeaux ♦ adj deep red

clar·i·fy /'klærə͜ˌfaɪ/ vt fml make more easily understood –**fication** /͜ˌklærəfə'keɪʃən/ n [C;U]

clar·i·net /͜ˌklærə'nɛt/ n kind of WOODWIND musical instrument ~**tist** n person who plays the clarinet

clar·i·ty /'klærət͜iʸ/ n [U] clearness

clash /klæʃ/ v **1** vi come into opposition **2** vi (of colors) look wrong together **3** vi (of events) be planned for the same time **4** vi/t make a loud metallic noise ♦ n **1** [C] disagreement **2** [S] metallic noise

clasp /klæsp/ n metal fastener ♦ vt **1** seize firmly **2** firm hold ♦ vt **1** seize firmly **2** fasten with a clasp

class /klæs/ n **1 a** [C] group of students taught together **b** [C] period of time they are taught for **2** [C] division; level: *a first-class carriage* **3** [U] high quality; elegance (ELEGANT) – see also FIRST CLASS ♦ vt put into a class; consider – **y** adj fashionable and of high class **4** [C] social group of a particular rank: *the ruling class* **5** [U] system of dividing society into such groups

class ac·tion /͜ˌ· '·͜·͜·/ n legal action by a group of people similarly interested

class-con·scious /͜ˌ· '·͜·͜·/ adj conscious of one's social position ~**ness** n [U]

clas·sic /'klæsɪk/ adj **1** of the highest quality **2** typical: *classic example* **3** having a long history; TRADITIONAL ♦ n piece of literature or art, a writer or artist of lasting importance **classics** n [P] ancient Greek and Roman literature

clas·si·cal /'klæsɪkəl/ adj **1** following ancient Greek or Roman models **2** (of music) with serious artistic intentions **3** TRADITIONAL

clas·si·fy /'klæsə͜ˌfaɪ/ vt arrange into classes –**fied** adj **1** divided into classes **2** officially secret –**fication** /͜ˌklæsəfə'keɪʃən/ n [C;U]

class·mate /'klæsmeʸt/ n child in the same class

class·room /'klæsruʷm, -rʊm/ n room in a school, etc., in which a class meets for a lesson

clat·ter /'klætəʳ/ n [S;U] noise of hard objects hitting each other: *a clatter of dishes* ♦ vi/t make a clatter

clause /klɔz/ n **1** gram group of words containing a subject and verb **2** law separate division of a piece of legal writing

claus·tro·pho·bi·a /͜ˌklɔstrə'foʷbiʸə/ n [U] fear of being closed in

claw¹ /klɔ/ n **1** sharp nail on an animal's or bird's toe **2** limb of a CRAB, etc. **3** curved end of some tools

claw² vi/t tear or pull with claws

clay /kleʸ/ n [U] earth from which bricks, pots, etc., are made

clean¹ /kliʸn/ adj **1** not dirty **2** not yet used: *clean piece of paper* **3** morally pure: *clean joke* **4** smooth; regular: *clean lines of a new car* **5** come clean tell the unpleasant truth ♦ n [S] act of cleaning ♦ adv completely: *I clean forgot.* | *They got clean away.*

clean² vt make clean ~**er** n person or thing that cleans –**ners** n **1** shop where clothes, etc., are cleaned with chemicals **2** take someone to the cleaners cause someone to lose all their money, etc.

clean out phr vt **1** make (the inside of a room, drawer, etc.) clean and tidy **2** take all someone's money

clean up phr vi/t **1** clean thoroughly **2** sl gain money as profit

clean-cut /͜ˌ· '·͜·͜/ adj **1** well shaped **2** neat and clean in appearance

clean·ly¹ /'kliʸnliʸ/ adv in a clean way

clean·ly² /'klɛnliʸ/ adj fml always clean –**liness** n [U]

cleanse /klɛnz/ vt make pure **cleanser** n chemical, etc., used for cleaning

clean-shav·en /͜ˌ· '·͜·͜/ adj with no beard

clean sweep /͜ˌ· '·͜/ n **1** complete change **2** complete victory

clear¹ /klɪəʳ/ adj **1** easy to see through: *clear glass* **2** without marks, etc.: *clear skin* | (fig.) *a clear conscience* **3** easy to hear or understand **4** certain: *I'm not certain where she lives.* | *a clear case of murder* **5** open; empty: *The road's clear of snow.* **6** free; no longer touching: *We're clear of danger now.* | *He swung clear of the wall.* **7** (of wages or profit) remaining after all taxes, etc. have been paid ♦ n [U] in the clear free from guilt, debt, etc. ♦ adv **1** in a clear way: *shout loud and clear* **2** completely: *The prisoner got clear away.* **3** out of the way: *jump clear of the train* ~**ly** adv **1** in a clear way: *speak clearly* **2** undoubtedly: *clearly wrong*

clear² v **1** vi/t become clear; remove

something unwanted: *The sky cleared.* | *clear snow from the road* **2** *vt* get past without touching: *clear a fence* **3** *vt* give official approval to **4** *vt* free from blame **5** *vt* earn as CLEAR (7) profit or wages: *She clears $10,000 a year.*

clear away *phr vt* make an area tidy by removing

clear off *phr vi* go away

clear out *phr v* **1** *vi* go away **2** *vt* empty

clear up *phr v* **1** *vt* explain: *clear up the mystery* **2** *vt/i* tidy

clear·ance /ˈklɪərəns/ *n* **1** [U] official approval **2** [C;U] distance between objects **3** [U] also **security clearance** — official acceptance that one is in no way an enemy of one's country **4** [C] also **clearance sale** /ˈ··ˌ·/ — time when a store sells goods cheaply so as to get rid of as many as possible

clear-cut /ˌ·ˈ·◄/ *adj* clear in meaning

clear·ing /ˈklɪərɪŋ/ *n* area cleared of trees

cleav·age /ˈkliːvɪdʒ/ *n* **1** division caused by splitting **2** space between a woman's breasts as seen when she is wearing a dress

cleave /kliːv/ *vt* **cleaved** or **cleft** /kleft/ or **clove** /kləʊv/, **cleaved** or **cleft** or **cloven** /ˈkləʊvən/ divide or make by a cutting blow **~·er** *n* tool for cutting meat

cleave to *phr vt lit* remain loyal to

clef /klef/ *n* sign at the beginning of a line of written music to show the PITCH[1] (of) notes

cleft /kleft/ *v past t. of* CLEAVE

clem·en·cy /ˈklemənsiː/ *n* [U] *fml* mercy **-ent** *adj fml* (of weather) not severe

clench /klentʃ/ *vt* close tightly: *clench one's fists*

cler·gy /ˈklɜːdʒiː/ *n* [P] priests

cler·gy·man /ˈklɜːdʒiːmən/ *n* **-men** /-mən/ Christian priest

cler·ic /ˈklerɪk/ *n* clergyman **~al** *adj* **1** of priests **2** of clerks

clerk /klɑːk/ *n* **1** office worker **2** official in charge of court records, etc.

clev·er /ˈklevər/ *adj* **1** quick at learning **2** intelligent but possibly deceitful: *clever response* **3** showing skill: *clever idea* **~·ly** *adv* **~·ness** *n* [U]

cli·ché /ˈkliːʃeɪ/ *n* expression or idea used so often it has lost much of its force

click /klɪk/ *n* slight sound, as of a camera ♦ *v* **1** *vi/t* make a click **2** *vi* fall into place; understand **3** *vi* be a success

cli·ent /ˈklaɪənt/ *n* **1** person who pays for advice from a professional person **2** customer

cli·en·tele /ˌkliːɒnˈtel, ˌkliː-/ *n* clients; customers

cliff /klɪf/ *n* steep rock face, esp. on a coast

cliff-hang·er /ˈklɪfˌhæŋər/ *n* **1** competition, etc., whose result is in doubt until the very end **2** story told in parts, each of which ends at a moment of exciting doubt as to what will happen next

cli·mac·tic /klaɪˈmæktɪk/ *adj* forming a climax

cli·mate /ˈklaɪmɪt/ *n* **1** average weather conditions **2** condition of opinions: *political climate* **-matic** /klaɪˈmætɪk/ *adj*

cli·max /ˈklaɪmæks/ *n* **1** most powerful part of a story, usu. near the end **2** ORGASM ♦ *vi/t* bring or come to a climax

climb /klaɪm/ *v* **1** *vi/t* move, esp. using hands and feet: *climb a ladder* | *go climbing in the Rockies* **2** *vi* rise: *The road climbs steeply.* **3** *vi* (of a plant) grow upwards ♦ *n* **1** journey by climbing **2** place to climb **~·er** *n* person or thing that climbs

clinch[1] /klɪntʃ/ *vt* settle (an agreement) firmly

clinch[2] *n* EMBRACE

cling /klɪŋ/ *vi* **clung** /klʌŋ/ hold tightly **~·ing** *adj* **1** (of clothes) fitting tightly **2** (of a person) too dependent

clin·ic /ˈklɪnɪk/ *n* place for general or specialized medical treatment **~al** *adj* **1** of clinics or hospitals **2** coldly scientific

clink /klɪŋk/ *vi/t* (cause to) make a sound like pieces of glass knocking together **clink** *n* [S]

clip[1] /klɪp/ *n* small esp. metal object for holding things together: *paper clip* ♦ *vt* **-pp-**

clip[2] *vt* **-pp-** **1** cut with scissors, etc. **2** *sl* hit ♦ *n* **1** cutting **2** *sl* quick blow: *a clip round the ear* **~·pers** *n* [P] tool with a scissors action **~·ping** *n* **1** piece cut off **2** piece cut from a newspaper

clique /kliːk, klɪk/ *n derog* closely united group of people

clit·o·ris /ˈklɪtərɪs/ *n* small front part of the female sex organ

cloak /kləʊk/ *n* loose outer garment without SLEEVES ♦ *vt* keep secret

cloak-and-dag·ger /ˌ··ˈ··◄/ *adj* (of stories, etc.) dealing with adventure and mystery

cloak·room /ˈkləʊk-ruːm, -rʊm/ *n* room where coats, etc., may be left

clob·ber /ˈklɒbər/ *vt sl* **1** attack severely **2** defeat completely

clock /klɒk/ *n* **1** instrument for measuring time **2 around the clock** all day and all night **3 put the clock back** return to old-fashioned ideas **4 watch the clock** think continually of how soon work will end **5 work against the clock** work very quickly in order to finish a job before a certain time ♦ *vt* record (time, speed, distance, etc.)

clock in/out *phr vi* record the time of arriving at/leaving work

clock up *phr vt infml* **1** record (a distance traveled, a speed reached, etc.) **2** succeed in getting

clock·wise /ˈklɑk-waɪz/ *adv* in the direction of the movement of a clock

clock·work /ˈklɑk-wɜrk/ *n* [U] **1** machinery wound up with a key **2 like clockwork** without trouble

clod /klɑd/ *n* lump or mass of clay or earth

clog[1] /klɑg/ *n* wooden shoe

clog[2] *vi/t* **-gg-** (cause to) become blocked or filled

clois·ter /ˈklɔɪstər/ *n* covered passage usu. forming part of a college, MONASTERY, etc. **~ed** *adj* sheltered from the world

clone /kloʊn/ *n* descendant of a single plant or animal produced by non-sexual means ♦ **clone** *vt*

close[1] /kloʊz/ *v* **1** *vt/i* shut: *close one's eyes* | *When does the store close?* **2** *vt* bring to an end: *close a bank account* **3 close a deal (with)** settle a business agreement ♦ *n* [S] *fml* end of a period of time: *at the close of day*

close down *phr vi/t* (of a factory, etc.) stop operating **closedown** /ˈkloʊzdaʊn/ *n*

close in *phr vi* surround gradually

close[2] /kloʊs/ *adj* **1** near: *close to the stores* | *a close friend* **2** thorough: *close inspection* **3** without fresh air; too warm **4** decided by a small difference: *a close finish to the race* ♦ *adv* **1** near: *close behind/together* **2 close on** almost **3 close to home** near the (usu. unpleasant) truth **~ly** *adv* **~ness** *n* [U]

close call /ˌkloʊs ˈkɔl/ *n infml* situation in which something dangerous or very unpleasant is only just avoided

closed shop /ˌ· ˈ·◂/ *n* place of work where one must belong to a particular LABOR UNION

close-knit /ˌkloʊs ˈnɪt◂/ also **closely-knit** /ˌ·· ˈ·◂/ — *adj* tightly bound together by social, political, etc., beliefs and activities

close-set /ˌkloʊs ˈsɛt◂/ *adj* set close together: *close-set eyes*

close shave /ˌkloʊs ˈʃeɪv/ *n infml* situation in which something dangerous or very unpleasant is only just avoided – see also CLOSE CALL

clos·et /ˈklɑzɪt/ *n* cupboard built into a wall – see also WATER CLOSET ♦ *adj* not publicly admitted; secret

♦ *vt* enclose (esp. oneself) in a private room

close-up /ˈkloʊs ʌp/ *n* photograph taken from very near

clo·sure /ˈkloʊʒər/ *n* [C;U] closing: *bank closures*

clot /klɑt/ *n* lump formed from liquid: *blood clot* ♦ *vi/t* **-tt-** form into clots

cloth /klɔθ/ *n* [C;U] (piece of) material made by weaving

clothe /kloʊð/ *vt* provide clothes for

clothes /kloʊz, kloʊðz/ *n* [P] things to cover the body; garments

clothes·horse /ˈkloʊzhɔrs, ˈkloʊðɔz-/ *n infml* person who is very interested in clothes and fashion

clothes·line /ˈkloʊzlaɪn, ˈkloʊðɔz-/ *n* wire hung outdoors for drying clothes

clothes·pin /ˈkloʊzpɪn, ˈkloʊðɔz-/ *n* wooden or plastic CLIP for hanging clothes on a clothesline

cloth·ing /ˈkloʊðɪŋ/ *n* [U] clothes

cloud /klaʊd/ *n* **1** [C;U] white or gray mass floating in the sky which is formed from very small drops of water **2** [C] similar floating mass: *clouds of smoke/mosquitoes* **3** [C] something threatening: *the clouds of war* **4 have one's head in the clouds** be impractical **5 under a cloud** out of favor ♦ *v* **1** *vt/i* cover with clouds **2** *vt* confuse: *cloud the issue* **~y** *adj* **1** full of clouds **2** not clear

clout /klaʊt/ *n* **1** [C] blow with the hand **2** [U] influence, esp. political ♦ *vt* strike, esp. with the hand

clove[1] /kloʊv/ *v* past t. of CLEAVE

clove[2] *n* dried flower of a tropical tree used in cooking

clove[3] *n* any of the smallest pieces into which the root of the GARLIC plant can be divided

clo·ven /ˈkloʊvən/ *v* past p. of CLEAVE

clo·ver /ˈkloʊvər/ *n* [C;U] **1** plant with 3 leaves on each stem, often grown as food for cattle **2 in clover** living in comfort

clown /klaʊn/ *n* **1** performer in a CIRCUS who makes people laugh **2** person acting like this ♦ *vi* behave foolishly

cloy /klɔɪ/ *vi/t* (of food) become unpleasant because too sweet: (fig.) *cloying sentimentality*

club[1] /klʌb/ *n* **1** society of people who meet for amusement or some purpose; building where they meet: *health/tennis club* **2** heavy stick used as a weapon **3** stick for striking the ball in GOLF **4** playing card with one or more black figures shaped like clovers on it – see also BOOK CLUB ♦ vt -bb- hit with a heavy stick

club² v **club together** phr vi share the cost of something with others

cluck /klʌk/ vi make the noise a hen makes **cluck** n

clue /kluː/ n **1** something that helps to find the answer to a problem **2 not have a clue** know nothing; be unable to understand

clump¹ /klʌmp/ n group of trees, etc.

clump² vi walk heavily

clum·sy /'klʌmziʸ/ adj **1** awkward in movement **2** TACTless –**sily** adv –**siness** n [U]

clung /klʌŋ/ v past t. and p. of CLING

clunk·er /'klʌŋkər/ n old car or machine that doesn't work well

clus·ter /'klʌstər/ n group of things close together ♦ vi form a close group

clutch¹ /klʌtʃ/ v **1** vt hold tightly **2** vi try to seize: He clutched at a branch. ♦ n **1** act of clutching **2** apparatus connecting and disconnecting the working parts of a car engine **clutches** n [P] control: in the clutches of the enemy

clutch² n (chickens born from) a number of eggs laid by one bird: (fig.) a whole clutch of new problems

clut·ter /'klʌtər/ vt make untidy ♦ n [U] scattered disorderly things

cm written abbrev. for: centimeter(s)

Co. /koʷ/ abbrev. for: COMPANY (1)

C.O. /ˌsiʸ 'oʷ/ n Commanding Officer; person in the armed forces in charge of others

coach /koʷtʃ/ n **1** person who trains people for sports, or gives private lessons ♦ vt train; teach **2** large carriage pulled by a horse or horses ♦ adj of a cheap travel ticket: I flew back coach.

co·ag·u·late /koʷˈægyəˌleʸt/ vi/t change from a liquid to a solid

coal /koʷl/ n [C;U] (piece of) black mineral that can be burned: a coalmine

co·a·lesce /ˌkoʷəˈles/ vi fml grow together; unite

coal·field /'koʷlfiʸld/ n area where there is coal under the ground

co·a·li·tion /ˌkoʷəˈlɪʃən/ n union of political parties or groups for a special purpose

coarse /kɔrs, koʷrs/ adj **1** not fine; lumpy **2** rough in manner; insensitive ~**ly** adv ~**ness** n [U] **coarsen** vi/t

coast /koʷst/ n **1** stretch of land by the sea **2 the coast is clear** all danger has gone ♦ vi go DOWNHILL on a bicycle, etc., without effort or power ~**al** adj

coast·guard /'koʷstgɑrd/ n **1** military organization responsible for the coast and sea near by **2** member of the coastguard

coast·line /'koʷstlaɪn/ n shape of a coast

coat /koʷt/ n **1** outer garment with SLEEVES, fastened at the front **2** animal's fur, etc. **3** covering on a surface: coat of paint ♦ vt cover (a surface) ~**ing** n thin covering

coat hang·er /'· ·,··/ n a HANGER

coat·room /'koʷtruːm, -rʊm/ n CLOAKROOM

coat of arms /ˌ· · '·/ n **coats of arms** patterns or pictures, usu. on a shield, used by a family, town, etc., as their special sign

coax /koʷks/ vt **1** persuade gently **2** obtain (something) by gently persuading

cob /kab/ n **1** long hard central part of an ear of corn **2** strong horse with short legs **3** male SWAN

cob·ble /'kabəl/ also **cobble-stone** /'kabəlˌstoʷn/ — n rounded stone used for road surfaces –**bled** adj covered with cobbles

cobble² vt put together quickly and roughly

cob·bler /'kablər/ n shoe repairer

co·bra /'koʷbrə/ n kind of poisonous snake

cob·web /'kabweb/ n a SPIDER's net of spun threads

co·caine /koʷˈkeʸn, 'koʷkeʸn/ n [U] drug used against pain, or for pleasure

cock /kak/ n **1** fully grown male bird, esp. a chicken **2** hammer of a gun **3** a TAP for controlling the flow of liquid in a pipe **4** sl PENIS ♦ **1** vt/i raise up: The horse cocked its ears. **2** vt set (the hammer of a gun) in the correct position for firing

cock·a·ma·mie /ˌkakəˈmeʸmiʸ/ adj sl making no sense

cock·a·too /'kakəˌtuʷ/ n -**toos** Australian bird with a large CREST (1) on its head

cock·er·el /'kakərəl/ n young cock

cock·eyed /'kakaɪd/ adj **1** stupid **2** CROOKed (1)

Cock·ney /'kakniʸ/ n [C] person from the industrial part of London

cock·pit /'kakˌpɪt/ n part of a plane where the pilot sits

cock·roach /'kak-roʷtʃ/ n large insect which lives esp. in dirty or old houses

cock·sure /ˌkakˈʃʊər/ adj having too much confidence in oneself

cock·tail /'kakteʸl/ n **1** mixed alcoholic drink **2** mixture of fruit or SEAFOOD – see also MOLOTOV COCK·TAIL

cock·y /ˈkɒkiʸ/ adj sl too sure of oneself

co·coa /ˈkoʷkoʷ/ n [U] 1 brown powder tasting of chocolate 2 hot drink made from this

co·co·nut /ˈkoʷkə‚nʌt, -nət/ n [C;U] (flesh of) a very large tropical nut

co·coon /kəˈkuʷn/ n silky covering that protects some insects in their inactive stage ♦ vt protect from hardship

cod /kɒd/ n cod or cods large sea fish

cod·dle /ˈkɒdl/ vt treat (someone) too tenderly

code /koʷd/ n 1 system of signs, or of secret writing: computer code 2 collection of laws or social customs ♦ vt translate into a code

co·ed /ˈkoʷˌɛd, ˌkoʷˈɛd/ n female student in a college open to both sexes ♦ adj coeducational

co·ed·u·ca·tion /ˌkoʷɛdʒəˈkeʸʃən/ n [U] education of boys and girls together –**al** adj

co·erce /koʷˈɜrs/ vt fml force to do something –**ercive** adj –**ercion** /koʷˈɜrʒən/ n [U]

co·ex·ist /ˌkoʷɪgˈzɪst/ vi exist at the same time ~**ence** n [U] (esp. of countries) existing together peacefully

cof·fee /ˈkɒfiʸ/ n [C;U] (drink made by pouring boiling water onto) the (crushed) berries of a tropical tree

coffee ta·ble /ˈ·· ‚··/ n low table

cof·fer /ˈkɒfər, ˈkɑ-/ n large chest for money, etc.

cof·fin /ˈkɒfɪn/ n box in which a dead person is buried

cog /kɒg/ n 1 tooth on the edge of a wheel that moves another wheel 2 **cog in the machine** unimportant person in a very large organization

co·gent /ˈkoʷdʒənt/ adj fml forceful; convincing (CONVINCE): cogent arguments **cogency** n

cog·i·tate /ˈkɒdʒəˌteʸt/ vi fml think carefully

co·gnac /ˈkoʷnyæk, ˈkɑn-, ˈkɒn-/ n [U] kind of BRANDY

cog·nate /ˈkɒgneʸt/ adj fml related: cognate languages

co·hab·it /ˌkoʷˈhæbɪt/ vi fml live together as though married ~**ation** /koʷˌhæbəˈteʸʃən/ n [U]

co·her·ent /koʷˈhɪərənt, -ˈhɛr-/ adj (of speech, ideas, etc.) reasonably connected; clear –**ence** n [U] ~**ly** adv

co·he·sive /koʷˈhiʸsɪv/ adj sticking together –**sion** /-ˈhiʸʒən/ n [U]

coil /kɔɪl/ vi/t twist into a circle ♦ n 1 connected set of twists: coil of rope 2 twisted wire that carries an electric current

coin /kɔɪn/ n piece of metal money ♦ vt 1 make (coins) 2 invent (new words)

co·in·cide /ˌkoʷɪnˈsaɪd/ vi 1 happen at the same time 2 (of opinions, etc.) agree

co·in·ci·dence /koʷˈɪnsədəns, -ˌdɛns/ n [C;U] accidental and surprising combination of events: By sheer coincidence, we have the same birthday. –**dental** /koʷˌɪnsəˈdɛntl/ adj

coke /koʷk/ n [U] 1 substance left after gas has been removed from coal 2 COCAINE

col·an·der /ˈkʌləndər, ˈkɑ-/ n bowl with holes, for separating liquid from food

cold¹ /koʷld/ adj 1 low in temperature: cold wind 2 unfriendly: a cold stare 3 (of cooked food) allowed to get cool 4 unconscious: I knocked him out cold. 5 **get/have cold feet** lose courage 6 **give/get the cold shoulder** treat/be treated unsympathetically ~**ly** adv ~**ness** n [U]

cold² n 1 [U] low temperature 2 [C;U] illness of the nose and throat 3 **(out) in the cold** not noticed; unwanted

cold-blood·ed /ˌ·ˈ···◂/ adj 1 (of snakes, etc.) having a body temperature that varies with the surroundings 2 cruel; without feeling: cold-blooded murder

cold-cuts /ˈkoʷldˈkʌts/ n [P] thin pieces of cold cooked meat

cold-heart·ed /ˌ·ˈ···◂/ adj unkind

cold tur·key /ˌ·ˈ··/ n [U] sl (the unpleasant sick feeling caused by) the sudden stopping of the use of a drug by an ADDICT

cold war /ˌ·ˈ·◂/ n severe political struggle without actual fighting

col·ic /ˈkɑlɪk/ n [U] severe pain in the stomach and bowels

col·lab·o·rate /kəˈlæbəˌreʸt/ vi 1 work together 2 help the enemy –**rator** n –**ration** /kəˌlæbəˈreʸʃən/ n [U]

col·lage /kəˈlɑʒ, koʷ-/ n picture made by gluing various materials or objects onto a surface

col·lapse /kəˈlæps/ v 1 vi fall down suddenly; The bridge collapsed under the weight of the train. 2 vi fall helpless 3 vi/t fold flat ♦ n [C;U] collapsing: (fig.) the collapse of the peace talks –**lapsible** adj that can be folded for packing, etc.

col·lar /ˈkɑlər/ n 1 part of a garment that fits around the neck 2 band put around an animal's neck ♦ vt seize and hold

col·lar·bone /ˈkɑlərˌboʷn/ n bone joining the RIBs to the shoulders

col·late /kəˈleʸt, kɑ-, ˈkoʷleʸt, ˈkɑ-/ vt fml 1 compare (copies of books, etc.) to find the differences 2 arrange (the sheets) of (esp. a book) in the proper order

col·lat·er·al /kəˈlætərəl/ n [S;U] property promised as SECURITY for a debt

col·league /ˈkaliyg/ n fellow worker

col·lect¹ /kəˈlɛkt/ v **1** vt/i gather together: *collect taxes* | *A crowd collected in the street.* **2** vt save (stamps, etc.) as a HOBBY **3** vt regain control of (oneself, one's thoughts, etc.) **4** vt get: *collect one's skirt from the cleaners* – **ed** adj controlled; calm ~**ive** adj shared by many people: *collective ownership* – **ive** n business owned and controlled by the people who work in it ~**ively** adv: *collectively responsible* – **or** n person who collects something: *coin collector* ~**ion** /kəˈlɛkʃən/ n **1** [U] collecting **2** [C] set of things, sum of money, etc., collected

collect² adj, adv to be paid for by the receiver: *Call me collect.*

collective bar·gain·ing /·ˌ··· ˈ····/ n [U] talks between unions and employers about working conditions, etc.

col·lege /ˈkalɪdʒ/ n **1** school for higher education; part of a university **2** group of people with a common profession or purpose: *the College of Arts and Sciences*

college boards /··· ˈ·/ n set of examinations demanded for a person to be admitted to many universities

col·lide /kəˈlaɪd/ vi **1** crash violently **2** be opposed: *The bosses collided with the unions.*

col·li·er /ˈkaliyər/ n coal MINEr

col·li·sion /kəˈlɪʒən/ n [C;U] colliding

col·lo·qui·al /kəˈlowkwiyəl/ adj (of words, style, etc.) suitable for informal conversation – **ly** adv ~**ism** n colloquial expression

col·lude /kəˈluwd/ vi fml act in collusion

col·lu·sion /kəˈluwʒən/ n fml secret agreement to deceive

co·logne /kəˈlown/ n [C;U] liquid with a pleasant smell, put on the skin

co·lon¹ /ˈkowlən/ n lower part of the bowels

colon² n the mark (:)

colo·nel /ˈkɜrnl/ n army or airforce officer of middle rank

co·lo·ni·al /kəˈlowniyəl/ adj **1** of or about colonies (COLONY (1)) **2** of the period, etc., before 1776: *colonial furniture* ♦ n person living or having lived in a COLONY (1) ~**ism** n [U] principle of having colonies

col·o·nize /ˈkalə,naɪz/ vt make into a colony: *colonize Australia* –**nist** n

person living in a new COLONY (1) –**nization** /ˌkalənəˈzeyʃən/ n [U]

col·on·nade /ˌkaləˈneyd/ n row of PILLARS

col·o·ny /ˈkaləniy/ n **1** place lived in and controlled by people from a distant country **2** group of people of the same kind, living together

col·or /ˈkʌlər/ n **1** [C;U] red, blue, green, etc. **2** [C;U] paint or DYE **3** [U] appearance of the skin **4** [U] interesting details of a place, thing, or person – see also OFF COLOR ♦ v **1** vt give color to **2** vi BLUSH **3** vt change; influence – **ed** adj **1** having colors; not just white, or black and white **2** (of people) black or brown ~**ful** adj **1** brightly colored **2** exciting ~**ing** n [C;U] **1** substance giving color **2** skin color, showing health ~**less** adj **1** without color **2** dull **colors** n [P] **1** official flag **2** something worn as the sign of a club, team, etc. **3** **show one's true colors** show one's real nature or character – see also FLYING COLORS

color-blind /ˈ··· ˌ·/ adj unable to see the difference between colors

color line /ˈ··· ·/ n customs or laws that prevent people of different colors from mixing

co·los·sal /kəˈlasəl/ adj extremely large

co·los·sus /kəˈlasəs/ n –**suses** or –**si** /-saɪ/ very large person or thing

colt /kowlt/ n young male horse

col·umn /ˈkaləm/ n **1** PILLAR **2** something this shape: *a column of figures* | *a marching column of soldiers* **3** a division of a page **4** newspaper article – see also FIFTH COLUMN ~**ist** /ˈkaləmnɪst, -ləmɪst/ n writer of a newspaper column

co·ma /ˈkowmə/ n unnatural deep sleep

co·ma·tose /ˈkowmə,tows, ˌka-/ adj **1** in a coma **2** inactive and sleepy

comb /kowm/ n **1** [C] toothed piece of plastic, etc., for tidying the hair or as an ornament **2** [S] act of combing **3** HONEYCOMB ♦ vt **1** tidy (hair) with a comb **2** search (a place) thoroughly

com·bat /ˈkambæt/ n [C;U] struggle; fight **combat** /kəmˈbæt, ˈkambæt/ vt/i –**t**- or –**tt**-: *to combat inflation* ~**ant** /kəmˈbætnt/ n person who fights ~**ive** adj fond of fighting

com·bi·na·tion /ˌkambəˈneyʃən/ n **1** [U] combining: *We worked well in combination.* **2** [C] people or things combined **3** [C] numbers needed to open a special lock: *combination lock*

com·bine¹ /kəmˈbaɪn/ vi/t join together; unite

com·bine² /ˈkambaɪn/ n **1** group of people, businesses, etc., acting together **2** also **combine harvester** /ˌ‥ ˈ‥‥/ machine that cuts and THRESHes grain

com·bo /ˈkambowˈ/ n infml **1** combination **2** group of musicians

com·bus·ti·ble /kəmˈbʌstəbəl/ adj burning easily

com·bus·tion /kəmˈbʌstʃən/ n [U] process of burning

come /kʌm/ vi came /keym/, **come 1** move towards the speaker; arrive **2** reach a particular point: *The water came up to my neck.* | *We came to an agreement.* | *The bill comes to $18.50.* **3** have a particular position: *Monday comes after Sunday.* **4** happen: *How did you come to be invited?* **5** begin: *I came to realize the truth.* **6** become: *come apart* | *come undone* | *My dream came true.* **7** be offered, produced, etc.: *Shoes come in different sizes.* | *Milk comes from cows.* **8** sl have an ORGASM **9** **come and go** pass or disappear quickly **10** **how come?** why? **11 to come** in the future **comer** n **1** person who appears likely to be successful in their job **2** **all comers** everyone who comes and tries **coming** n [S] arrival **coming** adj future: *the coming winter*

come about phr vi happen

come across/upon phr vt find by chance

come across phr vi be effective and well received

come along phr vi **1** improve; advance **2** arrive by chance **3** **Come along!** Hurry up!

come apart phr vi break into pieces without the need of force

come at phr vt advance towards in a threatening manner

come away phr vi become disconnected without being forced

come back phr vi return

come between phr vt cause trouble between

come by phr vt obtain; receive

come down phr vi **1** fall **2** **come down in the world** fall to a lower standard of living **3** **come down in favor of/on the side of** decide to support

come down on phr vt punish

come down to phr vt be no more than: *It all comes down to a question of money.*

come down with phr vt catch (an infectious illness)

come forward phr vi offer oneself to fill a position, give help to police, etc.

come from phr vt have (a place) as one's home

come in phr vi **1** become fashionable **2** **come in handy/useful** be useful

come in for phr vt receive (esp. blame)

come in on phr vt take part in

come into phr vt **1** INHERIT **2** begin to be in (a state or activity)

come of phr vt result from: *No good will come of it.*

come off phr v **1** vi happen as planned **2** vt **come off it!** stop lying or pretending

come on phr vi **1** improve; advance **2** (of weather, illness, etc.) begin **3** **Come on!** Hurry up!

come out phr vi **1** appear **2** become known **3** (of color, etc.) be removed **4** end up: *How did everything come out?* **5** (of a photograph) be successful **6** declare oneself to be HOMOSEXUAL

come out against phr vt declare one's opposition to

come out in phr vt be partly covered by (marks caused by an illness)

come out with phr vt say, esp. suddenly

come over phr v **1** vt (of feelings, etc.) influence suddenly: *What's come over you?* **2** vi make a short informal visit

come round phr vi **1** also **come to** — regain consciousness **2** change one's opinions **3** happen as usual

come through phr v **1** vi (of news, etc.) become known **2** vi/t SURVIVE

come to phr vt **1** enter the mind of: *The idea came to me suddenly.* **2** concern: *He's ignorant when it comes to politics.* **3** COME round

come under phr vt **1** be in (a particular class): *Rabbits come under the heading of pets.* **2** be governed or controlled by

come up phr vi **1** happen **2** come near

come up against phr vt meet (difficulties)

come up with phr vt think of (a plan, reply, etc.); produce

come·back /ˈkʌmbæk/ n return to strength or fame

co·me·di·an /kəˈmiˈdiˈyən/ n **1** **comedienne** /kəˌmiˈdiˈyˈen/ fem. — actor who makes people laugh **2** amusing person

come·down /ˈkʌmdawn/ n fall in importance

com·e·dy /ˈkamədiˈ/ n **1** [C;U] (type of) funny play, film, etc. **2** [U] amusing quality of something

com·et /ˈkamɪt/ n bright heavenly body with a tail

come-up·pance /ˌkʌm ˈʌpəns/ n punishment or misfortune that is richly deserved

com·fort /ˈkʌmfərt/ n **1** [U] lack of pain or anxiety; physical satisfaction **2** [C] something that satisfies physical needs **3** [C;U] (person or thing that brings) help for an unhappy person ♦ *vt* make less unhappy

com·for·ta·ble /ˈkʌmftəbəl, ˈkʌm-fərtəbəl/ *adj* **1** giving comfort: *a comfortable chair* **2** feeling comfort; not suffering or anxious **–bly** *adv*

com·for·ta·bly off /ˌ····· ˈ·/ *adj* fairly rich

com·fort·er /ˈkʌmfərtər/ *n* thick QUILTed bed cover

com·fy /ˈkʌmfiʸ/ *adj infml* comfortable

com·ic /ˈkɑmɪk/ *adj* **1** funny **2** of COMEDY ♦ *n* **1** children's magazine with sets of funny drawings **2** COME-DIAN **~al** *adj* funny **comics** *n* [P] part of a newspaper with funny drawings

comic strip /ˈ·· ·ˌ·/ *n* set of drawings telling a short funny story

com·ma /ˈkɑmə/ *n* the sign (,)

com·mand /kəˈmænd/ *v* **1** *vt/i* order; direct: *command them to attack | your commanding officer* **2** *vt* deserve and get: *command respect* **3** *vt* control (a place) from above ♦ *n* **1** [C] order, instruction **2** [U] control: *take command of the army* **3** [C] division of an army, air force, etc. **4** [S;U] ability to use something: *a good command of spoken English* **~er** *n* **1** naval officer of middle rank **2** any officer in command

com·man·dant /ˈkɑmənˌdænt/ *n* officer in charge of a military organization

com·man·deer /ˌkɑmənˈdɪər/ *vt* seize (private property) for public use

com·mand·ment /kəˈmændmənt/ *n* law given by God

command mod·ule /·ˈ· ˌ··/ *n* part of a space vehicle from which operations are controlled

com·man·do /kəˈmændoʷ/ *n* **–dos** *or* **–does** (member of) a fighting force trained to make quick RAIDS

com·mem·o·rate /kəˈmeməˌreʸt/ *vt* honor the memory of **–rative** *adj*: *commemorative stamps* **–ration** /kəˌmeməˈreʸʃən/ *n* [U]

com·mence /kəˈmens/ *vi/t fml* begin; start **~ment** *n* [U] ceremony when people finish school and are given DIPLOMAS

com·mend /kəˈmend/ *vt fml* **1** praise **2** put into someone's care **~able** *adj* worthy of praise **~ation** /ˌkɑmən-ˈdeʸʃən/ *n* **1** [U] praise **2** [C] official prize

com·men·su·rate /kəˈmensərɪt, -ʃərɪt, -tʃərɪt/ *adj fml* equal; suitable: *a job commensurate with his abilities*

com·ment /ˈkɑment/ *n* [C;U] written or spoken opinion ♦ *vi/t* make a comment

com·men·ta·ry /ˈkɑmənˌteriʸ/ *n* **1** [C] collection of opinions on a book, etc. **2** [C;U] description broadcast during an event: *football commentary*

com·men·tate /ˈkɑmənˌteʸt/ *vi* broadcast a description **–tator** *n*

com·merce /ˈkɑmərs/ *n* [U] buying and selling; business

com·mer·cial /kəˈmɜrʃəl/ *adj* **1** of or used in commerce: *commercial law/ vehicles* **2** producing profit **3** (of television or radio) paid for by charges made for advertisements ♦ *n* television or radio advertisement **~ly** *adv* **~ize** *vt* make into a matter of profit rather than religion, art, etc.

com·mis·e·rate /kəˈmɪzəˌreʸt/ *v* commiserate with *phr vt* express sympathy for **–ration** /kəˌmɪzə-ˈreʸʃən/ *n* [C;U]

com·mis·sion /kəˈmɪʃən/ *n* **1** [C;U] payment for selling goods, made to the salesman **2** [C] job or duty given to someone **3** [C] group officially appointed to find out and report on facts **4** [C] paper appointing an officer in the armed forces **5** out of commission** not working ♦ *vt* **1** give a COMMISSION (2, 4) to **2** place an order for: *commission a portrait* **~er** *n* **1** member of a COMMISSION (3) **2** government representative in certain countries

com·mit /kəˈmɪt/ *vt* **–tt–** **1** do (something wrong) **2** send (someone) to prison or a MENTAL hospital **3** commit oneself: **a** make oneself responsible **b** give a firm opinion **~ment** *n* responsibility to do something **~tal** *n* [C;U] committing someone to prison, etc.

com·mit·tee /kəˈmɪtiʸ/ *n* group chosen to do special business

com·mod·i·ty /kəˈmɑdətiʸ/ *n* article of trade; product

com·mo·dore /ˈkɑməˌdɔr, -ˌdoʷr/ *n* **1** naval officer of high rank **2** president of a sailing club

com·mon¹ /ˈkɑmən/ *adj* **1** ordinary; usual: *common salt | the common cold* **2** shared in a group: *common knowledge* **3** rough in manner; VULGAR **~ly** *adv*

common² *n* **1** area of grassland with no fences which all people are free to use **2 in common** in shared possession

common de·nom·i·na·tor /ˌ··· ·ˈ···ˌ·/ *n* quality or belief shared by all the members of a group

com·mon·er /ˈkɑmənər/ *n* ordinary person

common law /ˌ··· ˈ·/ *n* [U] unwritten law based on custom and court decisions ♦ **common-law** /ˈ··· ·/ *adj*

Common Mar·ket /ˌ·· ˈ···◂/ n [the] the EEC

com·mon·place /ˈkɑmənˌpleʸs/ adj ordinary; dull

common sense /ˌ·· ˈ·◂/ n [U] practical good sense gained from experience

com·mon·wealth /ˈkɑmənˌwɛlθ/ n **1** country which governs itself: *Puerto Rico is a commonwealth.* **2** official title of certain states, such as Massachusetts

com·mo·tion /kəˈmoʷʃən/ n [S;U] noisy confusion

com·mu·nal /kəˈmyuʷnl, ˈkɑmyənl/ adj shared by a group

com·mune¹ /ˈkɑmyuʷn, kəˈmyuʷn/ n **1** group who live and work together and share their possessions **2** local government division in France, etc.

com·mune² /kəˈmyuʷn/ vi exchange thoughts, ideas or feelings: *commune with nature*

com·mu·ni·ca·ble /kəˈmyuʷnɪkəbəl/ adj fml (esp. of ideas, thoughts, illnesses, etc.) that can be (easily) passed from one person to another

com·mu·ni·cate /kəˈmyuʷnəˌkeʸt/ v **1** vi/t make (opinions, etc.) known **2** vt pass on (a disease) **3** vi (of rooms) be connected –**cator** n person who communicates –**cation** /kəˌmyuʷnəˈkeʸʃən/ n **1** [U] communicating **2** [C] fml message, letter, etc. –**cations** n [P] ways of traveling or sending messages

com·mu·ni·ca·tive /kəˈmyuʷnɪkətɪv, -ˌkeʸt̬ɪv/ adj willing to give information

com·mun·ion /kəˈmyuʷnyən/ n [U] **1** fml sharing of beliefs, feelings, etc. **2** (cap.) Christian ceremony of sharing bread and wine

com·mu·ni·qué /kəˌmyuʷnəˈkeʸ, kəˈmyuʷnəˌkeʸ/ n official report

com·mu·nis·m /ˈkɑmyəˌnɪzəm/ n [U] **1** social and political system by which the state owns the means of production **2** (cap.) system of government on this principle with only one political party –**nist** n, adj

com·mu·ni·ty /kəˈmyuʷnət̬iʸ/ n **1** [C] group of people with shared interests **2** [S] people in general; the public **3** [U] shared possession

com·mute /kəˈmyuʷt/ v **1** vi travel regularly between home and work **2** vt make (a punishment) less severe –**muter** n person who commutes to work

com·pact¹ /kəmˈpækt, ˈkɑmpækt/ adj neatly packed into a small space

com·pact² /ˈkɑmpækt/ n **1** container for face powder **2** small car

compact³ n fml agreement between two or more parties, countries, etc.

compact disc /ˌ·· ˈ·/ also **CD** — n small circular piece of plastic on which sound, information, etc., can be stored

com·pan·ion /kəmˈpænyən/ n person who spends time with another ~**able** adj friendly ~**ship** n [U] friendly company

com·pa·ny /ˈkʌmpəniʸ/ n **1** [C] business; people working together: *a bus/theater company* **2** [C] group of about 120 soldiers **3** [U] **a** presence of companions: *I was grateful for her company.* **b** companions, esp. guests **4** be good/bad company be a good/bad person to be with **5** part company (with/from) finish a relationship

com·pa·ra·ble /ˈkɑmpərəbəl/ adj similar

com·par·a·tive /kəmˈpærət̬ɪv/ adj **1** gram expressing an increase in quality or quantity: *'Worse' is the comparative form of 'bad'.* **2** measured or judged by a comparison that is not stated: *She's a comparative newcomer to television.* (= has not been on television often) **3** making a comparison: *a comparative study of European languages* ♦ n gram comparative form of an adjective or adverb ~**ly** adv

com·pare /kəmˈpɛər/ v **1** vt judge (one thing) against another thing, to show likeness or difference **2** vt show the likeness between (2 things) **3** vi be worthy of comparison

com·pa·ri·son /kəmˈpærəsən/ n **1** [C;U] (statement of) comparing: *Boston is small in comparison with New York.* **2** [U] likeness: *There's no comparison between them.*

com·part·ment /kəmˈpɑrtmənt/ n separate division of a space; small room in a railroad car, etc.

com·pass /ˈkʌmpəs/ n **1** instrument for showing direction, with a needle that points to the north **2** fml range; limit: *outside the compass of this department* also **pair of compasses** instrument for drawing circles

com·pas·sion /kəmˈpæʃən/ n [U] sympathy; pity ~**ate** adj ~**ately** adv

com·pat·i·ble /kəmˈpæt̬əbəl/ adj able to exist or work together –**bly** adv –**bility** /kəmˌpæt̬əˈbɪlət̬iʸ/ n [U]

com·pat·ri·ot /kəmˈpeʸtriʸət/ n person of the same nationality as another

com·pel /kəmˈpɛl/ vt –ll– force to do something ~**ling** adj important; urgent: *compelling reasons*

com·pen·sate /ˈkɑmpənˌseʸt/ vt/i pay, or give something, to balance a loss –**sation** /ˌkɑmpənˈseʸʃən/ n [S;U] something given to compensate: *unemployment compensation*

–sa·to·ry /kəmˈpɛnsəˌtɔriʸ, -ˌtoʷriʸ/ adj

com·pete /kəmˈpiʸt/ vi try to win in a competition

com·pe·tence /ˈkɑmpətəns/ n [U] ability to do what is needed **–tent** adj **–tently** adv

com·pe·ti·tion /ˌkɑmpəˈtɪʃən/ n 1 [C] test of strength, skill, etc. 2 [U] trying to win: *tough competition between them* 3 [U] person or people against whom one competes

com·pet·i·tive /kəmˈpɛt̮ət̮ɪvʸ/ adj 1 decided by competition 2 liking to compete

com·pet·i·tor /kəmˈpɛt̮ət̮ər/ n person, firm, etc., that competes

com·pile /kəmˈpaɪl/ vt make (a book, etc.) from collected facts **–piler** n **–pilation** /ˌkɑmpəˈleʸʃən/ n 1 [U] act of compiling 2 [C] something compiled

com·pla·cen·cy /kəmˈpleʸsənsiʸ/ n [U] unreasonable feeling of satisfaction **–cent** adj **–cently** adv

com·plain /kəmˈpleʸn/ vi/t say that one is unhappy: *to complain that the room is too hot*

com·plaint /kəmˈpleʸnt/ n 1 [C;U] (statement of) complaining 2 [C] illness: *a liver complaint*

com·ple·ment /ˈkɑmpləmənt/ n 1 something that completes 2 full number needed 3 gram noun or adjective after a verb such as 'be' or 'become' ♦ /-ˌmɛnt/ vt make complete or perfect **–ary** /ˌkɑmpləˈmɛntəriʸ◂/ adj supplying what is needed

com·plete /kəmˈpliʸt/ adj 1 having all necessary parts; whole 2 finished; ended 3 total; thorough: *complete silence* ♦ vt 1 make whole 2 finish **–ly** adv in every way **–pletion** /-ˈpliʸʃən/ n [U]

com·plex¹ /ˌkəmˈplɛks, kɑm-, ˈkɑmplɛks/ adj 1 difficult to understand 2 made of many connected parts **~ity** /kəmˈplɛksət̮iʸ/ n [C;U]

com·plex² /ˈkɑmplɛks/ n 1 system of many connected parts: *new sports complex* 2 group of unconscious fears or feelings

com·plex·ion /kəmˈplɛkʃən/ n 1 natural appearance of the skin: *good/dark complexion* 2 general character of a situation

com·pli·ance /kəmˈplaɪəns/ n [U] fml complying (COMPLY) **–ant** adj

com·pli·cate /ˈkɑmpləˌkeʸt/ vt make difficult to deal with **–cated** adj COMPLEX **–cation** /ˌkɑmpləˈkeʸʃən/ n added difficulty

com·plic·i·ty /kəmˈplɪsət̮iʸ/ n [U] fml taking part with someone else in a crime

com·pli·ment¹ /ˈkɑmpləmənt/ n expression of praise **compliments** n [P] good wishes

com·pli·ment² /ˈkɑmpləˌmɛnt/ vt express admiration of **~ary** /ˌkɑmpləˈmɛntəriʸ◂/ adj 1 expressing admiration 2 given free: *complimentary tickets*

com·ply /kəmˈplaɪ/ vi fml agree to do something; obey

com·po·nent /kəmˈpoʷnənt/ n any part of a whole machine or system

com·pose /kəmˈpoʷz/ v 1 vi/t write (music, poetry, etc.) 2 vt get (oneself) under control 3 **be composed of** consist of **–posed** adj calm **–poser** n writer of music

com·pos·ite /kəmˈpɑzɪt, kɑm-/ adj, n (something) made up of different parts

com·po·si·tion /ˌkɑmpəˈzɪʃən/ n 1 [U] act of writing music, poetry, etc. 2 [C] something written 3 [U] mixture or arrangement of parts

com·post /ˈkɑmpoʷst/ n [U] decayed plant matter, used to improve the soil

com·po·sure /kəmˈpoʷʒər/ n [U] calmness

com·pound¹ /ˈkɑmpaʊnd/ adj consisting of 2 or more parts ♦ n: *chemical compounds*

com·pound² /kəmˈpaʊnd/ vt 1 make by combining parts 2 make worse: *compound an error*

com·pound³ /ˈkɑmpaʊnd/ n enclosed area containing buildings

com·pre·hend /ˌkɑmprɪˈhɛnd/ vt fml 1 understand 2 include

com·pre·hen·sion /ˌkɑmprɪˈhɛnʃən, -tʃən/ n [U] fml power of understanding **–sible** /-səbəl/ adj understandable **–sibly** adv

com·pre·hen·sive /ˌkɑmprɪˈhɛnsɪvʸ◂/ adj thorough; including a lot

com·press /kəmˈprɛs/ vt 1 force into less space 2 put (ideas, etc.) into fewer words **–ion** /-ˈprɛʃən/ n [U]

com·prise /kəmˈpraɪz/ v consist of; have as parts

com·pro·mise /ˈkɑmprəˌmaɪz/ n [C;U] agreement reached by each side agreeing to some of the other side's demands ♦ v 1 vi make a compromise 2 vt put into a dishonorable position

comp·trol·ler /kənˈtroʷlər/ n (state government) official who looks after income and spending

com·pul·sion /kəmˈpʌlʃən/ n 1 [U] force that makes a person do something 2 [C] strong desire **–sive** /-sɪvʸ/ adj caused by a compulsion: *compulsive drinking*

com·pul·so·ry /kəmˈpʌlsəriʸ/ adj that must be done by law, etc. **–rily** adv

com·punc·tion /kəmˈpʌŋkʃən/ n [U] feeling of guilt

cnt.

com·pute /kəmˈpyuʷt/ vt calculate

com·put·er /kəmˈpyuʷt̮ər/ n ELECTRONIC machine that stores, recalls, and deals with information ~**ize** vt use or begin to use a computer to control (an operation) ~**ization** /kəmˌpyuʷtərəˈzeʸʃ ən/ n [U]

com·rade /ˈkamræd/ n 1 fml close companion 2 fellow member of a union or political party 3 communist (COMMUNISM) ~**ship** n [U]

con /kan/ vt -nn- trick (a trusting person) ♦ n infml for CONFIDENCE GAME

con·cave /ˌkanˈkeʸv◂/ adj curved inwards

con·ceal /kənˈsiʷl/ vt hide ~**ment** n [U]

con·cede /kənˈsiʸd/ vt 1 admit as true 2 give as a right 3 end a game or match by admitting defeat

con·ceit /kənˈsiʸt/ n [U] too high an opinion of oneself ~**ed** adj

con·ceive /kənˈsiʸv/ v 1 vt think of; imagine 2 vi/t become PREGNANT ~**ceivable** adj imaginable; possible ~**ceivably** adv

con·cen·trate /ˈkansənˌtreʸt/ v 1 vi direct all one's attention: concentrate on the problem 2 vt/i bring or come together in one place 3 vt make (a liquid) stronger ♦ n [C;U] concentrated liquid

con·cen·tra·tion /ˌkansənˈtreʸʃ ən/ n 1 [U] close attention 2 [C] close gathering

concentration camp /··'·· ˌ·/ n large prison for political prisoners

con·cen·tric /kənˈsentrɪk/ adj (of circles) having the same center

con·cept /ˈkansept/ n general idea; NOTION ~**ual** /kənˈseptʃuʷəl/ adj of or based on the formation of) concepts ~**ualize** vi/t form a concept (of)

con·cep·tion /kənˈsepʃ ən/ n 1 [C;U] understanding 2 [U] forming of an idea 3 [C;U] fml starting of a new life by the union of a male and female sex cell

con·cern /kənˈsɜrn/ vt 1 be about (a subject) 2 be of importance to: problems which concern all of us 3 worry: I'm concerned about her. ♦ n 1 [C] something that matters to someone 2 [U] worry: no cause for concern 3 [C] business; company: a going concern ~**ing** prep about

con·cert /ˈkansərt, -sɜrt/ n 1 musical performance 2 in concert: a working together b playing at a concert

con·cert·ed /kənˈsɜrtɪd/ adj done together by agreement: a concerted effort

con·cer·ti·na /ˌkansərˈtiʸnə/ n small ACCORDION ♦ vi (of a vehicle)

become pressed together as the result of a crash

con·cer·to /kənˈtʃɛrtoʷ/ n -tos piece of music for one instrument supported by an ORCHESTRA

con·ces·sion /kənˈseʃ ən/ n 1 something CONCEDEd after a disagreement 2 official permission to do something 3 also **concession stand** space for a small business within a larger one ~**ary** given as a concession ~**aire** /kənˌsɛʃəˈnɛər/ n ~**er** n holder of a CONCESSION (3)

con·cierge /ˌkoʷnˈsyɛarʒ/ n hotel official who looks after guests' needs

con·cil·i·ate /kənˈsɪliʸˌeʸt/ vt remove the anger of ~**ation** /kənˌsɪliʸˈeʸʃ ən/ n [U] ~**atory** /kənˈsɪliʸəˌtɔriʸ, -ˌtoʷriʸ/ adj trying to conciliate

con·cise /kənˈsaɪs/ adj expressing a lot in a few words ~**ly** adv ~**ness** n [U]

con·clude /kənˈkluʷd/ v fml 1 vt/i bring or come to an end 2 vt come to believe 3 vt settle: conclude an agreement

con·clu·sion /kənˈkluʷʒən/ n 1 decision; settlement 2 end ~**sive** /-sɪv/ adj ending all doubt: conclusive proof

con·coct /kənˈkakt, kan-/ vt 1 make by mixing parts 2 invent (something false) ~**ion** /-ˈkakʃən/ n mixture

con·com·i·tant /kənˈkamətənt, kan-/ adj existing or happening together

con·cord /ˈkaŋkɔrd, ˌɔːrd/ n [U] friendly agreement

con·course /ˈkaŋkɔrs, -koʷrs/ n place where crowds can gather

con·crete /kanˈkriʸt, ˈkaŋkriʸt/ adj 1 real or solid; not ABSTRACT: A car is a concrete object. 2 clear; particular: concrete proposals n /ˈkaŋkriʸt, kanˈkriʸt/ [U] building material made of sand, cement, etc. ♦ vt cover (a path, wall, etc.) with concrete

con·cu·bine /ˈkaŋkyəˌbaɪn/ n fml or humor woman who has sex with, but is not married to, a man

con·cur /kənˈkɜr/ vi -rr- fml 1 agree 2 happen at the same time ~**rence** /kənˈkɜrəns, -ˈkʌr-/ n [C;U] ~**rent** adj ~**rently** adv

con·cus·sion /kənˈkʌʃən/ n damage to the brain by a heavy blow

con·demn /kənˈdem/ vt 1 express disapproval of 2 state the punishment for: condemn him to death | (fig.) She was condemned to life in a wheelchair. 3 declare (a building, etc.) unfit for use ~**ation** /ˌkandemˈneʸʃ ən, -dəm-/ n [C;U]

con·dense /kənˈdens/ vt/i 1 make (a gas) liquid 2 make (a liquid) thicker

3 put into fewer words –**denser** *n* –**densation** /ˌkandɪnˈseʸʃən, -dən-/ *n* [U] **1** act of condensing **2** drops of water formed when steam condenses

con·de·scend /ˌkandɪˈsend/ *vi* **1** do something unsuited to one's social or professional position **2** *derog* behave as though one is grander than others –**scension** /-ˈsenʃən/ *n* [U]

con·di·ment /ˈkandəmənt/ *n fml* something used for giving taste to food

con·di·tion¹ /kənˈdɪʃən/ *n* **1** [U] state; way of being: *a car in poor condition* **2** [C] something necessary for something else: *I'll come on condition that John comes too.* **3** [C] illness **4** in/out of condition thoroughly fit/not fit **5** on no condition never **conditions** *n* [P] surrounding facts: *better working conditions* –**tional** *adj* depending on conditions –**tionally** *adv*

condition² *vt* **1** control; DETERMINE **2** train to behave in a certain way ~**ing** *n* [U]

con·do·lence /kənˈdoʷləns/ *n* [C;U] expression of sympathy

con·dom /ˈkandəm, ˈkʌn-/ *n* usu. rubber covering worn over the male sex organ during SEXUAL INTERCOURSE, as a means of birth control and as a protection against disease

con·do·min·i·um /ˌkandəˈmɪniʸəm/ also **con·do** /ˈkandoʷ/ — *n infml* apartment which is owned by the people living in it

con·done /kənˈdoʷn/ *vt* forgive (wrong behavior)

con·du·cive /kənˈduʷsɪv, -ˈdyuʷ-/ *adj fml* likely to produce: *conducive to health*

con·duct¹ /kənˈdʌkt/ *v* **1** *vt* direct; lead **2** *vt/i* direct the playing of (musicians) **3** *vt* be the path for (electricity, etc.) **4** conduct oneself *fml* behave ~**ive** *adj* able to conduct electricity, etc. ~**ion** /-ˈdʌkʃən/ *n* [U] passage of electricity, etc.

con·duct² /ˈkandʌkt, -dəkt/ *n* [U] **1** *fml* behavior **2** management of something

con·duc·tor /kənˈdʌktər/ *n* **1** person who conducts musicians **2 conductress** /-trɪs/ *fem.* — person who collects payments on a bus or train **3** substance that conducts electricity, etc.

con·duit /ˈkanduʷət, -dyuʷət/ *n* pipe for water, gas, etc.

cone /koʷn/ *n* **1** hollow or solid object with a round base and pointed top **2** fruit of a PINE or FIR tree

con·fec·tion /kənˈfekʃən/ *n fml* food with a sweet taste ~**ery** *n* [U] candies, cakes, etc. ~**er** *n* person who sells these

con·fed·e·ra·cy /kənˈfedərəsiʸ/ also **con·fed·e·ra·tion** /kənˌfedəˈreʸʃən/ — *n* **1** union of people, parties, or states **2** the Confederacy – see CONFEDERATE STATES

con·fed·e·rate /kənˈfedərɪt/ *n* **1** ACCOMPLICE **2** member of a confederacy

Confederate states /·ˌ··· ˈ·/ *n* the 11 southern states that fought against the North in the CIVIL WAR

con·fer /kənˈfɜr/ *v* –**rr–** *fml* **1** *vi* talk together **2** *vt* give (a title, etc.) to

con·fe·rence /ˈkanfərəns/ *n* meeting for the exchange of ideas

con·fess /kənˈfes/ *vi/t* admit (one's faults) ~**or** *n* priest who hears one's confession ~**ion** /-ˈfeʃən/ *n* [C;U] telling of one's faults

con·fet·ti /kənˈfetiʸ/ *n* [U] bits of colored paper thrown at parties

con·fi·dant /ˈkanfəˌdænt, -ˌdant, ˌkanfəˈdænt,-ˈdant/ **confidante** *(same pronunciation) fem.* — *n* person to whom one tells secrets

con·fide /kənˈfaɪd/ *vt* tell (a secret) trustingly

confide in *phr vt* talk freely to

con·fi·dence /ˈkanfədəns/ *n* **1** [U] faith; trust **2** [U] belief in one's own ability **3** [C] something told secretly **4** in confidence secretly –**dent** *adj* sure

confidence game /ˈ··· ·/ *n* trick played in order to cheat a trusting person of money

con·fi·den·tial /ˌkanfəˈdenʃəl◂, -tʃəl◂/ *adj* **1** told in secret **2** trusted with secrets: *confidential secretary* ~**ly** *adv*

con·fig·u·ra·tion /kənˌfɪgyəˈreʸʃən/ *n* shape; arrangement

con·fine¹ /kənˈfaɪn/ *vt* **1** keep shut in: *confined to bed* **2** keep within the limits ~**ment** *n* **1** [U] being shut up **2** [C;U] giving birth to a child: *her 3rd confinement*

con·fine² /ˈkanfaɪn/ *n* [P] limits

con·firm /kənˈfɜrm/ *vt* **1** support; give proof of: *confirm a telephone message in writing* **2** admit (a person) to membership of the Christian church ~**ed** *adj* firmly settled; unlikely to change: *confirmed bachelor* ~**ation** /ˌkanfərˈmeʸʃən/ *n* **1** proof **2** religious service in which someone is confirmed

con·fis·cate /ˈkanfəˌskeʸt/ *vt* seize (private property) officially, without payment –**cation** /ˌkanfəˈskeʸʃən/ *n* [C;U]

con·fla·gra·tion /ˌkanfləˈgreʸʃən/ *n fml* large fire which causes much destruction

con·flate /kənˈfleʸt/ *vi/t* combine –**flation** /-ˈfleʸʃən/ *n* [C;U]

con·flict¹ /ˈkanflɪkt/ *n* **1** disagreement; argument **2** *fml* war

con·flict² /kən'flɪkt/ vi be in opposition

con·flu·ence /'kɒnflu°əns/ n place where two or more rivers flow together

con·form /kən'fɔrm/ vi obey established rules or customs ~ist n person who conforms ~ity n [U]

con·found /kən'faʊnd, kɑn-/ vt confuse and surprise

con·front /kən'frʌnt/ vt face; meet: confront problems ~ation /ˌkɑnfrən'teʸʃən/ n [C;U] angry opposition

con·fuse /kən'fyuʷz/ vt 1 cause to be mixed up in the mind: I'm confused. 2 be unable to tell the difference between: to confuse Jack and/with Paul 3 make less clear: confusing the issue –fusion /-'fyuʷʒən/ n [U]

con·fute /kən'fyuʷt/ vt prove to be wrong

con·geal /kən'dʒiʸl/ vi/t become solid: congealed blood

con·ge·nial /kən'dʒiʸnyəl/ adj pleasant; in agreement with one's tastes ~ly adv

con·gen·i·tal /kən'dʒenətḷ/ adj (of diseases) existing from one's birth

con·gest·ed /kən'dʒestəd/ adj too full; blocked –tion /-'dʒestʃən/ n [U]

con·glom·e·rate /kən'glɑmərɪt/ n large business firm producing many kinds of goods –ration /kənˌglɑmə'reʸʃən/ n

con·grat·u·late /kən'grætʃə,leʸt/ vt express pleasure at (someone's) success or good luck: I congratulated them on the birth of their daughter. –lations /kənˌgrætʃə'leʸʃənz/ interj, n [P] I congratulate you –latory /kən'grætʃələ,tɔriʸ, -ˌtoʷriʸ/ adj

con·gre·gate /'kɑŋgrə,geʸt/ vi gather together –gation /ˌkɑŋgrə'geʸʃən/ n group of people gathered together in church

con·gress /'kɑŋgrɪs/ n 1 (cap.) highest of the US bodies which make laws, consisting of the Senate and the House of Representatives: a congressman 2 formal meeting to exchange information ~ional /kən'grɛʃənəl/ adj

con·gru·ous /'kɑŋgruʷəs/ adj fml suitable; proper

con·i·cal /'kɑnɪkəl/ adj like a CONE in shape

co·ni·fer /'kɑnəfər, 'koʷ-/ n tree that bears cones (CONE (2))

con·jec·ture /kən'dʒektʃər/ vi/t fml guess ♦ n [C;U] –tural adj

con·ju·gal /'kɑndʒəgəl/ adj fml of marriage

con·ju·gate /'kɑndʒə,geʸt/ vt gram give the forms of (a verb) –gation /ˌkɑndʒə'geʸʃən/ n class of verbs conjugated in the same way

con·junc·tion /kən'dʒʌŋkʃən/ n 1 gram word such as 'but' or 'while' 2 in conjunction with in combination with

con·junc·ti·vi·tis /kənˌdʒʌŋktɪ'vaɪtɪs/ n painful eye disease

con·jure /'kɑndʒər/ v 1 vi do clever tricks that seem magical 2 vt cause to appear as if by magic: (fig.) conjure up memories of the past

conk /kɑŋk/ vi sl conk out 1 break or fail (esp. of a machine) 2 lose consciousness 3 die

con·nect /kə'nɛkt/ v 1 vt/i join together: connect 2 pipes 2 vt think of as related

con·nec·tion /kə'nɛkʃən/ n 1 [C;U] being connected; relationship 2 [C] plane, train, etc. planned to take passengers arriving by another one 3 [C] person connected to others by family or business 4 in connection with fml with regard to

con·nive /kə'naɪv/ v connive at phr vt have no attempt to stop (something wrong) –nivance n [U]

con·nois·seur /ˌkɑnə'sɜr, -'suər/ n person with special knowledge of art, wine, etc.

con·note /kə'noʷt/ vt fml (of a word) suggest something more than its ordinary meaning –notation /ˌkɑnə'teʸʃən/ n: 'Skinny' has bad connotations.

con·nu·bi·al /kə'nuʷbiʸəl, -'nyuʷ-/ adj fml of marriage

con·quer /'kɑŋkər/ vt 1 defeat (enemies): (fig.) conquer one's fear 2 take (a place) by force: a conquered city ~or n

con·quest /'kɑŋkwɛst/ n 1 [U] conquering 2 [C] something conquered, esp. land gained in war

con·science /'kɑnʃəns, -tʃəns/ n 1 [C;U] knowledge of right and wrong: to have a guilty conscience 2 on one's conscience causing one to feel guilty

con·sci·en·tious /ˌkɑnʃiʸ'ɛnʃəs◂, -tʃəs◂, -tʃiʸ-/ adj careful and honest: conscientious work/workers ~ly adv ~ness n [U]

conscientious ob·jec·tor /ˌ·····'·ˌ··/ n person who refuses to serve in the armed forces because of moral or religious beliefs

con·scious /'kɑnʃəs, -tʃəs/ adj 1 awake and able to think 2 knowing; AWARE 3 intentional: conscious effort ~ly adv ~ness n [S;U]

con·script¹ /kən'skrɪpt/ vt make someone serve in the armed forces ~ion /kən'skrɪpʃən/ n [U] practice of conscripting people

con·script² /'kɑnskrɪpt/ n conscripted person

con·se·crate /'kɑnsə,kreʸt/ vt 1 declare as holy: consecrated wine 2

con·se·cu·tion /ˌkɒnsɪˈkreɪ-ʃən/ n [U] set apart solemnly for a particular purpose: consecrate one's life to helping the poor –**cration** /ˌkɒnsəˈkreɪʃən/ n [U]

con·sec·u·tive /kənˈsɛkyətɪv/ adj following in unbroken order ~**ly** adv

con·sen·sus /kənˈsɛnsəs/ n general agreement

con·sent /kənˈsɛnt/ vi give permission ♦ n [U] permission

con·se·quence /ˈkɒnsə‚kwɛns, -kwəns/ n 1 [C] result 2 [U] fml importance: It's of no consequence to me.

con·se·quent /ˈkɒnsə‚kwɛnt, -kwənt/ adj fml following as a result ~**ly** adv

con·se·quen·tial /ˌkɒnsəˈkwɛn-ʃəl◂, -tʃəl/ adj fml 1 consequent 2 important

con·ser·va·tion /ˌkɒnsərˈveɪʃən/ n [U] 1 protection of animals, plants, ancient buildings, etc. 2 careful use of a limited supply, to prevent waste ~**ist** n ~**ism** n [U]

con·ser·va·tive /kənˈsɜrvətɪv/ adj 1 not liking change 2 kept rather low: a conservative estimate 3 of a political party opposed to sudden change ♦ n person who dislikes change ~**ly** adv –**tism** n [U]

con·ser·va·to·ry /kənˈsɜrvə‚tɔriᵉ, -‚toʷriᵉ/ n 1 GREENHOUSE connected to another building 2 school of music or acting

con·serve¹ /kənˈsɜrv/ vt use carefully; preserve: conserve one's energy

con·serve² /ˈkɒnsɜrv/ n fml fruit preserved by cooking in sugar; JAM

con·sid·er /kənˈsɪdər/ v 1 vi/t think about 2 vt take into account; remember: you have to consider your wife 3 vt believe to be: consider him suitable –**ed** reached after careful thought ~**ing** prep if one takes into account: She did well, considering her age.

con·sid·er·a·ble /kənˈsɪdərəbəl/ adj fairly large –**bly** adv much

con·sid·er·ate /kənˈsɪdərɪt/ adj kind and thoughtful ~**ly** adv

con·sid·er·a·tion /kən‚sɪdəˈreɪʃən/ n 1 [U] thoughtful attention 2 [C] fact to be remembered when deciding something 3 [C] payment; reward 4 **take something into consideration** remember when making a judgment

con·sign /kənˈsaɪn/ vt 1 send (goods) for sale 2 fml give into someone's care ~**ment** n 1 [C] goods consigned 2 [U] act of consigning

con·sist /kənˈsɪst/ v

consist in phr vt fml have as a base; depend on

consist of phr vt be made up of

con·sis·ten·cy /kənˈsɪstənsiᵉ/ n 1 [U] state of always behaving in the same way 2 [C] degree of thickness of a liquid –**tent** adj 1 not changing 2 in agreement –**tently** adv

con·sole¹ /kənˈsoʷl/ vt make less unhappy –**solation** /ˌkɒnsəˈleɪʃən/ n [C;U] (person or thing giving) comfort

con·sole² /ˈkɒnsoʷl/ n surface containing the controls for a machine or system

con·sol·i·date /kənˈsɑlə‚deɪt/ vi/t 1 (cause to) become stronger 2 combine into one –**dation** /kən‚sɑlə-ˈdeɪʃən/ n

con·som·mé /ˌkɒnsəˈmeɪ/ n [U] clear soup

con·so·nant¹ /ˈkɒnsənənt/ n (letter representing) a speech sound such as b, m, s, made by stopping or RESTRICTing the flow of air from the lungs

consonant² adj fml in agreement

con·sort¹ /ˈkɒnsɔrt/ n wife or husband of a ruler

con·sort² /kənˈsɔrt/ v **consort with** phr vi spend time in company

con·sor·ti·um /kənˈsɔrtiᵉəm, -ˈsɔrtiᵉəm/ n –**tiums** or –**tia** /-ʃiᵉə, -tiᵉə/ combination of a number of companies, banks, etc.

con·spic·u·ous /kənˈspɪkyuʷəs/ adj easily seen; noticeable ~**ly** adv

con·spir·a·cy /kənˈspɪrəsiᵉ/ n [C;U] (plan made by) conspiring

con·spir·a·tor /kənˈspɪrətər/ n person who conspires

con·spire /kənˈspaɪər/ vi 1 plan something bad together secretly 2 (of events) combine in a bad way

con·stant /ˈkɒnstənt/ adj 1 happening all the time 2 unchanging: a constant speed 3 continuous 4 loyal ♦ n something that never varies ~**ly** adv –**stancy** n [U] 1 freedom from change 2 fml loyalty

con·stel·la·tion /ˌkɒnstəˈleɪʃən/ n named group of stars

con·ster·na·tion /ˌkɒnstərˈneɪʃən/ n [U] great shock and fear

con·sti·pa·tion /ˌkɒnstəˈpeɪʃən/ n [U] being unable to empty the bowels properly –**ted** /ˈkɒnstə‚peɪtɪd/ adj

con·stit·u·en·cy /kənˈstɪtʃuʷənsiᵉ/ n (voters in) an area that elects a representative

con·stit·u·ent /kənˈstɪtʃuʷənt/ n 1 necessary part: the constituents of cement 2 voter ♦ adj helping to make a whole

con·sti·tute /ˈkɒnstə‚tuʷt, -‚tyuʷt/ vt 1 form when added together 2 establish

con·sti·tu·tion /ˌkɒnstəˈtuʷʃən, -ˈtyuʷ-/ n 1 laws and principles by which a country is governed **2** (*cap.*) **the Constitution** of the United States **3** person's physical condition **4** structure of something **~al** *adj* **1** by or of a political constitution **2** in agreement with the Constitution **3** of a person's constitution **~ally** *adv*

con·strain /kən'streɪn/ *vt fml* force (someone) to do something

con·straint /kən'streɪnt/ *n* [C;U] something that limits freedom: *acted under constraint*

con·strict /kən'strɪkt/ *vt* make narrower or tighter **~ion** /-'strɪkʃən/ *n* [C;U]

con·struct /kən'strʌkt/ *vt* make out of parts; build

con·struc·tion /kən'strʌkʃən/ *n* **1** [U] building; the building industry **2** [C] something built **3** [P] road repairing **4** [C] meaning given to something as of a law **–tive** /-tɪv/ *adj* helpful: *constructive suggestions*

con·strue /kən'struː/ *vt* place a certain meaning on

con·sul /'kɒnsəl/ *n* representative of a government in a foreign city **~ar** *adj* **~ate** *n* consul's office

con·sult /kən'sʌlt/ *vt* go to (a person, book, etc.) for advice **–ation** /ˌkɒnsəl'teɪʃən/ *n* [C;U]

con·sul·tant /kən'sʌltənt/ *n* person who gives professional advice **–tancy** *n* **–tative** *adj* giving advice

con·sume /kən'suːm/ *vt fml* **1** eat or drink **2** use up; destroy **–suming** *adj* main: *a consuming interest in trains* **–sumer** *n* person who buys goods

con·sum·mate¹ /kən'sʌmɪt, 'kɒnsə-/ *adj* perfect; complete

con·sum·mate² /'kɒnsəˌmeɪt/ *vt fml* **1** complete (a marriage) by having sex **2** make perfect **–mation** /ˌkɒnsə'meɪʃən/ *n* [C;U]

con·sump·tion /kən'sʌmpʃən/ *n* **1** [S;U] consuming; amount consumed **2** [U] TUBERCULOSIS **–tive** /-tɪv/ *adj* suffering from TUBERCULOSIS

cont *written abbrev. for:* continued

con·tact /'kɒntækt/ *n* **1** [U] meeting; relationship: *Have you been in contact with the disease?* **2** [C] person one knows who can help one: *some useful contacts in Spain* **3** [C] electrical part that touches another to carry electric current ♦ *vt* reach (someone) by telephone, etc.

contact lens /'·· ˌ·/ *n* plastic LENS (1) shaped to fit over the eye to improve eyesight

con·ta·gion /kən'teɪdʒən/ *n* **1** [U] spreading of a disease by touch **2** [C] harmful influence **–gious** *adj*

con·tain /kən'teɪn/ *vt* **1** have within itself: *Beer contains alcohol.* **2** keep under control: *I can't contain myself.*

con·tain·er /kən'teɪnər/ *n* **1** box, bottle, etc., used to contain something **2** large metal box in which goods are packed to be carried on ships, etc.

con·tam·i·nate /kən'tæməˌneɪt/ *vt* make impure or dirty: *contaminated water* **–nation** /kənˌtæmə-'neɪʃən/ *n* [U]

con·tem·plate /'kɒntəmˌpleɪt/ *vt* **1** think about; consider as possible **2** look solemnly at **–plation** /ˌkɒntəm'pleɪʃən/ *n* [U] deep thought **–plative** /kən'templətɪv, 'kɒntəmˌpleɪtɪv/ *adj*

con·tem·po·ra·ry /kən'tempəˌreɪriː/ *adj* **1** modern; of the present **2** of the same time ♦ *n* person of the same age, or living at the same time

con·tempt /kən'tempt/ *n* [U] complete lack of respect **~ible** *adj* deserving contempt **~uous** *adj* showing contempt

contempt of court /·ˌ· · ˈ·/ *n* [U] offense of disobeying a judge in court

con·tend /kən'tend/ *v* **1** *vi* compete; struggle **2** *vt fml* claim; declare **~er** *n* competitor

con·tent¹ /kən'tent/ *adj* satisfied; happy ♦ *vt* make happy **~ed** *adj* quietly happy **~edly** *adv* **~ment** *n* [U] quiet happiness

con·tent² /'kɒntent/ *n* **1** [U] subject matter of a book **2** [S] amount contained in something: *a high fat content* **contents** *n* [P] what something contains

con·ten·tion /kən'tenʃən, -tʃən/ *n* **1** [C] claim; point of view **2** [U] struggle **–tious** *adj* **1** causing argument **2** quarrelsome

con·test¹ /'kɒntest/ *n* struggle; competition

con·test² /kən'test, 'kɒntest/ *vt fml* **1** compete for **2** argue about the rightness of **~ant** *n* competitor

con·text /'kɒntekst/ *n* **1** words that surround a word or phrase **2** surrounding conditions

con·ti·nent /'kɒntən-ənt/ *n* **1** [C] large land mass; Europe, Asia, etc. **2** [*the*] (*cap.*) Europe without Britain **~al** /ˌkɒntən'entəl/ *adj* (*cap.*) of the 13 American **colonies**: *Continental Congress*

con·ti·nen·tal break·fast /ˌ····· '··/ *n* light breakfast usu. of bread, butter, JAM and coffee

con·tin·gen·cy /kən'tɪndʒənsiː/ *n* possible event that might cause problems

con·tin·gent¹ /kən'tɪndʒənt/ *adj* **1** dependent on something uncertain **2** happening by chance

contingent² *n* **1** part of a larger force of soldiers, ships, etc. **2** part of a larger gathering of people

con·tin·u·al /kənˈtɪnyuⁿəl/ adj regular; frequent ~**ly** adv

con·tin·ue /kənˈtɪnyuⁿ/ vi/t 1 go on doing something 2 start again after stopping **–uation** /kənˌtɪnyuⁿˈeʸʃən/ n 1 [U] act of continuing 2 [C] something which continues from something else

con·ti·nu·i·ty /ˌkɑntənˈuⁿəṭiʸ, -ˈyuⁿ-/ n [U] uninterrupted connection

con·tin·u·ous /kənˈtɪnyuⁿəs/ adj continuing unbroken: *The brain needs a continuous supply of blood.* ~ **ly** adv

con·tin·u·um /kənˈtɪnyuⁿəm/ n **–uums** or **–ua** /-yuⁿə/ 1 something which is without parts and the same from beginning to end 2 something that changes gradually without sudden breaks

con·tort /kənˈtɔrt/ vt twist out of shape **–ion** /-ˈtɔrʃən/ n [C;U]

con·tour /ˈkɑntʊər/ n 1 shape of the edges of something, such as a coast 2 line on a map showing the edges of areas above a certain height

con·tra·band /ˈkɑntrəˌbænd/ n [U] goods that cannot be brought legally into a country

con·tra·cep·tion /ˌkɑntrəˈsɛpʃən/ n [U] (methods for) preventing sex from resulting in pregnancy (PREGNANT) **–tive** /-ˈsɛptɪv◂/ n, adj (drug, etc.) used for contraception

con·tract¹ /ˈkɑntrækt/ n formal agreement to do something ~ **ual** /kənˈtræktʃuⁿəl/ adj

con·tract² /kənˈtrækt/ v 1 vi/t arrange by formal agreement 2 vi/t (cause) to become smaller 3 vt fml get (a disease) **–ion** /-ˈtrækʃən/ n 1 [U] process of getting smaller 2 [C] shortened form of a word 3 [C] strong tightening of a muscle

con·trac·tor /ˈkɑnˌtræktər, kənˈtræk-/ n firm that provides supplies and/or workers, esp. for building work

con·tra·dict /ˌkɑntrəˈdɪkt/ v 1 vt/i say the opposite of; declare to be wrong 2 vt (of a statement, fact, etc.) be opposite to (another) ~ **ory** adj: *contradictory reports* ~ **ion** /-ˈdɪkʃən/ n [C;U]

con·tral·to /kənˈtræltoʷ/ n **–tos** female ALTO

con·trap·tion /kənˈtræpʃən/ n apparatus with a strange appearance

con·tra·ry¹ /ˈkɑnˌtrɛriʸ/ n [S] 1 opposite 2 **on the contrary** no, not at all 3 **to the contrary** to the opposite effect ♦ adj completely different; opposed

con·tra·ry² /ˈkɑnˌtrɛəriʸ, kənˈtrɛəriʸ/ adj (of a person) unreasonable

con·trast¹ /kənˈtræst/ v 1 vt

compare so that differences are made clear 2 vi show a difference: *sharply contrasting attitudes*

con·trast² /ˈkɑntræst/ n [C;U] noticeable difference

con·tra·vene /ˌkɑntrəˈviʸn/ vt fml break (a law) **–vention** /-ˈvɛnʃən/ n [C;U]

con·tre·temps /ˈkɑntrəˌtɑn/ n fml **–temps** /-ˌtɑnz/ unlucky and unexpected event

con·trib·ute /kənˈtrɪbyuⁿt, -yət/ v 1 vt/i join with others in giving something 2 vi help in causing: *contribute to good health* 3 vt write (an article) for a magazine **–utor** n person who contributes **–utory** adj **–ution** /ˌkɑntrəˈbyuⁿʃən/ n [C;U]

con·trite /kənˈtraɪt, ˈkɑntraɪt/ adj fml sorry for having done wrong ~ **ly** adv **–trition** /kənˈtrɪʃən/ n [U]

con·trive /kənˈtraɪv/ vt succeed in doing something: *contrive to escape* **–trivance** n clever plan or invention **–trived** adj unnatural and forced

con·trol /kənˈtroʷl/ vt **–ll–** 1 direct; have power over 2 hold back; RESTRAIN ♦ n 1 [U] power to control: *lose control of oneself* 2 [C;U] means of controlling: *wage control(s)* 3 [C] place where something is controlled: *controls of a plane* 4 [C] standard against which the results of a study are measured 5 **out of control** in(to) a state of not being controlled 6 **under control** working properly ~ **ler** n person who directs something

con·tro·ver·sy /ˈkɑntrəˌvɜrsiʸ/ n [C;U] fierce argument **–sial** /ˌkɑntrəˈvɜrʃəl◂/ adj causing controversy **–sially** adv

co·nun·drum /kəˈnʌndrəm/ n 1 RIDDLE 2 difficult problem

con·ur·ba·tion /ˌkɑnɜrˈbeʸʃən/ n number of towns joined into one large city or network

con·va·lesce /ˌkɑnvəˈlɛs/ vi spend time getting well after an illness **–lescence** n [S;U] time spent getting well **–lescent** n, adj (person) spending time getting well

con·vene /kənˈviʸn/ v 1 vi meet together 2 vt call (a group) to meet **–vener**, **–venor** n person who convenes meetings

con·ve·nience /kənˈviʸnyəns/ n 1 [U] fitness; suitableness 2 [C] useful tool or apparatus 3 [U] personal comfort **–ent** adj 1 suited to one's needs 2 near **–ently** adv

convenience store /·ˈ···ˌ·/ n store that stays open longer than other stores and sells food, drugs, and things for the house

con·vent /ˈkɑnvɛnt, -vənt/ n place where NUNS live

con·ven·tion /kənˈvɛnʃən, -tʃən/ n 1 [C;U] accepted social custom 2 [C] meeting of a group with a shared purpose 3 [C] formal political agreement ~al adj following accepted customs ~ally adv

con·verge /kənˈvɜrdʒ/ vi come together and meet: roads converging at the station -vergence n [U]

con·ver·sant /kənˈvɜrsənt/ adj fml having knowledge or experience

con·ver·sa·tion /ˌkɑnvərˈseɪʃən/ n [C;U] informal talk ~al adj (of language) used in conversation

con·verse¹ /kənˈvɜrs/ vi fml talk informally

con·verse² /kənˈvɜrs, ˈkɑnvɜrs/ adj opposite: the converse opinion ~ly adv

con·ver·sion /kənˈvɜrʒən, -ʃən/ n [C;U] act of converting

con·vert¹ /kənˈvɜrt/ vt/i 1 change into another form: convert dollars into pounds 2 change to a particular religious belief, etc. ~er n apparatus that converts something, esp. information to be put into a computer ~ible adj (esp. of money) able to be converted ~ible n car with a roof that can be folded back

con·vert² /ˈkɑnvɜrt/ n person who has accepted a particular belief

con·vex /ˌkɑnˈvɛks◄, kənˈvɛks/ adj curved outwards

con·vey /kənˈveɪ/ vt 1 take; carry 2 make (feelings, etc.) known ~er, ~or n

con·vey·ance /kənˈveɪəns/ n 1 [C] fml vehicle 2 [U] legal paper giving the right to property

conveyor belt /·ˈ··· ·/ n endless moving belt carrying objects from one place to another

con·vict¹ /kənˈvɪkt/ vt prove (someone) to be guilty of a crime

con·vict² /ˈkɑnvɪkt/ n convicted person who is sent to prison

con·vic·tion /kənˈvɪkʃən/ n [C;U] 1 being convicted of a crime 2 firm belief

con·vince /kənˈvɪns/ vt cause to feel sure of something -vincing adj: a convincing argument -vincingly adv

con·viv·i·al /kənˈvɪviʲəl/ adj merry and friendly ~ity /kənˌvɪviʲˈælətiʲ/ n [U]

con·vo·lut·ed /ˈkɑnvəˌluʷtɪd/ adj fml 1 twisted 2 difficult to understand -lution /ˌkɑnvəˈluʷʃən/ n twist

con·voy /ˈkɑnvɔɪ/ n 1 group of ships or vehicles traveling together, esp. for safety 2 protecting force of fighting ships, etc. ♦ vt go with and protect

con·vulse /kənˈvʌls/ vt shake

violently -vulsive adj -vulsion /-ˈvʌlʃən/ n

coo /kuʷ/ v 1 vi make the soft cry of a DOVE 2 speak lovingly

cook /kʊk/ v 1 vi/t prepare (food) by using heat 2 vi (of food) be cooked 3 vt change (accounts, etc.) dishonestly ♦ n person who cooks food

cook·e·ry /ˈkʊkəriʲ/ n [U] art of cooking

cook·ie /ˈkʊkiʲ/ n 1 small sweet cake 2 person: a smart/tough cookie

cool¹ /kuʷl/ adj 1 pleasantly cold 2 calm; unexcited: a cool-headed decision 3 not very friendly 4 (used to add force to an expression): a cool $1,000 a month ♦ n 1 cool temperature: the cool of the evening 2 calmness: lose one's cool ♦ adv play it cool act calmly ~ness n [U] ~ly /ˈkuʷl-liʲ/ adv

cool² vi/t make or become cool

cool down/off/out phr vi become calmer

coon /kuʷn/ n infml 1 RACCOON 2 **coon's age** n long time

coop¹ /kuʷp/ n cage for small creatures

coop²

coop up phr vt shut into a small space

co·op·e·rate /koʷˈɑpəˌreɪt/ vi work together for a shared purpose -rative /-rətɪv/ adj helpful -rative n company, farm, etc., owned by its workers -ration /koʷˌɑpəˈreɪʃən/ n

co-opt /koʷˈɑpt/ vt (of an elected group) choose as a fellow member

co·or·di·nate /koʷˈɔrdnˌeɪt/ vt cause to work together effectively: coordinate our efforts -nation /koʷˌɔrdəˈneɪʃən/ n [U]

co·or·di·nates /koʷˈɔrdnɪts/ n [P] separate garments in matching colors that can be worn together

cop¹ /kɑp/ n sl policeman

cop² v

cop out phr vi sl avoid responsibility **cop-out** /ˈ· ·/ n

cope /koʷp/ vi deal with something successfully

cop·i·er /ˈkɑpiʲər/ n machine for making paper copies (COPY (1))

co·pi·ous /ˈkoʷpiʲəs/ adj present in great quantity ~ly adv

cop·per¹ /ˈkɑpər/ n 1 [U] a soft red-brown metal b its color 2 [C] copper coin

copper² n sl policeman

cop·pice /ˈkɑps/ n small group of trees

cop·u·late /ˈkɑpyəˌleɪt/ vi fml have sex -lation /ˌkɑpyəˈleɪʃən/ n [U]

cop·y /ˈkɑpiʲ/ n 1 thing made to be like another 2 single example of a book, newspaper, etc. see also HARD

COPY, SOFT COPY ♦ v 1 vt make a copy of 2 vt do the same as 3 vi/t cheat in an examination, etc., by copying

cop·y·cat /ˈkɑpiᵞˌkæt/ n derog infml person who copies other people's behavior, dress, work, etc.

cop·y·right /ˈkɑpiᵞˌraɪt/ n [C;U] legal right to be the only seller of a book, etc.

cor·al /ˈkɔrəl, ˈkɑrəl/ n [U] white, pink, or red substance formed by small sea creatures

cord /kɔrd/ n [C;U] 1 thick string or thin rope 2 electric wire 3 quantity of wood for burning

cor·dial¹ /ˈkɔrdʒəl/ adj warm and friendly ~ly adv in a cordial manner

cordial² n [U] nonalcoholic fruit drink

cor·don /ˈkɔrdn/ n ring of police, etc., surrounding an area ♦ v cordon off phr vt protect with a cordon

cords /kɔrdz/ n [P] infml pants made from corduroy

cor·du·roy /ˈkɔrdəˌrɔɪ, ˌkɔrdəˈrɔɪ/ n strong cotton cloth with raised lines

core /kɔr/ n 1 central part: core of an apple 2 to the core thoroughly ♦ vt remove the core of (a fruit)

cork /kɔrk/ n 1 [U] BARK of a tree (the **cork oak**) 2 [C] piece of this used for closing a bottle ♦ vt close with a cork

cork·screw /ˈkɔrkskruᵂ/ n metal tool for removing a cork from a bottle

corn¹ /kɔrn/ n [U] (seed of) a tall food plant with long bunches of yellow seeds

corn² n painful lump of hard skin on the foot

cor·ne·a /ˈkɔrniᵞə/ n protective covering on the front surface of the eye

corned beef /ˌ· ˈ·◄/ n [U] kind of cooked BEEF usu. sold in cans

cor·ner /ˈkɔrnər/ n 1 point where 2 lines, edges, or roads meet 2 part of the world: remote corners of America 3 around the corner near 4 cut corners use a shorter method 5 in a tight corner in a difficult position 6 turn the corner become better after a period of difficulties, etc. ♦ v 1 vt force into a difficult position 2 vt gain control of (by buying, selling, or production of goods) 3 vi (of a vehicle) turn a corner

corn meal /ˈ· ·/ n COARSE flour made of corn

cor·ner·stone /ˈkɔrnərˌstoᵂn/ n 1 stone set at one bottom corner of a building 2 something of great importance, on which everything else is based

cor·net /kɔrˈnɛt/ n musical instrument like a TRUMPET

corn·flakes /ˈkɔrnfleᵞks/ n [P] bits of crushed CORN¹ to be eaten with milk at breakfast

cor·nice /ˈkɔrnɪs/ n decorative border at top edge of the front of a building, a PILLAR, or the walls of a room

corn·y /ˈkɔrniᵞ/ adj sl too common; old-fashioned

co·rol·la·ry /ˈkɔrəˌlɛriᵞ, ˈkɑr-/ n fml something that naturally follows from something else

coronary throm·bo·sis /ˌkɔrənɛriᵞ θræmˈboᵂsɪs, ˌkɑr-/ also **coronary** — n stopping of the blood supply to the heart; kind of HEART ATTACK

cor·o·na·tion /ˌkɔrəˈneᵞʃən, ˌkɑr-/ n ceremony of crowning a king or queen

cor·o·ner /ˈkɔrənər, ˈkɑr-/ n official who inquires into the cause of a person's death if it is not clearly known

cor·o·net /ˌkɔrəˈnɛt, ˌkɑr-/ n small crown worn by nobles, etc.

cor·po·ral¹ /ˈkɔrpərəl/ adj fml of the human body: corporal punishment

corporal² n person of low rank in an army or other military force

cor·po·rate /ˈkɔrpərɪt/ adj 1 shared by a whole group: corporate responsibility 2 of a CORPORATION

cor·po·ra·tion /ˌkɔrpəˈreᵞʃən/ n large business organization

corps /kɔr, koᵂr/ n 1 a trained army group b branch of the army equal to 2 DIVISIONS 2 group with the same activity: the press corps

corpse /kɔrps/ n dead body

cor·pu·lent /ˈkɔrpyələnt/ adj very fat

cor·pus·cle /ˈkɔrpəsəl, -ˌpʌsəl/ n any of the red and white cells in the body

cor·ral /kəˈræl/ n enclosed area (esp. in the western states) for cattle and horses ♦ vt -ll- put in a corral

cor·rect¹ /kəˈrɛkt/ adj 1 without mistakes; true 2 proper: correct behavior ~ly adv ~ness n [U]

correct² vt make right; show the mistakes in –ive adj, n –ion /kəˈrɛkʃən/ n 1 [U] correcting 2 [C] change that improves something 3 [U] punishment

cor·re·late /ˈkɔrəˌleᵞt, ˈkɑr-/ vi/t (show to) have a close connection –ation /ˌkɔrəˈleᵞʃən, ˌkɑr-/ n close connection

cor·re·spond /ˌkɔrəˈspɑnd, ˌkɑr-/ vi 1 be equal; match 2 exchange letters ~ing adj matching; equal

cor·re·spon·dence /ˌkɔrəˈspɑndəns, ˌkɑr-/ n [S;U] 1 (of) writing letters 2 equality between things; likeness –dent n 1 person with whom one exchanges letters 2 someone employed by a newspaper, television or radio station, etc., to report news from a distant area

cor·ri·dor /ˈkɔrədər, -ˌdɔr, ˈkar-/ n passage between rows of rooms

cor·rob·o·rate /kəˈrabəˌreɪt/ vt support (an opinion, etc.) by proof –**ration** /kəˌrabəˈreɪʃən/ n [U]

cor·rode /kəˈroʷd/ vt/i destroy slowly, esp. by chemical action

cor·ro·sion /kəˈroʷʒən/ n [U] 1 corroding 2 RUST, etc., produced by corroding –**sive** /-sɪv/ adj

cor·ru·gated /ˈkɔrəˌgeʸtɪd, ˈkar-/ adj having wavelike folds –**gation** /ˌkɔrəˈgeʸʃən, ˌkar-/ n

cor·rupt /kəˈrʌpt/ adj 1 morally bad, esp. dishonest 2 containing mistakes ♦ vt/i make or become corrupt –**ly** adv ~**ion** /-ˈrʌpʃən/ n [U]

cor·sage /kɔrˈsaʒ, -ˈsadʒ/ n flowers worn on a woman's dress for a special occasion

cor·set /ˈkɔrsɪt/ also **corsets** pl. — n — tightly fitting undergarment formerly worn by women

cor·tege /kɔrˈtɛʒ, -ˈteʸʒ/ n funeral procession

cos·met·ic /kazˈmɛtɪk/ n cream, powder, etc., for the skin or hair ♦ adj 1 of, related to, or causing increased beauty 2 dealing only with the outside appearance rather than the central part of something

cos·mic /ˈkazmɪk/ adj of the whole universe

cos·mo·naut /ˈkazməˌnɔt/ n a Soviet ASTRONAUT

cos·mo·pol·i·tan /ˌkazməˈpalətn◂/ adj 1 consisting of people from many parts of the world 2 not narrow in one's attitudes ♦ n cosmopolitan person

cos·mos /ˈkazməs, -moʷs/ n the whole universe

cos·set /ˈkasɪt/ vt -**tt**- treat too kindly

cost¹ /kɔst/ n 1 [C] price of something 2 [U] what is needed to gain something 3 **at all costs** whatever it may cost 4 **to one's cost** from one's own unpleasant experience ~**ly** adj expensive **costs** [P] cost of taking a matter to a court of law

cost² vt 1 (past t. and p. **cost**) have as a price: It cost me $5. 1 (fig.) The mistake cost him his job. 2 (past t. and p. **costed**) calculate the price to be charged for (a job)

co-star /ˈkoʷ star/ n famous actor or actress who appears with another famous actor or actress in a film, etc. ♦ **co-star** vi

cost-ef·fec·tive /ˈ··ˌ··/ adj bringing the best possible profits or advantages for the lowest possible cost ~**ly** adv ~**ness** n [U]

cos·tume /ˈkastuʷm, -styuʷm/ n [C;U] clothes, esp. as worn in plays

costume jew·el·ry /ˈ·· ˌ···/ n [U] jewelry which looks valuable but is made from cheap materials

cot /kat/ n light narrow bed which folds flat

cot·tage /ˈkatɪdʒ/ n small house, used esp. for vacation

cot·ton¹ /ˈkatn/ n [U] 1 soft white hair of a southern crop plant 2 thread or cloth made from this 3 soft mass of cotton for cleaning wounds, etc.

cotton² v **cotton on** phr vi infml understand

couch¹ /kautʃ/ n long seat like a bed

couch² vt fml express: His refusal was couched in unfriendly terms.

cou·gar /ˈkuʷgər/ n large American wild cat; mountain lion

cough /kɔf/ v 1 vi push air out noisily from the lungs 2 vt produce by doing this: cough up blood ♦ n 1 [C] act of coughing 2 [S] illness that makes a person cough

cough up phr vt infml produce (money or information) unwillingly

could /kəd; strong kʊd/ v aux 1 (describes **can** in the past): He could read when he was 4. 2 (used to describe what someone has said): She asked if she could smoke. 3 (used to show what is possible): I think the accident could have been prevented. 4 (used to make a request): Could you help me?

could·n't /ˈkʊdnt/ v short for: could not

coun·cil /ˈkaʊnsəl/ n group of people appointed or elected to manage something ~**lor** n member of a council

coun·sel /ˈkaʊnsəl/ n **counsel** 1 [C] law legal advisor acting for someone 2 [C] fml advice ♦ v -**l**- fml advise ~**or** n advisor

count¹ /kaʊnt/ v 1 vt/n name (numbers) in order: count (to) 20 2 vt find the total of 3 vt include: 6 people, counting me 4 vt consider to be: count yourself lucky 5 vi have value: Every moment counts. ♦ n 1 act of counting; total 2 one of a number of crimes of which a person is thought to be guilty: guilty on all counts 3 **be out for the count** (in BOXING) be counted out; be unconscious 4 **keep/lose count** know/no longer know the exact number ~**able** adj that can be counted: Egg is a count-able noun. ~**less** adj very many

count down phr vt count backwards to zero, esp. before sending a spacecraft into space **countdown** /ˈkaʊntdaʊn/ n

count in phr vt include

count on/upon phr vt depend on; expect

count out *phr vt* **1** put down in turn while counting **2** not include **3** declare (a BOXER who fails to get up after 10 seconds) to be a loser of a fight

count² *n* European nobleman

coun·te·nance /ˈkaʊntən-əns/ *n fml* **1** [C] face **2** [U] support; approval ♦ *vt fml* give approval to

coun·ter¹ /ˈkaʊntər/ *n* **1** table where people in a store, etc., are served **2** over the counter (when buying drugs) without a PRESCRIPTION **3** under the counter secretly and often unlawfully

counter² *n* **1** object used in some games instead of money **2** machine that counts

coun·ter³ *vt/i* meet an attack; oppose: *counter her proposal*

counter⁴ *adv, adj* opposed; opposite: *act counter to all advice*

coun·ter·act /ˌkaʊntərˈækt/ *vt* reduce the effect of: *counteract a poison*

coun·ter·at·tack /ˈkaʊntərəˌtæk/ *vi/t, n* (make) an attack to oppose another

coun·ter·bal·ance /ˈkaʊntərˌbæləns/ *vt, n* (act as) a force that balances another

coun·ter·clock·wise /ˌkaʊntərˈklɑkwaɪz/ *adv* in the opposite direction to the movement of a clock

coun·ter·feit /ˈkaʊntərfɪt/ *n, adj* (thing) made as a copy of something else, to deceive: *counterfeit money* ♦ *vt* make a counterfeit of

coun·ter·mand /ˌkaʊntərˈmænd, ˈkaʊntərˌmænd/ *vt* declare (a command already given) ineffective

coun·ter·part /ˈkaʊntərˌpɑrt/ *n* person or thing that matches another, but in a different system

coun·ter·pro·duc·tive /ˌkaʊntərprəˈdʌktɪv/ *adj* having an opposite effect from the one intended

coun·ter·sign /ˈkaʊntərˌsaɪn/ *vt* add another signature to (a paper already signed)

count·er·vail·ing /ˌkaʊntərˈveɪlɪŋ/ *adj* acting with equal force but opposite effect

coun·tess /ˈkaʊntɪs/ *n* a woman who holds the rank of COUNT or EARL for herself **b** wife of a COUNT or EARL

coun·try /ˈkʌntriʲ/ *n* **1** [C] nation, with its land and population **2** [S;U] also **countryside** /ˈkʌntriʲˌsaɪd/ — land outside towns ♦ *adj* of, in or from the country

country and west·ern /ˌ… ·ˈ…/ also **country mu·sic** /ˌ… ·ˈ…/ — *n* [U] popular music in the style of the southern and western states

country club /ˈ… ·/ *n* club whose members can use outdoor sport

facilities (FACILITY), attend social activities, etc.

coun·try·man /ˈkʌntriʲmən/ **-woman** /-ˌwʊmən/ *fem.* — *n* **-men** /-mən/ **1** COMPATRIOT **2** person who does not live in a town

country mile /ˌ… ·/ *n* long way

coun·ty /ˈkaʊntiʲ/ *n* area divided from others for purposes of local government

county clerk /ˌ… ·ˈ·/ *n* elected official in most states who keeps records of property titles, etc.

coup /kuʷ/ *n* **1** clever effective action **2** also **coup d'é·tat** /ˌkuʷ deʲˈtɑ, -də-/ — sudden and violent seizure of state power by a small group

cou·pe /kuʷp, kuʷˈpeʲ/ *n* closed car with 2 doors and a sloping back

cou·ple /ˈkʌpəl/ *n* **1** two things of the same kind **2** two people, esp. a husband and wife **3** a few ♦ *v* **1** *vt* join (two things) together **2** *vi* (of animals) MATE **-pling** *n* something that joins two things, esp. two railroad cars

cou·pon /ˈkuʷpɑn, ˈkyuʷ-/ *n* ticket showing the right of the holder to receive something

cour·age /ˈkɜrɪdʒ, ˈkʌr-/ *n* [U] ability to control fear; bravery **-ageous** /kəˈreʲdʒəs/ *adj* brave **-ageously** *adv*

cou·ri·er /ˈkʊəriʲər, ˈkɜr-, ˈkʌr-/ *n* official messenger

course /kɔrs, koʷrs/ *n* **1** path along which something moves **2** area for races or certain sports: *a golf course* **3** plan of action **4 a** set of lessons, treatments, etc. **b** university studies: *a 4 year course* **5** any of several parts of a meal **6** a matter of course that which one expects to happen **7** in due course at the right time **8** in the course of during **9** of course certainly **10** run/take its/their course (of an illness, etc.) continue to its natural end **11** stay the course continue something through to the end in spite of difficulty ♦ *vi* (of liquid) flow quickly

court¹ /kɔrt, ˈkoʷrt-/ *n* **1 a** [C] room (courtroom) or building where law cases are judged **b** [U] people gathered there **2** [C] area for certain ball games such as BASKETBALL and tennis **3** [C] king or queen with the royal family, officials, etc. **4** [C] also **court·yard** /ˈkɔrtyɑrd, ˈkoʷrt-/ — open space surrounded by buildings or in the middle of a building

court² *vt fml* **1** try to win the favor of **2** visit and pay attention to (a woman a man hopes to marry) **3** risk foolishly: *to court disaster*

court·house /ˈkɔrthaʊs, ˈkoʷrt-/ *n* building with courtrooms and other offices

cour·te·ous /ˈkɜrtiⁱəs/ adj fml polite and kind ~ly adv

cour·te·sy /ˈkɜrtəsiⁱ/ n [C;U] polite behavior **2 by courtesy of** with the permission of

court-mar·tial /ˈ•ˌ•ⁱ/ n (trial before) a court for offenses against military law ♦ vt -l- try (someone) in a court-martial

court·ship /ˈkɔrt-ʃɪp, ˈkoʷrt-/ n [U] (period of) trying to attract someone to oneself, esp. with the aim of marriage

cous·in /ˈkʌzən/ n **1** child of one's uncle or aunt **2** related person or thing — see also FIRST COUSIN, SECOND COUSIN

cove /koʷv/ n small BAY¹

cov·e·nant /ˈkʌvənənt/ n formal agreement

cov·er¹ /ˈkʌvər/ **1** vt spread something over; hide in this way: *cover the body with a sheet* **2** vt lie on the surface of; spread over (something): *furniture covered in dust* | *The town covers five square miles.* **3** vt travel (a distance) **4** vt include: *a talk covering the whole history of medicine* **5** vt report (an event) for a newspaper **6** vt be enough money for **7** vt protect from loss; insure **8** vt keep a gun aimed at **9** vi/t act in place of (someone who is absent)

cover up phr vt prevent (something) from being noticed **cover-up** /ˈ•••ˌ•/ n

cover up for phr vt hide something wrong or shameful in order to save (someone else) from punishment, blame, etc.

cov·er² n **1** [C] anything that protects or hides by covering: *cushion covers* | (fig.) *The business is a cover for illegal activity.* **2** [C] outside of a book or magazine **3** [U] shelter; protection **4** [U] insurance against loss, etc. **5 take cover** find a safe place to hide **6 under plain/separate cover** in a plain/separate envelope ~ing n something that covers or hides

cov·er·age /ˈkʌvərɪdʒ/ n [U] time and space given to reporting an event

cov·er·alls /ˈkʌvərˌɔlz/ n [P] garment for the whole body, to protect one's clothes

cover charge /ˈ••• ˌ•/ n charge made by a restaurant etc. in addition to the cost of the food and drinks or of the service

cover let·ter /ˈ•• ˌ•/ n letter or note containing an explanation or additional information, sent with a parcel or another letter

cov·ert /ˈkʌvərt, ˈkoʷ-, koʷˈvɜrt/ adj hidden; secret ~ly adv

cov·et /ˈkʌvɪt/ vt desire (esp. someone else's possessions) eagerly ~ous adj

cow¹ /kaʊ/ n female of cattle and some other large animals

cow² vt frighten into obedience

cow·ard /ˈkaʊərd/ n person afraid of pain or danger ~ly adj

cow·ard·ice /ˈkaʊərdɪs/ n [U] lack of courage

cow·boy /ˈkaʊbɔɪ/ also **cow·hand** /ˈkaʊhænd/ — n man who looks after cattle on horseback

cow·er /ˈkaʊər/ vi bend low from fear or shame

cow·pat·tie /ˈkaʊˌpætiⁱ/ n lump of COW DUNG

cox·swain /ˈkɑksən, -sweⁱn/ n person who guides and controls a rowing boat or crew, esp. in races ♦ vi/t act as coxswain

coy /kɔɪ/ adj pretending not to be confident in one's own ability ~ly adv

coy·ote /kaɪˈoʷtiⁱ, ˈkaɪ-oʷt/ n small WOLF

co·zy /ˈkoʷziⁱ/ adj warm and comfortable –zily adv –ziness n [U]

CPU /ˌsiⁱ piⁱ ˈyuʷ/ abbrev. for CENTRAL PROCESSING UNIT

crab /kræb/ n SHELLFISH with 10 legs, that can be eaten

crab·by /ˈkræbiⁱ/ adj bad-tempered

crack¹ /kræk/ v **1** vi/t break without dividing into pieces: *cracked cups* **2** vi/t make a sudden explosive sound: *crack a whip* **3** vi/t cause to break open: *crack a safe* **4** vi (of a voice) change suddenly in level **5** vi/t hit suddenly **6** vi lose strength or control: *crack (up) under the strain* **7** make (a joke) **8** discover the secret of (a CODE (1)) **9** (cause to) strike with a sudden blow **10 cracked up to be** believed to be **11 get cracking** be or become busy doing something in a hurried way

crack down phr vi take strong action against something

crack² n **1** thin line caused by breaking **2** explosive sound: *crack of thunder* **3** sudden sharp blow **4** sudden change in the level of the voice **5** quick joke; clever remark **6 at the crack of dawn** very early in the morning ♦ adj very skillful: *crack troops*

crack³ n [U] sl extremely pure form of COCAINE, taken illegally for pleasure

cracked /krækt/ adj infml slightly crazy

crack·down /ˈkrækdaʊn/ n infml severe enforcement of laws or rules

crack·er /ˈkrækər/ n **1** unsweetened BISCUIT **2** paper container of explosive powder that makes a noise when pulled apart

crack·er·jack /ˈkrækərˌdʒæk/ n sl very clever person

crack·le /ˈkrækəl/ vi make small sharp sounds: *The fire crackled.* crackle n [S;U]

crack·pot /ˈkrækpɑt/ adj strange; crazy ♦ n crackpot person

cra·dle /ˈkreⁱdl/ n 1 small bed for a baby 2 origin of something: *the cradle of Western civilization* 3 frame to support something ♦ vt hold gently

craft¹ /kræft/ n trade needing skill, esp. with one's hands

craft² n **craft** boat, aircraft, or spacecraft

crafts·man /ˈkræftsmən/ **crafts·wo·man** /-ˌwʊmən/ fem. — n —**men** /-mən/ skilled worker ~**ship** n [U]

craft·y /ˈkræftiʲ/ adj cleverly deceitful —**ily** adv —**iness** n [U]

crag /kræg/ n high steep rock ~**gy** adj 1 steep and rough 2 (esp. of a man's face) rough in appearance

cram /kræm/ v -mm- 1 vt force into a small space; fill too full: *box crammed with letters* 2 vi study hard for a short time: *cram for an examination*

cramp /kræmp/ n [C;U] sudden painful tightening of a muscle ♦ vt 1 cause to have a cramp 2 prevent natural growth or development 3 **cramp someone's style** prevent someone from showing their abilities to the full —**ed** adj limited in space

cram·pon /ˈkræmpɑn/ n set of SPIKES fixed to a boot for climbing ice slopes

crane /kreⁱn/ n 1 machine with a movable arm for lifting heavy objects 2 tall waterbird with long legs ♦ vi/t stretch out (one's neck) to see better

cra·ni·um /ˈkreⁱniʲəm/ n bony part of the head, covering the brain **cranial** adj

crank /kræŋk/ n 1 handle for turning, shaped like an L 2 person with strange ideas ♦ vt 1 move by turning a crank 2 use a CRANK (1) to start a car ~**y** adj 1 (of people or ideas) peculiar 2 bad-tempered

crank out phr vt produce rapidly

cran·ny /ˈkræniʲ/ n small narrow opening in a wall, etc.

crap /kræp/ n [U] taboo sl 1 (act of passing) solid waste from the bowel 2 nonsense ♦ **crap** vi -pp-

crash /kræʃ/ v 1 vi/t fall or hit violently: *The car crashed into a tree.* 2 vi make a sudden loud noise 3 vi move violently and noisily: *The elephant crashed through the fence.* 4 vi fail suddenly in business ♦ n 1 violent vehicle accident: *a car/plane crash* 2 sudden loud noise 3 sudden business failure ♦ adj intended to get quick results: *a crash diet/course*

crash hel·met /ˈ· ˌ··/ n protective HELMET worn by people who ride motor cycles, etc.

crash-land /ˌ· ˈ·/ vi/t (cause a plane) to crash in a controlled way **crash landing** n

crass /kræs/ adj fml showing great stupidity and a complete lack of feeling or respect for others

crate /kreⁱt/ n large wooden or plastic box for bottles, etc.

cra·ter /ˈkreⁱtər/ n 1 mouth of a VOLCANO 2 hole made by a bomb, etc. 3 round hole with a flat bottom on the moon's surface

cra·vat /krəˈvæt/ n wide piece of cloth worn like a TIE

crave /kreⁱv/ vi/t have a very strong desire for (something) **craving** n

crawl /krɔl/ vi 1 move slowly, esp. with the body close to the ground: *crawling babies/(fig.) traffic* 2 be covered by crawling insects, etc. 3 have an unpleasant sensation, as of insects, etc., moving slowly over one's skin: *The idea makes my skin crawl.* 4 infml try to win the favor of someone by being too nice to them ♦ n [S] 1 very slow movement 2 rapid way of swimming ~**er** n 1 something, esp. a vehicle, that goes slowly 2 person who CRAWLS (4)

cray·on /ˈkreⁱɑn, -ən/ n pencil of colored chalk or wax crayon vi/t

craze /kreⁱz/ n popular fashion that lasts a short time ♦ vt make excited or crazy

cra·zy /ˈkreⁱziʲ/ adj 1 INSANE; foolish 2 wildly excited —**zily** adv —**ziness** n [U]

crazy bone /ˈ·· ·/ n FUNNY BONE

creak /kriʲk/ vi, n make the sound of a badly oiled door ~**y** adj

cream /kriʲm/ n [U] 1 thick liquid that rises to the top of milk 2 soft mixture like this: *face cream* 3 best part: *the cream of the students* ♦ adj yellow-white ♦ vt 1 make into a soft mixture: *creamed potatoes* 2 take cream from the surface of (milk) 3 sl defeat ~**y** adj 1 containing cream 2 like cream

cream off phr vt take the best part

cream·e·ry /ˈkriʲməriʲ/ n DAIRY

crease /kriʲs/ n line made by folding or pressing ♦ vi/t press into creases

cre·ate /kriʲˈeⁱt/ vt 1 cause (something new) to exist; make 2 appoint to a rank; create him a general —**ator** n 1 [C] a person who creates something 2 [the] (cap.) God —**ation** /-ˈeⁱʃən/ n 1 [U] act of creating 2 [C] something created 3 [U] the whole universe

cre·a·tive /kriˈeʸtɪv/ adj able to make new things; inventive ~**ly** adv ~**tivity** /ˌkriˈeʸˈtɪvətiʸ/ n [U]

crea·ture /ˈkriʸtʃər/ n person, animal, or being

creature com·fort /ˌ·· ˈ··/ n thing that makes one comfortable

cre·dence /ˈkriʸdns/ n fml acceptance as true; belief

cre·den·tials /krəˈdenʃəlz, -tʃəlz/ n [P] written proof of a person's ability and trustworthiness

cred·i·bil·i·ty gap /ˌ··ˈ··· ·/ n difference between what someone, esp. a politician, says and what they really mean or do

cred·i·ble /ˈkredəbəl/ adj that can be believed –**bly** adv –**bility** /ˌkredəˈbɪlətiʸ/ n [U]

cred·it¹ /ˈkredɪt/ n **1** [U] system of buying things and paying later: *buy on credit* **2** [U] quality of being likely to repay debts **3** [U] amount of money in someone's bank account **4** [U] belief; trust **5** [C;U] (cause of) public honor: *get credit for an invention* | *He's a credit to his team.* **6** [C] unit of a student's work **7 to someone's credit a** in someone's favor **b** to/in someone's name ~**able** adj deserving approval ~**ably** adv

credits n [P] names of actors, etc., which appear at the beginning or end of a film or television show

credit² vt **1** believe **2** add to an account

credit card /ˈ·· ·/ n plastic card allowing one to buy goods without paying in paper money or coin

cred·i·tor /ˈkredətər/ n person to whom money is owed

cred·u·lous /ˈkredʒələs/ adj too willing to believe –**lity** /krəˈduʷlətiʸ, -ˈdyuʷ-/ n [U]

creed /kriʸd/ n system of (esp. religious) beliefs

creek /kriʸk, krɪk/ n small stream **up the creek** sl in a difficult situation

creep¹ /kriʸp/ vi **crept** /krept/ **1** move slowly and quietly; CRAWL **2** (of a plant) grow along the ground or a surface X CRAWL (3) ~**er** n creeping plant ~**y** adj strange and frightening **creeps** n [P] feeling of fear and strangeness

creep² n infml unpleasant person

cre·mate /ˈkriʸmeʸt, krɪˈmeʸt/ vt burn (a dead person) –**mation** /krɪˈmeʸʃən/ n [C;U]

crem·a·to·ri·um /ˌkriʸməˈtoriʸəm, -ˈtoʷr-, ˌkre-/ n place where bodies are cremated

crepe /kreʸp/ n **1** [U] cloth, paper or rubber with a lined and folded surface **2** [C] very thin PANCAKE

crept /krept/ v past t. and p. of CREEP

cre·scen·do /krəˈʃendoʷ/ n –**dos** gradual increase of force or loudness, esp. in music

cres·cent /ˈkresənt/ n **1** curved shape of the new moon **2** something shaped like this, such as a curved street

crest /krest/ n **1** growth of feathers on a bird's head **2** decoration like this on a soldier's HELMET **3** top of a hill, wave, etc. **4** picture used as a personal mark on letters, etc.

crest·fal·len /ˈkrest͵fɔlən/ adj disappointed

cret·in /ˈkriʸtn/ n **1** sl very stupid person **2** med kind of IDIOT

cre·vasse /krəˈvæs/ n deep crack in ice

crev·ice /ˈkrevɪs/ n narrow crack in rock, etc.

crew /kruʷ/ n **1 a** all the people working on a ship or plane **b** all of these except the officers **2** group working together: *a camera crew* ♦ vi act as ship's crew

crew cut /ˈ· ·/ n very short hair style

crib /krɪb/ n **1** bed for a small child **2** book supplying a translation ♦ vt –**bb–** copy (someone's work) dishonestly

crib death /ˈ· ·/ n [C;U] unexplained death of a healthy baby

crick /krɪk/ n painful stiffening of the muscles, esp. in the back or the neck **crick** vt

crick·et /ˈkrɪkɪt/ n jumping insect that makes a loud noise

cried /kraɪd/ v past t. and p. of CRY

cries /kraɪz/ v pres. t. of CRY ♦ n pl. of CRY

crime /kraɪm/ n **1** [C;U] offense that is punishable by law **2** [S] a shame

crim·i·nal /ˈkrɪmənəl/ adj of crime ♦ n person who is guilty of crime ~**ly** adv

crim·son /ˈkrɪmzən/ n, adj [U] deep red

cringe /krɪndʒ/ vi **1** bend low from fear; COWER **2** behave towards someone in a way that shows no respect for oneself

crin·kle /ˈkrɪŋkəl/ n fold made by crushing ♦ vi/t make or get crinkles

crip·ple /ˈkrɪpəl/ n person who cannot use the limbs, esp. the legs, properly ♦ vt **1** make into a cripple **2** damage seriously: *crippling debts*

cri·sis /ˈkraɪsɪs/ n –**ses** /-siʸz/ moment of great danger or difficulty – see also MID-LIFE CRISIS

crisp /krɪsp/ adj **1** hard, dry, and easily broken: *crisp bacon* **2** (of weather) cold and dry **3** (of style, manners, etc.) brief and clear: *crisp reply* ♦ vi/t cook until crisp ~**ly** adv ~**ness** n [U] ~**y** adj

criss·cross /ˈkrɪskrɒs/ *vi/t, n* (make) a network of crossed lines

cri·te·ri·on /kraɪˈtɪəriˀən/ *n* **-ria** /-riˀə/ standard on which a judgment is based

crit·ic /ˈkrɪtɪk/ *n* **1** person who gives judgments about art, music, etc. **2** person who expresses disapproval ~**al** *adj* **1** finding fault **2** of a critic's work **3** of or at a CRISIS: *critical decisions* ~**ism** /ˈkrɪtə̩sɪzəm/ *n* [C;U] **1** work of a critic **2** disapproval ~**ize** *vi/t* **1** make judgments **2** find fault

cri·tique /krɪˈtiˀk/ *n* book or article criticizing the work of esp. a writer

crit·ter /ˈkrɪtər/ *n infml* CREATURE

croak /kroˀk/ *vi/t , n* **1** (make) the deep low noise a FROG makes **2** speak with a rough voice as if one has a sore throat **3** *sl* die

crock·e·ry /ˈkrakəriˀ/ *n* [U] EARTHENWARE

croc·o·dile /ˈkrakə̩daɪl/ *n* **1** [C] large tropical river REPTILE **2** [U] its skin, used as leather

crocodile tears /ˈkrakədaɪl ˌtɪərz/ *n* [P] insincere sorrow

cro·cus /ˈkroˀkəs/ *n* small spring plant with purple, yellow and white flowers

cro·ny /ˈkroˀniˀ/ *n infml* (old) friend or companion

crook /krʊk/ *n* **1** *infml* thief **2** bend or curve: *the crook of her arm* ♦ *vi/t* bend ~**ed** /ˈkrʊkɪd/ *adj* **1** not straight **2** dishonest

croon /kruˀn/ *vi/t* sing gently in a low soft voice ~**er** *n*

crop[1] /krɑp/ *n* **1** plant grown by a farmer **2** amount gathered in a season: (fig.) *this year's crop of students*

crop[2] *vt* **-pp- 1** (of animals) bite off the tops of (grass etc.) **2** cut (hair, etc.) short

crop up *phr vi* happen unexpectedly

crop·per /ˈkrɑpər/ *n infml* **come a cropper** fall heavily; fail

cro·quet /kroˀˈkeˀ/ *n* [U] outdoor game in which players knock wooden balls through HOOPS

cross[1] /krɒs/ *n* **1** the mark + **2** a upright post with a bar across it, esp. **a** that on which Christ died **b** this shape as a sign of the Christian faith **3** sorrow; pain **4** mixture of 2 things

cross[2] *v* **1** *vi/t* go or put across **2** *vt* oppose (someone's wishes, etc.) **3** *vi* (of letters) pass in opposite directions **4** *vt* mix different breeds of (animals or plants) **5** **cross oneself** make the sign of the cross with the hand **6** **cross one's mind** come into one's thoughts **7** **cross swords** argue **8** **keep one's fingers crossed** hope that nothing will

happen to upset one's plans ~**ing** *n* **1** journey across the sea **2** place where a road, etc., may be crossed

cross off/out *phr vt* draw a line through (writing)

cross[3] *adj* angry ~**ly** *adv* ~**ness** *n* [U]

cross·beam /ˈkrɒsbiˀm/ *n* beam supporting a floor

cross·bow /ˈkrɒsboˀ/ *n* weapon combining a BOW[2] (1) and a gun

cross·breed /ˈkrɒsbriˀd/ *n* animal or plant of mixed breed **-bred** /-bred/ *adj*

cross·check /ˌkrɒsˈtʃek, ˈkrɒstʃek/ *vt* test (a calculation, etc.) by using a different method

cross-coun·try /ˌ· ˈ··◂/ *adj, adv* across the fields or open country

cross-dress·ing /ˈ· ˌ··/ *n* transvestism (TRANSVESTITE)

cross-ex·am·ine /ˌ· ·ˈ··/ *vt* question (esp. a witness in court) closely, to test answers given before

cross-eyed /ˈ· ·/ *adj* with the eyes looking in towards the nose

cross·fire /ˈkrɒsfaɪər/ *n* [U] gunfire across one's direction of movement

cross-leg·ged /ˌkrɒs ˈlegɪd◂, -ˈlegd◂/ *adj* having the knees wide apart and ankles crossed

cross-pur·pos·es /ˌ· ˈ··/ *n* **be at cross-purposes** misunderstand one another

cross-ques·tion /ˌ· ˈ··/ *vt* CROSS-EXAMINE

cross-ref·er·ence /ˌ· ˈ··/ *n* note directing the reader to another place in the book

cross·roads /ˈkrɒsroˀdz/ *n* **-roads** **1** place where roads cross **2** point where a decision must be made

cross-sec·tion /ˈ· ˌ·/ *n* **1** (drawing of) a surface made by cutting across **2** typical example of a whole

cross·town /ˈkrɒstaʊn/ *adj* traveling in a direction in a place, or across a town or city: *a crosstown bus*

cross·walk /ˈkrɒswɔk/ *n* set of white lines across a road where people have a right to walk across

cross·word puz·zle /ˈkrɒswɔrd ˌpʌzəl/ *n* printed game in which words are fitted into numbered squares

crotch /krɑtʃ/ *n* place between the tops of a person's legs

crotch·et·y /ˈkrɑtʃəti̯/ *adj infml* bad-tempered

crouch /kraʊtʃ/ *vi* lower the body by bending the knees

crou·pi·er /ˈkruˀpiˀˌeˀ, -piˀər/ *n* person who collects and pays out money at a CASINO

crow[1] /kroˀ/ *n* **1** large shiny black bird **2** **as the crow flies** in a straight line **3 eat crow** admit one is wrong

crow² /·/ *vi* **1** make the loud cry of a COCK **2** speak proudly

crow·bar /ˈkroʷˌbɑr/ *n* iron bar for raising heavy objects

crowd /kraʊd/ *n* **1** large number of people together **2** particular social group: *the college crowd* ♦ *v* **1** *vi* come together in a crowd **2** *vt* (esp. of people) fill: *a crowded bus*

crown /kraʊn/ *n* **1** [C] circular head decoration, esp. for a king or queen **2** [*the*+S] royal power **3** [C] top of a head, hat, hill, etc. **4** artificial cap on a tooth ♦ *vt* **1** place a crown on the head of **2** cover the top of: *mountains crowned with snow* **3** complete worthily **4 to crown it all** to complete good or bad luck ~**ing** *adj* above all things

crow's feet /ˈ· ·/ *n* [P] line at the outer corner of a person's eye; WRINKLE

crow's nest /ˈ· ·/ *n* small shelter near top of a ship's MAST from which a person can watch for danger, etc.

cru·cial /ˈkruːʃəl/ *adj* of the greatest importance ~**ly** *adv*

cru·ci·ble /ˈkruːsəbəl/ *n* pot for melting metals in

cru·ci·fix /ˈkruʷsəˌfɪks/ *n* cross with a figure of Christ on it

cru·ci·fix·ion /ˌkruʷsəˈfɪkʃən/ *n* [C;U] death by nailing to a cross

cru·ci·fy /ˈkruʷsəˌfaɪ/ *vt* **1** kill by crucifixion **2** be very cruel to, esp. publicly

crud /krʌd/ *n* **1** dirt **2** unspecific illness usu. of stomach

crude /kruʷd/ *adj* **1** in a natural state; untreated **2** without sensitive feeling: *crude jokes* **3** badly made ♦ *n* [U] crude oil ~**ly** *adv* **crudity** *n* [C;U]

cru·el /ˈkruʷəl/ *adj* -ll- **1** liking to cause suffering **2** causing suffering: *cruel disappointment* ~**ly** *adv* ~**ty** *n* [C;U]

cru·et /ˈkruʷɪt/ *n* set of containers for oil, VINEGAR, etc., at meals

cruise /kruʷz/ *v* **1** *vi* sail slowly for pleasure **2** *vi* (of a car, etc.) move at a steady speed **3** *vi/t* look (in public places) for a sexual partner, esp. one of the same sex ♦ *n* sea voyage for pleasure **cruiser** *n* **1** fast fighting ship **2** motor boat with a CABIN

cruise mis·sile /ˈ· ˌ·/ *n* GUIDED MISSILE that flies low and can examine the ground

crumb /krʌm/ *n* small piece of dry food, esp. bread: (fig.) *crumbs of information*

crum·ble /ˈkrʌmbəl/ *v* **1** *vi/t* break into small pieces **2** *vi* come to ruin ~**bly** *adj* easily crumbled

crum·my /ˈkrʌmiʸ/ *adj* worthless

crum·ple /ˈkrʌmpəl/ **1** *vi/t* crush into irregular folds **2** *vi* lose strength

crunch /krʌntʃ/ *v* **1** *vt* crush (food) noisily with the teeth **2** *vi* make a crushing noise ♦ *n* [S] **1** crunching sound **2** CRISIS: *when it comes to the crunch*

cru·sade /kruʷˈseʸd/ *n* **1** Christian war against the Muslims in the Middle Ages **2** any united struggle: *a crusade for women's rights* ♦ *vi* take part in a crusade ~**sader** *n*

crush /krʌʃ/ *v* **1** *vi/t* break or spoil by pressure **2** *vi* press; push: *They crushed through the gates.* **3** *vt* destroy completely: (fig.) *He felt crushed by her cruel remark.* ♦ *n* **1** [S] crowd of people pressed together **2** [C] strong and foolish love for someone, but only temporary

crust /krʌst/ *n* [C;U] hard outer surface of something, esp. bread ~**y** *adj* **1** with a hard crust **2** bad-tempered

crus·ta·cean /krʌˈsteʸʃən/ *n* SHELLFISH

crutch /krʌtʃ/ *n* **1** stick to help someone to walk **2** something that gives moral support: *He uses religion as a crutch.* **3** CROTCH

crux /krʌks/ *n* central part of a problem

cry¹ /kraɪ/ *v* **1** *vi* produce tears from the eyes **2** *vi/t* call out loudly: '*Help!*' *he cried.* **3** *vi* (of a bird or animal) make its natural sound **4 cry one's eyes/heart out** cry very bitterly **5 for crying out loud** *sl* (used to give strength to a demand, etc.): *Oh, for crying out loud, shut that door!*

cry out for *phr vt* need very badly

cry² *n* **1** [C] shout expressing something: *cries of joy* | *a war cry* | *a cry for help* **2** [S] period of crying **3** bird's or animal's natural sound **4 a far cry from** a great deal different from (something)

cry·ba·by /ˈkraɪˌbeʸbiʸ/ *n* [C] person who cries too readily with little cause

crypt /krɪpt/ *n* room under a church

cryp·tic /ˈkrɪptɪk/ *adj* with a hidden meaning

crys·tal /ˈkrɪstəl/ *n* **1** [C;U] (piece of) transparent ice-like mineral **2** [U] expensive colorless glass **3** [C] regular shape formed naturally by some substances such as sugar **4** [C] transparent cover of a clock or watch face ~**lize** *v* **1** *vi/t* form into crystals **2** *vi/t* make (ideas, etc.) fixed in form **3** *vt* preserve (fruit) with sugar

crystal ball /ˌ·· ˈ·/ *n* ball used by FORTUNE-TELLERS to look into the future

cub /kʌb/ *n* young lion, bear, etc.

cub·by·hole /ˈkʌbiˌhoʷl/ n small room or cupboard

cube /kyuʷb/ n **1** solid object with 6 equal square sides **2** result of multiplying a number by itself twice ♦ vt multiply a number by itself twice: 3 cubed is 27.

cu·bic /ˈkyuʷbɪk/ adj multiplying length by width and height: a cubic foot

cu·bi·cle /ˈkyuʷbɪkəl/ n small division of a large room

cuck·oo /ˈkuʷkuʷ, ˈkʊ-/ n bird that lays its eggs in other birds' nests and makes a noise like its name

cu·cum·ber /ˈkyuʷkʌmbər/ n long green vegetable eaten raw

cud /kʌd/ n [U] **1** food swallowed and brought up again by cows, etc., for further eating **2** chew the cud think deeply before making a decision

cud·dle /ˈkʌdl/ v **1** vt hold lovingly in one's arms **2** vi lie close and comfortably ♦ n [S] cuddling; HUG –**dly** adj suitable for cuddling

cud·gel /ˈkʌdʒəl/ n CLUB (2)

cue¹ /kyuʷ/ n **1** signal for the next actor to speak in a play **2** example of how to behave

cue² n stick for pushing the ball in BILLIARDS or POOL² (2)

cuff¹ /kʌf/ n **1** end of a SLEEVE **2** off the cuff (of an answer, etc.) without preparation

cuff² vt hit lightly; SMACK **cuff** n

cuff link /ˈ·ˌ·/ n button-like object used for fastening cuffs

cui·sine /kwɪˈziʸn/ n [U] style of cooking

cul-de-sac /ˌkʌl də ˈsæk, ˌkʊl-/ n street closed at one end

cul·i·na·ry /ˈkʌləˌnɛriʸ, ˈkyuʷ-/ adj of, related to the kitchen or cooking

cull /kʌl/ **1** vt fml gather (information, etc.) **2** vi/t take the best parts from a group

cul·len·der /ˈkʌləndər/ n COLANDER

cul·mi·nate /ˈkʌlməˌneʸt/ v

    culminate in phr vt fml reach the last and highest point: The battle culminated in victory. –**nation** /ˌkʌlməˈneʸʃən/ n [S]

cul·pa·ble /ˈkʌlpəbəl/ adj fml deserving blame –**bly** adv –**bility** /ˌkʌlpəˈbɪlətiʸ/ n [U]

cul·prit /ˈkʌlprɪt/ n guilty person

cult /kʌlt/ n **1** system of worship **2** popular fashion: cult films

cul·ti·vate /ˈkʌltəˌveʸt/ vt **1 a** prepare (land) for crops **b** grow (crops) **2** improve or develop by careful attention, study, etc. **3** pay friendly attention to (people) –**vated** adj educated and having good manners –**vation** /ˌkʌltəˈveʸʃən/ n [U]

cul·ture /ˈkʌltʃər/ n **1** [C;U] art, thought, and customs of a society: tribal cultures **2** [U] high development in art and thought **3** [U] raising animals and growing plants –**tural** adj: cultural activities –**tured** adj **1** cultivated **2** produced by humans: cultured pearls

cum·ber·some /ˈkʌmbərsəm/ adj heavy and awkward to carry

cu·mu·la·tive /ˈkyuʷmyələtɪv, -ˌleʸ-/ adj increasing by one addition after another ~ **ly** adv

cun·ning /ˈkʌnɪŋ/ adj clever in deceiving ♦ n [U] quality of being cunning ~**ly** adv

cunt /kʌnt/ n taboo VAGINA

cup /kʌp/ n **1** container, usu. with a handle, to drink from **2** thing shaped like a cup: bra cups **3** gold or silver container given as a prize in competitions **4** HOLE in GOLF ♦ vt –**pp**– form (one's hands) into a cup shape

cup·board /ˈkʌbərd/ n place to keep dishes, plates, etc. in a kitchen

cup·cake /ˈkʌpkeʸk/ n small cake for one person

cu·ra·ble /ˈkyuʷrəbəl/ adj that can be cured

cu·rate /ˈkyuʷrɪt/ n priest of the lowest rank, who helps another

cu·ra·tor /kyuʷˈreʸtər, ˈkyuʷrˌeʸtər, -ətər/ n person in charge of a MUSEUM, etc.

curb /kɜrb/ n **1** stone edge of a SIDEWALK **2** controlling influence; CHECK (2) ♦ vt hold back; control

curd /kɜrd/ n [C;U] thick soft substance that separates from milk when it becomes sour

cur·dle /ˈkɜrdl/ vi/t (cause to) form into CURDS; (cause to) thicken

cure /kjuər/ vt **1 a** bring back to health: (fig.) a plan to cure the economy **b** make (a disease) go away **2** preserve (food, skin, tobacco) by drying, etc. ♦ n **1** something that cures a person or disease **2** a return to health after illness

cur·few /ˈkɜrfyuʷ/ n [C;U] time or signal for people to stay indoors

cu·ri·o /ˈkyuʷriʸˌoʷ/ n –**os** rare or beautiful small object

cu·ri·os·i·ty /ˌkyuʷriʸˈasətiʸ/ n **1** [S;U] desire to know **2** [C] interesting rare object

cu·ri·ous /ˈkyuʷriʸəs/ adj **1** eager to learn **2** peculiar ~**ly** adv

curl¹ /kɜrl/ n **1** hanging twist of hair **2** thing this shape: curls of smoke ~ y adj having curls

curl² vi/t twist; wind

    curl up phr vi/t (cause to) lie comfortably with the limbs drawn close to the body: curl up with a good book

cur·rant /ˈkɜrənt, ˈkʌr-/ n **1** dried GRAPE **2** kind of black, red, or white BERRY

cur·ren·cy /ˈkʌrənsiʸ, ˈkʌr-/ n 1 [C;U] money in use in a country 2 [U] state of being generally believed

cur·rent¹ /ˈkʌrənt, ˈkʌr-/ adj 1 of the present time: current fashion 2 commonly accepted 3 (of money) used as currency

current² n 1 flow of liquid, gas, or electricity 2 general tendency or course of events

cur·ric·u·lum /kəˈrɪkyələm /-lə/ or -lums course of study in a school, etc.

curriculum vi·tae /kəˌrɪkyələm ˈviˑtaɪ, -ˈvaɪtiʸ/ n a short written account of a person's education and past employment – see also RESUME

cur·ry¹ /ˈkɜriʸ, ˈkʌriʸ/ n [C;U] Indian dish of meat, vegetables, etc. with a hot taste ♦ vt make into curry

curry² v curry favor try to win approval dishonestly

curse /kɜrs/ n 1 words calling for evil to come to someone 2 cause of misfortune: Foxes are a curse to farmers. 3 word or words used in swearing ♦ vi/t 1 call down evil upon 2 use violent language (against) 3 be cursed with suffer from cursed /ˈkɜrsɪd/ adj hateful; annoying

cur·sor /ˈkɜrsər/ n mark which can move around a SCREEN connected to a computer to point to a particular position

cur·so·ry /ˈkɜrsəriʸ/ adj (of work, reading, etc.) not thorough –rily adv

curt /kɜrt/ adj (of speech) impolitely short –ly adv –ness n [U]

cur·tail /kərˈteʸl/ vt fml shorten; reduce ~ ment n [C;U]

cur·tain /ˈkɜrtn/ n 1 cloth hung over a window, or in front of a theater stage: (fig.) curtain of smoke 2 [P] sl the end, esp. of a person's life

curt·sy /ˈkɜrtsiʸ/ vi, n (make) a woman's act of bending the knees and lowering the head to show respect

cur·va·ture /ˈkɜrvətʃər, -ˌtʃʊər/ n [C;U] state of being curved

curve /kɜrv/ n line that is not straight and has no angles ♦ vi/t: The road curves to the right.

cush·ion /ˈkʊʃən/ n bag filled with something soft, for lying or sitting on; (fig.) a cushion of air ♦ vt 1 lessen the force of 2 protect from hardship

cush·y /ˈkʊʃiʸ/ adj (of a job, style of life, etc.) easy

cuss /kʌs/ vi/t CURSE (2) ♦ n difficult person

cus·tard /ˈkʌstərd/ n [U] sweet yellow mixture of eggs and milk

cus·to·di·an /kʌˈstoʷdiʸən/ n person in charge of a public building

cus·to·dy /ˈkʌstədiʸ/ n 1 right to look after someone: give him custody of his child 2 being guarded or imprisoned: in police custody

cus·tom /ˈkʌstəm/ n 1 [C;U] established social behavior 2 [C] something someone does regularly **customs** n [P] 1 taxes on goods entering or leaving a country 2 place where these taxes are collected

cus·tom·a·ry /ˈkʌstəˌmeriʸ/ adj established by custom; usual

custom-built /ˌ·· ˈ·◄/ also **custom-made** — adj made especially for one person or group of people

cus·tom·er /ˈkʌstəmər/ n person who buys things from a store

cus·tom·ized /ˈkʌstəˌmaɪzd/ adj changed to match the needs of one person or group of people

cut¹ /kʌt/ v cut, -tt- 1 vt/i use something sharp to divide, remove, shorten, make a hole, etc.: cut your fingers/your hair/the corn 2 vi a be able to be cut b (of a knife, etc.) be sharp 3 vt make shorter or smaller: cut a long speech 4 vt make (esp. a public service) less in size, amount, etc.: They're cutting postal deliveries/bus services. 5 vt stay away on purpose: cut a lecture 6 vt put (a film) into final form 7 vt hurt the feelings of (someone): cutting remarks 8 vt (of a line, path, etc.) cross 9 vi stop filming a scene 10 cut corners do something quickly and cheaply but not perfectly 11 cut it close leave oneself too little time or money 12 cut it out stop doing something 13 cut no/not much ice have no/little influence 14 cut one's losses stop doing something before one loses any more money 15 cut someone (dead) refuse to recognize them

  cut across phr vt 1 go across instead of around 2 make a different division in: cut across party lines

  cut back phr v 1 vt PRUNE (a plant) 2 vi/t reduce **cutback** /ˈkʌtbæk/ n planned reduction

  cut down phr vt 1 vt bring down by cutting 2 vi/t reduce: cut down (on) smoking 3 knock down or kill (someone) 4 cut down to size reduce from too great importance to true or suitable importance

  cut in phr vi 1 interrupt 2 drive between moving vehicles 3 vt include

  cut off phr vt 1 separate by cutting 2 disconnect (telephone, gas, electricity, etc.) 3 separate from others: cut off by floods 4 end unexpectedly 5 DISINHERIT

  cut out phr v 1 vt remove by cutting 2 vt make by cutting: cut out a *dress* **3** *vt/i* stop: *cut out smoking* | *The engine keeps cutting out.* **4 not cut out for** not suitable for

cut up *phr vt* **1** cut into little pieces **2** make unhappy **3** behave in a humorous way

cut² *n* **1** opening made by cutting **2** piece of meat, etc., cut off **3** reduction: *cuts in government spending* **4** way in which clothes, hair, etc., are shaped **5** *infml* someone's share of a profit **6 a** act of removing a part, to improve or shorten **b** part removed **7 a cut above** better

cut-and-dried /ˌ· · ˈ·◂/ *adj* unlikely to change; fixed

cute /kyuʷt/ *adj* **1** delightfully pretty **2** (too) clever

cu·ti·cle /ˈkyuʷtɪkəl/ *n* skin at the base of one's nails

cut·lass /ˈkʌtləs/ *n* short sword with a curved blade

cut·le·ry /ˈkʌtləriʸ/ *n* [U] *fml* SILVERWARE

cut·let /ˈkʌtlɪt/ *n* small piece of meat

cut-price /ˌ· ˈ·◂/ *adj* (of goods) cheap

cut·ter /ˈkʌtər/ *n* **1** person or tool that cuts **2** small fast boat

cut·throat /ˈkʌtθroʷt/ *adj* fierce; unprincipled: *cutthroat competition*

cut·ting /ˈkʌtɪŋ/ *n* piece cut from a plant to form a new one

cy·a·nide /ˈsaɪəˌnaɪd/ *n* [U] strong poison

cy·ber·net·ics /ˌsaɪbərˈnɛtɪks/ *n* [U] science of how information is dealt with by machines and the brain

cy·cle¹ /ˈsaɪkəl/ *n* (time needed for) a set of events in regularly repeated order: *a 50-minute cycle* **cyclical** /ˈsaɪklɪkəl, ˈsɪ-/ *adj fml* happening in cycles

cycle² *v, n* bicycle **cyclist** *n*

cy·clone /ˈsaɪkloʷn/ *n* very violent wind moving rapidly in a circle

cyl·in·der /ˈsɪləndər/ *n* **1** object or container with a circular base and straight sides **2** tube for a PISTON in an engine

cym·bal /ˈsɪmbəl/ *n* one of a pair of metal plates struck together to make a noise in music

cyn·ic /ˈsɪnɪk/ *n* person who sees little good in anything and shows it by making unkind remarks ~**al** *adj* ~**ally** /-kliʸ/ *adv* ~**ism** /ˈsɪnəˌsɪzəm/ *n* [U]

cy·press /ˈsaɪprəs/ *n* EVERGREEN tree with dark green leaves and hard wood

cyst /sɪst/ *n* hollow growth in the body, containing liquid

cyst·i·tis /sɪˈstaɪtɪs/ *n* [U] disease of the BLADDER

czar /zɑr/ *n* (until 1917) male ruler of Russia

czarina /zɑˈriʸnə/ *n* (until 1917) **1** female ruler of Russia **2** wife of the czar

D

D, d /diː/ the 4th letter of the English alphabet

D *written abbrev. for:* **1** died **2** DIAMETER **3** DEMOCRAT

DA /ˌdiː ˈeɪ/ *n* district attorney

dab /dæb/ *vi/t* -**bb**- touch or cover lightly ♦ *n* small quantity of paint, etc.

dab·ble /ˈdæbəl/ *v* **1** *vi* work at something not professionally: *dabble in politics* **2** *vt* move (one's feet, etc.) playfully about in water

dachs·hund /ˈdɑkshunt, -hʊnd/ *n* small dog with short legs and a long body

dad /dæd/ *n infml* father

dad·dy /ˈdædiː/ *n* (child's word for) father

daf·fo·dil /ˈdæfəˌdɪl/ *n* yellow spring flower shaped like a bell

daf·fy /ˈdæfiː/ *adj* crazy

daft /dæft/ *adj* silly ~**ly** *adv* ~**ness** *n* [U]

dag·ger /ˈdægər/ *n* **1** short knife used as a weapon **2 look daggers at** look angrily at

dah·lia /ˈdælyə/ *n* big bright garden flower

dai·ly /ˈdeɪliː/ *adj, adv* every day ♦ *n* newspaper sold every day but Sunday

dain·ty /ˈdeɪntiː/ *adj* small, pretty, and delicate –**tily** *adv* –**tiness** *n* [U]

dair·y /ˈdeəriː/ *n* place where milk, butter, cheese, etc., are produced or sold

dairy cat·tle /ˈ·· ˌ·· / *n* [P] cows kept for milk, not meat

da·is /ˈdeɪɪs, ˈdaɪ-ɪs/ *n* raised floor at one end of a hall

dai·sy /ˈdeɪziː/ *n* **1** common white flower with yellow center **2 as fresh as a daisy** not tired

dale /deɪl/ *n* valley

dal·li·ance /ˈdæliːəns/ *n lit* flirtation (FLIRT)

dal·ly /ˈdæliː/ *vi* waste time

　dally with *phr vt* play with (an idea)

dam¹ /dæm/ *n* wall built to keep back water

dam² /dæm/ *vt* -**mm**- make a dam across

　dam up *phr v* control (a feeling, esp. of anger) in an unhealthy way

dam·age /ˈdæmɪdʒ/ *n* [U] harm; loss: *brain damage* ♦ *vt* cause damage to **damages** *n* [P] money paid for damage done

dame /deɪm/ *n sl* woman

damn /dæm/ *vt* **1** (of God) punish **2** declare to be bad **3** ruin: *damning evidence* **4** Well, I'll be damned! *infml* I'm very surprised ♦ *n* not give a damn not care at all ♦ *interj* (used in curses): *Damn it!* **damn,** also ~ **ed** *adj, adv* (used for giving force to an expression): *run damned* (= very) *fast* | *He's a damn fool.* ~**able** /ˈdæmnəbəl/ *adj* very bad ~**ation** /dæmˈneɪʃən/ *n* [U] **1** act of damning **2 in damnation** (used for giving force to an expression of anger): *What in damnation do you mean?* **damnedest** /ˈdæmdɪst/ *n* **do one's damnedest** do everything possible

damp¹ /dæmp/ *adj* slightly wet ♦ *n* [U] slight wetness ~**ness** *n* [U]

damp² also **dampen** /ˈdæmpən/ *vt* **1** wet slightly **2** reduce (eagerness, etc.): *damp their spirits*

　damp down *phr vt* make (a fire) burn more slowly

damp·er /ˈdæmpər/ *n* **1** metal plate controlling the flow of air to a fire **2** influence reducing eagerness

damp proof·ing /ˈ· ·· / *n* material built into a wall to stop wetness from coming up

dam·sel /ˈdæmzəl/ *n old lit* **1** young unmarried woman of noble birth; young girl **2 damsel in distress** *humor* girl in trouble

dam·son /ˈdæmzən/ *n* kind of small PLUM

dance /dæns/ *n* **1** [C] (music for) a set of movements performed to music **2** [C] party with dances **3** [U] art of dancing – see also SONG AND DANCE ♦ *vi/t* do a dance **dancer** *n*

dan·de·li·on /ˈdændəlˌaɪən/ *n* common bright yellow flower

dan·druff /ˈdændrəf/ *n* bits of dead skin in the hair

dan·dy /ˈdændiː/ *n* man who is almost too well dressed ♦ *adj* good: *fine and dandy*

dan·ger /ˈdeɪndʒər/ *n* **1** [U] possibility of harm **2** [C] cause of danger ~**ous** *adj* not safe ~**ously** *adv*

dan·gle /ˈdæŋgəl/ *vi/t* **1** hang loosely **2 keep someone dangling** keep someone waiting and not knowing what the result will be

dan·ish /ˈdeɪnɪʃ/ *n* pastry with fruit center: *prune danish*

dank /dæŋk/ *adj* unpleasantly wet and cold

dap·per /ˈdæpər/ *adj* neatly dressed

dap·pled /ˈdæpəld/ *adj* having cloudy spots of color or shadow

dare /deər/ *v* **1** *vi* be brave enough (to): *He didn't dare (to) ask.* **2** *vt* CHALLENGE to do something: *I dared her to jump.* ♦ *n* CHALLENGE: *She jumped for a dare.*

dare·dev·il /ˈdeərˌdevəl/ *n* person foolishly fond of adventure

dar·ing /ˈdɛərɪŋ/ n [U] bravery ♦ adj 1 brave 2 shocking ~**ly** adv

dark /dɑrk/ adj 1 without (much) light: *dark room* 2 tending towards black: *dark green* 3 secret; hidden: *dark mysteries* 4 evil; sad ♦ n [U] 1 absence of light 2 after/before dark after/before night 3 in the dark not knowing something ~**en** vi/t make or become darker ~**ly** adv ~**ness** n [U]

Dark Ag·es /ˈ· ˌ··/ n [the+P] period in Europe between about AD 476 to AD 1000

dark horse /ˌ· ˈ·/ n unknown competitor who may win

dark·room /ˈdɑrkruːm, -rʊm/ n room where photographs are developed and printed

dar·ling /ˈdɑrlɪŋ/ adj, n dearly loved (person)

darn¹ /dɑrn/ vt/i mend (holes in cloth) ♦ n darned hole

darn² n, adj, interj DAMN

dart /dɑrt/ n 1 pointed object to throw, esp. in a game called **darts** 2 quick movement ♦ vi/t move or send suddenly

dart·board /ˈdɑrtbɔrd, -boʷrd/ n circular board at which darts are thrown

dash /dæʃ/ v 1 vi run quickly 2 vi/t strike violently: *The waves dashed the boat against the rocks.* 3 vt destroy (hopes, etc.) ♦ n 1 [C] sudden quick run or short race 2 [C] small amount added: *a dash of pepper* 3 [C] the mark (–) 4 [U] combination of bravery and style: *I admire his dash.* ~**ing** adj having a lot of DASH (4)

dash·board /ˈdæʃbɔrd, -boʷrd/ n instrument board in a car

da·ta /ˈdeʲtə, ˈdætə, ˈdɑtə/ n [P;U] facts; information, esp. as stored in a computer's **data bank** for **data processing**

da·ta·base /ˈdeʲtəˌbeʲs/ n computer's collection of data

date¹ /deʲt/ n 1 day, month, or year of an event 2 arrangement to meet 3 person of the opposite sex whom one arranges to meet socially 4 **out of date: a** old-fashioned **b** no longer VALID 5 **to date** up till now 6 **up to date** modern

date² v 1 vt guess the date of 2 vt write the date on 3 vi become old-fashioned 4 vi/t make a social date with **dated** adj old fashioned

   date from also **date back to** phr vt has lasted since

date³ n small tropical fruit with a long pit

daub /dɔb/ vt cover with something sticky

daugh·ter /ˈdɔtər/ n someone's female child

daughter-in-law /ˈ··· · ˌ·/ n **daughters-in-law** son's wife

daunt /dɔnt, dɑnt/ vt discourage ~**less** adj not discouraged

daw·dle /ˈdɔdl/ vi waste time; be slow

dawn¹ /dɔn/ n 1 [C;U] first light of morning 2 [S] first appearance: *the dawn of civilization*

dawn² vi begin to grow light

   dawn on phr vt become known to: *The truth dawned on me.*

day /deʲ/ n 1 [C] period of 24 hours 2 [C;U] time between sunrise and sunset: *the daylight hours | in the daytime* 3 [C] hours that one works 4 [C] period; time: *the present day* 5 [S] period of success 6 **call it a day** finish working for the day 7 **day after day** also **day in, day out** continuously 8 **make someone's day** make someone very happy 9 **one day** at some time 10 **one's days** one's life 11 **the other day** recently 12 **these days** now

day·break /ˈdeʲbreʲk/ n [U] DAWN (1)

day-care cen·ter /ˈdeʲkɛər ˌsɛntər/ n public NURSERY for babies

day·dream /ˈdeʲdriʷm/ vi, n (have) pleasant dreamlike thoughts

day·light sav·ing time /ˌdeʲlaɪt ˈseʲvɪŋ ˌtaɪm/ n time used in the summer when clocks move ahead one hour

day·lights /ˈdeʲlaɪts/ n [P] **beat/knock/scare the (living) daylights out of** hit/frighten (someone) very severely

day-to-day /ˌ· · ˈ·◂/ adj 1 happening each day: *We just live day-to-day.* 2 planning for one day at a time

daze /deʲz/ vt make unable to think clearly ♦ n dazed condition

daz·zle /ˈdæzəl/ vt 1 make unable to see because of too strong light 2 cause wonder to: *dazzled by success*

dea·con /ˈdiʲkən/ ~**ess** /-kənɪs/ fem. — Christian church officer below a priest

dead¹ /dɛd/ adj 1 no longer alive 2 no longer used or usable: *dead languages/battery | The telephone went dead.* 3 complete: *dead silence* 4 without activity: *the place seems dead* 5 NUMB: *My fingers went dead.* 6 (of sound or color) dull ♦ adv 1 completely: *stop dead* 2 directly: *dead ahead* ~**en** vt cause to lose (strength, feeling, brightness): *deaden pain/noise*

dead² n **in the dead of** in the greatest or least active period of

dead·beat /ˈdɛdbiːt/ n lazy aimless person

dead cen·ter /ˌ· ˈ··/ n exact center

dead end /ˌ· ˈ·/ n end of a street) with no way out: (fig.) *We've reached a dead end in our talks.*

dead heat /ˌ· ˈ·/ n race in which the competitors finish together

dead let·ter /ˌ· ˈ·/ n letter that can't be delivered because the address is wrong

dead·line /ˈdɛdlaɪn/ n fixed date for finishing something

dead·lock /ˈdɛdlɑk/ n disagreement that cannot be settled

dead·ly /ˈdɛdliʸ/ adj 1 likely to cause death 2 total: *deadly enemies* 3 *infml* very dull ♦ adv 1 like death: *deadly pale* 2 very: *deadly dull*

dead·pan /ˈdɛdpæn/ adj, adv with no show of feeling, esp. when telling jokes

dead ring·er /ˌ· ˈ··/ n someone who looks exactly like someone else

dead·weight /ˈdɛdˌweʸt/ n [S] whole weight of something that does not move

dead wood /ˈ· ·/ n [U] useless people or things

deaf /dɛf/ adj 1 unable to hear 2 **deaf to** unwilling to listen to ~**en** vt (of loud noises) make unable to hear: *The noise was deafening.* (= very loud) ~**ness** n [U]

deaf-mute /ˈ· ·/ n, adj (person) who is deaf and cannot speak

deal¹ /diʸl/ vi/t **dealt** /dɛlt/ 1 give out (esp. playing cards) as a share 2 strike: *deal someone a blow* ~**er** n 1 person who deals cards 2 person in business: *car dealer* ~**ing** n [U] methods of business or personal relations ~**ings** n [P] personal or business relations

deal in phr vt do business in; sell

deal with phr vt 1 do business with 2 take action about 3 be about: *a book dealing with Ireland*

deal² n 1 [C] business arrangement 2 [C] one's turn to deal cards 3 **a good/great deal** 1 [U] a fairly/very large amount: *work a good deal faster* 2 [C] something sold cheap

dean /diʸn/ n 1 important university official 2 Christian priest in charge of several others

dear /dɪər/ adj 1 loved; precious 2 (at the beginning of letters): *Dear Sir* ♦ n 1 loved person 2 (used when speaking to someone you love): *Yes, dear.* ♦ interj (expressing surprise, sorrow, etc.): *Oh dear!* ~**ly** adv 1 with much feeling 2 at terrible cost

dearth /dɜrθ/ n [S] fml lack

death /dɛθ/ n 1 [C;U] end of life: (fig.) *the death of our hopes* 2 [U] state of being dead 3 cause of death: *Drinking will be the death of him.* 4 **at death's door** in danger of dying; about to die 5 **like death warmed up** infml very ill or tired 6 **put to death** kill, esp. officially 7 **to death** beyond proper limits: *sick/*

bored/worried to death ~**less** adj unforgettable ~**ly** adj, adv like death

death row /ˌdɛθ ˈroʸ/ n prison area for those waiting for the death sentence

death tax /ˈ· ·/ n tax paid on property after death

death trap /ˈ· ·/ n very dangerous thing or place

dé·bâ·cle /deʸˈbɑkəl, dɪ-/ n sudden complete failure

de·bar /dɪˈbɑr/ v -rr- **debar from** phr vt officially prevent from

de·base /dɪˈbeʸs/ vt make lower in value ~**ment** n [C;U]

de·bate /dɪˈbeʸt/ n [C;U] (process of) discussion (DISCUSS) ♦ vi/t 1 hold a debate about 2 think about; wonder **debatable** adj doubtful; questionable

de·bauch /dɪˈbɔtʃ/ vt lead away from moral behavior, esp. in relation to sex and alcohol ♦ n ORGY ~**ed** adj ~**ery** n [U]

de·bil·i·tate /dɪˈbɪləˌteʸt/ vt make weak ~**ty** n [U] fml weakness

deb·it /ˈdɛbɪt/ n record of money owed ♦ vt charge against an account

deb·o·nair /ˌdɛbəˈnɛər◂/ adj cheerful and fashionably dressed

de·brief /diʸˈbriʸf/ vt find out information from (someone on one's own side) by thorough questioning after an action

deb·ris /dəˈbriʸ, deʸ-/ n [U] broken remains; ruins

debt /dɛt/ n [C;U] something owed; state of owing ~**or** n person who owes money

de·bug /diʸˈbʌg/ vt infml 1 remove the BUGs (3) from a room or building 2 search for and remove the BUGs (5) in (a computer PROGRAM)

de·bunk /diʸˈbʌŋk, dɪ-/ vt point out the truth about a wrong idea

de·but /deʸˈbyuʷ, dɪ-, ˈdeʸbyuʷ/ n first public appearance

dec·ade /ˈdɛkeʸd/ n period of 10 years

dec·a·dent /ˈdɛkədənt/ adj falling to a lower level of morals ~**dence** n [U]

de·cal /ˈdiʸkæl, ˈdɛkəl/ n picture for sticking or printing onto a surface

de·camp /dɪˈkæmp/ vi go away quickly and esp. secretly

de·cant /dɪˈkænt/ vt pour (liquid) into another container ~**er** n glass container for liquid, esp. wine

de·cap·i·tate /dɪˈkæpəˌteʸt/ vt BEHEAD

de·cath·lon /dɪˈkæθlɑn, -lən/ n ATHLETIC competition with 10 separate events

de·cay /dɪˈkeʸ/ vi 1 go bad: *decayed*

teeth **2** lose health, power, etc. ♦ *n* [U] process of decaying

de·ceased /dɪˈsiʲst/ *adj fml* dead ♦ *n fml* the dead person

de·ceit /dɪˈsiʲt/ *n* [U] dishonesty ~**ful** *adj* dishonest ~**fully** *adv*

de·ceive /dɪˈsiʲv/ *vt* cause to believe something false **deceiver** *n*

de·cel·e·rate /ˌdiʲˈsɛləˌreʲt/ *vi/t* (cause to) go slower

De·cem·ber /dɪˈsɛmbər/ *n* the 12th and last month of the year

de·cent /ˈdiʲsənt/ *adj* **1** socially acceptable; proper **2** good enough: *a decent meal* **3** kind **decency** *n* [U] being DECENT (1)

de·cen·tral·ize /ˌdiʲˈsɛntrəˌlaɪz/ *vi/t* move (a business, etc.) from a central office or place to several smaller ones

de·cep·tion /dɪˈsɛpʃən/ *n* **1** [U] deceiving **2** [C] trick **~tive** /-tɪv/ *adj* misleading **~tively** *adv*

dec·i·bel /ˈdɛsəˌbɛl, -bəl/ *n* unit of loudness

de·cide /dɪˈsaɪd/ *v* **1** *vi/t* make a choice or judgment: *She decided to go.* **2** *vt* make (someone) decide **3** *vi/t* end uncertain state **decided** *adj* **1** easily seen: *decided improvement* **2** sure of oneself **decidedly** *adv* certainly

    decide on *phr vt* decide in favor of

de·cid·u·ous /dɪˈsɪdʒuʷəs/ *adj* (of trees) losing their leaves in autumn

dec·i·mal /ˈdɛsəməl/ *adj* based on the number 10 ♦ *n* number such as .5 or .06 **~ize** *vi/t* change to a decimal system of money, etc.

dec·i·mate /ˈdɛsəˌmeʲt/ *vt* destroy a large part of

de·ci·pher /dɪˈsaɪfər/ *vt* read (something difficult, esp. a CODE)

de·ci·sion /dɪˈsɪʒən/ *n* **1** [C;U] deciding; choice: *reach a decision* **2** [U] firmness of judgment

de·ci·sive /dɪˈsaɪsɪv/ *adj* **1** firm in judgment **2** leading to a clear result ~**ly** *adv* ~**ness** *n* [U]

deck[1] /dɛk/ *n* **1** floor of a ship **2** PACK of playing cards **3** raised wooden PORCH

deck[2] *vt* **1** decorate **2** **decked out** dressed or decorated for a special occasion

deck·chair /ˈdɛktʃɛər/ *n* folding chair with a cloth seat (also **beach chair**)

de·claim /dɪˈkleʲm/ *vt fml* say loudly, like an actor

dec·la·ra·tion /ˌdɛkləˈreʲʃən/ *n* [C;U] **1** declaring **2** official statement

de·clare /dɪˈklɛər/ *vt* **1** make known officially: *declare war* **2** state clearly **3** tell CUSTOMS officials about (taxable goods)

de·clas·si·fy /ˌdiʲˈklæsəˌfaɪ/ *vt* declare (esp. political and military information) no longer secret

de·cline /dɪˈklaɪn/ *v* **1** *vi* become worse or less **2** *vt/i* refuse (an invitation, etc.) politely **3** process of declining (DECLINE (1)): *Interest in the arts is on the decline.*

de·code /ˌdiʲˈkoʷd/ *vt* read (something written in CODE)

de·col·o·nize, -ise /ˌdiʲˈkaləˌnaɪz/ *vt* give political independence to ~**nization** /ˌdiʲkalənəˈzeʲʃən/ *n* [U]

de·com·pose /ˌdiʲkəmˈpoʷz/ *vi* go bad; DECAY **-position** /ˌdiʲkampəˈzɪʃən/ *n* [U]

de·com·press /ˌdiʲkəmˈprɛs/ *vt/i* **1** reduce air pressure on **2** relax ~**ion** /-ˈprɛʃən/ *n* [U]

de·con·tam·i·nate /ˌdiʲkənˈtæməˌneʲt/ *vt* remove dangerous substances from ~**nation** /-ˌtæməˈneʲʃən/ *n* [U]

dé·cor /deʲˈkɔr, ˈdeʲkɔr/ *n* decoration and furnishings of a place

dec·o·rate /ˈdɛkəˌreʲt/ *v* **1** *vt* add something beautiful to **2** *vi/t* paint, put paper, etc., on rooms **3** *vt* give a mark of honor, such as a MEDAL, etc. to, **-rator** *n* person who decorates houses **-rative** /ˈdɛkərətɪv, ˈdɛkəreʲ-/ *adj* beautiful; attractive **-ration** /ˌdɛkəˈreʲʃən/ *n* **1** [U] decorating **2** [C] something that decorates **3** [C] mark of honor, MEDAL, etc.

dec·o·rous /ˈdɛkərəs/ *adj* (of appearance or behavior) correct

de·co·rum /dɪˈkɔrəm, -ˈkoʷr-/ *n* [U] *fml* correct behavior

de·coy /ˈdiʲkɔɪ, dɪˈkɔɪ/ *n* something used for getting a person or bird into a trap **decoy** /dɪˈkɔɪ/ *vt*

de·crease[1] /dɪˈkriʲs/ *vi/t* (cause to) become less

de·crease[2] /ˈdiʲkriʲs/ *n* **1** [U] process of decreasing **2** [C] amount by which something decreases

de·cree /dɪˈkriʲ/ *n* official command or decision ♦ *vt* order officially

de·crep·it /dɪˈkrɛpɪt/ *adj* weak from old age

de·cry /dɪˈkraɪ/ *vt fml* speak disapprovingly of

ded·i·cate /ˈdɛdəˌkeʲt/ *vt* **1** give to a serious purpose: *dedicate her life to medical research* | *a dedicated doctor* **2** declare (a book, etc.) to be in honor of someone, by printing their name at the front **-cation** /ˌdɛdəˈkeʲʃən/ *n* **1** [C;U] act of dedicating **2** [U] words used in dedicating a book

de·duce /dɪˈduʷs, dɪˈdyuʷs/ *vt* reach (a piece of knowledge) by reasoning

de·duct /dɪˈdʌkt/ vt take away (part) from a total ~ **ible** adj: expenses deductible from tax

de·duc·tion /dɪˈdʌkʃən/ n [C;U] **1** example of deducing; knowledge deduced: a brilliant deduction **2** process of deducting; something deducted: a salary of $20,000 after all deductions

deed /diːd/ n **1** lit something done; action **2** law signed agreement

deem /diːm/ vt fml consider; judge

deep /diːp/ adj **1** going far down from the top, or in from the outside: deep river/wound | ankle-deep in mud **2** (of color) dark **3** (of sound) low **4** strong; extreme: deep sleep | deep distrust | in deep trouble **5** difficult to understand **6** a wise: a deep thinker b mysterious: a deep secret **7** go off the deep end sl become confused **8** in/into deep water infml in/into serious trouble **9** thrown in at the deep end suddenly and unexpectedly faced with a difficult piece of work ♦ adv far down; far in. ~ **en** vi/t make or become deeper ~ **ly** adv ~ **ness** n [U]

deep freeze /ˌ· ˈ·/ vt freeze food quickly in order to preserve it ♦ n FREEZER

deep fry /ˈ· ·/ vt FRY completely under the surface of oil or fat

deep-root·ed /ˌ· ˈ··◂/ also **deep-seated** — adj strongly fixed: deep-rooted habits

deer /dɪər/ n large fast animal of which the males have ANTLERS

de·face /dɪˈfeɪs/ vt spoil the surface of ~ **ment** n [U]

de fac·to /ˌdeɪ ˈfæktoʊ, dɪ-/ adj, adv fml in actual fact, though not by law

de·fame /dɪˈfeɪm/ vt fml attack the good REPUTATION of **defamation** /ˌdefəˈmeɪʃən/ n [U] **defamatory** /dɪˈfæməˌtɔːriʸ, -ˌtoʊriʸ/ adj

de·fault /dɪˈfɔːlt/ n [U] failure to fulfil a contract, pay a debt, etc. **default** vi ~ **er** n

de·feat /dɪˈfiːt/ vt **1** win a victory over **2** cause to fail ♦ n [C;U] (example of) defeating ~ **ism** n [U] practice of thinking or behaving in expectation of defeat ~ **ist** n

def·e·cate /ˈdefəˌkeɪt/ vi fml pass waste matter from the bowels

de·fect[1] /ˈdiːfekt, dɪˈfekt/ n imperfection; fault ~ **ive** /dɪˈfektɪv/ adj

de·fect[2] /dɪˈfekt/ vi desert one's political party, country, etc. ~ **or** n ~ **ion** /-ˈfekʃən/ n [C;U]

de·fense /dɪˈfens/ n **1** [U] act or process of defending **2** [C] something used in defending **3** [C;U] law a arguments used in defending someone in court b lawyers who defend someone **4** players or part of a game that stops the other team from making points ~ **less** adj unable to defend oneself

de·fend /dɪˈfend/ vt **1** keep safe; protect **2** act as a lawyer for (someone charged with a crime) **3** argue in favor of

de·fen·dant /dɪˈfendənt/ n person against whom a legal charge or claim is brought

de·fen·si·ble /dɪˈfensəbəl/ adj that can be defended

de·fen·sive /dɪˈfensɪv/ adj **1** used in defense **2** (of someone) who always seems to be expecting attack ♦ n **on the defensive** prepared for attack ~ **ly** adv ~ **ness** n [U]

de·fer /dɪˈfɜr/ vt ‑rr‑ POSTPONE ~ **ment** n [C;U]

defer to phr vt fml accept the decision of

def·er·ence /ˈdefərəns/ n [U] fml respect for another's wishes

de·fi·ance /dɪˈfaɪəns/ n [U] open disobedience ~ **ant** adj ~ **antly** adv

de·fi·cien·cy /dɪˈfɪʃənsiʸ/ n [C;U] lack: vitamin deficiency ‑cient adj

def·i·cit /ˈdefəsɪt/ n amount by which something, esp. money, is too little

de·file /dɪˈfaɪl/ vt fml make dirty

de·fine /dɪˈfaɪn/ vt **1** give the meaning of; explain exactly **2** set, mark or show the limits of: a clearly-defined shape

def·i·nite /ˈdefənɪt/ adj clear; ~ **ly** adv **1** in a clear way **2** certainly

definite ar·ti·cle /ˌ··· ˈ···/ n (in English) the word THE

def·i·ni·tion /ˌdefəˈnɪʃən/ n **1** [C;U] (statement) defining something **2** [U] clearness of shape: The photograph lacks definition.

de·fin·i·tive /dɪˈfɪnətɪv/ adj that cannot be questioned; not needing change

de·flate /dɪˈfleɪt, diː-/ v **1** vt let air or gas out of (a tire, etc.) **2** vi/t reduce the supply of money in a country **deflation** /-ˈfleɪʃən/ n [U] **deflationary** adj

de·flect /dɪˈflekt/ vi/t turn aside from a straight course: (fig.) to deflect someone from their purpose ~ **ion** /-ˈflekʃən/ n [C;U]

de·form /dɪˈfɔːrm/ vt spoil the shape of ~ **ity** n [C;U] imperfection of the body

de·fraud /dɪˈfrɔːd/ vt deceive so as to get something: They defrauded him of $50.

de·fray /dɪˈfreɪ/ vt fml pay for

de·frost /dɪˈfrɔːst/ vt remove ice from; unfreeze

deft /deft/ adj effortlessly skillful ~ **ly** adv

de·funct /dɪˈfʌŋkt/ adj dead

de·fuse /diːˈfjuːz/ vt 1 remove the FUSE from (a bomb, etc.) 2 make harmless

de·fy /dɪˈfaɪ/ vt 1 refuse to obey a CHALLENGE to do something impossible 3 remain unreachable by all efforts at or from: *It defies description.*

de·gen·e·rate /dɪˈdʒenərɪt/ adj having become worse than before ♦ n degenerate person ♦ vi /-nəˌreɪt/ become worse **-rative** /-nərətɪv/ adj **-ration** /dɪˌdʒenəˈreɪʃən/ n [U]

de·grade /dɪˈgreɪd/ v 1 vt bring shame to 2 vi/t change to a simpler chemical form **degradation** /ˌdegrəˈdeɪʃən/ n [C;U]

de·gree /dɪˈgriː/ n 1 unit of measurement of angles, or of temperature 2 stage; level: *getting better by degrees* 3 title given to a university student – see also THIRD DEGREE

de·hy·drate /diːˈhaɪdreɪt/ vt remove water from

de·i·fy /ˈdiːəˌfaɪ, ˈdeɪ-/ vt make a god of

deign /deɪn/ vt derog CONDESCEND

de·i·ty /ˈdiːəti, ˈdeɪ-/ n god or goddess

de·jec·ted /dɪˈdʒektɪd/ adj low in spirits; sad **-tion** /-ˈdʒekʃən/ n

de·lay /dɪˈleɪ/ v 1 vt make later 2 vi act slowly ♦ n 1 [U] delaying 2 [C] example or time of being delayed

de·lec·ta·ble /dɪˈlektəbəl/ adj delightful; DELICIOUS

del·e·gate¹ /ˈdelɪgət/ n person chosen to act for others

del·e·gate² /ˈdeləˌgeɪt/ v 1 vi/t give (power, etc.) to someone else 2 vt appoint (someone) as a delegate **-gation** /ˌdeləˈgeɪʃən/ n 1 [U] act of delegating 2 [C] group of delegates

de·lete /dɪˈliːt/ vt take out (written words) **deletion** /-ˈliːʃən/ n [C;U]

del·e·te·ri·ous /ˌdeləˈtɪəriəs/ adj fml harmful

del·i /ˈdeli/ n, infml DELICATESSEN

de·lib·e·rate¹ /dɪˈlɪbərɪt/ adj 1 done on purpose 2 (of speech, movement, etc.) slow; unhurried **-ly** adv

de·lib·e·rate² /dɪˈlɪbəˌreɪt/ vi/t fml consider carefully **-ration** /dɪˌlɪbəˈreɪʃən/ n fml 1 [C;U] (process of) deliberating 2 [U] being slow and unhurried

del·i·ca·cy /ˈdelɪkəsi/ n 1 [U] being delicate 2 [C] something good to eat

del·i·cate /ˈdelɪkɪt/ adj 1 easily damaged, hurt, or made ill 2 soft and fine: *delicate silk* 3 needing careful treatment: *a delicate situation* 4 easily spoiled but not easy to recognize: *a delicate flavor* 5 sensitive: *delicate instruments* **-ly** adv

del·i·ca·tes·sen /ˌdelɪkəˈtesən/ also **deli** infml — n store that sells ready cooked foods and sandwiches

de·li·cious /dɪˈlɪʃəs/ adj (esp. of taste or smell) delightful **-ly** adv

de·light /dɪˈlaɪt/ n 1 [U] great pleasure; joy 2 [C] cause of great pleasure ♦ v 1 give delight to 2 vi find delight: *He delights in scandal.* **-ful** adj very pleasing **-fully** adv

de·lin·e·ate /dɪˈlɪniˌeɪt/ vt fml show by drawing

de·lin·quent /dɪˈlɪŋkwənt/ n, adj (person) who breaks a law **-quency** n [U]

de·lir·i·ous /dɪˈlɪəriəs/ adj excited and dreamy, esp. because of illness **-ly** adv **-ium** /-riəm/ n [U] excited dreamy state

de·liv·er /dɪˈlɪvər/ vt 1 take (goods, letters, etc.) to people's houses 2 help in the birth of 3 give (a blow, kick, etc.) 4 say (a speech, etc.) 5 fml rescue **-er** n fml rescuer **-ance** n [U] fml saving; rescue **-y** n 1 [C;U] delivering things; things delivered 2 [C] birth of a child 3 [C;U] style of public speaking

del·ta /ˈdeltə/ n land in the shape of a TRIANGLE at the mouth of a river

de·lude /dɪˈluːd/ vt mislead; deceive

del·uge /ˈdeljuːdʒ/ n heavy rain; flood **deluge** vt

de·lu·sion /dɪˈluːʒən/ n 1 [U] deluding 2 [C] false belief

de luxe /dɪ ˈlʌks, -ˈlʊks/ adj of very high quality

delve /delv/ vi search deeply

Dem /dem/ abbrev. for: DEMOCRAT

dem·a·gogue /ˈdeməˌgɒg, -ˌgɔːg/ n leader who gains power by exciting the crowds

de·mand /dɪˈmænd/ n 1 [C] demanding; claim 2 [S;U] desire for things that people can pay for: *a great demand for teachers* ♦ v 1 ask for firmly; claim 2 need: *problems demanding your attention* **-ing** adj needing a lot of attention or effort

de·mar·ca·tion /ˌdiːmɑːrˈkeɪʃən/ n [U] limits; separation

de·mean /dɪˈmiːn/ vt fml bring shame to; DEGRADE

de·mea·nor /dɪˈmiːnər/ n [U] fml behavior

de·ment·ed /dɪˈmentɪd/ adj crazy

de·mer·it /diːˈmerɪt/ n fml fault

de·mil·i·ta·rize /ˌdiːˈmɪlətəˌraɪz/ vt remove armed forces from (an area) **-rization** /ˌdiːˌmɪlətərəˈzeɪʃən/ n [U]

de·mise /dɪˈmaɪz/ n [U] law death

dem·o /ˈdemoʊ/ n infml demos DEMONSTRATION (2)

de·mo·bi·lize /diːˈmoʊbəˌlaɪz/ vi/t fml send home the members of (an armed force), usu. at the end of a war

de·moc·ra·cy /dɪˈmɑːkrəsi/ n 1 [U]

government by elected representatives of the people **2** [C] country governed in this way **3** [U] social equality

dem·o·crat /'demə,kræt/ n **1** person who believes in democracy **2** (cap.) member of the Democratic Party **~ic** /ˌdemə'krætɪk◄/ adj **1** of or favoring democracy **2** (cap.) of a US political party (the **Democratic Party**) **~ically** /-kliʸ/ adv

Democrat n member or supporter of the **Democratic Party**, one of the two largest political parties of the US **~ic** adj

de·mog·ra·phy /dɪ'mɑgrəfiʸ/ n [U] study of the numbers, types, habits and movement of human population **~phic** /ˌdemə'græfɪk, ˌdiʸ-◄/ adj

de·mol·ish /dɪ'mɑlɪʃ/ vt **1** pull down (buildings, etc.); destroy **2** infml eat up hungrily **~molition** /ˌdemə-'lɪʃən/ n [C;U]

de·mon /'diʸmən/ n **1** evil spirit **2** very active skillful person **~ic** /dɪ-'mɑnɪk/ adj of, by or like a demon

dem·on·stra·ble /dɪ'mɑnstrəbəl/ adj fml easily proved **~bly** adv

dem·on·strate /'demən,streʸt/ v **1** vt show clearly **2** vi take part in a public demonstration **~strator** n **~stration** /ˌdemən'streʸʃən/ n **1** [C;U] showing something **2** [C;U] also **demo** — a public show of opinion, by marching, etc. **b** showing of a product to attract buyers: software demo

de·mon·stra·tive /dɪ'mɑnstrətɪv/ adj showing feelings openly

de·mor·al·ize /dɪ'mɔrə,laɪz, -'mɑr-/ vt destroy the courage and confidence of **~ization** /dɪ,mɔrələ-'zeʸʃən, dɪ,mɑ-/ n [U]

de·mote /dɪ'moʷt/ vt reduce in rank **demotion** /dɪ'moʷʃən/ n [C;U]

de·mur /dɪ'mɜr/ vi **-rr-** fml show opposition to a plan

de·mure /dɪ'myʊər/ adj quiet and MODEST **~ly** adv

den /den/ n **1** home of a wild animal **2** secret or private place **3** small, quiet room in a house

de·na·tion·al·ize /diʸ'næʃənəl,aɪz/ vt remove from state ownership **~ization** /ˌdiʸnæʃənələ'zeʸʃən/ n [C;U]

de·ni·al /dɪ'naɪəl/ n **1** [U] denying (DENY) **2** [C] statement that something is false

den·i·grate /'denə,greʸt/ vt declare to be worthless

den·im /'denəm/ n [U] strong cotton cloth **denims** n [P] JEANS

den·i·zen /'denəzən/ n lit person that lives in a particular place

de·nom·i·na·tion /dɪ,nɑmə'neʸʃən/ n **1** religious group **2** unit of value

de·nom·i·na·tor /dɪ'nɑmə,neʸtər/ n see COMMON DENOMINATOR

de·note /dɪ'noʷt/ vt be the name or sign of; mean

de·noue·ment /ˌdeʸnuʷ'mɑŋ/ n end of a story, when everything is explained

de·nounce /dɪ'naʊns/ vt speak or write publicly against

dense /dens/ adj **1** closely packed **2** hard to see through: dense fog **3** stupid **~ly** adv **density** n [C;U]

dent /dent/ n **1** small hollow in a surface, made by a blow **2 make a dent in** make a first step towards success in ♦ vt make a dent

den·tal /'dentəl/ adj of the teeth

den·tist /'dentɪst/ n person trained to treat the teeth **~ry** n [U]

den·tures /'dentʃərz/ n [P] false teeth

de·nude /dɪ'nuʷd, dɪ'nyuʷd/ vt fml remove the covering from: a hill denuded of trees

de·nun·ci·a·tion /dɪ,nʌnsiʸ'eʸʃən/ n [C;U] act or example of denouncing (DENOUNCE)

de·ny /dɪ'naɪ/ vt **1** declare untrue **2** refuse to allow

de·o·do·rant /diʸ'oʷdərənt/ n [C;U] chemical that hides bad smells

de·part /dɪ'pɑrt/ vi fml leave; go away **2 depart this life** lit to die **~ed** adj gone for ever

depart from phr vt turn or move away from

de·part·ment /dɪ'pɑrtmənt/ n **1** division of a government, business, college, etc. **2** infml activity or subject for which a person is responsible **~al** /ˌdiʸpɑrt'mentl, dɪ,pɑrt-/ adj

department store /·'·· ˌ·/ n large store divided into departments

de·par·ture /dɪ'pɑrtʃər/ n [C;U] going away: (fig.) a new departure (= change from a usual course of action) in television

de·pend /dɪ'pend/ v **1** [it+vt] vary according to; be decided by: It depends how much you want to spend. **2 That (all) depends/It all depends** That/It has not yet been decided

depend on/upon phr vt **1** trust **2** be supported by **3** vary according to

de·pen·da·ble /dɪ'pendəbəl/ adj that can be trusted

de·pen·dant, -dent /dɪ'pendənt/ n person supported by another

de·pen·dence /dɪ'pendəns/ n [U] **1** being dependent: our dependence on oil **2** trust **3** need to have certain drugs regularly

de·pen·dent /dɪ'pendənt/ adj that depends on

de·pict /dɪˈpɪkt/ vt fml show in a picture, or in words

de·pil·a·to·ry /dɪˈpɪləˌtɔriʸ, -ˌtoʷriʸ/ n, adj (substance) that gets rid of unwanted hair

de·plete /dɪˈpliʸt/ vt fml lessen (supplies, etc.) greatly **depletion** /-ˈpliʸʃən/ n [U]

de·plore /dɪˈplɔr, dɪˈploʷr/ vt be very sorry about (and consider wrong) **deplorable** adj very bad

de·ploy /dɪˈplɔɪ/ vt arrange for effective action **~ment** n [U]

de·pop·u·late /ˌdiʸˈpɑpyəˌleʸt/ vt reduce greatly the population

de·port /dɪˈpɔrt, dɪˈpoʷrt/ vt send (an unwanted foreigner) out of the country **~ation** /ˌdiʸpɔrˈteʸʃən, -poʷr-/ n [C;U]

de·port·ment /dɪˈpɔrtmənt, -ˈpoʷrt-/ n [U] way a person stands and walks

de·pose /dɪˈpoʷz/ vt remove (a ruler) from power

de·pos·it¹ /dɪˈpɑzɪt/ vt **1** put down **2** (of a river, etc.) leave (soil, etc.) lying **3** put in a bank, etc., to be safe **~ or** n person who deposits money

deposit² n **1** [C;U] material deposited by a natural process **2** first part of a payment for something, to show that an agreement will be kept

dep·ot /ˈdiʸpoʷ/ n **1** building where goods are stored **2** bus garage **3** train station

de·praved /dɪˈpreʸvd/ adj wicked **depravity** /dɪˈprævətiʸ/ n [C;U]

dep·re·cate /ˈdeprəˌkeʸt/ vt fml express disapproval of

de·pre·ci·ate /dɪˈpriʸʃiʸˌeʸt/ vi (esp. of money) fall in value **–ation** /dɪˌpriʸʃiʸˈeʸʃən/ n [U]

dep·re·da·tions /ˌdeprəˈdeʸʃənz/ n [P] acts of destruction

de·press /dɪˈpres/ vt **1** sadden: *depressing news* **2** make less active **3** fml press down **~ed** adj **1** sad **2** suffering from low levels of business activity

de·pres·sion /dɪˈpreʃən/ n **1** [C;U] sad feeling **2** [C] period of reduced business activity **3** [C] hollow in a surface **4** [C] area of low air pressure

de·prive /dɪˈpraɪv/ vt prevent from having something: *deprive us of our rights* **deprivation** /ˌdeprəˈveʸʃən/ n [C;U]

depth /depθ/ n [C;U] **1** (degree of) being deep **2 in depth** done thoroughly **3 out of one's depth: a** in water deeper than one's height **b** beyond one's understanding **depths** n [the+P] deepest or most central part of: *the depths of winter/ despair*

dep·u·ta·tion /ˌdepyəˈteʸʃən/ n group sent to act on the part of others

dep·u·ty /ˈdepyətiʸ/ n **1** person given power to act for another **2** person working under a public official **–tize** vi act as a deputy

de·rail /dɪˈreʸl, diʸ-/ vt cause (a train) to run off the line **~ment** n [C;U]

de·ranged /dɪˈreʸndʒd/ adj unbalanced in the mind

der·by /ˈdɜrbiʸ/ n man's round hard hat

de·reg·u·late /diʸˈregyəˌleʸt/ vt remove from control by law **–lation** /ˌdiʸregyəˈleʸʃən/ n [U]

der·e·lict /ˈderəlɪkt/ adj fallen into ruin ♦ n person, esp. an alcoholic (ALCOHOL), who has no home and no legal means of support **~ion** /ˌderəˈlɪkʃən/ n **1** state of being derelict **2** failure to do one's duty

de·ride /dɪˈraɪd/ vt fml laugh unkindly at

de·ri·sion /dɪˈrɪʒən/ n [U] unkind laughter **–sive** /dɪˈraɪsɪv/ adj: *derisive laughter* **–sory** adj deserving derision; ABSURD

de·riv·a·tive /dɪˈrɪvətɪv/ adj derog not original or new

de·rive /dɪˈraɪv/ v **1** vt obtain from somewhere: *derive pleasure from one's work* **2** vi have something as an origin: *words that derive from Latin* **derivation** /ˌderəˈveʸʃən/ n [C;U]

der·ma·ti·tis /ˌdɜrməˈtaɪtɪs/ n [U] skin disease with redness and swelling

de·rog·a·to·ry /dɪˈrɑgətɔriʸ, -ˌtoʷriʸ/ adj fml (of words) showing disapproval

der·rick /ˈderɪk/ n **1** large CRANE (1) **2** tower over an oil well

de·scend /dɪˈsend/ vi/t **1** go down **2 be descended from** have as an ANCESTOR **~ant** n person descended from another

descend on/upon phr vt **1** arrive suddenly **2** attack suddenly

de·scent /dɪˈsent/ n **1** [C;U] going down **2** [C] downward slope **3** [U] family origins: *of German descent*

de·scribe /dɪˈskraɪb/ vt **1** say what something is like **2** fml draw the shape of: *describe a circle*

de·scrip·tion /dɪˈskrɪpʃən/ n **1** [C;U] statement that describes **2** [C] sort: *birds of every description* **–tive** /-tɪv/ adj **1** that describes **2** saying how a language is used

des·e·crate /ˈdesəˌkreʸt/ vt spoil (a holy thing or place) **–cration** /ˌdesəˈkreʸʃən/ n [S;U]

de·seg·re·gate /diʸˈsegrɪˌgeʸt/ vt end racial segregation (SEGREGATE) in

des·ert[1] /ˈdezərt/ n large area of dry sandy land

de·sert[2] /dɪˈzɜrt/ v 1 vt leave (a place) empty 2 vt leave (people) cruelly 3 vi leave military service without permission ~er n person who deserts (3) ~ion /-ˈzɜrʃən/ n [C;U]

de·serts /dɪˈzɜrts/ n [P] what someone deserves

de·serve /dɪˈzɜrv/ vt be worthy of: *She deserved to win.* **deservedly** /dɪˈzɜrvɪdliʲ/ adj rightly **deserving** adj

des·ic·cate /ˈdesəˌkeʲt/ vi/t fml dry up

de·sign /dɪˈzaɪn/ vt 1 draw a plan for (something to be made) 2 plan (something) for a purpose: *books designed for use in colleges* ♦ n 1 [C] plan drawn for making something 2 [U] art of designing things 3 [C] decorative pattern 4 [C] plan in the mind **designs** n [P] evil plans: *designs on your life*

des·ig·nate /ˈdezɪgˌneʲt/ vt choose for a particular job or purpose ♦ adj /-nət, -neʲt/ chosen for an office but not yet officially placed in it

de·sign·er[1] /dɪˈzaɪnər/ n person who makes plans or designs

designer[2] adj 1 made by a designer: *designer jeans* 2 humor or derog intended to make the user appear extremely fashionable: *designer stubble/drug*

de·sir·a·ble /dɪˈzaɪərəbəl/ adj worth having; attractive –**bly** adv –**bility** /dɪˌzaɪərəˈbɪlətiʲ/ n [U]

de·sire /dɪˈzaɪər/ vt wish for; want very much ♦ n 1 [C;U] strong wish 2 [C;U] strong wish for sexual relations with 3 [C] something desired **desirous** adj feeling or having a desire

de·sist /dɪˈzɪst, dɪˈsɪst/ vi stop doing

desk /desk/ n table at which one writes or does business: *airport information desk*

desk·top /ˈdesktɑp/ adj being or using a small computer: *desktop publishing*

des·o·late /ˈdesəlɪt/ adj sad and lonely –**lation** /ˌdesəˈleʲʃən/ n [U]

de·spair /dɪˈspeər/ vi lose all hope ♦ n loss of hope ~**ingly** adv

de·spatch /dɪˈspætʃ/ n, v DISPATCH

des·per·ate /ˈdespərɪt/ adj 1 ready for any wild act because of despair 2 very dangerous and without much hope of success ~**ly** adv ~**ation** /ˌdespəˈreʲʃən/ n [U]

des·pic·a·ble /dɪˈspɪkəbəl, ˈdespɪ-/ adj deserving to be despised

de·spise /dɪˈspaɪz/ vt regard as worthless

de·spite /dɪˈspaɪt/ prep in spite of

de·spon·dent /dɪˈspɑndənt/ adj without hope; discouraged –**dency** n [U]

des·pot /ˈdespət, -pɑt/ n ruler with total power who governs cruelly ~**ic** /deˈspɑtɪk, dɪ-/ adj

des·sert /dɪˈzɜrt/ n [C;U] sweet food served at the end of a meal

de·sta·bi·lize /diʲˈsteʲbəˌlaɪz/ vt make (a government, etc.) unsteady

des·ti·na·tion /ˌdestəˈneʲʃən/ n place to which someone or something is going

des·tined /ˈdestnd/ adj intended, esp. by fate: *He was destined to become famous.*

des·ti·ny /ˈdestəniʲ/ n [C;U] fate; what must happen

des·ti·tute /ˈdestəˌtuʷt, -ˌtyuʷt/ adj 1 without food, clothes, shelter, etc. 2 fml lacking in: *destitute of feeling* –**tution** /ˌdestəˈtuʷʃən, -ˈtyuʷ-/ n [U]

de·stroy /dɪˈstrɔɪ/ vt 1 make useless; ruin 2 kill (esp. an animal) ~**er** n 1 someone who destroys 2 small fast fighting ship

de·struc·tion /dɪˈstrʌkʃən/ n [U] destroying; ruin –**tive** /-tɪv/ adj 1 causing destruction 2 not helpful: *destructive criticism*

des·ul·to·ry /ˈdesəlˌtɔriʲ, -ˌtoʷriʲ/ adj fml passing from one thing to another without plan or purpose

de·tach /dɪˈtætʃ/ vt separate from something larger ~**ed** adj 1 (of a house) not joined to others 2 not influenced by personal feelings ~**ment** n 1 [U] being detached (2) 2 [C] group of soldiers, etc.

de·tail /dɪˈteʲl, ˈdiʲteʲl/ n 1 small fact about something 2 small working party of soldiers, etc. ♦ vt 1 describe fully: *a detailed account* 2 appoint (soldiers, etc.) for special work

de·tain /dɪˈteʲn/ vt prevent (someone) from leaving

de·tain·ee /ˌdiʲteʲˈniʲ/ n person detained officially in a camp or prison

de·tect /dɪˈtekt/ vt notice; discover ~**able** adj ~**ive** n person who catches criminals ~**or** n instrument for finding something: *a metal detector* ~**ion** /-ˈtekʃən/ n [U]

dé·tente /deʲˈtɑnt/ n [C;U] calmer political relations between unfriendly countries

de·ten·tion /dɪˈtenʃən, -tʃən/ n [U] act of preventing a person from leaving

detention home /·ˈ··· ˌ·/ n prison school for young offenders

de·ter /dɪˈtɜr/ vt –**rr**– discourage from doing something

de·ter·gent /dɪˈtɜrdʒənt/ n [C;U] (esp. soapless) product for washing things

dial

de·te·ri·o·rate /dɪˈtɪəriʲəˌreʲt/ vi become worse –**ration** /dɪˌtɪəriʲəˈreʲʃən/ n [U]

de·ter·mi·na·tion /dɪˌtɜrməˈneʲʃən/ n [U] **1** strong will to succeed **2** firm intention **3** finding out

de·ter·mine /dɪˈtɜrmɪn/ vt **1** form a firm intention **2** limit; fix **3** find out; calculate

de·ter·min·er /dɪˈtɜrmənər/ n gram word (such as 'his' in 'his new car') that describes a noun and comes before any adjectives that describe the same noun

de·ter·rent /dɪˈtɜrənt/ n, adj (something) that DETERS

de·test /dɪˈtɛst/ vt hate very much ~**able** adj

de·throne /dɪˈθroʷn/ vt remove (a king or queen) from power

det·o·nate /ˈdɛtnˌeʲt/ vi/t explode –**nator** n piece of equipment used for detonating –**nation** /ˌdɛtnˈeʲʃən/ n [C;U]

de·tour /ˈdiʲtuər/ n way around something

de·tract /dɪˈtrækt/ v **detract from** phr vt lessen the value of

de·trac·tor /dɪˈtræktər/ n person who says bad things about another

det·ri·ment /ˈdɛtrəmənt/ n [U] fml harm; damage ~**al** /ˌdɛtrəˈmɛntəl◂/ adj

deuce /duʷs, dyuʷs/ n [U] **1** playing card with number 2 or 2 spots **2** (in tennis) 40 points to each player

de·val·ue /diʲˈvælyuʷ/ vi/t **1** reduce the exchange value of (money) **2** make (a person or action) seem less valuable or important –**uation** /diʲˌvælyuʷˈeʲʃən/ n [C;U]

dev·a·state /ˈdɛvəˌsteʲt/ vt destroy completely –**station** /ˌdɛvəˈsteʲʃən/ n [U]

de·vel·op /dɪˈvɛləp/ v **1** vi/t (cause to) grow or become more advanced **2** vt use (land) for building on **3** vt begin to have: develop measles **4** vt cause (a photograph) to appear on paper –**er** n person who develops land –**ment** n **1** [U] developing **2** [C] new event **3** developed piece of land

de·vel·op·ing coun·try /·ˌ··· ˈ··/ n poor country that is trying to improve its industry and living conditions

de·vi·ant /ˈdiʲviʲənt/ adj different from an accepted standard –**ance** n [U]

de·vi·ate /ˈdiʲviʲˌeʲt/ vi turn away from what is usual –**ation** /ˌdiʲviʲˈeʲʃən/ n [C;U] noticeable difference

de·vice /dɪˈvaɪs/ n **1** instrument or tool **2** plan; trick **3 leave someone to their own devices** leave (someone) alone, without help

dev·il /ˈdɛvəl/ n **1** evil spirit **2** sl person: You lucky devil! ~**ish** adj evil; like the devil ~**ishly** adv very: devilishly hard work

devil's ad·vo·cate /ˌ·· ˈ···/ n person who opposes an idea or plan to test how good it is

devil's food cake /ˈ··· ·/ n chocolate cake with chocolate FROSTING

de·vi·ous /ˈdiʲviʲəs/ adj not direct; not very honest

de·vise /dɪˈvaɪz/ vt plan; invent

de·void /dɪˈvɔɪd/ adj **devoid of** fml empty of: a house devoid of furniture | devoid of human feeling

de·vo·lu·tion /ˌdɛvəˈluʷʃən/ n [U] giving of power to someone else

de·volve /dɪˈvɑlv/ v pass on work

de·vote /dɪˈvoʷt/ vt give completely to something **devoted** adj loyal; loving **devotion** /-ˈvoʷʃən/ n [U] **1** great love **2** devoutness **devotions** n [P] prayers

dev·o·tee /ˌdɛvəˈtiʲ, -ˈteʲ, -voʷ-/ n person who admires someone or something

de·vour /dɪˈvaʊər/ vt **1** eat up hungrily: (fig.) I devoured the book. **2** completely take up the attention of: devoured by hate

de·vout /dɪˈvaʊt/ adj **1** seriously religious **2** deeply felt: a devout hope ~**ly** adv

dew /duʷ, dyuʷ/ n [U] drops of water that form on cold surfaces in the night ~**y** adj wet as if with dew: a dewy-eyed look

dex·ter·i·ty /dɛkˈstɛrəṭiʲ/ n [U] quick cleverness, esp. with one's hands –**terous** /ˈdɛkstərəs/, –**trous** /-trəs/ adj

dex·trose /ˈdɛkstroʷz, -stroʷs/ n [U] form of sugar found in some fruits

di·a·be·tes /ˌdaɪəˈbiʲṭɪs, -ˈbiʲṭiʲz/ n [U] disease in which there is too much sugar in the blood –**tic** /-ˈbɛṭɪk◂/ n, adj (person) suffering from this

di·a·bol·i·cal /ˌdaɪəˈbɑlɪkəl/ adj very cruel or bad ~**ly** /-kliʲ/ adv

di·a·dem /ˈdaɪəˌdɛm/ n lit crown

di·ag·nose /ˈdaɪəgˌnoʷs, ˌdaɪəgˈnoʷs/ vt discover the nature of (a disease)

di·ag·no·sis /ˌdaɪəgˈnoʷsɪs/ n –**ses** /-siʲz/ [C;U] (judgment made by) diagnosing –**nostic** /-ˈnɑstɪk◂/ adj

di·ag·o·nal /daɪˈægənəl/ adj (of a straight line) joining opposite corners of a square, etc. ~**ly** adv

di·a·gram /ˈdaɪəˌgræm/ n plan drawn to explain a shape, idea, etc. ~**matic** /ˌdaɪəgrəˈmæṭɪk/ adj

di·al /ˈdaɪəl/ n **1** marked face of a clock, etc. **2** wheel with holes on a telephone ♦ vi/t –**l**– make a telephone call

di·a·lect /ˈdaɪəˌlɛkt/ n [C;U] variety of a language, spoken in one part of a country

di·a·lec·tic /ˌdaɪəˈlɛktɪk/ n [U] method of arguing according to certain rules

di·a·log /ˈdaɪəˌlɔg, -ˌlɑg/ n [C;U] **1** conversation in a book or play **2** exchange of opinion between leaders, etc.

di·am·e·ter /daɪˈæmətər/ n distance across a circle, measured through the center

di·a·met·ri·cal·ly /ˌdaɪəˈmetrɪkliʸ/ adv completely: *diametrically opposed/opposite*

di·a·mond /ˈdaɪəmənd/ n **1** [C;U] hard valuable precious stone **2** [C] figure with 4 equal sides, standing on one of its points **3** [C] red figure shaped like a diamond on a playing card **4** BASEBALL playing area **5 diamond in the rough** person with qualities needing more development

di·a·per /ˈdaɪəpər/ n cloth worn by a baby to take up waste matter from its body

di·a·phragm /ˈdaɪəˌfræm/ n **1** muscle separating the lungs from the stomach **2** thin plate in a telephone, camera, etc.

di·ar·rhe·a /ˌdaɪəˈriʸə/ n [U] illness in which the bowels are emptied too often

di·a·ry /ˈdaɪəriʸ/ n (book for) a daily record of events in one's life **–rist** n writer of a diary

di·a·tribe /ˈdaɪəˌtraɪb/ n fml violent attack in words

dice /daɪs/ n small 6-sided block with spots on it, used in games [P] – see also DIE² ♦ vt **1** cut (food) into small squares **2 dice with death** take a great risk **~y** adj risky and uncertain

di·chot·o·my /daɪˈkɑtəmiʸ/ n fml division into 2 opposite parts or groups

dick /dɪk/ n **1** sl DETECTIVE **2** taboo sl PENIS

dic·tate¹ /ˈdɪkteʸt, dɪkˈteʸt/ vi/t **1** say (words) for someone else to write down **2** give (orders)

dic·tate² /ˈdɪkteʸt/ n order (esp. from within ourselves): *the dictates of your own conscience*

dic·ta·tion /dɪkˈteʸʃən/ n **1** [U] dictating **2** [C] piece of writing dictated

dic·ta·tor /ˈdɪkteʸtər, dɪkˈteʸtər/ n ruler with complete power **~ship** n [C;U] (country with) government by a dictator **~ial** /ˌdɪktəˈtɔriʸəl, -ˈtoʷr-/ adj

dic·tion /ˈdɪkʃən/ n [U] way in which someone pronounces words

dic·tion·a·ry /ˈdɪkʃəˌneriʸ/ n book giving a list of words in alphabetical order, with their meanings

dic·tum /ˈdɪktəm/ n **-ta** /-tə/ or **-tums** formal statement of opinion

did /dɪd, d;*strong* dɪd/ v past t. of DO

di·dac·tic /daɪˈdæktɪk/ adj fml intending to teach

did·dle /ˈdɪdl/ vt infml **1** waste time **2** cheat

didn't /ˈdɪdnt/ v short for: did not

die¹ /daɪ/ vi **died**, pres p. **dying** /ˈdaɪ-ɪŋ/ **1** stop living; become dead: (fig.) *My love will never die.* | *His secret died with him.* **2 be dying for/to** want very badly **3 die hard** (of beliefs, customs, etc.) take a long time to disappear

die away phr vi fade and then cease

die down phr vi become less: *The excitement soon died down.*

die off phr vi die one by one

die out phr vi become EXTINCT

die² n **1** metal block for shaping coins, etc. **2** singular of DICE

die·hard /ˈdaɪhɑrd/ n person who strongly opposes change

die·sel /ˈdiʸzəl/ n [U] heavy oil used instead of gas, esp. in buses and trains

di·et /ˈdaɪət/ n **1** food and drink usually taken **2** limited list of food and drink that someone is allowed for medical reasons **3 (be/go) on a diet** (be/start) living on a limited list of food usu. in order to lose weight ♦ vi eat according to a DIET (2)

dif·fer /ˈdɪfər/ vi **1** be different **2** disagree

dif·fe·rence /ˈdɪfərəns/ n **1** [C;U] way or fact of being different **2** [C] slight disagreement **3 split the difference** agree on an amount exactly between

dif·fe·rent /ˈdɪfərənt/ adj **1** unlike **2** separate: *They go to different schools.* **3** various: *It comes in different colors.* **4** unusual **~ly** adv

dif·fe·ren·tial /ˌdɪfəˈrenʃəl, -ˈtʃəl/ n amount of difference between things: *pay differentials*

dif·fe·ren·ti·ate /ˌdɪfəˈrenʃiʸeʸt, -ˈtʃiʸ-/ vi/t see a difference (between)

dif·fi·cult /ˈdɪfɪˌkʌlt, -kəlt/ adj **1** hard to do, understand, etc. **2** (of people) not easily pleased

dif·fi·cul·ty /ˈdɪfɪˌkʌltiʸ, -kəl-/ n **1** [U] being difficult; trouble **2** [C] something difficult; problem

dif·fi·dent /ˈdɪfədənt/ adj lacking confidence in oneself **~ly** adv **–dence** n [U]

dif·fuse¹ /dɪˈfyuʷz/ vi/t fml spread freely in all directions **–fusion** /-ˈfyuʷʒən/ n [U]

dif·fuse² /dɪˈfyuʷs/ adj fml 1 diffused² 2 using too many words

dig /dɪg/ vi/t dug /dʌg/, pres p. **dig·ging** 1 break up and move (earth) 2 make (a hole) in this way: dig an underground tunnel 3 like or understand 4 dig someone in the ribs touch someone with one's elbow, as to share a joke ♦ n 1 quick push 2 place being uncovered by archaeologists (ARCHAEOLOGY) 3 unpleasant remark digs n [P] place to live

dig at phr vt speak to (someone) in an unpleasant way: Stop digging at me!

dig in phr v 1 vi/t dig a protective place for oneself; get firmly settled 2 vi start eating

dig out phr vt get out by digging

dig up phr vt find (something buried) by digging: (fig.) dig up an old scandal

di·gest¹ /daɪˈdʒest, dɪ-/ vt 1 change (food) so that the body can use it 2 arrange (facts) in one's mind ~ible adj ~ive adj of or helping in digesting food ~ion /-ˈdʒestʃən/ n ability to digest food

di·gest² /ˈdaɪdʒest/ n short SUMMARY

dig·it /ˈdɪdʒɪt/ n 1 any number from 0 to 9 2 fml finger or toe ~al adj using digits: digital watch ~ize vt use digits to express information

dig·ni·fied /ˈdɪgnəˌfaɪd/ adj having dignity

dig·ni·ta·ry /ˈdɪgnəˌteriʸ/ n fml person of high rank

dig·ni·ty /ˈdɪgnətiʸ/ n [U] 1 nobleness of character 2 formal grand behavior 3 beneath one's dignity below one's standard of moral or social behavior

di·gress /daɪˈgres, dɪ-/ vi fml (of a writer or speaker) move away from the subject ~ion /-ˈgreʃən/ n [C;U]

dike /daɪk/ n 1 bank to hold back water 2 ditch

di·lap·i·dat·ed /dəˈlæpəˌdeʸtɪd/ adj falling to pieces

di·late /daɪˈleʸt, ˈdaɪleʸt/ vi/t (cause to) become wider by stretching: eyes dilated with terror dilation /-ˈleʸʃən/ n [U]

dil·a·to·ry /ˈdɪləˌtoriʸ, -toʷriʸ/ adj too slow in action

di·lem·ma /dəˈlemə/ n difficult choice between 2 things

dil·et·tante /ˌdɪləˈtɑnt/ n, adj (person) who enjoys art or branch of study but does not take it seriously

dil·i·gence /ˈdɪlədʒəns/ n [U] steady effort ~gent adj ~gently adv

di·lute /daɪˈluʷt, dɪ-/ vt make (liquid) weaker and thinner dilution /-ˈluʷʃən/ n [C;U]

dim /dɪm/ adj –mm– 1 (of light) not bright 2 not easy to see 3 sl stupid 4 take a dim view of think badly of ♦ vi/t –mm– make or become dim ~ly adv ~ness n [U]

dime /daɪm/ n 1 coin of US and Canada worth 10 cents 2 a dime a dozen sl common

di·men·sion /dɪˈmenʃən, -tʃən, daɪ-/ n 1 measurement of breadth, length, or height 2 particular area or part of a problem, subject, etc. 3 –dimensional having (so many) dimensions: 2-dimensional dimensions n [P] size

di·min·ish /dɪˈmɪnɪʃ/ vi/t make or become smaller

dim·i·nu·tion /ˌdɪməˈnuʷʃən, -ˈnyuʷ-/ n [C;U] diminishing

di·min·u·tive /dɪˈmɪnyətɪv/ adj fml very small

dim·ple /ˈdɪmpəl/ n small hollow in the cheek, etc.

dim·wit /ˈdɪmwɪt/ n stupid person ~ted /dɪmˈwɪtɪd• / adj

din /dɪn/ n loud unpleasant noise

dine /daɪn/ vi fml eat dinner ♦ -er n 1 cheap restaurant with fast food 2 dining car

dine off phr vt eat for dinner

dine out phr v eat a meal in a restaurant, hotel, etc.

din·ghy /ˈdɪŋgiʸ, ˈdɪŋiʸ/ n small open boat

din·gy /ˈdɪndʒiʸ/ adj dirty and faded

dining car /ˈ·· ·/ also diner — n railroad car where meals are served

dining ta·ble /ˈ·· ˌ··/ n table for having meals on

dink·y /ˈdɪŋkiʸ/ n adj infml very small

din·ner /ˈdɪnər/ n [C;U] main meal of the day, eaten either at midday or in the evening

dinner jack·et /ˈ·· ˌ··/ n man's black (or white) coat for formal evening occasions

di·no·saur /ˈdaɪnəˌsɔr/ n 1 large REPTILE that no longer exists 2 something very large and old-fashioned that no longer works well

dint /dɪnt/ n by dint of by means of

di·o·cese /ˈdaɪəsɪs, -ˌsiʸs, -ˌsiʸz/ n area controlled by a BISHOP –cesan /daɪˈɑsəsən/ adj

dip¹ /dɪp/ v –pp– 1 vt put into a liquid for a moment 2 vi/t drop slightly: temperatures dipped overnight

dip into phr vt 1 use up (money) 2 read (a book) for a short time

dip² n 1 [C] quick swim 2 [C] downward slope 3 [U] liquid into which food is dipped at parties 4 [C] (liquid for) dipping animals: cattle dip

diph·ther·i·a /dɪfˈθɪəriʸə, dɪp-/ n

[U] serious infectious disease of the throat

diph·thong /'dɪfθɒŋ, -θɑŋ, 'dɪp-/ n compound vowel sound

di·plo·ma /dɪ'pləʊmə/ n official paper showing success in studying something: *high school diploma*

di·plo·ma·cy /dɪ'pləʊməsiʸ/ n [U] 1 management of relations between countries 2 skill at dealing with people

dip·lo·mat /'dɪpləˌmæt/ n person whose profession is DIPLOMACY (1) ~**ic** /ˌdɪplə'mætɪk◂/ adj of or having diplomacy ~**ically** /-kliʸ/ adv

diplomatic re·la·tions /ˌ···· · '··/ n [P] connection between 2 countries that each keep an EMBASSY in the other country

dire /daɪər/ adj terrible

di·rect¹ /də'rekt, daɪ-/ vt 1 tell (someone) the way to a place 2 control; manage 3 fml command; order 4 aim

direct² adj 1 going straight: *direct route* 2 with nothing coming between: *direct result* 3 honest; clearly expressed: *direct answer* 4 exact: *direct opposite* ♦ adv without turning aside ~**ly** adv in a direct way 2 at once ~**ness** n [U]

di·rec·tion /də'rekʃən, daɪ-/ n 1 [C] point towards which a person or thing moves or faces 2 [U] control; management **directions** n [P] instructions

di·rec·tive /də'rektɪv, daɪ-/ n official order

direct ob·ject /·ˌ· '··/ n the noun, noun phrase, or PRONOUN that is needed to complete the meaning of a TRANSITIVE verb: *In 'I saw Mary', 'Mary' is the direct object.*

di·rec·tor /də'rektər, daɪ-/ n 1 SENIOR manager of a firm 2 person who directs a play or movie ~**ship** n company director's position

di·rec·to·ry /də'rektəriʸ, daɪ-/ n book or list of names, facts, etc.: *telephone directory*

direct speech /·ˌ· '·/ n [U] gram actual words of a speaker

dirge /dɜrdʒ/ n slow sad song

dirt /dɜrt/ n [U] 1 unclean matter; mud, etc. 2 nasty talk 3 treat someone like dirt treat someone as worthless ~**y** adj 1 not clean 2 unpleasantly concerned with sex: *dirty jokes* 3 unpleasant: *dirty looks* ~**y** vt make dirty ~**ily** adv

dirt cheap /ˌ· '·◂/ adj extremely cheap

dis·a·bil·i·ty /ˌdɪsə'bɪlətiʸ/ n 1 [U] being disabled 2 [C] HANDICAP (1)

dis·a·ble /dɪs'eʸbəl/ vt make unable to use one's body properly –**abled** adj ~**ment** n [C;U]

dis·a·buse /ˌdɪsə'byuʷz/ vt fml free (someone) from a wrong idea

dis·ad·van·tage /ˌdɪsəd'væntɪdʒ/ n [C;U] unfavorable condition ~**ous** /ˌdɪsædvæn'teʸdʒəs, -vən-, dɪsˌæd-/ adj

dis·ad·van·taged /ˌdɪsəd'væntɪdʒd/ adj suffering from a disadvantage with regard to one's social position, family background, etc.

dis·af·fect·ed /ˌdɪsə'fektɪd/ adj lacking (esp. political) loyalty –**fection** /-'fekʃən/ n [U]

dis·a·gree /ˌdɪsə'griʸ/ vi 1 have different opinions 2 be different ~**able** adj unpleasant ~**ably** adv ~**ment** n [C;U] difference of opinion

disagree with phr vt (of food, etc.) make ill

dis·ap·pear /ˌdɪsə'pɪər/ vi 1 go out of sight 2 cease to exist ~**ance** n [C;U]

dis·ap·point /ˌdɪsə'pɔɪnt/ vt fail to fulfil hopes ~**ed** adj sad at not seeing hopes fulfilled ~**ing** adj ~**ingly** adv ~**ment** n 1 [U] being disappointed 2 [C] something disappointing

dis·ap·prove /ˌdɪsə'pruʷv/ vi have an unfavorable opinion –**proval** n [U]

dis·arm /dɪs'ɑrm/ v 1 vt take away weapons from 2 vi reduce a nation's military strength 3 vt drive away the anger of: *a disarming smile* ~**ingly** adv: *smile disarmingly*

dis·ar·ma·ment /dɪs'ɑrməmənt/ n [U] act or principle of DISARMING (2)

dis·ar·ray /ˌdɪsə'reʸ/ n [U] fml disorder

dis·as·so·ci·ate /ˌdɪsə'soʷʃiʸˌeʸt, -siʸ-/ vt DISSOCIATE

dis·as·ter /dɪ'zæstər/ n [C;U] sudden serious misfortune –**trous** adj –**trously** adv

disaster a·re·a /·'··· ·ˌ···/ n place which gets government help because of a disaster

dis·a·vow /ˌdɪsə'vaʊ/ vt fml refuse to admit (knowledge, etc.)

dis·band /dɪs'bænd/ vi/t break up (a group)

dis·be·lief /ˌdɪsbə'liʸf/ n [U] lack of belief

dis·be·lieve /ˌdɪsbə'liʸv/ vi/t refuse to believe

dis·card /dɪ'skɑrd/ vt get rid of; throw away

di·scern /dɪ'sɜrn, dɪ'zɜrn/ vt see or understand esp. with difficulty ~**ible** adj ~**ing** adj able to decide and judge; having good taste ~**ment** n [U]

dis·charge¹ /dɪs'tʃɑrdʒ, 'dɪstʃɑrdʒ/ v 1 vt send (a person) away 2 vt/i let out (gas, liquid, etc.) 3 vt perform (a duty or promise) **4** vt pay (a debt) **5** vt fire (a gun, etc.)

dis·charge² /'dɪstʃɑrdʒ, dɪs'tʃɑrdʒ/ n **1** [U] discharging **2** [C;U] something discharged

di·sci·ple /dɪ'saɪpəl/ n follower of a (religious) leader

dis·ci·pli·nar·i·an /ˌdɪsəpləˈnɛəriʸ-ən/ n person who can make others obey and believes in firm discipline

dis·ci·pli·na·ry /'dɪsəplə,neriʸ/ adj connected with punishment: take disciplinary action

dis·ci·pline /'dɪsəplɪn/ n **1** [U] training to produce obedience and self-control **2** [U] control gained by this training **3** [U] punishment **4** [C] branch of learning ♦ vt **1** train to be obedient **2** punish

dis·claim /dɪs'kleɪm/ vt say one does not own: disclaim responsibility ~**er** n written statement which disclaims

dis·close /dɪs'kloʷz/ vt make (a secret) known

dis·clo·sure /dɪs'kloʷʒər/ n **1** [U] act of disclosing **2** [C] disclosed secret

dis·co /'dɪskoʷ/ n —**cos** club where people dance to recorded music

dis·col·or /dɪs'kʌlər/ vi/t change color for the worse —**oration** /dɪs-ˌkʌlə'reʸʃən/ n [C;U]

dis·com·fort /dɪs'kʌmfərt/ n [C;U] (cause of) being uncomfortable

dis·con·cert /ˌdɪskən'sɜrt/ vt worry; upset ~**ingly** adv

dis·con·nect /ˌdɪskə'nɛkt/ vt undo the connection of ~**ed** adj (of thoughts and ideas) badly arranged

dis·con·so·late /dɪs'kɑnsəlɪt/ adj hopelessly sad

dis·con·tent /ˌdɪskən'tɛnt/ n [U] restless unhappiness ~**ed** adj

dis·con·tin·ue /ˌdɪskən'tɪnyuʷ/ vi/t fml stop; end

dis·cord /'dɪskɔrd/ n **1** [U] fml disagreement between people **2** [C;U] lack of musical HARMONY ~**ant** /dɪs'kɔrdənt/ adj

dis·co·theque /'dɪskə,tɛk, ˌdɪskə-'tɛk/ n fml for DISCO

dis·count¹ /'dɪskaʊnt/ n reduction in cost

dis·count² /dɪs'kaʊnt/ vt regard (information) as unimportant or untrue

discount cen·ter /'·· ˌ··/ n department store that sells goods cheaper than other stores

dis·cour·age /dɪ'skɜrɪdʒ, -'skʌr-/ vt **1** take away hope from **2** persuade not to do something ~**ment** n [C;U]

dis·course /'dɪskɔrs, -koʷrs/ n [C;U] fml serious conversation or speech

dis·cour·te·ous /dɪs'kɜrtiʸəs/ adj fml not polite ~**ly** adv

dis·cov·er /dɪ'skʌvər/ vt find; find out ~**er** n —**y** n **1** [U] discovering **2** [C] something found

dis·cred·it /dɪs'krɛdɪt/ vt stop people from believing in ~**able** adj bringing shame

di·screet /dɪ'skriʸt/ adj not saying too much; showing good sense and judgment: a discreet silence ~**ly** adv

dis·crep·an·cy /dɪs'krɛpənsiʸ/ n difference between amounts, etc.

di·screte /dɪ'skriʸt/ adj fml separate; not continuous

di·scre·tion /dɪ'skrɛʃən/ n [U] **1** being discreet **2** ability to decide what to do: use your own discretion ~**ary** adj

di·scrim·i·nate /dɪ'skrɪmə,neʸt/ v **1** vi/t recognize a difference **2** **dis-criminate against/in favor of** treat worse/better than others —**nating** adj (of a person) able to choose the best by seeing small differences —**natory** /-nə,tɔriʸ, -ˌtoʷriʸ/ adj —**nation** /dɪˌskrɪmə-'neʸʃən/ n [U]

dis·cus /'dɪskəs/ n heavy plate to be thrown as a sport

di·scuss /dɪ'skʌs/ vt talk about ~**ion** /-'skʌʃən/ n [C;U]

dis·dain /dɪs'deʸn/ n [U] fml CONTEMPT ♦ vt regard with disdain; be too proud to: She disdained to answer. ~**ful** adj

dis·ease /dɪ'ziʸz/ n [C;U] illness —**eased** adj: ill

dis·em·bark /ˌdɪsɪm'bɑrk/ vi/t (cause to) leave a ship

dis·em·bod·ied /ˌdɪsɪm'bɑdiʸd◂/ adj existing with no body: a disembodied voice

dis·en·chant·ed /ˌdɪsɪn'tʃæntɪd◂/ adj having lost belief in the value of something —**ment** n [U]

dis·en·fran·chise /ˌdɪsɪn'fræntʃaɪz/ vt DISFRANCHISE ~**ment** n [U]

dis·en·gage /ˌdɪsɪn'geʸdʒ/ vi/t **1** come loose and separate **2** stop fighting

dis·en·tan·gle /ˌdɪsɪn'tæŋgəl/ vt make free from knots: (fig.) disentangle truth from lies

dis·fa·vor /dɪs'feʸvər/ n [U] fml dislike; disapproval

dis·fig·ure /dɪs'fɪgyər/ vt spoil the beauty of ~**ment** n [C;U]

dis·fran·chise /dɪs'fræntʃaɪz/ vt take away the right to vote from ~**ment** n [U]

dis·gorge /dɪs'gɔrdʒ/ vi/t (cause to) flow out

dis·grace /dɪs'greʸs/ n [S;U] (cause of) shame or loss of respect ♦ vt bring disgrace to ~**ful** adj

dis·grun·tled /dɪsˈgrʌntəld/ *adj* annoyed and disappointed

dis·guise /dɪsˈgaɪz/ *vt* change the appearance of, to hide or deceive ♦ *n* **1** [C] something worn to disguise someone **2** [U] being disguised

dis·gust /dɪsˈgʌst/ *n* [U] dislike caused esp. by a bad smell or taste or bad behavior ♦ *vt* cause disgust in ~**ingly** *adv*

dish[1] /dɪʃ/ *n* **1** large plate **2** cooked food of one kind

dish[2] *v sl* talk with friends

dish out *phr vt* **1** serve out to several people **2 dish it out** punish or express disapproval of someone else, esp. thoughtlessly or unjustly

dish up *phr vi/t* put (a meal) onto dishes

dis·heart·en /dɪsˈhɑrtn/ *vt* discourage

di·shev·eled /dɪˈʃevəld/ *adj* (esp. of someone's hair) untidy

dis·hon·est /dɪsˈɑnɪst/ *adj* not honest ~**ly** *adv* ~**y** *n* [U]

dis·hon·or /dɪsˈɑnər/ *n* [S;U] *fml* (person or thing bringing) loss of honor ♦ *vt* **1** bring dishonor to **2** cause (a check) to BOUNCE (3) ~**able** *adj*

dish tow·el /ˈ· ··/ *n* cloth for drying washed cups, plates, etc.

dish·wash·er /ˈdɪʃˌwɑʃər, -ˌwɔ-/ *n* machine that washes dishes

dis·il·lu·sion /ˌdɪsəˈluʒən/ *vt* tell the unpleasant truth to ~**ed** *adj* ~**ment** *n* [U]

dis·in·cen·tive /ˌdɪsɪnˈsentɪv/ *n* something that discourages effort

dis·in·clined /ˌdɪsɪnˈklaɪnd/ *adj* unwilling

dis·in·fect /ˌdɪsɪnˈfekt/ *vt* make (things and places) free from infection ~**ant** *n* chemical that disinfects

dis·in·gen·u·ous /ˌdɪsɪnˈdʒenyuˠəs/ *adj* not sincere; slightly dishonest

dis·in·her·it /ˌdɪsɪnˈherɪt/ *vt* take away the right to INHERIT from

dis·in·te·grate /dɪsˈɪntəˌgreɪt/ *vi/t* break up into small pieces **-gration** /dɪsˌɪntəˈgreɪʃən/ *n* [U]

dis·in·terest·ed /dɪsˈɪntrəstɪd, -ˈɪntəˌrestɪd, -ˈɪntərəstɪd/ *adj* not influenced by personal advantage

dis·joint·ed /dɪsˈdʒɔɪntɪd/ *adj* (of words, ideas, etc.) not well connected ~**ly** *adv*

disk /dɪsk/ *n* **1** anything round and flat, such as a plate or record **2** flat piece of CARTILAGE in one's back: *a slipped disk* **3** flat circular piece of plastic used for storing computer information

disk drive /ˈ· ·/ *n* piece of electrical equipment used for passing information to and from a DISK (2)

disk jock·ey /ˈ· ˌ··/ also **DJ** — *n* broadcaster who introduces records of popular music

dis·like /dɪsˈlaɪk/ *vt* not like ♦ *n* [C;U]: *have a dislike of cats*

dis·lo·cate /ˈdɪsloʊˌkeɪt, dɪsˈloʊˌkeɪt/ *vt* **1** put (a bone) out of place **2** put (traffic, plans, etc.) into disorder **-cation** /ˌdɪsloʊˈkeɪʃən/ *n* [C;U]

dis·lodge /dɪsˈlɑdʒ/ *vt* force out of a position

dis·loy·al /dɪsˈlɔɪəl/ *adj* not loyal ~**ly** *adv* ~**ty** *n* [C;U]

dis·mal /ˈdɪzməl/ *adj* sad; hopeless ~**ly** *adv*

dis·man·tle /dɪsˈmæntəl/ *vt* take to pieces

dis·may /dɪsˈmeɪ/ *vt, n* [U] (fill with) great fear and hopelessness

dis·mem·ber /dɪsˈmembər/ *vt* cut or tear (a body) apart

dis·miss /dɪsˈmɪs/ *vt* **1** *fml* remove from a job **2** send away **3** refuse to think seriously about **4** (of a judge) stop (a court case) ~**al** *n* [C;U] ~**ive** *adj* contemptuous (CONTEMPT)

dis·o·be·di·ent /ˌdɪsəˈbiˠdiˠənt/ *adj* refusing to obey ~**ly** *adv* ~**ence** *n* [U]

dis·o·bey /ˌdɪsəˈbeɪˠ/ *vi/t* not obey

dis·or·der /dɪsˈɔrdər/ *n* **1** [U] confusion **2** [C;U] public violence **3** [C;U] illness of the body or mind ♦ *vt* put into disorder ~**ly** *adj*

disorderly con·duct /·ˌ··· ˈ··/ *n* [U] small offenses: *He was charged with disorderly conduct.*

dis·or·gan·ize /dɪsˈɔrgəˌnaɪz/ *vt* throw into confusion

dis·or·i·ent /dɪsˈɔriˠənt, -ˈoˠr-/ — *vt* cause (someone) to lose sense of time, direction, etc.; confuse

dis·own /dɪsˈoˠn/ *vt* say that one has no connection with

di·spar·age /dɪˈspærɪdʒ/ *vt* speak without respect of **-agingly** *adv*

dis·pa·rate /ˈdɪspərɪt/ *adj fml* that cannot be compared; quite different **-rity** /dɪˈspærətiˠ/ *n* [C;U] inequality

dis·pas·sion·ate /dɪsˈpæʃənɪt/ *adj* calm and fair; not taking sides ~**ly** *adv*

di·spatch, despatch /dɪˈspætʃ/ *vt* **1** send: *dispatch invitations* **2** finish (work, etc.) quickly **3** kill officially ♦ *n* **1** [C] message sent **2** [U] sending **3** [U] speed and effectiveness

di·spel /dɪˈspel/ *vt* -**ll**- drive away; scatter

dis·pen·sa·tion /ˌdɪspənˈseɪˠʃən, -pen-/ *n* **1** system of beliefs governing human affairs **2** [C;U] permission to disobey a rule **3** [U] *fml* dispensing

di·spense /dɪˈspens/ *vt* **1** give out to

people **2** prepare (medicines) **dis-pensary** *n* place where medicines are dispensed

dispense with *phr vt* do without
di·spens·er /dɪˈspɛnsər/ *n* container for holding and dispensing things in small amounts: *a paper cup dispenser*

di·sperse /dɪˈspɜrs/ *vi/t* scatter in different directions **dispersal** *n* [U]
di·spir·it·ed /dɪˈspɪrɪtɪd/ *adj lit* discouraged

dis·place /dɪsˈpleɪs/ *vt* **1** force out of the proper place **2** take the place of ~ **ment** *n* [U]

di·splay /dɪˈspleɪ/ *vt* show ♦ *n* [C;U]: *a display of skill*

dis·please /dɪsˈpliːz/ *vt fml* annoy –**pleasure** /-ˈplɛʒər/ *n* [U] annoyance

dis·po·sa·ble /dɪˈspoʊzəbəl/ *adj* **1** to be used once and then thrown away: *disposable plates* **2** able to be used: *disposable income*

dis·pos·al /dɪˈspoʊzəl/ *n* [U] **1** removal **2** at one's disposal for one to use

dis·pose /dɪˈspoʊz/ *v* **dispose of** *phr vt* get rid of

dis·posed /dɪˈspoʊzd/ *adj* **1** willing: *I don't feel disposed to help.* **2** having a tendency

dis·po·si·tion /ˌdɪspəˈzɪʃən/ *n fml* person's natural character

dis·pos·sess /ˌdɪspəˈzɛs/ *vt fml* take property away from

dis·pro·por·tion·ate /ˌdɪsprəˈpɔrʃənɪt, -ˈpoʷr-/ *adj* too much or too little ~**ly** *adv*

dis·prove /dɪsˈpruːv/ *vt* prove to be false

di·spute /dɪˈspyuːt/ *v* **1** *vi/t* argue (about) **2** *vt* question the truth of **3** *vt* struggle over or about (esp. in defense): *disputed territory* ♦ *n* [C;U] argument; quarrel

dis·qual·i·fy /dɪsˈkwɑləˌfaɪ/ *vt* make unfit to do something –**fication** /dɪsˌkwɑləfəˈkeɪʃən/ *n* [C;U]

dis·qui·et /dɪsˈkwaɪət/ *vt fml* make anxious ♦ *n* [U] anxiety

dis·re·gard /ˌdɪsrɪˈgɑrd/ *vt* pay no attention to ♦ *n* [U] lack of proper attention

dis·re·pair /ˌdɪsrɪˈpɛər/ *n* [U] need for repair

dis·rep·u·ta·ble /dɪsˈrɛpyətəbəl/ *adj* having a bad REPUTATION

dis·re·pute /ˌdɪsrɪˈpyuːt/ *n* [U] loss of people's good opinion

dis·re·spect /ˌdɪsrɪˈspɛkt/ *n* [U] rudeness ~**ful** *adj*

dis·rupt /dɪsˈrʌpt/ *vt* throw into disorder ~**ive** *adj*: *disruptive influence* ~**ion** /-ˈrʌpʃən/ *n* [U]

dis·sat·is·fy /dɪsˈsætɪsˌfaɪ, dɪsˈsætɪs-/ *vt* fail to satisfy; displease:

a dissatisfied customer –**faction** /dɪˌsætɪsˈfækʃən, dɪsˌsæ-/ *n* [U]

dis·sect /dɪˈsɛkt, daɪ-/ *vt* cut up (a body) so as to study it ~**ion** /-ˈsɛkʃən/ *n* [U]

dis·sem·i·nate /dɪˈsɛməˌneɪt/ *vt fml* spread (ideas, etc.) widely –**nation** /dɪˌsɛməˈneɪʃən/ *n* [U]

dis·sen·sion /dɪˈsɛnʃən, -tʃən/ *n* [C;U] disagreement; argument

dis·sent /dɪˈsɛnt/ *vi* disagree with an opinion ♦ *n* [U] refusal to agree ~**er** *n*

dis·ser·ta·tion /ˌdɪsərˈteɪʃən/ *n* long (written) account of a subject

dis·ser·vice /dɪˈsɜrvɪs, dɪsˈsɜr-/ *n* [U] harm or harmful action

dis·si·dent /ˈdɪsədənt/ *n, adj* (person) who disagrees: *political dissidents*

dis·sim·i·lar /dɪˈsɪmələr, dɪsˈsɪ-/ *adj* not similar

dis·si·pat·ed /ˈdɪsəˌpeɪtɪd/ *adj* wasting one's life in foolish or dangerous pleasure

dis·so·ci·ate /dɪˈsoʊʃiˌeɪt, -siˈ-/ also **disassociate** — *n* separate in one's mind –**ation** /dɪˌsoʊsiˈeɪʃən, -ʃiˈ-/ *n* [U]

dis·so·lute /ˈdɪsəˌluːt/ *n, adj* (person) who leads a bad or immoral life ~**ly** *adv* ~**ness** *n* [U]

dis·so·lu·tion /ˌdɪsəˈluːʃən/ *n* [U] breaking up of a group

dis·solve /dɪˈzɑlv/ *vi/t* **1** make (a solid) become liquid **2** cause (a group) to break up: *dissolve the socialist economy* **3** fade out or away gradually: *his strength/the clouds dissolved* **4** lose one's self-control under the influence of strong feeling: *dissolve into tears/laughter*

dis·so·nance /ˈdɪsənəns/ *n* **1** [C;U] combination of musical notes which do not sound pleasant together **2** [S;U] lack of agreement between beliefs and actions –**nant** *adj*

dis·suade /dɪˈsweɪd/ *vt* persuade not to –**suasion** /-ˈsweɪʒən/ *n* [U]

dis·tance /ˈdɪstəns/ *n* **1** [C;U] separation in space between places **2** [S] distant place: *watch from a distance* **3** go the distance (in sports) keep playing, etc. till the end of the match **4** keep one's distance stay far enough away **5** keep someone at a distance treat someone without much friendliness – see also MIDDLE DISTANCE ♦ *vt* separate (esp. oneself) esp. in the mind or feelings

dis·tant /ˈdɪstənt/ *adj* **1** far off **2** not close: *distant relations* **3** unfriendly ~**ly** *adv*

dis·taste /dɪsˈteɪst/ *n* [U] dislike ~**ful** *adj* unpleasant

dis·tem·per /dɪˈstɛmpər/ *n* [U] infectious disease of animals

dis·tend /dɪˈstɛnd/ vi/t fml swell

dis·till /dɪˈstɪl/ v 1 make (a liquid) into gas and then make the gas into liquid, as when making alcoholic drinks 2 get or take the most important part(s) of (a book, an idea, etc.) ~ery n place where WHISKEY, etc., is distilled ~ation /ˌdɪstəˈleɪʃən/ n [C;U]

dis·tinct /dɪˈstɪŋkt/ adj 1 different; separate 2 clearly noticed ~ly adv

dis·tinc·tion /dɪˈstɪŋkʃən/ n 1 [C;U] difference 2 [S;U] being unusually excellent 3 [C] mark of honor –**tive** /-tɪv/ adj showing a difference –**tively** adv

dis·tin·guish /dɪˈstɪŋgwɪʃ/ v 1 vi/t recognize a difference 2 vi/t see clearly 3 vt make different 4 **distinguish oneself** perform noticeably well ~able adj ~ed adj excellent; famous

dis·tort /dɪˈstɔrt/ vt 1 twist out of the natural shape 2 give a false account of ~ion /dɪˈstɔrʃən/ n [C;U]

dis·tract /dɪˈstrækt/ vt take (someone's attention) away ~ed adj anxious and confused ~ion /-ˈstrækʃən/ n 1 [C] amusement, etc., that distracts 2 [U] anxious confusion

dis·traught /dɪˈstrɔt/ adj very anxious and troubled

dis·tress /dɪˈstrɛs/ n [U] 1 great suffering or sorrow 2 serious danger ♦ vt cause suffering to: *distressing news*

dis·trib·ute /dɪˈstrɪbyət, -byuᵂt/ vt 1 give out: *distribute prizes* 2 scatter –**utor** n 1 person who distributes goods 2 instrument that distributes electric current in an engine –**ution** /ˌdɪstrəˈbyuᵂʃən/ n [C;U]

dis·trict /ˈdɪstrɪkt/ n area of a country or city

district at·tor·ney /ˌ··· ·ˈ···/ also **DA** —n lawyer from a particular area of a town or city etc.

dis·trust /dɪsˈtrʌst/ vt have no trust in ♦ n [S;U] lack of trust ~ful adj ~fully adv

dis·turb /dɪsˈtɜrb/ vt 1 interrupt 2 worry: *disturbing news* ~ance n [C;U] 1 act of disturbing 2 noisy disorder ~ed adj having or showing signs of an illness of the mind

dis·u·ni·ty /dɪsˈyuᵂnətiʸ/ n [U] disagreement; quarrelling

dis·use /dɪsˈyuᵂs/ n [U] state of no longer being used: *to fall into disuse* –**used** /ˌdɪsˈyuᵂzd◂/ adj

ditch /dɪtʃ/ n passage cut for water to flow through ♦ vt sl get rid of

dith·er /ˈdɪðər/ vi be unable to decide **dither** n [S]

dit·to /ˈdɪtoᵘ/ n –**tos** the same

dit·ty /ˈdɪtiʸ/ n short simple song

di·van /dɪˈvæn, ˈdaɪvæn/ n bed with no back

dive /daɪv/ vi **dived** or **dove** /doᵘv/ AmE, 1 jump head first into water 2 go under water 3 (of a plane or bird) go down steeply and swiftly 4 go down quickly: *dive under the table* 5 enter quickly into some matter or activity ♦ n 1 act of diving 2 not very respectable club, etc. **diver** n person who dives, or works on the sea bottom

di·verge /dəˈvɜrdʒ, daɪ-/ vi separate; get further apart **divergence** n [C;U]

di·verse /dəˈvɜrs, daɪ-/ adj of different kinds **diversity** n [S;U] variety

di·ver·si·fy /dəˈvɜrsəˌfaɪ, daɪ-/ vi/t make diverse: *diversify your range of products* –**fication** /dəˌvɜrsəfəˈkeɪ-ʃən, daɪ-/ n [U]

di·ver·sion /dəˈvɜrʒən, daɪ-/ n 1 [C;U] diverting 2 [C] something that amuses people ~ary adj intended to DIVERT: *diversionary tactics*

di·vert /dəˈvɜrt, daɪ-/ vt turn to another direction: *divert a river/my attention*

di·vest /dəˈvɛst, daɪ-/ vt take away from someone

di·ves·ti·ture /dəˈvɛstətʃər, -tʃᵘər, daɪ-/ n [U] reduction of investment (INVEST) by selling things, etc.

di·vide /dəˈvaɪd/ vi/t 1 separate into parts 2 find out how many times one number is contained in another 3 be an important cause of disagreement between ♦ n something that divides

div·i·dend /ˈdɪvəˌdɛnd, -dənd/ n 1 part of profit that is divided among the owners of SHARES (2) 2 **pay dividends** produce an advantage

di·vine¹ /dəˈvaɪn/ adj 1 of God or a god 2 excellent **divinity** /dəˈvɪnə-tiʸ/ n 1 [U] quality or state of being divine 2 [C] god or goddess 3 [U] THEOLOGY

divine² vi/t fml find out; guess 2 find (water or minerals) underground using a stick shaped like a Y **diviner** n

div·ing·board /ˈdaɪvɪŋˌbɔrd, -boᵘrd/ n high board off which people DIVE (1) into the water

di·vis·i·ble /dəˈvɪzəbəl/ adj that can be divided

di·vi·sion /dəˈvɪʒən/ n 1 [U] separation or sharing 2 [C] one of the parts into which a whole is divided: *the company's export division* 3 [C] something that separates 4 [C] disagreement 5 [U] process of dividing numbers ~al adj

di·vi·sive /dəˈvaɪsɪv, -ˈvɪ-/ adj causing disunity

di·vorce /dəˈvɔrs, -ˈvoᵘrs/ n 1 [C;U] legal ending of a marriage 2 [C] separation ♦ v 1 vt/i end a marriage by law **2** vt separate completely **divorcée, divorcé** masc. /dǝˌvɔrˈseɪ, -ˌvoʊˈr-/ — n divorced person

di·vulge /dǝˈvʌldʒ, daɪ-/ vt fml tell (a secret)

diz·zy /ˈdɪzɪ/ adj **1** feeling as if things are going round and round **2** causing this feeling: dizzy heights **3** silly —**zily** adv —**ziness** n [U]

DJ /ˈdiˈdʒeɪ/ n DISK JOCKEY

DNA /ˌdiˈɛn ˈeɪ/ n [U] acid which carries GENETIC information in a cell

do¹ /dǝ; strong duː/ v aux **did** /dɪd/, **done** /dʌn/ **1** (used with another verb): Do you like it? | Do be careful! **2** (used instead of another verb): He walks faster than I do. | She likes it, and so do I. | She sings, doesn't she?

do² v **1** vt perform (an action); work at or produce: do a chore/one's homework/ the cooking/business/ one's best/one's duty | do (= study) Science at school | do 80 miles an hour | It'll do you good. **2** vi a advance: do well/badly **b** behave: Do as you're told! **3** vi/t be enough or suitable (for): Will $5 do (you)? | That will do! **4** vt tour: Do Europe in two weeks. **5** do well by treat well **6** How do you do? (used when one is introduced to someone) **7** make do use (something) even though it may not be perfect or enough **8** nothing doing sl no **9** That does it! (expression showing that enough, or too much has been done) **10** What do you do (for a living)? What is your work?

do away with phr vt **1** cause to end **2** kill or murder (someone or oneself)

do for phr vt **1** kill or ruin **2** What will you do for (something)? What arrangements will you make for (something)?: What will you do for food?

do in phr vt **1** kill **2** tire completely

do out of phr vt cause to lose, by cheating

do over phr vt **1** redecorate **2** do again

do up phr vt **1** fasten or wrap **2** repair; improve

do with phr vt **1** need; want **2** cause (oneself) to spend time doing: I don't know what to do with myself since you've gone. **3** (in questions with 'what') to do with regard to: 'What have you done with my pen?' (=where have you put it?) **4** have/ be to do with connected with

do without phr vi/t succeed without

do³ n infml **1** hair style **2** dos and don'ts rules of behavior

do·cent /ˈdoʊsǝnt, doʊˈsɛnt/ n guide in a park or MUSEUM

do·cile /ˈdɑsǝl/ adj quiet and easily taught

dock¹ /dɑk/ n **1** place where ships are loaded and unloaded, or repaired **2** place in a British court of law where prisoner stands ♦ vi/t **1** (cause to) sail into, or remain at, a dock (1) **2** (cause spacecraft) to join in space ~ er n person who works at a dock, loading and unloading ships

dock² vt cut off the end of: (fig.) dock someone's wages

dock·yard /ˈdɑkyɑrd/ n SHIPYARD

doc·tor /ˈdɑktǝr/ n **1** person trained in medicine **2** person holding one of the highest university degrees ♦ vt **1** change dishonestly: doctor the accounts **2** make (an animal) unable to breed

doc·tor·ate /ˈdɑktǝrɪt/ n degree of a DOCTOR (2)

doc·tri·naire /ˌdɑktrǝˈnɛǝr◂/ adj not questioning a doctrine; not practical: doctrinaire science

doc·trine /ˈdɑktrɪn/ n [C;U] belief; set of teachings —**trinal** /ˈdɑktrǝnǝl/ adj

doc·u·ment /ˈdɑkyǝmǝnt/ n paper giving information, proof, etc. ♦ /-mɛnt/ vt prove or support with documents —**ation** /ˌdɑkyǝmɛnˈteɪʃǝn, -mǝn-/ n [U] documents used as proof

doc·u·men·ta·ry /ˌdɑkyǝˈmɛntǝriˈ◂/ adj **1** of documents **2** giving or teaching facts through art ♦ n film, broadcast, etc., dealing with facts

dodge /dɑdʒ/ v **1** vi/t avoid (something) by suddenly moving aside **2** vt avoid dishonestly ♦ n clever trick **dodger** n: tax dodger

doe /doʊ/ n female of esp. the deer, rat, and rabbit

does /dǝz; strong dʌz/ v 3rd pers. sing. pres. of DO

does·n't /ˈdʌzǝnt/ v short for: does not

dog /dɔg/ n **1** common animal with 4 legs, useful to humans **2** male of this and similar animals **3** a dog's life a very unhappy life **4** let sleeping dogs lie leave something alone — see also TOP DOG ♦ vt —**gg**- follow closely; PURSUE: dogged by bad luck **dogs** n [P] **1** dog races **2** go to the dogs be ruined

dog col·lar /ˈ· ˌ··/ n **1** neckband for a dog **2** infml priest's stiff collar

dog-eared /ˈ· ·/ adj (of pages) bent down with use

dog-eat-dog /ˌ· · ˈ·/ adj having, showing or marked by cruel self-interest

dog·ged /ˈdɔgɪd/ adj refusing to give up; determined ~**ly** adv

doggie bag /ˈ··· ·/ n bag to put food into from a restaurant

dog·gone /ˈdɒɡən, ˌdɒɡɒn/ adj euph DAMN

dog·house /ˈdɒɡhaus/ n **in the doghouse** in a state of disfavor or shame

dog·ma /ˈdɒɡmə, ˈdaɡmə/ n [C;U] (religious) belief to be accepted without reasoning ~ **tic** /dɒɡˈmætɪk, daɡ-/ adj trying to force one's beliefs on other people ~ **tically** /-kliʸ/ adv

do-good·er /ˈ·· ·/ n person who tries to do good things for others

dog's age /ˈ·· ·/ n infml very long time

dog-tired /ˌ· ·◂/ adj very tired

do-it-yourself /ˌ· ·· ·/ n [U] doing repairs, painting the house, etc., oneself, rather than paying workmen

dol·drums /ˈdoʷldrəmz, ˈdɑl-/ n [P] **in the doldrums** sad and dull

dole /doʷl/ v dole out phr vt give in small shares

dole·ful /ˈdoʷlfəl/ adj unhappy ~ **ly** adv

doll¹ /dɑl/ n **1** small toy figure of a person **2** sl person that one likes

doll² v doll up phr vt dress prettily

dol·lar /ˈdɑlər/ n **1** unit of money, as used in the US, Canada, and other countries **2** piece of paper, coin, etc., of this value

dollar di·plo·ma·cy /ˈ·· ·ˌ···/ n POLICY of the US government which encourages people to do business in other countries

dollar sign /ˈ·· ·/ n **1** the mark $ **2** **dollar signs in one's eyes** thinking about getting money

dol·lop /ˈdɑləp/ n shapeless mass, esp. of food

dol·phin /ˈdɑlfɪn, ˈdɔl-/ n sea animal, two to three meters long, which swims in groups

do·main /doʷˈmeʸn, də-/ n **1** area of interest or knowledge **2** land controlled by one ruler

dome /doʷm/ n **1** rounded roof **domed** adj like or covered with a dome

do·mes·tic /dəˈmɛstɪk/ adj **1** of the house, home, or family **2** not foreign: domestic policies **3** (of animals) not wild ♦ n house servant ~ **ally** /-kliʸ/ adv

dom·i·cile /ˈdɑmə·saɪl, -səl, ˈdoʷ-/ n fml place where one lives **domicile** vt

dom·i·nant /ˈdɑmənənt/ adj most noticeable or important; dominating –**nance** n [U] controlling influence; importance

dom·i·nate /ˈdɑməˌneʸt/ vi/t **1** have power (over); control **2** have the

most important place (in) **3** rise or be higher than: The castle dominated the whole town. –**nation** /ˌdɑməˈneʸʃən/ n [U]

dom·i·neer /ˌdɑməˈnɪər/ vi try to control others unpleasantly

do·min·ion /dəˈmɪnyən/ n **1** [U] lit power to rule **2** [C] land under one government

dom·i·no /ˈdɑməˌnoʷ/ n –**noes** small flat piece of wood with spots on it, used with others in a game (**dominoes**)

domino ef·fect /ˈ··· ·ˌ·/ n [S] situation in which one event causes similar ones to happen one after another

do·nate /ˈdoʷneʸt, doʷˈneʸt/ vt give (money, etc.), esp. for a good purpose **donation** /doʷˈneʸʃən/ n [C;U]

done /dʌn/ v **1** past p. of DO **2** finished **3** socially acceptable

don·key /ˈdɑŋkiʸ, ˈdʌŋ-, ˈdɒŋ-/ n **1** animal like a small horse, with long ears **2** fool

do·nor /ˈdoʷnər/ n person who gives or donates: blood donor

don't /doʷnt/ v short for: do not

doo·dle /ˈduʷdl/ vi/t draw lines, figures, etc., aimlessly while thinking of something else **doodle** n

doom /duʷm/ n **1** unavoidable destruction **2 doom and gloom** hopelessness ~ **ed** DESTINED to something bad

Dooms·day /ˈduʷmzdeʸ/ n **1** end of the world **2 till Doomsday** forever

door /dɔr, doʷr/ n **1** thing that closes an entrance: bedroom/cupboard/car door **2** DOORWAY **3** (in some fixed phrases) house or building: live next door/2 doors away **4 be on the door** have some duty at the door, such as collecting tickets **5 by the back door** secretly or by a trick **6 shut/close the door to/on** make impossible **7 out of doors** OUTDOORS

door·man /ˈdɔrmən, ˈdoʷr-/ n –**men** /-mən/ **1** man working at the door of a theater, hotel, etc. **2** bouncer (BOUNCE)

door·step /ˈdɔrstɛp, ˈdoʷr-/ n step in front of a door

door·way /ˈdɔrweʸ, ˈdoʷr-/ n opening for a door

dope /doʷp/ n **1** [U] harmful drug **2** [C] fool ♦ vt give dope to ~ **y** adj **1** sleepy and unable to think clearly, (as if) caused by drugs **2** stupid

dor·mant /ˈdɔrmənt/ adj inactive: dormant volcano

dor·mi·to·ry /ˈdɔrməˌtɔriʸ, -ˌtoʷriʸ/ n building belonging to a university where students live

dor·mouse /ˈdɔrmaʊs/ n –**mice** /-maɪs/ small mouse

dos·age /ˈdoʷsɪdʒ/ n fml amount of a dose

dose /dow s/ n measured amount of medicine to be taken at a time ♦ vt give medicine to

dos·si·er /ˈdɑsiⁱₑⁱ, ˈdɔ-/ n set of papers containing facts about a person or subject

dot /dɑt/ n 1 small spot 2 **on the dot** at the exact moment ♦ vt -tt- 1 mark with a dot 2 cover with dots 3 **dotted about** scattered 4 **sign on the dotted line** agree to something quickly and unconditionally ~**ty** adj slightly mad

do·tage /ˈdow tɪdʒ/ n [U] weakness of the mind caused by old age

dote /dow t/ v **dote on** phr vt be too fond of

doub·le¹ /ˈdʌbəl/ adj 1 with 2 parts or uses: double doors | a double meaning 2 for 2 people: a double bed ♦ adv, predeterminer twice: cloth folded double | buy double the amount **doubly** adv twice as: doubly careful

double² n 1 [C;U] twice the amount: I'll have a double (vodka) please. 2 [C] person who looks just like another 3 **on the double** quickly **doubles** n [P] match between 2 pairs of players

double³ v 1 vi/t make or become twice as much 2 vt fold in half

double as phr vt have as a second use or job

double back phr vi return along the same path

double up phr vi/t bend (the body) at the waist: doubled up with pain

double bass /ˌdʌbəl ˈbeⁱs/also **bass fiddle** — n largest musical instrument of the VIOLIN family, with a very deep sound

double bill /ˌ·· ˈ·/ n entertainment having two acts or performers

double-breast·ed /ˌ·· ˈ··◄/ adj (of a coat) crossing over in front, with 2 rows of buttons

double-check /ˌ·· ˈ·/ vi/t examine (something) twice for exactness or quality

double chin /ˌ·· ˈ·/ n fold of loose skin between the face and neck

double-cross /ˌ·· ˈ·/ vt cheat; BETRAY ~**er** n

double-deal·er /ˌ·· ˈ··/ n dishonest person -**ing** adj, n [U]

double-deck·er /ˌ·· ˈ··/ n 1 bus or ship with 2 levels 2 SANDWICH made with 3 pieces of bread

double head·er /ˌ·· ˈ··/ n two games between the same teams or 2 different pairs of teams played one after the other

double-joint·ed /ˌ·· ˈ··◄/ adj having joints that move backwards as well as forwards

double-quick /ˌ·· ˈ·◄/ adj, adv very quick(ly)

double take /ˈ·· ˌ·/ n late reaction of surprise to something unusual: He did a double take.

doubt /daʊt/ vt 1 feel uncertain about 2 consider unlikely: I doubt he'll come. ♦ n 1 [C;U] (feeling of) being uncertain 2 **in doubt** in a condition of being uncertain 3 **no doubt** probably ~**ful** adj 1 uncertain 2 not likely ~**less** adv 1 without doubt 2 probably

dough /dow/ n [U] 1 mixture for making bread 2 sl money

dough·nut, donut /ˈdow nʌt, -nət/ n circular cake cooked in fat

dour /daʊər, dʊər/ adj hard and cold in one's nature; unfriendly ~**ly** adv

douse /daʊs/ vt 1 throw water over 2 put out (a light)

dove¹ /dʌv/ n 1 kind of PIGEON 2 person in favor of peace

dove² /dow v/ v past t. of DIVE

dove·tail /ˈdʌvteⁱl/ n joint for two pieces esp. of wood ♦ v 1 vt join two pieces of wood with a dovetail 2 vi fit skillfully or perfectly together

dow·a·ger /ˈdaʊədʒər/ n grand old lady

dow·dy /ˈdaʊdiⁱ/ adj 1 dressed in a dull way 2 (of clothes) dull

down¹ /daʊn/ adv 1 to or at a lower level: The sun's going down. | Please sit down. 2 to the south: come down from Canada 3 on paper: write/copy it down 4 from the past: jewels handed down in the family 5 (shows reduction): Profits are down. | Turn the radio down. 6 **Down with…** Let's get rid of… ♦ prep 1 to or at a lower level on: run down the hill | swim down the river 2 along: They live down the road. 3 to: I'm just going down to the store. ♦ adj 1 at a lower level, esp. lying on the ground: The telephone wires are down. | Prices are down. 2 directed down: the down escalator 3 finished: 8 down and 2 to go 4 sad 5 not working: The computer/phone is down. 6 **down on** having a low opinion or dislike for ♦ vt 1 knock down; defeat 2 drink quickly ~**er** n sl 1 drug that reduces activity 2 experience or state of affairs which makes one sad

down² n [U] soft feathers or hair ~**y** adj

down-and-out /ˌ· · ˈ·◄/ adj, n (person who is) suffering from bad fortune, lack of money, etc.

down·cast /ˈdaʊnkæst/ adj 1 downhearted 2 (of eyes) looking down

down·fall /ˈdaʊnfɔl/ n sudden ruin

down·grade /ˈdaʊngreⁱd/ vt reduce to a lower position

down·heart·ed /ˌdaʊnˈhɑrtɪd/ adj low in spirits; sad

down·hill /ˌdaʊnˈhɪl◄/ adj, adv 1

down a slope **2 go downhill** become worse

down-home /ˈ· ·/ adj having nice, simple qualities: *down-home cooking*

down pay·ment /ˈ· ·· ·/ n part of the full price paid at the time of buying, with the rest to be paid later

down·pour /ˈdaʊnpɔr, -poʷr/ n heavy fall of rain

down·right /ˈdaʊnraɪt/ adj **1** plain; honest **2** (of something bad) complete ♦ adv: *downright ugly*

down·shift /ˈdaʊnʃɪft/ vi change to a lower GEAR (2)

down·stairs /ˌdaʊnˈstɛərz/ adv, adj on or to a lower floor

down·state /ˈdaʊnsteʸt/ adj, adv southern or country parts of a state: *downstate Illinois*

down·stream /ˌdaʊnˈstriʸm◂/ adv, adj moving with the current of a river

down·time /ˈdaʊntaɪm/ n [U] time during which a computer is not operating

down-to-earth /ˌ· · ·ˈ·◂/ adj practical; sensible

down·town /ˌdaʊnˈtaʊn◂/ adv, adj to or in the town center

down·trod·den /ˈdaʊnˌtrɑdn/ adj treated badly by those in power

down·ward /ˈdaʊnwərd/ adj going down **–wards** adv

down·wind /ˌdaʊnˈwɪnd◂/ adj, adv way the wind is blowing

dow·ry /ˈdaʊəriʸ/ n property that a woman's father gives to her husband when she marries

doze /doʷz/ vi sleep lightly **doze** n [S]

doz·en /ˈdʌzən/ determiner, n **dozen** or **dozens**

Dr written abbrev. for: Doctor

drab /dræb/ adj dull **~ness** n [U]

draft /dræft/ n **1** first rough plan of something **2** written order for money from a bank **3** current of air **4** depth of water a ship needs **5** practice of making someone serve in the armed forces ♦ vt **1** make a DRAFT (1) of **2** make someone serve in the armed forces

drafts·man /ˈdræftsmən/ **-woman** /-ˌwʊmən/ fem. — n **-men** /-mən/ **1** person who drafts new laws **2 a** person who draws parts of a new machine or building **b** person who draws well

drag /dræg/ v **1** vt pull (something heavy) along **2** vi move too slowly: *The meeting dragged on for hours.* **3** vt cause to come or go unwillingly: *They dragged me to a party.* **4** vi move along while touching the ground: *Her long dress dragged in the dust.* **5** vt search the bottom of

(water) with a net **6 drag one's feet/heels** act intentionally in a slow or ineffective way ♦ n **1** [C] someone or something that makes it hard to advance **2** [S] sl dull event or person **3** [U] sl the clothing of one sex worn by the other **4** [C] sl act of breathing in cigarette smoke

drag on phr vi last an unnecessarily long time

drag out phr v **1** vi/t (cause to) last an unnecessarily long time **2** vt force (something) to be told

drag up phr vt raise (a subject) unnecessarily

drag·on /ˈdrægən/ n **1** imaginary animal that breathes fire **2** fierce old woman

drain /dreʸn/ vi/t **1** (cause to) flow away **2** make or become dry by removing liquid: *drain a field* **3** empty by drinking the contents of **4** make weak and tired ♦ n **1** ditch or pipe to carry water away **2** hole in a bath, etc. where a PLUG (1) fits **3** something that uses up money, etc. **4 down the drain** used wastefully or brought to nothing **~age** n [U] system for draining

drain·rack /ˈdreʸnræk/ n container in which dishes are placed to dry

drake /dreʸk/ n male duck

dra·ma /ˈdrɑmə, ˈdræmə/ n **1** [C] theatrical play **2** [U] plays as a group **3** [C;U] exciting situation **~tic** /drəˈmætɪk/ adj **1** of the theater **2** exciting **~tically** /-kliʸ/ adv **~tist** /ˈdræmətɪst, ˈdrɑ-/ n writer of plays **~tize** vt **1** turn (a story, etc.) into a play **2** present (facts) in an exciting way

drank /dræŋk/ v past t. of DRINK

drape /dreʸp/ vt **1** hang (cloth) in folds **2** cause to hang or stretch out loosely or carelessly: *He draped his legs over the arm of the chair.* **~ry** /ˈdreʸpəriʸ/ also **drapes** — n [U] (cloth for) curtains, etc.

dras·tic /ˈdræstɪk/ adj sudden and violent **~ally** /-kliʸ/ adv

draw[1] /drɔ/ v **drew** /druʷ/, **drawn** /drɔn/ vi/t **1** make (pictures) with a pen or pencil **2** vt cause to come, go, or move by pulling: *get drawn into an argument | horse-drawn cart | She drew me aside.* **3** vt take or pull out: *draw his sword | draw $100 from the bank | draw blood* (= cause to flow) | *draw a bath* (= put water in the bathtub) **4** vt attract: *The play drew big crowds.* **5** vi move steadily: *The car drew ahead.* **6** vt make or get by reasoning: *draw a comparison/lesson/conclusion* **7** vi end a game without either side winning **8** vi/t take (breath) in **9 draw a blank** fail to find the information, etc. looked for **10 draw the curtains/the blinds** close the curtains or blinds

11 draw the line (at) refuse to do or accept **drawn** adj stretched out of shape: face drawn with sorrow **drawing** n 1 [U] art of drawing pictures **2** [C] picture

draw away phr v 1 vi/t move (something) away **2** vi get further and further ahead

draw back phr vi be unwilling to join others

draw in phr vi 1 (of days) become shorter **2** arrive

draw into phr vt encourage (someone unwilling) to join in

draw on phr vt 1 make use of **2** come near in time

draw out phr v 1 vi (of days) become longer **2** vt persuade to talk

draw up phr v 1 vt DRAFT (a plan, check etc.) **2** vi (of a vehicle) arrive and stop

draw² n 1 result with neither side winning **2** LOTTERY **3** person or thing that attracts the public **4** money a SALESMAN gets before he sells anything

draw-back /ˈdrɔːbæk/ n disadvantage

drawer /drɔːr/ n sliding container in a piece of furniture

drawl /drɔːl/ vi/t speak or say slowly **drawl** n

drawn /drɔːn/ v past p. of DRAW

dread /dred/ vt fear greatly ♦ n [S;U] great fear **-ful** adj terrible **-fully** adv

dream¹ /driːm/ n 1 image experienced during sleep **2** something hopefully desired **3** something very beautiful – see also WET DREAM **~less** adj (of sleep) peaceful

dream² vi/t **dreamed** or **dreamt** /dremt/ **1** have a dream **2** imagine (something) **3 not dream of** refuse to consider **~er** n 1 person who dreams **2** impractical person **~y** adj 1 seeming half asleep **2** peaceful and beautiful

dream up phr vt invent (esp. something silly)

drear-y /ˈdrɪəriˈ/ adj sad and dull **-ily** adv **-iness** n [U]

dredge /dredʒ/ vi/t bring up mud, etc. from the bottom of water

dredge up phr vt 1 bring to the surface of water **2** produce or bring up (usu. something unpleasant): dredge up the past

dregs /dregz/ n [P] 1 bits of matter that sink to the bottom of liquid **2** worthless part: the dregs of society

drench /drentʃ/ vt make thoroughly wet

dress /dres/ v 1 vi/t put clothes on **2** vi put on formal evening clothes **3** vt clean and cover (a wound) **4** vt arrange; prepare: dress a salad/a store window **5 dressed to kill** dressed in one's best clothes ♦ n 1 [C] woman's outer garment made in one piece **2** [U] clothing – see also EVENING DRESS **~ing** n 1 covering for a wound **2** SAUCE, etc. – see also WINDOW DRESSING **~y** showy or too ornamental

dress up phr v 1 vi/t put special clothes on **2** vt make (something or someone) seem different or more attractive

dres-ser /ˈdresər/ n chest of drawers

dressing gown /ˈ··ˌ·/ n loose coat for wearing indoors

dressing ta-ble /ˈ··ˌ··/ n table with a mirror, in a BEDROOM

dress-mak-er /ˈdresˌmeɪkər/ n person who makes clothes

drew /druː/ v past t. of DRAW

drib-ble /ˈdrɪbəl/ v 1 vi let SALIVA flow out slowly from the mouth **2** vi/t (liquid) flow slowly **3** vi/t move (a ball) by many short kicks or strokes **dribble** n

dried /draɪd/ v past t. and p. of DRY

drift /drɪft/ n 1 mass of something blown together: snowdrifts **2** aimless movement **3** general meaning: the drift of his argument ♦ vi 1 be driven by wind or water **2** move or live aimlessly **~er** person who DRIFTS (2)

drill¹ /drɪl/ n tool for making holes ♦ vi/t use a drill (on)

drill² n [C;U] training by repeating and following orders: army drill ♦ vi/t do or give drill

dri-ly /ˈdraɪliˈ/ adv in a DRY¹ (4) manner

drink /drɪŋk/ v **drank** /dræŋk/, **drunk** /drʌŋk/ **1** vi/t swallow (liquid) **2** vi take in (too much) alcohol ♦ n [C;U] **1** liquid to drink **2** alcohol to drink **~able** adj **~er** n person who drinks too much alcohol

drink to phr vt wish (someone or something) good health or success

drip /drɪp/ vi/t **1** fall or let fall in drops **2** overflow with or as if with liquid: (fig.) She was dripping with diamonds. ♦ n 1 (sound of) liquid falling in drops **2** dull person **~ping** adj very wet

drip-dry /ˌ· ˈ·◂/ adj (of clothes) that will dry smooth if hung while wet

drive¹ /draɪv/ v **drove** /droʊv/, **driven** /ˈdrɪvən/ **1** vi/t guide (a wheeled vehicle) **2** vt take (someone) in a vehicle **3** vt force (animals, etc.) to go **4** vt be the power for **5** vt send by hitting **6** vt force (someone) into a bad state: The pain's driving me mad. **7** vi (esp. of rain) move violently **8 be driving at** mean; HINT **driver** n person who drives vehicles or animals

drive² n 1 [C] journey in a vehicle

2 [C] a big road through a scenic area **3** [C] stroke in a ball game **4** [C] CAMPAIGN **5** [U] force of mind: *He lacks drive.* **6** [C] important natural need which must be fulfilled **7** journey for cows: *a cattle drive*

drive-in /ˈ· ·/ *n, adj* (place) that people can use while remaining in their cars: *a drive-in restaurant/movie/bank*

driv·el /ˈdrɪvəl/ *n* [U] nonsense

driz·zle /ˈdrɪzəl/ *n* [U] fine misty rain **drizzle** *vi*

droll /droʷl/ *adj* odd and amusing: *a droll person/expression*

drom·e·da·ry /ˈdrɑməˌdɛriʸ/ *n* camel with one HUMP (1)

drone /droʷn/ *vi* make a continuous low dull sound **drone** *n* [S]

drone on *phr vi* speak for a long time in an uninteresting manner

drool /druʷl/ *vi* let liquid flow from the mouth: (fig.) *Stop drooling* (= show pleasure in a foolish way) *over that singer.*

droop /druʷp/ *vi* hang downwards **droop** *n* [S]

drop¹ /drɑp/ *n* **1** [C] small round mass of liquid **2** [C] small round piece of candy **3** [S] a distance or fall straight down **b** fall in quantity: *a drop in sales* **4** at the drop of a hat suddenly **drops** *n* liquid medicine taken drop by drop

drop² *v* **-pp-** **1** *vi/t* fall or let fall **2** *vi/t* (cause to) become less: *The temperature dropped.* **3** *vt* let (someone) get out of a vehicle **4** *vt* stop; give up: *drop a subject* **5** *vt* say or write informally: *drop a hint/a note* **6** *vt* leave out (from a team)

drop back/behind *phr vi* get further away by moving more slowly

drop in/by *phr vi* make an unexpected visit

drop off *phr vi* **1** get less **2** fall asleep

drop out *phr vi* stop taking part **dropout** /ˈdrɑpaʊt/ *n* person who leaves high school, etc., without finishing

drop·pings /ˈdrɑpɪŋz/ *n* [P] waste matter from the bowels of animals or birds

dross /drɔs, drɑs/ *n* [U] waste or impure matter

drought /draʊt/ *n* [C;U] long period of dry weather when there is not enough water

drove¹ /droʷv/ *v past t.* of DRIVE

drove² *n* group; crowd: *droves of tourists*

drown /draʊn/ *v* **1** *vi/t* die or kill by being under water **2** *vt* cover completely with water **3** *vt* cover up (a sound) with a louder one **4 drown one's sorrows** drink alcohol in an attempt to forget one's troubles

drowse /draʊz/ *vi* fall into a light sleep **drowsy** *adj* sleepy **-sily** *adv* **-siness** *n* [U]

drudge /drʌdʒ/ *vi* do hard dull work ◆ *n* person who drudges **~ry** /ˈdrʌdʒəriʸ/ *n* [U] hard uninteresting work

drug /drʌg/ *n* **1** medicine **2** substance taken for pleasure: *a drug addict* ◆ *vt* **-gg-** **1** add harmful drugs to **2** give drugs to

drug·gist /ˈdrʌgɪst/ *n* person who sells medicines

drug·store /ˈdrʌgstɔr, -stoʷr/ *n* store that sells medicine, also paper products, food, etc.

drum¹ /drʌm/ *n* **1** musical instrument made of a skin stretched over a circular frame **2** container, etc., shaped like this: *oil drum*

drum² *vi* **-mm-** **1** beat a drum **2** make drumlike noises **3 drum something into someone** make someone remember something by saying it often **~mer** *n* person who plays a drum

drum out *phr vt* send away formally and disapprovingly

drum up *phr vt* obtain by continuous effort and esp. by advertising

drunk¹ /drʌŋk/ *v past p.* of DRINK

drunk² *adj* under the influence of alcohol

drunk³ *n* also **drunkard** /ˈdrʌŋkərd/ — person who is (habitually) drunk

drunk·en /ˈdrʌŋkən/ *adj* **1** DRUNK² **2** resulting from or connected with too much drinking: *a drunken sleep* **~ly** *adv* **~ness** *n* [U]

dry¹ /draɪ/ *adj* **1** not wet: *dry clothes/climate* **2** (of wine) not sweet **3** not allowing the sale of alcohol **4** amusing without appearing to be so; quietly IRONIC: *dry wit* **5** uninteresting **~ly, drily** *adv* **~ness** *n* [U]

dry² *v* **1** *vi/t* make or become dry **2** *vt* preserve (food) by removing liquid **~er, drier** *n* machine that dries

dry out *phr vi/t* **1** (cause to) give up dependence on alcohol **2** (cause to) become completely dry

dry up *phr vi* **1** (of a supply) stop coming **2** *sl* SHUT UP (1)

dry-clean /ˈ· ·, ˈ· ·/ *vt* clean (clothes) with chemicals instead of water **~ers** *n* cleaners (CLEAN) **~ing** *n* [U] **1** action or industry of dry-cleaning clothes **2** clothes that need to be or have just been dry-cleaned

dry dock /ˈ· ·/ *n* place where a ship is held while water is pumped out

dry law /ˈ· ·/ *n* law forbidding alcohol

dry run /ˌ· ˈ·/ *n* practice attempt made before the real thing

dry rot /ˌ· ˈ·/ n [U] disease that turns wood into powder

du·al /ˈduːəl, ˈdjuːəl/ adj having 2 parts; double: *dual citizenship* (= of 2 countries) ~**ity** /duːˈæləˌtiʸ, djuˈ-/ n [U]

dub /dʌb/ vt **-bb- 1** give (a name) to **2** change the spoken language of (a film)

du·bi·ous /ˈduːbiʸəs, ˈdjuː-/ adj feeling or causing doubt ~**ly** adv

duch·ess /ˈdʌtʃɪs/ n **a** wife of a DUKE **b** woman who holds the rank of DUKE in her own right

duck /dʌk/ n **1** [C] common swimming bird **2** [U] its meat **3 take to something like a duck to water** learn or get used to something very easily ◆ v **1** vi/t lower (one's head) quickly **2** vt push (someone) under water **3** vt try to avoid responsibility – see also LAME DUCK, SITTING DUCK

duck·ling /ˈdʌklɪŋ/ n young duck – see also UGLY DUCKLING

duct /dʌkt/ n tube that carries liquids, air, etc.

dud /dʌd/ n sl useless thing or person: *a dud check*

dude /duːd, djuːd/ n infml man

due /duː, djuː/ adj **1** owed **2** fml suitable; proper **3** expected: *The train is due any minute.* **4 due to** because of ◆ adv (before **north, south, east, west**) exactly ◆ n something that rightfully belongs to one: *give him his due* **dues** n [P] official payments

du·el /ˈduːəl, ˈdjuːəl/ n fight arranged between 2 people **duel** vi

du·et /duːˈɛt, djuːˈɛt/ n piece of music for 2 performers

duf·fel bag /ˈdʌfəl ˌbæg/ n large cloth bag used (by soldiers) to carry clothes, etc.

dug /dʌg/ v past t. and p. of DIG

dug·out /ˈdʌgaʊt/ n **1** boat made of a hollow log **2** shelter dug in the ground

duke /duːk, djuːk/ n British nobleman of the highest rank ~**dom** n rank or lands of a duke

dull /dʌl/ adj **1** not bright or shining **2** slow in thinking **3** not sharp: *a dull pain* **4** uninteresting ◆ vt make dull ~**ness** n [U]

du·ly /ˈduːliʸ, ˈdjuːliʸ/ adv properly; as expected

dumb /dʌm/ adj **1** unable to speak **2** unwilling to speak; silent **3** sl stupid ~**ly** adv ~**ness** n [U]

dumb·found /dʌmˈfaʊnd, ˈdʌmfaʊnd/ vt make dumb from surprise

dum·my /ˈdʌmiʸ/ n **1** object made to look like a real thing or person **2** sl stupid person

dump /dʌmp/ vt **1** drop carelessly **2** sell (goods) abroad more cheaply than at home ◆ n **1** place for dumping waste **2** stored supply **3** sl dirty untidy place **4 in the dumps** sad ~**truck** n large vehicle for carrying earth and stones ~**y** adj short and fat

dump·ling /ˈdʌmplɪŋ/ n ball of boiled DOUGH

dump·ster /ˈdʌmpstər/ n large container for carrying away unwanted things

dunce /dʌns/ n slow learner

dune /duːn, djuːn/ n long low sandhill piled up by the wind

dung /dʌŋ/ n [U] animal MANURE

dun·ga·rees /ˌdʌŋgəˈriːz, ˌdʌŋgəˌriʸz/ n [P] JEANS for working in

dun·geon /ˈdʌndʒən/ n underground prison

dunk /dʌŋk/ vt dip (esp. food) into liquid while eating

du·o /ˈduːoʷ, ˈdjuːoʷ/ n a pair, esp. of musicians

dupe /duːp, djuːp/ vt trick; deceive ◆ n fml person who is duped

du·plex /ˈduːplɛks, ˈdjuː-/ n pair of joined houses

du·pli·cate[1] /ˈduːpləkɪt, ˈdjuː-/ n, adj (something that is) exactly like another

du·pli·cate[2] /ˈduːpləˌkeʸt, ˈdjuː-/ vt copy exactly ~**cator** n machine that copies ~**cation** /ˌduːpləˈkeʸʃən, ˌdjuː-/ n [U]

du·plic·i·ty /duːˈplɪsətiʸ, djuː-/ n [U] fml dishonesty

du·ra·ble /ˈduʳərəbəl, ˈdjuʳər-/ adj lasting for a long time **durables** n [P] goods expected to last for years

du·ra·tion /duˈreʸʃən, dju-/ n [U] fml **1** time during which something lasts **2 for the duration** as long as something lasts

du·ress /duˈrɛs, dju-/ n [U] fml threats: *promise under duress*

dur·ing /ˈduʳərɪŋ, ˈdjuʳərɪŋ/ prep **1** all through (a length of time) **2** at some moment in: *die during the night*

dusk /dʌsk/ n [U] time when the light of day fades

dusk·y /ˈdʌskiʸ/ adj slightly dark in color

dust[1] /dʌst/ n [U] powder made of earth or other matter ~**y** adj covered with dust

dust[2] vt **1** clean the dust from: *dust books* **2** cover with powder: *dust crops* ~**er** n cloth, etc. for removing dust

dust off phr vt begin to use or practice again, after a period of not doing so

dust bowl /ˈ· ·/ n area with frequent DROUGHT

dust·cov·er /ˈdʌstkʌvər/ n large

sheet used to cover furniture, etc., to keep off dust

dust jack·et /'·· ¡··/ n loose paper cover on a hard cover book

dust·pan /'dʌstpæn/ n flat container into which house dust is swept

Dutch /dʌtʃ/ adj 1 of the Netherlands (Holland) 2 **go dutch (with someone)** share costs 3 **dutch treat** meal or entertainment where costs are shared 4 **in dutch** sl in trouble

du·ty /'duʷt̬iʸ, 'dyuʷ-/ n [C;U] 1 something one must do 2 tax: *customs duties* 3 **heavy duty** (of machines, etc.) able to do hard work 4 **on/off duty** having/not having to work **dutiful** adj showing respect and obedience **dutifully** adv

duty-free /ˌ··'··/ adj, adv (of goods) allowed to enter a country without tax

dwarf /dwɔrf/ n **dwarfs** or **dwarves** /dwɔrvz/ very small person, animal, or plant ♦ vt cause to look small

dwell /dwɛl/ vi **dwelled** or **dwelt** /dwɛlt/ lit live (in a place) ~**er** n person or animal that lives somewhere: *city-dwellers* ~**ing** n fml home

　dwell on phr vt think or speak a lot about

dwin·dle /'dwɪndl/ vi become gradu-ally fewer or smaller

dye /daɪ/ n [C;U] substance used to color cloth, etc. ♦ vi/t **dyes, dyed, dyeing** color with dye

dyed-in-the-wool /ˌ··· '·◂/ adj impossible to change (as to the stated or known quality): *a dyed-in-the-wool Republican*

dy·ing /'daɪ-ɪŋ/ v present p. of DIE

dyke /daɪk/ n sl LESBIAN

dy·nam·ic /daɪ'næmɪk/ adj 1 powerful and active 2 of force that causes movement ~**ally** /-kliʸ/ adv **dynamics** n [U] science that deals with matter in movement ~**ism** /'daɪnə-ˌmɪzəm/ n [U] being DYNAMIC (1)

dy·na·mite /'daɪnəˌmaɪt/ n [U] 1 powerful explosive 2 something or someone that will cause great shock, admiration, etc. ♦ vt blow up with dynamite

dy·na·mo /'daɪnəˌmoʷ/ n **-mos** machine that turns movement into electricity

dyn·a·sty /'daɪnəstiʸ/ n line of rulers of the same family

dys·en·te·ry /'dɪsənˌtɛriʸ/ n [U] painful bowel disease

dys·lex·i·a /dɪs'lɛksiʸə/ n [U] inability to read, from difficulty in recognizing letter shapes **-ic** adj

E

E, e /iʸ/ the 5th letter of the English alphabet

E written abbrev. for: east(ern)

each /iʸtʃ/ determiner, pron every one separately: each child | each of the children ♦ adv to or each: They cost fifty cents each.

each oth·er /ˌ·ˈ·ˈ·/ pron with each doing something to the other: kiss each other | hold each other's hands

ea·ger /ˈiʸgər/ adj keen; wanting very much ~ly adv ~ness n [U]

ea·gle /ˈiʸgəl/ n large bird with a hooked beak, that eats meat ~-eyed /ˌ·· ˈ·◄/ adj having very good eyesight

ear¹ /ɪər/ n 1 [C] either of the 2 parts of the head with which we hear 2 [S] good recognition of sounds: an ear for music 3 all ears listening eagerly 4 play by ear play music without written notes 5 up to one's ears in deep in; very busy with

ear² n head of a plant that produces grain: ear of corn

ear·ache /ˈɪəreʸk/ n [U] pain inside the ear

ear·drum /ˈɪərdrʌm/ n tight skin inside the ear which allows one to hear sound

earl /ɜrl/ n British nobleman of high rank ~dom n rank or lands of an earl

ear·ly /ˈɜrliʸ/ adv, adj 1 sooner than usual or expected: The train arrived early. | an early supper 2 near the beginning: It happened early in the morning/in the early morning. 3 at the earliest and not sooner

early bird /ˌ·· ˈ·/ n person who gets up or arrives early

ear·mark /ˈɪərmark/ vt set aside (money, time, etc.) for a particular purpose

earn /ɜrn/ v 1 vi/t get (money) by working 2 vt deserve (what one has worked for) ~er n ~ings n [P] money earned

ear·nest /ˈɜrnɪst/ adj determined and serious ♦ n in earnest: a in a determined way b not joking ~ly adv ~ness n [U]

ear·plug /ˈɪərplʌg/ n soft thing put into the ear to keep out noise, etc.

ear·ring /ˈɪərɪŋ, ˈɪərˌrɪŋ/ n decoration for the ear

ear·shot /ˈɪərʃɑt/ n within/out of earshot within/beyond the distance at which a sound can be heard

earth /ɜrθ/ n 1 [S;U] (often cap.) the world we live on: the planet Earth 2 [U] its surface, as opposed to the sky: The rocket fell to earth. 3 [U] soil: a bucket of earth ~ly adj 1 of this world, not heaven 2 possible: no earthly reason ~-y adj 1 like soil 2 concerned with the body, not the mind

earth·en·ware /ˈɜrθənˌwɛər/ n [U] (pots, etc., made of) baked clay

earth·quake /ˈɜrθkweʸk/ n sudden violent shaking of the earth's surface

earth·work /ˈɜrwɜrk/ n large structure of earth used as a protection against enemies

ear·wig /ˈɪərˌwɪg/ n insect with 2 curved parts on its tail

ease¹ /iʸz/ n [U] 1 ability to do something easily 2 state of being comfortable 3 ill at ease uncomfortable

ease² v 1 vi/t make or become less painful or difficult 2 vt make less anxious 3 vt move slowly and carefully into a different position

  ease off/up phr vi become less active or severe

ea·sel /ˈiʸzəl/ n wooden frame to support a picture or BLACKBOARD

east /iʸst/ n 1 [the+S] (often cap.) direction from which the sun rises 2 area of the US east of the Mississippi River ♦ adj 1 in the east 2 (of wind) from the east ♦ adv to the east ~ward adj, adv

Eas·ter /ˈiʸstər/ n Christian holy day in memory of Christ's death

eas·ter·ly /ˈiʸstərliʸ/ adj east

east·ern /ˈiʸstərn/ adj of the east part of the world or of a country

Eastern time /ˌ·· ˈ·/ n time used on the East coast of the US to the Ohio Valley

eas·y /ˈiʸziʸ/ adj 1 not difficult 2 comfortable; without worry ♦ adv go easy on: a be less severe with b not use too much of -ily adv 1 without difficulty 2 without doubt: easily the best

easy chair /ˈ·· ˌ·/ n an ARMCHAIR

eas·y·go·ing /ˌiʸziʸˈgoʷɪŋ◄/ adj pleasantly calm and unhurried

eat /iʸt/ v ate /eʸt/, eaten /ˈiʸtn/ 1 vi/t take in (food) through the mouth 2 vt ((away, into)) destroy by chemical action 3 be eaten up with be full of (violent feeling) 4 eat one's words admit that one was wrong 5 eat your heart out infml be very jealous – see also CROW¹ (3) ~able adj ~er n

eaves /iʸvz/ n [P] edges of a roof, beyond the walls

eaves·drop /ˈiʸvzdrɑp/ vi -pp- listen secretly to conversation ~per n

ebb /ɛb/ vi grow less or lower: His

courage ebbed away. ♦ *n* [S] **at a low ebb** in a bad state

ebb tide /ˌ·'·/ *n* [C;U] outward flow of the sea

eb·o·ny /'ebəniʸ/ *adj, n* [U] (of the color of) hard black wood

e·bul·lient /ɪ'bʌliʸənt, ɪ'bʊl-/ *adj fml* full of happy excitement **–lience** *n* [U]

EC /ˌiʸ 'siʸ/ *n* European Community; West European organization to encourage trade and friendly relations

ec·cen·tric /ɪk'sentrɪk/ *adj* **1** (of people) unusual; peculiar **2** (of circles) not having the same center ♦ *n* eccentric person **~ity** /ˌeksen-'trɪsəṭiʸ, -sən-/ *n* [C;U]

ec·cle·si·as·ti·cal /ɪˌkliʸziʸ'æstɪkəl/ *adj* of the Christian church

ech·e·lon /'eʃəˌlɑn/ *n* level within an organization

ech·o /'ekoʷ/ *n* **-oes** sound sent back from a surface ♦ *v* **1** *vi* come back as an echo **2** *vt* copy or repeat (words, ideas, etc.)

é·clair /eʸ'kleər, ɪ-, 'eʸkleər/ *n* cake shaped like a finger, with cream inside

e·clec·tic /ɪ'klektɪk/ *adj fml* using ideas from many different systems **~ism** /-təˌsɪzəm/ *n* [U]

e·clipse /ɪ'klɪps/ *n* disappearance of the sun's light (cut off by the moon) or of the moon's light (cut off by the Earth) ♦ *vt* **1** cause an eclipse of **2** make (something) less important by comparison

e·col·o·gy /ɪ'kɑlədʒiʸ/ *n* [U] relations of living things to their surroundings **-gist** *n* **-gical** /ˌiʸkə-'lɑdʒɪkəl◄, ˌek-/ *adj*

ec·o·nom·ic /ˌekə'nɑmɪk◄, ˌiʸ-/ *adj* **1** connected with business, industry, and wealth **2** profitable **~al** *adj* not wasteful **~ally** /-kliʸ/ *adv*

ec·o·nom·ics /ˌekə'nɑmɪks, ˌiʸ-/ *n* [U] study of the way in which wealth is produced and used **-nomist** /ɪ'kɑnəmɪst/ *n*

e·con·o·mize /ɪ'kɑnəˌmaɪz/ *vi* avoid waste

e·con·o·my /ɪ'kɑnəmiʸ/ *n* **1** [C] economic system of a country **2** [C;U] avoidance of waste – see also MIXED ECONOMY ♦ *adj* cheap: *an economy class air ticket*

e·co·sys·tem /'iʸkoʷˌsɪstəm/ *n* all the living things in an area and the relationship between them

ec·sta·sy /'ekstəsiʸ/ *n* [C;U] great joy **ecstatic** /ɪk'stætɪk, ek-/ *adj* **ecstatically** /-kliʸ/ *adv*

e·cu·men·i·cal /ˌekyə'menɪkəl◄/ *adj* favoring Christian unity

ec·ze·ma /'eksəmə, 'egzəmə, ɪg-'ziʸmə/ *n* [U] red swollen condition of the skin

ed·dy /'ediʸ/ *n* circular movement of water, smoke, etc. ♦ *vi* move in eddies

edge /edʒ/ *n* **1** cutting part of a knife, etc. **2** narrowest part along the outside of an object: *the edge of a coin* **3** place where something begins or ends: *the water's edge* **4 have the edge on** be better than **5 on edge** nervous **6 set someone's teeth on edge** *infml* give an unpleasant feeling to someone **7 take the edge off** *infml* make less severe ♦ *v* **1** *vt* put a border on **2** *vi/t* move gradually, esp. sideways **edging** *n* [C;U] border **edgy** *adj* nervous

ed·i·ble /'edəbəl/ *adj* that can be eaten

e·dict /'iʸdɪkt/ *n* official public command

ed·i·fice /'edəfɪs/ *n fml* large fine building

ed·it /'edɪt/ *vt* prepare (a newspaper, film, etc.) for printing or showing **~or** *n* person who edits

e·di·tion /ɪ'dɪʃən/ *n* **1** one printing, esp. of a book **2** form in which a book is printed: *a paperback edition*

ed·i·to·ri·al /ˌedə'tɔriʸəl, -'toʷr-/ *adj* of an editor ♦ *n* newspaper article giving the paper's opinion

ed·u·cate /'edʒəˌkeʸt/ *vt* teach; train ♦ **-or** *n* person who educates

ed·u·ca·tion /ˌedʒə'keʸʃən/ *n* [S;U] (knowledge resulting from) teaching or training **~al** *adj*

eel /iʸl/ *n* long snake-like fish

ee·rie /'ɪəriʸ/ *adj* frightening because of being strange: *an eerie silence* **eerily** *adv*

ef·face /ɪ'feʸs/ *vt fml* rub out

ef·fect /ɪ'fekt/ *n* [C;U] **1** result; what happens because of a cause **2 in effect: a** in operation **b** in fact **3 take effect** come into operation – see also SIDE EFFECT ♦ *vt fml* produce; cause **effects** *n* [P] **1** sounds, etc., produced in a film or play **2** *fml* personal belongings

ef·fec·tive /ɪ'fektɪv/ *adj* **1** producing the desired result: *very effective new laws* **2** *fml* actual: *the effective strength of our army* **~ly** *adv* **~ness** *n* [U]

ef·fem·i·nate /ɪ'femənɪt/ *adj* (of a man) too like a woman **~nacy** *n* [U]

ef·fer·vesce /ˌefər'ves/ *vi* form bubbles of gas **-vescence** *n* [U] **-vescent** *adj*

ef·fete /ɪ'fiʸt, ε-/ *adj* weak; EFFEMINATE

ef·fi·ca·cy /'efəkəsiʸ/ *n* [U] *fml* effectiveness

ef·fi·cient /ɪ'fɪʃənt/ *adj* working well; *an efficient secretary/machine* **~ly** *adv* **-ciency** *n* [U]

ef·fi·gy /'efədʒiʸ/ *n fml* wooden, stone, etc., likeness of someone

ef·flu·ent /ˈefluʷənt/ n [C;U] flowing out of liquid chemical or human waste

ef·fort /ˈefərt/ n 1 [U] use of strength 2 [C] attempt: *a good effort* ~**less** adj successful without effort ~**lessly** adv

ef·fron·te·ry /ɪˈfrʌntəriʸ/ n [U] rudeness without any feeling of shame

ef·fu·sive /ɪˈfjuʷsɪv/ adj showing too much feeling ~**ly** adv

EFL /ˌiʸ ef ˈel/ abbrev. for: English as a foreign language

e.g. /ˌiʸ ˈdʒiʸ/ abbrev. for: for example

e·gal·i·tar·i·an /ɪˌɡæləˈteəriʸən/ adj believing in social equality ~**ism** n [U]

egg[1] /eɡ/ n 1 [C] round object with a shell, containing a baby bird, snake, etc. 2 [C;U] (the contents of) an egg when used as food: *a boiled egg* 3 [C] female cell producing young 4 **have egg on one's face** seem foolish

egg[2] v **egg on** phr vt encourage someone, esp. to do wrong

egg·cup /ˈeɡ-kʌp/ n container for a boiled egg

egg·head /ˈeɡhed/ n derog a HIGH-BROW

egg·plant /ˈeɡplænt/ n large purple vegetable

e·go /ˈiʸɡoʷ/ n egos 1 one's opinion of oneself: *an enormous ego* 2 tech one's conscious self – see also ALTER EGO

e·go·cen·tric /ˌiʸɡoʷˈsentrɪk◂/ adj thinking only about oneself; selfish

e·go·is·m /ˈiʸɡoʷˌɪzəm/ n [U] selfishness -**ist** n

e·go·tis·m /ˈiʸɡəˌtɪzəm/ n [U] believing that one is more important than other people -**tist** n –**tistic** /ˌiʸɡəˈtɪstɪk◂/, –**tistical** adj

ego trip /ˈ···/ n act or set of acts done mainly because it makes one feel proud of oneself

e·gre·gious /ɪˈɡriʸdʒəs/ adj fml noticeably bad

ei·der·down /ˈaɪdərˌdaʊn/ also com-**forter** — n bed covering filled with feathers

eight /eɪt/ det, n, pron 8 **eighth** det, adv, n, pron 8th

eigh·teen /ˌeɪˈtiʸn◂/ det, n, pron 18 ~**th** det, adv, n, pron 18th

eigh·ty /ˈeɪtiʸ/ det, n, pron 80 -**tieth** det, adv, n, pron 80th

ei·ther[1] /ˈiʸðər, ˈaɪ-/ det, pron, conj 1 one or the other: *I haven't seen either John or Sam.* | *I haven't met either (of them).* | *He either drives or walks.* 2 each of two: *houses on either side of the road*

either[2] adv (used with negative expressions) also: *I haven't been to France, or Germany either.*

e·jac·u·late /ɪˈdʒækyəˌleɪt/ vi/t 1 throw out (SPERM) suddenly from the body 2 fml just suddenly -**lation** /ɪˌdʒækyəˈleɪʃən/ n [C;U]

e·ject /ɪˈdʒekt/ vt fml throw out ~**ion** /ɪˈdʒekʃən/ n [U]

ejection seat /·ˈ·· ˌ·/ n seat that throws one out of a plane that is burning, etc.

eke /iʸk/ v **eke out** phr vt 1 make (supplies) last as long as possible 2 work hard to earn little money: *eke out a living*

e·lab·o·rate[1] /ɪˈlæbərɪt/ adj full of detail ~**ly** adv

e·lab·o·rate[2] /ɪˈlæbəˌreɪt/ vi add more detail -**ration** /ɪˌlæbəˈreɪʃən/ n [C;U]

é·lan /eɪˈlɑn/ n [U] spirit; VIGOR

e·lapse /ɪˈlæps/ vi fml (of time) pass

e·las·tic /ɪˈlæstɪk/ adj able to spring back into shape after stretching or bending ♦ n elastic material ~**ity** /ɪˌlæˈstɪsətiʸ, ˌiʸlæ-/ [U]

e·lat·ed /ɪˈleʸtɪd/ adj proud and happy -**ion** /ɪˈleʸʃən/ n [U]

el·bow /ˈelboʷ/ n joint where the arm bends ♦ vt push with the elbows

elbow grease /ˈ··· ·/ n [U] hard work with the hands

elbow room /ˈ··· ·/ n [U] space to move freely

el·der[1] /ˈeldər/ adj (of a family member) older: *my elder sister* ♦ n 1 older of 2 people 2 person in a respected official position ~**ly** adj rather old

elder states·man /ˌ··· ˈ··/ n old and respected person who is asked for advice because of his or her experience

el·dest /ˈeldɪst/ n, adj (person who is) the oldest of 3 or more

e·lect /ɪˈlekt/ vt 1 choose by voting 2 fml decide: *She elected to go.* ♦ adj fml chosen, but not yet at work: *president elect* ~ **or** n 1 person with the right to vote 2 member of the electoral college ~**oral** adj ~**orally** adv

e·lec·tion /ɪˈlekʃən/ n [C;U] (occasion of) choosing representatives by voting

e·lec·tion·eer·ing /ɪˌlekʃəˈnɪərɪŋ/ n [U] activity of persuading people to vote for a political party

electoral col·lege /·ˌ··· ˈ··/ n group of representatives who elect the president

electoral vote /·ˌ··· ˈ·/ n formal vote of the electoral college

e·lec·to·rate /ɪˈlektərɪt/ n all the electors (1)

e·lec·tric /ɪˈlektrɪk/ adj 1 worked by or producing electricity: *an electric razor* 2 infml very exciting ~**al** adj concerned with or using electricity:

an electrical fault ~**ally** /-kliⁱ/ *adv*

electric chair /ı·,·· '·'/ *n* [*the*+S] punishment of electrocuting (ELECTROCUTE) a criminal

el·ec·tri·cian /ı,lɛk'trıʃən, ,iⁱlɛk-/ *n* person who fits and repairs electrical equipment

e·lec·tri·ci·ty /ı,lɛk'trısəṭiⁱ, ,iⁱlɛk-/ *n* [U] power supply, carried usu. by wires, for heating, lighting, etc.

e·lec·tri·fy /ı'lɛktrə,faı/ *vt* **1** use electric power for **2** excite greatly

e·lec·tro·cute /ı'lɛktrə,kyuʷt/ *vt* kill by passing electric current through the body **-cution** /ı,lɛktrə'kyuʷʃən/ *n* [C;U]

e·lec·trode /ı'lɛktroʷd/ *n* point at which current enters or leaves a BATTERY (1)

e·lec·trol·y·sis /ı,lɛk'trɑləsıs/ *n* [U] the use of electricity **a** for separation of a liquid into its chemical parts or **b** for destruction of hair roots

e·lec·tron /ı'lɛktrɑn/ *n* small piece of matter that moves around the NUCLEUS of an atom

el·ec·tron·ic /ı,lɛk'trɑnık, ,iⁱlɛk-/ *adj* of, using, or produced by equipment that works by means of an electric current passing through CHIPS¹ (4), TRANSISTORS, etc. (for example, televisions, computers, etc.): *electronic music/mail* ~**ally** /-kliⁱ/ *adv* **electronics** *n* [U] study or making of such equipment

el·e·gant /'ɛləgənt/ *adj* graceful; stylish ~**ly** *adv* **-gance** *n* [U]

el·e·ment /'ɛləmənt/ *n* **1** [C] simple substance consisting of only one kind of atom **2** [S] small amount: *an element of truth in what you say* **3** [C] part of a whole: *Honesty is an important element in his character.* **4** [C] heating part of a piece of electric equipment **5 in/out of one's element** doing/not doing what one is best at **elements** *n* [*the*+P] **1** (bad) weather **2** first things to study in a subject **elemental** /,ɛlə'mɛntəl◂/ *adj* of the forces of nature

el·e·men·ta·ry /,ɛlə'mɛntəriⁱ◂/ *adj* **1** easy: *elementary questions* **2** concerned with the beginning of something: *elementary arithmetic* **3** concerned with elementary school

elementary school /·'···· ,·/ *n* school for the first 6 to 8 years of a child's education

el·e·phant /'ɛləfənt/ *n* very large animal with TUSKS and a long round nose (TRUNK) – see also WHITE ELEPHANT ~**ine** /,ɛlə'fæntiⁱn, -taɪn/ *adj* heavy and awkward

el·e·vate /'ɛlə,veⁱt/ *vt fml* **1** raise **2** improve the mind of

el·e·va·tion /,ɛlə'veⁱʃən/ *n* **1** [U] *fml* act of elevating **2** [S] height

above sea level **3** [C] drawing of one side of a building

el·e·va·tor /'ɛlə,veⁱtər/ *n* **1** apparatus in a building for taking people and things from one floor to another **2** machine for raising grain, etc.

e·lev·en /ı'lɛvən/ *det, n, pron* 11 – **th** *det, adv, n, pron* 11th

eleventh hour /·,·· '·/ *n* [*the*+S] the very last moment

elf /ɛlf/ *n* **elves** /ɛlvz/ small usu. male fairy ~**in** *adj*

e·li·cit /ı'lısıt/ *vt fml* get (information, etc.) from someone

e·lide /ı'laıd/ *vt* leave out (a sound) in pronunciation

el·i·gi·ble /'ɛlədʒəbəl/ *adj* fulfilling the conditions; suitable **-bility** /,ɛlədʒə'bıləṭiⁱ/ *n* [U]

e·lim·i·nate /ı'lımə,neⁱt/ *vt* remove; get rid of **-nation** /ı,lımə'neⁱʃən/ *n* [U]

e·lite /ı'liⁱt, eⁱ-/ *n* favored powerful group in society **elitism** *n* [U]

elk /ɛlk/ *n* very large animal like a DEER

el·lipse /ı'lıps/ *n* OVAL shape

el·lip·ti·cal /ı'lıptıkəl/ *adj* **1** OVAL **2** (of speech) with hidden meaning

elm /ɛlm/ *n* large tree with broad leaves

el·o·cu·tion /,ɛlə'kyuʷʃən/ *n* [U] good clear speaking

e·lon·gate /ı'lɔŋgeⁱt, 'iⁱlɔŋ,geⁱt/ *vt* make longer

e·lope /ı'loʷp/ *vi* run away to get married ~**ment** *n* [C;U]

el·o·quent /'ɛləkwənt/ *adj* **1** able to influence people by using language well **2** *fml* showing something very strongly: *an eloquent reminder of the horrors of wars* ~**quence** *n* [U]

else /ɛls/ *adv* **1** more; as well: *What else can I say?* **2** apart from (what is mentioned): *He's here. Everyone else has gone home.* **3** otherwise: *You must go or else go to prison.*

else·where /'ɛls-hweər, -weər/ *adv* at, in, from, or to another place

ELT /,iⁱ ɛl 'tiⁱ/ *n* [U] English language teaching

e·lu·ci·date /ı'luʷsə,deⁱt/ *vt fml* explain **-dation** /ı,luʷsə'deⁱʃən/ *n* [U]

e·lude /ı'luʷd/ *vt* escape from

e·lu·sive /ı'luʷsıv/ *adj* hard to find or remember

elves /ɛlvz/ *pl.* of ELF

e·ma·ci·at·ed /ı'meⁱʃiⁱeⁱṭıd/ *adj* extremely thin **-ation** /ı,meⁱʃiⁱ-'eⁱʃən, -siⁱ-/ *n* [U]

em·a·nate /'ɛmə,neⁱt/ *v* **emanate from** *phr vi fml* come out (from somewhere) **-nation** /,ɛmə'neⁱʃən/ *n* [C;U]

e·man·ci·pate /ı'mænsə,peⁱt/ *vt* make (slaves, etc.) free **-pation** /ı,mænsə'peⁱʃən/ *n* [U]

e·mas·cu·late /ɪˈmæskyəˌleɪt/ vt **1** weaken **2** CASTRATE **-lation** /ɪˌmæskyəˈleɪʃən/ n [U]

em·balm /ɪmˈbɑm/ vt preserve (a dead body) with chemicals, etc. ~ **er** n

em·bank·ment /ɪmˈbæŋkmənt/ n wall that holds back water or carries a road or railroad

em·bar·go /ɪmˈbɑrɡoʷ/ n **-goes** official order forbidding trade ♦ vt put an embargo on

em·bark /ɪmˈbɑrk/ vi/t go or put onto a ship **~ation** /ˌɛmbɑrˈkeɪ-ʃən/ n [C;U]

embark on/upon phr vt start (something new)

em·bar·rass /ɪmˈbærəs/ vt make ashamed or socially uncomfortable: an embarrassing question/silence **~ingly** adv **~ment** n [C;U]

em·bas·sy /ˈɛmbəsiʸ/ n offices of an AMBASSADOR

em·bat·tled /ɪmˈbætld/ adj surrounded by enemies or difficulties

em·bed /ɪmˈbɛd/ vt **-dd-** fix firmly in surrounding material

em·bel·lish /ɪmˈbɛlɪʃ/ vt **1** decorate **2** add (esp. untrue) details to **~ment** n [C;U]

em·ber /ˈɛmbər/ n [usu. pl.] piece of very hot coal, etc., in a dying fire

em·bez·zle /ɪmˈbɛzəl/ vi/t steal (money placed in one's care) **~ment** n [U] **-zler** n

em·bit·ter /ɪmˈbɪtər/ vt make sad and angry

em·bla·zon /ɪmˈbleɪzən/ vt show (a decoration, etc.) noticeably

em·blem /ˈɛmbləm/ n sign representing something: The school's emblem is a knight.

em·bod·y /ɪmˈbɑdiʸ/ vt fml give physical expression to **-iment** n: She's the embodiment of evil.

em·boss /ɪmˈbɔs, ɪmˈbɑs/ vt decorate with a raised pattern

em·brace /ɪmˈbreɪs/ v **1** vi/t take (someone) lovingly in one's arms **2** vt fml include **3** vt fml become a believer in: embrace the Muslim faith ♦ n: a warm embrace

em·broi·der /ɪmˈbrɔɪdər/ vi/t **1** decorate (cloth) by sewing in colored thread **2** EMBELLISH **~y** n [U]

em·broiled /ɪmˈbrɔɪld/ adj mixed up in something troublesome: to get embroiled in an argument

em·bry·o /ˈɛmbriʸˌoʷ/ n **-os 1** creature in its first state before birth **2 in embryo** still incomplete **~nic** /ˌɛmbriʸˈɑnɪk◂/ adj

em·bry·ol·o·gy /ˌɛmbriʸˈɑlədʒiʸ/ n [U] study of embryos

em·cee /ˌɛm ˈsiʸ/ n MASTER OF CEREMONIES

e·mend /ɪˈmɛnd/ vt take mistakes out of (something written) **~ation** /ˌiʸmenˈdeɪʃən/ n [C;U]

em·e·rald /ˈɛmərəld/ n [C;U] (color of) a bright green precious stone

e·merge /ɪˈmɜrdʒ/ vi **1** come out **2** (of facts) become known **emergence** n [U] **emergent** adj beginning to develop: emergent nations

e·mer·gen·cy /ɪˈmɜrdʒənsiʸ/ n dangerous happening which must be dealt with at once

em·e·ry /ˈɛməriʸ/ n [U] hard powder used for polishing

em·i·grant /ˈɛməɡrənt/ n person who emigrates

em·i·grate /ˈɛməˌɡreɪt/ vi leave one's own country to live in another **-gration** /ˌɛməˈɡreɪʃən/ n [C;U]

é·mi·gré /ˈɛməˌɡreɪ/ n fml a REFUGEE

em·i·nence /ˈɛmənəns/ n [U] great importance

é·mi·nence grise /ˌɛmənɑns ˈɡriʸz/ n someone who secretly has great influence, but does not have an official position of power

em·i·nent /ˈɛmənənt/ adj (of a person) famous and admired **~ly** adv fml extremely

e·mir /əˈmɪər/ n Muslim ruler **~ate** /əˈmɪrɪt, -reʸt/ n lands, etc., of an emir

em·is·sa·ry /ˈɛməˌsɛriʸ/ n fml person sent with a message or to do special work

e·mis·sion /ɪˈmɪʃən/ n fml **1** [U] act of emitting **2** [C] something emitted

e·mit /ɪˈmɪt/ vt **-tt-** fml send out: to emit smoke/a humming sound

e·mol·u·ments /ɪˈmɑlyəmənts/ n [P] fml or pomp pay; wages

e·mo·tion /ɪˈmoʷʃən/ n **1** [C] strong feeling, such as love, sorrow, etc. **2** [U] strength of feeling: a voice shaking with emotion **~al** adj **1** concerning the emotions **2** having feelings that are (too) strong **~ally** adv

e·mo·tive /ɪˈmoʷtɪv/ adj causing strong feeling

em·pa·thy /ˈɛmpəθiʸ/ n [S;U] ability to imagine oneself in the position of another person **-thize** vi

em·pe·ror /ˈɛmpərər/ n ruler of an empire

em·pha·sis /ˈɛmfəsɪs/ n **-ses** /-siʸz/ [C;U] special force or attention given to something important

em·pha·size /ˈɛmfəˌsaɪz/ vt place emphasis on

em·phat·ic /ɪmˈfætɪk/ adj strongly emphasized **~ally** /-kliʸ/ adv

em·phy·se·ma /ˌɛmfəˈsiʸmə, -ˈziʸ-/ n serious lung illness, often resulting from smoking

em·pire /ˈɛmpaɪər/ n group of countries under one government

em·pir·i·cis·m /ɪmˈpɪrəˌsɪzəm, ɛm-/

n attitude to life, etc., based on practical experience, not on books **-cal** /-rɪkəl/ *adj*

em·ploy /ɪmˈplɔɪ/ *vt* 1 give paid work to 2 *fml* use **~able** *adj* suitable as a worker **~er** *n* person who employs others **~ment** *n* 1 [U] paid work 2 [C] *fml* useful activity

em·ploy·ee /ɪmˈplɔɪ-iʸ, ˌemplɔɪˈiʸ, ɪm-/ *n* employed person

em·pow·er /ɪmˈpaʊər/ *vt fml* give power to **~ment** *n*

em·press /ˈemprɪs/ *n* female ruler of an empire

emp·ty /ˈemptiʸ/ *adj* 1 containing nothing 2 insincere: *empty promises* ♦ *n* [*usu. pl.*] empty container ♦ *vt/i* make or become empty **-tiness** *n* [U]

empty-hand·ed /ˌ·· ˈ··/ *adj* having gained nothing

empty-head·ed /ˌ·· ˈ··◁/ *adj* silly

e·mu /ˈiʸmyuʷ/ *n* large Australian flightless bird

em·u·late /ˈemyəˌleʸt/ *vt* try to do as well as or better than **-lation** /ˌemyəˈleʸʃən/ *n*

e·mul·sion /ɪˈmʌlʃən/ *n* [U] creamy liquid mixture, esp. paint

en·a·ble /ɪˈneʸbəl/ *vt* make able: *to enable them to walk again*

en·act /ɪˈnækt/ *vt* make (a law)

en·am·el /ɪˈnæməl/ *n* [U] 1 glassy covering on metal, etc. 2 hard surface of the teeth ♦ *vt* –l– cover with enamel

en·am·ored /ɪˈnæmərd/ *adj* very fond of (an idea, etc.)

en bloc /ɑn ˈblɑk/ *adv* all together as a single unit

en·camp·ment /ɪnˈkæmpmənt/ *n* military camp

en·cap·su·late /ɪnˈkæpsəˌleʸt/ *vt* express in a short form

en·case /ɪnˈkeʸs/ *vt* cover completely

en·chant /ɪnˈtʃænt/ *vt* 1 delight 2 use magic on **~ing** *adj* delightful **~ingly** *adv* **~ment** *n* [C;U]

en·chi·la·da /ˌentʃəˈlɑdə/ *n* Mexican dish of meat, etc. inside a TORTILLA

en·cir·cle /ɪnˈsɜrkəl/ *vt* surround

en·clave /ˈenkleʸv, ˈɑn-/ *n* part of a country, etc. surrounded by another: *ethnic enclaves in Chicago*

en·close /ɪnˈkloʷz/ *vt* 1 surround with a fence, etc. 2 put (something else) into an envelope

en·clo·sure /ɪnˈkloʷʒər/ *n* 1 enclosed place 2 something put in with a letter 3 act of enclosing

en·com·pass /ɪnˈkʌmpəs/ *vt* include; be concerned with

en·core /ˈɑŋkɔr, ˈɑŋkoʷr, ˈɑn-/ *interj, n* (word calling for) a repeated performance

en·coun·ter /ɪnˈkaʊntər/ *vt fml* meet (something dangerous or unexpected) ♦ *n* sudden (esp. unpleasant) meeting

en·cour·age /ɪnˈkɜrɪdʒ, -ˈkʌr-/ *vt* give approval to; urge: *He encouraged her to try.* **~ment** *n* [C;U]

en·cour·aged /ɪnˈkɜrɪdʒd, -ˈkʌr-/ *adj* feeling new hope and confidence

en·cour·ag·ing /ɪnˈkɜrɪdʒɪŋ, -ˈkʌr-/ *adj* causing feelings of hope and confidence: *encouraging words*

en·croach /ɪnˈkroʷtʃ/ *vi* go beyond what is right or usual: *encroach on their territory* **~ment** *n* [C;U]

en·crust·ed /ɪnˈkrʌstɪd/ *adj* thickly covered: *encrusted with jewels/mud*

en·cum·ber /ɪnˈkʌmbər/ *vt* load; BURDEN **-brance** *n*

en·cy·clo·pe·di·a /ɪnˌsaɪkləˈpiʸdiʸə/ *n* book of many facts in alphabetical order **-dic** *adj* wide and full

end[1] /end/ *n* 1 point where something stops or finishes: *the end of the road/of August* 2 little piece remaining: *Throw away the ends.* 3 *fml* aim; purpose 4 **at a loose end** having nothing to do 5 **in the end** at last 6 **make ends meet** get just enough money 7 **no end of** an endless amount of 8 **on end a** continuously: *for hours on end* **b** upright 9 **put an end to** stop – see also SHARP END **~less** *adj* never finishing **~lessly** *adv*

end[2] *vi/t* finish **~ing** *n* end (of a story, etc.)

end up *phr vi* finish (one's journey, etc.): *Where did you end up staying last night?*

en·dan·ger /ɪnˈdeʸndʒər/ *vt* cause danger to

en·dear /ɪnˈdɪər/ *vt* **endear oneself to** make oneself loved by **~ment** *n* expression of love

en·deav·or /ɪnˈdevər/ *vi fml* try ♦ *n* [C;U] *fml* effort

en·dem·ic /enˈdemɪk, ɪn-/ *adj* (esp. of something bad) often happening in a place

en·dive /ˈendaɪv/ *n* [U] plant with leaves which are eaten as a vegetable

en·dorse /ɪnˈdɔrs/ *vt* 1 express approval of (opinions, etc.) 2 write one's name on (a check) **~ment** *n* [C;U]

en·dow /ɪnˈdaʊ/ *vt* 1 give a continuing income to (a school, etc.) 2 **be endowed with** *fml* have (a good quality) from birth **~ment** *n* [C;U]

en·dur·ance /ɪnˈdʊərəns, -ˈdyʊər-/ *n* [U] power of enduring

en·dure /ɪnˈdʊər, -ˈdyʊər/ *v* 1 *vt* suffer (pain, etc.) patiently 2 *vi* continue to exist

en·e·ma /ˈenəmə/ *n* putting of a liquid, esp. a medicine, into the bowels through the RECTUM

en·e·my /ˈenəmiʲ/ n 1 person who hates or opposes another person 2 country with which one is at war

en·er·get·ic /ˌenərˈdʒetɪk◂/ adj very active ~**ally** /-kliʲ/ adv

en·er·gy /ˈenərdʒiʲ/ n [U] 1 ability to be active and work hard 2 power that drives machines, etc.: *nuclear energy*

en·fant ter·ri·ble /ˌɑnfɑn teˈriʲblə/ n shocking but also often interesting and amusing person

en·fee·bled /ɪnˈfiʲbəld/ adj fml made weak

en·fold /ɪnˈfoʷld/ vt take into one's arms

en·force /ɪnˈfɔrs, ɪnˈfoʷrs/ vt cause (a law etc.) to be obeyed ~**able** adj ~**ment** n [U]

en·fran·chise /ɪnˈfræntʃaɪz/ vt give the right to vote to ~**ment** n [U]

en·gage /ɪnˈgeʲdʒ/ v fml 1 vt arrange to employ 2 vi/t lock (machine parts) together **engaged** adj 1 having agreed to marry 2 fml busy or in use ~**ment** n 1 agreement to marry 2 fml arrangement to meet someone 3 fml battle

  engage in phr vt fml make (someone) busy in

en·gag·ing /ɪnˈgeʲdʒɪŋ/ adj charming ~**ly** adv

en·gen·der /ɪnˈdʒendər/ vt fml cause; produce

en·gine /ˈendʒən/ n 1 machine that turns power into movement 2 machine that pulls a train

en·gi·neer /ˌendʒəˈnɪər/ n 1 person who plans machines, roads, bridges, etc. 2 person who controls engines ♦ vt cause by secret planning ~**ing** n [U] profession of an ENGINEER (1)

English break·fast /ˌɪŋglɪʃ ˈbrekfəst/ n a breakfast of esp. BACON and eggs, TOAST and MARMALADE

en·grave /ɪnˈgreʲv/ vt cut (words, etc.) on a hard surface **engraver** n **-engraving** n [C] picture printed from an engraved piece of metal 2 [U] work of an engraver

en·gross /ɪnˈgroʷs/ vt completely fill the attention of

en·gulf /ɪnˈgʌlf/ vt swallow up: *a house engulfed in flames*

en·hance /ɪnˈhæns/ vt increase (something good) ~**ment** n [C;U]

e·nig·ma /ɪˈnɪgmə/ n mystery ~**tic** /ˌenɪgˈmætɪk◂/ adj ~**tically** /-kliʲ/ adv

en·joy /ɪnˈdʒɔɪ/ vt 1 get pleasure from 2 fml possess (something good) 3 enjoy oneself be happy ~**able** adj pleasant ~**ably** adv ~**ment** n [C;U]

en·large /ɪnˈlɑrdʒ/ vt/i (cause to) become larger ~**ment** n [C; U]

  enlarge on/upon phr vt say more about

en·light·en /ɪnˈlaɪtn/ vt make free from false beliefs ~**ment** n [U]

en·list /ɪnˈlɪst/ v 1 vi/t (cause to) join the armed forces 2 vt obtain (help, etc.) ~**ment** n [C;U]

en·liv·en /ɪnˈlaɪvən/ vt to make more active or cheerful

en masse /ˌɑn ˈmæs/ adv all together

en·mesh /ɪnˈmeʃ/ vt catch as if in a net

en·mi·ty /ˈenmətiʲ/ n [C;U] fml hatred

e·nor·mi·ty /ɪˈnɔrmətiʲ/ n 1 [U] enormous size 2 [C;U] fml great wickedness

e·nor·mous /ɪˈnɔrməs/ adj very large ~**ly** adv extremely

e·nough /ɪˈnʌf/ determiner, pron, adv 1 as much or as many as is needed: *enough food/chairs* | *not big enough* 2 fair enough infml all right 3 oddly/strangely enough… and this is strange, but… 4 sure enough as expected

en·quire /ɪnˈkwaɪər/ vi/t INQUIRE **enquiry** n [C;U]

en·rage /ɪnˈreʲdʒ/ vt make very angry

en·rich /ɪnˈrɪtʃ/ vt 1 make rich 2 improve by adding something ~**ment** n [U]

en·roll /ɪnˈroʷl/ vi/t 1 (cause to) join a group officially ~**ment** n [C;U]

en route /ɑn ˈruʷt, ɛn-/ adv on the way; traveling

en·sconced /ɪnˈskɑnst/ adj comfortably seated

en·sem·ble /ɑnˈsɑmbəl/ n 1 small group of musicians 2 fml set of things

en·shrine /ɪnˈʃraɪn/ vt fml preserve as if holy

en·sign /ˈensən, -saɪn/ n 1 ship's flag 2 US naval officer of low rank

en·slave /ɪnˈsleʲv/ vt make into a slave ~**ment** n [U]

en·sue /ɪnˈsuʷ/ vi fml happen afterwards or as a result

en·sure /ɪnˈʃʊər/also **insure** — vt make (something) certain to happen

en·tail /ɪnˈteʲl/ vt make necessary

en·tan·gle /ɪnˈtæŋgəl/ vt cause to become twisted with something else ~**ment** n [C;U]

en·ter /ˈentər/ v 1 vi/t come or go in or into 2 vt become a member of 3 vt put into a book, list, etc.

  enter into phr vt take part in

  enter on/upon phr vt fml begin

en·ter·prise /ˈentərˌpraɪz/ n 1 [C] plan that needs courage 2 [U] willingness to take risks 3 [U] type of business organization: *private*

enterprise – see also FREE ENTERPRISE
-prising *adj* having ENTERPRISE (2)
en·ter·tain /ˌentəˈteɪn/ *v* **1** *vi/t* amuse and interest **2** *vi/t* provide food and drink for (guests) **3** *vt fml* be willing to consider (ideas) **~er** *n* person who amuses people professionally **~ment** *n* **1** [U] act of entertaining **2** [C] public amusement
en·thral /ɪnˈθrɔl/ *vt* hold the complete attention of
en·throne /ɪnˈθroʊn/ *vt* put a (ruler) on a THRONE
en·thuse /ɪnˈθuːz/ *vi* speak with enthusiasm
en·thu·si·as·m /ɪnˈθuːziˌæzəm/ *n* [C;U] great interest and admiration **-ast** *n* person who is very interested in something **-astic** /ɪnˌθuːziˈæstɪk◂/ *adj* full of enthusiasm **-astically** /-kliʸ/ *adv*
en·tice /ɪnˈtaɪs/ *vt* persuade, esp. to do wrong **~ment** *n* [C;U]
en·tire /ɪnˈtaɪər/ *adj* complete **~ly** *adv* **~ty** /ɪnˈtaɪərətiʸ/ *n* [U] *fml*
en·ti·tle /ɪnˈtaɪtl/ *vt* **1** give a right (to) **2** give a title to (a book, etc.) **~ment** *n* [U]
en·ti·ty /ˈentətiʸ/ *n* thing with separate existence
en·tou·rage /ˈɑntuˌrɑʒ/ *n* people who surround someone important
en·trails /ˈentreɪlz/ *n* bowels
en·trance¹ /ˈentrəns/ *n* **1** [C] door, etc., by which one enters **2** [C] act of entering **3** [U] right to enter
en·trance² /ɪnˈtræns/ *vt* fill with delight
en·trant /ˈentrənt/ *n* person who enters a race, profession, etc.
en·treat /ɪnˈtriːt/ *vt fml* beg; IMPLORE **~y** *n* [C;U] act of entreating
en·trée /ˈɑntreɪ/ *n* **1** main dish of a meal **2** freedom to enter
en·trenched /ɪnˈtrentʃt/ *adj* (of beliefs, etc.) firmly established
en·tre·pre·neur /ˌɑntrəprəˈnɜr, -ˈnʊər, -ˈnyʊər/ *n* person who starts a business, etc., and takes business risks **~ial** *adj*
en·trust /ɪnˈtrʌst/ *vt* give to someone to take care of
en·try /ˈentriʸ/ *n* **1** [C;U] act of coming or going in **2** place where one enters **3** [C] something written in a list
en·twine /ɪnˈtwaɪn/ *vt* twist together or around
e·nu·me·rate /ɪˈnuːməˌreɪt, ɪˈnyuː-/ *vt fml* name one by one **-ration** /ɪˌnuːməˈreɪʃən, -ˌnyuː-/ *n* [C;U]
e·nun·ci·ate /ɪˈnʌnsiʸˌeɪt/ *vt/i* pronounce (words) clearly **-ation** /ɪˌnʌnsiʸˈeɪʃən/ *n* [U]
en·vel·op /ɪnˈveləp/ *vt* cover completely; *enveloped in flames* **~ment** *n* [U]

en·ve·lope /ˈenvəˌloʷp, ˈɑn-/ *n* paper container for a letter
en·vi·a·ble /ˈenviʸəbəl/ *adj* very desirable **-bly** *adv*
en·vi·ous /ˈenviʸəs/ *adj* feeling ENVY **~ly** *adv*
en·vi·ron·ment /ɪnˈvaɪrənmənt, -ˈvaɪərn-/ *n* conditions in which people, animals, etc., live **~al** /ɪnˌvaɪrənˈmentl◂, -ˌvaɪərn-/ *adj* **~ally** *adv* **~alist** *n* person who tries to keep our natural surroundings from being spoiled
en·vis·age /ɪnˈvɪzɪdʒ/ also **envision** /ɪnˈvɪʒən/ — *vt* see in the mind; expect
en·voy /ˈenvɔɪ, ˈɑn-/ *n* messenger; representative
en·vy /ˈenviʸ/ *n* [U] **1** bad feeling one has towards someone who has better luck than oneself **2 the envy of (someone)** something which other people want to have or to be: *Her house is the envy of all her friends.* ♦ *vt* feel envy towards or because of
en·zyme /ˈenzaɪm/ *n* substance produced by living cells that causes chemical change
e·on /ˈiʸɑn/ *n* an AEON
ep·au·let, -lette /ˈepəˌlet, ˌepəˈlet/ *n* shoulder decoration on a uniform
e·phem·e·ral /ɪˈfemərəl/ *adj* lasting only a short time
ep·ic /ˈepɪk/ *n* **1** long poem, film, etc., about the deeds of gods or great men **2** *derog* event needing a lot of time and effort ♦ *adj* (of stories) full of bravery and excitement
ep·i·cu·re·an /ˌepɪkyʊˈriʸən/ *n* person who believes pleasure is very important
ep·i·dem·ic /ˌepəˈdemɪk◂/ *n* many cases of an infectious disease at the same time
ep·i·gram /ˈepəˌgræm/ *n* short amusing poem or saying
ep·i·lep·sy /ˈepəˌlepsiʸ/ *n* disease of the brain causing sudden unconsciousness **-leptic** /ˌepəˈleptɪk◂/ *adj, n*
ep·i·logue /ˈepəˌlɔg, -ˌlɑg/ *n* last part of a play or book
E·pis·co·pal·i·an /ɪˌpɪskəˈpeɪliʸən/ also **e·pis·co·pal** /ɪˈpɪskəpəl/ — *n, adj* **1** of or governed by BISHOPS **2** (of or being a) member of the Protestant Episcopal Church
ep·i·sode /ˈepəˌsoʷd/ *n* one separate event or period of time
ep·is·tle /ɪˈpɪsəl/ *n fml* LETTER (1)
ep·i·taph /ˈepəˌtæf/ *n* words written above a grave
ep·i·thet /ˈepəˌθet/ *adj* adjective, esp. used of a person
e·pit·o·me /ɪˈpɪtəmiʸ/ *n* something that perfectly shows a particular

quality: *My son is the epitome of laziness.* –**mize** *vt* be typical of

e·poch /ˈepək, ˈepak/ *n* period of historical time, esp. one in which some very important event happened ~-**making** *adj* extremely important

e·pox·y /iˈpaksiʸ/ *n* very strong glue

e·qua·ble /ˈekwəbəl, ˈiʸ-/ *adj* even and regular: *an equable climate* –**bly** *adv*

e·qual /ˈiʸkwəl/ *adj* **1** the same in size, value, etc. **2 equal to** having enough ability, etc., for ♦ *n* person equal to another ♦ *vt* **-l-** be the same as ~**ize** *vt* make equal – **ly** *adv*: *equally fit* | *to share the work equally* ~**ity** /iˈkwalətiʸ/ *n* [U]: *the equality of women*

equal sign /ˈ·· ·/ *n* the mark =

eq·ua·nim·i·ty /ˌiʸkwəˈnimətiʸ, ˌe-/ *n* [U] *fml* calmness of mind

e·quate /iˈkweʸt/ *vt* consider as equal

e·qua·tion /iˈkweʸʒən/ *n* statement that 2 quantities are equal: $2x + 1 = 7$ *is an equation.*

e·qua·tor /iˈkweʸt̬ər/ *n* [*the*+S] imaginary line around the world, equally distant from the North and South POLES –**ial** /ˌiʸkwəˈtoʸriʸəl◂, -ˈkwʳr-, ˌe-/ *adj*

e·ques·tri·an /iˈkwestriʸən/ *adj fml* concerned with riding horses

e·qui·lib·ri·um /ˌiʸkwəˈlibriʸəm/ *n* [U] *fml* BALANCE (1)

e·qui·nox /ˈiʸkwəˌnaks, ˈe-/ *n* time of year when day and night are of equal length

e·quip /iˈkwip/ *vt* **-pp-** provide with what is necessary ~**ment** *n* [U] things needed for an activity

eq·ui·ta·ble /ˈekwɪt̬əbəl/ *adj* fair and just: *an equitable division of the money* -**bly** *adv*

eq·ui·ties /ˈekwət̬iʸz/ *n* [P] *tech* business's ordinary stock, on which no fixed amount of interest is paid

eq·ui·ty /ˈekwət̬iʸ/ *n* [U] *fml* fairness

e·quiv·a·lent /iˈkwivələnt/ *n, adj* (something) the same in value

e·quiv·o·cal /iˈkwivəkəl/ *adj* doubtful in meaning; questionable -**cate** *vi fml* speak in an equivocal way on purpose

ERA /ˌiʸ ɑr ˈeʸ/ *n* Equal Rights Amendment (to the US Constitution) especially concerned with sexual equality but not yet a law

e·ra /ˈiʸərə, ˈerə/ *n* period of historical time, marked esp. by particular developments

e·rad·i·cate /iˈrædəˌkeʸt/ *vt* put an end to (something bad) -**cation** /iˌrædəˈkeʸʃən/ *n* [U]

e·rase /iˈreʸs/ *vt fml* rub out

e·ras·er /iˈreʸsər/ *n* piece of elastic substance for removing pencil marks

ere /eər/ *prep, conj old use* before

e·rect /iˈrekt/ *adj* upright ♦ *vt* **1** put upright: *erect a tent* **2** *fml* build: *erect a monument* ~**ly** *adv* ~**ness** *n* [U] ~**ion** /iˈrekʃən/ *n* **1** [U] the act of erecting something **2** [C] *fml* a building **3** [C;U] (an example of) the state of the PENIS when upright

er·go /ˈɜrgoʷ/ *adv* therefore

er·go·nom·ics /ˌɜrgəˈnamiks/ *n* [U] study of how people work best with machines -**ic** *adj* -**ically** /-kliʸ/ *adv*

e·rode /iˈroʷd/ *vt* (of acids, water, etc.) wear away; reduce **erosion** /iˈroʷʒən/ *n* [U]

e·ro·ge·nous /iˈradʒənəs/ *adj* sexually sensitive

e·rot·ic /iˈrat̬ik/ *adj* of sexual love ~**ism** /-t̬əˌsizəm/ *n* [U]

err /ɜr, er/ *vi fml* make a mistake

er·rand /ˈerənd/ *n* short journey to do or esp. buy something

er·rant /ˈerənt/ *adj fml* wandering away and misbehaving

er·rat·ic /iˈræt̬ik/ *adj* changeable; not regular ~**ally** /-kliʸ/ *adv*

er·ro·ne·ous /iˈroʷniʸəs/ *adj fml* (of a belief) incorrect ~**ly** *adv*

er·ror /ˈerər/ *n* **1** [C] mistake **2** [U] state of being mistaken

er·satz /ˈeərzats/ *adj derog* used instead of something else; artificial

erst·while /ˈɜrstwaɪl/ *adj lit* former

er·u·dite /ˈeryəˌdaɪt, ˈerə-/ *adj fml* full of learning

e·rupt /iˈrʌpt/ *vi* (of a VOLCANO) explode suddenly ~**ion** /iˈrʌpʃən/ *n* [C;U]

es·ca·late /ˈeskəˌleʸt/ *vi/t* (cause to) grow greater or more serious -**lation** /ˌeskəˈleʸʃən/ *n* [U]

es·ca·la·tor /ˈeskəˌleʸt̬ər/ *n* set of moving stairs

es·ca·pade /ˈeskəˌpeʸd/ *n* wild dangerous act

es·cape /iˈskeʸp/ *v* **1** *vi/t* get out; get free (from) **2** *vt* avoid (something dangerous): *to escape death* **3** *vt* be forgotten by: *His name escapes me.* ♦ *n* [C;U] (act of) getting free

es·cap·is·m /iˈskeʸpˌizəm/ *n* [U] activity providing escape from dull reality -**ist** *adj, n*

e·scarp·ment /iˈskarpmənt/ *n* long cliff

es·chew /isˈtʃuʷ/ *vt fml* avoid

es·cort¹ /ˈeskɔrt/ *n* **1** person or people who go with another as a protection or honor **2** social companion, esp. a man

es·cort² /iˈskɔrt/ *vt* go with as an escort

Es·ki·mo /ˈeskəmoʷ/ *n* member of a

race of people living in the icy far north of N America

ESL /ˌiˈes ˈel/ n, adj abbrev. for: English as a second language

ESOL /ˈiˈsɑl/ n, adj abbrev. for: English for speakers of other languages

e·soph·a·gus /ɪˈsɑfəgəs/ n med food tube from the mouth to the stomach

es·o·ter·ic /ˌesəˈterɪk◄/ adj having deep and secret meanings understood only by a few people ~ally /-kliʸ/ adv

ESP /ˌiʸ es ˈpiʸ/ n [U] extrasensory perception; knowledge obtained without using one's ordinary 5 senses

es·pe·cial·ly /ɪˈspeʃəliʸ/ adv 1 to a particularly great degree: *not especially hot* 2 in particular: *I like fruit, especially apples.*

es·pi·o·nage /ˈespiʸəˌnɑʒ, -nɪdʒ/ n [U] spying (SPY)

es·pouse /ɪˈspaʊz/ vt fml support (an aim, etc.) espousal n [C;U]

es·say /ˈeseʸ/ n short piece of writing on a subject ~ist n writer of essays

es·sence /ˈesəns/ n 1 [U] most important quality of something [C;U] 2 liquid, etc., with some particular strong taste or smell: *vanilla essence* 3 of the essence extremely important

es·sen·tial /ɪˈsenʃəl, -tʃəl/ adj 1 necessary 2 FUNDAMENTAL: *the essential difference between us* ♦ n [usu. pl.] something necessary ~ly adv deep down, at base: *She's essentially kind.*

es·tab·lish /ɪˈstæblɪʃ/ vt 1 begin; CREATE (an organization, set of rules, etc.) 2 settle (esp. oneself) firmly in a particular state or position: *the film which established her reputation as a director* 3 make certain of (a fact, etc.) ~ment n 1 [U] act of establishing 2 [C] fml place run as a business 3 [the+S] (cap.) often derog the powerful people who control public life

es·tate /ɪˈsteʸt/ n 1 piece of land in the country, with one owner 2 law whole of a person's property, esp. as left after death – see also REAL ESTATE

es·teem /ɪˈstiʸm/ n [U] fml respect: *I hold him in high esteem.* ♦ vt 1 respect greatly 2 fml consider to be estimable /ˈestəməbəl/ adj worthy of respect

es·ti·mate¹ /ˈestəˌmeʸt/ vt/i calculate; form an opinion about (cost, etc.) -mation /ˌestəˈmeʸʃən/ n [U] judgment; opinion

es·ti·mate² /ˈestəmɪt/ n calculation of cost, number, etc.

es·trange /ɪˈstreʸndʒ/ vt make

unfriendly: *estranged wife* (=not living with her husband) ~ment n [C;U]

es·tro·gen /ˈestrədʒən/ n [U] substance in females that makes the body ready to produce young

es·tu·ar·y /ˈestʃuˌeriʸ/ n mouth of a river, into which the sea flows

etc., etcetera /et ˈseṭərə, -trə/ adv and the rest; and other things

etch /etʃ/ vt/i draw with a needle and acid on metal ~ing n [C;U]

e·ter·nal /ɪˈtɜrnl/ adj lasting for ever ~ly adv

e·ter·ni·ty /ɪˈtɜrnəṭiʸ/ n 1 [U] endless time after death 2 [C] an extremely long time

e·ther /ˈiʸθər/ n [U] 1 liquid that easily changes to a gas 2 upper levels of the air

e·the·re·al /ɪˈθɪəriʸəl/ adj extremely light and delicate

eth·ic /ˈeθɪk/ n system of moral behavior: *the Christian ethic* ~al adj 1 of morals 2 morally good ~ally /-kliʸ/ adv ethics n 1 [U] science of morals 2 [P] moral rules

eth·nic /ˈeθnɪk/ adj of or related to a racial, national, or tribal group ~ally /-kliʸ/ adv

e·thos /ˈiʸθɑs/ n [S] characteristic moral beliefs of a person or group

et·i·quette /ˈeṭɪkɪt, -ˌket/ n [U] formal rules of manners

et·y·mol·o·gy /ˌeṭəˈmɑlədʒiʸ/ n [U] study of the origins of words

eu·ca·lyp·tus /ˌyuʷkəˈlɪptəs/ n tree whose oil is used as medicine for colds

eu·lo·gy /ˈyuʷlədʒiʸ/ n fml speech in praise of someone -gize vt praise highly -gistic /ˌyuʷləˈdʒɪstɪk◄/ adj full of praise

eu·nuch /ˈyuʷnək/ n man who has been castrated (CASTRATE)

eu·phe·mis·m /ˈyuʷfəˌmɪzəm/ n [C;U] (use of) a pleasanter, less direct word for something unpleasant -mistic /ˌyuʷfəˈmɪstɪk◄/ adj

eu·pho·ri·a /yuʷˈfɔriʸə, -ˈfoʷr-/ n [U] state of happiness and cheerful excitement -ric /yuʷˈfɔrɪk, -ˈfar-/ adj

eu·tha·na·si·a /ˌyuʷθəˈneʸʒə/ n [U] painless killing of very ill or very old people

e·vac·u·ate /ɪˈvækyuˌeʸt/ vt take all the people away from (a dangerous place) -ation /ɪˌvækyuʷˈeʸʃən/ n [C;U] -ee /-kyuʷˈiʸ/ n person who has been evacuated

e·vade /ɪˈveʸd/ vt avoid; escape from

e·val·u·ate /ɪˈvælyuʷˌeʸt/ vt calculate the value of -ation /ɪˌvælyuʷˈeʸʃən/ n [C;U]

e·van·gel·i·cal /ˌiʸvænˈdʒelɪkəl,

,evən- / n, adj (often cap.) **1** (member) of those Christian churches that believe in studying the Bible rather than in ceremonies **2** (person) showing very great eagerness in spreading Christian beliefs

e·van·ge·list /ɪ'vændʒəlɪst/ n traveling Christian religious teacher **-lism** n [U] — **-ic** /ɪ,vændʒə'lɪstɪk◂/ adj

e·vap·o·rate /ɪ'væpə,reɪt/ vi/t change into steam and disappear **-ration** /ɪ,væpə'reɪʃən/ n [U]

e·va·sion /ɪ've³ʒən/ n [C;U] the act of evading (EVADE): tax evasion **-sive** /-sɪv/ adj

eve /iːv/ n [S] **1** (usu. cap.) day before a (religious) holiday **2** time just before any event: on the eve of the election

e·ven¹ /'iːvən/ adv **1** (shows that something is unexpected and surprising): John's a very good swimmer, but even he doesn't swim in the river. (= so certainly nobody else does) **2** (makes comparisons stronger): It's even colder than yesterday. **3** even if it does not matter if **4** even now/so/then in spite of that: I explained, but even then he didn't understand. **5** even though though

even² adj **1** smooth and regular: an even surface/temperature **2** (of things that can be compared) equal: an even chance **3** (of numbers) that can be divided by two ~ly adv ~ness n [U]

even³ v even out phr vi/t (cause to) become level or equal

even-hand·ed /,·· '··◂/ adj giving fair and equal treatment to all sides

eve·ning /'iːvnɪŋ/ n time between afternoon and when most people go to bed

evening dress /'·· ,·/ n **1** [U] formal clothes for the evening **2** [C] woman's formal long dress

eve·nings /'iːvnɪŋz/ adv regularly in the evening: Tom works evenings.

e·vent /ɪ'vent/ n **1** (important) happening **2** one race, etc., in a day's sports **3** at all events in spite of everything **4** in the event of... if (something) happens ~ful adj full of important events

e·ven·tu·al /ɪ'ventʃuʷəl/ adj happening at last ~ly adv in the end: They eventually succeeded. ~ity /ɪ,ventʃuʷ'ælətiʸ/ n fml possible event

ev·er /'evər/ adv **1** at any time: Does it ever snow? | Nothing ever annoys him. **2** (in comparisons): ever since Christmas | the ever-increasing population **3** (gives force to a question): What ever is that? **4** (gives force to an EXCLAMATION): Was he

ever mad! **5** ever so/such infml very

ev·er·glade /'evər,gleɪd/ n low wet land with tall grass and branching WATERWAYS

ev·er·green /'evər,griːn/ n, adj (tree) that does not lose its leaves in winter

ev·er·last·ing /,evər'læstɪŋ◂/ adj lasting for ever

ev·ery /'evriʸ/ determiner **1** each: I enjoy every minute of it. **2** (of things that can be counted) once in each: I go every 3 days. **3** as much as is possible: I have every reason to trust him. **4** every other the 1st, 3rd, 5th, etc., or the 2nd, 4th, 6th, etc.: Take the pills every other day. **5** every now and then and every so often — sometimes, but not often

ev·ery·bod·y /'evriʸ,bɑdiʸ, -,bʌdiʸ, -bədiʸ/ pron everyone

ev·ery·day /'evriʸ,deɪʸ/ adj ordinary; common

ev·ery·one /'evriʸ,wʌn, -wən/ pron **1** every person: Everyone was pleased. **2** all the people usually here: Where is everyone?

ev·ery·thing /'evriʸ,θɪŋ/ pron **1** each thing: They've eaten everything. **2** all that matters: Money isn't everything.

ev·ery·where /'evriʸ,hwɛər, -,wɛər/ also **ev·ery·place** /-pleɪʸs/ — adv at or to every place

every which way /,·· '·· ·/ adv in every direction

e·vict /ɪ'vɪkt/ vt force to leave a house, etc., by law ~ion /ɪ'vɪkʃən/ n [C;U]

ev·i·dence /'evədəns/ n [U] **1** proof **2** answers given in a court of law **3** in evidence present and easily seen

ev·i·dent /'evədənt, -,dent/ adj plain and clear ~ly adv

e·vil /'iːvəl/ adj harmful; wicked ♦ n [C;U] fml wickedness or misfortune ~ly /'iːvəl-liʸ/ adv

e·voc·a·tive /ɪ'vɑkətɪv/ adj bringing memories: an evocative smell

e·voke /ɪ'voʷk/ vt fml produce (a memory)

ev·o·lu·tion /,evə'luʷʃən/ n [U] gradual development, esp. of living things from earlier and simpler forms

e·volve /ɪ'vɑlv/ vi/t develop gradually

ewe /yuʷ/ n female sheep

ex·a·cer·bate /ɪg'zæsər,beɪt/ vt fml make (something bad) worse

ex·act¹ /ɪg'zækt/ adj correctly measured; PRECISE: the exact time ~ly adv **1** correctly **2** (as a reply) I agree! **3** not exactly not really ~ness, also ~itude n [U]

exact² vt fml demand and obtain

by force ~**ing** adj demanding great effort

ex·ag·ge·rate /ɪgˈzædʒəˌreɪt/ vi/t make (something) seem larger, etc., than it is -**ration** /ɪgˌzædʒəˈreɪʃən/ n [C;U]

ex·al·ta·tion /ˌɛgzɔlˈteɪʃən, ˌɛksɔl-/ n great joy because of success

ex·alt·ed /ɪgˈzɔltɪd/ adj, fml of high rank

ex·am /ɪgˈzæm/ n test of knowledge

ex·am·i·na·tion /ɪgˌzæməˈneɪʃən/ n 1 [C] fml exam 2 [C;U] act of examining

ex·am·ine /ɪgˈzæmɪn/ vt 1 look carefully at: Has the doctor examined you yet? 2 ask questions, to find out something or to test knowledge -**iner** n

ex·am·ple /ɪgˈzæmpəl/ n 1 something that shows a general rule: a typical example 2 something to be copied: Her courage is an example to us all. 3 **for example** (abbrev. **e.g.**) here is one of the things just spoken of 4 **make an example of someone** punish someone to frighten others

ex·as·per·ate /ɪgˈzæspəˌreɪt/ vt annoy very much -**ratedly** adv -**ratingly** adv -**ration** /ɪgˌzæspəˈreɪʃən/ n [U]

ex·ca·vate /ˈɛkskəˌveɪt/ vt 1 dig (a hole) 2 uncover by digging -**vator** n person or machine that excavates -**vation** /ˌɛkskəˈveɪʃən/ n [C;U]

ex·ceed /ɪkˈsiːd/ vt 1 be greater than 2 do more than: to exceed the speed limit ~**ingly** adv fml extremely

ex·cel /ɪkˈsɛl/ vi -**ll**- fml be extremely good (at something)

Ex·cel·len·cy /ˈɛksələnsiː/ n (title of some people of high rank in some countries and churches)

ex·cel·lent /ˈɛksələnt/ adj very good -**lence** n [U]

ex·cept /ɪkˈsɛpt/ prep not including; but not: Everyone except John was tired. ♦ vt fml leave out; not include

ex·cep·tion /ɪkˈsɛpʃən/ n [C;U] (a case of) leaving out or being left out: Everyone, without exception, must attend. | I don't usually see people after 5:00, but I'll make an exception in your case. 2 **take exception to** be made angry by ~**al** adj unusual, esp. because very good ~**ally** adv

ex·cerpt /ˈɛksɜrpt/ n piece taken from a book, etc.

ex·cess /ɪkˈsɛs, ˈɛksɛs/ n, adj [S;U] (an amount that is) greater than is usual or allowed: an excess of violence in the film ~**ive** adj too much ~**ively** adv **excesses** n [P] extremely bad, cruel, etc., behavior

ex·change /ɪksˈtʃeɪndʒ/ vt give and receive in return: I exchanged my pounds for dollars. ♦ n 1 [C;U] act

of exchanging 2 [U] changing of money: the rate of exchange 3 [C] place where a telephone wires meet **b** business people meet: a stock exchange 4 [C] short period of fighting or talking – see also FOREIGN EXCHANGE

ex·cise¹ /ˈɛksaɪz/ n [U] tax on goods produced inside a country

ex·cise² /ɪkˈsaɪz/ vt fml remove by cutting

ex·cite /ɪkˈsaɪt/ vt 1 cause to have strong (pleasant) feelings: an excited little boy 2 fml cause (feelings): to excite interest ~**ment** n [C;U] **excitable** adj easily excited **exciting** adj: exciting films

ex·cla·ma·tion /ˌɛkskləˈmeɪʃən/ n word(s) exclaimed

exclamation point /··ˈ··ˌ·/ n PUNCTUATION MARK (!) written after an exclamation

ex·claim /ɪkˈskleɪm/ vi/t speak or say suddenly

ex·clude /ɪkˈskluːd/ vt 1 keep out or leave out 2 shut out from the mind: Don't exclude that possibility. **excluding** prep not including **exclusion** /ɪkˈskluːʒən/ n [U]

ex·clu·sive /ɪkˈskluːsɪv, -zɪv/ adj 1 keeping out unsuitable people 2 not shared ♦ n story appearing in only one newspaper ~**ly** adv only: exclusively for women

ex·com·mu·ni·cate /ˌɛkskəˈmyuːnəˌkeɪt/ vt exclude from the Christian Church -**cation** /ˌɛkskəˌmyuːnəˈkeɪʃən/ n [C;U]

ex·cre·ment /ˈɛkskrəmənt/ n [U] fml solid waste from the bowels

ex·crete /ɪkˈskriːt/ vt pass out (waste matter)

ex·cru·ci·at·ing /ɪkˈskruːʃiːˌeɪtɪŋ/ adj (of pain) very bad ~**ly** adv

ex·cul·pate /ˈɛkskʌlˌpeɪt/ vt fml free from blame

ex·cur·sion /ɪkˈskɜrʒən/ n short trip for pleasure

ex·cuse¹ /ɪkˈskyuːz/ vt 1 forgive: Please excuse my bad handwriting. 2 make (bad behavior) seem less bad 3 free from a duty 4 **Excuse me** (said when starting to speak to a stranger, or when one wants to get past a person, or to APOLOGIZE for something) 5 **excuse oneself** ask permission to be absent **excusable** adj that can be forgiven

ex·cuse² /ɪkˈskyuːs/ n reason given when asking to be excused

ex·e·cra·ble /ˈɛksɪkrəbəl/ adj fml very bad

ex·e·cute /ˈɛksɪˌkyuːt/ vt 1 kill as a legal punishment 2 fml carry out; perform: execute a plan -**cution** /ˌɛksɪˈkyuːʃən/ n 1 [C;U] legal killing 2 [U] fml carrying out;

performance **-cutioner** n official who executes criminals

ex·ec·u·tive /ɪgˈzɛkyəṭɪv/ adj concerned with managing, or carrying out decisions ♦ n 1 [C] person in an executive position in business 2 [the+S] branch of government that carries out the law

ex·ec·u·tor /ɪgˈzɛkyəṭər/ n person who carries out the orders in a WILL[2]

ex·em·pla·ry /ɪgˈzɛmpləri/ adj fml suitable to be copied

ex·em·pli·fy /ɪgˈzɛmpləˌfaɪ/ vt be or give an example of **-fication** /ɪgˌzɛmpləfəˈkeɪʃən/ n [C;U]

ex·empt /ɪgˈzɛmpt/ adj freed from a duty, etc. ♦ vt make exempt **-ion** /ɪgˈzɛmpʃən/ n [C;U]

ex·er·cise /ˈɛksərˌsaɪz/ n 1 [U] use of the powers of the body to improve it: go swimming for exercise 2 [C] something done for training: naval exercises 3 [C] written school work 4 [S;U] use (of a power or right) ♦ 1 vi/t take or give EXERCISE (1) 2 vt use (a power or right)

ex·ert /ɪgˈzɜrt/ vt 1 use (strength, etc.) 2 **exert oneself** make an effort **~ion** /ɪgˈzɜrʃən/ n [U]

ex gra·tia /ˌɛks ˈgreɪʃə/ adj, fml (of a payment) made as a favor, and not because one has a legal duty to make it

ex·hale /ɛksˈheɪl, ɛkˈseɪl/ vi/t breathe out **exhalation** /ˌɛkshəˈleɪʃən, ˌɛksə-/ n [U]

ex·haust /ɪgˈzɔst/ vt 1 tire out 2 use up completely ♦ n 1 pipe by which gases escape from an engine 2 [U] these gases **~ive** adj thorough **~ively** adv **~ion** /ɪgˈzɔstʃən/ n [U]

ex·hib·it /ɪgˈzɪbɪt/ vt 1 show publicly for sale, etc. 2 fml show that one has (a quality) ♦ n something shown in a MUSEUM, etc. **~or** n person showing exhibits

ex·hi·bi·tion /ˌɛksəˈbɪʃən/ n 1 public show of objects 2 act of exhibiting **~ism** n behavior of someone who wants to be looked at **~ist** n

ex·hil·a·rate /ɪgˈzɪləˌreɪt/ vt make cheerful and excited **-ration** /ɪgˌzɪləˈreɪʃən/ n [U]

ex·hort /ɪgˈzɔrt/ vt fml urge strongly **~ation** /ˌɛksɔrˈteɪʃən, ˌɛgzɔr-/ n [C;U]

ex·hume /ɪgˈzuʷm, ɪgˈzyuʷm, ɛksˈhyuʷm/ vt dig up (a dead body) **exhumation** /ˌɛkshyuˈmeɪʃən, ˌɛksyuʷ-/ n [C;U]

ex·i·gen·cy /ˈɛksədʒənsiʸ, ɪgˈzɪ-/ n fml urgent need

ex·ile /ˈɛksaɪl, ˈɛgzaɪl/ n 1 [U] unwanted absence from one's country 2 [C] someone forced into this ♦ vt send into exile

ex·ist /ɪgˈzɪst/ vi have life; be real:

The problems she talks about simply don't exist. **~ence** n 1 [U] state of being real 2 [S] way of living: *lead a miserable existence* **~ent** adj existing; present

ex·is·ten·tial /ˌɛgzɪˈstɛnʃəl◂/ adj related to existence

ex·it /ˈɛgzɪt, ˈɛksɪt/ n 1 way out of a building 2 act of leaving ♦ vi (used as a stage direction) he/she/it goes out

exit ramp /ˈ·· ˌ·/ n road for driving onto or off a HIGHWAY

ex·o·dus /ˈɛksədəs/ n [S] going away of many people

ex·on·e·rate /ɪgˈzɑnəˌreɪt/ vt fml free (someone) from blame **-ration** /ɪgˌzɑnəˈreɪʃən/ n [U]

ex·or·bi·tant /ɪgˈzɔrbəṭənt/ adj (of cost) too much **~ly** adv

ex·or·cize /ˈɛksɔrˌsaɪz, -sər-/ vt drive out (an evil spirit, etc.) by prayers **-cism** n act or art of exorcizing **-cist** n

ex·ot·ic /ɪgˈzɑṭɪk/ adj pleasantly strange: *exotic flowers/food* **~ally** /-kliʸ/ adv

ex·pand /ɪkˈspænd/ vi/t (cause to) grow larger or more detailed

expand on/upon phr vt make more detailed

ex·panse /ɪkˈspæns/ n wide open space

ex·pan·sion /ɪkˈspænʃən, -tʃən/ n [C;U] act of expanding **~ism** n intention of expanding one's land, etc. **~ist** n, adj

ex·pan·sive /ɪkˈspænsɪv/ adj friendly and willing to talk **~ly** adv

ex·pa·ti·ate /ɪkˈspeɪʃiʸˌeɪt/ v **expatiate on/upon** phr vt fml speak a lot about

ex·pat·ri·ate /ɛksˈpeɪtriʸɪt/ n, adj (person) living abroad

ex·pect /ɪkˈspɛkt/ vt think or believe that something will happen **~ing** adj infml PREGNANT **~ation** /ˌɛkspɛkˈteɪʃən/ n 1 [U] state of expecting 2 [C] something expected

ex·pec·tant /ɪkˈspɛktənt/ adj 1 waiting hopefully 2 PREGNANT **~ly** adv **-tancy** n [U] hope

ex·pec·to·rate /ɪkˈspɛktəˌreɪt/ vi fml SPIT

ex·pe·di·ent /ɪkˈspiʸdiʸənt/ adj (of an action) useful, esp. for one's own purposes ♦ n useful plan, esp. one thought of in a hurry because of urgent need **-ency** n [U]

ex·pe·dite /ˈɛkspəˌdaɪt/ vt fml make (a plan) go faster

ex·pe·di·tion /ˌɛkspəˈdɪʃən/ n (people making) a journey for a purpose: *an expedition to the North Pole* **~ary** adj (of an army) sent abroad to fight

ex·pel /ɪkˈspɛl/ vt -ll- 1 dismiss

officially from a school, etc. **2** *fml* force out from a container

ex·pend /ɪkˈspɛnd/ *vt* spend; use up ~**able** *adj* that can be used up without worrying

ex·pen·di·ture /ɪkˈspɛndətʃər, -ˌtʃʊər/ *n* [S;U] *fml* spending

ex·pense /ɪkˈspɛns/ *n* [U] **1** cost **2** at **someone's expense: a** with someone paying **b** (of a joke) against someone **expenses** *n* [P] money for a purpose: *We'll pay his traveling expenses.*

ex·pen·sive /ɪkˈspɛnsɪv/ *adj* costing a lot ~**ly** *adv*

ex·pe·ri·ence /ɪkˈspɪəriʲəns/ *n* **1** [U] knowledge gained by practice **2** [C] something that happens to: *a fascinating experience* ♦ *vt* suffer or learn by experience: *to experience defeat* -**enced** *adj* having EXPERIENCE (1)

ex·per·i·ment /ɪkˈspɛrəmənt/ *n* [C;U] test carried out to learn something ♦ /-ˌmɛnt, -mənt/ *vi* perform experiments ~**al** /ɪkˌspɛrəˈmɛntəl◂/ *adj* used for or based on experiments ~**ation** /ɪkˌspɛrəmɛnˈteʲʃən/ *n* [U]

ex·pert /ˈɛkspɜrt/ *n, adj* (person) with special skill or training ~**ly** *adv*

ex·per·tise /ˌɛkspərˈtiʲz/ *n* [U] skill in a particular field

expert sys·tem /ˈ·· ˌ···/ *n* computer system which contains information on a particular subject, used to find the answers to problems

ex·pi·ate /ˈɛkspiʲˌeʲt/ *vt fml* pay for (a crime) by accepting punishment -**ation** /ˌɛkspiʲˈeʲʃən/ *n* [U]

ex·pire /ɪkˈspaɪər/ *vi* **1** (of something that lasts for a time) come to an end **2** *lit* die **expiry**, also **expiration** /ˌɛkspəˈreʲʃən/ *n* [U]

ex·plain /ɪkˈspleʲn/ *v* **1** *vi/t* make (a meaning) clear **2** *vt* be the reason for

explain away *phr vt* give an excuse for (something) in order to avoid blame

ex·pla·na·tion /ˌɛkspləˈneʲʃən/ *n* **1** [U] act of explaining **2** [C] something that explains **explanatory** /ɪkˈsplænəˌtoriʲ, -ˌtoʷriʲ/ *adj* (of a statement) explaining

ex·ple·tive /ˈɛksplətɪv/ *n fml* word used for swearing

ex·pli·ca·ble /ɪkˈsplɪkəbəl, ˈɛksplɪ-/ *adj fml* (of behavior, etc.) understandable

ex·pli·cit /ɪkˈsplɪsɪt/ *adj* (of a statement, etc.) clearly and fully expressed ~**ly** *adv* ~**ness** *n* [U]

ex·plode /ɪkˈsploʷd/ *v* **1** *vi/t* blow up; burst **2** *vi* show violent feeling

ex·ploit¹ /ɪkˈsplɔɪt/ *vt* **1** use (people) unfairly for profit **2** use (things) fully for profit ~**er** *n* ~**ation** /ˌɛksplɔɪˈteʲʃən/ *n* [U] ~**ative** /ɪkˈsplɔɪtəˌtɪv/ *adj* tending to exploit

ex·ploit² /ˈɛksplɔɪt/ *n* brave successful act

ex·plore /ɪkˈsplɔr, ɪkˈsploʷr/ *vt* **1** travel through (a place) for discovery **2** examine (a subject) carefully **explorer** *n* **exploration** /ˌɛksplə-ˈreʲʃən/ *n* [C;U] **exploratory** /ɪkˈsplɔrəˌtoriʲ, ɪkˈsploʷrəˌtoʷriʲ/ *adj*

ex·plo·sion /ɪkˈsploʷʒən/ *n* **1** (noise of) exploding **2** sudden increase: *the population explosion*

ex·plo·sive /ɪkˈsploʷsɪv/ *n, adj* (substance) that explodes ~**ly** *adv*

ex·po·nent /ɪkˈspoʷnənt/ *n* someone who expresses or supports a belief

ex·port¹ /ɪkˈspɔrt, ɪkˈspoʷrt, ˈɛksport, ˈɛkspoʷrt/ *vi/t* send (goods) abroad for sale ~**er** *n*

ex·port² /ˈɛksport, ˈɛkspoʷrt/ *n* **1** [U] (business of) exporting **2** [C] something exported

ex·pose /ɪkˈspoʷz/ *vt* **1** uncover; leave without protection **2** make known (a secret crime, etc.) **3** uncover (photographic film) to the light **4** expose oneself show one's sexual parts on purpose, in the hope of shocking people **exposure** /ɪkˈspoʷʒər/ *n* [C;U]

ex·po·sé /ˌɛkspoʷˈzeʲ, -spə-/ *n* public statement of something shameful

ex·po·si·tion /ˌɛkspəˈzɪʃən/ *n* [C;U] *fml* explaining; explanation

ex·pos·tu·late /ɪkˈspɑstʃəˌleʲt/ *vi fml* complain loudly and firmly

ex·pound /ɪkˈspaʊnd/ *vt fml* describe (a belief, etc.) in detail

ex·press¹ /ɪkˈsprɛs/ *vt* **1** make known by words or looks: *She expressed surprise at his decision.* **2** **express oneself** speak or write one's thoughts or feelings

ex·press² *adj* **1** going quickly **2** clearly stated: *her express wish* ♦ *n* express train ♦ *adv* by an express method ~**ly** *adv* **1** clearly **2** on purpose

ex·pres·sion /ɪkˈsprɛʃən/ *n* **1** [C;U] act of expressing: *political expression* **2** [C] word or phrase: *an odd expression to use* **3** [C] look on someone's face: *a surprised expression* **4** [U] quality of showing feeling: *singing without much expression* ~**less** *adj* without EXPRESSION (4)

ex·pres·sive /ɪkˈsprɛsɪv/ *adj* showing feelings ~**ly** *adv*

ex·press·way /ɪkˈsprɛsˌweʲ/ *n* wide road for fast travel over long distances

ex·pro·pri·ate /ɛkˈsproʷpriʲˌeʲt/ *vt fml* take away for public use -**ation** /ɪkˌsproʷpriʲˈeʲʃən/ *n* [C;U]

ex·pul·sion /ɪkˈspʌlʃən/ n [C;U] act of expelling (EXPEL)

ex·punge /ɪkˈspʌndʒ/ vt remove completely from a list, etc.

ex·pur·gate /ˈekspərˌgeɪt/ vt fml remove improper words, etc., from

ex·qui·site /ɪkˈskwɪzɪt, ˈekskwɪ-/ adj beautifully made or done **~ly** adv

ex·tant /ɪkˈstænt/ adj fml still existing

ex·tend /ɪkˈstend/ v **1** vt make longer or larger: extend the parking lot **2** vt stretch out (part of one's body) to the limit **3** vt fml offer, give: extend a welcome **4** vi t((to)) (of land) reach

ex·ten·sion /ɪkˈstenʃən/ n **1** [U] act of extending **2** [C] part added **3** [C] telephone line inside a set of offices, etc.

ex·ten·sive /ɪkˈstensɪv/ adj large in amount or area **~ly** adv

ex·tent /ɪkˈstent/ n **1** [U] amount or length: the extent of the damage **2** [S] degree: to a large extent

ex·ten·u·at·ing /ɪkˈstenyuˌeɪtɪŋ/ adj giving good reasons (for bad behavior): extenuating circumstances

ex·te·ri·or /ɪkˈstɪəriʲər/ n outside of something **exterior** adj

ex·ter·mi·nate /ɪkˈstɜrməˌneɪt/ vt kill all of **-nation** /ɪkˌstɜrməˈneɪʃən/ n [U]

ex·ter·nal /ɪkˈstɜrnl/ adj outside **~ly** adv

ex·tinct /ɪkˈstɪŋkt/ adj **1** (of a kind of animal) no longer existing **2** (of a VOLCANO) no longer active **~ion** /ɪkˈstɪŋkʃən/ n [U] state of being or becoming extinct

ex·tin·guish /ɪkˈstɪŋgwɪʃ/ vt fml **1** put out (a fire, etc.) **2** destroy (hope, etc.) **~er** n apparatus for putting out fires

ex·tir·pate /ˈekstərˌpeɪt/ vt fml destroy completely

ex·tol /ɪkˈstoʷl/ vt -ll- praise highly

ex·tort /ɪkˈstɔrt/ vt obtain by force or threats **~ion** /ɪkˈstɔrʃən/ n [C;U] **~ionist** n

ex·tor·tion·ate /ɪkˈstɔrʃənɪt/ adj EXORBITANT

ex·tra /ˈekstrə/ adj, adv beyond what is usual or necessary: extra money | pay extra ♦ n **1** extra thing **2** film actor in a crowd scene **3** special EDITION (1) of a newspaper

ex·tract¹ /ɪkˈstrækt/ vt **1** pull out, esp. with difficulty **2** get (a substance) from another substance **~ion** /ɪkˈstrækʃən/ n **1** [C;U] act or example of extracting **2** [U] family origin: of Russian extraction

ex·tract² /ˈekstrækt/ n **1** piece of writing taken from a book, etc. **2** product obtained by extracting: almond extract

ex·tra·cur·ric·u·lar /ˌekstrəkəˈrɪkyələr◂/ adj outside the ordinary course of work in a school or college

ex·tra·dite /ˈekstrəˌdaɪt/ vt send (a foreign criminal) home for trial **-dition** /ˌekstrəˈdɪʃən/ n [C;U]

ex·tra·mar·i·tal /ˌekstrəˈmærətl◂/ adj (of sexual relationships) outside marriage

ex·tra·mu·ral /ˌekstrəˈmyuʳərəl◂/ adj **1** connected with but outside an organization **2** involving representatives from more than one school

ex·tra·ne·ous /ɪkˈstreɪniʲəs/ adj not directly connected

extra·or·di·na·ry /ɪkˈstrɔrdnˌeriʲ/ adj **1** very strange **2** beyond what is ordinary: a man of extraordinary ability **-narily** adv

ex·trap·o·late /ɪkˈstræpəˌleɪt/ vi/t guess facts already known

ex·tra·sen·so·ry per·cep·tion /ˌekstrəˌsensəriʲ pərˈsepʃən/ n [U] see ESP

ex·tra·ter·res·tri·al /ˌekstrətəˈrestriʲəl/ adj (from) outside the Earth

ex·trav·a·gant /ɪkˈstrævəgənt/ adj **1** wasteful of money, etc. **2** (of ideas, behavior, etc.) beyond what is reasonable **-gance** n [C;U]

ex·trav·a·gan·za /ɪkˌstrævəˈgænzə/ n very grand and expensive piece of entertainment

ex·treme /ɪkˈstriʲm/ adj **1** furthest or greatest possible: extreme cold | the extreme south of the country **2** often derog beyond the usual limits: extreme opinions ♦ n furthest possible degree: He's gone from one extreme to the other. **~ly** adv very

ex·trem·is·m /ɪkˈstriʲmɪzəm/ n derog holding of (politically) extreme opinions **-ist** n, adj

ex·trem·i·ty /ɪkˈstreməṭiʲ/ n [S;U] highest degree **extremities** n [P] hands and feet

ex·tri·cate /ˈekstrəˌkeɪt/ vt set free from something that is hard to escape from

ex·tro·vert, extravert /ˈekstrəˌvɜrt/ n cheerful person who likes to be with others

ex·u·be·rant /ɪgˈzuʷbərənt/ adj overflowing with life and excitement **~ly** adv **-rance** n [U]

ex·ude /ɪgˈzuʷd, ɪkˈsuʷd/ vi/t (cause to) flow out slowly in all directions

ex·ult /ɪgˈzʌlt/ vi fml show great delight **~ant** adj **~antly** adv **~ation** /ˌegzʌlˈteɪʃən, ˌekzʌl-/ n [U]

eye /aɪ/ n **1** either of the 2 parts of the head with which we see **2** way of seeing: an experienced eye **3** hole in a needle **4** ring into which a hook fits **5** be in the public eye be often seen by the public **6** have an eye

for be able to judge **7 in one's mind's eye** in one's imagination **8 in the eyes of** in the opinion of **9 keep an eye on** watch carefully **10 lay eyes on** *infml* catch sight of **11 see eye to eye** agree completely **12 up to one's eyes in** *infml* very busy with ◆ *vt* look at closely

eye·ball /ˈaɪbɔl/ *n* the whole of the EYE (1), including the part inside the head ◆ *v* look at closely

eye·brow /ˈaɪbraʊ/ *n* line of hairs above each eye

eye·catch·ing /ˈ· ˌ··/ *adj* unusual and attractive to look at

eye·lash /ˈaɪlæʃ/ *n* hair on the edge of the eyelid

eye·lid /ˈaɪˌlɪd/ *n* piece of skin that moves to close the eye

eye·o·pen·er /ˈ· ˌ···/ *n* something surprising that changes one's ideas about something

eye shad·ow /ˈ· ˌ··/ *n* [U] colored powder to decorate eyelids

eye·sight /ˈaɪsaɪt/ *n* [U] power of seeing

eye·sore /ˈaɪsɔr, -soʷr/ *n* something ugly to look at

eye·wit·ness /ˈaɪˌwɪtnɪs/ *n* person who sees something happen and can describe it

ey·rie, eyry /ˈɛəriʸ, ˈaɪəriʸ/ *n* high nest of an EAGLE

F, f /ɛf/ the 6th letter of the English alphabet

F *abbrev. for*: FAHRENHEIT

fa·ble /ˈfeɪbəl/ n short story that teaches a lesson **fabled** *adj* spoken of as true; famous

fab·ric /ˈfæbrɪk/ n [C;U] **1** woven cloth **2** structure of a building, etc.

fab·ri·cate /ˈfæbrəˌkeɪt/ vt invent (something false) –**cation** /ˌfæbrəˈkeɪʃən/ n [C;U]

fab·u·lous /ˈfæbyələs/ adj **1** existing in fables **2** unbelievable: *fabulous wealth* **3** excellent ~**ly** *adv* very: *fabulously rich*

fa·cade /fəˈsɑd/ n **1** front of a building **2** false appearance

face¹ /feɪs/ n **1** [C] front part of the head **2** [C] expression on the face **3** [C] front; surface: *face of a cliff* **4** [U] position of respect: *afraid of losing face* **5** **face to face** in someone's direct presence **6** **in the face of** in opposition to **7** **on the face of it** APPARENTly **8** **make a face/faces** make an expression with the face **9** **to someone's face** openly in their presence ~**less** *adj* with no clear character

face² /feɪs/ v **1** vi/t turn the face towards **2** vt meet and oppose: *face danger* **3** vt cover the front of: *a building faced with stone*

face up to *phr vt* be brave enough to deal with

face·cloth /ˈfeɪs-klɔθ/ n small cloth for washing the face

face-lift /ˈ·ˌ·/ n medical operation to make the face look younger

face-sav·ing /ˈ·ˌ·/ adj allowing one's respect for oneself to be kept

fac·et /ˈfæsɪt/ n **1** one of the flat sides of a cut jewel **2** ASPECT of a subject

fa·ce·tious /fəˈsiʸʃəs/ adj using silly jokes ~**ly** *adv*

face val·ue /ˌ·ˈ·/ n **1** [C;U] value shown on a postage stamp, etc. **2** [U] value of something as it first appears

fa·cial /ˈfeɪʃəl/ adj of the face ♦ n facial beauty treatment

fa·cile /ˈfæsəl/ adj (of words) too easy; not deep

fa·cil·i·tate /fəˈsɪləˌteɪt/ vt fml make easy

fa·cil·i·ty /fəˈsɪləti/ n [U] ability to do things easily –**ties** n [P] useful things: *shopping/sporting facilities*

fac·ing /ˈfeɪsɪŋ/ n [U] **1** outer covering of a wall, etc. **2** material sewn in to stiffen a garment

fac·sim·i·le /fækˈsɪməliʸ/ n exact copy of a picture, etc. **facsimile machine** n fml FAX

fact /fækt/ n **1** [C] something known to be true **2** [U] truth **3** **in fact** really

fac·tion /ˈfækʃən/ n group within a larger (political) one

fac·tor /ˈfæktər/ n influence that helps to produce a result

fac·to·ry /ˈfæktəriʸ/ n place where goods are made by machinery

facts of life /ˌ· ·ˈ·/ n [P] the details of sex and birth

fac·tu·al /ˈfæktʃuʷəl/ adj based on fact ~**ly** *adv*

fac·ul·ty /ˈfækəltiʸ/ n **1** natural power of the mind or body: *the faculty of hearing* **2 a** teachers in a school, university, etc. **b** university department

fad /fæd/ n temporary interest in something

fade /feɪd/ v **1** vi/t (cause to) lose color or freshness **2** vi disappear gradually

fade in/out *phr vi/t* (in film making and broadcasting) (cause to) appear/disappear slowly

fag /fæg/ n derog sl for HOMOSEXUAL

fag·got, fagot /ˈfægət/ n **1** bunch of sticks for burning **2** FAG

Fah·ren·heit /ˈfæɹənˌhaɪt/ n scale of temperature in which water freezes at 32° and boils at 212°

fail /feɪl/ v **1** vi/t be unsuccessful or unable to do what is wanted: *The crops/business failed.* **3** vt judge to be unsuccessful in a test **4** vt disappoint or leave (someone) at a bad time: *My courage failed me.* **5** vi lose strength: *His health is failing.* ♦ **without fail** certainly

fail·ing /ˈfeɪlɪŋ/ n fault; weakness ♦ *prep* in the absence of

fail-safe /ˈ·ˌ·/ adj **1** made so that any failure will stop the machine **2** certain to succeed: *a fail-safe plan*

fail·ure /ˈfeɪlyər/ n **1** [U] lack of success **2** [C] person or thing that fails **3** [C;U] non-performance; inability: *heart failure*

faint /feɪnt/ adj **1** likely to lose consciousness **2** lacking strength or courage **3** not clear or bright **4** slight: *faint chance* ♦ vi lose consciousness ♦ n act of fainting ~**ly** *adv* ~**ness** n [U]

faint-heart·ed /ˌ·ˈ··◂/ adj cowardly

fair¹ /feər/ adj **1** just and honest: *fair play* **2** between poor and good: *a fair knowledge of French* **3** having a good, clean appearance: *a fair copy of the report* **4** (of skin or hair) not dark **5** (of weather) not stormy ♦ *adv* **1** honestly: *play fair* **2 fair and square: a** honestly **b** directly **3 fair enough** *infml* all right ~**ly** *adv* **1** honestly **2** fairly warm

fair² n 1 competition for showing farm products, animals, etc., with amusements 2 large show of goods: *book fair*

fair game /ˌ· ˈ·/ n [U] a something that it is reasonable to attack **b** person, idea, etc., which can easily be laughed at or CRITICIZED

fair·ground /ˈfeərɡraʊnd/ n open space for a FAIR²(1)

fair sex /ˌ· ˈ·/ n [the] see GENTLE SEX

fair·way /ˈfeərweɪ/ n part of a GOLF course along which one hits the ball

fair-weath·er friend /ˌ·ˌ·· ˈ·/ n friend who is absent in times of trouble

fai·ry /ˈfeəriʲ/ n 1 small imaginary person with magical powers 2 *derog* HOMOSEXUAL man

fairy god·moth·er /ˌ·· ˈ···/ n person who helps, and esp. saves, someone who is in trouble

fai·ry·land /ˈfeəriʲˌlænd/ n [S] 1 land where fairies live 2 place of magical beauty

fairy tale /ˈ·· ·/ n 1 story about magic 2 untrue story **fairy-tale** *adj* magically wonderful

fait ac·com·pli /ˌfeɪt ækɑmˈpliʲ, ˌfeɪt ɑkɑmˈpliʲ/ n **faits accomplis** /ˌfeɪt ækɑmˈpliʲz, ˌfeɪz ɑkɑmˈpliʲ/ something that has happened and cannot now be changed

faith /feɪθ/ n 1 [U] confident trust 2 [C;U] religious belief 3 [U] loyalty to a promise: *keep faith with them* **~ful** *adj* 1 loyal 2 true to the facts: *faithful copy* ♦ n [the+P] religious people **~fully** *adv* **~less** *adj fml* disloyal

faith heal·ing /ˈ· ˌ··/ n [U] method of treating diseases by prayer, etc.

fake /feɪk/ n person or thing that is not what he/she/it looks like or pretends to be ♦ vt/i make or copy (e.g. a work of art) to deceive

fa·kir /fəˈkɪər, fɑ-/ n Hindu or Muslim holy man

fal·con /ˈfælkən, ˈfɔl-/ n bird that can be trained to hunt **~er** n person who trains falcons **~ry** n [U] hunting with falcons

fall¹ /fɔl/ vi **fell** /fel/, **fallen** /ˈfɔlən/ 1 come or go down freely: *She fell into the lake.* | *The house fell down.* 2 hang loosely: *Her hair falls over her shoulders.* 3 become lower: *The temperature fell.* 4 (of land) slope down 5 happen: *Christmas falls on a Friday.* 6 become: *fall asleep/in love* 7 be wounded or killed in battle 8 be defeated 9 (of the face) take on a look of sadness, etc. 10 **fall flat** produce no result 11 **fall into line** obey or CONFORM 12 **fall short** fail to reach a standard

fall back *phr vi* RETREAT

fall back on *phr vt* use when there

is failure or lack of other means

fall behind *phr vi/t* not keep level (with)

fall for *phr vt* **a** be attracted by **2** accept and be cheated by

fall off *phr vi* become less

fall on *phr vt* attack eagerly

fall out *phr vi* quarrel: *fall out with his boss*

fall through *phr vi* (of a plan) fail

fall² n 1 act of falling 2 something that has fallen: *a heavy fall of snow* 3 AUTUMN **falls** n [P] WATERFALL

fal·la·cy /ˈfæləsiʲ/ n [C;U] false belief or reasoning **–lacious** /fəˈleʲʃəs/ adj fml based on fallacy

fall guy /ˈ· ·/ n *infml for* SCAPEGOAT

fal·li·ble /ˈfæləbəl/ adj able to make mistakes **–bility** /ˌfæləˈbɪlətiʲ/ n [U]

falling star /ˌ·· ˈ·/ n SHOOTING STAR

fal·lo·pi·an tube /fəˈloʷpiʲən ˌtuʷb, -ˌtyuʷb/ n tube through which eggs pass to the WOMB

fall·out /ˈfɔlaʊt/ n [U] dangerous dust left in the air after a NUCLEAR explosion

fal·low /ˈfæloʷ/ adj (of land) dug but left unplanted

false /fɔls/ adj 1 not true or correct 2 disloyal: *false friend* 3 not real: *a false eye* 4 careless; unwise: *One false move and I'll shoot you!* **~ly** adv **~ness** n [U] **~hood** n [C;U] lying; lie

false a·larm /ˌ·· ·ˈ·/ n warning of something bad that does not happen

false bot·tom /ˌ·· ˈ··/ n something that looks like the bottom of a box, etc., but hides a secret space

false pre·ten·ces /ˌ·· ·ˈ··/ n [P] behavior intended to deceive

false start /ˌ·· ˈ·/ n unsuccessful beginning that means one must start again

fal·set·to /fɔlˈsetoʷ/ n [C;U] **–tos** (man with an) unnaturally high voice

fal·si·fy /ˈfɔlsəˌfaɪ/ vt make false **–fication** /ˌfɔlsəfəˈkeʲʃən/ n [C;U]

fal·si·ty /ˈfɔlsətiʲ/ n [U] fml falseness

fal·ter /ˈfɔltər/ vi 1 move or behave uncertainly 2 speak in an unsteady manner **~ingly** adv

fame /feʲm/ n [U] condition of being well known **famed** adj famous

fa·mil·ial /fəˈmɪlyəl/ adj fml of a family

fa·mil·iar /fəˈmɪlyər/ adj 1 often seen; common 2 too friendly 3 **familiar with** knowing thoroughly **~ly** adv **~ity** /fəˌmɪliʲˈyærətiʲ, -ˌmɪliʲˈær-/ n [C;U]

fa·mil·iar·ize /fəˈmɪlyəˌraɪz/ vt make well informed

fam·i·ly /ˈfæməliʲ/ n 1 one's parents, children, aunts, etc. 2 one's children 3 people descended from the same ANCESTOR 4 division of living creatures or languages: the cat family ♦ adj suitable for children: a family film

family plan·ning /ˌ···ˈ···/ n [U] controlling of the number of children in a family by CONTRACEPTION

family tree /ˌ···ˈ·/ n drawing showing the relationship of family members

family way /ˈ··· ˌ·/ n infml being PREGNANT: She's in the family way.

fam·ine /ˈfæmɪn/ n [C;U] serious lack of food

fam·ished /ˈfæmɪʃt/ adj very hungry

fa·mous /ˈfeʲməs/ adj very well known ~ly adv very well

fan¹ /fæn/ n instrument for making a flow of air ♦ v –nn– 1 vt send out air onto 2 vi spread in a half circle

fan² n enthusiastic supporter: football fans

fa·nat·ic /fəˈnætɪk/ n person who is too enthusiastic about something: religious fanatics ~al adj ~ally /-kliʲ/ adv ~ism /-təˌsɪzəm/ n [U]

fan belt /ˈ· ·/ n belt driving a FAN¹ to cool an engine

fan·ci·ful /ˈfænsɪfəl/ adj showing imagination rather than reason ~ly adv

fan·cy /ˈfænsiʲ/ n 1 [C] opinion not based on fact 2 lit [U] imagination 3 take a fancy to become fond of ♦ adj 1 decorative and unusual 2 higher than the usual or reasonable price

fan·fare /ˈfænfeər/ n short loud piece of TRUMPET music to introduce a person or event

fang /fæŋ/ n long sharp tooth

fan·light /ˈfænlaɪt/ n small window over a door

fan mail /ˈ· ·/ n [U] letters to a famous person from FANS²

fan·ny /ˈfæniʲ/ n sl BOTTOM¹ (2)

fan·tas·tic /fænˈtæstɪk/ adj 1 sl wonderful 2 (of ideas) not practical 3 wild and strange ~ally /-kliʲ/ adv

fan·ta·size /ˈfæntəˌsaɪz/ vi/t have fantasies (about)

fan·ta·sy /ˈfæntəsiʲ, -ziʲ/ n [C;U] (something made by) imagination: sexual fantasies

far /far/ adv, adj farther /ˈfarðər/ or further /ˈfɜrðər/, farthest /ˈfarðɪst/ or furthest /ˈfɜrðɪst/ 1 a long way: too far to walk | the far distance 2 very much: far better 3 (of a political position) very much to the LEFT OR RIGHT: the far left 4 as/so far as to the degree that: So far as I know, he's coming. 5 far and away by a great deal or amount: She's far and away the best actress. 6 far be it from me to (used esp. to show disagreement or disapproval) I certainly would not want to 7 far from: a very much not: I'm far from pleased. b instead of: Far from being angry, he's delighted. 8 how far to what degree 9 so far until now 10 So far, so good Things are satisfactory up to this point, at least

far·a·way /ˈfarəˌweʲ/ adj 1 distant 2 (of a look in someone's eyes) dreamy

farce /fars/ n 1 light funny play 2 set of silly events farcical adj

fare /feər/ n 1 [C] money charged for a journey 2 [U] fml food ♦ vi get on; succeed: fare badly

Far East /ˌ· ˈ·◂/ n [S] countries east of India

fare·well /ˌfeərˈwel/ interj, n fml goodbye

far·fetched /ˌfarˈfetʃt◂/ adj hard to believe

far·flung /ˌ· ˈ·◂/ adj spread over a great distance

far·gone /ˌ· ˈ·/ adj in an advanced state, esp. of something bad

farm /farm/ n area of land and buildings where crops are grown and animals raised ♦ vi/t use (land) as a farm

farm out phr vt send (work) for other people to do

farm·er /ˈfarmər/ n person who owns or manages a farm

farm·hand /ˈfarmhænd/ n worker on a farm

farm·house /ˈfarmhaʊs/ n 1 main house on a farm 2 house in this style

farm·yard /ˈfarmjard/ n yard surrounded by farm buildings

far·off /ˌ· ˈ·◂/ adj distant

far·reach·ing /ˌ· ˈ··◂/ adj having a wide influence

far·sight·ed /ˌfarˈsaɪtɪd◂, ˈfarˌsaɪtɪd/ adj 1 able to judge future effects 2 able to see things only when they are far away

fart /fart/ vi taboo send out air from the bowels fart n taboo 1 escape of air from the bowels 2 sl extremely unpleasant person

far·ther /ˈfarðər/ adv, adj FURTHER

far·thest /ˈfarðɪst/ adv, adj FURTHEST

fas·ci·nate /ˈfæsəˌneʲt/ vt attract and interest strongly –nating adj –nation /ˌfæsəˈneʲʃən/ n [S;U]

fas·cis·m /ˈfæʃɪzəm/ n [U] political system marked by total state control under a single leader, and support of one's own nation and race fascist n, adj

fash·ion /ˈfæʃən/ n 1 [C;U] way of dressing or behaving that is

popular at a certain time **2** [S] *fml*
manner of doing something: *in an
orderly fashion* **3 after a fashion**
not very well ♦ *vt fml* make; shape
~**able** according to the latest
fashion ~**ably** *adv*

fast¹ /fæst/ *adj* **1** quick: *fast cars* **2**
firmly fixed: *fast colors* **3** (of a clock)
showing time later than the right
time ♦ *adv* **1** quickly **2** firmly **3 fast
asleep** sleeping deeply **4 pull a fast
one (on)** *infml* deceive (someone)
with a trick

fast² *vi* eat no food, esp. for religious reasons ♦ *n* period of fasting

fas·ten /ˈfæsən/ *vi/t* make or become firmly fixed ~**er** *n* thing that
fastens things together ~**ing** *n*
something that holds things shut

   fasten on *phr vt* take eagerly and
use

fast food /ˈ· ·/ *n* [U] restaurant food
that is cooked and ready before
ordered

fas·tid·i·ous /fæˈstɪdiˠəs, fə-/ *adj*
difficult to please; disliking anything dirty or nasty ~**ly** *adv* ~**ness**
n [U]

fat /fæt/ *n* [U] **1** material under the
skins of animals and human beings
which helps keep them warm **2** this
substance used in cooking ♦ *adj* **1**
having a lot of FAT (1) on the body **2**
thick or tightly packed: *fat book*
~**ness** *n* [U]

fa·tal /ˈfeˠtl/ *adj* causing death or
ruin ~**ly** *adv*

fa·tal·is·m /ˈfeˠtlˌɪzəm/ *n* [U] belief
that events are controlled by FATE
(1) –**ist** *n*

fa·tal·i·ty /feˠˈtæləti̠ˠ, fə-/ *n* [C] **1**
violent death **2** [U] being fatal

fat cat /ˌ· ˈ·/ *n derog sl* wealthy person with a bad influence or way of
life

fate /feˠt/ *n* **1** [U] power beyond
human control that decides events
2 [C] end, esp. death **3** [S] the future
~**ful** *adj* important (esp. in a bad
way) for the future: *fateful decision*
~**fully** *adv* **fated** *adj* **1** caused by
fate **2** *infml* very unlucky

fat·head /ˈfæthed/ *n* fool

fa·ther /ˈfɑðər/ *n* **1** male parent **2**
(*usu. cap.*) priest ♦ *vt* become the
father of ~**hood** *n* [U] ~**less** *adj*
~**ly** *adj* like a good father **fathers**
n [P] FOREFATHERS

father fig·ure /ˈ·· ˌ··/ *n* older man
on whom one depends for advice

father-in-law /ˈ·· ˌ· ˌ/ *n* **fathers-in-
law** father of one's wife or husband

fa·ther·land /ˈfɑðərˌlænd/ *n* one's
native land

Father's Day /ˈ·· ˌ/ *n* third Sunday
in June, when fathers are given
presents and cards

fath·om /ˈfæðəm/ *n* unit of measurement (6 feet) for the depth of
water ♦ *vt* understand fully

fa·tigue /fəˈtiˠg/ *n* **1** [U] tiredness **2**
[U] weakness in metals caused by
repeated bending **3** [C] (in the army)
a job of cleaning or cooking — see
also **fatigues** ♦ *vt fml* make tired

fa·tigues /fəˈtiˠgz/ *n* [P] military
clothes

fat·ten /ˈfætn/ *vt* make fatter

fat·ty /ˈfæti̠ˠ/ *adj* containing fat ♦
n sl fat person

fat·u·ous /ˈfætʃuˠəs/ *adj* silly: *fatu-
ous remarks* ~**ly** *adv*

fau·cet /ˈfɔsɪt/ *n* apparatus with a
handle for controlling the flow of
water, etc. from a pipe, barrel, etc.

fault /fɔlt/ *n* **1** mistake or imperfection **2** crack in the Earth's surface
3 at fault in the wrong **4 find fault
with** complain about **5 one's fault**
something one can be blamed for **6
to a fault** (of good qualities) too; too
much ♦ *vt* find mistakes in ~**less**
adj perfect ~**y** *adj*

fau·na /ˈfɔnə/ *n* [U] animals of a particular area or period

faux pas /ˌfoˠ ˈpɑ/ *n* **faux pas** /ˌfoˠ
ˈpɑz/ social mistake

fa·vor /ˈfeˠvər/ *n* **1** [U] approval:
gain widespread favor **2** [C] kind
act: *do me a favor* **3 in favor of**: in
support of **4 in one's favor** to one's
advantage ♦ *vt* **1** approve of **2** be
unfairly fond of; treat with favor
~**able** *adj* **1** showing or winning
approval **2** advantageous ~**ably** *adv*

fa·vo·rite /ˈfeˠvərɪt/ *n* **1** person or
thing loved above all others **2** horse
expected to win a race ♦ *adj* most
loved –**ritism** *n* [U] unfairly generous treatment of one person

fawn¹ /fɔn/ *n* **1** [C] young deer **2** [U]
light yellow-brown color

fawn² *v* **fawn on** *phr vt* try to gain
the favor of, by being too attentive

fax /fæks/ *vt* send (copies of printed
material) in ELECTRONIC form along
a telephone line ♦ *n* also **fax
machine 1** apparatus that does this
2 paper sent by fax

faze /feˠz/ *vt* shock into silence

FBI /ˌef biˠ ˈaɪ/ *n* Federal Bureau of
Investigation; US police department
under central control for crimes involving more than one state

fear /fɪər/ *n* **1** [C;U] feeling that
danger is near **2** [U] danger **3 No
fear!** Certainly not! ♦ *vi/t fml* be
afraid (of) ~**ful** *adj* **1** terrible;
shocking **2** *fml* afraid ~**less** *adj* not
afraid ~**lessly** *adv* ~**some** *adj lit*
frightening

fea·si·ble /ˈfiˠzəbəl/ *adj* able to be
done; possible –**bility** /ˌfiˠzə-
ˈbɪləti̠ˠ/ *n* [U]

feast /fiˑst/ n **1** splendid meal **2** religious FESTIVAL ♦ vi **1** eat and drink very well **2 feast one's eyes on** look at with delight

feat /fiˑt/ n difficult action successfully done

fea·ther /ˈfeðər/ n **1** one of a bird's many light skin coverings **2 a feather in one's cap** honor to be proud of ♦ vt **1** put feathers on or in **2 feather one's nest** make oneself dishonestly rich while in a trusted position ~**y** adj soft and light

feath·er·bed /ˈfeðərˌbed/ vt/i have more workers than needed because of union demands

fea·ther·brained /ˈfeðərˌbreˑnd/ adj silly and thoughtless

fea·ture /ˈfiˑtʃər/ n **1** noticeable quality **2** part of the face **3** long newspaper article **4** film being shown at a cinema ♦ v **1** vt include as a performer **2** vi play an important part ~**less** adj uninteresting **features** n [P] face

featured ar·ti·cle /ˌ‥ ˈ‥‥/ n

Feb·ru·a·ry /ˈfebruˑˌeriˑ, ˈfebyuˑˌeriˑ/ n the 2nd month of the year

fe·ces /ˈfiˑsiˑz/ n [P] solid waste from the bowels

feck·less /ˈfeklɪs/ adj worthless and irresponsible

fec·und /ˈfekənd, ˈfiˑ-/ adj fml FERTILE

fed /fed/ v past t. and p. of FEED

fed·e·ral /ˈfedərəl/ adj **1** of or being a federation of the US government as opposed to the States

fed·e·ra·tion /ˌfedəˈreˑʃən/ n **1** [C] united group of states, organizations, etc. **2** [U] action or result of uniting in this way

fed up /ˌ‥ ˈ‥/ adj sl tired and discontented

fee /fiˑ/ n money paid for professional services, to join a club, etc.

fee·ble /ˈfiˑbəl/ adj weak **feebly** adv

fee·ble·mind·ed /ˌfiˑbəlˈmaɪndɪd◄/ adj with low INTELLIGENCE

feed /fiˑd/ v fed /fed/ **1** vt give food to **2** vi (esp. of animals) eat **3** vt supply; provide: feed information into a computer ♦ n **1** animal's meal **2** [U] food for animals **3** [C] pipe, etc., through which a machine is fed

feed·back /ˈfiˑdbæk/ n information about the results of an action, passed back to the person in charge

feel¹ /fiˑl/ v felt /felt/ **1** vt learn about with the fingers **2** vt experience (the touch of something): feel the wind **3** vi search with the fingers: feel for a pencil **4** to be consciously: feel hungry/happy **5** vt suffer because of: feel the cold **6** give

a sensation: This sheet feels wet. **7** vt believe without reasoning: I feel they won't come. **8 feel like** wish for; want

feel for phr vt be sorry for

feel² n [S] **1** sensation caused by touching **2** act of feeling **3 get the feel of** become used to and skilled at

feel·er /ˈfiˑlər/ n **1** thread-like part of an insect's head, with which it touches things **2** suggestion made to test opinion

feel·ing /ˈfiˑlɪŋ/ n **1** [S] consciousness of something felt **2** [S] belief not based on reason **3** [U] power to feel **4** [U] excitement of mind: cause ill feeling **5** [U] sympathy **feelings** n [P] EMOTIONS

feet /fiˑt/ n pl. of FOOT

feign /feˑn/ vt fml pretend to have or be

feint /feˑnt/ n false attack or blow ♦ vi make a feint

feist·y /ˈfaɪstiˑ/ adj excited and quarrelsome

fe·li·ci·ty /fɪˈlɪsətiˑ/ n [U] fml happiness

fe·line /ˈfiˑlaɪn/ adj of or like a cat

fell¹ /fel/ v past t. of FALL

fell² vt cut or knock down: fell a tree/a man

fel·ler /ˈfelər/ n sl fellow; man

fel·low /ˈfeloˑ/ n **1** man **2** member of a learned society or college **3** companion: schoolfellows ♦ adj another of the same group: fellow prisoners/ students ~**ship** n **1** [C] group or society **2** [U] companionship **3** [C] position of a college fellow

fellow feel·ing /ˌ‥ ˈ‥‥/ n [S;U] sympathy for someone like oneself

fellow trav·el·er /ˌ‥ ˈ‥‥/ n someone who is sympathetic to an idea or cause without actually joining in

fel·o·ny /ˈfeləniˑ/ n [C;U] serious crime (e.g. murder) **felon** n person guilty of felony

felt¹ /felt/ v past t. and p. of FEEL

felt² n [U] thick cloth made of pressed wool

felt-tip pen /ˌ‥ ‥ ˈ‥/ n pen with felt at the end instead of a NIB

fe·male /ˈfiˑmeˑl/ adj **1** of the sex that produces young **2** (of plants) producing fruits **3** having a hole into which something fits: female plug ♦ n woman or female animal

fem·i·nine /ˈfemənɪn/ adj **1** suitable for a woman **2** gram of the class of words for females ~**ninity** /ˌfeməˈnɪnətiˑ/ n [U] being feminine (1)

fem·i·nism /ˈfeməˌnɪzəm/ n [U] principle that women should have the same rights as men ~**nist** n, adj

femme fa·tale /ˌfem fəˈtæl, ˌfæm-, -ˈtɑl/ n beautiful woman who brings men to ruin

fence¹ /fɛns/ n 1 wall made of wood or wire 2 someone who buys and sells stolen goods 3 **sit on the fence** avoid taking sides in an argument ♦ vt surround or separate with a fence

fence² vi 1 fight with a long thin sword as a sport 2 avoid giving an honest answer **fencer** n

fenc·ing /'fɛnsɪŋ/ n [U] 1 fighting with a sword as a sport 2 material for making fences

fend /fɛnd/ vi
   fend for oneself look after oneself
   fend off phr vt push away

fend·er /'fɛndər/ n 1 side part of a car that covers the wheels 2 protective cover over a cycle wheel

fender ben·der /'·· ,··/ n car accident with little damage

fer·ment¹ /fər'mɛnt/ vi/t 1 change chemically so that sugar becomes alcohol 2 make or become excited ~**ation** /ˌfɜrmən'teɪʃən, -mɛn-/ n [U]

fer·ment² /'fɜrmɛnt/ n [U] trouble and excitement

fern /fɜrn/ n plant with feathery green leaves

fe·ro·cious /fə'roʊʃəs/ adj fierce; violent ~**ly** adv

fe·roc·i·ty /fə'rɑsəti/ n [U] ferociousness

fer·ret /'fɛrɪt/ n small fierce animal that hunts rats and rabbits ♦ vi/t search; find by searching

fer·rous /'fɛrəs/ adj of or containing iron

fer·ry /'fɛri/ also **fer·ry·boat** /'fɛriˌboʊt/ — n boat that carries people and things across a narrow piece of water ♦ vt carry (as if) on a ferry

fer·tile /'fɜrtl/ adj 1 producing young, crops, etc. 2 (of a person's mind) inventive ~**tility** /fər'tɪləti/ n [U]

fer·ti·lize /'fɜrtlˌaɪz/ vt make fertile ~**lizer** plant food ~**lization** /ˌfɜrtlə'zeɪʃən/ n [U]

fer·vent /'fɜrvənt/ adj feeling strongly: fervent hope/believer ~**ly** adv

fer·vid /'fɜrvɪd/ adj fml sharing too strong feeling

fer·vor /'fɜrvər/ n [U] quality of being fervent: ZEAL

fes·ter /'fɛstər/ vi 1 (of a wound) become infected 2 feel anger without expressing it

fes·ti·val /'fɛstəvəl/ n 1 time for public happiness: Christmas is a festival of the church. 2 group of musical, etc., performances held regularly

fes·tive /'fɛstɪv/ adj joyful

fes·tiv·i·ty /fɛ'stɪvəti/ n [C;U] festive activity

fes·toon /fɛ'stuːn/ vt decorate with chains of flowers, RIBBONS, etc.

fetch /fɛtʃ/ vt 1 go and get and bring back 2 be sold for: The house fetched $30,000. 3 **fetch and carry** do the small duties of a servant

fete /feɪt/ n day of public amusement held esp. to collect money ♦ vt honor publicly

fet·id /'fɛtɪd, 'fiː-/ adj smelling bad

fet·ish /'fɛtɪʃ/ n something to which one pays too much attention

fet·ter /'fɛtər/ n chain for a prisoner's foot: (fig.) the fetters of an unhappy marriage ♦ vt tie; prevent from moving

fe·tus, foetus /'fiːtəs/ n creature before birth, at a later stage than an EMBRYO

feud /fyuːd/ n violent continuing quarrel ♦ vi have a feud

feu·dal /'fyuːdl/ adj of the system of holding land in return for work, as practiced in Europe from the 9th to the 15th century ~**ism** n [U]

fe·ver /'fiːvər/ n [S;U] 1 (disease causing) high body temperature –see also YELLOW FEVER 2 excited state ~**ish** adj 1 of or having fever 2 unnaturally fast ~**ishly** adv

few /fyuː/ determiner, pron, n [P] 1 (with a) some: Let's invite a few friends. 2 (without a) not many: She has few friends.

fi·an·cé /ˌfiːɑn'seɪ, fiː'ɑnseɪ/ **fiancée** (same pronunciation) fem. — n person one is ENGAGEd to

fi·as·co /fiː'æskoʊ/ n –cos complete failure

fib /fɪb/ vi, n -bb- (tell) a small lie ~**ber** n

fi·ber /'faɪbər/ n 1 [C] thin thread-like plant or animal growth 2 [U] mass of threads 3 [U] person's inner character 4 substance in fruits and vegetables necessary for health: high-fiber diet **fibrous** adj

fi·ber·glass /'faɪbərˌglæs/ n [U] material of glass fibers used for making boats, etc.

fick·le /'fɪkəl/ adj not loyal; often changing

fic·tion /'fɪkʃən/ n 1 [U] stories 2 [S;U] untrue story ~**al** adj

fic·ti·tious /fɪk'tɪʃəs/ adj untrue: invented

fid·dle /'fɪdl/ n 1 VIOLIN 2 dishonest practice 3 **(as) fit as a fiddle** perfectly healthy 4 **play second fiddle (to)** play a less important part (than) ♦ vi 1 move things aimlessly 2 vi play the VIOLIN ~**dler** n

fid·dling /'fɪdlɪŋ/ adj small and silly

fi·del·i·ty /fə'dɛləti, faɪ-/ n 1 faithfulness 2 closeness to an original

fid·get /'fɪdʒɪt/ vi move one's body around restlessly ~**y** adj

field¹ /fiːld/ n 1 [C] piece of farming land 2 [C] open area: *a football field | an oilfield | a battlefield* 3 [C] branch of knowledge 4 [S] place where practical operations actually happen: *study tribal languages in the field* 5 [C] area where a force is felt: *gravitational field*

field² v 1 vi/t (in baseball, etc.) catch or stop (the ball) 2 vt produce (a team or army) ~**er** n

field day /ˈ· ·/ n 1 day for outdoor activities with a school, club, etc. 2 **have a field day** enjoy oneself very much

field e·vent /ˈ· ·, ·/ n sports event with competitions, such as throwing weights or jumping

field glass·es /ˈ· , ··/ n [P] BINOCULARS

field of vi·sion /ˌ· · ˈ··/ n whole space within seeing distance

field-test /ˈ· ·/ vt try (something) out in the FIELD¹ (4)

field·work /ˈfiːldwɜːrk/ n [U] study done in the FIELD¹ (4)

fiend /fiːnd/ n 1 devil 2 *infml* someone very enthusiastic about something ~**ish** adj ~**ishly** adv

fierce /fɪərs/ adj 1 angry, violent, and cruel 2 severe: *fierce heat/competition* ~**ly** adv ~**ness** n [U]

fi·er·y /ˈfaɪəriʲ/ adj 1 like fire 2 violent: *fiery temper*

fi·es·ta /fiˈestə/ n religious holiday with dancing, etc.

fif·teen /ˌfɪfˈtiːn◂/ det, n, pron 15 ~**th** det, adv, n, pron 15th

fifth /fɪfθ/ det, n, pron, adv 5th

Fifth A·mend·ment /ˌ· ·ˈ··/ n law that people do not have to make statements against themselves in a court

fifth col·umn /ˌ· ˈ··/ n group of people who secretly help the enemies of their country in war

fif·ty /ˈfɪftiʲ/ det, n, pron 50 ~**tieth** det, adv, n, pron 50th

fifty-fif·ty /ˌ·· ˈ··◂/ adj, adv (of a division or chances) equal(ly)

fig /fɪg/ n (tree that bears) a soft sweet fruit with small seeds

fig. written abbrev. for: 1 FIGURATIVE 2 FIGURE¹ (5)

fight¹ /faɪt/ vi/t fought /fɔːt/ 1 use violence (against); struggle 2 argue ~**er** n 1 person who fights professionally: (fig.) *a tireless fighter against racism* 2 small military aircraft

fight back 1 recover from a bad or losing position 2 defend oneself by fighting

fight off phr vt keep away with an effort

fight out phr vt settle (a quarrel) by fighting

fight² n 1 [C] battle 2 [U] power or wish to fight 3 [C] boxing (BOX²) match

fighting chance /ˌ·· ˈ·/ n small but real chance if great effort is made

fig leaf /ˈ· ·/ n something that hides something else, esp. dishonestly

fig·ment /ˈfɪgmənt/ n something not real: *a figment of his imagination*

fig·u·ra·tive /ˈfɪgyʊrətɪv/ adj (of words, phrases, etc.) used in some way other than the main or usual meaning, to suggest a picture in the mind or make a comparison ~**ly** adv: *She's up to her eyes in paperwork — figuratively speaking, of course!*

fig·ure¹ /ˈfɪgyər/ n 1 (shape of) a human body: *a good figure* 2 person: *a leading political figure* 3 (sign for) a number 4 price 5 DIAGRAM

figure² v 1 vi take a part 2 vt believe 3 **That figures** infml That seems reasonable

figure on phr vt plan on; include in one's plans

figure out phr vt discover by thinking

fig·ure·head /ˈfɪgyər,hed/ n someone who is the chief in name only

figure of speech /ˌ··· · ˈ·/ n figurative expression

fil·a·ment /ˈfɪləmənt/ n thin thread, esp. in an electric light BULB (2)

filch /fɪltʃ/ vt steal secretly; something of small value)

file¹ /faɪl/ n steel tool for rubbing or cutting hard surfaces ♦ vt rub or cut with a file: *file one's nails*

file² n 1 arrangement for storing papers 2 store of papers on one subject 3 unit of collected information in a computer

file³ vt put in a file

file for phr vt law request officially

file⁴ n line of people one behind the other ♦ vi walk in a file

fi·li·al /ˈfɪliʲəl/ adj fml suitable to a son or daughter

fil·i·bus·ter /ˈfɪlə,bʌstər/ vi delay Congressional action by making long speeches **filibuster** n

fil·i·gree /ˈfɪlə,griʲ/ n [U] decorative wire work

filing cab·i·net /ˈ·· ,··/ n piece of office furniture for storing papers in

fil·ings /ˈfaɪlɪŋz/ n [P] very small sharp bits that have been rubbed off a metal surface with a FILE¹

fill /fɪl/ v 1 vt/i make or become full 2 vt go or be put into: *fill a vacancy* 3 fulfil ♦ n full supply ~**er** n substance added to increase size ~**ing** n 1 material to fill a hole, esp. in a tooth 2 food mixture folded inside pastry, SANDWICHes, etc.

fill in *phr vt* **1** tell (what is necessary): *He filled me in about the accident.* **2** supply the most recent information **3** take someone's place

fill out *phr v* **1** *vi* get fatter **2** *vt* put in (what is necessary): *fill out a form*

fill up *phr vi/t* make or become full

fil·let /ˈfilᵉʲ, ˈfileʲ/ *n* piece of meat or fish without bones ♦ *vt* remove bones from

filling sta·tion /ˈ·· ˌ··/ GAS STATION

fil·ly /ˈfiliʲ/ *n* young female horse

film /film/ *n* **1** [C;U] (roll of) thin material used in photography **2** [C] *fml* cinema picture; MOVIE **3** [S;U] thin covering: *film of oil* ♦ *vi/t* make a FILM (2) (of) ~**y** *adj* very thin: *filmy silk*

film·strip /ˈfilmˌstrip/ *n* [C;U] length of photographic film that shows drawings, etc., separately as still pictures

fil·ter /ˈfiltər/ *n* **1** apparatus through which liquids are passed to clean or change them: *coffee filter* **2** glass that changes the color or amount of light ♦ *vi/t* go or send (as if) through a filter: *People filtered out of the gym.*

filter tip /ˈ·· ·/ *n* (cigarette with) an end that filters smoke

filth /filθ/ *n* [U] **1** very nasty dirt **2** something rude or unpleasant ~**y** *adj*

fin /fin/ *n* winglike part of a fish **2** thing shaped like this on a car, etc.

fi·nal /ˈfainl/ *adj* **1** last **2** (of a decision, etc.) that cannot be changed ♦ also **finals** *pl. n* **1** last of a set of matches **2** last and most important examinations in a college course ~**ly** *adv* **1** at last **2** allowing no further change ~**ist** *n* player in a final match or competition ~**ize** *vt* give final form to

fi·na·le /fiˈnæliʲ, -ˈnɑ-/ *n* last division of a piece of music, etc.

fi·nance /fᵊˈnæns, ˈfainæns/ *n* [U] **1** management of (public) money **2** money, esp. provided by a bank, to help run an organization or buy something ♦ *vt* provide money for **finances** *n* [P] money owned or provided **financial** /faᵊˈnænʃᵊl, faᵊ-, -tʃᵊl/ *adj* **financially** *adv*

financial year /·ˌ·· ·ˈ·/ *n* yearly period over which accounts are calculated

fi·nan·cier /ˌfinənˈsiᵊr, fᵊˈnæn-, ˌfainæn-/ *n* someone who controls large sums of money

finch /fintʃ/ *n* small bird with an attractive song

find /faind/ *vt* found /faʊnd/ **1** get (something lost or not known) by searching **2** learn by chance or effort: *find (out) where he lives* **3** obtain by effort: *find time to study* **4** (of a thing) arrive at: *Water finds its*

own level. **5** know to exist: *Elephants are found in Africa.* **6** *law* decide to be: *find someone guilty* **7 find fault with** criticize or blame ♦ *n* something good or valuable that is found ~**er** *n* **find·ing** *n* **1** what is learned by inquiry **2** *law* decision made in court **3** something learned as the result of an official inquiry

fine[1] /fain/ *adj* **1** good; beautiful **2** very thin or small: *fine thread/dust* | (fig.) *fine distinction* **3** (of weather) bright; not wet **4** healthy ♦ *adv* **1** very well **2** very thin ~**ly** *adv* **1** into small bits **2** delicately: *finely tuned*

fine[2] *n* money paid as a punishment ♦ *vt* take a fine from

fine arts /ˌ· ˈ·/ *n* [P] painting, music, etc.

fine print /ˌ· ˈ·/ *n* [U] small but important writing on a contract, etc.

fi·ne·ry /ˈfainəriʲ/ *n* [U] beautiful clothes

fi·nesse /fᵊˈnes/ *n* [U] delicate skill

fin·ger /ˈfingər/ *n* **1** any of the 5 end parts of the hand **2** part of a covering for the hand, covering a finger **3** object shaped like a finger **4** **(have) a finger in every pie** (have) a part in everything that is going on **5 keep one's fingers crossed** hope for the best **6 lay a finger on** harm **7 not lift a finger** make no effort to help **8 put one's finger on** find **9 twist around one's little finger** successfully influence ♦ *vt* feel with one's fingers ~**ing** *n* [U] use of the fingers when playing music

finger·nail /ˈfingərˌneᵉʲl/ *n* one of the hard flat pieces at the ends of the fingers

fin·ger·print /ˈfingərˌprint/ *n* mark made by a finger pressed onto a surface ♦ *vt* take (someone's) fingerprints

fin·ger·tip /ˈfingərˌtip/ *n* **1** end of a finger **2 have something at one's fingertips** know it well

fin·ick·y /ˈfinikiʲ/ *adj* disliking many things

fin·ish /ˈfiniʃ/ *v* **1** *vi/t* come or bring to an end **2** *vt* eat or drink the rest of **3** take all one's powers, hopes of success, etc. ♦ *n* **1** [C] last part **2** [S;U] appearance or condition of having been properly polished, painted, etc.

   finish off *phr vt* kill

   finish with *phr vt* have no more use for

finishing school /ˈ··· ·/ *n* private school where rich girls learn how to behave in social life

fi·nite /ˈfainait/ *adj* **1** limited **2** *gram* (of a verb) changing according to tense and subject ~**ly** *adv*

fi·ord /fyord, fyoᵂrd/ *n* FJORD

fir /fɜr/ n straight tree with leaves like needles

fire¹ /faɪər/ n 1 [U] condition of burning: *afraid of fire* 2 [C] something burning, on purpose or by accident: *light a fire* | *forest fires* 3 heat used for cooking: *Put the pan on the fire.* 4 [U] destruction by fire 5 [U] shooting from guns 6 **catch fire** start to burn 7 **on fire** burning 8 **open/cease fire** start/stop shooting 9 **set fire to** cause to burn 10 **under fire** being shot at – see also **hang fire** (HANG¹)

fire² v 1 vi/t shoot off (bullets or arrows) 2 vt dismiss from a job 3 vt excite: *fire one's imagination* 4 vt bake (clay things) in a KILN

fire a·larm /ˈ· ·ˌ·/ n signal that warns people of fire

fire·arm /ˈfaɪərɑrm/ n gun

fire·bomb /ˈfaɪərbɑm/ n INCENDIARY bomb

fire·brand /ˈfaɪərbrænd/ n person who causes trouble; agitator (AGITATE)

fire department /ˈ· ·ˌ·/ n company of men that put out fires

fire drill /ˈ· ·/ n [C;U] practice in leaving a burning building safely

fire en·gine /ˈ· ˌ··/ n vehicle that carries fire fighters and their equipment

fire es·cape /ˈ· ·ˌ·/ n outside stairs for leaving a burning building

fire fight·er /ˈ· ˌ··/ n person who puts out fires

fire fight·ing /ˈ· ˌ··/ n [U] 1 action to put out large fires 2 actions taken to discover and remove causes of sudden trouble in organizations, etc.

fire·place /ˈfaɪərpleɪs/ n opening for a fire in a room

fire·pow·er /ˈfaɪərˌpaʊər/ n [U] ability to deliver gunfire

fire·proof /ˈfaɪərpruwf/ adj unable to be damaged by fire fireproof vt

fire·screen /ˈfaɪərskriyn/ n protective framework around a fireplace

fire·side /ˈfaɪərsaɪd/ n area around the fireplace

fire sta·tion /ˈ· ˌ··/ n building for a FIRE DEPARTMENT

fire·wood /ˈfaɪərwʊd/ n [U] wood cut to be used on fires

fire·work /ˈfaɪərwɜrk/ n container of explosive powder, burned to make colored lights **fireworks** n [P] 1 show of FIREWORKS 2 show of anger

firing line /ˈ·· ·/ n [S] position of being the object of attack

firing squad /ˈ·· ˌ·/ n group of soldiers ordered to shoot an offender

firm¹ /fɜrm/ adj, adv 1 solidly fixed 2 not likely to change 3 determined; RESOLUTE ~**ly** adv ~**ness** n [U]

firm² n business company

fir·ma·ment /ˈfɜrməmənt/ n lit the sky

first /fɜrst/ determiner, adv 1 before the others 2 for the first time: *my first visit* 3 rather than do something else 4 **first thing** at the earliest time in the morning ♦ n, pron [S] 1 person or thing before others: *the first to arrive* 2 **at first** at the beginning ~**ly** adv before anything else

first aid /ˌ· ˈ·/ n [U] treatment given by an ordinary person to someone hurt in an accident, etc.

first base /ˌ· ˈ·/ n [U] first step of a course of action

first·born /ˈfɜrstbɔrn/ adj, n **firstborn** eldest (child)

first class /ˌ· ˈ·◄/ n [U] best traveling conditions on a plane, etc. **first-class** adj of the best quality

first cous·in /ˌ· ˈ··/ n child of one's aunt or uncle

first de·gree /ˌ· ·ˈ·◄/ adj of the highest level of seriousness: *first degree murder*

first fam·i·ly /ˌ· ˈ···/ n [the] President, his wife and children

first floor /ˌ· ˈ·◄/ n part of a building at ground level

first·hand /ˌfɜrstˈhænd◄/ adj, adv (of information) directly from its origin

first la·dy /ˌ· ˈ··/ n [the] wife of the President

first name /ˈ· ·/ n name that stands before one's family name

first-rate /ˌ· ˈ·◄/ adj of the best quality

first strike /ˌ· ˈ·◄/ n attack made on your enemy before they (can) attack you

fis·cal /ˈfɪskəl/ adj fml of public money, taxes, etc.

fish /fɪʃ/ n fish or fishes 1 [C] creature that has cold blood and lives in water 2 [U] its flesh as food 3 **drink like a fish** drink too much alcohol ♦ v 1 vi try to catch fish 2 vi search indirectly: *fish for compliments* 3 vt bring out or up: *He fished a key from his pocket.* ~**y** adj 1 like fish 2 seeming false: *a fishy story*

fish·er·man /ˈfɪʃərmən/ n -men /-mən/ man who catches fish, esp. as a job

fish·e·ry /ˈfɪʃəriy/ also -ries pl. part of the sea where fishing is practiced

fish·ing /ˈfɪʃɪŋ/ n [U] sport or job of catching fish

fis·sion /ˈfɪʃən/ n [U] splitting of a cell or atom

fis·sure /ˈfɪʃər/ n deep crack in rock

fist /fɪst/ n hand when closed tightly: *holding a fistful of coins*

fit¹ /fɪt/ v -tt- 1 vi/t be the right size and shape (for): *The lid doesn't fit.* 2 vt put in place: *fit a new lock* 3 vt make suitable for ♦ n [S] 1 quality of fitting well 2 way that something fits: *a tight fit* ~ted adj

fit in phr v 1 vi match; HARMONIZE 2 vt make room or time for

fit out phr vt supply; FURNISH

fit² adj 1 suitable, right: *fit to eat | Do as you think fit.* 2 physically healthy 3 ready to: *laugh fit to burst* 4 fit to be tied very angry ~ness n [U]

fit³ n 1 short attack of illness, etc.: *fit of coughing* 2 sudden loss of consciousness 3 by fits and starts not regularly 4 have a fit be very angry

fit·ful /ˈfɪtfəl/ adj restlessly irregular ~ly adv

fit·ting /ˈfɪtɪŋ/ adj fml suitable ♦ n 1 something fixed into a building 2 occasion of trying whether clothes fit

five /faɪv/ det, n, pron 1 5 2 $5 bill

fix¹ /fɪks/ vt 1 fasten firmly 2 arrange; decide on: *fix a price* 3 repair 4 tidy: *I must fix my hair.* 5 prepare (food or drink) 6 arrange the result of (something) dishonestly ~ative n chemical for sticking things in position ~ation /fɪkˈseɪʃən/ n OBSESSion

fix on phr vt choose

fix up phr vt 1 provide 2 repair, change or improve

fix² n 1 awkward situation 2 sl IN-JECTion of a drug 3 position calculated by looking at the stars, etc.

fix·er /ˈfɪksər/ n person who is good at arranging that something happens, esp. by using influence or dishonesty

fix·ture /ˈfɪkstʃər/ n 1 something fixed into a building 2 person long established in the same place

fizz /fɪz/ vi, n [S] (make) a sound of BUBBLES in a liquid ~y adj

fiz·zle /ˈfɪzəl/ v fizzle out phr vi end disappointingly

fjord /fjɔrd, fyoʳˈd/ n narrow arm of the sea between steep cliffs, esp. in Norway

flab /flæb/ n [U] infml soft loose flesh

flab·ber·gast·ed /ˈflæbərˌgæstɪd/ adj surprised and shocked

flab·by /ˈflæbiʲ/ adj 1 (of muscles) too soft 2 lacking force or effectiveness -biness n [U]

flac·cid /ˈflæksɪd, ˈflæsɪd/ adj not firm enough

flag¹ /flæg/ n piece of cloth used as the sign of a country, etc., or to make signals – see also WHITE FLAG ♦ vt -gg- put a flag on

flag down phr vt signal (a vehicle) to stop

flag² vi -gg- become weak

flag·on /ˈflægən/ n large container for liquids

flag·pole /ˈflægpoʷl/ n long pole to raise a flag on

fla·grant /ˈfleɪˈgrənt/ adj openly bad ~ly adv

flag·ship /ˈflægˌʃɪp/ n chief naval ship in a group

flag·staff /ˈflægstæf/ n flagpole

flag·stone /ˈflægstoʷn/ n flat stone for a floor or path

flag stop /ˈ· ·/ n place where a bus, etc. stops only if it is signalled

flag-wav·ing /ˈ· ˌ··/ n noisy expression of national military feeling

flail /fleɪl/ vi wave violently but aimlessly about

flair /fleər/ n [S] natural ability to do something

flak /flæk/ n 1 gunfire directed at enemy aircraft 2 severe opposition

flake¹ /fleʲk/ n small leaf-like bit: *soap flakes* flaky adj 1 made up of flakes or tending to flake 2 infml EC-CENTRIC flakiness n [U]

flake² vi fall off in flakes

flake out phr vi 1 fall asleep because of great tiredness 2 become crazy

flam·boy·ant /flæmˈbɔɪənt/ adj 1 brightly colored 2 (of a person) showy and bold

flame /fleʲm/ n [C;U] 1 (tongue of) burning gas 2 in flames burning – see also OLD FLAME ♦ vi 1 burn brightly 2 break out with sudden violence: (fig.) *in a flaming temper*

flam·ma·ble /ˈflæməbəl/ also in-flammable — adj easily set on fire and quick to burn

flan /flæn/ n open pastry case filled with fruit, etc.

flange /flændʒ/ n edge of a wheel, etc., that sticks out

flank /flæŋk/ n side of an animal, person, or moving army ♦ vt be placed beside

flan·nel /ˈflænl/ n [U] loosely woven woollen cloth

flap /flæp/ n 1 [C] flat part of anything that covers an opening 2 [S] sound of flapping ♦ 1 vi/t wave slowly up and down: *flap its wings* 2 get excited and anxious

flare¹ /fleər/ vi burn brightly but in an unsteady way ♦ n 1 [S] flaring light 2 [C] bright light used as a signal

flare up phr vi become suddenly hotter, more violent, etc. flare-up /ˈ· ·/ n

flare² vi/t widen towards the bottom: *flared skirt* flare n flares n [P] flared pants

flash¹ /flæʃ/ v 1 vi/t shine for a moment 2 vi move very fast 3 vt

flash² n 1 sudden bright light: (fig.) a flash of inspiration 2 short news report 3 FLASHLIGHT (1) 4 **in a flash** at once ♦ adj 1 sudden: flash flood 2 modern and expensive in appearance ~**y** adj unpleasantly big, bright, etc.

flash-back /'flæʃbæk/ n [C;U] scene in a film, etc., that goes back in time

flash-bulb /'flæʃbʌlb/ n bright electric light for photography

flash-light /'flæʃlaɪt/ n 1 small electric light carried in the hand 2 apparatus for taking photographs in the dark

flash point /'· ·/ n point or place at which violence may be expected

flask /flæsk/ n 1 bottle with a narrow neck 2 flat bottle for carrying drinks in one's pocket

flat¹ /flæt/ n 1 low level plain 2 flat part or side (of) 3 (in music) flat note 4 flat piece of stage scenery 5 a flat tire

flat² adj -tt- 1 smooth and level 2 spread out fully: lie down flat 3 not very thick: flat cakes 4 (of a tire) without enough air in it 5 (of beer, etc.) having lost its gas 6 dull and lifeless 7 (in music) below the right note 8 firm; with no more argument: a flat refusal

flat³ adv 1 into a flat or level position 2 below the right note: sing flat 3 no more: 3 minutes flat 4 flat broke with no money at all 5 flat out directly: He refused her flat out.

flat feet /₁· ·/ n feet that rest too flat on the ground **flat-footed** /₁· '···◂/ adj

flat rate /'· ·/ n one charge including everything

flat-ten /'flætn/ vi/t make or become flat

flat-ter /'flætər/ vt/i 1 praise too much or insincerely 2 give pleasure to 3 (of a picture) show (a person) as more beautiful ~**er** n ~**y** n [U] flattering remarks

flat-u-lence /'flætʃələns/ n [U] fml GAS (4)

flat-ware /'flætwɛər/ n — see SILVERWARE

flaunt /flɔnt, flɑnt/ vt derog show for admiration: flaunt her wealth

fla-vor /'fleɪvər/ n 1 [C;U] taste: 6 popular flavors | not much flavor 2 [S] particular feeling or character ♦ vt give taste to ~**ing** n [C;U] something added to improve the taste ~**less** adj

flaw /flɔ/ n fault or weakness ~**less** adj ~**lessly** adv ♦ vt make a flaw in

flax /flæks/ n [U] (thread made from the stem of) a plant with blue flowers used for making LINEN

flax-en /'flæksən/ adj lit (of hair) pale yellow

flay /fleɪ/ vt 1 remove the skin from 2 attack fiercely in words

flea /fliː/ n wingless jumping insect that feeds on blood

flea-bag /'fliːbæg/ n cheap, dirty hotel

flea mar-ket /'· ₁··/ n street market where used goods are sold

fleck /flɛk/ n small spot or grain ♦ vt mark with flecks

fledg-ling /'flɛdʒlɪŋ/ n 1 young bird learning to fly 2 inexperienced person

flee /fliː/ vi/t fled /flɛd/ fml hurry away (from); escape

fleece /fliːs/ n sheep's woolly coat ♦ vt rob by a trick; charge too much **fleecy** adj woolly

fleet /fliːt/ n 1 number of ships under one command 2 group of buses, etc. under one control

fleet-ing /'fliːtɪŋ/ adj not lasting long: fleeting glimpse

flesh /flɛʃ/ n 1 [U] soft part of a person or animal that covers the bones 2 [U] soft part of a fruit 3 [S] the body as opposed to the soul 4 **flesh and blood a** human beings **b** one's relatives 5 **in the flesh** in real life ~**y** adj fat

flew /fluː/ past t. of FLY

flex /flɛks/ vt bend or stretch (one's muscles)

flex-i-ble /'flɛksəbəl/ adj 1 easily bent 2 easily changed: flexible plans ~**bility** /₁flɛksə'bɪləṭiː/ n [U]

flex-i-time /'flɛksiːˌtaɪm/ n [U] system by which people can choose their hours of work

flick /flɪk/ n light sudden blow or movement ♦ vt touch or strike lightly

flick-er /'flɪkər/ vi 1 burn in an unsteady way 2 move backwards and forwards ♦ n [S] 1 flickering 2 temporary feeling: flicker of interest

fli-er, flyer /'flaɪər/ n 1 person (esp. a pilot) or thing that flies 2 LEAFLET

flight¹ /flaɪt/ n 1 [C;U] flying: birds in flight | (fig.) His account contained some amazing flights of fancy. 2 [C] journey by air 3 [C] aircraft making a journey: Flight Number 347 to Geneva 4 [C] group of birds or aircraft 5 [C] set of stairs ~**less** adj unable to fly

flight² n [C;U] (an example of) the act of running away; escape

flight attendant /'· ·,··/ n person on an aircraft who serves passengers

flight path /'· ·/ n course through the air of an aircraft, etc.

flight-y /'flaɪṭiː/ adj (of a person) too influenced by sudden desires or ideas

flim·sy /ˈflɪmziʸ/ adj light and thin; easily destroyed –**sily** adv

flinch /flɪntʃ/ vi move back in pain or fear

fling /flɪŋ/ vt flung /flʌŋ/ throw violently ♦ n [S] short time of enjoyment, often with no sense of responsibility

flint /flɪnt/ n 1 [C;U] hard stone that makes SPARKS (1) 2 bit of metal in a cigarette lighter that lights the gas

flip /flɪp/ 1 vt send spinning into the air 2 vi become mad or very angry ♦ n quick light blow

flip·pant /ˈflɪpənt/ adj disrespectful about serious subjects ~**ly** adv –**pancy** n [U]

flip·per /ˈflɪpər/ n 1 flat limb of a SEAL², etc. 2 rubber shoe shaped like this, for swimming

flip side /ˈ· ·/ n less interesting side of a record

flirt /flɜrt/ vi behave as if sexually attracted ♦ n person who flirts ~**ation** /flɜrˈteʸʃən/ n [C;U] ~**atious** adj liking to flirt

flirt with phr vt 1 consider, but not seriously 2 risk, esp. needlessly or lightly

flit /flɪt/ vi –tt– fly or move quickly and lightly

float /floʷt/ v vi/t (cause to) stay on the surface of liquid or be held up in air 2 vt establish (a business) by selling STOCK 3 vi/t (allow to) vary in exchange value: float the $ 4 suggest ♦ n 1 light object that floats 2 flat decorated vehicle drawn in a procession 3 money kept for use if an unexpected need arises ~**ing** adj not fixed

floating vot·er /ˌ·· ˈ··/ n person who does not always vote for the same political party

flock /flɑk/ n 1 group of sheep, goats, or birds 2 crowd 3 priest's congregation (CONGREGATE) ♦ vi move in large

flog /flɑg, flɔg/ vt –gg– 1 beat severely 2 **flog a dead horse** waste time with useless efforts

flood /flʌd/ also **floods** pl. — n 1 water covering a place that is low. dry 2 large quantity: floods of tears ♦ vi/t 1 fill or cover with water 2 overflow 3 arrive in large numbers

flood·gate /ˈflʌdgeʸt/ n 1 gate for controlling water 2 **open the floodgates** suddenly set loose something that was held back

flood·light /ˈflʌdlaɪt/ n powerful light thrown on the outside of buildings, etc. ♦ vt –**lit** /-lɪt/ light with floodlights

flood tide /ˈ· ·/ n [C;U] flow of the TIDE inwards

floor /flɔr, floʷr/ n 1 [C] surface one stands on indoors: dance floor 2 [C]

level of a building – see also FIRST FLOOR 3 [S] members of a body which makes laws 4 **go through the floor** infml (of a price) sink to a very low level 5 **take the floor: a** speak in a DEBATE **b** start dancing at a party, etc. ♦ vt 1 provide with a floor 2 knock down; defeat 3 confuse

floor·board /ˈflɔrbɔrd, ˈfloʷrboʷrd/ n board in a wooden floor

floor lamp /ˈ· ·/ n lamp on a tall base which stands on the floor

floor show /ˈ· ·/ n CABARET

flop /flɑp/ vi –pp– 1 fall awkwardly 2 fail ♦ n 1 [S] awkward fall 2 [C] failure –**py** adj soft and loose: floppy hat ~**piness** n [U]

flop·house /ˈflɑphaʊs/ n cheap hotel

flop·py disk /ˌ·· ˈ·/ n plastic circle on which computer information is stored

flo·ra /ˈflɔrə, ˈfloʷrə/ n [U] plants of a particular area or period

flo·ral /ˈflɔrəl, ˈfloʷrəl/ adj of flowers

flor·id /ˈflɔrɪd, ˈflɑrɪd/ adj 1 too highly decorated 2 having a red face

flor·ist /ˈflɔrɪst, ˈfloʷr-, ˈflɑr-/ n person who sells flowers

flo·ta·tion /floʷˈteʸʃən/ n [C;U] act of floating (FLOAT (2)) a business

flo·til·la /floʷˈtɪlə/ n group of small ships

flounce /flaʊns/ vi move violently to express anger or attract attention

floun·der /ˈflaʊndər/ vi 1 make wild movements, esp. in water 2 lose control when speaking, etc. ♦ n flat fish used for food

flour /flaʊər/ n [U] powder of crushed grain, used for making bread, etc.

flour·ish /ˈflɜrɪʃ, ˈflʌrɪʃ/ v 1 vi grow in a healthy manner: Business is flourishing. 2 vt BRANDISH ♦ n noticeable fancy movement

flout /flaʊt/ vt treat (rules, etc.) without respect

flow /floʷ/ vi (of liquid) move smoothly: (fig.)traffic flowed past ♦ n [S;U] steady stream or supply ~**ing** adj curving or hanging gracefully

flow·chart /ˈfloʷtʃɑrt/ n drawing showing how the parts of a process are connected

flow·er /ˈflaʊər/ n 1 [C] part of a plant that produces seeds 2 [S] lit best part: the flower of the nation's youth ~**less** adj ~**y** adj 1 decorated with flowers 2 (of language) FLORID (1) ♦ vi produce flowers

flow·er·bed /ˈflaʊərˌbed/ n small piece of ground where flowers are grown

flow·er·pot /ˈflaʊərˌpɑt/ n pot in which a plant is grown

flown /floʷn/ v past p. of FLY

flu /fluʷ/ also **influenza** fml — n [U] infectious disease like a bad cold but more serious

fluc·tu·ate /ˈflʌktfuʷˌeʸt/ vi fml (of levels, etc.) change continually **–ation** /ˌflʌktfuʷˈeʸʃən/ n [C;U]

flue /fluʷ/ n pipe through which smoke or heat passes

flu·ent /ˈfluʷənt/ adj 1 able to speak easily 2 (of speech) coming easily **~ly** adv **–ency** n [U]

fluff /flʌf/ n [U] 1 soft light pieces from woolly material 2 soft fur or hair on a young animal or bird ♦ vt 1 shake or brush out: *fluff out its feathers* 2 do (something) badly or unsuccessfully **~y** adv covered with fluff: *fluffy kitten* ~compare FUZZ

flu·id /ˈfluʷɪd/ adj 1 able to flow 2 unsettled: *Our ideas on the subject are still fluid.* ♦ n [C;U] liquid

fluke /fluʷk/ n [S] piece of accidental good luck

flum·mox /ˈflʌməks/ vt confuse completely

flung /flʌŋ/ v past t. and p. of FLING

flunk /flʌŋk/ vt 1 fail (an examination, etc.) 2 GRADE as unsatisfactory someone's examination answers

flunk out phr vi/t (cause to) leave school because of low GRADES

flu·o·res·cent /fluʷəˈresənt, flɔ-, floʷ-/ adj giving out bright light when certain waves have passed through

flu·o·ride /ˈfluʷəraɪd/ n [U] chemical compound said to protect teeth against decay **–ridate** /ˈfluʷərəˌdeʸt, ˈflɔ-, ˈfloʷ-/ vt add fluoride to **–ridation** /ˌfluʷərəˈdeʸʃən, ˌflɔ-, ˌfloʷ-/ n [U]

flur·ry /ˈflɜriʸ, ˈflʌriʸ/ n 1 [C] sudden rush of rain, snow, etc. 2 [S] nervous excitement ♦ vt make nervous

flush /flʌʃ/ n 1 [C] (cleaning with) a rush of water 2 [S] redness of the face 3 [S] feeling of eager excitement ♦ v 1 vt clean with a rush of water 2 vi BLUSH 3 vt make (something) leave a hiding place ♦ adj 1 level 2 sl having plenty of money **~ed** adj proud and excited

flus·ter /ˈflʌstər/ vt make nervous ♦ n [S] nervous state

flute /fluʷt/ n WOODWIND musical instrument played by blowing sideways across it

flut·ist /ˈfluʷtʃɪst/ n person who plays the flute

flut·ter /ˈflʌtər/ vi/t 1 a move (wings) quickly and lightly b fly by doing this 2 move in a quick irregular way: *flags fluttering* ♦ n 1 [S;U] fluttering or shaking movement 2 [S] state of excitement

flux /flʌks/ n [U] fml continual change

fly¹ /flaɪ/ v **flew** /fluʷ/, **flown** /floʷn/ 1 vi move through the air as a bird or aircraft does 2 vt control (an aircraft) 3 raise (a flag) 4 FLEE 5 vi go fast: *Time flies.* | *I have to fly.* (= I have to leave in a hurry) 6 **fly in the face of** DEFY 7 **fly into a rage/temper** become suddenly angry 8 **fly off the handle** infml become suddenly and unexpectedly angry 9 **let fly** attack with words, bullets or blows

fly² n 1 winged insect 2 hook that is made to look like a fly, used in fishing 3 **fly in the ointment** infml something that spoils the perfection of something 4 **like flies** infml in very large numbers

fly³ /flaɪ/ n covered front opening on pants

fly·blown /ˈflaɪbloʷn/ adj 1 covered with flies' eggs 2 old and worthless

fly·er /ˈflaɪər/ n FLIER

flying col·ors /ˌ·· ˈ··/ n [P] **with flying colors** very successfully; splendidly

flying sau·cer /ˌ·· ˈ··/ n spacecraft believed to come from another world

flying start /ˌ·· ˈ·/ n very good beginning

flying vis·it /ˌ·· ˈ··/ n very short visit

fly·leaf /ˈflaɪliʸf/ n **–leaves** /-liʸvz/ empty page at the beginning or end of a book

fly pa·per /ˈ· ˌ··/ n sticky paper used to catch flies

fly swat·ter /ˈ· ˌ··/ n instrument for hitting and killing flies

FM /ˌɛf ˈɛm/ n, adj abbrev for frequency modulation, a band of radio stations

foal /foʷl/ n young horse ♦ vi give birth to a foal

foam /foʷm/ n [U] 1 mass of BUBBLES 2 infml FOAM RUBBER ♦ vi produce foam **~y** adj

foam rub·ber /ˌ· ˈ··/ n [U] soft rubber full of BUBBLES

fob /fɑb/ v **-bb-** **fob off** phr vt deceive (someone) into accepting (something)

fo·cus /ˈfoʷkəs/ n **–cuses** or **–ci** /-saɪ/ 1 [C] point at which beams of light, etc., meet 2 [S] center of attention 3 **in/out of focus** (not) giving a clear picture because the LENS is not correctly placed ♦ vi/t **-s-** or **-ss-** 1 come or bring to a focus 2 direct (attention) **focal** adj

fod·der /ˈfɑdər/ n [U] 1 food for farm animals 2 anything that supplies a continuous demand

foe /foʷ/ n lit enemy

fog /fɑg, fɔg/ n [C;U] (period of) thick mist ♦ vi/t -**gg**- (cause to) become covered with fog -**gy** adj **1** misty **2** not clear: I haven't the foggiest idea.

fog·bound /ˈfɑgbaʊnd, ˈfɔg-/ adj prevented by fog from traveling

fog·horn /ˈfɑghɔrn, ˈfɔg-/ n horn used for warning ships in fog

fog lamp /ˈ··/ n bright lamp on a vehicle, for driving through fog

fo·gy /ˈfoʷgiʸ/ n derog slow uninteresting old person

foi·ble /ˈfɔɪbəl/ n foolish little personal habit

foil¹ /fɔɪl/ vt prevent (someone) from succeeding in a plan

foil² n **1** [U] thin sheet metal **2** [C] person or thing that provides a CONTRAST to another

foil³ n thin sword for fencing (FENCE² (1))

foist /fɔɪst/ vt force someone to accept: He tried to foist his company on them.

fold¹ /foʷld/ v **1** vt bend back on itself **2** vi be able to be folded: folding table **3** vt cross (one's arms) **4** vi (of a business) fail **5** vi stop taking part in a game of POKER ♦ n line made by folding -**er** n cardboard holder for papers

fold² n enclosure for sheep

fo·li·age /ˈfoʷliʸɪdʒ/ n [U] fml leaves

folk /foʷk/ n **1** [P] people **2** [U] folk music ♦ adj of music, etc. that has grown up among ordinary people: folk singer/concert/dancing folks n [P] one's relatives or parents

folk·lore /ˈfoʷk-lɔr, -loʷr/ n [U] beliefs long preserved among a tribe or nation

fol·low /ˈfɑloʷ/ v **1** vi/t come or go after **2** vt go along: follow the river **3** vt attend or listen to carefully **4** vi/t understand: I don't quite follow (you). **5** vt act according to: follow instructions **6** vi be a necessary result **7 as follows** as now to be told **8 follow suit** do what someone else has done -**er** n someone who follows or supports -**ing** adj **1** next: the following day **2** to be mentioned now -**ing** n group of supporters

follow through phr vt carry out to the end

follow up phr vt take action to continue or add to the effect of something done before **follow-up** /ˈ··/ n: The paper's doing a follow-up next week.

fol·ly /ˈfɑliʸ/ n [C;U] fml foolishness

fo·ment /foʷˈment/ vt fml help (something bad) to develop

fond /fɑnd/ adj **1** loving **2** foolishly hopeful: fond belief **3** having a great liking or love (for) -**ly** adv -**ness** n [C;U]

fon·dle /ˈfɑndl/ vt touch lovingly

font /fɑnt/ n **1** container for water for BAPTISM **2** all the characters in one style of TYPE (3)

food /fuʷd/ n [C;U] **1** something, esp. solid, that creatures eat **2 food for thought** something to think about carefully

food stamps /ˈ· ·/ n [P] notes supplied by the government that can be exchanged for food

food·stuff /ˈfuʷdstʌf/ n substance used as food

fool /fuʷl/ n **1** silly person **2 make a fool of oneself** behave in a silly way ♦ v **1** vt deceive **2** vi behave in a silly way **3** vi joke -**ish** adj silly -**ishly** adv -**ishness** n [U]

fool·har·dy /ˈfuʷlˌhɑrdiʸ/ adj taking unwise risks

fool·proof /ˈfuʷlpruʷf/ adj that cannot fail

fool's par·a·dise /ˌ· ˈ··/ n carelessly happy state in spite of a threat of change

foot¹ /fʊt/ n feet /fiʸt/ **1** [C] end part of the leg **2** [S] bottom: foot of the stairs **3** [C] (measure of length equal to) 12 inches (INCH) **4 a foot in the door** favorable position from which to advance, gain influence, etc. **5 on foot** walking **6 put one's feet up** rest **7 put one's foot down** speak firmly **8 put one's foot in one's mouth** infml say the wrong thing **9 set foot in/on** enter; visit -**age** n [U] length of news or movie film -**ing** n **1** firm placing of the feet: lose one's footing **2** position in relation to others: on an equal footing

foot² vt **foot the bill** infml pay the bill

foot·ball /ˈfʊtbɔl/ n **1** [U] game played between 2 teams of 11 players using an OVAL ball that can be handled or kicked **2** [C] ball used in this game

foot·bridge /ˈfʊtˌbrɪdʒ/ n narrow bridge to be used only by people walking

foot·hill /ˈfʊtˌhɪl/ n low hill at the foot of a mountain

foot·hold /ˈfʊthoʷld/ n **1** place where a foot can stand **2** position from which to advance

foot·lights /ˈfʊtlaɪts/ n [P] lights along the front of a stage floor

foot·loose /ˈfʊtluʷs/ adj free to go wherever one wants and do what one likes: footloose and fancy-free

foot·man /ˈfʊtmən/ n -**men** /-mən/ uniformed servant who opens doors, etc.

foot·note /ˈfʊtnoʷt/ n note at the bottom of a page

foot·path /ˈfʊtpæθ/ n -**paths** /-pæðz/ narrow path for walking on

foot·print /ˈfʊtˌprɪnt/ n mark made by a foot

foot·sore /ˈfʊtsɔr, -soʷr/ adj having sore feet from too much walking

foot·step /ˈfʊtstep/ n 1 sound of a person's step 2 **follow in someone's footsteps** follow an example set by someone else in the past

foot·wear /ˈfʊt-wɛər/ n [U] shoes, etc.

foot·work /ˈfʊt-wɜrk/ n [U] use of the feet in sports, etc.

for[1] /fər; strong fɔr/ prep 1 intended to be given to, used by, or used in: a present for you | cake for the party 2 to help: lift it for you | medicine for a cold 3 (shows purpose): What's this knife for? 4 in support of: play football for Miami 5 towards: set off for school 6 so as to get: wait for the bus | no demand for wheat 7 (shows price or amount): buy it for $1 8 meaning: Red is for danger. 9 (shows distance or time): stay for a week 10 because of: rewarded for his bravery 11 in regard to: an ear for music | good for his health 12 considering: tall for his age 13 (introducing phrases): no need for you to go

for[2] conj fml and the reason is that

for·age /ˈfɔrɪdʒ, ˈfar-/ n [U] food for horses and cattle ♦ vi search about

for·ay /ˈfɔreʸ, ˈfareʸ/ n sudden rush into enemy country: (fig.) his unsuccessful foray into politics

for·bear[1] /fɔrˈbɛər, fər-/ vi −bore /-ˈbɔr, -ˈboʷr/, −borne /-ˈbɔrn, -ˈboʷrn/ fml hold oneself back from doing something ~ance n [U] patient forgiveness

for·bear[2] /ˈfɔrbɛər, ˈfoʷr-/ n FOREBEAR

for·bid /fərˈbɪd, fɔr-/ vt −bade /-ˈbæd, -ˈbeʸd/ or −bad /-ˈbæd/, −bidden /-ˈbɪdn/ 1 refuse to allow 2 **God forbid (that)** I very much hope it will not happen (that) ~ding adj looking dangerous

force /fɔrs/ n 1 [U] strength; violence 2 [C;U] influence 3 [C] power that produces change: the force of gravity 4 [C] group of soldiers, police, etc. − see also FORCES 5 **in force** in large numbers 6 **in(to) force** in/into operation 7 **join forces (with)** unite (with) for a purpose ♦ vt 1 use (physical) force on 2 produce with effort: forced laughter 3 hasten the growth of (plants) 4 **force someone's hand** make someone act as one wishes or before they are ready ~ful adj (of plans, words, etc.) powerful ~fully adv **forcible** adj done by physical force **forcibly** adv

for·ceps /ˈfɔrseps, -seps/ n [P] medical instrument for holding objects

forc·es /ˈfɔrsɪz, ˈfoʷr-/ also **armed forces** — n [(the) P] (often cap.) the army, navy, and air force of a country

ford /fɔrd, foʷrd/ n place where one can cross a river without a bridge ♦ vt cross at a ford

fore /fɔr, foʷr/ adj front ♦ n **come to the fore** become well known; noticeable

fore·arm /ˈfɔrarm, ˈfoʷr-/ n arm between the hand and elbow

fore·bear /ˈfɔrbɛər, ˈfoʷr-/ n fml ANCESTOR

fore·bod·ing /fɔrˈboʷdɪŋ, foʷr-/ n [C;U] feeling of coming evil

fore·cast /ˈfɔrkæst, ˈfoʷr-/ vt −cast or −casted say in advance (what will happen in future) ♦ n statement of future events: weather forecast

fore·close /fɔrˈkloʷz, foʷr-/ vi/t take back property because a MORTGAGE has not been repaid

fore·fa·thers /ˈfɔrˌfaðərz, ˈfoʷr-/ n [P] ANCESTORS

fore·fin·ger /ˈfɔrˌfɪŋgər, ˈfoʷr-/ also **index finger** — n finger next to the thumb

fore·front /ˈfɔrfrʌnt, ˈfoʷr-/ n [S] leading position

fore·go /fɔrˈgoʷ, foʷr-/ vt FORGO

foregone con·clu·sion /ˌ··· ·ˈ··/ n result that is certain from the start

fore·ground /ˈfɔrgraund, ˈfoʷr-/ n nearest part of a view

fore·hand /ˈfɔrhænd, ˈfoʷr-/ n, adj (tennis stroke) with the inner part of hand and arm turned forward

fore·head /ˈfɔrɪd, ˈfarɪd, ˈfɔrhed, ˈfar-/ n face above the eyes

for·eign /ˈfɔrɪn, ˈfarɪn/ adj 1 of a country that is not one's own 2 coming or brought in from outside: a foreign body in her eye 3 **foreign to** not natural in ~er n foreign person

foreign af·fairs /ˌ··· ·ˈ·◄/ n [P] matters concerning international relations and the interests of one's own country in foreign countries

foreign ex·change /ˌ·· ·ˈ·/ n [U] (practice of buying and selling) foreign money

foreign serv·ice /ˌ·· ˈ··/ n [U] work in embassies (EMBASSY) abroad

fore·man /ˈfɔrmən, ˈfoʷr-/ **forewoman** /-ˌwʊmən/ fem. — n −men /-mən/ 1 worker in charge of others 2 leader of a JURY

fore·most /ˈfɔrmoʷst, ˈfoʷr-/ adj most important

fo·ren·sic /fəˈrensɪk, -zɪk/ adj used in the law and the tracking of criminals: forensic medicine

fore·run·ner /ˈfɔrˌrʌnər, ˈfoʷr-/ n person or thing that prepares the way for another

fore·see /fɔrˈsiʸ, foʷr-/ vt -saw /-ˈsɔ/, -seen /-ˈsiʸn/ see in advance ~able adj 1 that can be foreseen **2 in the foreseeable future** soon

fore·shad·ow /fɔrˈʃædoʷ, foʷr-/ vt be a sign of (what will happen)

fore·shore /ˈfɔrʃɔr, ˈfoʷrʃoʷr/ n [S] shore between the sea and ordinary land

fore·sight /ˈfɔrsaɪt, ˈfoʷr-/ n [U] ability to imagine the future; wise planning

for·est /ˈfɔrɪst, ˈfɑr-/ n [C;U] **1** area covered with trees **2 not see the forest for the trees** miss what is clear by looking too closely ~**er** n person who works in a forest ~**ry** n [U] work of planting and caring for trees

fore·stall /fɔrˈstɔl, foʷr-/ vt prevent (a person or plan) by acting first

fore·taste /ˈfɔrteʸst, ˈfoʷr-/ n [S] first experience of something that will come later

fore·tell /fɔrˈtel, foʷr-/ vt -told /-ˈtoʷld/ PROPHESY

fore·thought /ˈfɔrθɔt, ˈfoʷr-/ n [U] wise planning for the future

for·ev·er /fəˈrevər, fɔ-/ adv **1** for all future time **2** continually **3 take forever** take an extremely long time

fore·warn /fɔrˈwɔrn, foʷr-/ vt warn of coming danger

fore·went /fɔrˈwent, foʷr-/ past t. of FOREGO

fore·word /ˈfɔrwɜrd, -wərd, ˈfoʷr-/ n short introduction to a book

for·feit /ˈfɔrfɪt/ vt lose as a punishment ♦ n something forfeited

forge¹ /fɔrdʒ, foʷrdʒ/ vt **1** copy in order to deceive: a forged passport **2** form (metal) by heating and hammering: (fig.) forge a new agreement

forge ahead phr vi move with a sudden increase of speed and power

forge² n place where metal is forged

forg·er /ˈfɔrdʒər, ˈfoʷr-/ n person who forges papers, etc. ~**ry** /ˈfɔrdʒəriʸ, ˈfoʷr-/ n **1** [U] forging of papers, etc. **2** [C] forged paper, etc.

for·get /fərˈget/ vi/t -got /-ˈgɑt/, -gotten /-ˈgɑtn/ **1** fail to remember: Don't forget to lock the door. **2** stop thinking about: Let's just forget it. ~**ful** adj in the habit of forgetting

for·give /fərˈgɪv/ vi/t -gave /-ˈgeʸv/, -given /-ˈgɪvən/ stop blaming (someone for something) -**givable** adj: forgivable mistake -**giving** adj willing to forgive ~**ness** n [U] act of forgiving

for·go, fore- /fɔrˈgoʷ, foʷr-/ vt -went /-ˈwent/, -gone /-ˈgɔn/ fml give up

fork¹ /fɔrk/ n **1** instrument with points, for lifting food to the mouth **2** farm or gardening tool like this **3** place where a road, etc., divides; one of the divisions **4** main branch of a river

fork² v **1** vt lift, etc., with a fork **2** vi divide into branches —**ed** adj that divides into 2 or more points at the end

fork out phr vi/t pay (money) unwillingly

fork·lift truck /ˌfɔrklɪft ˈtrʌk/ n small vehicle with a movable apparatus for lifting goods

for·lorn /fərˈlɔrn, fɔr-/ adj lit alone and unhappy ~**ly** adv

form¹ /fɔrm/ n **1** [C;U] shape **2** [C] plan; kind: forms of government **3** [U] way in which a work of art is put together **4** [C] official paper with spaces for answering questions **5** [U] degree of skill, fitness, etc.: to be in form **6** [U] correct practice: a matter of form ~**less** adj shapeless

form² v **1** vi begin to exist: A cloud formed. **2** vt make from parts: form a committee **3** vt have the shape or substance of: The buildings form a square.

form·al /ˈfɔrməl/ adj **1** suitable for official occasions: formal dress/language **2** regular in shape: formal garden **3** stiff in manner and behavior ~**ly** adv —**ize** vt make formal —**ity** /fɔrˈmæləṭiʸ/ n **1** [U] attention to rules **2** [C] act in accordance with custom: legal formalities

for·mat /ˈfɔrmæt/ n size, shape, or arrangement of something ♦ vt -tt- arrange (a book, computer information, etc.) in a particular format

for·ma·tion /fɔrˈmeʸʃən/ n **1** [U] shaping of something **2** [C;U] arrangement; structure

for·ma·tive /ˈfɔrməṭɪv/ adj giving shape: a child's formative years

for·mer /ˈfɔrmər/ adj of an earlier period: her former husband ♦ n fml first of 2 things mentioned ~**ly** adv in earlier time

for·mi·da·ble /ˈfɔrmədəbəl, fɔrˈmɪdə-/ adj **1** large and frightening **2** hard to defeat —**bly** adv

for·mu·la /ˈfɔrmyələ/ n -las or -lae /-liʸ/ **1** rule expressed in a short form by letters, numbers, etc.: chemical formulae **2** list of substances used in making something: (fig.) a formula for trouble **3** combination of suggestions, plans, etc.: a peace formula **4** milk food for very young babies

for·mu·late /ˈfɔrmyəˌleʸt/ vt **1** express exactly **2** invent (a plan) —**lation** /ˌfɔrmyəˈleʸʃən/ n [C;U]

for·ni·cate /ˈfɔrnəˌkeʸt/ vi esp. law have sex outside marriage –**cation** /ˌfɔrnəˈkeʸʃən/ n [U]

for·sake /fərˈseʸk, fɔr-/ vt –**sook** /-ˈsʊk/ /, –**saken** /-ˈseʸkən/ lit DESERT² (2)

fort /fɔrt, foʷrt/ n 1 building for military defense 2 **hold the fort** look after everything while someone is away

forte /fɔrt, foʷrt, ˈfɔrteʸ/ n something someone does particularly well

forth /fɔrθ, foʷrθ/ adv lit 1 forward 2 **and (so on and) so forth** etc.

forth·com·ing /ˌfɔrθˈkʌmɪŋ◂, ˌfoʷrθ-/ adj 1 happening soon 2 supplied when needed: No answer was forthcoming. 3 ready to be helpful

forth·right /ˈfɔrθraɪt, ˈfoʷrθ-/ adj speaking plainly; direct

forth·with /ˌfɔrθˈwɪθ, -ˈwɪð, ˌfoʷrθ-/ adv fml at once

for·ti·eth /ˈfɔrtiʸəθ/ det, n, pron, adv 40th

for·ti·fy /ˈfɔrtəˌfaɪ/ vt 1 strengthen against attack 2 make stronger: fortified milk (=with VITAMINS added) –**fication** /ˌfɔrtəfəˈkeʸʃən/ n 1 [C] towers, etc., for defense 2 [U] act of fortifying

for·ti·tude /ˈfɔrtəˌtuʷd, -ˌtyuʷd/ n [U] uncomplaining courage

for·tress /ˈfɔrtrɪs/ n large fort

for·tu·i·tous /fɔrˈtuʷətəs/ adj fml accidental

for·tu·nate /ˈfɔrtʃənɪt/ adj lucky ~**ly** adv

for·tune /ˈfɔrtʃən/ n 1 [C;U] good or bad luck 2 [C] that which will happen to a person in the future: tell someone's fortune 3 [C] great sum of money: diamonds worth a fortune 4 **a small fortune** a lot of money

for·tune-tell·er /ˈfɔrtʃənˌtelər/ n person who claims to be able to tell people their future

for·ty /ˈfɔrtiʸ/ det, n, pron 40

forty winks /ˌ·· ˈ·/ n [P] short sleep in the day time

fo·rum /ˈfɔrəm, ˈfoʷrəm/ n place for public argument

for·ward /ˈfɔrwərd/ adj 1 toward the front or future 2 advanced in development 3 too bold often in sexual matters ♦ vt 1 send (letters, etc.) to a new address 2 fml send (goods) ♦ n player in BASKETBALL, etc. ~**ness** n [U] being FORWARD¹ (2, 3)

forward² also **forwards** — adv toward the front or future

for·went /fɔrˈwent, foʷr-/ past t. of FORGO

fos·sil /ˈfɑsəl/ n 1 part or print of an ancient animal or plant, preserved in rock, ice etc. 2 old person with

unchanging ideas ~**ize** vi/t 1 change into a fossil 2 (cause to) become very fixed (in ideas, etc.)

fos·ter /ˈfɑstər, ˈfɒ-/ vt 1 fml encourage to develop 2 take (a child) into one's home for a while

foster- see WORD BEGINNINGS, p 497

fought /fɔt/ v past t. and p. of FIGHT

foul¹ /faʊl/ adj 1 very unpleasant: foul smell/language/weather 2 **foul of** get into trouble with ~**ly** adv

foul² n act that is against the rules

foul³ vi/t 1 make dirty 2 be guilty of a FOUL²

foul out phv v stop playing BASKETBALL, etc., because of too many fouls

foul play /ˌ· ˈ·/ n [U] 1 (in sports) unfair play 2 criminal violence, esp. murder

foul up phr v infml spoil (an occasion, etc.) **foul-up** /ˈ· ·/ n

found¹ /faʊnd/ v past t. and p. of FIND

found² vt 1 establish; build 2 base: stories founded on fact ~**er** n person who establishes something

foun·da·tion /faʊnˈdeʸʃən/ n 1 [U] founding of an organization 2 [U] BASIS: rumors without foundation 3 [C] organization that gives out money **foundations** n [P] base that supports a building: (fig.) the foundations of her success

foundation stone /·ˈ·· ·/ n first stone of a new building, often laid with public ceremony

found·er /ˈfaʊndər/ vi lit (of a ship) fill with water and sink

foun·dry /ˈfaʊndriʸ/ n place where metal is melted and poured into shapes

fount /faʊnt/ n lit SOURCE

foun·tain /ˈfaʊntn/ n 1 decorative structure from which water springs up 2 flow of liquid

fountain pen /ˈ·· ·/ n refillable ink pen

four /fɔr, foʷr/ det, n, pron 4

four·teen /ˌfɔrˈtiʸn◂, ˌfoʷr-/ det, n, pron 14 ~**th** det, adv, n, pron 14th

fourth /fɔrθ, foʷrθ/ det, adv, n, pron 4th

fowl /faʊl/ n fowls or fowl 1 farmyard bird, esp. a hen 2 any bird

fox /fɑks/ n doglike wild animal, said to be clever ♦ vt confuse; deceive

fox·hole /ˈfɑkshoʷl/ n hole where soldiers hide from the enemy

fox·y /ˈfɑksiʸ/ adj 1 like a fox (e.g. clever, etc.) 2 attractive

foy·er /ˈfɔɪər/ n entrance hall of a theater, etc.

frac·as /ˈfreʸkəs, ˈfræ-/ n fml noisy quarrel

frac·tion /ˈfrækʃən/ n 1 division of a whole number (e.g. ⅓) 2 small part: *a fraction of the cost* – **al** *adj* so small as to be unimportant

frac·tious /ˈfrækʃəs/ *adj* restless and complaining

frac·ture /ˈfræktʃər/ n [C;U] *fml* breaking of a bone, etc. ♦ *vi/t fml* break

fra·gile /ˈfrædʒəl, -dʒaɪl/ *adj* 1 easily broken 2 having a small thin body or weak in health – **gility** /frəˈdʒɪləti/ n [U]

frag·ment¹ /ˈfrægmənt/ n piece broken off – **ary** *adj* incomplete

frag·ment² /ˈfrægment, frægˈment/ *vi/t* break into pieces – **ation** /ˌfrægmənˈteɪʃən, -men-/ n [U]

fra·grant /ˈfreɪɡrənt/ *adj* smelling sweet – **ly** *adv* – **grance** n [C;U]

frail /freɪl/ *adj* weak, esp. in body – **ty** n 1 [U] quality of being frail 2 [C] fault of character

frame /freɪm/ n 1 border into which something fits: *a window frame* 2 structure on which something is built 3 human or animal body 4 single photograph in a film 5 **frame of mind** state of mind at a particular time ♦ *vt* 1 put in a frame(1) 2 give shape to; express: *frame a question* 3 *infml* make a (guiltless person) seem guilty of a crime

frame-up /ˈ· ·/ n *infml* carefully prepared plan to frame (3) someone

frame·work /ˈfreɪmwɜrk/ n supporting structure

fran·chise /ˈfræntʃaɪz/ n 1 [S] the right to vote 2 [C] the right to sell a product

frank /fræŋk/ *adj* open and honest – **ly** *adv* – **ness** n [U]

frank·fur·ter /ˈfræŋkfɜrtər/ n also **frank** red smoked SAUSAGE

fran·tic /ˈfræntɪk/ *adj* wildly anxious, afraid, happy, etc. – **ally** /-kli/ *adv*

fra·ter·nal /frəˈtɜrnl/ *adj* BROTHER**ly**

fra·ter·ni·ty /frəˈtɜrnəti/ n 1 [C] people joined by common interests 2 [C] university club for men 3 [U] *fml* brotherly feeling

frat·er·nize, -ise /ˈfrætərˌnaɪz/ *vi* meet and be friendly (with someone) – **nization** /ˌfrætərnəˈzeɪʃən/ n [U]

frat·ri·cide /ˈfrætrəˌsaɪd/ n [U] *fml* murder of one's brother or sister

fraud /frɔd/ n 1 [C;U] criminal deceit to make money 2 [C] person who falsely claims to be something

fraud·u·lent /ˈfrɔdʒələnt/ *adj* deceitful; got or done by fraud – **ly** *adv*

fraught /frɔt/ *adj* 1 full of: *fraught with danger* 2 *infml* a (of a person) worried b (of conditions) difficult

fray¹ /freɪ/ *vi/t* develop loose threads by rubbing: *frayed collar* | (fig.) *frayed nerves*

fray² n [S] *lit* battle

freak /frik/ n 1 strange unnatural creature or event 2 person who takes a special interest in the stated thing: *a film freak* – **ish** *adj* unreasonable; unusual

freck·le /ˈfrekəl/ n small brown spot on the skin **freckled** *adj*

free /fri/ *adj* 1 able to act as one wants; not in prison or controlled by rules: *free speech* | *You are free to go.* 2 not busy or being used: *Is this seat free?* 3 *free time* 3 without payment: *free tickets* 4 (of a way or passage) not blocked 5 not fixed; loose 6 **free and easy** unworried 7 **free from/of** untroubled by; without: *free from dirt* | *tax free* 8 **free with** ready to give ♦ *adv* 1 without payment 2 without control 3 in a loose position ♦ *vt* **freed** /frid/ set free – **ly** *adv* 1 readily; openly 2 in great amounts

free·base /ˈ· ·/ *vi sl* smoke a specially prepared mixture of COCAINE

free·bie, -bee /ˈfribi/ n *infml* something that is given or received without payment

free·dom /ˈfridəm/ n [U] 1 state of being free 2 [*the*+S] certain rights, often given as a favor: *freedom to use the car*

freedom of speech /ˌ··· ˈ·/ n [U] FREE SPEECH

free en·ter·prise /ˌ· ····/ n [U] social system in which private trade, business, etc., is carried on without much government control

free-for-all /ˈ· · ˌ·/ n quarrel, etc., in which many people join

free-form /ˈ· ·/ *adj* not done or made according to usual rules: *free-form interview*

free·hand /ˈfrihænd/ *adj, adv* drawn without instruments

free hand /ˌ· ˈ·/ n [S] unlimited freedom of action

free·lance /ˈfrilæns/ *adj, adv, n* (done by) a writer, etc., who works for many employers **freelance** *vi* – **lancer** n

free·load /ˈfriloʊd/ *vi* live on another person's money – **er** n

free rein /ˌ· ˈ·/ n [U] complete freedom of action

free ride /ˌ· ˈ·/ n something got without paying

free speech /ˌ· ˈ·/ n [U] right to express one's ideas in public

free trade /ˌ· ˈ·/ n [U] system of allowing foreign goods freely into a country

free verse /ˌ· ˈ·/ n [U] poetry that does not follow the usual rules

free·way /ˈfriweɪ/ n EXPRESSWAY

free·wheel /ˌfriˈhwiˑl, -ˈwiˑl/ vi travel or move without effort or care ~**ing** adj infml not greatly worrying about rules, responsibilities, etc.

free will /ˌ· ˈ·/ n [U] **1** ability to decide freely what to do **2** belief that human effort can influence events, and they are not fixed in advance by God

freeze /friˑz/ v **froze** /froˑz/, **frozen** /ˈfroˑzən/ **1** vi/t harden into ice **2** vi (of weather) be at the temperature at which ice forms **3** vi/t stop working properly because of cold **4** vi feel very cold **5** vt preserve (food) at low temperatures **6** vi/t stop moving **7** vt fix (prices, wages, etc.) ♦ n [U] **1** period of freezing weather **2** fixing of prices or wages ~**er** n machine that freezes food

freeze out phr vt infml prevent from being included

freeze over phr vi/t (cause to) turn to ice on the surface

freight /freˑt/ n [U] goods carried by ship, plane, etc. ~**er** n ship or plane that carries goods

French doors /ˌ· ˈdɔrz, -ˈdoˌrz/ n [P] glass doors opening onto a garden, etc.

French fries /ˌ· ˈ·/ n [P] thin pieces of potato cooked in fat.

fre·net·ic /frəˈnetɪk/ adj too excited; feverish

fren·zy /ˈfrenziˑ/ n [S;U] violent excitement

fre·quen·cy /ˈfriˑkwənsiˑ/ n **1** [U] the happening of something a large number of times **2** [C;U] rate at which something happens or is repeated **3** [C] particular number of radio waves per second

fre·quent¹ /ˈfriˑkwənt/ adj happening often ~**ly** adv

fre·quent² /friˑˈkwent, ˈfriˑkwənt/ vt fml go to (a place) often

fres·co /ˈfreskoˑ/ n **-coes** or **-cos** picture painted on wet PLASTER¹(1)

fresh /freʃ/ adj **1** recently made, found, etc.; not STALE: fresh flowers **2** (of food) not frozen or canned **3** (of water) not salt **4** new and different: Make a fresh start. **5 a** (of wind) fairly strong **b** (of weather) cool and windy **6** not tired **7** too bold with someone of the opposite sex ♦ adv **1** just; newly **2 fresh out of** infml, having just used up one's supplies of ~**ly** adv ~**ness** n [U]

fresh·en /ˈfreʃən/ vi/t **1** make or become fresh **2** (of wind) become stronger

freshen up phr vi/t **1** (cause to) feel less tired, look more attractive, etc. **2** (of a drink) add more liquid, esp. alcohol, to it

fresh·man /ˈfreʃmən/ n **-men** /-mən/ student in the first year at high school, college or university

fresh·wa·ter /ˈfreʃˌwɔtər, -ˌwɑtər/ adj of a river or lake, not the sea

fret /fret/ vi/t **-tt-** worry about small things ~**ful** adj anxious and complaining ~**fully** adv

fret·saw /ˈfretsɔ/ n tool for cutting patterns in wood

fret·work /ˈfretwɜrk/ n [U] patterns cut with a fretsaw

fri·ar /ˈfraɪər/ n man belonging to a Christian religious group

fric·tion /ˈfrɪkʃən/ n [U] **1** rubbing of one surface against another **2** disagreement within a group

Fri·day /ˈfraɪdiˑ, -deˑ/ n the 5th day of the week – see also GOOD FRIDAY

fridge /frɪdʒ/ n infml REFRIGERATOR

friend /frend/ n **1** person whom one likes but who is not related **2** helper; supporter **3 make friends** form a friendship ~**less** adj without friends ~**ly** adj **1** acting as a friend **2** not causing unpleasant feelings in competitions, etc.: a friendly game ~**liness** n [U] ~**ship** n [C;U] friendly relationship

fries /fraɪz/ n see FRENCH FRIES

frieze /friˑz/ n decorative border along the top of a wall

frig·ate /ˈfrɪgɪt/ n small fast fighting ship

fright /fraɪt/ n [C;U] feeling of fear

fright·en /ˈfraɪtn/ vt fill with fear ~**ed** adj ~**ingly** adv

fright·ful /ˈfraɪtfəl/ adj terrible; very bad ~**ly** adv

fri·gid /ˈfrɪdʒɪd/ adj **1** (of a woman) disliking sex **2** very cold ~**ly** adv ~**gidity** /frɪˈdʒɪdətiˑ/ n [U]

frill /frɪl/ n **1** decorative wavy edge on cloth **2** unnecessary decoration ~**y** adj

fringe /frɪndʒ/ n **1** decorative edge of hanging threads on a curtain, etc. **2** edge: the fringe(s) of the crowd **3** not official; not CONVENTIONAL: fringe politics ♦ vt be the border of

fringe ben·e·fit /ˈ· ˌ···/ n something given with a job, besides wages

frisk /frɪsk/ v **1** vi jump about playfully **2** vt search (someone) with the hands, for hidden weapons ~**y** adj joyfully playful

fris·son /friˑˈsoˑn/ n feeling of excitement caused by fear

frit·ter /ˈfrɪtər/ n piece of cooked BATTER² with fruit, meat, etc., inside

fritter² v **fritter away** phr vt waste: He fritters away his money.

fri·vol·i·ty /frɪˈvɑlətiˑ/ n **1** [U] quality of being frivolous **2** [C] frivolous act or remark

friv·o·lous /ˈfrɪvələs/ adj not serious enough; silly ~**ly** adv

frizz·y /ˈfrɪziʸ/ *adj* (of hair) very curly, like wool

fro /froʷ/ *adv* see TO AND FRO

frog /frɔg, frɑg/ *n* **1** small jumping creature that lives on land and in water **2 a frog in the/one's throat** difficulty in speaking because of roughness in the throat or emotion

frog·man /ˈfrɔgmæn, -mən, ˈfrɑg-/ *n* **-men** /-mɛn, -mən/ skilled underwater swimmer who uses breathing apparatus

frol·ic /ˈfrɑlɪk/ *vi* **-ck-** jump about happily **frolic** *n* **~some** *adj* playful

from /frəm; *strong* frʌm, frɑm/ *prep* **1** starting at (a place or time): *fly from New York to Paris* | *work from Monday till Friday* **2** given or sent by: *a letter from John* **3** away: *subtract 10 from 15* **4** using: *Bread is made from flour.* **5** because of: *suffer from heart disease* **6** out of: *He took a knife from his pocket.* **7** in a state of protection or prevention with regard to: *She saved the child from drowning.* **8** judging by: *From what John tells me, they're very rich.*

frond /frɑnd/ *n* leaf of a FERN or PALM[1]

front /frʌnt/ *n* **1** [C] part in the direction that something moves or faces: *the front of the aircraft/of the house* | *his front teeth* **2** [C] line where fighting takes place in war **3** [*the*+S] road beside the sea in a tourist town **4** [C] line dividing cold from warmer air **5** [C] (often false) outward appearance: *present a smiling front* **6** [C] combined effort or movement against opposing forces: *present a united front* **7** [C] particular area of activity: *They have made little progress on the jobs front.* **8** [C] *infml* person, group or thing used for hiding the real nature of a secret or unlawful activity: *front for a gang of car thieves* **9 in front**: **a** ahead **b** in the most forward position **10 in front of**: **a** ahead of **b** in the presence of **11 up front** *infml* as payment in advance ♦ *vi/t* face (towards): *The hotel fronts onto the lake.* **~al** *adj* at, of, or from the front

front·age /ˈfrʌntɪdʒ/ *n* front width of a building or piece of land

fron·tier /frʌnˈtɪər/ *n* **1** edge of a country **2** part of a country that marks furthest point where people have settled **frontiers** *n* [P] furthest limit: *the frontiers of knowledge*

front line /ˌ· ˈ··◂/ *n* [S] **1** military FRONT (2) **2** most advanced position **front-line** *adj*

front man /ˈ· ·/ *n* someone who explains the views or future plans of esp. a large company to the public

front-page /ˈ· ·/ *adj* very interesting; worthy of being on the front page of a newspaper: *front-page news*

front room /ˈ· ·/ *n* LIVING ROOM

front-run·ner /ˌ· ˈ··/ *n* person who has the best chance of success in competing for something

frost /frɔst/ *n* **1** [U] white powder that forms on things below freezing point **2** [C;U] (period of) freezing weather ♦ *v* **1** *vi/t* (cause to) become covered with frost **2** *vt* **a** roughen the surface of (glass) **b** cover with frosting **~y** *adj* **1** very cold **2** unfriendly: *a frosty greeting*

frost·bite /ˈfrɔstbaɪt/ *n* [U] harmful swelling etc., of the limbs, caused by cold **-bitten** *adj*

frosting /ˈfrɔstɪŋ/ *n* mixture of powdery sugar with liquid, used to decorate cakes

froth /frɔθ/ *n* [U] **1** mass of small BUBBLEs on beer, etc. **2** *derog* light empty show of talk or ideas ♦ *vi* produce froth **~y** *adj* covered with froth

frown /fraʊn/ *vi* draw the EYEBROWs together in anger or effort **frown** *n*

froze /froʷz/ *v past t. of* FREEZE

fro·zen /ˈfroʷzən/ *v past p. of* FREEZE

fru·gal /ˈfruʷgəl/ *adj* **1** not wasteful **2** small and cheap: *frugal supper*

fruit /fruʷt/ *n* **1** [C;U] part of a plant containing the seed, often eatable **2** [C] also **fruits** *pl.* result or reward **3** male HOMOSEXUAL ♦ *vi* bear fruit **~ful** *adj* useful; successful **~fully** *adv* **~less** *adj* unsuccessful **~lessly** *adv* **~y** *adj* **1** like fruit **2** (of a voice) rich and deep **3** crazy

fruit·cake /ˈfruʷtkeʸk/ *n* **1** [C;U] cake containing small dried fruits, nuts, etc. **2** [C] *infml* a crazy, silly person **3 as nutty as a fruitcake** completely crazy

fru·i·tion /fruʷˈɪʃən/ *n* [U] *fml* fulfilment of plans, etc.

frus·trate /ˈfrʌstreʸt/ *vt* **1** disappoint and annoy **2** prevent the fulfillment of (plans) **-tration** /frʌˈstreʸʃən/ *n* [C;U]

fry /fraɪ/ *vi/t* cook in hot fat or oil **fry** *n* see FRENCH FRIES, SMALL FRY

fry·er /ˈfraɪər/ *n* chicken for frying

frying pan /ˈ·· ˌ·/ *n* **1** flat pan for frying **2 out of the frying pan into the fire** out of a bad position into an even worse one

ft *written abbrev. for*: FOOT[1] (3)

fuck /fʌk/ *vi/t taboo* have sex (with) ♦ *n taboo sl* **1** act of having sex **2 not give a fuck** not care at all

fuck off *phr vi taboo sl* go away

fuck over *phr vt taboo sl* treat badly

fuck up phr vt taboo sl spoil; ruin
♦ **fuck-up** /'· ·/ n

fudge¹ /fʌdʒ/ n [U] creamy brown candy made of sugar, milk, butter, etc.

fudge² v 1 vt put together roughly or dishonestly 2 vi/t avoid taking firm action (on)

fu·el /fyuʷəl/ n [C;U] material (e.g. coal) that produces heat or power ♦ v –l–1 vt provide with fuel 2 vi take in fuel

fu·gi·tive /'fyuʷdʒətɪv/ n person escaping from something

ful·crum /'fʊlkrəm, 'fʌl-/ n –crums or –cra /-krə/ point on which a LEVER turns

ful·fill /fʊl'fɪl/ vt 1 perform (a promise, duty, etc.) 2 develop fully the character and abilities of (oneself) ~ment n [U]

full /fʊl/ adj 1 holding as much or as many as possible: full bottle/bus 2 well fed 3 complete: your full name 4 highest possible: full speed 5 (of a garment) loose: full skirt 6 rounded; PLUMP 7 full of thinking only of ♦ n 1 in full completely 2 to the full thoroughly ♦ adv 1 straight; directly: The sun shone full on her face. 2 very: They knew full well he wouldn't keep his promise. ~ly adv 1 at least: It's fully an hour since he left. 2 completely ~ness, fulness n [U]

full-blown /ˌ· '·◂/ adj 1 (of a flower) completely open 2 fully developed: a full-blown war

full-fledged /ˌfʊl 'flɛdʒd◂/ adj 1 (of a bird) having grown all its feathers 2 completely trained

full-grown /ˌ· '·◂/ adj completely developed

full-length /ˌ· '·◂/ adj 1 (of a painting, etc.) showing someone from head to foot 2 not shorter than usual

full moon /ˌ· '·/ n the moon when seen as a circle

full-scale /ˌ· '·◂/ adj 1 (of a model, etc.) as big as the object represented 2 (of an activity) not lessened: full-scale war

full stop /ˌ· '·/ n come to a full stop stop completely

full-time /ˌ· '·◂/ adj working or studying all the usual hours

ful·some /'fʊlsəm/ adj praising too much

fum·ble /'fʌmbəl/ vi 1 use the hands awkwardly 2 vi/t drop (a football) ♦ n

fume /fyuʷm/ vi show great anger

fumes /fyuʷmz/ n [P] gas or smoke with a strong smell

fu·mi·gate /'fyuʷməˌgeʸt/ vt disinfect by means of smoke or gas

fun /fʌn/ n [U] 1 playfulness 2 (cause of) amusement; enjoyment 3 for fun also for the fun of it — for pleasure 4 in fun not seriously 5 make fun of laugh unkindly at

func·tion /'fʌŋkʃən/ n 1 natural purpose of something or someone 2 important social gathering ♦ vi be in action; work ~al adj 1 made for use, not decoration 2 functioning

fund /fʌnd/ n supply of money for a purpose ♦ vt provide money for

fun·da·men·tal /ˌfʌndə'mɛntəl◂/ adj central; very important: fundamental difference ♦ n important rule ~ly adv ~ism n [U] belief in the exact truth of the Bible ~ist n, adj

fu·ne·ral /'fyuʷnərəl/ n ceremony of burying or burning a dead person

funeral par·lor /'··· ˌ··/ n – see MORTUARY

fun·gi·cide /'fʌndʒəˌsaɪd, -gə-/ n [C;U] chemical for destroying fungus

fun·gus /'fʌŋgəs/ n –gi /-dʒaɪ, -gaɪ/ or –guses [C;U] leafless plant that grows on wood, etc.

fu·nic·u·lar /fyuʷ'nɪkyələr, fə-/ n mountain railway worked by a rope

funk·y /'fʌŋkiʸ/ adj infml (of JAZZ or similar music) having a simple direct style and feeling

fun·nel /'fʌnl/ n tube with a wide mouth for pouring liquids through ♦ vi/t –l– pass (as if) through a FUNNEL (1)

fun·ny /'fʌniʸ/ adj 1 amusing 2 strange –nily adv

funny bone /'··· ·/ also crazy bone — n tender part of the elbow

fur /fɜr/ n 1 [U] soft thick hair of a cat, rabbit, etc. 2 [C] (garment made of) the skin of an animal and the attached fur ~ry adj

fu·ri·ous /'fyuʷəriʸəs/ adj 1 very angry 2 wild; uncontrolled ~ly adv

furl /fɜrl/ vt roll or fold up (a sail, flag, etc.)

fur·long /'fɜrlɔŋ/ n a measure of length equal to 220 yards (201 meters)

fur·nace /'fɜrnɪs/ n 1 enclosed space where metals, etc., are heated 2 enclosed fire to heat a house

fur·nish /'fɜrnɪʃ/ vt 1 put furniture in 2 fml supply ~ings n [P] furniture, etc., for a room

fur·ni·ture /'fɜrnɪtʃər/ n [U] beds, chairs, etc.

fu·ror /'fyuʷərɔr/ n [S] sudden burst of public interest

fur·ri·er /'fɜriʸər, 'fʌr-/ n person who makes or sells fur garments

fur·row /'fɜroʷ, 'fʌroʷ/ n 1 track cut by a PLOW 2 WRINKLE ♦ vt make furrows in

fur·ther /'fɜrðər/ adv, adj 1 (comparative of FAR) at or to a greater distance or more distant point: *too tired to walk any further* **2** more: *any further questions* **3 further to** continuing the subject of **4 go further** give, do, or say more ♦ *vt* help to advance ~**ance** *n* [U] *fml* advancement ~**most** *adj* farthest

fur·ther·more /ˈfɜrðərˌmɔr, -ˌmoʷr/ *adv fml* also

fur·thest /ˈfɜrðɪst/ *adv, adj (superlative of* FAR) at or to the greatest distance or degree

fur·tive /ˈfɜrtɪv/ *adj* trying to escape notice ~**ly** *adv* ~ **ness** *n* [U]

fu·ry /ˈfyʊəriʸ/ *n* **1** [S;U] great anger **2** [U] wild force

fuse[1] /fyuʷz/ *n* wire that melts to break an electric connection ♦ *vi/t* **1** join by melting **2** stop working because a fuse has melted

fuse[2] *n* **1** pipe, etc., that carries fire to an explosive article **2** part of a bomb, etc., that makes it explode

fu·se·lage /ˈfyuʷsəˌlɑʒ, -lɪdʒ, -zə-/ *n* body of an aircraft

fu·sil·lade /ˈfyuʷsəˌleʸd, ˈfyuʷz-, -ˌlɑd/ *n* rapid continuous firing of shots

fu·sion /ˈfyuʷʒən/ *n* [C;U] join together by melting: (fig.) *a fusion of different styles of music*

fuss /fʌs/ *n* [S;U] **1** unnecessary show of excitement or annoyance **2 make a fuss of** pay loving attention to ♦ *vi* show unnecessary anxiety ~**y** *adj* **1** too concerned about details **2** (of dress, etc.) too highly decorated

fu·tile /ˈfyuʷt̬l, -taɪl/ *adj* unsuccessful; useless: *futile attempts* **futility** /fyuʷˈtɪlət̬iʸ/ *n* [U]

fu·ture /ˈfyuʷtʃər/ *n* **1** [S] time after the present: *in the future* **2** [C] that which will happen to someone or something: *an uncertain future* **3** [U] likelihood of success **4 in the future** from now on **future** *adj: his future wife* | *the future tense*

fu·tur·is·tic /ˌfyuʷtʃəˈrɪstɪk◂/ *adj* of strange modern appearance

fuzz /fʌz/ *n* [U] FLUFF ~**y** *adj* **1** (of hair) standing up in a light short mass **2** not clear in shape **3** (of cloth, etc.) having a raised soft hairy surface -**ily** *adv* -**iness** *n* [U]

FYI *abbrev. for*: for your information

G

G g /dʒiʸ/ the 7th letter of the English alphabet

g¹ *written abbrev. for:* GRAM(s)

g² *n* $1000

gab /gæb/ *vi* talk informally ◆ *n* see **the gift of the gab** (GIFT)

gab·ar·dine -erdine /ˈgæbərˌdiʸn/ *n* 1 [U] strong cloth 2 [C] type of coat made from this

gab·ble /ˈgæbəl/ *vi/t* speak or say too quickly to be heard **gabble** *n* [S]

ga·ble /ˈgeʸbəl/ *n* top of a wall with 3 corners, between sloping roofs

gad /gæd/ *v* **gad about** *phr vi* travel for enjoyment

gad·get /ˈgædʒɪt/ *n* small useful machine or tool ~**ry** *n* [U] gadgets

Gae·lic /ˈgeʸlɪk, ˈgælɪk/ *adj, n* [U] (of or being) any of the CELTIC languages, esp. those of Scotland, Ireland, or the Isle of Man

gaffe /gæf/ *n* social mistake

gaf·fer /ˈgæfər/ *n* 1 old man 2 man in charge of lighting for a movie

gag /gæg/ *n* 1 something put over someone's mouth to stop them from talking 2 joke ◆ *vt* -**gg**- put a GAG(1) on **gag on** *phr v* fail to swallow

ga·ga /ˈgɑgɑ/ *adj* SENILE

gage /geʸdʒ/ *n, v* see GAUGE

gag·gle /ˈgægəl/ *n* [S] 1 group of GEESE 2 group of noisy people: *gaggle of reporters*

gai·e·ty /ˈgeʸəti̯/ *n* [U] cheerfulness

gai·ly /ˈgeʸli̯/ *adv* cheerfully

gain¹ /geʸn/ *v* 1 *vi/t* obtain (something useful) 2 *vi* (of a clock) go too fast 3 *vt fml* reach (a place) with effort ~**er** *n*

gain on/upon *phr vt* get close to (someone ahead in a race)

gain² *n* [C;U] increase in wealth or amount ~**ful** *adj* paid for: *gainful employment* ~**fully** *adv*

gain·say /ˌgeʸnˈseʸ/ *vt* -**said** /-ˈsed/ *fml* DENY

gait /geʸt/ *n* way of walking

gai·ter /ˈgeʸt̯ər/ *n* covering for the lower leg

gal /gæl/ *n infml* woman

ga·la /ˈgeʸlə, ˈgælə, ˈgɑlə/ *n* special public entertainment

gal·ax·y /ˈgæləksi̯/ *n* large group of stars ~**actic** /gəˈlæktɪk/ *adj*

gale /geʸl/ *n* 1 strong wind 2 noisy burst of laughter, etc.

gall¹ /gɔl/ *n* [U] daring rudeness

gall² *vt* cause to feel annoyed disappointment or anger

gal·lant /ˈgælənt/ *adj* 1 brave 2 (of a man) polite to women ~**ly** *adv* ~**ry** *n* [U]

gall blad·der /ˈ· ˌ·· / *n* baglike organ in which BILE is stored

gal·le·on /ˈgæli̯ən/ *n* (esp. Spanish) sailing ship of the 15th to 18th centuries

gal·le·ry /ˈgæləri̯/ *n* 1 place where works of art are shown 2 upper floor of a hall or church 3 passage in a mine 4 top floor in a theater

gal·ley /ˈgæli̯/ *n* 1 ancient ship rowed by slaves 2 ship's kitchen

Gal·lic /ˈgælɪk/ *adj* typical of France

gal·li·vant /ˈgælə₁vænt, ₁gæləˈvænt/ *vi* GAD about

gal·lon /ˈgælən/ *n* (a measure for liquids equal to) 231 CUBIC inches or 4 QUARTS

gal·lop /ˈgæləp/ *n* [S] movement of a horse at its fastest speed **gallop** *vi/t*

gal·lows /ˈgæloʸz/ *n* **gallows** wooden frame on which criminals were once killed by hanging

gallows hu·mor /ˈ·· ˌ··/ *n* [U] *lit* jokes about the unpleasant side of life

gall·stone /ˈgɔlstoʸn/ *n* hard stone or grain that forms in the GALL BLADDER

ga·lore /gəˈlɔr, gəˈloʸr/ *adj* in plenty: *bargains galore*

gal·va·nize -nise /ˈgælvəˌnaɪz/ *vt* 1 cover (another metal) with ZINC 2 shock into action

gam·bit /ˈgæmbɪt/ *n* action done to produce a future advantage, esp. an opening move in a game, conversation, etc.

gam·ble /ˈgæmbəl/ *v* 1 *vi/t* BET (1) 2 *vi* take a risk ◆ *n* [S] risky matter ~**bler** *n*

gam·bol /ˈgæmbəl/ *vi lit* -**l**- jump about in play

game /geʸm/ *n* 1 [C] form of play or sport 2 [C] single part of a match in tennis, etc. 3 [U] wild animals and birds hunted for food and sport 4 [C] *infml* secret trick: *give the game away* (= let a secret plan be known) 5 [C] *infml* profession or activity: *the advertising game* – see also BIG GAME, FAIR GAME ◆ *adj* brave and willing ~**ly** *adv* **games** *n* [P] sport competitions

games·man·ship /ˈgeʸmzmənˌʃɪp/ *n* [U] art of winning by using rules to one's own advantage but without cheating

game·war·den /ˈgeʸmˌwɔrdn/ *n* man who looks after GAME (3)

gam·ut /ˈgæmət/ *n* [S] whole range of a subject

gan·der /ˈgændər/ *n* male GOOSE

gang¹ /gæŋ/ *n* 1 group of people

working together, esp. criminals **2** group of friends

gang² v **gang up** phr vi work together (against someone); CON-SPIRE

gang·ling /ˈgæŋglɪŋ/ adj tall, thin, and awkward

gang·plank /ˈgæŋplæŋk/ n movable bridge for getting into or out of a ship

gan·grene /ˈgæŋgriˀn, gæŋˈgriˀn/ n [U] decay of a body part because blood has stopped flowing there –**grenous** /-grənəs/ adj

gang·ster /ˈgæŋstər/ n member of a criminal GANG (1)

gang·way /ˈgæŋweˀ/ n large gangplank ♦ interj (said to make people clear a path)

gan·try /ˈgæntriˀ/ n frame supporting movable heavy machinery

gap /gæp/ n empty space between 2 things: (fig.) gaps in my knowledge

gape /geˀp/ vi **1** look hard in surprise **2** come apart: gaping hole

gar·age /gəˈrɑʒ, gəˈrɑdʒ/ n **1** building in which motor vehicles are kept **2** place that repairs them, and sells gas and oil

garage sale /ˈ·· ˌ·/ n sale of personal belongings from a family's garage

garb /gɑrb/ n [U] fml clothes

gar·bage /ˈgɑrbɪdʒ/ n [U] **1** waste material to be thrown away **2** nonsense

garbage can /ˈ·· ˌ·/ n container for waste materials

garbage man /ˈ·· ˌ·/ n person employed to empty garbage cans

garbage truck /ˈ·· ˌ·/ n vehicle that collects the contents of garbage cans

gar·ble /ˈgɑrbəl/ vt give a confused description of

gar·den /ˈgɑrdn/ n **1** piece of land for growing flowers and vegetables **2** also **gardens** pl. — public park **3** **lead someone up the garden path** trick someone into believing what is not true and acting on it ♦ vi work in a garden ~**er** n

garden par·ty /ˈ·· ˌ··/ n formal party held in a garden

gar·gan·tu·an /gɑrˈgæntʃuˀən/ adj extremely large

gar·gle /ˈgɑrgəl/ vi wash the throat by blowing through liquid ♦ n **1** [S] act of gargling **2** [C;U] liquid for gargling

gar·goyle /ˈgɑrgɔɪl/ n figure of an ugly creature on a church roof, etc.

gar·ish /ˈgeərɪʃ, ˈgærɪʃ/ adj unpleasantly bright ~**ly** adv

gar·land /ˈgɑrlənd/ n circle of flowers for decoration ♦ vt put garlands on

gar·lic /ˈgɑrlɪk/ n [U] plant like an onion, used in cooking

gar·ment /ˈgɑrmənt/ n fml article of clothing

gar·ner /ˈgɑrnər/ vt lit collect

gar·net /ˈgɑrnɪt/ n red jewel

gar·nish /ˈgɑrnɪʃ/ vt decorate (food) ♦ n something used to garnish

gar·ret /ˈgærɪt/ n lit small usu. unpleasant room at the top of a house

gar·ri·son /ˈgærəsən/ n **1** soldiers living in a town or fort **2** fort or camp where such soldiers live ♦ vt (send a group of soldiers to) guard (a place)

gar·rotte /gəˈrɑt/ vt STRANGLE, esp. with a metal collar or wire

gar·ru·lous /ˈgærələs, ˈgæryə-/ adj fml talking too much ~**ly** adv

gar·ter /ˈgɑrtər/ n elastic band to keep a STOCKING up

gas /gæs/ n –s- or –ss- **1** [C;U] substance like air **2** [U] gas used for heating, cooking, poisoning, etc. **3** [U] liquid obtained from PETROLEUM and used for producing power in engines **4** [U] (condition of having) gas in the stomach ♦ v **1** vt kill with gas **2** vi infml talk a long time ~**eous** /ˈgæsiəs/ adj of or like gas

gas up phr vi fill a vehicle with gas

gash /gæʃ/ vt, n (wound with) a long deep cut

gas·ket /ˈgæskɪt/ n flat piece of material placed between surfaces to prevent oil, etc., from escaping

gas·light /ˈgæs-laɪt/ n [U] light from burning gas

gas·man /ˈgæsmæn/ n –men /-men/ **1** official who visits houses to see how much gas has been used **2** workman who puts in gas pipes, repairs cookers, etc.

gas mask /ˈ· ·/ n breathing apparatus that protects the wearer against poisonous gas

gas·o·line -lene /ˌgæsəˈliˀn, ˈgæsəˌliˀn/ n [U] GAS (3)

gasp /gæsp/ v **1** vi breathe quickly and with effort **2** vt say while gasping **gasp** n

gas sta·tion /ˈ· ˌ··/ n place that sells gas and oil and may also do repairs

gas·sy /ˈgæsiˀ/ adj full of gas -**siness** n [U]

gas tank /ˈ· ·/ n **1** container inside a car that supplies gas (3) **2** large container from which gas is carried to buildings

gas·tric /ˈgæstrɪk/ adj of the stomach: gastric juices

gas·tri·tis /gæˈstraɪtɪs/ n [U] painful swelling of the inside of the stomach

gas·tro·en·te·ri·tis /ˌgæstroˀˌentə-ˈraɪtɪs/ n [U] swelling of the inside of the stomach and bowels

gas·tron·o·my /gæˈstrɒnəmiʸ/ n [U] art of good eating

gas·works /ˈgæswɜːks/ n gasworks place where gas is made from coal

gate /geʸt/ n 1 frame closing an opening in a wall, fence, etc. 2 way in or out at an airport 3 (money paid by) the number of people attending a match, etc.

gate·crash /ˈgeʸtkræʃ/ vi/t go to (a party, public event, etc.) uninvited or without a ticket ~ **er** n

gate·post /ˈgeʸtpoʷst/ n post from which a gate is hung

gate·way /ˈgeʸt-weʸ/ n 1 [C] opening for a gate 2 [S] way of finding: *the gateway to success*

gath·er /ˈgæðər/ v 1 vi/t come or bring together 2 vt obtain gradually: *gather facts/speed* 3 vt collect (flowers, crops, etc.) 4 vt understand: *I gather she's ill.* 5 vt draw (cloth) into small folds: *gathered skirt* ~**ing** n meeting

gauche /goʷʃ/ adj socially awkward

gau·dy /ˈgɔːdiʸ/ adj too bright; too highly decorated –**di·ly** adv

gauge, gage /geʸdʒ/ n 1 instrument for measuring 2 thickness or width of e.g. a gun barrel 3 distance between the RAILS of a railway ♦ vt 1 measure 2 make a judgment about

gaunt /gɔːnt, gɑːnt/ adj 1 thin, as if ill or hungry 2 (of a place) bare and unattractive ~**ness** n [U]

gaunt·let /ˈgɔːntlɪt, ˈgɑːnt-/ n long GLOVE protecting the wrist

gauze /gɔːz/ n [U] thin net-like cloth

gave /geʸv/ v past t. of GIVE

gav·el /ˈgævəl/ n small hammer used by a chairman, etc., to get attention

ga·votte /gəˈvɒt/ n fast French dance or its music

gawk /gɔːk/ vi look at something in a foolish way

gaw·ky /ˈgɔːkiʸ/ adj awkward in movement –**ki·ness** n [U]

gay /geʸ/ adj 1 HOMOSEXUAL 2 bright: *gay colors* 3 cheerful ♦ n GAY (1) person

gaze /geʸz/ vi look steadily ♦ n [S] steady fixed look

ga·zette /gəˈzet/ n official government newspaper giving important notices, etc.

gaz·et·teer /ˌgæzəˈtɪər/ n list of names of places

GDP /ˌdʒiʸ diʸ ˈpiʸ/ n [the+S] Gross Domestic Product; the total value of everything produced in a country, usu. in a single year, except for income received from abroad

gear¹ /gɪər/ n 1 [C;U] set of toothed wheels in a machine 2 [U] equipment: *football gear* 3 [U] apparatus

of wheels, etc.: *the landing gear of an aircraft*

gear² *v*

gear to phr vt allow (an activity or action) to be influenced by a (particular fact): *education geared to the needs of industry*

gear up phr vt infml put (esp. oneself) into a state of excited or anxious expectation

gear·box /ˈgɪərbɒks/ n case containing the gears of a vehicle

gear shift /ˈ· ·/ n rod that controls the gears of a vehicle

geese /giʸs/ n pl. of GOOSE

Gei·ger count·er /ˈgaɪgər ˌkaʊntər/ n instrument that measures RADIO-ACTIVITY

gel·a·tin /ˈdʒelətn/ n [U] gluey material used in making food and medicine

geld /geld/ vt remove the sexual organs of (certain male animals) ~**ing** n gelded animal, esp. a horse

gel·ig·nite /ˈdʒelɪgˌnaɪt/ n [U] powerful explosive

gem /dʒem/ n 1 jewel 2 very valuable thing or person

gen·der /ˈdʒendər/ n [C;U] 1 (in grammar) (division into) MASCULINE, FEMININE, or NEUTER 2 division into male and female; sex

gene /dʒiʸn/ n material in a cell controlling HEREDITY

ge·ne·al·o·gy /ˌdʒiʸniʸˈælədʒiʸ, -ˈælə-, ˌdʒeː-/ n [C;U] (study of) the history of a family, often shown in a drawing like a tree –**gi·cal** /ˌdʒiʸniʸəˈlɒdʒɪkəl, ˌdʒeː-/ adj

gen·e·ra /ˈdʒenərə/ n pl. of GENUS

gen·e·ral /ˈdʒenərəl/ adj 1 concerning all: *the general feeling* 2 not detailed: *a general idea* 3 (in titles) chief: *Attorney General* ♦ n 1 army or airforce officer of very high rank 2 **in general** usually ~**ly** adv 1 usually 2 by most people 3 without considering details –**ral·i·ty** /ˌdʒenəˈrælətiʸ/ n 1 [C] general statement 2 [U] being general

general e·lec·tion /ˌ··· ·ˈ··/ n final election for local, state or national officials

gen·e·ral·ize /ˈdʒenərəˌlaɪz/ vi make a general statement –**ization** /ˌdʒenərələˈzeʸʃən/ n [C;U] (statement formed by) generalizing

general prac·ti·tion·er /ˌ··· ·ˈ··ˑ/ n also **GP** doctor trained in general medicine

general strike /ˌ··· ˈ·/ n stopping of work by all trade unionists or closing of all businesses for political protest

gen·e·rate /ˈdʒenəˌreʸt/ vt produce: *generate heat* –**ra·tor** n machine that generates esp. electricity –**rative** /ˈdʒenərətɪv/ adj able to produce

gen·e·ra·tion /ˌdʒenəˈreɪʃən/ n 1 [C] length of time in which a child grows up and has children 2 [C] people of about the same age 3 [U] act of generating

ge·ner·ic /dʒəˈnerɪk/ adj not having a TRADEMARK (1) ~**ally** /-kliʸ/ adv

gen·e·ros·i·ty /ˌdʒenəˈrasətiʸ/ n 1 [U] quality of being generous 2 [C] generous act

gen·e·rous /ˈdʒenərəs/ adj 1 giving freely 2 more than enough ~**ly** adv

gen·e·sis /ˈdʒenəsɪs/ n [S] origin

ge·net·ics /dʒəˈnetɪks/ n [U] study of HEREDITY **genetic** adj -**ically** /-kliʸ/ adv

ge·nial /ˈdʒiʸnyəl, ˈdʒiʸniʸəl/ adj cheerful and kind ~**ly** adv

gen·i·tals /ˈdʒenətlz/ n [P] outer sex organs **genital** adj

ge·nius /ˈdʒiʸnyəs/ n 1 [U] great and rare powers of thought, skill, or imagination 2 [C] person with this ability 3 [S] special ability or skill: *She has a genius for saying the wrong thing.*

gen·o·cide /ˈdʒenəˌsaɪd/ n [U] killing of a whole race of people

gen·re /ˈʒanrə/ n fml class; kind

gent /dʒent/ n sl gentleman

gen·teel /dʒenˈtiʸl/ adj unnaturally polite

gen·tile /ˈdʒentaɪl/ n, adj (sometimes cap.) (person who is) not Jewish

gen·til·i·ty /dʒenˈtɪlətiʸ/ n [U] being genteel

gen·tle /ˈdʒentəl/ adj not rough or violent ~**ness** n [U] -**tly** adv

gen·tle·man /ˈdʒentəlmən/ n -**men** /-mən/ 1 man who behaves well and can be trusted 2 any man 3 lit man of good family ~**ly** adj like a GENTLEMAN (1)

gentleman's a·gree·ment /ˌ··· ·ˈ··/ n unwritten agreement made between people who trust each other

gentle sex /ˌ·· ·ˈ·/ n [the+S] females; women (now usu. considered offensive to women)

gen·tle·wo·man /ˈdʒentəlˌwʊmən/ n -**women** /-ˌwɪmɪn/ lady

gen·try /ˈdʒentriʸ/ n [P] wealthy people who live in the country: *the local gentry*

gen·u·flect /ˈdʒenyəˌflekt/ vi fml bend one's knee in worship ~**ion** /ˌdʒenyəˈflekʃən/ n [C;U]

gen·u·ine /ˈdʒenyuʷɪn/ adj real; true ~**ly** adv ~**ness** n [U]

ge·nus /ˈdʒiʸnəs/ n **genera** /ˈdʒenərə/ division of plants or animals

ge·og·ra·phy /dʒiʸˈagrəfiʸ/ n [U] study of the countries of the world and of seas, towns, etc. -**pher** n /-fər/ -**phical** /ˌdʒiʸəˈgræfɪkəl◂/ adj -**phically** /-kliʸ/ adv

ge·ol·o·gy /dʒiʸˈalədʒiʸ/ n [U] study of the Earth's history as recorded in rocks -**gist** n -**gical** /ˌdʒiʸəˈladʒɪkəl/ adj -**gically** /-kliʸ/ adv

ge·om·e·try /dʒiʸˈamətriʸ/ n [U] study of lines, angles, and surfaces and their relationships **geometric** /ˌdʒiʸəˈmetrɪk◂/ adj **geometrically** /-kliʸ/ adv

ge·ri·at·rics /ˌdʒeriʸˈætrɪks, ˌdʒiʸər-/ n [U] medical care of old people **geriatric** adj

germ /dʒɜrm/ n 1 bacterium carrying disease 2 beginning of an idea, etc.

ger·mane /dʒɜrˈmeʸn/ adj fml RELEVANT

Ger·man Shep·herd /ˌdʒɜrmən ˈʃepərd/ n large WOLF-like dog

ger·mi·cide /ˈdʒɜrməˌsaɪd/ n [C;U] chemical for killing germs

ger·mi·nate /ˈdʒɜrməˌneʸt/ vi/t cause (a seed) to start growing -**nation** /ˌdʒɜrməˈneʸʃən/ n [U]

ger·und /ˈdʒerənd/ n VERBAL NOUN

ges·ta·tion /dʒeˈsteʸʃən/ n [S;U] carrying of a young creature inside the mother's body

ges·tic·u·late /dʒeˈstɪkyəˌleʸt/ vi wave the hands and arms about to express something -**lation** /dʒeˌstɪkyəˈleʸʃən/ n [C;U]

ges·ture /ˈdʒestʃər/ n 1 [C;U] movement of the body to express something 2 [C] action done to show one's feelings

get /get/ v **got** /gat/, **gotten** /ˈgatn/ or **got** pres. p. **getting** 1 vt receive; obtain: *get a letter* | *get permission* 2 vt collect; bring 3 vt catch (an illness) 4 vi/t (cause to) go or arrive: *get home* | *get my boots off* 5 [+adj] become: *get sick/married* 6 vi come or bring to the stated degree of success: *Now we're getting somewhere.* 7 vt succeed in or be allowed: *He's nice when you get to know him.* | *I never get to drive the car.* 8 vt prepare (a meal) 9 vt hear or understand: *I don't get you.* 10 vt confuse; PUZZLE: *It's got me!* 11 vt annoy: *It's his attitude that gets me.* 12 vt infml **a** punish or harm (someone) in return for harm they have done you: *I'll get you for this!* **b** catch or attack: *The crocodiles will get them.* 13 **get (something) done:** **a** cause something to be done: *I must get these shoes mended.* **b** experience something that happens to one: *I got my hand caught in the door.* 14 **have got** have: *He's got red hair.* 15 **you get** infml there is/are

get around phr vi 1 be able to move again after an illness 2 travel 3 avoid; CIRCUMVENT 4 persuade to do something (of news, etc., spread)

get across/over *phr vi/t* (cause to) be understood

get along *phr vi* 1 make progress; manage 2 progress 3 be friendly: *They don't get along very well.*

get around to *phr vt* find time for; do at last

get at *phr vt* 1 reach 2 mean; IMPLY 3 say unkind things

get away *phr vi* escape

get away with *phr vt* escape punishment for

get back *phr vi* 1 return 2 return to power after having lost it 3 speak or write to a person at a later time: *I can't tell you now, but I'll get back to you tomorrow.* 4 **get back at someone** also **get one's own back on someone** — punish someone in return for a wrong done to oneself

get by *phr vi* 1 continue to live; SURVIVE 2 be acceptable; be good enough but not very good

get down *phr vt* 1 swallow: *get the medicine down* 2 write down 3 DEPRESS: *This weather gets me down.* 4 *vi* enjoy oneself at a party

get down to *phr vt* begin to work at

get in *phr v* 1 *vi* arrive: *The plane got in late.* 2 *vt* call (someone) to help 3 *vt* collect a supply of 4 *vt* enter (a vehicle) 5 *vt* say (something), esp. by interrupting a conversation

get into *phr vt* 1 develop (a bad condition): *get into trouble* 2 become accustomed to

get off *phr v* 1 *vi* leave; start 2 *vi/t* (cause to) escape punishment 3 *vt* leave (a public vehicle) 4 *vt* dis-MOUNT (1)

get onto *phr vt* 1 CONTACT 2 begin to talk about: *How did we get onto that subject?*

get out *phr v* 1 *vi/t* (cause to) escape 2 *vi* become known 3 gain from

get over *phr vt* 1 get better from (illness, etc.) 2 manage to deal with 3 reach the end of (usu. something unpleasant) 4 make clear; cause to be understood 5 **I can't/couldn't get over** I am/was very much surprised at

get through *phr v* 1 *vi/t* pass (an examination, etc.) 2 *vi* reach someone by telephone 3 *vi* finish 4 *vi/t* (cause to) be understood by someone

get together *phr vi* have a meeting or party

get up *phr vi* rise from bed

get up to *phr vt* 1 do (something bad) 2 reach

get·a·way /ˈgɛtəˌweɪ/ *n* [S] escape

get-to-geth·er /ˈ·· ·ˌ··/ *n* friendly informal meeting for enjoyment

get·up /ˈgɛtʌp/ *n* set of clothes

get-up-and-go /ˌ· ··· ·ˈ·/ *n* [U] *infml* forceful active quality of mind

gey·ser /ˈgaɪzər/ *n* natural spring of hot water

ghast·ly /ˈgæstliʲ/ *adj* 1 very bad; terrible 2 pale and looking very ill

gher·kin /ˈgɜrkɪn/ *n* small green CUCUMBER

ghet·to /ˈgɛtoʷ/ *n* -tos *or* -toes part of city where poor people or foreigners live

ghetto-blast·er /ˈ··ˌ··/ *n* large TAPE RECORDER that can be carried around

ghost /goʷst/ *n* 1 (spirit of) a dead person who appears again 2 also **ghost writer** /ˈ· ·ˌ··/ — person who writes material which another person gives out as their own 3 **give up the ghost** die 4 **the ghost of a** the slightest ~**ly** *adj* like a ghost ♦ *vt* write (something) as a GHOST (2)

ghost town /ˈ· ·/ *n* empty town that was once busy

ghoul /guʷl/ *n* person who likes thinking about dead bodies and nasty things ~**ish** *adj*

GI /ˌdʒiʲ ˈaɪ/ *n* US soldier ♦ *adj* military: *GI haircut*

gi·ant /ˈdʒaɪənt/ **giantess** /-tɛs/ *fem.* — *n* big strong person or creature ♦ *adj* very large

gib·ber /ˈdʒɪbər/ *vi* talk very fast and meaninglessly

gib·ber·ish /ˈdʒɪbərɪʃ, ˈgɪ-/ *n* [U] meaningless talk

gib·bet /ˈdʒɪbət/ *n* GALLOWS

gib·bon /ˈgɪbən/ *n* animal like a monkey with no tail and long arms

gibe, jibe /dʒaɪb/ *n* remark that makes someone look foolish ♦ *v* **gibe at** *phr vt*

gib·lets /ˈdʒɪblɪts/ *n* [P] bird's heart, etc., taken out before cooking

gid·dy /ˈgɪdiʲ/ *adj* 1 (causing a) feeling of unsteady movement 2 (of a person) not serious —**diness** *n* [U]

gift /gɪft/ *n* 1 something given freely 2 TALENT: *a gift for music* 3 **the gift of the gab** *infml* the ability to speak well continuously, and esp. to persuade people ~**ed** *adj* TALENTed

gift horse /ˈ· ·/ *n* **look a gift horse in the mouth** complain about a gift

gig /gɪg/ *n* popular musician's performance

gi·gan·tic /dʒaɪˈgæntɪk/ *adj* very large

gig·gle /ˈgɪgəl/ *vi* laugh in a silly way **giggle** *n* [C] act of giggling

gig·o·lo /ˈdʒɪgəˌloʷ, ˈʒɪ-/ *n* woman's paid lover and companion

gild /gɪld/ *vt* 1 cover with gold or gold paint 2 **gild the lily** to try to improve something that is already good enough, so spoiling the effect

gill¹ /gɪl/ n organ through which a fish breathes

gill² /dʒɪl/ n small measure of liquid

gilt /gɪlt/ n [U] material with which things are gilded

gim·let /ˈgɪmlət/ n alcoholic drink with LIME juice

gim·mick /ˈgɪmɪk/ n trick, phrase, etc., used to draw attention ~**y** adv

gin /dʒɪn/ n [U] colorless alcoholic drink

gin·ger /ˈdʒɪndʒər/ n [U] 1 plant whose root tastes hot and is used in cooking 2 orange-brown color: ginger hair

ginger ale /ˈ·· ·, ·, ·· ˈ·/ n [C;U] gassy non-alcoholic drink

gin·ger·bread /ˈdʒɪndʒər‚bred/ n [U] cake with ginger in it

gin·ger·ly /ˈdʒɪndʒərli²/ adv carefully ♦ adj careful

ging·ham /ˈgɪŋəm/ n [U] cotton cloth with a pattern of squares

gi·raffe /dʒəˈræf/ n African animal with a long neck

gird /gɜrd/ vt **girded** or **girt** /gɜrt/ fml 1 fasten with a belt 2 surround

gir·der /ˈgɜrdər/ n metal beam supporting a roof, bridge, etc.

gir·dle /ˈgɜrdl/ n 1 woman's UNDERWEAR that fits tightly round the stomach 2 lit something that surrounds something: a girdle of islands ♦ vt lit go all around

girl /gɜrl/ n young female person ~**hood** n time of being a girl ~**ish** adj like a girl

girl·friend /ˈgɜrlfrend/ n 1 man's female companion 2 woman's female friend

girt /gɜrt/ v past t. and p. of GIRD

girth /gɜrθ/ n 1 [C] band around a horse's middle to hold the SADDLE firm 2 [U] fml thickness measured around something: the girth of a tree

gist /dʒɪst/ n [S] main points of something

give¹ /gɪv/ v **gave** /geɪv/, **given** /ˈgɪvən/ 1 vt cause or allow someone to have: give him a present/a job | Give me time. 2 vt pay in exchange: I'll give $3000 for the car. 3 vi supply money: give generously to charity 4 vt provide: Cows give milk. 5 vt perform (an action): give an order/a sign 6 vt offer (an amusement, etc.): give a party 7 vi bend or stretch under pressure 8 vt fml cause to believe, esp. wrongly: I was given to understand that he was ill. 9 vt call on (people present) to drink a TOAST (2) to: I give you the President! 10 **give or take (a certain amount)** more or less (a certain amount) 11 **give rise to** cause to happen 12 **give way (to): a** admit defeat in an argument or fight **b** break **c** become

less useful or important than **d** allow oneself to show (esp. a feeling) **giver** n

give away phr vt 1 give freely 2 show the truth about

give back phr vt return (something) to the owner

give in phr v 1 vi SURRENDER 2 vt deliver

give off phr vt send out (a smell, etc.)

give out phr v 1 vt DISTRIBUTE 2 vi come to an end: My strength gave out.

give up phr v 1 vi/t stop: give up smoking 2 vi stop trying to guess, etc. 3 vt regard as lost or hopeless 4 vt offer as a prisoner 5 vt deliver to someone: give up one's seat in the train

give² n [U] quality of bending or stretching under pressure

give-and-take /ˌ· · ˈ·/ n [U] willingness to COMPROMISE (= give way to another's wishes)

give·a·way /ˈgɪvə‚weɪ/ n [S] something unintentional that makes a secret known ♦ adj (of a price) very low

giv·en /ˈgɪvən/ adj 1 fixed and stated: a given time 2 have a tendency to ♦ prep if one takes into account: Given her inexperience, she's done a good job.

given name /ˈ·· ‚·/ n FIRST NAME

giz·mo /ˈgɪzmoʷ/ n GADGET

gla·cial /ˈgleɪʃəl/ adj of ice or an ICE AGE

gla·cier /ˈgleɪʃər/ n mass of ice that flows slowly down a valley

glad /glæd/ adj 1 pleased 2 lit causing happiness ~**ly** adv willingly ~**ness** n [U]

glad·den /ˈglædn/ vt make glad

glade /gleɪd/ n lit open space in a forest

glad·i·a·tor /ˈglædiˤ‚eɪʳtər/ n (in ancient Rome) man who fought in public as an entertainment

glam·o·rize /ˈglæmə‚raɪz/ vt make (something) appear more attractive than it really is

glam·or /ˈglæmər/ n 1 the charm of something unusual or expensive 2 sexual attraction ~**ous** adj

glance /glæns/ vi give a rapid look ♦ n 1 rapid look 2 **at a glance** at once

glance off phr vi/t (of a blow, etc.) hit and move off at an angle

gland /glænd/ n body organ that treats materials in the blood to produce various liquid substances

glan·du·lar /ˈglændʒələr/ adj of the glands

glare /gleər/ vi 1 look fiercely 2 shine too strongly **glare** n [S]

glaring /ˈ/ adj 1 too bright 2 noticeably bad: *glaring injustice*

glass /glæs/ n 1 [U] hard transparent material used in windows, etc. 2 [C] something made of this, esp. a container for drinking from 3 [C] amount held by such a container – see also GLASSES ~y adj like glass: *a glassy stare*

glass·blow·er /ˈglæsˌbloʷər/ n person who shapes hot glass by blowing through a tube

glass·es /ˈglæsɪz/ n [P] two pieces of specially cut glass in a frame, worn in front of the eyes for improving a person's ability to see

glass·ware /ˈglæswɛər/ n [U] glass objects generally

glass·works /ˈglæswɜrks/ n **glass·works** factory where glass is made

glau·co·ma /glauˈkoʷmə, glɔ-/ n [U] eye disease marked by increased pressure within the centre part of the eye

glaze /gleʸz/ v 1 vt put a shiny surface on (pots, etc.) 2 vt fit (a window, etc.) with glass 3 vi (of the eyes) become dull ♦ n [U] shiny surface

gla·zier /ˈgleʸʒər/ n workman who fits glass into windows

gleam /gliʸ/ n 1 a gentle light 2 sudden sign of something: *a gleam of interest* ♦ n 1 send out a gleam

glean /gliʸn/ vt gather (facts, etc.) in small amounts

glee /gliʸ/ n [U] joyful satisfaction ~ful adj ~fully adv

glee club /ˈ· ·/ n men's CHORUS (1), usu. at a university

glen /glɛn/ n narrow valley

glib /glɪb/ adj –bb– speaking or spoken too easily: *glib excuses* ~ly adv ~ness n [U]

glide /glaɪd/ vi 1 move smoothly and noiselessly 2 fly in a glider **glider** n plane with no engine ♦ n gliding movement

glim·mer /ˈglɪmər/ vi shine faintly ♦ n 1 faint light 2 small uncertain sign: *a glimmer of hope*

glimpse /glɪmps/ n quick incomplete view of something ♦ vt see for a moment

glint /glɪnt/ vi, n (give out) a small flash of light

glis·ten /ˈglɪsən/ vi shine as if wet

glit·ter /ˈglɪtər/ vi flash brightly: *glittering diamonds* ♦ n [S;U] brightness

glit·te·ra·ti /ˌglɪtəˈratiʸ/ n [(the) P] fashionable people whose social activities are widely reported

gloat /gloʷt/ vi look at something with selfish satisfaction ~ingly adv

glo·bal /ˈgloʷbəl/ adj 1 of the whole world 2 taking account of all considerations ~ly adv

globe /gloʷb/ n 1 [C] object in the shape of a ball; esp. one with a map of the Earth painted on it 2 [the+S] the Earth

globe·trot·ter /ˈgloʷbˌtrɑtər/ n person who travels widely **-ting** adj, n

glob·u·lar /ˈglɑbyələr/ adj shaped like a ball

glob·ule /ˈglɑbyuʷl/ n drop of liquid

gloom /gluʷm/ n 1 [U] darkness 2 [S;U] sadness; hopelessness ~y adj ~ily adv

glo·ri·fy /ˈglɔrəˌfaɪ, ˈgloʷr-/ vt 1 praise; worship 2 cause to seem more important: *Her cabin is just a glorified hut.* –**fication** /ˌglɔrəfəˈkeʸʃən, ˌgloʷr-/ n [U]

glo·ri·ous /ˈglɔriʸəs, ˈgloʷr-/ adj 1 having great honor: *glorious victory* 2 splendid ~ly adv

glo·ry¹ /ˈglɔriʸ, ˈgloʷriʸ/ n [U] 1 great honor 2 splendid beauty

glory² v **glory in** phr vt enjoy, often selfishly

gloss /glɔs, glɑs/ n [S;U] 1 shiny brightness 2 pleasant but deceiving outer appearance 3 explanation of a piece of writing ♦ vt write an explanation of ~y adj shiny

gloss over phr vt hide (faults)

glos·sa·ry /ˈglɑsəriʸ, ˈglɔ-/ n list of explanations of words

glossy mag·a·zine /ˌ·· ·ˈ·/ n magazine printed on shiny paper with lots of pictures, esp. of clothes

glove /glʌv/ n 1 covering for the hand 2 **fit like a glove** fit perfectly – see also KID GLOVES

glow /gloʷ/ vi 1 give out heat or light without flames 2 be warm and red in the face ♦ n [S] glowing light ~ing adj strongly approving: *a glowing account*

glow·er /ˈglauʷər/ vi look with an angry expression ~ingly adv

glow·worm /ˈgloʷwɜrm/ n insect that gives out a greenish light

glu·cose /ˈgluʷkoʷs/ n [U] sugar found in fruit

glue /gluʷ/ n [U] sticky substance for joining things ♦ vt pres. p. **gluing** or **glueing** 1 join with glue 2 **glued to** close to: *children glued to the television* ~y adj

glue-snif·fing /ˈ· ˌ··/ n [U] harmful breathing in of FUMES of glue to produce a state of excitement

glum /glʌm/ adj –mm– sad; GLOOMy ~ly adv

glut /glʌt/ vt –tt– supply with too much: *stores glutted with imports* ♦ n [S] too large a supply

glu·ti·nous /ˈgluːⁿtn-əs/ *adj fml* sticky

glut·ton /ˈglʌtn/ *n* **1** person who eats too much **2** person who is always ready to do more of something hard or unpleasant: *a glutton for punishment* ~ **ous** *adj* GREEDY~ **y** *n* [U] *fml* habit of eating too much

gly·ce·rin /ˈglɪsərɪn/ *n* [U] colorless liquid used in making soap, medicines, and explosives

gm *written abbrev. for:* GRAM

gnarled /nɑrld/ *adj* rough and twisted: *gnarled tree trunks*

gnash /næʃ/ *n* strike (one's teeth) together

gnat /næt/ *n* small flying insect that stings

gnaw /nɔ/ *vi/t* bite steadily (at): (fig.) *gnawing anxiety*

gnome /noʊm/ *n* (in stories) little (old) man who lives under the ground

GNP /ˌdʒiː en ˈpiː/ *n* [*the*+S] Gross National Product; total value of everything produced in a country, usu. in a single year

go¹ /goʊ/ *v* **went** /went/, **gone** /ɡɔn, ɡɑn/ **1** *vi* leave a place: *I have to go now.* **2** *vi* move; travel: *go by bus* | *go shopping* **3** *vi* lead; reach: *This road goes to the West Coast.* **4** *vi* start an action: *Ready, set, go!* **5 a** become: *go crazy* | *This milk's gone bad.* **b** be or remain: *Her protests went unnoticed.* **6** *vi* match; fit: *Blue and green don't go (together).* | *4 into 3 won't go.* | *Your dress goes with your eyes.* **7** *vi* belong: *The knives go in this drawer.* **8** *vi* (of machines) work: *This clock doesn't go.* **9** *vi* be sold: *The house is going cheap.* **10** *vi* have (certain words or sounds): *Ducks go 'quack'.* **11** *vi* become weak or worn out: *My voice is going.* **12** *vi* lose one's usual powers of control: *let oneself go* | *He's pretty far gone.* **13** *vi* state or do up to or beyond a limit: *go too far* **14** *vi* be accepted or acceptable: *What she says goes.* **15** *vi* happen or develop in the stated way: *The party went well.* **16 as someone/something goes** compared with the average person or thing of that type: *He's not a bad cook, as cooks go, but he's no expert.* **17 be going to** (shows the future): *Is it going to rain?* **18 go all out for** be very enthusiastic about **19 go a long way** also *go far:* **a** (of money) buy a lot **b** (of a person) succeed **20 go and: a** go in order to: *go and get it* **b** (shows surprise): *She went and bought it!* **21 go for it** *infml* make every effort to succeed at something **22 go it alone** act independently **23 to go** left; remaining: *only 3 more days to go* **24 ~goer** person who goes somewhere regularly: *churchgoers*

go about *phr vt* perform; work at: *go about one's business*

go after *phr vt* try to get; chase

go against *phr vt* **1** oppose **2** be unfavorable to: *The case may go against you.*

go ahead *phr vi* **1** begin **2** continue

go along *phr vi* continue

go along with *phr vt* agree with

go around *phr vi* **1** (of an illness) spread **2** be enough for everyone: *not enough chairs to go around* **3** be often out in public (with someone)

go at *phr vt* attack; TACKLE

go back *phr vi* **1** return **2** stretch back in time

go back on *phr vt* break (a promise, etc.)

go by *phr v* **1** *vi* pass (in place or time): *A year went by.* **2** *vt* act according to **3** *vt* judge by **4 go by the name of** be called

go down *phr vi* **1** become lower **2** sink: *The sun/The ship went down.* **3** become less swollen **4** (of food) be swallowed **5** be accepted: *His speech went down well with the crowd.* **6** be recorded: *This day will go down in history.*

go for *phr vt* **1** attack **2** go after **3** like or be attracted by **4 go for nothing** be wasted

go in *phr vi* **1** (of the sun, etc.) become covered by clouds **2** join

go in for *phr vt* **1** enter (a competition) **2** have a habit of: *go in for football*

go into *phr vt* **1** enter (a profession) **2** explain or examine thoroughly

go off *phr v* **1** *vi* **a** explode **b** ring or sound loudly **2** *vi* succeed or fail: *The conference went off well.* **3** *vi* stop operating

go off with *phr vt* take away without permission

go on *phr v* **1** *vi* happen: *What's going on?* **2** *vi* (of time) pass **3** *vi* **a** continue: *go on with your work* **b** talk, complain, or behave in a certain way continually **4** *vi* be put into operation **5** *vt* use as proof, etc.: *I'm going on what you told me.* **6 go on!** *infml* I don't believe you!

go out *phr vi* **1** leave the house **2** spend time with someone **3** stop burning or shining: *The light went out.* **4** become unfashionable **5** (of the sea) go back to its low level **6** take part: *go out for football*

go over *phr vt* **1** examine **2** repeat

go through *phr v* **1** *vi* be approved officially **2** *vt* suffer or experience **3** *vt* finish; spend **4** *vt* search

go through with *phr vt* complete

go to *phr vt* make oneself have: *go to a lot of trouble*

go under *phr vi* 1 (of a ship) sink 2 fail

go up *phr vi* 1 rise 2 be built 3 be destroyed in fire, etc.

go with *phr vt* 1 match 2 be often found with

go without *phr vi/t* 1 DO without 2 it goes without saying it is clear without needing to be stated

go² n 1 [U] quality of being very active 2 [C] attempt 3 from the word go from the beginning 4 no go *infml* useless 5 It's all go. it's very busy 6 make a go of *infml* make a success of 7 on the go very busy

goad /goʷd/ *vt* urge by continuous annoyance ♦ *n* stick for driving cattle

go·a·head¹ /'·· ·,·/ *n* [(the)S] permission to take action

go-ahead² *adj* active in using new methods

goal /goʷl/ *n* 1 one's aim or purpose 2 a place where the ball must go to gain points in some games b point(s) gained by sending the ball there

goal·keep·er /'goʷl,kiʸpər/ *n* player responsible for keeping the ball out of a team's goal

goal·post /'goʷlpoʷst/ *n* one of the 2 posts between which the ball must go to gain a goal

goat /goʷt/ *n* 1 horned animal like a sheep 2 get one's goat annoy one

goa·tee /goʷ'tiʸ/ *n* small pointed beard

gob·ble /'gabəl/ *vi/t* eat quickly and often noisily

gob·ble·dy·gook /'gabəldiʸ,gʊk, -,guʷk/ *n* [U] meaningless official language

go-be·tween /'·· ·,·/ *n* person who takes messages, etc., from one person or side to another

gob·let /'gablɪt/ *n* glass or metal drinking cup with a stem and no handle

gob·lin /'gablɪn/ *n* unkind fairy that plays tricks on people

go-cart /'goʷ kart/ *n* small low racing car

god /gad/ **goddess** /'gadɪs/ *fem.* — *n* 1 [C] being who is worshipped 2 (*cap.*) (in the Christian, Jewish, and Muslim religions) the maker and ruler of the world ~ **less** *adj fml* wicked; not showing respect or belief in God ~ **like** *adj* like a god: *godlike beauty* ~ **ly** *adj fml* religious; leading a good life

god·child /'gadtʃaɪld/ *n* boy (**godson**) or girl (**goddaughter**) for whom someone makes promises at BAPTISM

god·fa·ther /'gad,faðər/ *n* male GODPARENT

god-fear·ing /'·· ·,··/ *adj fml* good and well behaved

god·for·sak·en /'gadfər,seʸkən, ,gadfər'seʸ-/ *adj* (of places) sad and empty

god·moth·er /'gad,mʌðər/ *n* female godparent

god·pa·rent /'gad,pɛərənt, -,pær-/ *n* person who takes responsibility for a new Christian at BAPTISM

god·send /'gadsɛnd/ *n* unexpected lucky chance or thing

goes /goʷz/ *v* 3rd person sing. present tense of GO

go·fer, gopher /'goʷfər/ *n* person whose job is to bring or take things for other people

go-get·ter /'·· ·,··/ *n* someone who is forceful and determined, and likely to succeed

gog·gle /'gagəl/ *vi* STARE with the eyes wide open **goggles** *n* [P] glasses to protect the eyes

go-go /'·· ·/ *adj* of or being a form of fast dancing with sexy movements

go·ing /'goʷɪŋ/ *n* [U] speed or condition of travel: *fast/rough going* ♦ *adj* operating at present: *the going rate* | *a going concern*

goings-on /,·· '·/ *n* [P] undesirable activities

goi·ter /'gɔɪtər/ *n* swelling in the neck caused by lack of certain chemicals

gold /goʷld/ *n* 1 [U] valuable yellow metal 2 [U] gold coins 3 [U] the color of gold: *gold paint* 4 [C] gold MEDAL 5 as good as gold very well behaved

gold·en /'goʷldən/ *adj* 1 of or like gold 2 very favorable: *a golden opportunity*

golden an·ni·ver·sa·ry /,·· ··'···/ *n* the date that is exactly 50 years after the date of an event

golden par·a·chute /,·· '···/ *n* large amount of money given to someone leaving a firm

golden rule /,·· '·/ *n* [S] very important rule of behavior

gold·fish /'goʷld,fɪʃ/ *n* **goldfish** small orange fish kept as a pet

gold leaf /,· '·/ *n* [U] thin sheets of gold

gold·mine /'goʷldmaɪn/ *n* 1 mine where gold is found 2 profitable business

gold rush /'·· ·/ *n* rush to newly discovered goldmines

gold·smith /'goʷld,smɪθ/ *n* person who makes things out of gold

golf /galf, gɔlf/ *n* game in which people hit a ball into holes with GOLF CLUBS ~ **er** *n*

golf ball /'·· ·/ *n* 1 small hard ball used in golf 2 ball used in an electric TYPEWRITER to press letters onto the paper

golf club /ˈ· ·/ n 1 stick with a long handle for hitting the ball in golf 2 club for golfers with buildings and land they can use

gone /gɔn, gɑn/ v past p. of GO: *George has gone to Iowa.* (= he is there now)

gong /gɔŋ, gɑŋ/ n round piece of metal that makes a ringing sound when struck

gon·or·rhe·a /ˌgɑnəˈriːə/ n [U] disease passed on during sexual activity

goo /guʷ/ n [U] 1 sticky material 2 SENTIMENTALISM

good¹ /gʊd/ adj **better** /ˈbɛt̬ər/, **best** /bɛst/ 1 satisfactory: *good food/brakes* 2 pleasant: *good news* | *have a good time* 3 useful; suitable: *Milk is good for you.* 4 clever: *good at math* 5 well-behaved 6 morally right: *good deeds* 7 fml kind: *Be good enough to hold this.* 8 thorough: *have a good cry* 9 **a good: a** at least: *a good 3 hours* **b** large in size, amount: *a good distance* 10 **a good deal a** quite a lot **b** something sold cheaply 11 **all in good time** (it will happen) at a suitable later time; be patient 12 **as good as** almost the same as 13 **Good!** I agree, I'm glad, etc. 14 **good and** … *infml* completely: *I'll do it when I'm good and ready.* 15 **good for: a** effective in use: *The ticket is good for a month.* **b** likely to produce: *She's always good for a few dollars/a laugh.* 16 **in good time** early 17 **make good** be successful

good² n [U] 1 something that is good 2 something that causes gain or improvement: *It'll do you good.* | *It's no good.* (= it's useless) | *What's the good of/What good is it having a car if you don't drive?* 3 **for good** forever 4 **Good for you!** (used to express approval and pleasure at someone's success, etc.) 5 **up to no good** doing or intending doing something bad – see also GOODS

good af·ter·noon /ˌ· ˌ·ˈ·/ interj (used when meeting someone in the afternoon)

good·bye /gʊdˈbaɪ/ interj (used when leaving someone)

good eve·ning /ˌ· ˈ··/ interj (used when meeting someone in the evening)

good-for-noth·ing /ˌ· · ˈ··, ˈ· · ˌ··/ adj, n useless (person)

Good Fri·day /ˌ· ˈ··/ n the Friday before EASTER

good-hu·mored /ˌ· ˈ··◄/ adj cheerful and friendly

good-look·ing /ˌ· ˈ··◄/ adj attractive; beautiful

good·ly /ˈgʊdliʸ/ adj fml 1 large 2 satisfying

good morn·ing /ˌ· ˈ··/ interj (used when meeting someone in the morning)

good-na·tured /ˌ· ˈ··◄/ adj kind

good·ness /ˈgʊdnɪs/ n [U] 1 quality of being good 2 the best part of food, etc. 3 (used in expressions of surprise and annoyance): *Goodness me!* | *for goodness' sake*

good·night /gʊdˈnaɪt/ interj (used when leaving someone at night, or going to sleep)

goods /gʊdz/ n [P] 1 things for sale 2 proof of guilt: *I've got the goods on him.* 3 possessions 4 **come up with/deliver the goods** produce in full what is expected

good Sa·mar·i·tan /ˌ· ·ˈ··/ n person who kindly helps people in trouble

good·will /ˌgʊdˈwɪl/ n [U] 1 kind feelings 2 popularity of a business, as part of its value

good·y /ˈgʊdiʸ/ n something very pleasant, esp. to eat

goo·ey /ˈguʷiʸ/ adj 1 sticky and sweet 2 SENTIMENTAL

goof /guʷf/ n infml 1 foolish person 2 silly mistake ♦ vi infml make a silly mistake ~y adj

  goof off phr vi infml waste time or avoid work

goose /guʷs/ n geese /giʸs/ 1 bird like a large duck 2 silly person

goose·ber·ry /ˈguʷsˌbɛriʸ, -bəriʸ, ˈguʷzˌ-/ n garden bush with hairy green berries

goose·flesh /ˈguʷsflɛʃ/ also **goose bumps** /ˈ· ·/ — n [U] condition in which the skin rises up in small points

goose-step /ˈguʷs-stɛp/ n [S] way of marching with stiff straight legs

GOP /ˌdʒiʸ oʷ ˈpiʸ/ n [the] the Republican Party

go·pher /ˈgoʷfər/ n 1 rat-like animal that lives in a hole 2 GOFER

gore¹ /gɔr, goʷr/ vt wound with horns or TUSKS

gore² n [U] lit (esp. thick) blood **gory** adj

gorge¹ /gɔrdʒ/ n 1 steep narrow valley 2 **make someone's gorge rise** make someone feel sickened

gorge² vi/t eat or feed eagerly

gor·geous /ˈgɔrdʒəs/ adj wonderful; beautiful ~ly adv

go·ril·la /gəˈrɪlə/ n the largest of the APES

gosh /gɑʃ/ interj (expressing surprise)

gos·pel /ˈgɑspəl/ n 1 [U] something completely true 2 [C] (cap.) any of 4 accounts of Christ's life in the Bible

gos·sa·mer /ˈgɑsəmər/ n [U] thin silky thread

gos·sip /ˈgɑsəp/ n 1 [S;U] talk about

other people's private lives **2** [C] person who likes this kind of talk ♦ *vi* spend time in gossip

got /gɑt/ *v* past *t.* and *p.* of GET

Goth·ic /ˈgɑθɪk/ *adj* **1** of a style of building common from the 12th to 16th centuries, with pointed arches and tall pillars **2** of a style of writing in the 18th century which produced NOVELs set in lonely fearful places

got·ten /ˈgɑtn/ *v* past *p.* of GET

gou·ache /guˈɑʃ, gwɑʃ/ *n* [C;U] (picture painted by) a method using colors mixed with water and a sort of glue

gouge /gaʊdʒ/ *v* get too much money for: *They gouged me on these tickets.* **gouge out** *phr vt* push or dig out violently

gourd /gɔrd, goʷrd, gʊərd/ *n* hard outer shell of a fruit

gour·met /gʊərˈmeʸ, ˈgʊərmeʸ/ *n* person who knows a lot about food and drink

gout /gaʊt/ *n* [U] disease that makes the toes and fingers swell badly

gov·ern /ˈgʌvərn/ *v* **1** *vi/t* rule (a country, etc.) **2** *vt* control: *The price is governed by the quantity produced.* ~**ance** *n* [U] *fml* governing

gov·ern·ess /ˈgʌvərnɪs/ *n* woman who teaches children in their home

gov·ern·ment /ˈgʌvərmənt, ˈgʌvərnmənt/ *n* **1** [C] group of people who govern: *the Swiss government* **2** [U] act or process of governing: *the art of government* **3** [U] form or method of governing: *a return to democratic government* ~**al** /ˌgʌvərənˈmentəl, -vərˈmen-/ *adj*

gov·er·nor /ˈgʌvənər, -vər-/ *n* elected official head of a state in the U.S.: *the governor of California* ~**ship** *n* [U]

gown /gaʊn/ *n* **1** woman's dress **2** outer garment worn by judges, members of universities, etc. **3** loose garment worn for some special purpose: *a nightgown/dressing gown*

GP /ˌdʒiʸ ˈpiʸ/ also **general practitioner** — *n* doctor who is trained in general medicine

grab /græb/ *vt/i* **-bb-** seize suddenly and roughly ♦ *n* **1** sudden attempt to seize something **2 up for grabs** ready for anyone to take or win

grace /greʸs/ *n* [U] **1** beauty of movement or shape **2** delay allowed as a favor: *give them a week's grace* **3** prayer of thanks before or after meals **4** God's favor towards people **5 a saving grace** pleasing quality for which the person's faults are forgiven him **6 with (a) good/bad grace** willingly/unwillingly ♦ *vt*

fml give honor or beauty to ~**ful** *adj* **1** having GRACE(1) **2** suitably expressed ~**fully** *adv* ~**less** *adj* awkward

gra·cious /ˈgreʸʃəs/ *adj* **1** polite and pleasant **2** having those qualities made possible by wealth: *gracious living* ~**ly** *adv* ~**ness** *n* [U]

gra·da·tion /greʸˈdeʸʃən/ *n fml* stage; degree: *gradations of color*

grade /greʸd/ *n* **1** level of quality **2** a class in an American school: *She's in third grade.* **b** mark given for school work **c** gradient **3 make the grade** succeed; reach the necessary standard ♦ *vt* separate into levels of quality

grade cross·ing /ˈ· ˌ··/ *n* place where two railroads cross

grade school /ˈ· ·/ *n* ELEMENTARY SCHOOL

gra·di·ent /ˈgreʸdiʸənt/ *n* degree of slope, as on a road

grad·u·al /ˈgrædʒuʷəl/ *adj* happening slowly; not sudden ~**ly** *adv* ~**ness** *n* [U]

grad·u·ate¹ /ˈgrædʒuʷɪt/ *n* **1** person with a university degree **2** person who has completed any school or college course

grad·u·ate² /ˈgrædʒuʷeʸt/ *v* **1** *vi* become a graduate **2** *vt* GRADE **3** *vt* mark with degrees for measurement –**ation** /ˌgrædʒuʷˈeʸʃən/ *n* **1** [U] (ceremony of) becoming a graduate **2** [C] mark of measurement

graf·fi·ti /grəˈfiʸtiʸ/ *n* [P;U] drawings or writings on a wall

graft /græft/ *n* **1** [C] piece from one plant fixed inside another to grow there **2** [C] piece of skin or bone similarly fixed into the body **3** [U] practice of obtaining money or advantage by the dishonest use of esp. political influence ♦ *vt* put onto as a graft

grain /greʸn/ *n* **1** [C] single seed of rice, wheat, etc. **2** [U] crops from food plants like these **3** [C] small hard piece: *grains of sand* … (fig.) *a grain of truth* **4** [U] natural arrangement of threads or FIBERs in wood, cloth, etc. **5 be/go against the grain** it is not what one wishes (to do, know, etc.)

gram /græm/ *n* (measure of weight equal to) 1/1000 of a kilogram

gram·mar /ˈgræmər/ *n* [U] (book that teaches) rules for the use of words

gram·mar·i·an /grəˈmɛəriʸən/ *n* person who studies and knows about grammar

grammar school /ˈ·· ˌ·/ *n* ELEMENTARY SCHOOL

gram·mat·i·cal /grəˈmætɪkəl/ *adj* **1** concerning grammar **2** correct according to the rules of grammar

gra·na·ry /'greʸnəriʸ, 'græ-/ n building where grain is stored

grand /grænd/ adj **1** splendid; IMPRESSive **2** (of people) important **3** pleasant; delightful ♦ n **1** GRAND PIANO **2** also **g** (pl. **grand**) sl 1,000 dollars

gran·dad /'grændæd/ n infml grandfather

grand·child /'græntʃaɪld/ n **grandchildren** /-ˌtʃɪldrən/ boy (**grandson**) or girl (**granddaughter**) who is the child of the stated person's son or daughter

gran·dee /græn'diʸ/ n Spanish or Portuguese nobleman

gran·deur /'grændʒər, -dʒʊər/ n [U] quality of being grand; magnificence (MAGNIFICENT)

grand·fa·ther /'græn,faðər, 'grænd-/ n male GRANDPARENT

grandfather clock /'··· ,·/ n tall clock that stands on the floor

gran·dil·o·quent /græn'dɪləkwənt/ adj using (too many) long words

gran·di·ose /'grændiʸˌoʷs, ˌgrændiʸ'oʷs/ adj intended to seem splendid and important

grand·ma /'grænma, 'græma, 'grændma/ n infml grandmother

grand·moth·er /'græn,mʌðər, 'grænd-/ n female grandparent

grand·pa /'grænpa, 'græmpa, 'grændpa/ n infml grandfather

grand·par·ent /'græn,peərənt, -ˌpær-, 'grænd-/ n parent of someone's father or mother

grand pi·a·no /ˌ·· ·'··/ n large piano with strings set parallel to the ground

grand slam /ˌ·· '·/ n **1** the winning of all of a set of important sports competitions **2** baseball HOME RUN when there is a player on every base

grand·stand /'grænstænd, 'grænd-/ n seats arranged in rising rows, for people watching races, etc.

grand to·tal /ˌ·· '··/ n complete amount

gran·ite /'grænɪt/ n [U] hard usu. grey rock

gran·ny, -nie /'græniʸ/ n infml grandmother ♦ adj for old people: a granny flat

gra·no·la /grə'noʷlə/ n [U] breakfast dish of grain, nuts, fruit, etc., eaten with milk

grant /grænt/ vt **1** fml give: grant permission **2** admit the truth of **3 take something for granted** accept it without question ♦ n money granted esp. officially

gran·u·lar /'grænyələr/ adj made of grains

gran·u·lat·ed /'grænyəˌleʸtɪd/ adj (of sugar) in the form of not very fine powder

gran·ule /'grænyuʷl/ n small grain

grape /greʸp/ n green or purple fruit from which wine is made – see also SOUR GRAPES

grape·fruit /'greʸpfruʷt/ n large yellow fruit like a sour orange

grape·vine /'greʸpvaɪn/ n [S] unofficial way of spreading news: hear about it through the office grapevine

graph /græf/ n drawing showing the relationship between 2 changing values

graph·ic /'græfɪk/ adj **1** clear and detailed: a graphic description **2** of drawing, printing, etc. ~**ally** /-kliʸ/ adv **1** clearly **2** using graphs

graphics /n [P] drawings, etc.

graph·ite /'græfaɪt/ n [U] black substance used in pencils, etc.

grap·ple /'græpəl/ v **grapple with** phr vt seize and struggle with: (fig.) grapple with a problem

grasp /græsp/ vt **1** take firm hold of **2** succeed in understanding ♦ n [S] **1** firm hold **2** understanding ~**ing** adj too eager for money

grass /græs/ n **1** [U] common wild green plants that cows, etc., eat **2** [C] one of these plants: tall grasses

grass·hop·per /'græs,hapər/ n insect which can jump high and makes a sharp noise by rubbing parts of its body together

grass roots /ˌ·· '·/ n [P] ordinary people, not those with political power ♦ adj: grass roots protest

grass wid·ow /ˌ·· '··/ n woman whose husband is away for a period of time

grate¹ /greʸt/ n metal frame in a fireplace

grate² v **1** vt rub into pieces on a rough surface: grated cheese **2** vi make a sharp unpleasant sound **grater** n tool for grating food, etc.

grate·ful /'greʸtfəl/ adj feeling or showing thanks ~**ly** adv ~**ness** n [U]

grat·i·fy /'grætəˌfaɪ/ vt please; satisfy ~**ing** adj pleasing –**fication** /ˌgrætəfə'keʸʃən/ n [C;U]

grat·ing /'greʸtɪŋ/ n network of bars to protect an opening

grat·is /'grætɪs, 'greʸ-, 'gra-/ adv, adj fml without payment; free

grat·i·tude /'grætəˌtuʷd, -ˌtyuʷd/ n [U] gratefulness

gra·tu·i·tous /grə'tuʷətəs, -'tyuʷ-/ adj fml not deserved or necessary: gratuitous insults ~**ly** adv

gra·tu·i·ty /grə'tuʷətiʸ, -'tyuʷ-/ n fml TIP³ for a service done

grave¹ /greʸv/ n hole where a dead person is buried

grave² adj serious; solemn ~**ly** adv

grav·el /'grævəl/ n [U] small stones

used for making paths, etc. ~ly adj
1 covered with gravel **2** having a
low rough hard sound

grave·stone /ˈgreɪvstəʊn/ n stone
over a grave

grave·yard /ˈgreɪvjɑːd/ n CEMETERY

graveyard shift /ˈ·· ˌ·/ n night
working hours

grav·i·tate /ˈgrævɪˌteɪt/ vi be attracted (as if) by gravity –tation
/ˌgrævɪˈteɪʃən/ n [U]

grav·i·ty /ˈgrævɪtiʲ/ n [U] **1** force by
which objects are drawn towards
each other and to the earth **2** seriousness: *the gravity of his illness*

gra·vy /ˈgreɪviʲ/ n [U] juice that
comes out of meat in cooking

gravy train /ˈ·· ˌ·/ n [the+S] something from which many people can
make money or profit without
much effort

gray, grey /greɪ/ adj **1** of the color
of black mixed with white **2** having
gray hair ♦ n [U] gray color ♦ vi become gray

graze[1] /greɪz/ vi (of animals) eat
growing grass

graze[2] vt **1** rub the skin from **2** rub
lightly while passing ♦ n surface
wound

grease /griːs, griːz/ n [U] soft fat or
oil ♦ vt **1** put grease on **2 grease
someone's palm** BRIBE **greasy** **3
like greased lightning** infml extremely fast **greasy** adj

great /greɪt/ adj **1** excellent and important: *great writers* **2** large: *great
pleasure* | *a great many people* **3** en-
thusiastic; active: *a great filmgoer*
4 to an extreme degree: *great friends*
5 very good: *a great film* **6 great-**:
a parent of someone's GRANDPARENT:
his great-grandfather **b** child of
someone's GRANDCHILD: *his great-
granddaughter* ~ly adv very much
~ness n [U]

Great Plains /ˌ· ·/ n dry, flat area
of land in North America

great white hope /ˌ· ·· ·/ n person
who is expected to bring great success

greed /griːd/ n [U] desire for too
much food, money, etc. ~y adj –ily
adv

green /griːn/ adj **1** of a color between yellow and blue; the color of
leaves and grass **2** pale and unhealthy in the face **3** (of fruit, plants,
etc.) young or unripe **4** inexperienced and easily deceived **5**
very jealous: *green with envy* ♦ n **1**
[U] green color **2** [C] smooth area
with grass: *village green* ~ness n
[U] **greens** n [P] green leafy vegetables

green·back /ˈgriːnbæk/ n dollar

green·e·ry /ˈgriːnəriʲ/ n [U] green
leaves and plants

green-eyed mon·ster /ˌ·· · ˈ··/ n
[the+S] jealousy

green·gage /ˈgriːngeɪdʒ/ n kind of
green PLUM

green·horn /ˈgriːnhɔːn/ n beginner

green·house /ˈgriːnhaʊs/ n glass
building for growing plants in

green thumb /ˌ· ·/ n [P] natural
skill in making plants grow

greet /griːt/ vt **1** welcome **2** be suddenly seen or heard ~**ing** n **1** words
used on meeting or writing to someone **2** a good wish: *Christmas greetings*

gre·gar·i·ous /grɪˈgeəriʲəs/ adj fond
of companionship

gre·nade /grəˈneɪd/ n small bomb
to be thrown by hand

grew /gruː/ v past t. of GROW

grey·hound /ˈgreɪhaʊnd/ n thin dog
with long legs, which can run
quickly

grey mat·ter /ˈ·· ˌ··/ n [U] **1** the brain
2 infml power of thought

grid /grɪd/ n **1** GRATING **2** system of
numbered squares on a map

grid·i·ron /ˈgrɪdaɪən/ n **1** frame for
cooking meat over a fire **2** field
marked for football

grief /griːf/ n [U] **1** (cause of) great
sorrow **2 come to grief** suffer harm;
fail **3 Good grief!** (expression of
surprise and some dislike)

griev·ance /ˈgriːvəns/ n cause for
complaint

grieve /griːv/ v **1** vi suffer grief **2** vt
make unhappy

griev·ous /ˈgriːvəs/ adj fml very
harmful; severe ~**ly** adv

grill /grɪl/ v **1** vi/t cook over direct
heat outside **2** vt question severely
♦ n BARBECUE

grille /grɪl/ n bars filling a space,
esp. for safety

grim /grɪm/ adj –**mm**- **1** serious;
terrible: *grim news* **2** showing determination: *grim smile* ~**ly** adv
~**ness** n [U]

gri·mace /ˈgrɪməs, grɪˈmeɪs/ vi
twist the face to express pain, etc.
grimace n

grime /graɪm/ n [U] black dirt on a
surface **grimy** adj

grim reap·er /ˌ· ˈ··/ n [the] (a name
for death, considered as a person)

grin /grɪn/ vi –**nn**- **1** smile widely **2
grin and bear it** suffer without
complaint **grin** n

grind /graɪnd/ vt ground /graʊnd/ **1**
crush into powder: *grind coffee
beans* **2** rub (the teeth) together **3**
make smooth or sharp by rubbing:
grind knives **4** press upon with a
strong twisting movement **5 grind
to a halt** stop noisily ♦ n infml [S]
hard dull work ~**er** n person or
machine that grinds

grind away _phr v_ study hard

grind down _phr vt_ keep in a state of suffering and hopelessness

grind out _phr vt derog_ produce (esp. writing or music) continually, but like a machine

grind·stone /ˈgraɪndstoʷn/ _n_ **1** round stone that is turned to sharpen tools **2 one's nose to the grindstone** in a state of continuous hard work

grin·go /ˈgrɪŋgoʷ/ _n often derog._ white American or European, esp. when in countries where the people speak Spanish

grip /grɪp/ _vi/t_ -pp- **1** seize tightly **2** hold someone's attention: _a gripping story_ ♦ _n_ **1** tight hold **2** thing that grips **3** traveler's small bag **4 come/get to grips with** deal seriously with

gripe /graɪp/ _vi sl_ complain continuously ♦ **gripe** _n_

gris·ly /ˈgrɪzliʸ/ _adj_ shocking and sickening

gris·tle /ˈgrɪsəl/ _n_ [U] CARTILAGE in cooked meat

grit /grɪt/ _n_ [U] **1** small stones and sand **2** lasting courage: determination ♦ _vt_ -tt- **1** put grit on (esp. a road) **2 grit one's teeth** show determination **-ty** _adj_

griz·zled /ˈgrɪzəld/ _adj_ having gray hair

griz·zly bear /ˈ·· ˌ·/ _n_ large strong bear

groan /groʷn/ _vi, n_ (make) a loud deep sound of suffering

gro·cer /ˈgroʷsər/ _n_ storekeeper who sells dry foods and other things for the home

gro·cer·ies /ˈgroʷsəriʸz/ _n_ [P] goods sold by a grocer

grog·gy /ˈgrɑgiʸ/ _adj_ weak and unsteady from illness, etc. **-giness** _n_ [U]

groin /grɔɪn/ _n_ place where the legs meet the front of the body

groom /gruʷm, grʊm/ _n_ **1** person who looks after horses **2** BRIDEGROOM ♦ _vt_ **1** brush and clean (horses) **2** make (oneself) neat and tidy **3** prepare (someone) for special work

groove /gruʷv/ _n_ long hollow in a surface

grope /groʷp/ _v_ **1** _vi_ search about with the hands as in the dark **2** _vt sl_ (try to) feel the body of (a person) to get sexual pleasure **grope** _n_

gross¹ /groʷs/ _adj_ **1** unpleasantly fat **2** rough; rude **3** clearly wrong: _gross negligence_ **4** total: _gross income_ ♦ _vt_ gain as total profit **~ly** _adv_ **~ness** _n_ [U]

gross² _determiner, n_ **gross** or **grosses** 144

gro·tesque /groʷˈtɛsk/ _adj_ strange and ugly **~ly** _adv_

grot·to /ˈgrɑtoʷ/ _n_ **-toes** or **-tos** cave

ground¹ /graʊnd/ _v past t. and p. of_ GRIND

ground² _n_ **1** [S;U] surface of the earth **2** [U] soil **3** [C] piece of land used for a particular purpose: _a playground_ **4** [U] **a** base for argument: _You're on safe ground as long as you avoid the subject of politics._ **b** area of knowledge or experience: _It was absurd to try to cover so much ground in such a short course._ **5** [U] position of advantage to be won or defended: _The army has lost ground._ | _The idea is gaining ground._ (= becoming more popular) **6** [C] safety wire carrying electricity to the ground **7 get off the ground** make a successful start **8 into the ground** more or further than is necessary – see also GROUNDS **~less** _adj_ without reason: _groundless fears_ **~lessly** _adv_

ground³ _v_ **1** _vi_ (of a boat) strike against the bottom of the sea, a river, etc. **2** _vt_ cause (a plane or pilot) to stay on the ground **3** _vt_ base: _arguments grounded on experience_ **~ing** _n_ [S] first necessary training in something

ground·cloth /ˈgraʊndklɔθ/ _n_ **-cloths** /-klɔðz, -klɔθs/ WATERPROOF sheet to spread on the ground

ground floor /ˌ· ˈ·/ _n_ **1** part of a building at ground level **2 get/be in on the ground floor** be part of an activity, business operation, etc., from the time it starts

grounds /graʊndz/ _n_ [P] **1** solid bits at the bottom of a liquid **2** gardens, etc., around a building **3** reason: _grounds for divorce_

ground·work /ˈgraʊndwɜrk/ _n_ [U] work on which further study, etc., is based

group /gruʷp/ _n_ connected set of people or things ♦ _vi/t_ form into groups

grouse¹ /graʊs/ _vi, n_ GRUMBLE

grouse² _n_ grouse small fat bird which is shot for food and sport

grove /groʷv/ _n lit_ small group of trees

grov·el /ˈgrɑvəl, ˈgrʌ-/ _vi_ -l- **1** lie flat in fear or obedience **2** be shamefully humble and eager to please **~ler** _n_

grow /groʷ/ _v_ **grew** /gruʷ/, **grown** /groʷn/ **1** _vi_ get bigger **2** _vi_ (of plants) live and develop **3** _vt_ cause (plants, etc.) to grow **4** _fml_ become: _grow old_ **grown** _adj_ ADULT: _grown men_

grow on _phr vt_ become more pleasing to: _This music will grow on you._

grow out of phr vt get too big or old for

grow up phr vi 1 develop from child to man or woman 2 start to exist: *customs that have grown up*

growl /graʊl/ vi, n (make) the threatening noise of an angry dog

grown-up /ˌ· ˈ·◂/ adj, n ADULT

growth /groʷθ/ n 1 [S;U] process of growing; increase 2 [C] something that has grown, esp. an unnatural lump in the body

grub¹ /grʌb/ n 1 [C] insect in the wormlike stage 2 [U] sl food

grub² vi/t -bb- dig with the hands or PAWS

grub·by /ˈgrʌbiʸ/ adj rather dirty –biness n [U]

grub·stake /ˈgrʌbˌsteʸk/ n money provided to develop a new business

grudge /grʌdʒ/ vt be unwilling to give: *He grudged paying so much.* ♦ n continuing feeling of anger against someone **grudgingly** adv

gru·el·ing /ˈgruʷəlɪŋ/ adj very tiring

grue·some /ˈgruʷsəm/ adj very shocking and sickening ~**ly** adv

gruff /grʌf/ adj (of the voice) deep and rough ~**ly** adv ~**ness** n [U]

grum·ble /ˈgrʌmbəl/ vi complain ♦ n complaint

grump·y /ˈgrʌmpiʸ/ adj bad-tempered –**ily** adv –**iness** n [U]

grunt /grʌnt/ vi, n (make) the short rough sound that pigs make

guar·an·tee /ˌgærənˈtiʸ/ n 1 written promise to replace an article if it is found to be imperfect 2 agreement to be responsible for a debt ♦ vt 1 give a guarantee about 2 promise: *I guarantee you'll enjoy it.*

guar·an·tor /ˈgærəntɔr, -tər/ n law person who agrees to be responsible for a debt

guard /gɑrd/ n 1 [U] state of watching against attack: *soldiers on guard* 2 a [C] person keeping guard b [S] group of these people 3 [C] protective apparatus or person: *a bodyguard* – see also OLD GUARD ♦ vt 1 defend 2 watch (prisoners) to prevent escape ~**ed** adj not saying too much

guard against phr vt prevent by care: *guard against infection*

guard·i·an /ˈgɑrdiʸən/ n person responsible for a child ~**ship** n [U]

gu·ber·na·to·ri·al /ˌguʷbərnəˈtɔriʸəl, -ˈtoʷr-, ˌgyuʷ-/ adj of a governor

guer·ril·la /gəˈrɪlə/ n member of an unofficial army which attacks in small groups

guess /ges/ v 1 vi/t form an opinion (on) without knowing all the facts 2 vt *infml* suppose; consider likely ♦

n 1 opinion formed by guessing 2 attempt to guess

guess·work /ˈgeswɜrk/ n [U] guessing

guest /gest/ n 1 person invited to someone's home, or staying in a hotel 2 person, esp. an entertainer, invited to take part in a show, etc. 3 **be my guest!** please feel free to do so ♦ vi take part as a guest performer

guest·house /ˈgesthaʊs/ n -houses /-ˈhaʊzɪz/ small house for guests

guf·faw /gəˈfɔ/ vi laugh loudly and esp. rudely **guffaw** n

guid·ance /ˈgaɪdns/ n [U] help; advice

guide /gaɪd/ n 1 person who shows the way 2 something that influences behavior 3 also **guide book** /ˈ· ·/ — book describing a place 4 instruction book ♦ vt act as a guide to

guided mis·sile /ˌ·· ˈ··/ n MISSILE whose flight is controlled by electrical means

guide·lines /ˈgaɪdlaɪnz/ n [P] main points on how to deal with something

guild /gɪld/ n association of people with the same interests

guile /gaɪl/ n [U] deceit ~**ful** adj ~**less** adj

guil·lo·tine /ˈgɪləˌtiʸn, ˈgɪyə-, ˌgɪlə-ˈtiʸn, ˌgɪyə-/ n 1 machine for cutting off the heads of criminals 2 machine for cutting paper ♦ vt use a GUILLOTINE (1) on

guilt /gɪlt/ n [U] 1 fact of having done wrong; blame 2 shame ~**y** adj having done wrong

guinea pig /ˈgɪniʸ ˌpɪg/ n 1 small tailless furry animal sometimes used in scientific tests 2 person on whom something is tested

guise /gaɪz/ n fml outer appearance

gui·tar /gɪˈtɑr/ n stringed musical instrument played with the fingers

gulch /gʌltʃ/ n narrow stony valley with steep sides made by a rushing stream

gulf /gʌlf/ n 1 piece of sea partly surrounded by land 2 division, esp. between opinions

gull /gʌl/ n any of several kinds of large birds that live on or near the sea

gul·ly /ˈgʌliʸ/ n small gulch

gul·let /ˈgʌlɪt/ n food pipe in the throat

gul·li·ble /ˈgʌləbəl/ adj easily tricked ~**bility** /ˌgʌləˈbɪlətiʸ/ n [U]

gulp /gʌlp/ vi/t swallow hastily **gulp** n

gum¹ /gʌm/ n flesh in which the teeth are fixed

gum² n **1** [U] sticky plant substance **2** [U] CHEWING GUM ♦ vt **-mm-** stick with GUM (1) **~my** adj sticky

gump·tion /'gʌmpʃən/ n [U] **1** practical good sense **2** courage

gum·shoe /'gʌmʃuʷ/ n DETECTIVE

gun¹ /gʌn/ n weapon that fires bullets or SHELLs through a tube – see also **stick to one's guns** (STICK²)

gun² v

gun down phr vt shoot, causing to fall to the ground dead or wounded

gun for phr vt **1** aim at **2** search for in order to attack

gun·boat /'gʌnboʷt/ n small heavily armed warship

gun·fire /'gʌnfaɪər/ n [U] (sound of) shooting

gung-ho /ˌgʌŋ 'hoʷ◂/ adj showing extreme, often foolish, eagerness, esp. to attack an enemy

gun·man /'gʌnmən/ n **-men** /-mən/ armed criminal

gun·ner /'gʌnər/ n soldier who uses heavy guns

gun·ny·sack /'gʌniʸˌsæk/ n cloth bag for storing potatoes, coal, etc.

gun·point /'gʌnpɔɪnt/ n **at gunpoint** under a threat of death by shooting

gun·pow·der /'gʌnˌpaʊdər/ n [U] explosive powder

gun·run·ner /'gʌnˌrʌnər/ n person who unlawfully and secretly brings guns into a country **-ning** n [U]

gur·gle /'gɜrgəl/ vi, n (make) the sound of water flowing unevenly

gu·ru /'guʷruʷ, 'guəruʷ, guʷ'ruʷ/ n **gurus 1** Eastern religious teacher **2** greatly respected person whose ideas are valued

gush /gʌʃ/ v **1** vi flow out: oil gushing from a pipe **2** vt send out (liquid) in large quantities **3** vi express admiration foolishly ♦ n [S] sudden flow

gust /gʌst/ n sudden rush of wind **-y** adj

gus·to /'gʌstoʷ/ n [U] eager enjoyment

gut /gʌt/ n [U] thread made from animal bowels ♦ vt **1** take out the inner organs of: gut a fish **2** destroy the inside of (a building) ♦ adj coming from feelings rather than thought: gut reactions **guts** n [P] **1** bowels **2** bravery and determination **gutsy** n brave

gut course /'·· ·/ n very easy college course

gut·ter /'gʌtər/ n **1** [C] ditch or pipe that carries away rainwater **2** [the+S] the lowest level of society

gutter press /'·· ˌ·/ n newspapers which tend to be full of shocking stories

gut·tur·al /'gʌtərəl/ adj (of speech) coming from deep in the throat

guy /gaɪ/ n sl **a** man **b** person, male or female: Come on, you guys!

guz·zle /'gʌzəl/ vi/t eat or drink eagerly

gym /dʒɪm/ n **1** [C] gymnasium **2** [U] gymnastics

gym·na·si·um /dʒɪm'neʸziʸəm/ n hall with apparatus for indoor exercise

gym·nas·tics /dʒɪm'næstɪks/ n [U] training of the body by physical exercises **-tic** adj

gy·ne·col·o·gy /ˌgaɪnə'kɑlədʒiʸ, ˌdʒaɪ-/ n [U] medical study and treatment of the female sex organs **-gist** n **-gical** /ˌgaɪnəkə'lɑdʒɪkəl, ˌdʒaɪ-/ adj **-gically** /-kliʸ/ adv

gyp·sy, gipsy /'dʒɪpsiʸ/ n person with no fixed home who travels with others, working in CARNIVALs, etc.

gy·rate /'dʒaɪreʸt, dʒaɪ'reʸt/ vi fml swing around and around **gyra·tion** /dʒaɪ'reʸʃən/ n [C;U]

gy·ro·scope /'dʒaɪrəˌskoʷp/ n wheel that spins inside a frame, used for keeping ships, etc., steady

H

H, h /eɪtʃ/ the 8th letter of the English alphabet

ha·be·as cor·pus /ˌheɪbiʲəs ˈkɔrpəs/ n [U] **1** written order that a person in prison must be brought before a court **2** law principle protecting people held by police without reason

hab·er·dash·er /ˈhæbərˌdæʃər/ n fml storekeeper who sells men's hats, GLOVES, etc. **~y** n [U] haberdasher's goods

hab·it /ˈhæbɪt/ n **1** [C;U] person's usual behavior **2** [C] clothes worn by a MONK or NUN

hab·it·a·ble /ˈhæbətəbəl/ adj fit to be lived in

hab·i·tat /ˈhæbəˌtæt/ n natural home of an animal or plant

hab·i·ta·tion /ˌhæbəˈteɪʃən/ n fml [U] living in: houses fit for habitation

ha·bit·u·al /həˈbɪtʃuʷəl/ adj **1** usual **2** (done) by habit **~ly** adv

ha·bit·u·é /həˈbɪtʃuʷeɪ/ n fml regular attender

hack¹ /hæk/ vi/t cut roughly

hack² n **1** writer who does a lot of poor quality work **2** old horse

hack·er /ˈhækər/ n someone who is able to use or change information in a computer system without permission

hacking cough /ˌ·· ˈ·/ n cough with a rough, unpleasant sound

hack·les /ˈhækəlz/ n **make someone's hackles rise** make someone very angry

hack·neyed /ˈhækniʲd/ adj (of a saying) meaningless because used too often

hack·saw /ˈhæksɔ/ n tool with a blade with fine teeth, used esp. for cutting metal

had /d, əd, həd; strong hæd/ v past t. and p. of HAVE

had·dock /ˈhædək/ n haddock common fish, used as food

had·n't /ˈhædnt/ v short for: had not

hag /hæg/ n derog ugly old woman

hag·gard /ˈhægərd/ adj (of the face) lined and hollow from tiredness

hag·gle /ˈhægəl/ vi argue over a price

hail¹ /heɪl/ n [U] frozen rain drops: (fig.) a hail of bullets ♦ vi (of hail) fall

hail² vi **1** call out to: hail a taxi **2** recognize (someone) as important: They hailed him king.

hail as phr vt recognize as (something good)

hail from phr vt come from: She hails from New Orleans.

hail·stone /ˈheɪlstoʷn/ n single piece of hail

hair /heər/ n **1** [C] threadlike growth from the skin **2** [U] mass of these growths **3 let one's hair down** behave as one likes after being formal **4 make someone's hair curl** infml shock someone **5 make one's hair stand on end** frighten one badly **6 tear one's hair out** show extreme grief or anger **~y** adj **1** covered with hair **2** infml exciting in a way that causes fear; dangerous **~iness** n [U]

hair·do /ˈheərduʷ/ n **-dos** style a person's hair is shaped into

hair·dress·er /ˈheərˌdresər/ n person who cuts and shapes hair

hair·piece /ˈheərpiʲs/ n piece of false hair used to make one's own hair seem thicker

hair·pin bend /ˌheərpɪn ˈbend/ n curve on a road in the shape of a U

hair-rais·ing /ˈ· ˌ··/ adj very frightening

hair's breadth /ˈ· ·/ n very short distance

hair·split·ting /ˈ· ˌ··/ n [U] derog act or habit of paying too much attention to unimportant differences and details

hal·cy·on /ˈhælsiʲən/ adj lit peaceful and happy: halcyon days

hale /heɪl/ adj **hale and hearty** very healthy

half¹ /hæf/ n **halves** /hævz/ **1** either of 2 equal parts; ½: Half of 50 is 25. **2** either of 2 parts into which something is divided: He's in the bottom half of the class. **3** coin, ticket, drink, etc., of ½ the value or amount: Just a half, please. **4 by halves** incompletely **5 go halves** share something equally **6 my/your/his/her better half** one's husband or wife

half² predeterminer, adj ½ in amount: She bought half a pound of rice.

half³ adv **1** partly: half cooked | half French **2 half and half** ½ one and ½ the other **3 not half** not at all: This food's not half bad. **4 not half** as not nearly as

half-and-half /ˌ·· ˈ·/ n [U] mixture of milk and cream, used in coffee, etc.

half-baked /ˌ· ˈ·◂/ adj (esp. of ideas) not sensible

half-broth·er /ˈ· ˌ··/ n brother related through only one parent

half-caste /ˈ· ·/ also **half-breed** — n, adj (person) with parents of different races

half-heart·ed /ˌ· ˈ·‹·‹/ adj showing not much interest

half-life /ˈ· ·/ n time it takes for half the atoms in a radioactive (RADIO-ACTIVE) substance to decay

half-mast /ˈ· ·/ n point near the middle of a FLAGPOLE where the flag flies as a sign of sorrow

half-sis·ter /ˈ· ˌ·‹/ n sister related through only one parent

half·way /ˌhæfˈweʸ‹/ adj, adv 1 at the middle point between 2 things 2 **meet someone halfway** make an agreement with someone which partly meets the demands of both sides

halfway house /ˈ·· ˌ·/ n home for people getting over criminal or drug problems

half-wit /ˈ· ·/ n stupid person or one with a weak mind — **ted** /ˌ· ˈ·‹·‹/ adj

hall /hɔl/ n 1 passage inside the entrance of a house 2 large room for meetings, etc.

hal·le·lu·ja /ˌhælɪˈluʷyə/ interj (expression of praise to God)

hall·mark /ˈhɔlmɑrk/ n mark proving that something is really silver or gold: (fig.) *Clear expression is the hallmark of a good writer.*

hal·lowed /ˈhælɵʷd/ adj fml holy

Hal·low·e'en /ˌhælɵˈwiʸn, ˌhɑ-/ n October 31, when children play tricks and dress in strange clothes

hal·lu·ci·nate /həˈluʷsəˌneʸt/ vi see things that are not there —**natory** /-sənəˌtɔriʸ, -ˌtoʷriʸ/ adj —**nation** /həˌluʷsəˈneʸʃən/ n [C;U] (experience of seeing) something which is not really there, because of illness or drugs

hall·way /ˈhɔlweʸ/ n HALL (1)

ha·lo /ˈheʸlɵʷ/ n —**loes** or —**los** 1 circle representing light around the heads of holy people in pictures 2 circle of light around the sun or moon

halt /hɔlt/ vi/t fml stop **halt** n [S]

hal·ter /ˈhɔltər/ n 1 rope for leading a horse 2 woman's shirt with an open back

halt·ing /ˈhɔltɪŋ/ adj stopping and starting uncertainly

halve /hæv/ vt 1 reduce by half: *halve the time* 2 divide into halves

halves /hævz/ n pl. of HALF

ham /hæm/ n 1 [C;U] (preserved meat from) the upper part of a pig's leg 2 [C] actor whose performance is unnatural 3 [C] non-professional radio operator ♦ vi/t perform like a HAM 2

ham·burg·er /ˈhæmˌbɜrgər/ n 1 flat round cake of small bits of meat, eaten in a BUN (2) 2 GROUND BEEF

ham-fist·ed /ˌ· ˈ·‹·‹/ adj awkward in using the hands

ham·mer¹ /ˈhæmər/ n 1 tool with a metal head for driving nails into wood 2 part of a piano, etc., that hits another part 3 **come under the hammer** be offered for sale at an AUCTION 4 **throwing the hammer** sport in which a heavy metal ball on a chain is thrown

hammer² v 1 vi/t hit with a hammer 2 vt defeat thoroughly 3 vi work continuously: *hammer away at the problem* 4 vt force: *hammer the facts into their heads*

hammer out phr vt talk about in detail and come to a decision about

ham·mock /ˈhæmək/ n cloth or net hung up to sleep in

ham·per¹ /ˈhæmpər/ vt cause difficulty in movement

hamper² n large basket with a lid

ham·ster /ˈhæmstər/ n small mouse-like animal often kept as a pet

ham·string /ˈhæmˌstrɪŋ/ n cordlike TENDON at the back of the leg ♦ vt —**strung** /-ˌstrʌŋ/ make powerless

hand¹ /hænd/ n 1 [C] movable part at the end of the arm 2 [C] pointer on a clock, etc. 3 [C] set of playing cards held by one player 4 [S] writing by hand 5 [C] worker; someone with a skill: *farm hands* – see also OLD HAND 6 [S] help: *give/lend a hand* 7 [C;U] control: *get out of hand | have the matter in hand | in the hands of the police* 8 [S] APPLAUSE: *Give the singer a big hand.* 9 **at first hand** by direct experience 10 **at hand** near in time or place 11 **at second/third/fourth hand** as information passed on through 1, 2, or 3 people 12 **by hand: a** not typed (TYPE) or printed **b** delivered directly, not by mail 13 **change hands** go from the possession of one person to that of another 14 **get/keep one's hand in** get/stay used to an activity 15 **get the upper hand (of)** get control or power (over something/somebody difficult) 16 **give someone a free hand** let them do things in their own way 17 **hand in glove (with)** closely connected (with someone), esp. in something bad 18 **hand in hand: a** holding each other's hands **b** in close connection 19 **hand over fist** very quickly and successfully 20 **have a hand in** be partly responsible for 21 **have one's hands full** be very busy 22 **in hand** ready for use 23 **live from hand to mouth** have just enough money, food, etc., to live 24 **on hand** ready for use or to take part 25 **on the one/other hand** (used for comparing 2 things) 26 **(out of/off) one's hands** (no longer) one's responsibility 27 **play into someone's hands** do something which gives (one's opponent) an advantage **28 raise one's hand to/against** (make a movement) to hit **29 show one's hand** make one's power or intentions clear, esp. after keeping them secret **30 throw up one's hand (at)** accept defeat **31 to hand** within reach **32 try one's hand (at)** attempt (an activity) **33 turn one's hand to** begin to practice (a skill) **34 wait on (someone) hand and foot** do every little thing for (someone) **35 with a heavy hand** in a firm manner

hand² *vt* **1** give with one's hand(s) **2 (have to) hand it to someone** (have to) admit the high quality or success of someone

hand down *phr vt* give (clothes) to a younger or smaller person

hand in *phr vt* deliver

hand on *phr vt* give to someone else

hand out *phr vt* **1** give out to several people **2** give freely: *He's always ready to hand out advice.*

hand over *phr vt* give control of: *We handed him over to the police.*

hand·bag /ˈhændbæg, ˈhæn-/ *n* woman's small bag for money and personal things

hand·book /ˈhændbʊk, ˈhæn-/ *n* book of instructions

hand·brake /ˈhændbreʸk, ˈhæn-/ *n* BRAKE worked by the driver's hand, not by the foot

hand·cuffs /ˈhændkʌfs, ˈhæn-/ *n* [P] pair of metal rings for fastening a criminal's wrists ♦ *vt* put handcuffs on

hand·ful /ˈhændfʊl, ˈhæn-/ *n* **1** as much as can be held in one hand **2** small number (of people) **3** *infml* person or animal that is hard to control

handgun /ˈhændɡʌn, ˈhæn-/ *n* small gun – see PISTOL

hand·i·cap /ˈhændiʸkæp/ *n* **1** disability of the body or mind **2** disadvantage given to the stronger competitors in a sport ♦ *vt* –**pp**- **1** give a disadvantage to **2** (of a disability of body or mind) prevent (someone) from acting or living as most people do

hand·i·craft /ˈhændiʸkræft/ *n* skill such as weaving, which uses the hands

hand·i·work /ˈhændiʸwɜrk/ *n* [U] **1** work demanding the skillful use of the hands **2** result of someone's action

hand·ker·chief /ˈhæŋkərtʃif, -ˌtʃiʸf/ *n* cloth or paper for drying the nose, etc.

han·dle¹ /ˈhændl/ *n* part of a door, cup, etc., that one holds

handle² *vt* **1** touch or move with the hands **2** control; deal with: *handle the accounts* **3** (of a car, boat, etc.) obey controlling movements in the stated way –**dler** *n* person who controls an animal

han·dle·bars /ˈhændlˌbɑrz/ *n* [P] curved bar above front wheel of a bicycle, etc., which controls the direction it goes in

hand·out /ˈhændaʊt/ *n* **1** something given free **2** printed sheet of information given out

hand·picked /ˌhændˈpɪkt◄, ˌhæn-/ *adj* carefully chosen

hand·shake /ˈhændʃeʸk, ˈhæn-/ *n* act of taking each other's hand as a greeting

hand·some /ˈhænsəm/ *adj* **1** of good appearance: *a handsome boy* **2** more than large enough: *a handsome reward* ~**ly** *adv*

hand·stand /ˈhændstænd, ˈhæn-/ *n* position in which the body is supported upside down on the hands

hand-to-mouth /ˌ· · ˈ·◄/ *adj* (of a way of life) with just enough food, money, etc., to live

hand·writ·ing /ˈhændˌraɪtɪŋ/ *n* [U] (style of) writing done by hand –**written** /ˈhændˌrɪtn/ *adj* written by hand

hand·y /ˈhændiʸ/ *adj* **1** useful **2** skillful with one's hands **3** easily reached **4 come in handy** be useful –**ily** *adv*

hand·y·man /ˈhændiʸˌmæn/ *n* –**men** /-ˌmɛn/ person who does small repairs

hang¹ /hæŋ/ *v* **hung** /hʌŋ/ **1** *vi/t* fix or be fixed from above so that the lower part is free **2** *vi/t* (of certain kinds of meat) be kept in this position until ready to eat **3** *vt* stick (WALLPAPER) on a wall **4** *vt* (*past t. and p.* **hanged**) kill by dropping with a rope around the neck **5 hang fire** be delayed **6 hang one's head** appear ashamed

hang around *phr vi* **1** wait without purpose **2** delay **3** spend time: *hang around with friends*

hang back *phr vi* be unwilling to move

hang on *phr vi* **1** keep hold of something **2** wait **3** pay close attention to **4** depend on

hang onto *phr vt* try to keep

hang out *phr vi infml* **1** live or spend a lot of time **2 let it all hang out** *sl* behave exactly as you want to

hang up *phr vi* **1** finish a telephone conversation **2** put something on a hook **3 be hung up on/about** *sl* be anxious or have a fixed idea about

hang² *n* **get/have the hang of something** understand how a machine, etc., works

han·gar /ˈhæŋər, ˈhæŋɡər/ n building where aircraft are kept

hang·er /ˈhæŋər/ n hook and bar to hang a garment from

hanger-on /ˌ·· ·ˈ·/ n **hangers-on** person who tries to be friendly in the hope of advantage

hang glid·ing /ˈ· ˌ··/ n [U] the sport of gliding (GLIDE (2)) using a large KITE (1) instead of a plane

hang·man /ˈhæŋmən/ n **-men** /-mən/ man whose work is hanging criminals

hang·o·ver /ˈhæŋˌoʷvər/ n **1** feeling of sickness, etc., the day after drinking too much alcohol **2** condition or effect resulting from an earlier event or state

hang-up /ˈhæŋʌp/ n sl something about which a person gets unusually worried

han·ker /ˈhæŋkər/ v **hanker after/for** phr vt desire strongly **hankering** n [S]

han·kie, -ky /ˈhæŋkiʸ/ n handkerchief

hank·y-pank·y /ˌhæŋkiʸ ˈpæŋkiʸ/ n [U] improper behavior, esp. deceit or sexual activity, of a not very serious kind

hap·haz·ard /ˌhæpˈhæzərd/ adj unplanned; disorderly

hap·less /ˈhæpləs/ adj lit unlucky

hap·pen /ˈhæpən/ vi **1** (of an event) take place: When did the accident happen? **2** be or do by chance: We happened to meet. **3** be true by or as if by chance: As it happens, we do know each other. **~ing** n event

happen on phr vt find by chance

hap·py /ˈhæpiʸ/ adj **1** pleased; contented **2** causing pleasure: a happy occasion **3** (of thoughts, etc.) suitable: a happy remark **4** (used in good wishes): Happy Birthday! **-pily** adv **-piness** n [U]

happy-go-luck·y /ˌ··· ·ˈ···/ adj unworried; CAREFREE

happy hour /ˈ·· ˌ·/ n limited period in the day when alcoholic drinks are sold at lower than usual prices in a bar, etc.

ha·rangue /həˈræŋ/ vt attack or try to persuade with a long angry speech **harangue** n

har·ass /həˈræs, ˈhærəs/ vt worry repeatedly **~ment** n [U]

har·bor /ˈhɑrbər/ n sheltered area where ships are safe ♦ vt **1** give protection to **2** keep (thoughts or feelings) in the mind

hard¹ /hɑrd/ adj **1** firm and stiff: hard skin **2** difficult: hard question **3** needing or using effort: hard work/worker **4** unpleasant; severe: hard winter | Don't be too hard on him. **5** (of water) containing minerals that stop soap from forming

LATHER easily **6** (of drugs) dangerous and ADDICTive **~ness** n [U]

hard² adv **1** with great effort: push hard **2** heavily: raining hard **3** hard at it working hard **4** hard by fml near **5** hard done by unfairly treated **6** hard hit suffering loss **7** hard put (to it) having great difficulty **8** hard up infml not having enough (esp. money) **9** take (it) hard suffer deeply

hard-and-fast /ˌ·· ·ˈ·◄/ adj (of rules) fixed

hard·back /ˈhɑrdbæk/ n book with a stiff cover

hard·ball /ˈhɑrdbɔl/ n [U] **1** baseball **2** play hardball use methods that are not gentle, and may be unfair

hard-bit·ten /ˌ·· ·ˈ··◄/ adj (of a person) made firm in argument and decision by hard experience

hard·board /ˈhɑrdbɔrd, -boʷrd/ n [U] stiff cardboard, used like wood

hard-boiled /ˌ·· ·ˈ·◄/ adj **1** (of eggs) boiled till the yellow part is hard **2** (of people) not showing feeling

hard ci·der /ˌ·· ˈ··/ n [U] alcoholic drink made from apples

hard cop·y /ˈ· ˌ··/ n [U] readable information from a computer, esp. printed on paper

hard-core /ˌhɑrdˈkɔr◄, -ˈkoʷr◄/ n [U] small unchanging group within an organization ♦ adj **1** very strongly following a particular belief or activity **2** showing or describing sexual activity in a very detailed way: hardcore pornography

hard cur·ren·cy /ˌ·· ·ˈ···/ n [C;U] money that can be freely exchanged

hard·en /ˈhɑrdn/ vi/t make or become hard or firm

harden to phr vt make (someone) less sensitive to (something or doing something)

hard·head·ed /ˌhɑrdˈhɛdɪd◄/ adj strong in mind, practical

hard-heart·ed /ˌ·· ·ˈ··◄/ adj not kind or gentle

hard la·bor /ˌ· ˈ··/ n [U] (punishment which consists of) hard physical work such as digging, etc.

hard-line /ˌhɑrdˈlaɪn◄/ n firm unchanging opinion or attitude **hard-liner** n

hard luck /ˌ·· ·ˈ·/ n [U] bad luck

hard·ly /ˈhɑrdliʸ/ adv **1** almost not: I can hardly wait. **2** not at all: You can hardly blame me.

hard-nosed /ˌ·· ·ˈ·◄/ adj infml determined to get what one wants

hard of hear·ing /ˌ·· · ˈ··/ adj partly DEAF

hard-pressed /ˌ·· ·ˈ·◄/ adj experiencing severe or continual difficulties

hard sell /ˌ· ˈ·◄/ n [U] method of selling by putting pressure on buyers

hard·ship /ˈhɑrdˌʃɪp/ n [C;U] difficult conditions of life, such as lack of money, food, etc.

hard·ware /ˈhɑrdwɛər/ n [U] 1 pans, tools, etc., for the home 2 machinery which makes up a COMPUTER 3 machinery used in war

hardware store /ˈ·· ˌ·/ n store that sells hardware

hard·wear·ing /ˌhɑrdˈwɛərɪŋ◄/ adj (of clothes, etc.) that last a long time

hard·wood /ˈhɑrdwʊd/ n [U] strong wood from trees that lose their leaves in the fall

har·dy /ˈhɑrdiʸ/ adj able to bear cold, hard work, etc. **–diness** n [U]

hare /hɛər/ n animal like a large rabbit that can run quickly

hare·brained /ˈhɛərbreʸnd/ adj impractical; foolish

hare·lip /ˈhɛərˌlɪp/ n top lip divided into 2 parts

har·em /ˈhɛərəm, ˈhærəm/ n (women living in) the women's part of a Muslim house

hark /hɑrk/ vi lit listen

hark back phr vi talk about the past

harm /hɑrm/ n [U] 1 damage; injury (INJURE) 2 **out of harm's way** safe ♦ vt cause harm to **~ful** adj **– less** adj not dangerous

har·mon·i·ca /hɑrˈmɑnɪkə/ n musical instrument played by moving the mouth up and down it and blowing

har·mo·ni·um /hɑrˈmoʷniʸəm/ n musical instrument like a piano, worked by pumped air

har·mo·nize /ˈhɑrməˌnaɪz/ vi/t 1 (cause to) be in agreement, esp. in style, color, etc. 2 sing or play in musical HARMONY

har·mo·ny /ˈhɑrməniʸ/ n 1 [C;U] musical notes pleasantly combined 2 [U] peaceful agreement 3 [C;U] pleasant combination of colors, etc.

har·ness /ˈhɑrnɪs/ n [C;U] 1 leather bands, etc., that fasten a horse to a cart 2 similar arrangement for tying someone to something: *safety harness* ♦ vt 1 fasten with a harness 2 use (wind, water, etc.) to produce esp. electrical power

harp¹ /hɑrp/ n large musical instrument with strings played with the fingers **~ist** n

harp² v **harp on** phr vt talk a lot about (one's misfortunes)

har·poon /hɑrˈpuʷn/ vt, n (strike with) a spear on a rope, for hunting WHALES, etc.

harp·si·chord /ˈhɑrpsɪˌkɔrd/ n kind of early piano

har·row·ing /ˈhæroʷɪŋ/ adj causing painful feelings

har·ry /ˈhæriʸ/ vt fml trouble continually

harsh /hɑrʃ/ adj 1 painful to the senses: *harsh light* 2 cruel **~ly** adv **~ness** n [U]

har·vest /ˈhɑrvɪst/ n 1 (time of) gathering the crops 2 amount of crops gathered ♦ vt gather (crops)

has /s, z, əz, həz; strong hæz/ v 3rd pers. sing. pres. t. of HAVE

has-been /ˈ· ·/ n derog person or thing no longer popular or respected

hash /hæʃ/ n [U] 1 meal of (recooked) cut up meat and potatoes 2 **make a hash of something** do something badly 3 infml HASHISH

hash-browns /ˌhæʃˈbraʊnz/ n [P] potatoes cut in very small thin pieces, cooked until brown

hash·ish /ˈhæʃiʸʃ, hæʃˈiʸʃ/ n [U] strongest form of the drug CANNABIS

has·n't /ˈhæzənt/ v short for: has not

has·sle /ˈhæsəl/ n infml a lot of trouble ♦ vi/t cause trouble or difficulties for

haste /heʸst/ n [U] quick movement, or action

has·ten /ˈheʸsən/ vi/t 1 fml hurry 2 be quick (to say): *I hasten to add that no one was hurt.*

hast·y /ˈheʸstiʸ/ adj 1 (too) quickly 2 (of people) too quick in acting or deciding **–ily** adv

hat /hæt/ n 1 covering for the head 2 **keep (something) under one's hat** keep (something) secret 3 **take one's hat off to** show admiration for 4 **talking through one's hat** saying something stupid – see also OLD HAT **–ter** n maker of hats

hatch¹ /hæʧ/ v 1 vi/t (cause to) be born from an egg 2 vt form (a plan)

hatch² n (cover over) a hole in a wall or floor

hatch·back /ˈhæʧbæk/ n car with a door at the back that opens upwards

hatch·et /ˈhæʧɪt/ n 1 small AX 2 **bury the hatchet** become friends again after a bad quarrel

hatchet job /ˈ·· ˌ·/ n cruel attack in speech or writing

hate /heʸt/ vt 1 dislike very much 2 be sorry: *I hate to tell you.* ♦ n [C;U] strong dislike **~ful** adj very unpleasant **~fully** adv

ha·tred /ˈheʸtrɪd/ n [S;U] hate

haugh·ty /ˈhɔtiʸ/ adj too proud; ARROGANT **–tily** adv **–tiness** n [U]

haul /hɔl/ vi/t 1 pull with effort 2 pull with a vehicle ♦ n 1 a amount of fish caught b amount of something gained, esp. stolen goods 2 distance that something travels or is carried: *the long haul home*

haul off *phr v* **1** prepare to strike: *He hauled off and punched him.* **2** take away

haul·age /ˈhɔːlɪdʒ/ *n* [U] **1** carrying of goods by road **2** charge for this

haunch /hɔːntʃ, hɑːntʃ/ *n* fleshy part of the body between the waist and knee

haunt /hɔːnt/ *vt* **1** (of a spirit) appear in **2** visit regularly **3** remain in the thoughts of: *haunted by the memory | haunting tune* ♦ *n* place often visited

have¹ /v, əv, həv; *strong* hæv/ *v aux, pres. t. I/you/we/they* **have**, *he/she/it* **has** /z, əz, həz; *strong* hæz/; *past t.* **had** /d, əd, həd; *strong* hæd/ **1 a** (forms perfect tenses): *I've/I have finished.* **b** Had (I, he, etc.) if (I, he, etc.) had: *Had I known, I would have stayed.* **2** had better (do/not do) ought (not) to: *You'd better tell him about it.* **3** have (got) to be forced to; must: *I'll have to wash it.* **4** have had it *infml* have experienced, worked, etc., all one can: *I've had it! Let's go home.*

have² *vt* **1** also **have got** — possess: *She has/has got two sisters.* **2** experience or enjoy: *to have a party/a vacation* **3** receive: *I had some good news today.* **4** eat, drink, or smoke: *I had a cigarette.* **5** ask (someone) to one's home: *We're having some people around/over for drinks.* **6** allow: *I won't have all this noise.* **7** cause to be done: *You should have your hair cut.* **8** give birth to: *to have twins* **9** have done with finish **10** have it in for be as unkind as possible to **11** have one's eyes on watch continuously **12** have to do with have a connection with

have on *phr vt* **1** be wearing **2** have arranged to do **3** have (unfavourable information) recorded against (someone) **4** have nothing on be not nearly as good as

have out *phr vt* **1** get (a tooth or organ) removed **2** settle by argument: *have the whole thing out with Bill*

ha·ven /ˈheɪvən/ *n* calm safe place

have·n't /ˈhævənt/ *v short for:* have not

hav·oc /ˈhævək/ *n* [U] widespread damage

hawk¹ /hɔːk/ *n* **1** bird that catches creatures for food **2** person who believes in use of force, esp. military

hawk² *vt* sell (goods) on the street or at the doors of houses

hay /heɪ/ *n* [U] dried grass for animal food

hay fe·ver /ˈ·ˌ··/ *n* [U] illness like a bad cold, caused by breathing in POLLEN from the air

hay·stack /ˈheɪstæk/ *n* large pile of stored hay

hay·wire /ˈheɪwaɪər/ *adj* go haywire (of plans, etc.) become badly disordered

haz·ard /ˈhæzərd/ *n* danger; risk ♦ *vt* **1** offer (a guess or suggestion) **2** put in danger ~ **ous** *adj* dangerous

haze /heɪz/ *n* [S;U] light mist **hazy** *adj* **1** misty **2** uncertain: *I'm hazy about the details.* ♦ *vt* play tricks on (a FRESHMAN)

ha·zel /ˈheɪzəl/ *n, adj* light greenish brown: *hazel eyes*

H-bomb /ˈeɪtʃ bɑːm/ *n* HYDROGEN BOMB

he /iː, *strong* hiː/ *pron* (used for the male subject of a sentence)

head¹ /hed/ *n* **1** [C] part of the body containing the eyes, mouth, and brain **2** [*the* S] end where this rests: *the head of the bed* **3** [C] mind: *Don't put ideas into his head.* **4** [S] **a** ability: *no head for figures* **b** the power to be in control of oneself: *to keep/lose one's head in a crisis* **5** ruler; chief: *heads of state* **6** [(*the*) S] **a** top: *head of a hammer/a page/the stairs* **b** front: *head of a procession* **7** [S] pressure of steam or water **8** **a/per head** for each person: *cost $5 a head* **9** above/over one's head too hard to understand **10** bring/come to a head reach a point where something must be done **11** eat/shout, etc., one's head off *infml* eat/shout, etc., too much, loudly, etc. **12** go to one's head: **a** make one drunk **b** make one (or someone) too excited **c** make someone too proud **13** head and shoulders above very much better than **14** head over heels: **a** turning over headfirst **b** completely: *head over heels in love* **15** make head or tail of manage to understand **16** out of one's head *infml* crazy **17** put our/your/their heads together think out a plan with other people **18** turn someone's head: **a** make someone too proud **b** make someone fall in love **heads** *n* [U] front of a coin

head² *v* **1** *vt* be at the top or front of: *head a procession* **2** *vt* be the best at something **3** *vi* go somewhere: *head north/towards Rome/for the bar* **4** be the chief, director, etc.: *to head the department*

head off *phr vt* **1** cause to change direction **2** prevent

head·ache /ˈhedeɪk/ *n* **1** pain in the head **2** problem

head·dress /ˈhed dres/ *n* decorative head covering

head·first /ˌhedˈfɜːrst/ *adj, adv* with the rest of the body following the head

head·gear /ˈhɛdgɪər/ n [U] covering for the head

head·hunt·er /ˈhɛdˌhʌntər/ n person who tries to find suitable people for important jobs

head·ing /ˈhɛdɪŋ/ n words written as a title at the top of a page

head·land /ˈhɛdlənd, -lænd/ n piece of land sticking out into the sea

head·light /ˈhɛdlaɪt/ n strong light on the front of a vehicle

head·line /ˈhɛdlaɪn/ n 1 heading above a newspaper story 2 main point of the news on radio

head·long /ˈhɛdlɔŋ, ˌhɛdˈlɔŋ◂/ adj, adv 1 HEADFIRST 2 in foolish haste

head-on /ˌ·ˈ·◂/ adv, adj with the front parts meeting, usu. violently: a head-on collision

head·phones /ˈhɛdfoʷnz/ n [P] listening apparatus that fits over the ears

head·quar·ters /ˈhɛdˌkwɔrtərz/ n –ters also HQ central office of an organization

head·rest /ˈhɛd-rɛst/ n support for the head

head·room /ˈhɛd-ruʷm, -rʊm/ n [U] space to stand or move under something

head start /ˌ· ˈ·/ n [S] advantage in a race or competition

head·stone /ˈhɛdstoʷn/ n stone marking the top end of a grave

head·strong /ˈhɛdstrɔŋ/ adj uncontrollable; impatient

head·way /ˈhɛdweʸ/ n make headway advance; make PROGRESS

head·wind /ˈhɛdˌwɪnd/ n wind blowing directly against one

head·y /ˈhɛdiʸ/ adj 1 making one drunk 2 exciting

heal /hiʸl/ vi/t make or become healthy again ~er n

health /hɛlθ/ n [U] 1 state of being well, without disease 2 condition of body or mind: in poor health 3 TOAST (2): to drink someone's health ~y adj 1 physically strong 2 producing good health 3 showing good health: (fig.) healthy profits

heap /hiʸp/ n untidy pile ♦ vt pile up: heap food on the plate **heaps** n [P] infml lots: heaps of time

hear /hɪər/ v **heard** /hɜrd/ 1 vi/t receive (sounds) with the ears 2 vt be told or informed: I hear they're married. 3 vt listen to with attention: A priest heard my confession. 4 consider (a case) officially as a judge 5 won't/wouldn't hear of refuse(s) to allow

hear from phr vt receive news from, esp. by letter

hear of phr vt know about: I've never heard of him.

hear out phr vt listen to, till the end

hear·ing /ˈhɪərɪŋ/ n 1 [U] ability to hear sound 2 [U] distance at which one can hear 3 [C;U] act or experience of hearing 4 [C] chance to explain 5 [C] law trial of a case

hearing aid /ˈ··ˌ·/ n small electric apparatus to improve hearing

hear·say /ˈhɪərseʸ/ n [U] things heard but unproved

hearse /hɜrs/ n car for carrying a body to a funeral

heart /hɑrt/ n 1 [C] organ that pumps blood around the body 2 [C] center of a person's feelings: a kind heart | My heart bled (= I was very sorry) for him. 3 [C] something shaped like a heart 4 [C] center: heart of a lettuce/of the city/of the matter 5 [C] red figure in the shape of a heart, on a playing card 6 [U] courage: take/lose heart 7 after one's own heart of the kind that one likes 8 break someone's/one's heart make/become very unhappy 9 by heart from memory 10 eat one's heart out be very troubled 11 from the (bottom of one's) heart with real feeling 12 have one's heart in the right place be a kind person 13 lose one's heart to fall in love with 14 set one's heart on want very much 15 take something to heart feel it deeply

heart·ache /ˈhɑrteʸk/ n [U] deep sorrow

heart at·tack /ˈ· ·ˌ·/ n dangerous condition in which the heart beats irregularly and painfully

heart·beat /ˈhɑrtbiʸt/ n [C;U] pumping movement of the heart

heart·break /ˈhɑrtbreʸk/ n terrible sorrow **–ing** adj causing heartbreak

heart·brok·en /ˈhɑrtˌbroʷkən/ adj BROKEN-HEARTED

heart·burn /ˈhɑrtbɜrn/ n [U] unpleasant feeling of burning in the chest, caused by INDIGESTION

heart·en /ˈhɑrtn/ vt encourage

heart·felt /ˈhɑrtfɛlt/ adj sincere

hearth /hɑrθ/ n area around the fire in a home

heart·land /ˈhɑrtlænd/ n 1 central and most important area 2 the MID-WEST

heart·less /ˈhɑrtlɪs/ adj cruel ~ly adv ~ness n [U]

heart-rend·ing /ˈhɑrtˌrɛndɪŋ/ adj causing great pity ~ly adv

heart·strings /ˈhɑrtˌstrɪŋz/ n [P] deepest feelings of love and pity

heart·throb /ˈhɑrtθrɑb/ n infml 1 person who is very attractive and with whom others fall in love 2 person whom one loves: his latest heartthrob

heart-to-heart /ˌ·· ˈ·◄/ n open talk about personal details **heart-to-heart** adj

heart·warm·ing /ˈhɑrtˌwɔrmɪŋ/ adj causing pleasant feelings: *heart-warming response*

heart·y /ˈhɑrtiʸ/ adj **1** friendly and cheerful **2** healthy **3** (of meals) large −**ily** adv in a hearty way

heat¹ /hiʸt/ n **1** (U) (degree of) hotness **2** (U) hot weather: *I don't like the heat much.* **3** (U) great excitement **4** (C) part of a race, those who win then racing against others **5 in heat** (of female dogs, etc.) in a state of sexual excitement − see also WHITE HEAT

heat² vi/t make or become hot ~**ed** adj excited and angry ~**er** n machine for heating air or water ~**ing** n (U) system for keeping rooms warm

hea·then /ˈhiʸðən/ n, adj (person) not belonging to one of the large established religions

heath·er /ˈhɛðər/ n (U) plant which has small pink or purple flowers

heat·stroke /ˈhiʸtstroʷk/ n (U) SUN-STROKE

heat wave /ˈ· ·/ n period of unusually hot weather

heave /hiʸv/ v **1** vi/t pull or lift with effort **2** vt throw (something heavy) **3** vi rise and fall regularly **4** vi VOMIT **5 heave a sigh** SIGH

heav·en /ˈhɛvən/ n **1** home of God or the gods **2** (usu. cap.) God: *Heaven help you!* | *Good heavens!* **3** (C usu. pl.) the sky **4** (U) wonderful place or state **5 move heaven and earth** do everything possible (to cause or prevent something) − see also SEVENTH HEAVEN

heav·en·ly /ˈhɛvənliʸ/ adj **1** of heaven: *The moon is a* **heavenly body**. **2** wonderful

heav·y¹ /ˈhɛviʸ/ adj **1** of great weight **2** of unusual amount: *heavy rain/traffic* | *a heavy smoker* (= someone who smokes a lot) **3** needing effort: *heavy work* **4** serious and dull: *heavy reading* **5** (of food) too solid **6** (of the sea) with big waves **7 find it heavy going** find it very difficult **8 make heavy weather of something** make a job or problem seem more difficult than it really is ♦ adv in a troublesome, dull way −**ily** adv −**iness** n (U)

heav·y² n serious usu. male part in a play, etc., esp. a bad character

heav·y-du·ty /ˌ·· ˈ··◄/ adj (of clothes, machines, etc.) strong enough for rough treatment

heav·y-hand·ed /ˌ·· ˈ··◄/ adj **1** severe **2** awkward; not careful

heav·y·heart·ed /ˌhɛviʸ ˈhɑrtɪd◄/ adj sad

heavy in·dus·try /ˌ·· ˈ···/ n (U) industry that produces large goods, or materials such as coal, steel, etc., that are used in the production of other goods

heav·y·weight /ˈhɛviʸˌweʸt/ n, adj **1** (a FIGHTER) of the heaviest class in boxing (BOX²) **2** (a person or thing) **a** of more than average weight **b** having great importance or influence

He·brew /ˈhiʸbruʷ/ n (U) language of the ancient Jews and of modern Israel

heck·le /ˈhɛkəl/ vi/t interrupt (a speaker) disapprovingly at a meeting −**ler** n

hec·tare /ˈhɛktɛər/ n (a measure of area of land equal to) 10,000 square meters

hec·tic /ˈhɛktɪk/ adj full of hurry and excitement

hec·tor /ˈhɛktər/ vt BULLY

he'd /hiʸd; *strong* hiʸd/ *short for:* **1** he would **2** he had

hedge /hɛdʒ/ n **1** row of bushes dividing gardens or fields **2** protection: *a hedge against inflation* ♦ v **1** vt make a hedge around **2** vi refuse to answer directly **3 hedge one's bets** protect oneself against loss by favoring or supporting more than one side in a competition, etc.

he·don·is·m /ˈhiʸdnˌɪzəm/ n (U) idea that pleasure is the only important thing in life −**ist** n −**istic** /ˌhiʸdnˈɪstɪk◄/ adj

heed /hiʸd/ vt fml give attention to ♦ n (U) fml attention ~**less** adj

heel /hiʸl/ n **1** back of the foot **2** part of a shoe, sock, etc., which covers this, esp. the raised part of a shoe under the foot **3** unpleasant person, who treats others badly **4 at/on one's heels** close behind one **5 cool one's heels** rest **6 down at heel** (of people) untidy and looking poor **7 kick one's heels** not have anything particular to do ♦ v **1** vt put a heel on (a shoe) **2** vi (of a dog) follow closely

hef·ty /ˈhɛftiʸ/ adj big and powerful

he·gem·o·ny /hɪˈdʒɛməniʸ, -ˈgɛmˈhɛdʒəˌmoʷniʸ/ n (U) fml power of one state over others

heif·er /ˈhɛfər/ n young cow

height /haɪt/ n **1** (C;U) (degree of) being high **2** (C) measurement from top to bottom **3** (C) also **heights** pl. — high place **4** (S) **a** highest degree: *the height of fashion* **b** the main or most active point: *the height of the storm*

height·en /ˈhaɪtn/ vi/t make or become greater in degree

hei·nous /ˈheʸnəs/ adj fml (of wickedness) extreme

heir /ɛər/ **heiress** /ˈɛərɪs/ fem. —

person with the legal right to receive property, etc., when the owner dies

heir·loom /ˈɛərluːm/ *n* valuable object given by older members of a family to younger ones over many years

held /held/ *v past t. and p. of* HOLD

hel·i·cop·ter /ˈhelɪˌkɑptər/ *n* aircraft that flies by means of blades on top, which turn quickly

he·li·um /ˈhiːlɪəm/ *n* [U] very light gas used in AIRSHIPs, etc.

hell /hel/ *n* **1** [U] place where the wicked are said to be punished after death **2** [C] terrible place **3** [U] *sl* (used in anger or to give force): *What the hell's that?* | *That's a hell of a good car.* **4 for the hell of it** for fun **5 give someone hell** treat them roughly **6 hell to pay** *sl* serious trouble or punishment **7 like hell: a** very much: *I worked like hell all week.* **b** not at all: *'He paid, didn't he?' 'Like hell he did.'* **8 play hell with** cause damage to ♦ *interj* (an expression of) anger or disappointment ~**ish** *adj* terrible

he'll /ɪl, iʲl, hɪl; *strong* hiʲl/ *short for:* he will

hel·lo /həˈloʷ, heˈloʷ, ˈheloʷ/ *interj, n* **-los** (used in greeting and answering a telephone)

helm /helm/ *n* **1** wheel or TILLER that guides a ship **2 at the helm** in control

hel·met /ˈhelmɪt/ *n* protective head covering

help¹ /help/ *v* **1** *vi/t* make it possible for (someone) to do something; be useful to (someone) **2** *vt* avoid; prevent: *I can't help laughing.* | *It can't be helped.* (= these things happen) **3** *vt* give food, etc., to: *Help yourself to sugar.* | *He just helped himself to the money.* (= took) ~ **er** *n* person who helps ~**ing** *n* serving of food

help out *phr vi/t* give help (to someone) at a time of need

help² *n* **1** [U] act of helping; AID **2** [C] someone or something that helps **3 so help me** I am speaking the truth **4 Help!** Please bring help. ~**ful** *adj* useful ~**fully** *adv* ~**less** *adj* unable to look after oneself ~**lessly** *adv*

hem¹ /hem/ *n* edge of a skirt, etc., turned under and sewn

hem² *vt* **-mm-** put a hem on

hem in *phr vt* surround closely

hem·i·sphere /ˈhemәˌsfɪər/ *n* **1** half a SPHERE **2** half of the Earth: *the southern hemisphere*

hem·line /ˈhemlaɪn/ *n* length of a skirt or dress

he·mo·phil·i·a /ˌhiʲməˈfɪliʲә, -ˈfiʲljә/ *n* [U] disease that makes the sufferer bleed badly after only a

small cut **-ic** /-iʲ, æk/ *n* person suffering from hemophilia

hem·or·rhage /ˈheməridʒ/ *n* [C;U] flow of blood, esp. long and unexpected

hem·or·rhoid /ˈheməˌrɔɪd/ *n* swollen blood vessel at the lower end of the bowel

hemp /hemp/ *n* [U] plant used for making rope, rough cloth, and the drug CANNABIS

hen /hen/ *n* female bird, esp. the kind kept for its eggs on farms

hence /hens/ *adv fml* **1** for this reason **2** from here or now

hence·forth /ˈhensfɔrθ, -foʷrθ, ˌhensˈfɔrθ, -ˈfoʷrθ/, **-for·ward** /ˌhensˈfɔrwərd/ *adv fml* from now on

hench·man /ˈhentʃmәn/ *n* **-men** /-mən/ faithful supporter who may use violent methods

hen·na /ˈhenә/ *n* [U] red-brown DYE

hen·pecked /ˈhenpekt/ *adj* (of a man) too obedient to his wife

hep·a·ti·tis /ˌhepəˈtaɪtɪs/ *n* [U] serious disease of the LIVER

her /ər, hər; *strong* hɜr/ *pron* (used for the female object of a sentence) ♦ *determiner* of her: *her car* **hers** *pron* of her; her one(s): *It's hers.*

her·ald /ˈherәld/ *n* (in former times) person who brought important news ♦ *vt fml* be a sign of (something coming)

her·ald·ry /ˈherәldriʲ/ *n* [U] study of COATS of arms

herb /ɜrb, hɜrb/ *n* any plant used in medicine or to improve the taste of food ~**al** *adj* of herbs ~**alist** *n* person who uses herbs, esp. to treat disease

her·ba·ceous /hɜrˈbeʲʃәs, ɜr-/ *adj* (of a plant) having soft (not woody) stems: *a herbaceous border* (= border of such plants)

her·biv·o·rous /hɜrˈbɪvәrәs, ɜr-/ *adj* (of animals) which eat grass or plants

Her·cu·le·an /ˌhɜrkyәˈliʲәn, hɜrˈkyuʷliʲәn/ *adj* needing great strength or determination

herd /hɜrd/ *n* **1** group of animals together **2** people generally, thought of as acting all alike ♦ *vt* drive in a herd: (fig.) *to herd tourists into a bus*

here /hɪər/ *adv* **1** εt, in, or to this place: *'It's Professor Worth here.'* (= speaking on the telephone) **2** at this point: *Here we agree.* **3 here and there** scattered about **4 Here goes!** Now I'm going to have a try. **5 Here's to** (said when drinking a TOAST (2)) **6 neither here nor there** not connected with the matter being talked about

here·a·bouts /ˈhɪərəˌbaʊts/ *adv* somewhere near here

here·af·ter /ˌhɪərˈæftər/ *adv fml* in

the future ♦ *n* [S] life after death

here·by /ˌhɪərˈbaɪ, ˈhɪərbaɪ/ *adv fml* by this means

he·red·i·ta·ry /həˈredəˌteriʲ/ *adj* passed down from parent to child

he·red·i·ty /həˈredətiʲ/ *n* [U] fact that qualities are passed on from parent to child

here·in /ˌhɪərˈɪn/ *adv fml* in this

her·e·sy /ˈherəsiʲ/ *n* [C;U] belief that goes against what is officially accepted

her·e·tic /ˈherətɪk/ *n* person guilty of heresy — **al** /həˈretɪkəl/ *adj*

here·with /ˌhɪərˈwɪθ, -ˈwɪð/ *adv fml* with this

her·i·tage /ˈherətɪdʒ/ *n* something passed down within a family or nation

her·mit /ˈhɜrmɪt/ *n* person who lives alone, esp. for religious reasons

her·mit·age /ˈhɜrmətɪdʒ/ *n* hermit's home

her·ni·a /ˈhɜrniʲə/ *n* [C;U] conditions in which an organ, esp. the bowel, pushes through its covering wall

he·ro /ˈhɪəroʷ/ **heroine** /ˈheroʷɪn/ *fem.* — *n* **-roes** **1** someone admired for bravery etc. **2** most important character in a story — **ic** /hɪˈroʷɪk/ *adj* very brave — **ically** /-kliʲ/ *adv* — **ics** *n* [P] grand speech or actions that mean nothing — **ism** /ˈheroʷˌɪzəm/ *n* [U] courage

her·o·in /ˈheroʷɪn/ *n* [U] drug made from MORPHINE

her·pes /ˈhɜrpiʲz/ *n* [U] very infectious skin disease

her·ring /ˈherɪŋ/ *n* sea fish used for food — see also RED HERRING

her·ring·bone /ˈherɪŋˌboʷn/ *n* [U] pattern of Vs, esp. in material

her·self /ərˈself; strong hərˈself/ *pron* **1** (*reflexive form of* **she**): She hurt herself. **2** (*strong form of* **she**):She ate it herself. **3** (**all**) **by herself**: **a** alone **b** without help **4 to herself** not shared

he's /iʲz; strong hiʲz/ short for: **1** he is **2** he has

hes·i·tant /ˈhezətənt/ *adj* tending to hesitate — **tancy** *n* [U]

hes·i·tate /ˈhezəˌteʲt/ *vi* **1** pause because one is uncertain **2** be unwilling — **tation** /ˌhezəˈteʲʃən/ *n* [C;U]

het·e·ro·dox /ˈhetərəˌdɑks/ *adj* (of beliefs, etc.) against accepted opinion

het·e·ro·ge·ne·ous /ˌhetərəˈdʒiʲniʲəs, -ˈdʒiʲnyəs/ *adj fml* of many different kinds

het·e·ro·sex·u·al /ˌhetərəˈsekʃuʷəl◂/ *adj* attracted to people of the other sex — **ity** /ˌhetərəˌsekʃuʷˈælətiʲ/ *n* [U]

het up /ˌhet ˈʌp/ *adj sl* nervous and excited

hew /hyuʷ/ *vi/t* **hewed**, **hewed** or **hewn** /hyuʷn/ *fml* cut with a heavy tool

hex·a·gon /ˈheksəˌgɑn/ *n* figure with 6 sides — **al** /hekˈsægənəl/ *adj*

hey·day /ˈheʲdeʲ/ *n* [S] time of greatest success

hi /haɪ/ *interj infml* HELLO (= informal greeting)

hi·a·tus /haɪˈeʲtəs/ *n fml* space where something is missing

hi·ber·nate /ˈhaɪbərˌneʲt/ *vi* (of some animals) sleep during the winter — **nation** /ˌhaɪbərˈneʲʃən/ *n* [U]

hic·cup, hiccough /ˈhɪkəp/ *n* sudden stopping of the breath with a sharp sound **hiccup** *vi*

hick /hɪk/ *n infml* foolish person from the country

hide[1] /haɪd/ *v* **hid** /hɪd/, **hidden** /ˈhɪdn/ **1** *vt* put out of sight **2** *vi* keep oneself from being seen

hide[2] *n* **1** animal's skin **2 hide or/nor hair of** *infml* any sign of

hide·bound /ˈhaɪdbaʊnd/ *adj* not willing to consider new ideas

hid·e·ous /ˈhɪdiʲəs/ *adj* very ugly; very unpleasant to look at — **ly** *adv*

hide·out /ˈhaɪdaʊt/ also **hide·a·way** /ˈhaɪdəˌweɪ/ — *n* place where one can go to avoid people

hid·ing[1] /ˈhaɪdɪŋ/ *n* beating

hid·ing[2] *n* [U] state of being hidden: go into hiding

hi·er·ar·chy /ˈhaɪəˌrɑrkiʲ/ *n* [C;U] organization with higher and lower ranks

hi·e·ro·glyph·ics /ˌhaɪərəˈglɪfɪks/ *n* [P] writing that uses pictures, as in ancient Egypt

hi·fi /haɪ ˈfaɪ/ *n* **hi-fis** equipment for playing recorded sound

high[1] /haɪ/ *adj* **1** far above the ground: a high mountain | 20 feet high **2** great: high cost **3** good: high standards **4** (of a musical note) not deep **5** (of time) as the middle point: high summer | It's high time we were going. (= We should go at once.) **6** *infml* under the influence of drink or drugs ♦ *n* **1** high point or level: Sales are at an all-time high. **2** state of great excitement: on a high — **ly** *adv* **1** very: highly amused **2** very well: highly paid

high[2] *adv* **1** to or at a high level: aim high **2** feelings ran high people got excited and angry **3 high and dry** deserted **4 high and low** everywhere

high-and-might·y /ˌ· · ˈ···◂/ *adj infml* too proud and certain of one's own importance

high·brow /ˈhaɪbraʊ/ *n, adj* (person) knowing a lot about art, books, etc.

high·chair /ˈhaɪtʃeər/ *n* seat for feeding a small child

high-class /ˌ· '·◂/ *adj* **1** of good quality **2** of high social position

higher ed·u·ca·tion /ˌ·· ·'···/ *n* [U] education at a university or college

higher-up /ˌ·· '·◂/ *n* more important official person

high fi·del·i·ty /ˌ·· ·'···/ also **hi-fi** — *adj* able to play sound almost perfectly

high-fli·er, -flyer /ˌ·· '··/ *n* **1** clever person who has high aims **2** stock of high value

high-grade /ˌ· '·◂/ *adj* of high quality

high-hand·ed /ˌ·· '···◂/ *adj* using power too forcefully

high horse /'·· ·, ·'·/ *n* **on one's high horse** *infml derog* behaving as if one knows best, or more than others

high jump /'·· ·/ *n* [S] sport of jumping over a bar

high-lev·el /ˌ·· '···◂/ *adj* in or at a position of high importance

high-life /'·· ·/ *n* enjoyable life of the rich and fashionable

high·light /'haɪlaɪt/ *n* **1** most important detail **2** lightest area on a picture, or in the hair ♦ *vt* throw attention onto

high point /'·· ·/ *n* most remembered part of an activity, esp. because pleasant

highly-strung /ˌ··· '·◂/ *adj* nervous; excitable

high-mind·ed /ˌ·· '···◂/ *adj* having high principles

High·ness /'haɪnɪs/ *n* (title of some royal persons)

high-pow·ered /ˌ·· '···◂/ *adj* having great force or ability

high-rise /'·· ·/ *adj, n* (building) with many floors

high school /'·· ·/ *n* school for children in GRADES 9-12

high seas /ˌ· '·/ *n* [the+P] oceans that do not belong to any particular country

high-sea·son /ˌ·· '···◂/ *n* [U] time of year when business is greatest and prices are highest

high-spir·it·ed /ˌ·· '····◂/ *adj* active and fond of adventure

high tech·nol·o·gy /ˌ·· ·'····◂/ *n* [U] use of the most modern machines, processes, etc., in business or industry **high tech**, **hi-tech** *adj*

high·way /'haɪweʸ/ *n* broad main road with rapid traffic

high·way·man /'haɪweʸmən/ *n* -**men** /-mən/ (in former times) man who used to stop people on the roads and rob them

hi·jack /'haɪdʒæk/ *vt* **1** take control of (esp. an aircraft) by force **2** stop and rob (a train, etc.) ~**er** *n*

hike /haɪk/ *vi, n* (go for) a long country walk ♦ *vt* increase: *They've hiked the prices.* **hiker** *n*

hi·lar·i·ous /hɪ'leəriʸəs, -'lær-/ *adj* full of or causing laughter ~**ly** *adv*

hi·lar·i·ty /hɪ'lærətiʸ, -'leər-/ *n* [U] cheerful laughter

hill /hɪl/ *n* **1** raised piece of land, not as high as a mountain **2** slope on a road, etc. ~**y** *adj*

hill·bil·ly /'hɪl,bɪliʸ/ *n* derog someone from a mountain area

hilt /hɪlt/ *n* **1** handle of a sword **2** (**up**) **to the hilt** completely

him /ɪm; *strong* hɪm/ *pron* (used for the male object of a sentence)

him·self /ɪm'self; *strong* hɪm'self/ *pron* **1** (*reflexive form of* **he**): *He shot himself.* **2** (*strong form of* **he**): *He made it himself.* **3** (**all**) **by himself:** **a** alone **b** without help **4 to himself** not shared

hind /haɪnd/ *adj* (of animals' legs) back

hin·der /'hɪndər/ *vt* delay the PROGRESS of ~**drance** *n* [C;U]

hind·most /'haɪndmoʷst/ *adj* furthest behind

hind·quar·ters /'haɪnd,kwɔrtərz/ *n* [P] animal's back legs

hind·sight /'haɪndsaɪt/ *n* [U] ability to understand the past, and esp. what went wrong

Hin·du /'hɪnduʷ/ *n* -**dus** person whose religion is Hinduism **Hindu** *adj*

Hin·du·is·m /'hɪnduʷ,ɪzəm/ *n* [U] chief religion of India, noted for its CASTE system and belief in reincarnation (REINCARNATE)

hinge¹ /hɪndʒ/ *n* metal joint on which a door, etc., swings

hinge² *vt* fix on hinge

hinge on/upon *phr vt* depend on

hint /hɪnt/ *n* **1** small or indirect suggestion: (fig.) *There's a hint of summer in the air.* **2** useful advice ♦ *vi/t* suggest indirectly

hin·ter·land /'hɪntər,lænd/ *n* [S] inner part of a country

hip /hɪp/ *n* fleshy part where the legs join the body

hip·pie -py /'hɪpiʸ/ *n* (young) person with long hair who is against the standards of ordinary society

hip·po·pot·a·mus /ˌhɪpə'pɒtəməs/ also **hip·po** /'hɪpoʷ/ — *n* -**muses** *or* -**mi** /-maɪ/ large African river animal

hire /haɪər/ *vt* get the use or services of something or someone for wages or payment: *hire a teacher* ♦ *n* person or thing hired: *new hires*

his /ɪz; *strong* hɪz/ *determiner* of him: *his shoes* ♦ *pron* of him; his one(s): *It's his.*

hiss /hɪs/ *vi/t* make a sound like 's', esp. to show disapproval **hiss** *n*

his·to·ri·an /hɪˈstɔriⁱən, -ˈstoʷr-/ n person who studies history

his·tor·ic /hɪˈstɔrɪk, -ˈstar-/ adj important in history: an historic event

his·tor·i·cal /hɪˈstɔrɪkəl, -ˈstar-/ adj about history: historical research/novels ~**ly** /-kliⁱ/ adv

his·to·ry /ˈhɪstəriⁱ/ n 1 [U] study of past events 2 [C] account of past events 3 [C] record of someone's past: her medical history 4 **make history** do something important which will be remembered – see also NATURAL HISTORY

his·tri·on·ics /ˌhɪstriⁱˈanɪks/ n [P] insincere behavior, like a theatrical performance **histrionic** adj

hit¹ /hɪt/ vt hit, pres. p. **hitting** 1 come, or bring something, hard against: He hit the ball with the bat.| The car hit the wall. 2 reach: hit the main road 3 have a bad effect on 4 **hit it off** have a good relationship 5 **hit the bottle** infml drink too much alcohol 6 **hit the nail on the head** say or do the right thing 7 **hit the road** infml start on a journey 8 **hit the roof** show or express great anger 9 **hit the spot** satisfy completely

hit back phr vi reply forcefully to an attack on oneself

hit on/upon phr vt find by chance

hit out at/against phr vt attack in words

hit up phr v infml (ask to) borrow: He hit me up for $10.

hit² n 1 blow 2 successful performance

hit-and-miss /ˌ·· ˈ·/ adj depending on chance

hitch /hɪtʃ/ v 1 vt fasten by hooking a rope or metal part on something 2 vi hitchhike 3 **get hitched** get married ♦ n 1 difficulty or delay 2 kind of knot

hitch up phr vt pull up into place

hitch·hike /ˈhɪtʃhaɪk/ vi travel by getting rides in other people's cars **hitchhiker** n

hi-tech /ˌhaɪ ˈtɛk/ adj of or using HIGH TECHNOLOGY

hith·er·to /ˌhɪðərˈtuʷ, ˈhɪðərˌtuʷ/ adv fml until now

hit list /ˈ· ·/ n infml list of people or organizations against whom some (bad) action is planned

hit man /ˈ· ·/ n criminal who is employed to kill someone

hit-or-miss /ˌ·· ˈ·/ adj HIT-AND-MISS

hit pa·rade /ˈ· ·ˌ·/ n list of popular songs in the order of the numbers which are sold of each

HIV /ˌeⁱtʃ aɪ ˈviⁱ/ n [(the) S] VIRUS carried in the blood that often develops into the disease AIDS: He's HIV positive. (=He has the HIV virus.)

hive¹ /haɪv/ n 1 box, etc., where bees are kept 2 very busy place

hive² v **hive off** phr vt make separate from a larger organization

HMO /ˌeⁱtʃ ɛm ˈoʷ/ n health maintenance organization, a kind of health care like insurance

hoard /hɔrd, hoʷrd/ n (secret) store of something valuable ♦ vt save; store, esp. secretly

hoarse /hɔrs, hoʷrs/ adj (of a voice) sounding rough ~**ly** adv ~**ness** n [U]

hoar·y /ˈhɔriⁱ, ˈhoʷriⁱ/ adj (of hair) white with age: (fig.) hoary old jokes

hoax /hoʷks/ n trick to deceive someone **hoax** vt

hob·ble /ˈhabəl/ n 1 vi walk with difficulty 2 vt tie 2 legs of (a horse)

hob·by /ˈhabiⁱ/ n pleasant activity for one's free time

hob·by·horse /ˈhabiⁱˌhɔrs/ n 1 children's toy like a horse's head on a stick 2 fixed idea to which a person keeps returning in conversation

hob·nail /ˈhabneⁱl/ n heavy nail in the SOLE of a boot or shoe

hob·nob /ˈhabnab/ vi -**bb**- have a social relationship (with)

ho·bo /ˈhoʷboʷ/ n person who has no home or work

hock¹ /hak/ n lower part of leg of a pig, horse, cow, etc.

hock² vt sl for PAWN²

hock·ey /ˈhakiⁱ/ n [U] game played by two teams of 11 players each, with sticks and a ball see also ICE HOCKEY, FIELD HOCKEY

ho·cus-po·cus /ˌhoʷkəs ˈpoʷkəs/ n derog [U] trick

hod /had/ n box on a stick, for carrying bricks

hodge-podge /ˈhadʒpadʒ/ n confused mixture

hoe /hoʷ/ n garden tool for breaking up the soil **hoe** vi/t

hog /hɔg, hag/ n 1 pig 2 person who eats too much 3 **go the whole hog** infml do something thoroughly – see also ROAD HOG ♦ vt take and keep (all of something) for oneself

hogs·head /ˈhɔgzhɛd, ˈhagz-/ n large barrel for beer, etc.

hog·wash /ˈhɔgwɔʃ, ˈhagwaʃ/ n [U] stupid talk; nonsense

hoist /hɔɪst/ vt pull up on a rope ♦ n 1 upward push 2 apparatus for lifting heavy goods

hold¹ /hoʷld/ v **held** /hɛld/ 1 vt keep in the hands, etc. 2 vt keep in a particular position: hold one's head up | Hold it! (= don't move) 3 vt support: The branch won't hold me. 4 vt not allow to leave: The police held 2 men. 5 vt not use: hold one's breath 6 vt defend against attack 7 vi remain unchanged: *What I said still holds.* **8** *vt* have room for: *The theater holds 500.* **9** *vt* possess: *hold the office of chairman* **10** *vt* believe **11** *vt* cause to happen: *hold an election* **12** *vt* keep (the interest or attention) of (someone) **13 hold court** receive admirers in a group **14 hold good** be true **15 Hold it!** *infml* Don't move. **16 hold one's own** keep one's (strong) position **17 hold one's tongue** not talk **18 hold the line** keep a telephone connection **19 hold water** seem to be true

    hold against *phr vt* allow (something bad) to influence one's feelings about (someone)

    hold back *phr v* **1** *vt* control **2** *vt* keep secret **3** *vi* be unwilling to act

    hold down *phr vt* **1** keep in a low position **2** keep (a job)

    hold forth *phr vi* talk at length

    hold off *phr v* **1** *vt* keep at a distance **2** *vi/t* delay

    hold on *phr vi* **1** wait (esp. on the telephone) **2** continue in spite of difficulties

    hold onto *phr vt* keep possession of

    hold out *phr vi* **1** continue to exist; last **2** offer

    hold out for *phr vt* demand firmly and wait in order to get

    hold over *phr vt* POSTPONE

    hold to *phr vt* keep to: *I'll hold you to your promise.*

    hold up *phr vt* **1** delay **2** rob by force

    hold with *phr vt* approve of

hold² *n* **1** [U] holding **2** [C] something to hold, esp. in climbing **3** [C] influence

hold³ *n* bottom of a ship, where goods are stored

hold·er /ˈhoʷldər/ *n* **1** person who possesses something **2** container

hold·ings /ˈhoʷldɪŋz/ *n* [P] land, etc., that one possesses

hold·up /ˈhoʷldʌp/ *n* **1** delay, as in traffic **2** attempt at armed robbery

hole¹ /hoʷl/ *n* **1** empty space in something solid **2 a** home of a small animal **b** small unpleasant space for living in **3** *infml* difficult position **4** (in GOLF) hollow place in the ground into which the ball must be hit: *an 18-hole golf course* **5 make a hole in** *infml* use up a large part of **6 pick holes in** find faults in – see also BLACK HOLE

hole² *vt* **1** make a hole in **2** *vi/t* hit (the ball) into a hole in GOLF

    hole up *phr vi sl* hide as a means of escape

hol·i·day /ˈhɑləˌdeʸ/ *n* day fixed by law or custom when people don't go to work because they are celebrating something

hol·i·er-than-thou /ˌ···ˈ·/ *adj derog* thinking oneself to be morally better than other people

hol·i·ness /ˈhoʷliʸnɪs/ *n* [U] **1** being holy **2** (*cap.*) (title of the Pope)

ho·lis·tic /hoʷˈlɪstɪk/ *adj* concerning the whole of something or someone, not just its parts: *holistic medicine*

hol·ler /ˈhɑlər/ *vi* shout

hol·low /ˈhɑloʷ/ *adj* **1** having an empty space inside **2** lacking flesh: *hollow cheeks* **3** (of sounds) as if made by striking an empty container **4** insincere ♦ *n* **1** wide hole **2** small valley ♦ *vt* make hollow

hol·ly /ˈhɑliʸ/ *n* [C;U] tree whose red berries are used for Christmas decoration

hol·o·caust /ˈhɑləˌkɔst, ˈhoʷ-/ *n* great destruction and the loss of many lives, esp. by burning

hol·o·gram /ˈhoʷləˌgræm, ˈhɑ-/ *n* picture made with LASER light so that it appears to be solid rather than flat

hol·o·graph·y /hoʷˈlɑgrəfiʸ/ *n* [U] science of producing holograms

hol·ster /ˈhoʷlstər/ *n* leather holder for a PISTOL

ho·ly /ˈhoʷliʸ/ *adj* **1** connected with, or serving, religion **2** leading a pure and blameless life

hom·age /ˈhɑmɪdʒ, ˈɑ-/ *n* [U] *fml* signs of great respect

hom·burg /ˈhɑmbɜrg/ *n* man's soft hat

home¹ /hoʷm/ *n* **1** [C] place where one lives **2** [C;U] one's house and family: *She came from a poor home.* **3** [S] **a** place where a plant or animal is found **b** place where something was originally discovered, made or developed **4** [C] place for the care of people or animals: *an old people's home* **5** [U] (in sports) place which a player must try to reach **6 be/feel at home** feel comfortable **7 make oneself at home** behave freely **8 nothing to write home about** nothing special ~**less** *adj*

home² *adv* **1** to or at one's home: *go home* **2** to the right place: *strike a nail home* **3 bring/come home to one** make/become clearly understood **4 home free** *infml* having safely or successfully completed something

home³ *adj* **1** of or related to one's home or origin **2** not foreign **3** prepared or made in the home: *home grown* **4** (of a sports match) played at the place, sports field, etc., of one's home area

home⁴ *v* **home in on** *phr vt* aim exactly towards – see also HOMING

home·bo·dy /ˈhoʷmˌbɑdiʸ/ *n* person who likes to stay home

home·com·ing /'ho^wm‚kʌmɪŋ/ n **1** arrival home, esp. after a long absence **2** yearly event at a school or university

home·land /'ho^wmlænd/ n country where one was born

home·ly /'ho^wmli^y/ adj not attractive

home·mak·er /'ho^wm‚me^ykər/ n woman who looks after her children and home; HOUSEWIFE

ho·me·op·a·thy, homoeo- /‚ho^wmi^y-'apəθi^y/ n [U] system of treating disease with small amounts of substances that in larger amounts would produce a similar illness –**opathic** /‚ho^wmi^yə'pæθ1k◂/ adj

home·room /'ho^wmru^wm, -rʊm/ n room in a school where students in the same GRADE meet at certain times of the day

home run /‚· '·/ also **hom·er** /'ho^wmər/ — n a point in BASEBALL, made by hitting the ball so far that it is possible to run to each base

home·sick /'ho^wm‚sɪk/ adj unhappy because away from home **~ness** n [U]

home·stead /'ho^wmsted/ n land and its buildings given to a farmer (in former times)

home·wards /'ho^wmwərdz/ also **homeward** — adj going towards home

home·work /'ho^wmwɜrk/ n [C] **1** school work done outside the school **2** preparations done before taking part in an important activity

hom·ey, homy /'ho^wmi^y/ adj infml pleasant, like home

hom·i·cide /'hamə‚sa1d/ n [C;U] fml murder –**cidal** /‚hamə'sa1dl◂/ adj

hom·i·ly /'haməli^y/ n long speech on moral behavior

hom·ing /'ho^wmɪŋ/ adj of or having the ability to **a** guide oneself home **b** (of machines) guide themselves towards the place they are aimed at

ho·mo·ge·ne·ous /‚ho^wmə'dʒi^y-ni^yəs, -'dʒi^ynyəs, ‚ha-/ adj formed of parts of the same kind

ho·mo·ge·nize, -nise /hə'madʒə-‚na1z/ vt make (the parts of a whole, esp. a mixture) become evenly spread

ho·mo·sex·u·al /‚ho^wmə'sekʃu^wəl/ n, adj (person) sexually attracted to people of the same sex **~ity** /‚ho^wmə‚sekʃu^w'æləti^y/ n [U]

hon·est /'anɪst/ adj **1** not likely to lie or cheat **2** (of actions, etc.) showing these qualities **~ly** adv **1** in an honest way **2** really

hon·es·ty /'anəsti^y/ n [U] quality of being honest

hon·ey /'hʌni^y/ n **1** [U] sweet substance that bees make **2** [C] dearly loved person

hon·ey·comb /'hʌni^y‚ko^wm/ n wax structure that bees make to store honey

hon·ey·moon /'hʌni^y‚mu^wn/ n **1** vacation taken by 2 people who have just gotten married **2** short period of good relations, etc., at the beginning of a period in office, etc. ♦ vi spend one's honeymoon **honeymooner** n

honk /haŋk, hɔŋk/ vi, n (make) the sound of a car horn

hon·ky /'haŋki^y, 'hɔŋki^y/ n derog sl white person

hon·or·ar·y /'anə‚reri^y/ adj **1** (of a rank, etc.) given as an honor **2** unpaid: honorary chairman

hon·or /'anər/ n **1** [U] great public respect **2** [U] high standards of behavior: men of honor **3** [S] person or thing that brings pride: He's an honor to his parents. **4** [C] (cap.) (used as a title for a judge) ♦ vt **1** bring honor to **2** keep (an agreement) **honors** n [P] **1** marks of respect: full military honors **2** a university degree

hon·or·a·ble /'anərəbəl/ adj **1** bringing or showing honor **2** (cap.) (title for certain high officials, judges, etc.) –**bly** adv

honor roll /'·· ‚·/ n list of students with high grades

hood /hʊd/ n **1** covering for the head and neck **a** except the face, so that it can be pushed back **b** including the face, to avoid recognition **2** folding cover over a BUGGY², etc. **3** lid over the front of a car **4** young male who makes trouble

hood·wink /'hʊd‚wɪŋk/ vt deceive

hoof /hʊf, hu^wf/ n hoofs or hooves /hʊvz, hu^wvz/ horny foot of a horse, etc.

hook /hʊk/ n **1** curved piece of metal or plastic for catching, hanging, or fastening things **2** (in boxing (BOX²)) blow given with the elbow bent **3 by hook or by crook** by any means possible **4 off the hook** no longer in a difficult situation ♦ vt catch, hang, or fasten with a hook **~ed** adj **1** shaped like a hook **2** dependent (on drugs, etc.)

hook·er /'hʊkər/ n infml PROSTITUTE

hook·y /'hʊki^y/ n infml **play hooky** stay away from school without permission

hoo·li·gan /'hu^wlɪgən/ n noisy violent person who breaks things, etc. **~ism** n [U]

hoop /hu^wp, hʊp/ n circular band of wood or metal

hoop·la /'hu^wpla, 'hʊp-/ n [U] BALLYHOO

hoo·ray /hʊ're^y, hə're^y/ interj, n HURRAY

hoot /hu^wt/ n **1** sound made by an

OWL **2** shout of dislike **3** not care/ give a hoot/two hoots not care at all **4** very funny situation ♦ *vi/t* (cause to) make a hoot

hooves /huvz, hu^wvz/ *pl. of* HOOF

hop¹ /hap/ *vi* -pp- **1** (of people) jump on one leg **2** (of small creatures) jump **3** get into or onto a vehicle **4** Hop to! Hurry! ♦ *n* **1** jump **2** distance flown by a plane without landing

hop² *n* climbing plant used for giving taste to beer

hope /ho^wp/ *n* **1** [C;U] expectation that something good will happen **2** [C] expectation or thing that may bring success **3** beyond/past hope with no chance of success **4** hold out hope give encouragement ♦ *vi/t* wish and expect ~**ful** *adj* feeling or giving hope ~**fully** *adv* **1** in a hopeful way **2** if our hopes succeed ~**less** *adj* **1** feeling or giving no hope **2** not skilled: *hopeless at math* ~**lessly** *adv*

hop·per /'hapər/ *n* large FUNNEL for grain or coal

horde /hord, ho^wrd/ *n* large moving crowd

ho·ri·zon /hə'raɪzən/ *n* **1** line where the sky seems to meet the earth or sea **2** broaden one's horizons increase the range of one's experience

hor·i·zon·tal /ˌhorə'zantəl◂, ˌhar-/ *adj* flat; level ♦ *n* [C;U] a horizontal line, surface or position ~**ly** *adv*

hor·mone /'hormo^wn/ *n* substance produced in the body that influences growth, etc.

horn /horn/ *n* **1** [C] pointed growth on an animal's head **2** [U] material that this is made of: *horn-rimmed glasses* **3** [C] apparatus, e.g. in a car, that makes a warning sound **4** [C] musical instrument played by blowing **5** blow one's own horn praise oneself ~**y** *adj* **1** *taboo sl* sexually excited **2** hard and rough

hor·net /'hornɪt/ *n* large stinging insect

hor·o·scope /'horəˌsko^wp, 'har-/ *n* set of ideas about someone's character, life and future gained by knowing the position of the stars or PLANETS at the time of their birth

hor·ren·dous /hə'rɛndəs, hɔ-, ha-/ *adj* really terrible ~**ly** *adv*

hor·ri·ble /'horəbəl, 'har-/ *adj* **1** causing HORROR **2** very unpleasant **-bly** *adv*

hor·rid /'horɪd, 'harɪd/ *adj* nasty

hor·rif·ic /hɔ'rɪfɪk, ha-, hə-/ *adj* horrifying ~**ally** /-kli^y/ *adv*

hor·ri·fy /'horəˌfaɪ, 'har-/ *vt* fill with horror: *horrifying news*

hor·ror /'horər, 'harər/ *n* **1** [C;U] (something causing) great shock and fear **2** [C] unpleasant person,

usu. a child **3** have a horror of hate ♦ *adj* frightening: *horror films* -**s** *n infml* [the+P] state of great fear, worry or sadness

horror-strick·en /'··· ,··/ also **horror-struck** /'··· ·/ — *adj* deeply shocked

hors d'oeu·vre /ɔr 'dɜrv/ *n* -**d'oeuvres** /'dɜrvz/ small things served at the beginning of a meal

horse¹ /hors/ *n* **1** large animal with four legs, that people ride on, etc. **2** apparatus for jumping over **3** eat like a horse eat a lot **4** (straight) from the horse's mouth (of information) directly from the person concerned – see also DARK HORSE, HIGH HORSE, TROJAN HORSE

horse² *v* horse around *phr vi infml* play roughly or waste time in rough play

horse·back /'horsbæk/ *n* on horseback riding a horse ♦ *adj, adv* on the back of a horse: *horseback riding*

horse·car /'horskar/ *n* vehicle in which a horse can travel

horse·man /'horsmən/ **horse·wom·an** /-ˌwumən/ *fem.* — *n* -**men** /-mən/ person riding a horse

horse·play /'hors-ple^y/ *n* [U] rough noisy behavior

horse·pow·er /'horsˌpauər/ *n* horsepower unit measuring the power of an engine

horse·shoe /'horʃ-ʃu^w, 'hors-/ *n* shoe in the shape of a U for a horse, believed to bring good luck

hors·y /'horsi^y/ *adj* **1** interested in horses **2** looking like a horse

hor·ti·cul·ture /'hortəˌkʌltʃər/ *n* [U] science of growing fruit, flowers, and vegetables -**tural** /ˌhortə-'kʌltʃərəl/ *adj*

hose¹ /ho^wz/ *n* tube used for watering gardens, etc. ♦ *vt* use a hose on

hose² *n* [U] socks and STOCKINGs

ho·sier·y /'ho^wʒəri^y/ *n* [U] socks, stockings, etc.

hos·pice /'haspɪs/ *n* **1** hospital for people with incurable illnesses **2** house made for travelers to rest

hos·pi·ta·ble /'haspɪtəbəl, ha'spɪ-/ *adj* offering a friendly welcome to guests -**bly** *adv*

hos·pi·tal /'haspɪtl/ *n* place where people who are ill or injured (IN-JURE) are treated ~**ize** *vt* put into a hospital

hos·pi·tal·i·ty /ˌhaspə'tæləti^y/ *n* [U] being hospitable

host¹ /ho^wst/ *n* **1** man who receives guests **2** person who introduces performers, e.g. on a television show ♦ *vt* act as a host

host² *n* large number: *a host of difficulties*

hos·tage /'hastɪdʒ/ *n* prisoner kept

hos·tel /ˈhɒstl/ n building where students, etc., can live and eat

host·ess /ˈhoʊstɪs/ n 1 female host 2 young woman who acts as companion, dancing partner, etc., in a social club

hos·tile /ˈhɒstl, ˈhɑstaɪl/ adj 1 unfriendly 2 belonging to an enemy

hos·til·i·ty /hɑˈstɪlɪtiʲ/ n [U] unfriendliness −ties n [P] war

hot[1] /hɑt/ adj -tt- 1 having a high temperature 2 having a burning taste: hot pepper 3 fierce; excitable: hot temper 4 (of news) very recent 5 knowledgeable about and interested in: She's very hot on jazz. 6 **hot and bothered** a worried by a feeling that things are going wrong b sexually excited 7 **hot on someone's trail** following someone closely 8 **not so hot** infml not very good −ly adv 1 angrily 2 eagerly: hotly pursued

hot[2] v -tt- **hot up** phr vi become more exciting or dangerous

hot air /ˌ· ˈ·/ n [U] meaningless talk

hot·bed /ˈhɑtbɛd/ n place where something bad can develop: a hotbed of crime

hot-blood·ed /ˌ· ˈ···◂/ adj PASSIONATE

hot dog /ˈ· ·/ n 1 FRANKFURTER in a long BUN (2) 2 person too confident of his abilities

ho·tel /hoʊˈtɛl/ n building where people can stay in return for payment

ho·tel·ier /hoʊˈtɛlyər, ˌoʊtlˈyeʲ/ n hotel manager

hot·foot /ˈhɑtfʊt/ adv fast and eagerly ♦ vi leave quickly

hot·head /ˈhɑthɛd/ n person who acts in haste, without thinking −ed /ˌhɑtˈhɛdɪd◂/ adj

hot·house /ˈhɑthaʊs/ n heated GREENHOUSE

hot line /ˈ· ·/ n 1 direct telephone line between heads of government 2 telephone line for a special purpose

hot·plate /ˈhɑtpleʲt/ n metal surface for cooking food that can be moved from place to place

hot seat /ˈ· ·/ n infml position of difficulty from which one must make important decisions

hot spot /ˈ· ·/ place where there is likely to be unrest and perhaps war

hot-tem·pered /ˌ· ˈ···◂/ adj easily made angry

hot wa·ter /ˌ· ˈ··/ n [U] trouble: get into hot water

hot-wa·ter bot·tle /ˌ· ˈ·· ˌ··/ n rubber container for hot water to reduce aches and pain

hound /haʊnd/ n hunting dog ♦ vt chase and worry

hour /aʊər/ n 1 period of 60 minutes 2 time when a new hour starts: arrive on the hour 3 distance one can travel in this period of time: It's only an hour away. 4 period of time: my lunch hour 5 **after hours** later than the usual times of work or business 6 **at all hours** (at any time) during the whole day and night – see also ELEVENTH HOUR, HAPPY HOUR ~ly adj, adv once every hour

hour·glass /ˈaʊərˌglæs/ n container in which sand drops through a narrow passage, formerly used to measure time

house[1] /haʊs/ n houses /ˈhaʊzɪz/ 1 a building for people to live in, esp. on more than one level b people in such a building: You'll wake the whole house. 2 building for a stated purpose: a hen house | the House of Representatives 3 (often cap.) noble or royal family 4 a division of a school b business firm: the house magazine 5 theater, or the people in it 6 **bring the house down** cause loud admiration 7 **get on like a house on fire** be very friendly 8 **keep house** do or control the cleaning, cooking, etc. 9 **on the house** (of drinks) paid for by the people in charge

house[2] /haʊz/ vt provide a home, or space, for

house·boat /ˈhaʊsboʊt/ n boat for living in

house·bound /ˈhaʊsbaʊnd/ adj unable to leave one's home

house·break·er /ˈhaʊsˌbreʲkər/ n thief who enters a house by force

house-bro·ken /ˈhaʊsˌbroʊkən/ adj (of pets) trained to empty the bowels and BLADDER outside the house

house·coat /ˈhaʊskoʊt/ n garment worn by women at home

house·hold /ˈhaʊshoʊld, ˈhaʊsoʊld/ n all the people living in a house ♦ adj concerned with the management of a house: household expenses ~er n person who owns or is in charge of a house

household name /ˌ·· ˈ·/ also **household word** — n person or thing that is very well known or talked about by almost everyone

house·keep·er /ˈhaʊsˌkiʲpər/ n person paid to run a house

house·keep·ing /ˈhaʊsˌkiʲpɪŋ/ n 1 work of running a house 2 money set aside for food, etc.

house·maid /ˈhaʊsmeʲd/ n female servant who does HOUSEWORK

House of Com·mons /ˌ·· ˈ··/ n [the] the lower but more powerful of the 2 parts of the British or Canadian PARLIAMENT

House of Lords /₁· · ·'·/ n [the] the upper but less powerful of the 2 parts of the British PARLIAMENT, the members of which are not elected

House of Rep·re·sen·ta·tives /₁· ·· '···/ n [the] the larger and lower of the 2 parts of the central body that makes the laws in such countries as New Zealand, Australia, and the US

house-proud /'· ·/ adj keeping one's home very clean and tidy

house-warm·ing /'haʊsˌwɔrmɪŋ/ n party given for friends when one has moved into a new house

house-wife /'haʊswaɪf/ n -wives /-waɪvz/ woman who works at home for her family, cleaning, cooking, etc.

house-work /'haʊswɜrk/ n [U] cleaning, etc., in a house

hous·ing /'haʊzɪŋ/ n 1 [U] places to live 2 [C] protective cover for a machine

housing proj·ect /'·· ˌ··/ n group of apartments built by the government for poor people

hov·el /'hʌvəl, 'hɑ-/ n dirty little house or hut

hov·er /'hʌvər, 'hɑ-/ vi 1 (of birds, etc.) stay in the air in one place 2 (of people) wait around

hov·er·craft /'hʌvərˌkræft, 'hɑ-/ n -craft or -crafts boat that moves over land or water supported by a strong force of air

how /haʊ/ adv 1 (used in questions) **a** in what way: How do you spell it? **b** in what state of health: How are you? **c** (in questions about number, size, etc.): How big is it? 2 (showing surprise): How kind of you! 3 **How come…?** infml Why is it that…? 4 **How do you do?** (used when formally introduced to someone; this person replies with the same phrase) ♦ conj the way in which; the fact that: I remember how they laughed.

how·dy /'haʊdiʸ/ interj infml (used to greet people) HELLO

how·ev·er /haʊ'ɛvər/ adv 1 in whatever degree or way: We'll go, however cold it is. 2 in spite of this 3 in what way (showing surprise): However did you get here?

howl /haʊl/ vi/t, n (make) a long loud cry ~er n silly mistake that makes people laugh

HP /ˌeɪʸtʃ 'piʸ/ abbrev. for: HORSE-POWER

HQ /ˌeɪʸtʃ 'kyuʷ/ n [C;U] HEAD-QUARTERS

hr, hrs written abbrev. for: hour(s)

hub /hʌb/ n 1 center of a wheel 2 center of activity

hub-bub /'hʌbʌb/ n [S] mixture of loud noises

hub·cap /'hʌbkæp/ n metal covering for the center of a wheel on a car

hud·dle /'hʌdl/ vi/t get or come together in a crowd ♦ n crowd

hue /hyuʷ/ n fml color

hue and cry /ˌ· · '·/ n expression of worry, anger, etc., by noisy behavior

huff /hʌf/ n [S] bad temper ~y adj

hug /hʌg/ vt -gg- 1 hold tightly in one's arms 2 travel along beside: The boat hugged the coast. **hug** n

huge /hyuʷdʒ/ adj very big ~ly adv very much

huh /hʌ/ interj (used for asking a question or for expressing surprise or disapproval)

hu·la /'huʷləʸ/ n Hawaiian dance

hulk /hʌlk/ n 1 old broken ship 2 heavy, awkward person or creature

hulk·ing /'hʌlkɪŋ/ adj big and awkward

hull /hʌl/ n body of a ship or aircraft

hum /hʌm/ v -mm- 1 vi BUZZ (1) 2 vi/t sing with closed lips 3 vi be full of activity ♦ n [U]

hu·man /'hyuʷmən/ adj 1 of people 2 kind, etc., as people should be: He's really very human. ♦ n person ~ism n [U] system of belief based on people's needs, and not on religion ~ize vt make human or humane ~ly adv according to human powers: not humanly possible

hu·mane /hyuʷ'meɪʸn/ adj 1 showing human kindness and the qualities of a civilized person 2 trying not to cause pain: a humane method of killing animals ~ly adv

hu·man·i·tar·i·an /hyuʷˌmænə'teəriʸən/ n, adj (person) trying to improve life for human beings by improving living conditions, etc. ~ism n [U]

hu·man·i·ty /hyuʷ'mænətiʸ/ n [U] 1 being human or humane 2 people in general

hum·ble /'hʌmbəl/ adj 1 low in rank; unimportant 2 having a low opinion of oneself and a high opinion of others; not proud ♦ vt make humble -bly adv

hum·bug /'hʌmbʌg/ n [U] insincere nonsense

hum·drum /'hʌmdrʌm/ adj dull and ordinary

hu·mid /'hyuʷmɪd/ adj (of air) DAMP ~ify /hyuʷ'mɪdəˌfaɪ/ vt make humid ~ity n [U]

hu·mil·i·ate /hyuʷ'mɪliʸˌeɪʸt/ vt cause to feel ashamed -ation /hyuʷˌmɪliʸ'eɪʸʃən/ n [C;U]

hu·mil·i·ty /hyuʷ'mɪlətiʸ/ n [U] quality of being HUMBLE (2)

hu·mor /'hyuʷmər, 'yuʷ-/ n [U] ability to be amused or cause amusement ♦ vt keep (someone) happy by acceptance of their foolish wishes, behavior, etc. **humor along** phr vt encourage in a joking or friendly way

hu·mor·ist /ˈhyuʷmərɪst, ˈyuʷ-/ n person who makes jokes in speech or writing

hu·mor·ous /ˈhyuʷmərəs, ˈyuʷ-/ adj funny **~ly** adv

hump /hʌmp/ n 1 [C] round lump, esp. on a CAMEL's back **2 over the hump** infml past the worst part of the work ♦ v 1 vt carry (something heavy), esp. with difficulty 2 vi/t taboo sl have sex with

hunch[1] /hʌntʃ/ n idea based on feeling rather than reason

hunch[2] vt pull (part of the body) into a rounded shape: hunched shoulders

hunch·back /ˈhʌntʃbæk/ n (person with) a back misshaped by a round lump **~ed** adj

hun·dred /ˈhʌndrɪd/ det, n, pron **–dred** or **–dreds** 100 **–th** det, adj, n, pron 100th

hun·dred·weight /ˈhʌndrɪdˌweʸt/ n **–weight** (a measure of weight equal to) 100 pounds

hung /hʌŋ/ v past t. and p. of HANG – see also **be hung up on** (HANG up)

hung ju·ry /ˌ· ˈ··/ n jury that can not agree on a VERDICT

hun·ger /ˈhʌŋgər/ n 1 [U] need for food 2 [S] strong wish ♦ vi feel hunger **–gry** adj feeling hunger

hunger strike /ˈ·· ˌ·/ n refusal to eat as a sign of strong dissatisfaction

hunk /hʌŋk/ n 1 thick piece of food, etc. 2 infml physically attractive man

hunt /hʌnt/ vi/t 1 chase (animals) for food or sport 2 search (for) ♦ n 1 chasing or searching 2 people hunting animals: a bear hunt **~er** n

hunt down/out/up phr vt find by searching

hur·dle /ˈhɜrdl/ n 1 frame to jump over in a race 2 difficulty to be dealt with

hurl /hɜrl/ vt throw violently: (fig.) He hurled abuse at the other driver.

hur·ly-bur·ly /ˌhɜrliʸ ˈbɜrliʸ/ n old fash. [S;U] noisy activity

hur·ray, hooray /həˈreʸ, hʊˈreʸ/ also **hurrah** /həˈrɑ, hɑˈrɑ, hʊ-/ — becoming rare interj, n (shout of joy or approval)

hur·ri·cane /ˈhɜrəˌkeʸn, ˈhʌr-/ n violent storm from the sea with a strong fast circular wind

hur·ry /ˈhɜriʸ, ˈhʌriʸ/ vi/t (cause to) go or do something (too) quickly: Hurry up! (= Be quick!) ♦ n [S;U] 1 quick activity 2 need to hurry **–ried** adj done (too) quickly **–riedly** adv

hurt /hɜrt/ v hurt 1 vt cause pain or

damage to 2 vt cause pain (to the feelings of (a person)) 3 vi feel pain 4 vi/t matter (to): It won't hurt (you) to wait. ♦ n [C;U] harm; damage **~ful** adj **~fully** adv

hur·tle /ˈhɜrtl/ vi move or rush with great force

hus·band /ˈhʌzbənd/ n man to whom a woman is married

hush /hʌʃ/ vi/t (cause to) be silent ♦ n [S;U] silence

hush up phr vt keep secret

husk /hʌsk/ n dry outer covering of some vegetables, fruits and seeds

hus·ky /ˈhʌskiʸ/ adj 1 (of a voice) HOARSE 2 (of a person) big and strong **–kily** adv

hus·tle /ˈhʌsəl/ vt 1 push or drive as if one is in a hurry 2 persuade someone forcefully, esp. to buy something ♦ n [U] hurried activity **hustler** n 1 infml busy, active person, esp. one who tries to persuade people to buy things, etc. 2 sl male PROSTITUTE

hut /hʌt/ n small simple building

hutch /hʌtʃ/ n cage for rabbits, etc.

hy·brid /ˈhaɪbrɪd/ n animal or plant of mixed breed

hy·drant /ˈhaɪdrənt/ n water pipe in the street, used to put out fires

hy·draul·ic /haɪˈdrɔlɪk/ adj using water pressure

hy·dro·e·lec·tric /ˌhaɪdroʷɪˈlektrɪk◂/ adj producing electricity by water power

hy·dro·foil /ˈhaɪdrəˌfɔɪl/ n large motor boat which raises itself out of the water as it moves

hy·dro·gen /ˈhaɪdrədʒən/ n [U] light gas that burns easily

hydrogen bomb /ˈ··· ˌ·/ n bomb made using hydrogen which explodes when the central parts of the atoms join together

hy·giene /ˈhaɪdʒiʸn/ n [U] cleanness, to prevent the spreading of disease **hygienist** /haɪˈdʒiʸnɪst, ˈhaɪdʒiʸn-/ person who knows a lot about hygiene **hygienic** /ˌhaɪdʒiʸˈɛnɪk, haɪˈdʒɛnɪk/ adj

hymn /hɪm/ n song of praise to God

hype /haɪp/ vt infml try to get a lot of public attention to, esp. more than is deserved **hype** n [U] attempts to do this

hyped up /ˌ· ˈ·/ adj infml very excited and anxious

hy·per·ac·tive /ˌhaɪpərˈæktɪv◂/ adj also **hyper** unable to rest or be quiet

hy·per·bo·le /haɪˈpɜrbəliʸ/ n exaggeration (EXAGGERATE)

hy·phen /ˈhaɪfən/ n the mark (-) joining words or word parts **~ate** vt join with a hyphen

hyp·no·sis /hɪpˈnoʷsɪs/ n [U] state similar to sleep in which a person can be influenced by the person who produced the state −**notic** /-'naṭɪk/ *adj* −**tism** /'hɪpnəˌtɪzəm/ *n* [U] production of hypnosis −**tist** *n* −**tize** *vt* produce hypnosis in

hy·po·chon·dri·ac /ˌhaɪpə'kɑndriˈ-ˌæk/ *n* someone who worries unnecessarily about their health

hy·poc·ri·sy /hɪ'pɑkrəsiˈ/ *n* [U] pretending to be different from and usu. better than one is

hyp·o·crite /'hɪpəˌkrɪt/ *n* person who practices hypocrisy −**critical** /ˌhɪpə'krɪṭɪkəl◂/ *adj*

hy·po·der·mic /ˌhaɪpə'dɜrmɪk◂/ *adj, n* (of) a needle for putting drugs into the body

hy·pot·e·nuse /haɪ'pɑtnˌuʷs, -ˌyuʷs, -ˌuʷz/ *n* longest side of a TRIANGLE with a 90-degree angle

hy·poth·e·sis /haɪ'pɑθəsɪs/ *n* idea that may explain facts −**etical** /ˌhaɪpə'θɛṭɪkəl/ *adj* not yet proved

hys·te·ri·a /hɪ'stɛriˈə, -'stɪər-/ *n* [U] uncontrolled nervous excitement −**rical** /hɪ'stɛrɪkəl/ *adj* −**rics** *n* [P] attack(s) of hysteria

I, i¹ /aɪ/ *n* the 9th letter of the English alphabet

I² *pron* (used for the person speaking, as the subject of a sentence)

ice¹ /aɪs/ *n* **1** [U] frozen water **2** [U] *sl* diamonds **3 skating on thin ice** taking risks **4 keep something on ice** take no immediate action about something

ice² *vt* **1** make cold with ice **2** cover with FROSTING

ice over/up *phr vi* become covered with ice

ice age /ˈ· ·/ *n* period when ice covered many northern countries

ice·berg /ˈaɪsbɜrg/ *n* **1** mass of floating ice in the sea **2 the tip of the iceberg** a small sign of a much larger situation, problem, etc.

ice·box /ˈaɪsbɑks/also **ice chest** — *n* **1** box where food is kept cool with ice **2** *old-fash. for* FRIDGE

ice·break·er /ˈaɪsˌbreɪkər/ *n* **1** ship that cuts through floating ice **2** action which makes people who have just met more relaxed

ice cap /ˈ· ·/ *n* lasting covering of ice, e.g. at the POLES² (1)

ice cream /ˈ· ·/ *n* [C;U] frozen creamy food mixture

ice floe /ˈ· ·/ *n* large area of floating ice

ice hock·ey /ˈ· ˌ··/ *n* [U] game like HOCKEY played on ice

ice pack /ˈ· ·/ *n* bag of ice to put on the body

ice pick /ˈ· ·/ *n* tool for breaking ice

ice-skate /ˈ· ·/ *n* SKATE (1) **ice-skate** *vi*

i·ci·cle /ˈaɪsɪkəl/ *n* pointed stick of ice, formed when water freezes as it runs down

ic·ing /ˈaɪsɪŋ/ *n* [U] – see FROSTING

i·con·o·clast /aɪˈkɑnəˌklæst/ *n* person who attacks established beliefs ~ **ic** /aɪˌkɑnəˈklæstɪk/ *adj*

ic·y /ˈaɪsi/ *adj* **1** very cold **2** covered with ice **icily** *adv*

I'd /aɪd/ *short for:* **1** I would **2** I had

ID card /ˌaɪ ˈdiː kɑrd/ *n* card that gives a person's name, address, age, etc. as proof of their IDENTITY

i·de·a /aɪˈdiːə/ *n* **1** [C] plan, thought, or suggestion for a possible course of action **2** [C;U] picture in the mind; CONCEPTION **3** [C] opinion or belief: *strange ideas* **4** understanding: *They've got no idea how to run a house.* **5** [C] guess; feeling of probability: *I've an idea she doesn't like him.*

i·de·al /aɪˈdiːəl/ *adj* **1** perfect **2** too good to exist ♦ *n* **1** [*often pl.*] (belief in) high principles or perfect standards **2** perfect example ~ **ist** *n* ~ **ize** *vt* imagine as perfect ~ **ly** *adv* **1** in an ideal way: *ideally suited* **2** if things were perfect

i·de·al·ism /aɪˈdiːəˌlɪzəm/ *n* [U] quality or habit of living according to one's ideals, or the belief that such a way of life is possible – **ist** *n* – **istic** *adj* /aɪˌdiːəˈlɪstɪk◂, aɪˌdiːəˈ- /-**istically** /-kli⸣/

i·den·ti·cal /aɪˈdɛntɪkəl, ɪ-/ *adj* **1** exactly alike **2** the same ~ **ly** /-kliʸ/ *adv*

i·den·ti·fy /aɪˈdɛntəˌfaɪ, ɪ-/ *vt* show the identity of – **fication** /aɪˌdɛntəfə- ˈkeɪʃən, ɪ-/ *n* [U] **1** identifying **2** also **ID** paper, etc., that proves who one is

identify with *phr vt* **1** consider (someone) to be connected with **2** feel sympathy for

i·den·ti·ty /aɪˈdɛntətiʸ, ɪ-/ *n* **1** [C;U] who or what a person or thing is **2** [U] sameness

i·de·ol·o·gy /ˌaɪdiʸˈɑlədʒiʸ, ˌɪdiʸ-/ *n* [C;U] set of (political or social) ideas –**ogical** /ˌaɪdiʸəˈlædʒɪkəl, ˌɪdiʸ-/ *adj*

id·i·o·cy /ˈɪdiʸəsiʸ/ *n* **1** [U] stupidity **2** [C] stupid act

id·i·om /ˈɪdiʸəm/ *n* phrase that means something different from the meanings of its separate words: *'Kick the bucket' is an idiom meaning 'die'.*

id·i·o·mat·ic /ˌɪdiʸəˈmætɪk◂/ *adj* typical of natural speech ~ **ally** /-kliʸ/ *adv*

id·i·o·syn·cra·sy /ˌɪdiʸəˈsɪŋkrəsiʸ/ *n* personal peculiarity –**tic** /ˌɪdiʸəsɪn- ˈkrætɪk/ *adj* –**tically** /-kliʸ/ *adv*

id·i·ot /ˈɪdiʸət/ *n* **1** fool **2** person with low mental ability ~ **ic** /ˌɪdiʸ- ˈɑtɪk◂/ *adj*

i·dle¹ /ˈaɪdl/ *adj* **1** not working **2** lazy **3** useless: *idle threats* ~ **ness** *n* [U] **idly** *adv*

idle² *vi* **1** waste time **2** (of an engine) run slowly because it is disconnected **idler** *n*

idle away *phr vt* waste (time)

i·dol /ˈaɪdl/ *n* **1** image worshiped as a god **2** someone greatly admired ~ **ize** *vt* worship as an idol

i·dol·a·try /aɪˈdɑlətriʸ/ *n* [U] worshiping of idols –**trous** *adj* **idolater** *n*

id·yll·ic /aɪˈdɪlɪk/ *adj* simple and happy

i.e. /ˌaɪ ˈiʸ/ that is; by which is meant: *open to adults, i.e. people over 18*

if /ɪf/ *conj* **1** on condition that: *I'll come if I can.* **2** even though: *It was nice, if expensive.* **3** whether: *I don't* *know if he'll come.* **4 if anything** perhaps even **5 if I were you** (used when giving advice): *If I were you, I'd burn it.* **6 it isn't/it's not as if** it's not true that ♦ *n* **ifs and buts** reasons given for delay ♦ **iffy** *adj* doubtful

ig·nite /ɪgˈnaɪt/ *vi/t fml* start to burn

ig·ni·tion /ɪgˈnɪʃən/ *n* [C] electrical apparatus that starts an engine **2** [U] *fml* action of igniting

ig·no·ble /ɪgˈnoʷbəl/ *adj fml* not honorable –**bly** *adv*

ig·no·mi·ny /ˈɪgnəˌmɪniʸ/ *n* [C;U] (act of) shame –**nious** /ˌɪgnəˈmɪniʸəs/ *adj*

ig·no·ra·mus /ˌɪgnəˈreʸməs, -ˈræ-/ *n* ignorant person

ig·no·rant /ˈɪgnərənt/ *adj* **1** without knowledge **2** rude, esp. because of lack of social training –**rance** *n* [U]

ig·nore /ɪgˈnɔr, ɪgˈnoʷr/ *vt* refuse to notice

ilk /ɪlk/ *n* kind: *people of that ilk*

ill /ɪl/ *adj* **worse** /wɜrs/, **worst** /wɜrst/ **1** sick **2** bad: *ill fortune* ♦ *adv* **1** badly: *The child was ill-treated.* **2** not enough: *ill fed* ♦ *n* bad thing: *the social ills of poverty and unemployment*

I'll /aɪl/ *short for:* I will or I shall

ill-ad·vised /ˌ· ·ˈ··◂/ *adj* unwise

ill-bred /ˌ· ˈ·◂/ *adj* badly behaved

il·le·gal /ɪˈliʸgəl/ *adj* against the law ~**ly** *adv* –**ity** /ˌɪliʸˈgæləṭiʸ/ *n* [C;U]

il·le·gi·ble /ɪˈlɛdʒəbəl/ *adj* impossible to read

il·le·git·i·mate /ˌɪlɪˈdʒɪṭəmɪt/ *adj* **1** born to unmarried parents **2** against the rules ~**ly** *adv*

ill-got·ten /ˌ· ˈ··◂/ *adj* dishonestly obtained

il·lic·it /ɪˈlɪsɪt/ *adj* against the law or the rules ~**ly** *adv*

il·lit·e·rate /ɪˈlɪṭərɪt/ *adj* unable to read or write –**racy** *n* [U]

ill-na·tured /ˌ· ˈ···◂/ *adj* bad-tempered

ill·ness /ˈɪlnɪs/ *n* [C;U] DISEASE

il·log·i·cal /ɪˈlɑdʒɪkəl/ *adj* against LOGIC; not sensible ~**ly** /-kliʸ/ *adv*

il·lu·mi·nate /ɪˈluʷməˌneʸt/ *vt* **1** give light to **2** decorate with lights **3** (esp. in former times) decorate with gold and bright colors –**nating** *adj* helping to explain: *illuminating remark* –**nation** /ɪˌluʷməˈneʸʃən/ *n* [U] act of illuminating or state of being illuminated

il·lu·sion /ɪˈluʷʒən/ *n* something seen wrongly; false idea –**sory** /ɪˈluʷsəriʸ/ *adj fml* unreal

il·lus·trate /ˈɪləˌstreʸt/ *vt* **1** add pictures to **2** explain by giving examples –**trator** *n* person who draws pictures for a book, etc. –**tration**

/ˌɪləˈstreʸʃən/ *n* [C] picture **2** [C] example **3** [U] act of illustrating –**trative** /ɪˈlʌstrətɪv/ *adj* used as an example

il·lus·tri·ous /ɪˈlʌstriʸəs/ *adj* famous

I'm /aɪm/ *short for:* I am

im·age /ˈɪmɪdʒ/ *n* **1** picture in the mind, or seen in a mirror **2** general opinion about a person, etc., that has been formed or intentionally planted in people's minds **3** copy; likeness: *He's the image of his father.* **4** IDOL (1) –**ry** *n* [U] METAPHORS, etc., in literature

i·ma·gi·na·ry /ɪˈmædʒəˌneriʸ/ *adj* unreal

i·ma·gine /ɪˈmædʒɪn/ *vt* **1** form (an idea) in the mind: *imagine a world without cars* **2** believe; suppose: *I imagine they've forgotten.* –**ginable** *adj* that can be imagined –**ginative** *adj* good at imagining –**gination** /ɪˌmædʒəˈneʸʃən/ *n* **1** [C;U] ability to imagine **2** [U] something only imagined

im·bal·ance /ɪmˈbæləns/ *n* lack of balance or equality

im·be·cile /ˈɪmbəsəl, -ˌsɪl/ *n* IDIOT –**cility** /ˌɪmbəˈsɪləṭiʸ/ *n* **1** [U] being an imbecile **2** [C] foolish act

im·bibe /ɪmˈbaɪb/ *vi/t fml* drink or take in

im·bro·gli·o /ɪmˈbroʷliʸˌoʷ/ *n* –**os** confused situation

im·bue /ɪmˈbyuʷ/ *v* imbue with *phr vt* fill with (a feeling, etc.)

im·i·tate /ˈɪməˌteʸt/ *vt* **1** copy (behavior) **2** take as an example –**tator** *n* –**tative** *adj* following an example; not inventive –**tation** /ˌɪməˈteʸʃən◂/ *n* **1** [C;U] act or act of imitating **2** [C] copy of the real thing

im·mac·u·late /ɪˈmækyəlɪt/ *adj* clean; pure ~**ly** *adv*

im·ma·te·ri·al /ˌɪməˈtɪriʸəl/ *adj* **1** unimportant **2** without physical substance

im·ma·ture /ˌɪməˈtʃʊər, -ˈtʊər, -ˈtyʊər/ *adj* not fully formed or developed –**turity** *n* [U]

im·mea·su·ra·ble /ɪˈmɛʒərəbəl/ *adj* too big to be measured –**bly** *adv*

im·me·di·ate /ɪˈmiʸdiʸɪt/ *adj* **1** done or needed at once: *an immediate reply* **2** nearest: *the immediate future* ~**ly** *adv* **1** at once **2** with nothing between: *immediately in front* –**acy** *n* [U] nearness or urgent presence of something

im·me·mo·ri·al /ˌɪməˈmɔriʸəl, -ˈmoʷr-/ *adj* see TIME IMMEMORIAL

im·mense /ɪˈmɛns/ *adj* very large ~**ly** *adv* very much **immensity** *n* [U]

im·merse /ɪˈmɜrs/ *vt* put deep into liquid: (fig.) *immersed in my work* **immersion** /ɪˈmɜrʒən, -ʃən/ *n* [U]

im·mi·grate /ˈɪməˌgreɪt/ vi come to live in a country –**grant** n person who does this –**gration** /ˌɪməˈgreɪʃən/ n [U]

im·mi·nent /ˈɪmənənt/ adj going to happen soon ~**ly** adv

im·mo·bile /ɪˈmoʷbəl, -ˌbiʸl/ adj unmoving; unable to move –**bility** /ˌɪmoʷˈbɪləṭiʸ/ n [U] –**bilize** /ɪˈmoʷbəˌlaɪz/ vt make immobile

im·mor·al /ɪˈmɔrəl, ɪˈmɑr-/ adj **1** not good or right **2** sexually improper ~**ity** /ˌɪməˈrælət̬iʸ/ n [C;U]

im·mor·tal /ɪˈmɔrt̬l/ adj living or remembered for ever ♦ n immortal being ~**ize** vt give endless life or fame to ~**ity** /ˌɪmɔrˈtælət̬iʸ/ n endless life

im·mune /ɪˈmyuʷn/ adj unable to be harmed; protected **immunity** n [U] **immunize** /ˈɪmyəˌnaɪz/ vt protect from disease

immune sys·tem /·ˈ· ˌ·/ n system in the body that fights substances that cause disease

imp /ɪmp/ n **1** little devil **2** troublesome child ~**ish** adj

im·pact /ˈɪmpækt/ n **1** force of one object hitting another **2** influence; effect **3 on impact** at the moment of hitting

im·pair /ɪmˈpeər/ vt spoil; weaken

im·pale /ɪmˈpeʸl/ vt turn something sharp through: impaled on the spikes

im·pal·pa·ble /ɪmˈpælpəbəl/ adj fml not easily felt or understood

im·part /ɪmˈpɑrt/ vt fml give (knowledge, etc.)

im·par·tial /ɪmˈpɑrʃəl/ adj fair; just ~**ly** adv –**ity** /ɪmˌpɑrʃiʸˈælət̬iʸ/ n [U]

im·pass·a·ble /ɪmˈpæsəbəl/ adj (of roads, etc.) impossible to travel over

im·passe /ˈɪmpæs, ɪmˈpæs/ n point where further movement is blocked

im·pas·sioned /ɪmˈpæʃənd/ adj full of deep feelings: impassioned speech

im·pas·sive /ɪmˈpæsɪv/ adj showing no feelings; calm ~**ly** adv

im·pa·tient /ɪmˈpeʸʃənt/ adj **1** not patient **2** eager: impatient to go ~**ly** adv –**tience** n [U]

im·peach /ɪmˈpiʸtʃ/ vt charge (a public official) with a crime against the state ~**ment** n [C;U]

im·pec·ca·ble /ɪmˈpɛkəbəl/ adj faultless –**bly** adv

im·pe·cu·ni·ous /ˌɪmpɪˈkyuʷniʸəs/ adj fml without money; poor

im·pede /ɪmˈpiʸd/ vt get in the way of

im·ped·i·ment /ɪmˈpɛdəmənt/ n something that makes action difficult or impossible: a speech impediment

im·pel /ɪmˈpɛl/ vt –**ll**– (of an idea, etc.) cause (someone) to act

im·pend·ing /ɪmˈpɛndɪŋ/ adj (esp. of something bad) about to happen

im·pen·e·tra·ble /ɪmˈpɛnətrəbəl/ adj **1** that cannot be gone through **2** impossible to understand

im·per·a·tive /ɪmˈpɛrət̬ɪv/ adj urgent; that must be done ♦ n gram verb form expressing a command (e.g. 'Come!') ~**ly** adv

im·per·fect /ɪmˈpɜrfɪkt/ adj not perfect ♦ n gram verb that shows incomplete action ~**ly** adv ~**ion** /ˌɪmpɜrˈfɛkʃən/ n **1** [U] imperfect state **2** [C] fault

im·pe·ri·al /ɪmˈpɪəriʸəl/ adj of an EMPIRE or its ruler ~**ly** adv ~**ism** n [U] (belief in) the making of an EMPIRE ~**ist** n, adj

im·per·il /ɪmˈpɛrəl/ vt –**l**– put in danger

im·pe·ri·ous /ɪmˈpɪəriʸəs/ adj fml (too) commanding; expecting obedience from others

im·per·son·al /ɪmˈpɜrsənəl/ adj without personal feelings: impersonal organizations ~**ly** adv

im·per·so·nate /ɪmˈpɜrsəˌneʸt/ vt pretend to be (another person) –**nation** /ɪmˌpɜrsəˈneʸʃən/ n [C;U]

im·per·ti·nent /ɪmˈpɜrtn-ənt/ adj not properly respectful ~**ly** adv –**nence** n [U]

im·per·tur·ba·ble /ˌɪmpərˈtɜrbəbəl/ adj unworried; calm –**bly** adv

im·per·vi·ous /ɪmˈpɜrviʸəs/ adj **1** not letting water, etc., through **2** not easily influenced: impervious to criticism

im·pet·u·ous /ɪmˈpɛtʃuʷəs/ adj acting quickly but without thought ~**ly** adv –**osity** /ɪmˌpɛtʃuʷˈæsəṭiʸ/ n [U]

im·pe·tus /ˈɪmpət̬əs/ n **1** [U] force of something moving **2** [S;U] STIMULUS: a fresh impetus to the negotiations

im·pinge /ɪmˈpɪndʒ/ v **impinge on/upon** phr vt have an effect on

im·pi·ous /ˈɪmpiʸəs, ɪmˈpaɪəs/ adj without respect for religion ~**ly** adv

im·pla·ca·ble /ɪmˈplækəbəl, -ˈpleʸ-/ adj impossible to satisfy or PLACATE

im·plant /ɪmˈplænt/ vt fix deeply into

im·plau·si·ble /ɪmˈplɔzəbəl/ adj seeming to be untrue or impossible

im·ple·ment¹ /ˈɪmpləmənt/ n tool or instrument

im·ple·ment² /ˈɪmpləˌmɛnt/ vt carry out (plans, etc.)

im·pli·cate /ˈɪmplɪˌkeʸt/ vt fml show (someone) to be concerned: a letter implicating him in the crime

im·pli·ca·tion /ˌɪmplɪˈkeʸʃən/ n **1** [C;U] (example of) the act of implying **2** [C] possible later effect of something 3 [U] act of implicating

im·pli·cit /ɪmˈplɪsɪt/ adj 1 meant though not expressed 2 unquestioning: *implicit trust* ~**ly** adv

im·plore /ɪmˈplɔr, ɪmˈploʳr/ vt beg; request strongly: *implore them to go*

im·ply /ɪmˈplaɪ/ vt 1 express indirectly: *He implied that he had not yet made a decision* 2 make necessary

im·pon·der·a·ble /ɪmˈpɑndərəbəl/ n, adj (thing) whose effects cannot be measured exactly

im·port¹ /ɪmˈpɔrt, -ˈpoʳrt, -pɔʳrt/ vt bring in (goods) from abroad ~**er** n ~**ation** /ˌɪmpɔrˈteɪʃən, -poʳrt/ n [C;U]

im·port² /ˈɪmpɔrt, -poʳrt/ n 1 [C] something imported 2 [U] fml importance

im·por·tant /ɪmˈpɔrtnt/ adj mattering very much ~**ly** adv –**tance** n [U]

im·pose /ɪmˈpoʳz/ v 1 vt establish (a tax, etc.) 2 vt force the acceptance of 3 vi take unfair advantage **imposing** adj large and IMPRESSIVE **imposition** /ˌɪmpəˈzɪʃən/ n [C;U] act of imposing

im·pos·si·ble /ɪmˈpɑsəbəl/ adj 1 not possible 2 hard to bear: *make life impossible* –**bly** adv –**bility** /ɪmˌpɑsəˈbɪləti²/ n [U]

im·pos·tor /ɪmˈpɑstər/ n someone who deceives by pretending to be someone else

im·po·tent /ˈɪmpətənt/ adj 1 powerless 2 (of a man) unable to perform the sex act ~**ly** adv –**tence** n [U]

im·pound /ɪmˈpaʊnd/ vt take away officially

im·pov·er·ish /ɪmˈpavərɪʃ/ vt make poor

im·prac·ti·ca·ble /ɪmˈpræktɪkəbəl/ adj fml that cannot be used in practice

im·prac·ti·cal /ɪmˈpræktɪkəl/ adj not practical; not sensible or reasonable

im·preg·na·ble /ɪmˈpregnəbəl/ adj impossible to enter by attack

im·preg·nate /ɪmˈpregˌneɪt/ vt 1 make wet; SATURATE: *cloth impregnated with polish* 2 fml make PREGNANT

im·pre·sa·ri·o /ˌɪmprəˈsɑriˌoʷ, -ˈsɛɑr-/ n –**os** person who arranges theater or concert performances

im·press /ɪmˈpres/ vt 1 fill with admiration 2 tell (someone) that something matters: *impress on them that they must work* –**ive** adj causing admiration ~**ively** adv ~**ion** /-ˈpreʃən/ n 1 effect produced on the mind 2 mark left by pressing 3 attempt to copy a person's appearance or behavior, esp. in theater, etc. ~**ionable** adj easily influenced

im·print¹ /ɪmˈprɪnt/ vt press (a mark) on

im·print² /ˈɪmprɪnt/ n 1 mark left on or on something 2 name of the PUBLISHer as it appears on a book

im·pris·on /ɪmˈprɪzən/ vt put in prison ~**ment** n [U]

im·prob·a·ble /ɪmˈprɑbəbəl/ adj unlikely –**bly** adv –**bility** /ɪmˌprɑbəˈbɪləti²/ n [C;U]

im·promp·tu /ɪmˈprɑmptuʷ, -tyuʷ/ adj, adv without preparation

im·prop·er /ɪmˈprɑpər/ adj 1 not suitable or correct 2 socially unacceptable ~**ly** adv

im·prove /ɪmˈpruʷv/ vi/t make or become better ~**ment** n [C;U] (sign of) improving

im·pro·vise /ˈɪmprəˌvaɪz/ vi/t 1 do (something one has not prepared for) 2 invent (music) while one plays –**visation** /ɪmˌprɑvəˈzeɪʃən, ˌɪmprəvə-/ n [C;U]

im·pu·dent /ˈɪmpyədənt/ adj shamelessly disrespectful ~**ly** adv –**dence** n [U]

im·pulse /ˈɪmpʌls/ n 1 [C;U] sudden urge 2 sudden force: *nerve impulse* **impulsive** /ɪmˈpʌlsɪv/ adj acting on IMPULSE (1)

im·pu·ni·ty /ɪmˈpyuʷnəti²/ n [U] **with impunity** without being punished

im·pure /ɪmˈpyʊər/ adj 1 mixed with something else 2 morally bad **impurity** n [C;U]

in¹ /ɪn/ prep 1 contained or surrounded by: *in a box | in a field | in France* 2 (of time) a during: *in the summer* b at the end of: *finish in 5 minutes* 3 included as part of: *people in a story* 4 wearing: *the girl in red* 5 using: *write in pencil | pay in cash* 6 (shows an area of employment): *a job in insurance* 7 (shows direction): *the sun in my eyes* 8 (shows the way something is done or happens): *in public | in a hurry | in danger* 9 divided or arranged: *in rows* 10 for each: *a 1 in 10 chance* 11 with regard to: *weak in judgment* 12 as a/an: *What did you give me in return?* 13 **in all** as the total

in² /ɪn/ adv 1 (in order to be) contained or surrounded; away from the outside: *Open the bag and put the money in.* 2 towards or at home or the usual place: *Let's stay in tonight.* 3 into a surface: *hammer a nail in* 4 available or complete: *Results aren't in yet.* 5 so as to be added: *Fill in your name.* 6 (in sport) a having completed a run b (of a ball) inside the line 7 fashionable: *Long hair is in again.* 8 so as to have a position of power: *The Democrats are sure to get in.* 9 **be in for** be about to have (esp. something bad) 10 **be in on** take part in **11 be in with** *infml* be friendly with

in³ *adj* **1** directed inwards: *a letter in my in tray* **2** *infml* fashionable: *the in place to go* **3** shared by only a few favored people: *an in joke*

in⁴ *n* **the ins and outs (of something)** *infml* the details (of a difficult situation, etc.)

in·a·bil·i·ty /ˌɪnəˈbɪlət̬i/ *n* [S;U] lack of power or skill

in·ac·ces·si·ble /ˌɪnəkˈsɛsəbəl/ *adj* impossible to reach

in·ac·cu·rate /ɪnˈækyərɪt/ *adj* not correct ~**ly** *adv* ~**racy** *n* [C;U]

in·ad·e·quate /ɪnˈædəkwɪt/ *adj* not good enough ~**ly** *adv*

in·ad·ver·tent /ˌɪnədˈvɝtɪnt/ *adj* done by accident ~**ly** *adv*

in·a·li·e·na·ble /ɪnˈeɪlyənəbəl/ *adj fml* (of rights, etc.) that cannot be taken away

i·nane /ɪˈneɪn/ *adj* stupid ~**ly** *adv* **inanity** /ɪˈnænət̬i/ *n* [C;U]

in·an·i·mate /ɪnˈænəmɪt/ *adj* not living: *Stones are inanimate.*

in·ap·pro·pri·ate /ˌɪnəˈproʷprɪɪt◂/ *adj* not suitable ~**ly** *adv* ~**ness** *n* [U]

in·ar·tic·u·late /ˌɪnɑrˈtɪkyəlɪt/ *adj* **1** (of speech) not clear **2** (of people) not speaking clearly ~**ly** *adv*

in·as·much as /ˌɪnəzˈmʌtʃ əz/ *conj fml* to the degree that; because

in·au·gu·rate /ɪˈnɔgyəˌreʸt, -gə-/ *vt* **1** start or introduce formally with a special ceremony **2** be the beginning of (a period of time) –**ral** *adj*: *his inaugural speech* –**ration** /ɪˌnɔgyəˈreʸʃən, -gə-/ *n* [C;U]

Inauguration Day /·'··⸳··· ⸳·/ the 20th of January following the election of a new president

in·board /ˈɪnbɔrd, -boʷrd/ *adj* inside a boat

in·born /ˌɪnˈbɔrn◂/ *adj* present from one's birth

in·bred /ˌɪnˈbrɛd◂/ *adj* **1** inborn **2** produced by inbreeding

in·breed·ing /ˈɪnˌbriʸdɪŋ/ *n* [U] breeding between closely related family members

Inc. /ɪŋk, ˈɪnˈkɔrpəˌreʸtɪd/ *adj* incorporated; (of a business) formed into a legal CORPORATION

in·cal·cu·la·ble /ɪnˈkælkyələbəl/ *adj* too great to be counted –**bly** *adv*

in·can·des·cent /ˌɪnkænˈdɛsənt◂, -kæn-/ *adj* shining brightly when heated –**cence** *n* [U]

in·can·ta·tion /ˌɪnkænˈteʸʃən/ *n* [C;U] words used in magic

in·ca·pac·i·tate /ˌɪnkəˈpæsəˌteʸt/ *vt* make unable (to do something) –**ty** *n* [S;U] lack of ability

in·car·ce·rate /ɪnˈkɑrsəˌreʸt/ *vt fml* put in prison –**ration** /ɪnˌkɑrsəˈreʸʃən/ *n* [U]

in·car·nate /ɪnˈkɑrnɪt, -ˌneʸt/ *adj* in human form: *the devil incarnate* –**nation** /ˌɪnkɑrˈneʸʃən/ *n* **1** [U] state of being incarnate **2** [C] any of a person's many lives: (fig.) *in her former incarnation as mayor* **3** [the] (*cap.*) the coming of God to Earth in the body of Jesus Christ

in·cen·di·a·ry /ɪnˈsɛndiˌɛriʸ/ *adj* **1** causing fires: *incendiary bomb* **2** causing violence: *incendiary speech*

in·cense /ˈɪnsɛns/ *n* [U] substance burned to make a sweet smell

in·censed /ɪnˈsɛnst/ *adj fml* extremely angry

in·cen·tive /ɪnˈsɛntɪv/ *n* [C;U] encouragement to get things done

in·cep·tion /ɪnˈsɛpʃən/ *n fml* beginning

in·ces·sant /ɪnˈsɛsənt/ *adj* (of something bad) never stopping ~**ly** *adv*

in·cest /ˈɪnsɛst/ *n* [U] sexual relationship between close relatives ~**uous** /ɪnˈsɛstʃuʷəs/ *adj*

inch /ɪntʃ/ *n* **1** a measure of length equal to 1/12 of a foot or 2.54 centimeters **2** small amount **3every inch** completely **4 within an inch of** very near ♦ *vi/t* move slowly

in·ci·dence /ˈɪnsədəns/ *n* [S] rate of happening: *a high incidence of disease*

in·ci·dent /ˈɪnsədənt/ *n* **1** event, esp. one that is unusual **2** event that includes or leads to violence, danger, or serious disagreement: *The spy scandal caused a diplomatic incident.*

in·ci·den·tal /ˌɪnsəˈdɛntl◂/ *adj* **1** happening in connection with something else: *incidental expenses* **2** something (esp. a fact or detail) that is unimportant ~**ally** *adv* (used to introduce a new subject in talking)

in·cin·e·rate /ɪnˈsɪnəˌreʸt/ *vt fml* burn (unwanted things) –**rator** *n* machine for burning things

in·cip·i·ent /ɪnˈsɪpiʸənt/ *adj fml* at an early stage

in·cise /ɪnˈsaɪz/ *vt* cut into **incisor** *n* front cutting tooth **incisive** /-sɪv/ *adj* going directly to the point: *incisive comments* **incision** /ɪnˈsɪʒən/ *n* [C;U] (act of making) a cut, done with a special tool

in·cite /ɪnˈsaɪt/ *vt* encourage (violence, or people to be violent) ~**ment** *n* [C;U]

in·cline¹ /ɪnˈklaɪn/ *v* **1** *vt* encourage to feel or think **2** *vi* tend: *I incline to take the opposite view.* **3** *vi/t* slope **4** *vt fml* (cause to) move downward: *He inclined his head (in greeting).* **inclined** *adj* **1** inclined to **2** inclined to stick. **inclination** /ˌɪnkləˈneʸʃən/ *n* **1** [C;U] liking **2** [C] tendency **3** [C] act of inclining

in·cline² /ˈɪnklaɪn/ *n* slope

in·clude /ɪn'kluʷd/ vt **1** have as a part **2** put in with something else **inclusion** /ɪn'kluʷʒən/ n [U] **inclusive** /-'kluʷsɪv/ adj including everything

in·cog·ni·to /ˌɪnkagˈniʸtoʷ, ɪnˈkagnə,toʷ/ adj, adv taking another name

in·co·her·ent /ˌɪnkoʷˈhɪərənt/ adj not clearly connected ~ly adv -ence n [U]

in·come /'ɪnkʌm, 'ɪŋ-/ n money received regularly

income tax /'··· ·/ n tax on one's income

in·com·ing /'ɪn,kʌmɪŋ/ adj coming in, starting a period in office

in·com·mu·ni·ca·do /ˌɪnkəˌmyuʷˈni'kadoʷ/ adv (of people) prevented from giving or receiving messages

in·com·pa·ra·ble /ɪnˈkɑmpərəbəl/ adj unequaled; very great –bly adv

in·com·pat·i·ble /ˌɪnkəmˈpætəbəl/ adj not suitable to be together –bility /ˌɪnkəmˌpætəˈbɪlət̮iʸ/ n [U]

in·com·pe·tent /ɪnˈkɑmpətənt/ adj not skillful –tence n [U]

in·com·pre·hen·si·ble /ˌɪnkɑmprɪˈhensəbəl, ɪn,kɑm-/ adj impossible to understand –sion /-'henʃən/ n [U] failure to understand –bility /ˌɪnkɑmprɪˌhensəˈbɪlət̮iʸ, ɪn,kɑm-/ n [U]

in·con·ceiv·a·ble /ˌɪnkənˈsiʸvəbəl/ adj impossible to imagine

in·con·gru·ous /ɪnˈkɑŋgruʷəs/ adj out of place -ity /ˌɪnkɑŋˈgruʷət̮iʸ, -kən-/ n [C;U]

in·con·se·quen·tial /ˌɪnkɑnsəˈkwenʃəl, -tʃəl, ɪn,kɑn-/ adj **1** unimportant **2** not RELEVANT ~ly adv

in·con·sid·er·ate /ˌɪnkənˈsɪdərɪt/ adj not thinking of other people ~ly adv

in·con·so·la·ble /ˌɪnkənˈsoʷləbəl/ adj too sad to be comforted –bly adv

in·con·ti·nent /ɪnˈkɑntən-ənt/ adj unable to control one's bowels and BLADDER –nence n [U]

in·con·tro·vert·i·ble /ˌɪnkɑntrə'vert̮əbəl, ɪn,kɑn-/ adj fml which cannot be disproved –bly adv

in·con·ven·ience /ˌɪnkənˈviʸnyəns/ n (cause of) state of difficulty when things do not suit one ♦ vt cause inconvenience to –ent adj causing inconvenience –ently adv

in·cor·po·rate /ɪnˈkɔrpəˌreʸt/ vt **1** form into a CORPORATION **2** include in something larger –ration /ɪn,kɔrpəˈreʸʃən/ n [U]

in·cor·ri·gi·ble /ɪnˈkɔrədʒəbəl, -'kar-/ adj bad, and impossible to improve –bly adv

in·crease /ɪnˈkriʸs/ vi/t (cause to) become larger **increasingly** adv more and more **increase** /'ɪŋkriʸs/ n rise in amount, numbers, or degree

in·cred·i·ble /ɪnˈkrɛdəbəl/ adj **1** unbelievable **2** infml wonderful –bly adv

in·cred·u·lous /ɪnˈkrɛdʒələs/ adj not believing ~ly adv -lity /ˌɪnkrə'duʷlət̮iʸ, -'dyuʷ-/ n [U] disbelief

in·cre·ment /'ɪnkrəmənt, 'ɪŋ-/ n increase in money or value

in·crim·i·nate /ɪnˈkrɪmə,neʸt/ vt cause (someone) to seem guilty of a crime or fault

in·cu·bate /'ɪŋkyə,beʸt, 'ɪn-/ vt keep (eggs) warm until they HATCH –bator n apparatus for keeping eggs warm, or for keeping PREMATURE babies alive –bation /ˌɪŋkyə'beʸʃən/ n [U] **1** act of incubating **2** period between infection and the appearance of a disease

in·cul·cate /ɪnˈkʌl,keʸt, 'ɪnkʌl,keʸt/ vt fix (ideas) in someone's mind

in·cum·bent /ɪnˈkʌmbənt/ adj **be incumbent on** fml be the moral duty of ♦ n person holding a (political) office

in·cur /ɪnˈkɜr/ vt -rr- bring (esp. something bad) on oneself: incur expenses

in·cur·a·ble /ɪnˈkyʊərəbəl/ adj that cannot be cured –bly adv

in·cur·sion /ɪnˈkɜrʒən/ n fml sudden entrance; invasion (INVADE)

in·debt·ed /ɪnˈdɛt̮ɪd/ adj grateful ~ness n [U]

in·de·cent /ɪnˈdiʸsənt/ adj **1** sexually offensive **2** unsuitable ~ly adv –cency n [U]

in·de·ci·sion /ˌɪndɪˈsɪʒən/ n [U] inability to decide

in·deed /ɪnˈdiʸd/ adv fml **1** certainly; really: 'Did you see him?' 'Indeed I did.' **2** (showing surprise): Did he, indeed?

in·de·fat·i·ga·ble /ˌɪndɪˈfæt̮ɪgəbəl/ adj tireless –bly adv

in·de·fen·si·ble /ˌɪndɪˈfensəbəl/ adj that cannot be defended: indefensible behavior

in·de·fi·na·ble /ˌɪndɪˈfaɪnəbəl/ adj impossible to describe –bly adv

in·def·i·nite /ɪnˈdɛfənɪt/ adj not clear or fixed ~ly adv for an unlimited period

indefinite ar·ti·cle /·,··· '····/ (in English) A or AN

in·del·i·ble /ɪnˈdɛləbəl/ adj that cannot be removed or washed out –bly adv

in·del·i·cate /ɪnˈdɛlɪkɪt/ adj not polite or modest ~ly adv –cacy n [U]

in·dem·ni·fy /ɪnˈdɛmnə,faɪ/ vt pay (someone) in case of loss –nity n [C;U] protection against loss; payment for loss

in·dent /ɪnˈdɛnt/ vi/t start (a line of writing) further into the page than

the others ♦ *n a half-inch indent*
~**ation** /ˌɪndenˈteɪʃən/ *n* **1** [C;U]
(act of making) a space at the beginning of a line of writing **2** space
pointing inwards: *the indentations
of a coastline*

in·de·pen·dent /ˌɪndɪˈpendənt◄/ *adj*
1 governing itself **2** not depending
on advice, money, etc., from others
♦ *n (often cap.)* person who does not
belong to an established political
party ~**ly** *adv* –**dence** *n* [U]

in-depth /ˈ· ·/ *adj* very thorough

in·de·scri·ba·ble /ˌɪndɪˈskraɪbəbəl/
adj that cannot be described –**bly**
adv

in·de·struc·ti·ble /ˌɪndɪˈstrʌktəbəl/
adj too strong to be destroyed

in·de·ter·mi·nate /ˌɪndɪˈtɜrmɪnɪt/
adj not fixed as one thing or another

in·dex /ˈɪndeks/ *n* –**dexes** *or* –**dices**
/-dəˌsiːz/ **1** alphabetical list of subjects mentioned in a book **2 a** sign
by which something can be measured **b** system of comparing prices
with their former level: *the cost of
living index* ♦ *vt* make, include in,
or provide with an INDEX (1)

index fin·ger /ˈ·· ˌ·/ *n* FOREFINGER

In·di·an /ˈɪndiːən/ *n, adj* **1** (member) of the original peoples of North,
South, or Central America except
the ESKIMO **2** (person) from India

in·di·cate /ˈɪndəˌkeɪt/ *vt* **1** point at;
show **2** show (the direction in which
one is turning in a vehicle) by hand
signals, lights, etc. –**cator** *n* needle
or pointer showing measurement
–**cation** /ˌɪndəˈkeɪʃən/ *n* [C;U] sign
or suggestion indicating something

in·dic·a·tive /ɪnˈdɪkətɪv/ *adj* showing ♦ *n gram* verb form expressing
a fact or action

in·di·ces /ˈɪndəˌsiːz/ *n* pl. of INDEX

in·dict /ɪnˈdaɪt/ *vt* charge officially
with a crime ~**able** *adj* for which
one can be indicted: *indictable
offense* ~**ment** *n* [C;U] *under indictment for murder*

in·dif·fer·ent /ɪnˈdɪfərənt/ *adj* **1** not
interested **2** not very good ~**ly** *adv*
–**ence** *n* [U]

in·di·ge·nous /ɪnˈdɪdʒənəs/ *adj*
NATIVE to a place: *indigenous flowers*

in·di·ges·tion /ˌɪndəˈdʒestʃən, -daɪ-/
n [U] illness from not being able to
DIGEST food

in·dig·nant /ɪnˈdɪgnənt/ *adj* angry,
esp. at something unjust ~**ly** *adv*
–**nation** /ˌɪndɪgˈneɪʃən/ *n* [U]
indignant feeling

in·dig·ni·ty /ɪnˈdɪgnəˌtiː/ *n* [C;U]
treatment that makes one feel
ashamed

in·di·rect /ˌɪndəˈrekt◄, -daɪ-/ *adj*
1 not straight; not directly connected
to: *indirect route* | *indirect result* **2** (of
taxes) paid by increasing the cost of

goods or services **3** meaning something which is not directly mentioned: *an indirect answer* ~**ly** *adv*

indirect ob·ject /ˌ··· ˈ··/ *n* person or
thing that the DIRECT OBJECT is given
to, made for, done to, etc.: *In 'I asked
him a question', 'him' is the indirect
object.*

indirect speech /ˌ··· ˈ·/ *n* [U] *gram*
speech reported without repeating
the actual words (e.g. *She said, 'I'm
coming.'* becomes *She said she was
coming.*)

in·dis·creet /ˌɪndɪˈskriːt/ *adj* not
acting carefully or politely ~**ly** *adv*
–**cretion** /-ˈskreʃən/ *n* **1** [U] state or
quality of being indiscreet **2** [C] indiscreet act: *youthful indiscretions*

in·dis·crim·i·nate /ˌɪndɪˈskrɪmɪnɪt/
adj not choosing or chosen carefully
~**ly** *adv*

in·dis·pen·sa·ble /ˌɪndɪˈspensəbəl/
adj necessary

in·dis·posed /ˌɪndɪˈspoʊzd/ *adj fml*
1 not very well **2** unwilling

in·dis·pu·ta·ble /ˌɪndɪˈspjuːtəbəl/
adj beyond doubt: *indisputable
proof* –**bly** *adv*

in·dis·tin·guish·a·ble /ˌɪndɪˈstɪŋ
gwɪʃəbəl/ *adj* impossible to tell
apart: *indistinguishable from silk*

in·di·vid·u·al /ˌɪndəˈvɪdʒuːəl/ *adj* **1**
single; separate **2** (of a manner,
style, or way of doing things) particular to a person, thing, etc. ♦ *n* single person (in a group) ~**ly** *adv*
separately ~**ism** *n* [U] belief in the
rights of each person in society ~**ist**
n, adj (person) independent and
unlike other people ~**istic** /ˌɪndə
ˌvɪdʒuːˈɪlɪstɪk/ *adj* ~**ity** /ˌɪndə
ˌvɪdʒuːˈælətiː/ *n* [U] qualities that
make a person unusual

in·doc·tri·nate /ɪnˈdɑktrəˌneɪt/ *vt*
train to accept ideas without question –**nation** /ɪnˌdɑktrəˈneɪʃən/ *n*
[U]

in·do·lent /ˈɪndələnt/ *adj fml* lazy
–**lence** *n* [U]

in·dom·i·ta·ble /ɪnˈdɑmətəbəl/ *adj*
too strong to be discouraged or controlled

in·door /ˈɪndɔr, ˈɪndoʊr/ *adj* inside
a building **indoors** *adv*

in·du·bi·ta·ble /ɪnˈduːbətəbəl,
-ˈdjuː-/ *adj fml* unquestionable
–**bly** *adv*

in·duce /ɪnˈduːs, ɪnˈdjuːs/ *vt* **1** persuade **2** cause; produce ~**ment** *n*
[C;U] (something, esp. money,
which provides) encouragement to
do something

in·duct /ɪnˈdʌkt/ *vt* introduce someone officially into an organization,
esp. the army

in·duc·tion /ɪnˈdʌkʃən/ *n* **1** [U] act or
ceremony of introducing a person to
a new job, organization, etc. **2** [C;U]

(action of causing) birth of a child which has been hastened by the use of drugs **3** [U] way of reasoning using known facts to produce general laws

in·dulge /ɪnˈdʌldʒ/ v **1** vt allow to do or have something nice **2** vi allow oneself pleasure: *indulge in a cigar* **indulgence** n [U] indulging **2** [C] something in which one indulges **indulgent** adj (too) kind

in·dus·tri·al /ɪnˈdʌstriəl/ adj of or having INDUSTRY (1) **~·ly** adv **~·ism** n [U] system in which industries are important **~ist** n owner or manager of an industry **~·ize** vi/t (cause to) become industrially developed

industrial park /·ˌ·· ˈ·/ n area where factories are built

in·dus·tri·ous /ɪnˈdʌstriəs/ adj working hard **~·ly** adv

in·dus·try /ˈɪndəstriʸ/ n **1** [C;U] (branch of) the production of goods for sale: *the clothing industry* **2** [U] continual hard work

i·ne·bri·at·ed /ɪˈniʸbriʸeʸtɪd/ adj fml drunk

in·ed·i·ble /ɪnˈedəbəl/ adj unsuitable for eating

in·ef·fec·tive /ˌɪnɪˈfektɪv/ adj unable to produce the right results **~·ly** adv **~·ness** n [U]

in·ef·fec·tu·al /ˌɪnəˈfektʃuʷəl/ adj which does not give a good enough effect, or who is not able to get things done **~·ly** adv

in·ef·fi·cient /ˌɪnəˈfɪʃənt◂/ adj not working well **~·ly** adv **–ciency** n [U]

in·el·i·gi·ble /ɪnˈelədʒəbəl/ adj not fulfilling the conditions **–bility** /ɪnˌelədʒəˈbɪləṭiʸ/ n [U]

in·ept /ɪˈnept/ adj **1** foolishly unsuitable **2** totally unable to do things **~·ly** adv **~·itude** n [C;U]

in·e·qual·i·ty /ˌɪnɪˈkwɒləṭiʸ/ n [C;U] lack of fairness or equality

in·ert /ɪˈnɜrt/ adj **1** unable to move **2** not acting chemically: *inert gases*

in·er·tia /ɪˈnɜrʃə/ n **1** force that keeps a thing in the same state until pushed **2** laziness

in·es·ca·pa·ble /ˌɪnəˈskeʸpəbəl/ adj unavoidable

in·es·ti·ma·ble /ɪnˈestəməbəl/ adj fml too good to be measured **–bly** adv

in·ev·i·ta·ble /ɪˈnevəṭəbəl/ adj **1** unavoidable **2** infml expected and familiar: *The principal made her inevitable joke about the school food.* **–bly** adv **–bility** /ɪˌnevəṭəˈbɪləṭiʸ/ n [U]

in·ex·cu·sa·ble /ˌɪnɪkˈskyuʷzəbəl/ adj unforgivable **–bly** adv

in·ex·o·ra·ble /ɪnˈeksərəbəl/ adj fml impossible to change or prevent **–bly** adv

in·ex·pli·ca·ble /ˌɪnɪkˈsplɪkəbəl, ɪnˈeksplɪkə-/ adj too strange to be explained **–bly** adv

in·ex·pres·si·ble /ˌɪnɪkˈspresəbəl/ adj too great to be expressed **–bly** adv

in·ex·tri·ca·ble /ɪnˈekstrɪkəbəl, ˌɪnɪkˈstrɪ-/ adj impossible to escape from, or to untie **–bly** adv

in·fal·li·ble /ɪnˈfæləbəl/ adj **1** never making mistakes **2** always effective: *infallible cure* **–bility** /ɪnˌfælə-ˈbɪləṭiʸ/ n [U]

in·fa·mous /ˈɪnfəməs/ adj wicked **–my** n [C;U] wickedness

in·fan·cy /ˈɪnfənsiʸ/ n [S;U] early childhood

in·fant /ˈɪnfənt/ n fml baby

in·fan·tile /ˈɪnfənˌtaɪl, -tɪl/ adj childish

in·fan·try /ˈɪnfəntriʸ/ n [U] foot soldiers

in·fat·u·at·ed /ɪnˈfætʃuʷˌeʸṭɪd/ adj foolishly loving **–ation** /ɪnˌfætʃuʷ-ˈeʸʃən/ n [C;U]

in·fect /ɪnˈfekt/ vt give disease to: (fig.) *She infected the whole class with her laughter.* (= everyone laughed) **~·ion** /-ˈfekʃən/ n [C;U] (disease spread by) infecting **~·ious** adj able to infect: (fig.) *infectious laughter*

in·fer /ɪnˈfɜr/ vt **-rr-** draw (meaning) from facts: *I inferred from his letter that he had not made a decision* **~·ence** /ˈɪnfərəns/ n [C;U]

in·fe·ri·or /ɪnˈfɪəriʸər/ adj less good; low(er) in rank ♦ n inferior person **~·ity** /ɪnˌfɪəriʸˈɔrəṭiʸ, -ˈɑrə-/ n [U]

in·fer·nal /ɪnˈfɜrnl/ adj terrible; like HELL

in·fer·no /ɪnˈfɜrnoʷ/ n **–nos** place of very great heat and large uncontrollable flames

in·fer·tile /ɪnˈfɜrṭl/ adj not FERTILE: *infertile eggs*

in·fest /ɪnˈfest/ vt (of something bad) be present in large numbers **~·ation** n

in·fi·del·i·ty /ˌɪnfəˈdeləṭiʸ/ n [C;U] **1** (act of) disloyalty **2** (act of) sex with someone other than one's marriage partner

in·fight·ing /ˈɪnˌfaɪtɪŋ/ n [U] disagreement between members of a group

in·fil·trate /ɪnˈfɪlˌtreʸt, ˈɪnfɪl-/ vt enter secretly, with an unfriendly purpose **–tration** /ˌɪnfɪlˈtreʸʃən/ n [U]

in·fi·nite /ˈɪnfənɪt/ adj without limits; endless **~·ly** adv

in·fin·i·tive /ɪnˈfɪnəṭɪv/ n main verb form that can follow other verbs and be used with *to* (e.g. 'go' in *I can go* and *I want to go*)

in·fin·i·ty /ɪnˈfɪnətiʸ/ n [U] endless space or quantity

in·firm /ɪnˈfɜrm/ adj fml weak in body or mind ~**ity** n [C;U]

in·fir·ma·ry /ɪnˈfɜrməriʸ/ n room where sick people are given treatment

in·flame /ɪnˈfleʸm/ vt make violent **inflamed** red and swollen: inflamed eye

in·flam·ma·ble /ɪnˈflæməbəl/ adj 1 which can easily be set on fire and which burns quickly 2 easily excited or made angry

in·flam·ma·tion /ˌɪnfləˈmeʸʃən/ n [C;U] inflamed condition

in·flam·ma·to·ry /ɪnˈflæməˌtoriʸ, -ˌtoʷriʸ/ adj likely to inflame: inflammatory speeches

in·flate /ɪnˈfleʸt/ v 1 vt blow up (a tire, etc.) with air 2 vi/t increase the supply of money in a country **inflated** adj 1 full of air 2 too big: inflated prices | an inflated opinion of oneself

in·fla·tion /ɪnˈfleʸʃən/ n [U] 1 act of inflating or state of being inflated 2 rise in prices caused by increased production costs or an increase in money supply ~**ary** adj likely to cause INFLATION (2)

in·flec·tion /ɪnˈflɛkʃən/ n [C;U] a gram change in the form of a word to show difference in its use b movement up or down of the voice

in·flex·i·ble /ɪnˈflɛksəbəl/ adj impossible to bend or change –**bly** adv –**bility** /ɪnˌflɛksəˈbɪlətiʸ/ n [U]

in·flict /ɪnˈflɪkt/ vt force (punishment, etc.) on ~**ion** /-ˈflɪkʃən/ n [C;U]

in·flow /ˈɪnfloʷ/ n [C;U] flowing in

in·flu·ence /ˈɪnfluʷəns/ n [C;U] 1 (power to have) an effect 2 someone with this power: She's a bad influence on you. 3 **under the influence** drunk ♦ vt have an influence on

in·flu·en·tial /ˌɪnfluʷˈɛnʃəl, -tʃəl/ adj having great influence

in·flu·en·za /ˌɪnfluʷˈɛnzə/ n [U] fml FLU

in·flux /ˈɪnflʌks/ n [C;U] arrival in large numbers or quantities

in·fo /ˈɪnfoʷ/ n infml for information

in·form /ɪnˈfɔrm/ vt fml give information to ~**ant** n person who gives information ~**ed** adj 1 knowing things: well-informed 2 having and using suitable knowledge: an informed guess ~**er** n person who tells the police about someone

inform against/on phr vt tell the police that (someone) is guilty

in·for·mal /ɪnˈfɔrməl/ adj not formal; without ceremony: an informal meeting | informal clothes ~**ly** adv ~**ity** /ˌɪnfɔrˈmælətiʸ/ n [U]

in·for·ma·tion /ˌɪnfərˈmeʸʃən/ n [U] 1 knowledge given; facts 2 service that provides telephone numbers: I got your number from information.

information tech·nol·o·gy /··,·· ·ˈ···/ n [U] science of collecting and using information by means of computer systems

in·for·ma·tive /ɪnˈfɔrmətɪv/ adj telling one useful things

in·fra·red /ˌɪnfrəˈrɛd◀/ adj of the light RAYS of longer WAVELENGTH than those we can see

in·fra·struc·ture /ˈɪnfrəˌstrʌktʃər/ n necessary BASIC systems (e.g. of power, roads, laws, banks) needed to keep a country going

in·fringe /ɪnˈfrɪndʒ/ vt/i fml go against (a law, or someone's rights) ~**ment** n [C;U]

in·fu·ri·ate /ɪnˈfyʊəriʸˌeʸt/ vt make very angry

in·fuse /ɪnˈfyuʷz/ vt 1 fill (someone) with a quality 2 put (tea, etc.) into hot water to make a drink **infusion** /-ˈfyuʷʒən/ n [C;U] (liquid made by) infusing

in·ge·nious /ɪnˈdʒiʸnyəs/ adj clever at making or inventing: ingenious person/excuse ~**ly** adv –**nuity** /ˌɪndʒəˈnuʷətiʸ, -ˈnyuʷ-/ n [U]

in·gen·u·ous /ɪnˈdʒɛnyuʷəs/ adj simple and inexperienced ~**ly** adv

in·glo·ri·ous /ɪnˈgloriʸəs, -ˈgloʷr-/ adj lit shameful ~**ly** adv

in·got /ˈɪŋgət/ n lump of metal shaped like a brick

in·grained /ɪnˈgreʸnd, ˈɪngreʸnd/ adj deeply fixed: ingrained dirt/ habits

in·gra·ti·ate /ɪnˈgreʸʃiʸˌeʸt/ vt make (oneself) pleasant, so as to gain favor –**ating** adj –**atingly** adv

in·grat·i·tude /ɪnˈgrætəˌtuʷd, -ˌtyuʷd/ n [U] ungratefulness

in·gre·di·ent /ɪnˈgriʸdiʸənt/ n one of a mixture of things, esp. in baking

in-group /ˈ· ·/ n group that treats members better than non-members

in·hab·it /ɪnˈhæbɪt/ vt fml live in (a place) ~**ant** n person living in a place

in·hale /ɪnˈheʸl/ vi/t breathe in **inhaler** n apparatus for inhaling medicine to make breathing easier **inhalation** /ˌɪnhəˈleʸʃən/ n [C;U]

in·her·ent /ɪnˈhɪərənt, -ˈhɛr-/ adj necessarily present; problems inherent in the system ~**ly** adv

in·her·it /ɪnˈhɛrɪt/ vi/t receive (property, etc.) from someone who has died: (fig.) He's inherited his father's meanness ~**ance** n 1 [C] something inherited 2 [U] inheriting ~**or** n person who inherits

in·hib·it /ɪnˈhɪbɪt/ vt prevent; HINDER ~**ion** /ˌɪnhɪˈbɪʃən/ n feeling of being unable to do what one really wants to

in·hu·man /ɪn'hyuːmən/ *adj* cruel ~**ity** /ˌɪnhyuː'mænətiʲ/ *n* [C;U]

in·hu·mane /ˌɪnhyuː'meʲn/ *adj* unkind; not HUMANE *n* [C;U] ~**ly** *adv*

in·im·i·ta·ble /ɪ'nɪmɪtəbəl/ *adj* too good or unusual to be copied –**bly** *adv*

in·iq·ui·tous /ɪ'nɪkwətəs/ *adj fml* very unjust or wicked ~**ly** *adv* –**ty** *n* [C;U]

i·ni·tial /ɪ'nɪʃəl/ *adj* at the beginning ♦ *n* first letter of someone's name ♦ *vt* –**l**– write one's initials on ~**ly** *adv* at first

i·ni·ti·ate[1] /ɪ'nɪʃiʲeʲt/ *vt* 1 start (something) working 2 introduce (someone) into a group, etc. –**ation** /ɪˌnɪʃiʲ'eʲʃən/ *n* [C;U]

i·ni·ti·ate[2] /ɪ'nɪʃiʲɪt/ *n* person instructed or skilled in some special field

i·ni·tia·tive /ɪ'nɪʃətɪv, -ʃiʲə-/ *n* 1 [U] ability to act without help or advice: *on his own initiative* 2 [C] first step: *initiatives to encourage investment*

in·ject /ɪn'dʒɛkt/ *vt* put (a drug, etc.) into someone with a needle: (fig.) *inject new life, interest, etc., into something* ~**ion** /-'dʒɛkʃən/ *n* [C;U]

in·junc·tion /ɪn'dʒʌŋkʃən/ *n fml* official order

in·jure /'ɪndʒər/ *vt* hurt; damage **injured** *adj*, *n* hurt (people) **injury** *n* 1 [U] harm; damage 2 [C] wound, etc.

in·jus·tice /ɪn'dʒʌstɪs/ *n* [C;U] (act of) unfairness

ink /ɪŋk/ *n* [C;U] colored liquid for writing, printing, etc. ~**y** *adj* black

ink·ling /'ɪŋklɪŋ/ *n* [S;U] slight idea

in·laid /'ɪnleʲd, ɪn'leʲd/ *adj* set or namentally in another substance: *inlaid gold*

in·land /'ɪnlənd/ *adj, adv* inside or into a country *travel inland*

in·laws /'· ·/ *n* [P] relatives by marriage

in·let /'ɪnlɛt, 'ɪnlɪt/ *n* narrow piece of water reaching into the land

in·mate /'ɪnmeʲt/ *n* person living in a prison, hospital, etc.

in·most /'ɪnmoʷst/ also **in·ner·most** /'ɪnərmoʷst/ — *adj* furthest inside; most well-hidden

inn /ɪn/ *n* small hotel or restaurant

in·nards /'ɪnərdz/ *n* [P] inside parts, esp. of the stomach

in·nate /ɪˌɪ'neʲt◂/ *adj* (of a quality) present from birth ~**ly** *adv*

in·ner /'ɪnər/ *adj* 1 on the inside; close to the middle 2 secret, esp. if of the spirit: *inner meaning*/*life*

inner ci·ty /ˌ·· '··◂/ *n* center of an old city where many poor people live

in·ning /'ɪnɪŋ/ *n* period of play in BASEBALL: *He scored a home run in the second inning.*

inn·keep·er /'ɪnˌkiʲpər/ *n* manager of an INN

in·no·cent /'ɪnəsənt/ *adj* 1 not guilty 2 harmless 3 unable to recognize evil; simple ~**ly** *adv* –**cence** *n*

in·noc·u·ous /ɪ'nɑkyuʷəs/ *adj* harmless

in·no·va·tion /ˌɪnə'veʲʃən/ *n* 1 [C] new idea 2 [U] introducing new things –**vate** /'ɪnəˌveʲt/ *vi* make changes –**tor** *n* –**tive** also –**tory** /'ɪnəvəˌtɔriʲ, -ˌtoʷriʲ/ *adj*

in·nu·en·do /ˌɪnyuʷˈɛndoʷ/ *n* –**does** or –**dos** [C;U] unpleasant indirect remark(s)

in·nu·me·ra·ble /ɪ'nuːmərəbəl, ɪ'nyuː-/ *adj* too many to count

i·noc·u·late /ɪ'nɑkyəˌleʲt/ *vt* introduce a weak form of a disease into (someone) as a protection –**lation** /ɪˌnɑkyə'leʲʃən/ *n* [C;U]

in·of·fen·sive /ˌɪnə'fɛnsɪv/ *adj* not causing dislike; not rude ~**ly** *adv*

in·op·por·tune /ɪnˌɑpər'tuʷn, -'tyuʷn, ˌɪnɑ-/ *adj fml* at the wrong time ~**ly** *adv*

in·or·di·nate /ɪn'ɔrdn-ɪt/ *adj fml* beyond reasonable limits ~**ly** *adv*

in·put /'ɪnpʊt/ *n* [S;U] something put in for use, esp. information into a computer ♦ *vt* –**tt**–; *past t. & p.* **inputted** or **input** put (information) into a computer

in·quest /'ɪnkwɛst/ *n* official inquiry, esp. when someone dies unexpectedly

in·quire /ɪn'kwaɪər/ *vi/t* ask for information (about) **inquiring** *adj* that shows an interest in knowing **inquiry** /ɪn'kwaɪəriʲ, 'ɪnˌkwaɪ-, 'ɪŋkwəriʲ/ *n* 1 [C;U] (act of) inquiring 2 [C] set of meetings, etc., to find out why something happened

inquire after *phr vt fml* ask about the health of

inquire into *phr vt* look for information about

in·qui·si·tion /ˌɪnkwə'zɪʃən/ *n* thorough and esp. cruel inquiry

in·quis·i·tive /ɪn'kwɪzətɪv/ *adj* asking too many questions ~**ly** *adv*

in·roads /'ɪnroʷdz/ *n* [P] 1 attack upon or advance into a new area 2 effort or activity that lessens the quantity or difficulty of what remains afterwards: *inroads in fighting a disease*

ins and outs /ˌ·· '··/ *n* [*the*+P] details (of a situation, problem, etc.)

in·sane /ɪn'seʲn/ *adj* crazy ~**ly** *adv* **insanity** /ɪn'sænətiʲ/ *n* [U]

in·san·i·ta·ry /ɪn'sænəˌteriʲ/ *adj* dirty enough to cause disease

in·sa·tia·ble /ɪnˈseɪʃəbəl, -ʃiˈə-/ adj impossible to satisfy –**bly** adv

in·scribe /ɪnˈskraɪb/ vt fml write (words) on **inscription** /ɪnˈskrɪpʃən/ n piece of writing inscribed, esp. on stone

in·scru·ta·ble /ɪnˈskruʷtəbəl/ adj mysterious: *inscrutable smile* –**bly** adv

in·sect /ˈɪnsɛkt/ n small creature with 6 legs

in·sec·ti·cide /ɪnˈsɛktɪˌsaɪd/ n [C;U] chemical used to kill insects

in·se·cure /ˌɪnsɪˈkyʊər/ adj 1 not safe 2 not sure of oneself ~**ly** adv –**curity** n [U]

in·sem·i·na·tion /ɪnˌsɛməˈneɪʃən/ n [U] putting of male seed into a female

in·sen·si·ble /ɪnˈsɛnsəbəl/ adj 1 unconscious 2 lacking feeling for –**bility** /ɪnˌsɛnsəˈbɪlətiʸ/ n [U]

in·sen·si·tive /ɪnˈsɛnsətɪv/ adj not SENSITIVE –**ly** adv –**tivity** /ɪnˌsɛnsə-ˈtɪvətiʸ/ n [S;U]

in·sep·a·ra·ble /ɪnˈsɛpərəbəl/ adj impossible to separate

in·sert[1] /ɪnˈsɜrt/ vt put into something: *insert a key in a lock* ♦ **insert** /ˈɪnsɜrt/ n written or printed material put in between pages of a book –**ion** /ɪnˈsɜrʃən/ n [C;U]

in-ser·vice /ˌ·ˈ··◂/ adj (taking place) during one's work: *in-service training*

in·set /ˈɪnsɛt/ n picture, etc., in the corner of a larger one

in·side /ɪnˈsaɪd, ˈɪnsaɪd/ n 1 [the+S] a part nearest to the middle, or that faces away from the open air b infml position in which one is able to know special or secret information 2 [C] also **insides** pl. — infml one's stomach 3 **inside out: a** with the inside parts on the outside b thoroughly: *know it inside out* ♦ adj 1 facing or at the inside: *the inside pages of a newspaper* 2 from someone closely concerned: *inside information* ♦ adv to or in the inside, esp. indoors: *The children are playing inside.* ♦ prep 1 to or on the inside of: *inside the car* 2 in less time than: *inside an hour* **insider** /ɪnˈsaɪdər/ n person accepted in a social group, esp. someone with special information or influence

insider deal·ing /·ˌ·· ˈ··◂/ — also **insider trading** n [U] illegal practice of buying and selling stock by people who use their knowledge of the business affairs of the companies they work for

in·sid·i·ous /ɪnˈsɪdiʸəs/ adj secretly harmful ~**ly** adv

in·sight /ˈɪnsaɪt/ n [C;U] understanding: *insight into their lives*

in·sig·ni·a /ɪnˈsɪgniʸə/ n [P] objects worn as signs of rank

in·sig·nif·i·cant /ˌɪnsɪgˈnɪfəkənt/ adj not important ~**ly** adv –**cance** n [U]

in·sin·u·ate /ɪnˈsɪnyuʷˌeʸt/ vt 1 suggest (something unpleasant) indirectly 2 gain acceptance for (esp. oneself) by secret means –**ation** /ɪn-ˌsɪnyuʷˈeʸʃən/ n [C;U]

in·sip·id /ɪnˈsɪpɪd/ adj derog lacking a strong character, taste, or effect

in·sist /ɪnˈsɪst/ vi/t 1 order: *insist that he should go* 2 declare firmly: *He insists he wasn't there.* ~**ent** adj repeatedly insisting ~**ence** n [U]

in si·tu /ˌɪn ˈsaɪtuʷ, -tyuʷ, -ˈsiˈ-/ adv in its original place

in so far as /ˌ· · ˈ· ·/ conj to the degree that

in·so·lent /ˈɪnsələnt/ adj disrespectful; rude –**lence** n [U]

in·sol·u·ble /ɪnˈsɑlyəbəl/ adj 1 impossible to answer 2 impossible to DISSOLVE

in·sol·vent /ɪnˈsɑlvənt/ n, adj (someone) unable to pay their debts –**vency** n [U]

in·som·ni·a /ɪnˈsɑmniʸə/ n [U] inability to sleep **insomniac** /-niʸˌæk/ n, adj (someone) who habitually cannot sleep

in·sou·ci·ance /ɪnˈsuʷsiʸəns/ n [U] not caring about anything –**ant** adj

in·spect /ɪnˈspɛkt/ vt examine closely ~**or** n 1 official who inspects something 2 police officer of middle rank ~**ion** /-ˈspɛkʃən/ n [C;U]

in·spire /ɪnˈspaɪər/ vt 1 encourage to act 2 fill with a feeling: *inspire them with confidence* **inspiration** /ˌɪn-spəˈreʸʃən/ n 1 [U] act of inspiring or state of being inspired 2 [C] something that inspires 3 [C] sudden good idea **inspired** /ɪnˈspaɪərd/ adj very clever

in·sta·bil·i·ty /ˌɪnstəˈbɪlətiʸ/ n [U] 1 state of being unsteady 2 (of people) tendency to act in changeable ways

in·stall /ɪnˈstɔl/ vt 1 put (a machine, etc.) somewhere 2 settle (someone) in a position ~**ation** /ˌɪnstəˈleʸʃən/ n 1 [U] installing 2 [C] apparatus, etc., installed

in·stall·ment /ɪnˈstɔlmənt/ n 1 single part of a story, etc., that appears in regular parts 2 single regular payment

installment plan /·ˈ·· ˌ·/ n [U] system of paying small sums regularly for goods already received

in·stance /ˈɪnstəns/ n 1 EXAMPLE (1) 2 **for instance** for example ♦ vt give as an example

in·stant /ˈɪnstənt/ n moment of time ♦ adj happening or produced at once ~**ly** adv at once

instant re·play /ˌ·· ˈ··/ n second showing of a sports event immediately after it happens

in·stan·ta·ne·ous /ˌɪnstənˈteɪnɪəs/ adj happening at once ~**ly** adv

in·stead /ɪnˈstɛd/ adv **1** in place of that **2 instead of** in place of: You go instead of me.

in·step /ˈɪnstɛp/ n upper surface of the foot

in·sti·gate /ˈɪnstəˌgeɪt/ vt fml cause to do or happen –**gator** n –**gation** /ˌɪnstəˈgeɪʃən/ n [U]

in·still /ɪnˈstɪl/ vt put (ideas) into someone's mind

in·stinct /ˈɪnstɪŋkt/ n [C;U] natural tendency to act in a certain way ~**ive** /ɪnˈstɪŋktɪv/ adj: instinctive fear of snakes ~**ively** adv

in·sti·tute /ˈɪnstəˌtuʷt, -ˌtyuʷt/ n society formed for a special purpose ♦ vt fml start; establish

in·sti·tu·tion /ˌɪnstəˈtuʷʃən, -ˈtyuʷ-/ n **1** [C] (building for) a hospital, school, prison, etc., where people are looked after **2** [C] established custom **3** [U] act of instituting ~ **al** adj ~**alize** **1** make into an INSTITUTION (2) **2** vt (of people) put into an INSTITUTION (1)

in·struct /ɪnˈstrʌkt/ vt **1** give orders to **2** teach **3** law inform officially ~**ive** adj teaching something useful

in·struc·tor /ɪnˈstrʌktər/ n university teacher who does not have a PhD (= doctor's degree)

in·struc·tion /ɪnˈstrʌkʃən/ n **1** [C] order **2** [U] act of instructing; teaching **instructions** n [P] advice on how to do something: Follow the instructions on the packet.

in·stru·ment /ˈɪnstrəmənt/ n **1** thing that helps in work **2** apparatus for playing music ~**al** /ˌɪnstrəˈmɛntəl/ adj **1** for musical instruments **2** helpful; causing: His information was instrumental in catching the thief. ~**alist** /ˌɪnstrəˈmɛntəl-ɪst/ n player of a musical instrument

in·sub·or·di·nate /ˌɪnsəˈbɔrdn-ɪt/ adj disobedient –**nation** /ˌɪnsəˌbɔrdn-ˈeɪʃən/ n [C;U]

in·sub·stan·tial /ˌɪnsəbˈstænʃəl, -tʃəl/ adj not firm or solid

in·suf·fe·ra·ble /ɪnˈsʌfərəbəl/ adj unbearable

in·suf·fi·cient /ˌɪnsəˈfɪʃənt◂/ adj not enough ~**ly** adv –**ciency** n [S;U]

in·su·lar /ˈɪnsələr, ˈɪnsyə-/ adj **1** having narrow attitudes; concerned mainly with oneself **2** of an island ~**ity** /ˌɪnsəˈlærətɪʸ, ˌɪnsyə-/ n [U]

in·su·late /ˈɪnsəˌleɪt, ˈɪnsyə-/ vt **1** cover, to prevent the escape of heat, electricity, etc. **2** protect from experiences –**lator** n thing that insulates –**lation** /ˌɪnsəˈleɪʃən, ˌɪnsyə-/ n [U] (material for) insulating

in·sult¹ /ɪnˈsʌlt/ vt be rude to

in·sult² /ˈɪnsʌlt/ n **1** rude remark or action **2 add insult to injury** do or say something more against someone when one has already harmed them anyway

in·su·pe·ra·ble /ɪnˈsuʷpərəbəl/ adj impossible to deal with

in·sup·por·ta·ble /ˌɪnsəˈpɔrtəbəl, -ˈpoʷr-/ adj unbearable

in·sur·ance /ɪnˈʃʊərəns/ n **1** [U] agreement to pay money in case of misfortune **2** [U] money paid by or to an insurance company for this **3** [S;U] protection against anything

in·sure /ɪnˈʃʊər/ vt **1** protect by insurance: insured against fire ENSURE

in·sur·gent /ɪnˈsɜrdʒənt/ n, adj REBEL –**gency** n [C;U]

in·sur·moun·ta·ble /ˌɪnsərˈmaʊntə-bəl/ adj too large, difficult, etc., to be dealt with

in·sur·rec·tion /ˌɪnsəˈrɛkʃən/ n [C;U] REBELLION

in·tact /ɪnˈtækt/ adj undamaged

in·take /ˈɪnteɪk/ n **1** [S] amount or number taken in **2** [C] pipe to let in gas, water, etc.

in·tan·gi·ble /ɪnˈtændʒəbəl/ adj **1** which cannot be known by the senses or described: an intangible quality **2** which is hidden or not material, but known to be real: intangible assets of the business, such as the loyalty of its customers –**bly** adv –**bility** /ɪnˌtændʒəˈbɪlətɪʸ/ n [U]

in·te·ger /ˈɪntədʒər/ n a whole number

in·te·gral /ˈɪntəgrəl/ adj necessary to complete something: an integral part of the argument

in·te·grate /ˈɪntəˌgreɪt/ vi/t (cause to) mix with other races or people –**gration** /ˌɪntəˈgreɪʃən/ n [U] –**grationist** n believer in integration

integrated cir·cuit /ˌ···· ˈ··/ n set of electrical connections printed esp. on a CHIP¹ (4)

in·teg·ri·ty /ɪnˈtɛgrətɪʸ/ n [U] **1** honesty; trustworthiness **2** wholeness

in·tel·lect /ˈɪntlˌɛkt/ n [C;U] ability to think ~**ual** /ˌɪntəlˈɛktʃuʷəl/ adj **1** of the intellect **2** clever and well-educated ~**ual** n intellectual person ~**ually** adv

in·tel·li·gence /ɪnˈtɛlədʒəns/ n [U] **1** ability to learn and understand **2** (people who gather) information about enemies –**gent** adj clever –**gently** adv

in·tel·li·gent·si·a /ɪnˌtɛləˈdʒɛntsɪʸə/ n [P] intellectuals as a social group

in·tel·li·gi·ble /ɪnˈtɛlədʒəbəl/ adj understandable –**bly** adv –**bility** /ɪnˌtɛlədʒəˈbɪlətɪʸ/ n [U]

in·tend /ɪnˈtend/ vt have as one's purpose; mean

in·tense /ɪnˈtens/ adj strong (in quality or feeling) ~**ly** adv **intensity** n [U] quality or appearance of being intense

in·ten·si·fy /ɪnˈtensəˌfaɪ/ vi/t make or become more intense –**fication** /ɪnˌtensəfəˈkeɪʃən/ n [U]

in·ten·sive /ɪnˈtensɪv/ adj giving a lot of attention ~**ly** adv

in·tent¹ /ɪnˈtent/ n [U] **1** purpose: *enter with intent to steal* **2 to all intents and purposes** in almost every way

intent² adj **1** with fixed attention **2** determined

in·ten·tion /ɪnˈtenʃən, -tʃən/ n **1** [C;U] plan; purpose **2 good intentions** wish to bring about a good result ~**al** adj done on purpose ~**ally** adv

in·ter /ɪnˈtɜr/ vt –**rr**– fml bury

in·ter·act /ˌɪntərˈækt/ vi have an effect on each other ~**ion** /-ˈækʃən/ n [C;U]

in·ter·ac·tive /ˌɪntərˈæktɪv/ adj **1** that interacts **2** allowing the exchange of information between a computer and a user while a program is in operation

in·ter·cede /ˌɪntərˈsiːd/ vi speak in favor of someone

in·ter·cept /ˌɪntərˈsept/ vt stop (someone or something moving between 2 places) ~**ion** /-ˈsepʃən/ n [C;U]

in·ter·ces·sion /ˌɪntərˈseʃən/ n **1** [U] act of interceding **2** [C;U] prayer which asks for other people to be helped

in·ter·change /ˌɪntərˈtʃeɪndʒ/ vi/t exchange ~**able** adj ♦ n /ˈɪntərˌtʃeɪndʒ/ **1** [C;U] (act of) interchanging **2** [C] system of smaller roads connecting main roads

in·ter·col·le·gi·ate /ˌɪntərkəˈliːdʒiːət, -dʒət/ adj between colleges or universities: *intercollegiate sports*

in·ter·com /ˈɪntərˌkɑm/ n system for talking through a machine to people fairly near

in·ter·con·ti·nen·tal /ˌɪntərˌkɑntənˈentl/ adj between CONTINENTS

in·ter·course /ˈɪntərkɔrs/ n [U] **1** SEXUAL INTERCOURSE **2** fml conversation, etc., between people

in·ter·de·pen·dent /ˌɪntərdɪˈpendənt/ adj depending on each other

in·terest /ˈɪntərɪst/ n **1** [S;U] willingness to give attention: *take an interest* **2** [U] quality that makes people give attention: *That's of no interest to her.* **3** [C] activity or subject that one likes to give time to **4** [C] also **interests** pl. — advantage: *It's in your interest to go.* **5** [U] money paid for the use of money: *10%*

interest 6 [C] share in a business ♦ vt cause to feel INTEREST (1) ~**ed** /ˈɪntərəstɪd, ˈɪntəˌrestɪd/ adj **1** feeling INTEREST (1) **2** personally concerned ~**ing** adj having INTEREST (2)

in·ter·face /ˈɪntərˌfeɪs/ n point where 2 systems meet and act on each other ♦ vi/t connect or be connected by means of an interface

in·ter·fere /ˌɪntərˈfɪər/ vi **1** enter into a matter that does not concern one and in which one is not wanted **2** prevent something from working properly –**ference** n [U] **1** act of interfering **2** noises, etc., that stop radio or television from working properly

interfere with phr vt **1** get in the way of **2** touch or move (something) in a way that is not allowed **3** annoy or touch sexually

in·ter·ga·lac·tic /ˌɪntərɡəˈlæktɪk/ adj between the galaxies (GALAXY)

in·ter·im /ˈɪntərɪm/ adj done as part of something to follow later: *interim report*

in·te·ri·or /ɪnˈtɪəriːər/ n inside of something **interior** adj

in·ter·ject /ˌɪntərˈdʒekt/ vi/t fml make (a sudden remark) between others ~**ion** /-ˈdʒekʃən/ n **1** [C] word or phrase, such as *'Good heavens!'* interjected **2** [U] act of interjecting

in·ter·lock /ˌɪntərˈlɑk/ vi/t fasten or be fastened together

in·ter·loc·u·tor /ˌɪntərˈlɑkyətər/ n fml person one is talking with

in·ter·lop·er /ˈɪntərˌloʷpər/ n person found in a place, esp. among others, with no right to be there

in·ter·lude /ˈɪntərˌluʷd/ n period of time between 2 parts or activities

in·ter·mar·ry /ˌɪntərˈmæriː/ vi (of groups of people) become connected by marriage –**marriage** n [U]

in·ter·me·di·a·ry /ˌɪntərˈmiːdiːˌeriː/ n person who persuaded opposing sides to agree

in·ter·me·di·ate /ˌɪntərˈmiːdiːɪt/ adj between 2 others; HALFWAY

in·ter·ment /ɪnˈtɜrmənt/ n [C;U] fml burial

in·ter·mi·na·ble /ɪnˈtɜrmənəbəl/ adj long and dull; (seeming) endless –**bly** adv

in·ter·mis·sion /ˌɪntərˈmɪʃən/ n time between the parts of a play, etc.

in·ter·mit·tent /ˌɪntərˈmɪtnt◂/ adj not continuous ~**ly** adv

in·tern¹ /ɪnˈtɜrn/ vt put in prison, esp. in time of war ~**ment** n [U]

in·tern² /ˈɪntɜrn/ n person who has recently completed professional training, esp. in medicine, and is gaining practical experience, esp. in a hospital

in·ter·nal /ɪnˈtɜrnl/ adj **1** inside **2** not foreign: *internal trade* ~**ly** adv

In·ter·nal Rev·e·nue Ser·vice /·ˌ··ˈ··· ·ˌ··/ n [the] office that collects taxes also **IRS**

in·ter·na·tion·al /ˌɪntərˈnæʃənəl◂/ adj between nations **~ly** adv **~ism** n [U] principle that nations should work together

in·ter·ne·cine /ˌɪntərˈniˈsən, -ˈnesiˈn/ adj fml (of fighting, etc.) inside a group

in·ter·play /ˈɪntərˌpleˈ/ n [U] INTER-ACTION

in·ter·po·late /ɪnˈtɜrpəˌleˈt/ vt fml put in (words); interrupt **-lation** /ɪnˌtɜrpəˈleˈʃən/ n [C;U]

in·ter·pose /ˌɪntərˈpoˈz/ vt fml put or say between things

in·ter·pret /ɪnˈtɜrprɪt/ v 1 vt understand or explain the meaning of 2 vi/t turn (spoken words) into another language ~ er n person who INTERPRETS (2) **~ation** /ɪnˌtɜrprəˈteˈʃən/ n [C;U] 1 explanation 2 (example of) a performance of music, theater, etc., by someone giving their own idea of the COMPOSER'S writer's, etc., intentions

in·ter·ro·gate /ɪnˈterəˌgeˈt/ vt 1 question formally esp. for a long time and often with the use of threats or violence 2 (try to) get direct information from: to interrogate a computer **-gation** /ɪnˌterəˈgeˈʃən/ n [C;U] **-gative** /ˌɪntəˈrɑgətɪv/ adj asking a question

in·ter·rupt /ˌɪntəˈrʌpt/ vi/t break the flow of (speech, etc.) **-ion** /-ˈrʌpʃən/ n [C;U]

in·ter·sect /ˌɪntərˈsekt/ vi/t cut across: intersecting paths **-ion** /-ˈsekʃən, ˈɪntərˌsekʃən/ n 1 [U] act of intersecting 2 [C] place where two or more roads meet

in·ter·sperse /ˌɪntərˈspɜrs/ vt put here and there among other things

in·ter·state /ˈɪntərˌsteˈt/ adj between states: interstate crime/ highway

in·ter·stice /ɪnˈtɜrstəs/ n small space or crack between things placed close together

in·ter·twine /ˌɪntərˈtwaɪn/ vi/t twist together

in·ter·val /ˈɪntərvəl/ n 1 time between events 2 distance between things

in·ter·vene /ˌɪntərˈviˈn/ vi 1 interrupt so as to stop something 2 (of time) happen between events **-vention** /-ˈvenʃən/ n [C;U]

in·ter·view /ˈɪntərˌvyuˈ/ n meeting where a person is asked questions ♦ vt ask (someone) questions in an interview **~ee** /ˌɪntərvyuˈˈiˈ/ n person who is being or is to be interviewed, esp. for a job **~er** n person who interviews

in·tes·tate /ɪnˈtesteˈt, -stɪt/ adj law not having made a WILL² (5)

in·tes·tine /ɪnˈtestɪn/ also **-tines** pl n bowels **-tinal** adj

in·ti·ma·cy /ˈɪntəməsiˈ/ n 1 [U] state of being intimate 2 [C] remark or action of a kind that happens only between people who know each other very well 3 euph [U] the act of sex

in·ti·mate¹ /ˈɪntəmɪt/ adj 1 having a close relationship: intimate friends 2 private: her intimate thoughts 3 resulting from close study: intimate knowledge **~ly** adv

in·ti·mate² /ˈɪntəˌmeˈt/ vt fml make known; suggest **-mation** /ˌɪntə-ˈmeˈʃən/ n [C;U]

in·tim·i·date /ɪnˈtɪməˌdeˈt/ vt frighten by threats **-dation** /ɪnˌtɪm-əˈdeˈʃən/ n [U]

in·to /ˈɪntə; before vowels ˈɪntu; strong ˈɪntuˈ/ prep 1 so as to be in: jump into the water | get into trouble 2 so as to be: translate it into French 3 against; bump into a tree 4 (used when dividing): 7 into 11 won't go.

in·tol·e·ra·ble /ɪnˈtɑlərəbəl/ adj unbearable **-bly** adv

in·tol·e·rant /ɪnˈtɑlərənt/ adj not tolerant (TOLERATE) **-rance** n [U]

in·to·na·tion /ˌɪntəˈneˈʃən, -toˈ-/ n [C;U] rise and fall of the voice in speech

in·tone /ɪnˈtoˈn/ vi/t say (a prayer, etc.) in a level voice

in·tox·i·cate /ɪnˈtɑksəˌkeˈt/ vt make drunk; (fig.) intoxicated by success **-cation** /ɪnˌtɑksəˈkeˈʃən/ n [U]

in·trac·ta·ble /ɪnˈtræktəbəl/ adj difficult to control or deal with

in·tra·mu·ral /ˌɪntrəˈmyʊərəl◂/ n happening within one school or college: intramural sports

in·tran·si·gent /ɪnˈtrænsədʒənt, -zədʒənt/ adj fml refusing to change; STUBBORN **-gence** n [U]

in·tran·si·tive /ɪnˈtrænsəṭɪv, -zə-/ adj (of a verb) having a subject but no object: 'Break' is intransitive in the sentence 'My cup fell and broke' but transitive in 'I broke my cup'.

in·tra·state /ˌɪntrəˈsteˈt/ adj within a state: an intrastate highway

in·tra·ve·nous /ˌɪntrəˈviˈnəs◂/ adj into a VEIN: intravenous injection

in·trep·id /ɪnˈtrepɪd/ adj fml fearless **~ly** adv

in·tri·ca·cy /ˈɪntrɪkəsiˈ/ n 1 [U] being intricate 2 [C] something intricate

in·tri·cate /ˈɪntrɪkɪt/ adj having many details; COMPLICATED **~ly** adv

in·trigue /ɪnˈtriˈg/ v 1 vt interest greatly 2 vi make PLOTS ♦ n /ˈɪntriˈg, ɪnˈtriˈg/ 1 [U] act or practice of secret planning 2 [C] PLOTS **intriguing** /ɪnˈtriˈgɪŋ/ adj very interesting, esp. because of some strange quality

in·trin·sic /ɪnˈtrɪnsɪk, -zɪk/ adj belonging naturally; INHERENT ~**ally** /-kliʸ/ adv

in·tro·duce /ˌɪntrəˈduʷs, -ˈdjuʷs/ vt **1** make (people) known to each other **2** bring or put in -**duction** /-ˈdʌkʃən/ n **1** [U] act of introducing **2** [C] occasion of telling people each other's names **3** [C] explanation at the beginning of a book, etc. **4** [C] simple book about a subject -**ductory** /-ˈdʌktəriʸ/ adj happening or said at the beginning

in·tro·spec·tion /ˌɪntrəˈspekʃən/ n [U] thinking about one's own thoughts and feelings -**tive** /-tɪv/ adj

in·tro·vert /ˈɪntrəˌvɜrt/ n quiet introspective person ~**ed** adj

in·trude /ɪnˈtruʷd/ vi come in when not wanted **intruder** n person who intrudes, esp. intending to steal **intrusive** /-ˈtruʷsɪv/ adj intruding **intrusion** /-ˈtruʷʒən/ n [C;U]

in·tu·i·tion /ˌɪntuʷˈɪʃən, -tyuʷ-/ n [U] power of knowing something without reasoning or learned skill **2** [C] something known in this way -**tive** /ɪnˈtuʷətɪv, -ˈtyuʷ-/ adj -**tively** adv

in·un·date /ˈɪnənˌdeʸt/ vt flood: (fig.) inundated with letters -**dation** /ˌɪnənˈdeʸʃən/ n [C;U]

in·ured /ɪˈnuərd, ɪˈnyuərd/ adj accustomed (by long experience): inured to the smell

in·vade /ɪnˈveʸd/ vt **1** attack and take control of (a country) **2** crowd into **invader** n **invasion** /-ˈveʸʒən/ n [C;U]

in·val·id¹ /ɪnˈvælɪd/ adj not VALID: invalid argument/ticket ~**ate** vt make invalid ~**ation** /ɪnˌvælə-ˈdeʸʃən/ n [U]

in·va·lid² /ˈɪnvəlɪd/ n person weakened by illness

in·val·ua·ble /ɪnˈvælyəbəl, -yuʷəbəl/ adj too valuable for the worth to be measured

in·var·i·a·ble /ɪnˈveəriʸəbəl/ adj unchanging -**bly** adv always

in·vec·tive /ɪnˈvektɪv/ n [U] fml angry language

in·veigh /ɪnˈveʸ/ v **inveigh against** phr vt fml attack in words

in·vei·gle /ɪnˈveʸgəl/ v **inveigle into** phr vt trick (someone) into (doing something)

in·vent /ɪnˈvent/ vt **1** produce for the first time **2** think of (something untrue) ~**ive** adj able to invent ~**or** n ~**ion** /-ˈvenʃən/ n [U] act of inventing **2** [C] something invented

in·ven·to·ry /ˈɪnvənˌtoriʸ, -ˌtoʊriʸ/ n list, esp. one of all the goods in a place ♦ v make such a list

in·verse /ɪnˈvɜrs, ˈɪnvɜrs/ n, adj opposite

in·vert /ɪnˈvɜrt/ vt fml turn upside down **inversion** /-ˈvɜrʒən, -ʃən/ n [C;U]

in·ver·te·brate /ɪnˈvɜrtəbrɪt, -ˌbreʸt/ n animal without a BACKBONE

in·vest /ɪnˈvest/ vt use (money) to make more money ~**ment** n **1** [U] act of investing **2** [C] (something bought with) money invested ~**or** n

invest in phr vt buy

invest with phr vt fml give officially to: power invested in him | (fig.) Don't invest his words with too much meaning! (= take them too seriously)

in·ves·ti·gate /ɪnˈvestəˌgeʸt/ vi/t inquire carefully (about): investigate a crime -**gator** n -**gative** adj -**gation** /ɪnˌvestəˈgeʸʃən/ n [C;U]

in·ves·ti·ture /ɪnˈvestətʃər, -ˌtʃuər/ n ceremony of investing someone with rank

in·vet·e·rate /ɪnˈvetərɪt/ adj fixed in a bad habit: inveterate habit

in·vid·i·ous /ɪnˈvɪdiʸəs/ adj tending to cause bad feeling or make people unnecessarily offended or jealous

in·vig·o·rate /ɪnˈvɪgəˌreʸt/ vt give health and strength: an invigorating swim

in·vin·ci·ble /ɪnˈvɪnsəbəl/ adj too strong to be defeated -**bly** adv

in·vi·o·la·ble /ɪnˈvaɪələbəl/ adj fml impossible to VIOLATE: inviolable rights

in·vis·i·ble /ɪnˈvɪzəbəl/ adj that cannot be seen -**bly** adv -**bility** /ɪn-ˌvɪzəˈbɪləˌtiʸ/ n [U]

in·vite /ɪnˈvaɪt/ vt **1** ask to come **2** ask politely for: invite questions **inviting** adj attractive invitingly adv **invitation** /ˌɪnvəˈteʸʃən/ n **1** [C] request to come: invitations to a wedding **2** [U] act of inviting: entrance by invitation only **3** [C] encouragement to an action

in vitro /ɪn ˈviʸtroʷ/ adj (done) outside a living body, in a piece of scientific equipment

in·vo·ca·tion /ˌɪnvəˈkeʸʃən/ n fml **1** [U] act of invoking **2** [C] prayer for help

in·voice /ˈɪnvɔɪs/ vt, n (send) a bill for goods received

in·voke /ɪnˈvoʷk/ vt fml **1** call to (God, the law) for help **2** beg for **3** cause to appear by magic

in·vol·un·ta·ry /ɪnˈvɑlənˌteriʸ/ adj done without intention: an involuntary smile -**rily** /ɪnˌvɑlənˈteərəliʸ/ adv

in·volve /ɪnˈvɑlv/ vt **1** have as a necessary result **2** cause to become concerned **involved** adj **1** COMPLICATED **2** (of a person) closely concerned in relationships and activities with others, esp. in a personal or sexual way –**ment** n [U]

in·vul·ne·ra·ble /ɪnˈvʌlnərəbəl/ adj that cannot be harmed

in·ward /ˈɪnwərd/ adj, adv **1** on or towards the inside **2** of the mind or spirit: inward peace ~**ly** adv **inwards** adv

i·o·dine /ˈaɪədaɪn, -dɪn/ n [U] chemical used to prevent infection in wounds

i·on /ˈaɪən, ˈaɪɑn/ n atom with an electrical CHARGE ~**izer** /ˈaɪəˌnaɪzər/ n machine that produces negative ions, believed to make the air more healthy

i·on·o·sphere /aɪˈɑnəˌsfɪər/ n [the+S] part of the ATMOSPHERE which is used in helping to send radio waves around the Earth

i·o·ta /aɪˈoʷtə/ n [S] very small amount

IOU /ˌaɪ oʷ ˈyuʷ/ n 'I owe you'; signed piece of paper saying one owes money

ip·so fac·to /ˌɪpsoʷ ˈfæktoʷ/ adv fml (proved) by the fact itself

IQ /ˌaɪ ˈkyuʷ/ n intelligence quotient; measure of INTELLIGENCE

IRA /ˈaɪrə/ n Individual Retirement Account, a PENSION for one person using their own money

i·ras·ci·ble /ɪˈræsəbəl, aɪ-/ adj fml easily made angry

i·rate /aɪˈreʲt/ adj angry ~**ly** adv

ir·i·des·cent /ˌɪrəˈdesənt/ adj changing color as light falls on it –**cence** n [U]

i·ris /ˈaɪrɪs/ n **1** tall yellow or purple flower **2** colored part of the eye

irk /ɜrk/ vt annoy ~**some** adj annoying

i·ron¹ /ˈaɪərn/ n **1** [U] common hard metal used in making steel, etc. **2** [C] heavy object for making cloth smooth **3 have several irons in the fire** have various different interests, activities, or plans at the same time

♦ adj very firm: iron will

iron² vt make smooth with an iron
iron out phr vt remove (difficulties, etc)

Iron Age /ˈ·· ·/ n [the] time in the history of mankind when iron was used for tools, etc.

Iron Cur·tain /ˌ·· ˈ··/ n preventing the flow of ideas between western Europe and the Communist (COMMUNISM) countries after the Second World War

i·ron·ic /aɪˈrɑnɪk/ also ~**al** –adj expressing IRONY ~**ally** /-kliʲ/ adv

ironing board /ˈ·· ·/ n narrow table for ironing clothes on

iron lung /ˌ·· ˈ·/ n machine fitted over the body which helps one breathe in and out

i·ron·y /ˈaɪrəniʲ/ n **1** [U] intentional use of words which are opposite to one's real meaning, in order to be amusing or to show annoyance **2** [C;U] event or situation which is the opposite of what one expected

ir·ra·di·ate /ɪˈreʲdiʲˌeʲt/ vt **1** fml throw bright light on **2** treat with X-RAYS or similar beams of force **3** treat (food) with X-RAYS to kill bacteria and make last longer

ir·ra·tion·al /ɪˈræʃənəl/ adj not reasonable ~**ly** adv

ir·rec·on·ci·la·ble /ɪˌrekənˈsaɪləbəl, ɪˈrekənˌsaɪ-/ adj impossible to bring into agreement –**bly** adv

ir·re·fu·ta·ble /ɪˈrefyətəbəl, ˌɪrɪˈfyuʷtə-/ adj fml too strong to be disproved

ir·reg·u·lar /ɪˈregyələr/ adj **1** uneven **2** fml against the usual rules **3** gram not following the usual pattern ~**ly** adv –**ity** /ˌɪ regyəˈlærəṭiʲ/ n [C;U]

ir·rel·e·vant /ɪˈreləvənt/ adj not RELEVANT –**vance** n [C;U]

ir·rep·a·ra·ble /ɪˈrepərəbəl/ adj too bad to be put right –**bly** adv

ir·re·place·a·ble /ˌɪrɪˈpleʲsəbəl/ adj too special for anything else to REPLACE it

ir·re·proa·cha·ble /ˌɪrɪˈproʷtʃəbəl/ adj fml faultless –**bly** adv

ir·re·sis·ti·ble /ˌɪrɪˈzɪstəbəl/ adj so nice, powerful, etc., that one cannot RESIST it –**bly** adv

ir·res·o·lute /ɪˈrezəˌluʷt/ adj fml unable to make decisions ~**ly** adv

ir·re·spec·tive /ˌɪrɪˈspektɪv/ adv irrespective of without regard to

ir·re·spon·si·ble /ˌɪrɪˈspɑnsəbəl/ adj not trustworthy; careless –**bly** adv –**bility** /ˌɪrɪˌspɑnsəˈbɪləṭiʲ/ n [U]

ir·re·trie·va·ble /ˌɪrɪˈtriʲvəbəl/ adj impossible to get back or put right –**bly** adv

ir·rev·e·rent /ɪˈrevərənt/ adj not respectful, esp. of holy things ~**ly** adv –**rence** n [U]

ir·rev·o·ca·ble /ɪˈrevəkəbəl/ adj unchangeable once made or started: irrevocable decision –**bly** adv

ir·ri·gate /ˈɪrəˌgeʲt/ vt supply water to (land) –**gation** /ˌɪrəˈgeʲʃən/ n [U]

ir·ri·ta·ble /ˈɪrəṭəbəl/ adj easily annoyed –**bly** adv –**bility** /ˌɪrəṭəˈbɪləṭiʲ/ n [U]

ir·ri·tate /ˈɪrəˌteʲt/ vt **1** annoy **2** make sore –**tation** /ˌɪrəˈteʲʃən/ n [C;U]

IRS /ˌaɪ ɑr ˈes/ n [the] INTERNAL REVENUE SERVICE

is /s, z, əz; strong ɪz/ v 3rd person sing. present tense of BE

Is·lam /ɪsˈlɑm, ˈɪslɑm, -ləm, ˈɪz-/ n (people and countries that practice) the Muslim religion ~**ic** /ɪsˈlɑmɪk, -ˈlæ-, ɪz-/ adj

is·land /ˈaɪlənd/ n **1** piece of land surrounded by water **2** raised place where people can wait in the middle of a road for traffic to pass ~**er** n person living on an island

isle /aɪl/ n lit island

is·n't /ˈɪzənt/ v short for: is not

i·so·late /ˈaɪsəˌleɪt/ vt keep separate from others −**lated** adj alone; only: an isolated case −**lation** /ˌaɪsəˈleɪʃən/ n [U]

is·sue /ˈɪʃuʷ/ n **1** [C] subject to be talked about or argued about – see also SIDE ISSUE **2** [C] printing at one time of a magazine, etc. **3** [U] law children ♦ vt produce or provide officially: issue a statement/new uniforms

isth·mus /ˈɪsməs/ n narrow piece of land joining 2 larger pieces

it /ɪt/ pron **1** that thing already mentioned: 'Where's my dinner?' 'The cat ate it.' **2** that person: 'Who's that?' 'It's me.' **3** (used in statements about weather, time, or distance): It's raining. | It's Thursday. | It's not far to Paris. **4** (used when the real subject comes later): It's too bad you forgot. **5** (making part of a sentence more important): It was Jane who told me. ♦ n **1** infml **a** very important person: He thinks he's it. **b** the important point: This is it, I have to decide. **2** That's it: **a** That's complete; there's nothing more to come. **b** That's right.

IT /ˌaɪ ˈtiʸ/ n INFORMATION TECHNOLOGY

i·tal·ics /ɪˈtælɪks, aɪ-/ n [P] sloping printed letters −**icize** /-ləˌsaɪz/ vt print in italics

itch /ɪtʃ/ vi **1** have the feeling of wanting to SCRATCH the skin **2** be itching to/for want very much ♦ n **1** itching feeling **2** strong desire – see also SEVEN-YEAR ITCH ~**y** adj

itchy feet /ˌ·· ˈ·/ n [P] infml desire to travel

itchy palm /ˌ·· ˈ·/ n infml great desire for money, esp. as payment for unfair favors

it'd /ˈɪtəd/ short for: **1** it would **2** it had

i·tem /ˈaɪtəm/ n **1** single thing on a list, etc. **2** piece of news ~**ize** vt make a detailed list of

i·tin·e·rant /aɪˈtɪnərənt/ adj traveling from place to place

i·tin·e·ra·ry /aɪˈtɪnəˌreriʸ/ n plan for a journey

it'll /ˈɪtl/ short for: it will

its /ɪts/ determiner of it: its ears

it's /ɪts/ short for: **1** it is **2** it has

it·self /ɪtˈself/ pron **1** (reflexive form of it): The cat washed itself. **2** (strong form of it): I had the copy, but the letter itself was missing. **3** (all) by itself: **a** alone **b** without help **4** in itself without considering the rest **5** to itself not shared

IUD /ˌaɪ yuʷ ˈdiʸ/ n plastic or metal object fitted inside a woman's WOMB as a form of CONTRACEPTION

I've /aɪv/ short for: I have

i·vo·ry /ˈaɪvəriʸ/ n [U] **1** hard white substance of which the TUSKS of ELEPHANTS are made **2** creamy white color of this

ivory tow·er /ˌ··· ˈ··/ n place where people avoid the difficult realities of ordinary life

i·vy /ˈaɪviʸ/ n [U] climbing plant with shiny leaves **ivied** adj covered with ivy

Ivy League /ˌ·· ˈ·◂/ adj belonging to or typical of a group of old and respected east coast universities

J

J, j /dʒeʸ/ the 10th letter of the English alphabet

jab /dʒæb/ vi/t -bb- push with force (something pointed) ♦ n sharp forceful push

jab·ber /ˈdʒæbər/ vi/t talk or say quickly **jabber** n [S;U]

jack¹ /dʒæk/ n 1 apparatus for lifting a car, etc. 2 playing card between the 10 and the queen

jack² v

  jack off phr vt taboo sl for MASTURBATE

  jack up phr vt lift with a JACK (1)

jack·al /ˈdʒækəl, -kɔl/ n kind of wild dog

jack·boot /ˈdʒækbuʷt/ n 1 [C] high military boot 2 [S] cruel military rule

jack·et /ˈdʒækɪt/ n 1 short coat with SLEEVES 2 cover for a machine, pipe, etc. 3 loose paper book cover

jack·ham·mer /ˈdʒækˌhæmər/ n power tool held in the hands, for digging up streets

jack knife /ˈ· ·/ n large pocket knife, the blade of which folds into the handle

jack-knife vi (of a vehicle) bend suddenly in the middle

jack·pot /ˈdʒækpɑt/ n biggest money prize to be won in a game

Ja·cuz·zi /dʒəˈkuʷziʸ/ n tdmk bath fitted with a system of hot water currents

jade /dʒeʸd/ n [U] (colour of) a green precious stone

ja·ded /ˈdʒeʸdɪd/ adj tired because of having had too much of something, esp. experience

jag·ged /ˈdʒægɪd/ adj with a rough uneven edge

jag·uar /ˈdʒægwɑr, ˈdʒægyuʷˌɑr/ n large spotted wild cat of S America

jail /dʒeʸl/ n [C;U] prison ♦ vt put in jail ~**er** n person in charge of prisoners

ja·lop·y /dʒəˈlɑpiʸ/ n old car

jam¹ /dʒæm/ n [U] fruit boiled in sugar, for spreading on bread

jam² v -mm- 1 vt crush or press tightly: jam clothes into a bag | jam the brakes on 2 vi get stuck: The door jammed. 3 vt block (radio messages) ♦ n 1 closely jammed mass: traffic jam 2 in a jam in a difficult situation

jam·bo·ree /ˌdʒæmbəˈriʸ/ n large party or gathering

jam-packed /ˌ· ˈ·◄/ adj with many people or things very close together

jan·gle /ˈdʒæŋgəl/ vi/t (cause to) make the noise of metal striking metal

jan·i·tor /ˈdʒænətər/ n CARETAKER

Jan·u·a·ry /ˈdʒænyuˌɛriʸ/ n the 1st month of the year

jar¹ /dʒɑr/ n short wide bottle

jar² vi/t -rr- 1 vi make a nasty sound 2 vt give a nasty shock to 3 vi go badly together: jarring colors

jar·gon /ˈdʒɑrgən/ n [U] language used by a particular group: computer jargon

jaun·dice /ˈdʒɔndɪs, ˈdʒɑn-/ n [U] disease that makes the skin yellow **jaundiced** adj mistrustful and CYNICal: jaundiced opinions

jaunt /dʒɔnt, dʒɑnt/ n short pleasure trip ~**y** adj cheerful and confident

jav·e·lin /ˈdʒævələn/ n light spear for throwing

jaw /dʒɔ/ n one of the 2 bony structures where the teeth are fixed ♦ vi/t infml talk (to) for a long time **jaws** n [P] 1 animal's mouth 2 two parts of a tool, etc., that hold things tightly: (fig.) the jaws of death

jay·walk /ˈdʒeʸwɔk/ vi cross streets carelessly

jazz¹ /dʒæz/ n [U] music with a strong beat, originated by black Americans ~**y** adj brightly coloured

jazz² v **jazz up** phr vt make brighter or more interesting

jeal·ous /ˈdʒɛləs/ adj 1 unhappy at not being liked as much as someone else: jealous husband 2 very ENVIous 3 wanting to keep what one has ~**ly** adv

jeal·ous·y /ˈdʒɛləsiʸ/ n [C;U] jealous feeling

jeans /dʒiʸnz/ n [P] strong cotton pants

jeep /dʒiʸp/ n (military) car for traveling on rough ground

jeer /dʒɪər/ vi/t laugh rudely (at) **jeer** n ~**ingly** adv

Jell-o /ˈdʒɛloʷ/ n [U] tdmk soft gluey food made with GELATIN

jel·ly /ˈdʒɛliʸ/ n 1 [C;U] fruit juice boiled with sugar to spread on bread 2 [S;U] any material between a liquid and a solid state

jeop·ar·dize, -dise /ˈdʒɛpərˌdaɪz/ vt fml put in danger

jeop·ar·dy /ˈdʒɛpərdiʸ/ n [U] fml danger: put one's future in jeopardy

jerk¹ /dʒɜrk/ n sudden quick pull or movement ♦ vi/t pull or move with a jerk ~**y** adj not smooth in movement

jerk² n sl person who is foolish and has bad manners

jer·ry-built /ˈdʒɛriʸ bɪlt/ adj built cheaply and badly

jer·sey /'dʒɜːrziʸ/ n (U) smooth material used in clothing

jest /dʒɛst/ vi fml joke **jest** n [C;U] ~ **er** n man kept formerly to amuse a ruler

jet¹ /dʒɛt/ n **1** narrow stream of gas or liquid forced out of a hole **2** hole from which this comes **3** aircraft whose engine (**jet engine**) works on this principle ♦ vi **1** come in a JET (1) **2** travel by JET (3)

jet² n (U) hard shiny black mineral: (fig.) **jet-black** hair

jet lag /'· ·/ n (U) tiredness after flying to a place where the time is different

jet set /'· ·/ n [S] international social group of rich fashionable people

jet·ti·son /'dʒɛtəsən, -zən/ vt throw away

jet·ty /'dʒɛtiʸ/ n small PIER

Jew /dʒuʷ/ n person descended from the people of ancient Israel whose history is told in the Bible ~ **ish** adj

jew·el /'dʒuʷəl/ n **1** (real or artificial) precious stone **2** very valuable person or thing ~ **er** n person who sells jewels ~ **ry** (U) jewels worn as decoration

jib /dʒɪb/ n long arm of a CRANE (1) from which the hook hangs down

jibe /dʒaɪb/ n, v GIBE

jif·fy /'dʒɪfiʸ/ n [S] moment: I'll come in a jiffy.

jig /dʒɪg/ n (music for) a quick merry dance ♦ vi jump up and down

jig·gle /'dʒɪgəl/ vi/t shake from side to side

jig·saw /'dʒɪgsɔː/ also **jigsaw puz·zle** /'·· ,··/ — n picture cut into pieces to be fitted together for fun

jilt /dʒɪlt/ vt unexpectedly refuse (an accepted lover)

Jim Crow /ˌdʒɪm ˈkroʷ/ n, adj (U) practice of treating black people unfairly: Jim Crow laws

jin·gle /'dʒɪŋgəl/ n **1** sound as of small bells ringing **2** simple poem used esp. for advertisement ♦ vi/t (cause to) sound with a jingle

jin·go·is·m /'dʒɪŋgoʷˌɪzəm/ n (U) derog extreme warlike NATIONAL-ism

jinx /dʒɪŋks/ n something that brings bad luck

jit·ters /'dʒɪtərz/ n [P] anxiety before an event —**tery** adj

jive /dʒaɪv/ n (U) **1** informal speech of black Americans **2** (dance performed to) a kind of popular music with a strong beat ♦ vi dance to jive music

job /dʒab/ n **1** [C] regular paid employment: out of a job (= unemployed) **2** [C] piece of work **3** [C] sl crime, esp. a robbery **4** [S] something hard to do: You'll have a job getting it open. **5** [S] one's affair; duty: It's not my job to interfere. **6** [C] infml example of a certain type: His new car is quite a job. **7** [C] infml a PLASTIC SURGERY operation: a nose job **8 make the best of a bad job** do as much or as well as possible in unfavorable conditions **9 on the job** while working; at work ~ **ber** n person who sells WHOLESALE ~ **less** adj unemployed

job ac·tion /'· ,··/ n slowing down of workers to protest

job lot /'· ·/ n group of things of different kinds bought or sold together

jock /dʒak/ n derog ATHLETE

jock·ey /'dʒakiʸ/ n professional rider in horse races ♦ vi/t try by all possible means to get into a good position: jockey for position

jock·strap /'· ·/ n supporter for male sex organs worn esp. while playing sports

joc·u·lar /'dʒakyələr/ adj fml joking; not serious ~ **ly** adv

joc·und /'dʒakənd, 'dʒoʷ-/ adj lit merry

jodh·purs /'dʒadpərz/ n [P] pants for horse riding

jog /dʒag/ v –**gg**- **1** vt knock slightly **2** vi run slowly for exercise **3 jog someone's memory** make someone remember ♦ n –**ger** n someone who JOGS (2)

jog along phr vi move slowly and uneventfully

join /dʒɔɪn/ v **1** vt fasten; connect: join 2 ropes **2** vi/t come together (with); meet: join me for a drink / The stream joins the river. **3** vt become a member of: join the army ♦ n place where 2 things are joined

join in phr vi take part in an activity

join up phr vi offer oneself for military service

join·er /'dʒɔɪnər/ n person who works in wood and makes doors, etc., inside buildings ~ **y** n (U) trade of a joiner

joint¹ /dʒɔɪnt/ n **1** place where things (esp. bones) join **2** sl public place for drinking, etc. **3** sl cigarette containing CANNABIS

joint² adj shared: joint bank account ~ **ly** adv

joist /dʒɔɪst/ n beam supporting a floor – see CROSSBEAM

joke /dʒoʷk/ n **1** something said or done to amuse people **2 play a joke on someone** do something to make other people laugh at someone ♦ vi tell jokes **joker** n **1** person who makes jokes **2** additional playing card with no fixed value

jol·ly[^1] /'dʒɑlɪ/ *adj* happy; pleasant

jolly[^2] *vt infml* persuade; urge gently

jolt /dʒoʷlt/ *vi/t* shake or shock **jolt** *n*

Jones·es /'dʒoʷnzɪz/ *n* **keep up with the Joneses** *derog* compete with one's neighbors socially, esp. by buying the same expensive new things that they buy

joss stick /'dʒɑs ˌstɪk/ *n* stick of IN-CENSE

jos·tle /'dʒɑsəl/ *vi/t* knock or push (against)

jot /dʒɑt/ *n* [S] very small bit: *not a jot of truth* ♦ *vt* **-tt-** write quickly **~ter** *n* notebook **~ting** *n* rough note

jour·nal /'dʒɜrnl/ *n* **1** magazine **2** DIARY **~ism** *n* profession of writing for newspapers **~ist** *n* person whose profession is journalism

jour·nal·ese /ˌdʒɜrnl'iʸz/ *n* [U] *derog* language of newspapers

jour·ney /'dʒɜrniʸ/ *n* long trip, esp. by land ♦ *vi lit* travel

jo·vi·al /'dʒoʷviʸəl/ *adj* friendly and cheerful **~ly** *adv*

jowl /dʒaʊl/ *n* lower part of the face

joy /dʒɔɪ/ *n* **1** [U] great happiness **2** [C] something that causes joy **~ful** *adj fml* full of or causing joy **~fully** *adv* **~ous** *adj lit* joyful

joy·ride /'dʒɔɪraɪd/ *n* ride for pleasure in a (stolen) car

JP /ˌdʒeʸ 'piʸ/ *n* Justice of the Peace

Jr *written abbrev. for:* JUNIOR

ju·bi·lant /'dʒuʷbələnt/ *adj fml* joyful; delighted **-lation** /ˌdʒuʷbə-'leʸʃən/ *n* [U] rejoicing

ju·bi·lee /'dʒuʷbəˌliʸ, ˌdʒuʷbə'liʸ/ *n* **1** time of rejoicing at an ANNIVER-SARY **2 diamond/golden/silver jubilee** 60th/50th/25th return of an important date

Ju·da·is·m /'dʒuʷdiʸˌɪzəm, -deʸ-, -də-/ *n* [U] religion and civilization of the Jews

judge /dʒʌdʒ/ *n* **1** public official who decides legal cases **2** person who decides in a competition, etc. **3** person who can give a valuable opinion: *I'm no judge of music.* ♦ *vi/t* act as a judge (in); form an opinion (about)

judg·ment, judgement /'dʒʌdʒ-mənt/ *n* **1** [U] ability to decide correctly: *a man of sound judgment* **2** [C] opinion **3** [C;U] decision of a judge or court of law: *She passed (= gave) judgment on the accused man.*

judgment day /'··· ˌ·/ *n* day when God will judge everyone

ju·di·cial /dʒuʷ'dɪʃəl/ *adj* of law courts and judges **~ly** *adv*

ju·di·ci·ar·y /dʒuʷ'dɪʃiʸˌeriʸ, -ʃəriʸ/ *n* **1** all the judges, as a group **2** branch

of government that includes the courts

ju·di·cious /dʒuʷ'dɪʃəs/ *adj fml* sensible **~ly** *adv*

ju·do /'dʒuʷdoʷ/ *n* [U] type of unarmed fighting for defense, from Asia

jug /dʒʌg/ *n esp.* container for liquids, with a handle and a lip for pouring

jug·gle /'dʒʌgəl/ *vi/t* **1** keep (objects) in the air by throwing and catching them **2** play tricks (with), esp. to deceive: *juggling the figures* **juggler** *n*

juice /dʒuʷs/ *n* [C;U] liquid from fruit, vegetables, or meat **juicy** *adj* **1** having a lot of juice **2** *infml* interesting esp. because providing details about improper behavior

juke·box /'dʒuʷkbɑks/ *n* music machine operated by coins

Ju·ly /dʒuʷ'laɪ, dʒə-/ *n* the 7th month of the year

jum·ble /'dʒʌmbəl/ *vi/t* mix in disorder ♦ *n* [S] disorderly mixture

jum·bo /'dʒʌmboʷ/ *adj* very large: *jumbo jet*

jump[^1] /dʒʌmp/ *v* **1** *vi* push oneself off the ground with one's leg muscles **2** *vt* cross in this way: *jump a stream* **3** *vi* move suddenly: *The noise made me jump.* **4** *vi* rise sharply: *Oil prices have jumped.* **5** *vt* attack suddenly **6** *vt* leave, pass or escape from (something) illegally **7 jump down someone's throat** *infml* attack someone in words, strongly and unexpectedly **8 jump the gun** start something too soon **9 jump all over someone** express disapproval firmly **10 jump to it!** hurry

jump at *phr vt* accept eagerly

jump on *phr vt infml* speak to sharply

jump[^2] *n* **1** act of jumping **2** thing to jump over **3 be/stay one jump ahead** do the right thing because one knows or guesses what one's competitors are going to do **~y** *adj* nervously excited

jump·er /'dʒʌmpər/ *n* **1** dress with no SLEEVES **2** horse or person that jumps

jump·suit /'dʒʌmpsuʷt/ *n* a garment combining top and pants in one piece

junc·tion /'dʒʌŋkʃən/ *n* place of joining: *railroad junction*

junc·ture /'dʒʌŋktʃər/ *n fml* point in time

June /dʒuʷn/ *n* the 6th month of the year

jun·gle /'dʒʌŋgəl/ *n* [C;U] thick tropical forest

ju·nior /'dʒuʷnyər/ *n, adj* **1** (someone) younger **2** (someone) of low or lower rank **3** third year student in a college or high school

Junior *adj* the younger (of two men in the same family with the same name)

junior college /ˌ·· ˈ··/ *n* two year college

junk /dʒʌŋk/ *n* [U] **1** old useless things **2** *sl* dangerous drug, esp. HEROIN ♦ *vt infml* get rid of as worthless

jun·ket /ˈdʒʌŋkɪt/ *n* **1** [C] *infml, often derog* trip, esp. one made by a government official and paid for with government money **2** [U] kind of thick sweet milk

junk food /ˈ· ·/ *n* [U] *infml* unhealthy food

junk·ie, **-y** /ˈdʒʌŋki/ *n sl* person who takes HEROIN: (fig.) *I'm a real sugar junkie.*

junk mail /ˈ· ·/ *n* [U] mail, usu. for advertising, sent to people although they have not asked for it

jun·ta /ˈhʊntə, ˈdʒʌntə/ *n* (military) government that has seized power by armed force

Ju·pi·ter /ˈdʒuːpətər/ *n* the largest PLANET, 5th in order from the sun

jur·is·dic·tion /ˌdʒuərəsˈdɪkʃən/ *n* [U] legal power

ju·ror /ˈdʒuərər/ *n* member of a jury

ju·ry /ˈdʒuəriʲ/ *n* **1** group of people chosen to decide questions of fact in a court of law **2** group of people chosen to judge a competition of any kind

just¹ /dʒəst; *strong* dʒʌst/ *adv* **1** exactly: *That's just right.* **2** completely: *It's just perfect.* **3** at this moment: *I'm just coming.* **4** only a short time (ago): *just after breakfast* | *I just* *finished it.* **5** almost not: *She arrived just in time.* **6** only: *no dinner, just coffee* **7** just about very nearly **8** **just as well: a** lucky or suitable: *It's just as well I brought my coat — it's freezing!* **b** with good reason, considering the situation: *Since there's no more work to do, we might just as well go home.* **9** **just now: a** at this moment: *We're having dinner just now — come back later.* **b** a moment ago: *Paul telephoned just now to say he'll be late.* **10** **just yet** quite yet

just² /dʒʌst/ *adj* fair; according to what is deserved ~**ly** *adv*

jus·tice /ˈdʒʌstɪs/ *n* **1** [U] quality of being just; fairness **2** [U] the law: *court of justice* **3** [C] JUDGE (1) esp. of the SUPREME COURT **4** **do justice to someone** also **do someone justice** — treat someone in a fair way

Justice of the Peace /ˌ··· · ˈ··/ *n* official who judges cases in the lowest law courts

jus·ti·fy /ˈdʒʌstəˌfaɪ/ *vt* give or be a good reason for **-fiable** /ˈdʒʌstəˌfaɪəbəl, ˌdʒʌstəˈfaɪ-/ *adj* **-fiably** *adv* **-fication** /ˌdʒʌstəfəˈkeɪʃən/ *n* [U] good reason

jut /dʒʌt/ *vi* **-tt-** stick out or up further than the things around it

ju·ve·nile /ˈdʒuːvəˌnaɪl, -nl/ *n* **1** young person **2** actor or actress who plays such a person ♦ *adj* **1** of or for juveniles **2** childish or foolish

juvenile de·lin·quen·cy /ˌ··· · ˈ···/ *n* [U] crimes by JUVENILES (1) **-quent** *n*

jux·ta·pose /ˈdʒʌkstəˌpoʷz, ˌdʒʌkstəˈpoʷz/ *vt fml* put side by side **-position** /ˌdʒʌkstəpəˈzɪʃən/ *n* [U]

K

K, k /keʸ/ the 11th letter of the English alphabet

K *written abbrev. for:* **1** 1024 BYTES of computer DATA **2** *infml* one thousand: *a $20K salary*

ka·bob /kəˈbɒb/ *n* small pieces of meat cooked on a stick

ka·lei·do·scope /kəˈlaɪdəˌskoʷp/ *n* tube containing mirrors, and often bits of colored glass, turned to produce changing patterns **-scopic** /kəˌlaɪdəˈskɒpɪk/ *adj* changing quickly and often

kan·ga·roo /ˌkæŋɡəˈruʷ/ *n* Australian animal that jumps along on its large back legs, and carries its baby in a pocket

ka·o·lin /ˈkeʸəlɪn/ *n* [U] fine white clay used in medicine, etc.

ka·pok /ˈkeʸpɑk/ *n* [U] material similar to cotton used to fill sleeping bags, etc.

kar·at /ˈkærət/ *n* CARAT

ka·ra·te /kəˈrɑṭiʸ/ *n* [U] Asian style of fighting using the hands and feet

ka·ty·did /ˈkeʸṭiʸˌdɪd/ *n* insect that makes a loud noise

kay·ak /ˈkaɪæk/ *n* light covered CANOE

ka·zoo /kəˈzuʷ/ *n* simple musical instrument that uses the voice

keel¹ /kiʸl/ *n* **1** bar along the bottom of a boat **2 on an even keel** steady

keel² *v* **keel over** *phr vi* fall over sideways

keen /kiʸn/ *adj* **1** (of the 5 senses) good, strong, quick, etc.: *keen eyesight* **2** (of edges) sharp; cutting: (fig.) *keen wind* ~**ly** *adv* ~**ness** *n* [U]

keep¹ /kiʸp/ *v* **kept** /kept/ **1** *vt* continue to have; not lose or give back **2** *vi/t* (cause to) continue being: *keep them warm | Keep off the grass!* **3** *vi* continually do something: *He keeps complaining.* **4** *vt* fulfil (a promise) **5** *vt* prevent: *keep them from knowing* **6** *vt* not tell (a secret) **7** *vt* make records of or in: *keep accounts/a diary* **8** *vt* support with money, etc. **9** *vt* own or manage: *keep chickens/a store* **10** *vi* remain fresh: *This fish won't keep.* **11** *vt* take suitable notice of (a holiday, etc): *keep Christmas* **12 keep (oneself) to oneself** not mix with or talk to other people very much **13 keep one's head** remain calm **14 keep one's shirt on** *infml* to remain calm; not to become upset or angry **15 keep someone company** remain with someone

keep at *phr vt* continue working at (something)

keep back *phr vt* not tell or give; WITHHOLD

keep down *phr vt* **1** prevent from increasing **2** OPPRESS

keep from *phr vt* **1** not to tell (someone) about something **2** prevent oneself from (doing something)

keep in (good) with *phr vt* remain friendly with

keep on *phr vi* **1** continue talking **2** continue to employ (someone) **3** continue to have (something)

keep on at *phr vt* ask repeatedly

keep out *phr vi/t* (cause to) stay away or not enter

keep to *phr vt* **1** stay in: *keep to the left* **2** limit oneself to: *keep to the point* **3** keep (something) private to (oneself)

keep up *phr v* **1** *vi* stay level **2** *vt* continue doing **3** *vt* prevent from going to bed **4** *vt* prevent from falling or dropping: *a belt to keep my pants up* | (fig.) *Keep your spirits up!* (= remain cheerful)

keep² *n* **1** [U] (cost of) necessary food, etc: *earn one's keep* **2** [C] central tower of a castle **3 for keeps** *infml* for ever

keep·er /ˈkiʸpər/ *n* person who guards or looks after: *zookeeper*

keep·ing /ˈkiʸpɪŋ/ *n* [U] **1** care; charge: *leave her jewels in my keeping* **2 in/out of keeping with** suitable/not suitable for

keep·sake /ˈkiʸpseʸk/ *n* thing kept to remind one of the giver

keg /keg/ *n* small barrel

ken /ken/ *n* **beyond one's ken** outside one's knowledge

ken·nel /ˈkenl/ *n* place where dogs are bred (BREED (2)) or looked after

kept /kept/ *v past t. and p. of* KEEP¹

ker·nel /ˈkɜrnl/ *n* **1** center of a nut, seed, etc. **2** important part of a subject

kerosene /ˈkerəˌsiʸn, ˌkerəˈsiʸn/ *n* sort of oil burned for lighting and heating

ketch·up /ˈketʃəp, ˈkæ-/ *also* **catsup** — *n* [U] thick liquid made from TOMATO juice

ket·tle /ˈketl/ *n* pot with a SPOUT, for boiling water

ket·tle·drum /ˈketlˌdrʌm/ *n* large metal drum

key¹ /kiʸ/ *n* **1** shaped piece of metal for locking a door, etc.: *car keys* **2** something that explains or helps one to understand **3** any of the parts of a piano, etc., to be pressed to produce the desired sound or effect: *typewriter keys* **4** musical notes starting at a particular base note: *the key of C* ♦ *adj* very important;

necessary: *key industries* | *a key position in the company*

key² vt 1 make suitable: *factories keyed to military needs* **2** keyboard (information) **3 keyed up** excited and nervous

key·board /ˈkiʸbɔrd, -boʷrd/ *n* row of KEYS (3) ♦ *vt* put (information) into a machine by working a keyboard

key·hole /ˈkiʸhoʷl/ *n* hole for a KEY (1)

key·note /ˈkiʸnoʷt/ *n* central idea (of a speech, etc.)

kg *written abbrev. for:* KILOGRAM(s)

kha·ki /ˈkækiʸ, ˈkɑ-/ *n* **1** [U] yellow-brown color **2** cloth of this color, esp. as worn by soldiers

kib·butz /kɪˈbʊts/ *n* –**zim** /ˌkɪbʊt-ˈsiʸm/ *or* –**zes** farm or other place in Israel where many families live and work together

kick¹ /kɪk/ *v* **1** *vt* hit with the foot **2** *vi* move the feet as if to kick **3** *vi* (of a gun) move violently when fired **4** *vt sl* stop or give up (a harmful activity) **5 kick someone in the teeth** *infml* discourage or disappoint someone very much **6 kick the bucket** *sl* die

kick around *phr v* **1** *vi/t* (of ideas) discuss **2** lie unnoticed in (a place) **3** *vt* beat roughly

kick in *phr vt* **1** contribute one's share of money **2** take effect

kick off *phr vi* begin

kick out *phr vt* remove or dismiss (someone), esp. violently

kick up *phr vt* make (trouble): *kick up a fuss*

kick² n 1 [C] act of kicking **2** [C] *sl* excitement; drive for kicks **3** [S;U] *infml* strength **4** [C] extremely strong new interest: *She's on a health food kick.*

kick·back /ˈkɪkbæk/ *n* BRIBE paid to government officials in exchange for a contract

kick-off /ˈ·· ·/ *n* first kick in football

kid¹ /kɪd/ *n* **1** [C] child or young person **2** [C;U] (leather from) a young goat

kid² *vi/t* –**dd**– *sl* pretend; deceive

kid gloves /ˌ· ˈ·/ *n* [P] gentle methods of dealing with people

kid·nap /ˈkɪdnæp/ *vt* –**pp**– take (someone) away by force, so as to demand money, etc. ~**per** *n*

kid·ney /ˈkɪdniʸ/ *n* organ that separates waste liquid from the blood

kidney ma·chine /ˈ·· ·ˌ·/ *n* hospital machine that can do the work of human kidneys

kill /kɪl/ *vt* **1** cause to die: (fig.) *My feet are killing me.* (= hurting very much) | (fig.) *The boss will kill me*

(= be very angry) *when she finds out.* **2** destroy; spoil **3 kill time** make time pass quickly **4 kill two birds with one stone** get two good results from one action ♦ *n* [S] **1** bird or animal killed **2** act or moment of killing ~**er** *n* ~**ing** *n* **1** murder **2 make a killing** make a lot of money suddenly

kill·joy /ˈkɪldʒɔɪ/ *n* person who spoils other people's pleasure

kiln /kɪln, kɪl/ *n* apparatus for baking pots, bricks, etc.

ki·lo /ˈkiʸloʷ/ *n* kilos kilogram

kil·o·byte /ˈkɪləˌbaɪt/ *n* 1000 or 1024 BYTES of computer information

kil·o·gram, –gramme /ˈkɪləˌɡræm/ *n* (a measure of weight equal to) 2.2 pounds

kil·o·me·ter, –metre /kɪˈlɑmətər, ˈkɪləˌmiʸtər/ *n* (a measure of length equal to) 0.62 of a mile

kil·o·watt /ˈkɪləˌwɑt/ *n* 1000 WATTS

kilt /kɪlt/ *n* short skirt worn esp. by Scotsmen

ki·mo·no /kəˈmoʷnə, -noʷ/ *n* –**nos 1** long loose Japanese garment **2** loose DRESSING GOWN

kin /kɪn/ *n* [P] **next of kin** one's closest relative(s) – see also KITH AND KIN

kind¹ /kaɪnd/ *n* **1** type; sort: *all kinds of people* **2 a kind of** unclear or unusual sort of: *I had a kind of feeling she'd phone.* **3 in kind** (of payment) in goods, not money **4 kind of** *infml* in a certain way; rather **5 of a kind: a** of the same kind: *They're two of a kind.* **b** of a not very good kind: *It was coffee of a kind, but we couldn't drink it.*

kind² *adj* helpful and friendly ~**ness** *n* **1** [U] quality of being kind **2** [C] kind act

kin·der·gar·ten /ˈkɪndərˌɡɑrtn, -ˌɡɑrdn/ *n* school for young children, usu. five-year olds

kind-heart·ed /ˌ· ˈ···◂/ *adj* having a kind nature ~**ly** *adv* ~**ness** *n* [U]

kin·dle /ˈkɪndl/ *vt/i* (cause to) start burning –**dling** [U] materials for starting a fire

kind·ly /ˈkaɪndliʸ/ *adv* **1** in a kind way **2** (showing annoyance) please **3 take kindly to** accept willingly ♦ *adj fml* kind

kin·dred /ˈkɪndrɪd/ *adj* **1** related **2 kindred spirit** person with almost the same habits, interests, etc.

ki·net·ic /kɪˈnɛtɪk, kaɪ-/ *adj fml* of or about movement

king /kɪŋ/ *n* **1** (title of) the male ruler of a country **2** most important man or animal **3** playing card with a picture of a king

king·dom /ˈkɪŋdəm/ *n* **1** country governed by a king or queen **2** any of the three divisions of natural objects: *the animal/plant/mineral kingdom*

king·pin /ˈkɪŋˌpɪn/ n most important person in a group

king-size /ˈ· ·/ adj larger than the standard size

kink /kɪŋk/ n 1 twist in hair, a pipe, etc. 2 strangeness of character ~**y** adj sexually unnatural

kins·man /ˈkɪnzmən/ **kins·wom·an** /-ˌwʊmən/ fem. — n —**men** /-mən/ fml relative

kip·per /ˈkɪpər/ n salt HERRING treated with smoke

kiss /kɪs/ vt/i touch with the lips as a sign of love or a greeting **kiss** n act of kissing

kiss of death /ˌ· · ˈ·/ n [the+S] infml something that makes failure certain

kit /kɪt/ n 1 necessary clothes, tools, etc.: *a sailor's/carpenter's kit* 2 set of pieces to be put together: *model airplane kit*

kit bag /ˈ· ·/ n bag for carrying a soldier's or sailor's kit

kitch·en /ˈkɪtʃən/ n room for cooking in

kitch·en·ette /ˌkɪtʃəˈnɛt/ n very small kitchen

kite /kaɪt/ n 1 frame covered with paper or cloth, for flying in the air 2 kind of HAWK[1] (1)

kith and kin /ˌkɪθ ən ˈkɪn/ n old fash one's friends and relatives

kitsch /kɪtʃ/ n objects, works of literature which pretend to be art but are considered silly, funny, or worthless

kit·ten /ˈkɪtn/ n 1 young cat 2 **have a kitten** infml be in a very nervous anxious condition

kit·ty /ˈkɪtiʲ/ n money collected by several people for an agreed purpose

kitty cor·ner /ˈ·· ˌ··/ adv across a street diagonally (DIAGONAL)

ki·wi /ˈkiʲwiʲ/ n 1 flightless New Zealand bird 2 infml New Zealander

KKK /ˌkeʲ keʲ ˈkeʲ/ see KU KLUX KLAN

Kleen·ex /ˈkliʲnɛks/ n [C;U] tdmk paper handkerchief

klep·to·ma·ni·a /ˌklɛptəˈmeʲniʲə/ n [U] disease of the mind that makes one steal —**ac** /-niʲˌæk/ n person with kleptomania

klutz /klʌts/ n CLUMSY, stupid person

km written abbrev. for: KILOMETER(S)

knack /næk/ n infml special skill

knap·sack /ˈnæpsæk/ n bag carried on the back containing clothes, etc.

knave /neʲv/ n old use dishonest man or boy

knead /niʲd/ vt mix (flour and water, etc.) by pressing with the

hands 2 press and rub (muscles) to cure pain, stiffness, etc.

knee /niʲ/ n 1 middle joint of the leg 2 part of a pair of pants, etc., that covers the knee 3 **bring someone to his knees** defeat someone completely ♦ vt hit with the knee

knee·cap /ˈniʲkæp/ n bone at the front of the knee

knee-deep /ˌ· ˈ·◂/ adj deep enough to reach the knees: (fig.) *knee-deep in debt* (= in trouble over debt)

knee-jerk /ˈ· ·/ adj derog (of opinion) held without thought

kneel /niʲl/ vi **knelt** /nɛlt/ or **kneeled** go down on one's knees

knell /nɛl/ n sound of a bell rung slowly for a death

knew /nuʷ, nyuʷ/ v past t. of KNOW[1]

knick·er·bock·ers /ˈnɪkərˌbakərz/ also **knickers** — n [P] short pants fitting tightly below the knees

knick-knack /ˈnɪknæk/ n small decorative object

knife /naɪf/ n **knives** /naɪvz/ 1 blade with a handle, for cutting 2 **have/get one's knife into someone** treat someone as an enemy and try to harm them ♦ vt wound with a knife

knife-edge /ˈ· ·/ n 1 something sharp and narrow 2 **on a knife-edge** in an extremely uncertain position

knight /naɪt/ n 1 (in former times) noble soldier 2 piece in CHESS ~**hood** n [C;U] rank of a knight ♦ vt make (someone) a KNIGHT (2)

knit /nɪt/ vi/t **knitted** or **knit** 1 make (clothes, etc.) by forming a network of threads with long needles (**knitting needles**) 2 join closely; grow together ~**ting** n something being knitted

knit·wear /ˈnɪt-wɛər/ n [U] knitted clothing

knives /naɪvz/ n pl. of KNIFE

knob /nab/ n 1 round handle or control button 2 round lump: *knob of wood* ~**by** /ˈnabiʲ/ adj having KNOBS (2): *knobby knees*

knock[1] /nak/ v 1 vi/t hit: *knock on the door* 2 vt sl say bad things about 3 (of a car engine) make a noise like hitting 4 **knock someone's block off** infml hit someone very severely 5 **knock on wood** knock on something wooden to keep away bad luck

knock around phr v 1 vi/t be present or active (in) 2 vt treat roughly 3 infml travel continuously

knock back phr vt 1 drink quickly 2 shock

knock down phr vt 1 destroy (a building) with blows 2 strike to the ground: *knocked down by a bus* 3 reduce (a price)

knock off *phr v* **1** *vi/t* stop (work) **2** *vt* take from a total payment: *knock $2 off the price* **3** *vt sl* rob **4** *vt* finish quickly **5** *vt sl* murder

knock out *phr vt* **1** make unconscious by hitting **2** (of a drug) make (someone) go to sleep **3** cause someone to be dismissed from a competition **4** *sl* fill with great admiration

knock up *phr v* **1** *vt sl* make PREGNANT

knock² *n* **1** sound of knocking **2** *infml* piece of bad luck

knock·down /ˈnɑkdaʊn/ *adj* strong enough to KNOCK DOWN (2)

knock·er /ˈnɑkər/ *n* instrument fixed to a door, for knocking

knock·ers /ˈnɑkərz/ *n* [P] *sl* a woman's breasts (usu. considered offensive to women)

knock-kneed /ˈ· ·/ *adj* with knees that touch when walking

knock·out /ˈnɑk-aʊt/ *n* **1** also **KO** — act of knocking a BOXer unconscious **2** person or thing causing admiration ♦ *adj infml* causing great admiration

knoll /noʊl/ *n* small round hill

knot /nɑt/ *n* **1** fastening made by tying rope, etc. **2** hard lump in wood, etc. **3** small group of people **4** a measure of the speed of a ship, about 1853 meters per hour **4 get tied (up) into knots (over)** become confused (about) ♦ *vt* **-tt-** make a knot in; join with a knot — **ty** *adj* **1** (of wood) with KNOTs (2) **2** difficult: *knotty problem*

know¹ /noʊ/ *v* **knew** /nuʷ, nyuʷ/, **known** /noʷn/ **1** *vi/t* have (information) in the mind **2** *vt* have learned **3** *vt* be familiar with: *Do you know Paris well?* **4** *vt* be able to recognize: *You'll know him by his red hair.* **5** [*only in past and perfect tenses*] see, hear, etc.: *I've known him to run 10 miles before breakfast.* – see also **let someone know** (LET)

know backwards *phr vt* know or understand perfectly

know of *phr vt* have heard of or about: *I know of him, but I've never met him.*

know² *n* **in the know** having knowledge or information (about a certain thing)

know-how /ˈ· ·/ *n* [U] practical ability

know·ing /ˈnoʷɪŋ/ *adj* having secret understanding ~**ly** *adv* **1** in a knowing way **2** intentionally

know-it-all /ˈ· · ˌ·/ *n* person who behaves as if he/she knew everything

knowl·edge /ˈnɑlɪdʒ/ *n* [S;U] **1** understanding **2** learning **3** information about something **4 to the best of one's knowledge** so far as one knows – see also WORKING KNOWLEDGE

knowl·edge·a·ble /ˈnɑlɪdʒəbəl/ *adj* having a lot of knowledge or information

known¹ /noʷn/ *past p. of* KNOW¹

known² *adj* **1** publicly recognized: *known criminals* **2 known as: a** generally recognized as **b** also publicly called

knuck·le¹ /ˈnʌkəl/ *n* finger joint

knuckle² *v*

knuckle down *phr vi* start working hard

knuckle under *phr vi* be forced to accept the orders of someone more powerful

KO /ˌkeyˈoʷ/ *n infml for* KNOCKOUT (1)

ko·a·la /koʷˈɑlə/ *n* type of small Australian animal like a bear

kook /kuʷk/ *n sl* **1** unusual person **2** crazy person

kook·y /ˈkuʷkiʸ/ *adj infml* behaving in a silly unusual manner

Ko·ran /kɔˈræn, -ˈrɑn, koʷ-, kə-/ *n* [*the*] the holy book of the Muslims

ko·sher /ˈkoʷʃər/ *adj* **1** (of food) prepared according to Jewish law **2** *infml* honest and trustworthy

kow·tow /ˌkaʊˈtaʊ, ˈkaʊtaʊ/ *vi* obey without question

Krem·lin /ˈkremlɪn/ *n* (buildings containing) the government of the former Soviet Union

ku·dos /ˈkuʷdɑs, -doʷs, ˈkyuʷ-/ *n* [U] public admiration and glory (for something done)

Ku Klux Klan /ˌkuʷ klʌks ˈklæn, ˌkyuʷ-/ also **KKK** — *n* [U] secret organization in the American south that hates black people

kung fu /ˌkʌŋ ˈfuʷ, ˌkʊŋ-/ *n* [U] Chinese style of fighting, like KARATE

kw *written abbrev. for*: KILOWATT(s)

L

L, l /ɛl/ the 12th letter of the English alphabet

l *written abbrev. for:* **1** (*often cap.*) lake **2** line **3** liter(s)

lab /læb/ *n* laboratory

la·bel /ˈleʸbəl/ *n* piece of paper, etc., fixed to something to say what it is, who owns it, etc. ♦ *vt* **1** fix a label on **2** describe as: *They labeled him a thief.*

la·bo·ra·to·ry /ˈlæbrəˌtoriʸ, -ˌtoʷriʸ/ *n* building or room where a scientist works

la·bo·ri·ous /ləˈbɔriʸəs, -ˈboʷr-/ *adj* needing great effort ~**ly** *adv*

la·bor[1] /ˈleʸbər/ *n* **1** [U] hard work **2** [U] workers as a group **3** [S;U] act of giving birth ♦ *adj* of the workers ~**er** *n* man who does heavy unskilled work

labor under *phr vt* suffer from: *labor under a delusion*

labor[2] *v* **1** *vi* work hard **2** *vt* work something out in too great detail: *labor the point*

Labor Day /ˈ·· ˌ·/ *n* legal holiday usu. the first Monday in September celebrating labor

labor u·nion /ˈ·· ˌ··/ *n* workers' organization to represent their interests and deal with employers

Lab·y·rinth /ˈlæbəˌrɪnθ/ *n* MAZE

lace /leʸs/ *n* **1** [U] netlike decorative cloth **2** [C] cord for fastening shoes, etc. ♦ *vt* **1** fasten with a lace **2** make (a drink) stronger by adding alcohol *adj* like LACE (1)

la·ce·rate /ˈlæsəˌreʸt/ *vt fml* cut; wound ~**ration** /ˌlæsəˈreʸʃən/ *n* [C]

lach·ry·mose /ˈlækrəˌmoʷs/ *adj fml* **1** in the habit of weeping **2** tending to cause weeping

lack /læk/ *vt* be without (enough of) ♦ *n* [S;U] absence; need ~**ing** *adj* missing **be lacking in** without the usual or needed amount of

lack·a·dai·si·cal /ˌlækəˈdeʸzɪkəl/ *adj* without enough effort; careless

lack·ey /ˈlækiʸ/ *n derog* person who obeys without question

lack·lus·ter /ˈlækˌlʌstər/ *adj* lifeless; dull

la·con·ic /ləˈkɑnɪk/ *adj fml* using few words ~**ally** /-kliʸ/ *adv*

lac·quer /ˈlækər/ *n* [U] transparent substance that makes a hard shiny surface, or keeps hair in place ♦ *vt* cover with lacquer

la·crosse /ləˈkrɔs/ *n* [U] field game for 2 teams, using sticks with nets at the end

la·cu·na /ləˈkuʷunə, -ˈkyuʷ-/ *n* –**nae** /-niʸ/ *or* -**nas** *fml* empty space, esp. in written matter or knowledge

lad /læd/ *n lit* boy; youth

lad·der /ˈlædər/ *n* bars joined to each other by steps, for climbing: (*fig.*) *the promotion ladder*

la·den /ˈleʸdn/ *adj* heavily loaded: (*fig.*) *laden with sorrow*

la·dle /ˈleʸdl/ *n* large spoon for serving liquids ♦ *vt* serve with a ladle

ladle out *phr vt* give out freely

la·dy /ˈleʸdiʸ/ *n* **1** woman **2** woman of good manners or high social rank **3** (*cap.*) (title for) a woman of noble rank ~ **like** *adj* (of a woman) behaving like a LADY (1) ~**ship** *n* (title for) a woman called LADY (3): *your ladyship*

lag /læg/ *vi* –**gg**– move too slowly: *lag behind the others*

la·ger /ˈlɑgər/ *n* [U] light kind of beer

la·goon /ləˈguʷn/ *n* lake of sea water, (partly) separated from the sea

laid /leʸd/ *v* past t. and p. of LAY[2]

laid-back /ˌ· ˈ·◄/ *adj infml* cheerfully informal and unworried

lain /leʸn/ *v* past p. of LIE[2]

lair /leər/ *n* home of a wild animal

la·i·ty /ˈleʸətiʸ/ *n* [P] LAY[3] people

lake /leʸk/ *n* large mass of water surrounded by land

lamb /læm/ *n* **1** [C] young sheep **2** [U] its meat **3** [C] harmless gentle person ♦ *vi* give birth to lambs

lam·bast /læmˈbeʸst/ *vt infml* beat or attack fiercely (in words)

lame /leʸm/ *adj* **1** unable to walk properly **2** (of excuses, etc.) weak ♦ *vt* make lame ~**ly** *adv* ~**ness** *n* [U]

lame duck /ˌ· ˈ·/ *n* political official whose period in office will soon end

la·ment /ləˈmɛnt/ *vi/t* **1** express grief or sorrow (for) **2** the late lamented the recently dead (person) ♦ *n* song, etc., expressing sorrow ~**able** /ləˈmɛntəbəl/ *adj fml* **1** unsatisfactory **2** worthy of blame ~**ation** /ˌlæmənˈteʸʃən/ *n* [C;U] *fml*

lam·i·nated /ˈlæməˌneʸtɪd/ *adj* made by joining thin sheets of a material

lamp /læmp/ *n* **1** apparatus for giving light **2** apparatus for producing sorts of heat that improve health: an INFRARED lamp

lam·poon /læmˈpuʷn/ *n* written attack that makes someone look foolish **lampoon** *vt*

lamp·post /ˈlæmpˌpoʷst, ˈlæmpˌoʷst/ *n* post supporting a street lamp

lamp·shade /ˈlæmpʃeʸd/ n cover for a lamp

lance /læns/ n long spearlike weapon ♦ vt cut open with a lancet

lan·cet /ˈlænsət/ n doctor's knife for cutting flesh

land[1] /lænd/ n 1 [U] solid dry part of the Earth's surface 2 [C] country; nation 3 [U] earth for farming 4 [U] also **lands** pl. — ground owned as property 5 **see how the land lies** try to discover the present state of affairs before taking action ~ed adj owning a lot of land

land[2] v 1 vi/t come or bring to land 2 vt succeed in getting: land the top job

land in phr vt bring (someone) into (an undesirable state or position): Her resignation landed us in a real mess.

land with phr vt give (someone) (something unwanted): I got landed with organizing the Christmas party.

land·fill /ˈlændfɪl/ n area filled in by buried waste materials

land·ing /ˈlændɪŋ/ n 1 level space at the top of a set of stairs 2 arrival on land: crash landing 3 place where people and goods are loaded, esp. from a ship

landing craft /ˈ·· ·/ n flat boat for landing soldiers and their vehicles on shore

landing gear /ˈ·· ·/ n [U] wheels and UNDERCARRIAGE of an aircraft

land·la·dy /ˈlænd‚leʸdiʸ, ˈlænleʸdiʸ/ n 1 woman a who runs a small hotel b from whom one rents a room 2 a female LANDLORD

land·locked /ˈlændlɑkt, ˈlænlɑkt/ adj surrounded by dry land

land·lord /ˈlændlɔrd, ˈlænlɔrd/ n person from whom one rents land or buildings

land·mark /ˈlændmɑrk, ˈlænmɑrk/ n 1 recognizable object from which one can tell one's position 2 important event, discovery, etc.

land·scape /ˈlændskeʸp, ˈlænskeʸp/ n (picture of) country scenery ♦ vt make (land) into a garden

land·slide /ˈlændslaɪd, ˈlænslaɪd/ n 1 sudden fall of earth and rocks 2 great success in an election

lane /leʸn/ n 1 narrow road 2 division of a wide road, to keep fast and slow vehicles apart 3 path used regularly by ships or aircraft 4 path marked for each competitor in a race

lan·guage /ˈlæŋgwɪdʒ/ n [C;U] 1 system of human expression by means of words: the origins of language 2 particular system as used by a people or nation: the English language 3 system of signs: computer languages 4 particular style or manner of expression: poetic language 5 words and phrases considered shocking: bad language

language la·bo·ra·tory /ˈ··· ‚····/ n room where foreign languages are taught using TAPE RECORDERS, etc.

lan·guid /ˈlæŋgwɪd/ adj lacking strength, will ~ly adv

lan·guish /ˈlæŋgwɪʃ/ vi fml 1 experience long suffering 2 become weak

lan·guor /ˈlæŋgər/ n 1 tiredness of mind or body 2 pleasant or heavy stillness

lank /læŋk/ adj (of hair) straight and lifeless

lank·y /ˈlæŋkiʸ/ adj ungracefully tall and thin

lan·tern /ˈlæntərn/ n container around the flame of a light

lap[1] /læp/ n front of a seated person between the waist and the knees

lap[2] v -pp- 1 vt drink as a cat does 2 vi (of water) move with soft sounds ♦ n act or sound of lapping

lap[3] n single journey around a racing track ♦ vt -pp pass (another racer) so as to be one lap ahead

la·pel /ləˈpɛl/ n part of the front of a coat that is joined to the collar and folded back

lapse /læps/ n 1 small fault or mistake 2 failure in correct behavior, belief, etc. 3 passing away of time ♦ vi 1 sink gradually: lapse into silence 2 (of time) pass 3 (of business agreements, etc.) come to an end **lapsed** adj 1 no longer practicing, esp. one's religion 2 law no longer in use

lar·ce·ny /ˈlɑrsəniʸ/ n [C;U] law (an act of) stealing

lard /lɑrd/ n [U] pig's fat used in cooking ♦ vt 1 put lard on 2 use lots of noticeable phrases in one's speech or writing

lar·der /ˈlɑrdər/ n storeroom or cupboard for food

large /lɑrdʒ/ adj 1 big 2 **at large: a** free **b** as a whole: the country at large ~ly adv mostly

lar·gess /lɑrˈdʒɛs, lɑrˈʒɛs/ n [U] money given generously

lark /lɑrk/ n 1 kind of bird 2 fun activity

lar·va /ˈlɑrvə/ n -vae /-viʸ/ wormlike young of an insect

lar·yn·gi·tis /‚lærənˈdʒaɪtɪs/ n [U] painful swelling of the larynx

lar·ynx /ˈlærɪŋks/ n hollow boxlike part in the throat, where voice is produced by the VOCAL CORDS

las·civ·i·ous /ləˈsɪviʸəs/ adj causing, showing or feeling uncontrolled sexual desire ~ly adv

la·ser /ˈleʸzər/ n apparatus producing a strong narrow beam of light

lash¹ /læʃ/ v 1 vi/t whip 2 vi/t move about violently 3 vt tie firmly

lash out phr vi attack violently

lash² n 1 (a hit with) the thin striking part of a whip: (fig.) the lash of the waves 2 EYELASH

lass /læs/ n lit girl

las·si·tude /ˈlæsəˌtuʷd, -ˌtyuʷd/ n [U] fml tiredness

las·so /ˈlæsoʷ, læˈsuʷ/ n -s rope for catching horses and cattle ♦ vt catch with a lasso

last¹ /læst/ determiner, adv 1 after the others 2 only remaining: my last $5 3 most recent(ly): When did we last meet? 4 least suitable or likely: He's the last person I'd have expected to see here. 5 every last every, not leaving out any ♦ n, pron [(the) S] 1 person or thing after all others: the last to leave 2 the only remaining: the last of the wine 3 the one or ones before the present one: the week before last (= 2 weeks ago) 4 at (long) last in the end ~ly adv in the end

last² v 1 vi continue 2 vi/t be enough (for): The food will last (us) a week. ~ing adj continuing for a long time

last-ditch /ˌ·ˈ·◄/ adj done as one last effort before accepting defeat

last name /ˈ· ·/ n person's family name; SURNAME

last straw /ˌ· ˈ·/ n [the+S] the difficulty, etc., that makes the total unbearable when it is added to one's present difficulties

last word /ˌ· ˈ·/ n [the+S] 1 remark that ends an argument 2 most modern example of something

latch¹ /lætʃ/ n 1 small bar for fastening a door, gate, window, etc. 2 spring lock for a house door which can be opened from outside with a key

latch² vt

latch on phr vi understand

latch onto phr vt 1 latch on 2 refuse to leave (someone)

late /leʸt/ adj, adv 1 after the usual time: The train was late. 2 near the end: in late September 3 recently dead: his late wife 4 recent: the latest fashions | Have you heard the latest? (= most recent news) 5 at the latest and not later 6 of late lately ~ly adv not long ago

la·tent /ˈleʸtnt/ adj existing but not yet noticeable or developed: latent talent latency n [U]

lat·e·ral /ˈlætərəl/ adj of, from, or to the side ~ly adv

lateral think·ing /ˌ··· ˈ··/ n [U] making of unusual connections in the mind to find a new and clever answer to a problem

la·tex /ˈleʸteks/ n [U] liquid from which natural rubber is made

lathe /leʸð/ n machine that turns a piece of wood or metal to be shaped

la·ther /ˈlæðər/ n [S;U] 1 FROTH made with soap and water 2 in a lather infml worried ♦ v 1 vi make a lather 2 vt cover with lather

Lat·in /ˈlætn/ n, adj (of) the language of the ancient Romans

Latin A·mer·i·can /ˌ·· ·ˈ···◄/ adj of the Spanish- or Portuguese-speaking countries of Central and S America

lat·i·tude /ˈlætəˌtuʷd, -ˌtyuʷd/ n [S;U] 1 distance north or south of the EQUATOR, measured in degrees 2 freedom of choice **latitudes** n [P] area at a particular latitude

la·trine /ləˈtriʸn/ n outdoor TOILET in a camp, etc.

lat·ter /ˈlætər/ adj of a later period: his latter years ♦ n fml second of 2 things mentioned ~ly adv recently

latter-day /ˈ·· ·/ adj modern

lat·tice /ˈlætɪs/ n wooden or metal frame with a network of crossing bars used as a fence, etc.

laud /lɔd/ vt lit praise ~able adj deserving praise

laugh /læf/ vi 1 express amusement, happiness, etc., by breathing out forcefully so that one makes sounds with the voice, usu. while smiling 2 no laughing matter serious ♦ n 1 act or sound of laughing 2 something done for a joke 3 have the last laugh win after earlier defeats 4 laugh up one's sleeve infml laugh secretly and often unkindly ~able adj foolish

laughing-stock /ˈ··· ·/ n someone or something regarded as foolish

laugh·ter /ˈlæftər/ n [U] laughing

launch /lɔntʃ, lɑntʃ/ vt 1 send (a newly built boat) into the water 2 send (a ROCKET, etc.) into the sky 3 begin (an activity): launch an attack/a company ♦ n 1 act of launching 2 large oat with a motor ~er n

launch into phr vt begin with eagerness, force, etc.

launch out phr vi begin something new

launch·ing pad /ˈ··· ·/ n base from which spacecraft, etc., are launched

laun·der /ˈlɔndər, ˈlɑn-/ vt 1 wash and iron (clothes) 2 hide (origins of money made from crime)

laun·dro·mat /ˈlɔndrəˌmæt, ˈlɑn-/ n place where the public pay to wash their clothes in machines

laun·dry /ˈlɔndriʸ, ˈlɑn-/ n 1 [C] place where clothes are laundered 2 [U] clothes (needing to be) laundered

laur·e·ate /ˈlɔriʸt, ˈlɑr-/ adj see POET LAUREATE

laur·el /ˈlɔrəl, ˈlɑrəl/ n EVERGREEN bush with shiny leaves **laurels** n

[P] **1** honor gained for something done **2** rest on one's laurels be satisfied with what one has done already, and not do any more

la·va /ˈlɑːvə, ˈlævə/ n [U] melted rock that flows from a VOLCANO

lav·a·to·ry /ˈlævəˌtɔriⁱ, -ˌtoʷriⁱ/ — n TOILET

lav·en·der /ˈlævəndər/ n [U] (pale purple color of) a plant having flowers with a strong smell

lav·ish /ˈlævɪʃ/ adj **1** generous **2** given or produced in (too) great quantity: *lavish praise* ♦ vt give freely: *She lavishes money on them.* ~**ly** adv

law /lɔ/ n **1** [C] rule made by a government **2** [U] all these rules: *Stealing is against the law.* **3** [C] statement of what always happens in certain conditions: *the laws of physics* **4** [*the*+S] *infml* police or a policeman **5** be a law unto oneself do exactly what one wishes **6** law and order respect for the law **7** lay down the law give an opinion in an unpleasant commanding manner ~**ful** adj allowed or recognized by law ~**fully** adv ~**less** adj not governed by laws ~**lessness** n [U]

law·a·bid·ing /ˈ· ·ˌ··/ adj obeying the law

lawn /lɔn/ n area of closely cut grass

lawn·bowls /ˈlɔnˌboʷlz/ n [U] outdoor game in which a big ball (**bowl**) is rolled on grass (**bowling green**)

lawn·mow·er /ˈlɔnˌmoʷər/ n machine that cuts grass

law·suit /ˈlɔsuʷt/ n non-criminal case in a law court

lax /læks/ adj careless and uncontrolled ~**ity** n [C;U]

lax·a·tive /ˈlæksətɪv/ n, adj (medicine) helping the bowels to empty

lay¹ /leⁱ/ v past t. of LIE²

lay² /leⁱ/ v laid /leⁱd/ **1** vt **a** put, carefully, in a flat position: *She laid his coat on the bed.* **b** set in proper order or position: *lay bricks* **2** vt arrange for use: *lay the table for dinner* **3** vt cause to settle or disappear: *lay his fears to rest* **4** vi/t (of a bird, insect, etc.) produce (eggs) **5** vt make (a statement, claim, etc.) in a serious or official way: *lay charges against someone* **6** vt sl have sex with: *He only goes to parties to get laid.* **7** lay hold of catch and hold firmly **8** lay waste destroy completely

lay down phr vt **1** state firmly: *lay down the law* **2** give up (one's life) **3** store (esp. wine) for the future

lay in phr vt get and store a supply of

lay into phr vt attack with words or blows

lay low phr vt **1** knock down **2** make ill **3** hide oneself for a short time

lay off phr vt **1** stop employing **2** give up

lay on phr vt lay it on tell something in a way that goes beyond the truth

lay out phr vt **1** arrange or plan: *lay out a garden* **2** knock (someone) down **3** spend (money) **4** prepare a dead person for the funeral

lay up phr vt **1** keep in bed with an illness: *laid up with flu* **2** collect and store for future use

lay³ adj **1** of or by people who are not priests **2** not professional

lay·a·bout /ˈleⁱəˌbaʊt/ n lazy person

lay·er /ˈleⁱər/ n **1** thickness of some substance laid over a surface: *layers of rock* **2** bird that lays eggs

lay·man /ˈleⁱmən/ n –men /-mən/ LAY³ person

lay·off /ˈ· ·/ n stopping of a worker's employment

lay·out /ˈleⁱaʊt/ n (planned) arrangement: *the layout of the room*

laze /leⁱz/ vi rest lazily

la·zy /ˈleⁱziⁱ/ adj **1** avoiding work **2** spent in inactivity lazily adv laziness n [U]

la·zy·bones /ˈleⁱziⁱˌboʷnz/ n lazy person

lb written abbrev. for: POUND¹ (1)

LCD /ˌɛl siⁱ ˈdiⁱ/ n liquid crystal display; part of an apparatus on which numbers, etc., are shown by passing an electric current through a special liquid

lead¹ /liⁱd/ v led /lɛd/ **1** vi/t guide, esp. by going first **2** vi (of a road, etc.) go somewhere: (fig.) *The plan led to trouble.* **3** vt influence: *What led you to do it?* **4** vt control or govern: *lead an army* **5** vi/t be ahead (of) in sports **6** vt experience (a kind of life) **7** vi (of a newspaper) have as a main story ~**ing** adj most important; chief

lead on phr vt influence (someone) to do something wrong or believe something untrue

lead up to phr vt be a preparation for

lead² /liⁱd/ n **1** [C] guiding suggestion **2** [S] **a** chief or front position **b** distance by which one competitor is ahead **2** [C] (person playing) the chief acting part in a play or film **4** [C] main or most important article in a newspaper **5** [C] wire carrying electrical power

lead³ /lɛd/ n **1** [U] heavy greyish metal used for water pipes, etc. **2** [C;U] (stick of) GRAPHITE used in pencils

lead·en /'ledn/ adj 1 dull grey 2 heavy and sad

lead·er /'liːdər/ n person who leads ~ **ship** n [U] position or qualities of a leader

leading light /ˌliːdɪŋ 'laɪt/ n person of importance

leading ques·tion /ˌliːdɪŋ 'kwestʃən/ n question formed so as to suggest the answer

leaf¹ /liːf/ n **leaves** /liːvz/ 1 flat green part of a plant, joined to its stem 2 sheet of paper or metal 3 part of a table top that can be slid or folded out 4 **turn over a new leaf** begin a new course of improved behavior, habits, etc. ~ **y** adj

leaf² v **leaf through** phr vt turn the pages (of a book, etc.) quickly without reading much

leaf·let /'liːflɪt/ n small sheet of printed matter ♦ vi give out (political) leaflets

league /liːg/ n 1 group of people, countries, etc., joined together for a shared aim 2 group of sports clubs that play against each other 3 level of quality: *They're not in the same league.* 4 **in league (with)** working together secretly

leak /liːk/ n 1 accidental hole through which something flows 2 spreading of secret news: *security leak* ♦ v 1 vi/t (allow to) pass through a leak 2 vt make (secrets) publicly known ~ **y** adj

leak·age /'liːkɪdʒ/ n [C;U] process or amount of leaking

lean¹ /liːn/ v **leaned** or **leant** 1 vi bend from an upright position 2 vi/t support or rest in a sloping position: *lean a ladder against a tree* 3 **lean over backwards** make every possible effort (to) ~ **ing** n tendency: *have artistic leanings*

lean on/upon phr vt 1 depend on 2 *infml* influence (someone) by threats

lean towards phr vt favor (a plan or opinion)

lean² adj 1 not fat 2 producing little profit: *a lean year for business*

leap /liːp/ v **leapt** /lept/ or **leaped** 1 jump 2 sudden increase in number, quantity, etc. 3 **by leaps and bounds** very quickly 4 **a leap in the dark** action or risk taken without knowing what will happen ♦ n sudden jump

leap·frog /'liːpfrɒg, -frag/ n [U] game in which players jump over each other ♦ vi/t -**gg**- go ahead of (each other) in turn

leap year /'· ·/ n a year, every 4th year, in which February has 29 days

learn /lɜːrn/ vi/t **learned** or **learnt** /lɜːrnt/ 1 gain (knowledge or skill): *learn French | learn to swim* 2 fix in the memory: *learn a poem* 3 become informed (of): *learn of his success* ~ **er** n -**ing** n [U] knowledge gained by study ~ **ed** /'lɜːrnɪd/ adj having great knowledge

lease /liːs/ n 1 contract for the use of a place in return for rent 2 **a new lease on life** new strength or desire to be happy, etc. ♦ vt give or take (a place) on a lease

leash /liːʃ/ n chain, etc. for leading a dog

least¹ /liːst/ determiner, pron 1 smallest number, amount, etc.: *Buy the one that costs (the) least.* 2 **at least: a** not less than: *at least $100* **b** if nothing else: *At least it's legal.* 3 **in the least** at all

least² adv (superlative of LITTLE) 1 less than anything else or than any others 2 **not least** partly, and quite importantly

leath·er /'leðər/ n preserved animal skin used for making shoes, etc. ~ **y** adj stiff like leather

leave¹ /liːv/ v **left** /left/ 1 vi/t go away (from) 2 vt allow to remain: *leave the door open | Is there any coffee left?* 3 vt fail to take or bring: *I've left my coat behind.* 4 vt give by a WILL² (5) 5 vt allow something to be the responsibility of (someone) *I'll leave you to buy the tickets.* 6 vt have remaining in a sum: *2 from 8 leaves 6.* 7 **leave go/hold of** stop holding 8 **leave it at that** do or say no more 9 **leave someone/something alone** stop behaving annoyingly in someone's presence or touching something 10 **leave someone/something standing** *infml* be much better than someone or something 11 **leave something up to someone** let someone decide

leave off phr vi/t stop (doing something)

leave out phr vt not include

leave² n 1 [C;U] time spent away from work 2 [U] *fml* permission 3 **take leave of** say goodbye to: *She must have taken leave of her senses.* (= gone crazy)

leaves /liːvz/ n pl. of LEAF¹

lech·er·ous /'letʃərəs/ adj derog wanting continual sexual pleasure ~ **ly** adv

lech·er·y /'letʃəriʲ/ n [U] derog being lecherous

lec·tern /'lektərn/ n sloping table to hold a book

lec·ture /'lektʃər/ n 1 speech given as a method of teaching 2 long solemn scolding or warning ♦ vi/t give a lecture (to) ~ **turer** n person who gives (university) lectures

led /led/ v. past t. and p. of LEAD¹

LED /ˌiː el iʲ 'diʲ/ n light-emitting diode, electronic apparatus used for making lighted numbers on clocks, etc.

ledge /lɛdʒ/ n shelf sticking out from a wall, rock, etc.

led·ger /'lɛdʒər/ n account book of a business

lee /liː/ n fml shelter from the wind ♦ adj on the side away from the wind

leech /liːtʃ/ n 1 wormlike creature that sucks blood 2 person who makes profit from others

leek /liːk/ n vegetable with long fleshy stem and broad leaves that tastes slightly of onions

leer /lɪər/ vi, n (look with) an unpleasant smile

lee·ward /'liːwərd, 'luːərd tech/ adj 1 with or in the direction of the wind: a leeward engine 2 away from the wind: the leeward side of the ship

lee·way /'liːweɪ/ n additional time, money, etc., allowing the chance of success

left[1] /lɛft/ past t. and p. of LEAVE[1]

left[2] adj 1 on the side of the body that contains the heart 2 in the direction of one's left side 3 belonging to or favoring the LEFT[3] (2) in politics

left[3] n [U] 1 left side or direction 2 political parties that favor more change and more state control ♦ adv towards the left ~ist n, adj (a supporter) of the political left

left field /ˌ· '·/ n 1 position in baseball 2 (way) out in left field impractical, not REALISTIC

left-hand /ˌ· '·◄/ adj on the left side ~ed adj using the left hand for most actions ~er left-handed person

left·o·vers /'lɛftˌoʊvərz/ n [P] food remaining uneaten after a meal

left wing /ˌ· '·/ n [U] LEFT[3] (2)

leg /lɛg/ n 1 limb that includes the foot, used for walking 2 part of a garment that covers this 3 support of a table, etc. 4 single stage of a journey 5 not have a leg to stand on have no good reason or excuse 6 on one's/its last legs: a very tired b nearly worn out c nearly dead 7 pull someone's leg make fun of a person in a playful way

leg·a·cy /'lɛgəsiː/ n 1 money, etc., left in someone's WILL 2 something left behind: Disease is often a legacy of war.

le·gal /'liːgəl/ adj of, allowed, or demanded by the law ~ly adv ~ize vt make legal ~ity /liː'gæləti/ n [U]

le·gal·ist·ic /ˌliːgə'lɪstɪk◄/ adj derog placing too great an importance on keeping exactly to what the law says

legal ten·der /ˌ·· '··/ n fml money that must by law be accepted in payment

le·ga·tion /lɪ'geɪʃən/ n offices of a minister below the rank of AMBASSADOR, representing one country in another country

le·gend /'lɛdʒənd/ n 1 [C] old story which may not be true 2 [U] such stories collectively 3 [C] famous person or act 4 [C] words that explain a picture, etc., in a book ~ary adj famous in legends

leg·gings /'lɛgɪŋz/ n [P] outer coverings to protect the legs

le·gi·ble /'lɛdʒəbəl/ adj that can be read easily ~bly adv ~bility /ˌlɛdʒə'brɪləti/ n [U]

le·gion /'liːdʒən/ n 1 division of an army, esp. in ancient Rome 2 large group of people ♦ adj fml very many ~ary n member of a legion (1)

le·gion·naire's dis·ease /ˌliːdʒə'nɛərz dɪˌziːz/ n [U] serious infectious disease of the lungs

le·gis·late /'lɛdʒəˌsleɪt/ vi make laws -lator n -lation /ˌlɛdʒə'sleɪʃən/ n [U] 1 law or set of laws 2 act of making laws

le·gis·la·tive /'lɛdʒəˌsleɪtɪv/ adj having the power and duty to make laws: a legislative assembly ♦ n [U] the branch of government that does this

le·gis·la·tor /'lɛdʒəˌsleɪtər/ n person who makes laws

le·gis·la·ture /'lɛdʒəˌsleɪtʃər/ n body of people who make the laws

le·git·i·mate /lə'dʒɪtəmɪt/ adj 1 legally correct 2 born of parents married to each other 3 reasonable: legitimate conclusion ~ly adv -macy n [U]

le·git·i·mize /lɪ'dʒɪtəˌmaɪz/ also legitimatize vt 1 make legal; make acceptable 2 make (a child) legitimate

leg·ume /'lɛgyuːm, lə'gyuːm/ n (seeds of) beans, PEAs etc., used as food

leg·work /'lɛgwɜrk/ n work that needs a lot of walking

lei·sure /'liːʒər, 'lɛ-/ n [U] 1 free time 2 at one's leisure at a convenient time leisured adj 1 having leisure 2 leisurely

lei·sure·ly /'liːʒərliː, 'lɛ-/ adj unhurried

lem·on /'lɛmən/ n 1 [C] sour fruit with a hard yellow skin 2 [U] light bright yellow 3 [C] sl something unsatisfactory or worthless esp. a car

lem·on·ade /ˌlɛmə'neɪd◄/ n [U] drink made of lemons, sugar, and water

lend /lɛnd/ v lent /lɛnt/ 1 vt/i give something for a limited time: lend him $10 till tomorrow 2 vt give; add: The flags lent color to the streets. 3 lend a hand give help 4 lend itself to be suitable for ~er n

length /lɛŋkθ, lɛŋθ/ n **1** [C;U] measurement of something from one end to the other or of its longest side **2** [U] quality or condition of being long: *the length of the exam paper* **3** [C] distance from front to back of a horse or boat in a race: *win by 3 lengths* **4** [C] amount of time from beginning to end **5** [C] piece of something: *a length of string* **6 at length: a** in many words **b** *fml* finally **7 go to any/great lengths** be prepared to do anything ~**y** *adj* (too) long

length·en /ˈlɛŋkθən, ˈlɛŋθən/ vi/t make or become longer

length·wise /ˈlɛŋkθwaɪz, ˈlɛŋθ-/ also **length·ways** /-weˈz/ — adv in the direction of the longest side

le·ni·ent /ˈliʸniʸənt, ˈliʸnyənt/ adj not severe in judgment ~**ly** adv −**ence**, −**ency** n [U]

lens /lɛnz/ n **1** curved piece of glass in a camera, microscope, etc. **2** part of the eye that can FOCUS light **3** CONTACT LENS

lent /lɛnt/ v past t. and p. of LEND

Lent n the 40 days before EASTER

len·til /ˈlɛntəl/ n small beanlike seed used for food

leop·ard /ˈlɛpərd/ **leopardess** /ˈlɛpərdɪs/ fem. n large spotted cat-like animal

le·o·tard /ˈliʸəˌtɑrd/ n close fitting garment made in one piece worn by dancers, etc.

lep·er /ˈlɛpər/ n **1** person with leprosy **2** person avoided by other people for social or moral reasons

lep·ro·sy /ˈlɛprəsiʸ/ n [U] disease in which the skin becomes rough, flesh and nerves are destroyed and fingers, toes, etc., drop off −**rous** adj

les·bi·an /ˈlɛzbiʸən/ adj, n (of or being) a woman HOMOSEXUAL ~**ism** n [U]

le·sion /ˈliʸʒən/ n fml wound

less¹ /lɛs/ determiner, pron, (comparative of LITTLE) n **1** smaller amount (than): *less noise* | *less than a mile* **2 less and less** (an amount) that continues to become smaller **3 less than no time** a very short time **4 none the less** but in spite of everything **5 think (the) less of** have a lower opinion of

less² adv **1** not so; to a smaller degree (than): *less cold* **2** not so much: *to work less* **3 less and less** increasingly rarely **4 much/still less** and certainly not

less³ prep but we subtract; MINUS: *I earned $100, less tax.*

les·see /lɛˈsiʸ/ n person who LEASES a property

less·en /ˈlɛsən/ vi/t make or become less

less·er /ˈlɛsər/ adj, adv smaller: *the lesser of 2 evils*

les·son /ˈlɛsən/ n **1** (period of) teaching something in school, etc. **2** experience from which to learn: *The accident taught him a lesson.* **3** short piece read from the Bible

lest /lɛst/ conj fml for fear that

let /lɛt/ vt let; pres. p. letting **1** allow (to do or happen): *He let his beard grow.* **2** (the named person) must, should, or can: *Let each man decide for himself.* | (when suggesting a plan) '*Let's have a party!*' **3** give the use of (a place) for rent **4 let alone** and certainly not: *He can't walk, let alone run.* **5 let go** stop holding **6 let oneself go: a** behave freely **b** stop taking care of one's appearance **7 let someone go: a** set someone free **b** dismiss someone from a job **8 let someone know** tell someone, esp. at a later date **9 let someone/something alone** stop behaving annoyingly in someone's presence or touching something **10 let well enough alone** allow existing conditions to remain as they are, for fear of making things worse

let down phr vt **1** make (clothes) longer **2** disappoint

let in for phr vt cause (esp. oneself) to have (something unwanted)

let into/in on phr vt allow to share (a secret)

let off phr vt **1** excuse from punishment **2** explode: *let off fireworks*

let on phr vi **1** tell a secret **2** pretend

let out phr v **1** give (a shout, etc.) **2** make (clothes) wider **3** finish: *School lets out at 3 o'clock*

let up phr vi lessen or stop

let·down /ˈlɛtdaʊn/ n disappointment

le·thal /ˈliʸθəl/ adj causing death

leth·ar·gy /ˈlɛθərdʒiʸ/ n [U] tiredness and laziness −**gic** /ləˈθɑrdʒɪk/ adj

let·ter /ˈlɛtər/ n **1** [C] written message sent to someone **2** [C] sign representing a sound **3** [(the) S] actual words of something: *the letter of the law* ~**ing** n [U] style and size of written letters **letters** n [U] fml literature

letter bomb /ˈ·· ·ˌ·/ n small bomb mailed in an envelope

let·ter·head /ˈlɛtərˌhɛd/ n name and address printed at the top of the owner's writing paper

let·tuce /ˈlɛtɪs/ n [C;U] green leafy vegetable, eaten raw

let·up /ˈlɛtʌp/ n [C;U] lessening of activity

leu·ke·mi·a /luʷˈkiʸmiʸə/ n [U] serious disease in which the blood has too many white cells

lev·el¹ /ˈlevəl/ adj **1** flat; HORIZON-TAL **2** equal: *Pete and Dan are level in math.* **3** one's level best all that one can do

level² n [C;U] **1** line or surface parallel with the ground; position of height in relation to a flat surface: *The garden is on 2 levels.* | (fig.) *The decision was made at the presidential level.* **2** standard of quality or quantity: *increase production levels* **3** apparatus for testing whether a surface is level ¹ (1) **4** on the level honest(ly)

level³ vt/i make or become level

level at/against phr vt **1** aim (a weapon) at **2** bring (a charge) against (someone)

level off/out phr vi stop rising or falling

level with phr vt infml speak truthfully to

level⁴ adv so as to be level: *a missile flying level with the ground*

level-head·ed /ˌ··ˈ··◄/ adj calm and sensible

le·ver /ˈlevər, ˈliˈ-/ n **1** bar that turns on its middle point, to lift things **2** rod that works a machine **3** something which may be used for influencing ♦ vt move with a lever: *Lever it into position.*

le·ver·age /ˈlevərɪdʒ, ˈliˈ-/ n [U] power of a lever: (fig.) *use political leverage*

lev·i·tate /ˈlevəˌteʸt/ vi rise into the air as if by magic –tation /ˌlevə-ˈteʸʃən/ n [U]

lev·i·ty /ˈlevəṭiʸ/ n [U] fml lack of proper seriousness

lev·y /ˈleviʸ/ vt demand and collect (esp. taxes) officially

lewd /luʷd/ adj sexually dirty: *lewd songs* ~ly adv ~ness n [U]

lex·i·cal /ˈleksɪkəl/ adj of words ~ly /-kliʸ/ adv

lex·i·cog·ra·phy /ˌleksəˈkɑgrəfiʸ/ n [U] writing of dictionaries –pher n

lex·i·con /ˈleksɪˌkɑn, -kən/ n dictionary or word list

li·a·bil·i·ty /ˌlaɪəˈbɪləṭiʸ/ n **1** [U] condition of being liable **2** [C] debt that must be paid **3** [C] someone or something that limits one's activities or freedom

li·a·ble /ˈlaɪəbəl/ adj **1** responsible in law **2** liable to have a tendency to

li·ai·son /ˈliʸəˌzɑn, liʸˈeʸzɑn/ n **1** [S;U] working association between groups **2** [C] sexual relationship between an unmarried man and woman

li·ar /ˈlaɪər/ n person who tells lies

lib /lɪb/ n [U] liberation (LIBERATE)

li·bel /ˈlaɪbəl/ n [C;U] damaging written statement about someone ♦ vt -l- make a libel against ~ous adj: *a libellous remark*

lib·e·ral /ˈlɪbərəl/ adj **1** willing to respect the opinions of others **2** (of education) leading to wide general knowledge **3** given freely: *liberal supplies* ~ism n [U] LIBERAL (1) opinions ~ize vt remove limits on freedom: *liberalize the divorce laws* ~ization /ˌlɪbərələˈzeʸʃən/ n [U]

liberal arts /ˌ··· ˈ·/ n course in college or university that gives a degree in social and human studies

lib·e·ral·i·ty /ˌlɪbəˈræləṭiʸ/ n [U] fml **1** generosity **2** broadness of mind

lib·e·rate /ˈlɪbəˌreʸt/ vt fml set free –rated adj socially and sexually free –rator n –ration /ˌlɪbə-ˈreʸʃən/ n [U]

lib·er·tar·i·an /ˌlɪbərˈteəriʸən/ n believer in freedom of thought ~ism n [U]

lib·er·tine /ˈlɪbərtiʸn/ n person with an unusual (or immoral) set of values

lib·er·ty /ˈlɪbərṭiʸ/ n [U] **1** personal or political freedom **2** chance or permission to do or use something **3** at liberty free **4** take liberties behave too freely

li·bid·i·nous /lɪˈbɪdənəs/ adj fml LASCIVIOUS ~ly adv

li·bi·do /lɪˈbiʸdoʷ/ n –dos tech the sexual urge

li·brar·i·an /laɪˈbreəriʸən/ n person in charge of a library ~ship n [U]

li·bra·ry /ˈlaɪˌbreriʸ, -brəriʸ, -briʸ/ n (room or building with) a collection of books, records, etc.

lice /laɪs/ n pl. of LOUSE

li·cense /ˈlaɪsəns/ n **1** [C;U] (paper showing) official permission to do something **2** [U] fml uncontrolled freedom

license vt give a LICENSE (1) to

licensee /ˌlaɪsənˈsiʸ/ n person with a license

li·cen·tious /laɪˈsɛnʃəs, -tʃəs/ adj sexually uncontrolled ~ly adv ~ness n [U]

licence plate /ˈ·· ˌ·/ n official number shown on a vehicle

lick /lɪk/ vt **1** move the tongue across **2** (of flames or waves) pass lightly over **3** infml defeat ♦ n **1** [C] act of licking **2** [C] small amount (of work etc.) **3** [S] infml speed

lic·o·rice, liquorice /ˈlɪkərɪs, -rɪʃ/ n [U] black substance used in medicine and candy

lid /lɪd/ n **1** movable cover of a container **2** EYELID

lie¹ /laɪ/ vi, n lied, pres. p. lying (make) a false statement – see also WHITE LIE

lie² vi lay /leʸ/, lain /leʸn/, pres. p. lying /ˈlaɪ-ɪŋ/ **1** be or remain in a flat position on a surface **2** be or remain in a particular position or state: *The town lies 2 miles to the* *east.| The machinery was lying idle.* **3** be the responsibility of: *The decision lies with you.* **4 lie low** be in hiding or avoid being noticed ♦ *n* [S] way something lies

lie about *phr vi* be lazy; do nothing

lie behind *phr vt* be the reason for

lie down *phr vi* **1 lie down on the job** do work that is not good enough in quantity or quality **2 take something lying down** suffer something bad without complaining or trying to stop it

lie over *phr vi* be POSTPONEd

lie de·tec·tor /'·· ·,··/ *n* instrument that is said to show when someone is telling LIES¹

lieu /luw/ *n* **in lieu (of)** instead (of)

lieu·ten·ant /luw'tenənt/ *n* officer of low rank in the armed forces

life /laɪf/ *n* **lives** /laɪvz/ **1** [U] active force that makes animals and plants different from stones or machines **2** [U] living things: *There is no life on the moon.* **3** [U] human existence: *Life is full of surprises.* **4** [C] period or way of being alive: *their busy lives* | (fig.) *during the life of this company* | (fig.) *The machine has a life of 10 years.* **5** [C] person: *No lives were lost.* **6** [U] activity; movement; strength: *full of life* **7** [U] existence as a collection of widely different experiences: *You see life in the navy.* **8** [U] also **life im·pris·on·ment** /,· ·'····/ — punishment of being put in prison for a long time **9** [C] BIOGRA-PHY **10** [*the*+S] person or thing that is the cause of enjoyment in a group: *the life and soul of the party* **11** [U] using a living person as the subject of a painting, etc.: *painted from life* **12 as large as life** unexpectedly, without any possibility of mistake, but the real person **13 come to life:** **a** regain one's senses after fainting **b** show or develop interest, excitement, etc. **14 for dear life** with the greatest effort **15 Not on your life!** Certainly not! **16 take one's life** kill oneself **17 take one's life in one's (own) hands** be in continual danger **18 take someone's life** kill them ~**less** *adj* **1** dead **2** not active; dull ~**lessly** *adv* ~**like** *adj* like a real person

life belt /'·· ·/ *n* belt worn to keep a person from sinking in water

life·blood /'laɪfblʌd/ *n* [U] something that gives continuing strength

life·boat /'laɪfbowt/ *n* boat for saving people in danger at sea

life buoy /'·· ·/ *n* floating ring to hold onto in the water

life cy·cle /'·· ,··/ *n* all the stages of development through which a creature passes during its life

life·guard /'laɪfgɑrd/ *n* swimmer employed to help other people in danger

life jack·et /'·· ,··/ *n* garment worn to support a person in water

life·line /'laɪflaɪn/ *n* **1** rope for saving life **2** something on which one's life depends

life·long /'laɪflɔŋ/ *adj* lasting all one's life

life of Ri·ley /,laɪf əv 'raɪliʸ/ *n* [*the*+S] *infml* a very easy untroubled life

life-size /,· '··◂/ **life-sized** — *adj* (of a work of art) as big as what it represents

life·span /'laɪfspæn/ *n* length of a creature's life

life·style /'laɪfstaɪl/ *n* way of living

life·time /'laɪftaɪm/ *n* time during which someone is alive

lift¹ /lɪft/ *v* **1** *vt* raise to a higher level **2** *vt* improve: *lift my spirits* **3** *vi* (of clouds, etc.) disappear **4** *vt* bring to an end: *lift a ban* **5** *vt* steal

lift off *phr vi* (of an aircraft or spacecraft) leave the ground **lift-off** /'·· ·/

lift² *n* **1** act of lifting **2** free ride in a vehicle **3** feeling of increased strength, higher spirits, etc.

lig·a·ment /'lɪgəmənt/ *n* band that joins bones together

lig·a·ture /'lɪgətʃər/ *n* **1** thread used for tying, esp. in medicine **2** 2 letters joined, such as ff, fi, etc.

light¹ /laɪt/ *n* **1** [U] force by which we see things: *sunlight* **2** [C] lamp, etc., that gives light **3** [C] (something that will make) a flame **4** [C] bright part of a painting, etc. **5** [S;U] brightness in the eyes **6** [C] way in which something is regarded: *see it in a different light* **7 bring/come to light** make or become known **8 in a good/bad light** in a favorable/unfavorable way **9 in light of** taking into account **10 see the light:** **a** be born **b** be made public **c** understand or accept an idea or truth **11 throw/shed light on** explain

light² *v* **lit** /lɪt/ or **lighted** **1** *vi/t* (cause to) start burning **2** *vt* give light to: *lighted streets* ~**ing** *n* system or quality of lights in a place

light up *phr v* **1** *vi/t* make or become bright **2** *vi* start smoking

light³ *adj* **1** not dark: *a light room* **2** pale: *light green*

light⁴ *adj* **1** not heavy **2** small in amount: *light lunch/traffic* **3** easy to bear or do: *light duties* **4** gentle: *light touch* **5** quick and graceful **6** (of wine, etc.) not very strong **7** not serious: *light reading* **8** (of sleep) not deep **9 make light of** treat as of little importance ♦ *adv* with few traveling cases or possessions: *to* *travel light* ~**ly** *adv* **1** gently **2** slightly **3** not seriously ~**ness** *n* [U]

light⁵ *vt* **lit** *or* **lighted** come down from flight and settle: (fig.) *I finally lit on the idea of going to Paris.*

light into *phr vt* attack strongly

light bulb /'· ·/ *n* BULB (2)

light·en /'laɪtn/ *vi/t* make or become **a** brighter **b** less heavy, or **c** (also **lighten up**) more cheerful

light·er /'laɪtər/ *n* instrument for lighting cigarettes, etc.

light-fin·gered /ˌ· '··◂/ *adj infml* having the habit of stealing small things

light-head·ed /ˌ· '·· ◂/ *adj* **1** unable to think clearly **2** not sensible

light-heart·ed /ˌ· '··◂/ *adj* cheerful

light·house /'laɪthɑʊs/ *n* tower with a powerful light to guide ships

light·ning /'laɪtnɪŋ/ *n* [U] **1** electric flash of light in the sky **2** very quick, short, or sudden: *a lightning visit*

lightning rod /'·· ˌ·/ *n* wire leading from the top of a building to the ground, as a protection against lightning

light·weight /'laɪt-weɪt/ *n* **1** person or thing of less than average weight **2** someone who does not think deeply or seriously **lightweight** *adj*

light year /'· ·/ *n* **1** distance that light travels in a year **2** *infml* a very long time

li·ka·ble, **likeable** /'laɪkəbəl/ *adj* (esp. of people) pleasant; attractive

like¹ /laɪk/ *vt* **1** regard with pleasure or fondness **2** be willing (to): *I don't like to ask.* **3** (with **would**) wish or choose (to have): *I'd like a boiled egg.* | *Would you like to read it?* | *How do you like...?* (used when asking for an opinion) **5** I'd **like to**... I would be surprised/interested to **6** I **like that!** That's very annoying! **7** if **you like** if that is what you want **liking** *n* [S] **1** fondness **2** to **one's liking** which suits one's ideas or expectations **likes** *n* [P] things that one likes

like² *prep* **1** in the same way as; similar to: *Do it like this.* **2** typical of: *It's not like her to be late.* **3** such as: *Houses like that are expensive.* **4** **something like** about ♦ *n* **1** something of the same kind: *running, swimming, and the like* **2** the **likes of** people or things of the stated type ♦ *adj fml* similar ♦ *conj* as: *Make it like you make tea.*

like·li·hood /'laɪkliˌhʊd/ *n* [U] probability

like·ly /'laɪkliʸ/ *adj* **1** probable **2** (**That's) a likely story!** *infml* (said to show that one disbelieves what someone has said) ♦ *adv* **1** **most/very likely** probably **2** Not **likely!** *infml* Certainly not!

like-mind·ed /ˌ· '···◂/ *adj* having the same ideas, interests, etc.

lik·en /'laɪkən/ *v* **liken to** *phr vt* compare to

like·ness /'laɪknɪs/ *n* [C;U] sameness in appearance: *a family likeness*

like·wise /'laɪk-waɪz/ *adv* similarly; also

li·lac /'laɪlək, -lɑk, -læk/ *n* **1** [C] bush with pinkish purple or white flowers **2** [U] pinkish purple

lilt /lɪlt/ *n* [S] pleasant pattern of rising and falling sound **lilt** *adj*

lil·y /'lɪliʸ/ *n* plant with large esp. white flowers: *her lily-white skin*

lily-liv·ered /ˌ·· '···◂/ *adj lit* cowardly

limb /lɪm/ *n* **1** leg, arm, or wing **2** branch of a tree **3** out on a **limb** alone without support **4** tear **limb from limb** tear (a person) apart

lim·ber /'lɪmbər/ *v* **limber up** *phr vi* exercise the muscles before a game, etc.

lim·bo /'lɪmboʷ/ *n* [U] state of being uncertain

lime¹ /laɪm/ *n* [U] white substance used in making cement

lime² *n* sour green fruit like a LEMON

lime·light /'laɪmlaɪt/ *n* [*the*+S] the center of public attention

lim·e·rick /'lɪmərɪk/ *n* funny poem with 5 lines

lim·ey /'laɪmiʸ/ *n derog* person from England

lim·it /'lɪmɪt/ *n* **1** farthest point or edge **2** *infml* someone or something too bad to bear **3** off **limits** where one is not allowed to go **4** within **limits** up to a reasonable point – see also TIME LIMIT ♦ *vt* keep below a limit ~**ed** *adj* **1** small; having limits **2** (*abbrev.* **Ltd**) (of a British company) having a reduced duty to pay back debts: *a limited company* ~**less** *adj* endless

lim·i·ta·tion /ˌlɪmɪ'teɪʃən/ *n* **1** [U] limiting **2** [C] condition that limits

lim·ou·sine /'lɪməˌziʸn, ˌlɪmə'ziʸn/ *n* long expensive car with the driver's seat separated from the back

limp¹ /lɪmp/ *vi, n* [S] (walk with) an uneven step

limp² *adj* lacking firmness; not stiff ~**ly** *adv*

lim·pet /'lɪmpɪt/ *n* kind of SHELLFISH that holds tightly to the rock: (fig.) *cling to him like a limpet*

lim·pid /'lɪmpɪd/ *adj lit* clear and transparent

linch·pin /'lɪntʃˌpɪn/ *n* person or thing that keeps something together

line¹ /laɪn/ *n* **1** long narrow mark on a surface: *a line drawing* (= done with pen or pencil **2** limit; border: *the finishing line in a race* **3** BOTTOM LINE **3 a** a row: *boys standing in (a) line* **b** row of words on a printed page: *The actor forgot his lines.* **4** row of military defenses **5** a direction followed: *the line of fire* **6** piece of string, wire, etc.: *fishing line* **7** telephone connection: *Hold the line, please.* **8** railroad **9** system of travel: *airline* **10** method of action: *new line of approach* | *You're on the right lines.* (= following the right method) **11** an official POLICY (1): *the party line* **12** trade or profession **13** family following one another: *line of politicians* **14** a short letter **15** area of interest **16** type of goods: *a new line in hats* **17 in line for** being considered for **18 in line with** in accordance with **19 (step) out of line** (act) differently from others or from what is expected **20 (reach) the end of the line** (reach) the last stages, esp. a point of failure **21 read between the lines** find hidden meanings

line² *vt* **1** mark with lines or WRINKLES: *lined paper* | *His face is very lined.* **2** form rows along: *crowds lining the streets*

line up *phr v* **1** *vi/t* form into a row esp. to wait for something **2** *vt* arrange (an event)

line³ *vt* **1** cover the inside of (something) with material: *fur-lined boots* **2 line one's pocket(s)/purse** make money for oneself **lining** *n* [C;U]: *brake linings*

lin·e·age /ˈlɪniʸ-ɪdʒ/ *n* [C;U] *fml* line of relationship from one person to another down through a family

lin·e·ar /ˈlɪniʸər/ *adj* **1** in lines **2** of length: *linear measurements*

line·back·er /ˈlaɪnˌbækər/ *n* player (in football) close behind the line of scrimmage

lin·en /ˈlɪnən/ *n* [U] **1** cloth made from FLAX, etc. **2** sheets, TABLECLOTHS, etc.

line of scrim·mage /ˌlaɪn əv ˈskrɪmɪdʒ/ *n* line where the football sits before each play begins

line print·er /ˈ· ˌ··/ *n* machine that prints computer information

lin·er /ˈlaɪnər/ *n* **1** large passenger ship **2** something used to LINE³ something

lines·man /ˈlaɪnzmən/ *n* **-men** /-mən/ (in sports) official who says whether a ball has gone outside the limits

line·up /ˈlaɪnʌp/ *n* **1** collection of people, esp. side by side in a line looking forward **2** competitors in a race or game **3** set of events

lin·ger /ˈlɪŋgər/ *vi* be slow to disappear; delay going: *lingering illness*

lin·ge·rie /ˌlɑnʒəˈreʸ, ˈlænʒəˌriʸ, -dʒə-/ *n* [U] *fml* women's underclothes

lin·go /ˈlɪŋgoʷ/ *n* **-goes** *sl* language

lin·guist /ˈlɪŋgwɪst/ *n* **1** person who studies and is good at foreign languages **2** person who studies language in general **~ic** /lɪŋˈgwɪstɪk/ *adj* of language **~ics** *n* [U] study of language

lin·i·ment /ˈlɪnəmənt/ *n* [U] liquid for rubbing on stiff muscles

link /lɪŋk/ *n* **1** connection **2** one ring of a chain – see also LINKS ♦ *vt/i* join; connect

link·age /ˈlɪŋkɪdʒ/ *n* [C;U] system or way of connection

links /lɪŋks/ *n* **links** GOLF course

li·no·le·um /lɪˈnoʷliʸəm/ *n* [U] smooth hard covering for floors

lint /lɪnt/ *n* [U] bits of cotton, FUZZ

li·on /ˈlaɪən/ **lioness** /ˈlaɪənɪs/ *fem.* — *n* **1** large yellow catlike animal **2** famous and important person: *a literary lion* **3 the lion's share** the biggest part **~ize** *vt* treat (someone) as important

lip /lɪp/ *n* **1** edge of the mouth **2** edge of a cup, etc. **3 lick/smack one's lips** think of or remember something (esp. food) with enjoyment – see also STIFF UPPER LIP

lip-read /ˈlɪp riʸd/ *vi/t* understand speech by watching lip movements

lip ser·vice /ˈ· ˌ··/ *n* [U] **pay lip service** to support in words, but not in fact

lip·stick /ˈlɪpˌstɪk/ *n* [C;U] (stick of) colored substance put on the lips

liq·ue·fy /ˈlɪkwəˌfaɪ/ *vi/t fml* make or become liquid **–faction** /ˌlɪkwəˈfækʃən/ *n* [U]

li·queur /lɪˈkɜr, lɪˈkuʊr/ *n* [C;U] strong sweet alcoholic drink

liq·uid /ˈlɪkwɪd/ *n* [C;U] a substance which is not a solid or a gas, which flows freely and is wet ♦ *adj* **1** in the form of a liquid **2** clear and looking wet **3** (of sounds) pure and flowing **4** easily exchanged for money: *liquid assets* **~ize** *vt* crush into juice

liq·ui·date /ˈlɪkwəˌdeʸt/ *v* **1** *vt* kill **2** *vi/t* arrange the end of (an unsuccessful company) **–dation** /ˌlɪkwəˈdeʸʃən/ *n* [U]

liq·uid·i·ty /lɪˈkwɪdət̬iʸ/ *n* [U] **1** state of being liquid **2** state of having LIQUID (4) money

liq·uor /ˈlɪkər/ *n* [U] alcoholic drink

liq·uo·rice /ˈlɪkərɪs, -rɪʃ/ *n* [U] LICORICE

liquor store /ˈ·· ·/ *n* store that sells alcohol to take away

lisp /lɪsp/ *vi* pronounce /s/ to sound like /θ/ also lisp *n* [S]

list¹ /lɪst/ *n* set of things written in order: *shopping list* – see also HIT LIST ♦ *vt* put into a list

list² *vi* (of a ship) lean or slope to one side *n*

lis·ten /ˈlɪsən/ *vi* **1** give attention in hearing **2 Don't listen to someone** Don't believe or do what someone says ~**er** *n*

  listen in *phr vt* **1** listen to (a broadcast on) the radio **2** listen to other people's conversation when one should not

list·less /ˈlɪstləs/ *adj* tired and not interested ~**ly** *adv* ~**ness** *n* [U]

list price /ˈ· ·/ *n* price suggested for an article by the makers

lit /lɪt/ *v past t. and p. of* LIGHT² or LIGHT⁵

lit·a·ny /ˈlɪtn-iⁱ/ *n* form of long Christian prayer: (fig.) *a long litany of complaints*

li·ter /ˈliⁱtər/ *n* metric measure of liquid slightly larger than a QUART

lit·e·ra·cy /ˈlɪtərəsiⁱ/ *n* [U] state or condition of being literate

lit·e·ral /ˈlɪtərəl/ *adj* **1** giving one word for each word: *a literal translation* **2** following the usual meaning of words ~**ly** *adv* **1** really **2** word by word

lit·e·ra·ry /ˈlɪtəˌreriⁱ/ *adj* of literature or writers

lit·e·rate /ˈlɪtərɪt/ *adj* **1** able to read and write **2** well educated

lit·e·ra·ture /ˈlɪtərətʃər, -ˌtʃʊər, ˈlɪtrə-/ *n* [U] **1** written works of artistic value **2** printed material giving information: *sales literature*

lithe /laɪð/ *adj* (of people or animals) able to bend easily

lith·o·graph /ˈlɪθəgræf/ *n* picture printed from stone or metal

lit·i·ga·tion /ˌlɪtəˈgeɪʃən/ *n* [U] *fml* process of taking action in law, in non-criminal matters

li·ti·gious /lɪˈtɪdʒəs/ *adj often derog* fond of litigation

lit·mus /ˈlɪtməs/ *n* [U] substance that turns red in acid and blue in ALKALI

lit·ter /ˈlɪtər/ *n* **1** [U] paper, etc., scattered untidily: *a litter basket* **2** [C] family of young animals ♦ *vt* scatter litter on

lit·tle¹ /ˈlɪtl/ *adj* **1** small: *little birds* **2** short: *a little while* **3** young **4** unimportant ♦ *adv* **1** not much: *little-known facts* **2** *fml* not at all: *They little knew that I was watching.*

little² *det, pron, n* **less, least 1** [U] (without **a** or **only**) not much: *I have very little (money) left.* **2** [S] (with **a** or **the**) a small amount, but at least some: *a little milk | stay a little longer* **3 little by little** gradually

little fin·ger /ˌ··· ˈ··/ *also* **pinkie** – *n* smallest finger on the hand

lit·ur·gy /ˈlɪtərdʒiⁱ/ *n* form of Christian worship –**gical** /lɪˈtɜrdʒɪkəl/ *adj*

live¹ /lɪv/ *v* **1** *vi* be alive **2** *vi* remain alive: *The doctor says he'll live.* **3** *vi* have one's home: *live in Paris* **4** *vi* lead (a kind of life) **5 live and let live** be tolerant (TOLERATE) **6 live it up** *infml* have a lot of fun

  live down *phr vt* cause (a bad action) to be forgotten, by later good behavior

  live off *phr vt* **1** produce one's food or income from **2** get money for one's needs from

  live on *phr v* **1** *vt* have as one's food or income **2** *vi* continue in life or use

  live out *phr v* **1** *vt* live till the end of **2** *vt* experience in reality: *live out one's fantasies*

  live through *phr vt* remain alive during: *live through 2 world wars*

  live together *phr vi* live as if married

  live up to *phr vt* keep to the high standards of

  live with *phr vt* **1** live as if married with **2** accept (an unpleasant thing)

live² /laɪv/ *adj* **1** alive **2** able to explode or shock: *live bomb/wire* **3** (of broadcasting) seen or heard as it happens

live·li·hood /ˈlaɪvliⁱˌhʊd/ *n* way one earns one's money

live·ly /ˈlaɪvliⁱ/ *adj* **1** full of quick movement and thought **2** bright: *lively colors* –**liness** *n* [U]

liv·en /ˈlaɪvən/ *v* **liven up** *phr vi/t* make or become lively

liv·er /ˈlɪvər/ *n* **1** [C] organ in the body that cleans the blood **2** [U] animal's liver as food

liv·e·ry /ˈlɪvəriⁱ/ *n* uniform worn by servants, etc.

lives /laɪvz/ *n pl. of* LIFE

live·stock /ˈlaɪvstɑk/ *n* [P] farm animals

live wire /ˌlaɪv ˈwaɪər/ *n* very active person

liv·id /ˈlɪvɪd/ *adj* **1** bluish grey **2** very angry

liv·ing¹ /ˈlɪvɪŋ/ *adj* **1** alive **2** still in use: *living language*

living² *n* **1** [S] LIVELIHOOD **2** [U] manner of life

living room /ˈ·· ˌ·/ *n* main room for general use in a house

liz·ard /ˈlɪzərd/ *n* REPTILE with 4 legs and a long tail

ll *abbrev. for:* lines

load /loʷd/ *n* **1** something being carried **2 a** amount the stated vehicle can carry **b** weight borne by the frame of a building **3** amount of work to be done **4 a load off someone's mind** the removing of a great worry **5 loads of** *infml* a lot of ♦ *v* **1** *vt/i* put a load on or in **2** *vt* put a bullet, etc., into (a gun) or film into (a camera) ~**ed** adj **1** containing a hidden trap: a loaded question **2** sl very rich **3** sl drunk

load line /'··/ n line on a ship showing the depth to which it can go down in the water when loaded

loaf[1] /loʷf/ n **loaves** /loʷvz/ **1** [C] single mass of baked bread **2** [C;U] food prepared in a solid piece: meat loaf

loaf[2] vi waste time ~**er** n **1** someone who loafs **2** men's shoe without LACES: pair of loafers

loan /loʷn/ n **1** something lent **2** amount of money lent **3 on loan** being borrowed ♦ vt lend

loan·shark /'loʷnʃɑrk/ n person who lends money at very high interest

loath, loth /loʷθ, loʷð/ adj unwilling

loathe /loʷð/ vt hate very much **loathing** n [S;U]

loath·some /'loʷðsəm, 'loʷθ-/ adj DISGUSTING

loaves /loʷvz/ n pl. of LOAF

lob /lɑb/ vt -**bb**- send (a ball) in a high curve ♦ n lobbed ball

lob·by /'lɑbiʸ/ n **1** hall or passage in a public building **2** group of people who try to influence those in power: the gun lobby ♦ vi/t **1** meet (a LEGISLATOR) in order to persuade him/her to support one's actions, etc. **2** be publicly active in trying to bring about change ~**ist** n

lobe /loʷb/ n **1** lower fleshy part of the ear **2** division of the brain or lungs

lob·ster /'lɑbstər/ n **1** [C] sea animal with CLAWS and 8 legs **2** [U] its meat as food

lo·cal /'loʷkəl/ adj **1** of a certain place: our local doctor **2** limited to one part: local anesthetic ♦ n **1** person living in a place **2** local train, bus, etc. ~**ly** adv

local gov·ern·ment /ˌ·· ·'··/ n group of people elected or paid to be the government of a particular area

lo·cal·i·ty /loʷˈkælətiʸ/ n fml place; area

lo·cal·ize /'loʷkəˌlaɪz/ vt keep inside a small area

lo·cate /'loʷkeʸt, loʷˈkeʸt/ vt fml **1** learn the position of **2** fix in a particular place: offices located in the town center **location** /loʷˈkeʸʃən/ n **1** [C] position **2** [U] act of locating **3 on location** in a town, country, etc., to make a film

lock[1] /lɑk/ n **1** apparatus for fastening a door, etc. **2** piece of water closed off by gates, so that the level can be raised or lowered **3 lock, stock, and barrel** completely

lock[2] v **1** vi/t fasten with a lock **2** vi become fixed or blocked

lock away phr vt keep safe or secret, as by putting in a locked place

lock in/out phr vt keep (a person or criminal) inside/outside a place by locking the door

lock onto phr vt (esp. of a MISSILE) find and follow (the object to be attacked) closely

lock up phr v **1** vi/t make (a building) safe by locking the doors **2** vt put in a safe place and lock the door: He should be locked up! (= in prison)

lock[3] n small piece of hair: his curly locks

lock·er /'lɑkər/ n small cupboard for clothes, etc., esp. at school, in a sports building, etc.

lock·et /'lɑkɪt/ n case for a small picture, etc., worn on a chain round the neck

lock·out /'lɑk-aʊt/ n closing of business because of disagreement over pay, hours, etc.

lo·co /'loʷkoʷ/ adj crazy

lo·co·mo·tion /ˌloʷkəˈmoʷʃən/ n [U] movement from place to place

lo·co·mo·tive /ˌloʷkəˈmoʷt̬ɪv/ adj of movement ♦ n fml train engine

lo·cust /'loʷkəst/ n large flying insect that destroys crops

lodge[1] /lɑdʒ/ v **1** vi stay somewhere and pay rent **2** vi/t (cause to) become fixed: The chicken bone lodged in his throat. **3** vt make (a report, etc.) officially: lodge a complaint

lodge[2] n **1** small house on the land of a larger one **2** house in wild country for hunters, etc.: skiing lodge **3** American Indian house **4** meeting place for an organization

lodg·ing /'lɑdʒɪŋ/ n [S;U] place to stay

loft /lɔft/ n ATTIC

loft·y /'lɔftiʸ/ adj **1** (of ideas, etc.) noble **2** proud **3** lit high -**ily** adv

log[1] /lɔg, lɑg/ n **1** thick piece of wood from a tree **2** official record of a journey **3 sleep like a log** sleep deeply without moving

log[2] vt -**gg**- record in a LOG[1] (2)

log in/on phr vi begin a period of using a computer system by performing a fixed set of operations

log off/out phr vi finish a period of using a computer system by performing a fixed set of operations

lo·gan·ber·ry /'loʷgənˌberiʸ, -bəriʸ/ n large dark red fruit used esp. for making wine

log·book /'lɔgbʊk, 'lɑg-/ n LOG[1] (2)

log·ger·heads /'lɔgərˌhedz, 'lɑ-/ n **at loggerheads** always disagreeing

lo·gic /'lɑdʒɪk/ n [U] **1** science of formal reasoning **2** good sense ~**al** adj ~**ally** /-kliʸ/ adv

lo·gis·tics /low'dʒɪstɪks, lə-/ n [P] detailed planning of an operation

log·o /'lowgow/ n –os sign, pattern, etc., representing a business or organization

log·jam /'lɔgdʒæm, 'lɑg-/ n situation that causes long delay

log·roll·ing /'lɔg,rowlɪŋ, 'lɑg-/ n doing favors for law makers in order to get favors in return

loin /lɔɪn/ n [C;U] (piece of) meat from the lower part of an animal

loins n [P] human body between the waist and legs

loin·cloth /'lɔɪnklɔθ/ n -cloths /-klɔðz, -klɔθs/ cloth worn around the loins

loi·ter /'lɔɪtər/ vi stand somewhere for no clear reason ~ **er** n

loll /lɑl/ vi 1 lie lazily 2 (allow to) hang down loosely

lol·li·pop /'lɑliˠ,pɑp/ n hard sweet made of boiled sugar

lone /lown/ adj fml alone; single

lone·ly /'lowniˠ/ adj 1 alone and unhappy 2 (of places) without people **-liness** n [U]

lone·some /'lownsəm/ adj LONELY (1)

long¹ /lɔŋ/ adj 1 large when measured from beginning to end: long hair | a long time | 2 miles long 2 **long on** with a lot of

long² adv 1 (for) a long time: long ago | Will you be long? 2 **as/so long as** on condition that 3 **no longer/(not) any longer** (not) any more 4 **so long** goodbye for now ♦ n 1 a long time: It won't take long. 2 **before long** soon 3 **the long and (the) short of it** infml the general result, expressed in a few words

long³ vi wish very much: longing to go ~ **ing** adj, n [C;U] (showing) a strong wish ~ **ingly** adv

long for phr vt want very much

long·dis·tance /,· '··◄/ adj covering a long distance ♦ adv to or from a distant point

long dis·tance call /,· '·· '·/ n a telephone call made over a long distance

lon·gev·i·ty /lɑn'dʒevətiˠ, lɔn-/ n [U] fml long life

long·hand /'lɔŋhænd/ n [U] ordinary writing by hand

lon·gi·tude /'lɑndʒə,tuˠd, -,tyuˠd/ n [C;U] distance east or west of Greenwich, England, measured in degrees **-tudinal** /,lɑndʒə'tuˠdn-əl, -'tyuˠd-/ adj going along, not across

long·range /,· '·◄/ adj covering a long distance or time

long·shore·man /,lɔŋ'ʃɔrmən, -'ʃowr-/, -/ʃowr,mən, -ʃowr-/ n man whose job is to load and unload ships

long shot /'· ,·/ n something not likely to happen

long·stand·ing /,lɔŋ'stændɪŋ◄/ adj having existed for a long time: long-standing rivalry

long·suf·fer·ing /,lɔŋ'sʌfərɪŋ◄/ adj patient under continued difficulties

long·term /,· '·◄/ adj for or in the distant future

long wave /,· '·◄/ n [U] radio broadcasting on waves of more than 1000 meters

long·wind·ed /,lɔŋ'wɪndɪd◄/ adj saying too much; dull

look¹ /luk/ v 1 vi use the eyes to see something 2 seem; appear: You look tired. 3 vi face: The window looks east. 4 **look as if/like** seem probably: It looks as if he's gone. 5 **(not) look oneself** (not) appear healthy

look after phr vt take care of

look ahead phr vi plan for the future

look around phr vi search

look at phr vt 1 watch 2 consider; examine 3 **not much to look at** not attractive in appearance

look back phr vi 1 remember 2 **never look back** continue to succeed

look down on phr vt DESPISE

look for phr vt try to find

look forward to phr vt expect to enjoy

look in phr vi infml make a short visit

look into phr vt examine; INVESTIGATE

look on phr v 1 vi watch 2 vt regard as

look out phr vi take care; keep watching

look over phr vt examine quickly

look around phr vi/t examine (a place)

look through phr vt examine for points to be noted

look to phr vt 1 depend on: I look to you for support. 2 pay attention to

look up phr v 1 vi improve 2 vt find (information) in a book 3 vt find and visit

look up to phr vt respect

look² n 1 act of looking 2 appearance 3 **I don't like the look of it/ the looks of this.** This (state of affairs, etc.) suggests something bad to me **looks** n [P] person's (attractive) appearance

look·ing glass /'··· ·/ n mirror

look·out /'luk-aut/ n [S] 1 state of watching 2 person who keeps watch 3 place from where one keeps watch

loom¹ /luwm/ n machine for weaving cloth

loom² vi appear in a threatening

way: *Fear of failure loomed large in his life.*

loon·y /'lu^wni^y/ *n, adj sl* LUNATIC

loop /lu^wp/ *n* (shape of) a piece of string, etc., curved back on itself ♦ *vi/t* make (into) a loop

loop·hole /'lu^wpho^wl/ *n* way of escape: *loopholes in the tax laws*

loose /lu^ws/ *adj* 1 not firmly fixed: *a loose tooth* 2 free from control: *loose cattle* 3 not packed together: *loose crackers* 4 (of clothes) too wide 5 not exact: *a loose translation* 6 without sexual morals: *loose living* 7 **cut loose** break away from a group or situation 8 **hang loose** keep calm ~**ly** *adv*

loose end /ˌ· '·/ *n* [*usu. pl.*] 1 part not properly completed 2 **at loose ends** having nothing to do

loos·en /'lu^wsən/ *vi/t* make or become looser **loosen up** *phr v* relax

loot /lu^wt/ *n* [U] 1 goods taken illegally by soldiers, etc. 2 money ♦ *vi/t* take loot (from) ~**er** *n*

lop /lɑp/ *vt* -**pp**- cut (branches) from a tree

lop-sid·ed /ˈ· ˌ··/ *adj* with one side lower than the other

lo·qua·cious /lo^wˈkwe^yʃəs/ *adj fml* talking a great deal ~**ly** *adv* –**city** /-ˈkwæsəti^y/ *n* [U]

lord /lɔrd/ *n* 1 ruler; master 2 nobleman: 3 (*cap.*) God

lord·ly /'lɔrdli^y/ *adj* proud; grand

lose /lu^wz/ *v* lost /lɔst/ 1 *vt* be unable to find: *lose a book/one's way* 2 *vt* have taken away: *lose one's job* 3 *vi/t* fail to win: *lose a battle* 4 *vt* have less of: *lose weight/money* 5 *vi* (of a clock) go too slowly 6 *vt* (cause to) fail to hear, see, or understand: *You've lost me; could you explain that again?* 7 **lose oneself in something** give all one's attention to something so as not to notice anything else 8 **lose sight of** forget **loser** *n* person who loses

lose out *phr vi* 1 make a loss 2 be defeated

loss /lɔs/ *n* 1 [U] act of losing; failure to keep 2 [C] person, thing, or amount lost: *The army suffered heavy losses.* 3 [C] failure to make a profit 4 **at a loss** uncertain what to do or say 5 **be a dead loss** *infml* have no worth or value

lost /lɔst/ *v past t. and p. of* LOSE

lost cause /ˌ· '·/ *n* something which has no chance of success

lot¹ /lɑt/ *n* 1 **a** a great number or amount: *a lot of people* | *lots (and lots) of money* 2 group or amount: *a new lot of students* 3 **a lot** much: *a lot better* 4 **a fat lot** *infml* none at all

lot² *n* 1 [C] piece of land 2 [C;U] (use of) different objects to make a decision by chance: *choose the winner by lot* 3 [S] *fml* one's fate 4 [C] article sold at an AUCTION 5 **a bad lot** a bad person

loth /lo^wθ/ *adj* LOATH

lo·tion /'lo^wʃən/ *n* [C;U] liquid mixture for the skin to make it clean and healthy

lot·te·ry /'lɑtəri^y/ *n* system of giving prizes to people who bought numbered tickets, chosen by chance

loud /laʊd/ *adj* 1 producing a lot of sound 2 unpleasantly colorful ♦ *adv* in a loud way ~**ly** *adv* ~**ness** *n* [U]

loud·speak·er /'laʊdˌspi^ykər/ *n* part of a radio or record player from which the sound comes out

lounge /laʊndʒ/ *vi* stand or sit lazily ♦ *n* comfortable room to sit in

lounge liz·ard /ˈ· ˌ··/ *n* man who is often in bars, trying to interest women

louse /laʊs/ *n* lice /laɪs/ 1 insect that lives on people's and animals' bodies 2 worthless person

lou·sy /'laʊzi^y/ *adj* 1 very bad: *lousy weather* 2 covered with lice

lout /laʊt/ *n* rough awkward man or boy ~**ish** *adj*

lov·a·ble /'lʌvəbəl/ *adj* deserving, causing or worthy of love

love /lʌv/ *n* 1 [U] great fondness for someone 2 [S;U] warm interest: *a love of music* 3 [C] loved person or thing 4 [U] (in tennis) NIL 5 **give/send someone one's love** send friendly greetings 6 **make love (to)** have sex (with) 7 **not for love or money** *infml* not by any means ♦ *v* 1 *vi/t* feel love (for) 2 *vt* like very much: *I'd love a drink.* **loving** *adj* fond

love af·fair /ˈ· ·ˌ·/ *n* sexual relationship: (fig.) *a love affair with Russian literature* (= a great interest and liking)

love child /ˈ· ·/ *n* child born outside marriage

love·ly /'lʌvli^y/ *adj* 1 beautiful: *lovely girl/view* 2 very pleasant: *lovely dinner*

lov·er /'lʌvər/ *n* 1 person who has a sexual relationship with another person outside marriage 2 person who is fond of the stated thing: *art lovers*

love·sick /'lʌvˌsɪk/ *adj* sad because of unreturned love

low /lo^w/ *adj* 1 not high: *low wall/cost/standards* 2 (of a supply) nearly finished 3 (of sounds) **a** deep **b** not loud 4 unhappy 5 not fair or honest: *a low trick* 6 for a slow speed: *a low gear* ♦ *adv* to or at a low level: *bend low* ♦ *n* low point or level

low·brow /ˈloʷbraʊ/ n, adj (person) not interested in art, books, etc.

low-down /ˈloʷdaʊn/ n [the+S] sl plain facts

low-down /ˌ· ·/ adj worthless; dishonorable

low·er¹ /ˈloʷər/ adj at or nearer the bottom: the lower leg

lower² vt 1 make less high 2 **lower oneself** bring oneself down in people's opinion

low·er³ /ˈlaʊər/ vi 1 be dark and threatening 2 FROWN severely

lower class /ˌloʷər ˈklæs◁/ n social class of lowest rank **lower-class** adj

low-key /ˌ· ˈ·◁/ adj quiet and controlled

low·lands /ˈloʷləndz/ n [P] land lower than its surroundings

low·ly /ˈloʷliʲ/ adj low in rank; HUMBLE **-liness** n [U]

low sea·son /ˌ· ˈ··/ n [U] time of year when business is least and prices are lowest

low-spir·it·ed /ˌ· ˈ···◁/ adj unhappy

lox /lɑks/ n [U] smoked SALMON

loy·al /ˈlɔɪəl/ adj faithful to one's friends, country, etc. **~ist** n person who remains loyal to a ruler **~ly** adv

loy·al·ty /ˈlɔɪəltiʲ/ n 1 [U] being loyal 2 [C] connection that binds one to someone or something to which one is loyal

loz·enge /ˈlɑzəndʒ/ n medical sweet: cough lozenge

LP /ˌɛl ˈpiʲ/ n record that plays for about 20 minutes each side

LSD /ˌɛl ɛs ˈdiʲ/ n [U] illegal drug that causes hallucinations (HALLUCINATE)

Ltd written abbrev. for: LIMITED (2)

lu·bri·cant /ˈluʷbrəkənt/ n [C;U] substance that lubricates; oil, etc.

lu·bri·cate /ˈluʷbrəˌkeʲt/ vt make (machine parts) work without rubbing

lu·cid /ˈluʷsɪd/ adj 1 easy to understand 2 able to think clearly **~ly** adv **~ity** /luʷˈsɪdətiʲ/ n [U]

luck /lʌk/ n [U] 1 what happens to someone by chance 2 success: wish them luck 3 **be down on one's luck** have bad luck, esp. be without money 4 **be in/out of luck** have/not have good fortune **~y** adj having or bringing good luck ♦ v **luck out** phr vi have an experience of good luck **~ily** adv

lu·cra·tive /ˈluʷkrətɪv/ adj profitable

lud·dite /ˈlʌdaɪt/ n (often cap.) derog someone who is opposed to change, esp. the introduction of new work methods and machinery

lu·di·crous /ˈluʷdɪkrəs/ adj causing laughter; foolish **~ly** adv

lug /lʌg/ vt **-gg-** pull or carry with difficulty ♦ n rough stupid person

lug·gage /ˈlʌgɪdʒ/ also **baggage** — n [U] bags, etc., of a traveler

lu·gu·bri·ous /ləˈguʷbriʲəs, -ˈgyuʷ-/ adj fml sorrowful **~ly** adv

luke·warm /ˈluʷkˈwɔrm◁/ adj 1 (of liquid) neither warm nor cold 2 not eager

lull /lʌl/ vt cause to rest ♦ n [S] calm period

lul·la·by /ˈlʌləˌbaɪ/ n song to make a child go to sleep

lum·ba·go /lʌmˈbeʲgoʷ/ n [U] pain in the lower back

lum·ber¹ /ˈlʌmbər/ v 1 vi move heavily and awkwardly 2 vt give (someone) an unwanted object or job

lumber² n 1 wood for building 2 useless articles stored away

lum·ber·jack /ˈlʌmbərˌdʒæk/ n man whose job is cutting down trees to make lumber

lu·mi·na·ry /ˈluʷməˌnɛriʲ/ n fml famous respected person

lu·mi·nous /ˈluʷmənəs/ adj shining in the dark **-nosity** /ˌluʷməˈnɑsətiʲ/ n [U]

lump /lʌmp/ n 1 solid mass: lump of coal/sugar 2 hard swelling 3 **lump in the throat** tight sensation in the throat caused by unexpressed pity, sorrow, etc. ♦ v **lump it** accept bad conditions without complaint **~y** adj: lumpy gravy

lump together phr vt consider (2 or more things) as a single unit

lump sum /ˌ· ˈ·/ n money given as a single payment rather than in parts

lu·na·cy /ˈluʷnəsiʲ/ n insanity (INSANE)

lu·nar /ˈluʷnər/ adj of the moon

lu·na·tic /ˈluʷnəˌtɪk/ adj, n crazy or foolish (person)

lunch /lʌntʃ/ also **lunch·eon** fml /ˈlʌntʃən/ — n [C;U] meal eaten at about noon **lunch** vi

lunch·eon·ette /ˌlʌntʃəˈnɛt/ n small restaurant that serves light meals usu. inside a store

lung /lʌŋ/ n either of the 2 breathing organs in the chest

lunge /lʌndʒ/ vi, n (make) a sudden forward movement

lurch¹ /lɜrtʃ/ vi move irregularly

lurch² n 1 lurching movement 2 **leave someone in the lurch** leave them when they are in difficulty

lure /lʊər/ n something that attracts: the lure of wealth ♦ vt attract into trouble

lu·rid /ˈlʊərɪd/ adj 1 unnaturally

bright: *lurid colors* **2** shocking; unpleasant

lurk /lɜrk/ *vi* wait in hiding, esp. for a bad purpose

lus·cious /ˈlʌʃəs/ *adj* **1** having a ripe sweet taste **2** sexually attractive

lush[1] /lʌʃ/ *adj* (of plants) growing thickly

lush[2] *n sl, esp.* alcoholic (ALCOHOL)

lust /lʌst/ *n* [C;U] strong (sexual) desire: *lust for power* **lust** *vi* ~**ful** *adj*

lus·ter /ˈlʌstər/ *n* [S;U] **1** brightness of a polished surface **2** glory

lust·y /ˈlʌstiʸ/ *adj* strong and healthy

lute /luʷt/ *n* old musical instrument with strings

lux·u·ri·ant /lʌgˈʒʊəriʸənt, lʌkˈʃʊər-/ *adj* growing well and thickly ~**ly** *adv* ~**ance** *n* [U]

lux·u·ri·ate /lʌgˈʒʊəriʸˌeʸt, lʌkˈʃʊər-/ *v* **luxuriate in** *phr vt* enjoy oneself lazily in

lux·u·ri·ous /lʌgˈʒʊəriʸəs, lʌkˈʃʊər-/ *adj* comfortable and esp. expensive

lux·u·ry /ˈlʌkʃəriʸ, ˈlʌgʒəriʸ/ *n* **1** [U] great comfort, as provided by wealth **2** [C] something pleasant, but not necessary and not often had or done

lye /laɪ/ *n* [U] chemical used in making soap

ly·ing /ˈlaɪ-ɪŋ/ *v pres. p. of* LIE[1] and LIE[2]

lynch /lɪntʃ/ *vt* (esp. of a crowd) kill without a legal trial

lyr·ic /ˈlɪrɪk/ *n, adj* (short poem) expressing strong feelings in songlike form ~**al** *adj fml* full of joyful feeling **lyrics** *n* [P] words of a popular song

M

M, m /ɛm/ the 13th letter of the English alphabet

m *written abbrev. for:* **1** mile(s) **2** meter(s) **3** million **4** married **5** male

ma /mɑ, mɔ/ *n sl* mother

ma'am /mæm/ *n* (polite way of addressing a woman)

ma·ca·bre /mə'kɑbrə, mə'kɑb, mə-'kɑbər/ *adj* causing fear, esp. because connected with death

ma·caw /mə'kɔ/ *n* large S American PARROT

mace /meᵉs/ *n* liquid used as a defensive weapon that causes tears and discomfort

Mach /mɑk/ *n* speed of an aircraft in relation to the speed of sound: *Mach 2* (= twice the speed of sound)

ma·chet·e /mə'ʃɛtⁱ, -'tʃɛ-/ *n* large heavy knife

Mach·i·a·vel·li·an /ˌmækⁱə'vɛl-ⁱ'ən◂/ *adj* skillful in using indirect means to get what one wants; CUNNING

mach·i·na·tions /ˌmækə'neⁱʃənz, ˌmæʃə-/ *n* [P] secret efforts or plans to do harm

ma·chine /mə'ʃiⁿ/ *n* **1** instrument or apparatus that uses power to work **2** group that controls and plans activities of a political party ♦ *vt* make or produce by machine

ma·chine-gun /mə'ʃiⁿgʌn/ *n* gun that fires continuously

machine-read·a·ble /·ˌ·'····/ *adj* in a form that can be understood and used by a computer

ma·chin·er·y /mə'ʃiⁿərⁱ/ *n* [U] **1** machines: *farm machinery* **2** working parts of a machine or engine **3** operation of a system or organization

ma·chis·mo /mɑ'tʃiⁿzmoʷ, mə-, -'tʃiz-, 'kiz-/ *n* [U] quality of being macho

ma·cho /'mɑtʃoʷ/ *adj often derog* (trying to appear) strong and brave

mack·er·el /'mækərəl/ *n* **mackerel** *or* **mackerels** sea fish, often eaten

mac·ro·bi·ot·ic /ˌmækroʷbaⁱ'ɑt̬ⁱk/ *adj* of a type of food (esp. vegetable products grown without chemicals) thought to produce good health

mad /mæd/ *adj* **-dd- 1** angry **2** very foolish **3** ill in the mind **4** filled with strong interest: *She's mad about politics.* **5 like mad** very hard, fast, loud, etc. **~ly** *adv*: *madly* (= very much) *in love* **~ness** *n* [U] **~den** *vt* annoy extremely

mad·am /'mædəm/ *n* (*often cap.*) **1** (polite way of addressing a woman) **2** woman who manages a house of PROSTITUTES

made /meⁱd/ *v past t. and p. of* MAKE

Mad·i·son Av·e·nue /ˌmædəsən 'ævənyuʷ, -nuʷ/ *n* [S] street in New York with many advertising companies

ma·don·na /mə'dɑnə/ *n* (in the Christian religion) (picture or figure of) Mary, the mother of Christ

mad·ri·gal /'mædrɪgəl/ *n* song for several singers without instruments

mael·strom /'meⁱlstrəm/ *n lit* **1** violent WHIRLPOOL **2** destroying force of events

maes·tro /'maⁱstroʷ/ *n* **-tros** great or famous musician

maf·i·a /'mɑfⁱə/ *n* **1** (*usu. cap.*) large US and Italian organization of criminals **2** influential group who support each other without any concern for people outside the group: *the medical mafia*

mag·a·zine /ˌmægə'ziⁿn, 'mægə-ˌziⁿn/ *n* **1** sort of book with a paper cover, which contains writing, photographs, and advertisements, that is printed every week or month and is of interest to a particular group of people **2** part of a gun in which bullets are stored

ma·gen·ta /mə'dʒɛntə/ *adj* dark purplish red

mag·got /'mægət/ *n* wormlike young of flies and other insects

mag·ic /'mædʒɪk/ *n* **1** use of strange unseen forces, or of tricks, to produce effects **2** special wonderful quality: *the magic of the theater* – see also BLACK MAGIC ♦ *adj* caused by or used in magic: *a magic trick/ring* **~al** *adj* strange and wonderful **~ally** /-kliʸ/ *adv*

ma·gi·cian /mə'dʒɪʃən/ *n* person who practices or entertains with magic

ma·gis·te·ri·al /ˌmædʒə'stⁱərⁱəl/ *adj fml* showing complete and undoubted control

ma·gis·trate /'mædʒɪˌstreⁱt, -strɪt/ *n* JUSTICE OF THE PEACE

mag·nan·i·mous /mæg'nænəməs/ *adj fml* very generous **~ly** *adv* **-mity** /ˌmægnə'nɪmət̬ⁱ/ *n* [U]

mag·nate /'mægneⁱt, -nɪt/ *n* wealthy and powerful person

mag·ne·si·um /mæg'niⁱzⁱəm, -ʒⁱəm/ *n* silver-white metal

mag·net /'mægnɪt/ *n* **1** piece of iron or steel that draws other metal objects towards it **2** person or thing that attracts or interests people greatly **~ism** *n* [U] magnetic force **~ize** *vt* **~ic** /mæg'nɛtⁱk/ *adj*: *a magnetic personality* **~ically** /-kliʸ/ *adv*

magnetic tape /·ˌ·· ·ˈ·/ *n* [C;U] TAPE on which sound or other information can be recorded

mag·nif·i·cent /mæɡˈnɪfəsənt/ *adj* extremely fine or good –**cence** *n* [U] ~**ly** *adv*

mag·ni·fy /ˈmæɡnəˌfaɪ/ *vt* cause to look or seem larger –**fication** /ˌmæɡnəfəˈkeɪʃən/ *n* [U]

magnifying glass /ˈ···· ˌ·/ *n* curved LENS (1) for magnifying things

mag·ni·tude /ˈmæɡnəˌtuʷd, -ˌtyuʷd/ *n* [U] *fml* degree of size or importance

mag·pie /ˈmæɡpaɪ/ *n* noisy black and white bird which likes to steal bright objects

ma·hog·a·ny /məˈhɑɡəniʸ/ *n* [U] dark reddish wood used for furniture

maid /meʸd/ *n* **1** female worker in a house or hotel **2** maiden – see also OLD MAID

maid·en /ˈmeʸdn/ *n lit* young unmarried woman ♦ *adj* **1** first: *the ship's maiden voyage* **2** unmarried: *my maiden aunts*

maiden name /ˈ··· ·/ *n* family name a woman had before marriage

mail¹ /meʸl/ *n* [U] **1** the official system for carrying letters, parcels, etc. **2** letters, etc., that one sends or receives ♦ *vt* send through this system

mail² *n* [U] soldiers' protective clothing in former times, made of small metal rings

mail·bag /ˈmeʸlbæɡ/ *n* **1** bag carried by a person delivering mail **2** mail received by a famous person, television program, etc.

mail·box /ˈmeʸlbɑks/ *n* box into which people put letters for mailing

maim /meʸm/ *vt* wound very seriously and usu. lastingly

main¹ /meʸn/ *adj* chief; most important: *its main function* ~**ly** *adv*: *His money comes mainly from investments.*

main² *n* **1** large pipe or wire supplying water, gas, or electricity **2 in the main** mainly; mostly

main·frame /ˈmeʸnfreʸm/ *n* the largest and most powerful kind of computer

main·land /ˈmeʸnlænd, -lənd/ *n* a land mass, considered without its islands **mainland** *adj*

main·line /ˈmeʸnlaɪn/ *vi/t* INJECT an illegal drug into one of the chief VEINS (= tubes carrying blood) of the body

main·spring /ˈmeʸnˌsprɪŋ/ *n* **1** chief spring in a watch **2** chief force or reason that makes something happen

main·stay /ˈmeʸnsteʸ/ *n* someone or something which provides the chief means of support

main·stream /ˈmeʸnstriʸm/ *n* main or usual way of thinking or acting in relation to a subject

Main Street /ˈ· ··/ *n* main street of a town

main·tain /meʸnˈteʸn/ *vt* **1** keep in good condition **2** support with money **3** continue to have or do **4** continue to say, believe, or argue

main·te·nance /ˈmeʸntənəns/ *n* [U] keeping in good condition

maintenance man /ˈ···· ˌ·/ *n* man whose job is to maintain (1) machines, etc.

ma·jes·ty /ˈmædʒəstiʸ/ *n* **1** (*cap.*) (used as a title for kings and queens) **2** [U] *fml* grandness –**tic** /məˈdʒɛstɪk/ *adj*: *majestic scenery* –**tically** /-kliʸ/ *adv*

ma·jor¹ /ˈmeʸdʒər/ *adj* of great importance or seriousness: *a major problem* | *major surgery*

major² *n* **1** army officer, above CAPTAIN **2** university student in a particular field of study: *an English major* – see also SERGEANT MAJOR

major³ *v* **major in** *phr vt* study as the chief subject(s) for a college degree

ma·jor·i·ty /məˈdʒɔrətiʸ, məˈdʒɑ-/ *n* **1** [(*the*) S] most **2** [C] difference in number between a large and small group: *win by a majority of 300 votes*

make¹ /meʸk/ *vt* **made** /meʸd/ **1** produce: *make a cake/ a noise: a decision* | *a bag made of leather* | *wine made from local grapes* **2** cause to be: *It made me happy.* **3** force; cause: *I can't make him understand.* **4** earn (money) **5** calculate or be counted as: *That makes the fourth glass you've had!* **6** add up to: *2 and 2 make 4* **7** tidy (a bed that has been slept in) **8** have the qualities of: *That story makes good reading.* **9** reach: *We made harbor by night fall.* **10** complete: *That picture really makes the room.* **11 make believe** pretend **12 make do** use something for lack of any better: *We had to make do with water.* **13 make it: a** arrive in time **b** succeed **14 make one's way** go: *I made my way home.* **15 make or break** which will cause success or complete failure **16 make a play for** try to get **17 make the most of** take advantage **18 make time** travel quickly **19 make tracks** leave quickly **maker** *n* **1** person who makes something: *a watchmaker* **2** (*usu. cap.*) God **making** *n* **1 be the making of** cause to improve greatly **2 have the makings of** have the possibility of developing into

make for *phr vt* **1** move in the

direction of: *I made for the exit.* **2** result in: *Large print makes for easy reading.*

make into *phr vt* use in making: *He made the bottle into an interesting ornament.*

make of *phr vt* **1** understand by: *I don't know what to make of the situation.* **2** give (the usu. stated importance) to: *She makes too much of her problems.*

make off *phr vi* leave in a hurry
make off with *phr vt* steal

make out *phr vt* **1** write (a check, etc.) in complete form **2** *vt* see, hear, or understand properly **3** *vt* claim; pretend **4** *vi* succeed **5** *vt* argue as proof: *make out a case* (= give good reasons) **6** *vi* kiss, etc.: *making out in the backseat of a car*

make over *phr vt* **1** remake **2** pass over to someone else, esp. legally

make up *phr v* **1** *vt* invent (a story, etc.), esp. to deceive **2** *vi/t* use special paint and powder on the face to look beautiful or change the appearance **3** *vt* prepare for use: *A pharmacist made up the doctor's prescriptions.* **4** *vt* form as a whole: *Oil makes up half of our exports.* **5** *vi* become friends again after a quarrel

make up for *phr vt* give something good to take away disappointment: *I bought him a present to make up for my bad behavior.*

make² n 1 type of product **2 on the make** searching for personal gain
make-be·lieve /'· ·ı·‹/ *n* [U] pretending
make·shift /'meʸkˌʃɪft/ *adj* used because there is nothing better
make-up /'·‹·/ *n* [C;U] **1** paint, powder, etc., worn on the face **2** combination of members or qualities
mal·ad·just·ed /ˌmælə'dʒʌstɪd‹/ *adj* not fitting in well with other people or with life generally
ma·laise /mæ'leʸz/ *n* [C;U] **1** failure to be active and successful **2** feeling of not being well
mal·a·prop·is·m /'mæləprɑpˌɪzəm/ *n* often amusing misuse of a word; use of a word that is similar to the intended word but means something completely different
ma·lar·i·a /mə'leəriʸə/ *n* [U] tropical disease spread by MOSQUITOes
mal·con·tent /ˈmælkən'tɛnt, 'mælkənˌtɛnt/ *n fml* dissatisfied person who is likely to make trouble
male /meʸl/ *n, adj* (person or animal) of the sex that does not give birth
male chau·vin·ist /ˌ·· '····‹/ *n derog* man who behaves unreasonably towards women because he thinks they are less able, strong, etc., than men

mal·e·fac·tor /'mæləˌfæktər/ *n fml or lit* person who does evil
ma·lev·o·lent /mə'lɛvələnt/ *adj lit* wishing to do evil to others ~**ly** *adv* –**lence** *n* [U]
mal·formed /ˌmæl'fɔrmd‹/ *adj* made or shaped badly: *a malformed limb* –**formation** /ˌmælfɔr'meʸʃən/ *n* [C;U]
mal·func·tion /mæl'fʌŋkʃən/ *n* fault in operation ♦ **malfunction** *vi*
mal·ice /'mælɪs/ *n* [U] desire to hurt or harm –**icious** /mə'lɪʃəs/ *adj*: *a malicious attack* –**iciously** *adv*
ma·lign /mə'laɪn/ *adj fml* bad; causing harm ♦ *vt* say bad things about
ma·lig·nant /mə'lɪgnənt/ *adj* **1** (of disease) likely to kill **2** *fml* malign ~**ly** *adv*
ma·lin·ger /mə'lɪŋgər/ *vi* avoid work by pretending to be ill ~**er** *n*
mall /mɔl/ *n* **1** area of streets with no cars, where one can shop **2** also **shopping mall** very large building with many stores and shops inside
mal·le·a·ble /'mæliʸəbəl/ *adj* (of metal) easy to shape; soft: (fig.) *a malleable personality*
mal·let /'mælɪt/ *n* wooden hammer
mal·nu·tri·tion /ˌmælnuʷ'trɪʃən, -nyuʷ-/ *n* [U] lack of (proper) food
mal·prac·tice /ˌmæl'præktɪs/ *n* [C;U] failure to do one's professional duty properly or honestly
malt /mɔlt/ *n* [U] partly grown grain used esp. for making beer and WHISKEY
mal·treat /mæl'triʸt/ *vt fml* treat roughly and/or cruelly ~**ment** *n* [U]
ma·ma /'mɑmə/ *n infml* mother
mam·mal /'mæməl/ *n* animal of the sort fed on the mother's milk when young
mam·moth /'mæməθ/ *adj* extremely large
man /mæn/ *n* **men** /mɛn/ **1** [C] adult male person **2** [U] the human race: *Man must change in a changing world.* **3** [C] person: *All men must die.* **4** [C] male of low rank: *officers and men* **5** [C] male member of a team **6** [C] object used in board games: *chess men* **7** *sl* form of address for a man (or woman) **8 a man of the world** man with a lot of experience **9 man and wife** *fml* married **10 one's own man** independent in action **11 the man in the street** the average person **12 to a man** every person: *They agreed, to a man.* – see also BEST MAN, FRONT MAN ♦ *vt* –**nn**– provide with people for operation ~**hood** *n* [U] quality or time of being a (brave) man
man-a·bout-town /ˌ·· ·· '·/ *n* (rich) man who spends a great deal of time

at fashionable social events, and often does not work

man·a·cle /ˈmænəkəl/ n metal ring for fastening a prisoner's hands or feet

man·age /ˈmænɪdʒ/ v 1 vt be in charge of; run 2 vi/t succeed in doing: I barely managed to get out of the way. 3 vi succeed in living, esp. on a small amount of money: We don't earn much, but we manage. ~**able** adj easy or possible to deal with ~**ment** n [U] 1 managing 2 the people in charge **manager** n person who runs a business, hotel, sports team, etc. ~**agerial** /ˌmænəˈdʒɪəriəl◂/ adj: managerial responsibilities

man·da·rin /ˈmændərɪn/ n 1 government official of high rank in the former Chinese empire 2 often derog official of high rank

man·date /ˈmændeʲt/ n government's right or duty to act according to the wishes of the electors

man·da·to·ry /ˈmændəˌtɔːriʲ, -ˌtoʷriʲ/ adj fml which must be done

man·di·ble /ˈmændəbəl/ n med jaw

man·do·lin /ˌmændəˈlɪn, ˈmændəl-ɪn/ n musical instrument with 8 strings

mane /meʲn/ n long hair on a horse's or lion's neck

ma·neu·ver /məˈnuʷvər/ n 1 skillful movement 2 secret trick to gain a purpose 3 **on maneuvers** doing battle training ♦ vt move or turn, esp. skillfully or deceivingly: The car maneuvers well in wet weather. -**verable** adj

man·ful·ly /ˈmænfəliʲ/ adv bravely and determinedly

man·ger /ˈmeʲndʒər/ n long open container for animals' food

man·gle /ˈmæŋgəl/ vt crush and tear so as to ruin

man·go /ˈmæŋgoʷ/ n -**goes** or -**gos** tropical fruit with sweet yellow flesh

mang·y /ˈmeʲndʒiʲ/ adj of bad appearance, esp. because of loss of hair or fur

man·han·dle /ˈmænˌhændl/ vt hold or move forcefully or roughly

man·hole /ˈmænhoʷl/ n opening in the road leading to underground pipes, wires, etc.

man·hour /ˈ· ·/ n amount of work one man can do in an hour, used to measure jobs: 200 man-hours went into the development.

ma·ni·a /ˈmeʲniʲə/ n [C;U] 1 madness 2 extreme interest or desire: a mania for collecting matchboxes | soccer mania **maniac** /-niæk/ n ~**cal** /məˈnaɪəkəl/ adj: maniacal laughter

man·i·cure /ˈmænɪˌkyʊər/ vt, n (give) treatment for the hands, esp. the nails, including cleaning, cutting, etc. -**curist** n

man·i·fest¹ /ˈmænəˌfest/ adj fml plain to see or understand; OBVIOUS ~**ly** adv

manifest² vt show plainly ~**ation** /ˌmænəfeˈsteʲʃən, -fə-/n [C;U]

man·i·fes·to /ˌmænəˈfestoʷ/ n -**tos** or -**toes** statement of intentions or opinions, esp. as made by a political party before an election

man·i·fold¹ /ˈmænəˌfoʷld/ adj many in number or kind

manifold² n tech pipe with holes, to allow gases to enter or escape from an engine, such as in a car

ma·nip·u·late /məˈnɪpyəˌleʲt/ vt 1 fml handle skilfully 2 control and influence for one's own purposes -**lative** /-ləˌtɪv, -ˌleʲtɪv/ adj -**lation** /məˌnɪpyəˈleʲʃən/ n [U]

man·kind /ˌmænˈkaɪnd/ n [U] human beings

man·ly /ˈmænliʲ/ adj having qualities (believed to be) suitable to a man -**liness** n [U]

man-made /ˌ· ˈ· ◂/ adj 1 produced by people 2 (of materials) not made from natural substances

man·ner /ˈmænər/ n 1 fml way: a meal prepared in the Japanese manner 2 way of behaving towards people: a rude manner 3 **all manner of** fml every sort of 4 -**mannered** /-mænərd/ having the stated way of behaving: bad-mannered 5 **(as) to the manner born** as if one is used to (something, esp. social position) from birth **manners** n [U] (polite) social practices: It's bad manners to make a noise while you eat.

man·ner·is·m /ˈmænəˌrɪzəm/ n (bad or strange) way of behaving that has become a habit

man·or /ˈmænər/ n area of land owned by the local lord in former times

man·pow·er /ˈmænˌpaʊər/ n [U] number of workers needed

man·qué /mɑŋˈkeʲ/ adj fml that failed to become the stated thing

man·sion /ˈmænʃən, -tʃən/ n large grand house

man-sized /ˈ· ·/ adj large

man·slaugh·ter /ˈmænˌslɔːtər/ n [U] crime of killing someone unintentionally

man·tel /ˈmæntl/ n mantelpiece.

man·tel·piece /ˈmæntəlˌpiʲs/ n shelf above a fireplace

mantle /ˈmæntl/ n 1 covering: a mantle of snow 2 (sign of) general or official recognition: He took over the mantle of world heavyweight champion

man-to-man /ˌ· · ˈ·◂/ adj, adv open(ly) and honest(ly)

man·u·al¹ /ˈmænyuʷəl/ adj of or using the hands ~ly adv

manual² n book giving information or instructions

man·u·fac·ture /ˌmænyəˈfæktʃər/ vt make in large quantities using machinery ♦ n [U] manufacturing: goods of foreign manufacture ~turer n

ma·nure /məˈnʊər, məˈnyʊər/ n [U] animal waste matter put on land to make crops grow ♦ vt put manure on

man·u·script /ˈmænyəˌskrɪpt/ n 1 first copy of a book, etc., written by hand or on a machine 2 old book written by hand

man·y /ˈmeniʸ/ determiner, pron 1 a large number (of): I don't have as many as you. | many people 2 a good/great many many 3 one too many infml too much (alcohol) to drink

map /mæp/ n 1 representation of (part of) the Earth's surface as if seen from above: a map of France 2 (put something) on the map (cause something to be) considered important ♦ vt -pp- make a map of

mar /mɑr/ vt fml spoil

mar·a·thon /ˈmærəˌθɑn/ n 1 running race of about 26 miles (42 kilometers) 2 (hard) activity that lasts a long time: a marathon speech of 6 hours

ma·raud·ing /məˈrɔdɪŋ/ adj moving around looking for things or people to attack -er n

mar·ble /ˈmɑrbəl/ n [U] 1 hard smooth usu. white stone used for STATUES or buildings 2 small glass ball rolled against others in a game (marbles)

march /mɑrtʃ/ v 1 vi walk with regular forceful steps like a soldier 2 vt force to go: They marched him off to prison. ♦ n act of marching: (fig.) the march (= steady advance) of history

March n the 3rd month of the year

mare /meər/ n female horse

mar·ga·rine /ˈmɑrdʒərɪn/ also **oleo** n — food substance like butter

mar·gin /ˈmɑrdʒɪn/ n 1 space down the edge of a page, with no writing or printing in it 2 amount by which one thing is greater than another: We won by a decisive margin. 3 area on the outside edge of a larger area: the margin of the stream

mar·gin·al /ˈmɑrdʒənl/ adj 1 small in importance or amount: a marginal difference 2 on the border ~ly adv

mar·i·jua·na /ˌmærəˈwɑnə, -ˈhwɑnə/ n [U] form of the drug CANNABIS

ma·ri·na /məˈriʸnə/ n small harbor for pleasure boats

mar·i·nade /ˌmærəˈneʸd, ˈmærəˌneʸd/ n [C;U] mixture of oil, wine, etc., into which food is put for a time before being cooked **-nate** /ˈmærəˌneʸt/ vt keep in a marinade

ma·rine /məˈriʸn/ adj 1 of the sea of ships and sailing ♦ n soldier who serves in one of the main branches of the US armed forces (the **Marine Corps**)

mar·i·ner /ˈmærənər/ n sailor

mar·i·o·nette /ˌmæriʸəˈnɛt/ n PUPPET with strings

mar·i·tal /ˈmærətl/ adj of marriage

mar·i·time /ˈmærəˌtaɪm/ adj 1 MARINE 2 near the sea

mark¹ /mɑrk/ n 1 something on or put onto a surface: dirty marks on the wall | tire marks in the snow 2 something that shows a quality: They all stood as a mark of respect. 3 a number that represents a judgment of quality: The top mark in the test was 8 out of 10. 4 printed or written sign: punctuation mark 5 particular type of machine: the new Mark 4 gun 6 make one's mark (on) gain success, fame, etc., (in) 7 short of the mark infml a slow in understanding or acting b not good enough 8 up to the mark: a of an acceptable standard b in good health 9 wide of the mark not correct or close to the subject

mark² 1 vi/t spoil with marks: Hot cups have marked the table. | The table marks easily. 2 vt give MARKS¹ (3) to 3 vt stay close to (an opposing player) to spoil their play 4 vt be a sign of: A cross marks his grave. | The election marks a turning point in our affairs. 5 mark time spend time on work, etc., without making any advance 6 (You) mark my words! You will see later that I am right. ~ed adj noticeable ~edly /ˈmɑrkɪdliʸ/ adv

mark down/up phr vt lower/raise the price of

mark out phr vt 1 also **mark off**— draw lines around (an area) 2 [(for)] show or choose as likely to become (successful) or gain (success)

mark³ n German unit of money

mark·er /ˈmɑrkər/ n 1 tool for making marks 2 object for marking a place

mar·ket¹ /ˈmɑrkɪt/ n 1 (place for) a gathering of people to buy and sell goods 2 desire to buy; demand: There's no market for coats at this time of year. 3 area where goods are sold: the foreign/domestic market 4 trade: the coffee market 5 in the market for wishing to buy 6 on the market (of goods) for sale 7 play

the market buy and sell stock to try to make a profit – see also BLACK MARKET, COMMON MARKET

market² /ʹ/ vt present and offer for sale ~**ing** n [U] skills of advertising, supplying, and selling goods ~**able** adj: (fig.) *marketable skills* ~**ability** /ˌmɑːkətəˈbɪlətiʲ/ n [U]

mar·ket·place /ʹmɑːkɪtˌpleʲs/ n 1 place where a market is held 2 activities of buying and selling

market re·search /ˌ·· ··ˈ··, ·· ·ˈ··/ n [U] study of what people buy and why

mark·ing /ʹmɑːkɪŋ/ n [C;U] (any of a set of) colored marks on an animal's fur or feathers

marks·man /ʹmɑːksmən/ **marks·woman**, /ˌ-ˌwʊmən/ fem. — n -**men** /-mən/ person who can shoot well ~**ship** n [U]

mark·up /ʹmɑːk-ʌp/ n price increase by a seller

mar·ma·lade /ʹmɑːməˌleʲd/ n [U] JAM made from oranges

ma·roon¹ /məˈruːn/ vt put or leave in a lonely or dangerous place, without help

maroon² /ʹ/ adj dark red

mar·quee /mɑːˈkiʲ/ n shelter made of glass or cloth over a path, SIDE-WALK, etc.

mar·riage /ʹmærɪdʒ/ n [C;U] 1 ceremony to marry people 2 state of being husband and wife ~**able** adj suitable for marriage

mar·row /ʹmærəʊ/ n [U] soft fatty substance inside bones

mar·ry /ʹmæriʲ/ v 1 vi/t take (as) a husband or wife: *He never married.* | *She married a soldier.* 2 vt join in marriage: *The priest married them.* 3 vt [(off)] cause to get married: *They married their daughter (off) to a young diplomat.* **married** adj 1 having a husband or wife: *a married man* 2 of MARRIAGE (2): *married life* 3 **married to** having as a husband or wife: *She's married to a doctor.*

Mars /mɑːz/ n the PLANET 4th in order from the sun

marsh /mɑːʃ/ n [C;U] (area of) soft wet land ~**y** adj

mar·shal¹ /ʹmɑːʃəl/ n 1 law official, like a SHERIFF (1) 2 military officer of very high rank 3 organizer (ORGANIZE) of an event, such as a ceremony or race

marshal² vt -l- 1 arrange (esp. facts) in good order 2 lead (people) carefully

marsh·mal·low /ˌmɑːʃˌmeləʊ, -ˌmæləʊ/ n type of soft round candy

mar·su·pi·al /mɑːˈsuːpiʲəl/ n animal, esp. Australian, that carries its young in a pocket of skin

mar·tial /ʹmɑːʃəl/ adj fml of war, soldiers, etc.

martial art /ˌ·· ·ˈ·/ n Eastern fighting sport: *Judo is a martial art.*

martial law /ˌ·· ·ˈ·/ n [U] government by the army under special laws

Mar·tian /ʹmɑːʃən/ n, adj (creature) from MARS

mar·ti·net /ˌmɑːtɪˈet/ n very STRICT person

mar·ti·ni /mɑːˈtiʲniʲ/ n alcoholic drink of GIN and VERMOUTH

mar·tyr /ʹmɑːtər/ n 1 someone who dies or suffers for their (religious) beliefs 2 **make a martyr of oneself** give up one's own wishes to help others, or in the hope of being praised ♦ vt kill as a martyr

mar·vel /ʹmɑːvəl/ n wonderful thing or example: *the marvels of modern science* ♦ vi -l- fml be filled with surprise and admiration ~**ous** adj very pleasing or good ~**lously** adv

Marx·is·m /ʹmɑːkˌsɪzəm/ n [U] teaching of Karl Marx on which COMMUNISM is based ~**ist** n, adj

mar·zi·pan /ʹmɑːzəˌpæn, ˌmɑːtsəˌpæn/ n [U] sweet paste made from ALMONDS

mas·ca·ra /mæˈskɑːrə/ n [U] dark substance for coloring the EYE-LASHes

mas·cot /ʹmæskət/ n object, animal, or person thought to bring good luck, used to represent a sports team

mas·cu·line /ʹmæskjʊlɪn/ adj 1 (in grammar) having to do with males 2 of or like a man -**linity** /ˌmæs-kjʊˈlɪnətiʲ/ n [U]

mash /mæʃ/ vt [(UP)] crush into a soft substance ♦ n [U] boiled grains fed to horses, cows, etc.

mask /mɑːsk/ n covering for the face, to hide or protect it ♦ vt hide ~**ed** adj wearing a mask

mas·o·chis·m /ʹmæsəˌkɪzəm/ n [U] 1 gaining pleasure from being hurt 2 wish to hurt so as to gain sexual pleasure -**chist** n -**chistic** /ˌmæsə-ˈkɪstɪk◂/ adj

Ma·son /ʹmeʲsən/ n man belonging to an ancient society whose members help each other ~**ic** /məˈsɑːnɪk/ adj

ma·son·ry /ʹmeʲsənriʲ/ n [U] stone building blocks

mas·que·rade /ˌmæskəˈreʲd/ vi pretend: *thieves masquerading as bank employees* ♦ n 1 hiding of the truth 2 party where people wear MASKS

mass /mæs/ n 1 [C] large lump, heap, or quantity: *a mass of clouds* 2 [C] also **masses** pl. — infml lots:

masses of work to do **3** [U] (in science) amount of matter in a body ♦ **matters** *n* [the+P] ordinary nary people in society

Mass *n* (in the Catholic and Orthodox churches) important religious ceremony

mas·sa·cre /'mæsəkər/ *n* killing of large numbers of people ♦ **massacre** *vt*

mas·sage /mə'saʒ, mə'sadʒ/ *n* [C;U] (act of) pressing and rubbing someone's body, esp. to cure pain or stiffness ♦ *vt* **1** give a massage to **2** change (facts, figures, etc.) usu. in a dishonest way

mas·seur /mə'sɜr, mæ-/ **masseuse** /mə'su*s, -'su*z, -'sɜz, mæ-/ *fem.* — *n* person who gives massages

mas·sive /'mæsɪv/ *adj* extremely big ~**ly** *adv* ~**ness** *n* [U]

mass me·di·a /ˌ· '··/ *n* [the+S] the MEDIA

mass-pro·duce /ˌ· ·'·/ *vt* produce (goods) in large numbers to the same pattern **mass production** *n* [U]

mast /mæst/ *n* long upright pole for carrying sails – see also HALF-MAST

mas·tec·to·my /mæ'stɛktəmiʸ/ *n* operation for the removal of a breast

mas·ter¹ /'mæstər/ *n* **1** mistress *fem.* — person in control of people, animals, or things **2** great artist, writer, etc. – see also OLD MASTER **3** captain of a ship **4** something from which copies are made: *a master tape* ~**ful** *adj* able or eager to control others –**fully** *adv* ~**ly** *adj* showing great skill

master² *vt* **1** learn or gain as a skill: *master the art of public speaking* **2** control and defeat: *He mastered his fear of heights.*

mas·ter·mind /'mæstərˌmaɪnd/ *vt* plan cleverly: *mastermind a crime* ♦ *n* very clever person

master of cer·e·mo·nies /ˌ· ·'···/ also **emcee, MC** *n* person who introduces speakers or performers at a public event

mas·ter·piece /'mæstərˌpiʸs/ *n* piece of work, esp. of art, done with extreme skill

mas·ter·y /'mæstəriʸ/ *n* [U] **1** power to control **2** great skill or knowledge

mas·tur·bate /'mæstərˌbeʸt/ *vi/t* excite the sex organs (of) by handling, rubbing, etc. –**bation** /ˌmæstər'beʸʃən/ *n* [U]

mat /mæt/ *n* **1** piece of strong material for covering part of a floor **2** small piece of material for putting under objects on a table

match¹ /mætʃ/ *n* **1** sports or other competition between two people or

sides; game: *a tennis match* **2** one who is equal to or better than another: *I'm no match for her at math.* **3** good combination: *The hat and shoes are a perfect match.* **4** marriage: *Both her daughters made good matches.* ♦ *v* **1** *vi/t* be similar (to) or combine well (with): *The curtains and carpets don't match.* **2** *vt* be equal to or find an equal for: *a restaurant that can't be matched for service*

match² *n* short thin stick that burns when its end is rubbed against a rough surface

match·box /'mætʃbaks/ *n* box for holding matches

match·mak·er /'mætʃˌmeʸkər/ *n* person who tries to arrange others' love affairs

mate¹ /meʸt/ *n* **1** friend, or person one works or lives with: *We're mates/schoolmates/roommates.* **2** either one of a male and female pair **3** officer on a non-navy ship

mate² *vi* (esp. of animals) join sexually to produce young

mate³ *n, v* CHECKMATE

ma·te·ri·al /mə'tɪriʸəl/ *n* **1** [C;U] substance of which things are or can be made **2** [U] cloth **3** [U] knowledge of facts from which a (written) work may be produced: *She's collecting material for a book.* ♦ *adj* **1** of matter or substance, not spirit **2** *fml* important or necessary ~**ly** *adv*

ma·te·ri·al·ism /mə'tɪriʸəˌlɪzəm/ *n* [U] (too) great interest in the pleasures of the world, money, etc. –**ist** *n* ~**istic** /məˌtɪriʸə'lɪstɪk◂/ *adj*

ma·te·ri·al·ize /mə'tɪriʸəˌlaɪz/ *vi* **1** become able to be seen **2** become real or actual: *Her hopes never materialized.* **3** come; arrive –**ization** /məˌtɪriʸələ'zeʸʃən/ *n* [U]

ma·ter·nal /mə'tɜrnl/ *adj* **1** of or like a mother **2** related through the mother's part of the family: *my maternal grandmother*

ma·ter·ni·ty /mə'tɜrnəṭiʸ/ *n* [U] motherhood ♦ *adj* for women who are going to give birth: *a maternity hospital/dress*

math·e·mat·ics /ˌmæθə'mæṭɪks/ also **math** /mæθ/ — *n* [U] science of numbers –**ical** *adj* –**ically** /-klɪʸ/ *adv* –**ician** /ˌmæθəmə'tɪʃən/ *n*

mat·i·née /ˌmætn'eʸ/ *n* afternoon performance of a play, movie, etc.

ma·tri·arch /'meʸtriʸˌɑrk/ *n* woman who controls a (family) group ~**al** /ˌmeʸtriʸ'ɑrkəl◂/ *adj* ruled by women

mat·ri·cide /'mætrəˌsaɪd/ *n* [C;U] murder of one's mother

ma·tric·u·late /mə'trɪkyəˌleʸt/ *vi*

become a member of a university –**ation** /məˌtrɪkyəˈleʸʃən/ n [U]

mat·ri·mo·ny /ˈmætrəˌmoʷniʸ/ n [U] being married –**nial** /ˌmætrəˈmoʷniʸəl◂/ adj

ma·tron /ˈmeʸtrən/ n 1 woman in charge of living arrangements in a school, prison, or other institution for girls or women 2 lit older married woman, esp. of quiet behavior ~**ly** adj 1 euph (of a woman) fat: a matronly figure 2 with the DIGNITY of a MATRON (3)

matte /mæt/ adj not shiny

mat·ted /ˈmætɪd/ adj twisted in a thick mass

mat·ter¹ /ˈmætər/ n 1 [C] subject; affair: several important matters to discuss 2 [the+S] trouble; cause of pain, illness, etc.: Is anything the matter? 3 [U] substance of which things are made: all the matter in the universe – see also GREY MATTER 4 [U] things of a particular kind or for a particular purpose: reading matter (= magazines, books, etc.) 5 a **matter of: a** a little more or less than: It's only a matter of hours before the doctor arrives. **b** needing as a part: Learning is a matter of concentration. 6 a **matter of course** a usual event 7 as a **matter of fact** in fact; really 8 **for that matter** (used when mentioning another possibility) 9 **no matter** … it makes no difference: No matter how hard I tried, I couldn't move it. 10 **That's a matter of opinion.** My opinion is different from yours.

matter² vi be important

matter-of-fact /ˌ··· ˈ·◂/ adj without feelings or imagination

mat·ting /ˈmætɪŋ/ n [U] rough woven material, esp. for the floor

mat·tress /ˈmætrɪs/ n large filled cloth case for sleeping on

ma·ture /məˈtʃʊər, məˈtʊər, məˈtyʊər/ adj 1 fully developed 2 fml sensible, like a mature person 3 carefully thought about ♦ vi/t become or make mature –**turity** n [U]

maud·lin /ˈmɔdlɪn/ adj stupidly sad, esp. when drunk

maul /mɔl/ vt hurt by handling roughly: mauled by a lion

mau·so·le·um /ˌmɔsəˈliʸəm, -zə-/ n grand building containing one or more graves

mauve /moʷv/ adj pale purple

mav·er·ick /ˈmævərɪk/ n person who acts differently from the rest of a group

mawk·ish /ˈmɔkɪʃ/ adj expressing ·love and admiration in a silly way

max·im /ˈmæksɪm/ n rule for sensible behavior

max·i·mize /ˈmæksəˌmaɪz/ vt make as big as possible

max·i·mum /ˈmæksəməm/ n, adj –**ma** /-mə/ or –**mums** largest (amount, number, etc.): our maximum offer | He smokes a maximum of 10 cigarettes a day. –**mal** adj

may /meʸ/ v aux 1 (shows a possibility): He may come and he may not. | She may have missed the train. (= perhaps she has missed it) 2 have permission to; be allowed to: You may come in now. | May we go home, please? 3 (used when expressing a wish): May you live happily ever after! 4 **may as well** have no strong reason not to: It's late, so I may as well go to bed.

May n the 5th month of the year

may·be /ˈmeʸbiʸ/ adv perhaps

may·hem /ˈmeʸhem/ n [U] violent disorder and confusion

may·on·naise /ˌmeʸəˈneʸz, ˈmeʸə-ˌneʸz/ n [U] thick liquid made from eggs and oil, added to food

may·or /ˈmeʸər, meər/ n person elected to be head of a city or town

maze /meʸz/ n arrangement of twisting paths in which one becomes lost

MC /ˌem ˈsiʸ/ n MASTER OF CEREMONIES – see also EMCEE

MD /ˌem ˈdiʸ/ abbrev. for: Doctor of Medicine

me /miʸ/ pron (object form of I)

mead·ow /ˈmedoʷ/ n field of grass

mea·ger /ˈmiʸgər/ adj not big enough ~**ly** adv ~**ness** n [U]

meal¹ /miʸl/ n (food eaten at) an occasion for eating

meal² n [U] crushed grain

mealy-mouthed /ˌ··· ˈ·◂/ adj expressing (unpleasant) things too indirectly

mean¹ /miʸn/ vt meant /ment/ 1 (of words, signs, etc.) represent an idea: 'Melancholy' means 'sad'. | The red light means 'stop'. 2 intend: He said Tuesday, but meant Thursday. | I said I'd help and I meant it. (= I am determined to do so) 3 be a sign of: This could mean war. 4 be of importance to the stated degree: Her work means a lot/everything to her. 5 **be meant to** be supposed to 6 **mean business** act with serious intentions 7 **mean well** act with good intentions ~**ing** n [C;U] 1 idea intended to be understood, esp. from words: 'Measure' has several meanings. 2 importance or value: His life lost its meaning when his wife died. ~**ing** adj suggesting a hidden thought: a meaning look ~**ingful** adj: a meaningful look ~**ingless** adj

mean² adj 1 unkind; nasty 2 bad-tempered 3 ungenerous 4 **no mean** very good: He's no mean cook.

mean³ n, adj average

me·an·der /mi³'ændər/ vi 1 wander 2 (of a stream) flow slowly and twistingly

means /mi³nz/ n means 1 [C] method; way 2 [P] money, esp. enough to live on 3 **by all means** (a polite way of giving permission) 4 **by means of** using; with 5 **by no means** fml not at all 6 **live beyond/within one's means** spend more than/not more than one can afford

means test /'··/ n inquiry into the amount of money someone has, esp. to find out if they need money from the state

meant /ment/ v past t. and p. of MEAN¹

mean·time /'mi³ntaɪm/ n **in the meantime** MEANWHILE (1)

mean·while /'mi³nhwaɪl, -waɪl/ adv 1 in the time between 2 events 2 during the same period of time

mea·sles /'mi³zəlz/ n [U] infectious disease in which the sufferer has small red spots on the skin

meas·ly /'mi³zli³/ adj sl too small

mea·sure¹ /'meʒər/ vt 1 find or show the size, amount, degree, etc., of: Measure the (height of the) cupboard first. | A clock measures time. 2 be of the stated size: The river measured 200 yards from side to side. **-surable** adj **-surably** adv

measure off/out phr vt take from a longer length or larger quantity

measure up phr vi show good enough qualities (for)

mea·sure² n 1 [U] measuring system 2 [C] unit in such a system 3 [S;U] fml amount: She's had a certain measure of success. 4 [C] act to bring about an effect: The police were forced to take strong measures. 5 **for good measure** in addition 6 **take someone's measure/get the measure of someone** judge what someone is like **-sured** adj careful and steady **~ment** n 1 [U] act of measuring 2 [C] length, height, etc., measured

meat /mi³t/ n [U] 1 flesh of animals (not fish) for eating 2 valuable matter, ideas, etc.: It was a clever speech, but there was no real meat to it. **~y** adj

mec·ca /'mekə/ n place that many people wish to reach

me·chan·ic /mɪ'kænɪk/ n person skilled in using or repairing machinery

me·chan·i·cal /mɪ'kænɪkəl/ adj 1 of or worked or produced by machinery 2 without new thought or strong feeling **~ly** /-kli³/ adv

me·chan·ics /mɪ'kænɪks/ n 1 [U] science of the action of forces on objects 2 [U] science of machinery 3 [P] way in which something works

mech·a·nis·m /'mekə₁nɪzəm/ n machine or the way it works: (fig.) the mechanism of the brain

mech·a·nize /'mekə₁naɪz/ vt (start to) use machines for or in **-ization** /₁mekənə'zeⁱʃən/ n [U]

med·al /'medl/ n usu. coinlike object given as a mark of honor, esp. for bravery **~ist** n person who has won a medal, esp. in sport

me·dal·li·on /mə'dælyən/ n large medal, or piece of jewelry like a medal

med·dle /'medl/ vi take action in a matter which does not concern one **~dler** n

me·di·a /'mi³di³ə/ n [U;P] television, radio, newspapers, etc. – see also MEDIUM²

me·di·ate /'mi³di³₁eⁱt/ vi act so as to bring agreement after a quarrel **-ator** n **-ation** /₁mi³di³'eⁱʃən/ n [U]

med·ic /'medɪk/ n infml doctor, esp. in the armed forces

med·ic·aid /'medɪ₁keⁱd/ n [U] (often cap.) system by which the government helps to pay the medical costs of people on low incomes

med·i·cal /'medɪkəl/ adj of or for the treatment of illness, esp. with medicine rather than operations ♦ n medical examination of the body **~ly** /-kli³/ adv

me·dic·a·ment /mɪ'dɪkəmənt, 'medɪ-/ n fml medicine

med·i·care /'medɪ₁keər/ n [U] (often cap.) system of medical care provided by the government, esp. for old people

med·i·ca·tion /₁medɪ'keⁱʃən/ n [C;U] medicine, a drug

me·di·ci·nal /mə'dɪsənəl/ adj as medicine; curing **~ly** adv

med·i·cine /'medəsən/ n 1 [C;U] substance for treating illness 2 [U] science of treating illness 3 **a taste/dose of one's own medicine** deserved punishment

medicine man /'···₁·/ n (in certain tribes) man with magical powers, esp. for curing people

med·i·e·val /₁mi³di³'i³vəl, ₁me-, ₁mi-/ adj of the MIDDLE AGES

me·di·o·cre /₁mi³di³'oⁱkər/ adj ordinary quality **-crity** /₁mi³di³-'akrəti³/ n [U]

med·i·tate /'medə₁teⁱt/ v 1 vi make the mind quiet, esp. to gain calmness or understanding 2 vt plan or consider carefully **-tation** /₁medə-'teⁱʃən/ n [C;U]

me·di·um¹ /'mi³di³əm/ adj of middle size, amount, quality, etc.

medium² n **-dia** /-di³ə/ or **-diums** 1 method of artistic expression or of giving information 2 condition or surroundings in which things exist

3 middle position: *a happy medium between eating all the time and not eating at all*

medium³ *n* –diums person who claims to receive messages from the spirits of the dead

med·ley /ˈmedliy/ *n* mass of different types mixed together

meek /miyk/ *adj* gentle and uncomplaining ~ly *adv* ~ness *n* [U]

meet¹ /miyt/ *v* met /met/ **1** *vi/t* come together (with): *I met an old friend in the street.* | *Our lips met (in a kiss).* **2** *vi/t* be introduced (to) **3** *vt fml* find or experience: *She met her death in a plane crash.* **4** *vt* follow (as if) in answer: *His speech was met with boos.* **5** *vt* satisfy: *Their offer meets all our needs.* **6** *vt* pay: *Have you enough money to meet your debts?* **7** **meet someone halfway** make an agreement which partly satisfies both sides **8** **more (in/to something) than meets the eye** hidden facts or reasons (in or for something) ~ing *n* occasion of coming together, esp. to talk

meet up *phr vi infml* meet, esp. by informal arrangements

meet with *phr vt* **1** experience: *I met with an accident.* **2** have a meeting with

meet² *n* gathering of people for sports events: *a track meet*

meg·a·bucks /ˈmegəˌbʌks/ *n infml* [P] lots of money

meg·a·lo·ma·ni·a /ˌmegəlowˈmeyniyə/ *n* [U] belief that one is more important, powerful, etc., than one really is -niac /-niyæk/ *n*

meg·a·phone /ˈmegəˌfown/ *n* instrument shaped like a horn, for making the voice louder

mel·an·chol·y /ˈmelənˌkaliy/ *adj, n* [U] sad(ness) -ic /ˌmelənˈkalik◄/ *adj*

mé·lange /meyˈlɑnʒ/ *n* mixture

mel·ee /ˈmeyley, meyˈley/ *n* struggling or disorderly crowd

mel·low /ˈmelow/ *adj* **1** suggesting gentle ripeness **2** (of color) soft and warm **3** (of people) relaxed and agreeable ♦ *vi/t* become or make mellow ~ness *n* [U]

mel·o·dra·mat·ic /ˌmelədrəˈmætɪk◄/ *adj* too full of excited feeling ~ally /-kliy/ *adv*

mel·o·dy /ˈmelədiy/ *n* **1** tune **2** song –dic /məˈlɑdik/ *adj* of or having melody -dious /məˈlowdiyəs/ *adj* tuneful

mel·on /ˈmelən/ *n* large round juicy fruit

melt /melt/ *v* **1** *vi/t* become or make liquid: *The sun melted the ice.* **2** *vi* go away: disappear **3** *vi* become more sympathetic

melt down *phr vt* make (a metal object) liquid by heating

melt·down /ˈmeltdaʊn/ *n* dangerous situation in which material burns through the bottom of an atomic REACTOR

melting pot /ˈ··· ˌ·/ *n* place where many different CULTUREs are mixed together

mem·ber /ˈmembər/ *n* **1** someone who belongs to a club, group, etc. **2** part of the body, such as an organ or limb ~**ship** *n* **1** [U] state of being a member (1) **2** [C] all the members of a club, society, etc.

mem·brane /ˈmembreyn/ *n* [C;U] soft thin skin

me·men·to /məˈmentow/ *n* –tos object that brings back pleasant memories

mem·o /ˈmemow/ *n* also **memorandum** — *n* -os note from one person or office to another within an organization

mem·oirs /ˈmemwarz/ *n* [P] AUTO-BIOGRAPHY

mem·o·ra·bil·i·a /ˌmemərəˈbɪliyə, -ˈbɪlyə, -ˈbiyl-/ *n* [P] interesting things connected with a famous person or event

mem·o·ra·ble /ˈmemərəbəl/ *adj* worth remembering, esp. because good –**bly** *adv*

mem·o·ran·dum /ˌmeməˈrændəm/ *n* –da /-də/ *fml* MEMO

me·mo·ri·al /məˈmoriyəl, -ˈmowr-/ *n* something, esp. a stone MONUMENT, in memory of a person, event, etc.

Memorial Day /·ˈ···· ˌ·/ *n* day for remembering all those who died fighting in wars; celebrated on the last Monday in May

mem·o·rize /ˈmeməˌraɪz/ *vt* learn and remember, on purpose

mem·o·ry /ˈmeməriy/ *n* **1** [C;U] ability to remember: *She's got a good memory.* **2** [C] example of remembering: *one of my earliest memories* **3** [U] time during which things happened which can be remembered: *within living memory* **4** [U] opinion held of someone after their death: *to praise his memory* **5** [C] part of a computer in which information is stored **6 in memory of** as a way of remembering or being reminded of

men /men/ *n pl. of* MAN

men·ace /ˈmenɪs/ *n* **1** [C;U] threat; danger **2** [C] troublesome person or thing ♦ *vt* threaten

mé·nage à trois /meyˌnɑʒ ɑ ˈtrwɑ/ *n* [S] relationship in which two people and the lover of one of them live together

me·na·ge·rie /məˈnædʒəriy, -ʒə-/ *n* collection of wild animals kept privately or for the public to see

mend /mend/ *v* **1** *vi/t* repair **2** *vi* regain one's health **3 mend one's ways** improve one's behavior ♦ *n*

1 repaired place 2 **on the mend** regaining one's health ~**er** *n*

me·ni·al /ˈmiːnɪəl, ˈmiːnjəl/ *adj* (of a job) humble and not interesting or important ♦ *n* someone who does menial work

men·in·gi·tis /ˌmenənˈdʒaɪtɪs/ *n* [U] serious brain illness

men·o·pause /ˈmenəˌpɔːz/ *n* [S] time of life when a woman's PERIOD¹ (3) stops

men·stru·al /ˈmenstruəl, -strəl/ *adj* of a woman's PERIOD

men·stru·ate /ˈmenstruˌeɪt/ *vi* have a PERIOD **–ation** /ˌmenstruˈeɪʃən/ *n* [U]

men·tal /ˈmentəl/ *adj* 1 of or in the mind: *mental illness* | *a mental picture* 2 of or for illness of the mind: *a mental hospital* 3 *infml* crazy ~**ly** *adv*

men·tal·i·ty /menˈtælətiː/ *n* 1 [U] abilities and powers of the mind 2 [C] person's character and way of thinking

men·thol /ˈmenθɒl, -θəl, -θoʊl/ *n* [U] substance which smells and tastes of MINT¹ ~**ated** /-θəˌleɪtɪd/ *adj*

men·tion /ˈmenʃən/ *vt* 1 tell of or about, esp. in a few words 2 **Don't mention it** (polite reply to thanks) 3 **not to mention** and in addition there's ... ♦ *n* 1 short remark about 2 naming of someone, esp. to honor them

men·tor /ˈmentɔːr, -tər/ *n* person who habitually advises another

men·u /ˈmenjuː/ *n* 1 list of food one can order in a restaurant 2 list of programs on computer SOFTWARE

meow /miˈaʊ/ *vi, n* (make) the crying sound a cat makes

mer·can·tile /ˈmɜːrkənˌtiːl, -ˌtaɪl/ *adj fml* of trade and business

mer·ce·na·ry /ˈmɜːrsəˌneriː/ *adj* influenced by the wish for money ♦ *n* soldier who fights for whoever will pay him

mer·chan·dise /ˈmɜːrtʃənˌdaɪz, -ˌdaɪs/ *n* [U] things for sale

mer·chant /ˈmɜːrtʃənt/ *n* person who buys and sells goods in large amounts ♦ *adj* used in trade, not war: *the merchant navy*

mer·cu·ry /ˈmɜːrkjəriː/ *n* [U] 1 silvery liquid metal 2 (*cap.*) the PLANET nearest the sun **–rial** /mɜːrˈkjʊəriːəl/ *adj* quick, active, and often changing

mer·cy /ˈmɜːrsiː/ *n* [U] 1 willingness to forgive, not to punish; kindness and pity 2 fortunate event 3 **at the mercy of** defenseless against **merciful** *adj* **merciless** *adj*

mere /mɪər/ *adj* only; nothing more than: *a mere child* ~**ly** *adv* only

mer·e·tri·cious /ˌmerəˈtrɪʃəs/ *adj fml* (seeming) attractive but of no real value ~**ly** *adv* ~**ness** *n* [U]

merge /mɜːrdʒ/ *v* 1 *vi* combine, esp. gradually, so as to become a single thing 2 *vi/t* join together: *The two companies merged.* **merger** *n* joining together of 2 or more companies

me·rid·i·an /məˈrɪdiːən/ *n* 1 imaginary line over the Earth's surface from the top to the bottom, used on maps 2 highest point, esp. of a star

me·ringue /məˈræŋ/ *n* [C;U] a mixture of sugar and the white part of eggs which is cooked for a short time

mer·it /ˈmerɪt/ *n* [C;U] good quality ♦ *vt fml* deserve

mer·i·toc·ra·cy /ˌmerəˈtɑːkrəsiː/ *n* social system which gives the highest positions to those with the most ability

mer·maid /ˈmɜːrmeɪd/ *n* (in stories) woman with a fish's tail

mer·ry /ˈmeriː/ *adj* full of or causing laughter and fun **–rily** *adv* **–riment** *n* [U]

merry-go-round /ˈ··ˌ·/ *n* machine with large model animals on which children ride around and around

me·sa /ˈmeɪsə/ *n* mountain with a flat top

mesh¹ /meʃ/ *n* [C;U] 1 net, esp. with small holes 2 threads in such a net

mesh² *vi* (of the teeth of GEARs) to connect: (fig.) *Their characters just don't mesh.* (= fit together suitably)

mes·mer·ize /ˈmezməˌraɪz/ *vt* hold the complete attention of, as if by a strong force

mess¹ /mes/ *n* 1 [S;U] (state of) untidiness or dirt 2 [S] bad situation; trouble 3 [C] room where soldiers, etc., eat 4 **make a mess of** ruin; spoil ~**y** *adj*

mess² *v*

mess around *phr v* 1 *vi* act or speak stupidly 2 *vi* spend time with no particular plan or purpose 3 **mess around with** *euph* have sexual relations with

mess up *phr vt* ruin; spoil

mes·sage /ˈmesɪdʒ/ *n* 1 piece of information passed from one person to another 2 main moral idea of a story, picture, etc. 3 **get the message** understand what is meant

mes·sen·ger /ˈmesəndʒər/ *n* person who brings a message

mes·si·ah /məˈsaɪə/ *n* 1 new leader in a religion 2 (*cap.*) Jesus Christ

met /met/ *v* past t. and p. of MEET¹

me·tab·o·lis·m /məˈtæbəˌlɪzəm/ *n* process by which a body lives, esp. by changing food into ENERGY **–lic** /ˌmetəˈbɑːlɪk/ *adj*

met·al /'metl/ n [C;U] usu. solid shiny material, such as iron, copper, or silver ~ **lic** /ˌme'tælɪk/ adj

met·al·lur·gy /'metlˌɜrdʒiʸ/ n [U] scientific study of metals adj –**gist** n –**gical** /ˌmetl'ɜrdʒɪkəl/

met·al·work /'metlˌwɜrk/ n [U] making of metal objects

met·a·mor·pho·sis /ˌmetə'mɔrfəsɪs/ n –**ses** /-siʸz/ complete change from one form to another

met·a·phor /'metəˌfɔr/ n [C;U] (use of) a phrase which describes one thing by stating another thing with which it can be compared (as in *the roses in her cheeks*) – see also MIXED METAPHOR ~ **ical** /ˌmetə'fɔrɪkəl, -'far-/ adj ~ **ically** /kliʸ/ adv

met·a·phys·i·cal /ˌmetə'fɪzɪkəl◂/ adj 1 concerned with the science of being and knowing 2 (of ideas) at a high level and difficult to understand

mete /miʸt/ v

mete out phr vt fml or lit give (esp. punishment)

me·te·or /'miʸtiʸər/ n small piece of matter that flies through space and can be seen burning if it comes near the Earth ~ **ic** /ˌmiʸtiʸ'ɔrɪk◂, -'arɪk◂/ adj very fast: *a meteoric rise to fame* ~ **ically** /-kliʸ/ adv

me·te·or·ite /'miʸtiʸəˌraɪt/ n meteor that lands on the Earth

me·te·or·ol·o·gy /ˌmiʸtiʸə'ralədʒiʸ/ n [U] scientific study of weather –**gist** n –**gical** /ˌmiʸtiʸərə'lədʒɪkəl/ adj

me·ter[1] /'miʸtər/ n machine that measures something: *a gas meter*

meter[2] n .1 a measure of length equal to 39.37 inches

meter[3] n [C;U] arrangement of beats in poetry

me·thane /'meθeʸn/ n [U] gas that burns easily

meth·od /'meθəd/ n 1 [C] way of doing something 2 [U] proper planning and arrangement 3 **method to one's madness** good reason for doing something that appears strange ~ **ical** /mə'θadɪkəl/ adj careful; using an ordered system ~ **ically** /-kliʸ/ adv

meth·o·dol·o·gy /ˌmeθə'dalədʒiʸ/ n set of methods

me·tic·u·lous /mə'tɪkyələs/ adj very careful, with great attention to detail ~ **ly** adv

mé·ti·er /me'tyeʸ, 'metyeʸ/ n fml one's type of work

met·ric /'metrɪk/ adj using a measured system (**metric system**) based on the meter and kilogram ~ **ation** /ˌmetri'keʸʃən/ n [U] changing to a metric system

met·ro /'metroʷ/ n –**ros** underground railway in France, Canada, Washington DC, and certain other places

me·trop·o·lis /mə'trapəlɪs/ n main or capital city –**litan** /ˌmetrə'palətn◂/ adj

met·tle /'metl/ n fml will to continue bravely in spite of difficulties

mez·za·nine /'mezəˌniʸn/ n 1 floor that comes between 2 other floors of a building 2 lowest BALCONY in a theater

mg written abbrev. for MILLIGRAM(s)

MIA /ˌɛm aɪ 'eʸ/ n soldier who is missing after a battle but is not known to be dead or a prisoner

mice /maɪs/ pl. of MOUSE

Mick·ey Finn /ˌmɪkiʸ 'fɪn/ n very strong alcoholic drink that has had a drug added to it

Mickey Mouse /ˌ·· ˌ·/ adj infml small and unimportant, not to be taken seriously

mi·crobe /'maɪkroʷb/ n bacterium

mi·cro·bi·ol·o·gy /ˌmaɪkroʷbaɪ'alədʒiʸ/ n [U] scientific study of very small living creatures –**gist** n

mi·cro·chip /'maɪkroʷˌtʃɪp/ n CHIP[1] (4)

mi·cro·com·put·er /'maɪkroʷkəmˌpyuʷtər/ also **mi·cro** /'maɪkroʷ/ infml — n the smallest type of computer, used esp. in the home, in schools, or by small businesses

mi·cro·cosm /'maɪkrəˌkazəm/ n something small that represents all the qualities, activities, etc., of something larger

mi·cro·film /'maɪkroʷˌfɪlm/ n [C;U] film for photographing something in a very small size ♦ vt photograph on microfilm

mi·cro·or·gan·ism /ˌmaɪkroʷ'ɔrgəˌnɪzəm/ n bacterium

mi·cro·phone /'maɪkrəˌfoʷn/ n electrical instrument for collecting sound, so as to make it louder or broadcast it

mi·cro·pro·ces·sor /ˌmaɪkroʷ'praˌsesər/ n central controlling CHIP[1] (4) in a small computer

mi·cro·scope /'maɪkrəˌskoʷp/ n scientific instrument that makes things look larger, used for studying extremely small things –**scop·ic** /ˌmaɪkrə'skapɪk◂/ adj 1 very small 2 using a microscope –**scopically** /-kliʸ/ adv

mi·cro·wave ov·en /ˌmaɪkrəweʸv 'ʌvən/ also **microwave** — n box that cooks food using very short electric waves

mid·air /ˌmɪd'eər◂/ n [U] point up in the sky

Mi·das touch /'maɪdəs ˌtʌtʃ/ n [the+S] ability to make everything one does successful

mid·dle /'mɪdl/ adj, n [S;U] (in or at) the center or a point half of the distance between 2 ends

middle age /ˌ·· '·◂/ n [U] period between youth and old age **middle-aged** adj

middle aged spread /ˌ··· '·/ n [U] increase of flesh around the waist which tends to happen as people grow older

Middle Ag·es /ˌ·· '··/ n [the+P] period between about AD 1100 and 1500 in Europe

mid·dle·brow /'mɪdlbraʊ/ n person who likes books, paintings, etc., that are of average quality but not too difficult ♦ **middlebrow** adj

middle class /ˌ·· '·◂/ n social class of business and professional people, office workers, etc. **middle-class** adj

middle dis·tance /ˌ·· '··◂/ n [U] part of a view between what is close and what is far away

Middle East /ˌ·· '·◂/ n [the+S] countries in Asia west of India ~**ern** adj

mid·dle·man /'mɪdlˌmæn/ n –**men** /-mɛn/ someone who buys from a producer and sells to a customer

middle name /ˌ·· '·/ n 1 name coming between the FIRST NAME and the SURNAME 2 infml something for which a person is well known: Generosity's my middle name.

middle-of-the-road /ˌ··· '·◂/ adj favoring a course of action that most people would agree with

mid·dling /'mɪdlɪŋ/ adj average

midge /mɪdʒ/ n small winged insect that bites

midg·et /'mɪdʒɪt/ adj, n very small (person)

mid-life cri·sis /ˌ· · '··/ n continuing feeling of unhappiness, lack of confidence, etc., suffered by someone in the middle years of life

mid·night /'mɪdnaɪt/ n [U] 12 o'clock at night

mid·riff /'mɪdrɪf/ n front of the body below the chest

midst /mɪdst/ n **in the midst of** in the middle of; among

mid·town /'mɪdtaʊn/ adj in the center of a town or city: the midtown bus

mid·way /ˌmɪd'weɪ◂/ adj, adv (at a point) half the distance between 2 ends or places

Mid·west /ˌmɪd'wɛst/ n [the+S] part of the US east and west of the Mississippi River

mid·wife /'mɪdwaɪf/ n –**wives** /-waɪvz/ nurse who helps women giving birth –**wifery** /'mɪdˌwaɪfəriᵛ/ n [U]

miffed /mɪft/ adj infml slightly angry

might¹ /maɪt/ v aux 1 (used for expressing slight possibility): He might come, but it's unlikely. 2 past t. of MAY: I thought it might rain. 3 ought; should: You might have offered to help! 4 **might as well** have no strong reason not to 5 **might well** be likely to

might² /maɪt/ n [U] power; strength ~**y** adj very great: a mighty blow

mi·graine /'maɪgreᵛn/ n [C;U] very severe headache

mi·grant /'maɪgrənt/ n migrating person or bird: migrant workers

mi·grate /'maɪgreᵛt/ vi 1 (of birds or fish) travel regularly from one part of the world to another, according to the season 2 move from one place to another, esp. for a limited period –**gration** /maɪ'greᵛʃən/ n [C;U] –**gratory** /'maɪgrəˌtɔriᵛ, -ˌtoᵘriᵛ/ adj

mike /maɪk/ n sl for MICROPHONE

mild /maɪld/ adj not strong, forceful, or severe; gentle ~**ly** adv ~**ness** n [U]

mil·dew /'mɪlduᵛ, -dyuᵛ/ n [U] gray or whitish growth on plants and on things kept a long time in slightly wet conditions ~**ed** adj

mile /maɪl/ n a measure of length equal to 1.609 kilometres or 5280 feet

mile·age /'maɪlɪdʒ/ n [C;U] 1 distance traveled, measured in miles 2 fixed amount of money paid for each mile traveled 3 amount of use: The newspapers are getting a lot of mileage out of the inauguration.

mile·stone /'maɪlstoᵘn/ n 1 stone beside the road, saying how far to the next town 2 important event

mi·lieu /mɪl'yuᵛ, -'yɜ, miᵛl-/ n –**s** or –**x** (same pronunciation) [usu. sing] person's social surroundings

mil·i·tant /'mɪlətənt/ n, adj (person) taking a strong active part in a struggle ~**ly** adv ~**tancy** n [U]

mil·i·ta·ris·m /'mɪlətəˌrɪzəm/ n [U] derog belief in the use of armed force –**rist** n –**ristic** /ˌmɪlətə'rɪstɪk◂/ adj

mil·i·ta·ry /'mɪləˌtɛriᵛ/ adj of, for, or by soldiers, armies, or war ♦ n [the+P] the army

mil·i·tate /'mɪləˌteᵛt/ v **militate against** phr vt act, serve, or have importance as a reason against

mi·li·tia /mə'lɪʃə/ n force trained to be soldiers in time of special need

milk /mɪlk/ n [U] 1 white liquid produced by human or animal females to feed their young 2 white liquid produced by certain plants: coconut milk ♦ v 1 vt take milk from (a cow, etc.) 2 vi (of a cow, etc.) give milk 3 vt get money, knowledge of a secret, etc., from (someone or something) by clever or dishonest

means *vt* get poison from (a snake) ~**y** *adj*

milk·maid /ˈmɪlkmeɪd/ *n* (esp. in former times) woman who milks cows

milk·man /ˈmɪlkmæn/ *n* –**men** /-men/ person who delivers milk to houses

milk shake /ˈ·ˌ·/ *n* drink of milk and ice cream with an added taste of fruit, chocolate, etc.

mill¹ /mɪl/ *n* 1 (building containing) a machine for crushing grain to flour 2 factory: *a cotton mill* 3 small machine for crushing: *a coffee mill* 4 **put someone through/go through the mill** (cause someone to) pass through (a time of) hard training, hard experience, etc. ♦ *vt* crush or produce in a mill ~**er** person who owns or works a flour mill

mill² *v* **mill around** *phr vi* move purposelessly in large numbers

mill³ *n* 1/10 of a CENT (1/1000 of a dollar), used to fix levels of tax

mil·len·ni·um /mɪˈleniʲəm/ *n* –**nia** /-niʲə/ 1 [C] 1,000 years 2 **the millennium** future age in which everyone will be happy

mil·let /ˈmɪlɪt/ *n* [U] small seeds of a grasslike plant, used as food

mil·li·gram, -gramme /ˈmɪləgræm/ *n* a measure of weight equal to 0.001 GRAMS

mil·li·me·ter /ˈmɪləˌmiʲtər/ *n* a measure of length equal to 0.001 METERS (2)

mil·li·ner /ˈmɪlənər/ *n* maker of women's hats ~**y** *n* [U] articles made and sold by a milliner

mil·lion /ˈmɪlyən/ *determiner, n, pron* million or **millions** 1 1,000,000 2 also **millions of** — very large number ~**th** *det, n, pron, adv*

mil·lion·aire /ˌmɪlyəˈneər/ **millionairess** /-rɪs/ *fem.* — *n* person who has a million or more dollars; very wealthy person

mil·li·pede /ˈmɪləˌpiʲd/ *n* small wormlike creature with many legs

mill·stone /ˈmɪlstoʷn/ *n* 1 circular crushing stone in a flour mill 2 cause of great trouble and anxiety

mime /maɪm/ *n* [C;U] use of actions without language to show meaning, esp. as a performance ♦ *n* actor who does this ♦ *vi/t* act in mime

mim·e·o·graph /ˈmɪmiʲəˌgræf/ *n* machine that makes copies from a specially prepared original

mim·ic /ˈmɪmɪk/ *vt* –**ck**– 1 copy (someone or something) amusingly 2 appear very like (something else) ♦ *n* person who mimics others ♦ *adj* not real

min·a·ret /ˌmɪnəˈret, ˈmɪnəˌret/ *n* tall thin tower in a MOSQUE

mince /mɪns/ *vi/t* 1 *vt* cut into very small pieces 2 *vi* walk in a silly unnatural way 3 **not to mince one's words** speak of something sad or unpleasant using plain direct language

mince·meat /ˈmɪnsmiʲt/ *n* [U] 1 mixture of dried fruit used as a filling for pastry 2 **make mincemeat of** defeat or destroy (a person, belief, etc.) completely

mind¹ /maɪnd/ *n* 1 [C;U] person's (way of) thinking or feeling; thoughts: *She has a very quick mind.* 2 [U] memory: *I'll bear/keep it in mind.* (= not forget it) | *I can't call it to mind.* (= remember it) 3 [C] attention: **Keep your mind on** *your work.* | *You need something to* **take your mind off** *the problem.* 4 [C;U] intention: *Nothing was further from my mind.* | *I've* **got a good mind to** (= I think I may) *report you.* 5 [C;U] opinion: *We are of one/ of the same mind on this matter.* | **To my mind** (= in my opinion) *you're quite wrong.* 6 [C] person considered for his/her ability to think well: *She's one of the finest minds in the country.* 7 **be in two minds (about something)** be unable to reach a decision 8 **change one's mind** change one's intentions or opinions 9 **have half a mind** have a desire or intention that is not firmly formed 10 **in one's right mind** not crazy 11 **know one's own mind** know what one wants 12 **make up one's mind** reach a decision 13 **mind over matter** control over events or material objects by the power of the mind 14 **on one's mind** causing anxiety 15 **out of one's mind** crazy 16 **speak one's mind** express plainly one's thoughts and opinions ~**ful** *adj* giving attention ~**less** *adj* not needing or using thought; stupid ~**lessly** *adv* ~**lessness** *n* [U]

mind² *v* 1 *vi/t* be opposed to (a particular thing): *'Coffee or tea?' 'I don't mind.'* (= I'd like either) | *Would you mind opening* (= please open) *the window?* 2 *vi/t* be careful (of): *Mind your manners!* 3 *vt* take care of; look after 4 **Do you mind?** I am offended and annoyed 5 **mind one's own business** not INTERFERE 6 **mind you** also **mind** — take this into account also 7 **never mind: a** don't worry **b** it doesn't matter 8 **never you mind** it is not your business

mind-bog·gling /ˈ· ·ˌ··/ *adj sl* very surprising

mind's eye /ˌ· ˈ·/ *n* [U] imagination; memory

mine¹ /maɪn/ *pron* of me; my one's: *This pen's mine, not yours.*

mine² *n* 1 place where coal or metal are dug from the ground: *a* goldmine | (fig.) *He's a mine of information.* (= can tell you a lot) **2** sort of bomb placed just under the ground or in the sea ♦ *v* **1** *vi/t* dig or get from a MINE² (1) **2** *vt* put MINES² (2) in or under **3** *vt* destroy by MINES² (2) **miner** *n* worker in a MINE² (1)

mine·field /'maɪnfiːld/ *n* **1** place where MINES² (2) have been put **2** something full of hidden dangers

min·er·al /'mɪnərəl/ *n* substance formed naturally in the earth, such as stone, metal, coal, salt, or oil

min·er·al·o·gy /ˌmɪnə'rælədʒiˠ, -'ræ-/ *n* [U] scientific study of minerals **-gist** *n*

mineral wa·ter /'··· ˌ··/ *n* [U] water from a spring, containing minerals

mine·sweep·er /'maɪnˌswiːpər/ *n* ship for finding and destroying MINES² (2)

min·gle /'mɪŋɡəl/ **1** *vi/t* mix so as to form an undivided whole **2** *vi infml* talk to different people at a party

min·i /'mɪniˠ/ *n* anything that is smaller than other things of the same kind: *a miniskirt*

min·i·a·ture /'mɪniˠətʃər, 'mɪnətʃər, -ˌtʃʊər/ *adj, n* very small (thing, esp. a copy of a bigger one) **-turize** *vt*

min·i·bus /'mɪniˠˌbʌs/ *n* small bus for between 6 and 12 people

min·i·mal /'mɪnəməl/ *adj* as little as possible **-ly** *adv*

min·i·mize /'mɪnəˌmaɪz/ *vt* **1** reduce as much as possible **2** treat as if not serious

min·i·mum /'mɪnəməm/ *n, adj* **-ma** /-mə/ *or* **-mums** smallest (amount, number, etc.)

min·ing /'maɪnɪŋ/ *n* [U] digging minerals out of the earth

min·ion /'mɪnyən/ *n* slavelike helper

min·is·cule /'mɪnəsˌkyuːl/ *adj* extremely small

min·is·ter¹ /'mɪnəstər/ *n* **1** politician in charge of a foreign government department: *the Minister of Defense* **2** Christian priest **-ial** /ˌmɪnə'stɪəriˠəl◄/ *adj*

minister² *v* minister to *phr vt fml* help: *ministering to the sick*

min·is·tra·tion /ˌmɪnə'streɪʃən/ *n* [C;U] giving of help and service

min·is·try /'mɪnəstriˠ/ *n* [C] **1** foreign government department **2** *[the+S]* job of being a priest: *to enter the ministry* (= become a priest)

mink /mɪŋk/ *n* mink [C;U] (valuable brown fur of) a small fierce animal

mi·nor¹ /'maɪnər/ *adj* of small importance or seriousness: *a minor problem / minor surgery*

minor² *n law* person too young to be held responsible

mi·nor·i·ty /mə'nɔrətiˠ/ *n* **1** [C] less than half: *A minority of people favor it.* **2** [C] small part of a population different from the rest: *minority rights / minority interest* (= supported by a small number of people) **3** [U] *law* state or time of being a minor

min·strel /'mɪnstrəl/ *n* traveling singer in former times

mint¹ /mɪnt/ *n* **1** [C] PEPPERMINT **2** [U] plant with leaves that smell fresh, used in food **-y** *adj*

mint² *n* **1** place where coins are made **2** make a mint earn a lot of money ♦ *vt* make (a coin) ♦ *adj* (of a stamp, coin, etc.) unused and in perfect condition

min·u·et /ˌmɪnyuˈwˠɛt/ *n* (music for) a slow graceful dance

mi·nus /'maɪnəs/ *prep* **1** made less by: *10 minus 4 is 6.* **2** below freezing point: *It was minus 10 today.* (= -10°) **3** *infml* without ♦ *n* also **minus sign** /'·· ·/ — a sign (-) showing a number less than zero, or that one number is to be taken away from another ♦ *adj* less than zero

min·us·cule, miniscule /'mɪnəˌskyuːl/ *adj* extremely small

min·ute¹ /'mɪnɪt/ *n* **1** 60th part of an hour **2** short time: *Wait a minute!* **3** 60th part of a degree of angle **4** short note of an official nature, such as on a report – see also MINUTES **5** **the minute (that)** as soon as

mi·nute² /maɪ'nuːt, -'nyuːt/ *adj* very small **-ness** [U]

min·utes /'mɪnɪts/ *n* [(the)P] written record of a meeting

mi·nu·ti·ae /maɪ'nuːʃiˠˌiˠ, -ˌaɪ, -'nyuː-/ *n* [P] small exact details

mir·a·cle /'mɪrəkəl/ *n* **1** unexplainable but wonderful act or event, esp. as done by a holy person: (fig.) *It's a miracle the explosion didn't kill her.* **2** wonderful example (of a quality, ability, etc.): *a miracle of modern science* **-culous** /mɪ'rækyələs/ *adj*

mi·rage /mɪ'rɑːʒ/ *n* something seen that is not really there, esp. as caused by the hot desert air

mire /maɪər/ *n* [U] *esp. lit* deep mud

mir·ror /'mɪrər/ *n* piece of glass in which one can see oneself ♦ *vt* show truly (as if) in a mirror

mirror im·age /'·· ˌ··/ *n* image in which the right side appears on the left, and the left side on the right

mirth /mɜrθ/ *n* [U] laughter

mis·ad·ven·ture /ˌmɪsəd'vɛntʃər/ *n* [C;U] *esp. lit* accident or piece of bad luck

mis·an·throp·ic /ˌmɪsən'θrɑpɪk/ *adj* disliking everyone **-ally** /-kliˠ/ *adv* **-ist** /mɪs'ænθrəpɪst/ *n*

mis·ap·pre·hen·sion /ˌmɪsæprɪ-ˈhenʃən, -tʃən/ n fml mistaken belief; misunderstanding

mis·ap·pro·pri·ate /ˌmɪsəˈprəʷprɪ-ˌeʲt/ vt take dishonestly (and use)

mis·be·have /ˌmɪsbɪˈheʲv/ vi/t behave (oneself) badly

misc. written abbrev. for: MISCEL-LANEOUS

mis·cal·cu·late /ˌmɪsˈkælkjəˌleʲt/ vi/t calculate wrongly; form a wrong judgment of something –**lation** /ˌmɪsˌkælkjəˈleʲʃən/ n

mis·car·riage /ˌmɪsˈkærɪdʒ, ˈmɪs-ˌkærɪdʒ/ n giving birth to a child too early for it to live

miscarriage of jus·tice /·ˌ···ˈ···, ˌ···· ˈ··/ n unjust legal decision

mis·car·ry /ˌmɪsˈkæriʲ/ vi **1** have a miscarriage **2** fml (of a plan) go wrong

mis·cel·la·ne·ous /ˌmɪsəˈleʲniʲəs◂/ adj of many different kinds

mis·cel·la·ny /ˈmɪsəˌleʲniʲ/ n mixture of various kinds

mis·chance /ˌmɪsˈtʃæns/ n [C;U] fml (piece of) bad luck

mis·chief /ˈmɪstʃɪf/ n **1** slightly bad behavior, esp. by children **2** damage; harm

mis·chie·vous /ˈmɪstʃəvəs/ adj **1** playfully troublesome **2** causing harm, esp. intentionally – **ly** adv

mis·con·ceive /ˌmɪskənˈsiʲv/ vt **1** make (a plan) badly **2** misunderstand

mis·con·cep·tion /ˌmɪskənˈsepʃən/ n case of wrong understanding

mis·con·duct /ˌmɪsˈkɑndʌkt/ n [U] fml bad behavior, esp. sexual

mis·con·struc·tion /ˌmɪskənˈstrʌk-ʃən/ n [C;U] wrong understanding

mis·deed /ˌmɪsˈdiʲd/ n fml wrong act

mis·de·mea·nor /ˌmɪsdɪˈmiʲnər/ n crime or wrong act which is not very serious

mi·ser /ˈmaɪzər/ n person who loves money and hates spending it ~ **liness** n [U] ~ **ly** adj

mis·e·ra·ble /ˈmɪzərəbəl/ adj **1** very unhappy **2** causing lack of cheerfulness: miserable weather **3** very low in quality or very small in amount: a few miserable pennies –**bly** adv

mis·e·ry /ˈmɪzəriʲ/ n [C;U] great unhappiness or suffering

mis·fire /ˌmɪsˈfaɪər/ vi **1** (of a gun) not fire properly **2** (of a plan or joke) not have the intended effect

mis·fit /ˈmɪsˌfɪt/ n someone who cannot live or work happily in their surroundings

mis·for·tune /mɪsˈfɔrtʃən/ n [C;U] **1** bad luck, esp. of a serious nature **2** very unfortunate event, condition, etc.

mis·giv·ing /mɪsˈgɪvɪŋ/ n [C;U] feeling that it might be better not to do a thing

mis·guid·ed /mɪsˈgaɪdɪd/ adj showing bad judgment; foolish ~ **ly** adv

mis·hap /ˈmɪshæp/ n slight unfortunate happening

mis·judge /ˌmɪsˈdʒʌdʒ/ vt judge wrongly, esp. form a wrong or unfairly bad opinion –**judgment** n [C;U]

mis·lay /mɪsˈleʲ/ vt –**laid** /-ˈleʲd/ lose for a short time

mis·lead /mɪsˈliʲd/ vt –**led** /-ˈled/ cause to think or act mistakenly

mis·man·age /ˌmɪsˈmænɪdʒ/ vt control or deal with (private, public or business affairs) badly ~ **ment** n [U]

mis·no·mer /ˌmɪsˈnoʷmər/ n unsuitable name

mi·so·gy·nist /mɪˈsɑdʒənɪst/ n person who hates women

mis·place /ˌmɪsˈpleʲs/ vt **1** put in the wrong place: (fig.) misplaced trust **2** mislay

mis·print /ˈmɪsˌprɪnt/ n mistake in printing

mis·rep·re·sent /ˌmɪsreprɪˈzent/ vt give an intentionally untrue account or explanation of ~ **ation** /ˌmɪsreprɪzenˈteʲʃən/ n [C;U]

miss¹ /mɪs/ v **1** vi/t fail to hit, catch, meet, see, hear, etc.: He shot at me, but missed. | I missed the train. | She narrowly missed being killed. **2** vt feel unhappy at the absence or loss of ♦ n failure to hit, etc. – see also NEAR MISS ~ **ing** adj not in the proper place; lost

miss out phr v vi lose a chance to gain advantage or enjoyment

miss² /mɪs/ n (usu. cap.) (title of a girl or unmarried woman): Miss Brown

mis·sile /ˈmɪsəl/ n **1** explosive flying weapon **2** object or weapon thrown: They threw bottles and other missiles at the police.

mis·sion /ˈmɪʃən/ n **1** special job, duty, or purpose: He felt his mission in life was to help others. | They were sent on a secret mission. **2** group of people sent abroad: a peace mission **3** place where missionaries work

mis·sion·a·ry /ˈmɪʃəˌneriʲ/ n person sent abroad to teach and spread religion

mis·sive /ˈmɪsɪv/ n fml or lit letter

mis·spent /ˌmɪsˈspent◂/ adj wasted

mist /mɪst/ n [C;U] thin FOG: (fig.) lost in the mists of time – **y** (fig.) misty memories

mis·take /mɪˈsteʲk/ v –**took** /mɪˈstʊk/, –**taken** /mɪˈsteʲkən/ **1** have a wrong idea about: He mistook my meaning. **2** fail to recognize ♦ n [C;U] something done through carelessness, lack of knowledge or skill, etc.: *I made a terrible mistake.* | *I did it by mistake.*

mistake for *phr vt* think wrongly that (a person or thing) is (someone or something else): *I mistook him for his brother.*

mis·tak·en /mɪ'steɪkən/ *adj* wrong; incorrect **– ly** *adv*

mis·tle·toe /'mɪsəl‚toʷ/ *n* [U] plant with white berries, used for Christmas decorations

mis·took /mɪ'stʊk/ *past t.* of MISTAKE

mis·tress /'mɪstrɪs/ *n* **1** woman in control **2** man's unmarried female sexual partner

mis·trust /mɪs'trʌst/ *vt* not trust ♦ *n* [U] lack of trust **– ful** *adj*

mis·un·der·stand /‚mɪsʌndər-'stænd/ *vi/t* **-stood** /-'stʊd/ understand wrongly **– ing** *n* [C;U] lack of correct understanding, esp. with slight disagreement

mit·i·gate /'mɪtə‚geɪt/ *vt fml* lessen the severity of **–gation** /‚mɪtə-'geɪʃən/ *n* [U]

mi·ter /'maɪtər/ *n* BISHOP's tall pointed hat

mitt /mɪt/ *n* type of protective mitten

mit·ten /'mɪtn/ *n* GLOVE without separate finger parts

mix /mɪks/ *vi/t* combine so that the parts no longer have a separate shape, appearance, etc.: *Oil and water don't mix.* | *Mix blue and yellow to make green.* | *She mixed herself a cocktail.* **2** *vi* be or enjoy being in the company of others **– ed** *adj* **1** of different kinds **2** for both sexes **3** mixed up in connected with (something bad) **– er** *n* ♦ *n* [C;U] MIXTURE (1): *cake mix*

mixed bag /‚· '·/ *n* [S] collection of things of many different kinds (and qualities)

mixed bles·sing /‚· '··/ *n* [S] something that is bad as well as good

mixed e·con·o·my /‚· ·'···/ *n* operation of a country's money supply, industry, and business by a mixture of principles from CAPITALISM and SOCIALISM

mixed met·a·phor /‚· '···/ *n* use of 2 METAPHORS together with a foolish or funny effect

mix·ture /'mɪkstʃər/ *n* **1** [C;U] set of substances (to be) mixed together **2** [S] combination: *a mixture of amusement and disbelief* **3** [U] act of mixing

mix-up /'· ·/ *n* state of disorder and confusion

mm *written abbrev. for* MILLIMETERS

mne·mon·ic /nɪ'mɑnɪk/ *adj, n* (something) used for helping one to remember

MO /‚ɛm 'oʷ/ **1** medical officer **2** MODUS OPERANDI

moan /moʷn/ *vi, n* (make a) **a** a low sound of pain **b** discontented complaint

moat /moʷt/ *n* long deep hole around esp. a castle usu. filled with water

mob /mɑb/ *n* **1** noisy (violent) crowd **2** group of criminals ♦ *vt* **-bb-** gather around a **a** to attack **b** because of interest or admiration

mo·bile /'moʷbəl/ *adj* (easily) movable; not fixed **–bility** /moʷ'bɪlətiʸ/ *n* [U]

mobile home /‚·· '·/ *n* long, narrow house on wheels

mo·bil·ize /'moʷbə‚laɪz/ *vt* bring into action, esp. ready for war **–ization** /‚moʷbələ'zeɪʃən/ *n* [U]

moc·ca·sin /'mɑkəsən/ *n* simple soft leather shoe

mock[1] /mɑk/ *vt* laugh at unkindly or unfairly

mock[2] *adj* not real; pretended: *a mock battle*

mock·e·ry /'mɑkəriʸ/ *n* **1** [U] mocking **2** [S] something unworthy of respect **3** make a mockery of show to be foolish or untrue

mock·ing·bird /'mɑkɪŋ‚bɜrd/ *n* bird that copies the songs of other birds

mock-up /'· ·/ *n* FULL-SIZE model of something to be built

mo·dal aux·il·ia·ry /‚moʷdl ɔg'zɪlyəriʸ, -'zɪləriʸ/ *n* verb that goes in front of another, such as *can, may,* or *would*

mode /moʷd/ *n* way of doing something

mod·el /'mɑdl/ *n* **1** small copy: *a model airplane* **2** person who models clothes **3** person to be painted or photographed **4** person or thing of the highest quality: *a model student* **5** type of vehicle, machine, weapon, etc.: *His car is the latest model.* ♦ *v* **-l-** **1** *vt* make a small copy **2** *vi/t* wear (clothes) to show them to possible buyers

model after *phr vt* form as a copy of: *She modeled herself after her mother.*

mo·dem /'moʷ‚dɛm/ *n* electronic apparatus for changing information from a form which a computer understands into a form which can be sent along a telephone line, etc., to another computer

mod·e·rate[1] /'mɑdərɪt/ *adj* **1** neither too much nor too little; middle **2** not politically extreme **– ly** *adv* not very **–ration** /‚mɑdə-'reɪʃən/ *n* [U] **1** self-control **2** reduction in force or degree **3** in moderation within sensible limits

mod·e·rate[2] /'mɑdə‚reɪt/ *vi/t* lessen in force, degree, etc.

mod·e·rate[3] /'mɑdərɪt/ *n* person whose opinions are MODERATE[1] (2)

mod·ern /'madərn/ adj 1 of the present time 2 new and different from the past ~ize v 1 vt make suitable for modern use 2 vi start using more modern methods ~ization /,madərnə'zeʸʃən/ n [C;U]

mod·est /'madıst/ adj 1 not too proud 2 not large 3 not sexually improper ~ly adv ~y n [U]

mod·i·cum /'madıkəm/ n small amount

mod·i·fy /'madə,faı/ vt 1 change, esp. slightly 2 make (a claim, condition, etc.) less hard to accept or bear 3 (esp. of an adjective or adverb) go with and describe (another word) –fication /,madəfə'keʸʃən/ n [C;U]

mod·u·late /'madʒə,leʸt/ vt vary the strength, nature, etc., of (a sound) –lation /,madʒə'leʸʃən/ n [C;U]

mod·ule /'madʒuʷl/ n 1 standard part used in building, making furniture, etc. 2 part of a spacecraft for independent use –ular /'madʒələr/ adj

mo·dus op·e·ran·di /,moʷdəs apə'rændiʸ/ n [S] method of doing something

modus vi·ven·di /,moʷdəs vı'vendiʸ/ n [S] way of living (together)

mo·gul /'moʷgəl/ n person of very great power and wealth, esp. in the film industry

mo·hair /'moʷhɛər/ n [U] (cloth from) the long silky hair of a sort of goat

Mo·ham·me·dan /moʷ'hæmədən/ n, adj Muslim

moist /mɔıst/ adj slightly wet ~en /'mɔısən/ vi/t make or become moist ~ure /'mɔıstʃər/ n [U] liquid in or on something ~urize vt remove the dryness from

mo·lar /'moʷlər/ n large back tooth

mo·las·ses /mə'læsız/ n [U] any of the sweet substances produced during the refining (REFINE) of sugar

mold¹ /moʷld/ n container into which a soft substance is poured, to take on the shape of the container when it sets ♦ vt shape or form (something solid): (fig.) *influences that molded her character* ~ing n [C;U] decorative stone, plastic, or wood band(s)

mold² n [U] soft often greenish growth on old food, etc. ~y adj: *moldy cheese*

mol·der /'moʷldər/ vi decay gradually

mole¹ /moʷl/ n small furry animal that lives underground

mole² n small, dark brown mark on the skin

mol·e·cule /'malə,kyuʷl/ n very small piece of matter, made of 2 or more atoms –cular /mə'lɛkyələr/ adj

mole·hill /'moʷl,hıl/ n small pile of earth thrown up by a mole – see also **make a mountain out of a mole-hill** (MOUNTAIN)

mo·lest /mə'lɛst/ vt 1 attack; harm 2 attack (esp. a woman or child) sexually

mol·li·fy /'malə,faı/ vt make less angry

mol·lusk /'maləsk/ n any of a class of limbless animals with soft bodies, usu. with a shell

mol·ly·cod·dle /'maliʸ,kadl/ vt take too much care of (a person or animal)

Mol·o·tov cock·tail /,malətəf 'kakteʸl, ,mɔl-/ n bottle filled with gasoline, used as a bomb

molt /moʷlt/ vi (of a bird or animal) lose most of its feathers, fur, etc.

mol·ten /'moʷltən/ adj (of metal or rock) melted

mom /mam/ n mother

mo·ment /'moʷmənt/ n 1 very short period of time 2 particular point in time 3 *fml* importance: *a matter of great moment* 4 **the moment (that)** as soon as ~ary adj lasting a moment ~arily /,moʷmən'tɛriliʸ/ adv 1 for just a very short time 2 very soon; in a moment

moment of truth /,··· '·/ n moment when something important will happen

mo·men·tous /moʷ'mentəs, mə-/ adj extremely important ~ness n [U]

mo·men·tum /moʷ'mentəm, mə-/ n [U] measurable quantity of movement in a body: (fig.) *The campaign had lost its momentum.*

mom·my /'mamiʸ/ n (child's word for) mother

mon·arch /'manərk, 'manark/ n non-elected ruler; king, queen, etc. ~y /'manərkiʸ/ n 1 [U] rule by a monarch 2 [C] country ruled by a monarch

mon·as·te·ry /'manəs,teriʸ/ n building in which MONKs live

mo·nas·tic /mə'næstık/ adj of MONKs or monasteries

Mon·day /'mʌndiʸ, -deʸ/ n the 1st day of the week, between Sunday and Tuesday

mon·e·ta·ris·m /'manətə,rızəm/ n [U] (in ECONOMICS) belief that the best way of controlling the ECONOMY of a country is to control its money supply -rist n, adj

mon·e·ta·ry /'manə,teriʸ/ adj of or about money

mon·ey /'maniʸ/ n [U] 1 something used for paying, esp. coins or paper notes **2** wealth: *We're in the money.* (= rich) **3 for my money** in my opinion **4 one's money's worth** full value for the money one has spent

money-grub·ber /ˈmʌniˌɡrʌbər/ *n* person unpleasantly determined to gain money

money order /ˈ·· ˌ··/ *n* check available at post offices that can be used as money

money-spin·ner /ˈ·· ˌ··/ *n* something that brings in a lot of money

money sup·ply /ˈ·· ·ˌ·/ *n* [*the*+S] all the money that exists and is being paid and spent in a country in the form of coins, notes, and CREDIT

mon·grel /ˈmʌŋɡrəl, ˈmʌn-/ *n* **1** dog of mixed breed **2** person or thing of mixed race or origin

mon·i·tor /ˈmɑnətər/ *vt* watch or listen to carefully for a special purpose ♦ *n* **1** television used to show the view seen by a television camera **2** instrument for monitoring a physical condition: *a heart monitor* **3** a SCREEN for use with a computer **a** SCREEN for use with a computer operation that make sure that the computer system is working properly **4** person who listens to foreign radio news, etc., and reports on its content

monk /mʌŋk/ *n* member of a male religious group that lives together

mon·key¹ /ˈmʌŋkiʸ/ *n* **1** small animal with a long tail, that climbs trees **2** *infml* child full of playful tricks **3 make a monkey (out) of someone** *infml* make someone appear foolish

monkey² *v* **monkey around** *phr vi* play foolishly

monkey busi·ness /ˈ·· ˌ··/ *n* [U] *infml* secret behavior which causes trouble

mon·o /ˈmɑnoʷ/ *adj* (of sound) coming from only one place: *a mono record* ♦ *n* MONONUCLEOSIS

mon·o·chrome /ˈmɑnəˌkroʷm/ *adj* **1** in only one color **2** in black and white only

mon·o·cle /ˈmɑnəkəl/ *n* LENS for one eye only, to help the sight

mo·nog·a·my /məˈnɑɡəmiʸ/ *n* [U] having only one husband or wife at a time –**mous** *adj*

mon·o·gram /ˈmɑnəˌɡræm/ *n* combined letters, esp. someone's INITIALS –**med** *adj*

mon·o·lith·ic /ˌmɑnlˈɪθɪk◂/ *adj* **1** like a large stone pillar **2** *often derog* forming a large unchangeable whole

mon·o·logue /ˈmɑnlˌɔɡ, -ˌɑɡ/ *n* long speech by one person

mon·o·nu·cle·o·sis /ˌmɑnoʷˌnuʷ-kliʸˈoʷsɪs, -ˌnyuʷ-/ *n* infectious

illness causing sleeping and fever

mo·nop·o·ly /məˈnɑpəliʸ/ *n* unshared control or right to do or produce something: (fig.) *He thinks he's got a monopoly on brains.* (=that he alone is clever) -**lize** *vt* keep unshared control of

mon·o·rail /ˈmɑnəˌreʸl/ *n* railroad with one RAIL

mon·o·sod·i·um glu·tam·ate /ˌmɑnəˌsoʷdiʸəm ˈɡluʷtəˌmeʸt/ *n* also **MSG** [U] chemical compound added to certain foods, to make their taste stronger

mon·o·syl·la·ble /ˈmɑnəˌsɪləbəl/ *n* word of one SYLLABLE –**bic** /ˌmɑnə-sɪˈlæbɪk◂/ *adj*

mon·o·tone /ˈmɑnəˌtoʷn/ *n* [S] way of speaking or singing in which the voice continues on the same note: *to speak in a monotone*

mo·not·o·ny /məˈnɑtniʸ/ *n* [U] dull sameness –**onous** *adj* dull; boring (BORE²) –**onously** *adv*

mon·soon /mɑnˈsuʷn/ *n* (time of) very heavy rains in and near India

mon·ster /ˈmɑnstər/ *n* **1** strange usu. large and frightening creature **2** very evil person ♦ *adj* unusually large: *a monster potato* – see also GREEN-EYED MONSTER

mon·stros·i·ty /mɑnˈstrɑsəṭiʸ/ *n* something very ugly and usu. large

mon·strous /ˈmɑnstrəs/ *adj* **1** extremely bad; shocking **2** unnaturally large, strange, etc. –**ly** *adv*

mon·tage /mɑnˈtɑʒ/ *n* [C;U] picture made from separate parts combined

Mon·te·rey Jack /ˌmɑntəreʸ ˈdʒæk/ *n* white slightly soft cheese used esp. for Mexican food

month /mʌnθ/ *n* 12th part of a year; ~**ly** *adj*

mon·u·ment /ˈmɑnyəmənt/ *n* **1** something built in honor of a person or event **2** historical old building or place **3** work, esp. a book, worthy of lasting fame ~**al** /ˌmɑnyəˈmen-təl◂/ *adj* **1** intended as a monument **2** very large **3** (esp. of something bad) very great in degree ~**ally** *adv* extremely

moo /muʷ/ *vi, n* (make) the sound of a cow

mooch /muʷtʃ/ *vt sl* get by asking **mooch from** *phr vt* get from someone by asking

mood¹ /muʷd/ *n* **1** state of feeling: *in a cheerful mood* **2** state of feeling in which one is bad-tempered or angry ~**y** *adj* often having bad moods ~**ily** *adv*

mood² *n* (in English) any of the three sets of verb forms that express **a** a fact or action (INDICATIVE), **b** a command (IMPERATIVE), or **c** a doubt, wish, etc. (SUBJUNCTIVE)

moon[1] /muːn/ n 1 large body that moves around the Earth and shines at night 2 body that moves around a PLANET other than the Earth – see also BLUE MOON

moon·beam /ˈmuːnbiːm/ n beam of light from the moon

moon·light[1] /ˈmuːnlaɪt/ [U] light of the moon

moonlight[2] vi -ed have a second job in addition to a regular one

moon·shine /ˈmuːnʃaɪn/ n WHISKEY made and sold secretly

moonshine n alcohol made illegally

moor /mʊər/ vi/t fasten (a boat) to land, etc., by means of ropes, etc. ~ings n [P] 1 ropes, ANCHORS, etc., for mooring 2 also **mooring** — place where a boat is moored

moose /muːs/ n moose large North American animal like a deer

moot point /ˌmuːt ˈpɔɪnt/ n 1 matter which is no longer important 2 undecided matter, on which people have different opinions

mop[1] /mɒp/ n 1 long stick with thick string or a SPONGE at one end, for washing floors 2 thick untidy mass of hair

mop[2] vt -pp- wash or dry (as if) with a mop: She mopped her brow.

mop up phr vt 1 remove liquid, dirt, etc., with a mop 2 finish dealing with: mop up small enemy groups

mope /moʊp/ vi be continuously sad

mo·ped /ˈmoʊˈpɛd/ n small motorcycle

mor·al /ˈmɒrəl, ˈmɑːrəl/ adj 1 of or based on the difference between good and evil or right and wrong: She has high moral principles. 2 pure and honest in character and behavior ♦ n lesson that can be learned from a story or event ~ize vi give one's opinions on right and wrong, esp. when unwelcome

morals n [P] standards of (sexual) behavior ~ity /məˈrælətiː/ n [U] rightness or pureness of behavior or of an action

mo·rale /məˈræl/ n [U] pride and confidence, esp. in relation to a job to be done

moral ma·jor·i·ty /ˌ··· ·ˈ···/ n [the+S] a movement that favors very severe Christian religious principles and is against political change

moral sup·port /ˌ··· ·ˈ·/ n [U] encouragement

mo·rass /məˈræs/ n [C] a situation that is difficult or impossible to escape from

mor·a·to·ri·um /ˌmɒrəˈtɔːriːəm, -ˈtoʊr-, ˌmɑːr-/ n -ria /-riːə/ official period during which a particular thing is not done

mor·bid /ˈmɔːrbɪd/ adj interested in death in an unhealthy way ~ly adv ~ity /mɔːrˈbɪdətiː/ n [U]

mor·dant /ˈmɔːrdnt/ adj fml cruel and cutting in speech

more[1] /mɔːr, moʊr/ adv 1 (forms COMPARATIVES): more difficult 2 to a greater degree: He likes this one more than that one. 3 again: Do it just once more.

more[2] determiner, pron (comparative of **many, much**) 1 a greater or additional number or quantity (of): He wants more food. | I can't eat any more. 2 **more and more** increasingly 3 **more or less: a** nearly **b** about

more·o·ver /mɔːrˈoʊvər, moʊr-/ adv fml in addition; besides

mo·res /ˈmɔːreɪz/ n [P] fml fixed moral customs in a social group

morgue /mɔːrg/ n place where dead bodies are kept until a funeral

mor·i·bund /ˈmɒrəbʌnd, ˈmɑː-/ adj completely inactive and near to the end of existence

morn·ing /ˈmɔːrnɪŋ/ n 1 time between sunrise and noon 2 **in the morning** tomorrow morning 3 **mornings** [P] in the morning: She works mornings.

morning-af·ter pill /ˌ··· ·ˈ· ˌ·/ n drug taken by mouth by a woman within 72 hours of having sex, to prevent her from having a baby

mo·ron /ˈmɔːrɒn, ˈmoʊrɑːn/ n derog very stupid person ~ic /məˈrɑːnɪk/ adj

mo·rose /məˈroʊs/ adj angry and silent ~ly adv

mor·phine /ˈmɔːrfiːn/ n [U] powerful drug for stopping pain

Morse code /ˌmɔːrs ˈkoʊd/ n [U] system of sending messages with letters represented by combinations of long and short signals

mor·sel /ˈmɔːrsəl/ n small piece, esp. of food

mor·tal /ˈmɔːrtl/ adj 1 that will die 2 of human beings 3 causing death: a mortal wound ♦ n human being ~ly adv 1 so as to cause death 2 very much: mortally offended ~ity /mɔːrˈtælətiː/ n [U] 1 rate or number of deaths 2 state of being mortal

mor·tar[1] /ˈmɔːrtər/ n [U] mixture of LIME, sand, and water, used in building

mortar[2] n 1 apparatus for firing small bombs 2 thick bowl in which things are crushed

mort·gage /ˈmɔːrgɪdʒ/ n 1 agreement to borrow money to buy esp. a house, which belongs to the lender until the money is repaid 2 the amount borrowed ♦ vt give up the ownership of (a house, etc.) for a time in return for money lent

mor·ti·cian /mɔr'tɪʃən/ UNDERTAKER

mor·ti·fy /'mɔrtə,faɪ/ vt make ashamed –**fication** /,mɔrtəfə'keɪ-ʃən/ n [U]

mor·tu·a·ry /'mɔrtʃuˈˌɛriʲ/ n 1 FUNERAL PARLOR 2 MORGUE

mo·sa·ic /mowˈzeɪɪk/ n pattern or picture formed by small pieces of colored stone or glass

Mos·lem /'mazləm, 'mas-/ n, adj Muslim

mosque /mask/ n building in which Muslims worship

mos·qui·to /məˈskiˈtoʷ/ n –**tos** or –**toes** small flying insect that sucks blood from whatever it bites

moss /mɔs/ n [U] (thick flat mass of) a small usu. green plant of wet places

most¹ /moʷst/ adv 1 (forms SUPER-LATIVES): the most difficult question 2 more than anything else: He likes bananas most of all. 3 fml very: I was most upset.

most² determiner, pron (superlative of **many, much**) 1 nearly all: Most people dislike him. 2 at (the) most not more than 3 for the most part mainly 4 make the most of get the best advantage from ~ **ly** adv mainly

mo·tel /moʷˈtɛl/ n hotel specially built for people traveling by car

moth /mɔθ/ n moths /mɔðz, mɔθs/ insect with large wings that flies mainly at night

moth·ball /'mɔθbɔl/ n 1 ball of chemical with a strong smell for keeping moths away from clothes 2 in mothballs stored and not used

moth·eat·en /'···,··/ adj 1 (of clothes) eaten by the young of moths 2 very worn out

moth·er /'mʌðər/ n 1 female parent 2 (usu. cap.) female head of a CON-VENT: mother superior ♦ vt care for or protect (too) lovingly –**hood** n [U] ~ **ly** adj like a good mother

mother coun·try /'··,··/ n country one was born in or came from originally

mother-in-law /'···,·/ n mothers-in-law wife's or husband's mother

mother-of-pearl /,··· ··'·/ n [U] shiny substance from inside certain shells, used for decoration

Mother's Day /'·· ,·/ n second Sunday in May, when mothers are celebrated

mother tongue /,·· '·/ n first language one spoke

mo·tif /moʷˈtiʲf/ n (repeated) artistic or musical pattern

mo·tion /'moʷʃən/ n 1 [U] act, way, or process of moving: the ship's rolling motion 2 [C] single movement 3 [C] suggestion formally made at a meeting 4 go through the motions do something without care or interest 5 put/set in motion start (a machine or process) ♦ vi/t signal or direct by a movement of esp. the hand ~ **less** adj unmoving

motion pic·ture /,·· '··/ n fml FILM (2): the motion picture industry

mo·ti·vate /'moʷtə,veʲt/ vt 1 give (someone) a (strong) reason for doing something; encourage 2 be the reason why (something) was done –**vation** /,moʷtə'veʲʃən/ n [U]

mo·tive /'moʷtɪv/ n reason for action

mot·ley /'matliʲ/ adj usu. derog. of many different kinds and qualities

mo·to·cross /'moʷtoʷˌkrɔs/ n [U] motorcycle racing across rough country

mo·tor /'moʷtər/ n machine that changes power into movement: an electric motor ♦ adj 1 driven by an engine: a motor boat 2 of cars, etc.: a motor mechanic 3 of movement: motor control ♦ vi go by car ~ **ist** n car driver

mo·tor·cycle /'moʷtər,saɪkəl/ n also **motorbike** /-ˌbaɪk/ infml — large heavy bicycle driven by an engine

motor lodge /'·· ,·/ n MOTEL

motor scoot·er /'·· ,··/ n SCOOTER (2)

mot·tled /'matld/ adj irregularly marked with colors and/or shapes

mot·to /'matoʷ/ n –**toes** or –**tos** phrase or short sentence used as a guiding principle

mound /maʊnd/ n 1 pile 2 small hill

mount¹ /maʊnt/ v 1 vi rise: Costs mounted. 2 vt get on (a horse, bicycle, etc.) 3 vt provide with a horse, etc.: the mounted police 4 vt prepare and produce: mount an exhibition/an attack 5 vt fix on a support or in a frame 6 vt go up; climb ♦ n animal for riding

mount² n (usu. cap.) (used before names of mountains): Mount Everest

moun·tain /'maʊntn/ n 1 very high rocky hill 2 very large amount 3 make a mountain out of a mole-hill make a problem seem more difficult than it is ~ **ous** adj 1 full of mountains 2 extremely large

moun·tain·eer /,maʊntn'ɪər/ n mountain climber ~ **ing** n [U]

Mountain time /'·· ,·/ n [U] the time used in the Rocky Mountain area of the US, two hours earlier than Eastern time

mourn /mɔrn, moʷrn/ vi/t feel or express grief (for), esp. when someone dies – **er** n – **ful** adj (too) sad ~ **ing** n [U] 1 grief 2 funeral clothes, usu. black

mouse /maʊs/ n **mice** /maɪs/ **1** furry animal with a long tail, like a rat but smaller **2** quiet nervous person **3** small box connected to a computer by a wire which, when moved by hand, causes a CURSOR to move around on a MONITOR (3) so that choices can be made within the PROGRAM in use **mousy** adj **1** (of a person) unattractively plain and quiet **2** (of hair) dull brown

mous·er /ˈmaʊsər/ n cat skilled at catching mice

mousse /muːs/ n [C;U] **1** sweet dish made from cream and eggs **2** FOAM used in hair to hold a style

mous·tache /ˈmʌstæʃ, məˈstæʃ/ n hair on the upper lip

mouth¹ /maʊθ/ n **mouths** /maʊðz/ **1** opening in the face for eating and speaking **2** opening; entrance: *the mouth of the cave* **3 down in the mouth** not cheerful **4 keep one's mouth shut** keep silent

mouth² /maʊð/ vt **1** say by moving the lips soundlessly **2** repeat without understanding or sincerity

mouth·ful /ˈmaʊθfʊl/ n **1** amount put into the mouth **2** long word or phrase, difficult to say

mouth·piece /ˈmaʊθpiːs/ n **1** part of a musical instrument, telephone, etc., held in or near the mouth **2** person, newspaper, etc., that only expresses the opinions of others

mouth-wa·ter·ing /ˈ··,····/ adj (of food) very attractive

move¹ /muːv/ v **1** vi/t (cause to) change place or position: *Sit still and don't move!* **2** vi act: *I had to move fast to clinch the deal.* **3** vi change one's home **4** vt cause to have strong feelings, esp. of pity: *a very moving story* **5** vi/t make (a formal suggestion) at a meeting ~**ment** n **1** [C;U] (act of) moving: *Police are watching his movements.* (= activities) **2** [C] group of people in a united effort: *a religious movement* – see also WOMEN'S MOVEMENT **3** [C] separate part of a large piece of music

move in phr vi **1** take possession of a new home **2** (prepare to) take control, attack, etc.

move on phr v **1** vi change (to something new) **2** vi/t go away to another place or position

move out phr vi leave one's former home

move over phr vi change position in order to make room for someone or something else

move² n **1** change of position or place, esp. in games like CHESS **2** set of actions to bring about a result: *new moves to settle the dispute* **3 get a move on** infml hurry up **4 make**

a move: a (start to) leave **b** begin to take action **5 on the move: a** travelling around **b** having started to move or happen

mov·ie /ˈmuːviː/ n FILM(2) **movies** n [the+P] CINEMA: *What's on at the movies? Let's go to the movies.*

movie star /ˈ·· ,·/ n popular actor or actress often seen in films

mow /moʊ/ vt **mowed**, **mowed** or **mown** /moʊn/ cut (grass, corn, etc.) ~**er** n

mow down phr vt knock down or kill, esp. in large numbers

mpg written abbrev. for: miles per GALLON

mph written abbrev. for: miles per hour

Mr. /ˈmɪstər/ n (ordinary man's title): *Mr. Smith*

Mrs. /ˈmɪsɪz/ n (married woman's title)

Ms. /mɪz/ n (unmarried or married woman's title)

MSG /ˌem es ˈdʒiː/ n [U] MONOSODIUM GLUTAMATE

Mt. written abbrev. for: MOUNT²

much¹ /mʌtʃ/ adv **1** a lot: *much better* | *much too small* **2** to the stated degree: *I liked it very much.* | *She would so much like to go.* **3** in most ways: *much the same as usual*

much² determiner, pron more, most **1** large amount or part (of): *He gave me too much cake.* | *How much is it?* (= What does it cost?) | *I didn't get much.* | (fig.) *I don't think much of that.* (= I have a low opinion of it) **2 I thought as much** I had expected that the stated usu. bad thing would happen **3 make much of: a** treat as important **b** understand **4 much as** although **5 not much of a** not a very good **6 not up to much** not very good **7 so much for** that is the end of **8 too much for** too difficult to

muck¹ /mʌk/ n [U] **1** dirt **2** worthless or improper material **3** MANURE ~**y** adj

muck² v

muck out /ˌ· ·ˈ·/ phr vt clean (room an animal lives in)

muck·rak·ing /ˈmʌk-reɪkɪŋ/ n [U] derog finding and telling unpleasant stories about famous or important people ~**ing** adj ~**er** n

mu·cous mem·brane /ˌmjuːkəs ˈmembreɪn/ n [U] smooth wet skin, as inside the mouth

mu·cus /ˈmjuːkəs/ n [U] slippery body liquid, as produced in the nose

mud /mʌd/ n [U] **1** very wet earth **2 one's name is mud** one is spoken badly of after causing trouble ~**dy** adj

mud·dle¹ /ˈmʌdl/ n state of confusion and disorder

muddle² /vt/ **1** put into disorder **2** confuse the mind of

muddle along /phr vi/ continue confusedly, with no plan

muddle through /phr vi/ succeed in spite of having no plan or good method

mud·pack /'mʌdpæk/ n health treatment in which mud is put on the face

mud·sling·ing /'mʌd,slɪŋɪŋ/ n attempt to persuade voters not to vote for an opponent by saying bad things about that person

mues·li /'myuˀzliˀ/ n [U] breakfast dish of grain, nuts, fruit, etc., with milk

muff¹ /mʌf/ n fur or cloth cover to keep the hands or ears warm

muff² /vt/ spoil a chance to do (something) well

muffin /'mʌfɪn/ n type of small cake, often made with fruit, etc.

muf·fle /'mʌfəl/ vt make (sound) less easily heard

muf·fler /'mʌflər/ n **1** woollen piece of clothing worn to keep one's neck warm **2** (a car) apparatus for reducing noise

mug¹ /mʌg/ n **1 a** large drinking cup with straight sides and a handle **b** the contents of this: *a mug of coffee* **2** sl face

mug² /vt –gg–/ rob violently ~**ger** n

mug·gy /'mʌgiˀ/ adj (of weather) unpleasantly warm with heavy wet air

mug·wump /'mʌg-wʌmp/ n derog person who tries to be independent of the leaders in politics

Mu·ham·ma·dan /muˈhæmədən, mo°-/ adj, n MUSLIM

mu·lat·to /məˈlætoʊ, -ˈlɑ-, myuˀ-/ n –tos or –toes lit person with one black parent and one white parent

mule /myuˀl/ n animal that is the young of a donkey and a horse **mulish** adj unwilling to change or agree; STUBBORN

mull /mʌl/ vt heat (wine) with sugar, SPICES, etc.

mull over /phr vt/ consider carefully

mul·ti·far·i·ous /ˌmʌltəˈfeəriˀəs◂/ adj fml of many different types

mul·ti·lat·e·ral /ˌmʌltɪˈlætərəl◂/ adj including more than 2 groups, countries, etc. **–ly** adv

mul·ti·na·tion·al /ˌmʌltɪˈnæʃənəl◂/ adj having factories, offices, etc., in many different countries **multinational** n

mul·ti·ple /'mʌltəpəl/ adj of many different types or parts ♦ n number which contains a smaller number an exact number of times: *Please order in multiples of 10.*

multiple scle·ro·sis /ˌ··· ·ˈ··/ n [U] serious nerve disease in which one can no longer control one's physical movements and actions

mul·ti·pli·ci·ty /ˌmʌltəˈplɪsətiˀ/ n [S;U] large number or great variety

mul·ti·ply /'mʌltə,plaɪ/ v **1** vt add (a number) to itself the stated number of times: *2 multiplied by 3 is 6.* **2** vi/t increase in number or amount **3** vi breed **–plication** /ˌmʌltəpləˈkeɪʃən/ n [C;U]

mul·ti·tude /'mʌltə,tuˀd, -,tyuˀd/ n **1** large number **2** large crowd

mum¹ /mʌm/ n infml CHRYSANTHEMUM

mum² adj infml not saying or telling anything: *Mum's the word.* (= silence must/will be kept about this)

mum·ble /'mʌmbəl/ vi/t speak or say unclearly

mum·bo jum·bo /ˌmʌmboʊ ˈdʒʌmboʊ/ n [U] derog meaningless talk or actions, esp. in religion

mum·mi·fy /'mʌmə,faɪ/ vt preserve as a MUMMY

mum·my /'mʌmiˀ/ n dead body preserved from decay, esp. in ancient Egypt

mumps /mʌmps/ n [U] infectious illness with swelling in the throat

munch /mʌntʃ/ vi/t eat (something hard) with a strong jaw movement

munch·ies /'mʌntʃiˀz/ n [P] **1** small pieces of food eaten between meals **2** feeling of hunger for these

mun·dane /mʌnˈdeɪnˀ/ adj ordinary; with nothing exciting or interesting in it

mu·ni·ci·pal /myuˀˈnɪsəpəl/ adj of a town or its local government

mu·ni·ci·pal·i·ty /myuˀˌnɪsəˈpæl-ətiˀ/ n town, city, etc., with its own local government

mu·nif·i·cent /myuˀˈnɪfəsənt/ adj fml very generous **–cence** n [U]

mu·ni·tions /myuˀˈnɪʃənz/ n [P] bombs, guns, etc.; war supplies

mu·ral /'myuərəl/ n painting done directly on a wall

mur·der /'mɜrdər/ n [C;U] **1** crime of killing someone intentionally **2** very difficult or tiring experience – see also BLOODY MURDER ♦ vt kill illegally and intentionally ~**er** n ~**ous** adj **1** intending or likely to cause murder **2** violent (in appearance)

murk·y /'mɜrkiˀ/ adj unpleasantly dark

mur·mur /'mɜrmər/ n **1** [C] soft low continuous sound **2** [S] complaint ♦ vi/t make or express in a murmur: *She murmured her approval.*

Mur·phy's Law /ˌmɜrfiˀz ˈlɔ/ n [S] idea that anything that can go wrong will go wrong

mus·cle¹ /ˈmʌsəl/ n 1 [C;U] (one of) the pieces of elastic material in the body which can tighten to produce movement 2 [U] strength 3 **not move a muscle** stay very still

muscle² v **muscle in** phr vi force one's way into (esp.) a group activity, so as to gain a share in what is produced

muscle-bound /ˈ·· ·/ adj having large stiff muscles

mus·cu·lar /ˈmʌskyələr/ adj 1 of muscles 2 with large muscles; strong

muse¹ /myuʷz/ vi think deeply

muse² n 1 (often cap.) any of 9 ancient Greek goddesses representing an art or science 2 force or person that seems to help someone write, paint, etc.

mu·se·um /myuʷˈziʸəm/ n building where objects of historical, scientific, or artistic interest are kept and shown

mush /mʌʃ/ n [U] soft mass of half liquid, half solid material –**y** adj

mush·room /ˈmʌʃruʷm, -rʊm/ n type of FUNGUS that is often eaten ♦ vi grow and develop fast

mu·sic /ˈmyuʷzɪk/ n [U] 1 sounds arranged in patterns, usu. with tunes 2 art of making music 3 printed representation of music 4 **face the music** admit to blame, responsibility, etc., and accept the results, esp. punishment or difficulty –**ian** /myuʷˈzɪʃən/ n

mu·sic·al /ˈmyuʷzɪkəl/ adj 1 of music 2 skilled at music ♦ n play or film with songs and usu. dances –**ly** /-kliʸ/ adv

musical chairs /ˌ··· ˈ·/ n [U] party game in which people have to find seats when the music stops

music hall /ˈ·· ·/ n [C] hall for musical entertainment

musk /mʌsk/ n [U] substance with a strong smell used in PERFUMEs ~**y** adj

mus·ket /ˈmʌskɪt/ n early type of gun with a long BARREL

Mus·lim /ˈmʌzləm, ˈmʊz-, ˈmʊs-/ n, adj (follower) of the religion started by Mohammed

mus·lin /ˈmʌzlɪn/ n [U] very fine thin cotton

mus·sel /ˈmʌsəl/ n sea animal with a black shell, often eaten

must /məst; strong mʌst/ vi 3rd person sing. **must 1** (shows what is necessary): It's an order; you must obey. **2** (shows what is certain): You must be cold. ♦ n /mʌst/ something that should be done, seen, etc.

mus·tache /ˈmʌstæʃ, məˈstæʃ/ n MOUSTACHE

mus·tang /ˈmʌstæŋ/ n wild horse

mus·tard /ˈmʌstərd/ n [U] yellow or brown substance with a hot taste, made from a plant and usu. eaten with meat

mus·ter /ˈmʌstər/ vt gather; collect

must·n't /ˈmʌsənt/ short for: must not

must·y /ˈmʌstiʸ/ adj with an unpleasant smell as if old –**iness** n [U]

mu·tant /ˈmyuʷtnt/ n creature having a strange, ABNORMAL shape

mu·ta·tion /myuʷˈteʸʃən/ n [C;U] (example or result of) a process of change in living cells, causing a new part or type

mute /myuʷt/ adj not speaking or spoken; silent ♦ n 1 person who cannot speak 2 object put on or in a musical instrument to make it sound softer –**ly** adv **muted** adj (of sound or color) softer than usual

mu·ti·late /ˈmyuʷtl̩ˌeʸt/ vt wound and make ugly or useless –**lation** /ˌmyuʷtl̩ˈeʸʃən/ n [C;U]

mu·ti·neer /ˌmyuʷtn̩ˈɪər/ n person who mutinies

mu·ti·ny /ˈmyuʷtn̩-iʸ/ n [C;U] (an example of) the act of taking power from the person in charge, esp. on a ship –**nous** adj 1 taking part in a mutiny 2 eagerly disobedient –**nously** adv ♦ vi take part in a mutiny

mutt /mʌt/ n dog of no particular breed

mut·ter /ˈmʌtər/ vi/t speak or say quietly and unclearly

mut·ton /ˈmʌtn̩/ n [U] meat from a sheep

mu·tu·al /ˈmyuʷtʃuʷəl/ adj 1 equal for both sides: their mutual dislike (= they dislike each other) 2 shared by both: mutual interests/friends ~**ly** adv

mutual fund /ˌ··· ˈ·/ n company through which one can buy STOCK in various other companies

mu·zak /ˈmyuʷzæk/ n [U] tdmk recorded music played continuously though usu. not loudly in restaurants, etc.

muz·zle /ˈmʌzəl/ n 1 animal's nose and mouth 2 covering for an animal's muzzle, to stop it biting 3 front end of a gun barrel ♦ vt 1 put a muzzle on (an animal) 2 force to keep silent

my /maɪ/ determiner of me: my parents ♦ interj (expresses surprise)

my·o·pi·a /maɪˈoʷpiʸə/ n [U] inability to see distant objects clearly –**pic** /maɪˈɑpɪk/ adj

myr·i·ad /ˈmɪriʸəd/ n, adj large and varied number (of)

my·self /maɪˈself/ pron 1 (reflexive form of I): I hurt myself. **2** (strong form of I): I'll do it myself. **3** (in) my usual state of mind or body: *I'm not myself today.* (= I feel ill) **4 (all) by myself: a** alone **b** without help **5 to myself** not shared

mys·te·ry /ˈmɪstəriʸ/ *n* **1** [C] something which cannot be explained or understood **2** [U] strange secret quality **–rious** /mɪˈstɪəriʸəs/ *adj* **1** unexplainable: *his mysterious disappearance* **2** hiding one's intentions **–riously** *adv* **-riousness** *n* [U]

mys·tic /ˈmɪstɪk/ *n* person who practices mysticism

mys·ti·cis·m /ˈmɪstəˌsɪzəm/ *n* gaining of secret religious knowledge

mystical, mystic *adj* **mystically** /-kliʸ/ *adv*

mys·ti·fy /ˈmɪstəˌfaɪ/ *vt* cause (someone) to wonder or be unsure: *her mystifying disappearance*

mys·tique /mɪˈstiʸk/ *n* special quality that makes a person or thing seem mysterious and different, esp. causing admiration

myth /mɪθ/ **1** story from ancient times **2** widely believed false story or idea **~ical** *adj* **1** of myths **2** not real

my·thol·o·gy /mɪˈθɑlədʒiʸ/ *n* [U] myths: *heroes of Greek mythology* **–gical** /ˌmɪθəˈlɑdʒɪkəl◂/ *adj*

N

N, n /ɛn/ the 14th letter of the English alphabet

N *written abbrev. for:* north(ern)

nab /næb/ *vt* -**bb**- *sl* **1** ARREST **2** get; take

na·dir /ˈneɪdɪər, -dər/ *n* lowest point of misfortune, failure, etc.

nag[1] /næg/ *vi/t* -**gg**- continuously complain (at) ~**ging** *adj* continuously hurting or worrying: *a nagging headache*

nag[2] *n* old horse

nail[1] /neɪl/ *n* **1** thin pointed piece of metal for hammering into a piece of wood **2** hard flat piece at the end of each finger and toe **3 hard as nails** without any tender feelings **4 hit the nail on the head** do or say exactly the right thing

nail[2] *vt* **1** fasten with a nail **2** *sl* catch; trap

nail down *phr vt* force to tell plans or wishes clearly

nail-bit·ing /ˈ· ˌ··/ *adj* causing excitement and anxiety

nail pol·ish /ˈ· ˌ··/ *n* [U] liquid for giving a hard shiny surface on finger and toe nails

na·ive /naɪˈiːv/ *adj* **1** without experience of life **2** too willing to believe without proof ~**ly** *adv* ~**ty** /naɪˈiːvəṭi/ *n* [U] quality of being naive

na·ked /ˈneɪkɪd/ *adj* **1** with no clothes on **2** uncovered: *a naked light* | (fig.) *the naked truth* **3 with the naked eye** without a microscope, TELESCOPE, etc. ~**ness** *n* [U]

nam·by-pam·by /ˌnæmbiˈ ˈpæmbiˈ◄/ *adj* too weak, childish, or easily frightened

name /neɪm/ *n* **1** [C] what someone (or something) is called: *Her name is Mary.* **2** [C] usu. offensive title for someone: *to call someone names* **3** [S;C] opinion others have of one; REPUTATION: *The restaurant has a good name.* | *He made a name for himself* (= became famous) *in show business.* **4** [C] *sl* famous or important person: *There were several big names* (= famous people) *at the party.* **5 in name only** in appearance or by title but not in fact **6 in the name of** by the right or power of: *Open up, in the name of the law!* **7 the name of the game** quality or object which is most necessary or important **8 to one's name** (of money) as one's property: *He hasn't a penny to his name.* ♦ *vt* **1** give a

name to: *They named their daughter Mary.* **2** say what the name of (someone or something) is: *Can you name this plant?* **3** appoint; choose ~**less** *adj* **1** whose name is not known or told **2** too terrible to mention ~**ly** *adv* and that is/they are: *There are two factors, namely cost and availability.*

name·drop /ˈneɪmdrɑp/ *vi* -**pp**- mention famous people as if one knew them well ~**per** *n*

name·sake /ˈneɪmseɪk/ *n* person with the same name

nan·ny /ˈnæniˈ/ *n* woman employed to take care of children

nanny goat /ˈ·· ·/ *n* female goat

nap[1] /næp/ *n* short sleep ♦ *vi* **1** have a nap **2 catch someone napping** find or take advantage of someone unprepared

nap[2] *n* soft furry surface of cloth

na·palm /ˈneɪpɑm, -pɑlm/ *n* [U] fiercely burning gasoline jelly, used in bombs

nape /neɪp/ *n* back (of the neck)

nap·kin /ˈnæpkɪn/ *n* piece of cloth or paper used at meals for protecting clothes and cleaning the lips and fingers

nar·cis·sis·m /ˈnɑrsəˌsɪzəm/ *n* [U] too great love for one's own appearance or abilities ~**sist** *n* ~**sistic** /ˌnɑrsəˈsɪstɪk◄/ *adj*

nar·cot·ic /nɑrˈkɑṭɪk/ *n* drug that produces sleep, harmful in large amounts

nar·rate /ˈnæreɪt, næˈreɪt/ *vt* tell (a story) or describe (events) ~**rator** *n* ~**ration** /næˈreɪʃən/ *n* [C;U]

nar·ra·tive /ˈnærəṭɪv/ *n* **1** [C;U] *fml* story **2** [U] art of narrating

nar·row[1] /ˈnæroʷ/ *adj* **1** small from one side to the other **2** limited **3** only just successful: *a narrow escape* **4** not open to new ideas: *a narrow mind* – see also STRAIGHT AND NAR- ROW ~**ly** *adv* only just ~**ness** *n* [U]

nar·row[2] *vi/t* become or make narrower

narrow down *phr vt* reduce, limit

narrow-mind·ed /ˌ··· ˈ···◄/ *adj* unwilling to respect the opinions of others when different from one's own ~**ness** *n* [U]

na·ry /ˈneəriˈ/ *adj* usu. *humor* not one single: *nary a person in sight*

na·sal /ˈneɪzəl/ *adj* of the nose

nas·cent /ˈnæsənt/ *adj* starting to develop

nas·ty /ˈnæstiˈ/ *adj* **1** not nice; unpleasant **2** dangerous or painful: *a nasty cut* ~**tily** *adv* ~**tiness** *n* [U]

na·tion /ˈneɪʃən/ *n* (all the people belonging to) a country

na·tion·al /ˈnæʃənəl/ *adj* **1** of or being a nation, esp. as opposed to a any of its parts: *a national news-paper* (= one read everywhere in the country) **b** another nation or other nations: *The national news comes after the international news.* **2** owned or controlled by the central government of a country: *a national bank | the National Weather Service* ♦ *n* person from a usu. stated country **~ly** *adv* **~ism** *n* [U] **1** love of and pride in one's country **2** desire to become a separate independent country **~ist** *adj, n* **~istic** /,næʃə-nəlʔıstık◂/ *adj* showing too great nationalism **~ity** /,næʃəʔnælʔtiʲ/ *n* [U] being from a particular country: *a man of Italian nationality*

National Guard /,··· ʼ·ʼ/ *n* state military forces that become part of the army in time of war

na·tion·al·ize /ʹnæʃənəl,aız/ *vt* take (a business or industry) into government control **-ization** /,næʃənələʹzeʲʃən/ *n* [U]

na·tion·wide /,neʲʃənʹwaıd◂/ *adj, adv* happening over the whole country

na·tive /ʹneʲt̬ıv/ *adj* **1** of or being one's place of birth **2** found naturally in a place: *native species* **3** not learned: *native ability* ♦ *n* **1** person born in a place **2** local person **3** native animal or plant

Native A·mer·i·can /,··· ·ʼ···/ *n* member of the peoples living in the Americas before European settlers came

Na·tiv·i·ty /nəʹtıvətiʲ/ *n* the birth of Christ

NATO /ʹneʲt̬oʷ/ *n* the North Atlantic Treaty Organization; a group of countries which give military help to each other

nat·ty /ʹnætiʲ/ *adj sl* neat in appearance **-tily** *adv: nattily dressed*

nat·u·ral /ʹnætʃərəl/ *adj* **1** existing or happening ordinarily in the world, esp. not made by people: *death from natural causes* **2** usual: *It's natural to feel nervous.* **3** existing from birth; not learned: *a natural talent* **4** having natural skill: *a natural musician* **5** ordinary; not AFFECTED ♦ *n* person with natural skill **~ly** *adv* **1** as a natural skill: *Swimming comes naturally to her.* **2** in an ordinary way **3** of course **~ist** *n* person who studies animals and plants **~istic** /,nætʃərəʹlıstık◂/ *adj* showing things exactly as they are: *a naturalistic painting* **~istically** /-kliʲ/ *adv*

nat·u·ral·ize /ʹnætʃərə,laız/ *vt* make (someone born elsewhere) a citizen of a country **-ization** /,nætʃərələ-ʹzeʲʃən/ *n* [U]

natural his·to·ry /,··· ʼ···/ *n* [U] study of animals and plants

natural se·lec·tion /,··· ·ʼ·/ *n* [U] process by which creatures well suited to their conditions live and those less well suited die

na·ture /ʹneʲtʃər/ *n* **1** [U] everything that exists in the world independently of people, such as animals and plants, the land, and the weather **2** [C;U] character: *She has a very kind nature.* – see also SECOND NATURE **3** [S] *fml* kind; sort

naugh·ty /ʹnɔtiʲ/ *adj* **1** (esp. of a child) behaving badly **2** sexually improper **-tily** *adv* **-tiness** *n* [U]

nau·se·a /ʹnɔziʲə, ʹnɔʒə, ʹnɔsiʲə, ʹnɔʃəl/ *n* [U] feeling of sickness and desire to VOMIT **-ate** /ʹnɔziʲeʲt, -ʒiʲ-, -siʲ-, -ʃiʲ-/ *vt* cause to feel nausea: *(fig.) nauseating hypocrisy*

nau·ti·cal /ʹnɔtıkəl/ *adj* of ships or sailing

na·val /ʹneʲvəl/ *adj* of a navy or fighting ships

nave /neʲv/ *n* long central part of a church

na·vel /ʹneʲvəl/ *n* small sunken place in the middle of the stomach

nav·i·ga·ble /ʹnævıgəbəl/ *adj* (of a river, etc.) deep and wide enough to let ships pass

nav·i·gate /ʹnævə,geʲt/ *vi/t* direct the course of (a ship, aircraft, etc., or a car) **-gator** *n* **-gation** /,nævə-ʹgeʲʃən/ *n* [U]

na·vy /ʹneʲviʲ/ *n* ships and sailors for fighting

navy blue /,·· ʼ·◂/ *n* [U] dark blue

NB (used in writing) take notice of (this)

NCO /,ɛn siʲ ʼoʷ/ *n* NON-COMMISSIONED OFFICER

near /nıər/ *adj* **1** at a short distance; close: *Christmas / My office is near.* **2** nearest and dearest one's family ♦ *adv, prep* not far (from): *Don't go near the edge.* ♦ *vi/t* come closer (to) **~ly** *adv* **1** almost **2** not nearly not at all **~ness** *n* [U]

near·by /,nıərʹbaı◂/ *adj, adv* near

Near East /,· ʼ·/ *n* [the+S] countries around the Eastern Mediterranean Sea, including Turkey and North Africa

near miss /,· ʼ·/ *n* something that comes close to succeeding or (of a bomb) hitting

near·sight·ed /,nıərʹsaıtıd◂, ʹnıər-,saıtıd/ *adj* unable to see distant things clearly **-ness** *n* [U]

neat /niʲt/ *adj* **1** tidy **2** simple and effective: *a neat trick* **3** pleasing: *a really neat new car* **4** (of an alcoholic drink) with no water, etc., added **~ly** *adv* **~ness** *n* [U]

neb·u·lous /ʹnɛbyələs/ *adj* not clear, esp. in meaning or expression **~ly** *adv*

ne·ces·sa·ry /'nɛsə,sɛri/ adj that is needed or must be done –**rily** adv in a way that must be so: *Food that looks good doesn't necessarily taste good.*

ne·ces·si·tate /nə'sɛsə,teɪt/ vt fml make necessary

ne·ces·si·ty /nə'sɛsəti/ n 1 [S;U] condition of being necessary; need: *There's no necessity to stay.* 2 [C] something necessary, esp. for life

neck¹ /nɛk/ n 1 part of the body joining the head to the shoulders 2 part of a garment that goes around this 3 narrow part sticking out from a broader part: *the neck of a bottle* 4 **neck and neck** doing equally well in a competition 5 **neck of the woods** infml area or part of the country 6 **up to one's neck (in)** deeply concerned (with or by): *He's up to his neck in debt.* (= he owes a lot of money)

neck² vi infml kiss and CUDDLE

neck·lace /'nɛk-lɪs/ n decorative chain or string of jewels, worn around the neck

neck·tie /'nɛktaɪ/ n TIE¹ (1)

nec·tar /'nɛktər/ n [U] 1 sweet liquid collected by bees from flowers 2 sweet drink that tastes wonderful

née /neɪ/ adj (used to show a woman's name before she married): *Sheila Smith, née Brown*

need¹ /niːd/ n 1 [S;U] condition in which something necessary or desirable is missing: *a need for better medical services* 2 [S;U] necessary duty: *There's no need for you to come.* 3 [C] something one must have 4 [U] state of lacking food, money, etc.: *children in need* 5 **if need be** if necessary ~**less** adj 1 unnecessary 2 **needless to say** of course ~**lessly** adv ~**y** adj poor

need² vt have a need for; want: *To survive, plants need water.*

need³ v have to; must: *Do you think I need to go to the meeting?*

nee·dle /'niːdl/ n 1 thin pointed pin or rod used in sewing or knitting (KNIT) 2 something long, thin, and sharp, such as a leaf, a pointer on a compass, or the part of a HYPODERMIC which is pushed into someone's skin 3 STYLUS ♦ vt annoy

nee·dle·work /'niːdl,wɜrk/ n [U] decorative sewing

ne'er-do-well /'nɛər duːˌwɛl/ n lit useless lazy person

ne·far·i·ous /nɪ'fɛəriəs/ adj fml wicked ~**ly** adv

ne·gate /nɪ'geɪt/ vt cause to have no effect **negation** /nɪ'geɪʃən/ n [U]

neg·a·tive /'nɛgətɪv/ adj 1 saying or meaning 'no': *a negative reply* 2 not useful or encouraging: *negative advice* 3 less than zero 4 (of electricity) of the type carried by ELECTRONS ♦ n 1 word, expression, or statement saying or meaning 'no': *The answer was in the negative.* 2 film showing dark areas as light and light as dark

ne·glect /nɪ'glɛkt/ vt 1 give too little attention or care to 2 fail (to do something) esp. because of carelessness ♦ n [U] neglecting or being neglected ~**ful** adj tending to neglect things ~**fully** adv ~**fulness** n [U]

neg·li·gee /ˌnɛglɪ'ʒeɪ, 'nɛglɪˌʒeɪ/ n light thin NIGHTGOWN

neg·li·gent /'nɛglɪdʒənt/ adj not taking enough care ~**ly** adv –**gence** n [U]

neg·li·gi·ble /'nɛglɪdʒəbəl/ adj too slight or unimportant to worry about

ne·go·ti·a·ble /nɪ'goʊʃiʲəbəl, -ʃəbəl/ adj 1 that can be settled or changed by being negotiated 2 infml that can be traveled through, along, etc.

ne·go·ti·ate /nɪ'goʊʃiʲeɪt/ v 1 vi/t talk to someone in order to try to get (an agreement) 2 vt travel safely along or through –**ator** n –**ation** /nɪˌgoʊʃiʲ'eɪʃən/ n [C;U]

Ne·gro /'niʲgroʷ/ **Negress** /'niʲgrɪs/ fem. — n –**es** tech or not polite black person

neigh /neɪ/ vi, n (make) the sound of a horse

neigh·bor /'neɪbər/ n someone who lives next door, or near ~**hood** n 1 area in a town 2 the area around a point or place: (fig.) *a price in the neighborhood of* (= about) *$500* ~**ing** adj (of a place) near ~**ly** adj friendly

nei·ther /'niːðər, 'naɪ-/ determiner, pron, conj not one and not the other: *Neither book/Neither of the books is very good.* ♦ adv also not: *I can't swim and neither can my brother.*

nem·e·sis /'nɛməsɪs/ n [U] lit (force bringing) just and unavoidable punishment

ne·o·clas·si·cal /ˌniʲoʷ'klæsɪkəl/ adj done recently, but in the style of ancient Greece and Rome

ne·o·co·lo·ni·al·is·m /ˌniʲoʷkə'loʷniʲəˌlɪzəm/ n [U] derog indirect control of smaller countries by more powerful ones

ne·o·lith·ic /ˌniʲə'lɪθɪk/ adj of a period about 10,000 years ago

ne·ol·o·gis·m /niʲ'ɑləˌdʒɪzəm/ n new word or expression

ne·on /'niʲɑn/ n [U] gas used in making bright electric lights

neph·ew /'nɛfjuʷ/ n son of one's brother or sister

nep·o·tis·m /'nɛpəˌtɪzəm/ n [U] giving unfair favor and advantages to one's relatives

Nep·tune /'neptuʷn, -tyuʷn/ n the PLANET 8th in order from the sun

nerd /nɜrd/ n infml unpleasant person

nerve /nɜrv/ n 1 [C] threadlike part in the body that carries feelings and messages to and from the brain 2 [U] courage: *I meant to do it, but I lost my nerve.* 3 [S;U] disrespectful rudeness: *He had the nerve to say I was a fool!* ♦ vt give courage to (someone, esp. oneself) **nerves** n [P] 1 great nervousness 2 **get on someone's nerves** make someone annoyed or bad-tempered **nervous** adj 1 a rather frightened b easily excited and worried 2 of the nerves: *The brain is at the center of the nervous system.* **nervously** adv **nervousness** n [U]

nerve cen·ter /'· ,··/ n place from which a system, organization, etc., is controlled

nerve-rack·ing /'· ,··/ adj that causes great worry or fear

nervous break·down /,·· '··/ n serious medical condition of deep worrying, anxiety, and tiredness which stops one working

nest /nɛst/ n 1 hollow place built or used by a bird as a home and a place to keep its eggs 2 quiet place where one can go to rest ♦ vi build or use a nest

nest egg /'· ·/ n amount of money saved for special future use

nes·tle /'nɛsəl/ vi/t settle, lie, or put in a close comfortable position: *She nestled down (into the big chair) and began to read.*

nest·ling /'nɛstlɪŋ/ n very young bird

net¹ /nɛt/ n [C;U] (piece of) material made of strings, wires, etc., tied together with regular spaces between them: *the fisherman's nets* ♦ vt **-tt-** catch in a net **~ting** n string, wire, etc., made into a net

net² adj left after nothing further is to be taken away: *a net profit* ♦ vt **-tt-** gain as a profit

neth·er /'nɛðər/ adj lit lower; under

net·tle /'nɛtl/ n wild plant with stinging leaves

net·work¹ /'nɛtwɜrk/ n 1 large system of lines, wires, etc., that cross or meet each other 2 group of radio or television stations – see also OLD-BOY NETWORK

network² vi/t 1 connect (computers) to form a NETWORK¹ (1), to share information 2 form new relationships with people for personal or professional advantage

neu·rol·o·gy /nʊ'rɑlədʒiʸ, nyʊ-/ n [U] scientific study of nerves and their diseases **-gist** n

neu·ro·sis /nʊ'roʷsɪs, nyʊ-/ n **-ses** a disorder of the mind in which one suffers from strong unreasonable fears and has troubled relations with other people **-rotic** /nʊ'rɑtɪk, nyʊ-/ adj of or suffering from a neurosis

neu·ter /'nuʷtər, 'nyuʷ-/ adj (in grammar) belonging to the class of words that mainly includes things rather than males or females ♦ vt remove part of the sex organs of (an animal)

neu·tral¹ /'nuʷtrəl, 'nyuʷ-/ adj 1 not supporting either side in a war, argument, etc. 2 having no strong or noticeable qualities: *a neutral color* **~ize** vt cause to have no effect **~ity** /nuʷ'trælətiʸ, nyuʷ-/ n [U]

neutral² n 1 [U] the position of a car's GEARs in which the engine is not connected with the wheels 2 [C] a neutral person or country

neu·tron /'nuʷtrɑn, 'nyuʷ-/ n a very small piece of matter that is part of an atom and carries no electricity

nev·er /'nɛvər/ adv not ever: *It never snows in the desert.*

nev·er·the·less /,nɛvərðə'lɛs◂/ adv in spite of that; yet: *It was a cold day but nevertheless very pleasant.*

new /nuʷ, nyuʷ/ adj 1 only recently made or begun: *a new film* 2 different from the one before: *She's looking for a new job.* 3 having only recently arrived or started: *I'm new here.* 4 **new** newly; recently: *new-mowed lawn* 5 **new to** just beginning to know about or do; unfamiliar with **~ly** adv that has just happened or been done; recently: *a newly-built house* **~ness** n [U]

new blood /,· '·/ n [U] new members of a group, bringing new ideas, ENERGY, etc.

new·com·er /'nuʷ,kʌmər, 'nyuʷ-/ n someone who has just arrived

new·fan·gled /,nuʷ'fæŋgəld◂, ,nyuʷ-/ adj new but neither necessary nor better

new·ly·wed /'nuʷliʸ,wɛd, 'nyuʷ-/ n recently married person

new moon /,· '·/ n time once every month when the moon doesn't appear

news /nuʷz, nyuʷz/ n 1 [U] facts that are reported about a recent event: *a piece of news* 2 [the+S] regular report of recent events on radio or television

news·cast·er /'nuʷz,kæstər, 'nyuʷz-/ n person who reads the news on television

news·pa·per /'nuʷz,peʸpər, 'nyuʷz-/ n paper printed with news, notices, advertisements, etc., that comes out every day or every week

new·speak /'nuʷspiʸk, 'nyuʷ-/ n [U]

language whose meanings are slightly changed to make people believe things that are not quite true

news·print /'nuʷzˌprɪnt, 'nyuʷz-/ n [U] paper on which newspapers are printed

news·wor·thy /'nuʷzˌwɜrðiʸ, 'nyuʷz-/ adj important or interesting enough to be reported as news

newt /nuʷt, nyuʷt/ n animal with 4 legs, living both on land and water

new wave /ˌ· '·◂/ n recent and fashionable change (in the Arts)

new year /ˌ· '·◂/ n (often caps.) a year which has just begun or will soon begin

next /nɛkst/ adj 1 with nothing before or between; nearest: the house next to mine 2 the one following or after: I'm coming next week. ♦ adv 1 just afterwards: First, heat the oil; next, add the onions. 2 the next time: when next we meet 3 next to almost: next to impossible

next door /ˌ· '·/ adv 1 in the next building: She lives next door. 2 next door to almost the same as

nib /nɪb/ n pointed piece on the end of a pen, out of which ink flows

nib·ble /'nɪbəl/ vi/t eat with small bites ♦ n small bite

nice /naɪs/ adj 1 good; pleasant: have a nice day 2 showing or needing careful understanding; SUBTLE: a nice distinction 3 infml bad: He got us into a nice mess. 4 nice and pleasantly; as was wanted: The soup was nice and hot. ~ly adv ~ness n [U]

ni·ce·ty /'naɪsəṭiʸ/ n fine or delicate point; detail

niche /nɪtʃ/ n 1 hollow place in a wall, where something is put 2 suitable place, job, etc.

nick[1] /nɪk/ n 1 small cut 2 **in the nick of time** only just in time; almost too late ♦ vt make a small cut in

nick·el /'nɪkəl/ n 1 [C] US coin worth 5 cents 2 [U] hard silver-white metal

nickel-and-dime /ˌ··· '·◂/ adj 1 not important 2 (of a business or operation) small

nick·name /'nɪkneʸm/ n informal name used instead of someone's real name ♦ vt: They nicknamed him 'Baldy'.

nic·o·tine /'nɪkəˌtiʸn/ n [U] poisonous chemical found in tobacco

niece /niʸs/ n daughter of one's brother or sister

nif·ty /'nɪftiʸ/ adj infml very good, attractive, or effective

nig·gard·ly /'nɪgərdliʸ/ adj very ungenerous

nig·gle /'nɪgəl/ vi be continually annoying or troubling

nigh /naɪ/ adj lit near ♦ adv lit nearly

night /naɪt/ n 1 [C;U] dark part of the day, between sunset and sunrise 2 **at night: a** during the night **b** at the end of the day 3 **by night** during the night 4 **make a night of it** spend all or most of the night in enjoyment 5 **night after night** every night 6 **night and day** also **day and night** —all the time 7 **nights** every night: I work nights.

night·cap /'naɪtkæp/ n drink before going to bed

night·club /'naɪtklʌb/ n restaurant open late at night where people may drink, dance, and see a show

night·fall /'naɪtfɔl/ n [U] beginning of night

night·gown /'naɪtgaʊn/ also **night·ie** /'naɪtiʸ/ — n woman's garment worn in bed

night·hawk /'naɪt-hɔk/ n NIGHTOWL

nigh·tin·gale /'naɪtnˌgeʸl, 'naɪtɪŋ-/ n bird with a beautiful song

night·life /'naɪtlaɪf/ n [U] evening entertainment or social activity

night·ly /'naɪtliʸ/ adj, adv (happening, done, etc.) every night

night·mare /'naɪtmɛər/ n 1 frightening dream 2 terrible experience or event

night·owl /'naɪtaʊl/ n person who likes to be awake at night

night·shirt /'naɪt-ʃɜrt/ n man's long loose shirt worn in bed

night watch·man /ˌ· '·◂/ n man who guards a building at night

ni·hil·is·m /'naɪəˌlɪzəm/ n [U] belief that nothing has meaning or value **-ist** n

nil /nɪl/ n nothing; zero

nim·ble /'nɪmbəl/ adj 1 quick, light, and neat in movement 2 quick in thought or understanding **-bly** adv **~ness** n [U]

nin·com·poop /'nɪnkəmˌpuʷp, 'nɪŋ-/ n foolish person

nine /naɪn/ det, n, pron 9 **ninth** det, adv, n, pron 9th

nine·teen /ˌnaɪn'tiʸn◂/ det, n, pron 19 **—th** det, adv, n, pron 19th

nine·ty /'naɪntiʸ/ det, n, pron 90 **-tieth** det, adv, n, pron 90th

nip /nɪp/ v **-pp-** 1 vt catch in a sharp tight usu. painful hold 2 **nip something in the bud** stop something before it has properly started ♦ n [S] 1 sharp tight hold or bite 2 coldness: a nip in the air

nip·ple /'nɪpəl/ n 1 round pointed area of dark skin on a breast 2 rubber object through which a baby sucks milk, etc. from a bottle

nip·py /'nɪpiʸ/ adj cold

nir·va·na /nɪərˈvɑːnə, nɜr-/ n [U] (usu. cap.) (in Buddhism and Hinduism) state of complete escape from suffering

nit·pick·ing /ˈnɪtˌpɪkɪŋ/ n [U] habit of paying too much attention to small unimportant details **nit-picking** adj

ni·trate /ˈnaɪtreʸt/ n chemical used esp. to improve the soil for growing crops

ni·tric ac·id /ˌnaɪtrɪk ˈæsɪd/ n [U] powerful acid which destroys other materials

ni·tro·gen /ˈnaɪtrədʒən/ n [U] gas that forms most of the Earth's air

ni·tro·gly·ce·rine /ˌnaɪtrəˈɡlɪsərɪn, -troʷ-/ n [U] powerful liquid explosive

nit·ty-grit·ty /ˌnɪtiʸ ˈɡrɪtiʸ/ n **get down to the nitty-gritty** sl deal with the difficult, practical, and important part of a matter

nit·wit /ˈnɪtˌwɪt/ n silly person

nix /nɪks/ adv infml no ♦ vt infml say no to

no /noʷ/ adv **1** (used for refusing or disagreeing): 'Do you like it?' 'No!' **2** not any: He felt no better. ♦ determiner **1** not a; not any: She felt no fear. | I'm no fool! **2** (shows what is not allowed): No smoking (on a sign) ♦ n answer or decision of no: a clear no

no. written abbrev. for: number

no·bil·i·ty /noʷˈbɪləti̊/ n [U] **1** people of high social rank with titles **2** state of being noble

no·ble /ˈnoʷbəl/ adj **1** of high moral quality; fine and unselfish **2** grand **3** of high social rank ♦ n lord in former times **–bly** adv

no·ble·man /ˈnoʷbəlmən/ **–wom·an** /-ˌwʊmən/ fem. — n **–men** /-mən/ member of the nobility

no·bod·y /ˈnoʷˌbɑdiʸ, -ˌbʌdiʸ/ pron no one ♦ n unimportant person

noc·tur·nal /nɑkˈtɜrnl/ adj happening or active at night

nod /nɑd/ vi/t **-dd-** bend (one's head) forward and down, esp. to show agreement or give a sign ♦ n act of nodding

nod off phr vi fall asleep unintentionally

nodding ac·quaint·ance /ˌ··· ˈ···/ n [S] slight familiarity

nod·ule /ˈnɑdʒuʷl/ n small round lump or swelling

nog·gin /ˈnɑɡɪn/ n sl head

noise /nɔɪz/ n [C;U] sound, esp. loud and unpleasant **noisy** adj making a lot of noise **noisily** adv **noisiness** n [U]

no·mad /ˈnoʷmæd/ n member of a tribe that does not settle long in one place **~ic** /noʷˈmædɪk/ adj

no-man's-land /ˈ·· ·ˌ·/ n [S;U] **1** land no one owns or controls, esp. between two armies or borders **2** any place far away where there are no people

no·men·cla·ture /ˈnoʷmənˌkleʸtʃər/ n [C;U] system of naming things

nom·i·nal /ˈnɑmənl/ adj **1** not really what the name suggests: He's only the nominal head of the business; his son really runs it. **2** (of an amount of money) very small **3** of or being a noun **~ly** adv

nom·i·nate /ˈnɑməˌneʸt/ vt to suggest officially that (someone) should be chosen or elected **–nation** /ˌnɑməˈneʸʃən/ n [C;U]

nom·i·nee /ˌnɑməˈniʸ/ n person who has been nominated

non-a·ligned /ˌnɑnəˈlaɪnd◂/ adj (of a country) not supporting any particular powerful nation

non·cha·lant /ˌnɑnfəˈlɑnt, -tʃə-/ adj calm and usu. uninterested **~ly** adv **–lance** n [U]

non·com·mis·sion·ed of·fi·cer /ˌnɑnkəˌmɪʃənd ˈɔfəsər, ˈɑfə-/ also **NCO** — n person in the army, navy, etc., below the rank of officer but with some power to command others

non·com·mit·tal /ˌnɑnkəˈmɪtl◂/ adj not showing what you really think or intend **~ly** adv

non·con·form·ist /ˌnɑnkənˈfɔrm-ɪst◂/ n, adj (person) not following customary ways of living, thinking, etc.

non·de·script /ˌnɑndɪˈskrɪpt◂/ adj looking very ordinary and dull

none /nʌn/ pron not any: She has several, but I have none. | None of the wine was drinkable. ♦ adv **1 none** the not at all: My car is none the worse for (= not damaged by) the accident. **2 none too** not very

non·en·ti·ty /nɑnˈentəti̊/ n person without much ability, character, or importance

none·the·less /ˌnʌnðəˈles◂/ adv in spite of that; NEVERTHELESS

non-e·vent /ˌnɑnɪˈvent/ n something much less important, interesting, etc., than expected

non·fic·tion /ˌnɑnˈfɪkʃən/ n [U] writing about facts, not stories

no-non·sense /ˌ· ˈ···/ adj practical and direct

non·per·son /ˌnɑnˈpɜrsən/ n person whose influence, importance or rights are ignored

non·plus /ˌnɑnˈplʌs/ vt **-ss-** or **-s-** to surprise (someone) so much that they do not know what to think or do

non·sense /ˈnɑnsens, -səns/ n [U] **1** meaningless words **2** foolish words,

ideas, or actions –**sensical** /nan-
'sɛnsɪkəl/ adj foolish

non se·qui·tur /ˌnɑn ˈsɛkwɪtər/ n
statement that does not follow by
correct reasoning from what has
been said before

non-start·er /ˌnɑnˈstɑrtər/ n person
or idea with no chance of success

non-stick /ˌnɑnˈstɪk◂/ adj with a
special surface that food will not
stick to when cooked

non-stop /ˌnɑnˈstɑp◂/ adj, adv
without a pause or interruption

noo·dle /ˈnuⁿdl/ n long thin piece
of PASTA made from flour, cooked in
soup or boiling water

nook /nʊk/ n 1 sheltered private
place 2 **nooks and crannies** places
that are hidden or that few people
know

noon /nuⁿn/ n [U] 12 o'clock in the
middle of the day

no one /ˈ· ·/ pron not anyone; no
person

noose /nuⁿs/ n ring formed by the
end of a rope, which closes tighter
as it is pulled

nope /noʊp/ adv infml no

nor /nər; strong nɔr/ conj 1 (used
after **neither** or **not**) also not; or:
neither hot nor cold — just warm 2
and also not: She didn't call, nor did
she write.

norm /nɔrm/ n usual or average way
of happening or behaving

nor·mal /ˈnɔrməl/ adj according to
what is usual, expected, or average
~ **ly** adv: Normally I go to bed at 11
o'clock. –**ity** /nɔrˈmæləţiʸ/ also
~ **cy** /ˈnɔrməlsiʸ/ n [U]

nor·mal·ize /ˈnɔrməˌlaɪz/ vi/t (cause
to) become normal, esp. to bring or
come back to a good or friendly state
–**ization** /ˌnɔrmələˈzeʸʃən/ n [U]

north /nɔrθ/ n (often cap.) direction
which is on the left of a person facing the rising sun ♦ adj 1 in the
north 2 (of wind) from the north ♦
adv 1 towards the north 2 **up north**
to or in the north ~ **ward** adj, adv

north-east /ˌnɔrθˈiʸst◂/ n, adj, adv
(direction) exactly between north
and east –**ern** adj

nor·ther·ly /ˈnɔrðərliʸ/ adj towards
or in the north

nor·thern /ˈnɔrðərn/ adj of the north
part of the world or of a country ~ **er**
n person who lives in or comes from
the northern part of a country

north-west /ˌnɔrθˈwest◂/ n, adj, adv
(direction) exactly between north
and west ~ **ern** adj

nos. written abbrev. for: numbers

nose /noʊz/ n 1 [C] the part of the
face above the mouth that is used for
breathing and smelling 2 [C]
(pointed) front end: the nose of the

rocket 3 [S] ability to find out: I have
a nose for trouble. | Just follow your
nose. (= use this ability) 4 [C] too
great an interest in things which do
not concern one: Stop poking your
nose into my affairs! 5 **keep one's
nose clean** keep out of trouble 6
pay through the nose (for) pay a
great deal too much money (for) 7
put someone's nose out of joint
make someone jealous by taking
their place as the center of attention
8 **turn one's nose up at** consider
(something) not good enough to
enjoy 9 **under someone's (very)
nose** quite openly in front of someone ♦ vi 1 move ahead slowly and
carefully 2 try to find out about
things that do not concern you

nose-bleed /ˈnoʊzbliʸd/ n case of
bleeding from the nose

nose-cone /ˈnoʊzkoʊn/ n pointed
front part of a spacecraft or MISSILE

nose-dive /ˈnoʊzdaɪv/ vi 1 (of a
plane) drop suddenly, front end first
2 fall suddenly and greatly: Prices
nosedived. **nosedive** n

nose-gay /ˈnoʊzgeʸ/ n lit small
bunch of flowers

nose-job /ˈnoʊzdʒɑb/ n infml medical operation on the nose to improve its appearance

nosh /nɑʃ/ vi eat between meals

no-show /ˌ· ˈ·/ n expected person
who doesn't appear

nos·tal·gia /nɑˈstældʒə, nə-/ n [U]
fondness for past things –**gic** adj

nos·tril /ˈnɑstrəl/ n either of the 2
openings in the nose

nos·y, nosey /ˈnoʊziʸ/ adj interested in things that do not concern one

not /nɑt/ adv 1 (used for showing the
opposite meaning): He's happy, but
I'm not. | It's a cat, not a dog! | Will
he come, or not? | Not one (= none) re-
mained. 2 **not at all** (a polite answer
to thanks) 3 **not that** I don't mean
that: Not that it matters, but where
were you last night?

no·ta·ble /ˈnoʊţəbəl/ adj unusual
or good enough to be especially noticed –**bly** adv particularly

no·ta·ry /ˈnoʊţəriʸ/ also **Notary
Pub·lic** /ˌ··· ˈ··/ — n public official
who watches the signing of written
statements and makes them official
–**rise** vt have a notary watch and
sign (a document)

no·ta·tion /noʊˈteʸʃən/ n [C;U] system of signs for writing something
down: musical notation

notch /nɑtʃ/ n cut in the shape of a
V ♦ vt make a notch in

note /noʊt/ n 1 [C] short written
record to remind one of something
2 [C] short piece of additional
information in a book 3 [C] short

informal letter **4** [C] (in some countries) piece of paper money **5** [C] (sign representing) a musical sound **6** [S] stated quality or feeling: *a note of anger in his voice* **7** [U] *fml* fame; importance: *a composer of some note* **8 compare notes** tell one's experiences and opinions of something to **9 take note of** pay attention to ♦ *vt* **1** record in writing: *The policeman noted down his address.* **2** notice and remember **noted** *adj* famous

note·book /ˈnoʷtbʊk/ *n* book of plain paper in which one writes NOTES¹ (1)

note·pa·per /ˈnoʷtˌpeʸpər/ *n* [U] paper for writing letters on

note·wor·thy /ˈnoʷtˌwɜrðiʸ/ *adj* NOTABLE

noth·ing /ˈnʌθɪŋ/ *pron* **1** not any thing: *There's nothing in this box — it's empty.* **2** something of no importance: *My debts are nothing to* (= much less than) *his.* **3 for nothing** **a** free **b** with no good result **4 nothing but** nothing other than: *He's nothing but a criminal.* **5 nothing doing:** I won't. **b** no result, interest, etc. **6 nothing for it** no other way **7 nothing like** not nearly: *It's nothing like as cold as yesterday.* **8 think nothing of** treat as easy or unimportant

no·tice /ˈnoʷtɪs/ *n* **1** [C] written or printed sign giving information **2** [U] information that something is going to happen; warning: *The rules may be changed without notice.* **3** [U] attention: *Don't take any notice of* (= pay no attention to) *him.* ♦ *vi/t* see, hear, etc., so as to be conscious of: *She was wearing a new dress, but he didn't even notice (it).* ~**able** *adj* big enough to be noticed ~**ably** *adv*

no·ti·fy /ˈnoʷtəˌfaɪ/ *vt* tell (someone), esp. formally **–fication** /ˌnoʷtəfəˈkeʸʃən/ *n* [U]

no·tion /ˈnoʷʃən/ *n* idea; opinion

no·to·ri·e·ty /ˌnoʷtəˈraɪətiʸ/ *n* [U] state of being notorious

no·to·ri·ous /noʷˈtɔriʸəs, -ˈtoʷr-/ *adj* famous for something bad: *a notorious liar* **–ly** *adv*

not·with·stand·ing /ˌnɑtwɪθˈstændɪŋ, -wɪð-/ *adv fml* in spite of that

nou·gat /ˈnuʷgət/ *n* [U] candy made of sugar, nuts, fruit, etc.

noun /naʊn/ *n* word that is the name of a thing, quality, action, etc., and can be used as the subject or object of a verb

nour·ish /ˈnɜrɪʃ, ˈnʌrɪʃ/ *vt* **1** keep alive and healthy by giving food **2** keep (a feeling, plan, etc.) alive ~**ment** *n* [U] food

nou·velle cuis·ine /ˌnuʷvɛl kwɪˈziʸn/ *n* [U] style of cooking that

tries to bring out the true taste of food and to present it attractively, often thought of as being served in amounts which are (too) small

nov·el¹ /ˈnɑvəl/ *n* long written story ~**ist** *n* novel writer

novel² *adj* new and interesting

nov·el·ty /ˈnɑvəltiʸ/ *n* **1** [U] interesting newness **2** [C] something new and unusual **3** [C] small cheap object, usu. not very useful

No·vem·ber /noʷˈvɛmbər, nə-/ *n* the 11th month of the year

nov·ice /ˈnɑvɪs/ *n* person who has just begun and has no experience

now /naʊ/ *adv* **1** at this present time: *He used to be fat, but now he's slim.* **2** next; at once: *Now for* (= now we will have) *the next question.* **3** (used for attracting attention or giving a warning): *Now then, what's all this?* **4 (every) now and again/then** at times; sometimes **5 from now on** starting now and continuing ♦ *conj* because: *Now that you've arrived, we can begin.*

now·a·days /ˈnaʊəˌdeʸz/ *adv* in these modern times

no way /ˌ· ˈ·/ *adv, interj sl* no; certainly not

no·where /ˈnoʷhwɛər, ˈnoʷwɛər/ *adv* **1** not anywhere **2 nowhere near** not at all near or nearly

nox·ious /ˈnɑkʃəs/ *adj* harmful; poisonous

noz·zle /ˈnɑzəl/ *n* short tube at the end of a pipe for controlling the flow of a liquid

nth /ɛnθ/ *adj* **to the nth degree** to the highest, greatest, furthest, etc., degree or form: *dull to the nth degree*

nu·ance /ˈnuʷɑns, ˈnyuʷ-, nuʷˈɑns, nyuʷ-/ *n* slight delicate difference in meaning, color, etc.

nub /nʌb/ *n* most important point

nu·bile /ˈnuʷbəl, -baɪl, ˈnyuʷ-/ *adj* (of a young woman) sexually attractive

nu·cle·ar /ˈnuʷkliʸər, ˈnyuʷ-/ *adj* being, using, or producing the great power got by breaking up atoms: *nuclear energy | nuclear warfare* (= with nuclear bombs)

nuclear fam·i·ly /ˌ···ˈ···/ *n* family unit that consists only of husband, wife, and children, without grandmothers, uncles, etc.

nuclear win·ter /ˌ···ˈ···/ *n* period which, according to scientists, would follow a nuclear explosion, when there would be no light, warmth, or growth because the sun would be hidden by dust

nu·cle·us /ˈnuʷkliʸəs, ˈnyuʷ-/ *n* **–clei** /-kliʸaɪ/ **1** central part of **a** an atom **b** a CELL (2) **2** original part around which the rest is built

nude /nuʷd, nyuʷd/ *adj* with no

clothes on ♦ *n* **1** (piece of art showing a) nude person **2 in the nude** with no clothes on

nudge /nʌdʒ/ *vt* push gently, esp. with the elbow **nudge** *n*

nud·is·m /ˈnuʷdɪzəm, ˈnyuʷ-/ *n* [U] practice of going around with no clothes on, usu. in a special place (**nudist camp**) **nudist** *n*

nu·di·ty /ˈnuʷdəti̯, ˈnyuʷ-/ *n* [U] state of being nude

nug·get /ˈnʌgɪt/ *n* small rough lump: *gold nuggets* | (fig.) *a nugget of information*

nui·sance /ˈnuʷsəns, ˈnyuʷ-/ *n* annoying person, animal, thing, or situation

nuke /nuʷk, nyuʷk/ *vt infml* attack with NUCLEAR weapons

null and void /ˌnʌl ən ˈvɔɪd/ *adj* having no legal effect

nul·li·fy /ˈnʌləˌfaɪ/ *vt* cause to have no effect

numb /nʌm/ *adj* unable to feel: *fingers numb with cold* **numb** *vt* ~**ness** *n* [U]

num·ber /ˈnʌmbər/ *n* **1** [C] (written sign for) a member of the system used in counting and measuring: *1, 2 and 3 are numbers.* **2** [C;U] quantity; amount: *A large number of people came.* **3** [C] piece of music **4 have someone's number** have knowledge useful in annoying or defeating someone ♦ *vt* **1** give a number to: *numbered pages* **2** reach as a total: *The audience numbered over 5000.* **3** *fml* include: *I number him among my friends.* **4 someone's days are numbered** someone cannot continue or live much longer ~**less** *adj* too many to count

number one /ˌ·· ˈ·/ *n* **1** chief person or thing **2** oneself and no one else: *Look out for number one.*

nu·me·ral /ˈnuʷmərəl, ˈnyuʷ-/ *n* sign that represents a number – see also ROMAN NUMERAL

nu·me·rate /ˈnuʷmərɪt, ˈnyuʷ-/ *adj* able to calculate with numbers

nu·mer·i·cal /nuʷˈmerɪkəl, nyuʷ-/ *adj* of or using numbers ~**ly** /-kli̯/ *adv*

nu·me·ro u·no /ˌnuʷmərowˈuʷnow, ˌnyuʷ-/ *n* NUMBER ONE

nu·me·rous /ˈnuʷmərəs, ˈnyuʷ-/ *adj* many

nun /nʌn/ *n* member of a female religious group that lives together ~**nery** building where they live

nurse /nɜrs/ *n* person who takes care of sick, hurt, or old people, esp. in hospital ♦ *vt* **1** take care of as or like a nurse **2** hold in the mind:

nurse a grudge **3** handle carefully or lovingly: *He nursed the battered plane home.* **4** feed (a baby) with breast milk **nursing** *n* [U] job of being a nurse

nurse·maid /ˈnɜrsmeʸd/ *n* woman employed to take care of a young child

nur·se·ry /ˈnɜrsəri̯/ *n* **1** place where young children are taken care of **2** place where garden plants are grown to be sold

nursery rhyme /ˈ··· ˌ·/ *n* song or poem for young children

nursery school /ˈ··· ˌ·/ *n* school for young children of 2 to 4 years of age

nursing home /ˈ·· ˌ·/ *n* place where old or sick people can live and be looked after

nur·ture /ˈnɜrtʃər/ *vt lit* give care and food to, so as to help development

nut /nʌt/ *n* **1** fruit with a hard shell and a softer dry seed inside which is eaten **2** small piece of metal with a hole through it for screwing onto a BOLT (2) **3** *sl* crazy person **4 a hard/tough nut to crack** a difficult question, person, etc., to deal with **nuts** *adj sl* crazy ♦ *n* [P] *taboo sl* TESTICLES ~**ty** *adj* **1** like or full of nuts **2** *sl* crazy

nut·case /ˈnʌtkeʸs/ *n sl* crazy person

nut·crack·er /ˈnʌtˌkrækər/ *n* tool for cracking the shell of a nut

nu·tri·ent /ˈnuʷtri̯ənt, ˈnyuʷ-/ *n, adj* (a chemical or food) providing for life or growth

nu·tri·tion /nuʷˈtrɪʃən, nyuʷ-/ *n* [U] process of giving or getting food ~**tious** *adj* valuable to the body as food

nuts and bolts /ˌ·· ˈ·/ *n* [(the) P] the simple facts or skills of a subject or job

nut·shell /ˈnʌtˌʃel/ *n* **in a nutshell** described in as few words as possible

nuz·zle /ˈnʌzəl/ *vi/t* press closely, esp. with the nose

ny·lon /ˈnaɪlɑn/ *n* [U] strong artificial material made into cloth, plastic, etc.

nymph /nɪmf/ *n* (in Greek and Roman literature) goddess of nature living in trees, streams, mountains, etc.

nym·pho·ma·ni·a /ˌnɪmfəˈmeʸni̯ə/ *n* [U] strong sexual desire in a woman to a degree considered as unhealthy or socially unacceptable ~**niac** /-ni̯ˌæk/ *n* woman with nymphomania

O

O, o /oʷ/ **1** the 15th letter of the English alphabet **2** (in speech) zero

oaf /oʷf/ n rough stupid awkward person

oak /oʷk/ n large broad tree with hard wood and curly leaves

oar /ɔr, oʷr/ n long pole with a flat blade, used for rowing a boat

oar·lock /'ɔrlɑk, 'oʷr-/ n fastener for an oar on the side of a boat

OAS /ˌoʷ eʸ 'ɛs/ n Organization of American States; economic, political and military organization of parts of North and South America

o·a·sis /oʷ'eʸsɪs/ n —ses /-si·z/ place with water and trees in a desert

oath /oʷθ/ n oaths /oʷðz/ **1** solemn promise **2** use of bad angry words; curse **3 be on/under oath** have promised to tell the truth

oat·meal /'oʷtmiʸl/ n [U] raw or cooked crushed oats

oats /oʷts/ n [P] sort of grain used as food – see also WILD OATS

ob·du·rate /'ɑbdərɪt, -dyər-, -dʒər-/ adj fml unwilling to think or act differently –**ly** adv –**racy** n [U]

o·be·di·ent /ə'biʸdiʸənt, oʷ-/ adj doing what one is told to do –**ly** adv –**ence** n [U]

o·bei·sance /oʷ'beʸsəns, ə-/ n [C;U] fml show of respect and obedience, esp. by bowing (BOW[1])

ob·e·lisk /'ɑbəlɪsk/ n tall pointed stone pillar

o·bese /oʷ'biʸs/ adj fml fat to an unhealthy degree **obesity** n [U]

o·bey /ə'beʸ, oʷ-/ vi/t do what one is told to do (by someone in a position of power)

o·bit·u·a·ry /ə'bɪtʃuʷˌɛriʸ, oʷ-/ n report in a newspaper, etc., of someone's death

ob·ject¹ /'ɑbdʒɪkt, -dʒɛkt/ n **1** thing that can be seen or felt **2** purpose **3** gram word or words that represent **a** the person or thing (the **direct object**) that something is done to (such as *door* in *She closed the door.*) or **b** the person (the **indirect object**) who is concerned in the result of an action (such as *her* in *I gave her the book.*) **4** person or thing that produces the stated feeling: *She has become an object of pity.* **5 be no object** not be a difficulty

ob·ject² /əb'dʒɛkt/ vi be against something or someone: *I object to paying so much.*

ob·jec·tion /əb'dʒɛkʃən/ n **1** statement or feeling of dislike or opposition **2** reason or argument against

ob·jec·tio·na·ble /əb'dʒɛkʃənəbəl/ adj unpleasant –**bly** adv

ob·jec·tive¹ /əb'dʒɛktɪv/ adj **1** not influenced by personal feelings; fair **2** existing outside the mind; real –**tivity** /ˌɑbdʒɛk'tɪvəṭiʸ/ n [U]

objective² n purpose of a plan

object les·son /'·· ˌ··/ n event or story from which one can learn how or how not to behave

ob·jet d'art /ˌɔbʒeʸ 'dɑr, ˌɑb-/ **objets d'art** (same pronunciation) small object of some value as art

ob·li·ga·tion /ˌɑblə'geʸʃən/ n [C;U] duty: *You're under* **no obligation** *to buy.* (= you don't have to) –**tory** /ə'blɪgəˌtɔriʸ, -ˌtoʷriʸ/ adj

o·blige /ə'blaɪdʒ/ vt fml **1** make it necessary for (someone) to do something: *We were obliged to* (= had to) *leave.* **2** do a favor for **3 (I'm) much obliged (to you)** (used for thanking someone politely)

o·blig·ing /ə'blaɪdʒɪŋ/ adj kind and eager to help ~**ly** adv

o·blique /ə'bliʸk, oʷ-/ adj **1** indirect: *an oblique hint* **2** sloping

o·blit·er·ate /ə'blɪtəˌreʸt/ vt remove all signs of; destroy –**ation** /əˌblɪtə'reʸʃən/ n [U]

o·bliv·i·on /ə'blɪviʸən/ n [U] **1** state of being completely forgotten **2** state of being unconscious or not noticing one's surroundings

o·bliv·i·ous /ə'blɪviʸəs/ adj not noticing: *He was oblivious of/to the danger.*

ob·long /'ɑblɔŋ/ n figure with 4 angles of 90 degrees, and 4 sides, 2 long and 2 shorter ones **oblong** adj

ob·nox·ious /əb'nɑkʃəs/ adj extremely unpleasant ~**ly** adv

o·boe /'oʷboʷ/ n musical instrument made of a black wooden tube, played by blowing **oboist** n player of an oboe

ob·scene /əb'siʸn, ɑb-/ adj very offensive or shocking, esp. sexually **obscenity** /əb'sɛnəṭiʸ/ n [C;U] obscene word or behavior

ob·scure /əb'skyuər/ adj **1** hard to understand; not clear **2** not well known ♦ vt hide **obscurity** n [U] state of being obscure

ob·se·qui·ous /əb'siʸkwiʸəs/ adj fml too eager to obey or serve –**ly** adv ~**ness** n [U]

ob·ser·vance /əb'zɜrvəns/ n fml **1** [U] doing something in accordance with a law, custom, etc. **2** [C] part of a religious ceremony

ob·ser·vant /əb'zɜrvənt/ adj quick at noticing things

ob·ser·va·tion /ˌɑbzər'veʸʃən, -sər-/ n **1** [C;U] action of noticing **2** [U] ability to notice things **3** [C] fml remark, esp. about something noticed **4 under observation** being carefully watched during a period of time

ob·ser·va·to·ry /əbˈzɜrvəˌtɔriʸ, -ˌtoʷriʸ/ n place where scientists look at and study the stars, moon, etc.

ob·serve /əbˈzɜrv/ vt **1** watch carefully **2** fml act in accordance with (a law, custom, etc.) **3** fml say **ob-server** n **1** someone who observes **2** someone who attends meetings, etc., only to listen, not take part

ob·sess /əbˈses/ v **1** vt completely fill (someone's) mind, so they cannot think about anything else: *She was obsessed by the fear of failure.* **2** think about (something) all the time: *He's always obsessing about his marriage.* **~ive** adj that is an obsession **~ion** /-ˈseʃən/ n fixed and often unreasonable idea or pattern of behavior

ob·so·les·cent /ˌɑbsəˈlesənt◂/ adj becoming obsolete **-cence** n [U]

ob·so·lete /ˌɑbsəˈliʸt, ˈɑbsəˌliʸt/ adj no longer used; out of date

ob·sta·cle /ˈɑbstɪkəl/ n something that prevents action, movement, or success

obstacle course /ˈ··· ˌ·/ n area of land on which soldiers train by climbing or jumping over objects in order to develop their fitness and courage

ob·ste·tri·cian /ˌɑbstəˈtrɪʃən/ n doctor concerned with obstetrics

ob·stet·rics /əbˈstetrɪks/ n [U] branch of medicine concerned with the birth of children

ob·sti·nate /ˈɑbstənɪt/ adj **1** not willing to obey or change one's opinion **2** difficult to control or defeat: *obstinate resistance* **~ly** adv **-nacy** n [U]

ob·strep·er·ous /əbˈstrepərəs/ adj noisy and uncontrollable **~ly** adv **~ness** n [U]

ob·struct /əbˈstrʌkt/ vt **1** block **2** put difficulties in the way of **~ive** adj intentionally obstructing **~ion** /əbˈstrʌkʃən/ n **1** [C] act of obstructing **2** [U] something that obstructs

ob·tain /əbˈteʸn/ vt fml get: *How did you obtain this information?* **~able** adj

ob·tru·sive /əbˈtruʷsɪv/ adj fml unpleasantly noticeable **~ly** adv

ob·tuse /əbˈtuʷs, əbˈtyuʷs, ɑb-/ adj **1** fml annoyingly slow to understand **2** (of an angle) more than 90° **~ly** adv **~ness** n [U]

ob·verse /ˈɑbvɜrs/ n **1** front side of a coin, etc. **2** opposite

ob·vi·ate /ˈɑbviʸˌeʸt/ vt fml make unnecessary

ob·vi·ous /ˈɑbviʸəs/ adj easy to see and understand; clear: *an obvious lie* **~ly** adv

oc·ca·sion /əˈkeʸʒən/ n **1** [C] time when something happens: *May I take this occasion* (= this chance) *to thank you for your help.* **2** [U] fml reason: *He had no occasion to be so rude.* **3** [C] special event or ceremony **4 on occasion** fml occasionally – see also SENSE OF OCCASION ♦ vt fml cause

oc·ca·sion·al /əˈkeʸʒənəl/ adj happening sometimes; not regular **~ly** adv

oc·ci·den·tal /ˌɑksəˈdentəl◂/ n (person) of the western part of the world

oc·cult /əˈkʌlt, ɑ-, ˈɑkʌlt/ adj magical and mysterious ♦ n [the+S]

oc·cu·pant /ˈɑkyəpənt/ n person who is living in a house, room, etc. **-pancy** n [U] (period of) being an occupant

oc·cu·pa·tion /ˌɑkyəˈpeʸʃən/ n **1** [C] job **2** [C] something done to pass time **3** [U] taking possession of **~al** adj of one's job

oc·cu·py /ˈɑkyəˌpaɪ/ vt **1** be in: *The seat was occupied.* (= someone was sitting in it) **2** fill (space or time): *Writing occupies most of my spare time.* **3** take possession of: *an occupied country* **4** keep busy **-pant** n

oc·cur /əˈkɜr/ vi **-rr- 1** happen **2** be found; exist: *a disease that occurs in children* **~rence** /əˈkɜrəns, əˈkʌr-/ n **1** [C] event **2** [U] process of occurring

occur to phr vt (of an idea) come to (someone's) mind

o·cean /ˈoʷʃən/ n **1** [U] great mass of salt water that covers most of the Earth **2** [C] any of the large areas into which this is divided: *the Atlantic Ocean* **~ic** /ˌoʷʃiʸˈænɪk◂/ adj

o'clock /əˈklɑk/ adv (used in telling the time when it is exactly a numbered hour): *at 5 o'clock*

oc·ta·gon /ˈɑktəˌgɑn/ n flat figure with 8 sides and 8 angles

oc·tane /ˈɑkteʸn/ n substance added to increase the power and quality of gasoline: *high-octane fuel*

oc·tave /ˈɑktɪv/ n space of 8 degrees between musical notes

Oc·to·ber /ɑkˈtoʷbər/ n the 10th month of the year

oc·to·ge·nar·ian /ˌɑktədʒəˈnɛəriʸən/ n a person who is between 80 and 90 years old

oc·to·pus /ˈɑktəpəs/ n creature with 8 limbs that lives deep under the sea

odd /ɑd/ adj **1** strange; unusual **2** (of a number) that cannot be exactly divided by two **3** separated from its pair or set: *an odd shoe* **4** not regular: *doing odd jobs* **5** rather more than the stated number: *20-odd years ago* **~ly** adv strangely **~ity** n **1** [C] strange thing, person, etc. **2** [U] strangeness

odd·ball /ˈɒdbɔl/ n strange person

odd man out /ˌ· · ˈ·/ n person or thing different from or left out of a group

odd·ment /ˈɒdmənt/ n something left over: *a few oddments of cloth*

odds /ɒdz/ n [P] **1** probability of something happening: *The odds are* (= it is likely) *that she will fail.* **2 at odds** in disagreement

odds and ends /ˌ· · ˈ·/ n [P] small articles of various kinds

ode /oʷd/ n long poem

o·di·ous /ˈoʷdiʸəs/ adj fml very unpleasant

o·di·um /ˈoʷdiʸəm/ n [U] fml widespread hatred

o·dom·e·ter /oʷˈdɑmətər/ n instrument that tells how far a car, etc. has traveled

o·dor /ˈoʷdər/ n fml smell

of /əv, ə; strong ʌv, ɑv/ prep **1** belonging to: *the wheels of the car* **2** made from: *a crown of gold* **3** containing: *a bag of potatoes* **4** (shows a part or amount): *2 pounds of sugar* **5** a that is/are: *a friend of mine* | *some fool of a boy* (= some foolish boy) **b** happening in or on: *the Battle of Bunker Hill* **6** in relation to; in connection with: *a teacher of English* | *fond of swimming* **7** a done by: *the plays of Shakespeare* **b** done about: *a picture of Shakespeare* **8** with; having: *a matter of no importance* **9** (shows what someone or something is or does): *the laughter of the children* | *How kind of you!* **10** (used in dates): *the 27th of February* **11** during: *We often go there of an evening.*

off¹ /ɔf/ adv, adj **1** disconnected; removed: *The handle fell off.* **2** (esp. of electrical apparatus) not lit or working: *The TV is off.* **3** away: *She drove off.* | *2 miles off* **4** away or free from work: *She's taken this week off.* **5** so as to be finished or destroyed: *They were all killed off.* **6** not going to happen after all: *The party's off!* **7** incorrect: *off in his calculations* **8** provided with what you need: *They're not well off.* (= have not got much money) | *You'd be better off with a bike than that old car!* **9** not as usual: **a** *having an off day* **b** quiet and dull: *the off season* **10 off and on** sometimes **11 on the off chance** just in case **12 right/straight off** at once

off² prep **1** away from: *I jumped off the bus.* | *I cut a piece off the loaf.* | *The ship was blown off course.* **2** (of a road) turning away from (a larger one) **3** in the sea near: *an island off the coast*

of·fal /ˈɔfəl, ˈɑfəl/ n [U] the inside organs of an animal used as food

off·beat /ˌɔfˈbiʸt◂/ adj not conventional (CONVENTION)

off col·or /ˌ· ˈ··◂/ adj **1** sexually improper **2** slightly ill

of·fense /əˈfens/ n **1** [C] wrong act, esp. a crime **2** [U] cause for hurt feelings: *Don't take offense.* (= feel offended) **3** /ˈɔfens/ concerned with making points in a game: *a good offense*

of·fend /əˈfend/ v **1** vt hurt the feelings of; upset **2** vt displease greatly **3** vi do wrong: *to offend against good manners* ~ **er** n person who offends, esp. a criminal: *a first offender* (= someone found guilty of a crime for the first time) ~ **ing** adj causing displeasure, discomfort, or inconvenience

of·fen·sive /əˈfensɪv/ adj **1** extremely unpleasant **2** for attacking or making points in a game: *an offensive player* ♦ n **1** continued military attack **2 on the offensive** attacking ~ **ly** adv ~ **ness** n [U]

of·fer /ˈɔfər, ˈɑfər/ v **1** vt/i say one will give or do: *The police are offering a big reward.* | *She offered to drive me there.* **2** vt provide; give: *The situation doesn't offer much hope.* | *He offered no resistance.* **3** give (to God): *She offered (up) a prayer.* ♦ n **1** statement offering something **2** what is offered ~ **ing** n something offered

off·hand /ˌɔfˈhænd◂/ adv, adj **1** careless; disrespectful **2** without time to think or prepare

of·fice /ˈɔfɪs, ˈɑ-/ n **1** [C] room or building where written work is done **2** [C] place where a particular service is provided: *a ticket office* **3** [C] government department: *the Office of the Management of the Budget* **4** [C;U] important job or position of power: *the office of president*

of·fi·cer /ˈɔfəsər, ˈɑ-/ n **1** person in command in the army, navy, etc. **2** person in a government job: *a probation officer* **3** policeman

of·fi·cial /əˈfɪʃəl/ adj of, from, or decided by someone in a position of power and responsibility: *official permission* ♦ n person who holds an OFFICE (4) ~ **ly** adv **1** formally by an official **2** as stated publicly (but perhaps not really) ~ **dom** n [U] officials as a group ~ **ese** /əˌfɪʃʸˈliʸz/ n [U] infml language of government officials, considered unnecessarily hard to understand

of·fi·ci·ate /əˈfɪʃiʸˌeʸt/ vi perform official duties

of·fi·cious /əˈfɪʃəs/ adj too eager to give orders ~ **ly** adv ~ **ness** n [U]

of·fing /ˈɔfɪŋ/ n **in the offing** coming soon

off·load /ˌ· ˈ·/ vt get rid of (something unwanted)

off-peak /ˌ· ˈ·◂/ *adj* **1** less busy **2** existing during less busy periods

off-put·ting /ˈ· ˌ··/ *adj* unpleasant and making one not want to continue

off·set /ˈɔfsɛt, ˌɔfˈsɛt/ *vt* **-set**; *present p.* **-setting** make up for; balance: *They offset the cost by charging higher prices.*

off·shoot /ˈɔfʃuʷt/ *n* new stem or branch: (fig.) *an offshoot of a large company*

off·shore /ˌɔfˈʃɔr◂, -ˈʃoʷr◂/ *adv, adj* **1** in the sea near the coast: *offshore islands* **2** away from the coast: *offshore winds*

off·side /ˌɔfˈsaɪd◂/ *adj, adv* also **offsides** (in certain sports) ahead of the ball, which is against the rules

off·spring /ˈɔfˌsprɪŋ/ *n* **offspring** *fml* someone's child or children

off-the-rec·ord /ˌ· · ˈ··◂/ *adj, adv* unofficial and not to be formally recorded

off-the-wall /ˌ·· ˈ·◂/ *adj* amusingly foolish

off-white /ˌ· ˈ·◂/ *adj* grayish or yellowish white

of·ten /ˈɔfən/ *adv* **1** many times: *He was often ill.* **2** in many cases: *Very fat people are often unhealthy.* **3 as often as not** at least half of the time **4 every so often** sometimes **5 more often than not** more than half of the time

o·gle /ˈoʷgəl/ *vi/t* look (at) with great sexual interest

o·gre /ˈoʷgər/ **ogress** /ˈoʷgrɪs/ *fem.* — *n* **1** fierce creature in fairy stories, like a very large person **2** frightening person

oh /oʷ/ *interj* (expresses surprise, fear, etc.)

oil /ɔɪl/ *n* [U] thick fatty liquid that burns easily, esp. PETROLEUM ♦ *vt* put oil on or into **~y** *adj* **1** like or covered with oil **2** too polite **oils** *n* [P] paints containing oil

oil·field /ˈɔɪlfiʸld/ *n* area with oil underneath it

oil paint·ing /ˈ· ˌ··/ *n* [C;U] painting done using paint made with oil: *She's/he's no oil painting.* (= is not beautiful)

oil·rig /ˈɔɪlˌrɪg/ *n* large apparatus for getting oil up from under the sea

oil·skin /ˈɔɪlˌskɪn/ *n* [C;U] (garment made of) cloth treated with oil so as not to let water through

oil well /ˈ· ·/ *n* hole made in the ground to get oil

oint·ment /ˈɔɪntmənt/ *n* **1** [C;U] oily usu. medicinal substance rubbed on the skin **2 a/the fly in the ointment** one small unwanted thing that spoils the happiness of an occasion

o·kay, OK /oʷˈkeʸ/ *adj, adv* **1** all right; satisfactory **2** (expresses agreement or permission) ♦ *n* approval; permission ♦ *vt* give permission for

old /oʷld/ *adj* **1** having lived or existed a long time **2** of a particular age: *The baby is 2 years old.* **3** having been so a long time: *an old friend* **4** former: *He got his old job back.* | *an old boyfriend/girlfriend* **5 of old:** **a** in the past **b** for a long time ♦ *n* [*the*+S] old people

old age /ˌ· ˈ·◂/ *n* [U] part of one's life when one is old

old-boy net·work /ˈ·· ˌ··/ *n* profession or group in society made up of powerful men who help each other gain advantages

old·en /ˈoʷldən/ *adj lit* past; long ago: *in olden times*

old-fash·ioned /ˌ· ˈ··◂/ *adj* once usual or fashionable but now less common

old flame /ˌ· ˈ·/ *n* someone with whom one used to be in love

Old Glo·ry /ˌ· ˈ··/ *n* US flag

old guard /ˈ· ˌ·/ *n* [*the*+S] group of people with old-fashioned ideas who are against change

old hand /ˌ· ˈ·/ *n* very experienced person

old hat /ˌ· ˈ·/ *adj* old-fashioned

old maid /ˌ· ˈ·/ *n* old unmarried woman

old mas·ter /ˌ· ˈ··/ *n* (picture by) an important painter of esp. the 15th to 18th centuries

old tim·er /ˌ· ˈ··/ *n* **1** person who has been somewhere or done something for a long time **2** old man

old wives' tale /ˌ· ˈ· ·/ *n* ancient and not necessarily true belief

o·le·o /ˈoʷliʸˌoʷ/ *n* MARGARINE

ol·fac·to·ry /ɑlˈfæktəriʸ, oʷl-/ *adj med* of the sense of smell

ol·i·gar·chy /ˈɑləˌgɑrkiʸ/ *n* **1** [U] government by a small usu. unrepresentative group **2** [C] state governed in this way

ol·ive /ˈɑlɪv/ *n* **1** [C] small fruit of the **olive tree**, grown in Mediterranean countries and eaten raw or made into **olive oil** for cooking **2** [U] dull pale green

olive branch /ˈ·· ˌ·/ *n* sign of a wish for peace

om·buds·man /ˈɑmbʊdzmən/ *n* **-men** /-mən/ person who deals with complaints about an organization

ome·lette /ˈɑməlɪt/ *n* flat round mass of eggs beaten together and cooked

o·men /ˈoʷmən/ *n* sign of something that will happen

om·i·nous /ˈɑmənəs/ *adj* seeming to

show that something bad will happen ~**ly** adv

o·mis·sion /o‿ʷmɪʃən, ə‿-/ n 1 [U] act of omitting 2 [C] something left out

o·mit /o‿ʷmɪt, ə‿-/ vt 1 not include: *An important detail was omitted.* 2 *fml* not do; fail: *They omitted to tell me.*

om·ni·bus /ˈɑmnɪbəs/ n 1 book containing several works, esp. by one writer 2 *old use for* BUS

om·nip·o·tent /ɑmˈnɪpətənt/ adj fml having unlimited power –**tence** n [U]

om·nis·ci·ent /ɑmˈnɪʃənt/ adj knowing everything –**ence** n [U]

om·niv·o·rous /ɑmˈnɪvərəs/ adj (esp. of an animal) eating anything

on¹ /ɑn, ɔn/ prep 1 touching, supported by, hanging from, or connected with: *a lamp on the table* 2 towards; in the direction of 3 directed towards: *a tax on beer* 4 in (a large vehicle): *on a train* 5 (shows when something happens): *She's coming on Tuesday.* 6 about: *a book on golf* 7 by means of: *A car runs on gas.* 8 in a state of: *on fire* | *on vacation* 9 working for; belonging to: *She's on the committee.* 10 directly after and because of: *I acted on your advice.* 11 paid for by: *The drinks are on me!*

on² adv, adj 1 continuously, instead of stopping: *He kept on talking.* 2 further; forward: *We walked on to the next one.* 3 (so as to be) wearing: *He put his coat on.* | *He had nothing on.* 4 with the stated part in front: *They crashed head on.* 5 in(to) a vehicle: *The bus stopped and we got on.* 6 (esp. of electrical apparatus) lit or working: *The TV was on.* 7 (of something arranged) happening or going to happen: *What's on at the cinema?* | *I've got nothing on on Tuesday.* (= I'm not doing anything) 8 with the stated part forward: *Look at it head on.* 9 **and so on** etc. 10 **on the hour** every hour exactly at 3:00, 4:00, etc. 11 **on and off** from time to time 12 **on and on** without stopping

once /wʌns/ adv 1 one time: *We've only met once.* 2 formerly: *He was once a famous singer.* 3 **all at once** suddenly 4 **at once:** a now; without delay: *Come at once!* b together: *Don't all speak at once!* 5 **for once** for this one time only: *Just for once he was telling the truth.* 6 **once and for all** now, so as to be settled, with no further change 7 **once in a while** sometimes, but not often 8 **once more** again ♦ *conj* from the moment that: *Once he's arrived, we can start.*

once-o·ver /ˈˈ ˌˈˈ/ n infml a quick look or examination

on·com·ing /ˈɑnˌkʌmɪŋ, ˈɔn-/ adj coming towards one: *oncoming traffic*

one¹ /wʌn/ determiner, n 1 (the number) 1 2 a certain: *They'll come back one day.* | *The victim was one Roy Malkin.* 3 the same: *They all ran in one direction.* 4 particular type or example (of): *He can't tell one tree from another.* 5 **at one** *fml* in agreement 6 **be one up (on)** have the advantage (over) 7 **for one** as one (person, thing, reason, etc.) out of several: *If for one, see no reason to continue.* 8 **in one** combined: *It's a table and desk all in one.* 9 **one and all** every one 10 **one and the same** exactly the same 11 **one of** a member of: *Our dog's like one of the family.* 12 **one or two** a few

one² pron 1 single thing or person of the sort mentioned: *Have you any books on gardening? I'd like to borrow one.* 2 *fml* any person; you: *One should do one's duty.*

one an·oth·er /ˌˈ ˈˈ·ˈˈ/ pron EACH OTHER: *They hit one another.*

one-man band /ˌˈ · ˈ·ˈ/ n 1 a street musician who plays different instruments all at one time 2 activity which someone does all on their own

one-night stand /ˌˈ · ˈ·ˈ/ n 1 performance (of music or a play) given only once in each of a number of places by a (group of) performers 2 sexual relationship which lasts only one night

one-off /ˌˈ ˈ·◂/ adj 1 happening or done only once 2 made as a single example

one-piece /ˈˈ · ·/ adj made in one piece only

on·er·ous /ˈɑnərəs, ˈoʷ-/ adj fml difficult; hard to bear: *an onerous duty*

one·self /wʌnˈsɛlf/ pron fml 1 (reflexive form of ONE² (2)): *to wash oneself* 2 (strong form of ONE² (2)): *One shouldn't try and do everything oneself.* 3 **(all) by oneself** a alone b without help 4 **to oneself** not shared

one-shot /ˈˈ ·/ adj 1 happening or done only once 2 made as a single example

one-sid·ed /ˌˈ ˈ·◂/ adj with one side stronger or more favored than the other: *a one-sided football game*

one-time /ˈwʌntaɪm/ adj former

one-to-one /ˌˈ · · ˈ·◂/ adj, adv 1 matching one another exactly 2 between only two people

one-up·man·ship /ˌwʌnˈʌpmənˌʃɪp/ also **-ups-** n [U] art of getting an advantage without actually cheating

one-way /ˌˈ ˈ·◂/ adj moving or

allowing movement in one direction only: *a one-way street*

on·go·ing /ˈɑnˌgoʷɪŋ, ˈɔn-/ *adj* continuing: *an ongoing problem*

on·ion /ˈʌnyən/ *n* round white vegetable with a strong smell

on·line /ˈɑnlaɪn, ˈɔn-/ *adj* directly connected to and/or controlled by a computer **online** *adv*

on·look·er /ˈɑnˌlʊkər, ˈɔn-/ *n* person watching something happen

on·ly¹ /ˈoʷnli²/ *adj* **1** with no others in the same group: *my only friend | an only child* (=with no brothers or sisters) **2** best: *She's the only person for this job.*

only² *adv* **1** and no one or nothing else: *There were only 5 left.* **2** if only (expresses a strong wish): *If only she were here!* **3** only too very; completely: *I'm afraid it's only too true.*

only³ *conj* except that; but: *She wants to go, only she doesn't have enough money.*

on·rush /ˈɑnrʌʃ, ˈɔn-/ *n* strong movement forward

on·set /ˈɑnset, ˈɔn-/ *n* start, esp. of something bad

on·shore /ˌɑnˈʃɔrx, -ˈʃoʷrx, ˌɔn-/ *adv, adj* towards the coast: *onshore winds*

on·slaught /ˈɑnslɔt, ˈɔn-/ *n* fierce attack

on·to /ˈɑntə, ˈɔn-; *before vowels* -tʊ; *strong* -tuʷ/ *prep* **1** to a position or point on: *He jumped onto the train.* **2** be onto have found out about (someone or something wrong or illegal)

o·nus /ˈoʷnəs/ *n* [S] duty; responsibility: *The onus is on you to do it.*

on·ward /ˈɑnwərd, ˈɔn-/ *adj, adv* forward in space or time

oo·dles /ˈuʷdlz/ *n* [P] *infml* lots

ooze /uʷz/ *v* **1** *vi* (of thick liquid) pass or flow slowly **2** *vt* have (liquid) oozing out of: (fig.) *He oozes charm.* ♦ *n* [U] mud or thick liquid

o·pac·i·ty /oʷˈpæsəţi²/ *n* [U] opaqueness

o·pal /ˈoʷpəl/ *n* white precious stone with colors in it

o·paque /oʷˈpeʸk/ *adj* which you cannot see through ~ **ness** *n* [U]

OPEC /ˈoʷpek/ *n* Organization of Petroleum Exporting Countries

o·pen¹ /ˈoʷpən/ *adj* **1** not shut: *an open window/book* | (fig.) *an open mind* (= not closed to new ideas) **2** not surrounded by anything: *open country* **3** without a roof: *an open boat* **4** not fastened or folded: *with his shirt open* **5** not completely decided or answered: *an open question* **6** that one can go into as a visitor or customer: *Is the bank open yet?* **7** (of a job) not filled **8** not hiding or

hidden; honest **9** that anyone can enter: *an open competition* **10** spread out: *The flowers are open.* **11** keep open house encourage visitors to come at any time **12 open to: a** not safe from: *open to criticism* **b** willing to receive: *open to suggestions* **13 with open arms** in a very friendly way ~ **ly** *adv* not secretly ~ **ness** *n* [U]

open² *vi/t* **1** make or become open: *Open your mouth!* **2** spread; unfold: *open a map* **3** (cause to) start: *The story opens in a country village.* **4** (cause to) begin business: *The stores open at 9 o'clock.* **5 open fire** start shooting **6 open someone's eyes (to something)** make someone know or understand something ~ **er** *n*

open into/onto *phr vt* provide a means of entering or reaching

open out *phr vi* speak more freely

open up *phr v* **1** *vt* make possible the development of **2** *vi* open the door **3** *vi* speak more freely

open³ *n* [*the*+S] **1** the outdoors **2** in(to) the open (of opinions, secrets, etc.) in(to) the consciousness of the people around one

open-air /ˌ·· ˈ·◄/ *adj* of or in the outdoors: *an open-air theatre*

open-and-shut /ˌ·· ˈ·◄/ *adj* easy to prove

open-door pol·i·cy /ˌ·· ˈ···/ *n* idea of allowing businesses from all countries to trade freely in a certain country

open-end·ed /ˌ·· ˈ···◄/ *adj* with no limit set in advance

open-hand·ed /ˌ·· ˈ···◄/ *adj* generous

o·pen·ing /ˈoʷpənɪŋ/ *n* **1** hole or clear space **2** favorable set of conditions **3** unfilled job ♦ *adj* first; beginning

open-plan /ˌ·· ˈ·◄/ *adj* (of a large room) not divided into a lot of little rooms

op·e·ra /ˈɑpərə/ *n* musical play in which (most of) the words are sung ~ **tic** /ˌɑpəˈræţɪk◄/ *adj*

op·e·ra·ble /ˈɑpərəbəl/ *adj* (of a disease, etc.) that can be cured by an operation

op·e·rate /ˈɑpəˌreʸt/ *v* **1** *vi/t* (cause to) work: *learning to operate the controls* **2** *vi* carry on business: *We operate throughout Europe.* **3** *vi* cut the body to cure or remove diseased parts, usu. in a special room (**operating room**) **4** *vi* produce effects: *The new law operates in our favor.*

operating sys·tem /ˈ···· ˌ··/ *n* set of PROGRAMS inside a computer that controls the way it works and helps it to handle other programs

op·e·ra·tion /ˌɑpəˈreʸʃən/ *n* **1** [U]

condition or process of working **2** [C] thing (to be) done; activity **3** [C] cutting of the body to cure or remove a diseased part **4** [C] planned military movement ~**al** *adj* of operations: *operational costs* **2** ready for use

op·e·ra·tive /ˈɑpərətɪv, ˈɑpəˌreɪ-/ *adj* **1** (of a plan, law, etc.) working; producing effects **2** most important: *'Fast' is the operative word.* ♦ *n fml* worker

op·e·ra·tor /ˈɑpəˌreɪtər/ *n* person who works a machine, apparatus, or esp. telephone SWITCHBOARD

o·pin·ion /əˈpɪnyən/ *n* **1** [C] what someone thinks about something, based on personal judgment rather than facts: *In my opinion, it's crazy.* **2** [U] what people in general think about something **3** [C] professional judgment or advice ~**ated** *adj* too sure that what one thinks is right

o·pi·um /ˈoʷpiəm/ *n* [U] addictive (ADDICT) drug that produces sleep

op·po·nent /əˈpoʷnənt/ *n* **1** person who takes the opposite side in a competition or fight **2** person who opposes someone or something

op·por·tune /ˌɑpərˈtuʷn, -ˈtyuʷn/ *adj fml* **1** (of time) right for a purpose **2** coming at the right time ~**ly** *adv*

op·por·tun·is·m /ˌɑpərˈtuʷˌnɪzəm, -ˈtyuʷ-/ *n* [U] taking advantage of every chance for success, sometimes to other people's disadvantage –**ist** *n*

op·por·tu·ni·ty /ˌɑpərˈtuʷnətiʸ, -ˈtyuʷ-/ *n* [C;U] favorable moment; chance

op·pose /əˈpoʷz/ *vt* be or act against

op·posed /əˈpoʷzd/ *adj* **1** against: *I'm opposed to abortion.* **2** **as opposed to** and not

op·po·site /ˈɑpəzɪt, -sɪt/ *adj* **1** as different as possible from: *at opposite ends of the room* **2** facing: *the houses opposite* ♦ *n* opposite thing or person: *Black and white are opposites.* ♦ *prep* facing: *She sat opposite me.*

op·po·si·tion /ˌɑpəˈzɪʃən/ *n* **1** [U] act or state of opposing **2** [U] people who are against one

op·press /əˈprɛs/ *vt* **1** rule in a hard cruel way **2** cause to feel ill or sad ~**ive** *adj* **1** cruel; unjust **2** causing feelings of illness and unhappiness: *oppressive heat* ~**or** *n* ~**ion** *n* [U] /əˈprɛʃən/

opt /ɑpt/ *vi* make a choice: *I opted for the smaller one.*

    opt out *phr vi* decide not to take part

op·tic /ˈɑptɪk/ *adj* of the eyes: *the optic nerve*

op·ti·cal /ˈɑptɪkəl/ *adj* **1** of or about the sense of sight: *She thought she saw it, but it was an optical illusion.* (= something that deceives the sense of sight) **2** of or using light: *optical character recognition*

op·ti·mist /ˈɑptəˌmɪst/ *n* person who expects good things to happen –**mism** *n* [U] –**ic** /ˌɑptəˈmɪstɪk•/ *adj*

op·ti·mize /ˈɑptəˌmaɪz/ *vt* make as perfect or effective as possible

op·ti·mum /ˈɑptəməm/ also **optimal** /ˈɑptəməl/ — *adj* most favorable: *optimum conditions for growing rice*

op·tion /ˈɑpʃən/ *n* **1** [U] freedom to choose: *I had to do it; I had no option.* **2** [C] possible course of action that can be chosen **3** [C] right to buy or sell something at a stated time in the future – see also SOFT OPTION ~**al** *adj* which you can choose to have or not to have

op·tom·e·trist /ɑpˈtɑmətrɪst/ *n* person who makes and sells glasses, etc., for people's eyes

op·u·lent /ˈɑpyələnt/ *adj* **1** showing great wealth **2** in good supply –**lence** *n* [U]

o·pus /ˈoʷpəs/ *n* piece of work done, esp. a piece of music written

or /ər; *strong* ɔr/ *conj* **1** (shows different possibilities): *Will you have tea or coffee?* **2** if not: *Wear your coat or you'll be cold.* **3** (describes the same thing in a different way): *a yard, or three feet* **4** **or else** *infml* (used as a threat) or something bad will happen **5** **or so** about: *We waited for 5 minutes or so.*

or·a·cle /ˈɔrəkəl, ˈɑr-/ *n* **1** (in ancient Greece) person through whom a god answered human questions **2** person thought to be, or who believes himself to be, wise and able to give good advice

o·ral /ˈɔrəl, ˈoʷrəl/ *adj* **1** spoken, not written: *an oral exam* **2** *med* of the mouth ~**ly** *adv*

or·ange /ˈɔrɪndʒ, ˈɑr-/ *n* common round red-yellow fruit ♦ *adj* of the color of an orange

o·rang·u·tan /əˈræŋəˌtæŋ/ *n* large monkey with reddish hair and no tail

o·ra·tion /ɔˈreɪʃən, oʷ-, ə-/ *n* solemn formal public speech

or·a·tor /ˈɔrətər, ˈɑr-/ *n* public speaker

or·a·to·ry /ˈɔrəˌtɔriʸ, -ˌtoʷriʸ, ˈɑr-/ *n* [U] language highly decorated with long or formal words

or·bit /ˈɔrbɪt/ *n* **1** path of something going around something else, esp. in space **2** area of power or influence ♦ *vi/t* go around in an orbit: *The satellite orbits the Earth.* ~**al** *adj*

or·chard /ˈɔrtʃərd/ n place where fruit trees are grown

or·ches·tra /ˈɔrkɪstrə, ˈɔrˌkɛstrə/ n large group of musicians playing different instruments **orchestral** /ɔrˈkɛstrəl/ adj

or·ches·trate /ˈɔrkəˌstreʸt/ vt 1 arrange (music) to be played by an orchestra 2 plan (something with many parts) for best effect –**tration** /ˌɔrkəˈstreʸʃən/ n [C;U]

or·chid /ˈɔrkɪd/ n plant with bright flowers that have strange shapes

or·dain /ɔrˈdeʸn/ vt 1 make (someone) a priest 2 fml (of God, the law, etc.) order

or·deal /ɔrˈdiʸl, ˈɔrdiʸl/ n difficult or painful experience

or·der¹ /ˈɔrdər/ n 1 [U] way in which things are arranged: in alphabetical order | in order of importance | Leave everything in good order. (= tidily) 2 [U] fitness for use: The phone's out of order. (= doesn't work) 3 [U] condition in which laws and rules are obeyed: That new teacher can't keep order in his class. | Your papers are in order. (= acceptable according to the rules) 4 [C] command: An officer gives orders. 5 [C] request to supply goods: The waiter took our order. 6 [C] religious or social organization: The Benedictine order 7 [C] fml kind; sort: courage of the highest order 8 [P] state of being a priest, etc.: to take (holy) orders 9 **in order that** fml so that 10 **in order to** with the purpose of 11 **in the order of** about 12 **on order** asked for but not yet supplied – see also TALL ORDER

order² v 1 vt command: He ordered them to attack. 2 vt/i ask for (something) to be supplied: I ordered chicken soup. 3 vt arrange

order about phr vt give many commands to, unpleasantly

or·der·ly /ˈɔrdərliʸ/ adj 1 well arranged 2 liking tidy arrangement 3 peaceful and well behaved: an orderly crowd ♦ n helper in a hospital –**liness** n [U]

or·di·nal num·ber /ˌɔrdn-əl ˈnʌmbər, ˌɔrdnəl-/ n one of the numbers (1st, 2nd, 3rd, etc.) that show order rather than quantity

or·di·nary /ˈɔrdnˌɛriʸ, ˈɔrdˌnɛriʸ/ adj 1 not unusual; common 2 **out of the ordinary** unusual –**narily** /ˌɔrdnˈɛrəliʸ/ adv usually

or·di·na·tion /ˌɔrdnˈeʸʃən/ n [U;C] act of ORDAINing a priest

ore /ɔr, oʷr/ n [U] rock from which metal is obtained

or·gan /ˈɔrgən/ n 1 part of an animal or plant that has a special purpose, such as the heart 2 organization with a special purpose within a larger one: Congress is an organ of government. 3 large musical instrument played by blowing air through pipes ~**ist** n ORGAN (2) player

or·gan·ic /ɔrˈgænɪk/ adj 1 of living things or physical organs 2 made of parts with related purposes 3 (of food) grown without chemicals ~**ally** /-kliʸ/ adv

or·gan·ism /ˈɔrgəˌnɪzəm/ n 1 living creature 2 whole made of related parts

or·gan·i·za·tion /ˌɔrgənəˈzeʸʃən/ n 1 [C] group of people with a special purpose, such as a business or club 2 [U] organizing; arrangement

or·gan·ize /ˈɔrgəˌnaɪz/ vt 1 arrange into a good system: a well-organized office 2 make necessary arrangements for: to organize a party -**izer** n

or·gas·m /ˈɔrˌgæzəm/ n [C;U] highest point of sexual pleasure

or·gy /ˈɔrdʒiʸ/ n 1 wild party where people get drunk and have sex 2 infml a set of (usu. pleasant activities) close together in time

O·ri·ent /ˈɔriʸənt, -ˌɛnt, ˈoʷr-/ n esp. lit [the] the eastern part of the world; Asia

o·ri·ent² /ˈɔriʸˌɛnt, -ənt, ˈoʷr-/ vt 1 arrange or direct with a particular purpose: an export-oriented company 2 find out where you are -**ation** /ˌɔriʸənˈteʸʃən, ˌoʷr-/

o·ri·en·tal /ˌɔriʸˈɛntəl◄, ˌoʷr-/ n, adj (person) of or from the Orient

o·ri·en·tate /ˈɔriʸənˌteʸt, ˈoʷr-/ vt 1 arrange or direct with a particular purpose: an export-orientated company 2 find out where you are -**tation** /ˌɔriʸənˈteʸʃən, ˌoʷr-/ n [C;U]

or·i·fice /ˈɔrəfɪs, ˈar-/ n fml opening, esp. in the body

or·i·gin /ˈɔrədʒɪn, ˈar-/ n 1 [C;U] starting point 2 [U] also origins pl. — parents and conditions of early life: a woman of humble origin

o·rig·i·nal /əˈrɪdʒənəl/ adj 1 first; earliest 2 new and different 3 not copied ♦ n the one from which copies have been made ~**ly** adv 1 in the beginning, before changing 2 in a new and different way ~**ity** /əˌrɪdʒəˈnælətiʸ/ n [U] quality of being ORIGINAL (2)

o·rig·i·nate /əˈrɪdʒəˌneʸt/ vi/t (cause to) begin –**nator** n

or·na·ment /ˈɔrnəmənt/ n [C;U] decorative object(s) ♦ vt /-ˌment/ decorate –**al** /ˌɔrnəˈmentl◄/ adj ~**ation** /ˌɔrnəmenˈteʸʃən/ n [U]

or·nate /ɔrˈneʸt/ adj having (too) much ornament

or·ner·y /ˈɔrnəriʸ/ adj bad-tempered

or·ni·thol·o·gy /ˌɔrnəˈθɑlədʒiʸ/ n [U] scientific study of birds –**gist** n

or·phan /ˈɔrfən/ n child with no parents ♦ vt cause to be an orphan ~**age** n place where orphans live

or·tho·dox /ˈɔrθəˌdɑks/ adj 1 generally or officially accepted or used: orthodox methods 2 holding orthodox opinions ~**y** n [U]

or·tho·pe·dic /ˌɔrθəˈpidɪk◂/ adj of the branch of medicine (**orthopedics**) that puts bones straight

Os·car /ˈɑskər/ n yearly prize for best work in films

os·cil·late /ˈɑsəˌleɪt/ vi 1 move regularly from side to side 2 vary between opposing choices –**lation** /ˌɑsəˈleɪʃən/ n [C;U]

os·mo·sis /ɑzˈmoʊsɪs/ n [U] gradual passing of liquid through a skinlike wall –**tic** /ɑzˈmɑtɪk/ adj

os·ten·si·ble /ɑˈstɛnsəbəl/ adj (of a reason) seeming or pretended, but perhaps not really true –**bly** adv

os·ten·ta·tion /ˌɑstənˈteɪʃən, -tɛn-/ n [U] unnecessary show of wealth, knowledge, etc. –**tious** adj

os·te·o·path /ˈɑstiˈəˌpæθ/ n doctor with special knowledge to treat diseases by moving and pressing bones and muscles

os·tler /ˈɑslər/ n (in former times) man who took care of guests' horses at a small hotel

os·tra·cize, -cise /ˈɑstrəˌsaɪz/ vt stop accepting (someone) into one's group –**cism** n [U]

os·trich /ˈɑstrɪtʃ, ˈɑ-/ n extremely large African bird with long legs that cannot fly

OTB /ˌoʊ tiʸ ˈbiʸ/ n Off-Track Betting; officially arranged system for betting esp. on horses when it is not possible to go to the race

oth·er /ˈʌðər/ determiner, pron 1 the remaining one of a set; what is left as well as that mentioned: She held on with one hand and waved with the other. 2 additional: Do you have any other questions? 3 not this, not oneself, not one's own, etc.: He likes spending other people's money. 4 **one after the other** first one, then the next, etc. 5 **other than** a except: no one other than me b anything but: I can't be other than grateful. 6 **the other day/night/afternoon/evening** on a recent day/night/afternoon/evening

oth·er·wise /ˈʌðərˌwaɪz/ adv 1 differently 2 apart from that: The soup was cold, but otherwise the meal was excellent. 3 if not: Go faster, otherwise we'll be late.

ouch /aʊtʃ/ interj (expresses sudden pain)

ought /ɔt/ v aux 1 have a (moral) duty: You ought to look after them better. 2 (shows what is right or sensible): You ought to see a doctor. 3 will probably: Prices ought to come down soon.

ounce /aʊns/ n 1 [C] a measure of weight equal to 28.35 grams or 1/16 of a pound 2 [S] a small amount

our /aʊər, ɑr/ determiner of us: our house

ours /aʊərz, ɑrz/ pron of us; our one(s)

our·selves /aʊərˈsɛlvz, ɑr-/ pron 1 (reflexive form of **we**): We saw ourselves on TV. 2 (strong form of **we**): We built the house ourselves. 3 (**all**) **by ourselves**: a alone b without help 4 **to ourselves** not shared

oust /aʊst/ vt force (someone) out ~**er** n action of doing this

out¹ /aʊt/ adv 1 away from the inside: Open the bag and take the money out. 2 away from home or the usual place: Let's go out tonight. 3 away from a surface: The nail stuck out. 4 to lots of people or places: Hand out the drinks. 5 (of a fire or light) no longer burning 6 completely: I'm tired out. 7 aloud: Call the names out. 8 so as to be clearly seen, understood, etc.: Their secret is out. | Are the daffodils out (= in flower) yet? 9 wrong in guessing, etc.: I was 2 years out in my estimation. 10 (of the ball in a game, e.g. tennis) outside the line 11 no longer fashionable 12 (of the TIDE) away from the coast 13 **out of**: a from the inside; away from: I jumped out of bed. | (fig.) We're out of danger (= safe) now. | (fig.) It's out of sight. (= can't be seen) b from among: 4 out of 5 people preferred it. c not having; without: We're out of gas. d because of: I came out of interest. e (shows what something is made from): made out of wood 14 **out of it**: a lonely and unhappy because one is not included in something b infml not thinking clearly 15 **out to** trying to

out² adj 1 directed outward 2 openly HOMOSEXUAL 3 **out-and-out** complete; total

out³ vt make oneself known as a HOMOSEXUAL

out·board mo·tor /ˌaʊtbɔrd ˈmoʊtər, -boʷrd-/ n motor fixed to the back end of a small boat

out·break /ˈaʊtbreɪk/ n sudden appearance or start of something bad

out·burst /ˈaʊtbɜrst/ n sudden powerful expression of feeling

out·cast /ˈaʊtkæst/ n someone forced from their home or friendless

out·class /aʊtˈklæs/ vt be very much better than

out·come /ˈaʊtkʌm/ n effect; result

out·crop /ˈaʊtkrɑp/ n rock or rocks on the surface of the ground

out·cry /ˈaʊtkraɪ/ n public show of anger

out·dat·ed /ˌaʊtˈdeɪtɪd/ adj no longer in general use

out·do /aʊtˈduː/ vt –**did** /-ˈdɪd/, –**done** /-ˈdʌn/, *3rd person sing. pres. t.* –**does** /-ˈdʌz/ do or be better than

out·door /ˈaʊtdɔːr, -doʷr/ adj existing, happening, or used outside **outdoors** /ˌaʊtˈdɔːrz, -ˈdoʷrz/ adv

out·er /ˈaʊtər/ adj on the outside; furthest from the middle

outer space /ˌ·· ·/ n [U] area where the stars and other heavenly bodies are

out·field /ˈaʊtfiʳld/ n area of baseball diamond farthest from the BATTER

out·fit /ˈaʊtˌfɪt/ n 1 set of things esp. clothes for a particular purpose 2 group of people working together ♦ vt –**tt**– provide with a set of esp. clothes ~**ter** n

out·flank /aʊtˈflæŋk/ vt go around the side of (an enemy) to attack

out·go·ing /ˈaʊtˌɡoʊɪŋ/ adj 1 finishing a period in office 2 friendly

out·grow /aʊtˈɡroʊ/ vt –**grew** /-ˈɡruː/, –**grown** /-ˈɡroʊn/ grow too big, too old, or too fast for

out·house /ˈaʊthaʊs/ n –**houses** /-haʊzɪz/ 1 small building near a larger main building 2 outdoor TOILET

out·ing /ˈaʊtɪŋ/ n 1 [C] short journey for pleasure, esp. by a group 2 [U;C] practice of making secret HOMOSEXUALS known

out·land·ish /aʊtˈlændɪʃ/ adj strange and unpleasing ~**ly** adv ~**ness** n [U]

out·last /aʊtˈlæst/ vt last longer than

out·law /ˈaʊtlɔ/ n (in former times) criminal being hunted ♦ vt declare (something) illegal

out·lay /ˈaʊtleɪ/ n money spent on something

out·let /ˈaʊtlet, -lɪt/ n 1 way out for liquid or gas: (fig.) *an outlet for his energy* 2 electrical SOCKET 3 store which sells goods cheaply: *a factory outlet*

out·line /ˈaʊtlaɪn/ n 1 line showing the shape of something 2 main ideas or facts, without details ♦ vt : *She outlined her plans.*

out·live /aʊtˈlɪv/ vt live longer than

out·look /ˈaʊtlʊk/ n 1 view from a place 2 future probabilities 3 one's general point of view

out·ly·ing /ˈaʊtˌlaɪ-ɪŋ/ adj distant; far from a city, etc.

out·mod·ed /aʊtˈmoʊdɪd/ adj no longer in fashion or use

out·num·ber /aʊtˈnʌmbər/ vt be more in numbers than: *outnumbered by the enemy*

out-of-bounds /ˌ· · ˈ·◁/ adj 1 (in sports) outside the playing area 2 (of behavior) unacceptable

out-of-date /ˌ· · ˈ·◁/ adj no longer in use or in fashion

out-of-the-way /ˌ· · · ˈ·◁/ adj 1 distant 2 unusual

out·pa·tient /ˈaʊtˌpeɪʃənt/ n person treated at a hospital but not staying there

out·post /ˈaʊtpoʊst/ n group of people or settlement far from the main group or settlement

out·put /ˈaʊtpʊt/ n 1 [C;U] production: *The factory's output is 200 cars a day.* 2 information produced by a computer

out·rage /ˈaʊtreɪdʒ/ n 1 [C] very wrong or cruel act 2 [U] anger caused by such an act ♦ vt offend greatly ~**ous** /aʊtˈreɪdʒəs/ adj 1 very offensive 2 wildly unexpected and unusual

out·right /ˌaʊtˈraɪt◁/ adv 1 completely: *She won outright.* 2 without delay: *He was killed outright.* 3 openly: *Tell him outright what you think.* ♦ adj complete and clear: *an outright lie*

out·set /ˈaʊtset/ n beginning: *There was trouble from/at the outset.*

out·shine /aʊtˈʃaɪn/ vt –**shone** /-ˈʃoʷn/ 1 shine more brightly than 2 be much better than

out·side /ˌaʊtˈsaɪd◁, ˈaʊtsaɪd/ n 1 [(the) S] the part furthest from the middle, or that faces away from one or towards the open air: *to paint the outside of a house* 2 **At the outside** at the most ♦ adj 1 facing or at the outside: *the outside wall* 2 from elsewhere: *an outside broadcast* 3 (of a chance or possibility) slight ♦ adv 1 to or on the outside, esp. in the open air: *go outside* ♦ prep 1 to or on the outside of: *Wait just outside the door.* 2 beyond the limits of: *outside my experience*

out·sid·er /aʊtˈsaɪdər/ n 1 person not accepted in a social group 2 person or animal not expected to win

out·size /ˈaʊtsaɪz/ adj larger than the standard sizes

out·skirts /ˈaʊtskɜrts/ n [P] outer areas or limits of a town

out·smart /aʊtˈsmɑrt/ vt defeat by being more clever

out·spo·ken /aʊtˈspoʷkən/ adj expressing thoughts or feelings openly ~**ly** adv ~**ness** n [U]

out·stand·ing /aʊtˈstændɪŋ/ adj 1 much better than others 2 not yet done or paid ~**ly** adv

out·stay /aʊtˈsteɪ/ vt stay longer than: *to outstay one's welcome* (= stay too long as a guest so as to be no longer welcome)

out·strip /aʊtˈstrɪp/ vt –pp– do better than: *to outstrip one's competitors*

out·ward /ˈaʊt·wərd/ adj, adv 1 away: *the outward journey* 2 on the outside but perhaps not really: *outward cheerfulness* ~ly adv **outwards** adv

out·weigh /aʊtˈweʲ/ vt be more important than

out·wit /aʊtˈwɪt/ vt –tt– defeat by being more clever

out·worn /ˌaʊtˈwɔrn, -ˈwoʳrn/ adj (of an idea, custom, etc.) no longer used or useful

o·val /ˈoʷvəl/ n, adj (something) shaped like an egg

o·va·ry /ˈoʷvəriʲ/ n part of a female that produces eggs

o·va·tion /oʷˈveʲʃən/ n joyful expression of public approval

ov·en /ˈʌvən/ n closed box for cooking, baking clay, etc.: *It's like an oven in here.* (= uncomfortably hot)

over[1] /ˈoʷvər/ prep 1 higher than but not touching: *the clock over the fireplace* 2 so as to cover: *Put a cloth over the jug.* 3 from side to side of, esp. by going up and down: *to climb over a wall* | *a bridge over the river* 4 down across the edge of: *It fell over the cliff.* 5 in; through: *There's snow over most of the Rockies.* 6 in control of: *I don't want anyone over me, telling me what to do.* 7 more than: *over 10 years ago* 8 while doing, eating, etc.: *We held a meeting over lunch.* 9 by means of: *I heard it over the radio.* 10 about: *an argument over money* 11 **over and above** as well as

over[2] adv 1 downwards from an upright position: *I fell over.* 2 across an edge or distance: *The milk boiled over.* | *We flew over to Europe.* 3 so that another side is seen: *Turn the page over.* 4 beyond: *children of 7 and over* (= older) 5 so as to be covered: *The windows are boarded over.* 6 remaining: *Was there any money left over?* 7 (shows something is repeated): *I had to do it (all) over again.* 8 in all details: *Think it over carefully.* ♦ adj ended: *The party's over.*

o·ver·all /ˌoʷvərˈɔl◂/ adj, adv including everything: *overall costs*

o·ver·alls /ˈoʷvərˌɔlz/ n [P] garment for the whole body, to protect one's clothes

o·ver·awe /ˌoʷvərˈɔ/ vt make quiet because of respect and fear

o·ver·bal·ance /ˌoʷvərˈbæləns/ vi become balanced and fall over

o·ver·bear·ing /ˌoʷvərˈbeərɪŋ/ adj forcefully trying to tell others what to do

o·ver·board /ˈoʷvərˌbɔrd, -ˌboʷrd/ adv 1 over the side of a boat into the water 2 **go overboard** become very or too enthusiastic

o·ver·cast /ˌoʷvərˈkæst◂/ adj dark with clouds

o·ver·coat /ˈoʷvərˌkoʷt/ n long warm coat

o·ver·come /ˌoʷvərˈkʌm/ vt –came /-ˈkeʲm/, –come 1 defeat 2 make helpless: *overcome with grief*

o·ver·crowd /ˌoʷvərˈkraʊd/ vt put or allow too many people or things in (one place)

o·ver·do /ˌoʷvərˈduʷ/ vt –did /-ˈdɪd/, –done /-ˈdʌn/, 3rd person sing. pres. t. –does /-ˈdʌz/ do, decorate, perform, etc., too much: *I've been overdoing it* (= working too hard) *lately.*

o·ver·dose /ˈoʷvərˌdoʷs/ n too much of a drug

o·ver·draft /ˈoʷvərˌdræft/ n money lent by a bank to an overdrawn person

o·ver·drawn /ˌoʷvərˈdrɔn◂/ adj having taken more money from your bank account than it contains

o·ver·drive /ˈoʷvərˌdraɪv/ n [U] GEAR that allows a car to go fast on less than full power

o·ver·due /ˌoʷvərˈduʷ◂, -ˈdyuʷ◂/ adj late

o·ver·flow /ˌoʷvərˈfloʷ/ vi/t 1 flow over the edge (of): *The water's/The bathtub's overflowing.* 2 go beyond the limits (of): *The crowd overflowed into the street.* ♦ n /ˈoʷvərˌfloʷ/ (pipe for carrying away) something that overflows

o·ver·grown /ˌoʷvərˈgroʷn◂/ adj 1 covered with plants growing uncontrolled 2 grown too large

o·ver·hang /ˌoʷvərˈhæŋ/ vi/t –hung /-ˈhʌŋ/ hang or stick out over (something) ♦ n /ˈoʷvərˌhæŋ/ overhanging rock, roof, etc.

o·ver·haul /ˈoʷvərˌhɔl/ n thorough examination: *The car needs an overhaul.*

o·ver·head /ˌoʷvərˈhed◂, ˈoʷvərˌhed/ adj, adv above one's head: *overhead cables* ♦ n /ˈoʷvərˌhed/ money spent regularly to keep a business running

o·ver·hear /ˌoʷvərˈhɪər/ vi/t –heard /-ˈhɜrd/ hear (what others are saying) without them knowing

o·ver·joyed /ˌoʷvərˈdʒɔɪd/ adj extremely pleased

o·ver·kill /ˈoʷvərˌkɪl/ n [U] something that goes beyond the desirable or safe limits

o·ver·la·den /ˌoʷvərˈleʲdn/ past p. of OVERLOAD

o·ver·land /ˈoʷvərˌlænd/ adj, adv across land and not by sea or air

o·ver·lap /ˌoʷvərˈlæp/ vi/t –pp– cover (something) partly and go beyond it: (fig.) *Our interests over-lap.* (= are partly the same) ♦ *n* /ˈoʷvərˌlæp/ part that overlaps

o·ver·leaf /ˈoʷvərˌliʸf/ *adv* on the other side of the page

o·ver·load /ˌoʷvərˈloʷd/ *vt* –**loaded** *or* –**laden** /-ˈleʸdn/ **1** load too heavily **2** put too much electricity through **overload** /ˈoʷvərˌloʷd/ *n*

o·ver·look /ˌoʷvərˈlʊk/ *vt* **1** give a view from above **2** not notice; miss **3** forgive

o·ver·manned /ˌoʷvərˈmænd/ *adj* having more workers than are needed for a job -**manning** *n* [U]

o·ver·much /ˌoʷvərˈmʌtʃ◂/ *adv, determiner, pron* *fml* too much **2** very much: *I don't like him over-much.*

o·ver·night /ˌoʷvərˈnaɪt◂/ *adj, adv* **1** for or during the night **2** suddenly: *an overnight success*

o·ver·pass /ˈoʷvərˌpæs/ *n* place where two roads cross at different levels

o·ver·play /ˌoʷvərˈpleʸ/ *vt* make (something) appear more important than it really is

o·ver·pow·er /ˌoʷvərˈpaʊər/ *vt* defeat by greater power ~**ing** *adj* very strong: *an overpowering desire*

o·ver·ran /ˌoʷvərˈræn/ *past tense of* OVERRUN

o·ver·rate /ˌoʷvərˈreʸt/ *vt* give too high an opinion of

o·ver·re·act /ˌoʷvər-riʸˈækt/ *vi* act too strongly as a result of (something)

o·ver·ride /ˌoʷvərˈraɪd/ *vt* –**rode** /-ˈroʷd/, –**ridden** /-ˈrɪdn/ forbid obedience to or acceptance of (and take the place of): *My orders were overridden.* -**riding** *adj* greater than anything else: *of overriding importance*

o·ver·rule /ˌoʷvərˈruʷl/ *vt* decide against (something already decided) by official power

o·ver·run /ˌoʷvərˈrʌn/ *v* –**ran** /-ˈræn/, –**run 1** *vt* spread over and cause harm **2** *vi/t* continue beyond (a time limit)

o·ver·seas /ˌoʷvərˈsiʸz◂/ *adv, adj* in, to, or from a foreign country across the sea

o·ver·see /ˌoʷvərˈsiʸ/ *vt* –**saw** /-ˈsɔ/, –**seen** /-ˈsiʸn/ watch to see that work is properly done -**seer** /ˈoʷvərˌsiʸər, -ˌsɪər/ *n*

o·ver·shad·ow /ˌoʷvərˈʃædoʷ/ *vt* **1** make worried and sadder **2** make appear less important

o·ver·shoot /oʷvərˈʃuʷt/ *vi/t* –**shot** /-ˈʃɑt/ go too far or beyond, and miss

o·ver·sight /ˈoʷvərˌsaɪt/ *n* unintended failure to notice or do something

o·ver·sleep /ˌoʷvərˈsliʸp/ *vi* –**slept** /-ˈslɛpt/ wake up too late

o·ver·step /ˌoʷvərˈstɛp/ *vt* –**pp**– go beyond (the limits of what is proper or allowed)

o·vert /oʷˈvɜrt, ˈoʷvɜrt/ *adj* not hidden; open: *overt resistance* ~**ly** *adv*

o·ver·take /ˌoʷvərˈteʸk/ *v* –**took** /-ˈtʊk/, –**taken** /-ˈteʸkən/ **1** *vi/t* pass (a vehicle in front) **2** *vt* (of something unpleasant) reach suddenly and unexpectedly

over-the-hill /ˌ·· ·ˈ·◂/ *adj* (too) old

o·ver·throw /ˌoʷvərˈθroʷ/ *vt* –**threw** /-ˈθruʷ/, –**thrown** /-ˈθroʷn/ remove from power ♦ *n* /ˈoʷvərˌθroʷ/ the violent overthrow of the government

o·ver·time /ˈoʷvərˌtaɪm/ *n, adv* [U] (money paid for or time spent working) beyond the usual working time: *to work overtime to do something* (= use much effort)

o·ver·tones /ˈoʷvərˌtoʷnz/ *n* [P] things suggested but not stated clearly

o·ver·took /ˌoʷvərˈtʊk/ *past tense of* OVERTAKE

o·ver·ture /ˈoʷvɜrtʃər, -ˌtʃʊər/ *n* musical introduction, esp. to an OPERA **overtures** *n* [P] offer to begin talks

o·ver·turn /ˌoʷvərˈtɜrn/ *v* **1** *vi/t* turn over **2** *vt* bring to an end suddenly

o·ver·view /ˈoʷvərˌvyuʷ/ *n* usu. short account (of something) which gives a general picture but no details

o·ver·weight /ˌoʷvərˈweʸt/ *adj* weighing too much

o·ver·whelm /ˌoʷvərˈhwɛlm, -ˈwɛlm/ *vt* **1** defeat or make powerless by much greater numbers **2** (of feelings) make completely helpless

o·ver·wrought /ˌoʷvərˈrɔt/ *adj* too nervous and excited

ov·u·late /ˈɑvyəˌleʸt/ *vi* produce eggs from the OVARY –**lation** /ˌɑvyəˈleʸʃən/ *n* [U]

ow /aʊ/ *interj* (expresses sudden slight pain)

owe /oʷ/ *vt* **1** have to pay: *I owed her $5.* **2** feel grateful for: *We owe a lot to our parents.*

ow·ing /ˈoʷɪŋ/ *adj* **1** still to be paid **2 owing to** /ˈ·· ·/ because of

owl /aʊl/ *n* night bird with large eyes

own¹ /oʷn/ *determiner, pron* **1** belonging to the stated person and no one else: *At last I had my own room/ a room of my own.* **2 come into one's own** begin to be properly respected for one's qualities **3 have/get one's own back (on someone)** succeed in doing harm (to someone) in return for harm

done to oneself **4 hold one's own (against)** avoid defeat (by) **5 on one's own: a** alone **b** without help
own² *vt* possess, esp. by legal right ~**er** *n* ~**ership** *n* [U]

   own to *phr vt* admit

   own up *phr vi* admit a fault or crime
ox /ɑks/ *n* **oxen** /'ɑksən/ large animal of the cattle type, esp. male
ox·y·gen /'ɑksədʒən/ *n* [U] gas

present in the air, necessary for life
oy·ster /'ɔɪstər/ *n* **1** flat shellfish, often eaten **2 the world is one's/someone's oyster** there are no limits on where one/someone can go, etc.

oz *written abbrev. for:* OUNCE(s)

o·zone /'oʷzoʷn/ *n* [U] **1** type of oxygen in a LAYER high above the earth **2** sea air that is pleasant to breathe

P

P, p /piʸ/ **1** the 16th letter of the English alphabet **2** mind one's p's and q's be careful in what one says so as to avoid displeasing others

p *abbrev. for:* page

pace /peʸs/ n **1** speed, esp. of walking or running: *She works so fast I can't keep pace with* (= go as fast as) *her.* **2** (distance moved in) a single step **3** **put someone through his/her paces** make someone do something in order to show his/her abilities, qualities, etc. **4 set the pace** fix the speed for others to copy **5 show one's paces** show one's abilities/qualities ♦ v **1** vi/t walk (across) with slow regular steps **2** vt set the speed of movement for

pace out/off phr vt measure by taking steps

pace·mak·er /ˈpeʸsˌmeʸkər/ n **1** person who sets a speed or example for others to follow **2** machine used to make weak or irregular HEARTBEATS regular

Pa·cif·ic time /pəˈsɪfɪk ˌtaɪm/ n [U] time used on the West Coast of the US, 3 hours earlier than Eastern time

pa·ci·fi·er /ˈpæsəˌfaɪər/ n baby's rubber NIPPLE for sucking

pac·i·fist /ˈpæsəfɪst/ n person who believes war is wrong and refuses to fight **–fism** n [U]

pac·i·fy /ˈpæsəˌfaɪ/ vt make calm and quiet, esp. less angry **–fication** /ˌpæsəfəˈkeʸʃən/ n [U]

pack¹ /pæk/ n **1** number of things wrapped or tied together or put in a case **2** packet **3** group of hunting animals **4** collection, group: *a pack of lies/thieves*

pack² v **1** vi/t put (things) into cases, boxes, etc., for taking somewhere or storing **2** vi/t fit or push into a space: *Crowds of people packed into the hall.* **3** vt cover, fill, or surround closely with protective material **4 pack a (hard) punch** infml **a** (of a fighter) able to give a strong hard blow **b** use very forceful language in an argument **5 send someone packing** infml cause someone undesirable to leave quickly **~ed** adj full of people

pack in phr vt infml attract in large numbers: *That film is really packing them in.*

pack off phr vt infml BUNDLE off

pack up phr v infml **1** vi finish work **2** gather one's possessions: *pack up and leave*

pack·age /ˈpækɪdʒ/ n **1** number of things packed together; parcel **2** set of related things offered as a unit ♦ vt **1** make into a package **2** put in a special container for selling

package deal /ˈ·· ˌ·/ n offer or agreement where a number of things must all be accepted together

package tour /ˈ·· ˌ·/ n vacation where all travel, hotels, food, etc., are paid for together

pack·et /ˈpækɪt/ n small container or parcel: *a packet of sugar*

pack·ing /ˈpækɪŋ/ n [U] **1** putting things in cases or boxes **2** protective material for packing things

pack rat /ˈpækræt/ n person who saves things that appear useless

pact /pækt/ n solemn agreement

pad¹ /pæd/ n **1** something made or filled with soft material, for protection or to give shape **2** many sheets of paper fastened together: *a writing pad* **3** LAUNCHING PAD **4** sl one's house or home **5** bottom part of foot, usu. with thick skin, of some animals that have 4 feet ♦ vt **–dd– 1** protect, shape, or make more comfortable with a pad or pads **2** make longer by adding unnecessary words **~ding** n [U] **1** material used to pad something **2** unnecessary words or sentences

pad² vi **–dd–** walk steadily and usu. softly

pad·dle¹ /ˈpædl/ n short pole with a wide blade at one end or both ends, for rowing a small boat ♦ vi/t **1** row with a paddle **2 paddle one's own canoe** infml depend on oneself and no one else

paddle² vi walk about in water a few inches deep ♦ n [S] act of paddling

pad·dock /ˈpædək/ n small field where horses are kept

pad·dy /ˈpædiʸ/ n field where rice is grown in water

paddy wag·on /ˈ·· ˌ··/ n infml police vehicle for carrying prisoners

pad·lock /ˈpædlɑk/ n lock that can be removed, fastened with a bar in the shape of a U, for locking gates, bicycles, etc. ♦ vi/t fasten or lock with a padlock

pa·gan /ˈpeʸgən/ n person who does not believe in one's religion, or in any of the main religions ♦ adj: *pagan tribes* **~ism** n [U]

page¹ /peʸdʒ/ n one or both sides of a sheet of paper in a book, newspaper, etc.

page² n **1** boy servant at a hotel, club, etc. **2** boy attendant at a wedding

pag·eant /ˈpædʒənt/ n splendid public show or ceremony **~ry** n [U] splendid show of ceremonial grandness

pa·go·da /pə'gowʷdə/ n temple (esp. Buddhist or Hindu) built on several floors

paid /peʸd/ past t. and p. of PAY – see also **put paid to** (PUT)

paid-up /ˌ·ˈ◂/ adj having paid in full (esp. so as to continue being a member)

pail /peʸl/ n bucket

pain /peʸn/ n 1 (U) suffering in body or mind; hurting: Are you in pain? 2 (C) case of such suffering in a particular part: a pain in my stomach 3 (S) also **pain in the neck** /ˌ··· ˈ·/ —sl person, thing, or happening that makes one angry or tired 4 **on/under pain of** /fml at the risk of suffering (a punishment) if something is not done ♦ vt fml cause pain to ~**ed** adj displeased or hurt in one's feelings ~**ful** adj: a painful cut ~**less** adj **pains** n [P] effort; trouble: I went to great pains to get the one you wanted.

painstaking /'peʸnsˌteʸkɪŋ/ adj very careful and thorough

paint /peʸnt/ n (U) liquid coloring matter for decorating surfaces or making pictures ♦ vi/t 1 put paint on (a surface) 2 make a picture (of) with paint 3 describe in clear, carefully chosen words 4 **paint the town red** go out and have a good time ~**ing** n 1 (U) act or art of painting 2 (C) painted picture – see also OIL PAINTING **paints** n [P] set of small containers of paints of different colors, for painting pictures

paint·er¹ /'peʸntər/ n person who paints pictures, or houses, rooms, etc.

painter² n rope for tying up a small boat

paint·work /'peʸntwɜrk/ n (U) painted surface

pair /peər/ n 1 two of the same kind: a pair of gloves 2 something made of two similar parts: a pair of scissors 3 two people closely connected ♦ vi/t form into one or more pairs: Jane and David paired off at the party.

pair up phr vi/t (cause to) join in pairs, esp. for work or sport

pa·ja·mas /pə'dʒɑməz, -'dʒæ-/ n pants and shirt that fit loosely, worn in bed

pal /pæl/ n infml friend

pal·ace /'pælɪs/ n large grand house, esp. where a king or president lives

palace rev·o·lu·tion /ˌ··· ··ˈ··/ n removal of a president, king, etc., from power by people who worked closely with him/her

pal·a·ta·ble /'pælətəbəl/ adj fml

good to taste 2 acceptable; pleasant: not a palatable suggestion

pal·ate /'pælɪt/ n 1 the top inside part of the mouth 2 ability to judge good food or wine

pa·la·tial /pə'leʸʃəl/ adj (of a building) large and splendid

pa·la·ver /pə'lævər/ n (U) trouble over unimportant matters; FUSS

pale¹ /peʸl/ adj 1 not bright or dark: pale blue 2 (of a face) rather white ♦ vi 1 become pale 2 seem less important, clever, etc., when compared with

pale² n limit of proper behavior: beyond the pale

pal·e·on·tol·o·gy /ˌpeʸliʸɑn'tɑlədʒiʸ/ n (U) study of FOSSILS –**gist** n

pal·ette /'pælɪt/ n board on which a painter mixes colors

pal·ings /'peʸlɪŋz/ n [P] (fence made of) pointed pieces of wood

pall¹ /pɔl/ vi become uninteresting or dull

pall² n 1 (S) heavy or dark covering: a pall of smoke 2 (C) cloth spread over a COFFIN

pall·bear·er /'pɔlˌbeərər/ n person who walks beside or helps carry a COFFIN

pal·let /'pælɪt/ n large flat frame used with a FORKLIFT TRUCK for lifting heavy goods

pal·li·ate /'pæliʸeʸt/ vt fml cause to be or seem less unpleasant or wrong –**ative** /'pæliʸeʸtɪv, 'pæliʸətɪv/ n, adj: only a palliative, not a cure

pal·lid /'pælɪd/ adj (of skin) pale to an unhealthy degree ~**ness** n (U)

pal·lor /'pælər/ n (S) pallidness

palm¹ /pɑm/ n tall tropical tree with no branches and a mass of large leaves at the top

palm² n inside surface of the hand

palm³ v **palm off** phr vt 1 get rid of by deception 2 deceive into accepting

palm·ist /'pɑmɪst/ n person who tells someone's future by looking at their PALM² ~**ry** n (U) palmist's art

palm·y /'pɑmiʸ/ adj (of past periods) most pleasant and successful

pal·pa·ble /'pælpəbəl/ adj fml easily and clearly known: a palpable lie –**bly** adv

pal·pi·tate /'pælpəˌteʸt/ vi (of the heart) beat fast and irregularly –**tations** /ˌpælpə'teʸʃənz/ n [P]

pal·try /'pɔltriʸ/ adj worthlessly small or unimportant

pam·pas /'pæmpəz, -pəs/ n (U) wide treeless plains in South America

pam·per /'pæmpər/ vt treat too kindly

pam·phlet /'pæmflɪt/ n small book with paper covers

pan¹ /pæn/ n 1 round metal container for cooking, usu. with a long handle **2** container with holes in the bottom used for separating precious metals from other material

pan² /v/ **-nn-** **1** *vt infml* CRITICIZE very severely **2** *vi/t* move (a camera) to follow the action being recorded on film or television **3** *vi/t* use a pan (2) to search for valuable metals: *pan for gold*

pan out *phr vi* happen in a particular way

pan·a·ce·a /ˌpænəˈsiʲə/ *n* something that will put right all troubles

pa·nache /pəˈnæʃ, pəˈnɑʃ/ *n* [U] showy splendid way of doing things

Pan A·mer·i·can·is·m /ˌpæn əˈmerɪkəˌnɪzəm/ *n* idea supporting unity among all north, south, and central American countries

pan·cake /ˈpænkeʲk/ *n* flat cake cooked in a pan

pan·cre·as /ˈpæŋkriʲəs/ *n* bodily organ that helps in changing food chemically for use by the body

pan·da /ˈpændə/ *n* black and white bearlike animal from China

pan·de·mo·ni·um /ˌpændəˈmoʷniʲəm/ *n* [U] wild and noisy disorder

pan·der /ˈpændər/ *v* **pander to** *phr vt* satisfy in an unworthy way: *The newspapers pander to people's interest in sex scandals.*

Pan·do·ra's box /pænˌdɔrəz ˈbɑks, -ˌdoʷr-/ *n* **open Pandora's box** unintentionally cause, by taking some action, a large number of problems that did not exist or were not known about before

pane /peʲn/ *n* sheet of glass in a window

pan·e·gyr·ic /ˌpænəˈdʒɪrɪk/ *n infml* speech or writing full of great praise

pan·el /ˈpænl/ *n* **1** flat piece of wood in a door or on a wall **2** board with instruments fixed in it: *an aircraft's control panel* **3** small group of people who answer questions on esp. a radio or television show **4** piece of cloth of a different color or material, set in a dress – see also SOLAR PANEL ♦ *vt* **-l-** decorate with PANELS (1): *oak-paneled walls* **~ing** *n* [U] PANELS (1)

pang /pæŋ/ *n* sudden sharp feeling of pain

pan·han·dle /ˈpænˌhændl/ *vi* beg on the street **~r** *n*

pan·ic /ˈpænɪk/ *n* [C;U] sudden uncontrollable fear or terror which spreads quickly ♦ *vi/t* **-ck-** (cause to) feel panic **~ky** *adj* suddenly afraid

panic-strick·en /ˈ·· ˌ··/ *adj* filled with panic

pan·nier /ˈpænyər, ˈpæniʲər/ *n*

basket, esp. either of a pair on a bicycle

pan·o·ply /ˈpænəpliʲ/ *n* [U] splendid ceremonial show or dress

pan·o·ra·ma /ˌpænəˈræmə, -ˈrɑ-/ *n* **1** complete view of a wide stretch of land **2** general representation in words or pictures **–ramic** /-ˈræmɪk/ *adj*

pan·sy /ˈpænziʲ/ **1** small garden plant with flowers **2** *infml derog* **a** EFFEMINATE young man **b** male HOMOSEXUAL

pant /pænt/ *vi* breathe quickly, with short breaths ♦ *n* quick short breath

pan·the·is·m /ˈpænθiʲˌɪzəm/ *n* [U] religious idea that God and the universe are the same thing **–ist** *n*

pan·ther /ˈpænθər/ *n* LEOPARD, esp. a black one

pan·ties /ˈpæntiʲz/ *n* [P] women's short undergarment worn below the waist

pan·to·mime /ˈpæntəˌmaɪm/ *n* MIME

pan·try /ˈpæntriʲ/ *n* small room with shelves where food is kept

pants /pænts/ *n* [P] **1** outer garment with 2 legs, covering the body from the waist downwards **2 with one's pants down** *sl* awkwardly unprepared **3 by the seat of one's pants** *infml* guided by one's experience rather than by a formal plan

pap /pæp/ *n* [U] **1** soft liquid food for babies or sick people **2** reading matter or entertainment intended only for amusement, which does not instruct or contain ideas of any value

pap·a /ˈpɑpə/ *n* father

pa·pa·cy /ˈpeʲpəsiʲ/ *n* power and office of the POPE

pa·pal /ˈpeʲpəl/ *adj* of the POPE

pap·a·raz·zo /ˌpæpəˈrætsoʷ/ *n* **–zi** /-tsiʲ/ newspaper writer or photographer who follows famous people about hoping to find out interesting or shocking stories about them

pa·per /ˈpeʲpər/ *n* **1** [U] material in thin sheets for writing or printing on, wrapping things in, etc. **2** [C] newspaper **3** [C] set of questions to be answered in an examination **4** [C] piece of writing for specialists, often read aloud **5 on paper** as written down, but not yet tried out in reality ♦ *vt* cover with WALLPAPER

papers *n* [P] pieces of paper written on or printed, esp. used for official purposes

pa·per·back /ˈpeʲpərˌbæk/ *n* book with a thin cardboard cover

pa·per·boy /ˈpeʲpərˌbɔɪ/ *n* boy who delivers newspapers

paper clip /ˈ·· ˌ·, ˌ·· ˈ·/ *n* piece of curved wire for holding papers together

paper ti·ger /ˌ·· ˈ··/ *n* enemy that seems or wishes to seem powerful or threatening but is really not so

pa·per·weight /ˈpeɪpər.weɪt/ *n* heavy object put on papers to stop them being scattered

pa·per·work /ˈpeɪpər.wɜrk/ *n* (U) writing reports and letters, keeping records, etc.

pap·ri·ka /pæˈpriːkə, ˈpæprɪkə/ *n* (U) red powder with a hot taste, from a plant and used in cooking

par /pɑr/ *n* 1 (S) (nearly) equal level: *Her skill is on a par with mine.* 2 (U) average number of hits in GOLF 3 **under par** *infml* not in the usual or average condition of health

par·a·ble /ˈpærəbəl/ *n* short simple story which teaches a moral lesson

pa·rab·o·la /pəˈræbələ/ *n* curved line, like a thrown ball rising and falling **-bolic** /ˌpærəˈbɑlɪk◂/ *adj*

par·a·chute /ˈpærəʃuːt/ *n* piece of cloth on long ropes, fastened to someone to allow them to fall slowly and safely from an aircraft ♦ *vi/t* drop by means of a parachute

pa·rade /pəˈreɪd/ *n* 1 informal procession 2 ceremonial gathering of soldiers to be officially looked at – see also HIT PARADE ♦ *v* 1 *vi* walk or gather in a parade 2 *vi* walk showily 3 *vt* show in order to be admired: *parading her knowledge*

par·a·dise /ˈpærəˌdaɪs, -ˌdaɪz/ *n* 1 (U)(*usu. cap.*) Heaven 2 (S;U) place or state of perfect happiness – see also FOOL'S PARADISE

par·a·dox /ˈpærəˌdɑks/ *n* 1 statement that says 2 opposite things but has some truth in it 2 strange combination of opposite qualities, ideas, etc. **~ical** /ˌpærəˈdɑksɪkəl/ *adj* **~ically** /-kliʸ/ *adv* 1 in a paradoxical way 2 it is a paradox that

par·af·fin /ˈpærəfɪn/ *n* (U) type of wax used to make CANDLES

par·a·gon /ˈpærəˌgɑn, -gən/ *n* person who is or seems to be a perfect model to copy

par·a·graph /ˈpærəˌgræf/ *n* division of a piece of writing that begins a new line

par·a·keet /ˈpærəˌkiʸt/ *n* small brightly colored Australian bird

par·al·lel /ˈpærəˌlel, -ləl/ *adj* 1 (of lines) always the same distance apart 2 comparable ♦ *n* 1 (C;U) comparable person or thing 2 (C) similarity (point of) 3 (C) line of LATITUDE ♦ *vt* **-l-** be similar to

par·al·lel·o·gram /ˌpærəˈleləˌgræm/ *n* figure with 4 sides, having opposite sides equal and parallel

pa·ral·y·sis /pəˈræləsɪs/ *n* (U) loss of movement in (some) of the body muscles **paralytic** /ˌpærəˈlɪtɪk◂/ *adj* suffering from paralysis

par·a·lyze /ˈpærəˌlaɪz/ *vt* 1 cause paralysis in 2 cause to stop working: *The strike paralyzed the industry.*

par·a·med·ic /ˌpærəˈmedɪk/ *n* someone, such as an AMBULANCE driver, who helps in the care of sick people but is not a doctor or nurse

pa·ram·e·ter /pəˈræmətər/ *n* (*usu. pl.*) any of the established limits within which something must operate

par·a·mil·i·tary /ˌpærəˈmɪləˌteriʸ/ *adj* acting like an army, esp. illegally

par·a·mount /ˈpærəˌmaʊnt/ *adj fml* greater than all others in importance

par·a·noi·a /ˌpærəˈnɔɪə/ *n* (U) disease of the mind in which you think esp. that other people are trying to harm you **-noid** /ˈpærəˌnɔɪd/ *adj* (as if) suffering from paranoia

par·a·pet /ˈpærəˌpɪt, -ˌpet/ *n* low protective wall at the edge of a roof, bridge, etc.

par·a·pher·na·lia /ˌpærəfərˈneʸlyə, -fəˈneʸl-/ *n* (U) small articles of various kinds

par·a·phrase /ˈpærəˌfreʸz/ *vt, n* (make) a re-expression of (something written or said) in different words

par·a·site /ˈpærəˌsaɪt/ *n* 1 animal or plant that lives and feeds on another 2 useless person supported by others' efforts **-sitic** /ˌpærəˈsɪtɪk◂/ *adj*

par·a·sol /ˈpærəˌsɔl, -ˌsɑl/ *n* SUNSHADE

par·a·troops /ˈpærəˌtruʷps/ *n* (P) soldiers who drop from aircraft using PARACHUTES

par·cel¹ /ˈpɑrsəl/ *n* 1 something wrapped up in paper and fastened 2 **part and parcel of** a most important part that cannot be separated from the whole of

parcel² *v* **-l-** **parcel out** *phr vt* divide into parts or shares

parch /pɑrtʃ/ *vt* make hot and dry

parch·ment /ˈpɑrtʃmənt/ *n* (C;U) treated animal skin, used formerly for writing on

par·don /ˈpɑrdn/ *n* 1 (C;U) (act of) forgiving, esp. of a guilty person, so they will no longer be punished 2 **I beg your pardon**, also **pardon me** —**a** 'Please excuse me for having accidentally touched/pushed you.' **b** 'Please repeat what you said.' ♦ *vt* give pardon to ♦ *interj* (ask for something not fully heard to be repeated) **~able** *adj* that can be forgiven

pard·ner /ˈpɑrdnər/ *n infml* partner or friend

pare /peər/ *vt* cut off the edge or thin

covering of: (fig.) *We must pare
down* (= reduce) *costs.*

par·ent /ˈpeərənt, ˈpær-/ n father or
mother ~**tal** /pəˈrentəl/ adj

pa·ren·the·sis /pəˈrenθəsɪs/ n -**ses**
/-ˌsiˑyz/ fml **1** (usu. pl.) either of the
marks (or) used to enclose a piece
of information **2** words introduced
as an added explanation or thought

pa·ri·ah /pəˈraɪə/ n fml person not
accepted by society

par·ish /ˈpærɪʃ/ n area for which a
priest has responsibility: *the parish
church*

pa·rish·ion·er /pəˈrɪʃənər/ n person
who lives in a parish

par·i·ty /ˈpærətiˑy/ n [U] fml being
equal

park¹ /pɑrk/ n large usu. grassy enclosed piece of land in a town, used
by the public for pleasure and rest

park² vi/t put (a vehicle) for a time:
(fig.) *He just came in and parked
himself on the sofa.*

par·ka /ˈpɑrkə/ n short coat with a
HOOD

parking lot /ˈ·· ˌ·/ n open or enclosed place where cars and other
vehicles may be left

parking me·ter /ˈ·· ˌ··/ n apparatus
into which one puts one's money, allowing one to park near it for a time

park·way /ˈpɑrkweˑy/ n large road
through a park

par·lance /ˈpɑrləns/ n [U] fml particular way of speaking or use of words

par·ley /ˈpɑrliˑy/ vi, n (hold) a talk,
esp. with an enemy to make peace

par·lia·ment /ˈpɑrləmənt/ n body of
people elected or appointed to make
laws in Britain and Commonwealth
countries ~**ary** /ˌpɑrləˈmentəriˑy◂/
adj

par·lor /ˈpɑrlər/ n **1** LIVING ROOM **2**
business place: *an ice-cream parlor*

parlor game /ˈ·· ·/ n game played
sitting down indoors

pa·ro·chi·al /pəˈroˑwkiˑyəl/ adj **1** only
interested in one's own affairs **2** of
a PARISH

par·o·dy /ˈpærədiˑy/ n [C;U] copy of
a writer's or musician's style, made
to amuse ♦ vt make a parody of

pa·role /pəˈroˑwl/ n [U] letting someone out of prison before their official period in prison has ended ♦ vt
let out of prison on parole

par·ox·ys·m /ˈpærəkˌsɪzəm/ n sudden sharp expression of feeling or
attack of pain

par·quet /pɑrˈkeˑy/ n [U] small wooden blocks making a floor

par·rot /ˈpærət/ n tropical bird with
a curved beak and usu. brightly
colored feathers ♦ vt repeat (someone else's words or actions) without
thought or understanding

par·ry /ˈpæriˑy/ vt turn aside (a blow
or weapon): (fig.) *parrying awkward questions*

par·si·mo·ni·ous /ˌpɑrsəˈmoˑwniˑyəs/
adj unwilling to spend money;
STINGY ~**ly** adv ~**ness** n [U]

par·si·mo·ny /ˈpɑrsəˌmoˑwniˑy/ n [U]
fml ungenerousness; state of being
parsimonious

pars·ley /ˈpɑrsliˑy/ n [U] small plant
used in cooking

pars·nip /ˈpɑrsnɪp/ n plant with a
long white root used as a vegetable

par·son /ˈpɑrsən/ n priest in charge
of a PARISH

par·son·age /ˈpɑrsənɪdʒ/ n parson's
house

part¹ /pɑrt/ n **1** [C] any of the pieces
into which something is divided: *an
engine with 100 moving parts* | *The
travel is the best part of my job* **2**
[S;U] share in an activity: *Did you
take part in the fighting?* **3** [U] side;
position: *He took my part* (= supported me) *in the quarrel.* **4** [C]
(words of) a character acted in a
play or film **5** [C] line on the head
when the hair is parted **6 for my
part** as far as I am concerned **7 for
the most part**: a mostly **b** in most
cases **8 in part** partly **9 on the part
of** of or by (someone) **10 play a part
in** have an influence on **11 in good
part** without being offended ♦ adv
partly: *The exams are part written,
part practical* ~**ly** adv **1** not completely **2** in some degree **parts** n [P]
area of a country: *We don't have
much rain in these parts.*

part² v **1** vi/t separate: *They parted
as friends.* | *She parted the curtains.*
2 vt separate (hair on the head)
along a line **3 part company
(with):** a end a relationship (with)
b no longer be together (with) **c** disagree (with) ~**ing** n [U] leaving

part with phr vt give away; stop
having

par·take /pɑrˈteˑyk/ vi -**took** /-ˈtʊk/,
-**taken** /-ˈteˑykən/ fml eat or drink
something offered

par·tial /ˈpɑrʃəl/ adj **1** not complete
2 (unfairly) favoring one more than
another **3 partial to** very fond of
~**ly** adv ~**ity** /ˌpɑrʃiˈælətiˑy/ n **1**
[U] being PARTIAL (2) **2** [S] fondness:
a partiality for cream cakes

par·tic·i·pant /pɑrˈtɪsəpənt, pər-/ n
person who participates

par·tic·i·pate /pɑrˈtɪsəˌpeˑyt, pər-/ vi
take part or have a share in an activity -**pation** /pɑrˌtɪsəˈpeˑyʃən,
pər- n [U]

par·ti·ci·ple /ˈpɑrtəˌsɪpəl, -səpəl/ n
PAST PARTICIPLE or PRESENT PARTI-
CIPLE

par·ti·cle /ˈpɑrtɪkəl/ n very small
piece

particle board /'··· ,·/ n [U] building material made from small pieces of wood glued together

par·tic·u·lar /pər'tɪkyələr/ adj 1 special; unusual: of no particular importance 2 single and different from others: this particular case 3 showing (too) much care over small matters 4 in particular especially ♦ n small single part of a whole; detail ~ly adv especially

parting shot /ˌ··'·/ n remark or action made when leaving

par·ti·san /'pɑrʔəzən, -sən/ n, adj 1 (person) giving strong unconditioned support to one side 2 member of an armed group that fights in secret against an enemy that has conquered its country

par·ti·tion /pɑr'tɪʃən, pər-/ n 1 [C] thin wall indoors 2 [U] division, esp. of a country ♦ vt divide up

partition off phr vt separate with a partition

part·ner /'pɑrtnər/ n person you are with, doing something together: a dancing/business/marriage partner ♦ vt act as a partner to ~ship n 1 [U] being a partner 2 [C] business owned by 2 or more partners

part of speech /ˌ· · '·/ n class of word, such as 'noun' or 'verb'

par·took /pɑr'tʊk/ v past t. of PARTAKE

part-time /ˌ· '·◄/ adj, adv (working) during only part of the regular working time

par·ty /'pɑrʔi/ n 1 gathering of people for food and amusement: a birthday party 2 association of people with the same political aims: the Democratic party 3 group of people doing something together: a search party – see also WORKING PARTY 4 esp. law person or group concerned in a matter 5 be (a) party to take part in or know about (some action or activity) 6 (follow) the party line act according to the official opinion of a political party – see also THIRD PARTY ♦ vi infml, enjoy oneself, esp. at a party or parties

pass¹ /pæs/ v 1 vi/t reach and move beyond: Several cars passed (us). 2 vi/t go through or across: A cloud passed across the sun. 3 vi/t (cause to) go: I passed a rope around the tree. 4 vi come to an end: Summer is passing. 5 vt give: Please pass me the salt. 6 vt (in sports) kick, throw, etc., (esp. a ball) to a member of one's own side 7 vi (of time) go by b vt spend (time) 8 vt accept officially: Congress passed a new law. 9 vi/t succeed in (an examination) 10 vt give (a judgment, opinion, etc.): The judge passed a heavy sentence on him. 11 let something pass leave (a wrong statement, mistake, etc.)

without putting it right 12 pass the hat collect money for a cause 13 pass the time of day (with) give a greeting (to), and/or have a short conversation (with)

pass away phr vi die

pass by phr vt disregard

pass for phr vt be (mistakenly) accepted or considered as

pass off phr v vt present falsely: passing herself off as a doctor

pass on phr vi 1 pass away 2 move on

pass out phr vi faint

pass over phr vt fail to choose

pass up phr vt fail to take advantage of; miss

pass² n 1 successful result in an examination 2 official paper showing that one is allowed to do something: a travel pass 3 act of giving the ball to someone else in sports 4 way by which one can travel through or over a place, esp. a range of mountains 5 act of trying to interest someone sexually: He made a pass at me.

pass·a·ble /'pæsəbəl/ adj 1 (just) good enough 2 a (of a road) fit to be used b (of a river) fit to be crossed –bly adv

pas·sage /'pæsɪdʒ/ n 1 [C] long narrow connecting way, esp. a CORRIDOR 2 [C] way through: We forced a passage through the crowd. 3 [U] fml going across, through, etc.: the bill's passage through the House 4 [U] onward flow (of time) 5 [S] (cost of) a journey by sea or air 6 [C] short part of a speech, piece of music, etc.

pas·sé /pæ'seɪ/ adj old-fashioned

pas·sen·ger /'pæsəndʒər/ n person being taken in a vehicle

pass·er·by /ˌpæsər'baɪ/ n passersby person who is going past a place

pass·ing /'pæsɪŋ/ n [U] 1 going by 2 ending; disappearance 3 death 4 in passing while talking about something else ♦ adj 1 moving or going by: passing traffic 2 not lasting long: I didn't give it a passing thought.

pas·sion /'pæʃən/ n 1 [C;U] strong deep feeling, esp. of love or anger 2 [S] a strong liking: a passion for tennis 3 the Passion the suffering and death of Christ

pas·sion·ate /'pæʃənɪt/ adj filled with passion ~ly adv

pas·sive¹ /'pæsɪv/ adj 1 suffering something bad without (enough) opposition 2 (of verbs or sentences) expressing an action which is done to the subject of a sentence ~ly ~ness, also n [U] –sivity /pæ'sɪvəʔi/

passive² n [the+S] passive form of a verb

pass·key /ˈpæs-kiʸ/ n 1 key given to only a few people 2 key that will open many different locks

pass·port /ˈpæspɔrt, -poʷrt/ n 1 small official book allowing one to enter foreign countries 2 something that lets one get something else easily: Is money a passport to happiness?

pass·word /ˈpæswɜrd/ n secret word which one has to know to be allowed into a building, etc.

past¹ /pæst/ adj 1 (of time) earlier than the present: the past few days 2 ended: Winter is past. 3 gram expressing past time: the past tense ♦ former: a past president of our club ♦ n [S] 1 (what happened in) the time before the present: It happened in the past. | our country's glorious past 2 derog secret former life containing wrongs of some kind: a woman with a past

past² prep 1 up to and beyond: They rushed past us. 2 beyond in time or age: It's 10 minutes past four. 3 beyond the possibility of: I'm past caring. (= no longer care) 4 past it infml no longer able to do the things one could formerly do ♦ adv by: The children ran past.

pas·ta /ˈpæstə/ n [U] food made in different shapes from flour paste

paste /peʸst/ n [U] 1 soft mixture of powder and liquid 2 liquid mixture, usu. with flour, for sticking paper together ♦ vt fasten with paste

pas·tel /pæˈstel/ adj soft and light in color

pas·teur·ize /ˈpæstʃəraɪz, -stə-/ vt heat (a liquid) to destroy bacteria –ization /ˌpæstʃərəˈzeʸʃən, -stə-/ n [U]

pas·tiche /pæˈstiʸʃ/ n work of art made of, or in the style of, other works of art

pas·tille /pæˈstiʸl/ n small hard candy esp. containing throat medicine

pas·time /ˈpæs-taɪm/ n something done to pass one's time pleasantly

past mas·ter /ˌ· ˈ··/ n very skilled person

pas·tor /ˈpæstər/ n Christian priest in charge of a church

pas·tor·al /ˈpæstərəl/ adj 1 of a priest's duties amongst his religious group 2 of simple country life

past par·ti·ci·ple /ˌ· ·ˈ····/ n form of a verb used in compounds to show the passive or the PERFECT¹ (5) tenses (such as broken in The cup was broken.)

past per·fect /ˌ· ˈ··/ n verb tense that expresses action completed

before a particular time, formed in English with had

pas·try /ˈpeʸstriʸ/ n 1 [U] a mixture of flour, fat, and liquid, eaten when baked 2 [C] article of food made from this

pas·ture /ˈpæstʃər/ n [C;U] (piece of) grassy land where farm animals feed ♦ vt put in a pasture to feed

past·y /ˈpeʸstiʸ/ adj (of the face) white to an unhealthy degree

PA sys·tem /ˌpiʸ ˈeʸ ˌsɪstəm/ n way of talking to a large group of people at once or to people in many different places or rooms

pat¹ /pæt/ vt -tt- strike gently and repeatedly with a flat hand ♦ n 1 light friendly stroke with the hand 2 small shaped mass of butter 3 a pat on the back expression of praise or satisfaction for something done

pat² adj, adv (too) easily or quickly answered or known

patch /pætʃ/ n 1 irregularly shaped part of a surface different from the rest: damp patches on the wall 2 small piece of material to cover a hole 3 small piece of ground: a cabbage patch 4 piece of material worn to protect a damaged eye ♦ vt put a PATCH (2) on

patch up phr vt 1 repair 2 become friends again after (a quarrel)

patch·work /ˈpætʃwɜrk/ n [C;U] (piece of) sewn work made by joining small bits of different materials: (fig.) the patchwork of fields seen from an airplane

patch·y /ˈpætʃiʸ/ adj 1 in or having patches (PATCH (1)): patchy fog 2 incomplete or only good in parts –ily adv –iness n [U]

pât·é /pɑˈteʸ, pæ-/ n [U] food made by crushing meat, esp. LIVER, into a soft mass

pa·tent /ˈpeʸtnt, ˈpæ-/ n (official paper giving someone) the unshared right to make or sell a new invention ♦ adj 1 protected by a patent 2 fml clear to see: his patent annoyance ♦ vt obtain a patent for ~ly adv fml clearly

patent leath·er /ˌpætnt ˈleðər◂, ˌpæt n-/ n [U] very shiny leather, usu. black

pa·ter·nal /pəˈtɜrnl/ adj 1 of or like a father 2 protecting people like a father but allowing them no freedom 3 related to a person through the father's side of the family ~ly adv

pa·ter·nal·ism /pəˈtɜrnlˌɪzəm/ n [U] a PATERNAL (2) way of controlling people -istic /pəˌtɜrnlˈɪstɪk/ adj ~istically /-kliʸ/ adv

pa·ter·ni·ty /pəˈtɜrnətiʸ/ n [U] esp. law origin from the male parent

path /pæθ/ n **paths** /pæðz/ **1** track or way where you can walk **2** line along which something moves: *the path of an arrow*

pa·thet·ic /pəˈθeţɪk/ adj **1** causing pity or sorrow **2** derog hopelessly unsuccessful ~**ally** /-kliʸ/ adv

pa·thol·o·gy /pəˈθalədʒiʸ, pæ-/ n [U] study of disease –**gist** n specialist in pathology, esp. one who examines a dead body to find out how the person died -**gical** /ˌpæθəˈladʒɪkəl◂/ adj **1** of pathology **2** caused by disease, esp. of the mind **3** great and unreasonable: *pathological jealousy* -**gically** /-kliʸ/ adv

pa·thos /ˈpeʸθas, -θɔs/ n [U] quality that causes pity and sorrow

path·way /ˈpæθweʸ/ n PATH (1)

pa·tience /ˈpeʸʃəns/ n [U] ability to wait calmly, to control oneself when angered, or to accept unpleasant things without complaining

pa·tient¹ /ˈpeʸʃənt/ adj showing patience ~**ly** adv

patient² n person being treated medically

pat·i·na /pəˈtiʸnə/ n pleasingly smooth shiny surface

pat·i·o /ˈpæţiʸˌoʷ/ n –**os** space with a stone floor next to a house, for sitting out on in fine weather

pa·tois /ˈpætwa/ n –**tois** /-twaz/ [C;U] local form of speech

pa·tri·arch /ˈpeʸtriʸˌark/ n **1** old man who is much respected **2** chief BISHOP of the Eastern Churches ~**al** /ˌpeʸtriʸˈarkəl◂/ adj **1** ruled only by men **2** of a patriarch

pat·ri·cide /ˈpætrəˌsaɪd/ n [U] **1** murder of one's father **2** person guilty of this

pat·ri·mo·ny /ˈpætrəˌmoʷniʸ/ n [S;U] property one gets from one's dead father, grandfather, etc.

pa·tri·ot /ˈpeʸtriʸət, -ˌat/ n someone who loves their country ~**ism** n [U] ~**ic** /ˌpeʸtriʸˈaţɪk◂/ adj -**ically** /-kliʸ/ adv

pa·trol /pəˈtroʷl/ n **1** [U] (period of) patrolling: *warships on patrol in the Atlantic* **2** [C] small group on patrol ♦ vi/t go around (an area, building, etc.) repeatedly to see that there is no trouble

pa·tron /ˈpeʸtrən/ n **1** person who gives money for support: *a patron of the arts* **2** fml customer in a store, bar, etc., esp. regularly ~**age** /ˈpeʸtrənɪdʒ, ˈpæ-/ n [U] **1** support given by a PATRON (1) **2** right to appoint people to important positions **3** [U] regular support given to a business by its customers

pat·ron·ize /ˈpeʸtrəˌnaɪz, ˈpæ-/ vt **1** act towards (someone) as if you were better or more important than them **2** fml be a PATRON (2) of

patron saint /ˌ·· ·ˈ·/ n SAINT giving special protection to a particular place, activity, etc.

pat·sy /ˈpætsiʸ/ n infml someone who is easily deceived or taken advantage of

pat·ter¹ /ˈpæţər/ vi, n (run with or make) the sound of something striking lightly, quickly, and repeatedly

patter² n [U] fast continuous amusing talk

pat·tern /ˈpæţərn/ n **1** regularly repeated arrangement, esp. with a decorative effect: *cloth with a pattern of red and white squares* **2** way in which something develops: *the usual pattern of the illness* **3** shape used as a guide for making something: *a dress pattern* ♦ vt **1** make a decorative pattern on **2** make according to a PATTERN (3)

pat·ty /ˈpæţiʸ/ n small flat piece of food or candy: *hamburger patties*

pau·ci·ty /ˈpɔsəţiʸ/ n [S] fml less than is needed; lack

paunch /pɔntʃ, pantʃ/ n fat stomach ~**y** adj

pau·per /ˈpɔpər/ n very poor person

pause /pɔz/ n short but noticeable break in activity, speech, etc. ♦ vi make a pause

pave /peʸv/ vt **1** cover with a hard level surface **2 pave the way (for/to)** prepare for or make possible

pave·ment /ˈpeʸvmənt/ n hard flat road surface

pa·vil·ion /pəˈvɪlyən/ n large public building usu. put up for only a short time, used for EXHIBITIONS, etc.

paw /pɔ/ n **1** animal's foot with CLAWS **2** infml human hand: *Keep your paws off me!* ♦ vi/t **1** (of an animal) touch or strike with the foot **2** handle rudely or roughly

pawn¹ /pɔn/ n **1** least valuable piece in CHESS **2** unimportant person used for someone else's advantage

pawn² vt leave with a pawnbroker in return for money lent ♦ n [U]: *My watch is in pawn.*

pawn·bro·ker /ˈpɔnˌbroʷkər/ n person who lends money in return for things one brings, which he keeps if one does not repay the money

pay /peʸ/ v **paid** /peʸd/ n **1** vi/t give (money) to (someone) in return for goods bought, work done, etc. **2** vt settle (a bill, debt, etc.) **3** vi/t be profitable (to); be worth the trouble (to): *It doesn't pay (you) to argue with him.* **4** vt give, offer, or make: *Pay attention to what I say.* | *We paid them a visit.* **5 pay one's way** pay money for things as one wants them so as not to get into debt **6 pay through the nose (for)** infml pay far too much (for) ♦ n [U] **1** money received for work **2 in the pay of** employed by ~ **er** n

pay back phr vt **1** return (what is owing) to (someone) **2** return bad treatment, rudeness, etc., to

pay for phr vt receive suffering or punishment for

pay off phr v **1** vt pay all of (a debt) **2** vt pay and dismiss **3** vt pay (someone) to keep silent about a wrong act **4** vi be successful

pay out phr v make (a large payment)

pay up phr vi pay a debt in full, esp. unwillingly or late

pay·a·ble /ˈpeⁱəbəl/ adj that must or can be paid

pay·check /ˈpeⁱtʃek/ n weekly or monthly wages in check form

pay dirt /ˈ· ·/ n [U] valuable discovery

pay·ee /peⁱˈiⁱ/ n tech person to whom money is or should be paid

pay·load /ˈpeⁱloʷd/ n amount carried in a vehicle, esp. a spacecraft

pay·mas·ter /ˈpeⁱˌmæstər/ n person who pays someone, and can therefore control their actions

pay·ment /ˈpeⁱmənt/ n **1** [U] act of paying **2** [C] amount of money (to be) paid – see also BALANCE OF PAYMENTS, DOWN PAYMENT

pay·off /ˈpeⁱˌɔf/ n **1** payment made to settle matters **2** ending to something, when everything is explained

pay pack·et /ˈ· ˌ··/ n (envelope containing) wages

pay phone /ˈ· ·/ n telephone that works when money is put in it

pay·roll /ˈpeⁱroʷl/ n **1** list of workers employed **2** total amount of wages paid in a particular company

PC /ˌpiⁱˈsiⁱ/ n personal computer, for use at home or in businesses: an IBM PC/PC-based software

PE /ˌpiⁱˈiⁱ/ n [U] physical education; development of the body by games, exercises, etc.

pea /piⁱ/ n large round green seed used as food

peace /piⁱs/ n [U] **1** period free of war **2** calmness; quietness **3** good order in a country: The job of the police is to keep the peace. **4** lack of anxiety: peace of mind **5 hold one's peace** remain silent **6 make one's peace with** settle a quarrel with ~**ful** adj **1** quiet; untroubled **2** without war ~**fully** adv ~**fulness** n [U]

peace·time /ˈpiⁱs-taⁱm/ n [S] time when at nation is not at war

peach /piⁱtʃ/ n round soft juicy yellow-red fruit

pea·cock /ˈpiⁱkɑk/ n large bird with long beautifully colored tail feathers

peak /piⁱk/ n **1** highest point, level, etc. **2** sharply pointed mountain top ♦ n highest; greatest: at peak fitness ♦ vi reach a PEAK (1)

peal /piⁱl/ n **1** loud long sound: peals of laughter **2** sound of bells ringing ♦ vi (of a bell) ring loudly

pea·nut /ˈpiⁱnʌt/ n nut that grows in a shell underground **peanuts** n [P] sl very little money

peanut but·ter /ˈ·· ˌ··/ n [U] spreadable food made from crushed peanuts: peanut butter and jelly

pear /peər/ n sweet, juicy fruit, narrow at the stem end and wide at the other

pearl /pɜrl/ n round silver-white jewel formed in the shell of OYSTERS

pearly gates /ˌ·· ˈ·/ n [the+P] gates of Heaven

peas·ant /ˈpezənt/ n **1** person who works on the land in a poor country or in former times **2** infml derog person who is uneducated or has bad manners

peas·ant·ry /ˈpezəntriⁱ/ n all the PEASANTS (1) in a place

peat /piⁱt/ n [U] partly decayed plant material in the earth, used for growing things or burning ~**y** adj

peb·ble /ˈpebəl/ n small stone –**bly** adj

pe·can /pɪˈkæn, -ˈkæn, ˈpiⁱkæn/ n kind of nut with a hard shell: pecan pie

pec·ca·dil·lo /ˌpekəˈdɪloʷ/ n –loes or –los unimportant wrong

peck /pek/ v **1** vi/t (of a bird) strike with the beak **2** vt kiss hurriedly ♦ n **1** stroke or mark made by pecking **2** hurried kiss

peck·ing or·der /ˈ·· ˌ··/ n social order, showing who is more and less important

pe·cu·liar /pɪˈkyuʷlyər/ adj **1** strange, esp. in a displeasing way **2** belonging only to a particular place, time, etc.: a plant peculiar to these islands **3** crazy **4** a little ill ~**ly** adv **1** especially **2** strangely ~**ity** /pɪˌkyuʷliⁱˈærətiⁱ/ n **1** [U] being peculiar **2** [C] something PECULIAR (2) **3** [C] strange or unusual habit, etc.

ped·a·gog·i·cal /ˌpedəˈgɑdʒɪkəl, -ˈgoʷ-/ adj of teaching or the study of teaching methods ~**ly** /-kliⁱ/ adv

ped·a·gogue /ˈpedəˌgɑg/ n teacher who is too much concerned with rules

ped·al /ˈpedl/ n part pushed with the foot to drive or control a machine: a bicycle pedal ♦ v –**ll**- **1** vi work pedals **2** vi/t ride (a bicycle)

ped·ant /ˈpednt/ n person who gives too much value to small details and formal rules ~**ic** /pəˈdæntɪk/ adj ~**ically** /-kliⁱ/ adv

ped·dle /ˈpedl/ vt try to sell by going from place to place

ped·dler /ˈpedlər/ n 1 person who peddles illegal drugs 2 person who peddles small articles

ped·es·tal /ˈpedəstl/ n 1 base on which a pillar or STATUE stands 2 **put someone on a pedestal** treat someone as better or nobler than anyone else

pe·des·tri·an¹ /pəˈdestriˈən/ n walker

pedestrian² adj 1 dull and ordinary 2 for pedestrians: a pedestrian crossing

pedestrian cros·sing /·ˌ··· ˈ··/ n place where pedestrians (2) can cross the road legally

pe·di·at·rics /ˌpiˈdiˈætriks/ n [U] branch of medicine concerned with children –**rician** /ˌpiˈdiˈəˈtriʃən/ n children's doctor

ped·i·gree /ˈpedəˌgriˈ/ n [C;U] (an official description of) the set of people or animals from whom a person or animal is descended ♦ adj (of an animal) specially bred from a family of animals of high quality

pee /piˈ/ vi infml for urinate (URINE) ♦ n infml 1 [S] act of peeing 2 [U] URINE

peek /piˈk/ vi, n (take) a quick look

peel /piˈl/ v 1 vt remove (the outer covering) from (esp. a fruit or vegetable): (fig.) They peeled off their clothes and jumped in the water. 2 vi come off in small pieces: My skin is peeling. 3 **keep one's eyes peeled** keep careful watch ♦ n [U] outer covering of fruits and vegetables

peep¹ /piˈp/ vi, n (take) a quick look often secret look

peep² n 1 [C] short weak high sound 2 [S] sound, esp. something spoken

peer¹ /piər/ n fml one's equal in rank, quality, etc.

peer² vi look very carefully or hard: peering through the mist

peer·less /ˈpiərləs/ adj fml better than any other

peeve /piˈv/ vt annoy

peev·ish /ˈpiˈviʃ/ adj bad-tempered ~**ly** adv ~**ness** n [U]

peg¹ /peg/ n short piece of wood, metal, etc., for hanging things on, etc.

peg² vt -**gg**- 1 decide or think that someone is as stated: She had him pegged as a cheater. 2 fasten with a peg: (fig.) Prices have been pegged at this year's levels.

pe·jo·ra·tive /pəˈdʒɔrətɪv, -ˈdʒɑr-/ adj (of a word or expression) saying that something is bad or worthless

pe·kin·ese /ˌpiˈkəˈniˈz, -ˈniˈs/ n small dog with long silky hair

pel·i·can /ˈpelikən/ n large water bird with a large beak in which it stores fish to eat

pel·let /ˈpelit/ n 1 small ball of soft material 2 small metal ball fired from a gun

pelt¹ /pelt/ v 1 vt attack by throwing things 2 vi (of rain) fall very heavily

pelt² n animal's skin with its fur

pel·vis /ˈpelvis/ n frame of bones in a bowl shape at the base of the SPINE –**vic** adj

pen¹ /pen/ n instrument for writing with ink

pen² n enclosed piece of land for keeping animals in ♦ vt –**nn**- shut in a pen or small space

pe·nal /ˈpiˈnl/ adj of or being legal punishment, esp. in prison

pe·nal·ize /ˈpiˈnlˌaɪz, ˈpen-/ vt put in an unfavorable or unfair situation

pen·al·ty /ˈpenltiˈ/ n 1 punishment or disadvantage suffered, esp. for doing wrong 2 (in sports) disadvantage suffered by a player or team for breaking a rule

pen·ance /ˈpenəns/ n [U] willing punishment of oneself, to show one is sorry for doing wrong

pen·chant /ˈpentʃənt/ n liking for something

pen·cil¹ /ˈpensəl/ n narrow pointed writing instrument containing a thin stick of black material

pencil² v –**l**- **pencil in** phr vt include for now, with the possibility of being changed later

pen·dant /ˈpendənt/ n hanging piece of jewelry, esp. around the neck

pend·ing /ˈpendɪŋ/ adj waiting to be decided ♦ prep until

pen·du·lous /ˈpendʒələs, -dyə-/ fml hanging down loosely

pen·du·lum /ˈpendʒələm, -dyə-/ n weight hanging so as to swing freely, esp. as used to control a clock

pen·e·trate /ˈpenəˌtreˈt/ v 1 vi/t go (into or through): The knife didn't penetrate his skin. 2 vt see into or through –**trating** adj 1 (of sight, a question, etc.) sharp and searching 2 able to understand clearly and deeply –**tration** /ˌpenəˈtreˈʃən/ n [U] 1 act of penetrating 2 ability to understand clearly and deeply

pen·guin /ˈpeŋgwin, ˈpen-/ n black and white sea bird of the ANTARCTIC that cannot fly

pen·i·cil·lin /ˌpenəˈsilin/ n [U] medicine that kills bacteria

pe·nin·su·la /pəˈninsələ, -syə-/ n piece of land almost surrounded by water

pe·nis /ˈpiˈnis/ n male sex organ

pen·i·tent /ˈpenətənt/ adj feeling

sorry and intending not to do wrong again –**tence** n [U]

pen·i·ten·tia·ry /ˌpenəˈtenʃəriʸ, -tʃəriʸ/ n prison

pen·knife /ˈpen-naɪf/ n –**knives** /-naɪvz/ small knife with a folding blade

pen·man·ship /ˈpenmənˌʃɪp/ n practice of HANDWRITING

pen name /ˈ· ·/ n false name used by a writer instead of his/her real name

pen·nant /ˈpenənt/ n 1 long narrow pointed flag 2 CHAMPIONship in a sports division

pen·ni·less /ˈpenɪlɪs, ˈpenl-ɪs/ adj having no money

pen·ny /ˈpeniʸ/ n **pennies** 1 unit of money equal to 1/100th of a dollar 2 **a pretty penny** a fairly large amount of money

pen pal /ˈ· ·/ n usu. foreign friend that you write to but have usu. never met

pen·sion[1] /ˈpenʃən/ n money paid regularly to someone who can no longer earn (enough) money by working esp. because of old age or illness – **er** person receiving a pension

pen·sion[2] /ˌpɑnsˈyoʷn/ n house in a non-English speaking country where one can get a room and meals

pen·sive /ˈpensɪv/ adj deeply or sadly thoughtful – **ly** adv – **ness** n [U]

pen·tath·lon /penˈtæθlən, -ˌlɑn/ n sports event in which the competitors take part in 5 different sports

pent·house /ˈpenthaʊs/ n set of rooms built on top of a tall building

pent up /ˌpent ˈʌp/ adj not allowed to be free or freely expressed: pent-up emotions

pe·nul·ti·mate /pɪˈnʌltəmɪt/ adj next to the last

pe·num·bra /pəˈnʌmbrə/ n fml slightly dark area between full darkness and full light

pen·u·ry /ˈpenyəriʸ/ n fml being very poor –**rious** /pəˈnʊəriʸəs, -ˈnyʊə-/ adj

peo·ple /ˈpiʸpəl/ n 1 [P] persons other than oneself; persons in general: How many people were at the meeting? | That sort of thing annoys people. 2 [(the) P] all the ordinary members of a nation 3 [C] race; nation: the peoples of Africa 4 [P] persons from whom one is descended ♦ vt 1 live in (a place) 2 fill with PEOPLE (1)

pep[1] /pep/ n [U] infml enthusiastic activity and forcefulness

pep[2] v –**pp**– **pep up** sl make more active or interesting

pep·per[1] /ˈpepər/ n 1 [U] powder

that tastes hot, made from the fruit of a tropical plant 2 [C] hollow vegetable that tastes slightly hot: green peppers

pepper[2] vt hit repeatedly with shots

pep·per·mint /ˈpepərˌmɪnt/ n 1 [U] MINT[1] (2) plant with a special strong taste 2 [C] candy with this taste

pep·pe·ro·ni /ˌpepəˈroʷniʸ/ n [U] SAUSAGE with a hot taste used esp. for PIZZA

pep pill /ˈ· ·/ n PILL (1) taken to make one quicker or happier for a short time

pep talk /ˈ· ·/ n talk intended to make people work harder, more quickly, etc.

per /pər; strong pɜr/ prep 1 for each: apples at 90 cents per pound 2 infml according to: as per your instructions

per an·num /pər ˈænəm/ adv each year

per·ceive /pərˈsiʸv/ vt fml (come to) have knowledge of, esp. by seeing or understanding

per·cent /pər ˈsent/ n, adv, adj (one part) in or for each 100: a 10 percent pay raise

per·cen·tage /pərˈsentɪdʒ/ n 1 [C] number stated as if it is part of a whole which is 100: a high percentage of babies [U] infml advantage; profit

per·cep·ti·ble /pərˈseptəbəl/ adj fml noticeable –**bly** adv

per·cep·tion /pərˈsepʃən/ n [U] fml 1 action of perceiving (PERCEIVE) 2 keen mental understanding

per·cep·tive /pərˈseptɪv/ adj having or showing PERCEPTION (2) ~**ly** adv

perch /pɜrtʃ/ n 1 branch, rod, etc., where a bird sits 2 high position or place ♦ v 1 vi (of a bird) sit 2 vi/t put or be in a high or unsafe place: a house perched on top of the cliff

per·cip·i·ent /pərˈsɪpiʸənt/ adj fml perceptive –**ence** n [U]

per·co·late /ˈpɜrkəˌleʸt/ vi pass slowly through a material with small holes: (fig.) The news gradually percolated through to us. –**lator** n pot in which coffee is made by hot water percolating through the crushed beans

per·cus·sion /pərˈkʌʃən/ n [U] musical instruments played by being struck: The drum is a percussion instrument.

per·di·tion /pərˈdɪʃən/ n [U] fml punishment after death that lasts for ever

pe·remp·to·ry /pəˈremptəriʸ/ adj fml 1 impolitely quick and unfriendly 2 (of a command) that must be obeyed –**rily** adv

pe·ren·ni·al /pəˈrɛniəl/ adj 1 lasting forever or for a long time 2 (of a plant) living for more than 2 years ♦ n perennial plant ~ly adv

per·fect¹ /ˈpɜrfɪkt/ adj 1 of the very best possible kind, standard, etc. 2 as good or suitable as possible: Your English is almost perfect. 3 with nothing missing; full: a perfect set of teeth 4 complete: a perfect fool 5 gram expressing an action that has happened and finished: The perfect tense is formed with 'have' in English. ~ly adv

per·fect² /pərˈfɛkt/ vt make perfect ~ible adj

per·fec·tion /pərˈfɛkʃən/ n [U] 1 being perfect 2 making perfect 3 perfect example: His performance was sheer perfection.

per·fec·tion·ist /pərˈfɛkʃənɪst/ n someone not satisfied with anything not perfect

per·fid·i·ous /pərˈfɪdiəs/ adj fml disloyal ~ly adv ~ness n [U]

per·fo·rate /ˈpɜrfəˌreɪt/ vt 1 make a hole through 2 make a line of holes in (paper) to make it easier to tear ~ration /ˌpɜrfəˈreɪʃən/ n [C;U]

per·form /pərˈfɔrm/ v 1 vt do (a piece of work, ceremony, etc.): to perform an operation 2 vi/t act or show (a play, piece of music, etc.), esp. in public 3 vi work or carry out an activity in (the stated way): a car that performs well in the mountains ~ance n 1 [U] action or manner of performing 2 [C] (public) show of music, a play, etc. ~er n actor, musician, etc.

per·fume /ˈpɜrfyum, pərˈfyum/ n [C;U] (liquid having) a pleasant smell ♦ vt /pərˈfyum, ˈpɜrfyum/ cause to smell pleasant

per·func·to·ry /pərˈfʌŋktəriy/ adj fml done hastily and without interest or care

per·haps /pərˈhæps, præps/ adv it may be; possibly

per·il /ˈpɛrəl/ n [C;U] (something that causes) great danger ~ous adj

pe·rim·e·ter /pəˈrɪmətər/ n (length of) the border around an enclosed area, esp. a camp or AIRFIELD

pe·ri·od¹ /ˈpɪəriyəd/ n 1 stretch of time 2 division of a school day 3 monthly flow of blood from a woman's body 4 a mark (.) showing esp. the end of a sentence ~ic /ˌpɪəriyˈɑdɪk/ adj repeated and regular ~ical n magazine that comes out regularly ~ically /-kliy/ adv

period² adv infml (used at end of a sentence) and that is all I'm going to say on the matter: I'm not going, period.

per·i·pa·tet·ic /ˌpɛrəpəˈtɛtɪk/ adj fml traveling about, esp. to work

pe·riph·e·ry /pəˈrɪfəriy/ n outside edge ~ral adj 1 on the periphery 2 slight: of peripheral interest

per·i·scope /ˈpɛrəˌskowp/ n long tube with mirrors so that people lower down can see what is above them, esp. in SUBMARINES

per·ish /ˈpɛrɪʃ/ vi fml 1 die 2 (cause to) decay or lose natural qualities ~able adj (of food) that will decay quickly ~ing, ~ed adj very cold

per·jure /ˈpɜrdʒər/ vt perjure oneself tell lies in a court of law ~jury n [U] lying in court

perk¹ /pɜrk/ n money, goods, etc., that one gets from an employer in addition to one's pay: Having Tuesdays free is one of the perks of the job.

perk² v perk up phr vi/t make or become more cheerful

perk·y /ˈpɜrkiy/ adj confidently cheerful ~iness n [U]

perm /pɜrm/ n act of putting artificial curls into hair ♦ vt give a perm to

per·ma·nent /ˈpɜrmənənt/ adj lasting a long time or forever ~ly adv ~ence n [U]

per·me·a·ble /ˈpɜrmiyəbəl/ adj that can be permeated

per·me·ate /ˈpɜrmiyˌeɪt/ vt spread or pass through or into every part of

per·mis·si·ble /pərˈmɪsəbəl/ adj fml allowed ~bly adv

per·mis·sion /pərˈmɪʃən/ n [U] act of allowing

per·mis·sive /pərˈmɪsɪv/ adj allowing (too) much freedom, esp. in sexual matters ~ly adv ~ness n [U]

per·mit¹ /pərˈmɪt/ vi/t ~tt~ allow

per·mit² /ˈpɜrmɪt/ n official paper allowing something

per·mute /pərˈmyuwt/ vt rearrange in a different order ~mutation /ˌpɜrmyuwˈteɪʃən/ n [C;U]

per·ni·cious /pərˈnɪʃəs/ adj fml very harmful ~ly adv ~ness n [U]

per·nick·e·ty /pərˈnɪkətiy/ adj worrying too much about small things

per·o·ra·tion /ˌpɛrəˈreɪʃən/ n fml 1 last part of a speech 2 grand, long, but meaningless speech

per·pen·dic·u·lar /ˌpɜrpənˈdɪkyələr/ adj 1 exactly upright 2 at an angle of 90° to another line or surface ♦ n [C;U] perpendicular line or position

per·pe·trate /ˈpɜrpəˌtreɪt/ vt fml be guilty of ~trator n

per·pet·u·al /pərˈpɛtʃuwəl/ adj lasting (as if) for ever ~ly adv

per·pet·u·ate /pərˈpɛtʃuwˌeɪt/ vt fml make (something) continue to exist for a long time ~ation /pərˌpɛtʃuwˈeɪʃən/ n [U]

per·pe·tu·i·ty /ˌpɜrpə'tuːəti̯ʸ, -'tyuːʷ-/ n **in perpetuity** fml for ever

per·plex /pər'pleks/ vt make (someone) feel confused by being difficult to understand: a perplexing problem ~**ity** n [U]

per se /ˌpɜr 'seɪ/ adv considered alone and not in connection with other things

per·se·cute /'pɜrsɪˌkyuːt/ vt **1** cause to suffer, esp. for religious beliefs **2** trouble or harm continually –**cutor** n –**cution** /ˌpɜrsɪ'kyuːʃən/ n [C;U]

per·se·vere /ˌpɜrsə'vɪər/ vi continue firmly in spite of difficulties –**verance** n [U]

per·sist /pər'sɪst, -'zɪst/ vi **1** continue firmly in spite of opposition or warning: Do not persist in this unwise action. **2** continue to exist ~**ent** adj persisting: persistent rudeness/coughing ~**ently** adv ~**ence** n [U]

per·son /'pɜrsən/ n **1** single human being **2** gram form of verb or PRONOUN, showing the speaker (**first person**), the one spoken to (**second person**), or the one spoken about (**third person**) **3** in person personally; oneself **4** on one's person carried around with one

per·so·na /pər'soʷnə/ n outward character a person takes on

per·son·a·ble /'pɜrsənəbəl/ adj fml attractive and friendly

per·son·age /'pɜrsənɪdʒ/ n character in a play or book, or in history

per·son·al /'pɜrsənəl/ adj **1** of, for, or by a particular person: It's a personal (= private) matter. **2** of the body: personal cleanliness ~**ly** adv **1** directly and not through a representative **2** giving one's own opinion **3** privately

personal ad /'··· ˌ·/ n advertisement in a newspaper that gives or asks for messages, news, etc., about particular people

per·son·al·i·ty /ˌpɜrsə'næləti̯ʸ/ n **1** [C;U] whole nature or character of a person **2** [U] unusual, strong, exciting character: She's got lots of personality. **3** [C] person who is well known

personality cult /·····ˌ·/ n practice of giving too great admiration to a particular person, esp. a political or religious leader

personal pro·noun /ˌ··· '··/ n PRONOUN showing the PERSON (2), such as I or you

personal ster·e·o /ˌ··· '···/ n small machine for playing CASSETTES, which has EARPLUGS and is carried around with the user

per·son·i·fy /pər'sɑnəˌfaɪ/ vt **1** be a good example of (a quality) **2** represent as being human –**fica·tion** /pərˌsɑnəfə'keɪʃən/ n [C;U]

per·son·nel /ˌpɜrsə'nel/ n **1** [P] all employed people in a company, army, etc. **2** [U] department that deals with these people and their problems

per·spec·tive /pər'spektɪv/ n **1** [U] effect of depth, distance, and solidity in drawing and painting **2** [C;U] proper relationship of each part of a matter: We must get the problem in perspective; it's not really that serious.

per·spi·ca·cious /ˌpɜrspɪ'keɪʃəs/ adj fml showing good judgment and understanding ~**ly** adv ~**ness** n [U]

per·spire /pər'spaɪər/ vi fml for SWEAT –**spiration** /ˌpɜrspə'reɪʃən/ n [U] fml **1** sweat **2** act of sweating

per·suade /pər'sweɪd/ vt make (someone) do something by reasoning, arguing, begging, etc.

per·sua·sion /pər'sweɪʒən/ n **1** [U] (skill in) persuading **2** [C] particular belief: her political persuasions

per·sua·sive /pər'sweɪsɪv/ adj able to persuade others ~**ly** adv ~**ness** n [U]

pert /pɜrt/ adj amusingly disrespectful ~**ly** adv ~**ness** n [U]

per·tain /pər'teɪn/ v **pertain to** phr vt fml be about or connected with

per·ti·na·cious /ˌpɜrtn'eɪʃəs/ adj fml holding firmly to an opinion or action

per·ti·nent /'pɜrtn-ənt/ adj fml directly connected; RELEVANT ~**ly** adv –**nence** n [U]

per·turb /pər'tɜrb/ vt fml worry ~**ation** /ˌpɜrtər'beɪʃən/ n [C;U]

pe·ruse /pə'ruːz/ vt fml read carefully perusal n [C;U]

per·vade /pər'veɪd/ vt fml spread all through

per·va·sive /pər'veɪsɪv/ adj pervading; widespread ~**ly** adv ~**ness** n [U]

per·verse /pər'vɜrs/ adj **1** purposely doing wrong or unreasonable things **2** awkward and annoying ~**ly** adv

per·ver·sion /pər'vɜrʒən, -ʃən/ n **1** [C] perverted form of what is true, reasonable, etc. **2** [C] unnatural sexual act **3** [U] act of perverting

per·ver·si·ty /pər'vɜrsəti̯ʸ/ n **1** [U] being perverse **2** [C] perverse act

per·vert¹ /pər'vɜrt/ vt **1** lead into wrong or unnatural (sexual) behavior **2** use for a bad purpose

per·vert² /'pɜrvərt/ n person who does unnatural sexual acts

pes·si·mist /'pesəmɪst/ n person who expects bad things to happen –**mism** n [U] –**mistic** /ˌpesə'mɪstɪk◁/ adj

pest /pest/ n **1** animal or insect that harms food products **2** annoying person

pes·ter /'pestər/ vt annoy continually, esp. with demands

pes·ti·cide /'pestə₁saɪd/ n [C;U] chemical to kill PESTS (1)

pes·ti·lence /'pestələns/ n fml terrible disease killing many people

pes·ti·lent /'pestələnt/ adj **1** fml causing a pestilence **2** unpleasantly annoying

pes·tle /'pesəl, 'pestl/ n instrument for crushing things in a thick bowl

pet /pet/ n **1** animal kept as a companion: my pet cat **2** person especially favored ♦ v –tt– **1** vi touch sexually **2** vt touch lovingly

pet·al /'petl/ n colored leaflike part of a flower

pet·er /'piʸtər/ v peter out phr vi gradually end

pe·tite /pə'tiʸt/ adj (esp. of a woman) having a small and neat figure

pe·ti·tion /pə'tɪʃən/ n request or demand to a government, etc., signed by many people ♦ vi/t make or send a petition ~**er** n

pet name /₁· '·/ n name for someone you like, instead of their real name

pet peeve /₁· '·/ n small thing that one complains about often

pet·ri·fy /'petrə₁faɪ/ vt **1** frighten very much **2** turn into stone

pet·ro·dol·lar /'petroʷ₁dɑlər/ n US dollar earned by the sale of oil, esp. by countries in the Middle East that produce oil

pe·tro·le·um /pə'troʷliʸəm/ n [U] mineral oil obtained from below the ground

pet·ti·coat /'petiʸ₁koʷt/ n skirtlike undergarment

pet·ty /'petiʸ/ adj **1** unimportant (by comparison) **2** showing a narrow and ungenerous mind –**tiness** n [U]

petty cash /₁·· '·/ n [U] money kept for small payments

petty of·fi·cer /₁·· '···◄/ n person of middle rank in the navy

pet·u·lant /'petʃələnt/ adj showing childish bad temper ~**ly** adv –**lance** n [U]

pew /pyuʷ/ n seat in a church: (fig.) Take a pew. (= Sit down.)

pew·ter /'pyuʷtər/ n [U] grayish metal made from lead and tin

PG /₁piʸ 'dʒiʸ/ abbrev. for: parental guidance; (of a film) which may in parts be unsuitable for children under 15

pha·lanx /'feʸlæŋks/ n group packed closely together, esp. for attack or defense

phal·lus /'fæləs/ n image of the male sex organ –**lic** adj

phan·tom /'fæntəm/ n **1** GHOST **2** something that is not really there

pha·raoh /'feəroʷ, 'feʸroʷ/ n ruler of ancient Egypt

phar·ma·ceu·ti·cal /₁fɑrmə'suʷtɪkəl/ adj of (the making of) medicine

phar·ma·cist /'fɑrməsɪst/ n **1** person who makes medicines **2** DRUGGIST

phar·ma·col·o·gy /₁fɑrmə'kɑlədʒiʸ/ n [U] study of medicine and drugs –**gist** n

phar·ma·cy /'fɑrməsiʸ/ n **1** [C] DRUGSTORE **2** [U] making or giving out of medicines

phar·ynx /'færɪŋks/ n med throat

phase /feʸz/ n **1** stage of development **2** way the moon looks at a particular time ♦ vt arrange in separate phases

phase in/out phr vt introduce/ remove gradually

pheas·ant /'fezənt/ n large bird often shot for food

phe·nom·e·nal /fɪ'nɑmənl/ adj very unusual ~**ly** adv: phenomenally strong

phe·nom·e·non /fɪ'nɑmə₁nɑn, -nən/ n –**na** /-nə/ **1** fact or event in the world as it appears or is experienced by the senses, esp. an unusual one **2** very unusual person, thing, etc.

phil·an·der·er /fɪ'lændərər/ n oldfash man who has too many love affairs

phil·an·thro·pist /fɪ'lænθrəpɪst/ n kind person who gives money to those who are poor or in trouble –**py** n [U] –**pic** /₁fɪlən'θrɑpɪk◄/ adj

phi·lat·e·ly /fɪ'lætl-iʸ/ n [U] stamp collecting –**list** n

phil·is·tine /'fɪlə₁stiʸn/ n person who does not understand and actively dislikes art, music, beautiful things, etc.

phi·los·o·pher /fɪ'lɑsəfər/ n **1** person who studies philosophy **2** philosophical (2) person

philosopher's stone /·₁··· '·/ n imaginary substance thought in former times to change any metal into gold

phi·los·o·phize /fɪ'lɑsə₁faɪz/ vi talk or write like a philosopher

phi·los·o·phy /fɪ'lɑsəfiʸ/ n **1** [U] study of the nature and meaning of existence, reality, morals, etc. **2** [C] system of thought –**ophical** /₁fɪlə'sɑfɪkəl◄/ adj **1** of philosophy **2** accepting things with calm courage –**ophically** /-kliʸ/ adv

phlegm /flem/ n [U] **1** thick liquid produced in the nose and throat **2** fml calmness

phleg·mat·ic /fleg'mætɪk/ *adj* calm and difficult to excite ~**ally** /-klɪʸ/ *adv*

pho·bi·a /'foʷbiʸə/ *n* strong (unreasonable) fear and dislike

phoe·nix /'fiʸnɪks/ *n* imaginary bird that burnt itself up and was born again from its ashes

phone /foʷn/ *n, vi/t* telephone

phone book /'· ·/ *n* book with a list of all telephone numbers in an area

phone booth /'· ·/ *n* hut containing a public telephone

phone-in /'· ·/ *n* show in which telephoned questions, etc., from the public are broadcast

phone-tap·ping /'· ·ˌ··/ *n* [U] listening secretly to other people's telephone conversations by means of special electronic equipment

pho·net·ic /fə'netɪk/ *adj* **1** of the sounds of human speech **2** (of a language) with all the sounds spelled very much as they sound ~**ally** /-klɪʸ/ *adv*

pho·net·ics /fə'netɪks/ *n* [U] study and science of speech sounds –**ician** /ˌfoʷnə'tɪʃən, ˌfan-/ *n*

pho·no·graph /'foʷnəˌgræf/ *n old-fash* RECORD PLAYER

pho·nol·o·gy /fə'nalədʒiʸ/ *n* [U] study of the system of speech sounds in a language –**ogical** /ˌfanə'ladʒɪkəl/ *adj*

pho·ny /'foʷniʸ/ *n, adj sl* (someone or something) pretended or false

phos·phate /'fasfeʸt/ *n* [C;U] chemical found naturally or made from phosphoric acid, esp. as used for making plants grow better

phos·pho·res·cent /ˌfasfə'resənt/ *adj* shining faintly in the dark by a natural process –**cence** *n* [U]

phos·pho·rus /'fasfərəs/ *n* [U] yellowish waxlike chemical that burns when brought into the air –**phoric** /fas'fɔrɪk, fas'fa-, 'fasfərɪk/ *adj*

pho·to /'foʷtoʷ/ *n* –tos photograph

pho·to·cop·y /'foʷtəˌkapiʸ, 'foʷtoʷ-/ *vi/t, n* (make) a photographic copy –**ier** machine that does this

photo fin·ish /ˌ·· '··/ *n* very close finish to a race, etc., where a photograph is needed to show which competitor won

pho·to·gen·ic /ˌfoʷtə'dʒenɪk◄/ *adj* that looks good when photographed

pho·to·graph /'foʷtəgræf/ *n* picture taken with a camera and film ♦ *vt* take a photograph of ~**er** /fə'tagrəfər/ *n* ~**y** *n* [U] art or business of producing photographs or films ~**ic** /ˌfoʷtə'græfɪk◄/ *adj*

pho·to·sen·si·tive /ˌfoʷtoʷ'sensə-tɪv/ *adj* changing under the action of light

pho·to·syn·the·sis /ˌfoʷtoʷ'sɪnθə-sɪs/ *n* [U] process by which plants make food using sunlight

phras·al /'freʸzəl/ *adj* of or being a phrase

phrasal verb /ˌ·· '·/ *n* group of words that acts like a verb and consists usu. of a verb with an adverb and/or a PREPOSITION: 'Set off' and 'put up with' are phrasal verbs.

phrase /freʸz/ *n* **1** group of words without a FINITE verb **2** short (suitable) expression in the stated way ♦ *vt* express in the stated way

phrase·book /'freʸzbʊk/ *n* book explaining foreign phrases, for use abroad

phra·se·ol·o·gy /ˌfreʸziʸ'alədʒiʸ/ *n fml* choice and use of words

phys·i·cal /'fɪzɪkəl/ *adj* **1** of or being matter or material things (not the mind, etc.) **2** of the body: physical strength ~**ly** /-klɪʸ/ *adv* **1** with regard to the body **2** according to the laws of nature: physically impossible

phy·si·cian /fɪ'zɪʃən/ *n fml* doctor

phys·i·cist /'fɪzəsɪst/ *n* person who studies or works in physics

phys·ics /'fɪzɪks/ *n* [U] science dealing with matter and natural forces

phys·i·ol·o·gy /ˌfɪziʸ'alədʒiʸ/ *n* [U] science of how living bodies work –**gist** *n* –**gical** /ˌfɪziʸə'ladʒɪkəl/ *adj*

phys·i·o·ther·a·py /ˌfɪziʸoʷ'θerəpiʸ/ *n* [U] exercises, rubbing, etc., to treat sick people –**pist** *n*

phy·sique /fɪ'ziʸk/ *n* shape and quality of a person's body

pi·an·o /piʸ'ænoʷ/ *n* –os large musical instrument with wire strings, played by pressing black and white bars

pi·az·za /piʸ'ætsə/ *n* public square, esp. in Italy

pic·a·resque /ˌpɪkə'resk◄/ *adj* (of a story) dealing with a character of whom one disapproves but who is not usu. wicked

pic·co·lo /'pɪkəˌloʷ/ *n* –los small FLUTE

pick[1] /pɪk/ *vt* **1** choose **2** pull off from a plant: picking fruit **3** take up with the fingers, a beak, or a pointed instrument **4** remove unwanted pieces from: picking her teeth **5** steal from: I had my pocket picked. **6** open (a lock) without a key **7** cause (a fight, etc.) intentionally **8** pick and choose choose very carefully **9** pick holes in find the weak points in **10** pick one's way walk carefully **11** pick someone's brains make use of someone's knowledge ~**er** *n* ~**ings** *n* [P] additional money or profits

pick at *phr vt* eat (a meal) with little interest

pick off *phr vt* shoot one by one

pick on *phr vt* choose unfairly for punishment or blame

pick out *phr vt* **1** choose specially **2** see among others, esp. with difficulty

pick up *phr v* **1** *vt* take hold of and lift up **2** *vt* gather together: *Pick up your toys.* **3** *vi/t* (cause to) start again **4** *vt* get: *I picked up a cold last week.* **5** *vt* go and meet or collect: *I'll pick you up at the station.* **6** *vi* improve, esp. in health **7** *vt* become friendly with for sexual purposes **8** *vt* catch: *The police picked up the criminals at the airport.* **9** *vt* be able to hear or receive (on a radio)

pick² *n* [U] **1** choice: *Take your pick!* **2** best: *It's the pick of the new films.*

pick³ *n* **1** PICKAXE **2** sharp, pointed, usu. small instrument **3** small piece of metal, plastic, etc. for picking the strings of a GUITAR etc.

pick·axe, -ax /'pɪk-æks/ *n* large tool with 2 sharp points, for digging up roads, etc.

pick·et /'pɪkɪt/ *n* **1** person or group outside a place of work trying to persuade others not to work there during a quarrel with employers **2** soldier guarding a camp **3** strong pointed stick fixed in the ground ♦ *vt* surround with or as PICKETS (1)

pick·le /'pɪkəl/ *n* **1** [C;U] CUCUMBER preserved in VINEGAR or salt water **2** [U] vinegar or salt water for preserving foods **3** [S] dirty, difficult or confused condition: *in a pickle* ♦ *vt* preserve in pickle **-led** *adj infml* drunk

pick-me-up /'·· ‚·/ *n infml* something, esp. a drink or medicine, that makes one feel stronger, happier, etc.

pick·pock·et /'pɪk‚pɑkɪt/ *n* person who steals from people's pockets

pick·up /'·· ·/ *n* **1** light VAN having an open body with low sides **2** person of the opposite sex who one meets informally, esp. for sexual relations

pic·nic /'pɪknɪk/ *n* **1** informal outdoor meal **2** enjoyable experience ♦ *vi* **-ck-** have a picnic

pic·to·ri·al /pɪk'tɔriəl, -'toʷr-/ *adj* having or expressed in pictures ~ **ly** *adv*

pic·ture /'pɪktʃər/ *n* **1** [C] representation made by painting, drawing, or photography **2** [C] what is seen on a television: *We don't get a very good picture.* **3** *old-fash* [C] cinema film **4** [C] image in the mind **5** [S] person or thing that is beautiful **6** [S] perfect example: *He's the picture of health.* (= very healthy) **7 in the picture: a** knowing all the facts **b**

receiving much attention ♦ *vt* **1** imagine: *Just picture the frightful scene.* **2** paint or draw **pictures** *n* [P] **1** the cinema **2** the film industry

pic·tur·esque /‚pɪktʃə'resk◄/ *adj* **1** charming to look at **2** (of language) unusually forceful and descriptive

pid·dling /'pɪdlɪŋ/ *adj infml* small and unimportant

pid·gin /'pɪdʒən/ *n* language which is a mixture of other languages

pie /paɪ/ *n* baked dish of pastry filled with fruit or meat

pie·bald /'paɪbɔld/ *n, adj* (horse) colored black and white

piece¹ /piʸs/ *n* **1** separate part or bit: *Just picture the frightful 2* single object that is an example of its kind or class: *a piece of paper/music/*(fig.) *advice* **3** small object used in board games: *a chess piece* **4** *sl* small gun **5 give someone a piece of one's mind** *infml* tell someone angrily what you think of them **6 go to pieces** *infml* lose the ability to think or act clearly **7 in one piece** unharmed **8 of a piece** similar; in agreement **9 say one's piece** say what one wants to or has planned to, esp. in a way that is annoying or unwelcome to others

piece² *v* **piece together** *phr vt* complete by finding all the bits and putting them together

pi·èce de ré·sis·tance /piʸ‚es də rəzi'stɑns, -reʸ-/ *n* **pièces de résistance** (*same pronunciation*) the best or most important thing or event

piece·meal /'piʸsmiʸl/ *adj, adv* (done) only one part at a time

piece of cake /‚·· · '·/ *n* [S] *infml* something very easy to do

piece·work /'piʸswɜrk/ *n* [U] work paid for by the amount done rather than by the hours worked

pie chart /'·· ·/ *n* circle divided into several parts showing the way in which something, e.g. money or population, is divided up

pied /paɪd/ *adj* marked with different colors

pi·ed-à-terre /piʸ‚eʸd ə 'tɛər/ *n* **pieds-à-terre** (*same pronunciation*) small additional home

pier /pɪər/ *n* **1** long structure built out into the sea **2** supporting pillar

pierce /pɪərs/ *vt* make a hole in or through with a point: (fig.) *A cry of fear pierced the silence.* **piercing** *adj* **1** (of wind) very strong and cold **2** (of sound) unpleasantly sharp and clear **3** searching: *a piercing look*

pi·e·ty /'paɪətiʸ/ *n* [U] *fml* deep respect for God and religion

pif·fling /'pɪflɪŋ/ *adj infml* useless; worthless

pig /pɪg/ *n* **1** fat animal with short

legs and no fur, kept on farms for food **2** *infml* person who is dirty or rude or eats too much **3 make a pig of oneself** *infml* eat (or drink) too much

pig out *phr v infml* eat too much at one meal

pi·geon /ˈpɪdʒən/ *n* **1** fairly large, light gray bird **2** *sl* person who is easily deceived

pi·geon·hole /ˈpɪdʒənhoʊl/ *n* **1** box-like division for putting papers in **2** neat division which separates things too simply ♦ *vt* **1** put aside and do nothing about **2** put in a PIGEONHOLE (2)

pigeon-toed /ˈ·· ˌ·/ *adj* having feet that point inwards

piggy·back /ˈpɪgiˌbæk/ *adv* on the back and shoulders: *He carried his son piggyback.* | *riding piggyback*

pig·gy·bank /ˈpɪgiˌbæŋk/ *n* small container, usu. shaped like a pig, used by children for saving coins

pig·head·ed /ˈpɪgˌhedɪd/ *adj* very unwilling to agree or obey

pig·let /ˈpɪglɪt/ *n* young pig

pig·ment /ˈpɪgmənt/ *n* **1** [C;U] dry colored powder for making paint **2** [U] natural coloring matter in plants and animals ~**ation** /ˌpɪg-mənˈteʲʃən/ *n* [U]

pig·my /ˈpɪgmiʲ/ *n* PYGMY

pig·sty /ˈpɪgstaɪ/ *n* **1** small building for pigs **2** very dirty room or house

pig·swill /ˈpɪgˌswɪl/ *n* [U] waste food given to pigs

pig·tail /ˈpɪgteʲl/ *n* length of hair in a BRAID hanging down the back

pike¹ /paɪk/ *n* **pikes** *or* **pike** large river fish that eats smaller fish

pike² *n* spear with a long handle

pil·chard /ˈpɪltʃərd/ *n* small sea fish, often eaten

pile¹ /paɪl/ *n* **1** tidy heap: *a pile of books* **2** also **piles** *pl*. — *infml* lots: *I've got piles of work to do.* **3** *infml* very large amount of money **4** large tall building – see also PILES **♦** *v* **1** *vt* make a pile of **2** *vi* come or go in a (disorderly) crowd: *The children piled into the car.*

pile up *phr vi* form into a mass or large quantity

pile² *n* [C;U] soft surface of short threads on CARPETs or cloth

pile³ *n* heavy supporting post hammered into the ground

piles /paɪlz/ *n* [P] HEMORRHOIDS

pile-up /ˈpaɪlʌp/ *n* traffic accident with many vehicles

pil·fer /ˈpɪlfər/ *vi/t* steal (small things)

pil·grim /ˈpɪlgrəm/ *n* person on a journey to a holy place ~**age** *n* [C;U] pilgrim's journey

pill /pɪl/ *n* **1** [C] small ball of medicine **2** [*the*+S] (*often cap.*) pill taken for birth control

pil·lage /ˈpɪlɪdʒ/ *vi/t fml* steal things violently from (a place taken in war)

pil·lar /ˈpɪlər/ *n* **1** tall upright round post, usu. of stone, used esp. as a support for a roof **2** important member and active supporter: *a pillar of the church*

pill·box /ˈpɪlbɑks/ *n* **1** small round box for PILLs (1) **2** CONCRETE shelter with a gun inside it

pil·lion /ˈpɪlyən/ *n* passenger seat on a motorcycle

pil·lo·ry /ˈpɪləriʲ/ *vt* attack with words, esp. in public

pil·low /ˈpɪloʷ/ *n* filled cloth bag for supporting the head in bed ♦ *vt* rest (esp. one's head) on something

pil·low·case /ˈpɪloʷˌkeʲs/ *n* cloth cover for a pillow

pi·lot /ˈpaɪlət/ *n* **1** person who flies a plane **2** person who guides ships into a HARBOR, etc. ♦ *adj* intended to try something out: *a pilot survey* ♦ *vt* act as the pilot of

pilot light /ˈ·· ˌ·/ *n* **1** small gas flame to light a main flame **2** small electric light to show an apparatus is turned on

pimp /pɪmp/ *n* man who controls and gets money from PROSTITUTEs

pim·ple /ˈpɪmpəl/ *n* small raised diseased spot on the skin

pin /pɪn/ *n* **1** short thin pointed piece of metal for fastening things **2** BROOCH ♦ *vt* -**nn**- **1** fasten with a pin **2** keep in one position, esp. by weight from above **3 pin one's hopes on someone** depend on someone for help, etc.

pin down *phr vt* **1** force to give clear details, make a firm decision, etc. **2** prevent from moving

pin·cer /ˈpɪnsər/ *n* footlike part of a CRAB, LOBSTER, etc., for seizing things **pincers** *n* [P] tool for holding things tightly

pinch /pɪntʃ/ *v* **1** *vt* press tightly between 2 surfaces or between finger and thumb **2** *vi* hurt by being too tight **3** *vt infml* steal **4 pinch pennies** not spend money ♦ *n* **1** [C] act of pinching **2** [C] amount picked up with finger and thumb: *a pinch of salt* **3** [*the*+S] suffering through not having enough esp. of money: *We're beginning to feel the pinch.* **4 in a pinch** if necessary **5 with a pinch of salt** as being untrue or not dependable: *Take everything he says with a pinch of salt.*

pin·cush·ion /ˈpɪnˌkuʃən/ *n* small filled bag for sticking pins into until needed

pine¹ /paɪn/ *n* tall tree with thin

sharp leaves that do not drop off in winter

pine² /paɪn/ vi 1 lose strength and health through grief 2 have a strong desire, esp. that is impossible to fulfil

pine·ap·ple /'paɪnˌæpəl/ n [C;U] large tropical fruit with sweet juicy yellow flesh

ping /pɪŋ/ vi, n (make) a short sharp ringing sound

ping-pong /'pɪŋpɒŋ, -pɒŋ/ n [U] TABLE TENNIS

pin·ion¹ /'pɪnyən/ vt prevent from moving by tying or holding the limbs

pinion² n small wheel fitting against a larger one for turning

pink /pɪŋk/ adj pale red ♦ n **in the pink** in perfect health

pink eye /'·· ·/ n [S] CONJUNCTIVITIS

pink·ie /'pɪŋkiʸ/ n smallest finger

pink slip /ˌ· '·/ n notice of being fired from a job

pin mon·ey /'·· ˌ··/ n [U] money earned by doing small jobs

pin·na·cle /'pɪnəkəl/ n highest point or degree: *the pinnacle of success*

pin·point /'pɪnpɔɪnt/ vt find or describe exactly

pins and nee·dles /ˌ· · '··/ n [P] slight pricking pains in a limb

pin·stripe /'pɪnstraɪp/ n 1 [C] one of a pattern of parallel pale lines on dark cloth 2 [P] also **pinstripe suit** /ˌ·· '·/ — suit made of cloth with a pattern of pinstripes

pint /paɪnt/ n a measure of liquids equal to 16 fluid OUNCEs

pin-up /'pɪnʌp/ n picture of an attractive or admired person such as a popular singer, esp. as stuck up on a wall

pi·o·neer /ˌpaɪə'nɪər/ n person who does something first, preparing the way for others, esp. one who helped settle the western US ♦ vt act as a pioneer in

pi·ous /'paɪəs/ adj 1 having deep respect for God and religion 2 unlikely to be fulfilled: *a pious hope* ~**ly** adv

pipe /paɪp/ n 1 tube carrying liquid or gas 2 small tube with a bowl-like container, for smoking tobacco 3 simple tubelike musical instrument **pipes** n [P] BAGPIPES

pipe² vt 1 carry in pipes 2 play music on a PIPE (3) or PIPEs **piper** n player of BAGPIPES

pipe down phr vi infml stop talking or being noisy

pipe up phr vi suddenly start to speak

piped mu·sic /ˌ· '··/ n [U] quiet recorded music played continuously in public places

pipe dream /'· ·/ n impossible hope, plan, or idea

pipe·line /'paɪp-laɪn/ n 1 line of joined pipes, esp. for carrying oil or gas 2 **in the pipeline** about to arrive or appear; being prepared

pi·pette /pɪ'pet/ n small glass tube for sucking up and measuring liquids

pip·ing /'paɪpɪŋ/ n [U] PIPES¹ (1)

piping² adv **piping hot**

pi·quant /'piʸkənt, 'piʸkɑnt, piʸ-'kɑnt/ adj 1 having a pleasant sharp taste 2 interesting and exciting to the mind –**quancy** /'piʸkənsiʸ/ n [U]

pique /piʸk/ n [U] annoyance and displeasure because of hurt pride ♦ vt offend

pi·ra·cy /'paɪrəsiʸ/ n [U] robbery by pirates

pi·ra·nha /pə'rɑnyə, -'ræn-, -'rɑnə/ n fierce S. American river fish that eats flesh

pi·rate /'paɪrɪt/ n 1 person who sails around robbing ships 2 person who pirates things ♦ vt make and sell (a book, record, etc., by someone else) without permission or payment

pir·ou·ette /ˌpɪruʷ'et/ n very fast turn on one foot by a dancer **pirouette** vi

piss¹ /pɪs/ vi taboo sl urinate (URINE)

piss off phr v taboo sl annoy

pissed off adj angry

piss² n taboo sl URINE

pis·tol /'pɪstl/ n small gun held in one hand

pis·ton /'pɪstən/ n short part of an engine shaped like a pipe, that goes up and down inside a tube and sends power to the engine

pit¹ /pɪt/ n 1 hole in the ground 2 coal mine 3 small hollow mark on a surface 4 space in front of a stage where musicians sit 5 hard central part of certain fruit 6 **pit of the stomach** place where fear is thought to be felt **pits** n [P] 1 place beside the track where cars are repaired during a race 2 infml the worst possible example of something

pit² vt –tt– mark with PITS¹ (3)

pit against phr vt set against in competition or fight

pitch¹ /pɪtʃ/ v 1 set up (a camp or tent) 2 vi (of a ship or aircraft) move along with the front and back going up and down 3 vt set the PITCH² (2) of (a sound, music, etc.) 4 vt throw 5 vi/t (cause) fall suddenly forwards 6 vi play the position of PITCHER² in baseball

pitch in phr vi 1 start eagerly 2 add one's help or support

pitch² n 1 degree of highness and lowness of a (musical) sound 2 level;

degree: *a high pitch of excitement* **3** *infml* seller's special way of talking about goods he/she is trying to sell: *a good sales pitch* **4** action of pitching (pitch(1)(6)): *a slow/fast pitch*

pitch³ /ˌ/ *n* [U] black substance used for keeping out water: (fig.) *a* **pitch-black** (= very dark) *night*

pitched bat·tle /ˌ· ˈ··/ *n infml* fierce and long quarrel or argument

pitch·er¹ /ˈpɪtʃər/ *n* container for holding and pouring liquids

pitcher² *n* (in baseball) player who throws the ball towards the BATTER³

pitch·fork /ˈpɪtʃfɔrk/ *n* fork with a long handle for lifting dried grass on a farm

pit·e·ous /ˈpɪtiⁱəs/ *adj fml* causing pity ~**ly** *adv*

pit·fall /ˈpɪtfɔl/ *n* unexpected difficulty or danger

pith /pɪθ/ *n* [U] soft white substance in the stems of some plants and under the skin of oranges, etc. ~**y** *adj* full of pith **2** strongly and cleverly stated in few words

pit·i·a·ble /ˈpɪtiⁱəbəl/ *adj* **1** deserving pity **2** PITIFUL ~**bly** *adv*

pit·i·ful /ˈpɪtɪfəl/ *adj* **1** causing or deserving pity **2** worthless; weak ~**ly** *adv*

pit·i·less /ˈpɪtɪlɪs/ *adj* merciless; cruel ~**ly** *adv*

pit stop /ˈpɪtstɑp/ *n* **1** stop at pits (PIT¹) **2** stop for food, etc. while traveling

pit·tance /ˈpɪtns/ *n* very small amount of pay or money

pi·tu·i·ta·ry /pəˈtuⁱəˌteriⁱ/ *n* small organ near the brain which helps to control growth

pit·y /ˈpɪtiⁱ/ *n* **1** [U] sympathy and sorrow for others' suffering or unhappiness: *We took pity on* (= felt pity for and helped) *the homeless family.* **2** [S] unfortunate state of affairs: *It's a pity you have to go now.* **3 for pity's sake** (used to add force to a request) please **4 more's the pity** unfortunately ♦ *vt* feel pity for

piv·ot /ˈpɪvət/ *n* central point on which something turns ♦ *vi/t* turn on or provide with a pivot ~**al** *adj*

pix·el /ˈpɪksəl, -ˌsel/ *n* tech one small dot of light on a television or computer SCREEN

pix·ie, pixy /ˈpɪksiⁱ/ *n* small fairy that plays tricks

piz·za /ˈpiⁱtsə/ *n* [C;U] flat round pastry baked with cheese, TOMATOes, etc., on top

pizz·azz /pəˈzæz/ *n* [U] *sl* exciting, forceful quality

plac·ard /ˈplækɑrd, -kərd/ *n* board put up or carried around publicly, with information on it

pla·cate /ˈpleⁱkeⁱt, ˈplæ-/ *vt* cause to stop feeling angry

place¹ /pleⁱs/ *n* **1** [C] particular position in space: *the place where the accident happened* | (fig.) *Sports never had a nice place in his life.* **2** [C] particular town, building, etc.: *Is San Diego a nice place to live in?* **3** [C] usual or proper position: *Put it back in its place.* **4** position in the result of a competition, race, etc.: *I got first place in the exam.* **5** [C] position of employment, in a team, etc.: *She got a place on the Board of Directors.* **6** [S] numbered point in an argument, etc.: *In the first place, I can't afford it.* **7** [S] duty: *It's not my place to tell them what to do.* **8** [C] space or seat for a person: *save our places; we'll be right back.* **9** [S] *infml* home: *Come back to my place.* **10 go places** *infml* be increasingly successful **11 in/out of place: a** in/not in the usual or proper position **b** suitable/unsuitable **12 in place of** instead of **13 know one's place** consider oneself of low rank and behave respectfully **14 set a place** put knives, forks, spoons, etc., in position on the dinner table (for one person) **15 put someone in his/her place** show someone that he/she is not as important as he/she would like to be **16 take place** happen **17 take the place of** act or be used instead of; REPLACE

place² *vt* **1** put in the stated place **2** make (an order for goods one wants to buy) **3** remember fully who (someone) is ~**ment** *n* [U] act or example of placing someone or something in position

pla·ce·bo /pləˈsiⁱboʷ/ *n* -**bos** or -**boes** substance given instead of real medicine, without the person who takes it knowing that it is not real

pla·cen·ta /pləˈsentə/ *n* -**tas** or -**tae** -tiⁱ/ thick mass inside the WOMB joining the unborn child to its mother

plac·id /ˈplæsɪd/ *adj* not easily angered or excited ~**ly** *adv*

pla·gia·rize /ˈpleⁱdʒəˌraɪz/ *vt* take (words, ideas, etc.) from (someone else's work) and use them in one's own writings without admitting that one has done so ~**rism** *n* [U]

plague /pleⁱg/ *n* **1** [C;U] quickly spreading disease that kills many people **2** [C] widespread uncontrollable mass or number: *a plague of locusts* ♦ *vt* trouble or annoy continually

plaid /plæd/ *n* (piece of) thick cloth with a pattern of colored squares

plain¹ /pleⁱn/ *adj* **1** without decoration or pattern; simple **2** easy to see, hear, or understand **3** expressing thoughts clearly, honestly, and exactly **4** fairly ugly ♦ *adv* completely: *plain stupid* **~ly** *adv* **~ness** *n* [U]

plain² *n* large stretch of flat land

plain-clothes /ˌpleⁱnˈkloʷz◂, -kloʷðz◂/ *adj* wearing ordinary clothes and not a uniform: *a plain-clothes policeman*

plain sail·ing /ˌ· ˈ··/ *n* [U] something easy to do

plain-spo·ken /ˌpleⁱnˈspoʷkən◂/ *adj* (too) direct and honest in speech

plain·tiff /ˈpleⁱntɪf/ *n* person who brings a legal charge or claim

plain·tive /ˈpleⁱntɪv/ *adj* sounding sad **~ly** *adv*

plan /plæn/ *n* **1** arrangement for carrying out a (future) activity **2** (maplike drawing showing) an arrangement of parts in a system ♦ *vi/t* **-nn-** make a plan (for) **~ner** *n*

plane¹ /pleⁱn/ *n* **1** aircraft **2** level; standard: *Let's keep the conversation on a friendly plane.* **3** *math* flat surface ♦ *adj math* completely flat

plane² *n* tool with a sharp blade for making wood smooth ♦ *vt* use a plane on

plan·et /ˈplænɪt/ *n* large body in space that moves around a star, esp. the sun **~ary** *adj*

plan·gent /ˈplændʒənt/ *adj fml* (of a sound) expressing sorrow

plank /plæŋk/ *n* **1** long narrow wooden board **2** main principle of a political party's stated aims **~ing** *n* [U] (floor) planks

plank·ton /ˈplæŋktən/ *n* [U] extremely small sea animals and plants

plant¹ /plænt/ *n* **1** [C] living thing with leaves and roots **2** [C] factory or other industrial building **3** [U] industrial machinery **4** [C] *infml* **a** person placed secretly in a group in order to discover facts about them **b** thing hidden on a person to make him seem guilty

plant² *vt* **1** put (plants or seeds) in the ground **2** *infml* hide (illegal goods) on someone to make them seem guilty **3** *infml* put (a person) secretly in a group **4** place firmly or forcefully **~er** *n*

plan·ta·tion /plænˈteⁱʃən/ *n* area where large plants are grown as a business, esp. in the old South: *a cotton plantation*

plaque /plæk/ *n* flat metal or stone plate with writing on it, usu. fixed to a wall

plas·ma /ˈplæzmə/ *n* [U] liquid part of blood, containing the cells

plas·ter¹ /ˈplæstər/ *n* **1** [U] mixture of lime, water, sand, etc., which hardens when dry

plaster² *vt* **1** put plaster on (a wall, etc.) **2** cover too thickly **~ed** *adj infml* drunk

plaster cast /ˌ·· ˈ·/ *n* copy of a STATUE in plaster

plas·tic /ˈplæstɪk/ *n* [C;U] light artificial material used for making various things ♦ *adj fml* **1** easily formed into various shapes **2** connected with the art of shaping forms in clay, wood, etc. **3** *infml* not sincere **~ity** /plæsˈtɪsəti/ *n* [U]

plastic sur·ge·ry /ˌ·· ˈ···/ *n* [U] repair of body parts with pieces of skin or bone taken from other parts

plate /pleⁱt/ *n* **1** [C] **a** flat dish from which food is eaten or served **b** also **plate·ful** /-fʊl/ — amount of food this will hold **2** [C] flat, thin, usu. large piece of something hard **3** [U] metal covered with gold or silver **4** [C] picture in a book, usu. colored **5** **on a plate** with too little effort ♦ *vt* cover (a metal article) with gold, silver, or tin

plat·eau /plæˈtoʷ/ *n* **-eaus** or **-eaux** /-ˈtoʷz/ **1** large area of level high land **2** steady unchanging level, period, or condition

plate glass /ˌ· ˈ·◂/ *n* [U] clear glass in large thick sheets

plat·form /ˈplætfɔrm/ *n* **1** raised area beside the track at a train station **2** raised floor for speakers or performers **3** main ideas and aims of a political party, esp. as stated before an election

plat·i·num /ˈplætn-əm, ˈplatnəm/ *n* [U] very valuable gray-white metal

plat·i·tude /ˈplætəˌtuʷd, -ˌtyuʷd/ *n* statement that is true but not new or interesting

pla·ton·ic /pləˈtɑnɪk/ *adj* (of friendship, esp. between a man and woman) not sexual

pla·toon /pləˈtuʷn/ *n* small group of soldiers

plat·ter /ˈplætər/ *n* large dish for serving food

plat·y·pus /ˈplætəpəs/ *n* small Australian animal that has a beak and lays eggs

plau·dits /ˈplɔdɪts/ *n* [P] show of pleased approval

plau·si·ble /ˈplɔzəbəl/ *adj* seeming true; believable **-bly** *adv*

play¹ /pleⁱ/ *n* **1** [U] activity for fun, esp. by children **2** [C] story written to be acted **3** [U] action in a sport: *Rain stopped play.* **4** [U] action; effect: *He had to bring all his experience* **into play.** (= use it)

play² *v* **1** *vi* amuse oneself with a game, toys, etc. **2** *vi/t* produce sounds or music (from) **3** *vi/t* take part in (a sport or game) **4** *vi/t* perform (in): *Who played the part of Hamlet?* **5** *vt* plan and carry out:

They played a trick on me. **6** pretend to be: *Stop playing the fool!* (= being foolish) **7** *vt* strike and send (a ball) **8** *vt* place (a playing card) face upwards on the table **9** *vt* aim; direct: *The firemen played their hoses on the blaze.* **10** *vi* move lightly and irregularly: *A smile played across her lips.* **11** **play ball** *infml* COOPERATE **12** **play for time** delay in order to gain time **13** **play into someone's hands** behave in a way that gives someone an advantage over one **14** **play it by ear** act according to changing conditions, rather than making fixed plans in advance **15** **play (it) safe** act so as to avoid trouble **16** **play possum** pretend to sleep **17** **play the field** have many love affairs **18** **play the game** do what others expect ~ **er** *n* person playing a sport or a musical instrument

play along *phr vi* pretend to agree, esp. to avoid trouble

play at *phr vt* **1** PLAY² (6) **2** do in a way that is not serious

play back *phr vt* listen to or look at (something just recorded) **play·back** /ˈpleɪbæk/ *n* playing of something just recorded, esp. on television

play down *phr vt* cause to seem less important

play off *phr v* **1** *vt* set (people or things) in opposition, esp. for one's own advantage **2** *vi* play another game in order to decide who wins **play-off** /ˈ· ·/ *n* second game played to decide who wins

play on *phr vt* try to use or encourage (others' feelings) for one's own advantage

play up *phr v* **1** *vi/t* cause trouble or suffering (to) **2** *vt* give special importance to

play up to *phr vt* act so as to win the favor of

play with *phr vt* **1** consider (an idea) not very seriously **2** play with oneself MASTURBATE **3** to play with that one can use; AVAILABLE

play-act /ˈ· ·/ *vi* behave with an unreal show of feeling

play·boy /ˈpleɪbɔɪ/ *n* wealthy (young) man who lives for pleasure

play-doh /ˈpleɪdoʊ/ *n tdmk* U.S. colored claylike substance played with by children

play·ful /ˈpleɪfəl/ *adj* **1** full of fun **2** not intended seriously ~ **ly** *adv* ~ **ness** *n* [U]

play·ground /ˈpleɪɡraʊnd/ *n* piece of ground for children to play on

playing card /ˈ·· ˌ·/ *n fml for* CARD (1a)

play·mate /ˈpleɪmeɪt/ *n* child's friend who shares in games

play·pen /ˈpleɪpen/ *n* enclosed frame for a baby to play in

play·thing /ˈpleɪˌθɪŋ/ *n* **1** toy **2** person treated without consideration

play·wright /ˈpleɪraɪt/ *n* writer of plays

pla·za /ˈplɑːzə, ˈplæzə/ *n* **1** public square or market place **2** small group of stores with one parking lot

plea /pliː/ *n* **1** *fml* urgent or serious request **2** *law* statement by someone in a court saying whether they are guilty or not

plea bar·gain·ing /ˈ· ˌ···/ *n* [U] practice of agreeing to say in a court of law that one is guilty of a small crime in exchange for not being charged with a greater one

plead /pliːd/ *v* **1** *vi* make continual and deeply felt requests **2** *vt law* say officially in court that one is (guilty or not guilty) **3** *vt* offer as an excuse: *He pleaded ignorance.*

pleas·ant /ˈplezənt/ *adj* pleasing; nice ~ **ly** *adv*

pleas·ant·ry /ˈplezəntriː/ *n fml* politely amusing remark

please /pliːz/ *v* **1** *vi/t* make (someone) happy or satisfied **2** *vi* want; like: *They can appoint whoever they please.* ♦ *interj* (used when asking politely for something) **pleased** *adj* happy; satisfied: *Are you pleased with your new car?*

plea·sur·a·ble /ˈpleʒərəbəl/ *adj fml* enjoyable – **bly** *adv*

plea·sure /ˈpleʒər/ *n* **1** [U] happy feeling; enjoyment **2** [C] something that gives one pleasure **3** [S] something that is not inconvenient and that one is pleased to do: *'Thank you for helping me.' 'My pleasure.'*

pleat /pliːt/ *n* flat narrow fold in cloth ♦ *vt* make pleats in

ple·be·ian /plɪˈbiːən/ *n, adj* (member) of the ordinary people

pleb·is·cite /ˈplebəˌsaɪt/ *n* vote by the people of a country to decide a matter

pledge /pledʒ/ *n* **1** solemn promise **2** something valuable left with someone as a sign that one will fulfil an agreement **3** something given as a sign of love ♦ *vt* make a solemn promise of

ple·na·ry /ˈpliːnəriː, ˈple-/ *adj fml* **1** (of powers or rights) full; limitless **2** attended by all members: *a plenary session of Congress*

plen·i·po·ten·ti·a·ry /ˌplenəpəˈtenʃəriː, -tʃəriː, -ʃiːˌeriː, -tʃiːˌeriː/ *n fml* official or representative with full powers

plen·ti·ful /ˈplentɪfəl/ *adj* in large enough quantities: *plentiful supplies* ~ **ly** *adv*

plen·ty /ˈplentiː/ *pron* as much as

or more than is needed: *There's plenty (of food) for everyone.*

pleth·o·ra /'plεθərə/ *n* [S] *fml* too much

Plex·i·glas /'plεksiʸˌglæs/ *n tdmk* [U] strong glasslike plastic

pli·a·ble /'plaɪəbəl/ *adj* 1 easily bent 2 able and willing to change; ADAPTable 3 PLIANT (1) **–bility** /ˌplaɪə'bɪl-əṭiʸ/ *n* [U]

pli·ant /'plaɪənt/ *adj* 1 (too) easily influenced 2 PLIABLE (1) **–ancy** *n* [U]

pli·ers /'plaɪərz/ *n* [P] small tool for holding small things or cutting wire

plight /plaɪt/ *n* bad or serious condition or situation

plinth /plɪnθ/ *n* square block which a STATUE stands on

plod /plɑd/ *vi* **–dd–** 1 walk slowly and with effort 2 work steadily, esp. at something dull **~der** *n* slow, steady, not very clever worker

plonk /plɑŋk, plɔŋk/ *vt infml* put, esp. heavily or with force

plop /plɑp/ *vi, n* **–pp–** [S] (make or fall with) a sound like something falling smoothly into liquid

plot¹ /plɑt/ *n* 1 set of connected events on which a story is based 2 secret plan to do something bad 3 small piece of ground for building or growing things

plot² *v* **–tt–** 1 *vi/t* plan together secretly (something bad) 2 *vt* mark (the course of a ship or aircraft) on a map 3 *vt* mark (a line showing facts) on special paper with squares **~ter** *n*

plow /plaʊ/ *n* farming tool for breaking up earth and turning it over ♦ *v* 1 *vi/t* break up and turn over (earth) with a plow 2 *vi* go forcefully or roughly

plow back *phr vt* put (money earned) back into a business

ploy /plɔɪ/ *n* something done to gain an advantage, sometimes deceivingly

pluck¹ /plʌk/ *vt* 1 pull the feathers off (a bird to be cooked) 2 pull out or pick up sharply 3 play an instrument by pulling (its strings) 4 *esp. lit.* pick (a flower)

pluck up *phr vt* show (courage) in spite of fear

pluck² *n* [U] courage **~y** *adj* brave

plug /plʌg/ *n* 1 small usu. round thing for blocking a hole, esp. in a BATHTUB, etc. 2 small object for connecting an apparatus with a supply of electricity 3 publicly stated favorable opinion about a product on radio, television, etc., intended to make people want to buy it ♦ *vt* **–gg–** 1 block or fill with a PLUG (1) 2 give a PLUG (3) to

plug in *phr vt* connect to a supply of electricity

plum /plʌm/ *n* roundish usu. dark red fruit with a hard seed in the middle ♦ *adj* very desirable: *a plum job*

plum·age /'pluʷmɪdʒ/ *n* [U] feathers on a bird

plumb¹ /plʌm/ *vt* 1 (try to) find the meaning of 2 put in plumbing 3 **plumb the depths** reach the lowest point

plumb² *adv* exactly: *plumb in the center*

plumb·er /'plʌmər/ *n* person who fits and repairs water pipes

plumb·ing /'plʌmɪŋ/ *n* [U] 1 all the water pipes and containers in a building 2 work of a plumber

plumb line /'· ·/ *n* string with a weight on it, for finding the depth of water or whether something is upright

plume /pluʷm/ *n* 1 (large or showy) feather 2 rising feathery shape: *a plume of smoke* **plumed** *adj*

plummet /'plʌmɪt/ *vi* fall steeply or suddenly

plump /plʌmp/ *adj* pleasantly fat **~ness** *n* [U]

plump up *phr vt* make rounded and soft by shaking

plun·der /'plʌndər/ *vi/t* steal or rob in time of war ♦ *n* [U] (goods seized by) plundering **~er** *n*

plunge /plʌndʒ/ *vi/t* 1 move suddenly forwards and/or downwards 2 (of the neck of a woman's garment) have a low front or in a V shape showing a large area of chest: *a plunging neckline* ♦ *n* 1 act of plunging 2 **take the plunge** at last do something one had delayed

plunger *n* 1 tool for clearing a stopped TOILET or DRAIN 2 part of a machine that moves up and down

plu·per·fect /ˌpluʷ'pɜrfɪkt/ *n* PAST PERFECT

plu·ral /'plʊərəl/ *n, adj* (word or form) that expresses more than one

plus /plʌs/ *prep* with the addition of: *3 plus 2 is 5.* ♦ *adj* 1 greater than zero 2 additional and desirable ♦ *n* 1 sign (+) for adding 2 *infml* welcome or favorable addition

plush /plʌʃ/ *adj* looking very splendid and expensive

Plu·to /'pluʷtoʷ/ *n* the PLANET 9th in order from the sun

plu·to·crat /'pluʷtəˌkræt/ *n* powerful wealthy person **~ic** /ˌpluʷtə'kræṭɪk◂/ *adj*

plu·to·ni·um /pluʷ'toʷniʸəm/ *n* [U] substance used in producing atomic power

ply¹ /plaɪ/ *n* [U] measure of the number of threads in wool, rope, etc., or the number of sheets in plywood

ply² v **1** vi travel regularly for hire or other business **2** vt work at (a trade)

ply with phr vt keep giving (esp. food) to

ply·wood /ˈplaɪwʊd/ n [U] material made of thin sheets of wood stuck together

pm, PM /ˌpiːˈem/ abbrev. for: post meridiem = (Latin) after noon (used after numbers expressing time)

pneu·mat·ic /nʊˈmætɪk, njʊ-/ adj **1** worked by air pressure **2** filled with air: a pneumatic tire

pneu·mo·nia /nʊˈmoʊnjə, njʊ-/ n [U] serious lung disease

P.O. /ˌpiːˈoʊ/ abbrev. for: post office

poach¹ /poʊtʃ/ vi/t catch or kill (animals) illegally on someone else's land: (fig.) poaching (= stealing) my ideas ~**er** n

poach² vt cook in gently boiling water

pock·et /ˈpɑkɪt/ n **1** small baglike part in or on a garment **2** container for thin things in a case, inside a car door, etc. **3** small separate area or group: pockets of mist **4** (supply of) money: beyond my pocket (= too expensive) **5** in one's pocket in one's control **6** out of pocket having spent money without any good result ♦ adj small enough to put into one's pocket: a pocket camera ♦ vt **1** put into one's pocket **2** take (money) dishonestly

pock·et·book /ˈpɑkɪtˌbʊk/ n **1** small notebook **2** handbag

pocket mon·ey /ˈ·· ˌ··/ n [U] money given regularly to a child by its parents – see also allowance

pock·mark /ˈpɑkmɑrk/ n hollow mark on the skin where a diseased spot has been ~**ed** adj

pod /pɑd/ n long narrow seed container of peas and beans

po·di·um /ˈpoʊdiəm/ n –**ums** or –**dia** /-diʲə/ raised part for a speaker or performer to stand on

po·em /ˈpoʊɪm/ n piece of writing in patterns of lines and sounds

po·et /ˈpoʊɪt/ n writer of poetry ~**ic** /poʊˈetɪk/ adj **1** of poetry **2** graceful ~**ical** adj **1** written as poetry **2** poetic ~**ically** /-kliʲ/ adv

poetic jus·tice /·ˌ·· ˈ··/ n [U] something suitably bad happening to a person who does something wrong

poetic li·cence /·ˌ·· ˈ··/ n [U] poet's freedom to change facts, not to obey the usual rules of grammar, etc.

poet lau·re·ate /ˌ·· ˈ···/ n (often caps.) poet who represents his/her country or state

po·et·ry /ˈpoʊɪtriʲ/ n [U] **1** art of a poet **2** poems **3** graceful quality

pog·rom /ˈpoʊˈgrɑm, pəˈgrɑm/ n planned killing of large numbers of people

poi·gnant /ˈpɔɪnjənt/ adj sharply sad ~**ly** adv **poignancy** n [U]

poin·set·ti·a /pɔɪnˈsetiʲə/ n plant with red flowers, having associations with Christmas

point¹ /pɔɪnt/ n **1** [C] sharp end: the point of a needle **2** [C] particular place or moment: a weak point in the plan | At that point I left. **3** [C] unit for recording the score in a game **4** [C] single particular idea or part of an argument or statement: You've made (= expressed) an important point. **5** [C] main idea, which gives meaning to the whole: That's beside the point. (= is unimportant) **6** [U] purpose; advantage: There's no point in waiting any longer. **7** [C] place on a measuring system: the boiling point of water | the 32 points of the compass **8** [C] particular quality or ability: Spelling isn't her strong point. **9** [C] sign (·) to the left of decimals: 4·2 is read as '4 point 2'. **10** case in point something that proves or is an example of the subject under consideration **11** in point of fact actually **12** make a point of take particular care to **13** on the point of just about to **14** to the point of so as to be almost **15** when it comes/came to the point when the moment for action or decision comes/came

point² v **1** vi show or draw attention to something by holding out a finger, stick, etc., in its direction **2** vi/t aim or be aimed: The gun was pointed/pointing at his head. **3** vt fill in and make smooth the spaces between bricks (of a wall, etc.) with cement ~**ed** adj **1** having a sharp end **2** directed against a particular person: a pointed remark ~**edly** adv

point out phr vt draw attention to

point-blank /ˌ· ˈ·◄/ adj, adv **1** fired from a very close position **2** forceful and direct: a point-blank refusal

point·er /ˈpɔɪntər/ n **1** stick for pointing at things **2** thin piece that points to numbers on a measuring apparatus **3** piece of helpful advice **4** type of hunting dog

point·less /ˈpɔɪntlɪs/ adj meaningless; useless ~**ly** adv ~**ness** n [U]

point of view /ˌ· · ˈ·/ n particular way of considering something

poise /pɔɪz/ n [U] **1** quiet confidence and self-control **2** balanced way of moving ♦ vt put lightly in a place where it is hard to be steady **poised** adj ready: poised to attack **2** showing poise

poi·son /ˈpɔɪzən/ n [C;U] substance that can kill or cause illness ♦ vt **1** give poison to or put poison in **2**

have a damaging or evil effect on ~**ous** *adj*

poke /powk/ *vi/t* **1** push out sharply: *She poked her head around the corner.* **2** push a pointed thing (into) **3 poke fun at** cause (unkind) laughter at **4 poke one's nose into something** inquire into something which does not concern one ♦ *n* act of poking

pok·er¹ /'powkər/ *n* thin metal rod for poking a fire to make it burn better

pok·er² *n* [U] card game played for money

poker face /'·· ,·/ *n* face that hides someone's thoughts or feelings

pok·y /'powkiʸ/ *adj* uncomfortably small and unattractive

po·lar /'powlər/ *adj* of or near the North or South Poles

polar bear /'·· ,·/ *n* large white bear that lives near the North Pole

po·lar·i·ty /pow'læriṭiʸ, pə-/ *n* [C;U] *fml* having or developing 2 opposite qualities

po·lar·ize /'powlə,raɪz/ *vi/t* form into groups based on 2 directly opposite principles –**ization** /,powlərə'zeʸʃən/ *n* [U]

Po·lar·oid /'powlə,rɔɪd/ *n tdmk* **1** [U] substance that makes sunshine less bright, used in SUNGLASSES **2** [C] camera that produces finished photographs in seconds

pole¹ /powl/ *n* long straight thin stick or post

pole² *n* **1** (*often cap.*) point furthest north and south on the Earth: *the North Pole* **2** either end of a MAGNET **3** either of the points on a BATTERY where wires are fixed **4** either of 2 positions that are as far apart as they can be **5 poles apart** widely separated in opinion, etc.

pole·cat /'powlkæt/ *n* small fierce animal with an unpleasant smell

po·lem·ic /pə'lemɪk/ *n* [C;U] *fml* fierce argument defending or attacking ideas or opinions –**al** *adj*

pole vault /'· ·/ *n* jump over a high bar using a long pole

po·lice /pə'liʸs/ *n* [P] official body for making people obey the law, catching criminals, etc. ♦ *vt* control or keep a watch on with policemen: (fig.) *a new committee to police the nuclear industry*

police of·fi·cer /·'· ,···/ also **po·lice·man** /pə'liʸsmən/ *masc* **police·wom·an** /pə'liʸs,wʊmən/ *fem* — *n* member of the police

police state /·'· ,·/ *n* country where people are controlled by (secret) political police

pol·i·cy /'pɑləsiʸ/ *n* **1** what a government, company, political party,

etc., intends to do about a particular matter **2** insurance contract

po·li·o /'powliʸ,ow/ *n* [U] serious infectious nerve disease, esp. of the SPINE, which often prevents movement

pol·ish¹ /'pɑlɪʃ/ *vt* **1** make smooth and shiny by rubbing **2** make as perfect as possible: *a polished performance* ♦ *n* **1** [U] liquid, paste, etc., for polishing **2** [S] act of polishing **3** [U] fine quality ~**ed** *adj* **1** (of a piece of artistic work, a performance, etc.) done with great skill and control **2** polite and graceful ~**er** *n*

polish off *phr vt* finish (food, work, etc.) quickly or easily

polish up *phr vt* improve by practicing

po·lite /pə'laɪt/ *adj* having good manners ~**ly** *adv* ~**ness** *n* [U]

pol·i·tic /'pɑlə,tɪk/ *adj fml* sensible; having advantage

po·lit·i·cal /pə'lɪtɪkəl/ *adj* **1** of or concerning government and public affairs **2** of (party) politics **3** very interested or active in politics ~**ly** /-kliʸ/ *adv*

political a·sy·lum /·,··· ·'··/ *n* [U] official protection given to someone who has left their country because they oppose its government

pol·i·ti·cian /,pɑlə,tɪʃən/ *n* person whose business is politics

pol·i·tics /'pɑlə,tɪks/ *n* **1** [U] the activity of winning and using government power, in competition with other parties: *active in local politics* **2** [U] art and science of government: *studying politics at university* **3** [P] political opinions **4** [U] activity within a group by which some members try to gain an advantage: *office politics*

pol·ka /'powlkə, 'powkə/ *n* quick simple dance for people dancing in pairs

polka dot /'·· ,·/ *n* (one of a) pattern of round spots on a background of a different color: *a polka dot dress*

poll /powl/ *n* **1** [C] also **opinion poll** — attempt to find out the general opinion about something by questioning a number of people chosen by chance **2** [C;U] election **3** [S] number of votes given ♦ *vt* **1** receive (a stated number of votes) **2** question in a POLL (1)

pol·len /'pɑlən/ *n* [U] yellow dust that makes plants produce seeds

pol·li·nate /'pɑlə,neʸt/ *vt* bring pollen to (a flower) –**nation** /,pɑlə-'neʸʃən/ *n* [U]

poll·ster /'powlstər/ *n* person who carries out POLLS (1)

pol·lute /pə'luʸt/ *vt* make dangerously impure or unfit for use:

polluted rivers **–lution** /pə'luʷʃən/ *n* [U] **1** act of polluting **2** polluting substance

po·lo /'poʷloʷ/ *n* [U] game played on horses by hitting a ball with a hammer that has a long handle – see also WATER POLO

polo neck /'·· ˌ·/ *n* round rolled collar

pol·ter·geist /'poʷltərˌgaɪst/ *n* spirit that makes noises and throws things around

pol·y·es·ter /ˌpaliʸˈɛstər, ˈpaliʸˌɛstər/ *n* [U] artificial material used for cloth

po·lyg·a·my /pəˈlɪgəmiʸ/ *n* [U] having 2 or more wives at one time **–mist** *n* **–mous** *adj*

pol·y·glot /ˈpaliʸˌglat/ *adj fml* speaking or including many languages

pol·y·gon /ˈpaliʸˌgan/ *n* figure with 5 or more straight sides

pol·y·graph /ˈpaliʸˌgræf/ *n* LIE DETECTOR

pol·y·math /ˈpaliʸˌmæθ/ *n fml* person who knows a lot about many subjects

pol·y·mer /ˈpaləmər/ *n* simple chemical compound with large MOLECULES

pol·yp /ˈpalɪp/ *n* **1** very simple small water animal **2** small diseased growth in the body

pol·y·sty·rene /ˌpaliʸˈstaɪriʸn/ *n* [U] light plastic that keeps heat in

pol·y·tech·nic /ˌpaliʸˈtɛknɪk/ *n* place of higher education giving training in science, industry, etc.

pol·y·the·is·m /ˈpaliʸˌθiʸˌɪzəm/ *n* [U] belief in many gods

pol·y·thene /ˈpaləˌθiʸn/ *n* [U] strong plastic used for making many common articles

pol·y·un·sat·u·ra·ted /ˌpaliʸʌnˈsætʃərəˌt̬ɪd/ *adj* (of fat or oil) having chemicals combined in a way that is thought to be good for the health when eaten

pom·e·gran·ate /ˈpaməˌgrænɪt, ˈpamə-/ *n* fruit with small red seeds inside

pom·mel /ˈpamʌl/ *n* rounded part at the front of a SADDLE

pomp /pamp/ *n* [U] grand solemn ceremonial show

pom·pom /ˈpampam/ *n* **1** small decorative woollen ball **2** large decoration made from colored paper, used by CHEERleaders

pom·pous /ˈpampəs/ *adj* foolishly solemn and thinking oneself important **~ly** *adv* **–ness**, **–posity** /pamˈpasət̬iʸ/ *n* [U]

pon·cho /ˈpantʃoʷ/ *n* **–chos** cloth worn over the shoulders, with a hole for the head

pond /pand/ *n* small area of still water

pon·der /ˈpandər/ *vi/t* spend time considering

pon·der·ous /ˈpandərəs/ *adj* **1** heavy, slow, and awkward **2** dull and solemn

pon·tiff /ˈpantɪf/ *n* POPE

pon·tif·i·cate /panˈtɪfəˌkeʸt/ *vi* give one's opinion as if it were the only right one

pon·toon /panˈtuʷn/ *n* floating hollow container connected with others to support a floating bridge

po·ny /ˈpoʷniʸ/ *n* small horse

po·ny·tail /ˈpoʷniʸˌteʸl/ *n* hair tied in a bunch at the back of the head

pooch /puʷtʃ/ *n infml* dog

poo·dle /ˈpuʷdl/ *n* dog with curling hair, often cut in shapes

pooh-pooh /ˌpuʷ ˈpuʷ/ *vt* treat as not worth considering

pool¹ /puʷl/ *n* **1** small area of water in a hollow place **2** small amount of liquid on a surface **3** SWIMMING POOL

pool² *n* **1** [C] shared supply of money, goods, workers, etc. – see also CAR POOL **2** [U] game played with 15 balls on a table with holes in corners and sides ♦ *vt* put esp. money into a common pot to share

poor /puər/ *adj* **1** having very little money **2** less or worse than usual or than expected: *a poor harvest/ essay | poor weather/health* **3** unlucky; deserving pity: *Poor David has failed his exams.* **~ness** *n* [U] low quality

poor·ly /ˈpuərliʸ/ *adv* not well; badly: *poorly paid*

poor re·la·tion /ˌ·· ·ˈ··/ *n* one regarded as the least important among a group of similar ones

pop¹ /pap/ *vi/t* **–pp– 1** (cause to) make a small explosive sound **2** come, go, or put quickly: *A button popped off his shirt.* **3 pop the question** *infml* make an offer of marriage

pop up *phr vi* happen or appear suddenly

pop² *n* **1** [C] small explosive sound **2** [U] sweet FIZZY drink

pop³ *n* [U] modern popular music with a strong beat: *a pop group/concert*

pop⁴ *n* **1** father **2** (used as a form of address to an old man)

pop⁵ *abbrev. for*: population

pop art /ˈ· ·/ *n* [U] modern art showing objects from daily life

pop·corn /ˈpapkɔrn/ *n* [U] special CORN seeds heated so that they swell

pope /poʷp/ *n* (*often cap.*) the head of the Roman Catholic Church

pope's nose /ˌ· ˈ·/ *n* fleshy piece at the tail end of a cooked chicken, etc.

pop-eyed /ˌ·'·◂/ adj with eyes that are wide open

pop·ish /'pᵂpɪʃ/ adj derog Roman Catholic

pop·lar /'pɑplər/ n tall straight thin tree

pop·lin /'pɑplɪn/ n [U] strong cotton cloth

pop·py /'pɑpiʸ/ n plant with bright flowers, usu. red

pop·py·cock /'pɑpiʸˌkɑk/ n [U] nonsense

pop·si·cle /'pɑpsɪkəl/ n tdmk piece of ICE¹(2) on a stick

pop·u·lace /'pɑpyələs/ n fml [U] all the (ordinary) people of a country

pop·u·lar /'pɑpyələr/ adj 1 liked by many people: a popular restaurant 2 common; widespread: a popular name 3 of the general public: popular opinion ~ ly adv by most people ~ ize, -ise vt ~ity /ˌpɑpyə'lærəti̯/ n [U]

pop·u·late /'pɑpyəˌleʸt/ vt live in as a population

pop·u·la·tion /ˌpɑpyə'leʸʃən/ n (number of) people (or animals) living in a particular area or country

pop·u·list /'pɑpyəlɪst/ n person who claims to support the aims of ordinary people in politics

pop·u·lous /'pɑpyələs/ adj fml having a large population

porce·lain /'pɔrsəlɪn, 'pᵂr-/ n [U] (cups, plates, etc., made from) fine hard thin claylike substance

porch /pɔrtʃ, pᵂrtʃ/ n roofed entrance built out from a house or church

por·cu·pine /'pɔrkyəˌpaɪn/ n animal with long needle-like hairs on its back that are used in defense

pore¹ /pɔr/ n small hole in the skin, through which SWEAT passes

pore² v pore over phr vt read with close attention

pork /pɔrk, pᵂrk/ n [U] meat from pigs

porn /'pɔrn/ n [U] infml pornography

por·nog·ra·phy /pɔr'nɑgrəfiʸ/ n [U] law or derog (books, films, etc.) showing or describing sexually exciting scenes –**graphic** /ˌpɔrnə'græfɪk◂/ adj

po·rous /'pɔrəs, 'pᵂrəs/ adj allowing liquid to pass slowly through

por·poise /'pɔrpəs/ n large fishlike sea animal

port¹ /pɔrt/ n waterside city where ocean ships come and go

port² n [U] left side of a ship or aircraft

port³ n [U] strong sweet red wine from Portugal

por·ta·ble /'pɔrtəbəl, 'pᵂr-/ adj that can be carried

por·tals /'pɔrtlz/ n [P] grand entrance to a building

port·cul·lis /pɔrt'kʌlɪs, pᵂrt-/ n castle gate that can be raised and lowered

por·tend /pɔr'tɛnd, pᵂr-/ vt fml be a sign of (a future undesirable event)

por·tent /'pɔrtɛnt, 'pᵂr-/ n fml sign of a future strange or undesirable event

por·ten·tous /pɔr'tɛntəs, pᵂr-/ adj fml 1 threatening 2 solemnly important concerning oneself

por·ter /'pɔrtər, 'pᵂr-/ n 1 person who carries loads, esp. travelers' bags, or goods in a train station 2 person in charge of the entrance to a hotel, hospital, etc.

port·fo·li·o /pɔrt'foʷliʸˌoʷ, pᵂrt-/ n 1 a flat case for carrying drawings, etc. b drawings, etc., carried in this 2 collection of business shares owned

port·hole /'pɔrthoʷl, 'pᵂrt-/ n window in a ship or aircraft

por·ti·co /'pɔrtɪˌkoʷ, 'pᵂr-/ n -coes or -cos grand pillared (PILLAR) entrance to a building

por·tion¹ /'pɔrʃən/ n 1 part: the front portion of the train 2 share 3 quantity of food for one person

portion² v portion out phr vt share

port·ly /'pɔrtliʸ, 'pᵂr-/ adj (of a person) fat

port·man·teau /pɔrt'mæntoʷ, pᵂrt-/ n -teaus or -teaux /-toʷz/ large case for carrying clothes

port of call /ˌ·'·'·/ n 1 port where a ship stops 2 place one visits

por·trait /'pɔrtrɪt, -treʸt, 'pᵂr-/ n 1 picture of a person 2 lifelike description in words

por·tray /pɔr'treʸ, pᵂr-/ vt 1 represent, describe 2 act the part of ~al n [C;U]

pose /poʷz/ v 1 vi stand or sit in a particular position to be drawn, photographed, etc. 2 vt cause (a problem) 3 vt ask (a question) ♦ n 1 position when posing (POSE (1)) 2 pretended way of behaving

pose as phr vt pretend to be

pos·er /'poʷzər/ n poseur

po·seur /poʷ'zɜr/ n person who behaves unnaturally to produce an effect

posh /pɑʃ/ adj fashionable and splendid

pos·it /'pɑzɪt/ vt fml suggest as being possible

po·si·tion /pə'zɪʃən/ n 1 [C;U] place where something is 2 [U] proper place: Is everyone in position? 3 [C] way in which something is placed or stands, sits, etc. 4 [C] situation;

state: *the company's current financial position* **5** [C] place in a rank or group: *He finished in second position.* **6** [C] *fml* job **7** [C] *fml* opinion
♦ *vt* place

pos·i·tive /ˈpazətɪv/ *adj* **1** leaving no possibility of doubt: *positive proof* **2** having no doubt; sure **3** effective; actually helpful **4** more than zero **5** (of electricity) of the type carried by PROTONS **6** complete; real: *a positive delight* ~**ly** *adv* **1** in a POSITIVE (1,2) way **2** really; indeed

pos·se /ˈpasiⁱ/ *n* group of people gathered together to help find a criminal

pos·sess /pəˈzɛs/ *vt* **1** *fml* have; own **2** (of a feeling or idea) seem to control all (someone's) actions ~**ed** *adj* wildly mad ~**or** *n*

pos·ses·sion /pəˈzɛʃən/ *n* **1** [U] state of possessing; ownership **2** [C] something one owns **3** [U] control by an evil spirit

pos·ses·sive /pəˈzɛsɪv/ *adj* **1** unwilling to share one's own things **2** *gram* showing ownership: *'My' is a possessive adjective.* ~**ly** *adv* ~**ness** *n* [U]

pos·si·bil·i·ty /ˌpasəˈbɪləti̥ⁱ/ *n* **1** [S;U] (degree of) likelihood **2** [U] fact of being possible **3** [C] something possible: *The house is in bad condition but it has possibilities.* (= can be improved)

pos·si·ble /ˈpasəbəl/ *adj* **1** that can exist, happen, or be done **2** acceptable; suitable ♦ *n* **1** [*the*+S] that which can exist, happen, or be done **2** [C] person or thing that might be suitable ~**bly** *adv* **1** in accordance with what is possible: *I'll do all I possibly can.* **2** perhaps

pos·sum /ˈpasəm/ *n* small animal that climbs trees

post[1] /ˈpoʷst/ *n* **1** strong thick upright pole fixed in position **2** finishing place in a race ♦ *vt* **1** put up a notice about **2** report as being: *The ship was posted missing.*

post[2] *n* send by MAIL[1]

post[3] *n* **1** job **2** special place of duty, esp. of a soldier **3** military base ♦ *vt* **1** place (soldiers, policemen, etc.) on duty **2** send to a job, esp. abroad

post·age /ˈpoʷstɪdʒ/ *n* [U] charge for carrying a letter, parcel, etc., by post

postage stamp /ˈ·· ˌ·/ *n fml* for STAMP

post·al /ˈpoʷstl/ *adj* **1** of the POST OFFICE **2** sent by mail

post·card /ˈpoʷstkɑrd/ *n* card for sending messages by mail without an envelope

post·date /ˌpoʷstˈdeⁱt/ *vt* write a

date later than the actual date of writing on (esp. a check)

post·er /ˈpoʷstər/ *n* large printed notice or picture

pos·te·ri·or /paˈstɪəriⁱər, poʷ-/ *adj fml* nearer the back ♦ *n* BOTTOM[1] (2)

pos·ter·i·ty /paˈstɛrəti̥ⁱ/ *n* [U] people or times after one's death

post·grad·u·ate /ˌpoʷstˈgrædʒuʷɪt/ *n, adj* (person doing university studies) after getting a BACHELOR'S DEGREE

post·haste /ˌpoʷstˈheⁱst/ *adv fml* very quickly

post·hu·mous /ˈpastʃəməs/ *adj* after death ~**ly** *adv*

post·man /ˈpoʷstmən/ *n* -**men** /-mən/ MAILMAN

post·mark /ˈpoʷstmɑrk/ *n* official mark on a letter, etc., showing where and when it was posted **postmark** *vt*

post·mas·ter /ˈpoʷstˌmæstər/ *n* director of a post office

post·mor·tem /ˌpoʷstˈmɔrtəm/ *n* **1** tests to find out why someone died **2** finding out why something failed

post of·fice /ˈ· ˌ·/ *n* place where stamps are sold, letters can be mailed, and various sorts of government business are done

post·pone /poʷstˈpoʷn, poʷsˈpoʷn/ *vt* move to a later time ~**ment** *n* [C;U]

post·script /ˈpoʷstˌskrɪpt, ˈpoʷs-ˌskrɪpt/ *n* remark(s) added at the end of a letter

pos·tu·late /ˈpastʃəˌleⁱt/ *vt fml* accept as true, as a base for reasoning

pos·ture /ˈpastʃər/ *n* **1** physical position **2** manner of behaving or thinking on some occasion *vi* **1** place oneself in fixed physical positions, esp. in order to make other people admire one **2** pretend to be something one is not

po·sy /ˈpoʷziⁱ/ *n* small bunch of flowers

pot[1] /pat/ *n* **1** [C] large round container esp. for cooking and serving: *a soup pot/pots and pans* **2** [U] *sl for* MARIJUANA **3** **go to pot** *infml* become ruined or worthless

pot[2] *v* -**tt**- *vt* plant in a pot ~**ted** *adj* **1** (of meat, fish, etc.) made into a paste **2** (of a book) in a short simple form

pot·ash /ˈpatæʃ/ *n* [U] sort of potassium used in farming and industry

po·tas·si·um /pəˈtæsiⁱəm/ *n* [U] soft silver-white metal common in nature and necessary for life

po·ta·to /pəˈteⁱtoʷ, -tə/ *n* -**toes** common brown or yellowish vegetable that grows underground

potato chip /·ˈ·· ˌ·/ *n* thin piece of dry cooked potato

pot·bel·ly /ˈpɑtˌbeliʸ/ n infml fat stomach

pot·boil·er /ˈpɑtˌbɔɪlər/ n book, etc., produced quickly just to earn money

po·tent /ˈpoʷtnt/ adj powerful: a potent drug ~ly adv potency n [U]

po·ten·tial /pəˈtɛnʃəl/ adj that may become so; not (yet) actual: potential danger ♦ n [U] possibility for developing ~ly adv ~ity /pəˌtɛnʃiʸˈæləti̯ʸ/ n [C;U]

pot·hole /ˈpɑthoʷl/ n 1 deep hole going far underground 2 unwanted hole in the road

po·tion /ˈpoʷʃən/ n liquid mixture intended as a medicine, poison, or magic charm

pot·luck /ˌpɑtˈlʌk•/ adj (of a meal) to which everyone brings a dish: potluck dinner ♦ n take potluck choose without enough information; take a chance

pot·shot /ˈpɑt-ʃɑt/ n carelessly aimed shot

potted plant /ˌ•• ˈ•/ n plant grown (indoors) in a pot

pot·ter¹ /ˈpɑtər/ n person who makes pottery

potter² vi move or act slowly or purposelessly

potter about/around phr vi spend time in activities that demand little effort

pot·ter·y /ˈpɑtəri̯ʸ/ n [U] (pots, dishes, etc., made of) baked clay

pot·ty /ˈpɑti̯ʸ/ n pot for children to urinate (URINE) into

pouch /paʊtʃ/ n 1 small leather bag 2 baglike part of an animal

poul·tice /ˈpoʷltɪs/ n soft wet heated mass placed on the skin to lessen pain

poul·try /ˈpoʷltri̯ʸ/ n [U] (meat from) farmyard birds such as hens, ducks, etc.

pounce /paʊns/ vi fly down or jump suddenly to seize

pounce on phr vt seize or accept eagerly

pound¹ /paʊnd/ n 1 standard unit of money in Britain 2 a measure of weight equal to 0.4536 kilograms or 16 OUNCES

pound² v 1 vt crush 2 vi/t strike repeatedly and heavily 3 vi move with quick heavy steps

pound into phr vi/t repeat (something) forcefully over and over again to (someone)

pound³ n place where lost animals and cats are kept until their owners take them back

pour /pɔr, poʷr/ v 1 vi/t (cause to) flow fast and steadily 2 vi rush together in large numbers 3 vi (of rain) fall hard

pour out phr vt tell freely and with feeling

pout /paʊt/ vi push the lips forwards, esp. to show displeasure pout n

pov·er·ty /ˈpɑvərti̯ʸ/ n [U] 1 being poor 2 fml lack

poverty line /ˈ••• ˌ•/ n [S] level of income for deciding who is poor, determined by the government: living below the poverty line

poverty-strick·en /ˈ••• ˌ••/ adj extremely poor

POW /ˌpiʸ oʷ ˈdʌbəlyuʷ/ n PRISONER OF WAR

pow·der /ˈpaʊdər/ n 1 [C;U] very fine dry grains 2 [U] substance like this with a pleasant smell, used on the skin 3 [U] gunpowder ♦ vt put POWDER (2) on ~ed adj produced in the form of powder: powdered sugar ~y adj

powder puff /ˈ•• •/ n soft ball for putting on POWDER (2)

powder room /ˈ•• ˌ•/ n women's public TOILET

pow·er /ˈpaʊər/ n 1 [U] strength 2 [U] force used for driving machines, producing electricity, etc.: nuclear power 3 [S;U] control over others; influence 4 [U] what one can do; (natural) ability: the power of speech 5 [C;U] right to act: The police now have the power to search people in the street. 6 [C] person, nation, etc., that has influence or control 7 the powers that be infml the unknown people in important positions who make decisions that have an effect on one's life – see also BLACK POWER ♦ vt supply power to (a machine)

pow·er·boat /ˈpaʊərˌboʷt/ n fast boat for racing

pow·er·ful /ˈpaʊərfəl/ adj 1 full of force: a powerful engine 2 great in degree: a powerful smell 3 having much control or influence 4 having a strong effect: powerful drugs ~ly adv

pow·er·house /ˈpaʊərˌhaʊs/ n infml person who is very enthusiastic and able

pow·er·less /ˈpaʊərlɪs/ adj lacking strength or ability: powerless to help

power of at·tor·ney /ˌ••• •ˈ••/ n [U] right to act for someone else in business or law

power plant /ˈ••• •/ n engine supplying power to a factory, aircraft, etc.

power sta·tion /ˈ•• ˌ••/ n building where electricity is made

pow·wow /ˈpaʊˌwaʊ/ n important meeting esp. of Native Americans

pp abbrev. for: pages

PR /ˌpiʸ ˈɑr/ n [U] PUBLIC RELATIONS

prac·ti·ca·ble /ˈpræktɪkəbəl/ adj that can be done –bility /ˌpræktɪkəˈbɪləti̯ʸ/ n [U]

prac·ti·cal /ˈpræktɪkəl/ adj **1** concerned with action or actual conditions, rather than ideas **2** effective or convenient in actual use: *a practical uniform* **3** clever at doing things and dealing with difficulties; sensible ~**ly** /-kli⁹/ adv **1** usefully; suitably **2** almost ~**ity** /ˌpræktɪˈkæləṭi⁹/ n [C;U]

practical joke /ˌ··· ˈ·/ n trick played on someone to amuse others

prac·tice /ˈpræktɪs/ n **1** [C;U] regular or repeated doing of something, to gain skill **2** [U] experience gained by this **3** [U] actual doing of something: *to put a plan into practice* **4** [C] business of a doctor or lawyer **5** [C;U] something regularly done **6** **in/out of practice** having/not having practiced enough ♦ v **1** vi/t do (an action) or perform on (esp. a musical instrument) repeatedly to gain skill **2** vi/t do (the work of a doctor, lawyer, etc.) **3** vt act in accordance with (a religion): *a practicing Jew* **4** vt find out (habitually) **5** **practice what one preaches** do what you advise others to do –**ticed** adj skilled through practice

prac·ti·tion·er /prækˈtɪʃənər/ n person who works in a profession, esp. a doctor – see also GENERAL PRACTITIONER

prae·sid·i·um /prɪˈsɪdi⁹əm, -ˈzɪ-/ n –**iums** or –**ia** /-di⁹ə/ PRESIDIUM

prag·mat·ic /prægˈmæṭɪk/ adj concerned with actual effects rather than general principles ~**ally** /-kli⁹/ adv

prai·rie /ˈpreəri⁹/ n wide grassy plain

praise /pre⁹z/ vt **1** speak of with admiration **2** worship ♦ n [U] expression of admiration

praise·wor·thy /ˈpre⁹zˌwɜrði⁹/ adj deserving praise

prance /præns/ vi **1** (of an animal) jump on the back legs **2** move happily or showily

prank /præŋk/ n playful but foolish trick

prat·tle /ˈpræṭl/ vi talk continually about unimportant things ♦ n [U] foolish or unimportant talk

pray /pre⁹/ vi **1** speak to God or a god, often silently, often asking for something **2** wish or hope strongly: *We're praying for fine weather.*

prayer /preər/ n **1** [C] (form of words used in) a solemn request to God or a god **2** [U] praying

preach /pri⁹tʃ/ v **1** vi/t make (a religious speech) in public **2** vt urge others to accept: *preaching revolution* **3** vi offer unwanted advice on matters of right and wrong ~**er** n

pre·am·ble /ˈpri⁹ˌæmbəl, pri⁹ˈæmbəl/ n something said or written before getting to the main part

pre·car·i·ous /prɪˈkeəri⁹əs/ adj not firm or steady; full of danger ~**ly** adv

pre·cau·tion /prɪˈkɔʃən/ n action done to avoid possible trouble ~**ary** adj

pre·cede /prɪˈsi⁹d/ vt come (just) before –**ceding** adj: *the preceding day*

pre·ce·dence /ˈpresədəns, prɪˈsi⁹dns/ n [U] (right to) a particular place before others, esp. because of importance

pre·ce·dent /ˈpresədənt/ n **1** [U] what has usu. been done before **2** [C] earlier act which shows what may be done now

pre·cept /ˈpri⁹sept/ n fml guiding rule of behavior

pre·cinct /ˈpri⁹sɪŋkt/ n division of a town for election or police purposes **precincts** n [P] space around a large (old) building, usu. inside walls

pre·cious /ˈpreʃəs/ adj **1** of great value **2** fml (of words, manners, etc.) unnaturally fine or perfect ♦ adv very: *precious few* ~**ness** n [U]

pre·ci·pice /ˈpresəpɪs/ n very steep side of a mountain or cliff

pre·cip·i·tate¹ /prɪˈsɪpəˌte⁹t/ vt **1** fml make (an unwanted event) happen sooner **2** fml throw down suddenly **3** separate (solid matter) from liquid chemically ♦ n [C;U] precipitated matter –**tation** /prɪˌsɪpəˈte⁹ʃən/ n [U] fml **1** precipitating **2** rain, snow, etc. **3** unwise speed

pre·cip·i·tate² /prɪˈsɪpəṭɪt/ adj fml too hasty ~**ly** adv

pre·cip·i·tous /prɪˈsɪpəṭəs/ adj fml **1** dangerously steep **2** precipitate ~**ly** adv ~**ness** n [U]

pré·cis /pre⁹ˈsi⁹, ˈpre⁹si⁹/ n fml **précis** /-si⁹z/ shortened form of something written or said

pre·cise /prɪˈsaɪs/ adj **1** exact **2** (too) careful and correct about small details ~**ly** adv **1** exactly **2** yes, that is correct

pre·ci·sion /prɪˈsɪʒən/ n [U] exactness ♦ adj **1** done with exactness: *precision bombing* **2** giving exact results: *precision instruments*

pre·clude /prɪˈklu⁹d/ vt fml prevent

pre·co·cious /prɪˈko⁹ʃəs/ adj developing unusually early ~**ly** adv ~**ness** n [U]

pre·cog·ni·tion /ˌpri⁹kɑgˈnɪʃən/ n [U] fml knowing about things before they happen

pre·con·cep·tion /ˌpri⁹kənˈsepʃən/ n opinion formed in advance without (enough) knowledge –**ceived** /-kənˈsi⁹vd◄/ adj: *preconceived notions*

pre·con·di·tion /ˌpri⁹kənˈdɪʃən/ n

thing that must be agreed to if something is to be done

pre·cur·sor /prɪˈkɜrsər, ˈpriʸˌkɜrsər/ n one that came before and led to a later thing

pred·a·to·ry /ˈpredəˌtoriʸ, -ˌtoʷriʸ/ adj 1 killing and eating other animals 2 living by attacking and robbing **predator** n predatory animal

pre·de·ces·sor /ˈpredəˌsesər/ n one that came before: my predecessor as principal

pre·des·ti·na·tion /ˌpriʸdestəˈneyʃən, priʸˌdes-/ n [U] belief that everything in the world has been decided by God, and that no human effort can change it

pre·des·tine /priʸˈdestɪn/ vt settle in advance, esp. as if by fate or the will of God

pre·de·ter·mine /ˌpriʸdɪˈtɜrmɪn/ vt 1 fix unchangeably from the beginning 2 arrange in advance

pre·de·ter·min·er /ˌpriʸdɪˈtɜrmənər/ n word that can be used before a DETERMINER (such as the, that, his, etc.): In the phrase 'all the boys', 'all' is a predeterminer

pre·dic·a·ment /prɪˈdɪkəmənt/ n difficult situation

pred·i·cate /ˈpredɪkɪt/ n part of a sentence which makes a statement about the subject

pred·i·ca·tive /ˈpredɪˌkeʸtɪv, -kətɪv/ adj coming after a verb

pre·dict /prɪˈdɪkt/ vt say in advance (what will happen) ~**able** adj 1 that can be predicted 2 not doing anything unexpected ~**ably** adv ~**ion** /prɪˈdɪkʃən/ n [C;U] predicting or something predicted

pre·di·lec·tion /ˌpredlˈekʃən, ˌpriʸ-/ n special liking for something

pre·dis·pose /ˌpriʸdɪˈspoʷz/ vt fml make (someone) likely to do or have ~**position** /ˌpriʸdɪspəˈzɪʃən/ n

pre·dom·i·nant /prɪˈdamənənt/ adj most powerful, noticeable, important, etc. ~**ly** adv ~**nance** n [U]

pre·dom·i·nate /prɪˈdaməˌneʸt/ vi 1 have the main power or influence 2 be greatest in numbers

pre·em·i·nent /priʸˈemənənt/ adj better than any others ~**ly** adv ~**nence** n [U]

pre·empt /priʸˈempt/ vt prevent by taking action in advance ~**ive** adj

preen /priʸn/ vi/t (of a bird) clean (itself or its feathers) with its beak

pre·fab·ri·cate /priʸˈfæbrəˌkeʸt/ vt make (the parts of a building, ship, etc.) in advance in a factory and put them together later

pref·ace /ˈprefɪs/ n introduction to a book ♦ vt introduce (speech or writing) in the stated way

pref·a·to·ry /ˈprefəˌtoriʸ, -ˌtoʷriʸ/ adj fml acting as a preface

pre·fect /ˈpriʸfekt/ n (esp. in France) public official with government or police duties

pre·fer /prɪˈfɜr/ vt -rr- 1 like better; choose rather: I prefer wine to beer. 2 law make (a charge) officially ~**erable** /ˈprefərəbəl/ adj better, esp. because more suitable ~**ably** adv

pref·er·ence /ˈprefərəns/ n [C;U] 1 liking for one thing rather than another 2 special favor shown to one person, group, etc.

pref·e·ren·tial /ˌprefəˈrenʃəl, -tʃəl/ adj giving or showing PREFERENCE (2) ~**ly** adv

pre·fix /ˈpriʸfɪks/ n wordlike part added at the beginning of a word to change its meaning (as in untie) ♦ vt 1 add a prefix to 2 add (something) to the beginning (of)

preg·nant /ˈpregnənt/ adj 1 having an unborn child or young in the body 2 full of hidden meaning ~**nancy** n [C;U]

pre·hen·sile /priˈhensəl, -ˌsaɪl/ adj able to hold things: a monkey's prehensile tail

pre·his·tor·ic /ˌpriʸhɪˈstorɪk, -ˈstar-/ adj of times before recorded history ~**ally** /-kliʸ/ adv

pre·judge /ˌpriʸˈdʒʌdʒ/ vt form an opinion about before knowing all the facts

prej·u·dice /ˈpredʒədɪs/ n 1 [C;U] unfair feeling against something 2 [U] fml damage; harm ♦ vt 1 cause to have a prejudice 2 weaken; harm: It may prejudice your chances of success.

prej·u·di·cial /ˌpredʒəˈdɪʃəl/ adj harmful

prel·ate /ˈprelɪt/ n priest of high rank

pre·lim·i·na·ry /prɪˈlɪməˌneriʸ/ adj coming before (and preparing for) esp. the main one ♦ n preliminary act or arrangement

prel·ude /ˈprelyuʷd, ˈpreʸluʷd, ˈpriʸluʷd/ n 1 something that is followed by something larger or more important 2 short piece of music introducing a large musical work

pre·mar·i·tal /priʸˈmærətl/ adj happening before marriage

pre·ma·ture /ˌpriʸməˈtʃuʷər, -ˈtuʷər, -ˈtyuʷər/ adj happening before the proper time ~**ly** adv

pre·med /ˈpriʸˌmed/ also **premedical** /priʸˈmedɪkəl/ — adj of university courses for those planning to be doctors: a premed student

pre·med·i·tat·ed /priʸˈmedəˌteʸtɪd/ adj planned in advance ~**tation** /priʸˌmedəˈteʸʃən/ n [U]

prem·ier /pɪˈmɪər, -ˈmjɪər, ˈprɪ-mɪər/ n PRIME MINISTER ♦ adj fml first in importance

pre·miere, -mière /pɪˈmɪər, -ˈmjɪər, -ˈmjɛər/ n first public performance of a film or play ♦ vt give a premiere of (a play or film)

prem·ise /ˈpremɪs/ n fml statement or idea on which reasoning is based

prem·is·es /ˈpremɪsɪz/ n [P] building and its land, considered as a piece of property

pre·mi·um /ˈpriˑmiˑəm/ n 1 money paid for insurance 2 additional charge 3 **at a premium** rare or difficult to obtain 4 **put a premium on** cause to be an advantage ♦ adj best: premium quality

pre·mo·ni·tion /ˌpriˑvməˈnɪʃən, ˌpre-/ n feeling that something is going to happen

pre·na·tal /ˌpriˑˈneˑtl/ adj existing or happening before birth: prenatal care

pre·oc·cu·pa·tion /priˑˌɒkyəˈpeˑʃən, priˑˌɒk-/ n 1 [U] being preoccupied 2 [C] something that takes up all one's attention

pre·oc·cu·py /priˑˈɒkyəˌpaɪ/ vt fill (someone's) thoughts, taking attention away from other things

prep·a·ra·tion /ˌprepəˈreˑʃən/ n 1 [U] act or process of preparing 2 [C] arrangement for a future event 3 [C] fml (chemical) mixture for a certain purpose

pre·par·a·to·ry /prɪˈpærəˌtɔriˑ, -ˌtoˑriˑ, -ˈpeər-, ˈprepərə-/ adj done to get ready

preparatory school /·ˈ··· ·ˌ·/ also **prep school** /ˈprep skuˑl/ — n private school that makes pupils ready for college

pre·pare /prɪˈpeər/ vi/t 1 get or make ready 2 put (oneself) into a suitable state of mind —pared adj willing: not prepared to help

pre·pon·de·rance /prɪˈpɒndərəns/ n [S] fml larger number; state of being more

prep·o·si·tion /ˌprepəˈzɪʃən/ n word (such as in or by) used with a noun or PRONOUN to show its connection with another word ~al adj

pre·pos·sess·ing /ˌpriˑpəˈzesɪŋ/ adj fml very pleasing; charming

pre·pos·ter·ous /prɪˈpɒstərəs/ adj foolishly unreasonable or improbable ~ly adv

prep·py /ˈprepiˑ/ adj infml typical of (former) students of expensive private schools, esp. in being neat and well dressed

prep school n PREPARATORY SCHOOL

pre·req·ui·site /priˑˈrekwəzɪt/ n fml something needed before something else can happen

pre·rog·a·tive /prɪˈrɒgətɪv/ n special right belonging to someone

pres·age /ˈpresɪdʒ, prɪˈseˑdʒ/ vt fml be a warning or sign of (a future event)

Pres·by·te·ri·an /ˌprezbəˈtɪəriˑən, ˌpres-/ n, adj (member) of a Protestant church governed by a body of officials of equal rank

pre·school /ˈpriˑskuˑl/ n school for very young children

pre·sci·ent /ˈpreʃiˑənt, -ʃənt/ adj fml seeming to know in advance —ence n [U]

pre·scribe /prɪˈskraɪb/ vt 1 order as a medicine or treatment 2 fml state (what must be done)

pre·scrip·tion /prɪˈskrɪpʃən/ n 1 [C] (doctor's written order for) a particular medicine or treatment 2 [U] act of prescribing

pre·scrip·tive /prɪˈskrɪptɪv/ adj saying how a language ought to be used

pres·ence /ˈprezəns/ n [U] 1 fact of being present 2 fml personal appearance and manner, as having a strong effect on others

presence of mind /ˌ··· ·ˈ·/ n [U] ability to act quickly, calmly, and wisely when necessary

pres·ent¹ /ˈprezənt/ n gift

pre·sent² /prɪˈzent/ vt 1 give, esp. as part of a ceremony 2 be the cause of: That presents no difficulties. 3 offer for consideration: to present a report 4 provide for the public to see in a theatre, cinema etc. 5 introduce and take part in (a radio or television show) 6 introduce (someone) esp. to someone of higher rank 7 **present itself** (of something possible) happen ~er n

pres·ent³ /ˈprezənt/ adj 1 here/there: I was not present at the meeting. 2 existing or being considered now: my present address 3 gram expressing an existing state or action: the present tense

present⁴ n 1 [the+S] the PRESENT³ (2) time 2 **at present** at this time 3 **for the present** now, but not necessarily in the future

pre·sen·ta·ble /prɪˈzentəbəl/ adj fit to be seen publicly —bly adv

pre·sen·ta·tion /ˌprezənˈteˑʃən, ˌpriˑ-/ n [C;U] act of presenting 2 [U] way something is shown, explained, etc., to others

present-day /ˌ··· ·ˈ·◄/ adj existing now; modern

pre·sen·ti·ment /prɪˈzentəmənt/ n strange feeling that something (bad) is going to happen

pres·ent·ly /ˈprezəntliˑ/ adv 1 soon 2 now: I'm presently working for IBM.

present par·ti·ci·ple /ˌ··· ·ˈ····/ n (in grammar) a participle that is formed in English by adding –ing to the verb and can be used in compound forms of the verb to show PROGRESSIVE tenses, or sometimes as an adjective

pres·er·va·tion /ˌprɛzərˈveʸʃən/ n [U] **1** act of preserving **2** condition after a long time

pre·ser·va·tive /prɪˈzɜrvətɪv/ n, adj [C;U] (substance) used to PRESERVE (2) food

pre·serve /prɪˈzɜrv/ vt **1** keep from decaying or being destroyed or lost: *preserving old customs/one's health* **2** treat (food) so it can be kept a long time ♦ n **1** [P] JAM (1,2) **2** [C] something limited to one person or group

pre·side /prɪˈzaɪd/ vi be in charge, esp. at a meeting

pres·i·den·cy /ˈprɛzədənsiʸ/ n office of president

pres·i·dent /ˈprɛzədənt/ n **1** head of state (and government) in countries that do not have a king or queen **2** head of a business firm, government department, club, etc. ~ial /ˌprɛzəˈdɛnʃəl◂/ adj

pre·sid·i·um /prɪˈsɪdiʸəm, -ˈzɪ-/ n –iums or –ia /-diʸə/ ruling political committee, esp. in Communist (COMMUNISM) countries

press[1] /prɛs/ v **1** vt push firmly and steadily **2** vt hold firmly as a sign of friendship, etc.: *He pressed my hand warmly.* **3** vt direct weight onto to make flat, shape, get liquid out, etc. **4** vi move strongly, esp. in a mass **5** vt give (clothes) a smooth surface and a sharp fold by using a hot iron **6** vt urge strongly: *She pressed her guests to say a little longer.* **7** vi make quick action necessary **8 press the flesh** shake hands with many people, esp. to win votes ~ed adj not having enough: *pressed for time* ~ing adj urgent

press for phr vt demand urgently

press on phr vi continue with determination

press[2] n **1** [U] (writers for) the newspapers **2** [S] treatment given in the newspapers: *The play got good press.* **3** [S] act of pushing steadily **4** [C] printing machine **5** [C] business for printing (and sometimes also selling) books, etc. **6** [C] apparatus for pressing something **7** [C] act of making a garment smooth with a hot iron **8 go to press** (of a newspaper, etc.) start being printed

press box /ˈ· ·/ n place where newspaper reporters sit at sports events

press con·fer·ence /ˈ· ˌ···/ n meeting where someone answers reporters' questions

press-gang /ˈprɛsgæŋ/ vt force to do something unwillingly

pres·sure /ˈprɛʃər/ n **1** [C;U] (force

produced by) pressing: *Water pressure burst the dam.* **2** [C;U] (force of) the weight of the air **3** [U] forcible influence; strong persuading **4** [C;U] conditions of anxiety in life or work ♦ vt (try to) make (someone) do something by forceful demands

pressure cook·er /ˈ·· ˌ··/ n closed metal pot in which food is cooked quickly in hot steam

pres·sur·ize /ˈprɛʃəˌraɪz/ vt control the air pressure inside

pres·tige /prɛˈstiʸʒ, -ˈstiʸdʒ/ n [U] quality of being widely admired, esp. because of being the best or connected with high rank **–tigious** /prɛˈstɪdʒəs, -ˈstiʸ-/ adj having or bringing prestige

pre·su·ma·bly /prɪˈzuʷməbliʸ, -ˈzyuʷ-/ adv it may reasonably be supposed that

pre·sume /prɪˈzuʷm, -ˈzyuʷm/ v **1** vt take as true without proof **2** vi fml be disrespectful enough; dare: *I wouldn't presume to argue.*

pre·sump·tion /prɪˈzʌmpʃən/ n [U] **1** act of supposing **2** fml disrespectful behavior

pre·sump·tive /prɪˈzʌmptɪv/ adj law probable

pre·sump·tu·ous /prɪˈzʌmptʃuʷəs/ adj disrespectful and with too high an opinion of oneself ~ly adv

pre·sup·pose /ˌpriʸsəˈpoʷz/ vt **1** accept as true in advance without proof **2** need according to reason: *A child presupposes a mother.* **–position** /ˌpriʸsʌpəˈzɪʃən/ n [C;U]

pre·tend /prɪˈtɛnd/ v **1** vi/t give an appearance of (something untrue), to deceive or as a game **2** vi attempt; dare

pre·tend·er /prɪˈtɛndər/ n person who makes a (doubtful or unproved) claim to some high position

pre·tense /ˈpriʸtɛns, prɪˈtɛns/ n **1** [S;U] false appearance or reason **2** [U] claim to possess: *little pretense to fairness*

pre·ten·sion /prɪˈtɛnʃən, -tʃən/ n fml claim to possess a skill, quality, etc.

pre·ten·tious /prɪˈtɛnʃəs, -tʃəs/ adj claiming importance, rank, or artistic value one does not have ~ly adv ~ness n [U]

pre·ter·nat·u·ral /ˌpriʸtərˈnætʃərəl/ adj fml beyond what is usual or natural ~ly adv

pre·text /ˈpriʸtɛkst/ n false reason

pret·ty /ˈprɪtiʸ/ adj pleasing to look at ♦ adv **1** fairly; quite **2 pretty well** almost: *pretty well finished* **–tily** adv – see also **a pretty penny** (PENNY)

pre·vail /prɪˈveʸl/ vi fml **1** win **2** exist; be widespread ~ing adj **1** (of wind) that usu. blows **2** common or general (in some place or time)

prevail upon phr vt fml persuade
prev·a·lent /'prevələnt/ adj fml common in a place or at a time ~ly adv –**lence** n [U]

pre·var·i·cate /prɪ'værɪˌkeɪt/ vi fml try to hide the truth –**cation** /prɪˌværə'keɪʃən/ n [C;U]

pre·vent /prɪ'vent/ vt stop (something) happening or (someone) doing something ~**ion** /prɪ'venʃən/ n [U]

pre·ven·tive /prɪ'ventɪv/ adj that prevents esp. illness

pre·view /'priːvjuː/ n private showing or short description of film, show, etc., before it is publicly seen ♦ vt give a preview of

pre·vi·ous /'priːvɪəs/ adj before this one: my previous employer ~**ly** adv

prey¹ /preɪ/ n [U] 1 animal hunted and eaten by another 2 such hunting and eating: The eagle is a bird of prey.

prey² v **prey on** phr vt 1 hunt and eat as prey 2 trouble greatly

price /praɪs/ n 1 money (to be) paid for something: (fig.) the price of freedom 2 **at a price** at a high price 3 **not at any price** not at all ♦ vt fix the price of

price·less /'praɪslɪs/ adj 1 extremely valuable 2 infml very funny

price tag /'· ·/ n 1 small ticket showing the price of an article 2 a (fixed or stated) price: The government has not yet put a price tag on the plan.

pric·ey /'praɪsɪ/ adj infml expensive

prick¹ /prɪk/ v 1 vt make a small hole in with something with a sharp point 2 vi/t (cause to) feel a light sharp pain on the skin 3 **prick up one's ears** start to listen carefully

prick² n 1 small sharp pain 2 mark made by pricking 3 taboo PENIS 4 taboo sl foolish worthless man

prick·le /'prɪkəl/ n 1 [C] small sharp point on an animal or plant 2 [S] pricking sensation on the skin ♦ vi/t PRICK¹ (2) –**ly** adj 1 covered with prickles 2 that gives you a prickling sensation 3 difficult to deal with

prickly pear /ˌ·· '·/ n CACTUS that bears fruit which can be eaten

pride¹ /praɪd/ n 1 [S;U] pleasure in what you (or someone connected with you) can do or have done well 2 [U] reasonable respect for oneself 3 [U] too high an opinion of yourself 4 [S] most valuable one: the pride of my collection 5 **pride of place** esp. BrE highest or best position

pride² v **pride oneself on** phr vt be proud of (oneself) because of

priest /priːst/ n 1 (in the Christian Church, esp. in the ROMAN CATHOLIC Church) specially trained person who performs religious ceremonies and other religious duties 2 **priestess** /'priːstes/ fem. — specially trained person in certain non-Christian religions ~**hood** n [U] 1 position of being a priest 2 all the priests

prig /prɪg/ n unpleasantly moralistic person ~**gish** adj

prim /prɪm/ adj –**mm**– easily shocked by rude things ~**ly** adv

pri·ma·cy /'praɪməsɪ/ n [U] fml being first in importance, rank, etc.

prima don·na /ˌpriːmə 'dɒnə, ˌprɪmə-/ n 1 main female OPERA singer 2 someone who thinks they are very important and often gets excited and angry

pri·ma fa·cie /ˌpraɪmə 'feɪʃiː/ adj, adv law based on what seems true

pri·mal /'praɪməl/ adj belonging to the earliest times

pri·ma·ri·ly /praɪ'meərəliː/ adv mainly

pri·ma·ry¹ /'praɪˌmeriː, -məriː/ adj 1 chief; main: the primary purpose of his visit 2 earliest in time or order of development: primary education

primary² n election in which the members of a political party in a particular area vote for the person they would like to see as their party's CANDIDATE for a political office

primary col·or /ˌ··· '··/ n red, yellow, or blue

primary school /ˌ··· ·/ n ELEMENTARY SCHOOL

pri·mate /'praɪmeɪt/ n member of the most highly developed group of MAMMALS which includes human beings, monkeys, and related animals

prime¹ /praɪm/ n [S] time when someone is at their best

prime² adj 1 main 2 best

prime³ vt 1 put PRIMER¹ (1) on 2 instruct in advance 3 put explosive powder into (a gun)

prime min·is·ter /ˌ· '···/ n chief minister and government leader

prime num·ber /ˌ· '··/ n number that can only be divided by itself and 1

prim·er¹ /'praɪmər/ n 1 [U] paint put on before the main painting 2 [C] tube containing explosive, esp. to set off a bomb

prim·er² /'prɪmər/ n simple book for beginners

prime rate /ˌ· '·/ n lowest interest rate a bank charges, on which it bases other rates

prime time /'· ·/ n [U] time when most people are thought to watch television

pri·me·val /praɪˈmiːvəl/ *adj* very ancient

prim·i·tive /ˈprɪmətɪv/ *adj* **1** of the earliest stage of development **2** roughly made or done **3** old-fashioned and inconvenient *n* member of a PRIMITIVE (1) race or tribe ~**ly** *adv*

pri·mo·gen·i·ture /ˌpraɪmoʊˈdʒɛnə-tʃər/ *n* [U] system by which a dead man's property goes to his eldest son

pri·mor·di·al /praɪˈmɔːrdiəl/ *adj* existing from or at the beginning of time

prim·rose /ˈprɪmroʊz/ *n* pale yellow spring flower

prince /prɪns/ *n* **1** king's son **2** royal ruler of a small country ~**ly** *adj* **1** of a prince **2** splendid; generous

Prince Charm·ing /ˌ· ˈ··/ *n* [S] wonderful male lover

prin·cess /ˈprɪnsɪs, -sɛs/ *n* **1** king's daughter **2** prince's wife

prin·ci·pal /ˈprɪnsəpəl/ *adj* main ◆ *n* **1** [C] head of a school, etc. **2** [S] money lent, on which interest is paid ~**ly** *adv*

prin·ci·pal·i·ty /ˌprɪnsəˈpælətiy/ *n* country ruled by a prince

prin·ci·ple /ˈprɪnsəpəl/ *n* **1** [C] general truth or belief: *the principle of free speech* **2** [C;U] moral rule which guides behavior: *She resigned on a matter of principle.* **3** [U] high personal standard of right and wrong: *a man of principle* **4** [P] general rules on which a skill, etc., is based: *Archimedes' principle* **5 in principle** as an idea, if not in fact **6 on principle** because it would be morally wrong to do otherwise

print¹ /prɪnt/ *n* **1** [U] printed letters, words, etc. **2** [C] mark made on a surface: *a thumbprint* **3** [C] photograph printed on paper **4** [C] picture printed from a metal sheet **5 in/out of print** (of a book) that can still/no longer be obtained — see also SMALL PRINT

print² *v* **1** *vi/t* press (letters or pictures) on (esp. paper) with shapes covered with ink or paint **2** *vt* make (a book, magazine, etc.) by doing this **3** *vt* cause to be included in or produced as a newspaper, etc. **4** *vt* copy (a photograph) from film onto paper **5** *vi/t* write without joining the letters ~**able** *adj* suitable for reading by anyone ~**er** *n* **1** person who prints books, etc. **2** copying machine

print·out /ˈprɪntˌaʊt/ *n* [C;U] printed record produced by a computer

pri·or¹ /ˈpraɪər/ *adj* **1** earlier **2** more important **3 prior to** before

prior² *n* head of a priory

pri·or·i·tize /praɪˈɔrəˌtaɪz/ *vt* give (something) priority

pri·or·i·ty /praɪˈɔrətiy/ *n* **1** [U] (right of) being first in position or earlier in time **2** [C] something that needs attention before others

pri·o·ry /ˈpraɪəriy/ *n* (building for) a religious group

prism /ˈprɪzəm/ *n* transparent block with 3 sides that breaks up light into different colors

pris·on /ˈprɪzən/ *n* [C;U] large building where criminals are kept for punishment

prison camp /ˈ·· ·/ *n* guarded camp for prisoners of war

pris·on·er /ˈprɪzənər/ *n* person kept in prison

prisoner of war /ˌ··· · ˈ·/ also POW *n* soldier, etc., caught by the enemy in war

pris·sy /ˈprɪsiy/ *adj infml* annoyingly exact or proper

pris·tine /ˈprɪstiyn/ *adj fml* fresh and clean

pri·va·cy /ˈpraɪvəsiy/ *n* [U] **1** the (desirable) state of being away from other people **2** secrecy

pri·vate /ˈpraɪvɪt/ *adj* **1** not (to be) shared with others; secret **2** just for one person or a small group, not everyone **3** not connected with or paid for by government: *private school* **4** not connected with one's work or rank; unofficial **5** quiet; without lots of people ◆ *n* soldier of the lowest rank ~**ly** *adv*

private de·tec·tive /ˌ··· ·ˈ··/ *n* person, not a policeman, hired to follow people, report on their actions, etc.

private en·ter·prise /ˌ··· ˈ···/ *n* [U] CAPITALISM

private eye /ˌ·· ˈ·/ *n infml* private DETECTIVE

private parts /ˌ·· ˈ·/ *n* [P] outer sexual organs

private sec·tor /ˌ·· ˈ···◂/ *n* [the+S] those industries and services that are owned and run by private companies, not by the state

pri·va·tion /praɪˈveyʃən/ *n* [C;U] *fml* lack of things necessary for life

pri·vat·ize /ˈpraɪvəˌtaɪz/ *vt* sell (an industry or organization owned by the government) into private ownership **-ization** /ˌpraɪvətəˈzey-ʃən/ *n* [U]: *the privatization of public services*

priv·et /ˈprɪvɪt/ *n* [U] bush often used for HEDGEs

priv·i·lege /ˈprɪvəlɪdʒ/ *n* **1** [C] special advantage limited to a particular person or group **2** [U] (unfair) possession of such advantages because of wealth, social rank, etc. **-leged** *adj* having (a) privilege

priv·y¹ /ˈprɪviy/ *adj fml* sharing secret knowledge (of)

prize /praız/ n something you are given for winning, doing well, etc. ♦ vt value highly adj **1** that is gained or is worthy of a prize: *a prize hen* **2** given as a prize: *prize money*

prize·fight /ˈpraızfaıt/ n professional BOXING match ~**er** n

pro¹ /prow/ n pros infml a PROFESSIONAL

pro² n argument or reason in favor (of something)

prob·a·bil·i·ty /ˌprabəˈbıləṭiʸ/ n **1** [S;U] likelihood **2** [C] probable event or result

prob·a·ble /ˈprabəbəl/ adj that has a good chance of happening or being true; likely –**bly** adv

pro·bate /ˈprowˈbeʸt/ n [U] legal process of declaring someone's WILL(5) properly made

pro·ba·tion /prowˈbeʸʃən/ n [U] **1** (period of) testing someone's suitability **2** system of not sending criminals to prison if they behave well for a time

probation of·fi·cer /·ˈ··· ˌ··/ n person who watches and advises criminals on probation (2)

probe /prowb/ vi/t search or examine carefully (as if) with a long thin instrument ♦ n **1** metal tool for probing **2** spacecraft for searching through space **3** thorough inquiry

pro·bi·ty /ˈprowbəṭiʸ/ n [U] fml perfect honesty

prob·lem /ˈprabləm/ n difficulty that needs attention and thought

prob·lem·at·ic /ˌprabləˈmæṭık/ adj full of problems or causing problems

pro·bos·cis /prəˈbasıs/ n long movable nose of certain animals

pro·ce·dure /prəˈsiʸdʒər/ n **1** [C] set of actions for doing something **2** [U] way a meeting, trial, etc., is (to be) run –**dural** adj

pro·ceed /prəˈsiʸd, prow-/ vi fml **1** begin or continue in a course of action **2** walk or travel in a particular direction

pro·ceed·ings /prəˈsiʸdıŋz, prow-/ n [P] legal action taken against someone

pro·ceeds /ˈprowsiʸdz/ n [P] money gained from the sale of something

pro·cess /ˈprases, ˈprow-/ n **1** set of actions that produce continuation, change, or something new **2** method, esp. for producing goods **3 in the process of** actually doing (the stated thing) at the time ♦ vt **1** treat and preserve (food): *processed cheese* **2** print a photograph from (film) **3** deal with; examine

pro·ces·sion /prəˈseʃən/ n [C;U] line of people or vehicles moving along, esp. during a ceremony

pro·ces·sor /ˈprasesər, ˈprow-/ n MICROPROCESSOR – see also WORD PROCESSOR

pro·claim /prowˈkleʸm, prə-/ vt declare publicly and officially

proc·la·ma·tion /ˌprakləˈmeʸʃən/ n **1** [C] official public statement **2** [U] act of proclaiming

pro·cliv·i·ty /prowˈklıvəṭiʸ/ n fml strong natural liking or tendency

pro·cras·ti·nate /prowˈkræstəˌneʸt, prə-/ vi fml delay (annoyingly) –**nation** /prowˌkræstəˈneʸʃən, prə-/ n [U]

pro·cre·ate /ˈprowkriʸˌeʸt/ vi fml produce young –**ation** /ˌprowˈkriʸˈeʸʃən/ n [U]

proc·tor /ˈpraktər/ n teacher who watches over students during an examination ♦ vi to do this

pro·cure /prowˈkyuər, prə-/ v **1** vt fml obtain **2** vi/t provide (a woman) for sexual pleasure –**curer** n

prod /prad/ v –**dd** **1** vi/t push with a pointed object **2** vt urge sharply **prod** n

prod·i·gal /ˈpradıgəl/ adj fml **1** carelessly wasteful, esp. of money **2** giving or producing (something) freely and in large amounts ~**ity** /ˌpradıˈgæləṭiʸ/ n [U]

pro·di·gious /prəˈdıdʒəs/ adj wonderfully large, powerful, etc. ~**ly** adv

prod·i·gy /ˈpradədʒiʸ/ n **1** person with wonderful abilities: *child prodigy* **2** a wonder in nature

pro·duce¹ /prəˈduʷs, -ˈdyuʷs/ vt **1** bring into existence; give: *These trees produce rubber.* | *Poverty produces ill-health.* **2** make (goods for sale) **3** give birth to **4** bring out and show **5** prepare and bring before the public

prod·uce² /ˈpraduʷs, -dyuʷs, ˈprow-/ n [U] something produced, esp. on a farm

pro·duc·er /prəˈduʷsər, -ˈdyuʷ-/ n **1** person, company, etc., that produces goods **2** person in charge of the business of putting on a play, film, etc.

prod·uct /ˈpradʌkt, -dəkt/ n **1** something made or produced **2** result

pro·duc·tion /prəˈdʌkʃən/ n **1** [U] act of producing **2** [U] process of making products **3** [U] amount produced: *a cut in production* **4** [C] play, film, or broadcast that is produced

production line /·ˈ··· ·/ n arrangement of factory workers and machines for producing goods

pro·duc·tive /prəˈdʌktıv/ adj **1** that produces a lot **2** causing or producing (a result) ~**ly** adv

pro·duc·tiv·i·ty /ˌprowˈdʌkˈtıvəṭiʸ,

ˌprɑdək-/ *n* [U] rate of producing goods, crops, etc.

prof /prɑf/ *n infml for* PROFESSOR

pro·fane /proʷˈfeʸn, prə-/ *adj* **1** showing disrespect, esp. for holy things **2** (esp. of language) socially shocking **3** *fml* concerned with human life in this world; SECULAR: *profane art* ♦ *vt* treat disrespectfully ~**ly** *adv*

pro·fan·i·ty /prəˈfænəṭiʸ/ *n* [C;U] profane behavior or speech

pro·fess /prəˈfɛs, proʷ-/ *vt fml* **1** declare openly **2** claim, usu. falsely **3** have as one's religion ~**ed** *adj* **1** declared by oneself to be (the stated thing) **2** pretended

pro·fes·sion /prəˈfɛʃən/ *n* **1** form of employment, esp. a socially respected one like law or medicine **2** people in a particular profession **3** *fml* open declaration

pro·fes·sion·al /prəˈfɛʃənəl/ *adj* **1** working in a profession **2** doing for payment what others do for fun **3** showing high standards of work ♦ *n* professional person ~**ism** *n* [U] skill or quality of professionals

pro·fes·sor /prəˈfɛsər/ *n* university teacher of highest rank ~**ial** /ˌproʷfəˈsɔriʸəl, ˌprɑ-, -ˈsoʷr-/ *adj*

prof·fer /ˈprɑfər/ *vt fml* offer

pro·fi·cient /prəˈfɪʃənt/ *adj* very good at doing something ~**ly** *adv* ~**ciency** *n* [U]

pro·file /ˈproʷfaɪl/ *n* **1** side view, esp. of someone's head **2** state of being noticed by other people around me: *The management is trying to keep a* **low profile** *on this issue.* | *a* **high** *political* **profile** **3** short description ♦ *vt* draw or write a profile of

prof·it¹ /ˈprɑfɪt/ *n* **1** [C;U] money gained from some action **2** [U] advantage gained from some action

prof·it² *v* profit **by/from** *phr vt* gain advantage or learn from

prof·it·a·bil·i·ty /ˌprɑfəṭəˈbɪləṭiʸ/ *n* [U] state of being profitable or the degree to which a business is profitable

prof·it·a·ble /ˈprɑfəṭəbəl/ *adj* producing profit –**bly** *adv*

prof·it·eer /ˌprɑfəˈtɪər/ *n* person who makes unfairly large profits **profiteer** *vi*

profit mar·gin /ˈ·· ˌ··/ *n* difference between production cost and selling price

profit shar·ing /ˈ·· ˌ··/ *n* [U] workers sharing the profits of a business

prof·li·gate /ˈprɑfləgɪt, -ˌgeʸt/ *adj fml* **1** foolishly wasteful **2** shamelessly immoral

pro·found /prəˈfaʊnd/ *adj* **1** very strongly felt; deep **2** having

thorough knowledge and understanding ~**ly** *adv* –**fundity** /prəˈfʌndəṭiʸ/ *n* [C;U]

pro·fuse /prəˈfyuʷs/ *adj* produced in great quantity ~**ly** *adv* –**fusion** /prəˈfyuʷʒən/ *n* [S;U] (too) great amount

pro·gen·i·tor /proʷˈdʒenəṭər, prə-/ *n* one in the past from which someone or something is descended

prog·e·ny /ˈprɑdʒəniʸ/ *n* [U] *fml* **1** descendants (DESCEND) **2** children

pro·ges·ter·one /proʷˈdʒestəˌroʷn/ *n* [U] substance in the body that prepares the UTERUS for its work

prog·no·sis /prɑgˈnoʷsɪs/ *n* –**ses** /-siʸz/ **1** doctor's opinion of how an illness will develop **2** description of the future

prog·nos·ti·cate /prɑgˈnɑstəˌkeʸt/ *vt fml* say (what is going to happen) –**cation** /prɑgˌnɑstəˈkeʸʃən/ *n* [C;U]

pro·gram¹ /ˈproʷgræm, -grəm/ *n* **1** list of performers or things to be performed **2** television or radio show **3** plan for future action **4** set of instructions for making a computer do something

program² *vt* –**mm-** or –**m-** supply (a computer) with a program ~**able** *adj* controllable by means of a program ~**mer** *n*

pro·gress¹ /ˈprɑgrɛs, -grəs/ *n* [U] **1** continual improvement or development **2** forward movement in space **3** **in progress** happening or being done

pro·gress² /prəˈgrɛs/ *vi* make progress

pro·gres·sion /prəˈgrɛʃən/ *n* **1** [S;U] progressing **2** [C] set of numbers that vary in a particular way

pro·gres·sive /prəˈgrɛsɪv/ *adj* **1** developing continuously or by stages **2** favoring change or new ideas **3** (of a verb form) showing action that is continuing ♦ *n* person with progressive ideas, esp. about social change ~**ly** *adv*

pro·hib·it /proʷˈhɪbɪt, prə-/ *vt fml* **1** forbid by law or rule **2** prevent

pro·hi·bi·tion /ˌproʷəˈbɪʃən/ *n* **1** [U] act of prohibiting something, esp. the sale of alcohol **2** [C] *fml* order forbidding something **3** (*cap*) period from 1920 to 1933 when sale of alcohol was forbidden in the US

pro·hib·i·tive /proʷˈhɪbəṭɪv, prə-/ *adj* preventing or tending to discourage: *prohibitive prices* (= too high) ~**ly** *adv*

proj·ect¹ /ˈprɑdʒɛkt, -dʒɪkt/ *n* long piece of planned work

pro·ject² /prəˈdʒɛkt/ *v* **1** *vi/t* stick out beyond a surface **2** *vt fml* aim and throw through the air **3** *vt* direct (sound or light) into space or onto a surface **4** *vt* make plans for:

our projected visit to Mexico **5** *vt* judge or calculate using the information one has: *projected sales figures* **6** *vi/t* express (oneself or one's beliefs, etc.) outwardly: *pro. to have a favorable effect on others*

pro·jec·tile /prə'dʒɛktəl, -ˌtaɪl/ *n fml* object or weapon thrown or fired

pro·jec·tion /prə'dʒɛkʃən/ *n* **1** [U] act of projecting **2** [C] something that sticks out **3** [C] guess of future possibilities based on known facts **-lifer** *n*

pro·jec·tion·ist /prə'dʒɛkʃənɪst/ *n* person who works a PROJECTOR, esp. in a cinema

pro·jec·tor /prə'dʒɛktər/ *n* apparatus for projecting films, etc.

pro·lapse /proʷ'læps/ *vi fml* (of an inner body organ) slip out of its right place

pro·le·tar·i·at /ˌproʷlə'tɛəriʲət/ *n fml* class of unskilled workers who earn wages

pro-life /ˌ•• '•◂/ *adj* opposed to ABOR-TION **-lifer** *n*

pro·lif·e·rate /prə'lɪfəˌreʲt, proʷ-/ *vi* increase rapidly in numbers **-ration** /prəˌlɪfə'reʲʃən, proʷ-/ *n* [S;U]

pro·lif·ic /prə'lɪfɪk, proʷ-/ *adj* producing a lot **~ally** /-kliʲ/ *adv*

pro·lix /proʷ'lɪks/ *adj fml* using too many words

pro·logue, -log /'proʷlɔg, -lɑg/ *n* **1** introduction to a play, long poem, etc. **2** event that leads up to another, bigger one

pro·long /prə'lɔŋ/ *vt* lengthen **~ed** *adj* long

prom /prɑm/ *n* formal dance at a school or college

prom·e·nade /ˌprɑmə'neʲd, -'nɑd/ *n* **1** wide path along the coast in a tourist town **2** *fml* unhurried walk ♦ *vi* walk slowly up and down

prom·i·nent /'prɑmənənt/ *adj* **1** sticking out **2** noticeable **3** famous **~ly** *adv* **-nence** *n* **1** [U] fact or quality of being prominent **2** [C] *fml* part that sticks out

pro·mis·cu·ous /prə'mɪskyuəs/ *adj* **1** not limited to one sexual partner **2** *fml* being of many sorts mixed together **-cuity** /ˌprɑmə'skyuʷət̬iʲ/ *n* [U]

prom·ise /'prɑmɪs/ *n* **1** [C] statement, which one wishes to be believed, of what one will do **2** [U] signs of future success, good results, etc. ♦ *v* **1** *vi/t* make a promise: *I promise I won't tell them.* **2** *vt* cause one to expect or hope for **-ising** *adj* showing PROMISE (2)

Promised Land /ˌ•• '•/ *n* [(the) S] **1** heaven **2** condition which one hopes for because it will bring happiness

prom·on·to·ry /'prɑmənˌtɔriʲ, -ˌtoʷriʲ/ *n* point of land stretching out into the sea

pro·mote /prə'moʷt/ *vt* **1** raise to a higher position or rank **2** help to arrange (a business, concert, etc.) **3** advertise **4** *fml* help to bring about **-moter** *n* person whose job is to promote events, activities, etc.

pro·mo·tion /prə'moʷʃən/ *n* [C;U] **1** raising of rank or position **2** advertising activity

prompt¹ /prɑmpt/ *vt* **1** cause; urge **2** remind (an actor) of forgotten words **prompt, ~er** *n* person who prompts actors

prompt² *adj* acting or done quickly or at the right time **~ly** *adv* **~ness** *n* [U]

prom·ul·gate /'prɑməlˌgeʲt/ *vt fml* **1** bring (a law, etc.) into effect by official public declaration **2** spread (a belief, etc.) widely

prone /proʷn/ *adj* **1** likely to suffer: *prone to colds* | *accident-prone* **2** lying face downwards

prong /prɔŋ, prɑŋ/ *n* pointed part of a fork: (fig.) *a 3-pronged attack* (= from 3 directions)

pro·nom·i·nal /proʷ'nɑmənl/ *adj* of a pronoun

pro·noun /'proʷnaʊn/ *n* word used instead of a noun, such as *he* or *it*

pro·nounce /prə'naʊns/ *vt* **1** make the sound of (a letter, word, etc.) **2** *fml* declare officially **-ment** *n* solemn declaration **-nounced** *adj* very strong or noticeable

pro·nun·ci·a·tion /prəˌnʌnsiʲ'eʲʃən/ *n* [C;U] way in which a language or word is pronounced

proof¹ /pruʷf/ *n* **1** [C;U] way of showing that something is true **2** [C] a test or trial **3** [C] test copy of something to be printed **4** [U] standard of strength for certain alcoholic drinks

proof² *adj* having or giving protection: *proof against temptation* | *waterproof*

proof·read /'pruʷfˌriʲd/ *vi/t* read and put right mistakes in (PROOFS (3)) **~er** *n*

prop¹ /prɑp/ *n* support for something heavy ♦ *vt* **-pp-** support or keep in a leaning position

prop² *n* small article used on stage **prop·a·gan·da** /ˌprɑpə'gændə/ *n* [U] information spread to influence public opinion

prop·a·gate /'prɑpəˌgeʲt/ *v* **1** *vi/t* (cause to) increase in number by producing young **2** *vt fml* spread (ideas, etc.) **-gation** /ˌprɑpə'geʲʃən/ *n* [U]

pro·pel /prə'pɛl/ *vt* **-ll-** move or push forward

pro·pel·lant /prə'pelənt/ n [C;U] explosive for firing a bullet or ROCKET

pro·pel·ler /prə'pelər/ n 2 or more blades on a central bar that turns to drive an aircraft or ship

pro·pen·si·ty /prə'pensəti⁷/ n fml natural tendency

prop·er /'prapər/ adj 1 right; suitable; correct 2 socially acceptable ~ly adv

proper noun /,·· '·/ n name of a particular thing or person, spelled with a CAPITAL letter

prop·er·ty /'prapərti⁷/ n 1 [U] something owned; possession(s) 2 [C;U] (area of) land and/or building(s) 3 [C] natural quality or power

proph·e·cy /'prafəsi⁷/ n [C;U] (statement) telling what will happen in the future

proph·e·sy /'prafə,sai/ vi/t say (what will happen in the future)

proph·et /'prafit/ n 1 person who makes known and explains God's will 2 person who tells about the future ~ic /prə'fɛtɪk/ adj

pro·phy·lac·tic /,prafə'læktɪk/ adj fml for preventing disease ♦ n something prophylactic, esp. a CONDOM

pro·pin·qui·ty /prə'pɪŋkwəti⁷/ n [U] fml nearness

pro·pi·ti·ate /prə'pɪʃi⁷,e⁷t, proʷ-/ vt fml make (an angry or unfriendly person) more friendly –ation /prə,pɪʃi⁷'e⁷ʃən, proʷ-/ n [U]

pro·pi·tious /prə'pɪʃəs/ adj fml favorable; offering advantage

pro·po·nent /prə'poʷnənt/ n fml person who advises the use of something

pro·por·tion /prə'pɔrʃən, -'poʷr-/ n 1 [C;U] relationship between one thing or part and another in size, importance, etc. 2 [C] part of a whole 3 **in/out of proportion** according/not according to real importance ♦ vt fml make in or put into suitable proportion ~al adj in correct proportion **proportions** n [P] size and shape

proportional rep·re·sen·ta·tion /·,··· ···'·-·/ n [U] system of voting in elections by which parties are given LEGISLATIVE representation according to the proportion of votes they receive, rather than having to get most of the votes in each voting area

pro·pos·al /prə'poʷzəl/ n 1 plan; suggestion 2 offer of marriage

pro·pose /prə'poʷz/ v 1 vt suggest 2 vt intend 3 vi/t make an offer of (marriage)

prop·o·si·tion /,prapə'zɪʃən/ n 1 statement giving an unproved judgment 2 suggested offer or arrangement 3 person or situation to be dealt with 4 suggested offer to have

sex with someone vt infml make a PROPOSITION (esp. 4) to (someone)

pro·pound /prə'paʊnd/ vt fml put forward (an idea)

pro·pri·e·ta·ry /prə'praɪə,teri⁷/ adj 1 privately owned: a proprietary brand name 2 of or like an owner

pro·pri·e·tor /prə'praɪətər/ n owner of a business

pro·pri·e·ty /prə'praɪəti⁷/ n [U] fml 1 social or moral correctness 2 rightness or reasonableness

pro·pul·sion /prə'pʌlʃən/ n [U] force that PROPELs –sive /-sɪv/ adj

pro ra·ta /,proʷ 're⁷tə, -'ratə/ adv, adj according to a fair share for each

pro·sa·ic /proʷ'ze⁷ɪk/ adj dull ~ally /-kli⁷/ adv

pros and cons /,proʷz ən 'kanz/ n [P] reasons for and against

pro·sce·ni·um /proʷ'si⁷ni⁷əm/ n front arch of a theater stage

pro·scribe /proʷ'skraɪb/ vt fml forbid, esp. by law

prose /proʷz/ n [U] ordinary written language (not poetry)

pros·e·cute /'prasə,kyuʷt/ vi/t bring a criminal charge (against) in court –cutor n –cution /,prasə'kyuʷʃən/ n 1 [C;U] prosecuting 2 [the+S] group of people prosecuting someone in court 3 [U] fml the carrying out of something that needs to be done

pros·e·lyte /'prasə,laɪt/ n fml new member of a religion

pros·e·lyt·ize /'prasələ,taɪz/ vi fml try to persuade people to become proselytes

pros·o·dy /'prasədi⁷, 'praz-/ n [U] arrangement of sounds and beats in poetry

pros·pect¹ /'praspekt/ n 1 [C;U] reasonable hope of something happening 2 [S;U] something which is likely soon 3 [C] wide or distant view

pros·pect² /prə'spekt/ vi try to find gold, oil, etc. ~or n

pro·spec·tive /prə'spektɪv/ adj likely to become

pro·spec·tus /prə'spektəs/ n small book advertising a product, college, new business, etc.

pros·per /'praspər/ vi 1 become successful and esp. rich 2 grow well ~ous adj successful and rich ~ity /prə'sperəti⁷/ n [U] success and wealth

pros·tate /'praste⁷t/ n organ in the male body producing a liquid that carries seed

pros·the·sis /pras'θi⁷sɪs/ n artificial body part

pros·ti·tute /'prastə,tuʷt, -,tyuʷt/ n someone who has sex with people for money ♦ *vt fml* use dishonorably for money **-tution** /ˌprɑstə-ˈtyuʷʃən, -ˈtyuʷ-/ *n* [U]

pros·trate /ˈprɑstreʸt/ *adj* **1** lying face downwards, esp. in worship **2** without any strength or courage ♦ *vt* make prostrate

pro·tag·o·nist /proʷˈtægənɪst/ *n* **1** main supporter of a new idea **2** someone taking part

pro·te·an /ˈproʷtiʸən, proʷˈtiʸən/ *adj fml* continually changing

pro·tect /prəˈtɛkt/ *vt* keep safe ~ **or** *n* ~**ion** /prəˈtɛkʃən/ *n* **1** [U] act of protecting or state of being protected **2** [C] something that protects

pro·tec·tion·ism /prəˈtɛkʃəˌnɪzəm/ *n* [U] helping one's own country's trade by taxing foreign goods

protection rack·et /·ˈ·· ˌ·ˈ·/ *n* getting money from store owners, etc., by threatening to damage their property

pro·tec·tive /prəˈtɛktɪv/ *adj* **1** that protects **2** wishing to protect ~**ly** *adv*

pro·tec·tor·ate /prəˈtɛktərɪt/ *n* country controlled and protected by another country

prot·é·gé /ˈproʷtəˌʒeʸ, ˌproʷtəˈʒeʸ/ *n* person guided and helped by another

pro·tein /ˈproʷtiʸn/ *n* [C;U] food substance that builds up the body and keeps it healthy

pro tem /ˌproʷ ˈtɛm/ *adv* for the present time only

pro·test¹ /ˈproʷtɛst/ *n* [C;U] **1** strong expression of disapproval, opposition, etc. **2 under protest** unwillingly

pro·test² /prəˈtɛst, proʷ-, ˈproʷtɛst/ *v* **1** *vi* make a protest **2** *vt* declare strongly against opposition ~**er** *n*

Prot·es·tant /ˈprɑtɪstənt/ *n, adj* (member) of a branch of the Christian church that separated from the Roman Catholic Church in the 16th century

prot·es·ta·tion /ˌprɑtɪˈsteʸʃən, ˌproʷ-/ *n fml* **1** [C] solemn declaration **2** [U] protesting

pro·to·col /ˈproʷtəˌkɔl, -ˌkɑl/ *n* [U] fixed rules of behavior

pro·ton /ˈproʷtɑn/ *n* very small piece of matter that is part of an atom and carries POSITIVE (5) electricity

pro·to·plasm /ˈproʷtəˌplæzəm/ *n* [U] substance from which all plants and creatures are formed

pro·to·type /ˈproʷtəˌtaɪp/ *n* first form of a machine, afterwards developed

pro·tract /proʷˈtrækt, prə-/ *vt* cause to last an (unnecessarily) long time ~**ion** /proʷˈtrækʃən, prə-/ *n* [U]

pro·trac·tor /proʷˈtræktər, prə-/ *n* instrument for measuring and drawing angles

pro·trude /proʷˈtruʷd/ *vi fml* stick out **-trusion** /proʷˈtruʷʒən/ *n* [C;U]

pro·tu·ber·ance /proʷˈtuʷbərəns, -ˈtyuʷ-/ *n fml* swelling; BULGE

proud /praʊd/ *adj* **1** showing proper and reasonable respect for oneself **2** having too high an opinion of oneself **3** having or expressing personal pleasure in something connected with oneself: *proud of her new car* **4** splendid; glorious ♦ *adv*: **do someone proud** make someone feel proud ~**ly** *adv*

prove /pruʷv/ *v* **1** *vt* show to be true **2** be (later) found to be: *These revelations could prove highly embarrassing.*

prov·en /ˈpruʷvən/ *adj* tested and shown to be true

prov·e·nance /ˈprɑvənəns/ *n fml* (place of) origin

prov·erb /ˈprɑvɜrb/ *n* short wise saying that is often heard ~**ial** /prəˈvɜrbiʸəl/ *adj* **1** widely known and spoken of **2** of, concerning, or like a proverb

pro·vide /prəˈvaɪd/ *vt* arrange for someone to get; supply **-vided** *conj* on condition that **-viding** *conj* provided

   provide for *phr vt* **1** supply with necessary things **2** (of the law) make possible

prov·i·dence /ˈprɑvədəns/ *n* [U] the kindness of fate

prov·i·dent /ˈprɑvədənt/ *adj fml* careful to save for future needs

prov·i·den·tial /ˌprɑvəˈdɛnʃəl◂, -tʃəl◂/ *adj fml* lucky

prov·ince /ˈprɑvɪns/ *n* **1** main division of a country **2** area of knowledge, activity, etc. **-incial** /prəˈvɪnʃəl, -tʃəl/ *adj* **1** of a province **2** narrow or old-fashioned in interest, customs, etc. **provinces** /ˈprɑvɪnsɪz/ *n* [*the*+P] parts of a country far from the main city

prov·ing ground /·ˈ·· ˌ·/ *n* **1** place for scientific testing **2** situation where something new is tried out

pro·vi·sion /prəˈvɪʒən/ *n* **1** [U] act of providing **2** [U] preparation against future risks or needs **3** [C] condition in an agreement or law **provisions** *n* [P] food supplies

pro·vi·sion·al /prəˈvɪʒənəl/ *adj* for use now, but likely to be changed ~**ly** *adv*

pro·vi·so /prəˈvaɪzoʷ/ *n* **-sos** condition made in advance

prov·o·ca·tion /ˌprɑvəˈkeʸʃən/ *n* **1** [U] act of provoking **2** [C] something annoying

pro·voc·a·tive /prəˈvɑkətɪv/ *adj*

likely to cause **a** anger **b** sexual interest ~**ly** adv

pro·voke /prə'vo^wk/ vt **1** make angry **2** cause (a feeling or action)

prow /prau/ n front part of a ship

prow·ess /'prauɪs/ n [U] fml great ability or courage

prowl /praul/ vi/t move about quietly and threateningly **prowl** n [S] ~**er** n

prox·im·i·ty /prɑk'sɪməti/ n [U] fml nearness

prox·y /'prɑksi/ n **1** [U] right to act for another person, esp. as a voter **2** [C] person given this right

prude /pru^wd/ n person easily offended by rude things, esp. connected with sex **prudish** adj

pru·dent /'pru^wdnt/ adj sensible and careful ~**ly** adv –**dence** n [U]

prune¹ /pru^wn/ n dried PLUM

prune² vt **1** cut off parts of (a tree or bush) to improve shape and growth **2** remove unwanted parts of

pruning shears /'·· ‚·/ n [P] strong garden scissors

pru·ri·ent /'pruəriənt/ adj fml interested in an unhealthy way in sex –**ence** n [U]

pry¹ /praɪ/ vi try to find out about someone's private affairs

pry² vt lift or force with a tool or metal bar

P.S. /‚pi^y 'ɛs/ n note added at the end of a letter

psalm /sɑm/ n religious song or poem, esp. as in the Bible

pseu·do·nym /'su^wdnₐɪm/ n invented name, esp. of a writer

psst /ps/ interj (used for quietly gaining someone's attention)

psych /saɪk/ v sl
psych out phr vt **1** understand by INTUITION **2** frighten
psych up phr vt make (esp. oneself) enthusiastic and ready

psy·che /'saɪki^y/ n fml human mind or spirit

psy·che·del·ic /‚saɪkə'delɪk◄/ adj **1** (of a drug) causing strange and powerful feelings **2** having strong patterns of color, lines, moving lights, noise, etc.

psy·chi·a·try /saɪ'kaɪətri^y, sɪ-/ n [U] study and treatment of diseases of the mind –**trist** n –**tric** /‚saɪki^y-'ætrɪk◄/ adj

psy·chic /'saɪkɪk/ adj **1** having strange powers, such as the ability to see into the future **2** of the mind **3** connected with the spirits of the dead ~**ally** /-kli^y/ adv

psy·cho·a·nal·y·sis /‚saɪko^wə'næl-əsɪs/ n [U] way of treating disorders of the mind by finding their causes in the patient's past life –**analyze**

/‚saɪko^w'ænl‚aɪz/ vt –**analyst** /-'ænl-ɪst/ n

psy·cho·log·i·cal /‚saɪkə'lɑdʒɪkəl/ adj **1** of or connected with the way the mind works **2** infml not real

psy·cho·log·i·cal war·fare /····,··· '··/ n [U] spreading fear, different political beliefs, etc., among the enemy

psy·chol·o·gy /saɪ'kɑlədʒi^y/ n [U] study of how the mind works –**gist** n

psy·cho·path /'saɪkə‚pæθ/ n crazy person who may be violent ~**ic** /‚saɪkə'pæθɪk◄/ adj

psy·cho·sis /saɪ'ko^wsɪs/ n –**ses** /-si^yz/ serious disorder of the mind –**chotic** /saɪ'kɑtɪk/ n, adj

psy·cho·so·mat·ic /‚saɪko^wsə-'mætɪk/ adj (of an illness) caused by anxiety, not a real disorder of the body

psy·cho·ther·a·py /‚saɪko^w'θerəpi^y/ n [U] treatment of mind disorders by psychological methods (not drugs, etc.) –**pist** n

pt written abbrev. for: **1** part **2** PINT(s) **3** point **4** port

PTA /‚pi^y ti^y 'e^y/ n Parent Teacher Association, local organization to involve parents in their children's schools

pu·ber·ty /'pyu^wbərti^y/ n period of change from childhood to the adult state in which one can produce children

pu·bic /'pyu^wbɪk/ adj of or near the sexual organs

pub·lic /'pʌblɪk/ adj **1** of or for people in general or everyone; not private: public opinion **2** of the government: public money **3** not secret **4** go public (of a company) offer stock for sale to the public **5** in the public eye often seen in public or on television, or mentioned in newspapers ◆ n [S] **1** people in general **2** people interested in the stated thing **3** in public openly ~**ly** adv

pub·li·ca·tion /‚pʌblə'ke^yʃən/ n **1** [U] act of publishing (PUBLISH) **2** [C] book, magazine, etc.

public com·pa·ny /·,·· '··/ n business that offers stock in itself for sale on a STOCK EXCHANGE

public de·fend·er /··· ·'··/ n lawyer paid by the state to defend poor people in court

pub·li·cist /'pʌbləsɪst/ n person who publicizes something, esp. products

pub·lic·i·ty /pʌ'blɪsəti^y/ n [U] **1** public notice or attention: unwelcome publicity **2** business of publicizing things; advertising

pub·li·cize /'pʌblə‚saɪz/ vt bring to public notice

public re·la·tions /·,·· ·'··/ n also PR — **1** [U] forming of a favorable public opinion of an organization **2** [P] good relations between an organization and the public

public school /ˌ·· ˌ·/ n school run by the state

public sec·tor /ˌ·· ˈ··/ n [the+S] those industries and services that are owned and run by the state

public ser·vant /ˌ·· ˈ··/ n person elected to or employed in government

public spir·it /ˌ·· ˈ··/ n [U] willingness to do what is helpful for everyone ~ ed adj

pub·lish /ˈpʌblɪʃ/ vt 1 bring out (a book, newspaper, etc.) 2 make known generally: publishing the victim's name ~ er n

puce /pyuʷs/ adj dark brownish purple

puck /pʌk/ n hard flat piece of rubber used in ICE HOCKEY

puck·er /ˈpʌkər/ vi/t tighten into folds

puck·ish /ˈpʌkɪʃ/ adj harmlessly playful

pud·ding /ˈpudɪŋ/ n [C;U] thick soft sweet food made from flour, milk, eggs, etc.

pud·dle /ˈpʌdl/ n small amount of water, esp. rain, lying in a hollow place in the ground

pudg·y /ˈpʌdʒiʸ/ adj short and fat

pu·er·ile /ˈpyuərəl, -raɪl/ adj fml childish; silly

puff¹ /pʌf/ v 1 vi breathe rapidly and with effort 2 vi/t send out or come out as little clouds of smoke or steam

puff out/up phr vi/t swell

puff² n 1 sudden light rush of air, smoke, etc. 2 hollow piece of light pastry filled with a soft, sweet mixture 3 infml piece of writing praising a person or entertainment ~ y adj rather swollen

puff·ball /ˈpʌfbɔl/ n ball-like FUNGUS

puf·fin /ˈpʌfɪn/ n seabird with a large brightly colored beak

puff pas·try /ˌ· ˈ··/ also **puff paste** — n [U] light pastry filled with air

pu·gi·list /ˈpyuʷdʒəlɪst/ n fml boxer (BOX²)

pug·na·cious /pʌgˈneʸʃəs/ adj fml fond of quarreling and fighting

puke /pyuʷk/ vi infml for VOMIT

pull¹ /pul/ v 1 vi/t bring (something) along behind one: The horses pulled the plow. 2 vi/t move (someone or something) towards oneself: She pulled the door open. 3 vt take with force: He had a tooth pulled (out). 4 vt stretch and damage: pull a muscle 5 vi move in or as a vehicle: The train pulled out. (= left) 6 vt attract 7 **pull someone's leg** tell someone something that is not true as a joke 8 **pull a fast one (on)** get

the advantage (over) by a trick 9 **pull a gun** take out a gun and aim it (at someone) 10 **pull the rug from under** stop supporting

pull away phr vi (esp. of a road vehicle) start to move off

pull down phr vt destroy (a building, etc.)

pull in phr vi (of a train) arrive at a station

pull off phr vt succeed in doing (something difficult)

pull out phr vi/t 1 (cause to) stop taking part 2 (of a train) leave a station

pull over phr vi/t (of a vehicle) move to one side and (cause to)

pull through phr vi/t 1 (cause to) live in spite of illness or wounds 2 (help to) succeed in spite of difficulties

pull together phr v 1 vi work together to help a shared effort 2 vt control the feelings of (oneself)

pull up phr vi (of a vehicle) stop

pull² n 1 [C;U] (act of) pulling 2 [C] rope, handle, etc. for pulling something 3 [S] difficult steep climb 4 [U] special (unfair) influence

pul·let /ˈpulɪt/ n young hen

pul·ley /ˈpuliʸ/ n apparatus for lifting things with a rope

pull·o·ver /ˈpulˌoʷvər/ n article of clothing, esp. a SWEATER pulled on over the head

pul·mo·na·ry /ˈpulməˌneriʸ, ˈpʌl-/ adj of the lungs

pulp /pʌlp/ n 1 [S;U] soft almost liquid mass, esp. of plant material 2 [U] book, magazine, etc., cheaply produced and containing matter of bad quality ♦ vt advise into pulp

pul·pit /ˈpulpɪt, ˈpʌl-/ n raised enclosure from which a priest speaks in church

pul·sar /ˈpʌlsɑr/ n starlike object that sends out regular radio signals

pul·sate /ˈpʌlseʸt/ vi 1 shake very rapidly and regularly 2 pulse –**sation** /pʌlˈseʸʃən/ n [C;U]

pulse /pʌls/ n 1 regular beating of blood in the body's blood tubes 2 strong regular beat 3 short sound or electrical charge ♦ vi move or flow with a strong beat

pul·ver·ize /ˈpʌlvəˌraɪz/ vt 1 crush to a powder 2 defeat thoroughly

pu·ma /ˈpyuʷmə, ˈpuʷmə/ n –mas or –ma large fierce wild cat

pum·mel /ˈpʌməl/ vt –l– hit repeatedly

pump¹ /pʌmp/ n machine for forcing liquid or gas into or out of something ♦ 1 vt empty or fill with a pump 2 vt put in or remove with a pump 3 vi a work a pump b work like a pump: My heart was pumping *fast.* **4** *vt* try to get information from with questions

pump² *n* light shoe for dancing, etc.

pump·kin /ˈpʌmpkɪn, ˈpʌŋkɪn/ *n* [C;U] extremely large round orange vegetable

pun /pʌn/ *n* amusing use of a word or phrase with 2 meanings

punch¹ /pʌntʃ/ *vt* **1** hit hard with the closed hand **2** cut a hole in with a special tool: *The inspector punched my ticket.* ♦ *n* **1** [C] hard blow with the closed hand **2** [U] forcefulness **3 pull one's punches** express an unfavorable opinion of someone or something less strongly than is deserved

punch² *n* [U] mixed sweet fruit drink usu. made with alcohol

punch³ *n* [C] steel tool for cutting holes

punch-drunk /ˈ· ·/ *adj* suffering brain damage from blows in boxing (BOX²)

punch line /ˈ· ·/ *n* funny part at the end of a joke

punc·til·i·ous /pʌŋkˈtɪliʲəs/ *adj fml* very exact about details, esp. of behavior ~**ly** *adv*

punc·tu·al /ˈpʌŋktʃuʷəl/ *adj* coming, happening, etc., at exactly the right time ~**ly** *adv* ~**ality** /ˌpʌŋktʃuʷˈælətiʲ/ *n* [U]

punc·tu·ate /ˈpʌŋktʃuʷˌeʲt/ *vt* **1** divide into sentences, phrases, etc., with punctuation marks **2** repeatedly break the flow of −**ation** /ˌpʌŋktʃuʷˈeʲʃən/ *n* [U] **1** act or system of punctuating **2** punctuation marks

punctuation mark /··· ·ˈ· ˌ·/ *n* sign used in punctuating, e.g. a PERIOD¹(4), or a COMMA

punc·ture /ˈpʌŋktʃər/ *n* small hole, esp. in a tire ♦ *vi/t* (cause to) get a puncture

pun·dit /ˈpʌndɪt/ *n* EXPERT who is often asked to give an opinion

pun·gent /ˈpʌndʒənt/ *adj* (of a taste or smell) strong and sharp

pun·ish /ˈpʌnɪʃ/ *vt* **1** cause (someone) to suffer for (a crime or fault) **2** deal roughly with ~**ment** *n* **1** [U] act of punishing **2** [C] way in which someone is punished

pun·ish·ing /ˈpʌnɪʃɪŋ/ *adj* that makes one thoroughly tired and weak

pu·ni·tive /ˈpyuʷnətɪv/ *adj* **1** intended as punishment **2** very severe

punk /pʌŋk/ *n* (since the 1970s) young person with strange clothes and often colored hair who likes loud violent music

punt /pʌnt/ *n* kick used in football when the ball is dropped towards the foot -**er** person who punts

pu·ny /ˈpyuʷniʲ/ *adj* small and weak

pup /pʌp/ *n* PUPPY

pu·pa /ˈpyuʷpə/ *n* −**pas** or −**pae** /-piʲ/ form of an insect in a covering preparing to become an adult **pupal** *adj*

pu·pil¹ /ˈpyuʷpəl/ *n* child being taught

pupil² *n* small round black opening in the middle of the eye

pup·pet /ˈpʌpɪt/ *n* **1** toylike figure of a person or animal that is made to move as if it were alive **2** person or group that is controlled by someone else: *a puppet government*

pup·py /ˈpʌpiʲ/ *n* young dog

puppy love /ˈ·· ·/ *n* [U] young boy's or girl's love that doesn't last long

pur·chase /ˈpɜrtʃəs/ *vt fml* buy ♦ *n fml* **1** [U] act of buying **2** [C] something bought **3** [U] firm hold on a surface

pur·dah /ˈpɜrdə/ *n* [U] system of keeping women out of public view, esp. among Muslims

pure /pyʊr/ *adj* **1** not mixed with anything else **2** clean **3** free from evil **4** complete; thorough: *by pure chance* ~**ly** *adv* wholly; only

pu·ree /pyuʷˈreʲ, ˈpyuʷəreʲ/ *n* [C;U] soft partly liquid mass of food ♦ *vt* make (fruit or vegetable) into a puree

pur·ga·tive /ˈpɜrgətɪv/ *n* medicine that empties the bowels

pur·ga·to·ry /ˈpɜrgəˌtoriʲ, -ˌtoʷriʲ/ *n* [U] **1** (in the Roman Catholic Church) place where the soul of a dead person is made pure and fit to enter heaven **2** situation of great suffering

purge /pɜrdʒ/ *vt* **1** get rid of (an unwanted person) from (a state, group, etc.) by driving out, killing, etc. **2** make clean and free from (something evil) **3** empty the bowels with medicine ♦ *n* act of purging (PURGE (1))

pu·ri·fy /ˈpyʊərəˌfaɪ/ *vt* make pure −**fication** /ˌpyʊərəfəˈkeʲʃən/ *n* [U]

pur·ist /ˈpyʊərɪst/ *n* someone who tries to make sure things are always done correctly and not changed, esp. in matters of grammar

pu·ri·tan /ˈpyʊərətn/ *n* **1** person with hard fixed standards of behavior who thinks pleasure is wrong **2** (*cap.*) member of a former Christian group that wanted to make religion simpler and less ceremonial ~**ical** /ˌpyʊərəˈtænɪkəl/ *adj*

pu·ri·ty /ˈpyʊərətiʲ/ *n* [U] being pure

purl /pɜrl/ *n* [U] knitting (KNIT) stitch done backwards ♦ *vi/t* use a purl stitch (on)

pur·loin /pər'lɔɪn, 'pɜrlɔɪn/ vt fml steal

pur·ple /'pɜrpəl/ adj of a color that is a mixture of red and blue

pur·port /'pɜrpɔrt, -poʷrt/ n [U] fml meaning ♦ /pər'pɔrt, -'poʷrt/ vt have an intended appearance of being

pur·pose /'pɜrpəs/ n 1 [C] reason for doing something 2 [C] use; effect; result: *It has served its purpose.* (= done what is needed) 3 [U] determined quality; power of will 4 **on purpose** intentionally ~**ful** adj determined ~**ly** adv intentionally

purr /pɜr/ vi make the low continuous sound of a pleased cat

purse¹ /pɜrs/ n 1 small bag for carrying coins 2 woman's HANDBAG 3 amount of money offered, esp. as a prize

purse² vt draw (esp. the lips) together in little folds

purs·er /'pɜrsər/ n ship's officer responsible for money and travelers' arrangements

purse strings /'· ·/ n **hold the purse strings** control the spending of money

pur·su·ance /pər'suʷəns/ n **in the pursuance of** fml doing

pur·su·ant /pər'suʷənt/ adj **pursuant to** fml in accordance with

pur·sue /pər'suʷ/ vt 1 follow in order to catch 2 fml continue steadily with: *pursuing a policy of neutrality* **-suer** n

pur·suit /pər'suʷt/ n 1 [U] act of pursuing 2 [C] fml activity, esp. for pleasure

pur·vey /pər'veʸ/ vt fml supply (food or other goods) ~**or** n

pur·view /'pɜrvyuʷ/ n [U] fml limit of one's concern, activity, or knowledge

pus /pʌs/ n [U] thick yellowish liquid produced in an infected part of the body

push¹ /pʊʃ/ v 1 vi/t use sudden or steady pressure to move (someone or something) forward, away from oneself, or to a different position: *He pushed the drawer shut.* 2 vt try to force (someone) by continual urging 3 vt sell (illegal drugs) 4 **be pushing** infml be nearly (a stated age) 5 **push one's luck** take a risk ~**ed** adj not having enough: *pushed for time* ~**er** n seller of illegal drugs

push around phr vt treat roughly and unfairly

push for phr vt demand urgently and forcefully

push off phr vi infml go away

push² n 1 act of pushing 2 large planned attack and advance 3 **at a push** if necessary 4 **if/when push**

comes to the shove if action must be taken 5 **give/get the push** infml dismiss/be dismissed from a job

push-but·ton /'· ,·/ n small button pressed to operate something

push·o·ver /'pʌʃ,oʷvər/ n [S] infml 1 something very easy to do or win 2 someone easily influenced or deceived

push-up /'· ·/ n form of exercise where one lies face down and pushes with one's arms

push·y /'pʊʃiʸ/ adj too forceful in getting things done, esp. for one's own advantage

pu·sil·lan·i·mous /,pyuʷsə'lænəməs/ adj fml cowardly

pus·sy¹ /'pʊsiʸ/ also **puss** /pʊs/, **pus·sy·cat** /'pʊsiʸ,kæt/ — n (child's name for) a cat

pussy² n taboo sl the female sex organ

pus·sy·foot /'pʊsiʸ,fʊt/ vi act too carefully

pus·tule /'pʌstʃuʷl/ n med small raised diseased spot on the skin

put /pʊt/ vt put, pres. p. **-tt-** 1 move, place, or fix to, on, or in the stated place 2 cause to be: *She put her books in order.* | *Put your mistakes right at once.* 3 express in words 4 express officially for judgment: *I'll put your suggestions to the committee.* 5 write down

put around phr vt spread (bad or false news)

put across phr vt cause to be understood

put aside phr vt save (money)

put away phr vt 1 remove to its usual storing place 2 infml eat (usu. large quantities of food) 3 place (someone) in prison or a hospital for crazy people

put back phr vt delay

put by phr vt PUT **aside**

put down phr vt 1 control; defeat: *put down a rebellion* 2 record in writing 3 embarrass: *He really put her down.* 4 kill (an old or sick animal) 5 cause to feel unimportant 6 pay (an amount) as part of the cost of something with a promise to pay the rest over a period of time n

put down to phr vt state that (something) is caused by

put forward phr vt suggest

put in phr vt 1 do (work) or spend (time) on work 2 interrupt by saying 3 (of a ship) enter a port

put in for phr vt make a formal request for

put into phr vt add (something) to (something): *Put more effort into your work!*

put off phr vt 1 delay 2 discourage 3 cause to dislike

put on *phr vt* **1** cover (part of) the body with (esp. clothing) **2** operate (a radio, light, etc.) by pressing or turning a button **3** increase: *She's put on weight.* **4** provide: *They're putting on another train.* **5** perform (a play, show, etc.) on stage **6** pretend to have (a feeling, quality, etc.) **7** deceive playfully

put onto *phr vt* give information about

put out *phr vt* **1** cause to stop burning or shining **2** trouble or annoy **3** broadcast or print **4 put oneself out** take trouble

put over *phr vt* PUT across

put over on *phr vt* put one over on deceive

put through *phr vt* **1** connect (a telephone caller) **2** cause to suffer or experience

put to *phr vt* **1** ask (a question) of or make (an offer) to **2** suggest to (someone) that **3 be hard put to** find it difficult to

put up *phr vt* **1** raise **2** put in a public place: *put up a notice* **3** provide food and a bed for **4** make; offer: *He didn't put up much of a fight.* **5** offer for sale **6** supply (money needed)

put up to *phr vt* give the idea of doing (esp. something bad)

put up with *phr vt* suffer without complaining

pu·ta·tive /ˈpyuˑtətɪv/ *adj fml* generally supposed to be or to become

put-down /ˈ· ·/ *n infml* words that make someone feel unimportant or hurt

put-on /ˈ· ·/ *n infml* something not intended seriously or sincerely

pu·tre·fy /ˈpyuˑtrəˌfaɪ/ *vi fml* decay –**faction** /ˌpyuˑtrəˈfækʃən/ *n* [U]

pu·tres·cent /pyuˈtresənt/ *adj fml* decaying

pu·trid /ˈpyuˑtrɪd/ *adj* **1** very decayed and smelling bad **2** worthless; greatly disliked

putsch /pʊtʃ/ *n* sudden attempt to remove a government by force

putt /pʌt/ *vi/t* (in GOLF) hit (the ball) along the ground towards or into the hole ~**er** *n* **1** CLUB¹ (3) for putting **2** person who putts

put·ty /ˈpʌtiʸ/ *n* [U] soft oily paste, esp. for fixing glass to window frames

put-up /ˈ· ·/ *adj infml* dishonestly arranged in advance

put-up·on /ˈ· ˌ··/ *adj* (of a person) used for someone else's advantage

puz·zle /ˈpʌzəl/ *v* **1** *vt* cause (someone) difficulty in the effort to understand **2** *vi* try hard to find the answer ♦ *n* **1** game or toy to exercise the mind **2** something that puzzles one

puzzle out *phr vt* find the answer to by thinking hard

PVC /ˌpiʸ viʸ ˈsiʸ/ *n* [U] type of plastic

pyg·my /ˈpɪgmiʸ/ *n* **1** (*usu. cap.*) member of an African race of very small people **2** very small person

py·lon /ˈpaɪlɑn/ *n* tall structure supporting wires that carry electricity

pyr·a·mid /ˈpɪrəmɪd/ *n* **1** solid figure with 4 sides, each having 3 angles, that slope up to meet at a point **2** large stone building in this shape, used as the burial place of kings, etc., in ancient Egypt

pyre /paɪər/ *n* high mass of wood for burning a dead body

Py·rex /ˈpaɪreks/ *n* [U] *tdmk* strong glass used in making cooking containers

py·ro·tech·nics /ˌpaɪərəˈtekniks/ *fml* [P] a splendid show of FIREWORKS

py·thon /ˈpaɪθɑn, -θən/ *n* large tropical snake that crushes the animals it eats

Q

Q, q /kyuʷ/ the 17th letter of the English alphabet

QED /ˌkyuʷ iʸ ˈdiʸ/ there is the proof of my argument

qua /kwɑ/ *prep fml* thought of only as

quack¹ /kwæk/ *vi, n* (make) the sound ducks make

quack² *n* person dishonestly claiming to be a doctor

quad¹ /kwɑd/ *n* square open space with four buildings around it as on a CAMPUS

quad² *n* QUADRUPLET

quad·ran·gle /ˈkwɑdræŋgəl/ *n* **1** QUADRILATERAL **2** *fml for* QUAD¹ **–rangular** /kwɑˈdræŋgyələr/ *adj*

quad·rant /ˈkwɑdrənt/ *n* **1** quarter of a circle **2** instrument for measuring angles

quad·ra·phon·ic /ˌkwɑdrəˈfɑnɪk◂/ *adj* giving sound from 4 different places

quad·ri·lat·er·al /ˌkwɑdrəˈlætərəl◂/ *n, adj* (flat figure) with 4 straight sides

quad·ru·ped /ˈkwɑdrəˌpɛd/ *n* creature with 4 legs

quad·ru·ple /kwɑˈdruʷpəl, ˈkwɑdrʊpəl/ *vi/t* multiply by 4 ♦ *adj, adv* 4 times as big

quad·ru·plet /kwɑˈdrʌplɪt, -ˈdruʷ-, ˈkwɑdrʊplɪt/ *n* any of 4 children born at the same time

quaff /kwɑf, kwæf/ *vt fml* drink deeply

quag·mire /ˈkwægmaɪər, ˈkwɑg-/ *n* **1** soft wet ground **2** bad situation that is difficult to escape from

quail¹ /kweʸl/ *n* quail *or* quails (meat of) a type of small bird

quail² *vi fml* be afraid; tremble

quaint /kweʸnt/ *adj* attractively old-fashioned **–ly** *adv*

quake /kweʸk/ *vi* shake; tremble

Quak·er /ˈkweʸkər/ *n* member of a Christian religious group that opposes violence

qual·i·fi·ca·tion /ˌkwɑləfəˈkeʸʃən/ *n* **1** [C] something that limits the force of a statement **2** [U] act of qualifying **3** [C *often pl.*] proof that one has passed an examination **qualifications** *n* [P] (proof of having) the necessary ability, experience, or knowledge, esp. for a job

qual·i·fy /ˈkwɑləˌfaɪ/ *v* **1** *vi/t* (cause to) reach a necessary standard **2** *vt* limit the force or meaning of (a statement) **–fied** *adj* **1** having suitable qualifications **2** limited: *qualified approval*

qual·i·ta·tive /ˈkwɑləˌteʸt̬ɪv/ *adj* of or about quality

qual·i·ty /ˈkwɑlət̬iʸ/ *n* **1** [C;U] (high) degree of goodness **2** [C] something typical of a person or thing

qualm /kwɑm, kwɔm/ *n* uncomfortable feeling of unsureness

quan·da·ry /ˈkwɑndəriʸ/ *n* feeling of not knowing what to do

quan·ti·fi·er /ˈkwɑnt̬əˌfaɪər/ *n* (in grammar) a word or phrase that is used with a noun to show quantity, such as *much*, *few*, and *a lot of*

quan·ti·fy /ˈkwɑnt̬əˌfaɪ/ *vt fml* measure **–fiable** *adj*

quan·ti·ta·tive /ˈkwɑnt̬əˌteʸt̬ɪv/ *adj* of or about quantity

quan·ti·ty /ˈkwɑnt̬ət̬iʸ/ *n* **1** [U] the fact of being measurable, and amount **2** [C] amount; number – see also UNKNOWN QUANTITY

quan·tum /ˈkwɑnt̬əm/ *n* **–ta** /-t̬ə/ (in PHYSICS) fixed amount

quantum leap /ˌ·· ˈ·/ *n* very large and important advance or improvement

quantum the·o·ry /ˈ·· ˌ···/ *n* [U] idea that ENERGY travels in quanta

quar·an·tine /ˈkwɔrənˌtiʸn, ˈkwɑr-/ *n* [U] period when a sick person or animal is kept away from others so the disease cannot spread ♦ *vt* put in quarantine

quark /kwɔrk, kwɑrk/ *n* smallest possible piece of material forming the substances which atoms are made

quar·rel¹ /ˈkwɔrəl, ˈkwɑ-/ *n* **1** angry argument **2** cause for or point of disagreement

quarrel² *vi* **1**– have an ARGUMENT (1) ~ **some** *adj* likely to argue

quarrel with *phr vt* disagree with

quar·ry¹ /ˈkwɔriʸ, ˈkwɑ-/ *n* place where stone, sand, etc., are dug out ♦ *vt* dig from a quarry

quarry² *n* person or animal being hunted

quart /kwɔrt/ *n* a measure of amount equal to two pints

quar·ter /ˈkwɔrt̬ər/ *n* **1** [C] a 4th part of a whole: *a quarter of a mile* **2** [C] 15 minutes: *quarter to 10* **3** [C] coin equal to one fourth of a dollar; 25 cents **4** [C] 3 months of the year **5** [C] part of a town: *the student quarter* **6** [C] person or place from which something comes: *no help from that quarter* **7** [U] *fml* giving of life to a defeated enemy ♦ *vt* **1** divide into 4 parts **2** provide lodgings for **quarters** *n* [P] (1) accommodation (ACCOMMODATE) **2 at close quarters** near together

quar·ter·back /ˈkwɔrt̬ərˌbæk/ *n* football player who directs the offense

quar·ter·deck /ˈkwɔrt̬ərˌdɛk/ *n* top part of a ship, used only by officers

quar·ter·fi·nal /ˌkwɔrtərˈfaɪnl/ n any of 4 matches where those that win play in SEMIFINALs

quar·ter·ly /ˈkwɔrtərliʲ/ adj, adv (happening) 4 times a year ♦ n quarterly magazine

quar·ter·mas·ter /ˈkwɔrtərˌmæstər/ n military officer in charge of supplies

quar·tet /kwɔrˈtɛt/ n (music for) 4 musicians

quar·to /ˈkwɔrtoʷ/ n large size of paper for books

quartz /kwɔrts/ n [U] hard mineral used in making very exact clocks

qua·sar /ˈkweʲzɑr/ n very bright very distant starlike object

quash /kwɑʃ/ vt 1 officially refuse to accept 2 put an end to: quash a rebellion

quat·er·cen·ten·a·ry /ˌkwɑtərsɛnˈtɛnəriʲ/ n 400 years after a particular event

quat·rain /ˈkwɑtreʲn/ n 4 lines of poetry

qua·ver /ˈkweʲvər/ vi (of a voice or music) shake ♦ n a shaking in the voice ~y adj

quay /kiʲ/ n place in a HARBOR by which ships stop and unload

quea·sy /ˈkwiʲziʲ/ adj 1 feeling one is going to be sick 2 uncertain about the rightness of doing something

queen /kwiʲn/ n 1 a female ruler b king's wife 2 leading female: a beauty queen 3 leading female insect in a group: a queen bee 4 sl male HOMOSEXUAL ~ly adj like, or suitable for, a queen

queer /kwɪər/ adj 1 strange 2 infml slightly ill 3 infml derog for HOMOSEXUAL ♦ n infml derog male HOMOSEXUAL

quell /kwɛl/ vt defeat; crush

quench /kwɛntʃ/ vt 1 satisfy (thirst) by drinking 2 put out (flames)

quer·u·lous /ˈkwɛrələs, ˈkwɛryə-/ adj fml complaining

que·ry /ˈkwɪəriʲ/ n question or doubt ♦ vt express doubt or unsureness about

quest /kwɛst/ n fml long search

ques·tion¹ /ˈkwɛstʃən/ n 1 [C] sentence or phrase asking for information 2 [C] matter to be settled; problem 3 [C;U] doubt: His honesty is beyond question. 4 in question being talked about 5 out of the question impossible 6 there's no question of there's no possibility of

question² vt 1 ask (someone) questions 2 have doubts about ~able adj 1 uncertain 2 perhaps not true or honest ~er n

question mark /ˈ·· ˌ·/ n mark (?) written at the end of a question

ques·tion·naire /ˌkwɛstʃəˈnɛər/ n set of questions asked to obtain information

quib·ble /ˈkwɪbəl/ vi argue about small unimportant points **quibble** n

quiche /kiʲʃ/ n flat pastry case filled with eggs, cheese, vegetables, etc.

quick¹ /kwɪk/ adj 1 fast 2 easily showing anger: a quick temper ♦ adv ~ly adv ~en vi/t make or become quicker ~ness n [U]

quick² n 1 [U] flesh to which the nails of fingers and toes are joined 2 cut (a person) to the quick hurt a person's feelings deeply

quick·ie /ˈkwɪkiʲ/ n something made or done in a hurry

quick·sand /ˈkwɪksænd/ n [U] wet sand which sucks things down

quick·step /ˈkwɪkstɛp/ n dance with fast steps

quick-wit·ted /ˌ·ˈ···◄/ adj swift to understand and act

quid pro quo /ˌkwɪd proʷ ˈkwoʷ/ n something given in fair exchange

qui·es·cent /kwaɪˈɛsənt, kwiʲ-/ adj fml inactive (for the present)

qui·et /ˈkwaɪət/ adj 1 with little noise 2 calm; untroubled: a quiet life ♦ n [U] 1 quietness 2 keep something quiet keep something a secret ♦ vi/t make or become quiet ~ly adv ~ness n [U]

qui·e·tude /ˈkwaɪəˌtuʷd, -ˌtyuʷd/ n [U] fml calmness; stillness

quill /kwɪl/ n 1 long feather 2 pen made from this 3 sharp prickle on some animals, esp. the PORCUPINE

quilt /kwɪlt/ n cloth covering for a bed, filled with feathers, etc. ~ed made with cloth containing soft material with stitching across it

quince /kwɪns/ n hard fruit like an apple

qui·nine /ˈkwaɪnaɪn/ n [U] drug used for treating MALARIA

quin·tes·sence /kwɪnˈtɛsəns/ n fml perfect type or example –**tessential** /ˌkwɪntəˈsɛnʃəl, -tʃəl/ adj

quint /kwɪnt/ n QUINTUPLET

quin·tet /kwɪnˈtɛt/ n (music for) 5 musicians

quin·tu·plet /kwɪnˈtʌplɪt, -ˈtuʷ-, -ˈtyuʷ-, ˈkwɪntʊplɪt/ n any of 5 children born at the same time

quip¹ /kwɪp/ n clever amusing remark ♦ vi –pp– make a quip

quirk /kwɜrk/ n 1 strange happening or accident 2 strange habit or way of behaving ~y adj

quit /kwɪt/ vi/t quitted or quit, pres. p. –tt– stop (doing something) and leave ~ter n person who lacks the courage to finish things when he/ she meets difficulties

quite /kwaɪt/ predeterminer, adv 1

completely; perfectly: *not quite right*
2 very; rather: *quite cold* **3 quite
a/an** unusual: *quite a party* | *It's
quite something to be a senator at 30.*

quits /kwɪts/ *adj* back on an equal
level with someone after an argument, repaying money, etc.

quiv·er¹ /'kwɪvər/ *vi/t* (cause to)
tremble a little **quiver** *n*

quiver² *n* container for ARROWS

quix·ot·ic /kwɪk'sɑtɪk/ *adj* doing
foolishly brave things in order to be
helpful

quiz /kwɪz/ *n* **-zz-** **1** short examination **2** game where questions are
asked ♦ *vt* **-zz-** ask questions of
(someone), esp. repeatedly

quiz·mas·ter /'kwɪzˌmæstər/ *n* person who asks questions in a quiz
game

quiz·zi·cal /'kwɪzɪkəl/ *adj* (of a
smile or look) suggesting a question
or secret knowledge **~ly** /-kliʸ/ *adv*

quoit /kwɔɪt, kɔɪt/ *n* ring to be
thrown over a small post in a game

quo·rate /'kwɔrɪt, 'kwoʷrɪt/ *adj* (of
a meeting) having a quorum
present

quo·rum /'kwɔrəm, 'kwoʷrəm/ *n*
number of people who must be
present for a meeting to be held

quo·ta /'kwoʷt̬ə/ *n* amount officially to be produced, received, etc.,
as one's share

quo·ta·tion /kwoʷ'teʸʃən/ *n* **1** [C]
words QUOTEd (1) **2** [U] act of quot-
ing **3** [C] amount QUOTEd (2)

quotation marks /·'··· ·/ *n* marks
(' or ') showing the start or end of
a QUOTATION (1)

quote /kwoʷt/ *v* **1** *vi/t* repeat the
words of (a person, book, etc.) in
speech or writing **2** *vt* offer as a
price for work to be done ♦ *n* **1**
infml QUOTATION (1, 3) **2 in quotes**
in QUOTATION MARKS

quo·tient /'kwoʷʃənt/ *n* number
got by dividing

q.v. (used for telling readers to look
in another place in the same book to
find something out)

R

R, r /ɑr/ the 18th letter of the English alphabet – see also THREE R'S

R *written abbrev. for:* **1** river **2** (of a film) restricted; that can only be seen by persons under 17 if an adult comes with them

rab·bi /ˈræbaɪ/ *n* Jewish priest

rab·bit /ˈræbɪt/ *n* common small animal with long ears, often kept as a pet or eaten

rab·ble /ˈræbəl/ *n* disordered noisy crowd

rabble-rous·ing /ˈ··ˌ···/ *adj* causing hatred and violence among a crowd of listeners

Ra·be·lai·si·an /ˌræbəˈleɪʒən, -ziˈən/ *adj* full of jokes about sex and the body that are shocking but harmless

rab·id /ˈræbɪd/ *adj* **1** suffering from rabies **2** (of feelings or opinions) unreasoningly violent

ra·bies /ˈreɪbiz/ *n* [U] disease passed on by the bite of an infected animal and causing madness and death

rac·coon /ræˈkuʷn/ *n* small North American animal with a tail with black and white rings round it

race[1] /reɪs/ *n* competition in speed: *a horse race* | (fig.) *a race against time* ♦ *vi/t* **1** compete in a race (against) **2** (cause to) go very fast

race[2] *n* **1** [C;U] (any of) the main divisions of human beings, each of a different physical type **2** [C] group of people with the same history, language, etc.: *the German race* **3** [C] breed or type of animal or plant

race·course /ˈreɪs-kɔrs, -koʷrs/ *n* RACETRACK

ra·cial /ˈreɪʃəl/ *adj* **1** of a RACE[2] **2** between RACES[2]: *racial tension* ~**ly** *adv*

ra·cis·m /ˈreɪsɪzəm/ *n* [U] **1** belief that one's own RACE[2] is best **2** dislike or unfair treatment of other races **racist** *adj, n*

rack[1] /ræk/ *n* **1** frame or shelf with bars, hooks, etc., for holding things **2** instrument for hurting people by stretching their bodies **3** bar with teeth, moved along by a wheel with similar teeth

rack[2] *vt* **1** cause great pain or anxiety to **2** **rack one's brains** think very hard

rack[3] *n* **rack and ruin** ruined condition, esp. of a building

rack·et[1], **racquet** /ˈrækɪt/ *n* instrument with a netlike part for hitting the ball in games like tennis

racket[2] *n* **1** [S] loud noise **2** [C] dishonest business

rack·e·teer /ˌrækəˈtɪər/ *n* someone who works a RACKET[2] (2)

rac·on·teur /ˌrækɑnˈtɜr/ *n fml* someone good at telling stories

rac·y /ˈreɪsiʸ/ *adj* (of a story, etc.) amusing, full of life, and perhaps dealing with sex

ra·dar /ˈreɪdɑr/ *n* [U] apparatus or method of finding solid objects by receiving and measuring the speed of radio waves seen as a SCREEN

ra·di·al[1] /ˈreɪdiʸəl/ *adj* like a wheel

radial[2] also **radial tire** /ˌ··· ˈ·/ — *n* car tire with cords inside the rubber that go across the edge of the wheel rather than along it, so as to give better driving control

ra·di·ant /ˈreɪdiʸənt/ *adj* **1** sending out light or heat in all directions **2** (of a person) showing love and happiness ~**ly** *adv* -**ance** *n* [U]

ra·di·ate /ˈreɪdiʸeɪt/ *vi/t* send out light, heat, etc.:(fig.) *She radiates happiness.*

ra·di·a·tion /ˌreɪdiʸˈeɪʃən/ *n* [U] **1** (act of) radiating **2** RADIOACTIVITY

ra·di·a·tor /ˈreɪdiʸeɪtər/ *n* **1** apparatus, esp. of hot water pipes, for heating a building **2** apparatus that keeps a car's engine cool

rad·i·cal /ˈrædɪkəl/ *adj* **1** (of a change) thorough and complete **2** in favor of complete political change ♦ *n* RADICAL (2) person ~**ly** -kliʸ *adv*

rad·i·i /ˈreɪdiʸaɪ/ *pl. of* RADIUS

ra·di·o /ˈreɪdiʸoʷ/ *n* **1** [U] sending or receiving sounds through the air by electrical waves **2** [C] apparatus to receive such sounds **3** [U] radio broadcasting industry **4 on the radio: a** (of a sound) broadcast **b** (of a person) broadcasting

ra·di·o·ac·tiv·i·ty /ˌreɪdiʸoʷækˈtɪvətiʸ/ *n* [U] **1** quality, harmful in large amounts to living things, that some ELEMENTS have of giving out ENERGY by the breaking up of atoms **2** the energy given out in this way: *exposed to radioactivity* -**tive** /ˌreɪdiʸoʷˈæktɪv◂/ *adj*

ra·di·og·ra·phy /ˌreɪdiʸˈɑgrəfiʸ/ *n* [U] taking of photographs made with X-RAYS, usu. for medical reasons -**pher** *n* [C] person who practices radiography

ra·di·ol·o·gy /ˌreɪdiʸˈɑlədʒiʸ/ *n* [U] study and medical use of radioactivity -**gist** *n* [C]

radio tel·e·scope /ˌ··· ˈ···/ *n* radio receiver for following the movements of stars and other objects in space

rad·ish /ˈrædɪʃ/ n small plant with a round red root, eaten raw

ra·di·um /ˈreɪdiəm/ n [U] radioactive (RADIOACTIVITY) metal used in the treatment of diseases

ra·di·us /ˈreɪdiəs/ n –**dii** /-diˌaɪ/ **1** (length of) a straight line from the center of a circle to its side **2** stated circular area measured from its center point: *houses within a ten-mile radius of the town*

raf·fi·a /ˈræfiə/ n [U] soft string-like substance from leaves of a PALM tree, used to make baskets, etc.

raf·fish /ˈræfɪʃ/ adj (of a person) happy, wild, and not very respectable

raf·fle /ˈræfəl/ n way of getting money by selling chances to win prizes ♦ vt offer as a raffle prize

raft /ræft/ n flat, usu. wooden, floating structure, used esp. as a boat

raf·ter /ˈræftər/ n large sloping beam that holds up a roof

rag /ræg/ n **1** small piece of old cloth **2** old worn article of clothing **3** infml derog newspaper

rag·bag /ˈrægbæg/ n confused mixture

rage /reɪdʒ/ n [C;U] **1** (sudden feeling of) extreme anger **2** all the rage very fashionable ♦ vi **1** be in a rage **2** (of bad weather, pain, etc.) be very violent

rag·ged /ˈrægɪd/ adj **1** old and torn **2** dressed in old torn clothes **3** rough; uneven: *a ragged beard* | (fig.) *a ragged performance* ~**ly** adv

rag·lan /ˈræglən/ adj (of an arm of a garment) joined at the neck rather than at the shoulder

rag·time /ˈrægtaɪm/ n [U] popular music of the 1920s, in which the strong notes of the tune come just before the main beats

raid /reɪd/ n **1** quick attack on an enemy position **2** unexpected visit by the police in search of crime ♦ vi/t make a raid (on): (fig.) *The children raided the kitchen for food.* ~**er** n

rail¹ /reɪl/ n **1** [C] fixed bar, esp. to hang things on or for protection **2** [C] line of metal bars which a train runs on **3** [U] railroad ♦ vt enclose or separate with rails ~**ing** n rail in a fence

rail² vi fml curse or complain angrily

rail·road /ˈreɪlroʊd/ vt **1** hurry (someone) unfairly **2** pass (a law) or carry out (a plan) quickly in spite of opposition ♦ n **1** track for trains **2** system of such tracks

rain¹ /reɪn/ n **1** [U] water falling from the clouds **2** [S] thick fall of anything: *a rain of questions* **3** as right as rain in perfect health **4**

(come) **rain or shine** whatever happens ~**y** adj **1** with lots of rain **2** for a rainy day for a time when money may be needed

rain² v **1** vi (of rain) fall **2** vi/t (cause to) fall thickly, like rain **3** rain cats and dogs rain very heavily

rain out /ˌ· ˈ·/ phr v stop because of rain: *The game was rained out.*

rain·bow /ˈreɪnboʊ/ n arch of different colors that appears in the sky after rain

rain check /ˈ· ·/ n request to claim later something offered now

rain·fall /ˈreɪnfɔːl/ n [C;U] amount of rain that falls in a certain time

rain for·est /ˈ· ˌ··/ n wet tropical forest

raise /reɪz/ vt **1** lift **2** make higher in amount, size, etc. **3** collect together: *raise an army* **4** produce and look after (children, animals, or crops) **5** mention or introduce (a subject) for consideration **6** a make (a noise) **b** cause people to make (a noise) or have feelings: *raise a laugh/raise doubts* **7** bring to an end (something that controls or forbids): *raise a siege* **8** raise Cain/hell/the roof infml become very angry ♦ n wage increase

rai·sin /ˈreɪzən/ n dried GRAPE

rai·son d'e·tre /ˌreɪzoʊn ˈdɛtrə/ n reason for existing

rake¹ /reɪk/ n gardening tool with a row of points at the end of a long handle

rake² vt **1** gather, loosen, or level with a rake **2** examine or shoot in a continuous sweeping movement

rake in phr vt infml earn or gain a lot of (money)

rake up phr vt **1** produce with difficulty by searching **2** remember and talk about (something that should be forgotten)

rake³ n man who leads a wild life with regard to drink and women

rake-off /ˈ· ·/ n infml usu. dishonest share of profits

rak·ish /ˈreɪkɪʃ/ adj wild and informal ~**ly** adv

ral·ly¹ /ˈræli/ n **1** large esp. political public meeting **2** motor race over public roads **3** long exchange of hits in tennis

rally² v **1** vi/t come or bring together (again) for a shared purpose **2** vi recover

rally around phr vi help in time of trouble

ram /ræm/ n **1** adult male sheep that can be the father of young **2** any machine that repeatedly drops or pushes a weight onto or into something ♦ vt –**mm**- **1** run into (something) very hard **2** force into place with heavy pressure: (fig.) *My father keeps ramming his ideas down my throat.*

RAM /ræm/ n [U] Random-Access Memory; computer memory holding information that is needed by the computer for a limited period, and can be searched in any order one likes

ram·ble¹ /ˈræmbəl/ n (long) country walk for pleasure

ramble² vi 1 go on a ramble 2 talk or write in a disordered wandering way –**bler** n –**bling** adj 1 (of speech or writing) disordered and wandering 2 (of a street, house, etc.) of irregular shape; winding 3 (of a plant) growing loosely in all directions

ram·bunc·tious /ræmˈbʌŋkʃəs/ adj too eager or active

ram·i·fi·ca·tion /ˌræməfəˈkeɪʃən/ n 1 branch of a system with many parts 2 any of the results that may follow from an action or decision

ramp /ræmp/ n 1 artificial slope connecting 2 levels 2 way onto or off of an EXPRESSWAY

ram·page /ˈræmpeɪdʒ, ræmˈpeɪdʒ/ vi rush about wildly or angrily ♦ n **on the rampage** rampaging

ram·pant /ˈræmpənt/ adj (of crime, disease, etc.) widespread and uncontrollable

ram·part /ˈræmpɑrt/ n wide bank or wall protecting a fort or city

ram·rod /ˈræmrɑd/ n stick for pushing explosive powder into or cleaning a gun

ram·shack·le /ˈræmˌʃækəl/ adj (of a building or vehicle) falling to pieces

ran /ræn/ past t. of RUN

ranch /ræntʃ/ n 1 large farm where animals are raised 2 style of house all on one floor

ran·cid /ˈrænsɪd/ adj (of butter, cream, etc.) unpleasant because not fresh

ran·cor /ˈræŋkər/ n [U] fml bitter unforgiving hatred –**corous** adj

R and D /ˌɑr ən ˈdiˀ/ n [U] research and development; part of a business concerned with studying new ideas, planning new products, etc.

ran·dom /ˈrændəm/ adj without any fixed plan ♦ n **at random** in a random way ~**ly** adv ~**ness** n [U]

rang /ræŋ/ past t. of RING

range¹ /reɪndʒ/ n 1 [S;U] distance over which something has an effect or limits between which it varies: *He shot her at close range.* | *a wide range of temperature* 2 [C] area where shooting is practiced or MISSILEs are tested 3 [C] connected line of mountains or hills 4 [the+S] stretch of grassy land where cattle feed 5 [C] set of different objects of

the same kind, esp. for sale 6 large STOVE: *a gas range*

range² v 1 vi vary between limits 2 vi wander freely: *The conversation ranged over many topics.* 3 vt put in position

rang·er /ˈreɪndʒər/ n forest or park guard

rank¹ /ræŋk/ n 1 [C;U] position in the army, navy, etc.: *the rank of colonel* 2 [C;U] (high) social position 3 [C] line of people or things 4 **keep/break rank(s)** (of soldiers) stay in line/fail to stay in line 5 **of the first rank** among the best 6 **pull rank (on someone)** use unfairly the advantage of one's higher position ♦ v 1 vi/t be or put in a certain class 2 vt arrange in regular order **ranks** n [P] ordinary soldiers below the rank of SERGEANT

rank² adj 1 (of smell or taste) very bad and unpleasant 2 (of something bad) complete: *a rank beginner at the job* 3 (of a plant) too thick and widespread

rank and file /ˌ· · ˈ·/ n [S] ordinary people in an organization, not the leaders

ran·kle /ˈræŋkəl/ vi continue to be remembered with bitterness and anger

ran·sack /ˈrænsæk/ vt 1 search thoroughly and roughly 2 search and rob

ran·som /ˈrænsəm/ n money paid to free a prisoner ♦ vt free by paying a ransom

rant /rænt/ vi talk wildly and loudly ♦ n [U]

rap¹ /ræp/ n 1 quick light blow 2 **take the rap (for)** infml receive the punishment (for someone else's crime) 3 **beat the rap** avoid punishment ♦ v -pp- 1 vi/t strike quickly and lightly 2 vt say sharply and suddenly

rap² vi sl -pp- a talk b speak the words of a song to a musical ACCOMPANIMENT with a steady beat

ra·pa·cious /rəˈpeɪʃəs/ adj fml taking all one can, esp. by force ~**ness**, –**pacity** /rəˈpæsət̬iˀ/ n [U]

rape¹ /reɪp/ vt have sex with (someone) against their will ♦ n [C;U] 1 act of raping 2 spoiling **rapist** n

rape² n [U] plant grown for the oil produced from its seeds

rap·id /ˈræpɪd/ adj fast ~**ly** adv ~**ity** /rəˈpɪdət̬iˀ/ n [U]

rapid-fire /ˈ··· ·/ adj (of a gun) able to fire shots quickly one after the other: (fig.) *rapid-fire jokes/questions*

rap·ids /ˈræpɪdz/ n [P] quickly flowing rocky part of a river

ra·pi·er /ˈreɪpiˀər/ n long thin sharp sword

rap·port /ræˈpɔr, ræˈpoʷr, rə-/ n [U] close agreement and understanding

rapt /ræpt/ adj having one's whole mind: *rapt attention*

rap·ture /ˈræptʃər/ n [U] fml great joy and delight **–turous** adj

rare¹ /reər/ adj uncommon **~ly** adv not often **~ness** n [U]

rare² adj (of meat) lightly cooked

rar·e·fied /ˈreərəˌfaɪd/ adj 1 (of air in high places) with less oxygen than usual 2 very high or grand

rar·ing /ˈreərɪŋ/ adj very eager: *We're raring to go.*

rar·i·ty /ˈreərəti/ n 1 [U] being uncommon 2 [C] something uncommon

ras·cal /ˈræskəl/ n 1 misbehaving child 2 dishonest person

rash¹ /ræʃ/ adj without thinking enough of the (possibly bad) results **~ly** adv **~ness** n [U]

rash² n red spots on the skin, caused by illness: *He broke out in* (= became covered in) *a rash.* (fig.) *a rash* (= sudden large number) *of complaints*

rasp /ræsp/ vt 1 rub with something rough 2 say in a rough voice ♦ 1 [C] tool for making metal, wood, etc. smooth 2 [S] rasping sound **–ing** adj (of a sound) unpleasantly rough

rasp·ber·ry /ˈræzˌberi, -bəri/ n 1 red berry, often eaten 2 rude sound made by putting one's tongue out and blowing

ras·ta·fa·ri·an /ˌræstəˈfeəriʲən◂/ also **ras·ta** /ˈræstə/ — n (often cap.) follower of a religion from Jamaica **~ism** n

rat /ræt/ n 1 animal like a large mouse 2 worthless disloyal person ♦ v **–tt-**

rat on phr vt infml act disloyally; BETRAY

ratch·et /ˈrætʃɪt/ n toothed wheel or bar that allows a part of a machine to move past it in one direction only

rate¹ /reʲt/ n 1 amount measured in relation to another: *a death rate of 500 a year* 2 payment fixed according to a standard scale 3 of the (numbered) quality: *a first-rate performer* 4 **at any rate** in any case 5 **at this/that rate** if events continue in the same way – see also FLAT RATE

rate² vt 1 have the stated opinion about 2 deserve 3 infml have a good opinion of: *I really rate her as a singer.*

rath·er /ˈræðər/ predeterminer, adv 1 fml to some degree: *a rather cold day* 2 more willingly: *I'd rather have tea than coffee.* 3 more exactly: *He's done it, or rather he says he has.*

rat·i·fy /ˈrætəˌfaɪ/ vt approve (a formal agreement) and make it official **–fication** /ˌrætəfəˈkeʲʃən/ n [U]

rat·ing /ˈreʲtɪŋ/ n statement of the quality of a thing in comparison to others of its kind: *Buyers gave the new model a high rating.* **ratings** n [P] list of the positions of popularity given to television shows

ra·ti·o /ˈreʲʃiʲoʷ, ˈreʲʃoʷ/ n **–os** way one amount is related to another: *The ratio of adults to children was 4 to 1.*

ra·tion /ˈræʃən, ˈreʲ-/ n amount of something allowed to one person for a period ♦ vt 1 limit (someone) to a fixed ration 2 limit and control (supplies) **rations** n [P] supplies of food

ra·tion·al /ˈræʃənəl/ adj 1 (of ideas and behavior) sensible 2 (of a person) able to reason **~ly** adv **~ity** /ˌræʃəˈnæləti/ n [U]

ra·tio·nale /ˌræʃəˈnæl/ n [C;U] reasons and principles on which a practice is based

ra·tion·al·ize /ˈræʃənəˌlaɪz/ vi/t 1 give or claim a rational explanation for (esp. strange behavior) **–ization** /ˌræʃənələˈzeʲʃən/ n [C;U]

rat race /ˈ· ·/ n endless competition for success in business

rat·tle /ˈrætl/ v 1 vi/t (cause to) make continuous quick hard noises 2 vi move quickly while making these noises 3 vt make anxious or afraid ♦ n 1 [C] toy or other instrument that rattles 2 [S] rattling noise

rattle off phr vt repeat quickly and easily from memory

rattle on/away phr vi talk quickly and continuously

rattle through phr vt perform quickly

rat·tle·snake /ˈrætlˌsneʲk/ n poisonous North American snake that rattles its tail

rat·ty /ˈræti/ adj untidy or in bad condition

rat trap /ˈ· ·/ n dirty old building that is in very bad condition

rau·cous /ˈrɔkəs/ adj unpleasantly loud and rough **~ly** adv **~ness** n [U]

raunch·y /ˈrɔntʃiʲ, ˈrɑn-/ adj infml 1 dirty, SLOVENLY 2 OBSCENE **–ily** adv **–iness** n [U]

rav·age /ˈrævɪdʒ/ vt 1 ruin and destroy 2 rob (an area) violently **ravages** n [P] destroying effects

rave /reʲv/ vi 1 talk wildly as if crazy 2 talk with extreme admiration ♦ n full of very eager praise: *rave reviews in the papers* **raving** adj, adv wildly (crazy)

ra·ven /ˈreʲvən/ n large black bird of the CROW family

rav·e·nous /ˈrævənəs/ adj very hungry **~ly** adv

ra·vine /rəˈviʲn/ n deep narrow valley with steep sides

rav·ish /ˈrævɪʃ/ vt fml 1 lit RAPE[1] 2 fill with delight ~**ing** adj very beautiful

raw /rɔ/ adj 1 not cooked 2 not yet treated for use: raw materials 3 not yet trained or experienced 4 (of skin) painful; sore 5 (of weather) cold and wet ~**ness** n [U]

raw deal /ˌ· ˈ·/ n unfair treatment

ray /reɪ/ n narrow beam of light or other force: (fig.) a ray (= small bit) of hope

ray·on /ˈreɪɒn/ n [U] silk-like material made from plant substances

raze /reɪz/ vt fml make (buildings, cities, etc.) flat

ra·zor /ˈreɪzər/ n sharp instrument for removing hair, esp. from a man's face

raz·zle-daz·zle /ˌræzəl ˈdæzəl/ n infml [U] confusion resulting from too much noise or sensation

razz·ma·tazz /ˌræzməˈtæz/ n [U] infml noisy showy activity

Rd written abbrev. for: Road

re /riː, reɪ/ prep fml on the subject of; with regard to

-'re /ər/ short for: are: We're ready.

reach /riːtʃ/ v 1 vt arrive at 2 vi stretch out an arm or hand for some purpose 3 vi/t touch by doing this: It's too high; I can't reach it. 4 vt get by doing this: Reach me my hat. 5 vi/t stretch (as far as): The garden reaches down to the lake. 6 vt get a message to ♦ n 1 [S;U] distance one can reach 2 [C] part of a river

re·act /riˈækt/ vi 1 act or behave as a result 2 change when mixed with another substance

re·ac·tion /riˈækʃən/ 1 [C;U] (way of) reacting 2 [S;U] change back to a former condition 3 [U] quality of being reactionary

re·ac·tion·a·ry /riˈækʃəˌneriː/ n, adj (person) strongly opposed to change

re·ac·tor /riˈæktər/ n large machine that produces ENERGY from atoms

read /riːd/ v read read /red/ 1 vi/t look at and understand (something printed or written): read a newspaper 2 vi/t say (written words) to others: Read me a story. 3 vi (of something written) have (the stated form or meaning) or give (the stated idea): The letter reads as follows... | Her letters always read well. 4 vt (of a measuring instrument) show 5 vt understand from things seen or felt: I can't read his moods very well. 6 **read between the lines** find hidden meanings 7 **take something as read** accept something as true without any need to consider it further ~**able** adj interesting or easy to read

read·er /ˈriːdər/ n 1 someone who reads 2 schoolbook for beginners ~**ship** n [S] number or type of READERS (1)

read·ing /ˈriːdɪŋ/ n 1 [U] act or practice of reading 2 [C] opinion about the meaning of something 3 [C] figure shown by a measuring instrument 4 [U] something to be read: It makes (= is) interesting reading. 5 [U] knowledge gained through books

read·out /ˈriːdaʊt/ n [U] information produced from a computer in readable form

read·y /ˈrediː/ adj 1 prepared and fit for use 2 willing 3 (of thoughts or their expressions) quick: a ready wit ♦ adv in advance: ready-made clothes ~**ily** adv 1 willingly 2 easily ~**iness** n [U]

ready mon·ey /ˌ·· ˈ··/ n [U] coins and paper money that can be paid at once

re·a·gent /riˈeɪdʒənt/ n chemical that shows the presence of a particular substance

re·al /riːəl/ adj 1 actually existing 2 complete: a real idiot 3 **for real** serious(ly) ♦ adv very ~**ly** adv 1 in fact; truly 2 very 3 (shows interest, doubt, or displeasure)

real es·tate /ˈ·· ˌ·/ n [U] houses or land to be bought

re·a·lism /ˈriːəˌlɪzəm/ n [U] 1 accepting the way things really are in life 2 (in art and literature) showing things as they really are ~**list** n ~**lis·tic** /ˌriːəˈlɪstɪk/ adj

re·al·i·ty /riˈælətiː/ n 1 [U] real existence 2 [C;U] something or everything real 3 **in reality** in fact

re·a·lize /ˈriːəˌlaɪz/ v 1 vi/t (come to) have full knowledge and understanding (of) 2 vt make (a purpose, fear, etc.) real 3 vt be sold for ~**lization** /ˌriːələˈzeɪʃən/ n [U]

realm /relm/ n 1 fml kingdom 2 area of activity; world

real-time /ˈ· ·/ adj of or being very quick information handling by a computer

Real·tor /ˈriːəltər/ n tdmk person in the REAL ESTATE business who is a member of the National Association of Realtors

ream /riːm/ n 500 pieces of paper **reams** n [P] a lot of writing

reap /riːp/ vi/t cut and gather (a crop of grain): (fig.) He reaped (= gained) the benefit of all his hard work. ~**er** n – see also GRIM REAPER

rear[1] /rɪər/ n, adj [U] 1 back (part) 2 **bring up the rear** be last

rear[2] v 1 vt care for until fully grown 2 vi rise upright on the back legs 3 vt raise (the head)

rear·guard /ˈrɪərgɑrd/ n soldiers protecting the rear of an army

rearguard ac·tion /ˌ··· ˈ··/ n fight by the rearguard of an army being driven back by a victorious enemy

re·ar·ma·ment /riˈɑrməmənt/ n [U] providing a nation with weapons again, or with new weapons

rea·son¹ /ˈriʸzən/ n 1 [C;U] why something is or was done; cause 2 [U] power to think, understand and form opinions 3 [U] healthy mind that is not crazy: *to lose one's reason* (= go crazy) 4 [U] good sense 5 **stand to reason** be clear to all sensible people 6 **within reason** not beyond sensible limits

reason² v 1 vi use one's REASON¹ (2) 2 vt give as an opinion based on REASON¹ (2) ~**ing** n [U] steps in thinking about or understanding something

   reason with phr vt try to persuade by fair argument

rea·so·na·ble /ˈriʸznəbəl/ adj 1 showing fairness or good sense 2 not expensive –**bly** adv 1 sensibly 2 quite: *in reasonably good health*

re·as·sure /ˌriʸəˈʃʊər/ vt comfort and make free from worry –**surance** n [C;U]

re·bate /ˈriʸbeʸt/ n official return of part of a payment

reb·el¹ /ˈrebəl/ n person who rebels

re·bel² /rɪˈbel/ vi -ll- oppose or fight against someone in control

re·bel·lion /rɪˈbelyən/ n [C;U] (act of) rebelling –**lious** adj

re·birth /riʸˈbɜrθ, ˈriʸbɜrθ/ n [S] fml renewal (RENEW) of life; change of spirit

re·born /riʸˈbɔrn/ adj fml as if born again

re·bound /rɪˈbaʊnd/ vi fly back after hitting something ♦ n /ˈriʸbaʊnd/ **on the rebound: a** while rebounding **b** while in an unsettled state of mind as a result of failure in a relationship

   rebound on phr vt (of a bad action) harm (the doer)

re·buff /rɪˈbʌf/ n rough or cruel answer or refusal ♦ vt

re·buke /rɪˈbyuʷk/ vt fml speak to angrily and giving blame to ♦ n

re·but /rɪˈbʌt/ vt fml prove the falseness of ~**tal** n [C;U]

re·cal·ci·trant /rɪˈkælsətrənt/ adj fml refusing to obey –**trance** n [U]

re·call /rɪˈkɔl/ vt 1 remember 2 send for or take back ♦ /rɪˈkɔl, ˈriʸkɔl/ n 1 [U] ability to remember 2 [S;U] call to return

re·cant /rɪˈkænt/ vi/t fml say publicly that one no longer holds (a religious or political opinion) ~**ation** /ˌriʸkænˈteʸʃən/ n [C;U]

re·cap /ˈriʸkæp/ vi/t -pp- repeat (the chief points of something said) ♦ n

re·ca·pit·u·late /ˌriʸkəˈpɪtʃəleʸt/ vi/t fml recap –**lation** /ˌriʸkəˌpɪtʃəˈleʸʃən/ n [C;U]

re·cede /rɪˈsiʸd/ vi move back or away

re·ceipt /rɪˈsiʸt/ n 1 [C] written statement that one has received money 2 [U] fml receiving **receipts** n [P] money received from a business

re·ceive /rɪˈsiʸv/ vt 1 get; be given: *receive a letter/a nasty shock* 2 accept as a visitor or member 3 turn (radio waves) into sound or pictures –**ceived** adj generally accepted –**ceiver** n 1 part of a telephone that is held to the ear 2 radio or television set 3 official who looks after the affairs of a BANKRUPT person 4 person who buys and sells stolen property 5 football player in a position to catch a pass

re·cent /ˈriʸsənt/ adj that happened or started only a short time ago ~**ly** adv not long ago

re·cep·ta·cle /rɪˈseptəkəl/ n fml container

re·cep·tion /rɪˈsepʃən/ n 1 [C] welcome: *a friendly reception* 2 [C] large formal party 3 [U] place where visitors to a hotel or other large building are welcomed 4 [U] quality of radio or television signals ~**ist** n person who welcomes and deals with visitors to a hotel, store, etc.

re·cep·tive /rɪˈseptɪv/ adj willing to consider new ideas ~**ness**, –**tivity** /ˌriʸsepˈtɪvəṭiʸ/ n [U]

re·cess /ˈriʸses, rɪˈses/ n 1 pause for rest during a working period, esp. for school children 2 space in an inside wall for shelves, cupboards, etc. 3 secret inner place ♦ /rɪˈses/ vt make or put into a RECESS (2)

re·ces·sion /rɪˈseʃən/ n 1 period of reduced business activity 2 act of receding (RECEED)

re·cher·ché /rəˌʃeərˈʃeʸ/ adj rare and strange

re·ci·pe /ˈresəpiʸ/ n set of cooking instructions

re·cip·i·ent /rɪˈsɪpiʸənt/ n fml person who receives something

re·cip·ro·cal /rɪˈsɪprəkəl/ adj fml given and received in return; MUTUAL ~**ly** /-kliʸ/ adv

re·cip·ro·cate /rɪˈsɪprəˌkeʸt/ vi/t fml give or do (something) in return –**cation** /rɪˌsɪprəˈkeʸʃən/ n [U]

re·cit·al /rɪˈsaɪṭl/ n performance of music or poetry by one person or a small group

re·cite /rɪˈsaɪt/ v 1 vi/t say (something learned) aloud in public 2 vt

fml give a detailed account or list of
recitation /ˌresə'teʸʃən/ *n* [C;U]

reck·less /'reklɪs/ *adj* not caring about danger **~ly** *adv* **~ness** *n* [U]

reck·on /'rekən/ *vt* **1** calculate; add up **2** consider; regard **3** guess; suppose **~ing** *n* [U] **1** calculation **2** punishment: *a day of reckoning*

reckon *phr vt* **1** take account of in one's plans **2** have to deal with **3 to be reckoned with** to be taken seriously as a possible opponent, competitor, etc.

re·claim /rɪ'kleʸm/ *vt* **1** ask for the return of **2** make (land) fit for use
reclamation /ˌreklə'meʸʃən/ *n* [U]

re·cline /rɪ'klaɪn/ *vi fml* lie back or down; rest **recliner** *n* chair that folds back

re·cluse /'rekluʷs, rɪ'kluʷs/ *n* someone who lives alone on purpose

rec·og·nize /'rekəgˌnaɪz/ *vt* **1** know again (as someone or something one has met before) **2** accept as being legal or real **3** be prepared to admit **4** show official gratefulness for **~nizable** /'rekəgˌnaɪzəbəl, ˌrekəg-'naɪ-/ *adj* **~nition** /ˌrekəg'nɪʃən/ *n* [U]

re·coil /rɪ'kɔɪl/ *vi* **1** move back suddenly in fear or dislike **2** (of a gun) spring back when fired **recoil** /'riʸkɔɪl, rɪ'kɔɪl/ *n* [S;U]

rec·ol·lect /ˌrekə'lekt/ *vi/t* remember **~ion** /-'lekʃən/ *n* [C;U] memory

rec·om·mend /ˌrekə'mend/ *vt* **1** praise as being good for a purpose **2** advise: *I'd recommend caution.* **3** (of a quality) to make (someone or something) attractive: *A hotel with little to recommend it.* **~ation** /ˌrekəmen'deʸʃən, -men-/ *n* [C;U]

rec·om·pense /'rekəmˌpens/ *n* [S;U] *fml* reward or payment for trouble or suffering ♦ *vt fml* give recompense to

rec·on·cile /'rekənˌsaɪl/ *vt* **1** make friendly again **2** find agreement between (2 opposing things) **~ciliation** /ˌrekənˌsɪliʸ'eʸʃən/ *n* [U]

reconcile to *phr vt* cause (someone) to accept (something unpleasant)

re·con·di·tion /ˌriʸkən'dɪʃən/ *vt* repair and bring back into working order: *a reconditioned engine*

re·con·nais·sance /rɪ'kɑnəsəns, -zəns/ *n* [C;U] (act of) reconnoitering

re·con·noi·ter /ˌriʸkə'nɔɪtər, ˌre-/ *vi/t* go near (the place where an enemy is) to find out information

re·con·sid·er /ˌriʸkən'sɪdər/ *vi/t* think again and change one's mind (about)

re·con·struc·tion /ˌriʸkən'strʌkʃən/ *n* **1** [C] repeating of events in a crime, etc. to find new information

2 [U] (cap.) period in American history after the Civil War

re·cord¹ /rɪ'kɔrd/ *v* **1** *vt* write down so that it will be known **2** *vi/t* preserve (sound or a television show) so that it can be heard or seen again **3** *vt* (of an instrument) show by measuring

re·cord² /'rekərd/ *n* **1** written statement of facts, events, etc. **2** known facts about past behavior: *his criminal record* **3** best yet done: *the world record for the long jump* **4** circular piece of plastic on which sound is stored for playing back **5 for the record** to be reported as official **6 off the record** unofficial(ly) **7 on the record: a** (of facts or events) (ever) recorded: *the coldest winter on record* **b** (of a person) having publicly said, as if for written records ♦ *adj* better, faster, etc., than ever before: *finished in record time*

re·cord·er /rɪ'kɔrdər/ *n* **1** simple musical instrument played by blowing **2** TAPE RECORDER

re·cord·ing /rɪ'kɔrdɪŋ/ *n* recorded performance, speech, or piece of music

record play·er /'·· ˌ··/ *n* machine for producing sounds from RECORDS² (4)

re·count¹ /ˌriʸ'kaʊnt/ *vt* count (esp. votes) again **recount** /'riʸkaʊnt/ *n*

re·count² /rɪ'kaʊnt/ *vt fml* tell

re·coup /rɪ'kuʷp/ *vt* get back (something lost, esp. money)

re·course /'riʸkɔrs, -koʷrs, rɪ'kɔrs, rɪ'koʷrs/ *n* **have recourse to** *fml* make use of

re·cov·er /rɪ'kʌvər/ *v* **1** *vt* get back (something lost or taken away) **2** *vi* return to the proper state of health, strength, ability, etc. **~able** *adj* **~y** *n* [U]

rec·re·a·tion /ˌrekriʸ'eʸʃən/ *n* [C;U] (form of) amusement; way of spending free time **~al** *adj*

recreation room /ˌ··'·· ˌ·/ *n* also **rec room** room in the house esp. for games

recreation ve·hi·cle /ˌ··'·· ˌ··/ *n* RV

re·crim·i·na·tion /rɪˌkrɪmə'neʸʃən/ *n* [C;U] (act of) quarreling and blaming one another

re·cruit /rɪ'kruʷt/ *n* new member of an organization, esp. the army, navy, etc. ♦ *vi/t* get recruits or as a recruit **~ment** *n* [U]

rec·tan·gle /'rekˌtæŋgəl/ *n* flat shape with four straight sides forming four 90° angles **~gular** /rek-'tæŋgyələr/ *adj*

rec·ti·fy /'rektəˌfaɪ/ *vt fml* put right

rec·ti·tude /'rektəˌtuʷd, -ˌtyuʷd/ *n* [U] *fml* moral properness

rec·tor /'rektər/ *n* priest in charge of a PARISH **~y** *n* rector's home

rec·tum /ˈrɛktəm/ n med lowest end of the bowel, where food waste passes out

re·cum·bent /rɪˈkʌmbənt/ adj fml lying down on the back or side

re·cu·pe·rate /rɪˈkuʷpəˌreʸt, -ˈkyuʷ-/ vi get well again after illness [U] −**rative** adj helping one to recuperate −**ration** /rɪˌkuʷpəˈreʸʃən, -ˌkyuʷ-/ n

re·cur /rɪˈkɜr/ vi −**rr**− happen again −**currence** /rɪˈkɜrəns, -ˈkʌr-/ n [C;U]: frequent recurrence of the fever −**current** adj

re·cy·cle /ˌriʸˈsaɪkəl/ vt treat (a used substance) so that it is fit to use again −**clable** adj

red /rɛd/ adj −**dd**− **1** of the color of blood **2** (of hair) brownish orange **3** (of skin) pink **4** (cap.) infml COMMUNIST **5 see red** become angry suddenly and lose control of oneself ♦ n **1** [C;U] red color **2** [U] red clothes **3 in the red** in debt **4** infml a COMMUNIST **5 Reds under the bed** (imaginary) danger that secret COMMUNISTS are hiding in one's country ~**den** vi/t make or become red

red car·pet /ˌ· ˈ·· / n [S] special ceremonial welcome to a guest

Red Cross /ˌ· ˈ· / n [the] international organization that looks after the sick and wounded

re·deem /rɪˈdiʸm/ vt **1** buy back (something given for money lent) **2** fml make (something bad) slightly less bad **3** fml fulfil (a promise, etc.)

Redeemer n [the, our+S] Christ

re·demp·tion /rɪˈdɛmpʃən/ n [U] redeeming

re·de·ploy /ˌriʸdɪˈplɔɪ/ vt rearrange (soldiers, workers in industry, etc.) in a more effective way ~**ment** n

red-hand·ed /ˌ· ˈ··◂/ adj in the act of doing wrong

red·head /ˈrɛdhɛd/ n person with RED (2) hair

red her·ring /ˌ· ˈ··/ n something introduced to draw people's attention away from the main point

red-hot /ˌ· ˈ·◂/ adj so hot that it shines red: (fig.) red-hot enthusiasm

red-let·ter day /ˌ· ˈ·· ·/ n specially good day

red-light dis·trict /ˌ· ˈ· ˌ··/ n area where PROSTITUTES work

red·neck /ˈrɛdnɛk/ n derog person who lives in the country, esp. one who is uneducated and has strong unreasonable opinions

red·o·lent /ˈrɛdl-ənt/ adj fml making one think (of); suggesting

re·dou·ble /riʸˈdʌbəl/ vi/t increase greatly

re·doubt /rɪˈdaʊt/ n fml small fort

re·doub·ta·ble /rɪˈdaʊtəbəl/ adj greatly respected and feared

re·dound /rɪˈdaʊnd/ v **redound to** phr vt fml increase (fame, honor, etc.)

re·dress /rɪˈdrɛs/ vt fml **1** put right (a wrong, injustice, etc.) **2 redress the balance** make things equal again ♦ n [U] something, such as money, that puts right a wrong

red tape /ˌ· ˈ·/ n [U] silly detailed unnecessary rules

re·duce /rɪˈduʷs, rɪˈdyuʷs/ vt **1** make less **2** (of a person) lose weight on purpose −**duction** /rɪˈdʌkʃən/ n [C;U]: price reductions

reduce to phr vt **1** bring to (a less favorable state): The child was reduced to tears. (= made to cry) **2** bring (something) to (a smaller number or amount)

re·dun·dant /rɪˈdʌndənt/ adj **1** unnecessarily repeating **2** no longer needed −**dancy** n [C;U]

red·wood /ˈrɛdwʊd/ n extremely tall American CONIFERous tree

reed /riʸd/ n **1** grasslike plant growing in wet places **2** thin piece of wood or metal in certain musical instruments, blown across to produce sound ~**y** adj **1** full of reeds **2** (of a sound) thin and high

reef /riʸf/ n line of sharp rocks or CORAL at or near the surface of the sea

reef·er /ˈriʸfər/ n infml cigarette containing the drug MARIJUANA

reek /riʸk/ vi, n (have) a strong unpleasant smell

reel[1] /riʸl/ n **1** round object on which cotton, cinema film, etc., can be wound **2** length of time it takes to show this amount of film ♦ vt bring, take, etc., by winding

reel off phr vt say quickly and easily from memory

reel[2] vi **1** walk in an unsteady way as if drunk **2** be shocked or confused **3** seem to go around and around

re-en·try /riʸˈɛntriʸ/ n [C;U] entering again, esp. into the Earth's ATMOSPHERE

ref /rɛf/ n infml for REFEREE (1)

refer /rɪˈfɜr/ v −**rr**−

refer to phr vt **1** mention; speak about **2** be about or directed towards **3** look at for information **4** send to (a person or place) for information, a decision, etc.

ref·er·ee /ˌrɛfəˈriʸ/ n **1** person in charge of a game **2** person who gives a REFERENCE (3)

ref·er·ence /ˈrɛfərəns/ n **1** [C;U] (act of) mentioning **2** [C;U] (act of) looking at something for information **3** [C] **a** information about someone's character and ability, job, esp. when they are looking for a job **b** person who gives such information **4 in/with reference to** fml about

reference book /'··· ͵·/ n book for finding information

ref·e·ren·dum /ˌrefəˈrendəm/ n –da /-də/ or –dums direct vote by all the people to decide something

re·fine /rɪˈfaɪn/ vt make pure –**refined** adj 1 made pure 2 showing education, delicateness of feeling, and good manners ~**ment** n 1 [C] clever addition or improvement 2 [U] act of refining 3 [U] quality of being refined

re·fin·er·y /rɪˈfaɪnəriʸ/ n place where oil, sugar, etc., is refined

re·fit /ˌriˈfɪt/ vt –tt– repair and put new machinery into (a ship) **refit** /ˈriʸfɪt/ n

re·flate /riʸˈfleʸt/ vi/t increase the supply of money in (a money system) –**flation** /-ˈfleʸʃən/ n [U]

re·flect /rɪˈflekt/ v 1 vt throw back (heat, sound, or an image) 2 vt give an idea of; express 3 vi think carefully ~**ive** adj thoughtful ~**or** n

reflect on phr vt 1 consider carefully 2 cause to be considered in a particular way

re·flec·tion /rɪˈflekʃən/ n 1 [C] reflected image 2 [U] reflecting of heat, sound, etc. 3 [C;U] deep and careful thought

re·flex /ˈriʸfleks/ n unintentional movement made in reply to an outside influence: quick/slow reflexes

re·flex·ive /rɪˈfleksɪv/ n, adj (word) showing effect on oneself: In 'I enjoyed myself', 'enjoy' is a reflexive verb.

re·form /rɪˈfɔrm/ vi/t make or become (morally) right; improve ♦ n [C;U] action to improve conditions, remove unfairness, etc. ~**er** n

re-form /ˌriʸˈfɔrm/ vi/t (cause to) form again, esp. into ranks

ref·or·ma·tion /ˌrefərˈmeʸʃən/ n [U] 1 (moral) improvement 2 (cap.) religious movement of the 16th century leading to the establishment of Protestant churches

reform school /·' ͵·/ also **reformatory** /rɪˈfɔrməˌtɔriʸ, -ˌtoʷriʸ/ — n special school for children who have broken the law

re·fract /rɪˈfrækt/ vt bend (light passing through) ~**ion** /-ˈfrækʃən/ n [U]

re·frac·to·ry /rɪˈfræktəriʸ/ adj fml disobedient and troublesome

re·frain[1] /rɪˈfreʸn/ vi fml not do something

refrain[2] n part of a song that is repeated

re·fresh /rɪˈfreʃ/ vt 1 cause to feel fresh or active again 2 **refresh one's memory** help oneself to remember again ~**ing** adj 1 producing comfort and new strength 2 pleasingly new and interesting ~**ment** n [U] ~**ments** n [P] food and drink

re·fri·ge·rate /rɪˈfrɪdʒəˌreʸt/ vt make (food, drink, etc.) cold to preserve or (of political) danger –**ration** /rɪˌfrɪdʒəˈreʸʃən/ n [U]

re·fri·ge·ra·tor /rɪˈfrɪdʒəˌreʸtər/ n electric cupboard where food is kept cold

ref·uge /ˈrefyuʷdʒ/ n [C;U] (place providing) protection or shelter

ref·u·gee /ˌrefyuˈdʒiʸ, ˈrefyuˌdʒiʸ/ n person forced to leave their country because of (political) danger

re·fund /ˈriʸfʌnd/ n repayment ♦ /rɪˈfʌnd/ vt pay (money) back

re·fur·bish /ˌriʸˈfɜrbɪʃ/ vt make fit for use again

re·fus·al /rɪˈfyuʷzəl/ n [C;U] (a case of) refusing

re·fuse[1] /rɪˈfyuʷz/ vi/t not accept, do, or give: She refused my offer.

ref·use[2] /ˈrefyuʷs/ n [U] waste material; GARBAGE

re·fute /rɪˈfyuʷt/ vt fml prove that (someone or something) is mistaken **refutation** /ˌrefyuˈteʸʃən/ n [C;U]

re·gain /rɪˈgeʸn/ vt get or win back

re·gal /ˈriʸgəl/ adj fml like a king or queen; very splendid ~**ly** adv

re·gale /rɪˈgeʸl/ v **regale with** phr vt entertain with

re·ga·lia /rɪˈgeʸlyə/ n [U] ceremonial clothes and decorations

re·gard[1] /rɪˈgard/ vt 1 look at or consider in the stated way: I regard him as the finest lawyer in the country. 2 fml pay respectful attention to ~**ing** prep fml in connection with

regard[2] n [U] 1 respect 2 respectful attention; concern 3 **in/with regard to** in connection with ~**less** adv 1 whatever may happen 2 **regardless of** without worrying about **regards** n [P] good wishes

re·gat·ta /rɪˈgatə, -ˈgæ-/ n meeting for boat races

re·gen·e·rate /rɪˈdʒenəˌreʸt/ vi/t grow again –**ration** /rɪˌdʒenəˈreʸʃən/ n [U]

re·gent /ˈriʸdʒənt/ n 1 person who governs in place of a king or queen who is ill, still a child, etc. 2 member of a governing board of a state university

reg·gae /ˈregeʸ/ n [U] West Indian popular dance and music

re·gi·cide /ˈredʒəˌsaɪd/ n [U] 1 killing a king or queen 2 person who does this

re·gime /reʸˈʒiʸm, rɪ-/ n 1 (system of) government 2 regimen

re·gi·men /ˈredʒəmən/ n fml fixed plan of food, exercise, etc., to improve health

re·gi·ment /ˈredʒəmənt/ n large

military group ♦ *vt* control too firmly ~**al** /ˌredʒəˈmentl◂/ *adj*

re·gion /ˈriʸdʒən/ *n* **1** quite large area or part **2** in the region of about ~**al** *adj*

reg·is·ter¹ /ˈredʒəstər/ *n* **1** (book containing) a record or list **2** range of the voice or a musical instrument **3** words, style, etc., used by speakers and writers in particular conditions

register² *v* **1** *vt* put into a REGISTER¹ (1) **2** *vi* put one's name on a list, esp. of those who will take part **3** *vt* (of a measuring instrument) show **4** *vt* (of a person or face) express **5** *vt* send by registered mail **6** *vi* have an effect (on a person)

registered mail /ˌ··· ˈ·/ *n* [U] system for posting things, which protects the sender against loss

re·gis·trar /ˈredʒəˌstrɑr/ *n* **1** keeper of official records **2** official at a college who keeps student records and sends out GRADES and official papers

re·gis·tra·tion /ˌredʒəˈstreʸʃən/ *n* [U] registering (REGISTER² (2))

re·gress /rɪˈgres/ *vi fml* go back to a former and usu. worse condition, way of behaving, etc. ~**ion** /-ˈgreʃən/ *n*

re·gret¹ /rɪˈgret/ *vt* -tt- be sorry about: *I've never regretted my decision to leave.* ~**table** *adj* that one should regret ~**tably** *adv*

regret² *n* [C;U] unhappiness at the loss of something, because of something one has done or not done, etc. ~**ful** *adj*

re·group /ˌriˈgruʷp/ *vi/t* form into new groups

reg·u·lar /ˈregyələr/ *adj* **1** usual or customary **2** not varying: *a regular pulse* | *a regular customer* **3** happening (almost) every time: *regular church attendance* **4** correct or usual **5** evenly shaped **6** employed continuously: *a regular soldier* **7** gram following the standard pattern: *regular verbs* **8** *infml* complete; thorough **9** pleasant and honest: *a regular guy* ♦ *n* regular visitor, customer, etc. ~**ly** *adv* at regular times ~**ize** *vt* make lawful –**larity** /ˌregyəˈlærəṭiʸ/ *n* [U]

reg·u·late /ˈregyəˌleʸt/ *vt* **1** control, esp. by rules **2** make (a machine) work in a certain way –**latory** /-ləˌtoriʸ, -ˌtoʷriʸ/ *adj fml* having the purpose of regulating

reg·u·la·tion /ˌregyəˈleʸʃən/ *n* **1** [C] (official) rule **2** [U] control

re·gur·gi·tate /rɪˈgɜrdʒəˌteʸt/ *vt fml* **1** bring back (swallowed food) through the mouth **2** repeat (something heard or read) in one's own work, without thought or change

re·hab /ˈriʸhæb/ *n infml* rehabilitate (2) ~**bed** *adj: a rehabbed house*

re·ha·bil·i·tate /ˌriʸhəˈbɪləˌteʸt, ˌriʸə-/ *vt* **1** make able to live an ordinary life again **2** put back into good condition **3** put back to a former high rank, position, etc. –**tation** /ˌriʸhəˌbɪləˈteʸʃən, ˌriʸə-/ *n* [U]

re·hash /riʸˈhæʃ/ *vt* use (old ideas) again **rehash** /ˈriʸhæʃ/ *n*

re·hearse /rɪˈhɜrs/ *vi/t* practice for later performance **rehearsal** *n* [C;U]

reign /reʸn/ *n* period of reigning ♦ *vi* **1** be the king or queen **2** exist (noticeably): *Silence reigned.*

reign of ter·ror /ˌ·· ˈ···/ *n* period of widespread official killing

re·im·burse /ˌriʸɪmˈbɜrs/ *vt* pay (money) back to ~**ment** *n* [C;U]

rein /reʸn/ *n* **1** also **reins** *pl.* — long narrow (leather) band for controlling a horse **2** give (free) rein to give freedom to (feelings or desires) **3** keep a tight rein on control firmly – see also FREE REIN **reins** *n* [P] means of control: *take the reins* (= become the leader)

re·in·car·nate /ˌriʸɪnˈkɑrˌneʸt/ *vt* cause to return to life in a new form after death –**nation** /ˌriʸɪnkɑrˈneʸʃən/ *n* [C;U]

rein·deer /ˈreʸndɪər/ *n* reindeer large deer from northern parts of the world

re·in·force /ˌriʸɪnˈfɔrs, -ˈfoʷrs/ *vt* strengthen with additions ~**ment** *n* [U] ~**ments** *n* [P] more soldiers sent to reinforce an army

reinforced con·crete /ˌ··· ˈ··/ *n* [U] CONCRETE strengthened by metal bars

re·in·state /ˌriʸɪnˈsteʸt/ *vt* put back into a position formerly held ~**ment** *n* [C;U]

re·it·e·rate /riʸˈɪṭəˌreʸt/ *vt fml* repeat several times –**ration** /riʸˌɪṭəˈreʸʃən/ *n* [C;U]

re·ject /rɪˈdʒekt/ *vt* refuse to accept ♦ /ˈriʸdʒekt/ *n* something thrown away as useless or imperfect ~**ion** /rɪˈdʒekʃən/ *n* [C;U]

re·joice /rɪˈdʒɔɪs/ *vi* feel or show great joy **rejoicing** *n* [C;U] (public) show of joy

re·join¹ /ˌriʸˈdʒɔɪn/ *vi/t* join again **re·join²** /rɪˈdʒɔɪn/ *vt* answer, esp. angrily

re·join·der /rɪˈdʒɔɪndər/ *n* (rude) answer

re·ju·ve·nate /rɪˈdʒuʷvəˌneʸt/ *vt* make young again –**nation** /rɪˌdʒuʷvəˈneʸʃən/ *n* [U]

re·lapse /rɪˈlæps/ *vi* return to a bad state of health or way of life **relapse** *n*

re·late /rɪˈleɪt/ vt **1** see or show a connection between **2** fml tell (a story) –**related** adj of the same family or kind; connected

relate to phr vt **1** connect (one thing) with (another) **2** infml understand and accept

re·la·tion /rɪˈleɪʃən/ n **1** [C] member of one's family **2** [C;U] connection **3** in/with relation to fml with regard to ~**ship** n **1** [C] friendship or connection between people **2** [C;U] dealings between (and feelings towards) each other

rel·a·tive /ˈrelətɪv/ n RELATION (1) ♦ adj compared to each other or something else: now living in relative comfort ~**ly** adv quite

relative clause /ˌ··· ˈ·/ n CLAUSE joined on by a RELATIVE PRONOUN

relative pro·noun /ˌ··· ˈ··/ n PRONOUN which joins a CLAUSE to the rest of a sentence, such as who, which, or that

rel·a·tiv·i·ty /ˌreləˈtɪvəti/ n [U] relationship between time, ENERGY, and mass, said to change with increased speed

re·lax /rɪˈlæks/ vi/t make or become **a** less active and worried **b** less stiff, tight, or severe ~**ation** /ˌriˈlæk-ˈseɪʃən/ n **1** [C;U] (something done for) rest and amusement **2** [U] act of making or becoming less severe

re·lay /ˈriˈleɪ/ n [C;U] **1** group that takes the place of another to keep work going continuously: In a relay (race), each member of each team runs part of the distance. **2** (broadcast sent out by) an electrical connection for receiving and passing on signals

re·lease /rɪˈliˈs/ vt **1** set free **2** allow to be seen or read publicly **3** press (a handle) so as to let something go ♦ n **1** [S;U] setting free **2** [C] new film, record, or piece of information that has been released

rel·e·gate /ˈreləˌgeɪt/ vt put into a lower or worse place –**gation** /ˌreləˈgeɪʃən/ n [U]

re·lent /rɪˈlent/ vi become less cruel or severe ~**less** adj continuously cruel or severe

rel·e·vant /ˈreləvənt/ adj directly connected with the subject ~**ly** adv –**vance** n [U]

re·li·a·ble /rɪˈlaɪəbəl/ adj that may be trusted –**ably** adv –**ability** /rɪˌlaɪəˈbɪləti/ n [U]

re·li·ant /rɪˈlaɪənt/ adj dependent (on) –**ance** n [U] **1** dependence **2** trust

rel·ic /ˈrelɪk/ n **1** something old that reminds us of the past **2** part of or something that belonged to a dead holy person

re·lief /rɪˈliˈf/ n **1** [S;U] comfort at the ending of anxiety, pain, or dullness **2** [U] help for people in trouble **3** [C] person who takes over another's duty **4** [C;U] decoration that stands out above the rest of the surface it is on **5** [U] part of one's income on which one does not have to pay tax **6** light relief pleasant and amusing change

relief map /·ˈ· ·/ n map showing the height of land

re·lieve /rɪˈliˈv/ vt **1** lessen (pain or trouble) **2** take over duties from **3** give variety or interest to **4** relieve oneself urinate (URINE) or empty the bowels **relieved** adj no longer worried

relieve of phr vt free from

re·li·gion /rɪˈlɪdʒən/ n [C;U] (system of) belief in and worship of one or more gods

re·li·gious /rɪˈlɪdʒəs/ adj **1** of religion **2** obeying the rules of a religion **3** performing the stated duties very carefully ~**ly** adv regularly

re·lin·quish /rɪˈlɪŋkwɪʃ/ vt fml for GIVE up (5)

rel·ish /ˈrelɪʃ/ n [U] **1** great enjoyment **2** substance eaten with a meal, to add taste and interest ♦ vt enjoy

re·live /ˌriˈlɪv/ vt experience again in the imagination

re·lo·cate /ˌriˈloʊˌkeɪt, ˌriˈloʊˈkeɪt/ vi (of a business) move [1] (3)

re·luc·tant /rɪˈlʌktənt/ adj unwilling ~**ly** adv –**tance** n [U]

re·ly /rɪˈlaɪ/ v **rely on** phr vt **1** trust **2** depend on

re·main /rɪˈmeɪn/ v **1** vi stay or be left behind after others have gone **2** continue to be: remain calm/a prisoner **remains** n [P] **1** parts which are left **2** fml dead body

re·main·der /rɪˈmeɪndər/ n what is left over ♦ vt sell (esp. books) cheap so as to get rid of them quickly

re·mark /rɪˈmɑrk/ n spoken or written opinion ♦ vt say

remark on phr vt fml mention

re·mar·ka·ble /rɪˈmɑrkəbəl/ adj unusual or noticeable –**bly** adv

re·me·di·al /rɪˈmiˈdiəl/ adj **1** providing a remedy **2** intended to improve one's skill in a particular field: remedial math

rem·e·dy /ˈremədi/ n [C;U] way of curing something ♦ vt put (something bad) right

re·mem·ber /rɪˈmembər/ v **1** vt call back into the mind **2** vi/t take care not to forget **3** vt give money or a present to

remember to phr vt send greetings from (someone) to: Remember me to your wife.

re·mem·brance /rɪˈmɛmbrəns/ n [U] 1 act of remembering 2 something given or kept to remind one

re·mind /rɪˈmaɪnd/ vt cause to remember ~**er** n something to make one remember

remind of phr vt cause to remember by seeming the same

rem·i·nisce /ˌrɛməˈnɪs/ vi talk pleasantly about the past –**niscence** n [U] –**niscences** n [P] written or spoken account of one's past life –**niscent** adj that reminds one (of); like

re·miss /rɪˈmɪs/ adj fml careless about a duty

re·mis·sion /rɪˈmɪʃən/ n [C;U] 1 lessening of the time someone has to stay in prison 2 fml period when an illness is less severe

re·mit /rɪˈmɪt/ vt -**tt**- fml 1 send (money) by mail 2 free someone from (a debt or punishment) ~**tance** n 1 [C] money remitted 2 [U] fml act of remitting money

rem·nant /ˈrɛmnənt/ n 1 part that remains 2 end of a roll of cloth, sold cheaply

re·mod·el /ˌriˈmɑdl/ vt repair, improve (esp. a house)

re·mon·strate /rɪˈmɑnˌstreɪt/ vi fml express disapproval

re·morse /rɪˈmɔrs/ n [U] sorrow for having done wrong ~**ful** adj ~**less** adj 1 showing no remorse 2 threatening and not able to be stopped

re·mote /rɪˈmoʊt/ adj 1 far distant in space or time 2 quiet and lonely: a remote village 3 widely separated; not close: a remote connection 4 slight: a remote chance of success 5 not showing interest in others ~**ly** adv at all: not remotely interested ~**ness** n [U]

remote con·trol /·ˌ· ·ˈ·/ n [U] controlling machinery by radio signals

re·move /rɪˈmuːv/ vt 1 take away; get rid of 2 fml dismiss 3 removed from distant or different from ♦ n stage; degree: Their action was only (at) one remove from (= was nearly) revolution. **removal** n [C;U] –**mover** n [C;U]

re·mu·ne·rate /rɪˈmyuːnəˌreɪt/ vt fml pay –**rative** /-ˌreɪtɪv, -rətɪv/ adj well paid –**ration** /rɪˌmyuːnəˈreɪʃən/ n [S;U]

re·nais·sance /ˌrɛnəˈsɑns◂, -ˈzɑns◂/ n rebirth of interest in art, literature, etc., esp. (cap.) in Europe between the 14th and 17th centuries

Renaissance man /ˌ··· ·ˈ·/ n man with many skills and deep knowledge

re·nal /ˈriːnl/ adj med of the KIDNEYS

rend /rɛnd/ vt rent /rɛnt/ lit 1 split 2 pull violently

ren·der /ˈrɛndər/ vt fml 1 cause to be

2 give 3 perform ~**ing** also **rendi·tion** /rɛnˈdɪʃən/ — n performance

ren·dez·vous /ˈrɑndəˌvuː◂, -deɪ-/ n -**vous** /-ˌvuːz/ 1 (arrangement for) a meeting 2 meeting place ♦ vi meet by arrangement

ren·e·gade /ˈrɛnəˌgeɪd/ n person who disloyally leaves one country or belief to join another

re·nege /rɪˈnɪg, rɪˈnɛg/ vi fml break a promise

re·new /rɪˈnuː◂, rɪˈnyuː◂/ vt 1 repeat: They renewed their attack. 2 give new life and freshness to 3 get something new of the same kind to take the place of: renew a driver's license ~**al** n [C;U]

ren·net /ˈrɛnɪt/ n [U] substance for thickening milk to make cheese

re·nounce /rɪˈnaʊns/ vt say formally that one does not own or has no more connection with

ren·o·vate /ˈrɛnəˌveɪt/ vt put back into good condition –**vation** /ˌrɛnəˈveɪʃən/ n [C;U]

re·nown /rɪˈnaʊn/ n [U] fame ~**ed** adj famous

rent[1] /rɛnt/ n [C;U] money paid regularly for the use of a house, garage, etc. ♦ vt 1 pay rent for the use of 2 allow to be used in return for rent ~**al** sum of money fixed to be paid as rent

rent[2] n large tear

rent[3] past t. & p. of REND

re·nun·ci·a·tion /rɪˌnʌnsiˈeɪʃən/ n [C;U] (act of) renouncing (RE-NOUNCE) something

re·or·gan·ize /ˌriˈɔrgəˌnaɪz/ vi/t ORGANIZE in a new and better way –**ization** n /ˌriˌɔrgənəˈzeɪʃən/ n [C;U]

rep[1] /rɛp/ n infml for SALES REPRESENTATIVE

rep[2] n [C;U] REPERTORY (company)

Rep written abbrev. for: REPUBLICAN

re·pair /rɪˈpɛər/ vt mend ♦ n 1 [C;U] (act or result of) mending 2 [U] condition: in good repair **repairs** [P] work done on roads to make them smoother

rep·a·ra·tion /ˌrɛpəˈreɪʃən/ n [C;U] fml repayment for loss or damage

rep·ar·tee /ˌrɛpɑrˈtiː, -ˈteɪ, ˌrɛpɑr-/ n [U] quick amusing talk

re·past /rɪˈpæst/ n fml meal

re·pat·ri·ate /riˈpeɪtriˌeɪt/ vt send (someone) back to their own country –**ation** /riˌpeɪtriˈeɪʃən/ n [C;U]

re·pay /rɪˈpeɪ/ vt **repaid** /-ˈpeɪd/ 1 pay (money) back to (someone) 2 reward ~**ment** n [C;U]

re·peal /rɪˈpiːl/ vt end (a law) repeal n [U]

re·peat /rɪˈpiːt/ vt 1 say or do again 2 repeat oneself keep saying the same thing ♦ also n 1 musical passage played a second time 2 performance broadcast a second time ~ed *adj* done again and again ~edly *adv*

re·pel /rɪ'pel/ *vt* -ll- **1** drive away (as if) by force **2** cause feelings of extreme dislike in ~lent *adj* extremely nasty ~lent *n* [C;U] substance that repels esp. insects

re·pent /rɪ'pent/ *vi/t fml* be sorry for (wrongdoing) ~ant *adj* ~ance *n* [U]

re·per·cus·sion /ˌriːpər'kʌʃən/ *n* effect felt over a wide area

rep·er·toire /'repərˌtwɑr, -ˌtwɔr/ *n* set of things one can perform

rep·er·to·ry /'repərˌtɔri, -ˌtoʷriʸ/ *n* [U] performing several plays one after the other on different days with the same actors

rep·e·ti·tion /ˌrepə'tɪʃən/ *n* [C;U] repeating -tious, -tive /rɪ'pețəțɪv/ *adj* containing parts that are repeated too much

re·phrase /riʸ'freʸz/ *vt* put into different (clearer) words

re·place /rɪ'pleʸs/ *vt* **1** put back in the right place **2** take the place of **3** get another (better) one instead of ~ment *n* **1** [U] act of replacing **2** [C] that replaces someone or something

re·plen·ish /rɪ'plenɪʃ/ *vt* fill up again

re·plete /rɪ'pliʸt/ *adj fml* very full, -pletion /-'pliʸʃən/ *n* [U]

rep·li·ca /'replɪkə/ *n* close copy

rep·li·cate /'replɪˌkeʸt/ *vt fml* copy exactly

re·ply /rɪ'plaɪ/ *vi, n* answer

re·port¹ /rɪ'pɔrt/ *n* **1** [C] account of events, business affairs, etc. **2** [C;U] what is said generally but unofficially **3** [C] noise of an explosion

report² *v* **1** *vi/t* provide information (about); give an account of, esp. for a newspaper or radio or television **2** *vi* go somewhere and say that one is there (and ready for work) **3** *vt* make a complaint about ~er *n* person who reports news

re·port·age /rɪ'pɔrtɪdʒ, -'poʷr-, ˌrepər'tɑʒ/ *n* [U] (writing, film, etc., in) the style of reporters

report card /·'· ˌ·/ *n* periodic written report of a child's behavior and work at school

re·port·ed·ly /rɪ'pɔrtɪdliʸ/ *adv* according to what is said

reported speech /·'· ·· '·/ *n* [U] IN-DIRECT SPEECH

re·pose /rɪ'poʷz/ *n* [U] *fml* rest ♦ *vt fml* rest; lie

repose in *phr vt fml* place (trust, hope, etc.) in

re·pos·i·to·ry /rɪ'pɑzəˌtɔriʸ, -ˌtoʷriʸ/ *n* place where things are stored

re·pos·sess /ˌriʸpə'zes/ *vt* take back, esp. when rent has not been paid

rep·re·hen·si·ble /ˌreprɪ'hensəbəl/ *adj fml* deserving blame; bad ~bly *adv*

rep·re·sent /ˌreprɪ'zent/ *v* **1** *vt* act or speak officially for (someone else) **2** *vt* be a picture or STATUE of; show **3** *vt* be a sign of; stand for **4** be: *This represents a considerable improvement.* ~ation /ˌreprɪzen'teʸʃən, -zən-/ *n* **1** [U] act of representing or state of being represented **2** [C] something which REPRESENTS (2,3) something else

rep·re·sen·ta·tive /ˌreprɪ'zentəțɪv/ *adj* **1** typical **2** (of government) in which the people and their opinions are represented ♦ *n* person who REPRESENTS (1) others, esp. in Congress – see also HOUSE OF REPRESENTATIVES

re·press /rɪ'pres/ *vt* control; hold back – ive *adj* hard and cruel ~ion /-'preʃən/ *n* [U] pushing unwelcome feelings into one's unconscious mind, with odd effects on behavior

re·prieve /rɪ'priʸv/ *vt* give a reprieve to ♦ *n* official order not to carry out the punishment of death (yet)

rep·ri·mand /'reprəˌmænd/ *vt* express severe official disapproval of reprimand *n*

re·pri·sal /rɪ'praɪzəl/ *n* [C;U] (act of) punishing others for harm done to oneself

re·prise /rɪ'priʸz/ *n* repeating of a piece of music

re·proach /rɪ'proʷtʃ/ *n* [C;U] **1** (word of) blame **2** above/beyond reproach perfect ♦ *vt* blame, not angrily but sadly ~ful *adj*

rep·ro·bate /'reprəˌbeʸt/ *n fml* person of bad character

re·pro·duce /ˌriʸprə'duʷs, -'dyuʷs/ *vi/t* **1** produce the young of (oneself or one's kind) **2** produce a copy (of) -duction /-'dʌkʃən/ *n* [C;U] -ductive /-'dʌktɪv/ *adj* concerned with producing young

re·proof /rɪ'pruʷf/ *n* [C;U] *fml* (expression of) blame or disapproval

re·prove /rɪ'pruʷv/ *vt fml* speak blamingly or disapprovingly to

rep·tile /'reptəl, 'reptaɪl/ *n* animal, such as a snake, with blood that changes temperature -tilian /rep-'tɪliʸən/ *adj*

re·pub·lic /rɪ'pʌblɪk/ *n* state ruled by a president and usu. an elected LEGISLATURE, not a king

re·pub·li·can¹ /rɪ'pʌblɪkən/ *adj* belonging to or supporting a republic

republican² *n* person who favors republics ~ism *n* [U] beliefs or practices of republicans

Republican *n* member or supporter of the **Republican Party**, one of the two largest political parties of the US

re·pu·di·ate /rɪˈpjuːdiˌeɪt/ vt fml **1** state that (something) is untrue **2** refuse to accept **–ation** /rɪˌpjuːdiˈeɪʃən/ n [U]

re·pug·nant /rɪˈpʌgnənt/ adj fml causing extreme dislike; nasty **–nance** n [U]

re·pulse /rɪˈpʌls/ vt **1** refuse coldly **2** drive back (an attack) **–pulsive** adj extremely unpleasant **–pulsion** /-ˈpʌlʃən/ n [U] **1** extreme dislike **2** natural force by which one body drives another away from it

rep·u·ta·ble /ˈrepjətəbəl/ adj having a good reputation **–bly** adv

rep·u·ta·tion /ˌrepjəˈteɪʃən/ n [C;U] opinion which people in general have about someone or something

re·pute /rɪˈpjuːt/ n [U] fml **1** reputation **2** good reputation **reputed** adj generally supposed, but with some doubt **reputedly** adv

re·quest /rɪˈkwest/ n **1** [C;U] polite demand **2** [C] something asked for ♦ vt demand politely

re·qui·em /ˈrekwiəm/ n (music for) a Christian ceremony for a dead person

re·quire /rɪˈkwaɪər/ vt **1** need **2** fml order, expecting obedience: You are required to (= must) do it. **~ment** n something needed or demanded

req·ui·site /ˈrekwəzɪt/ adj needed for a purpose

req·ui·si·tion /ˌrekwəˈzɪʃən/ n [C;U] formal demand ♦ vt demand or take officially

re·run /ˈriːrʌn/ n performance or television program broadcast more than once

re·scind /rɪˈsɪnd/ vt end (a law) or take back (a decision, order, etc.)

res·cue /ˈreskjuː/ vt save or set free from harm or danger **rescue** n **–cuer** n

re·search /rɪˈsɜːtʃ, ˈriːsɜːtʃ/ n [C;U] advanced and detailed study, to find out (new) information ♦ vi/t do research (on or for) **~er** n

re·sem·ble /rɪˈzembəl/ vt look or be like **–blance** n [C;U] likeness

re·sent /rɪˈzent/ vt feel hurt and angry because of **~ful** adj **~ment** n [U]

res·er·va·tion /ˌrezərˈveɪʃən/ n **1** [C;U] limiting condition(s): I accepted every point, without reservation. **2** [C] private doubt in one's mind **3** [C] arrangement to have or use something: a hotel reservation **4** [C] area set apart for particular people to live in

re·serve /rɪˈzɜːrv/ vt **1** keep apart for a special purpose **2** arrange to have or use: reserve hotel rooms ♦ n [C] quantity kept for future use **2** [C]

piece of land kept for the stated purpose **3** [C] player who will play if another cannot **4** [C] being reserved **5** [the+S] also **reserves** pl. — military forces kept for use if needed **6 in reserve** for future use **7 without reserve** fml completely **reserved** adj not liking to show one's feelings or talk about oneself

reserve bank /·ˈ· ˌ·/ n any of the 12 Federal Reserve Banks that hold the money of other banks

Reserve Of·fic·ers Train·ing Corps /·ˌ· ˌ··· ˈ·· ˌ·/ also **ROTC** — n special course of study to prepare university students for the armed services

res·er·voir /ˈrezərvwɑːr, -ˌvwɔːr/ n **1** artificial lake for storing water **2** large supply (still unused)

re·shuf·fle /riːˈʃʌfəl/ vt change around the positions of people working in an organization **reshuffle** /riːˈʃʌfəl, ˈriːʃʌfəl/ n

re·side /rɪˈzaɪd/ vi fml have one's home

res·i·dence /ˈrezədəns/ n fml **1** [C] (large grand) house **2** [U] state of residing **3 in residence** actually living in a place

res·i·dent /ˈrezədənt/ n, adj **1** (person) who lives in a place **2** doctor employed by a hospital while receiving training **~ial** /ˌrezəˈdenʃəl◀/ adj **1** consisting of private houses **2** for which one must live in a place: a residential course

re·sid·u·al /rɪˈzɪdʒuˈəl/ adj left over; remaining

res·i·due /ˈrezəˌduː, -ˌdjuː/ n what is left over

re·sign /rɪˈzaɪn/ vi/t leave (one's job or position) **~ed** adj calmly suffering without complaint **~edly** /rɪˈzaɪnədliː/ adv

resign to phr vt cause (oneself) to accept calmly (something which cannot be avoided)

res·ig·na·tion /ˌrezɪgˈneɪʃən/ n **1** [C;U] (act or written statement of) resigning **2** [U] state of being resigned

re·sil·i·ent /rɪˈzɪliənt/ adj **1** able to spring back to its former shape **2** able to recover quickly from misfortune **–ence** n [U]

res·in /ˈrezən/ n **1** [U] thick sticky liquid from trees **2** [C] artificial plastic substance

re·sist /rɪˈzɪst/ vt **1** oppose; fight against **2** remain unharmed by **3** force oneself not to accept

re·sist·ance /rɪˈzɪstəns/ n [S;U] **1** act of resisting or ability to resist **2** [U] force opposed to movement: wind resistance **3** (the) U] secret army fighting against an enemy in control of its country **4 the line/path**

of least resistance the easiest way –**ant** adj showing resistance

re·sis·tor /rɪˈzɪstər/ n piece of wire, etc., for reducing the power of an electrical current

res·o·lute /ˈrezəˌluʷt/ adj firm; determined in purpose ~**ly** adv

res·o·lu·tion /ˌrezəˈluʷʃən/ n 1 [C] formal decision at a meeting 2 [C] firm decision: a New Year's resolution to stop drinking 3 [U] quality of being resolute 4 [U] action of resolving (RESOLVE (1))

re·solve /rɪˈzɑlv/ vt 1 find a way of dealing with (a problem); settle 2 decide firmly 3 make a RESOLUTION (1, 2) ♦ n [C;U] fml for RESOLUTION (2, 3)

res·o·nant /ˈrezənənt/ adj 1 (of a sound) full, clear, and continuing 2 producing resonance (2) –**nance** n [U] 1 quality of being resonant 2 sound produced in a body by sound waves from another

res·o·nate /ˈrezəˌneʸt/ vi 1 produce resonance (2) 2 be resonant

re·sort¹ /rɪˈzɔrt/ n 1 vacation place 2 as a/in the last resort if everything else fails

resort² v resort to phr vt make use of, esp. when there is nothing else **re·sound** /rɪˈzaʊnd/ vi 1 be loud and clearly heard 2 be filled (with sound) ~**ing** adj very great: a resounding victory

re·source /ˈriʸsɔrs, -soʷrs, rɪˈsɔrs, -ˈsoʷrs/ n 1 [C] something that one can use or possess 2 [U] resourcefulness 3 **leave someone to his own resources** leave someone alone to pass the time as he wishes ♦ vt provide resources (1) for ~**ful** adj able to find a way around difficulties ~**fully** adv

re·spect /rɪˈspɛkt/ n 1 [U] great admiration and honor 2 [U] attention; care 3 [C] detail; point: In some respects (= ways) it is worse. 4 **with respect to** with regard to; about ♦ vt feel or show respect for ~**ing** prep in connection with **respects** n [P] polite formal greetings

re·spec·ta·ble /rɪˈspɛktəbəl/ adj 1 socially acceptable 2 quite good; a respectable income –**bly** adv –**bility** /rɪˌspɛktəˈbɪlətiʸ/ n [U]

re·spect·ful /rɪˈspɛktfəl/ adj feeling or showing RESPECT (1) ~**ly** adv

re·spec·tive /rɪˈspɛktɪv/ adj particular and separate ~**ly** adv each separately in the order mentioned

res·pi·ra·tion /ˌrespəˈreʸʃən/ n [U] fml breathing –**piratory** /ˈrespərəˌtɔriʸ, -ˌtoʷriʸ, rɪˈspaɪrə-/ adj: the respiratory system (=lungs, etc.)

res·pi·ra·tor /ˈrespəˌreʸtər/ n apparatus to help people breathe

res·pite /ˈrespɪt/ n [C;U] 1 short rest from effort, pain, etc. 2 delay before something unwelcome happens

re·splen·dent /rɪˈsplɛndənt/ adj gloriously bright and shining ~**ly** adv

re·spond /rɪˈspɑnd/ vi 1 answer 2 act in answer

respond to phr vt (esp. of a disease) get better as a result of

re·sponse /rɪˈspɑns/ n 1 [C] answer 2 [C;U] action done in answer

re·spon·si·bil·i·ty /rɪˌspɑnsəˈbɪlətiʸ/ n 1 [U] condition or quality of being responsible: I take full responsibility for losing it. 2 [C] something for which one is RESPONSIBLE (2) 3 [U] trustworthiness

re·spon·si·ble /rɪˈspɑnsəbəl/ adj 1 having done or caused something (bad); guilty 2 having a duty to do or look after something 3 trustworthy 4 (of a job) needing a trustworthy person to do it 5 **be responsible for** be the cause of –**bly** adv

re·spon·sive /rɪˈspɑnsɪv/ adj answer readily with words or feelings: (fig.) a disease responsive to treatment

rest¹ /rest/ n [C;U] (period of) freedom from action or something tiring 2 [U] not moving: It came to rest (= stopped) just here. 3 [C] support, esp. for the stated thing: a headrest 4 **set someone's mind/fears at/to rest** free someone from anxiety ~**ful** adj peaceful; quiet

rest² v 1 vi/t (allow to) take a rest 2 vt lean; support 3 vi lie buried: Let him rest in peace. 4 rest assured be certain

rest on phr vt 1 (of a proof, argument, etc.) depend on 2 lean on 3 (of eyes) be directed towards

rest with phr vt be the responsibility of

rest³ n 1 **the rest** ones that still remain; what is left 2 **for the rest** apart from what has already been mentioned

res·tau·rant /ˈrestərənt, -ˌrɑnt/ n place where meals are sold and eaten

res·tau·ra·teur /ˌrestərəˈtɜr/ n also **restauranter** restaurant owner

res·ti·tu·tion /ˌrestɪˈtuʷʃən, -ˈtyuʷ-/ n [U] fml giving something back to its owner, or paying for damage

res·tive /ˈrestɪv/ adj unwilling to keep still or be controlled ~**ly** adv

rest·less /ˈrestlɪs/ adj 1 giving no rest or sleep 2 unable to stay still, esp. from anxiety or lack of interest ~**ly** adv

res·to·ra·tion /ˌrestəˈreʸʃən/ n [C;U] restoring

re·sto·ra·tive /rɪˈstɔrətɪv, -ˈstoʷr-/ n, adj (food, medicine, etc.) that brings back health and strength

re·store /rɪˈstɔr, rɪˈstoʷr/ vt **1** give back **2** bring back into existence **3** bring back to a proper state, esp. of health **4** put back into a former position **5** repair (an old painting, building, etc.) **restorer** n

re·strain /rɪˈstreʸn/ vt prevent from doing something; control ~**ed** adj calm and controlled **restraint** n **1** [U] quality of being restrained or act of restraining oneself **2** [C] something that restrains: *the restraints of life in a small town*

re·strict /rɪˈstrɪkt/ vt keep within a certain limit ~**ive** adj that restricts one ~**ion** /-ˈstrɪkʃən/ n [C;U]

re·struc·ture /ˌriʸˈstrʌktʃər/ vt arrange (a system or organization) in a new way

rest·room /ˈrestruʷm, -rʊm/ n public TOILET

rest stop /ˈ· ·/ n **1** place along the road where people in cars can stop to rest, etc. **2** act of doing this

re·sult /rɪˈzʌlt/ n **1** [C;U] what happens because of an action or event **2** [C;U] (a) noticeable good effect **3** [C] situation of defeat or victory at the end of a game **4** [C] answer to a calculation ♦ vi happen as an effect or RESULT (1) ~**ant** adj resulting **result in** phr vt cause

re·sume /rɪˈzuʷm, rɪˈzyuʷm/ v **1** vi/t begin again after a pause **2** vt fml return to

ré·su·mé, resume /ˈrezəˌmeʸ, ˈreʸ-, ˌrezəˈmeʸ, ˌreʸ-/ n **1** shortened form of a speech, book, etc. **2** short written account of a person's education and past employment

re·sump·tion /rɪˈzʌmpʃən/ n [U] act of resuming

re·sur·gence /rɪˈsɜrdʒəns/ n [U] becoming active again

res·ur·rect /ˌrezəˈrekt/ vt bring back into use or fashion ~**ion** /-ˈrekʃən/ n [U] fig. rebirth **2** [the+S] return of dead people to life at the end of the world **3** [the] (cap.) return of Christ to life after his death

re·sus·ci·tate /rɪˈsʌsəˌteʸt/ vt bring a person back to life –**tation** /rɪ-ˌsʌsəˈteʸʃən/ n [U]

re·tail[1] /ˈriʸteʸl/ n [U] sale of goods in stores to customers, not for reselling to anyone else ♦ adv ~**er** n ♦ /rɪˈteʸl/ vi/t sell by retail

re·tain /rɪˈteʸn/ vt **1** keep; avoid losing **2** hold in place **3** employ (esp. a lawyer)

re·tain·er /rɪˈteʸnər/ n **1** servant **2** wires used to keep teeth in position **3** money paid in advance for services to a lawyer, etc.

re·tal·i·ate /rɪˈtæliʸˌeʸt/ vi pay back evil with evil –**atory** /-ˈliʸəˌtɔriʸ, -ˌtoʷriʸ/ adj –**ation** /rɪˌtæliʸˈeʸʃən/ n [U]

re·tard /rɪˈtard/ vt make slow or late ~**ed** adj slow in development of the mind

retch /retʃ/ vi try to be sick

re·ten·tion /rɪˈtenʃən, -tʃən/ n [U] state or action of retaining (RETAIN)

re·ten·tive /rɪˈtentɪv/ adj able to remember things well

re·think /ˌriʸˈθɪŋk/ vt **rethought** /-ˈθɔt/ think again and perhaps change one's mind about **rethink** /ˈriʸθɪŋk/ n [S]

ret·i·cent /ˈretəsənt/ adj unwilling to say much –**cence** n [U]

ret·i·na /ˈretn-ə/ n area at the back of the eye which receives light

ret·i·nue /ˈretn-ˌuʷ, -ˌyuʷ/ n group traveling with and helping an important person

re·tire /rɪˈtaɪər/ vi **1** leave one's job, usu. because of age **2** leave a place of action **3** fml go away, esp. to a quiet place **4** fml go to bed ♦ vt dismiss from work and pay a PENSION to ~**ment** n [U] **retired** adj having stopped working **retiring** adj liking to avoid company

re·tort[1] /rɪˈtɔrt/ n quick or angry reply ♦ vt make a retort

retort[2] n bottle with a long neck, for heating chemicals

re·touch /ˌriʸˈtʌtʃ/ vt improve (a picture) with small additions

re·trace /rɪˈtreʸs, riʸ-/ vt go back over: *She retraced her steps.* (= went back the way she had come)

re·tract /rɪˈtrækt/ vi/t **1** draw back or in: *The cat retracted its claws.* **2** take back (a statement or offer one has made) ~**able** adj ~**ion** /-ˈtrækʃən/ n [U]

re·tread /ˈriʸtred/ n tire with a new covering of rubber ♦ vt make (a retread)

re·treat /rɪˈtriʸt/ vi **1** move backwards, esp. when forced **2** escape (from something unpleasant) ♦ n **1** [C;U] (act of) retreating **2** [the+S] military signal for this **3** [C] place one goes to for peace and safety

re·trench /rɪˈtrentʃ/ vi fml arrange to lessen (one's spending) ~**ment** n [C;U]

re·tri·al /ˌriʸˈtraɪəl/ n new trial of a law case

ret·ri·bu·tion /ˌretrəˈbyuʷʃən/ n fml deserved punishment

re·trieve /rɪˈtriʸv/ vt **1** find and bring back **2** fml put right **retrieval** n [U] **retrieving retriever** n dog that retrieves shot birds

ret·ro·grade /ˈretrəˌɡreʸd/ adj moving back to an earlier and worse state

ret·ro·gres·sion /ˌretrəˈɡreʃən/ n [U] fml going back to an earlier and worse state –**sive** /-ˈɡresɪv/ adj

ret·ro·spect /ˈretrəˌspekt/ n **in retrospect** looking back to the past ~**ive** /ˌretrəˈspektɪv◂/ adj 1 thinking about the past 2 (of a law) having an effect on the past 3 also **retrospective ex·hi·bi·tion** /ˌ···ˌ·····'··/ — n a show of the work of a painter, SCULPTOR, etc., from his or her earliest years up to the present time

re·turn¹ /rɪˈtɜrn/ v 1 vi come or go back 2 vt give or send back 3 vt give (a VERDICT) 4 **return a favor** do a kind action in return for another

return² n 1 [C;U] (act of) coming or giving back 2 [C] profit 3 [C] official statement or set of figures: a tax return 4 **in return for** in exchange (for) 5 **Many happy returns (of the day)!** (used as a birthday greeting) ♦ adj (of a ticket) for the return part of a trip

Reu·ben sand·wich /ˌruˈbən ˈsændwɪtʃ, -ˈsænwɪtʃ/ n sandwich made with RYE bread, meat, cheese, SAUERKRAUT, and dressing

re·un·ion /riˈyunyən/ n 1 [C] meeting of former fellow workers, students, or friends after a separation 2 [U] state of being brought together again

rev /rev/ vt –vv– increase the speed of (an engine) ♦ sl for REVOLUTION (3)

re·vamp /riˈvæmp/ vt give a new and improved form to

re·veal /rɪˈviʲl/ vt allow to be seen or known

re·veil·le /ˈrevəliʲ/ n [U] signal to waken soldiers in the morning

rev·el /ˈrevəl/ v –l– lit pass the time in dancing, etc. ~**er** n person taking part in revelry ~**ry** n [U] wild noisy dancing and feasting

revel in phr vt enjoy greatly

rev·e·la·tion /ˌrevəˈleʲʃən/ n 1 [U] making known of something secret: forced to resign by the revelation of his unpleasant activities 2 [C] (surprising) fact made known

re·venge /rɪˈvendʒ/ n [U] punishment given in return for harm done to oneself ♦ vt do something in revenge

rev·e·nue /ˈrevəˌnuʷ, -ˌnyuʷ/ n [U] income, esp. received by the government

re·ver·be·rate /rɪˈvɜrbəˌreʲt/ vi (of sound) be continuously repeated in waves –**ration** /rɪˌvɜrbəˈreʲʃən/ n [C;U]

re·vere /rɪˈvɪər/ vt fml respect and admire greatly

rev·e·rence /ˈrevərəns/ n [U] fml great respect and admiration

Rev·e·rend /ˈrevərənd/ n (title of respect for) a Christian priest

rev·e·rent /ˈrevərənt/ adj showing (religious) reverence ~**ly** adv

rev·e·ren·tial /ˌrevəˈrenʃəl◂/ adj showing reverence ~**ly** adv

rev·e·rie /ˈrevəriʲ/ n [C;U] pleasant dreamlike state while awake

re·ver·sal /rɪˈvɜrsəl/ n 1 [C;U] (case of) being reversed 2 [C] defeat or piece of bad luck

re·verse /rɪˈvɜrs/ adj opposite in position: the reverse side | in reverse order ♦ n 1 [U] opposite 2 [U] position of a vehicle's controls that causes backward movement 3 [C] REVERSAL(2) 4 [C] back side of a coin, etc. ♦ v 1 vi/t go or cause (a vehicle) to go backwards 2 vt change around or over to the opposite: reverse the order | reverse a decision 3 **reverse the charges** make a telephone call to be paid for by the receiver

reverse dis·crim·i·na·tion /·ˌ· ····'··/ n [U] practice or principle of favoring people who are often treated unfairly, esp. because of their sex or race

re·ver·sion /rɪˈvɜrʒən/ n [U] return to a former condition or habit

re·vert /rɪˈvɜrt/ v **revert to** phr vt go back to (a former condition, habit, or owner)

re·view /rɪˈvyuʷ/ vt 1 consider and judge (an event or situation) 2 hold a REVIEW (2) 3 give a REVIEW (3a) of ♦ n 1 [C;U] (act of) REVIEWing (1) 2 a [C] (written) expression of judgment on a new book, play, etc. b magazine containing such judgments ~**er** n 3 grand show of armed forces, in the presence of a leader, general, etc.

re·vile /rɪˈvaɪl/ vt fml say bad things about

re·vise /rɪˈvaɪz/ v 1 vt improve and make correct (written material) 2 vt change (an opinion, intention, etc.)

re·vi·sion /rɪˈvɪʒən/ n 1 [C;U] (act of) revising 2 [C] revised piece of writing

re·vi·sion·is·m /rɪˈvɪʒənˌɪzəm/ n [U] questioning of the main beliefs of a (Marxist) political system –**ist** n

re·vi·tal·ize /riʲˈvaɪtlˌaɪz/ vt put new strength or power into

re·vive /rɪˈvaɪv/ v 1 vi/t become or make conscious or healthy again: (fig.) The photo revived (= brought to mind) old memories. 2 vi/t come or bring back into use or existence 3 vt perform (an old play) again after many years **revival** n 1 [C;U] rebirth 2 [C] new performance of an old play

rev·o·ca·tion /ˌrevəˈkeʲʃən/ n [U] revoking

re·voke /rɪˈvoʷk/ vt put an end to (a law, decision, permission, etc.)

re·volt /rɪˈvoʷlt/ v 1 vi (try to) take

power violently from those in power **2** vt (cause) to feel sick and shocked ♦ n [C;U] (example of) the act of REVOLTing (1) ~ing adj extremely nasty –**ingly** adv: *revoltingly dirty*

rev·o·lu·tion /ˌrevəˈluːʃən/ n **1** [C;U] (time of) great social change esp. of a political system by force **2** [C] complete change in ways of thinking or acting **3** [C] one complete circular movement –**ary** adj **1** of a REVOLUTION (1) **2** completely new and different ♦ n person who favors or joins in a REVOLUTION (1) ~**ize** vt cause a REVOLUTION (2) in

re·volve /rɪˈvɑlv/ vi/t spin around on a central point

  revolve around phr vt have as a center or main subject

re·volv·er /rɪˈvɑlvər/ n small gun with a revolving container for bullets

revolving cred·it /·,·· ˈ··/ n [U] CREDIT available up to a limit while payments are being made

re·vue /rɪˈvyuː/ n theatrical show with short acts, songs, jokes, etc.

re·vul·sion /rɪˈvʌlʃən/ n [U] feeling of being REVOLTed (2)

re·ward /rɪˈwɔrd/ n **1** [C;U] (something gained in) return for work or service **2** [C] money given for helping the police ♦ vt give a reward to or for ~**ing** adj giving personal satisfaction

re·wind /ˌriːˈwaɪnd/ vt go back to the beginning of (a TAPE, film, etc.)

re·work /ˌriːˈwɜrk/ vt put (music, writing, etc.) into a new or different form (in order to use again)

rhap·so·dy /ˈræpsədiː/ n **1** expression of too great praise and excitement **2** piece of music of irregular form –**dic** /ræpˈsɑdɪk/ adj

rhet·o·ric /ˈretərɪk/ n [U] **1** art of speaking to persuade **2** word which sound fine but have no meaning ~**al** /rɪˈtɔrɪkəl, -ˈtɑr-/ adj **1** asked or asking only for effect, and not expecting an answer: *a rhetorical question* **2** of or showing rhetoric –**ally** /-kliː/ adv

rheu·ma·tism /ˈruːmətɪzəm/ n [U] disease causing joint or muscle pain -**matic** /ruːˈmætɪk/ adj of, suffering from, or being rheumatism

rheu·ma·toid ar·thri·tis /ˌruːmətɔɪd ɑrˈθraɪtɪs/ n [U] disease that lasts a long time, causing pain and stiffness in the joints

rhine·stone /ˈraɪnstoʊn/ n diamond-like jewel made from glass or a transparent rock

rhi·no /ˈraɪnoʊ/ n –**nos** rhinoceros

rhi·no·ce·ros /raɪˈnɑsərəs/ n large African or Asian animal with thick skin and either 1 or 2 horns on its nose

rho·do·den·dron /ˌroʊdəˈdendrən/ n large bush with large bright flowers

rhom·bus /ˈrɑmbəs/ n figure with 4 equal straight sides

rhu·barb /ˈruːbɑrb/ n [U] plant with large leaves and thick red stems that are eaten

rhyme /raɪm/ v **1** vi (of words or lines in poetry) end with the same sound: *'Cat' rhymes with 'mat'.* **2** vt put together (words) ending with the same sound ♦ n **1** [U] (use of) rhyming words at ends of lines in poetry **2** [C] word that rhymes with another **3** [C] short simple rhyming poem **4 rhyme or reason** (any) sense or meaning

rhythm /ˈrɪðəm/ n [C;U] regular repeated pattern of sounds or movements: (fig.) *the rhythm of the seasons* -**mic** /ˈrɪðmɪk/, –**mical** adj –**mically** /-kliː/ adv

rhythm and blues /ˌ··· ˈ·/ n popular form of Black music

rhythm meth·od /ˈ·· ˌ··/ n [the+S] method of CONTRACEPTION which depends on having sex only at a time when the woman is not likely to CONCEIVE

rib /rɪb/ n **1** any of the curved bones enclosing the chest **2** curved rod for strengthening a frame **3** thin raised line in a pattern ♦ vt -**bb**- laugh at (someone) ~**bed** adj having a pattern of RIBS (3)

rib·ald /ˈrɪbəld/ adj fml (of jokes or laughter) rude and disrespectful

rib·bon /ˈrɪbən/ n long narrow band of cloth

rib cage /ˈ· ·/ n all one's RIBS (1)

rice /raɪs/ n [U] (plant with) a seed that is widely eaten

rice pa·per /ˈ· ˌ··/ n [U] sort of eatable paper

rich /rɪtʃ/ adj **1** having a lot of money or property **2** having a lot: *a city rich in ancient buildings* **3** expensive, valuable, and beautiful **4** (of food) containing a lot of cream, eggs, sugar, etc. **5** (of a sound or color) deep, strong, and beautiful **6** infml amusing but often rather annoying ♦ n [(the) P] rich people ~**ly** adv **1** splendidly **2** fully: *richly deserved* ~**ness** n [U]

rich·es /ˈrɪtʃɪz/ n [U] esp. lit wealth

rick /rɪk/ n large pile of dried grass

rick·ets /ˈrɪkɪts/ n [U] children's disease in which bones become soft and bent

rick·et·y /ˈrɪkətiː/ adj weak and likely to break

rick·shaw /ˈrɪkʃɔ/ n small East Asian carriage pulled by a man

ric·o·chet /ˈrɪkəˌʃeɪ/ n sudden change of direction of a bullet, stone, etc., when it hits a hard surface ♦ *vi* –t– change direction in a ricochet

rid /rɪd/ *v* (**rid** or **ridded**, *pres. p.* **-dd-**) **rid of** *phr vt* **1** make free of **2 get rid of: a** free oneself from **b** drive or throw away or destroy

rid·dance /ˈrɪdns/ *n* **good riddance** (said when one is glad that someone or something has gone)

rid·dle¹ /ˈrɪdl/ *n* **1** difficult and amusing question **2** mystery

riddle² *v* **riddle with** *phr vt* make full of holes

ride¹ /raɪd/ *v* **rode** /roʷd/, **ridden** /ˈrɪdn/ **1** *vi/t* travel along on (a horse, etc.), a bicycle, or a motorcycle) **2** *vi* travel on a bus **3** *vt* remain safe (and floating) through: *a ship riding a storm* **4 let something ride** let something continue, taking no action **5 ride high** have great success **6 ride roughshod over** act in a hurtful way towards **rider** *n* **1** person riding esp. a horse **2** statement added to esp. an official declaration or judgment

ride out *phr vt* come safely through (bad weather, trouble)

ride up *phr vi* (of clothing) move upwards or out of place

ride² *n* **1** journey on an animal, in a vehicle, etc. **2 take someone for a ride** deceive someone

ridge /rɪdʒ/ *n* long narrow raised part, where 2 slopes meet

rid·i·cule /ˈrɪdəˌkjuʷl/ *n* [U] unkind laughter ♦ *vt* laugh unkindly at

ri·dic·u·lous /rɪˈdɪkyələs/ *adj* silly ~**ly** *adv*

rife /raɪf/ *adj* (of a bad thing) widespread; common

rif·fle /ˈrɪfəl/ *v* **riffle through** *phr vt* turn over (papers, etc.) quickly, searching

riff-raff /ˈrɪfræf/ *n* [U] *derog* worthless, badly behaved people

ri·fle¹ /ˈraɪfəl/ *n* gun with a long barrel, fired from the shoulder

rifle² *vt* search through and steal from

rift /rɪft/ *n* crack: (fig.) *a rift in their friendship*

rig¹ /rɪg/ *vt* -**gg**- fit (a ship) with sails, ropes, etc.

rig out *phr vt* dress in special or funny clothes

rig up *phr vt* make quickly and roughly

rig² *n* **1** way a ship's sails and MASTS are arranged **2** apparatus: *a drilling rig* ~**ging** *n* [U] all the ropes, etc., holding up a ship's sails

rig³ *vt* -**gg**- arrange dishonestly for one's own advantage

right¹ /raɪt/ *adj* **1 a** on the side of the body away from the heart **b** in the direction of one's right side: *the*

right bank of the river **2** just; proper; morally good **3** correct **4** in a proper or healthy state; *to put the trouble right* | *Are you all right?*

right² *n* **1** [U] RIGHT¹ (1) side or direction **2** [U] what is RIGHT¹ (2) **3** [C;U] morally just or legal claim: *You've no right to* (= should not) *say that*. **4** [U] political parties that favor less change and less state control **5 in one's own right** because of a personal claim that does not depend on anyone else **6 in the right** not wrong or deserving blame ~**ness** *n* [U]: *the rightness of their claim* – see also RIGHTS

right³ *adv* **1** towards the RIGHT² (1,2) **2** correctly **3** exactly: *right in the middle* **4** completely: *Go right back to the beginning!* **5** yes; I will: *'See you tomorrow.' 'Right!'* – see also ALL RIGHT **6 right away** at once

right⁴ *vt* put back to a correct position or condition

right an·gle /ˌ· ˈ··/ *n* angle of 90 degrees

right·eous /ˈraɪtʃəs/ *adj* **1** morally good **2** having just cause: *righteous indignation* ~**ly** *adv* ~**ness** *n* [U]

right·ful /ˈraɪtfəl/ *adj* according to a just or legal claim ~**ly** *adv*

right-hand /ˈ· ·/ *adj* on the right side ~**ed** *adj* using the right hand for most actions ~**er** *n* right-handed person

right-hand man /ˌ· · ˈ·/ *n* most useful and valuable helper

right·ly /ˈraɪtliʸ/ *adv* **1** correctly **2** justly

right-mind·ed /ˌ· ˈ··◂/ *adj* having the right opinions, principles, etc.

right of way /ˌ· · ˈ·/ *n* **1** [U] right of a vehicle to go first **2** [C] (right to follow) a path across private land

rights /raɪts/ *n* [P] **1** political, social, etc., advantages with which someone has a just claim, morally or in law **2 by rights** in justice; if things were done properly **3 set/put someone/ something to rights** make someone/something just, healthy, etc. **4 the rights and wrongs of** the true facts of **5 within one's rights** not going beyond one's just claims

right-to-life /ˌ· · ˈ·/ *adj* opposing ABORTION -**lifer** *n*

right wing /ˌ· ˈ·/ *n* [U] of a political party of the RIGHT² (4)

ri·gid /ˈrɪdʒɪd/ *adj* **1** stiff **2** not easy to change ~**ly** *adv* ~**ity** /rɪˈdʒɪdətiʸ/ *n* [U]

rig·ma·role /ˈrɪgməˌroʷl/ *n* [S;U] long confused story or set of actions

rig·or /ˈrɪgər/ *n* [U] **1** severity **2** *fml* exactness and clear thinking

rig·or mor·tis /ˌrɪgər ˈmɔrtɪs/ *n* [U] stiffening of the muscles after death

rig·or·ous /ˈrɪgərəs/ adj **1** careful and exact **2** severe ~**ly** adv

rile /raɪl/ vt infml annoy

Ri·ley /ˈraɪliʸ/ n see LIFE OF RILEY

rim /rɪm/ n edge, esp. of a round object ♦ vt -**mm**- be around the edge of

rime /raɪm/ n [U] lit white FROST

rind /raɪnd/ n [C;U] thick outer covering of certain fruits, cheese, etc.

ring¹ /rɪŋ/ n **1** (metal) circle worn on the finger **2** circular band: smoke rings **3** circular mark or arrangement: a ring of troops around the building **4** enclosed space where things are shown, performances take place, or esp. people BOX or WRESTLE **5** group of people who work together, esp. dishonestly: a drug ring **6 run rings around** do things much better and faster than ♦ vt form or put a ring around

ring² v rang /ræŋ/, rung /rʌŋ/ **1** vi/t cause (a bell) to sound **2** vi (of a bell, telephone, etc.) sound **3** vi be filled with sound **4 ring a bell** remind one of something **5 ring the changes** introduce variety in **6 ring true/false** sound true/untrue ♦ n **1** [C] (making) a bell-like sound **2** [S] certain quality: It had a ring of truth. (= sounded true) **3** [S] esp. BrE telephone call: give me a ring later (= call me)

ring out phr vi (of a voice, bell, etc.) sound loudly and clearly

ring up phr vt **1** record (money paid) on a CASH REGISTER

ring·er /ˈrɪŋər/ n see DEAD RINGER

ring fin·ger /ˈ· ˌ··/ n the finger next to the smallest finger, esp. on the left hand

ring·lead·er /ˈrɪŋˌliʸdər/ n person who leads others to do wrong

ring·let /ˈrɪŋlɪt/ n long hanging curl of hair

ring·mas·ter /ˈrɪŋˌmæstər/ n person who directs CIRCUS performances

ring·side /ˈrɪŋsaɪd/ adj, adv, n (at) the edge of a RING¹ (4)

ring·worm /ˈrɪŋwɜrm/ n [U] disease causing red rings on the skin

rink /rɪŋk/ n specially prepared surface for skating (SKATE)

rink·y-dink /ˈrɪŋkiʸ ˌdɪŋk/ adj small and unimpressive

rinse /rɪns/ vt wash in clean water, so as to get rid of soap, dirt, etc. ♦ n **1** [C] act of rinsing **2** [C;U] liquid hair coloring

ri·ot /ˈraɪət/ n **1** [C] noisy violent crowd behavior **2** [S] large, impressive show: The garden is a riot of color. **3** [S] infml very funny and successful occasion or person **4 run riot**: **a** become violent and uncontrollable **b** (of a plant) grow too thick

and tall ♦ vi take part in a riot ~**er** n ~**ous** adj wild and disorderly

rip /rɪp/ vi/t **1** tear quickly and violently **2 let something rip** infml remove control and let things develop in their own way ♦ n long tear

rip off phr vt infml **1** charge too much **2** steal **rip-off** /ˈ· ·/ n something for which too much is charged or paid

RIP /ˌɑr aɪ ˈpiʸ/ abbrev. for: rest in peace (= words written on the stone over a grave)

rip·cord /ˈrɪpkɔrd/ n cord pulled to open a PARACHUTE

ripe /raɪp/ adj **1** (fully grown and) ready to be eaten: a ripe apple **2** ready; suitable: land ripe for industrial development **3** grown-up and experienced: He's reached the ripe old age of 90. ~**ness** n [U]

rip·en /ˈraɪpən/ vi/t make or become ripe

ri·poste /rɪˈpoʷst/ vi, n (make) a quick clever (unfriendly) reply

rip·ple /ˈrɪpəl/ vi/t **1** move in small waves **2** make a sound like gently running water ♦ n [C] **1** very small wave or gentle waving movement **2** sound of or like gently running water

rip-roar·ing /ˌ· ˈ··◂/ adj noisy and exciting

rise¹ /raɪz/ vi rose /roʷz/, risen /ˈrɪzən/ **1** go up; get higher: (fig.)My spirits rose. (= I became happier) **2** (of the sun, etc.) come above the horizon **3** (of land) slope upward **4** stand up **5** fml get out of bed **6** (of wind) get stronger **7** increase in size or number: Let the bread rise./rising crime rate **8** REBEL¹: They rose up against their leaders. **9** come back to life after being dead **10** (esp. of a river) begin **11** move up in rank **12 rise to the occasion** show that one can deal with a difficult matter **rising** n UPRISING

rise² n **1** [C] increase **2** [U] act of becoming greater or more powerful **3** reaction **4** [C] upward slope **5 give rise to** cause

ris·i·ble /ˈrɪzəbəl/ adj fml deserving to be laughed at

risk /rɪsk/ n [C;U] **1** chance that something bad may happen **2** (in insurance) a person or thing that is) a danger **3 at risk** in danger **4 at one's own risk** agreeing to bear any loss or danger **5 run/take a risk** do dangerous things ♦ vt **1** place in danger **2** take the chance of: Are you willing to risk failure? ~**y** adj dangerous

ri·sot·to /rɪˈsɒtoʷ, -ˈzɒt-/ n [C;U] rice dish with chicken, vegetables, etc.

ris·qué /rɪˈskeɪ/ adj (of a joke, etc.) slightly rude

rite /raɪt/ n ceremonial (religious) act with a fixed pattern

rit·u·al /ˈrɪtʃuˈəl/ n [C;U] (ceremonial) act or acts always repeated in the same form ♦ adj done as a rite: *ritual murder*

ritz·y /ˈrɪtsiʸ/ adj showy and expensive

ri·val /ˈraɪvəl/ n person with whom one competes ♦ adj competing ♦ vt -l- be as good as ~ry n [C;U] competition

riv·en /ˈrɪvən/ adj fml split violently apart

riv·er /ˈrɪvər/ n wide natural stream of water

riv·et /ˈrɪvɪt/ n metal pin used for fastening heavy metal plates together ♦ vt 1 fasten with rivets 2 attract and hold (someone's attention) strongly ~ing adj very interesting

ri·vi·e·ra /ˌrɪviʸˈɛərə/ n stretch of coast where people vacation

riv·u·let /ˈrɪvyəlɪt/ n lit very small stream

roach /roʷtʃ/ n COCKROACH

road /roʷd/ n 1 smooth prepared track for vehicles with wheels: (fig.) *We're on the road to* (= on the way to) *success.* **2 on the road** traveling

road·block /ˈroʷdblɑk/ n something placed across a road to stop traffic

road hog /ˈ· ·/ n fast selfish careless driver

road·house /ˈroʷdhaʊs/ n restaurant or bar on a road outside a town

road·run·ner /ˈroʷdˌrʌnər/ n bird that can run very quickly

roadside /ˈroʷdsaɪd/ adj near the side of the road: *roadside cafe*

road·way /ˈroʷdweɪ/ n middle part of a road, where vehicles drive

road·wor·thy /ˈroʷdˌwɜrðiʸ/ adj (of a vehicle) in safe condition to drive ~thiness n [U]

roam /roʷm/ vi/t wander around with no clear purpose

roan /roʷn/ n, adj (horse) of mixed color

roar /rɔr/ n deep loud continuing sound: *roars of laughter* ♦ v 1 vi give a roar 2 vt say forcefully 3 vi laugh loudly ~ing adj, adv 1 very great: *We're doing a roaring trade.* (= doing very good business) 2 very: *roaring drunk*

roast /roʷst/ vt cook (esp. meat) in an OVEN or over a fire ♦ adj roasted ♦ n large piece of roasted meat

rob /rɑb/ vt -bb- steal something from ~ber n ~bery n [C;U] (example of) the crime of robbing

robe /roʷb/ n long flowing garment

rob·in /ˈrɑbɪn/ n small brown bird with a red front

ro·bot /ˈroʷbɑt, -bət/ n machine that can do some of the work of a human being ~ics /roʷˈbɑtɪks/ n [U] study of the making and use of robots

ro·bust /roʷˈbʌst, ˈroʷbʌst/ adj strong (and healthy) ~ly adv ~ness n [U]

rock¹ /rɑk/ n 1 [C;U] stone forming part of the Earth's surface 2 [C] (large piece of) stone 3 emotionally strong person 4 [C] a diamond 5 [U] ROCK'N'ROLL 6 **on the rocks**: a (of a marriage) likely to fail soon b (of a drink) with ice but no water

rock² v 1 vi/t move regularly backwards and forwards or from side to side 2 vt shock greatly 3 **rock the boat** spoil the existing good situation

rock and roll /ˌ· · ·ˈ·/ n [U] ROCK'N'ROLL

rock bot·tom /ˌ· ˈ··◂/ n [U] the lowest point

rock can·dy /ˌ· ˈ··/ n hard sugar candy

rock·er /ˈrɑkər/ n 1 curved piece of wood on which something rocks 2 ROCKING CHAIR 3 **off one's rocker** infml crazy

rock·et /ˈrɑkɪt/ n object shaped like a tube driven through the air by burning gases, used for traveling into space, or as a MISSILE or FIREWORK ♦ vi rise quickly and suddenly

rock gar·den /ˈ· ˌ··/ n (part of a) garden laid out with rocks and small plants

rock·ing chair /ˈ·· ˌ·/ n chair with ROCKERS

rocking horse /ˈ·· ˌ·/ n wooden horse with ROCKERS, for a child to ride on

rock 'n' roll /ˌrɑk ən ˈroʷl/ n [U] popular modern music with a strong loud beat

rock·y /ˈrɑkiʸ/ adj 1 full of rocks 2 infml unsteady; not firm

ro·co·co /rəˈkoʷkoʷ/ adj with much curling decoration

rod /rɑd/ n long thin stiff pole or bar

rode /roʷd/ past t. of RIDE

ro·dent /ˈroʷdnt/ n small animal with long front teeth, such as a mouse, rat, or rabbit, that eats plants

ro·de·o /ˈroʷdiʸˌoʷ, roʷˈdeʸoʷ/ n -os public performance of COWBOY skills with horse riding, cattle catching, etc.

roe /roʷ/ n [C;U] mass of fish eggs, often eaten

ro·ger /ˈrɑdʒər/ interj (used in radio and signaling to say one has understood)

rogue /rəʷg/ n old-fash dishonest person ♦ adj 1 (of a wild animal) bad-tempered and dangerous 2 not following the usual or accepted standards **roguish** adj playful and fond of playing tricks

rogues' gal·ler·y /ˌˌ ˈˌˌˌ/ n collection of (pictures of) criminal or unpleasant people

role /rəʷl/ n 1 character played by an actor 2 part someone plays in an activity

roll¹ /rəʷl/ v 1 vi/t turn over and over or from side to side: *The ball rolled into the hole.* 2 vt form into esp. a tube by curling round and round 3 vi move steadily and smoothly (as if) on wheels 4 vi swing from side to side on the sea 5 vt make flat with a ROLLER (1) or ROLLING PIN 6 vi make a long deep sound 7 vt cause (esp. film cameras) to begin working 8 vt cause (the eyes) to move round and round 9 **roll in the aisles** (esp. of people at the theater) laugh uncontrollably 10 **roll one's r's** pronounce the sound /r/ with the tongue beating rapidly against the roof of the mouth 11 **roll one's own** infml make one's own cigarettes instead of buying them ~**ing** adj 1 (of land) with long gentle slopes 2 **rolling in dough** infml extremely rich

roll in phr vi arrive in large quantities

roll out phr vi 1 get out of bed 2 vt UNROLL

roll up phr vi 1 arrive 2 (used esp. asking people to see a show at a CIRCUS, etc.) come in

roll² n 1 act of rolling 2 rolled tube 3 small loaf of bread for one person 4 long deep sound (as if) of a lot of quick strokes: *a roll of drums* 5 official list of names 6 **on a roll** having several successes in a row: *He's on a roll.*

roll call /ˈˌ ·/ n calling a list of names to see who is there

roll·er /ˈrəʷlər/ n 1 apparatus shaped like a tube for pressing, making smooth, shaping, etc. 2 long heavy wave on the coast

roller coast·er /ˈˌˌ ˌˌˌ/ n small railway with sharp slopes and curves, found in amusement parks

roller der·by /ˈˌˌ ˌˌˌ/ n competition between two teams on roller skates

roller skate /ˈˌˌ ˌˌ/ n arrangement of 4 small wheels on a shoe, for moving along on **roller-skate** vi

rol·lick·ing /ˈrɑlɪkɪŋ/ adj noisy and merry

rolling pin /ˈˌˌ ˌ/ n piece of wood, etc. shaped like a tube, for making pastry flat

rolling stone /ˌˌˌ ˈˌ/ n person with no fixed home or responsibilities

ro·ly-po·ly /ˌrəʷliˈ ˈpəʷliˈ◄/ adj infml (of a person) fat and round

ROM /rɑm/ n read-only memory; computer memory holding information that is continuously needed by the computer

Ro·man /ˈrəʷmən/ n, adj (citizen) of Rome, esp. ancient Rome

Roman Cath·o·lic /ˌˌ ˈˌˌˌ/ n, adj (member) of the branch of the Christian religion led by the POPE ~**ism** /ˌˌ ·ˈˌˌˌˌ/ n [U]

ro·mance /rəʷˈmæns, ˈrəʷmæns/ n 1 [C] love affair 2 [U] ROMANTIC (3) quality 3 [C] story of love, adventure, etc. ♦ adj (cap.) of a group of Western European languages descended from Latin

Roman nu·me·ral /ˌˌ ˈˌˌˌ/ n any of the signs (such as I, II, V, X, L) used for numbers in ancient Rome and sometimes now

ro·man·tic /rəʷˈmæntɪk/ adj 1 showing warm feelings of love 2 of or suggesting love, adventure, strange happenings, etc. 3 having much imagination; not practical: *romantic notions* 4 showing romanticism ♦ n romantic person ~**ally** /-kliˈ/ adv ~**ism** /-təˌsɪzəm/ n [U] admiration of feeling rather than thought in art and literature ~**ize** vt make (something) seem more interesting or ROMANTIC (2) than it really is

Ro·ma·ny /ˈrəʷməniˈ/ n 1 [C] GYPSY 2 [U] gypsies' language

Ro·me·o /ˈrəʷmiˈˌəʷ/ n -os romantic male lover

romp /rɑmp/ vi play noisily and roughly ♦ n 1 occasion of romping 2 infml piece of amusing entertainment with plenty of action

romp through phr vt succeed in, quickly and easily

romp·ers /ˈrɑmpərz/ n [P] article of clothing made in one piece for babies

roof /ruʷf, rʊf/ n 1 top covering of a building, vehicle, etc. 2 upper part of the inside (of the mouth) ♦ vt put or be a roof on ~**ing** n [U] roof material

roof·top /ˈruʷftɑp, ˈrʊf-/ vt 1 roof 2 **from the rooftops** loudly, so that everyone can hear

rook¹ /rʊk/ n 1 large black bird, like a CROW 2 one of the powerful pieces in the game of CHESS

rook² vt sl cheat

rook·e·ry /ˈrʊkəriˈ/ n group of rooks' nests

rook·ie /ˈrʊkiˈ/ n 1 new soldier or policeman 2 first year professional ATHLETE

room /ruʷm, rʊm/ n 1 [C] division of a building, with its own floor, walls, and CEILING 2 [U] (enough) space **3** [U] need or possibility for something to happen: *room for improvement* ♦ *vi* have a place to live; have a room or rooms **—y** *adj* with plenty of space inside

room·mate /ˈruʷm‑meʸt, ˈrʊm‑/ *n* MATE¹ (1)

room ser·vice /ˈ· ‚·‚/ *n* [U] hotel service providing food, etc., in people's rooms

roost /ruʷst/ *n* **1** place where a bird sleeps **2 rule the roost** be the leader ♦ *vi* **1** (of a bird) sit and sleep **2 come home to roost** (of a bad action) have a bad effect on the doer, esp. after a period of time

roost·er /ˈruʷstər/ *n* fully grown male bird, esp. a chicken

root¹ /ruʷt/ *n* **1** part of a plant that goes down into the soil for food **2** part of a tooth, hair, etc., that holds it to the body **3** cause; beginning; origin **4** (in grammar) base part of a word to which other parts can be added **5** a number that when multiplied by itself a stated number of times gives another stated number **6 take root** (of plants or ideas) become established and begin to grow **—less** *adj* without a home **roots** *n* [P] **1** (one's connection with) one's place of origin **2 pull up one's roots** move to a new place from one's settled home **3 put down (new) roots** establish a (new) place, by making friends, etc. **—** see also GRASS ROOTS

root² *v* **1** *vi/t* (cause to) form roots: (fig.) *rooted to the spot* (= unable to move) | *deeply rooted* (= firmly fixed) **2** *vi* search by turning things over

root for *phr vt* support strongly

root out *phr vt* get rid of completely

root beer /ˈruʷtbɪər/ *n* gassy non-alcoholic drink

rope¹ /roʷp/ *n* **1** [C;U] (piece of) strong thick cord **2** [C] fat twisted string (of the stated kind) **3 give someone (plenty of) rope** allow someone (plenty of) freedom to act **4 ropes** *n* [P] rules, customs, and ways of operating

rope² *vt* tie with a rope

rope in *phr vt* *infml* persuade or force to join an activity

rope off *phr vt* separate or enclose with ropes

ro·sa·ry /ˈroʷzəriʸ/ *n* string of BEADS used by Roman Catholics for counting prayers

rose¹ /roʷz/ *past t. of* RISE

rose² *n* **1** (brightly colored flower with a sweet smell growing on) a bush with prickly stems **2** pale to dark pink color **3 —** see also BED OF ROSES

ro·sé /roʷˈzeʸ/ *n* [U] light pink wine

ro·se·ate /ˈroʷziʸət/ *adj lit* pink

rose-col·ored /ˈ· ‚·‚/ also **rose-tinted —** *adj* **look at/see/view the world through rose-colored glasses** see the world, life, etc., as better and more pleasant than they really are

ro·sette /roʷˈzɛt/ *n* flat flower-like arrangement of cloth, worn as a sign of something

rose win·dow /ˈ· ‚·‚/ *n* circular decorative church window

ros·in /ˈrazɪn/ *n* [U] substance rubbed on the BOWS² (2) of musical instruments with strings

ros·ter /ˈrastər/ *n* list of people's names and duties

ros·trum /ˈrastrəm/ *n* **—trums** or **—tra** /‑trə/ raised place for a public performer

ros·y /ˈroʷziʸ/ *adj* **1** (esp. of skin) pink **2** (esp. of future) giving hope

rot /rat/ *vi/t* **—tt‑** decay ♦ *n* [U] **1** decay **2** process of getting worse or going wrong **3** *infml* foolish nonsense

ro·ta·ry /ˈroʷtəriʸ/ *adj* rotating (ROTATE (1)) ♦ *n* area of circular traffic flow where several roads meet

ro·tate /ˈroʷteʸt/ *vi/t* **1** turn round a fixed point **2** (cause to) take turns or come round regularly **rotation** /roʷˈteʸʃən/ *n* **1** [U] action of rotating **2** [C] one complete turn **3 in rotation** taking regular turns

ROTC /ˈratsiʸ/ *n* RESERVE OFFICERS TRAINING CORPS

rote /roʷt/ *n* [U] *fml* repeated study using memory rather than understanding

rot·gut /ˈratgʌt/ *n* [U] *infml* strong alcoholic drink of low quality

ro·tor /ˈroʷtər/ *n* **1** rotating (ROTATE) part of a machine **2** set of HELICOPTER blades

rot·ten /ˈratn/ *adj* **1** decayed; gone bad **2** *infml* nasty or unpleasant **3 feel rotten** feel ill, tired, or unhappy

ro·tund /roʷˈtʌnd/ *adj fml* (of a person) fat and round

rou·ble /ˈruʷbəl/ *n* unit of money in the former USSR and its republics

rouge /ruʷʒ/ *n* [U] red substance for coloring the cheeks

rough¹ /rʌf/ *adj* **1** having an uneven surface **2** stormy and violent: *rough weather* **3** lacking gentleness, good manners, or consideration: *rough handling at the airport* **4** (of food and living conditions) not delicate; simple **5** not detailed or exact **6** unfortunate and/or unfair **7** *infml* unwell **8 rough and ready** simple and without comfort **—ly** *adv* **1** in a rough manner **2** about; not exactly

~**en** *vi/t* make or become rough
~**ness** *n* [U]

rough² /rʌf/ *n* **1** areas of long grass on a GOLF course **2 take the rough with the smooth** accept bad things as well as good things uncomplainingly

rough³ *v* **rough it** *infml* live simply and rather uncomfortably

rough up *phr vt infml* attack roughly, usu. as a threat

rough·age /ˈrʌfɪdʒ/ *n* [U] coarse matter in food, which helps the bowels to work

rough·cast /ˈrʌfkæst/ *n* [U] surface of little stones on the outside of a building

rough-hewn /ˌ·ˈ·◂/ *adj* (of wood or stone) roughly cut

rough·house /ˈrʌfhaʊs/ *vi* disorderly, noisy play esp. indoors –**housing** *n* [U]

rough·neck /ˈrʌfnɛk/ *n* unpleasant person with bad manners, esp. a boy or man

rough·shod /ˈrʌfʃɒd/ *adv* see **ride roughshod over** (RIDE¹)

rough stuff /ˈ· ·/ *n* [U] violent behavior esp. in sports

rou·lette /ruˈlɛt/ *n* [U] game of chance played with a small ball and a spinning wheel – see also RUSSIAN ROULETTE

round¹ /raʊnd/ *adj* **1** circular **2** shaped like a ball **3** (of parts of the body) fat and curved **4** (of a number) expressed to the nearest 10, 100, 1000, etc. ~**ness** *n* [U]

round² *adv* **1** around **2** with a circular movement: *The wheels went round.* **3** surrounding a central point: *Gather round.* **4** year round during the whole year **5 round about** a little bit more or less than

round³ *prep.* around

round⁴ *n* **1** number or set (of events): *a continual round of parties* **2** regular delivery journey: *do one's rounds* (= make one's usual visits) **3** number of esp. alcoholic drinks bought for everyone present: *I'll get the next round.* (= I'm paying) **4 a** (in GOLF) complete game **b** (in boxing (BOX²)) period of fighting in a match **c** (in tennis, football, etc.) stage in a competition **d** one single shot from a gun **5** long burst: *a round of applause* **6** type of song for 3 or 4 voices, in which each sings the same tune, one starting a line after another has just finished it

round⁵ *vt* **1** go around: *rounding the corner* **2** make round: *rounding his lips*

round off *phr vt* **1** reduce or increase to a whole number **2** end suitably and satisfactorily

round on *phr vt* turn and attack

round up *phr vt* **1** gather together (scattered things) **2** increase (an exact figure) to the next highest whole number

round·a·bout /ˈraʊndəˌbaʊt/ *adj* indirect

round·ly /ˈraʊndliʲ/ *adv fml* **1** completely **2** forcefully

round rob·in /ˌ· ˈ··/ *n* (sports) competition in which every team or player meets every other

round-ta·ble /ˌ· ˈ···◂/ *adj* at which everyone can meet and talk equally

round-the-clock /ˌ··· ·ˈ·◂/ *adj* happening both day and night

round trip /ˌ· ˈ·◂/ *n* journey to a place and back again **round-trip** *adj*: *round-trip ticket*

round-up /ˈraʊndʌp/ *n* gathering together of scattered things, animals, or people

rouse /raʊz/ *vt* **1** waken **2** make more active, interested, or excited **rousing** *adj* that makes people excited

rous·ta·bout /ˈraʊstəˌbaʊt/ *n* man who does heavy unskilled work

rout /raʊt/ *n* complete defeat ♦ *vt* defeat completely

route /ruːt, raʊt/ *n* way from one place to another – see also EN ROUTE ♦ *vt* send by a particular route

rou·tine /ruːˈtiʲn/ *n* **1** [C;U] regular fixed way of doing things **2** [C] set of dance steps, songs, etc. ♦ *adj* **1** regular; not special **2** dull ~**ly** *adv* –**ize** *vt*

rove /roʊv/ *vi esp. lit* wander

row¹ /roʊ/ *n* **1** neat line of people or things **2 in a row** one after the other without a break

row² *vi/t* move (a boat) through the water with OARs

row·dy /ˈraʊdiʲ/ *adj* noisy and rough ♦ *n* –**dily** *adv* –**diness** *n* [U] ~**ism** *n* [U] rowdy behavior

row house /ˈ· ·/ *n* house in a row of houses connected to each other

roy·al /ˈrɔɪəl/ *adj* of a king or queen ♦ *n* member of the royal family ~**ly** *adv* splendidly

royal blue /ˌ·· ˈ·/ *adj* of a purple-blue color

roy·al·ist /ˈrɔɪəlɪst/ *n* supporter of rule by kings and queens

roy·al·ty /ˈrɔɪəltiʲ/ *n* **1** [U] people of the royal family **2** [C] payment made to the writer of a book, piece of music, etc., out of the money from its sales

rpm /ˌɑr piʲ ˈɛm/ *abbrev. for:* revolutions per minute

RSVP /ˌɑr ɛs viʲ ˈpiʲ/ please reply (written on invitations)

rub /rʌb/ *vi/t* –**bb**- **1** press against (something or each other) with a repeated up and down or round and round movement **2 rub it in** *infml* keep talking about something that another person wants to forget **3 rub salt in the wound** make someone's suffering even worse **4 rub shoulders with** *infml* meet socially and treat as equals **5 rub someone the wrong way** *infml* annoy ♦ *n* [C] act of rubbing **2** [*the*+S] cause of difficulty: *There's the rub.* ~**bing** *n* copy made by rubbing paper laid over the top

rub down *phr vt* **1** dry by rubbing **2** make smooth by rubbing

rub in *phr vt* make (liquid) go into a surface by rubbing

rub off *phr vi* come off a surface (onto another) by rubbing: (fig.) *I hope some of her good qualities rub off on you.*

rub·ber¹ /ˈrʌbər/ *n* **1** [U] elastic substance used for keeping out water, making tires, etc. **2** [C] CONDOM ~**y** *adj*

rubber² *n* competition, esp. in cards, which usu. consists of an odd number of games

rubber band /ˌ·· ˈ·, ˈ·· ˌ·/ *n* thin circle of rubber for fastening things together

rub·ber·neck /ˈrʌbərˌnɛk/ *vi/t* look at continuously with great interest ♦ *n* person who does this

rubber plant /ˈ·· ·/ *n* decorative house plant with large leaves

rubber-stamp /ˌ·· ˈ·/ *n* piece of rubber with raised letters or figures, for printing ♦ *vt* approve or support (a decision) officially, without really thinking about it

rub·bish /ˈrʌbɪʃ/ *n* [U] **1** waste material to be thrown away **2** nonsense

rub·ble /ˈrʌbəl/ *n* [U] broken stone and bricks, esp. from a destroyed building

ru·bi·cund /ˈruːbɪkənd/ *adj fml* fat, red, and healthy looking

ru·ble /ˈruːbəl/ *n* ROUBLE

ru·bric /ˈruːbrɪk/ *n fml* set of printed instructions

ru·by /ˈruːbiʸ/ *n* deep red precious stone

ruck·sack /ˈrʌksæk, ˈrʊk-/ *n* BACK-PACK

ruck·us /ˈrʌkəs/ *n* [S] noisy angry argument or disagreement

rud·der /ˈrʌdər/ *n* blade at the back of a boat or aircraft to control its direction

rud·dy /ˈrʌdiʸ/ *adj* **1** (of the face) pink and healthy looking **2** *lit* red

rude /ruːd/ *adj* **1** not polite; having bad manners **2** concerned with sex: *a rude joke* **3** sudden and violent: *a rude shock* **4** *old use* roughly made ~**ly** *adv* ~**ness** *n* [U]

ru·di·men·ta·ry /ˌruːdəˈmɛntəriʸ◄/ *adj* **1** (of facts, knowledge, etc.) at the simplest level **2** small and not fully usable: *rudimentary wings*

ru·di·ments /ˈruːdəmənts/ *n* [*the*+P] simplest parts of a subject, learned first

rue /ruː/ *vt* be very sorry about ~**ful** *adj* feeling or showing that one is sorry about something

ruff /rʌf/ *n* stiff white collar shaped like a wheel

ruf·fi·an /ˈrʌfiʸən/ *n* unpleasant violent man

ruf·fle /ˈrʌfəl/ *vt* **1** make uneven **2** trouble; upset

rug /rʌg/ *n* thick decorative floor mat

rug·by /ˈrʌgbiʸ/ *n* [U] type of European football played with an OVAL ball which can be handled

rug·ged /ˈrʌgɪd/ *adj* large, rough, and looking strong ~**ly** *adv* ~**ness** *n* [U]

ru·in /ˈruːɪn/ *n* **1** [U] destruction **2** [C] also **ruins** *pl.* — remains of a building that has fallen down or been (partly) destroyed ♦ *vt* **1** spoil **2** cause total loss of money to ~**ed** *adj* (of a building) partly or wholly destroyed ~**ous** *adj* causing destruction or total loss of money

ru·in·a·tion /ˌruːʷəˈneʸʃən/ *n fml* [U] (cause of) being ruined

rule¹ /ruːl/ *n* **1** [C] something that tells one what must be done: *the rules of the game* **2** [U] period or way of ruling: *under foreign rule* **3** [C] RULER (2) **4 as a rule** usually **ruling** *n* official decision

rule² *v* **1** *vi/t* be in charge of (a country, people, etc.) **2** *vi* give an official decision **3** *vt* draw (a line) with a ruler

rule out *phr vt* **1** remove from consideration **2** make impossible

rule of thumb /ˌ·· ·ˈ·/ *n* [C;U] quick inexact way of calculating or judging

rul·er /ˈruːlər/ *n* **1** person who rules **2** narrow flat rod for measuring or drawing straight lines

rum /rʌm/ *n* [U] strong alcoholic drink made from sugar

rum·ba /ˈrʌmbə/ *n* Latin American dance with quick movements

rum·ble¹ /ˈrʌmbəl/ *vi* a deep continuous rolling sound

rumble² *n* **1** [S] deep rolling sound **2** [C] street fight

ru·mi·nant /ˈruːmənənt/ *n, adj* (animal) that RUMINATES (2)

ru·mi·nate /ˈruːməˌneʸt/ *vi* **1** think deeply **2** (of an animal) bring food back from the stomach and CHEW it again ~**native** *adj* seeming thoughtful

rum·mage /ˈrʌmɪdʒ/ vi turn things over untidily in searching

rummage sale /ˈ·· ·/ n sale of used articles, esp. to raise money for CHARITY

rum·my /ˈrʌmiʸ/ n [U] simple card game

ru·mor /ˈruʷmər/ n [C;U] (piece of) information, perhaps untrue, spread from person to person ~ed adj reported unofficially

rump /rʌmp/ n part of an animal above the back legs: rump steak

rum·ple /ˈrʌmpəl/ vt make untidy; disarrange

run¹ /rʌn/ v ran /ræn/, run, pres. p. -nn- **1** vi (of people and animals) move faster than a walk **2** vi take part in (a race) by running **3** vi/t (cause to) move quickly: The car ran into a tree. **4** vi/t (cause to) work: This machine runs on/by electricity. **5** vi (of a public vehicle) travel as arranged **6** vt control (an organization or system) **7** vi go; pass: The road runs south. **8** vi continue in operation, performance, etc.: The play ran for 2 years in L.A. **9** vi (cause liquid) to flow: run a bath | running water **10** vi pour out liquid: The baby's nose is running. **11** vi (melt and) spread by the action of heat or water **12** become: Supplies are running low. **13** vi try to get elected **14** vt print in a newspaper **15** vt bring into a country illegally and secretly **16** vi to appear often: Intelligence runs in that family. **17** vt take (someone or something) to somewhere in a vehicle: I'll run you home. **18** run for it escape by running **19** run short: **a** use almost all one has and not have enough left **b** become less than enough

run across phr vt meet or find by chance

run after phr vt **1** chase **2** try to gain the attention and company of

run along phr vi go away

run away phr vi go away (as if) to escape

run away/off with phr vt **1** gain control of: Don't let your temper run away with you. **2** go away with (a lover) **3** steal

run down phr v **1** vt knock down and hurt with a vehicle **2** vt chase and catch **3** vi (esp. of a clock or BATTERY) lose power and stop working **4** vt say unfair things about

run into phr vt **1** meet by chance **2** cause (a vehicle) to meet (something) with force

run off phr vt print (copies)

run on phr vi continue (for too long)

run out phr vi **1** come to an end,

so there is none left **2** have none left: We've run out of gas.

run over phr v **1** vt knock down and drive over **2** vi overflow

run through phr vt **1** repeat for practice **2** read or examine quickly **3** push one's weapon right through

run to phr vt reach (the stated amount): the total runs to $55.60.

run up phr vt **1** raise (a flag) **2** cause oneself to have (bills or debts)

run up against phr vt be faced with (a difficulty)

run² n **1** [C] act of running **2** [C] ship or train journey **3** [S] continuous set of similar events, performances, etc.: a run of bad luck | The play had a run of 3 months. **4** [S] a eager demand to buy: a big run on ice cream **b** general desire to sell money or take one's money out: a run on a bank **5** [S] freedom to use: He gave me the run of his library. **6** [C] animal enclosure: a chicken run **7** point won in baseball **8** [C] sloping course: a ski run **9** [C] fault in a stocking, etc. **10** a (good) run for one's money: **a** plenty of opposition in a competition **b** good results for money spent or effort made **11** in the long run after a long period; in the end **12** on the run trying to escape **13** the common/ordinary run (of) the usual sort (of)

run·a·bout /ˈ·· ·,·/ n small light car

run·a·round /ˈ·· ·,·/ n [the+S] sl delaying or deceiving treatment

run·a·way /ˈrʌnəˌweʸ/ adj **1** out of control: runaway prices **2** having escaped by running: a runaway child

run·down /ˈrʌndaʊn/ n detailed report

run-down /ˌ· ˈ·◄/ adj **1** tired, weak, and ill **2** in bad condition

rune /ruʷn/ n letter in an alphabet formerly used in Northern Europe **runic** adj

rung¹ /rʌŋ/ past p. of RING²

rung² n sideways bar in a ladder or on a chair

run-in /ˈ· ·/ n infml quarrel or disagreement, esp. with the police

run·ner /ˈrʌnər/ n **1** person or animal that runs **2** smuggler (SMUGGLE): a gunrunner **3** thin blade on which something slides on ice or snow **4** stem with which a plant spreads itself along the ground

runner-up /ˌ·· ˈ·/ n runners-up one that comes second in a race, etc.

run·ning¹ /ˈrʌnɪŋ/ n **1** act or sport of running **2** in/out of the running with some/no hope of winning

running² adj **1** (of water) flowing **2** continuous: a running battle | a running commentary **3** (of money) spent or needed to keep something working: running costs **4** in running

order (of a machine) working properly **5 take a running jump** run to a point where one starts a jump ♦ *adv* in a row: *I won 3 times running.*

running-mate /'··· ·/ *n* (in politics) person with whom one is trying to get elected for a pair of political positions of greater and lesser importance

run·ny /'rʌnɪ/ *adj* **1** in a more liquid form than usual **2** (of the nose or eyes) producing liquid

run-of-the-mill /ˌ· · · '·◄/ *adj* ordinary; dull

run-on sen·tence /'· · ˌ··/ *n* sentence with too many CLAUSES

runt /rʌnt/ *n* **1** small animal that is poorly developed physically **2** *derog* small unpleasant person

run-through /'·· ·/ *n* act of repeating (something) for practice

run-up /'· ·/ *n* sudden increase

run·way /'rʌnweɪ/ *n* surface on which aircraft land and take off

ru·pee /ruˈpiʸ, 'ruʷpiʸ/ *n* unit of money in India, Pakistan, etc.

rup·ture /'rʌptʃər/ *n* **1** [C;U] *fml* sudden breaking **2** [C] HERNIA ♦ *v* **1** *vi/t fml* break suddenly **2** *vt* give (oneself) a HERNIA

ru·ral /'rʊərəl/ *adj* of the country (not the town)

ruse /ruʷz, ruʷs/ *n* deceiving trick

rush¹ /rʌʃ/ *v* **1** *vi/t* go or take suddenly and very quickly **2** *vi* hurry **3** *vt* deal with (too) hastily **4** *vt* force (someone) to eat hastily **5** *vt* attack suddenly and all together **6 rush someone off his/her feet** make someone hurry too much or work too hard ♦ *n* **1** [C] sudden rapid movement **2** [U] (need for) (too much) hurrying **3** [S] sudden demand **4** [U] period of great and

hurried activity: *the Christmas rush*

rush² *n* grasslike water plant

rush·es /'rʌʃɪz/ *n* [P] (in film making) the first print of a film

rush hour /'· ·/ *n* busy period when most people are traveling to or from work

rusk /rʌsk/ *n* ZWIEBACK

rus·set /'rʌsɪt/ *adj esp. lit* brownish red ♦ *n* kind of potato

Rus·sian rou·lette /ˌrʌʃən ruʷ'let/ *n* [U] dangerous game in which one fires a gun at one's head without knowing whether it is loaded

rust /rʌst/ *n* [U] **1** reddish brown surface formed on iron, steel, etc., that has been wet **2** the color of this ♦ *vi/t* (cause to) become covered with rust ~**y** *adj* **1** covered with rust **2** *infml* lacking recent practice

rus·tic /'rʌstɪk/ *adj* typical of the country, esp. in being simple ♦ *n usu. derog* person from the country

rus·tle /'rʌsəl/ *v* **1** *vi/t* (cause to) make slight sounds like dry leaves moving **2** *vt* steal (cattle or horses) **-tler** *n*

rustle up *phr vt* provide quickly

rut¹ /rʌt/ *n* **1** [C] deep narrow track left by a wheel **2** [S] dull fixed way of life ~**ted** *adj* having ruts

rut² *n* (season of) sexual excitement in some animals ♦ *vi* **-tt-** (of an animal) be in a rut

ru·ta·ba·ga /ˌruʷtəˈbeʸgə/ *n* large round yellow root vegetable

ruth·less /'ruʷθlɪs/ *adj* doing cruel things without pity ~**ly** *adv* ~**ness** *n* [U]

RV /ˌɑr 'viʸ/ also **recreational vehicle** — *n* large vehicle for traveling and sleeping in while on vacation

rye /raɪ/ *n* [U] grass plant with grain used esp. for flour

S

S, s /es/ the 19th letter of the English alphabet

S *written abbrev. for*: south(ern)

Sab·bath /'sæbəθ/ n [S] religious day of rest, esp. Saturday (for Jews) or (for Christians) Sunday

sab·bat·i·cal /sə'bætɪkəl/ n, adj period with pay when one is free to leave one's ordinary job to travel and study

sa·ble /'seɪbəl/ n [C;U] (dark fur from) a small animal

sab·o·tage /'sæbətaʒ/ n [U] intentional damage carried out secretly ♦ vt perform sabotage against

sab·o·teur /ˌsæbə'tɜr/ n person who practices sabotage

sa·ber /'seɪbər/ n heavy military sword, usu. curved

saber-rat·tling /'··ˌ··/ n [U] talking about (military) power in a threatening way

sac·cha·rin /'sækərɪn, 'sækəˌraɪn, -ˌriʲn/ n [U] chemical that tastes very sweet and is used instead of sugar

sach·et /sæ'ʃeʲ/ n small plastic bag holding an amount of liquid, etc.

sack¹ /sæk/ n 1 [C] large simple bag of strong material 2 [the+S] infml bed 3 hit the sack infml go to bed ~ing n [U] sackcloth

sack² vt destroy and rob (a defeated city) **sack** n [U]: *the sack of ancient Rome*

sack·cloth /'sæk-klɔθ/ n [U] 1 also **sacking** /'sækɪŋ/ — rough cloth for making sacks 2 **sackcloth and ashes** lit sign of sorrow for what one has done

sac·ra·ment /'sækrəmənt/ n important Christian ceremony, such as BAPTISM or marriage ~**al** /ˌsækrə'mentl◁/ adj

sa·cred /'seɪkrɪd/ adj 1 connected with religion 2 holy because connected with God or gods 3 that is solemn and must be respected ~**ness** n [U]

sacred cow /ˌ·· '·/ n derog thing so much accepted that no even honest doubts about it are allowed

sac·ri·fice /'sækrəˌfaɪs/ n 1 (an offering) to gods, esp. of an animal killed as part of a ceremony 2 loss or giving up of something of value ♦ v 1 vi/t offer (something or someone) as a SACRIFICE (1) 2 vt give up or lose, esp. for some good purpose –**ficial** /ˌsækrə'fɪʃəl◁/ adj

sac·ri·lege /'sækrəlɪdʒ/ n [C;U]

treating a holy place or thing without respect –**legious** /ˌsækrə-'lɪdʒəs◁/ adj

sac·ro·sanct /'sækroʷˌsæŋkt/ adj often derog or humor too holy or important to be treated disrespectfully or harmed

sad /sæd/ adj –**dd**- 1 unhappy 2 unsatisfactory ~**ly** adv –**den** vt make or become SAD (1) ~**ness** n [U]

sad·dle¹ /'sædl/ n 1 rider's seat on a horse, bicycle, etc. 2 **in the saddle**: **a** sitting on a SADDLE (1) **b** in control (of a job)

saddle² vt put a saddle on (a horse)

saddle with phr vt give (someone) (an unpleasant or difficult duty, responsibility, etc.)

sa·dis·m /'seʲˌdɪzəm, 'sæ-/ n [U] unnatural fondness for cruelty to others, (sometimes to gain sexual pleasure) –**dist** n –**distic** /sə'dɪstɪk/ adj

sa·do·mas·o·chis·m /ˌseʲdoʷ-'mæsəˌkɪzəm/ n [U] the gaining of (sexual) pleasure from hurting oneself (or other people)

sa·fa·ri /sə'fɑriʲ, sə'færiʲ/ n [C;U] journey to hunt or photograph animals, esp. in Africa

safe¹ /seʲf/ adj 1 out of danger 2 not likely to cause danger or harm 3 (in baseball) having reached base without being put out 4 **safe and sound** unharmed 5 **on the safe side** being more careful than may be necessary 6 **play it safe** take no risks ~**ly** adv ~**ness** n [U]

safe² n thick metal box with a lock; for keeping valuable things in

safe-con·duct /ˌ· '··/ n [C;U] official protection given to someone passing through an area

safe-de·pos·it box /·ˌ··ˌ· ·/ n small box for storing valuable objects, esp. in a bank

safe·guard /'seʲfgɑrd/ n means of protection against something unwanted ♦ vt protect

safe·keep·ing /ˌseʲf'kiʲpɪŋ/ n [U] protection from harm or loss

safe·ty /'seʲftiʲ/ n [U] condition of being safe

safety pin /'·· ˌ·/ n bent pin with a cover at one end, used for fastening things

safety valve /'·· ˌ·/ n 1 means of getting rid of possibly dangerous forces (in a machine) 2 something that allows strong feelings to be expressed in a non-violent way

saf·fron /'sæfrən/ n [U] 1 deep orange substance obtained from a flower, used for giving color and taste to food 2 orange-yellow color

sag /sæg/ vi –**gg**- 1 sink or bend downwards out of the usual position 2 become less active, happy, etc.: *My* *spirits sagged when I saw all the work I had to do.* **sag** *n* [S;U]

sa·ga /ˈsɑgə/ *n* **1** old story, esp. about adventure **2** long story

sa·ga·cious /səˈgeɪʃəs/ *adj fml* wise ~ **ly** *adv* **-city** /səˈgæsəti/ *n* [U]

sage /seɪdʒ/ *adj lit* wise, esp. from long experience ♦ *n* wise person, esp. an old man

sa·go /ˈseɪgoʷ/ *n* [U] white plant substance used for making sweet dishes

said /sɛd/ *v past t. and. p. of* SAY ♦ *adj* just mentioned

sail /seɪl/ *n* **1** piece of strong cloth that allows the wind to move a ship through the water **2** trip in a boat **3** blade of a WINDMILL, for catching the wind **4 set sail** begin a trip at sea **5 under sail** driven by sails and wind ♦ *v* **1** *vi/t* travel (across) by boat **2** *vt* direct or command (a boat) on water **3** *vi* be able to control a sailing boat: *Can you sail?* **4** *vi* begin a voyage **5** *vi* move smoothly or easily – see also **sail close to the wind** (CLOSE²) ~ **ing** *n* [U] sport of riding in or directing a small boat with sails

sail·board /ˈseɪlbɔrd, -boʷrd/ *n* flat board with a sail used in the sport of WINDSURFING

sail·or /ˈseɪlər/ *n* person who works on a ship

saint /seɪnt/ *n written abbrev.* St. **1** person officially recognized after death as especially holy by the Christian church **2** *infml* a very good and completely unselfish person ~ **ly** *adj* very holy

sake /seɪk/ *n* **1 for the sake of: a** in order to help, improve, or bring advantage to **b** for the purpose of **2 for Christ's/God's/goodness/pity's sake** *infml* (used to give force to urgent request or sometimes an expression of annoyance): *For goodness sake, stop arguing!* | *For God's sake, what do you want from me!*

sa·la·cious /səˈleɪʃəs/ *adj fml* showing a strong (improper) interest in sex

sal·ad /ˈsæləd/ *n* [C;U] a mixture of usu. raw vegetables served cold

salad days /ˈ·· ·/ *n* [P] one's time of youth and inexperience

sal·a·man·der /ˈsæləmændər/ *n* small animal like a LIZARD

sa·la·mi /səˈlɑmiʸ/ *n* [U] large salty SAUSAGE usu. eaten cold

sal·a·ry /ˈsæləriʸ/ *n* [C;U] fixed regular pay each month for a job, esp. for workers of higher rank – **ried** *adj* receiving a salary (as opposed to wages)

sale /seɪl/ *n* **1** [C;U] (act of) selling **2** [C] special offering of goods at low prices **3 for sale** offered to be sold,

esp. privately **4 on sale: a** offered to be sold, esp. in a store **b** at or in a SALE (2) **salable** *adj*

sales /seɪlz/ *adj* of or for selling: *a sales forecast*

sales·clerk /ˈseɪlzklɜrk/ *n* person who serves customers in a store

sales·man /ˈseɪlzmən/ *n* **-men** /-mən/ a male salesperson

sales·man·ship /ˈseɪlzmənʃɪp/ *n* [U] skill in selling

sales·per·son /ˈseɪlzˌpɜrsən/ *n* **-people** /-ˌpiʸpəl/1 a sales representative **2** SALESCLERK, esp. a skilled one

sales rep·re·sen·ta·tive /ˈ· ···,···/ *n* person who goes from place to place, usu. within a particular area, selling and taking orders for their company's goods

sales talk /ˈ· ·/ *n* [U] talking intended to persuade people to buy

sales tax /ˈ· ·/ *n* tax added onto the price of goods at the time of buying them

sales·wo·man /ˈseɪlzˌwʊmən/ *n* **-women** /-ˌwɪmɪn/ a female salesperson

sa·li·ent /ˈseɪliʸənt/ *adj fml* most noticeable or important

sa·line /ˈseɪliʸn, -laɪn/ *adj* containing salt

sa·li·va /səˈlaɪvə/ *n* [U] natural liquid produced in the mouth ~ **ry** *adj*

sal·low /ˈsæloʷ/ *adj* (of the skin) yellow and looking unhealthy ~ **ness** *n* [U]

sal·ly¹ /ˈsæliʸ/ *n* **1** quick short attack **2** sharp, clever remark

sally² *v* **sally forth** *phr vi often humor* go out, esp. to meet a difficulty

salm·on /ˈsæmən/ *n* salmon [C;U] large fish with pink flesh of great value as food

sal·mo·nel·la /ˌsælməˈnelə◄/ *n* [U] bacteria that causes food poisoning

sal·on /səˈlɑn/ *n* stylish or fashionable small shop: *a hairdressing salon*

sa·loon /səˈluʷn/ *n* **1** large grandly furnished room for use of ship's passengers **2** public drinking place, esp. in the old West

salt¹ /sɔlt/ *n* **1** [U] common white substance used for preserving food and improving its taste: *salt water* **2** [C] chemical compound of an acid and a metal **3** [C] *infml* an old, experienced sailor: *an old salt* **4 the salt of the earth** person or people regarded as worthy of admiration and dependable **5 take something with a pinch/grain of salt** not necessarily believe all of something – see also **worth one's salt** (WORTH)

salt² *vt* put salt on

salt away /phr vt save money (esp. for the future)

salt·pe·ter /ˌsɔltˈpiˠtɚr/ n [U] chemical used in making GUNPOWDER and matches

salt·shaker /ˈsɔltˌʃeˠkɚr/ n small bottle with holes for shaking salt on to food

salt·y /ˈsɔltiˠ/ adj containing or tasting of salt

sa·lu·bri·ous /səˈluʷbriˠəs/ adj 1 socially desirable or RESPECTABLE 2 fml giving health

sal·u·ta·ry /ˈsælyəˌteriˠ/ adj causing an improvement in character, future behavior, health, etc.

sal·u·ta·tion /ˌsælyəˈteˠʃən/ n 1 [C;U] fml expression of greeting by words or actions 2 [C] word or phrase such as 'Ladies and Gentlemen', 'Dear Sir', 'Dear Miss Jones', at the beginning of a speech or letter

sa·lute /səˈluʷt/ n 1 military sign of recognition, esp. raising the hand to the forehead 2 ceremonial firing of guns to honor someone 3 **take the salute** (of a person of high rank) to stand while being SALUTEd by soldiers marching past ♦ v 1 vi/t make a SALUTE (1) (to) 2 vt fml honor and praise 3 vt fml greet

sal·vage /ˈsælvɪdʒ/ vt save (goods or property) from wreck or destruction ♦ n [U] act or process of salvaging

sal·va·tion /sælˈveˠʃən/ n [U] 1 (esp. in the Christian religion) the saving or state of being saved from SIN 2 something or someone that saves one from loss or failure

Salvation Ar·my /ˌ·,·· ˈ··/ n Christian organization with military uniforms and ranks, that helps poor people

salve /sæv/ n [C;U] medicinal paste for putting on a wound, sore place, etc. ♦ vt fml make (esp. feelings) less painful

sal·ver /ˈsælvɚr/ n fine metal plate for serving food, drink, etc., formally

sal·vo /ˈsælvoʷ/ n **-vos** or **-voes** firing of several guns together

Sa·mar·i·tan /səˈmærətn/ n see GOOD SAMARITAN

sam·ba /ˈsæmbə, ˈsɑmbə/ n quick dance of Brazilian origin

same¹ /seˠm/ adj 1 not changed or different; not another or other 2 alike in (almost) every way 3 **one and the same** exactly the same 4 **same here** infml me too 5 **by the same token** in the same way 6 **in the same boat** in the same unpleasant situation

same² pron 1 the same thing, person, condition, etc. 2 **just/all the same** in spite of this 3 **same to**

you I wish you the same (a greeting or sometimes an angry wish) ~**ness** n [U] 1 very close likeness 2 lack of variety

same³ adv **the same (as)** in the same way (as)

sam·o·var /ˈsæməˌvɑːr/ n Russian water boiler for making tea

sam·ple /ˈsæmpəl/ n small part representing the whole ♦ vt take and examine a sample of

sam·pler /ˈsæmplɚr/ n piece of cloth with pictures, etc., stitched on it with thread, done to show one's skill at sewing

san·a·to·ri·um /ˌsænəˈtɔriˠəm, -ˈtoʷriˠəm/ n **-ums** or **-a** /riˠə/ sort of hospital for sick people who are getting better but still need treatment, rest, etc.

sanc·ti·fy /ˈsæŋktəˌfaɪ/ vt make holy

sanc·ti·mo·ni·ous /ˌsæŋktəˈmoʷniˠəs/ adj fml disapproving of others because one thinks one is good, right, etc., and they are not ~**ly** adv ~**ness** n [U]

sanc·tion /ˈsæŋkʃən/ n 1 [U] fml formal or official permission, approval, or acceptance 2 [C] action taken against a person or country that has broken a law or rule 3 [C] something that forces people to keep a rule: a moral sanction ♦ vt fml 1 accept, approve, or permit, esp. officially 2 make acceptable: a custom sanctioned by long usage

sanc·ti·ty /ˈsæŋktətiˠ/ n [U] holiness

sanc·tu·a·ry /ˈsæŋktʃuʷˌeriˠ/ n 1 [C] part of a (Christian) church considered most holy 2 [C;U] (place of) protection for someone being hunted by officers of the law 3 [C] area where animals are protected

sanc·tum /ˈsæŋktəm/ n 1 holy place inside a temple 2 infml private place or room where one can be quiet and alone

sand /sænd/ n [U] 1 loose material of very small grains, found on sea coasts and in deserts 2 **build on sand** plan or do something with no good reason to believe in its success ♦ vt 1 make smooth by rubbing with esp. SANDPAPER 2 put sand on, esp. to stop slipping **sands** n [P] 1 area of sand 2 moments in time (as if measured by sand in an HOURGLASS): The sands of time are running out. ~**y** adj 1 consisting of sand or having sand on the surface 2 (of hair) yellowish brown

san·dal /ˈsændl/ n light shoe with a flat bottom and bands to hold it to the foot

sand·bag /ˈsændbæɡ/ n bag filled with sand, esp. for forming a protective wall

sand·blast /ˈsændblæst/ vt clean or cut with a very fast stream of sand

sand·cas·tle /ˈsænd.kæsəl/ n 1 small model, esp. of a castle, built of sand 2 **sandcastles in the air** [P] impossible or impractical ideas or plans

S and L, S & L /ˌɛs ənd ˈɛl/ n SAVINGS AND LOAN ASSOCIATION

sand·pa·per /ˈsænd.peʸpər/ n [U] paper covered with fine grainy material, for rubbing surfaces to make them smoother ♦ vt rub with sandpaper

sand·stone /ˈsændstoʷn/ n [U] soft rock formed from sand

sand·storm /ˈsændstɔrm/ n desert storm in which sand is blown about

sand·wich /ˈsændwɪtʃ, ˈsænwɪtʃ/ n 2 pieces of bread with other food between them ♦ vt fit (with difficulty) between 2 other things

sandwich board /ˈ·· ˌ·/ n advertising signs hung at the front and back of someone who walks about in public

sane /seʸn/ adj 1 healthy in mind; not crazy 2 sensible ~**ly** adv ~**ness** n [U]

sang /sæŋ/ v past t. of SING

san·guine /ˈsæŋgwɪn/ adj fml quietly hopeful

san·i·ta·ry /ˈsænəˌteriʸ/ adj 1 concerned with preserving health, esp. by removing dirt 2 not dangerous to health; clean

sanitary nap·kin /ˌ····· ˈ··/ n small mass of soft paper worn to take up MENSTRUAL blood

san·i·ta·tion /ˌsænəˈteʸʃən/ n [U] methods of protecting public health, esp. by removing and treating waste

san·i·tize /ˈsænəˌtaɪz/ vt 1 make sanitary 2 derog make less unpleasant, dangerous, strongly expressed, etc., in order not to offend people

san·i·ty /ˈsænət̬iʸ/ n [U] quality of being SANE

sank /sæŋk/ v past t. of SINK[1]

San·ta Claus /ˈsæntə ˌklɔz, ˈsæntiʸ-/ n imaginary old man believed by children to bring presents at Christmas

sap[1] /sæp/ n [U] watery liquid that carries food in plants

sap[2] vt -pp- weaken or destroy, esp. over a long time

sap·ling /ˈsæplɪŋ/ n young tree

sap·py /ˈsæpiʸ/ adj 1 foolish 2 too full of expressions of tender feelings

sap·phire /ˈsæfaɪər/ n [C;U] bright blue precious stone

sar·casm /ˈsɑrˌkæzəm/ n [U] saying the clear opposite of what is meant, in order to be (amusingly) offensive −**castic** /sɑrˈkæstɪk/ adj −**tically** /-kliʸ/ adv

sar·coph·a·gus /sɑrˈkɑfəgəs/ n −**gi** /-gaɪ/ or −**guses** stone box for a dead body

sar·dine /sɑrˈdiʸn/ n 1 small young fish often preserved in oil for eating 2 **like sardines** packed very tightly together

sar·don·ic /sɑrˈdɑnɪk/ adj seeming to regard oneself as too important to consider a matter, person, etc., seriously ~**ally** /-kliʸ/ adv

sarge /sɑrdʒ/ n infml for SERGEANT

sa·ri /ˈsɑriʸ/ n dress consisting of a length of cloth, worn by Hindu women

sa·rong /səˈrɔŋ, səˈrɑŋ/ n Malayan skirt consisting of a length of cloth

sar·to·ri·al /sɑrˈtɔriʸəl, -ˈtoʷr-/ adj fml of (the making of) men's clothes

SASE /ˌɛs eʸ ɛs ˈiʸ/ n self-addressed stamped envelope

sash[1] /sæʃ/ n length of cloth worn around the waist or over one shoulder

sash[2] n window frame, esp. in a sort of window with 2 frames that slide up and down

sass /sæs/ n rude, disrespectful talk ♦ vt

SAT /sæt/ n Scholastic Aptitude Test, taken by those wishing to attend US universities

sat /sæt/ past t. and p. of SIT

Sa·tan /ˈseʸtn/ n the Devil

sa·tan·ic /səˈtænɪk/ adj 1 very evil or cruel 2 of satanism ~**ally** /-kliʸ/ adv

sat·an·is·m /ˈseʸtn.ɪzəm/ n [U] worship of the devil −**ist** n

satch·el /ˈsætʃəl/ n small bag carried over the shoulders

sate /seʸt/ vt fml satisfy with more than enough of something

sat·el·lite /ˈsætlˌaɪt/ n 1 heavenly body that moves around a larger one 2 artificial object moving around the Earth, moon, etc. 3 country or person that depends on another

sa·ti·ate /ˈseʸʃiʸˌeʸt/ vt fml satisfy (too) fully

sat·in /ˈsætn/ n [U] smooth shiny cloth made mainly from silk

sat·ire /ˈsætaɪər/ n [C;U] (piece of writing, etc.) showing the foolishness or evil of something in an amusing way −**irical** /səˈtɪrɪkəl/ adj −**irize** /ˈsætəˌraɪz/ vt

sat·is·fac·tion /ˌsætɪsˈfækʃən/ n 1 [C;U] (something that gives) a feeling of pleasure 2 [U] fml fulfilment of a need, desire, etc. 3 [U] fml certainty: It has been proved to my satisfaction. 4 [U] fml chance to defend one's honor

sat·is·fac·to·ry /ˌsætɪsˈfæktəriʸ/ adj 1 pleasing 2 good enough −**rily** adv

sat·is·fy /ˈsætɪsˌfaɪ/ vt **1** please **2** fulfil (a need, desire, etc.) **3** fml fit (a condition, rule, standard, etc.) **4** persuade fully

sat·u·rate /ˈsætʃəˌreɪt/ vt **1** make completely wet **2** fill completely: *The house market is saturated.* –**rated** adj (of fat or oil) having chemicals combined in an unhealthy way -**ration** /ˌsætʃəˈreɪʃən/ n [U]

Sat·ur·day /ˈsætərdiː, -ˌdeɪ/ n the 6th day of the week, between Friday and Sunday

Sat·urn /ˈsætərn/ n the PLANET 6th in order from the sun, with large rings around it

sat·ur·nine /ˈsætərˌnaɪn/ adj fml sad and solemn, often in a threatening way

sauce /sɔs/ n [C;U] **1** quite thick liquid put on food [C] **2** cooked fruit eaten with meat: *cranberry sauce*

saucy adj **1** amusingly disrespectful or rude **2** producing sexual interest in an amusing way

sauce·pan /ˈsɔs-pæn/ n metal cooking pot with a handle

sau·cer /ˈsɔsər/ n small plate for putting a cup on – see also FLYING SAUCER

sau·er·kraut /ˈsauərˌkraut/ n sour CABBAGE

sau·na /ˈsɔnə, ˈsaunə/ n (a room or building for) a Finnish type of bath in steam

saun·ter /ˈsɔntər, ˈsɑn-/ vi walk in a slow, calm manner

saus·age /ˈsɔsɪdʒ/ n [C;U] finely cut meat in a tube of thin skin

sav·age /ˈsævɪdʒ/ adj **1** forcefully cruel or violent **2** uncivilized ♦ n member of an uncivilized tribe ♦ vt attack and bite fiercely ~**ly** adv

sav·age·ry /ˈsævɪdʒriː/ n [C;U] (act of) savage behavior

sa·van·na /səˈvænə/ n [U] flat grassy land in a warm part of the world

save¹ /seɪv/ v **1** vt make safe from danger or destruction **2** vi/t keep and add to an amount of (money) for later use **3** vt avoid the waste of (money, time, etc.) **4** vt keep for future use or enjoyment later **5** vt make unnecessary **6** vt (of a GOALKEEPER) stop one's opponents from getting the ball in the net **7** **save one's skin/neck** infml escape from a serious danger **8** **to save one's life** infml even with the greatest effort: *I can't play the piano to save my life.* ♦ n act of saving (SAVE (6)) **saver** n [P] money saved, esp. in a bank

save² prep fml except

saving grace /ˌ··· ˈ·/ n the one good thing that makes something acceptable

savings account /ˈ··· ·ˌ·/ n bank account for saving

savings and loan as·so·ci·a·tion /ˌ··· ˈ· ···ˌ··/ also **S & L** — n business organization into which people pay money in order to save it and gain interest, and which lends money to people who want to buy houses

savings bond /ˈ··· ˌ·/ n BOND (2) sold by the government in amounts up to $1000, on which it pays interest

sa·vior /ˈseɪvyər/ n **1** one who saves from danger or loss **2** (usu. cap.) Jesus Christ

sa·voir-faire /ˌsævwɑr ˈfɛər/ n [U] ability to do or say the proper thing on every social occasion

sa·vor /ˈseɪvər/ n [S;U] **1** taste or smell **2** (power to excite) interest ♦ vt enjoy slowly and purposefully

sa·vor·y /ˈseɪvəriː/ adj **1** not sweet; tasting of meat, cheese, etc. **2** fml morally good

sav·vy /ˈsæviː/ n [U] practical understanding or skill

saw¹ /sɔ/ past t. of SEE

saw² n tool with a thin blade and teeth for cutting hard materials ♦ vi/t **sawed** sawed, or **sawn** /sɔn/ cut (as if) with a saw

saw³ n short common saying

saw·buck /ˈsɔbʌk/ n sl $10 BILL

saw·dust /ˈsɔdʌst/ n [U] wood dust made by a saw in cutting

sax·o·phone /ˈsæksəˌfoʷn/ also **sax** /sæks/ infml — n metal musical instrument of the WOODWIND family, used esp. in JAZZ

say¹ /seɪ/ **said** /sed/ **1** vt pronounce (a sound, word, etc) **2** vi/t express (a thought, opinion, etc.) in words **3** vt give as a general opinion; claim **4** vt suppose; suggest: *Let's say they accept your idea — what then?* | *Would you accept, say,* (= for example) *$500?* **5** **go without saying** be clear; not need stating **6** **hard to say** difficult to judge **7** **say for oneself/something** offer as an excuse or defense: *You're late again. What have you got to say for yourself?* | *The place has little to be said for it.* **8** **say no more!** infml your/the meaning is clear **9** **say to oneself** think **10** **that is to say** expressed another (more exact) way **11** **they say** it is usually thought **12** **to say nothing of** including **13** **when all is said and done** it must be remembered that **14** **you don't say!** (an expression of slight surprise)

say² n [S;U] **1** power or right of (sharing in) acting or deciding **2** **have one's say** (have the chance to) express one's opinion

say·ing /ˈseɪɪŋ/ n common wise statement

say-so /'· ·/ n **1** personal statement without proof **2** permission

scab /skæb/ n **1** hard mass of dried blood formed over a wound **2** derog one who works while others are on STRIKE

scab-bard /'skæbərd/ n tube for holding a sword, knife, etc.

sca-bies /'skeʸbiʸz/ n [U] skin disease

sca-brous /'skeʸbrəs/ adj fml improper; SALACIOUS

scaf-fold /'skæfəld, -foʷld/ n raised stage for the official killing of criminals ~ing n [U] structure of poles and boards around a building for workmen to stand on

scal-a-wag /'skæləˌwæg/ n child who makes trouble

scald /skɔld/ vt burn with hot liquid **scald** n

scale[1] /skeʸl/ n **1** [C] set of marks on an instrument, used for measuring **2** [C] set of figures for measuring or comparing: a temperature scale **3** [C;U] relationship between a map or model and the thing it represents: a scale of 1 inch to the mile **4** [C;U] size or level in relation to other or usual things: a large-scale business operation **5** [C] set of musical notes at fixed separations **6** to scale according to a fixed rule for reducing the size of something in a drawing, etc.

scale[2] also **scales** pl. — n weighing apparatus

scale[3] n **1** any of the small flat stiff pieces covering fish, snakes, etc. **2** greyish material formed inside hot water pipes, pots in which water is boiled, etc. ♦ vt remove the scales from

scale[4] vt **1** climb up **2** increase/reduce, esp. by a fixed rate

scal-lop /'skaləp, 'skæləp/ n small sea animal (MOLLUSK) with a shell, used for food

scalp /skælp/ n skin on top of the head: (fig.) He wants the Mayor's scalp. (= wants to see him punished for doing wrong) ♦ vt cut off the scalp of

scal-pel /'skælpəl/ n small sharp knife used by doctors in operations

scalp-er /'skælpər/ n derog person who offers tickets for the theater, etc., at very high prices

scam /skæm/ n sl clever and dishonest plan or course of action

scamp /skæmp/ n playful child who makes trouble

scam-per /'skæmpər/ vi run quickly and usu. playfully

scam-pi /'skæmpiʸ/ n [U] (dish of) large SHRIMPS

scan /skæn/ v -nn- **1** vt examine closely, esp. making a search **2** vt look at quickly without careful reading **3** vi (of poetry, etc.) have a regular pattern of repeated beats ♦ n act of scanning ~ner n instrument for scanning (1): a brain scanner

scan-dal /'skændl/ n **1** [C] (something causing) a public shock **2** [U] talk which brings harm or disrespect to someone ~ize vt offend (someone's) feelings of what is right or proper ~ous adj morally shocking

Scan-di-na-vi-an /ˌskændə'neʸviʸən/ adj of Denmark, Norway, Sweden, Finland, and/or Iceland

scan-sion /'skænʃən/ n [U] way a line of a poem SCANS (3)

scant /skænt/ adj hardly enough

scant-y /'skæntiʸ/ adj hardly (big) enough -ily adv

scape-goat /'skeʸpgoʷt/ n one who takes the blame for others' faults

scar /skɑr/ n mark left when a wound gets better ♦ vt -rr- mark with a scar

scarce /skeərs/ adj **1** less than is wanted; hard to find **2** make oneself scarce infml go away or keep away, esp. in order to avoid trouble ~ly adv hardly; almost not **2** (almost) certainly not **scarcity** n [C;U] being scarce; lack

scare /skeər/ vt frighten ♦ n **1** [S] sudden fear **2** [C] (mistaken or unreasonable) public fear: scare stories about war in the newspapers **scary** adj frightening

scare-crow /'skeərkroʷ/ n figure dressed in old clothes set up in a field to scare birds away from crops

scare-mon-ger /'skeərˌmʌŋgər, -ˌmɑŋ-/ n person who spreads reports causing public anxiety

scarf /skɑrf/ n scarves /skɑrvz/ or scarfs piece of cloth worn around the neck or head

scar-let /'skɑrlɪt/ adj bright red

scarlet fe-ver /ˌ·· '··/ n [U] serious disease marked by a painful throat and red spots on the skin

scat /skæt/ vi -tt- (usu. imperative) infml go away fast

scath-ing /'skeʸðɪŋ/ adj bitterly cruel in judgment ~ly adv

sca-tol-o-gy /skæ'tɑlədʒiʸ/ n [U] (writing with) OBSCENE interest in body waste -ogical /ˌskætʒ'lɑ-dʒɪkəl/ adj

scat-ter /'skætər/ v **1** vi/t separate widely **2** vt spread widely (as if) by throwing ~ed adj far apart; irregularly separated

scat-ter-brain /'skætərˌbreʸn/ n careless or forgetful person ~ed adj

scav-enge /'skævɪndʒ/ vi/t **1** (of an animal) feed on (waste or decaying flesh) **2** search for or find (usable objects) among unwanted things ~**enger** n

sce·na·ri·o /sɪˈnɛəriˌoᵘ, -ˈnær-, -ˈnɑr-/ n -**os** 1 written description of the action in a film or play 2 description of a possible course of events

scene /siːn/ n 1 (in a play) division (within an act) 2 single piece of action in one place in a play or film 3 background for action of a play: *There are few scene changes.* 4 place where something happens: *the scene of the crime* 5 event regarded as like something in a play or film: *scenes of merrymaking* 6 show of angry feelings esp. between 2 people in public 7 an area of activity: *He's new to the film/political scene.* 8 **behind the scenes** secretly 9 **on the scene** present: *a report from our man on the scene in Africa* 10 **set the scene** prepare 11 **steal the scene** get all the attention and praise expected by someone else at a show, party, etc.

sce·ner·y /ˈsiːnəriʸ/ n [U] 1 natural surroundings, esp. in the country 2 painted background and other articles used on stage

sce·nic /ˈsiːnɪk/ adj showing attractive natural scenery

scent /sɛnt/ n 1 [C] pleasant smell 2 [C] smell followed by hunting animals ◆ vt 1 tell the presence of by smelling 2 get a feeling of the presence of 3 fill with pleasant smells

scep·ter /ˈsɛptər/ n ceremonial rod carried by a ruler

sched·ule /ˈskɛdʒuᵘl, -dʒəl/ n 1 planned list or order of things to be done 2 a timetable of trains, buses, etc. b list of prices 3 **ahead of/on/behind schedule** before/at/after the planned or expected time ◆ vt plan for a certain future time -**uled** adj 1 being a regular service 2 planned for a particular time

sche·mat·ic /skiʸˈmætɪk, skɪ-/ adj showing the main parts but leaving out details ~**ally** /-kliʸ/ adv

scheme /skiːm/ n 1 plan in simple form; system 2 clever dishonest plan ◆ vi make SCHEMES (3)

scher·zo /ˈskɛərtsoᵘ/ n -**zos** quick piece of music

schis·m /ˈsɪzəm, ˈskɪzəm/ n [C;U] separation between parts originally together, esp. in the church ~**atic** /sɪzˈmætɪk, skɪz-/ adj

schiz·oid /ˈskɪtsɔɪd/ adj of schizophrenia

schiz·o·phre·ni·a /ˌskɪtsəˈfriʸniʸə/ n [U] disorder in which the mind becomes separated from the feelings -**phrenic** /-ˈfrɛnɪk/ adj, n (of) someone with schizophrenia

schlep /ʃlɛp/ v -**pp**- infml 1 vt carry or drag (something heavy) 2 vi spend a lot of time and effort in getting from one place to another

schlock /ʃlɑk/ adj cheap and of poor quality

schmaltz, schmalz /ʃmɑlts, ʃmɔlts/ n [U] infml art or esp. music which brings out feelings in a too easy, not serious or delicate, way ~**y** adj

schmuck /ʃmʌk/ n infml fool

schol·ar /ˈskɑlər/ n 1 person with great knowledge of a (non-science) subject 2 holder of a SCHOLARSHIP (1) ~**ly** adj 1 concerned with serious detailed study 2 of or like a SCHOLAR(1)

schol·ar·ship /ˈskɑlərˌʃɪp/ n 1 [C] payment so that someone can attend a college 2 [U] exact and serious study

scho·las·tic /skəˈlæstɪk/ adj of schools and teaching

school[1] /skuːl/ n 1 [C;U] (attendance or work at) a place of education for people under 18 years 2 [C] body of students (and teachers) at such a place: *She was liked by the whole school.* 3 [C;U] teaching establishment: *a barber school* 4 [C;U] (in some universities) department concerned with one subject: *the School of Law* 5 [C;U] infml UNIVERSITY *Where did you to to school?* 6 [C] group of people with the same methods, style, etc: *Rembrandt and his school* ◆ vt fml teach, train, or bring under control

school[2] n large group of fish swimming together

school board /ˌ· ˈ·/ n local committee in charge of education

school of thought /ˌ· · ˈ·/ n group with the same way of thinking, opinion, etc.

school·teach·er /ˈskuːlˌtiʸtʃər/ n teacher at a school below college level

schoo·ner /ˈskuːnər/ n 1 large fast sailing ship 2 tall drinking glass esp. for BEER

schwa /ʃwɑ/ n vowel sound shown in this dictionary as /ə/ or /ʌ/

sci·at·i·ca /saɪˈætɪkə/ n [U] pain in the lower back

sci·ence /ˈsaɪəns/ n 1 [U] (study of) knowledge which depends on testing facts and stating general natural laws 2 [C] a branch of such knowledge, such as PHYSICS, chemistry, or BIOLOGY b anything which may be studied exactly

science fic·tion /ˌ· ·ˈ·/ n [U] stories about imaginary future (scientific) developments

sci·en·tif·ic /ˌsaɪənˈtɪfɪk◂/ adj 1 of science 2 needing or showing exact knowledge or use of a system ~**ally** /-kli²/ *adv*

sci·en·tist /ˈsaɪəntɪst/ *n* person who works in a science

sci-fi /ˈsaɪ faɪ/ *n infml* science fiction

scim·i·tar /ˈsɪmətər/ *n* curved sword

scin·til·late /ˈsɪntəlˌeɪt/ *vi* 1 (esp. of conversation) quick, clever and interesting 2 throw out quick flashes of light

scis·sors /ˈsɪzərz/ *n* [P] cutting tool with 2 joined blades

scle·ro·sis /skləˈroˠsɪs/ *n* [U] *med* hardening of some usu. soft organ in the body — see also MULTIPLE SCLEROSIS

scoff /skɒf, skɑf/ *vi* speak laughingly and disrespectfully

scoff·law /ˈskɒflɔ, ˈskɑf-/ *n* someone who disobeys laws about parking, etc.

scold /skoˠld/ *vt* speak angrily and complainingly to (a person doing wrong)

scoop /skuˠp/ *n* 1 sort of deep spoon for lifting and moving liquids or loose material 2 news report printed, broadcast, etc., before one's competitors can do so ♦ *vt* 1 take up or out (as if) with a SCOOP (1) 2 make a news report before (another newspaper)

scoot /skuˠt/ *vi* go quickly and suddenly

scoot·er /ˈskuˠtər/ *n* 1 child's vehicle with 2 wheels, pushed along by one foot 2 low vehicle with two small wheels, an enclosed engine, and usu. a wide curved part at the front to protect the legs

scope /skoˠp/ *n* [U] 1 area within the limits of a question, subject, etc. 2 space or chance for action or thought

scorch /skɔrtʃ/ *v* 1 *vt* burn the surface (of something) without destroying completely 2 *vt infml* travel very fast ♦ *n* something very exciting, angry, fast, etc.

scorched earth po·li·cy /ˌ·ˈ· ˈ· ···/ *n* destruction by an army of all useful things, esp. crops, in an area before leaving it to an advancing army

score¹ /skɔr/ *n* 1 number of points won in a game, examination, etc. 2 **a** written copy of a piece of music **b** music for a film or play 3 reason: *Don't worry on that score.* 4 old disagreement or hurt kept in the mind: *to have a score to settle with someone* 5 **know the score** understand the true and usu. unfavorable facts of a situation

score² *v* 1 *vi/t* make (a point) in a game 2 *vi* record the points made in a game 3 *vt* gain (a success, victory, etc.) 4 *vi/t* make (a clever point) esp.

in an argument: *She always tries to score (points) off other people in a conversation.* 5 *vt* arrange (music) for a particular combination of instruments 6 *vt* cut one or more lines on 7 *sl* (usu. of a man) have sex with someone 8 *sl* obtain and use unlawful drugs **scorer** *n* person who SCORES² (1, 2)

score³ *determiner, n* score *esp. lit* 20 scores *n* [P] a lot

score·board /ˈskɔrbɔrd, ˈskoˠrbˠrd/ *n* board on which a SCORE¹ (1) is recorded

scorn /skɔrn/ *n* [U] strong (angry) disrespect ♦ *vt* refuse to accept or consider because of scorn or pride ~**ful** *adj* ~**fully** *adv*

scor·pi·on /ˈskɔrpiˠən/ *n* small animal with a long poisonous stinging tail

scotch /skɒtʃ/ *vt fml* put an end to

Scotch *adj* Scottish ♦ *n* [U] WHISKY made in Scotland

Scotch tape /ˌ· ˈ·/ *n tdmk* band of thin clear sticky material ♦ *vt* put together with Scotch tape

scot-free /ˌskɑt ˈfriˠ/ *adj* without harm or esp. punishment

Scots /skɑts/ *adj* Scottish

Scot·tish /ˈskɑtɪʃ/ *adj* of Scotland

scoun·drel /ˈskaʊndrəl/ *n* wicked, selfish, or dishonest man

scour¹ /skaʊər/ *vt* search (an area) thoroughly

scour² *vt* clean by hard rubbing with a rough material ~**er** *n* piece of rough nylon for cleaning pots and pans

scourge /skɜrdʒ/ *n* cause of great harm or suffering ♦ *vt* cause great harm or suffering to

scout /skaʊt/ *n* 1 member of an association (the **Boy Scouts** or **Girl Scouts**) for training boys or girls in character and helping themselves 2 soldier sent ahead of an army to find out about the enemy 3 person who looks for good young sports people, actors, etc., for new teams, shows, etc.: *a talent scout* ♦ *vi* go looking for something

scowl /skaʊl/ *n* angry FROWN ♦ *vi* make a scowl

scrab·ble /ˈskræbəl/ *vi* SCRAMBLE (1, 2)

scrag·gy /ˈskrægiˠ/ *adj* thin and bony

scram /skræm/ *vi* —**mm**— [*often imperative*] *infml* get away fast

scram·ble /ˈskræmbəl/ *v* 1 *vi* move or climb quickly and untidily 2 *vi* struggle or compete eagerly or against difficulty 3 *vt* cook (an egg) with the white and yellow parts mixed together 4 *vt* mix up (a radio or telephone message) so that it cannot be understood ♦ *n* 1 [S] act of

scrambling (SCRAMBLE (1)) **2** [C]
motorcycle race over rough ground

scrap[1] /skræp/ n **1** [C] small piece **2**
[U] unwanted material (to be)
thrown away: *She sold the car for
scrap.* (= as metal to be used again)
♦ *vt* **-pp-** get rid of ~ **py** *adj* not
well arranged or planned

scrap[2] n sudden short fight or
quarrel ♦ *vi* **-pp-** fight or quarrel

scrap·book /'skræpbʊk/ n book of
empty pages on which pictures cut
from magazines, etc., are stuck

scrape /skreɪp/ v **1** *vi/t* (cause to)
rub roughly against a surface **2** *vt*
remove or clean by pulling or pushing an edge repeatedly across a surface **3** *vi* live, keep a business, etc.,
with no more than the necessary
money **4** *vi* succeed by doing work
of the lowest acceptable quality: *She
scraped through the exam.* **5 scrape
a living** get just enough food or
money to stay alive **6 scrape the
bottom of the barrel** take, use, suggest, etc., something of the lowest
quality ♦ n **1** act or sound of scraping **2** mark or wound made by
scraping **3** difficult situation

  scrape up/together *phr vt* gather
(enough money) with difficulty

scrap heap /'· ·/ n **1** pile of waste
material, esp. metal **2** imaginary
place where unwanted things, people, or ideas go

scrap pa·per /'· ‚··/ also **scratch
paper** — n [U] used paper for making notes, shopping lists, etc.

scratch /skrætʃ/ *vi/t* **1** rub and tear
or mark with something pointed or
rough **2** rub (a part of the body)
lightly and repeatedly **3** remove
(oneself, a horse, etc.) from a race or
competition **4 scratch a living** get
just enough food or money to stay
alive **5 scratch someone's back** do
someone a favor, expecting they
will return it **6 scratch the surface**
deal with only the beginning of a
matter or only a few of many cases
♦ n **1** [C] mark or sound made by
scratching **2** [S] act of SCRATCHing
(2) **3 from scratch** (starting) from
the beginning **4 up to scratch** at/to
an acceptable standard **5** without a
scratch without even the smallest
amount of hurt or damage ~ **y** *adj*
1 (of a record, etc.) spoiled by
scratches **2** (of clothes) hot, rough,
and uncomfortable

scrawl /skrɔl/ *vt* write carelessly or
awkwardly ♦ n (piece of) careless
or irregular writing

scraw·ny /'skrɔni/ *adj* unpleasantly thin

scream /skriʲm/ *vi/t* **1** cry out in a
loud high voice: (fig.) *The wind
screamed around the house.* **2** draw

attention, as if by such a cry ♦ n **1**
[C] sudden loud cry **2** [S] *infml* very
funny person, thing, etc.

scree /skriʲ/ n [U] small loose
stones on the side of a mountain

screech /skriʲtʃ/ *vi* **1** make an unpleasant high sharp sound, esp. in
terror or pain **2** (of machines,
BRAKES, etc.) make such a noise **3**
screech to a halt/standstill stop
very suddenly (as if) making this
noise ♦ n very high unpleasant
noise

screen /skriʲn/ n **1** something, esp.
a movable upright frame, that protects, shelters, or hides **2** surface on
which a cinema film is shown **3** the
MOTION PICTURE industry: *star of
stage, screen and radio* | *screen test*
(= test of one's ability to act in a
film) | *She first appeared on the
screen* (= acted in her first film) *last
year.* **4** front glass surface of an electrical instrument, esp. a television,
on which pictures or information
appear ♦ *vt* **1** shelter, protect, or
hide (as if) with a screen **2** test so as
to remove those that do not reach
the proper standard **3** show or
broadcast (a film or television
show) – see also SMALL SCREEN ~ **ing**
n **1** [C;U] (a) showing of a film **2** [U]
process of SCREEN (2) ing

screen·play /'skriʲnpleɪ/ n story
written for a film or television

screw /skruʷ/ n **1** metal pin having
a head with a cut across it, a point
at the other end, and a raised edge
winding round it so that when
twisted into wood, etc. it holds
firmly **2** act of turning one of these
3 PROPELLER, esp. on a ship **4** *taboo
sl* a act of having sex **b** someone considered as a person to have sex with
5 have a screw loose *humor* be
slightly crazy **6 put the screws on
someone** *infml* to force someone to
do as one wishes, esp. by threatening ♦ v **1** *vt* fasten with one or more
screws **2** *vi/t* tighten or fasten by
turning **3** *vi/t taboo sl* have sex
(with) **4** *sl* cheat: *We really got
screwed by that salesman.*

  screw up *phr vt* **1** twist (a part of
the face) to express disapproval or
uncertainty: *She screwed up her eyes
to read the sign.* **2** *vt* confuse or
annoy **3** *vi/t sl* **a** ruin **b** deal with
badly: *He really screwed up on that
job.* **4 screw up one's courage** stop
oneself from being afraid **5
screwed up** *infml* very worried and
confused

screw·ball /'skruʷbɔl/ n **1** SCREWY
person **2** type of throw with a BASE-
BALL

screw·driv·er /'skruʷ‚draɪvər/ n
tool with a blade that fits into the top
of a screw, for turning it

screw·y /ˈskruʷiʸ/ *adj infml* strange or slightly crazy

scrib·ble /ˈskrɪbəl/ *v* **1** *vi* write (meaningless marks) **2** *vt* write carelessly or hastily ♦ *n* [S;U] meaningless or careless writing

scribe /skraɪb/ *n* person employed to copy things in writing

scrimp /skrɪmp/ *vi* **scrimp and save** save money slowly and with great difficulty

script /skrɪpt/ *n* **1** [C] written form of a play, film, or broadcast **2** [C;U] particular alphabet: *Arabic script* **3** [S;U] *fml* writing by hand **~ed** *adj* having a SCRIPT (1)

scriptwriter /ˈskrɪptraɪt̬ər/ *n* writer of SCRIPTS (1)

scrip·ture /ˈskrɪptʃər/ also **scrip·tures** *pl.* — *n* [U] **1** the Bible **2** holy book(s) of the stated religion **-tural** *adj*

scrod /skrɑd/ *n* baby COD fish used for food

scroll /skroʷl/ *n* **1** rolled piece of paper, esp. containing official writing **2** decoration or shape like this in stone or wood

scrooge /skruʷdʒ/ *n* extremely ungenerous person

scro·tum /ˈskroʷt̬əm/ *n* **-ta** /-t̬ə/ *or* **-tums** bag of flesh holding the TESTICLES

scrounge /skraʊndʒ/ *vi/t* get (something) without work or payment or by persuading others **scrounger** *n*

scrub /skrʌb/ *v* **-bb-** **1** *vi/t* clean or remove by hard rubbing **2** *vt* no longer do or have; CANCEL ♦ *n* [S] act of scrubbing

scrub² *n* [U] low plants covering the ground thickly

scruff /skrʌf/ *n* flesh at the back (of the neck)

scruf·fy /ˈskrʌfiʸ/ *adj* dirty and untidy

scrump·tious /ˈskrʌmpʃəs/ *adj infml* (of food) extremely good

scrunch /skrʌntʃ/ *vt* crush

scrunch up *phr vt* press together closely

scru·ple /ˈskruʷpəl/ *n* **1** [C] moral principle which keeps one from doing something **2** [U] conscience

scru·pu·lous /ˈskruʷpyələs/ *adj* **1** *fml* very exact **2** exactly honest **~ly** *adv*

scru·ti·ny /ˈskruʷtn-iʸ/ *n* [U] careful and thorough examination **-nize** *vt* examine closely

scud /skʌd/ *vi* **-dd-** (esp. of clouds and ships) move along quickly

scuff /skʌf/ *vt* make rough marks on the smooth surface of (shoes, a floor, etc.) ♦ *n* mark made by scuffing

scuf·fle /ˈskʌfəl/ *n* disorderly fight among a few people **scuffle** *vi*

scull /skʌl/ *vi/t* row (a small light boat) **~er** *n*

scul·le·ry /ˈskʌləriʸ/ *n* room next to a kitchen, where pots and dishes are washed

sculp·tor /ˈskʌlptər/ *n* artist who makes sculptures

sculp·ture /ˈskʌlptʃər/ *n* **1** [U] art of shaping solid representations **2** [C;U] (piece of) work produced by this ♦ *vt* make by shaping

scum /skʌm/ *n* **1** [S;U] (unpleasant) material formed on the surface of liquid **2** [P] *often taboo* worthless immoral people: *the scum of the earth*

scurf /skɜrf/ *n* [U] small bits of dead skin, esp. in the hair

scur·ri·lous /ˈskɜrələs, ˈskʌr-/ *adj fml* containing very rude, improper, and usu. untrue statements **~ly** *adv* **~ness** *n* [U]

scur·ry /ˈskɜriʸ, ˈskʌriʸ/ *vi* hurry, esp. with short quick steps ♦ *n* [U] movement or sound of scurrying

scur·vy /ˈskɜrviʸ/ *n* [U] disease caused by lack of VITAMIN C

scut·tle¹ /ˈskʌt̬l/ *n* sort of bucket for holding and carrying coal

scuttle² *vi* rush with short quick steps

scuttle³ *vt* sink (a ship) by making holes in the bottom

scuz·zy /ˈskʌziʸ/ *adj sl* dirty or of low quality

scythe /saɪθ/ *n* tool with a long curving blade fixed to a handle, for cutting grass ♦ *vt* cut (as if) with a scythe

SDI /ˌɛs diʸ ˈaɪ/ *n* Strategic Defense Initiative; a US government plan for the use of special weapons to destroy enemy MISSILES from space

sea /siʸ/ *n* **1** [U] great body of salty water that covers much of the Earth's surface **2** [C] **a** particular (named) part of this: *the Caribbean Sea* **b** body of water (mostly) enclosed by land: *the Mediterranean Sea* **3** [C] any of a number of broad plains on the Moon: *the Sea of Tranquillity* **4** [C] large quantity spread out in front of one: *a sea of faces* **5 at sea**: **a** on a voyage **b** *infml* not understanding **6 by sea** on a ship **7 go to sea** become a sailor **8 put to sea** start a voyage

sea a·nem·o·ne /ˈ· ·ˌ···/ *n* simple flower-like sea animal

sea·board /ˈsiʸbɔrd, -boʷrd/ *n* the part of a country along a sea coast

sea change /ˈ· ·/ *n lit* a complete but usu. gradual change

sea·far·ing /ˈsiʸˌfɛərɪŋ/ *adj* connected with the sea and sailing

sea·food /ˈsiʸfuʷd/ *n* [U] fish and fishlike animals from the sea which can be eaten, esp. SHELLFISH

sea·front /ˈsiᵞfrʌnt/ n part of a town on the edge of the sea, often with a broad path along it

sea·gull /ˈsiᵞgʌl/ n GULL

sea·horse /ˈsiᵞhɔːs/ n small fish with a head and neck like those of a horse

seal¹ /siᵞl/ n 1 official mark put on an official paper, often by pressing a pattern into it 2 something fastened across an opening to protect it 3 tight connection to keep gas or liquid in or out 4 **set the seal on** bring to an end in a suitable way ♦ vt 1 fix a SEAL (1) onto 2 fasten or close (as if) with a SEAL (2, 3): (fig.) My lips are sealed. 3 make (more) certain, formal, or solemn 4 **seal someone's fate** fml make someone's death or punishment certain

seal off phr vt close tightly so as not to allow entrance or escape

seal² n large sea animal with a smooth body and broad flat limbs for swimming

sea legs /ˈ· ·/ n [P] ability to walk comfortably on a moving ship

sea lev·el /ˈ· ˌ··/ n the average height of the sea, used as a standard for measuring heights on land

sealing wax /ˈ·· ˌ·/ n hard easily melted substance used for sealing containers, etc.

sea li·on /ˈ· ˌ··/ n large SEAL² of the Pacific Ocean

seam /siᵞm/ n 1 line of stitches joining 2 pieces of cloth, etc. 2 narrow band of minerals between other rocks 3 **burst at the seams** infml be very full

sea·man /ˈsiᵞmən/ n -men /-mən/ 1 sailor, esp. of low rank 2 man skilled in handling ships at sea ~**ship** n [U] skill in handling a ship and directing its course

seam·stress /ˈsiᵞmstrɪs/ n woman who sews and makes clothes

seam·y /ˈsiᵞmiᵞ/ adj unpleasant and immoral -**iness** n [U]

sé·ance /ˈseᵞʌns/ n meeting where people try to talk to the spirits of the dead

sear /sɪər/ vt burn with sudden powerful heat ~**ing** adj 1 burning 2 causing or describing very strong feelings esp. of a sexual kind

search /sɜːtʃ/ vi/t 1 look through or examine (a place or person) carefully and thoroughly to try to find something 2 **search me!** infml I don't know! ♦ n 1 act of searching 2 **in search of** searching for ~**ing** adj sharp and thorough: a searching look ~**er** n

search·light /ˈsɜːtʃlaɪt/ n large powerful light that can be turned in any direction

search par·ty /ˈ· ˌ··/ n group of searchers, esp. for a lost person

search war·rant /ˈ· ˌ··/ n official written order allowing the police to search a place

sea·shore /ˈsiᵞʃɔː, -ʃoʷr/ n [U] land along the edge of the sea

sea·sick /ˈsiᵞˌsɪk/ adj sick because of a ship's movement ~**ness** n [U]

sea·side /ˈsiᵞsaɪd/ n [the+S] coast

sea·son /ˈsiᵞzən/ n 1 spring, summer, autumn, or winter 2 period of the year marked by a particular thing: the rainy/holiday/football season 3 **in/out of season** (of food) at/not at the best time of year for eating 4 **Season's Greetings!** (a greeting on a Christmas card) ♦ vt 1 give a special taste to (a food) by adding salt, pepper, a SPICE, etc. 2 dry (wood) gradually for use ~**able** adj fml suitable or useful for the time of year ~**al** adj happening or active only at a particular season ~**ed** adj having much experience ~**ing** n [C;U] something that seasons food

season tick·et /ˌ·· ˈ··/ n ticket usable for a number of sports events, journeys, performances, etc., during a fixed period of time

seat /siᵞt/ n 1 place for sitting 2 the part on which one sits 3 place as a member of an official body: to lose one's seat in the House 4 place where a particular activity happens 5 **in the driver's seat** infml in control 6 **take a back seat (to someone)** infml allow someone else to take control or have the more important job 7 **take/have a seat** please sit down ♦ vt 1 cause or help to sit: be seated (= please sit down) 2 have room for seats for ~**ing** n [U] seats

seat belt /ˈ· ·/ n protective belt around a seated person in a car, plane, etc.

sea ur·chin /ˈ· ˌ··/ n small sea animal with a prickly shell, shaped like a ball

sea·weed /ˈsiᵞwiᵞd/ n [U] plant that grows in the sea

sea·wor·thy /ˈsiᵞˌwɜːðiᵞ/ adj (of a ship) fit for a sea voyage

se·cede /sɪˈsiᵞd/ vi formally leave an official group or organization **secession** /-ˈseʃən/ n [U]

se·clude /sɪˈkluʷd/ vt fml keep (esp. oneself) away from other people **secluded** adj very quiet and private **seclusion** /sɪˈkluʷʒən/ n [U]

sec·ond¹ /ˈsɛkənd/ determiner, adv, pron 2nd

second² n 1 length of time equal to 1/60 of a minute 2 infml moment

second³ n 1 [C] imperfect article sold cheaper 2 [C] helper of a fighter in a boxing match (BOX²) or DUEL 3

second to none *infml* the best **seconds** [P] *infml* 2nd servings of food at a meal

second⁴ *vt* support formally (a formal suggestion at a meeting) ~ **er** *n*

sec·ond·a·ry /ˈsɛkənˌdɛriʸ/ *adj* **1** (of education or a school) for children past sixth grade **2** not main: *of secondary importance* **3** developing from something earlier: *a secondary infection* ~**rily** *adv*

second best /ˌ·· ˈ·◄/ *adj* not as good as the meal

second class /ˌ·· ˈ·◄/ *n* [U] traveling conditions cheaper than FIRST CLASS on a plane, etc. **second-class** *adj* below the highest quality

second cous·in /ˌ·· ˈ··/ *n* the child of one's parent's COUSIN

second fid·dle /ˌ·· ˈ··/ *n* position of having to report to the person in control

second-guess /ˌ·· ˈ·/ *vt infml* **1** make a judgment about (someone or something) only after an event has taken place **2** try to say in advance what (someone) will do, how (something) will happen, etc.

second-hand /ˌ·· ˈ·◄/ *adj, adv* **1** owned or used by someone else before; not new **2** (of information) not directly from its origin

second na·ture /ˌ·· ˈ··/ *n* [U] very firmly fixed habit

second-rate /ˌ·· ˈ·◄/ *adj* of low quality

second sight /ˌ·· ˈ·/ *n* [U] supposed ability to know about future or distant things

second thought /ˌ·· ˈ·/ *n* [C;U] thought that a past decision or opinion may not be right: *On second thoughts I think I will have a drink.*

second wind /ˌ·· ˈ·/ *n* [S] return of one's strength during hard physical activity, when it seemed one had become too tired to continue

se·cre·cy /ˈsiʸkrəsiʸ/ *n* [U] **1** keeping secrets **2** being secret

se·cret /ˈsiʸkrɪt/ *adj* **1** that no one else knows or must know about **2** undeclared ♦ *n* **1** matter kept hidden or known only to a few **2** special way of doing something well: *the secret of baking perfect bread* **3** mystery **4** **in secret** in a private way or place ~**ly** *adv*

secret a·gent /ˌ·· ˈ··/ *n* person gathering information secretly esp. for a foreign government

sec·re·tar·i·at /ˌsɛkrəˈtɛəriʸət/ *n* official office or department concerned with the running of a large organization

sec·re·ta·ry /ˈsɛkrəˌtɛriʸ/ *n* **1** person who prepares letters, keeps records, arranges meetings, etc., for another **2** government official or high non-elected official: *the Secretary of State* **3** officer of an organization who keeps records, writes official letters, etc. ~**rial** /ˌsɛkrəˈtɛəriʸəl/ *adj*

se·crete¹ /sɪˈkriʸt/ *vt* (esp. of an animal or plant organ) produce (a usu. liquid substance) **secretion** /sɪˈkriʸʃən/ *n* [C;U] (production of) a usu. liquid substance

secrete² *vt fml* hide **secretion** /-ˈkriʸʃən/ *n* [U]

se·cre·tive /ˈsiʸkrətɪv, sɪˈkriʸtɪv/ *adj* hiding one's thoughts or plans ~**ly** *adv* ~**ness** *n* [U]

secret ser·vice /ˌ·· ˈ··/ *n* government department dealing with special police work, esp. protecting high government officers

sect /sɛkt/ *n* small group within or separated from a larger (esp. religious) group

sec·tar·i·an /sɛkˈtɛəriʸən/ *adj* of or between sects, esp. as shown in great strength and narrowness of beliefs ~**ism** *n* [U]

sec·tion /ˈsɛkʃən/ *n* **1** [C] separate part of a larger object, place, group, etc. **2** [C;U] representation of something cut through from top to bottom ~**al** *adj* **1** in sections (to be) put together **2** limited to one particular group or area

sec·tor /ˈsɛktər/ *n* **1** part of a field of activity, esp. in business or trade – see also PRIVATE SECTOR, PUBLIC SECTOR **2** area of military control

sec·u·lar /ˈsɛkyələr/ *adj* not connected with or controlled by a church

se·cure /sɪˈkyuər/ *adj* **1** protected against danger or risk **2** fastened firmly **3** certain: *a secure job* **4** having no anxiety ♦ *vt* **1** close tightly **2** make safe *fml* get ~**ly** *adv*

se·cu·ri·ty /sɪˈkyuərʈiʸ/ *n* **1** [U] state of being secure **2** [U] (department concerned with) protection, esp. against law breaking, violence, enemy acts, escape from prison, etc.: *strict security measures* | *a maximum security prison* **3** [U] property of value promised to a lender in case repayment is not made **4** [C] document giving the owner the right to some property: *government securities*

se·dan /sɪˈdæn/ *n* large car with a fixed roof and 2 or 4 doors

sedan chair /·ˌ· ˈ·/ *n* seat carried through the streets on poles in former times

se·date /sɪˈdeʸt/ *adj* calm or quiet ♦ *vt* make sleepy or calm, esp. with a drug **sedation** /-ˈdeʸʃən/ *n* [U]

sed·a·tive /ˈsɛdəʈɪv/ *n* drug that makes one calm, esp. by causing sleep

sed·en·ta·ry /ˈsɛdnˌtɛriʸ/ *adj fml*

used to or needing long periods of sitting and only slight activity

sed·i·ment /'sedəmənt/ n [S;U] solid material that settles to the bottom of a liquid ~**ary** adj

se·di·tion /sɪ'dɪʃən/ n [U] speaking, actions, etc., encouraging people to disobey the government –**tious** adj

se·duce /sɪ'djuːs, sɪ'djuːs/ vt **1** persuade to have sex with someone **2** persuade to do esp. something bad by making it seem attractive **seducer** n **seduction** /sɪ'dʌkʃən/ n [C;U] **seductive** /sɪ'dʌktɪv/ adj very desirable or attractive

sed·u·lous /'sedʒələs/ adj fml showing steady attention, care, and determination ~**ly** adv

see¹ /siː/ v **saw** /sɔː/, **seen** /siːn/ **1** vi have or use the power of sight **2** vt notice, recognize, or examine by looking **3** vi/t come to know or understand: I can't see why you don't like it. **4** vt form an opinion or picture of in the mind: I see little hope of any improvement. **5** vt visit, meet, or receive as a visitor **6** vi/t (try to) find out: I'll see if he's there. **7** vt make sure; take care: See that you're ready at 8 o'clock. **8** vt go with: I'll see you home. **9** vt be the occasion of (an event or course in history) **10** vt have experience of: We've seen some good times together. | That sofa has seen better days. **11** (I'll) see you/be seeing you (soon/later/next week, etc.) (used when leaving a friend) **12** let me see (used for expressing a pause for thought) **13** see fit decide to **14** seeing is believing: **a** I'll believe it when I see it, but not before **b** Now I've seen it, so I believe it **15** see one's way (clear) to feel able or willing to **16** see red become very angry **17** see the back/last of someone have no more to do with someone **18** see the light: **a** understand or accept an idea **b** have a religious experience which changes one's belief **c** come into existence **19** see things think one sees something that is not there **20** so I see what you say is already clear **21** (you) see (used in explanations)

see about phr vt **1** deal with **2** consider further **3** We'll see about that! infml I will prevent that happening (or continuing)!

see in phr vt find attractive in: I don't know what she sees in him.

see off phr vt go to the airport, station, etc., with (someone who is starting a trip)

see out phr vt **1** last until the end of **2** go to the door with (someone who is leaving)

see through phr vt **1** not be deceived by **2** provide for, support, or help until the end of (esp. a difficult time)

see to phr vt attend to; take care of

see² n area governed by a BISHOP

seed /siːd/ n [C;U] **1** usu. small hard plant part that can grow into a new plant **2** [C] something from which growth begins: seeds of future trouble **3** [U] lit SEMEN **4** [C] SEEDed (3) player **5** go to seed: **a** (of a plant) produce seed after flowers have been produced **b** (of a person) lose one's freshness, esp. by becoming lazy, careless, old, etc. ♦ vt **1** (of a plant) grow and produce seed **2** plant seeds in (a piece of ground) **3** place (esp. tennis players at the start of a competition) in order of likelihood to win ~**less** adj

seed·ling /'siːdlɪŋ/ n young plant grown from a seed

seed mon·ey /'· ,··/ n [U] money needed to start up a business, program, etc.

seed·y /'siːdiʲ/ adj **1** looking poor, dirty, and uncared for **2** infml slightly unwell and/or in low spirits –**iness** n [U]

see·ing /'siːɪŋ/ also **seeing that** /'··· ·/ –conj as it is true that; since

seek /siːk/ v **sought** /sɔːt/ fml or lit **1** vi/t search (for) **2** vt ask for **3** vt try

seem /siːm/ v give the idea or effect of being; appear: She seems happy. ~**ing** adj that seems to be, but perhaps is not real: his seeming calmness ~**ingly** adv according to what seems to be so (but perhaps is not)

seem·ly /'siːmliʲ/ adj fml (socially) suitable –**liness** n [U]

seen /siːn/ v past p. of SEE

seep /siːp/ vi (of liquid) flow slowly through small openings in a material ~**age** n [S;U] slow seeping flow

seer /sɪər/ n lit someone who knows about the future

see·saw /'siːsɔː/ n **1** board balanced in the middle for people to sit on at opposite ends so that when one end goes up the other goes down **2** up and down movement ♦ vi move up and down esp. between opponents or opposite sides: seesawing prices

seethe /siːð/ vi **1** be in a state of anger or unrest **2** (of a liquid) move about as if boiling

see-through /'· ·/ adj (esp. of a garment) that can be (partly) seen through

seg·ment /'segmənt/ n any of the parts into which something may be cut up or divided ♦ vt /seg'ment/ divide into segments ~**ation** /ˌsegmənˈteʲʃən/ n [U]

seg·re·gate /'segrəˌgeʲt/ vt separate or set apart, esp. from a different social or racial group **-gation** /ˌsɛɡrəˈgeɪʃən/ n [U]

seis·mic /ˈsaɪzmɪk/ adj of or caused by EARTHQUAKES

seis·mo·graph /ˈsaɪzməˌɡræf/ n instrument for measuring the force of EARTHQUAKES

seize /siːz/ vt **1** take possession of by force or official order: (fig.) *She was seized by a sudden idea.* **2** take hold of eagerly, quickly, or forcefully **seizure** /ˈsiːʒər/ n **1** [U] act of seizing **2** [C] sudden attack of illness

seize up phr vt (of part of a machine) become stuck and stop working

sel·dom /ˈsɛldəm/ adv not often; rarely

se·lect /sɪˈlɛkt/ vt choose as best, most suitable, etc., from a group ♦ adj **1** limited to members of the best quality or class **2** of high quality ~ **or** n ~ **ion** /-ˈlɛkʃən/ n **1** [U] act of selecting or fact of being selected **2** [C] something or someone selected **3** [C] collection of things to choose from – see also NATURAL SELECTION

se·lec·tive /sɪˈlɛktɪv/ adj **1** careful in choosing **2** having an effect only on certain things ~ **ly** adv **-tivity** /sɪˌlɛkˈtɪvəti/ n ~ **ness** /sɪˈlɛktɪv-nɪs/ n [U]

selective ser·vice /·ˌ·· ˈ··/ n [S] system of choosing men for military service

self /sɛlf/ n **selves** /sɛlvz/ [C;U] whole being of a person, including their nature, character, abilities, etc.

self-ab·sorbed /ˌ·· ·ˈ·◄/ adj paying all one's attention to oneself and one's own affairs

self-ap·point·ed /ˌ·· ·ˈ··◄/ adj chosen by oneself to do something, unasked and usu. unwanted

self-as·sured /ˌ·· ·ˈ·◄/ adj confident **-surance** n [U]

self-cen·tered /ˌ·· ˈ··◄/ adj interested only in oneself ~ **ness** n [U]

self-con·fi·dent /ˌ·· ˈ··◄/ adj sure of one's own power to succeed ~ **ly** adv **-dence** n [U]

self-con·scious /ˌ·· ˈ··/ adj nervous and uncomfortable about oneself as seen by others ~ **ly** adv ~ **ness** adj [U]

self-con·tained /ˌ·· ·ˈ·◄/ adj **1** complete in itself; independent **2** not showing feelings or depending on others' friendship

self-con·trol /ˌ·· ·ˈ·/ n [U] control over one's feelings **-trolled** adj

self-de·fense /ˌ·· ·ˈ·/ n [U] act or skill of defending oneself: *He shot the man in self-defense.* (= only to protect himself)

self-de·ter·mi·na·tion /ˌ·· ···ˈ··/ n

[U] country's right to govern itself

self-em·ployed /ˌ·· ·ˈ·◄/ adj earning money from one's own business, rather than being paid by an employer

self-es·teem /ˌ·· ·ˈ·/ n [U] one's good opinion of one's own worth

self-ev·i·dent /ˌ·· ˈ···◄/ adj plainly true without need of proof ~ **ly** adv

self-ex·plan·a·to·ry /ˌ·· ·ˈ···/ adj easily understood

self-ful·fill·ing proph·e·cy /ˌ·· ·ˌ·· ˈ···/ n statement about what may happen in the future which causes that thing to happen

self-im·age /ˌ·· ˈ··/ n idea about oneself, esp. in comparison to others: *a positive self-image*

self-im·port·ant /ˌ·· ·ˈ··◄/ adj having too high an opinion of one's own importance **-ance** n [U]

self-in·dul·gent /ˌ·· ·ˈ··◄/ adj too easily allowing oneself pleasure or comfort **-gence** n [U]

self-in·terest /ˌ·· ˈ···, ·ˈ···/ n [U] concern for what is best for oneself ~ **ed** adj

self·ish /ˈsɛlfɪʃ/ adj concerned with one's own advantage without care for others ~ **ly** adv ~ **ness** n [U]

self·less /ˈsɛlflɪs/ adj concerned with others' advantage without care for oneself ~ **ly** adv ~ **ness** n [U]

self-made /ˌ·· ˈ·◄/ adj having gained success and wealth by one's own efforts alone

self-pos·sessed /ˌ·· ·ˈ·◄/ adj calm and confident **-session** n [U]

self-re·li·ant /ˌ·· ·ˈ··◄/ adj not depending on others' help **-ance** n [U]

self-re·spect /ˌ·· ·ˈ·/ n [U] proper pride in oneself ~ **ing** adj

self-right·eous /ˌ·· ˈ··/ adj (too) proudly sure of one's own rightness or goodness ~ **ly** adv ~ **ness** n [U]

self-sac·ri·fice /ˌ·· ˈ···/ n [U] the giving up of things that one cares deeply about, esp. in order to help others

self·same /ˈsɛlfseɪm/ adj lit exactly the same

self-sat·is·fied /ˌ·· ˈ···/ adj too pleased with oneself

self-seek·ing /ˌ·· ˈ··◄/ n, adj (someone) working only for their own advantage

self-ser·vice /ˌ·· ˈ··◄/ adj, n [U] (working by) the system in which buyers collect what they want and pay at a special desk

self-start·er /ˌ·· ˈ··/ n **1** a usu. electrical apparatus for starting a car engine **2** a person able to work alone on their own ideas

self-styled /ˌ·· ˈ·◄/ adj given the stated title by oneself, usu. without any right to it

self-suf·fi·cient /ˌ·· ·'···◂/ *adj* able to provide everything one needs without outside help **-ciency** *n* [U]

self-will /ˌ· '·/ *n* [U] strong unreasonable determination to follow one's own wishes ~ *ed adj*

sell[1] /sel/ *v* **sold** /soʷld/ **1** *vi/t* give (property or goods) to someone in exchange for money **2** *vt* help or cause (something) to be bought: *Bad news sells newspapers.* **3** *vt* offer (goods) for sale **4** *vi* be bought: *The magazine sells for $5.* **5** *vt* make acceptable or desirable by persuading **6 sell oneself: a** make oneself or one's ideas seem attractive to others **b** give up one's principles for money or gain **7 sell one's soul (to the devil)** act dishonorably in exchange for money, power, etc. **8 sell someone down the river** put someone in great trouble by being disloyal to them **9 sell something/someone short** value something or someone too low ~ **er** *n*

  sell off *phr vt* get rid of by selling, usu. cheaply

  sell out *phr v* **1** *vi/t* (cause to) sell all of (what was for sale): *The tickets are all sold out; there are none left.* **2** *vi* be disloyal or unfaithful, esp. for payment **sell-out** /'· ·/ *n* **1** performance, match, etc., for which all tickets have been sold **2** act of disloyalty or unfaithfulness

  sell up *phr vi* sell something (esp. a business) completely

sell[2] *n* [S] deception – see also HARD SELL, SOFT SELL

selves /selvz/ *pl. of* SELF

se·man·tic /sɪˈmæntɪk/ *adj* of meaning in language ~ **ally** /-kliʸ/ *adv* **-tics** *n* [U] study of meaning

sem·a·phore /ˈsɛməˌfɔr, -ˌfoʷr/ *n* [U] system of sending messages with flags

sem·blance /ˈsɛmbləns/ *n* [S] appearance; outward form or seeming likeness: *a semblance of order*

se·men /ˈsiʸmən/ *n* [U] liquid carrying SPERM, passed through the male sex organs

se·mes·ter /səˈmɛstər/ *n* either of the 2 teaching periods in the year in some schools

sem·i·cir·cle /ˈsɛmiʸˌsɜrkəl/ *n* half a circle

sem·i·co·lon /ˈsɛmiʸˌkoʷlən/ *n* mark (;) used to separate independent parts of a sentence

sem·i·con·duc·tor /ˌsɛmiʸkənˈdʌktər/ *n* substance which allows the passing of an electric current more easily at high temperatures

sem·i·fi·nal /ˈsɛmiʸˌfaɪnl, ˈsɛmaɪ-, ˌsɛmiʸˈfaɪnl◂, ˌsɛmaɪ-/ *n* either of 2 matches, those who win play in a FINAL

sem·i·nal /ˈsɛmənəl/ *adj* **1** *fml* influencing future development in a new way **2** containing or producing SEMEN

sem·i·nar /ˈsɛməˌnɑr/ *n* small study group

sem·i·na·ry /ˈsɛməˌnɛriʸ/ *n* college for training esp. Roman Catholic priests

Se·mit·ic /səˈmɪtɪk/ *adj* of a race of people including Jews and Arabs

sem·o·li·na /ˌsɛməˈliʸnə/ *n* [U] crushed wheat used esp. for PASTA and cooked milky dishes

sen·ate /ˈsɛnɪt/ *n* (*usu. cap.*) **1** higher of the 2 parts of the body that makes laws in the US, France, etc. **2** highest council of state in ancient Rome **3** governing council in some universities **-ator** *n* member of a senate **-atorial** /ˌsɛnəˈtɔriʸəl, -ˈtoʷr-/ *adj*

send /sɛnd/ **sent** /sɛnt/ **1** *vt* cause to go or be taken, without going oneself: *He sent her a birthday card.* **2 send packing** send away quickly **3 send word** send a message ~ **er** *n*

  send away *phr vt* **1** send to another place **2** order goods to be sent by mail

  send down *phr vt* **1** cause to go down

  send for *phr vt* ask or order to come: *Send for a doctor!*

  send off *phr vt* **1** mail (a letter, parcel, etc.) **2** send **away/send-off** /'· ·/ *n* show of good wishes at the start of a journey, new business, etc.

  send on *phr vt* **1** send (a letter) to the receiver's next address **2** send (belongings) in advance to a point on a journey

  send out *phr vt* **1** send from a central point **2** (of an object) produce: *The sun sends out light.* **3** obtain something from somewhere else: *We can send out for coffee later.*

  send up *phr vt* **1** cause to go up **2** send someone to prison

se·nile /ˈsiʸnaɪl, ˈsɛnaɪl/ *adj* of or showing old age, esp. in weakness of mind **senility** /sɪˈnɪlətiʸ/ *n* [U]

sen·ior /ˈsiʸnyər/ *n, adj* **1** (someone) older **2** person in the last year of high school or college **3** (someone) of high or higher rank ~ **ity** /siʸnˈyɔrətiʸ, -ˈyɑr-/ *n* [U] **1** being senior **2** official advantage gained by length of service in an organization

Senior *adj* the older, esp. of two men in the same family who have the same name

senior cit·i·zen /ˌ··· '···/ *n* older person, esp. one over 65 and RETIREd

sen·sa·tion /sɛnˈseʸʃən/ *n* **1** [C;U] feeling, such as of heat or pain, coming from the senses **2** [C] general feeling in the mind or body **3** [C] (cause of) excited interest ~**al** adj **1** wonderful **2** causing excited interest or shock ~**ally** adv

sen·sa·tion·al·ism /sɛnˈseɪʃənəlˌɪzəm/ n [U] the intentional producing of excitement or shock, esp. by books, magazines, etc., of low quality

sense /sɛns/ n **1** [C] intended meaning **2** [U] good and esp. practical understanding and judgment **3** [C] any of the 5 natural powers of sight, hearing, feeling, tasting, and smelling – see also SIXTH SENSE **4** [C;U] power to understand and judge a particular thing: *a poor sense of direction* **5** [S] feeling, esp. one that is hard to describe **6 in a sense** partly; in one way of speaking **7 make sense: a** have a clear meaning **b** be a wise course of action **8 make sense (out) of** understand **9 (there's) no sense (in)** no good reason for ♦ vt feel in the mind: *I could sense danger.* **senses** n [P] powers of (reasonable) thinking: *He must have taken leave of his senses.* (= gone crazy) ~**less** adj **1** showing a lack of meaning, thought, or purpose **2** unconscious

sense of oc·ca·sion /ˌ· · ·ˈ··/ n [S] **1** natural feeling that tells one how one should behave at a particular social event **2** suitable feeling produced in someone by an important event

sense or·gan /ˈ· ˌ··/ n eye, nose, tongue, ear, etc.

sen·si·bil·i·ty /ˌsɛnsəˈbɪlətiʲ/ also **sensibilities** pl. — n [U] delicate feeling about style or what is correct, esp. in art or behavior

sen·si·ble /ˈsɛnsəbəl/ adj **1** having or showing good sense; reasonable **2** sensible of fml recognizing; conscious of –**bly** adv

sen·si·tive /ˈsɛnsətɪv/ adj **1** quick to feel or show the effect of: *sensitive to light* **2** easily offended **3** showing delicate feelings or judgment: *a sensitive performance* **4** knowing or being conscious of the feelings and opinions of others **5** (of an apparatus) measuring exactly **6** needing to be dealt with carefully so as not to cause trouble or offense: *a sensitive issue* ~ **ly** adv –**tivity** /ˌsɛnsəˈtɪvətiʲ/ n [U]

sen·si·tize /ˈsɛnsətaɪz/ vt make sensitive

sen·sor /ˈsɛnsər/ n apparatus for discovering the presence of something, such as heat or sound

sen·so·ry /ˈsɛnsəriʲ/ adj fml of or by the physical senses

sen·su·al /ˈsɛnʃuʷəl, -tʃuʷ-/ adj **1** of physical feelings **2** interested in or

suggesting physical, esp. sexual, pleasure ~**ity** /ˌsɛnʃuʷˈælətiʲ, -tʃuʷ-/ n [U]

sen·su·ous /ˈsɛnʃuʷəs, -tʃuʷ-/ adj **1** giving pleasure to the senses **2** SENSUAL (2) ~ **ly** adv ~ **ness** n [U]

sent /sɛnt/ v past t. and p. of SEND

sen·tence /ˈsɛntəns/ n **1** group of words forming complete statement, command, question, etc. **2** (order given by a judge which fixes) a punishment for a criminal found guilty in court **3 give/pass/pronounce sentence** (of a judge) say the order for a punishment **4 under sentence of death** having received a death sentence ♦ vt (of a judge) give a punishment to

sen·ten·tious /sɛnˈtɛnʃəs/ adj fml full of supposedly wise moral remarks ~**ly** adv

sen·tient /ˈsɛnʃənt/ adj fml having feelings and consciousness

sen·ti·ment /ˈsɛntəmənt/ n **1** [U] tender feelings of pity, love, sadness, etc., or remembrance of the past **2** [C] fml thought or judgment caused by a feeling ~**al** /ˌsɛntəˈmɛntl◂/ adj **1** caused by sentiment **2** showing too much sentiment, esp. of a weak or unreal kind ~**ally** adv ~**ality** /ˌsɛntəmenˈtælətiʲ/ n [U]

sentiments /ˈsɛntəmənts/ n fml [P] opinion

sen·ti·nel /ˈsɛntən-əl/ n lit guard; sentry

sen·try /ˈsɛntriʲ/ n soldier guarding a building, entrance, etc.

se·pal /ˈsɛpəl/ n small leaf underneath a flower

sep·a·ra·ble /ˈsɛpərəbəl/ adj fml that can be separated –**bly** adv

sep·a·rate¹ /ˈsɛpəˌreɪt/ v **1** vi/t move, set, keep, or break apart **2** vi stop living together as husband and wife –**ration** /ˌsɛpəˈreɪʃən/ n **1** [C;U] the act of separating or the fact of being separated **2** [C;U] (a time of) being or living apart **3** [U] law a formal agreement by a husband and wife to live apart

sep·a·rate² /ˈsɛpərɪt/ adj **1** different: *a word with 3 separate meanings* **2** not shared: *We have separate rooms.* **3** apart ~ **ly** adv

sep·a·rat·ism /ˈsɛpərəˌtɪzəm/ n [U] belief that a particular political or religious group should be separate, not part of a larger whole –**ist** n

se·pi·a /ˈsiʲpiʲə/ n [U] red-brown color

Sep·tem·ber /sɛpˈtɛmbər/ n the 9th month of the year

sep·tet /sɛpˈtɛt/ n (music for) 7 musicians

sep·tic /ˈsɛptɪk/ adj infected with bacteria

sep·ti·ce·mi·a /ˌsɛptəˈsiʲmiʲə/ n [U]

dangerous infection spread through the body in the blood

septic tank /'··· ·/ n large container in which body waste matter is broken up and changed by bacteria

sep·ul·cher /'sepəlkər/ n lit burial place –**chral** /sɪ'pʌlkrəl/ adj fml or lit like or suitable for a grave

se·quel /'siʸkwəl/ n **1** something that follows, esp. as a result **2** film etc., which continues where an earlier one ended

se·quence /'siʸkwəns/ n **1** [C] group following each other in order **2** [U] order in which things follow each other **3** [C] scene in a film

se·ques·tered /sɪ'kwestərd/ adj **1** lit quiet and hidden **2** law (of a JURY) kept away from the public

se·ques·trate /'siʸkwə,streʸt, siʸ'kwes-/ vt seize (property) by legal order until claims on it are settled –**tration** /,siʸkwə'streʸʃən/ n [U]

se·quin /'siʸkwɪn/ n small round shiny piece sewn on a garment for decoration

se·ra·glio /sə'rælyoʷ, -'ral-/ n –os HAREM

se·ra·pe /sə'rapiʸ, -'ræp-/ n brightly colored woolen BLANKET worn around the shoulders by Latin Americans

se·raph·ic /sə'ræfɪk/ adj like an ANGEL, esp. in beauty or purity ~**ally** /-kliʸ/ adv

ser·e·nade /,serə'neʸd/ n piece of music played or sung to a woman by a lover ♦ vt sing or play a serenade to

ser·en·dip·i·ty /,serən'dɪpətiʸ/ n [U] ability to make useful discoveries by chance

se·rene /sə'riʸn/ adj completely calm and peaceful ~**ly** adv **serenity** /sə'renətiʸ/ n [U]

serf /sɜrf/ n slave-like farm worker in former times ~**dom** n [U] state or fact of being a serf

serge /sɜrdʒ/ n [U] strong woolen cloth

ser·geant /'sardʒənt/ n **1** army officer above a CORPORAL **2** policeman of middle rank

sergeant ma·jor /,·· '··/ n officer of high rank

se·ri·al¹ /'sɪəriʸəl/ adj of, happening or arranged in a SERIES

serial² n written or broadcast story appearing in parts at fixed times ~**ize** vt print or broadcast as a serial

serial num·ber /'··· ,··/ n number marked on something to show which one it is in a series

se·ries /'sɪəriʸz/ n series group of the same or similar things coming one after another or in order

se·ri·ous /'sɪəriʸəs/ adj **1** causing worry and needing attention **2** not cheerful or funny **3** needing or having great skill or thought ~**ly** adv ~**ness** n [U]

ser·mon /'sɜrmən/ n talk given by a priest as part of a church service

ser·pent /'sɜrpənt/ n lit snake

ser·rat·ed /sə'reʸtɪd, 'sereʸtɪd/ adj having (an edge with) a row of V shapes like teeth

se·rum /'sɪərəm/ n serums or sera /-rə/ [C;U] liquid containing substances that fight sickness, put into a sick person's blood

ser·vant /'sɜrvənt/ n person paid to do personal services for someone, esp. in their home – see also PUBLIC SERVANT

serve /sɜrv/ v **1** vi/t do work (for); give service (to): to serve in the army **2** vt provide with something necessary or useful: The pipeline serves the whole town. **3** vt offer (food, a meal, etc.) for eating **4** vt attend to (a customer in a store) **5** vt spend (a period of time): She served (2 years) in prison. **6** vi/t be good enough or suitable for (a purpose) **7** vi/t (esp. in tennis) begin play by hitting (the ball) to one's opponent **8** vt law deliver (an official order to appear in court) **9** if my memory serves me (right) if I remember correctly **10** serve someone right be suitable punishment ♦ n act or manner of serving (SERVE (7)) **server** n **1** something used in serving food **2** player who serves in tennis – see also TIME SERVER

ser·vice /'sɜrvɪs/ n **1** [C;U] act or work done for someone **2** [U] attention to guests in a hotel, restaurant, etc., or to customers in a store **3** [C;U] (operation of) an organization doing useful work: a bus service | telephone service **4** [C;U] (duty in) the army, navy, etc. **5** [C] religious ceremony **6** [C;U] examination of a machine to keep it in good condition **7** [C] SERVE **8** [C] set of dishes, etc.: a dinner service **9** at your service fml willing to help **10** of service fml useful; helpful ♦ vt repair or put in good condition ♦ adj something for the use of people working in a place, rather than the public: service stairs

ser·vi·cea·ble /'sɜrvɪsəbəl/ adj fit for (long or hard) use; useful

service charge /'·· ·/ n amount added to a bill to pay for a particular service

ser·vice·man /'sɜrvɪs,mæn, -mən/ –**woman** /-,wʊmən/ fem. — n –**men** /-mɛn, -mən/ member of the army, navy, etc.

service sta·tion /'·· ,··/ n GARAGE

ser·vile /'sɜrvəl, -vaɪl/ adj behaving

like a slave –**vility** /sɜrˈvɪləti/ n [U]

serv·ing /ˈsɜrvɪŋ/ n amount of food for 1 person

ser·vi·tude /ˈsɜrvəˌtuʷd, -ˌtyuʷd/ n [U] lit state of being a slave or one who is forced to obey another

ses·sion /ˈsɛʃən/ n 1 formal meeting or group of meetings of a LEGISLATURE or court 2 period of time used for a particular purpose: a recording/drinking session

set[1] /sɛt/ v set, pres. p. –**tt**- 1 vt put (to stay) in the stated place: to set a ladder against a wall 2 vt fix; establish: set a date for the wedding 3 vt put into the correct condition for use: set the clock/the table 4 vt cause to be: set a prisoner free | Her words set me thinking. 5 vt put: set a load down 6 vi APPLY oneself: set to work 7 vt put the action of (a film, story, etc.) in the stated place and time 8 vi/t (cause to) become solid: The jelly has set. 9 vi (of the sun, moon, etc.) go below the horizon 10 vt write or provide music for (a poem or other words to be sung) 11 vt fix (a precious stone) into (a piece of jewelry) 12 vt put (a broken bone) into a fixed position to mend 13 vt arrange (hair) when wet to be in a particular style when dry 14 vt arrange for printing 15 **set an example** offer a standard for others to follow 16 **set eyes on** see 17 **set light/fire to** cause (something) to burn 18 **set one's heart/hopes on** want very much 19 **set one's mind against** oppose 20 **set one's mind to** decide firmly on

set about phr vt begin

set back phr vt 1 place at esp. the stated distance behind something: The house is set back 15 feet from the road. 2 delay 3 cost (a large amount)

set in phr vi (of bad weather, disease, etc.) begin (and continue)

set off phr v 1 vi begin a journey 2 vt cause to explode (a sudden activity) 4 vt make (one thing) look better by putting it near something different: A white belt set off her blue dress.

set out phr v 1 vt arrange or spread out in order 2 vi begin a journey 3 vt begin with a purpose

set to phr vi begin eagerly or determinedly

set up phr vt 1 put into position 2 prepare (a machine, instrument, etc.) for use 3 establish or arrange (an organization, plan, etc.) 4 provide with what is necessary or useful

set[2] adj 1 given or fixed for study: a set program 2 determined: He's very set on going. 3 fixed;

PRESCRIBED: set hours 4 unmoving: a set smile 5 at a fixed price: a set dinner 6 infml ready: I'm all set, so we can go.

set[3] n 1 group forming a whole: a set of gardening tools 2 television or radio receiving apparatus 3 a scenery, etc., representing the place of action in a stage play b place where a film is acted 4 group of games in a tennis match 5 group of people of a particular social type: the smart set 6 act of setting (SET[1](13)) one's hair

set·back /ˈsɛtbæk/ n something that delays or prevents successful PROGRESS

set piece /ˌ· ˈ·◂/ n something carried out using a common formal pattern or plan

set·square /ˈsɛtskwɛər/ n plate with 3 sides and one 90 degree angle, for drawing or testing angles

set·tee /sɛˈtiʸ/ n SOFA

set·ter /ˈsɛtər/ n dog with long hair, used by hunters

set·ting /ˈsɛtɪŋ/ n 1 the going down (of the moon, sun, etc.) 2 way or position in which an instrument is prepared for use 3 a set of surroundings b time and place where the action of a book, film, etc., happens 4 set of articles (dishes, knives, forks, etc.) arranged at one place on a table for eating: a place setting

set·tle /ˈsɛtl/ v 1 vi start to live in a place 2 vi/t (place so as to) stay or be comfortable 3 vi/t come or bring to rest, esp. from above: Dust had settled on the furniture. 4 vi/t make or become quiet, calm, etc.: Settle down, children! 5 vt decide on firmly; fix: That settles it! (= That has decided the matter.) 6 vt provide people to live in (a place) 7 vi/t bring (a matter) to an agreement 8 vt pay (a bill) **settled** adj **settler** n member of a new population

settle down phr vi 1 (cause to) sit comfortably 2 give one's serious attention (to a job, etc.): I must settle down to some work today. 3 establish a home and live a quiet life 4 become used to a way of life, job, etc.

settle for phr vt accept (something less than hoped for)

settle in phr vi/t (help to) get used to a new home, job, etc.)

settle on phr vt decide or agree on; choose

settle up phr vi pay what is owed

set·tle·ment /ˈsɛtlmənt/ n 1 [U] movement of a new population into a new place to live there 2 [C] area of houses built recently, with few people 3 [C;U] agreement or decision ending an argument 4 [C;U] payment of money claimed 5 [C] a formal gift or giving of money: *He made a settlement on his daughter when she married.*

set-to /ˈ· ·/ *n infml* [S] short fight or quarrel

set-up /ˈ· ·/ *n* 1 arrangement; organization 2 competition deliberately made easy

sev·en /ˈsevən/ *determiner, n, pron* 7 ~ **th** *determiner, adv, n, pron* 7th

sev·en·teen /ˌsevənˈtiːn◂/ *determiner, n, pron* 17 ~ **th** *determiner, adv, n, pron* 17th

seventh heav·en /ˌ·· ˈ··/ *n* complete happiness

sev·en·ty /ˈsevəntiʸ/ *determiner, n, pron* 70 **–tieth** *determiner, adv, n, pron* 70th

seventy-eight /ˌ··· ˈ·/ *n* record played at 78 turns a minute

seven-year itch /ˌ· · ˈ·/ *n* dissatisfaction after 7 years of marriage

sev·er /ˈsevər/ *vt fml* divide in 2, esp. by cutting: (fig.) *sever diplomatic relations* ~ **ance** *n* [U]

sev·er·al /ˈsevərəl/ *determiner, pron* more than a few but not very many; some *adj fml* separate: *They went their several ways.*

severance pay /ˈ··· ·/ *n* [U] money paid by a company to a worker losing his job through no fault of his own

se·vere /səˈvɪər/ *adj* 1 causing serious harm, pain, or worry 2 not kind or gentle 3 completely plain and without decoration ~ **ly** *adv* **severity** /səˈverətiʸ/ *n* [U]

sew /soʷ/ *vi/t* sewed, sewn /soʷn/ join (esp. cloth) with thread

sew up *phr vt* 1 close or repair by sewing 2 settle satisfactorily

sew·age /ˈsuːɪdʒ/ *n* [U] waste material and water carried in sewers

sew·er /ˈsuːər/ *n* large underground pipe for carrying away human waste and water, esp. in a city

sew·er·age /ˈsuːərɪdʒ/ *n* [U] system of removing waste material through sewers

sex /seks/ *n* 1 [U] condition of being male or female 2 [C] set of all male or female people 3 [U] (activity connected with) SEXUAL INTERCOURSE: *to have sex (with someone)* ♦ *vt* find out whether (an animal) is male or female

sex ap·peal /ˈ· ·ˌ·/ *n* [U] power of being sexually exciting to other people

sex·is·m /ˈseksˌɪzəm/ *n* [U] (unfair treatment coming from) the belief that one sex is better, cleverer, etc., than the other ~ **ist** *adj, n*

sex or·gan /ˈ· ˌ··/ *n* part of the body used in producing children

sex·tant /ˈsekstənt/ *n* instrument for measuring angles between stars, to find out where one is

sex·tet /seksˈtet/ *n* (music for) 6 musicians

sex·ton /ˈsekstən/ *n* someone who takes care of a church building

sex·tu·plet /sekˈstʌplɪt, -ˈstuː-, -ˈstjuʷ-/ *n* any of 6 children born together

sex·u·al /ˈsekʃuʷəl/ *adj* of or connected with sex ~ **ly** *adv*: *sexually active* ~ **ity** /ˌsekʃuʷˈælətiʸ/ *n* [U] interest in, the expression of, or the ability to take part in sexual activity

sexual in·ter·course /ˌ··· ˈ··/ *n* [U] physical act between 2 people in which the sex organs are brought together

sex·y /ˈseksiʸ/ *adj* sexually exciting **–ily** *adv* **–iness** *n* [U]

SF *written abbrev. for:* SCIENCE FICTION

sh, shh /ʃ/ *interj* (used for demanding silence)

shab·by /ˈʃæbiʸ/ *adj* 1 untidy, not cared for, and worn out 2 unfair and ungenerous **–bily** *adv* **–biness** *n* [U]

shack¹ /ʃæk/ *n* small roughly built house or hut

shack² ** *v* **shack up *phr vi infml* (of a person, or persons) live together without being married

shack·le /ˈʃækəl/ *n* metal band for fastening the arms or legs: (fig.) *the shackles of slavery* ♦ *vt* fasten (as if) with shackles

shade /ʃeʸd/ *n* 1 [U] slight darkness, made esp. by blocking of direct sunlight 2 [C] something which provides shade or reduces light: *a lamp-shade* 3 [C] degree or variety of color: *shades of blue* 4 [C] slight difference: *shades of meaning* 5 [S] slightly: *a shade too loud* 6 [C] *lit* GHOST 7 **put someone/something in the shade** make someone/something seem much less important by comparison ♦ *v* 1 *vt* shelter from direct light 2 *vt* represent shadow on (an object in a picture) 3 *vi* change gradually **shady** *adj* 1 in or producing shade 2 probably dishonest

shades /ʃeʸdz/ *n* [P] 1 *infml* SUNGLASSES 2 **shades of** this reminds me of

shad·ow /ˈʃædoʷ/ *n* 1 [U] SHADE (1): *Most of the room was in shadow.* 2 [C] dark shape made on a surface by something between it and direct light: *The tree cast a long shadow across the lawn.* 3 [C] dark area: *shadows under her eyes* 4 [S] slightest bit: *not a shadow of a doubt* 5 [C] a form from which the real substance has gone: *After his illness he*

was only a shadow of his former self.
6 be afraid of one's own shadow be habitually afraid of everything ♦ *vt* **1** make a shadow on **2** follow and watch closely, esp. secretly ~**y** *adj* **1** hard to see or know about clearly **2** full of shade

shadow-box /'ʃædoʷ,bɑks/ *vi* fight with an imaginary opponent ~**ing** *n* [U]

shaft¹ /ʃæft/ *n* **1** thin rod forming the body of a weapon or tool, such as a spear or ax **2** bar which turns to pass power through a machine: *a propeller shaft* **3** long passage going down: *a mine shaft* **4** either of 2 poles that an animal is fastened between to pull a vehicle **5** beam (of light) **6** *lit* something shot like an arrow: *shafts of wit*

shaft² *vt sl* treat unfairly and very severely

shag /ʃæg/ *n* **1** shaggy style of hair **2** [U] rough strong tobacco

shag·gy /'ʃægiʸ/ *adj* being or covered with long uneven untidy hair ~**giness** *n* [U]

shaggy-dog sto·ry /,·· '· ,··/ *n* long joke with a purposely pointless ending

shake /ʃeʸk/ *v* **shook** /ʃʊk/, **shaken** /'ʃeʸkən/ **1** *vi/t* move up and down and from side to side with quick short movements **2** *vi/t* hold (someone's right hand) and move it up and down, to show esp. greeting or agreement **3** *vt* trouble; upset **4** *vi* (of a voice) tremble **5** *vt* get rid of: *shake a feeling/habit* **6 shake one's head** move one's head from side to side to answer 'no' ♦ *n* **1** [C] act of shaking **2** [C] *infml* moment **3** [C] *infml* MILK SHAKE **4** [S] *infml* treatment of the stated type: *a fair shake* – see also SHAKES **shaky** *adj* shaking; unsteady **shakily** *adv*

shake off *phr vt* get rid of; escape from

shake up *phr vt* **1** make big changes in (an organization), esp. to improve it **2** mix by shaking **3** upset **shake-up** /'· ·/ *n* rearrangement of an organization

shake-down /'ʃeʸkdaʊn/ *n infml* **1** act of getting money dishonestly **2** place prepared as a bed **3** last test operation of a new ship or aircraft

shakes /ʃeʸks/ *n infml* **1** [*the*+P] nervous shaking of the body from disease, fear, etc. **2 no great shakes** not very good

shale /ʃeʸl/ *n* [U] soft rock which splits naturally

shall /ʃəl/; *strong* ʃæl/ *v aux fml* (used with I and we) **1** (expresses the future tense) **2** (used in questions or offers): *Shall I* (= would you like me to) *go?*

shal·low /'ʃæloʷ/ *adj* **1** not deep **2** lacking deep or serious thinking **shallows** *n* [P] shallow area in a river, lake, etc.

sham /ʃæm/ *n* **1** [C] something that is not what it appears or is said to be **2** [U] falseness: PRETENSE ♦ *adj* not real ♦ *vi/t* -**mm**- put on a false appearance

sha·man /'ʃɑmən, 'ʃeʸ-/ *n* tribal medicine man

sham·ble /'ʃæmbəl/ *vi* walk awkwardly, dragging the feet

sham·bles /'ʃæmbəlz/ *n* [P] (place or scene of) great disorder

shame /ʃeʸm/ *n* **1** [U] painful feeling caused by knowledge of guilt, inability, or failure **2** [U] ability to feel this **3** [U] loss of honor **4** [S] something one is sorry about: *It's a shame you can't come.* **5 put someone/something to shame** show someone/something to be less good by comparison ♦ *vt* **1** bring dishonor to **2** cause to feel shame ~**ful** *adj* which one ought to feel ashamed of ~**fully** *adv* ~**fulness** *n* [U] ~**less** *adj* not feeling suitably ashamed: *a shameless liar* **2** done without shame ~**lessly** *adv* ~**lessness** *n* [U]

shame-faced /'ʃeʸmfeʸst/ *adj* showing suitable shame ~**ly** /'ʃeʸm-'feʸsɪdliʸ/ *adv*

sham·poo /ʃæm'puʷ/ *n* -**poos** [C;U] liquid soap for washing the hair ♦ *vt* -**pooed**, *present p.* -**pooing** wash with shampoo

sham·rock /'ʃæmrɑk/ *n* [U] plant with 3 leaves on each stem that is the national sign of Ireland

shang·hai /ʃæŋ'haɪ/ *vt* trick or force into doing something unwilling

Shan·gri-La /,ʃæŋgriʸ 'lɑ/ *n* distant beautiful imaginary place where everything is pleasant

shank /ʃæŋk/ *n* **1** cut of meat from the leg of an animal **2** smooth end of a SCREW (1) or DRILL

shan·ty¹ /'ʃæntiʸ/ *n* small roughly built house

shan·ty² *n* song sung by working sailors

shan·ty·town /'ʃæntiʸ,taʊn/ *n* (part of) a town where poor people live in shanties

shape /ʃeʸp/ *n* **1** [C;U] outer form of something: *a cake in the shape of a heart* **2** [U] general character or nature of something **3** [U] (proper) condition, health, etc. **4 get/put something into shape** arrange or plan something properly **5 in any shape or form** of any kind; at all **6 take shape** begin to be or look like the finished form ♦ *v* **1** *vt* give a particular shape to: *the influences that shape one's character* **2** *vi* develop in the stated way ~·less *adj* ~·ly *adj* (of a person) having an attractive shape

shape up *phr vi* **1** develop well or in the stated way **2** (usu. used threateningly or angrily) begin to perform more effectively, behave better, etc.

shard /ʃɑrd/ *n* broken piece of a bowl, cup, etc.

share /ʃeər/ *n* **1** part belonging to, owed to, or done by a particular person **2** part of the ownership of a business company, offered for sale to the public ♦ *v* **1** *vi/t* have, use, pay, etc., with others or among a group **2** *vt* divide and give out in shares **3 share and share alike** have an equal share in everything

share·crop·per /'ʃeərˌkrɑpər/ *n* farmer who rents the land he works

shark /ʃɑrk/ *n* **1 shark** or **sharks** large dangerous fish with sharp teeth **2** *infml* a person clever at getting money from others in dishonest ways

sharp /ʃɑrp/ *adj* **1** having or being a thin cutting edge or fine point: *a sharp knife* **2** not rounded: *a sharp nose* **3** causing a sensation like that of cutting, pricking, biting, or stinging: *a sharp wind | the sharp taste of lemon juice* **4** quick and strong: *a sharp pain | a sharp blow to the head* **5** sudden: *a sharp turn* **6** clear in shape or detail: *a sharp photo* **7** quick and sensitive in thinking, seeing, etc. **8** angry **9** (in music) above the right note **10** *infml* attractive ♦ *adv* exactly at the stated time ♦ *n* (in music) sharp note ~·ly *adv* ~·en *vi/t* become or make sharp or sharper ~·en·er *n*: *a pencil sharpener* ~·ness *n* [U]

sharp end /'· ·/ *n* [*the*+S] *infml* part of a job, organization, etc., where the most severe problems are experienced

sharp·shoot·er /'ʃɑrpˌʃuʷtər/ *n* person skilled in shooting

shat·ter /'ʃæt̬ər/ *v* **1** *vi/t* break suddenly into very small pieces **2** *vt* shock very much **3** *vt infml* tire very much

shave /ʃeɪv/ *v* **1** *vi/t* cut off (a beard or face hair) with a RAZOR or shaver **2** *vt* cut hair from (a part of the body) **3** *vt* cut off (very thin pieces) from (a surface) **4** *vt* come close to or touch in passing ♦ *n* act of shaving – see also CLOSE SHAVE **shaver** *n* **1** electric shaving tool **2** *infml* small boy **shaving** *n* very thin piece cut off from a surface

shaving cream /'·· ·/ *n* [U] soapy paste put on the face to make shaving easier

shawl /ʃɔl/ *n* large piece of cloth worn over the head or shoulders or wrapped around the body

she /ʃiʲ/ *pron* (used for the female subject of a sentence) ♦ *n* a female: *a she-goat*

sheaf /ʃiʲf/ *n* **sheaves** /ʃiʲvz/ **1** bunch of grain plants tied together **2** many things held or tied together: *a sheaf of notes*

shear /ʃɪər/ *v* **sheared, sheared** or **shorn** /ʃɔrn, ʃoʷrn/ **1** *vt* cut off wool from (a sheep) **2** *vi/t* break under a sideways or twisting force **3 be shorn of** have (something) completely removed from one **shears** *n* [P] large cutting tool like scissors

sheath /ʃiʲθ/ *n* **sheaths** /ʃiʲðz/ **1** narrow case for a blade **2** cover or garment that fits closely

sheathe /ʃiʲð/ *vt* put away in a SHEATH (1)

she·bang /ʃɪˈbæŋ/ *n* **the whole shebang** *infml* everything

shed[1] /ʃed/ *n* lightly built (wooden) building on one floor

shed[2] *vt* **shed; pres. p. -dd- 1** cause to flow out: *shedding tears* (= crying) **2** get rid of (outer skin, leaves, hair, etc.) naturally **3** get rid of (something not wanted or needed) **4** shed blood cause wounding or esp. killing **5** shed light on help to explain

she'd /ʃiʲd/ *short for*: **1** she would **2** she had

sheen /ʃiʲn/ *n* [S;U] shiny surface

sheep /ʃiʲp/ *n* **sheep 1** animal that eats grass, farmed for its wool and meat **2** person who is easily led – see also BLACK SHEEP ~·ish *adj* **1** like a sheep (2) **2** uncomfortable because one knows one has done something wrong or foolish ~·ish·ly *adv* ~·ish·ness *n* [U]

sheep·dog /'ʃiʲpdɔg/ *n* dog trained to control sheep

sheer[1] /ʃɪər/ *adj* **1** pure; nothing but: *He won by sheer luck.* **2** very steep **3** (of cloth) very thin ♦ *adv* straight up or down

sheer[2] *vi* change direction quickly

sheet /ʃiʲt/ *n* **1** large piece of cloth used on a bed **2** broad regularly shaped piece of a thin or flat material: *a sheet of glass/paper* **3** a broad stretch of something: *a sheet of ice* **4** moving or powerful wide mass: *The rain came down in sheets.*

sheet mu·sic /'· ˌ··, ˌ· '··/ *n* [U] music printed on folding sheets of paper

sheikh /ʃiʲk, ʃeɪk/ *n* Arab chief or prince ~·dom *n*

shek·els /'ʃekəlz/ *n* [P] unit of Israeli money

shelf /ʃelf/ *n* **shelves** /ʃelvz/ **1** flat (narrow) board fixed against a wall or in a frame, for putting things on

2 narrow surface of rock under water **3 on the shelf** delayed for an uncertain time

shelf life /ˈ· ·/ n length of time a product stays fresh in a store

shell¹ /ʃel/ n **1** [C;U] hard outer covering of a nut, egg, fruit, or certain types of animal: a snail shell **2** [C] outer surface or frame of something: (fig.) He's only a shell of a man. **3** [C] explosive for firing from a large gun **4 come out of one's shell** begin to be friendly or interested in others

shell² vt **1** remove from a SHELL¹(1) or POD **2** fire SHELLs¹ (3) at

shell out phr vt infml pay

she'll /ʃil; strong ʃiːl/ short for: **1** she will **2** she shall

shel·lac /ʃəˈlæk/ n [U] shiny paint-like coat for wood, etc.

shel·lack·ing /ʃəˈlækɪŋ/ n infml severe defeat

shell·fish /ˈʃel₁fɪʃ/ n –fish **1** [C] water animal with a soft body inside a shell: Oysters and lobsters are shellfish. **2** [U] such animals as food

shell-shock /ˈʃelʃak/ n (U) illness of the mind, esp. in soldiers caused by the experience of war –shocked adj

shel·ter /ˈʃeltər/ n **1** [C] building or enclosure giving protection **2** [U] protection, esp. from bad weather ♦ v **1** vt give shelter to **2** vi take shelter

shelve /ʃelv/ v **1** vt put aside until a later time **2** vi slope gradually

shelves /ʃelvz/ pl. of SHELF

she·nan·i·gans /ʃəˈnænɪɡənz/ n [P] infml **1** slightly dishonest practices **2** MISCHIEF

shep·herd /ˈʃepərd/ shepherdess /ˈʃepərdɪs/ fem. — n person who takes care of sheep ♦ vt lead or guide like sheep

sher·bet /ˈʃɜrbɪt/ n [C;U] dish of ice with a usu. fruit taste

sher·iff /ˈʃerɪf/ n elected law officer in a local area

sher·ry /ˈʃeriʲ/ n [U] pale or dark brown strong wine (originally from Spain

she's /ʃiʲz/ short for: **1** she is **2** she has

shib·bo·leth /ˈʃɪbələθ, -ˌleθ/ n **1** word used to test to which party, class, etc., a person belongs **2** once important custom or phrase which no longer has much meaning

shield /ʃiʲld/ n **1** something carried as a protection from being hit **2** representation of this, used for a COAT OF ARMS, BADGE, etc. **3** protective cover ♦ vt protect

shift /ʃɪft/ v **1** vi/t move from one place to another **2** vt get rid of; remove **3 shift for oneself** take care of oneself ♦ n **1** change in position

or direction **2** (period worked by) a group of workers which takes turns with others: the night shift **3** loose fitting simple dress ~less adj lazy and lacking in purpose ~y adj looking dishonest; not to be trusted ~ily adv ~iness n [U]

shift key /ˈ· ·/ n KEY on a TYPE-WRITER, etc., pressed to print a capital letter

shim·mer /ˈʃɪmər/ vi shine with a soft trembling light

shim·my /ˈʃɪmiʲ/ vi shake or VIBRATE

shin /ʃɪn/ n the part of the leg below the knee

shin·dig /ˈʃɪndɪɡ/ n infml party

shine /ʃaɪn/ v shone /ʃoʷn/ **1** vi/t (cause to) give off light (past t. and p. **shined**) polish **3** vi be clearly excellent ♦ n [S] **1** brightness **2** act of polishing **3 (come) rain or shine** whatever happens **4 take a shine to** start to like **shiny** adj bright

shin·gle /ˈʃɪŋɡəl/ n unit of roof covering –gly adj

shin·gles /ˈʃɪŋɡəlz/ n [U] disease producing painful red spots, esp. around the waist

shin·ny /ˈʃɪniʲ/ vi climb using hands and legs esp. quickly and easily

ship /ʃɪp/ n **1** large boat **2** large aircraft or space vehicle **3 when one's ship comes in/home** when one becomes rich ♦ vt –pp- **1** send by ship **2** send over a large distance by road, air, etc. ~per n dealer who ships goods ~ping n [U] ships as a group

ship·board /ˈʃɪpbɔrd, -boʷrd/ n on shipboard on a ship

ship·mate /ˈʃɪpmeʲt/ n fellow sailor on the same ship

ship·ment /ˈʃɪpmənt/ n **1** [C] load of goods sent by sea, road, or air **2** [C;U] sending, carrying, and delivering goods

ship·shape /ˈʃɪpʃeʲp/ adj clean and neat

ship·wreck /ˈʃɪp-rek/ n [C;U] destruction of a ship, by hitting rocks or by sinking ♦ vt **1** cause to suffer shipwreck **2** ruin

ship·yard /ˈʃɪp-yard/ n place where ships are built or repaired

shirk /ʃɜrk/ vi/t avoid (unpleasant work) because of laziness, lack of determination, etc. ~er n

shirt /ʃɜrt/ n **1** cloth garment for the upper body with SLEEVES and usu. a collar **2 keep one's shirt on** not lose one's temper **3 lose one's shirt** to lose all one has

shirt·sleeves /ˈʃɜrtˌsliʲvz/ n in (one's) shirtsleeves wearing nothing over one's shirt

shit /ʃɪt/ n [U] taboo **1** solid waste from the bowels **2** something of no value: *I don't give a shit.* (= I don't care) **2** worthless or unpleasant person ♦ *vi* -**tt**- *taboo* pass solid waste from the bowels ♦ *interj taboo* (expressing anger or annoyance) ~**ty** *adj taboo sl* unpleasant

shit list /'·· ·/ *n taboo* (group of) people that one strongly dislikes or has a grievance against

shiv·er /'ʃɪvər/ *vi* shake, esp. from cold or fear ♦ *n* feeling of shivering ~**y** *adj*

shoal[1] /ʃoʷl/ *n* dangerous bank of sand near the surface of water

shoal[2] *n* large group of fish swimming together

shock[1] /ʃɑk/ *n* [C;U] **1** (state or feeling caused by) an unexpected and usu. very unpleasant event **2** violent force from a hard blow, crash, explosion, etc., or from electricity ♦ *vt* cause unpleasant or angry surprise to ♦ *adj* very surprising: *shock tactics* ~**ing** *adj* **1** very offensive, wrong, or upsetting **2** very bad: *I've got a shocking cold.*

shock[2] *n* thick mass (of hair)

shock ab·sorb·er /'·· ̦·‚·/ *n* apparatus fitted to a vehicle to lessen the effect of violent movement

shod /ʃɑd/ *past t. and p. of* SHOE

shod·dy /'ʃɑdiʸ/ *adj* **1** cheaply and badly done **2** ungenerous; dishonorable –**dily** *adv* –**diness** *n* [U]

shoe /ʃuʷ/ *n* **1** covering worn on the foot **2** fill someone's shoes take the place and do the job of someone **3** in someone's shoes in someone's position: *I'd hate to be in your shoes.* ♦ *vt* **shod** fix a HORSESHOE on

shoe·lace /'ʃuʷleʸs/ *n* thin cord for fastening a shoe

shoe·string /'ʃuʷ‚strɪŋ/ *n* **on a shoestring** with a very small amount of money

shone /ʃoʷn/ *v past t. and p. of* SHINE

shoo /ʃuʷ/ *interj* (used for driving away esp. birds and animals) ♦ *vt* drive away (as if) by saying 'shoo'

shook /ʃʊk/ *v past t. of* SHAKE

shoot /ʃuʷt/ *v* **shot** /ʃɑt/ **1** *vi* fire a weapon **2** *vt* (of a person or weapon) send out (bullets, etc.) with force: (fig.) *She shot him an angry glance.* **3** *vt* hit, wound, or kill with a bullet, etc. **4** *vi* move very quickly or suddenly: *The car shot past us.* | *Pain shot up my arm.* | (fig.) *Prices have shot up.* **5** *vi/t* make (a photograph or film) (of) **6** *vi* kick, throw, etc., a ball to make a point in a game **7** *vi* play (a game of BILLIARDS, POOL, etc.) **8** shoot one's mouth off talk foolishly about what one does not know about or should not talk about **9** shoot the bull/the breeze *infml* have an informal not very serious conversation ♦ *n* **1** new growth

from a plant **2** occasion for shooting, esp. of animals

shoot down *phr vt* **1** bring down (a flying aircraft) by shooting **2** REJECT (an idea)

shoot up *phr v* **1** *vi* go upwards, increase, or grow quickly **2** *vt infml* damage or wound by shooting **3** *vi/t sl* take (a drug) directly into the blood using a needle

shooting star /‚·· '·/ *n* METEOR

shoot-out /'·· ·/ *n* battle between fighters with hand guns, usu. to decide a quarrel

shop[1] /ʃɑp/ *n* **1** [C] small building or room where goods are sold **2** a small department in a large store **3** [U] subjects connected with one's work: *Let's not talk shop.*

shop[2] *v* -**pp**- *vi* visit stores to buy things ~**per** *n* ~**ping** *n* [U] goods bought when visiting stores

shop around *phr vt* compare prices or values in different stores before buying: (fig.) *Shop around before deciding which club to join.*

shop floor /‚· '·◁/ *n* area, esp. in a factory, where the ordinary workers work

shop·keep·er /'ʃɑp‚kiʸpər/ *n* person in charge of a small store

shop·lift /'ʃɑp‚lɪft/ *vi* steal from a shop ~**er** *n*

shopping cen·ter /'·· ̦·/ *n* group of stores all built in one style

shopping mall /'·· ‚·/ *n* – see MALL

shop·worn /'ʃɑpwɔrn, -woʷrn/ *adj* slightly damaged or dirty from being kept in a store for a long time

shop stew·ard /‚· '·◁/ *n* trade union officer representing members in a place of work

shore[1] /ʃɔr, ʃoʷr/ *n* [C;U] **1** land along the edge of a sea, lake, etc. **2 on shore** on land; away from one's ship

shore[2] *v* **shore up** *phr vt* support (something in danger of falling), esp. with wood

shorn /ʃɔrn, ʃoʷrn/ *past p. of* SHEAR

short[1] /ʃɔrt/ *adj* **1** measuring a small or smaller than average amount in distance, length, or height **2** lasting only a little time, or less time than usual or expected **3** a shorter (and often more usual) way of saying: *The word 'disco' is short for 'discotheque'.* **4** not having or providing what is needed: *I'm short of money.* **5** rudely impatient **6 in short order** quickly **7 make short work of** deal with or defeat quickly **8 short and sweet** short and direct in expression **9 short of: a** not quite reaching **b** except for **10 short on** without very much or enough (of): *He's a nice fellow but short on brains.*

short² *adv* **1** suddenly: *He stopped short.* **2 fall short (of)** be less than (good) enough (for) **3 go short (of)** be without enough (of) **4 run short (of):** a not have enough left b become less than enough

short³ *n* **1** result; UPSHOT **2** short film shown before the main film at a cinema **3** SHORT CIRCUIT **4 for short** as a shorter way of saying it **5 in short** all I mean is; to put it into as few words as possible – see also SHORTS

short·age /ˈʃɔrtɪdʒ/ *n* [C;U] amount lacking; not enough

short·bread /ˈʃɔrtbred/ *n* [U] sweet buttery COOKIE

short·cake /ˈʃɔrtkeɪk/ *n* [C;U] sweet cake eaten with fruit and cream

short·change /ˌ·ˈ·/ *vt* **1** give back less than enough money to a buyer **2** fail to reward fairly

short cir·cuit /ˌ·ˈ··/ *n* faulty electrical connection where the current flows the wrong way and usu. puts the power supply out of operation **short-circuit** *vi/t* (cause to) have a short circuit

short·com·ing /ˈʃɔrtˌkʌmɪŋ/ *n* fault; failing

short cut /ˈ·· ·/ *n* quicker more direct way

short·en /ˈʃɔrtn/ *vi/t* make or become shorter

short·en·ing /ˈʃɔrtn-ɪŋ/ *n* [U] fat for cooking

short·fall /ˈʃɔrtfɔl/ *n* amount by which something fails to reach the expected total

short·hand /ˈʃɔrthænd/ *n* [U] system of special signs for fast writing

short·hand·ed /ˌʃɔrtˈhændɪd◄/ *adj* without enough workers or helpers

short-lived /ˌʃɔrtˈlaɪvd, -ˈlɪvd◄/ *adj* lasting only a short time

short or·der /ˌ·ˈ··◄/ *n* order for a quick meal in a small restaurant: *short order cook*

short·ly /ˈʃɔrtliʸ/ *adv* **1** soon **2** impatiently **3** in a few words

shorts /ʃɔrts/ *n* [P] **1** short pants **2** men's short UNDERPANTS

short shrift /ˌ·ˈ·/ *n* [U] unfairly quick or unsympathetic treatment

short·sight·ed /ˌʃɔrtˈsaɪtɪd/ *adj* not considering what may happen in the future ~**ly** *adv* ~**ness** *n* [U]

short·stop /ˈʃɔrtstɑp/ *n* baseball player between 2nd and 3rd base

short-term, short term /ˌ·ˈ·◄/ *adj, n* (concerning) a short period of time; (in or for) the near future: *short-term planning*

short wave /ˌ·ˈ·◄/ *n* [U] radio broadcasting on waves of less than 60 meters

shot¹ /ʃɑt/ *v past t. and p. of* SHOOT

shot² *n* **1** [C] (sound of) shooting a weapon **2** [C] hit, kick, etc., of a ball in sport **3** [C] person who shoots with the stated skill **4** [C] attempt: *I'll have a shot at it.* **5** [U] metal balls for shooting from shotguns or CANNONS **6** [C] a photograph b single part of a film made by one camera without interruption **7** [C] INJECTION: *a shot of penicillin* **8** [C] sending up of a spacecraft or ROCKET: *a moon shot* **9** [C] a small drink (esp. of WHISKEY) all swallowed at once **10 a shot in the arm** something which acts to bring back a better, more active condition **11 a shot in the dark** a wild guess unsupported by arguments **12 like a shot** quickly and eagerly – see also BIG SHOT

shot·gun /ˈʃɑtgʌn/ *n* gun fired from the shoulder, usu. having two barrels, used esp. to kill birds ♦ *adv infml* in the front seat on the passenger side of a car: *riding shotgun*

shotgun wed·ding /ˌ··ˈ··/ *n* wedding that has to take place, esp. because the woman is going to have a baby

should /ʃəd; *strong* ʃʊd/ *v aux* **1** a ought to b will probably **2** (used after *that* in certain expressions of feeling): *It's odd that you should mention him.* (= The fact that you have mentioned him is odd.) **3** *fml* (used instead of **shall** in conditional sentences with I and we as the subject and a past tense verb): *I should be surprised if he came.* **4** (to express humor or surprise): *As I left the house, who should I meet but my old friend Sam.* **5 I should think** I believe **6 I should think so!/not!** of course!/of course not!

shoul·der /ˈʃoʷldər/ *n* **1** a the part of the body at each side of the neck where the arms are connected b part of a garment which covers this part of the body **2** part where something widens slopingly: *the shoulder of a bottle* **3** side of the road **4 head and shoulders above** very much better than **5 rub shoulders with** meet socially **6 shoulder to shoulder:** a side by side b together; with the same intentions ♦ *vt* accept (a heavy responsibility, duty, etc.)

shoulder blade /ˈ·· ˌ·/ *n* either of 2 flat bones in the upper back

should·n't /ˈʃʊdnt/ *v short for:* should not

shout /ʃaʊt/ *vi/t* speak or say very loudly ♦ *n* loud cry or call

shout down *phr vt* prevent a speaker being heard by shouting

shouting dis·tance /ˈ·· ˌ··/ *n* short distance

shove /ʃʌv/ *vi/t* **1** push, esp. roughly or carelessly **2** *infml* move oneself: *Shove over and let me sit down.* ♦ *n* strong push

shov·el /ˈʃʌvəl/ *n* tool with a long handle and a broad blade for lifting loose material ♦ *vi/t* –1– move or work (as if) with a shovel

show¹ /ʃoʷ/ *v* showed, shown /ʃoʷn/ 1 *vt* allow or cause to be seen: *Show me your ticket.* 2 *vi* be able to be seen: *The stain won't show.* 3 *vt* go with and guide or direct: *May I show you to your seat?* 4 *vt* explain, esp. by actions: *Show me how to do it.* 5 *vt* make clear; prove: *This piece of work shows what you can do when you try.* 6 *vt* cause to be felt in one's actions: *They showed their enemies no mercy.* 7 *vi sl* for SHOW **up** (2) **8 it goes to show** it proves the point **9 to show for** as a profit or reward from

show off *phr v* 1 *vi derog* behave so as to try to get attention and admiration 2 *vt* show proudly or to the best effect

show up *phr v* 1 *vt* make clear the (esp. unpleasant) truth about 2 *vi* arrive; be present

show² *n* 1 [C] performance, esp. in a theater, cinema or on television or radio 2 [C] collection of things for the public to look at: *a flower show* 3 [S] showing of some quality; DISPLAY: *a show of temper* 4 [S] outward appearance: *a show of interest* 5 [U] (seemingly) splendid appearance or ceremony 6 [S] effort; act of trying: *They've put up a very good/poor show this year.* 7 **get this show on the road** *infml* start to work **8 on show** being shown to the public – see also **steal the show** (STEAL) ~**y** *adj* (too) colorful, bright, etc.

show busi·ness /ˈ· ˌ··/ *n* [U] job of people who work in television, films, the theater, etc.

show·case /ˈʃoʷkeˑs/ *n* a set of shelves enclosed in glass on which objects are placed for looking at in a store, etc.: (fig.) *The factory is a showcase for American industry.*

show·down /ˈʃoʷdaʊn/ *n* settlement of a quarrel in an open direct way

show·er /ˈʃaʊər/ *n* 1 short fall of rain (or snow) 2 fall or sudden rush of many small things: *a shower of sparks* 3 (apparatus for) washing the body by standing under running water 4 party for a stated purpose: *bridal shower* ♦ *v* 1 *vi* fall in showers 3 *vt* scatter or cover in showers 3 *vi* take a SHOWER (3) ~**y** *adj* with showers of rain

show·ing /ˈʃoʷɪŋ/ *n* 1 [S] performance: *a poor showing* 2 [C] act of putting on view

show·man /ˈʃoʷmən/ *n* -men /mən/

1 person whose business is producing public entertainments, etc. 2 person who is good at gaining public attention ~**ship** *n* [U]

shown /ʃoʷn/ *past p.* of SHOW

show-off /ˈ· ·/ *n* person who SHOWS **off** (1)

show·piece /ˈʃoʷpiˑs/ *n* fine example fit to be admired

show room /ˈ· ·/ *n* room where things to be sold are shown to the public: *a Chevrolet show room*

shrank /ʃræŋk/ *past t.* of SHRINK

shrap·nel /ˈʃræpnəl/ *n* [U] metal scattered from an exploding bomb

shred /ʃred/ *n* 1 small narrow piece torn or roughly cut off 2 slightest bit: *not a shred of evidence* ♦ *vt* –dd– cut or tear into shreds

shrew /ʃruʷ/ *n* 1 very small mouse-like animal 2 bad-tempered angry woman ~**ish** *adj*

shrewd /ʃruʷd/ *adj* 1 showing good practical judgment 2 likely to be right: *a shrewd estimate* ~**ly** *adv*

shriek /ʃriʸk/ *vi/t, n* (cry out with) a wild high cry

shrift /ʃrɪft/ *n* see SHORT SHRIFT

shrill /ʃrɪl/ *adj* (of a sound) high and (painfully) sharp **shrilly** /ˈʃrɪl-liʸ, ˈʃrɪliʸ/ *adv* ~**ness** *n* [U]

shrimp /ʃrɪmp/ *n* small sea creature with 10 legs, that is often eaten

shrine /ʃraɪn/ *n* 1 holy place, where one worships 2 box containing the remains of a holy person's body

shrink¹ /ʃrɪŋk/ *v* **shrank** /ʃræŋk/, **shrunk** /ʃrʌŋk/ 1 *vi/t* (cause to) become smaller 2 *vi* move back and away ~**age** *n* [U] loss in size

shrink from *phr vt* avoid, esp. from fear

shrink² *n infml* PSYCHOANALYST or PSYCHIATRIST

shrinking vi·o·let /ˌ·· ˈ···/ *n* SHY person

shriv·el /ˈʃrɪvəl/ *vi/t* –l– (cause to) become smaller by drying and twisting into small folds

shroud /ʃraʊd/ *n* 1 cloth for covering a dead body 2 something that covers and hides ♦ *vt* cover and hide

shrub /ʃrʌb/ *n* low bush

shrub·be·ry /ˈʃrʌbəriʸ/ *n* [C;U] mass or group of shrubs

shrug /ʃrʌg/ *vi/t* –gg– raise (one's shoulders), esp. showing doubt or lack of interest ♦ *n* act of shrugging

shrug off *phr vt* treat as unimportant or easily dealt with

shrunk /ʃrʌŋk/ *past p.* of SHRINK

shrunk·en /ˈʃrʌŋkən/ *adj* having been shrunk

shuck /ʃʌk/ *vt* remove the outer covering of (CORN, OYSTERS, etc.)

shud·der /'ʃʌdər/ vi shake uncontrollably for a moment ♦ n act of shuddering

shuf·fle /'ʃʌfəl/ v 1 vi/t mix up (playing cards) so as to produce a chance order 2 vi walk by dragging one's feet slowly along ♦ n 1 [C] act of shuffling cards 2 [S] slow dragging walk

shun /ʃʌn/ vt -nn- avoid with determination

shunt /ʃʌnt/ vt move from one place to another 2 move around or away: *Smith has been shunted to a smaller office.*

shush /ʃʌʃ, ʃuʃ/ interj (used for demanding silence)

shut /ʃʌt/ v shut, pres. p. -tt- 1 vi/t close: *Shut the door.* 2 vt keep or hold by closing a door, window, etc.: *He shut himself in his room.*

   shut down phr vi/t stop operation, esp. for a long time or forever **shutdown** /'ʃʌtdaun/ n

   shut off phr vi/t 1 stop in flow or operation, esp. by turning a handle or pressing a button 2 keep separate or away

   shut out phr vt defeat completely

   shut up phr v 1 vi/t (cause to) stop talking 2 vt keep enclosed

shut-in /'· ·/ n person too ill or old to go outside

shut·out /'ʃʌtaut/ n game in which one side makes no points

shut·ter /'ʃʌtər/ n 1 part of a camera which opens to let light fall on the film 2 movable cover for a window 3 **put up the shutters** infml close a business at the end of the day or forever ♦ vt close (as if) with SHUTTERS (2)

shut·tle /'ʃʌtl/ n 1 (vehicle used on) a regular short journey: *a shuttle service between downtown and the university* | *the Boston to New York air shuttle* 2 reusable spacecraft 3 part that carries thread in weaving ♦ vt move by a SHUTTLE (1)

shut·tle·cock /'ʃʌtl̩ˌkɑk/ n light feathered object struck in BADMINTON

shuttle di·plo·ma·cy /'·· ·ˌ··/ n [U] international talks carried out by someone who travels between the countries concerned taking messages and suggesting answers to problems

shy[1] /ʃaɪ/ adj 1 nervous in the company of others 2 (of animals) unwilling to come near people 3 **once bitten, twice shy** a person who has been tricked will be more careful in the future ~**ly** adv ~**ness** n [U]

shy[2] vi (esp. of a horse) make a sudden (frightened) movement

   shy away from phr vt avoid something unpleasant

shys·ter /'ʃaɪstər/ n infml dishonest person, esp. a lawyer

Si·a·mese twin /ˌsaɪəmiˈz 'twɪn/ n either of 2 people whose bodies are joined from birth

sib·i·lant /'sɪbələnt/ n fml (making or being) a sound like s or sh

sib·ling /'sɪblɪŋ/ n fml brother or sister

sick /sɪk/ adj 1 ill 2 throwing or about to throw food up out of the stomach: *We felt sick as soon as the ship began to move.* 3 feeling annoyance, dislike, and loss of patience: *I'm sick of your complaints.* | *His hypocrisy makes me sick!* 4 cruel in an unnatural or unhealthy way: *a sick joke* 5 **worried sick** very worried ~**ness** n 1 [C;U] illness 2 [U] feeling SICK (2)

sick·bay /'sɪkbeɪ/ n room with beds for sick people

sick·en /'sɪkən/ v 1 vt cause to feel SICK (3) 2 vi become ill ~**ing** adj extremely displeasing or unpleasant

sick·le /'sɪkəl/ n small tool with a curved blade for cutting long grass

sick·ly /'sɪkli/ adj 1 weak and unhealthy 2 pale to an unhealthy degree 3 causing a sick feeling

sick pay /'· ·/ n infml money received from an employer when one is too ill to work

sick·le cell a·ne·mi·a /ˌsɪkəl sɛl əˈniˑmiˑə/ n med illness caused by problems with the blood, esp. in black people

side[1] /saɪd/ n 1 surface that is not the top, bottom, front, or back 2 edge; border: *A square has 4 sides.* 3 either of the 2 surfaces of a thin flat object 4 part in relation to a central line: *I live on the other side of town.* 5 place or area next to something: *On one side of the window was a mirror, and on the other a painting.* | *He never leaves his mother's side.* 6 part or quality to be considered: *Try to look at both sides of the question.* 7 (group holding) a position in a quarrel, war, etc.: *I'm on your side.* | *I never take sides.* (= support one side against the other) 8 sports team 9 part of a line of a family that is related to a particular person: *an uncle on my father's side* (= my father's brother) 10 **get on the right/wrong side of someone** infml win/lose someone's favor 11 **on the right/wrong side of** younger/older than (a stated age) 12 **on the side** as a (sometimes dishonest) additional activity: *She does some teaching on the side.* 13 **on the big/small/etc. side** rather; too big/small/etc. side 14 **on/to one side: a** out of consideration or use for the present **b** away from other people for a private talk **15 side by side** next to (one) another **16 -sided** having the stated number or kind of sides

side² /saɪd/ *vi* support the stated SIDE¹ (7): *She sided with me.*

side·board /'saɪdbɔːrd, -boʷrd/ *n* long table-like cupboard for dishes, glasses, etc.

side·burns /'saɪdbɜːrnz/ *n* [P] hair on the sides of a man's face

side·car /'saɪdkɑːr/ *n* small seat with wheels fastened to the side of a motorcycle

side ef·fect /'·· ·ˌ·/ *n* effect in addition to the intended one

side is·sue /'· ˌ··/ *n* question or subject apart from the main one

side·kick /'saɪdˌkɪk/ *n infml* a (less important) helper or companion

side·light /'saɪdlaɪt/ *n* piece of additional (not very important) information

side·line /'saɪdlaɪn/ *n* **1** activity in addition to one's regular job **2** line marking the limit of play on a sports field

side·long /'saɪdlɒŋ/ *adj* directed sideways: *a sidelong glance*

side·sad·dle /'saɪdˌsædl/ *adv, n* (on) a woman's SADDLE on which one puts both one's legs on the same side

side·show /'saɪdʃoʷ/ *n* separate small show at a fair or CIRCUS

side·split·ting /'saɪdˌsplɪtɪŋ/ *adj* very funny

side·step /'saɪdstep/ *vi/t* **-pp-** **1** step aside to avoid (esp. a blow) **2** avoid (an unwelcome question, problem, etc.)

side·swipe /'saɪdswaɪp/ *vt* hit while passing the side of ♦ *n*

side·track /'saɪdtræk/ *vt* cause to leave one subject or activity and follow another (less important) one

side·walk /'saɪdwɔːk/ *n* PAVEd path at the side of a road

side·ways /'saɪdweʲz/ *adv* **1** with one side (not the back or front) forward or up **2** towards one side

side·wind·er /'saɪdˌwaɪndər/ *n* RATTLESNAKE

sid·ing /'saɪdɪŋ/ *n* **1** piece of railroad track where cars are parked **2** protective covering usu. metal on the outside of houses

si·dle /'saɪdl/ *v* sidle up *phr vi* walk secretively or nervously up (to someone)

siege /siʲdʒ/ *n* operation by an army surrounding a city, etc., to force the people inside to accept defeat

si·es·ta /siʲˈɛstə/ *n* short sleep in the afternoon

sieve /sɪv/ *n* **1** tool with a net or holes for letting liquid or small objects through **2** head/memory

like a sieve a mind that forgets quickly ♦ *vt* put through or separate with a sieve

sift /sɪft/ *v* **1** *vt* put (something non-liquid) through a sieve **2** *vi/t* examine (things in a mass or group) closely: *sifting the evidence*

sigh /saɪ/ *vi* let out a deep breath slowly and with a sound, usu. expressing sadness, satisfaction, or tiredness: *The wind sighed in the trees.* (= made a sound like sighing) ♦ *n* act or sound of sighing

sight /saɪt/ *n* **1** [U] power of seeing **2** [S;U] the seeing of something: *I caught sight of her* (= noticed her) *in the crowd.* **3** [C] something seen **4** [U] range of what can be seen: *The train came into sight.* **5** [C] something worth seeing: *the sights of San Francisco* **6** [C] part of an instrument or weapon which guides the eye in aiming **7** [S] something which looks very bad or laughable **8** [S] *infml* a lot: *She earns a sight more than I do.* **9 a sight for sore eyes** a person or thing that one is glad to see **10 at first sight** at the first time of seeing or considering **11 at/on sight** as soon as seen or shown **12 in sight: a** in view **b** near **13 know someone by sight** recognize someone without knowing them personally or without knowing their name **14 set one's sights on** direct one's efforts (towards) – see also SECOND SIGHT ♦ *vt* see for the first time – **ed** *adj* able to see – **ing** *n*: case of someone or something being sighted: *several sightings of rare birds* ~**less** *adj* blind

sight·see·ing /'saɪtˌsiʲɪŋ/ *n* [U] visiting places of interest –**seer** *n*

sign /saɪn/ *n* **1** mark which represents a known meaning: + *is the plus sign.* **2** movement of the body intended to express a meaning **3** notice giving information, a warning, etc. **4** something that shows the presence or coming of something else: *There are signs that the economy may be improving.* **5** also **star sign** — any of the 12 divisions of the year represented by groups of stars (Leo, Taurus, etc.) **6 a sign of the times** something that is typical of the way things are just now ♦ *vi/t* **1** write (one's name) on (a written paper), esp. officially or to show that one is the writer **2** SIGNAL (1) **3** SIGN up ~**er** *n*

sign away *phr vt* give up (ownership, etc.) formally by signing a paper

sign on *phr vi/t* (cause to) join a working force by signing a paper

sign up *phr vi/t* (cause to) sign an agreement to take part in something or take a job

sig·nal /ˈsɪgnəl/ n 1 sound or action which warns, commands, or gives a message: *a danger signal* 2 action which causes another to happen 3 apparatus by a railroad track to direct train drivers 4 message sent by radio or television waves ♦ vi -l- give a signal

sig·nal·man /ˈsɪgnəlmən/ n -men /-mən/ someone who works giving signals as on a railroad or in the army

sig·na·to·ry /ˈsɪgnəˌtɔriʸ, -ˌtoʷriʸ/ n fml signer of an agreement, esp. among nations

sig·na·ture /ˈsɪgnətʃər/ n person's name written by himself or herself – see also TIME SIGNATURE

sig·nif·i·cant /sɪgˈnɪfəkənt/ adj 1 of noticeable importance or effect 2 having a special meaning, indirectly expressed ~ly adv -cance n [S;U]

sig·ni·fy /ˈsɪgnəˌfaɪ/ v fml 1 vt mean 2 vi/t make known (esp. an opinion) by an action 3 vi matter

sign lan·guage /ˈ· ˌ··/ n language of hand movements, used by DEAF people

sign·post /ˈsaɪnpoʷst/ n sign showing directions and distances

si·lage /ˈsaɪlɪdʒ/ n [U] plants preserved as winter cattle food

si·lence /ˈsaɪləns/ n 1 [C;U] (period of) absence of sound 2 [U] not speaking or making a noise 3 [U] failure to mention a particular thing ♦ vt cause or force to be silent

si·lent /ˈsaɪlənt/ adj 1 free from noise 2 not speaking 3 failing or refusing to express an opinion, etc. 4 (of a letter) not pronounced ~ly adv

silent part·ner /ˌ·· ˈ··/ n business partner who does no active work in the business

sil·hou·ette /ˌsɪluʷˈɛt/ n dark shape seen against a light background ♦ vt cause to appear as a silhouette

sil·i·con /ˈsɪlɪˌkɑn, -kən/ n [U] simple non-metal substance found commonly in natural compounds

silicon chip /ˌ··· ˈ·/ n a CHIP¹ (4) in a computer or other ELECTRONIC machinery

silk /sɪlk/ n [U] (smooth cloth from) fine thread produced by silkworms ~en adj 1 silky 2 made of silk ~y adj soft, smooth, and/or shiny

silk·worm /ˈsɪlkˌwɜrm/ n CATERPILLAR which produces silk

sill /sɪl/ n shelflike part at the bottom of a window

sil·ly /ˈsɪliʸ/ adj not serious or sensible; foolish –liness n [U]

si·lo /ˈsaɪloʷ/ n 1 round tower-like enclosure for storing SILAGE 2 underground base for firing MISSILES

silt /sɪlt/ n [U] loose mud brought by a river or current ♦ v silt up phr vi/t fill or become filled with silt

sil·ver /ˈsɪlvər/ n 1 [U] soft whitish precious metal 2 [U] spoons, forks, dishes, etc., made of silver 3 [U] coins made of, or colored, silver 4 [C] silver MEDAL ♦ adj 1 made of silver 2 of the color of silver ~y adj 1 like silver in shine and color 2 having a pleasant metallic sound

silver an·ni·ver·sa·ry /ˌ··· ···ˈ···/ n the date that is exactly 25 years after the date of an event

sil·ver·smith /ˈsɪlvərˌsmɪθ/ n maker of jewelery, etc., in silver

sil·ver·ware /ˈsɪlvərˌweər/ n forks, knives, and spoons even if they are not silver

sim·i·lar /ˈsɪmələr/ adj almost but not exactly the same; alike ~ly adv ~ity /ˌsɪməˈlærəṭiʸ/ n 1 [U] quality of being similar 2 [C] way in which things are similar

sim·i·le /ˈsɪməliʸ/ n expression which describes one thing by comparing it with another (as in *as white as snow*)

sim·mer /ˈsɪmər/ vi/t cook gently in (nearly) boiling liquid: (fig.) *simmering with anger/excitement*

    simmer down phr vi become calmer

sim·per /ˈsɪmpər/ vi smile in a silly unnatural way

sim·ple /ˈsɪmpəl/ adj 1 without decoration; plain 2 easy 3 consisting of only one thing or part 4 (of something non-physical) pure: *the simple truth* 5 easily tricked; foolish –ply adv 1 in a simple way 2 just; only: *I simply don't know.* 3 really; completely: *a simply gorgeous day*

simple-mind·ed /ˌ·· ˈ··◂/ adj 1 foolish 2 simple and unthinking in mind

sim·ple·ton /ˈsɪmpəltən/ n mentally weak trusting person

sim·plic·i·ty /sɪmˈplɪsəṭiʸ/ n [U] 1 quality of being simple 2 **simplicity itself** very easy

sim·pli·fy /ˈsɪmpləˌfaɪ/ vt make simpler –fication /ˌsɪmpləfəˈkeʸʃən/ n [C;U]

sim·plis·tic /sɪmˈplɪstɪk/ adj derog treating difficult matters as if they were simple –ally /-kliʸ/ adv

sim·u·late /ˈsɪmyəˌleʸt/ vt give the appearance or effect of –lation /ˌsɪmyəˈleʸʃən/ n [U]

si·mul·cast /ˈsaɪməlˌkæst/ vt broadcast at the same time over television and radio ♦ n

sim·ul·ta·ne·ous /ˌsaɪməlˈteʸniʸəs/ adj happening or done at the same moment ~ly adv

sin /sɪn/ n [C;U] **1** offense against God or a religious law **2** *infml* something that should not be done: *He thinks it's a sin to stay in bed after 8 o'clock.* **3 live in sin** *old-fashioned or humor* (of 2 unmarried people) live together as if married ♦ *vi* **-nn-** do wrong ~**ful** *adj* wicked ~**ner** n

since /sɪns/ *adv* **1** at a time between then and now: *She left in 1979, and I haven't seen her since.* **2** from then until now: *He came here 2 years ago and has lived here ever since.* **3** ago: *I've long since forgotten his name.* ♦ *prep* from (a point in past time) until now: *I haven't seen her since 1979.* ♦ *conj* **1 a** after the past time when: *I haven't seen her since she left.* **b** continuously from the time when: *We've been friends since we met at school.* **2** because: *Since you can't answer, I'll ask someone else.*

sin·cere /sɪnˈsɪər/ *adj* free from deceit or falseness; honest and true ~**ly** *adv* –**cerity** /sɪnˈsɛrətɪ̯/ n [U]

si·ne·cure /ˈsaɪnɪˌkyʊər, ˈsɪ-/ n paid job with few or no duties

sin·ew /ˈsɪnyuˌ/ n [C;U] strong cord connecting a muscle to a bone ~**y** *adj*

sing /sɪŋ/ v sang /sæŋ/, sung /sʌŋ/ **1** *vi/t* produce (music, songs, etc.) with the voice **2** *vi* make or be filled with a ringing sound: *It made my ears sing.* ♦ n gathering of many people to sing ~**er** n

singe /sɪndʒ/ *vt* burn slightly

sin·gle¹ /ˈsɪŋgəl/ *adj* **1** being (the) only one: *a single sheet of paper* **2** considered by itself; separate: *He understands every single word I say.* **3** unmarried **4** for the use of only one person: *a single bed* ♦ n **1** record with only one short song on each side **2** \$1 BILL– see also SINGLES –**gly** *adv* one by one; not in a group

single² v **single out** *phr vt* choose from a group for special attention

single file /ˌ·· ˈ·/ *adv, n* (in) a line of people, vehicles, etc., one behind another

single-hand·ed /ˌ·· ˈ··◂/ *adj* without help from others ~**ly** *adv*

single-mind·ed /ˌ·· ˈ··◂/ *adj* having one clear aim or purpose ~**ly** *adv*

sin·gles /ˈsɪŋgəlz/ n **singles** (tennis) match between 2 players

sing·song /ˈsɪŋsɔŋ/ n [S] repeated rising and falling of the voice in speaking

sin·gu·lar /ˈsɪŋgyələr/ *adj* **1** (of a word) representing only one thing **2** *fml* unusually great ♦ n SINGULAR (1) word or form ~**ly** *adv fml* particularly

sin·is·ter /ˈsɪnɪstər/ *adj* threatening or leading to evil

sink¹ /sɪŋk/ v sank /sæŋk/, sunk /sʌŋk/ **1** *vi* (cause to) go down below a surface, out of sight, or to the bottom (of water) **2** *vi* get smaller **3** *vi* fall from lack of strength: *He sank into a chair.* **4** *vi* lose confidence or hope: *My heart sank.* **5** *vt* make by digging: *sink a well* **6** *vt* put (money, labor, etc.) into

sink in *phr vi* become fully and properly understood

sink² n kitchen or bathroom BASIN for washing

sinking feel·ing /ˈ·· ˌ··/ n [S] *infml* uncomfortable feeling in stomach raised by fear or helplessness, esp. because something bad is about to happen

sin·u·ous /ˈsɪnyuʷəs/ *adj* full of curves; winding ~**ly** *adv*

si·nus /ˈsaɪnəs/ n any of the spaces filled with air in the bones behind the nose

sip /sɪp/ *vi/t* **-pp-** drink with very small mouthfuls ♦ n very small amount drunk

si·phon /ˈsaɪfən/ n **1** tube for removing liquid by natural pressure **2** bottle for holding and forcing out a drink filled with gas ♦ *vt* remove with a siphon: (fig.) *The new road will siphon off traffic from the business district.*

sir /sər; *strong* sɜr/ n **1** (used respectfully when speaking to an older man or one of higher rank) **2** (used at the beginning of a formal letter): **Dear Sir,** …

sire /saɪər/ n **1** horse's male parent **2** *lit* (used when speaking to a king) ♦ *vt* (esp. of a horse) be the father of

si·ren /ˈsaɪərən/ n **1** apparatus for making a loud long warning sound: *a police/air-raid siren* **2** dangerous beautiful woman

sir·loin /ˈsɜrlɔɪn/ n [U] BEEF cut from the best part of the lower back

sis·sy /ˈsɪsiˌ/ n girlish or cowardly boy ♦ *adj* like a sissy

sis·ter /ˈsɪstər/ n **1** female relative with the same parents **2** female member of a religious group **3** female member of the same group (used esp. by supporters of the WOMEN'S MOVEMENT) belonging to the same group: *our sister organization* ~**hood** n **1** [U] being (like) sisters **2** [C] society of women leading a religious life ~**ly** *adj* like a sister

sister-in-law /ˈ··· ·ˌ·/ n sisters-in-law sister of one's husband or wife; one's brother's wife

sit /sɪt/ v sat /sæt/, *present p.* **-tt- 1** *vi* rest on a seat or on the ground with the upper body upright **2** *vi/t* (cause to) take a seat **3** *vi* (of an official body) have one or more meetings **4** *vi* (take up a position to) be painted or photographed **5 be sitting pretty** be in a very good position **6 sit tight** keep in the same position; not move

sit around *phr vt* do nothing, esp. while waiting or while others act

sit back *phr vi* rest and take no active part

sit down *phr vi* SIT (2)

sit in *phr vi* take another's regular place, e.g. in a meeting

sit in on *phr vi* attend without taking an active part

sit on *phr vt* **1** be a member of (a committee, etc.) **2** delay taking action on

sit out *phr vt* not take part

sit up *phr v* **1** *vi/t* (cause or help to) rise to a sitting position from a lying one **2** *vi* sit properly upright in a chair **3** *vi* stay up late; not go to bed **4** *vi* show sudden interest, surprise, or fear: *Her speech really made them sit up (and take notice).*

sit·com /ˈsɪtkɑm/ *n* [C;U] SITUATION COMEDY

site /saɪt/ *n* place where a particular thing happened or is done ♦ *vt* put or esp. build in a particular position

sit-in /ˈ· ·/ *n* method of expressing dissatisfaction and anger in which a group of people enter a public place, stop its usual services, and refuse to leave

sit·ter /ˈsɪtər/ *n* BABYSITTER

sit·ting /ˈsɪtɪŋ/ *n* **1** serving of a meal for a number of people at one time **2** act of having one's picture made **3** meeting of an official body

sitting duck /ˈ·· ·/ *n* one easy to attack or cheat

sitting room /ˈ·· ·/ *n fml* LIVING ROOM

sit·u·at·ed /ˈsɪtʃuˌweɪtɪd/ *adj* **1** in the stated place or position **2** in the stated situation: *How are you situated for money?* (= have you got enough?)

sit·u·a·tion /ˌsɪtʃuˈweɪʃən/ *n* **1** set of conditions, facts, and/or events **2** *fml* position with regard to surroundings **3** *fml* job

situation com·e·dy /ˌ···· ˈ···/ *n* [C;U] humorous television show typically having a number of standard characters who appear in different situations every week

six /sɪks/ *determiner, n, pron* 6 **–th** *determiner, adv, n, pron* 6th

six-pack /ˈ· ·/ *n* six drinks sold together: *six-pack of beer*

six·teen /ˌsɪkˈstiʸn◄/ *determiner, n, pron* 16 **–th** *determiner, adv, n, pron* 16th

sixth sense /ˌ· ˈ·/ *n* ability to know

things without using any of the 5 ordinary senses

six·ty /ˈsɪksti◄/ *determiner, n, pron* 60 **–tieth** *determiner, adv, n, pron* 60th

size¹ /saɪz/ *n* **1** [C;U] (degree of) bigness or smallness **2** bigness: *A town of some size.* **3** [C] standard measurement: *These shoes are size 9.* **4 -sized** of the stated size **5 cut someone down to size** show someone to be really less good, important, etc. **6 that's about the size of it** that's a fair statement of the matter

size² *v* **size up** *phr vt* form an opinion or judgment about

size·a·ble /ˈsaɪzəbəl/ *adj* quite large

siz·zle /ˈsɪzəl/ *vi* make a sound like food cooking in hot fat

skate¹ /skeɪt/ *n* **1** blade fixed to a shoe for moving along on ice **2** ROLLER SKATE **3 get/put one's skates on** *infml* move, act, or work quickly; hurry

skate² *vi* **1** move on skates **2** **(skate) on thin ice** *infml* (to be) doing something risky **skater** *n*

skate over/around *phr vt* avoid treating seriously

skate·board /ˈskeɪtbɔrd, -boʸrd/ *n* short board with 2 small wheels at each end for standing on and riding

skel·e·ton /ˈskelətn/ *n* **1** structure consisting of all the bones in the body **2** structure on which more is built or added **3 skeleton in the closet** a secret of which a person or family is ashamed ♦ *adj* enough simply to keep an operation going: *a skeleton staff* **–tal** *adj*

skeleton key /ˈ··· ·/ *n* key that fits an old-fashioned lock

skep·tic /ˈskeptɪk/ *n* skeptical person **~al** *adj* unwilling to believe **~ally** /-kliʸ/ *adv* **–ticism** /-tɪˌsɪzəm/ *n* [U] doubt

sketch /sketʃ/ *n* **1** simple quickly made drawing **2** short description **3** short humorous scene ♦ *vi/t* draw a sketch (of) **~y** *adj* not thorough or complete

skew /skyuʷ/ *vt* cause to be not straight or exact: DISTORT

skew·er /ˈskyuʷər/ *n* long pin put through meat for cooking

ski /skiʸ/ *n* skis long piece of wood, plastic, etc., fixed to boots for traveling on snow ♦ *vi* **skied,** present *p.* **skiing** travel on skis **–er** *n*

skid /skɪd/ *vi* **–dd–** (of a vehicle or wheel) slip sideways out of control ♦ *n* act of skidding

skill·ful /ˈskɪlfəl/ *adj* having or showing skill **~ly** *adv*

skill /skɪl/ *n* [C;U] special ability to do something well **~ed** *adj* having or needing skill: *a skilled job*

skim /skɪm/ v -mm- **1** vt remove from the surface of a liquid **2** vi/t read quickly to get the main ideas **3** vi/t (cause to) move quickly (nearly) touching (a surface)

skimp /skɪmp/ vi/t spend, provide, or use less (of) than is needed ~**y** adj not enough

skin /skɪn/ n **1** [U] natural outer covering of the body **2** [C] skin of an animal for use as leather, etc. **3** [C] natural outer covering of some fruits and vegetables: *banana skins* **4** [C;U] the solid surface that forms over some liquids **5 by the skin of one's teeth** only just **6 get under someone's skin** annoy or excite someone deeply **7 no skin off someone's nose** *infml* not something that upsets or causes disadvantage to someone **8 save one's skin** save oneself, esp. in a cowardly way, from death, etc. **9 skin and bone(s)** very thin ♦ vt -nn- remove the skin from ~**ny** adj very thin

skin-deep /ˌ· ˈ·◄/ adj on the surface only

skin-dive /ˈ· ·/ vi swim under water without heavy breathing apparatus **skin diver** n

skin·flint /ˈskɪnˌflɪnt/ n someone who dislikes giving or spending money

skin-tight /ˌ· ˈ·◄/ adj (of clothes) fitting tightly against the body

skint /skɪnt/ adj BrE infml having no money

skinny-dip /ˈskɪniʸ ˌdɪp/ vi swim without clothes

skip /skɪp/ v -pp- **1** vi move in a light dancing way **2** vi/t leave out (something in order); not deal with (the next thing) **3** vi move in no fixed order **4** vi jump over a rope passed repeatedly beneath one's feet **5** vi/t leave hastily and secretly: *The thieves have skipped the country.* **6** vt fail to attend or take part in (an activity) ♦ n light quick stepping and jumping movement

skip·per /ˈskɪpər/ n captain of a ship or sports team ♦ vt act as captain; lead

skir·mish /ˈskɜrmɪʃ/ n short military fight, not as big as a battle

skirt /skɜrt/ n woman's outer garment that hangs from the waist

skirt² vi/t **1** be or go around the outside (of) **2** avoid (a difficult subject)

skit /skɪt/ n short acted scene making fun of something

skit·tish /ˈskɪtɪʃ/ adj (esp. of a cat or horse) easily excited and frightened

skiv·vies /ˈskɪviʸz/ n infml men's UNDERWEAR

skulk /skʌlk/ vi hide or move about slowly and secretly, through fear or shame or for some evil purpose

skull /skʌl/ n head bone, enclosing the brain

skunk /skʌŋk/ n **1** small North American animal which gives out an unpleasantly smelly liquid when attacked **2** infml person who is bad, unfair, etc.

sky /skaɪ/ n **1** space above the Earth, where clouds and the sun, moon, and stars appear **2 the sky's the limit** there is no upper limit, esp. to the amount of money that can be spent

sky-div·ing /ˈskaɪˌdaɪvɪŋ/ n [U] sport of falling by PARACHUTE

sky-high /ˌ· ˈ·◄/ adj, adv at or to a very high level

sky·jack /ˈskaɪdʒæk/ vt HIJACK (an aircraft)

sky·light /ˈskaɪlaɪt/ n window in a roof

sky·line /ˈskaɪlaɪn/ n shape or view of esp. city buildings against the sky

sky·rock·et /ˈskaɪˌrɑkɪt/ vi increase suddenly and steeply

sky·scrap·er /ˈskaɪˌskreɪʸpər/ n very tall city building

sky·way /ˈskaɪweɪʸ/ n road that carries a lot of traffic above another road

slab /slæb/ n thick flat piece with usu. 4 sides: *a stone slab*

slack /slæk/ adj **1** (of a rope, etc.) not pulled tight **2** not careful or quick **3** not firm; weak: *slack discipline* **4** not busy ♦ n **take up the slack** tighten a rope, etc. ♦ vi **1** be lazy **2** reduce in speed, effort, etc. **slacks** n [P] informal pants ~**en** vi/t make or become slack ~**ness** n [U]

slag /slæg/ n [U] waste material left when metal is separated from its rock

slain /sleɪʸn/ past p. of SLAY

slake /sleɪʸk/ vt lit satisfy (thirst) with a drink

sla·lom /ˈslɑləm/ n SKI race down a very winding course

slam /slæm/ v -mm- **1** vi/t shut loudly and forcefully **2** vt push or put in a hurried and forceful way: *She slammed on the brakes.* **3** vt attack with words ♦ n noise of a door being slammed – see also GRAND SLAM

slan·der /ˈslændər/ n [C;U] (act of) saying something false and damaging about someone ♦ vt harm by making a false statement ~**ous** adj

slang /slæŋ/ n [U] very informal language that includes new and sometimes not polite words and meanings and is often used among particular groups of people, and not usu. in serious speech or writing

slant /slænt/ v 1 vi/t (cause to) be at an angle 2 vt usu. derog express in a way favorable to a particular opinion ♦ n 1 [S] slanting direction or position 2 [C] particular way of looking at or expressing facts or a situation

slap /slæp/ n 1 hit with the flat hand 2 **slap in the face** an action (seeming to be) aimed directly against someone else ♦ vt –pp– 1 give a slap to 2 place quickly, roughly, or carelessly ♦ adv also **slap-bang** /¦·ˌ·/ — directly; right: slap in the middle of lunch

slap-dash /ˈslæpˌdæʃ/ adj careless

slap·stick /ˈslæpˌstɪk/ n [U] humorous acting with fast violent action and simple jokes

slash /slæʃ/ v 1 vi/t cut with long sweeping violent strokes: (fig.) a slashing attack on the government 2 vt reduce very greatly ♦ n 1 long sweeping cut or blow 2 straight cut making an opening in a garment

slat /slæt/ n thin narrow flat piece of wood, plastic, etc. ~ted adj

slate[1] /sleɪt/ n 1 [U] dark grey easily split rock 2 [C] piece of this used in rows for covering roofs 3 [C] small board of this, used for writing on with chalk 4 [C] imaginary record of (mistakes of) the past: a clean slate ♦ vt place on a SCHEDULE

slaugh·ter /ˈslɔtər/ n 1 kill (many people) cruelly or wrongly 2 kill (an animal) for food 3 infml defeat severely in a game ♦ n [U] slaughtering

slaugh·ter·house /ˈslɔtərˌhaʊs/ n building where animals are killed for food

slave /sleɪv/ n 1 person who is owned by (and works for) another 2 person completely in the control of: a slave to drink ♦ vi work hard with little rest

slave driv·er /ˈ· ˌ··/ n person who makes one work very hard

slav·er /ˈslævər, ˈslɑ-, ˈsleɪ-/ vi 1 let SALIVA run out of the mouth 2 be unpleasantly eager or excited

slav·ery /ˈsleɪvəriʲ/ n [U] 1 system of having slaves 2 condition of being a slave

slav·ish /ˈsleɪvɪʃ/ adj 1 showing complete obedience to and willingness to work for others 2 copied too exactly, without being at all original ~ly adv

slay /sleɪ/ vt esp. lit slew /sluʷ/, slain /sleɪn/ kill

slea·zy /ˈsliʲziʲ/ adj dirty, looking poor, and suggesting immorality

sled /slɛd/ vi, n –dd– (travel on) a vehicle for sliding along snow on 2 metal blades

sledge·ham·mer /ˈslɛdʒˌhæmər/ n heavy hammer with a long handle

sleek /sliʲk/ adj 1 (of hair or fur) smooth and shining 2 stylish and without unnecessary decoration ~ly adv

sleep /sliʲp/ n 1 [U] natural unconscious resting state 2 [S] act or period of sleeping 3 **get to sleep** succeed in sleeping 4 **go to sleep:** a begin to sleep b (of an arm, leg, etc.) become unable to feel, or feel PINS AND NEEDLES 5 **put to sleep** kill (a suffering animal) mercifully ♦ vi slept /slɛpt/ 1 rest in sleep 2 provide beds or places for sleep (for a number of people): The house sleeps 6. ~er n 1 sleeping person 2 train with beds 3 book, play, record, etc., that has a delayed or unexpected success ~y adj 1 tired 2 inactive or moving slowly ~ily adv

sleep around phr vi derog have sex with a lot of different people

sleep in phr vi sleep late in the morning

sleep off phr vt get rid of (a feeling or effect) by sleeping: Sleep it off. (= sleep until one is no longer drunk)

sleep on phr vt delay deciding on (a matter) until next day

sleep through phr vt fail to be woken by

sleep together phr vi (of 2 people) have sex

sleep with phr vt have sex with

sleeping bag /ˈ·· ˌ·/ n large cloth bag for sleeping in

sleeping car /ˈ·· ·/ n railroad carriage with beds for passengers

sleeping pill /ˈ·· ˌ·/ n PILL which helps a person to sleep

sleeping sick·ness /ˈ·· ˌ··/ n [U] serious African disease which causes great tiredness

sleep·less /ˈsliʲplɪs/ adj 1 not providing sleep: a sleepless night 2 unable to sleep ~ly adv ~ness n [U]

sleep·walk·er /ˈsliʲpˌwɔkər/ n person who walks while asleep ~ing n [U]

sleet /sliʲt/ n [U] partly frozen rain ♦ vi (of sleet) fall

sleeve /sliʲv/ n 1 part of a garment for covering (part of) an arm 2 stiff envelope for keeping a record in 3 **have/keep something up one's sleeve** kept something secret for use at the right time in the future

sleigh /sleɪ/ n large SLED pulled by a horse or horses

sleight of hand /ˌslaɪt əv ˈhænd/ n [U] 1 skill and quickness of the hands in doing tricks 2 clever deception

slen·der /ˈslɛndər/ adj 1 gracefully or pleasingly thin 2 small and hardly enough: slender resources

slept /slept/ *v past t. and p.* of SLEEP

sleuth /sluːθ/ *n* DETECTIVE

slew¹ /sluː/ *v past t.* of SLAY

slew² /sluː/ *vi/t* turn or swing violently

slice /slaɪs/ *n* **1** thin flat piece cut off: *a slice of bread* | (fig.) *a slice of the profits* **2** kitchen tool with a broad blade for serving food **3 a slice of life** a representation of life as it really is ♦ *v* **1** *vt* cut into slices **2** *vi/t* hit (a ball) so that it moves away from a straight course

slick¹ /slɪk/ *adj* **1** smooth and slippery **2** skilful and effective, so as to seem easy **3** clever and able to persuade, but perhaps not honest ~**ly** *adv*

slick² *n* area of oil floating on esp. the sea

slick·er /ˈslɪkər/ *n* **1** *infml* an expensively dressed, confident, but probably untrustworthy person: *a city slicker* **2** coat made to keep out the rain

slide /slaɪd/ *v* **slid** /slɪd/ **1** *vi/t* go or send smoothly across a surface **2** *vi* move quietly and unnoticed **3 let something slide** let a situation or condition continue, esp. getting worse, without taking action, usu. because of laziness *n* **1** slipping movement **2** fall: *a slide in living standards* **3** apparatus for sliding down **4** piece of film through which light is passed to show a picture on a surface **5** small piece of thin glass to put an object on for seeing under a microscope

slide rule /ˈ· ·/ *n* ruler with a middle part that slides along, for calculating numbers

sliding scale /ˌ·· ˈ·/ *n* system of pay, taxes, etc., calculated by rates which may vary according to changing conditions

slight¹ /slaɪt/ *adj* **1** small in degree: *a slight improvement* **2** thin and delicate **3 in the slightest** at all ~**ly** *adv* **1** a little: *slightly better* **2** in a SLIGHT (2) way: *He's very slightly built.*

slight² *vt* treat disrespectfully or rudely ♦ *n* INSULT

slim /slɪm/ *adj* –**mm**– **1** attractively thin **2** (of probability, hope, etc.) very small ♦ *vi* –**mm**– try to make oneself thinner ~**ly** *adv* ~**mer** *n*

slime /slaɪm/ *n* unpleasant thick sticky liquid **slimy** *adj* **1** unpleasantly slippery **2** *derog* trying to please in order to gain advantage for oneself

sling /slɪŋ/ *vt* **slung** /slʌŋ/ **1** throw roughly or with effort **2** hang **3 sling mud at** say unfair and damaging things about (esp. a political opponent) ♦ *n* piece of cloth hanging from the neck to support a damaged arm

sling·shot /ˈslɪŋʃɑt/ *n* stick shaped like a Y, with a rubber band, for shooting small stones

slink /slɪŋk/ *vi* **slunk** /slʌŋk/ move quietly and secretly, as if in fear or shame

slip¹ /slɪp/ *v* –**pp**– **1** *vi* slide out of place unexpectedly or by accident **2** *vi/t* move or put smoothly and unnoticed **3** *vi/t* put on or take off (a garment) quickly **4** *vi* get worse or lower: *slipping standards* **5** *vi* make a mistake **6** *vt* fail to be remembered by: *It slipped my mind.* (= I forgot) **7** give secretly: *I slipped the waiter some money.* **8 let slip: a** fail to take (a chance) **b** make known accidentally ♦ *n* **1** small mistake **2** woman's undergarment like a skirt or loose dress **3** young, attractively SLIM person: *a slip of a girl* **4 give someone the slip** escape from someone

slip² *n* small or narrow piece of paper

slip·page /ˈslɪpɪdʒ/ *n* [C;U] (amount of) slipping

slipped disc /ˌ· ˈ·/ *n* painful displacement of one of the connecting parts between the bones of the SPINE

slip·per /ˈslɪpər/ *n* light soft shoe worn indoors

slip·per·y /ˈslɪpəriˈ/ *adj* **1** very smooth or wet, so one cannot easily hold or move on it **2** not to be trusted

slip·shod /ˈslɪpʃɑd/ *adj* carelessly done

slip·stream /ˈslɪpstriˈm/ *n* **1** area of low air pressure behind a vehicle which is moving quickly **2** stream of air driven backwards by an aircraft engine

slip-up /ˈ· ·/ *n* usu. slight mistake

slip·way /ˈslɪpweˈ/ *n* sloping track for moving ships into or out of water

slit /slɪt/ *n* long narrow cut or opening ♦ *vt* **slit**; *present p.* –**tt**– make a slit in

slith·er /ˈslɪðər/ *vi* **1** move smoothly and twistingly **2** slide in an unsteady manner

sliv·er /ˈslɪvər/ *n* small thin piece cut or broken off

slob /slɑb/ *n* rude, dirty, lazy, or carelessly dressed person

slob·ber /ˈslɑbər/ *vi* let SALIVA come out of the mouth; DROOL

slo·gan /ˈsloˈgən/ *n* short phrase expressing a political or advertising message

sloop /sluːp/ *n* small sailing ship

slop¹ /slɑp/ *vi/t* –**pp**– go or cause (a liquid) to go over the side of a container: *You're slopping paint everywhere!*

slop around *phr vi infml* play in or move about in anything wet or dirty slop | 390

slop² n [U] 1 [usu. P] food waste, esp. for feeding animals 2 derog tasteless liquid food

slope /sloʊp/ vi lie neither completely upright nor completely flat ♦ n 1 piece of sloping ground 2 degree of sloping

slop·py /ˈslɑpi/ adj 1 (of clothes) loose, informal and careless 2 not careful or thorough enough 3 silly in showing feelings −pily adv −piness n [U]

slosh /slɑʃ/ v, vi/t move or cause (liquid) to move about roughly and noisily, making waves ~ed adj infml drunk

slot /slɑt/ n 1 long straight narrow hole 2 place or position in a list, system, organization, etc. ♦ vi/t -tt- 1 (be) put into a SLOT (1) 2 fit into a SLOT (2)

sloth /sloʊθ, sloʊᵏθ/ n 1 [U] esp. lit laziness 2 [C] animal of S America that moves very slowly ~ful adj lazy

slot ma·chine /ˈ· ·ˌ·/ n machine with a long handle, into which people put money to try to win more money

slouch /slaʊtʃ/ vi walk, stand, or sit with round shoulders, looking tired ♦ n vague, useless person: She's no slouch when it comes to tennis. (= she's very good)

slough¹ /slʌf/ v slough off phr vt 1 (esp. of a snake) throw off (dead outer skin) 2 esp. lit get rid of as something worn out or unwanted

slough² /sluᵂ, slaʊ/ n lit bad condition that is hard to get free from

slov·en·ly /ˈslʌvənli/ adj 1 untidy 2 very carelessly done −liness n [U]

slow /sloʊ/ adj 1 having less than a usual speed; not fast 2 taking a long time: a slow job 3 (of a clock) showing a time that is earlier than the right time 4 not quick in understanding 5 not active: Business is slow. ♦ vi/t make or become slower ♦ adv slowly: slow-moving traffic ~ly adv ~ness n [U]

slow·down /ˈsloʊdaʊn/ n 1 lessening of speed or activity 2 decision to work slowly as a kind of STRIKE² (1)

slow·poke /ˈsloʊkoʊᵏtʃ/ n infml person who acts slowly

sludge /slʌdʒ/ n [U] thick soft mud

slug¹ /slʌg/ n small soft limbless creature, like a SNAIL with no shell

slug² vt -gg- hit hard

slug³ n 1 bullet 2 infml amount of strong alcoholic drink taken at one swallow

slug·gish /ˈslʌgɪʃ/ adj not very active or quick ~ly adv −ness n [U]

sluice /sluᵂs/ n passage for controlling the flow of water ♦ vt wash with a large flow of water

slum /slʌm/ n city area of bad living conditions and old unrepaired buildings ♦ vi amuse oneself by visiting a place on a much lower social level: go slumming ~my adj

slum·ber /ˈslʌmbər/ vi, n lit sleep

slump /slʌmp/ vi 1 drop down suddenly and heavily 2 decrease suddenly ♦ n 1 sudden decrease, esp. in business 2 time of seriously bad business conditions and high unemployment

slung /slʌŋ/ v past t. and p. of SLING

slunk /slʌŋk/ v past t. and p. of SLINK

slur¹ /slɜr/ vt -rr- pronounce unclearly

slur² vt -rr- make unfair damaging remarks about ♦ n: a slur on my reputation

slurp /slɜrp/ vt drink noisily **slurp** n

slush /slʌʃ/ n [U] 1 partly melted snow 2 books, films, etc., full of silly love stories ~y adj

slush fund /ˈ· ·/ n money secretly kept for dishonest payments

slut /slʌt/ n derog 1 sexually immoral woman 2 untidy, lazy woman ~tish adj

sly /slaɪ/ adj 1 secretly deceitful or tricky 2 playfully knowing: a sly joke 3 on the sly secretly ~ly adv ~ness n [U]

smack¹ /smæk/ vt 1 hit with the flat hand 2 open and close (one's lips) noisily in eagerness to eat ♦ n 1 blow with the open hand 2 sl [U] HEROIN ♦ adv exactly; right: smack in the middle

smack² v smack of phr vt have a taste or suggestion of

smack·er /ˈsmækər/ n sl dollar

small /smɔl/ adj 1 of less than usual size, amount, importance, etc. 2 young: small children 3 doing only a limited amount of business 4 slight: small hope of success 5 feel small feel ashamed or humble ♦ n [the+S] narrow middle part (of the back) ~ness n [U]

small arms /ˌ· ·/ n [P] guns made to be carried in one or both hands for firing

small for·tune /ˌ· ˈ··/ n [S] very large amount of money

small fry /ˈ· ·/ n young or unimportant person

small-mind·ed /ˌ· ˈ···◁/ adj having narrow or ungenerous views

small po·ta·toes /ˌ· ·ˌ··/ n [U] infml person or thing of little importance

small·pox /ˈsmɔlpɑks/ n [U] serious infectious disease which leaves marks on the skin

small print /ˈ· ˌ·/ n [the+U] something that is purposely made difficult to understand or is easy not to notice, such as part of an agreement or CONTRACT

small screen /ˈ· ˌ·/ n [the+S] television

small talk /ˈ· ·/ n [U] light conversation on non-serious subjects

small-time /ˌ· ˈ·◂/ adj limited in activity, ability, profits, etc.

smarm·y /ˈsmɑrmiʸ/ adj unpleasantly and falsely polite

smart¹ /smɑrt/ adj 1 clever 2 quick or forceful: a smart blow on the head ~**ly** adv ~**ness** n [U]

smart² vi, n (cause or feel) a stinging pain: (fig.) She was still smarting over his unkind words.

smart al·eck /ˈsmɑrt ˌælɪk/ n annoying person who pretends to know everything

smart·en /ˈsmɑrtn̩/ v **smarten up** phr vi/t grow wise esp. after some bad luck

smash /smæʃ/ v 1 vi/t break into pieces violently 2 vi/t go, drive, hit forcefully: The car smashed into a lamppost. 3 vt put an end to: The police have smashed the drugs ring. 4 vt hit (the ball) with a SMASH (2) ♦ n 1 (sound of) a violent breaking 2 hard downward, attacking shot, as in tennis 3 very successful new play, film, etc.: a smash hit 4 SMASH-UP

smash-up /ˈ· ·/ n serious road or railroad accident

smat·ter·ing /ˈsmætərɪŋ/ n limited knowledge: a smattering of German

smear /smɪər/ vt 1 spread (a sticky or oily substance) untidily across (a surface) 2 make unproved charges against (someone) in order to produce unfavorable public opinion ♦ n 1 mark made by smearing 2 unfair unproved charge against someone: a smear campaign

smear test /ˈ· ·/ n medical test on material from inside the body, esp. for discovering CANCER

smell /smel/ v **smelled** or **smelt** /smelt/ 1 vi have or use the sense of the nose 2 vt notice, examine, etc., (as if) by this sense: I think I smell gas! I could smell trouble coming. 3 vi have a particular smell: The bread smells stale. 4 vi have a bad smell 5 **smell a rat** guess that something wrong or dishonest is happening ♦ n 1 [U] power of using the nose to discover the presence of gases in the air 2 [C] quality that has an effect on the nose: a flower with a sweet smell 3 [C] bad smell ~**y** adj smelling bad

smelt /smelt/ vt melt (ORE) for removing the metal

smid·gin /ˈsmɪdʒɪn/ n [S] infml small amount

smile /smaɪl/ n pleased or amused expression in which the mouth is turned up at the ends ♦ vi make a smile **smilingly** adv

smirk /smɜrk/ vi, n (make) a silly SELF-SATISFIED smile

smite /smaɪt/ vt **smote** /smoʷt/, **smitten** /ˈsmɪtn̩/ lit strike hard

smith /smɪθ/ n maker of metal things: a silversmith

smith·e·reens /ˌsmɪðəˈriʸnz/ n (in)**to smithereens** into extremely small pieces

smit·ten /ˈsmɪtn̩/ v past p. of SMITE ♦ adj suddenly in love

smock /smɑk/ n long loose shirtlike garment, esp. for a woman expecting a baby

smog /smɑg, smɔg/ n [U] thick dark unpleasant mist in towns

smoke /smoʷk/ n 1 [U] usu. white, grey, or black gas produced by burning 2 [S] act of smoking tobacco 3 **go up in smoke** end or fail without results, esp. suddenly ♦ v 1 vi/t suck in smoke from (a cigarette, pipe, etc.) 2 vi give off smoke: smoking chimneys 3 vt preserve (fish, meat, etc.) with smoke **smoker** n 1 person who smokes 2 railroad car where smoking is allowed **smoky** adj 1 filled with smoke 2 tasting of or looking like smoke **smoking** n [U] practice or habit of smoking cigarettes, etc.

smoke out phr vt fill a place with smoke to force (a person, animal, etc.) to come out from hiding

smoke·screen /ˈsmoʷkskriʸn/ n 1 cloud of smoke produced to hide something 2 something that hides one's real intentions

smoke·stack /ˈsmoʷkstæk/ n 1 tall chimney of a factory or ship 2 chimney on a steam engine or ship

smokestack in·dus·try /ˈ· · ˌ···/ n the branch of industry that produces cars, ships, steel, etc.

smol·der /ˈsmoʷldər/ vi 1 burn slowly with (almost) no flame 2 have violent but unexpressed feelings

smooch /smuʷtʃ/ vi kiss and hold lovingly

smooth¹ /smuʷð/ adj 1 having an even surface; not rough 2 (of a liquid mixture) without lumps 3 even in movement, without sudden changes: a smooth flight 4 (too) pleasant or polite ~**ly** adv ~**ness** n [U]

smooth² vt make smooth(er)

smooth over phr vt make (difficulties) seem small or unimportant

smooth·y /ˈsmuʷðiʸ/ n infml person who is smooth¹ (4)

smote /smoʷt/ v past t. of SMITE

smoth·er /ˈsmʌðər/ vt 1 cover thickly or in large numbers: a face *smothered in/with spots* **2** die or kill from lack of air **3** keep from developing or happening: *smother a yawn*

smudge /smʌdʒ/ *n* dirty mark with unclear edges ♦ *vi/t* make or become dirty with a smudge

smug /smʌg/ *adj* **-gg-** too pleased with oneself **~ly** *adv* **~ness** *n* [U]

smug·gle /'smʌgəl/ *vt* take in or out secretly or illegally **-gler** *n* **-gling** *n* [U] taking goods to another country without paying the necessary tax

smut /smʌt/ *n* **1** [U] morally offensive talk, stories, etc. **2** [C] small piece of dirt **~ty** *adj* rude

snack /snæk/ *n* amount of food smaller than a meal ♦ *vi* eat a snack **~ bar** small restaurant for quick meals

snag /snæg/ *n* **1** hidden or unexpected difficulty **2** rough or sharp part of something that may catch and hold things passing it ♦ *vt* **-gg-** catch on a SNAG(2)

sna·fu /snæˈfuᵂ/ *n* confused situation

snail /sneʸl/ *n* small limbless creature with a soft body and a shell on its back, that moves slowly

snake /sneʸk/ *n* **1** long thin limbless creature, often with a poisonous bite **2** deceitful person **3 a snake in the grass** a false friend ♦ *vi* move twistingly

snake charm·er /'·· ¦··/ *n* person who controls snakes by playing music

snap /snæp/ *v* **-pp- 1** *vi/t* close the jaws quickly (on): *The dog snapped at my ankles.* **2** *vi/t* break suddenly and sharply **3** *vi/t* move with a sharp sound: *The lid snapped shut.* **4** *vi* speak quickly and angrily **5** *vt infml* to photograph **6 snap one's fingers** make a noise by moving the second finger quickly along the thumb **7 snap out of it** free oneself quickly from a bad state of mind **8 snap someone's head off** answer someone in a short rude way ♦ *n* **1** act or sound of snapping **2** informal photograph ♦ *adj* done without warning or long consideration: *snap judgments* **~py** *adj* **1** stylish; fashionable **2** hasty; quick: *Make it snappy!* (= Hurry up!)

snap up *phr vt* take or buy quickly and eagerly

snap·shot /'snæpʃɑt/ *n* informal photograph taken quickly

snare /'sneər/ *n* **1** trap for small animals **2** deceiving situation ♦ *vt* catch in a snare

snarl¹ /snɑrl/ *vi* **1** (of an animal) make a low angry sound **2** speak angrily ♦ *n* act or sound of snarling

snarl² *v* **snarl up** *phr vt* mix together so as to make movement difficult: *The traffic had got snarled up.* **snarl-up** /'· ·¦/ *n* confused state, esp. of traffic

snatch /snætʃ/ *vi/t* take (something) quickly and often violently or wrongfully ♦ *n* **1** act of snatching **2** short incomplete part: *overhearing snatches of conversation*

snaz·zy /'snæziʸ/ *adj infml* stylishly attractive **-zily** *adv*

sneak /sniʸk/ *vi/t* **snuck** /snʌk/ go or take quietly and secretly ♦ *n derog sl* school child who gives information about the wrongdoings of others **~er** *n* light shoe with a cloth top **~ing** *adj* **1** secret: *a sneaking admiration* **2** not proved but probably right: *a sneaking suspicion* **~y** *adj* acting or done secretly or deceitfully

sneak pre·view /ˌ· ˈ·¦/ *n* a chance to see something new, esp. a film, before anyone else has done so

sneer /snɪər/ *vi* express proud dislike and disrespect, esp. with an unpleasant curling smile ♦ *n* sneering look or remark

sneeze /sniʸz/ *vi, n* (have) a sudden uncontrolled burst of air from the nose

snick·er /'snɪkər/ *vi* laugh quietly or secretly in a disrespectful way **snicker** *n*

snide /snaɪd/ *adj* indirectly but unpleasantly expressing a low opinion **~ly** *adv*

sniff /snɪf/ *v* **1** *vi* breathe in loudly, esp. in short repeated actions **2** *vi/t* do this to discover a smell (in or on) **3** *vt* take (a harmful drug) through the nose ♦ *n* act or sound of sniffing **~er** *n*

sniff at *phr vt* dislike or refuse proudly

sniff out *phr vt* discover or find out (as if) by smelling

snip /snɪp/ *vt* **-pp-** cut with quick short strokes, esp. with scissors ♦ *n* **1** act of snipping **2** small amount

snipe /snaɪp/ *vi* **1** shoot from a hidden position **2** make an unpleasant indirect attack in words **sniper** *n*

snip·pet /'snɪpɪt/ *n* small bit: *a snippet of information*

sniv·el /'snɪvəl/ *vi* **-l-** act or speak in a weak complaining crying way

snob /snɑb/ *n* person who pays too much attention to social class, and dislikes people of a lower class **~bery** *n* [U] behavior of snobs **~bish** *adj*

snoop /snuᵂp/ *vi* search around or concern oneself with other people's affairs without permission **~er** *n*

snoot·y /'snuᵂtiʸ/ *adj infml* proudly rude **-ily** *adv* **-iness** *n* [U]

snooze /snuˮz/ *vi, n* (have) a short sleep

snore /snɔr/ *vi* breathe noisily while asleep ♦ *n* act or sound of snoring

snor·kel /ˈsnɔrkəl/ *n* breathing tube for swimmers under water ♦ *vi* go snorkeling

snort /snɔrt/ 1 *vi* make a rough noise by forcing air down the nose, often in impatience or anger 2 *vt* SNIFF (3) ♦ *n* act or sound of snorting

snot·ty-nosed /ˌsnɑtiʸ ˈnoˮzd◂/ *adj* (esp. of a young person) trying to act as if one is important; rude

snout /snaʊt/ *n* animal's long nose: *a pig's snout*

snow¹ /snoˮ/ *n* frozen rain that falls in white pieces (FLAKES) and often forms a soft covering on the ground ~y *adj*

snow² *vi* (of snow) fall

snow in *phr vt* prevent from traveling by a heavy fall of snow

snow under *phr vt* cause to have more of something than one can deal with: *snowed under with work*

snow·ball /ˈsnoˮbɔl/ *n* ball of pressed snow, as thrown by children ♦ *vi* increase faster and faster

snowbound /ˈsnoˮbaʊnd/ *adj* snowed in

snow·drift /ˈsnoˮˌdrɪft/ *n* deep mass of snow piled up by the wind

snow·drop /ˈsnoˮdrɑp/ *n* plant of early spring with a small white flower

snow·job /ˈsnoˮdʒɑb/ *n* act of deceiving, esp. by use of too much information

snow·man /ˈsnoˮmæn/ *n* –men /-men/ figure of a person made out of snow

snow·mo·bile /ˈsnoˮməˌbiʸl/ *n* motor vehicle for traveling over snow

snow·plow /ˈsnoˮplaʊ/ *n* apparatus or vehicle for clearing away snow

snow·storm /ˈsnoˮstɔrm/ *n* very heavy fall of snow

snow·suit /ˈsnoˮsuˮt/ *n* article of clothing made in one piece, covering legs and arms, worn in winter

snub /snʌb/ *vt* -bb- treat (someone) rudely, esp. by paying no attention to them ♦ *n* act of snubbing

snub² *adj* (of a nose) short and flat

snuck /snʌk/ *v past t. and p. of* SNEAK

snuff¹ /snʌf/ *n* [U] powdery tobacco for breathing into the nose

snuff² *vt* put out (a candle) by pressing the burning part

snuff out *phr vt* put a sudden end to

snug /snʌg/ *adj* -gg- 1 giving warmth, comfort, protection, etc. 2 (of clothes) fitting closely and comfortably

snug·gle /ˈsnʌgəl/ *vi* settle into a warm comfortable position

so¹ /soˮ/ *adv* 1 to such a (great) degree: *It was so dark I couldn't see.* 2 (used instead of repeating something): *He hopes he'll win and I hope so too.* 3 also: *He hopes he'll win and so do I.* 4 very: *We're so glad you could come!* 5 in this way 6 yes; it is true: *'There's a fly in your soup.' 'So there is!'* 7 *fml* therefore 8 and so on/forth and other things of that kind 9 or so more or less: *It'll only cost 15c or so.* 10 so as to: a in order to b in such a way as to 11 so long! *infml* goodbye 12 so many/much: a a certain number/amount: *a charge of so much a day* b an amount equal to: *These books are just so much waste paper!*

so² *conj* 1 with the result that: *It was dark, so I couldn't see.* 2 therefore: *He had a headache, so he went to bed.* 3 with the purpose (that): *I gave him an apple so (that) he wouldn't go hungry.* 4 (used at the beginning of a sentence) a (with weak meaning): *So here we are again.* b (to express discovery): *So that's how they did it!* 5 so what? Why is that important?; Why should I care?

so³ *adj* 1 true: *Is that really so?* 2 just so arranged exactly and tidily

soak /soˮk/ *vi/t* 1 (cause to) remain in liquid, becoming completely wet 2 (of liquid) enter (a solid) through the surface 3 *vt sl* make (a customer) pay too much ♦ *n* [C;U] (act of) soaking ~ed *adj* thoroughly wet, esp. from rain ~ing *adv, adj* very (wet)

soak up *phr vt* draw in (a liquid) through a surface: (fig.) *to soak up the sun | to soak up information*

so-and-so /ˈ· · ·ˌ·/ *n* 1 one not named 2 unpleasant or annoying person

soap /soˮp/ *n* 1 [U] usu. solid substance used with water for cleaning esp. the body 2 [C] *infml* SOAP OPERA ~y *adj*

soap·box /ˈsoˮpbɑks/ *n* on one's soapbox stating one's opinions loudly and forcefully

soap op·e·ra /ˈ· ·ˌ···/ *n* continuing television story about the daily life and troubles of the same set of characters

soar /sɔr, soˮr/ *vi* 1 (of a bird) fly high without moving the wings 2 rise steeply: *Prices soared.*

SOB /ˌɛs oˮ ˈbiʸ/ *n infml derog* SON-OF-A-BITCH (used in INSULTS(2))

sob /sɑb/ *vi* -bb- cry while making short bursts of sound breathing in ♦ *n* act or sound of sobbing

so·ber /ˈsoˮbər/ *adj* 1 not drunk 2 *fml* thoughtful, serious, or solemn;

not silly ♦ *vi/t* make or become
SOBER (2): *a sobering thought* **~ly**
adv

 sober up *phr vi/t* make or become
SOBER (1)

so·bri·e·ty /sə'braɪəti̯, soʷ-/ *n fml*
being sober

so·bri·quet /'soʷbrɪkeɪ, -kɛt, ˌsoʷ-
brɪ'keɪ/ *n fml for* NICKNAME

sob sto·ry /'·ˌ··/ *n* story intended
to make the hearer or reader cry,
feel pity, or feel sorry

so-called /ˌ· '··◂/ *adj* (undeservedly
but) commonly described in the
stated way

soc·cer /'sakər/ *n* [U] game played
with a round ball between 2 teams
of 11 players

so·cia·ble /'soʷʃəbəl/ *adj* fond of
being with others; friendly **–bly** *adv*
–bility /ˌsoʷʃə'bɪləti̯/ *n* [U]

so·cial /'soʷʃəl/ *adj* **1** of human society or its organization **2** living
together by nature **3** based on rank
in society: *social class* **4** for or spent
in time or activities with friends
(rather than work): *an active social
life* | *a social club* **n** informal gather-
ing: *ice-cream social* **~ly** *adv*

social climb·er /ˌ·· '··/ *n derog* person who tries to get accepted into a
higher social class

so·cial·is·m /'soʷʃəˌlɪzəm/ *n* [U] political system aiming at establishing a society in which everyone is
equal **–ist** *adj, n*

so·cia·lite /'soʷʃəˌlaɪt/ *n* person
who goes to many fashionable parties

so·cial·ize /'soʷʃəˌlaɪz/ *vi* spend
time with others in a friendly way

social sci·ence /ˌ·· '··/ *n* [C;U]
study of people in society, including
SOCIOLOGY, ECONOMICS, etc.

social se·cu·ri·ty /ˌ··· ·'···/ *n* [U]
money for old people paid to the
government by workers and employers

social serv·ic·es /ˌ·· '···/ *n* [P]
government services to help people,
such as education, health care, etc.

social work /'·· ·/ *n* [U] work done
to help the old, sick, unemployed,
etc. **~er** *n*

so·ci·e·ty /sə'saɪəti̯/ *n* **1** [U] everyone considered as a whole: *Society
has a right to expect obedience to the
law.* **2** [C;U] group of people who
share laws, organization, etc.:
modern Western society **3** [C] organization of people with similar aims
or interests: *She joined the university film society.* **4** [U] fashionable
people **5** [U] *fml* being with other
people **–tal** *adj of* society

so·ci·o·ec·o·nom·ic /ˌsoʷsiʷoʷˌɛkə-
'namɪk, ˌsoʷʃiʷoʷ-, -ˌiʸkə-/ *adj*

based on a combination of social
and money conditions

so·ci·ol·o·gy /soʷsiʸ'aləd͡ʒiʸ, ˌsoʷʃiʸ-/
n [U] study of society and group behavior **–ogist** *n* **–ogical** /ˌsoʷsiʸə-
'lad͡ʒɪkəl, ˌsoʷʃiʸə-/ *adj*

sock[1] /sak/ *n* cloth covering for the
foot

sock[2] *vt sl* strike hard ♦ *n* forceful
blow

sock·et /'sakɪt/ *n* hole into which
something fits esp. an electrical
PLUG

sod /sad/ *n* [C;U] (piece of) earth
with grass and roots growing in it

so·da /'soʷdə/ *n* [U] **1** SODA WATER: *a
whiskey and soda* **2** SODA drink **3**
FIZZY fruit drink with ice cream **4**
SODIUM

soda foun·tain /'··· ˌ··/ *n* place in a
store at which fruit drinks, ice
cream, etc., are served

soda pop /'·· ˌ·/ *n* sweet non-
alcoholic FIZZY drink

soda wa·ter /'·· ˌ··/ *n* [U] water
filled with gas esp. for mixing with
other drinks

sod·den /'sadn/ *adj* very wet

so·di·um /'soʷdiʸəm/ *n* [U] silver-
white metal found naturally only in
compounds

sod·o·my /'sadəmiʸ/ *n* [U] *fml or
law* any of various sexual acts, esp.
ANAL sex between males

so·fa /'soʷfə/ *n* comfortable seat for
2 or 3 people

soft /sɔft/ *adj* **1** not hard or stiff **2**
smooth to the touch: *soft skin* **3** quiet
4 restful and pleasant: *soft colors* **5**
with little force; gentle: *a soft breeze*
6 easy: *a soft job* **7** too kind **8** not in
good physical condition **9** dealing
with ideas not facts: *one of the soft
sciences like* PSYCHOLOGY **10** not of
the worst or most harmful kind:
Cannabis is a soft drug. **11** (of a
drink) containing no alcohol and
usu. sweet and served cold **12** (in
English pronunciation) **a** (of the letter *c*) having the sound /s/ and not
/k/ **b** (of the letter *g*) having the
sound /d͡ʒ/ and not /g/ **13** (of water)
free from minerals that stop soap
forming LATHER easily **14** *infml* foolish: *He's soft in the head.* **~ly** *adv*
~ness *n* [U]

soft·ball /'sɔftbɔl/ *n* (ball used in) a
game like baseball

soft-boiled /ˌ· '··◂/ *adj* (of an egg)
boiled not long enough for the yellow part to become solid

soft cop·y /'· ˌ··/ *n* [U] information
stored in a computer's memory or
shown on a SCREEN, rather than in
printed form

soft drink /'·· ·/ *n* any non-alcoholic
drink

soft·en /'sɔfən/ *vi/t* (cause to)

become soft(er) or more gentle ~ **er** *n*: *a water softener*

soften up *phr vt* break down opposition of (someone)

soft·heart·ed /ˌsɔftˈhɑtɪd◂/ *adj* easily made to act kindly or feel sorry for someone

soft op·tion /ˌ· ˈ··/ *n* course of action which will give one less trouble

soft-ped·al /ˈ· ˌ··/ *vt* make (a subject, fact, etc.) seem unimportant

soft sell /ˌ· ˈ·◂/ *n* [U] selling by gentle persuading

soft should·er /ˌ· ˈ··/ *n* hard surface beside a HIGHWAY where cars may stop if in difficulty

soft soap /ˌ· ˈ·/ *n* [U] saying nice things about people, esp. as a means of persuading **soft-soap** /ˈ· ·/ *vt* use soft soap on

soft spot /ˈ· ·/ *n* fondness

soft touch /ˌ· ˈ·/ *n infml* someone from whom it is easy to get what one wants because they are kind, easily deceived, etc.

soft·ware /ˈsɔftweər/ *n* [U] set of PROGRAMs that control a computer

soft·wood /ˈsɔftwʊd/ *n* [U] cheap easily cut wood from trees such as PINE and FIR

sog·gy /ˈsɑgi/ *adj* completely (and unpleasantly) wet **-giness** *n* [U]

soil¹ /sɔɪl/ *n* [U] top covering of the earth in which plants grow; ground

soil² *vt fml* make dirty

soi·rée /swɑˈreɪ/ *n* evening party, often including an artistic performance

so·journ /ˈsoʊdʒɜrn/ *vi lit* live for a time in a place

sol·ace /ˈsɑlɪs/ *n* [C;U] (something that gives) comfort for someone full of grief or anxiety

so·lar /ˈsoʊlər/ *adj* of or from the sun

solar cell /ˌ··· ˈ·/ *n* apparatus for producing electric power from sunlight

so·lar·i·um /soʊˈlɛəriʲəm/ *n* -ia /-riʲə/ *or* -iums room with glass walls, for sitting in the sunshine

solar pan·el /ˌ·· ˈ··/ *n* number of SOLAR CELLs working together

solar plex·us /ˌsoʊlər ˈplɛksəs/ *n* 1 system of nerves between the stomach and the BACKBONE 2 *infml* stomach

solar sys·tem /ˈ··· ˌ··/ *n* sun and the PLANETs going around it

sold /soʊld/ *v past t. and p. of* SELL

sol·der /ˈsɑdər/ *n* [U] easily meltable metal used for joining metal surfaces ♦ *vt* join with solder

sol·dier¹ /ˈsoʊldʒər/ *n* member of an army

sol·dier² *v* **soldier on** *phr vi*

continue working steadily in spite of difficulties

sole¹ /soʊl/ *n* bottom surface of the foot or of a shoe

sole² *n* flat fish often used for food

sole³ *adj* 1 only 2 unshared: *sole responsibility* ~**ly** *adv* only

so·le·cis·m /ˈsɑləˌsɪzəm/ *n fml* doing something wrong, esp. in grammar or social behavior

sol·emn /ˈsɑləm/ *adj* 1 without humor or lightness; serious 2 (of a promise) made sincerely and meant to be kept 3 of the grandest most formal kind ~**ly** *adv* ~**ness** *n* [U] ~**ity** /səˈlɛmnətiʲ/ *n* 1 [U] solemnness 2 [C] formal act proper for a grand event

sol-fa /ˌsoʊl ˈfɑ/ *n* system of names given to different musical notes

so·li·cit /səˈlɪsɪt/ *v* 1 *vt fml* ask for 2 ask people on the street to buy goods 3 *vi esp. law* advertise oneself as a PROSTITUTE

so·lic·i·tous /səˈlɪsətəs/ *adj fml* helpful and kind ~**ly** *adv* ~**ness** *n* [U]

so·lic·i·tude /səˈlɪsəˌtuʷd, -ˌtyuʷd/ *n* [U] *fml* solicitousness

sol·id /ˈsɑlɪd/ *adj* 1 not liquid or gas 2 not hollow 3 firm and well made 4 that may be depended on 5 in or showing complete agreement: *The strike was 100 per cent solid.* 6 not mixed with any other (metal): *a watch of solid gold* 7 *infml* continuous: *waiting for 4 solid hours* 8 having length, width and height ♦ *n* solid object or substance ~**ly** *adv* ~**ity** /səˈlɪdətiʲ/ *n* [U] quality or state of being solid

sol·i·dar·i·ty /ˌsɑləˈdærətiʲ/ *n* [U] loyalty within a group

so·lid·i·fy /səˈlɪdəˌfaɪ/ *vi/t* (cause to) become solid or hard

solid-state /ˌ·· ˈ·◂/ *adj* having electrical parts, esp. TRANSISTORs, that run without heating or moving parts

sol·il·o·quy /səˈlɪləkwiʲ/ *n* speech made by an actor alone on stage

sol·i·taire /ˈsɑləˌteər/ *n* [U] 1 card game for one player 2 (piece of jewelry having) a single jewel, esp. a diamond

sol·i·ta·ry /ˈsɑləˌteriʲ/ *adj* 1 (fond of being) alone 2 in a lonely place 3 single

sol·i·tude /ˈsɑləˌtuʷd, -ˌtyuʷd/ *n* [U] *fml* state of being alone

so·lo /ˈsoʊloʷ/ *n* **solos** something done by one person alone, esp. a piece of music for one performer ♦ *adj, adv* 1 without a companion or esp. instructor 2 as or being a musical solo ~**ist** *n* performer of a musical solo

sol·stice /ˈsɑlstɪs, ˈsoʊl-/ *n* time of

the longest and shortest days of the year

sol·u·ble /ˈsɑlyəbəl/ adj **1** that can be dissolved (DISSOLVE) **2** fml solvable –**bility** /ˌsɑlyəˈbɪləti̯/ n [U]

so·lu·tion /səˈluʷʃən/ n **1** [C] answer to a problem or question **2** [C;U] liquid with a solid mixed into it

solve /sɑlv/ vt find an answer to or explanation of **solvable** adj

sol·vent¹ /ˈsɑlvənt/ adj not in debt –**vency** n [U]

solvent² n [C;U] liquid that can turn solids into liquids

som·ber /ˈsɑmbər/ adj sadly serious or dark ~**ly** adv – **ness** n [U]

some¹ /sʌm/ determiner **1** an unknown or unstated number: She went to work for some computer firm (or other). **2** quite a large number or amount of: The fire lasted for some time. **3** infml no kind of: Some friend you are! **4** fine or important: That was some speech you made! **5** some ... or (an)other one or several which the speaker cannot or does not care to state exactly: He's staying with some friend or other. ♦ pron **1** an amount or number of the stated thing(s) **2** certain ones but not all ♦ adv **1** about (the stated number): Some 50 people came. **2** rather; a little: 'Are you feeling better?' 'Some, I guess.' **some more** an additional amount (of)

some² /səm; strong sʌm/ determiner a certain number or amount of: I bought some bread. | Some people like tea, others prefer coffee

some·bod·y /ˈsʌmˌbɑdiʸ, -ˌbʌdiʸ, -bədiʸ/ pron someone ♦ n [U] a person of some importance: He thinks he's really somebody.

some·how /ˈsʌmhaʊ/ adv **1** in some way not yet known or stated **2** for some reason: Somehow I don't believe her.

some·one /ˈsʌmwʌn/ pron **1** a person (but not a particular or known one) **2** or someone or a person like that: We need a builder or someone.

some·place /ˈsʌmpleʸs/ adv SOMEWHERE

som·er·sault /ˈsʌmərˌsɔlt/ n rolling jump in which the feet go over the head and then land on the ground **somersault** vi

some·thing /ˈsʌmθɪŋ/ pron **1** some unstated or unknown thing **2** better than nothing: At least we have the car, that's something. **3** make something of oneself/one's life be successful **4** or something (to show that the speaker is not sure): He's a director or something. **5** something of a(n) rather a(n); a fairly good **6** something like: a rather like b

infml about: There were something like 1000 people there. **7** something over/under rather more/less than **8** something to do with (having) a connection with

some·time /ˈsʌmtaɪm/ adv at some uncertain or unstated time ♦ adj fml former

some·times /ˈsʌmtaɪmz/ adv on some occasions but not all

some·what /ˈsʌmhwʌt, -hwɑt, wʌt, -wɑt/ adv a little; rather

some·where /ˈsʌmhwɛər, -wɛər/ adv **1** (at or to) some place **2** get somewhere begin to succeed

son /sʌn/ n **1** someone's male child **2** (used by an older man to a much younger man or boy): What's your name, son?

so·nar /ˈsoʷnɑr/ n apparatus for finding objects under water with sound waves

so·na·ta /səˈnɑtə/ n piece of music in usu. 3 or 4 parts, for 1 or 2 instruments

song /sɔŋ/ n **1** [C] short piece of music with words for singing **2** [U] act or art of singing **3** [C;U] music-like sound of birds **4** for a song very cheaply

song and dance /ˌ· · ˈ·/ n [S;U] infml an unnecessary or unwelcome expression of excitement, anger, etc.

son·ic /ˈsɑnɪk/ adj of or concerning the speed of sound or sound

son-in-law /ˈ· · ˌ·/ n sons-in-law daughter's husband

son·net /ˈsɑnɪt/ n poem of 14 lines

son·ny /ˈsʌniʸ/ n (used in speaking to a young boy)

son-of-a-bitch /ˌ· · · ˈ·/ n sons-of-bitches, son-of-a-bitches taboo also **SOB** someone strongly disliked

so·nor·ous /səˈnɔrəs, -ˈnoʷr-, ˈsɑn-ərəs/ adj having a pleasantly full loud sound ~**ly** adv –**ity** /səˈnɔr-əti̯, -nɑr-/ n [U]

soon /suʷn/ adv **1** within a short time **2** quickly; early: How soon can you finish it? **3** willingly: I'd sooner stay here. **4** as soon as at once after; when **5** no sooner ... than ... at once: No sooner had she arrived than it was time to go. **6** sooner or later certainly, although one cannot be sure when

soot /sʊt/ n [U] black powder produced by burning ~**y** adj ~**iness** n [U]

soothe /suʷð/ vt **1** make less angry or excited **2** make less painful **soothingly** adv

sooth·say·er /ˈsuʷθˌseʸər/ n lit person who tells the future

sop¹ /sɑp/ n something offered to gain someone's favor or stop them complaining

sop² v -pp- **sop up** phr vt take up (liquid) into something solid

soph·is·m /ˈsɑfɪzəm/ n fml **1** [U] SOPHISTRY **2** [C] argument that sounds correct but is false

so·phis·ti·cat·ed /səˈfɪstɪˌkeɪtɪd/ adj **1** experienced in and understanding the ways of society **2** highly developed and including the best or most modern systems –**ion** /səˌfɪstɪˈkeɪʃən/ n [U]

soph·ist·ry /ˈsɑfəstriʲ/ n [U] fml use of false deceptive arguments

soph·o·more /ˈsɑfəˌmɔr, -ˌmoʷr, ˈsɑfmɔr, ˈsɑfmoʷr/ n student in 10th grade of high school or the second year of high school or college

sop·o·rif·ic /ˌsɑpəˈrɪfɪk◂/ adj causing sleep

sop·ping /ˈsɑpɪŋ/ adv, adj very (wet)

so·pra·no /səˈprænoʷ, -ˈprɑ-/ n -nos **1** (someone, esp. a woman, with) the highest human singing voice **2** instrument which plays notes in the highest range

sor·cer·y /ˈsɔrsəriʲ/ n [U] doing of magic with the help of evil spirits **sorcerer, sorceress** fem. — n

sor·did /ˈsɔrdɪd/ adj **1** completely lacking fine or noble qualities; low **2** dirty and badly cared for ~**ly** adv ~**ness** n [U]

sore /sɔr, soʷr/ adj **1** painful, esp. from a wound or hard use **2** likely to cause offense: Don't joke about his weight: it's a sore point with him. **3** angry ♦ n painful usu. infected place on the body ♦ adv lit sorely ~**ly** adv fml very much ~**ness** n [U]

so·ror·i·ty /səˈrɔrətiʲ, -ˈrɑr-/ n society of women in a college with their own RESIDENCE

sor·row /ˈsɑroʷ, ˈsɔr-/ n [C;U] sadness; grief ♦ vi grieve ~**ful** adj ~**fully** adv ~**fulness** n [U]

sor·ry /ˈsariʲ, ˈsɔriʲ/ adj **1** feeling sadness, pity, or sympathy **2** ashamed of or unhappy about an action and wishing one had not done it **3** causing pity mixed with disapproval: You look a sorry sight. ♦ interj **1** (used for excusing oneself or expressing polite refusal, disagreement, etc.) **2** (used for asking someone to repeat something one has not heard)

sort² vi/t put (things) in order

sort out phr vt separate from a mass or group

sor·tie /ˈsɔrtiʲ/ n **1** short trip into

an unfamiliar place **2** short attack by an army

SOS /ˌɛs oʷ ˈɛs/ n urgent message for help

so-so /ˈ· ·/ adj, adv neither very bad(ly) nor very good/well

sot·to vo·ce /ˌsɑtoʷ ˈvoʷtʃiʲ/ adv fml quietly

souf·flé /suʷˈfleɪʲ/ n [C;U] light airy baked dish of eggs and flour

sought /sɔt/ v past t. and p. of SEEK

sought-af·ter /ˈ· ˌ··/ adj wanted because of rarity or high quality

soul /soʷl/ n **1** part of a person that is not the body and is thought not to die **2** person: Not a soul (= no one) was there. **3** perfect example: Your secret is safe with him; he's the soul of discretion. **4** most active part or influence: She's the life and soul of any party. **5** attractive quality of sincerity: The performance lacks soul. **6** SOUL MUSIC **7 heart and soul** (with) all one's power and feeling **8 keep body and soul together** have enough money, etc., to live –**ful** adj expressing deep feeling ~**fully** adv ~**less** adj having no attractive or tender human qualities ~**ly** adv

soul-des·troy·ing /ˈ· ·ˌ··/ adj (esp. of a job) very uninteresting

soul food /ˈ· ·/ n [U] old-fashioned cooking of the southern US

soul mu·sic /ˈ· ˌ··/ n [U] type of popular music usu. performed by black singers

soul-search·ing /ˈ· ˌ··/ n deep examination of one's mind and conscience

sound¹ /saʊnd/ n **1** [C;U] what is or may be heard **2** [S] idea produced by something read or heard: From the sound of it, I'd say the matter was serious. ♦ v **1** vi seem when heard: His explanation sounded suspicious. **2** vi/t (cause to) make a sound: Sound the trumpets. **3** vt signal by making sounds: Sound the alarm. **4** vt pronounce **5** vt measure the depth of (water, etc.) using a line with a weight on the end

sound off phr vi express an opinion freely and forcefully

sound out phr vt try to find out the opinion or intention of

sound² adj **1** not damaged or diseased **2** showing good sense or judgment: sound advice **3** thorough **4** (of sleep) deep and untroubled **5 as sound as a bell** in perfect condition ~**ly** adv ~**ness** n [U]

sound³ adv sound asleep deeply asleep

sound bar·ri·er /ˈ· ˌ···/ n point at which an aircraft, etc., reaches the speed of sound

sound ef·fects /ˈ· ·ˌ·/ n [P] sounds produced to give the effect of natural sounds in a radio or television broadcast or film

sounding board /'·· ·/ n means used for testing thoughts, opinions, etc.

sound·ings /'saʊndɪŋz/ n [P] 1 measurements made by sounding (SOUND¹ (5)) water 2 carefully quiet or secret enquiries

sound·proof /'saʊndpruːf/ adj that sound cannot get through or into ♦ vt make soundproof

sound·track /'saʊndtræk/ n recorded music from a film

soup /suːp/ n [U] liquid cooked food often containing pieces of meat or vegetables ♦ v **soup up** phr vt increase the power of (an engine, etc): soup up an old car

sour /saʊər/ adj 1 tasting acid: sour green apples 2 tasting bad because of chemical action by bacteria: sour milk 3 bad-tempered; unfriendly 4 **go/turn sour** go wrong ♦ vi/t (cause to) become sour ~**ly** adv ~**ness** n [U]

source /sɔːs, soʊrs/ n where something comes from; cause

sour grapes /ˌ· '·/ n [U] pretending to dislike what one really desires, because it is unobtainable

sour·puss /'saʊərˌpʊs/ n complaining humorless person

south /saʊθ/ n (often cap.) 1 the direction which is on the right of a person facing the rising sun 2 [the+S] a part of a country which is further south than the rest b the southeastern states of the US ♦ adj 1 in the south 2 (of wind) from the south ♦ adv towards the south ~**ward** adj, adv

south·east /ˌsaʊθ'iːst◂/ n, adj, adv (direction) exactly between south and east ~**ern** /-'iːstərn/ adj

south·er·ly /'sʌðərli/ adj south

south·ern /'sʌðərn/ adj of the south part of the world or of a country ~**er** n (often cap.) person who lives in or comes from the southern part of a country

south·west /ˌsaʊθ'west◂/ n, adj, adv (direction) exactly between south and west ~**ern** /-'westərn/ adj

sou·ve·nir /ˌsuːvə'nɪər, 'suːvəˌnɪər/ n object kept as a reminder of an event, journey, place, etc.

sou'west·er /saʊ'westər/ n hat of shiny material to keep off the rain, worn esp. by sailors

sove·reign /'sɒvrɪn/ n fml king, queen, etc. ♦ adj (of a country) independent and governing itself ~**ty** n [U] 1 complete freedom and power to act or govern 2 quality of being a sovereign state

So·vi·et /'soʊviˈət, -viˌɛt/ adj of the former USSR or its people

sow¹ /soʊ/ vi/t sowed, sown /soʊn/ or sowed plant (seeds) on (a piece of ground) ~**er** n

sow² /saʊ/ n female pig

soy·bean /'sɔɪbiːn/ n bean of an Asian plant which produces oil and is made into a special dark liquid used in Chinese cooking (**soy sauce**)

spa /spɑː/ n place with a spring of mineral water where people come to be cured

space /speɪs/ n 1 [U] something measurable in length, width, or depth; room: There's not enough space in the cupboard for all my clothes. 2 [C;U] quantity or bit of this: looking for a parking space 3 [U] what is outside the Earth's air; where the stars and PLANETS are 4 [U] what surrounds all objects and continues outwards in all directions: staring into space 5 [C;U] period of time: within the space of a few years ♦ vt place apart; arrange with spaces between

space out phr vt forget

space-age /'· ·/ adj very modern

space·craft /'speɪs-kræft/ n vehicle able to travel in SPACE (3)

spaced-out /ˌ· '·/ adj confused

space·ship /'speɪsˌʃɪp/ n (esp. in stories) spacecraft for carrying people

space sta·tion /'· ˌ··/ large spacecraft intended to stay above the Earth and act as a base for scientific tests, etc.

space·suit /'speɪs-suːt/ n special garment worn in SPACE (3), covering the whole body

spa·cious /'speɪʃəs/ adj having a lot of room: a spacious office ~**ness** n [U]

spack·le /'spækəl/ vt/i fill in the cracks (in walls, etc.) before painting

spade¹ /speɪd/ n 1 tool with a broad blade for digging 2 **call a spade a spade** speak the plain truth without being delicate or sensitive

spade² n playing card with one or more figures shaped like black leaves on it

spa·ghet·ti /spə'ɡɛti/ n [U] long round thin form of PASTA: spaghetti and meatballs

spake /speɪk/ v old use, past tense of SPEAK

span /spæn/ n 1 length between 2 limits, esp. of time: over a span of 3 years 2 length of time over which something continues: concentration span 3 (part of) a bridge, arch, etc., between supports 4 distance from the end of the thumb to the little finger in a spread hand ♦ vt -**nn-**

1 form an arch or bridge over **2** include in space or time

span·gle /ˈspæŋgəl/ n small shiny piece sewn on for decoration ♦ vt decorate with spangles

span·iel /ˈspænyəl/ n dog with long ears and long wavy hair

spank /spæŋk/ vt hit (esp. a child) with the open hand for punishment, esp. on the BUTTOCKS **spank** n

spar¹ /spɑr/ vi -rr- **1** practice boxing **2** fight with words

spar² n pole supporting a ship's ropes or sails

spare /spɛər/ vt **1** give up (something that is not needed): We have no money to spare. (= we have only just enough) **2** keep from using, spending, etc.: No expense was spared. (= a lot of money was spent) **3** not give (something unpleasant): Spare me the gory details. **4** esp. lit not punish or harm **5** spare a thought stop and consider ♦ adj **1** kept for use if needed: a spare tire **2** free: spare time **3** rather thin ♦ n SPARE PART

spare part /ˌ· ˈ·/ n machine part to take the place of one that is damaged

spare part sur·ge·ry /ˌ· ˈ· ···/ n [U] infml fixing of organs (such as a heart) from dead people in sick people to take the place of diseased organs

spare·ribs /ˈspɛərˌrɪbz/ n [P] (dish of) pig's RIBS with their meat

spark /spɑrk/ n **1** small bit of burning material flying through the air: (fig.) His murder was the spark that set off the war. **2** electric flash passing across a space **3** very small but important bit: not a spark of humor ♦ vi **1** produce a spark **2** lead to (esp. something unpleasant) **3** esp. AmE encourage

spark off phr vt cause (esp. something violent or unpleasant)

spar·kle /ˈspɑrkəl/ vi shine in small flashes: (fig.) Her conversation sparkled with wit. (= was bright and interesting) ♦ n [C;U] act or quality of sparkling **-kling** adj **1** full of life and brightness **2** (of wine) giving off gas in small BUBBLES

spark plug /ˈ· ·/ n part inside an engine that makes a SPARK (2) to light the gas and start the engine

spar·row /ˈspæroʷ/ n very common small brownish bird

sparse /spɑrs/ adj scattered; not filled with crowds ~**ly** adv ~**ness** n [U]

spar·tan /ˈspɑrtn/ adj simple, severe, and without attention to comfort

spas·m /ˈspæzəm/ n **1** sudden uncontrolled tightening of muscles **2** sudden short period of uncontrolled activity: spasms of coughing

spas·mod·ic /spæzˈmɑdɪk/ adj happening irregularly or non-continuously: spasmodic interest ~**ally** /-kliʸ/ adv

spas·tic /ˈspæstɪk/ n person with a disease in which some parts of the body will not move

spat /spæt/ v past t. and p. of SPIT

spate /speʸt/ n [S] large number or amount coming together at the same time

spa·tial /ˈspeʸʃəl/ adj fml of or in SPACE (1) ~**ly** adv

spat·ter /ˈspætər/ vi/t scatter (drops of liquid) or be scattered on (a surface)

spat·u·la /ˈspætʃələ/ n (kitchen) tool with a wide flat blade for spreading, mixing, etc.

spawn /spɔn/ n [U] eggs of water animals like fishes and FROGS ♦ vi **1** produce spawn **2** produce esp. in large numbers

speak /spiʸk/ v **spoke** /spoʷk/, **spoken** /ˈspoʷkən/ **1** vi say things; talk **2** vi express thoughts, ideas, etc., in some other way than this: Actions speak louder than words. **3** vt say; express: Is he speaking the truth? **4** vt be able to talk in (a language) **5** vi make a speech **6** vi mean in the stated way what is said: generally/personally speaking, I agree **7** on speaking terms willing to talk and be polite to another **8** so to speak as one might say **9** speak one's mind express one's thoughts (too) directly **10** to speak of worth mentioning **-er** n **1** person making a speech **2** person who speaks a language **3** LOUDSPEAKER

speak for phr vt express the thoughts, opinions, etc., of

speak out phr vi speak boldly, freely and plainly

speak up phr vi **1** speak more loudly **2** SPEAK out

speak·eas·y /ˈspiʸkˌiʸziʸ/ n (esp. in the 1920s and 1930s) place for going to buy and drink alcohol illegally

spear /spɪər/ n weapon consisting of a pole with a sharp point ♦ vt push or throw a spear into

spear·head /ˈspɪərhɛd/ n forceful beginner and/or leader of an attack or course of action ♦ vt lead forcefully

spear·mint /ˈspɪərˌmɪnt/ n [U] common MINT plant with a fresh taste

spe·cial /ˈspeʃəl/ adj **1** of a particular kind; not ordinary **2** particularly great or fine: a special occasion ♦ n **1** something not of the regular kind **2** infml an advertised reduced pri-- in a store ~**ly** adv **1** for on-- ular purpose **2** unusu--

spe·cial·ist /ˈsp--- with skill o---

subject **2** doctor who specializes in a particular sort of disease, etc.

spe·cial·ty /ˈspeʃəltiʲ/ n **1** person's particular field of work or study **2** finest product

spe·cial·ize /ˈspeʃəˌlaɪz/ vi limit one's study, business, etc., to one particular area **–ization** /ˌspeʃələˈzeʲʃən/ n [C;U]

spe·cies /ˈspiʲʃiʲz/ n **–cies** group of similar types of animal or plant

spe·cif·ic /spɪˈsɪfɪk/ adj **1** detailed and exact: *specific instructions* **2** particular; fixed or named: *a specific tool for each job* **–ally** /-kliʲ/ adv

spe·ci·fi·ca·tion /ˌspesəfəˈkeʲʃən/ n **1** [C] detailed plan or set of descriptions or directions **2** [U] act of specifying

spe·ci·fy /ˈspesəˌfaɪ/ vt state exactly

spe·ci·men /ˈspesəmən/ n **1** single typical thing or example **2** piece or amount of something to be shown, tested, etc.: *The doctor needs a specimen of your blood.*

spe·cious /ˈspiʲʃəs/ adj fml seeming correct but in fact false **–ly** adv **–ness** n [U]

speck /spek/ n very small piece or spot: *a speck of dust*

speck·le /ˈspekəl/ n any of a number of small irregular marks **–led** adj

spec·ta·cle /ˈspektəkəl/ n **1** something unusual that one sees, esp. something grand and fine **2** object of laughing, disrespect, or pity **spectacles** n old-fash [P] GLASSES

spec·tac·u·lar /spekˈtækyələr/ adj unusually interesting and grand ♦ n spectacular entertainment **~ly** adv

spec·ta·tor /ˈspekˌteʲtʲər/ n person watching an event or sport

spec·ter /ˈspektər/ n fml or lit for GHOST **–tral** adj

spec·trum /ˈspektrəm/ n **–tra** /-trə/ **1** set of bands of different colors into which light may be separated by a PRISM **2** broad and continuous range: *both ends of the political spectrum*

spec·u·late /ˈspekyəˌleʲt/ vi **1** make guesses **2** buy things to sell later in the hope of profit **–lator** n **–lative** /-lətɪv, -ˌleʲtɪv/ adj **–lation** /ˌspekyəˈleʲʃən/ n [C;U]

sped /sped/ v past t. and p. of SPEED

speech /spiʲtʃ/ n **1** [U] act, power, or way of speaking **2** [C] set of words spoken formally to a group of listeners – see also FREE SPEECH **~less** adj unable to speak because of strong feeling, shock, etc.

speed /spiʲd/ n **1** [C] rate of movement: *a speed of 2000 miles an hour* **2** [U] quickness of movement or ~~traveling~~ at speed (= fast) **3**

[U] sl for AMPHETAMINE ♦ v **speeded** or **sped** /sped/ **1** vi/t go or take quickly **2** vi drive illegally fast **~y** adj fast

speed up phr vi/t (cause to) go faster

speed·om·e·ter /spɪˈdɑmətər/ n instrument showing how fast a vehicle is going

speed·way /ˈspiʲdweʲ/ n **1** [U] sport of racing motorcycles on a closed track **2** [C] place where this is done

spell¹ /spel/ v **spelled 1** vi form words (correctly) from letters **2** vt name in order the letters of (a word) **3** vt (of letters) form (a word): *B-O-O-K spells 'book'.* **4** vt have as an effect: *His disapproval spells defeat for our plan.* **~er** n **~ing** n way a word is spelled

spell out phr vt explain in the clearest possible way

spell² n **1** unbroken period of time: *spells of sunshine* **2** quickly passing attack of illness: *a dizzy spell* ♦ vt replace someone while they rest: *I'll spell you for a while.*

spell³ n (words producing) a condition produced by magical power: (fig.) *The first time we saw Venice, we fell under its spell.*

spell·bind /ˈspelbaɪnd/ vt hold the complete attention of

spelling bee /ˈ·· ˌ·/ n competition in or between schools to find the best spellers

spend /spend/ vt **spent** /spent/ **1** pay (money) for goods or services **2** pass or use (time): *He spent 3 years in prison.* **~er** n **spent** adj **1** already used; no longer for use **2** worn out

spend·thrift /ˈspendˌθrɪft/ n person who wastes money

sperm /spɜrm/ n male sex cell which unites with the female egg to produce new life

spew /spyuʷ/ vi/t (cause to) come out in a rush or flood

sphere /sfɪər/ n **1** mass in the shape of a ball **2** area or range of existence, meaning, action, etc.: *this country's sphere of influence* **spherical** /ˈsfɛrɪkəl, ˈsfɪər-/ adj ball-shaped

sphinx /sfɪŋks/ n **1** ancient Egyptian image of a lion with a human head **2** person who behaves or speaks in a mysterious way

spice /spaɪs/ n **1** [C;U] vegetable product used for giving taste to food **2** [S;U] (additional) interest or excitement ♦ vt add spice to **spicy** adj **1** containing (much) spice **2** slightly improper or rude

spick-and-span /ˌspɪk ən ˈspæn/ adj completely clean and tidy

spi·der /ˈspaɪdər/ n small creature with 8 legs, of which many types make WEBS to catch insects **~y** adj long and thin like a spider's legs

spike /spaɪk/ n 1 pointed piece, esp. of metal 2 metal point fixed to the bottom of a (sports) shoe 3 group of grains or flowers on top of a stem 4 high thin heel of a woman's shoe ♦ vt 1 drive a spike into 2 add a strong alcoholic drink to (a weak or non-alcoholic one) 3 stop (esp. an article in a newspaper) from being printed or spread **spiky** adj

spill /spɪl/ vi/t **spilled** (cause to) pour out accidentally and be lost: I've spilled some coffee on the carpet.| (fig.) The crowd spilled into the streets. 2 **spill the beans** infml tell a secret too soon or to the wrong person ♦ n fall from a horse, bicycle, etc.

spin /spɪn/ v **spun** /spʌn/, pres. p. **-nn-** vi/t 1 turn around and around fast 2 vi/t make (thread) by twisting (cotton, wool, etc.): (fig.) spin a yarn (= tell a story) 3 vt produce in threadlike form: a spider spinning a web ♦ n 1 [C] act of spinning 2 [S;U] fast turning movement 3 [C] short trip (in a car) for pleasure 4 [S] a steep drop: The news sent prices into a spin. 5 **in a spin** in a confused state of mind **~ner** n

spin out phr vt cause to last long enough or too long

spin·ach /'spɪnɪtʃ/ n [U] vegetable with large soft leaves

spin·al cord /ˌ·· '·/ n thick cord of important nerves enclosed in the SPINE (1)

spin·dle /'spɪndl/ n 1 machine part around which something turns 2 pointed rod onto which thread is twisted **-dly** adj long, thin, and looking weak

spine /spaɪn/ n 1 row of bones down the center of the back 2 prickly animal or plant part 3 side of a book along which the pages are fastened **~less** adj weak and cowardly **spiny** adj prickly

spine-chil·ling /'·ˌ··/ adj very frightening

spin-off /'·· ·/ n (useful) indirect product of a process

spin·ster /'spɪnstər/ n unmarried woman

spi·ral /'spaɪərəl/ n, adj 1 (curve) winding around and around a central line or away from a central point 2 process of continuous upward or downward change ♦ vi **-l-** move in a spiral

spire /spaɪər/ n tall thin pointed roof of a church tower

spir·it /'spɪrɪt/ n 1 [C] person's mind or soul 2 [C] a being without a body, such as a GHOST 3 [U] quality of enthusiastic determination or brave effort: a woman with spirit | team spirit 4 [C] person of the stated kind of temper: a free spirit 5 [C] central quality or force: the spirit of the law (= its real intention) 6 [S;U] feeling in the mind towards something: AT-TITUDE: Please take my remarks in the spirit in which they were intended, and don't be offended. 7 **in spirit** in one's thoughts 8 **-spirited** having the stated feelings or spirits: high-spirited ♦ vt take secretly or mysteriously **spirits** n 1 [P] state of one's mind: in high spirits (= cheerful) 2 strong alcoholic drink **~ed** adj full of SPIRIT (3) **~edly** adv **~less** adj without SPIRIT (3) **~less-ness** n [U]

spir·i·tu·al /'spɪrɪtʃuˀəl/ adj 1 of the spirit rather than the body 2 religious ♦ n religious song originally sung by blacks **~ly** adv

spit¹ /spɪt/ v **spat** /spæt/; pres. p. **-tt-** 1 vi/t throw out (liquid or other contents) from the mouth with force 2 vt say with effort or anger 3 vi rain very lightly ♦ n [U] SALIVA

spit² /spɪt/ n 1 thin rod on which meat is cooked over a fire 2 small usu. sandy point of land running out into a stretch of water

spit and pol·ish /ˌ·· '··/ n [U] great military attention to a clean and shiny appearance

spite /spaɪt/ n [U] 1 desire to annoy or harm 2 **in spite of** taking no notice of: They continued, in spite of my warning. ♦ vt annoy or harm intentionally **~ful** adj

spitting im·age /ˌ·· '··/ n exact likeness

spit·tle /'spɪtl/ n [U] SALIVA

splash /splæʃ/ v 1 vi/t a (cause to) fall or move about in drops or waves, esp. wildly or noisily: Rain splashed against the window. b throw a liquid against (something): He splashed his face with cold water. 2 vt report as if very important, esp. in a newspaper ♦ n 1 (sound or mark made by) splashing 2 forceful effect: make a splash in society

splash down phr vi (esp. of a spacecraft) land in the sea **splash-down** /'splæʃdaʊn/ n [C;U]

splash·y /'splæʃiˀ/ adj big, bright, and very noticeable

splay /spleɪ/ vi/t spread out or become larger at one end

spleen /spliˀn/ n 1 organ that controls the quality of the body's blood supply 2 **vent one's spleen** express one's annoyance

splen·did /'splendɪd/ adj 1 grand in appearance or style 2 very fine; excellent **~ly** adv

splen·dor /'splendər/ n [U] excellent or grand beauty

splice /splaɪs/ vt fasten end to end to make one continuous length

splint /splɪnt/ n flat piece for keeping a broken bone in place

splin·ter /'splɪntər/ n small sharp piece, esp. of wood, broken off ♦ vi/t break into splinters

splinter group /'·· ,·/ n group of people that has separated from a larger body

split /splɪt/ v **split**; pres. p. **-tt-** 1 vi/t divide along a length, esp. by a blow or tear 2 vi/t divide into separate parts 3 vt share 4 vi/t separate into opposing groups or parties: Did you know John and Mary had split up? (= their marriage or relationship had ended) 5 **split hairs** concern oneself with unimportant differences ♦ n 1 cut, break, or division made by splitting – see also SPLITS **-ting** adj (of a headache) very bad

split per·son·al·i·ty /ˌ· ··'····/ n set of 2 very different ways of behaving present in one person

split tick·et /ˌ· '··/ n voting for members of different political parties

splits /splɪts/ n [the + P] movement in which a person's legs are spread wide and touch the floor along their whole length

split sec·ond /ˌ· '···◂/ n very short moment

splurge /splɜrdʒ/ vi/t spend more than one can usu. afford

splut·ter /'splʌtər/ vi 1 talk quickly, as if confused 2 make a wet spitting (SPIT) noise **splutter** n

spoil /spɔɪl/ v **spoiled** or **spoilt** /spɔɪlt/ 1 vt destroy the value, worth, or pleasure of; ruin 2 vt treat very or too well: Go on, spoil yourself, have another cake. 3 vi decay **spoils** n [P] fml or lit things taken without payment

spoil for phr vt 1 be very eager for 2 cause to be unsatisfied with: Fine French wine spoils you for cheaper kinds. 3 **be spoiled for choice** find it difficult to decide or choose

spoil·sport /'spɔɪlspɔrt, -spɔrt/ n person who ruins others' fun

spoke[1] /spoʊk/ v past t. of SPEAK

spoke[2] n any of the bars connecting the outer ring of a wheel to the center

spok·en /'spoʊkən/ v past p. of SPEAK

spoken for /'··· ·/ adj infml closely connected with a person of the opposite sex

spokes·per·son /'spoʊks,pɜrsən/ **spokes·man** /-mən/ masc., **spokes·wom·an** /-,wʊmən/ fem. — n person chosen to speak officially for a group

sponge /spʌndʒ/ n 1 [C] simple sea creature with a rubber-like body 2 [C;U] piece of this or plastic like it, which can suck up water and is used for washing ♦ v 1 vt clean with a sponge 2 vi derog get things from people free by taking advantage of their generosity **sponger** n person who SPONGES (2) **spongy** adj not firm

sponge cake /'·· ·/ n [U;C] light cake made from eggs, sugar, and flour

spon·sor /'spɑnsər/ n 1 company or person giving money to help others to do something 2 person who takes responsibility for a person or thing ♦ vt act as a sponsor for: a concert sponsored by American Express **~ship** n [U]

spon·ta·ne·ous /spɑn'teɪniːəs/ adj happening naturally, without planning or another's suggestion **~ly** adv **-taneity** /ˌspɑntə'niːʔəṭiʸ,-'neɪʸ-/ n [U]

spoof /spuʷf/ n funny untrue copy or description

spook /spuʷk/ vt cause (esp. an animal) to be suddenly afraid ♦ n infml for GHOST

spook·y /'spuʷkiʸ/ adj causing fear in a strange way **-ily** adv

spool /spuʷl/ n wheel-like object onto which things are wound

spoon /spuʷn/ n kitchen tool consisting of a small bowl with a handle, used esp. for eating ♦ vt take up with a spoon

spoon-feed /'· ·/ vt 1 feed with a spoon 2 teach (people) in very easy lessons

spo·rad·ic /spə'rædɪk/ adj happening irregularly **~ally** /-kliʸ/ adv

spore /spɔr, spoʷr/ n very small cell that acts like a seed: a mushroom's spores

sport /spɔrt, spoʷrt/ n 1 [C;U] activity needing physical effort and skill and usu. done as a competition according to rules 2 [C] friendly or kind person ♦ vt wear or show publicly: sporting a brand new coat **~ing** adj fair and generous **~y** infml right for sport

sports·cas·ter /'spɔrts,kæstər, 'spoʷrts-/ n person who talks about sports on television or radio

sports car /'· ·/ n low fast car

sports·man /'spɔrtsmən, 'spoʷr-/ **sports·wom·an** /-,wʊmən/ fem. — n **-men** /-mən/ person who plays sport(s) **~ship** n [U] fairness to one's opponent, esp. in sport

spot /spɑt/ n 1 usu. round part different from the main surface: a black spot on his white shirt 2 small diseased mark on the skin 3 place: a beautiful spot for a picnic 4 small or limited part of something: one of the brighter spots in the news 5 a specific position in a SEQUENCE **6** *infml* difficult situation **7** SPOTLIGHT **8** place in a broadcast: *a guest spot on TV* **9 hit the spot** *sl* satisfy a want or need **10 on the spot: a** at once **b** at the place of the action **c** in a position of having to make the right action or answer: *The question really put me on the spot.* – see also SOFT SPOT ♦ *vt* **-tt- 1** see; recognize **2** mark with spots **3** allow as an advantage in a game **~less** *adj* completely clean **~ter** *n* military person who watches for the fall of shots **~ty** *adj* with some parts less good than others

spot check /'· ,·/ *n* examination of a few chosen by chance to represent all **spot-check** *vt*

spot·light /'spotlaɪt/ *n* **1** (light from) a large lamp with a directable beam **2** public attention ♦ *vt* direct attention to

spouse /spaʊs, spaʊz/ *n fml or law* husband or wife

spout /spaʊt/ *n* **1** opening from which liquid comes out: *the spout of a teapot* **2** forceful (rising) stream of liquid **3** *infml* **up the spout** ruined ♦ *v vi/t* come or throw out in a forceful stream **spout off** *phr vi derog* pour out in a stream of words

sprain /spreɪn/ *vt* damage (a joint in the body) by sudden twisting **sprain** *n*

sprang /spræŋ/ *v past t. of* SPRING

sprawl /sprɔl/ *vi/t* spread out awkwardly or ungracefully ♦ *n* sprawling position or area

spray /spreɪ/ *vi/t* send or come out in a stream of small drops (onto) ♦ *n* **1** [U] water blown in very small drops **2** [C;U] liquid to be sprayed out from a container under pressure: *hair spray* (= to keep hair in place) **3** [C] small branch with its leaves and flowers

spread /spred/ *v* **spread 1** *vi/t* (cause to) become longer, broader, wider, etc. **2** *vi/t* (cause to) have an effect or influence or become known over a wider area: *The fire/news soon spread.* **3** *vi* cover a large area or period **4** *vt* put over (a surface): *Spread butter on the bread.* ♦ *n* **1** [U] act or action of spreading **2** [U] soft food for spreading on bread: *cheese spread* **3** [C] large or grand meal

spread-ea·gle /'· ,··/ *vt* put into a position with arms and legs spread wide

spread·sheet /'spredʃiːt/ *n* type of computer PROGRAM that allows figures (e.g. about sales, taxes, and profits) to be shown in groups on a SCREEN(4) so that quick calculations (CALCULATE) can be made

spree /spriː/ *n* period of much wild fun, spending, drinking, etc.

sprig /sprɪg/ *n* small end of a stem with leaves

spright·ly /'spraɪtliʲ/ *adj* cheerful and active **-liness** *n* [U]

spring¹ /sprɪŋ/ *v* **sprang** /spræŋ/, **sprung** /sprʌŋ/ **1** *vi* move quickly and suddenly as if by jumping: *The soldiers sprang to attention.* | (fig.) *The engine sprang into life.* **2** *vi/t* open or close with a SPRING (2): *The box sprang open.* (= opened suddenly) | *to spring a trap* **3** *vt* produce (as) (a surprise): *She sprang the news on us.* **4 spring a leak** (of a ship, container, etc.) begin to let liquid through a hole, etc.

spring from *phr vt* have as its origin

spring up *phr vi* come into existence suddenly

spring² *n* **1** [C;U] season between winter and summer **2** [C] length of wound metal that comes up again after being pressed down **3** [C] place where water comes naturally from the ground **4** [U] elastic quality **5** [C] act of springing **~y** *adj* elastic

spring·board /'sprɪŋbɔːd, -boʷrd/ *n* **1** bendable board for people who DIVE **2** strong starting point

spring-clean /ˌ· '·◄/ *vi/t* clean (a house, etc.) thoroughly **spring-cleaning** /ˌ· '··/ *n* [U]

sprin·kle /'sprɪŋkəl/ *vt* scatter (small drops or bits) on or over (a surface) **-kler** *n* apparatus for sprinkling drops of water

sprint /sprɪnt/ *vi* run very fast **sprint** *n* **~er** *n*

sprout /spraʊt/ *vi/t* send or come out as new growth ♦ *n* new growth on a plant

spruce¹ /spruʷs/ *adj* neat and clean ♦ **spruce up** *phr vt* make (esp. oneself) spruce

spruce² *n* tree of northern countries with short leaves shaped like needles

sprung /sprʌŋ/ *v past p. of* SPRING

spry /spraɪ/ *adj* (esp. of older people) active

spud /spʌd/ *n infml* potato

spun /spʌn/ *v past t. and p. of* SPIN

spunk·y /'spʌŋkiʲ/ *adj* very enthusiastic

spur /spɜːr/ *n* **1** sharp object fitted to a rider's boot, used to make a horse go faster **2** event or influence leading to action **3** length of high ground coming out from a mountain range **4 on the spur of the moment** without preparation or planning ♦ *vt* **-rr-** urge or encourage forcefully

spu·ri·ous /'spyʊəriʲəs/ *adj* **1** based on incorrect reasoning **2** pretended; false **~ly** *adv* **~ness** *n* [U]

spurn /spɜrn/ vt refuse or send away with angry pride

spurt /spɜrt/ vi/t 1 make a SPURT (1) 2 (cause to) flow out suddenly or violently ♦ n 1 sudden short increase of effort or speed 2 spurting of liquid or gas

sput·ter /'spʌtər/ vi make repeated soft explosive sounds

spu·tum /'spyuʷtəm/ n [U] liquid coughed up

spy /spaɪ/ n 1 person employed to find out secret information 2 person who watches secretly ♦ v 1 vi watch or search secretly 2 vt catch sight of

sq written abbrev. for: square

squab·ble /'skwabəl/ vi, n (have) a quarrel about unimportant things

squad /skwad/ n group of people working as a team

squad·ron /'skwadrən/ n large group of soldiers with TANKS (2), of fighting ships, or of aircraft in the airforce

squal·id /'skwalɪd/ adj 1 very dirty and unpleasant 2 of low moral standards ~**ly** adv

squall /skwɔl/ n sudden strong wind usu. with rain or snow ♦ vi cry violently ~**y** adj

squal·or /'skwalər/ n [U] SQUALID (1) conditions

squan·der /'skwandər/ vt spend foolishly and wastefully

square¹ /skwɛər/ n 1 shape with 4 straight equal sides forming 4 right angles 2 broad open area with buildings around it in a town 3 result of multiplying a number by itself ♦ adj 1 being a SQUARE (1) 2 of an area equal to a square with sides of the stated length: 1 square foot 3 forming (nearly) a right angle: a square jaw 4 fair; honest: a square deal 5 having paid and settled what is owed

square² v 1 vt put into a square shape 2 vt divide into squares 3 vt multiply by itself: 2 squared is 4. 4 vi/t (cause to) fit a particular explanation or standard 5 vt cause (totals of points or games won) to be equal 6 vt pay or pay for 7 vt pay or settle dishonestly: There are government officers who will have to be squared. ♦ adv squarely ~**ly** adv directly: He looked her squarely in the eye.

square up phr vi settle a bill

square knot /'··/ n double knot that will not undo easily

square meal /ˌ·'·/ n infml good satisfying meal

square one /ˌ·'·/ n [U] the starting point

square root /ˌ·'·/ n number which when squared (SQUARE² (3)) equals a particular number: 2 is the square root of 4.

squash /skwaʃ, skwɔʃ/ v 1 vt make flat; crush 2 vi/t push or fit into a small space 3 vt force into silence or inactivity ♦ n 1 [S] act or sound of squashing 2 [U] game played in a court with 4 walls with RACKETS and a small ball 3 [C;U] any of a group of vegetables with hard skins, including ZUCCHINI and PUMPKINS ~**y** adj soft and easy to squash

squat /skwat/ vi –tt– 1 sit with the legs drawn up under the body 2 live in an empty building without permission ♦ adj ungracefully short or low and thick ~**ter** n person who SQUATS (2)

squaw /skwɔ/ n native American woman

squawk /skwɔk/ vi 1 (of a bird) make a loud rough cry 2 complain loudly **squawk** n

squeak /skwiʸk/ vi, n (make) a short very high quiet sound ~**y** adj: a squeaky door

squeal /skwiʸl/ n a long very high cry ♦ vi 1 make a squeal 2 sl give secret information about one's criminal friends to the police ~**er** n

squeam·ish /'skwiʸmɪʃ/ adj easily shocked or upset by unpleasant things ~**ly** adv ~**ness** n [U]

squeeze /skwiʸz/ v 1 vt press firmly (together), esp. from opposite sides 2 vt get or force out (as if by) pressure: squeeze the juice from an orange 3 vi/t fit or go by forcing or pushing: She squeezed through the narrow opening. 4 vt cause many difficulties to: Higher lending rates are squeezing small businesses. ♦ n 1 act of squeezing 2 difficult situation caused by high costs or not enough supplies

squelch /skwɛltʃ/ v 1 vt prevent completely from acting; SUPPRESS 2 vi, n (make) the sound of soft mud being pressed ~**y** adj

squib /skwɪb/ n small toy explosive

squid /skwɪd/ n squid or squids sea creature with 10 arms at the end of its long body used for food

squig·gle /'skwɪgəl/ n short wavy or twisting line

squint /skwɪnt/ vi 1 look with almost closed eyes 2 have a SQUINT (1) ♦ n 1 condition in which the eyes look in different directions 2 act of SQUINTing (1)

squirm /skwɜrm/ vi twist the body about, esp. from discomfort, shame, or nervousness

squir·rel /'skwɜrəl/ n small furry animal that climbs trees

squirt /skwɜrt/ vi/t, n (force or be forced out in) a thin stream

squish·y /'skwɪʃiʸ/ adj infml pastelike; soft and wet

Sr written abbrev. for: SENIOR

SS /ˈɛs ˈɛs/ abbrev. for: STEAMSHIP

ssh /ʃ/ interj (used for asking for less noise)

St written abbrev. for: **1** Street **2** SAINT

stab /stæb/ vi/t -bb- strike forcefully (into) with a pointed weapon ♦ n **1** act of stabbing **2** try: I'll have a stab at it. **3 a stab in the back** an attack from someone supposed to be a friend ~ **bing** adj (of pain) sharp and sudden ~ **bing** n [C;U]: a big increase in the number of stabbings reported to police

sta·ble[1] /ˈsteɪbəl/ adj not easily moved, upset, or changed –**bilize** vi/t –**bilizer** n –**bility** /stəˈbɪlət̬i/ n [U]

stable[2] n **1** building where horses are kept **2** group of things with one owner ♦ vt keep in a stable

stac·ca·to /stəˈkɑt̬oʊ/ adj, adv played with very short notes

stack /stæk/ n **1** neat pile: a stack of dishes **2** large pile of dried grass stored outdoors **3** also **stacks** pl. — large amount ♦ vt **1** make into a neat pile (on) **2 blow one's stack** sl become very angry and shout

stack up phr vi measure, esp. in comparison to some others: How does your new car stack up?

sta·di·um /ˈsteɪdiəm/ n –**diums** or –**dia** /-diə/ large building containing a sports field and seats for SPECTATORS

staff /stæf/ n **1** the workers in a place **2** long thick stick or pole ♦ vt provide workers for

stag /stæɡ/ n **1** fully grown male deer **2** for men only: a stag night/party

stage /steɪdʒ/ n **1** raised floor on which plays are performed: He wants to go on the stage. (= become an actor) **2** a center of action or attention: on the center of the political stage **3** state reached at a particular time in a course of events: The project was canceled at an early stage. **4** part of a journey or long race **5** any of the separate driving parts of a ROCKET ♦ vt **1** perform or arrange for public show **2** cause to happen, esp. for public effect

stage·coach /ˈsteɪdʒkoʊtʃ/ n (in former times) carriage pulled by horses, providing a regular passenger service

stage-man·age /ˈ·· ˌ·ˌ·/ vt arrange for public effect, so that a desired result will happen as if naturally

stage man·ag·er /ˈ·· ˌ·ˌ·/ n person in charge of a theater stage

stage-struck /ˈsteɪdʒstrʌk/ adj in love with the theater and esp. wishing to be an actor

stage whis·per /ˌ·· ˈ··/ n loud

whisper intended to be heard by everyone

stag·ger /ˈstæɡər/ v **1** vi/t walk in an unsteady manner, almost falling **2** vt shock greatly **3** vt arrange so as to happen at different times ♦ n unsteady movement, as if about to fall

stag·nant /ˈstæɡnənt/ adj **1** (esp. of water) not flowing or moving, and often smelling bad **2** not developing or growing –**nate** /ˈstæɡneɪt/ vi become STAGNANT (2) –**nation** /stæɡˈneɪʃən/ n [U]

staid /steɪd/ adj serious and dull by habit ~ **ness** n [U]

stain /steɪn/ vi/t discolor in a way that is hard to repair ♦ n **1** stained place or spot **2** mark of guilt or shame

stained glass /ˌ· ˈ·◄/ n [U] colored glass for making patterns in windows

stain·less steel /ˌ·· ˈ·◄/ n [U] steel that does not RUST

stair /steər/ n step in a set of stairs **stairs** n [P] number of steps for going up or down, esp. indoors: a flight of stairs

stair·case /ˈsteərkeɪs/ n set of stairs with its supports and side parts

stake /steɪk/ n **1** pointed post for driving into the ground **2** share in something so that one is interested in whether it succeeds or fails **3** money risked on the result of something **4** post to which a person was tied for being killed, esp. by burning **5 at stake** at risk ♦ vt **1** risk the loss of (something) on a result **2 stake a claim** state that something should belong to one

stake out phr vt carefully watch (a building, etc.), expecting that some criminal activity will be seen **stakeout** /ˈsteɪkaʊt/ n act of doing this

stal·ac·tite /stəˈlækˌtaɪt/ n sharp point of rock hanging from a cave roof

stal·ag·mite /stəˈlæɡˌmaɪt/ n sharp point of rock standing on a cave floor

stale /steɪl/ adj **1** no longer fresh: stale bread/(fig.) news **2** no longer interesting or new ~ **ness** n [U]

stale·mate /ˈsteɪlmeɪt/ n **1** (in CHESS) position in which neither player can win **2** situation in which neither side in a quarrel can get an advantage

stalk[1] /stɔk/ n thin plant part with 1 or more leaves, fruits, or flowers on it

stalk[2] v **1** vt hunt by following closely and secretly **2** vi walk stiffly or proudly

stall[1] /stɔl/ n **1** small shop with an open front or other selling place in a market **2** indoor enclosure for an animal

stall² /vi/t **1** (cause to) stop because there is not enough speed or engine power **2** delay ♦ *n* act of stalling

stal·lion /ˈstælyən/ *n* male horse kept for breeding

stal·wart /ˈstɔlwərt/ *adj, n* strong and dependable (person)

sta·men /ˈsteɪmən/ *n* male part of a flower that produces POLLEN

stam·i·na /ˈstæmənə/ *n* [U] strength to keep going

stam·mer /ˈstæmər/ *vi/t* speak or say with pauses and repeated sounds ♦ *n* habit of stammering

stamp /stæmp/ *v* **1** *vi/t* put (the feet) down hard **2** *vt* mark by pressing: *The title was stamped in gold on the book.* | (fig.) *His manners stamped him as a military man.* **3** *vt* stick a stamp onto ♦ *n* **1** small piece of paper for sticking onto esp. a letter, parcel, etc., to be posted **2** tool for pressing or printing onto a surface: *a date-stamp* **3** mark made by this: (fig.) *a remark which bears the stamp of truth* **4** act of stamping the foot

stamp out *phr vt* put an end to

stam·pede /stæmˈpiːd/ *n* **1** sudden rush of frightened animals **2** sudden mass movement **3** RODEO ♦ *vi/t* (cause to) go in a stampede or unreasonable rush

stamping ground /ˈ··· ·/ *n* a favorite very familiar place

stance /stæns/ *n* **1** way of standing **2** way of thinking; ATTITUDE

stanch /stɔntʃ, stæntʃ/ *vt* stop the flow of (blood)

stan·chion /ˈstæntʃən/ *n* strong upright supporting bar

stand¹ /stænd/ *v* stood /stʊd/ **1** *vi* support oneself on one's feet in an upright position **2** *vi* rise to a position of doing this: *They stood (up) when he came in.* **3** *vi* be in height: *He stands 5 feet 10 inches.* **4** *vi/t* (cause to) rest in a position, esp. upright or on a base: *The clock stood on the shelf.* **5** *vi* be in a particular state of affairs: *How do things stand at the moment?* **6** *vi* be in a position to gain or lose): *He stands to win a fortune if his number's called.* **7** *vt* like; bear: *I can't stand* (= don't like) *whiskey.* **8** *vi* remain true or in force: *My offer still stands.* **9** *vt* pay the cost of (something) for (someone else): *He stood them a wonderful meal.* **10 know how/where one stands (with someone)** know how someone feels about one **11 stand a chance** have a chance **12 standing on one's head** with no difficulty at all: *I could do the job standing on my head.* **13 stand on one's hands/**

head support oneself on the hands/head and hands, with the feet in the air **14 stand on one's own two feet** be able to do without help from others **15 stand something on its head** change or upset violently **16 stand to reason** be clear to all sensible people

stand by *phr v* **1** *vt* remain loyal to **2** *vt* keep (a promise, agreement, etc.) **3** *vi* be present or near **4** *vi* remain inactive when action is needed **5** *vi* wait in readiness

stand down *phr vi* leave the witness box in court

stand for *phr vt* **1** represent; mean: *GB stands for Great Britain.* **2** have as a principle **3** accept without complaining

stand in *phr vi* take the place of the usual person for a time

stand out *phr vi* **1** have an easily-seen shape, color, etc. **2** be clearly the best

stand up *phr vt* **1** remain in good condition in spite of: *Will it stand up to continuous use?* **2** be accepted as true: *The charges will never stand up in court.* **3** fail to meet (someone, esp. of the opposite sex) as arranged

stand up for *phr vt* defend; support

stand² *n* **1** place for selling or showing things **2** piece of furniture for putting things on: *a hatstand* **3** building with an open front for watchers at a sports ground **4** raised stage: *the judge's stand* **5** strong effort of defense **6** place from which people called to a court speak; WITNESS STAND – see also ONE-NIGHT STAND

stan·dard /ˈstændərd/ *n* **1** level of quality that is considered proper or acceptable **2** something fixed as a rule for measuring weight, value, etc. **3** ceremonial flag ♦ *adj* of the usual kind; ordinary ~ize *vt* make all the same in accordance with a single STANDARD (2) –ization /ˌstændərdəˈzeɪʃən/ *n* [U]

standard of liv·ing /ˌ··· · ˈ··/ *n* degree of wealth and comfort in daily life that a person, country, etc., has

standard time /ˈ··· ·/ *n* [U] time used in the US from autumn to spring, one hour earlier than DAYLIGHT (SAVING) TIME

stand·by /ˈstændbaɪ/ *n* **1** one kept ready for use **2 on standby: a** ready for action **b** able to travel, esp. in a plane, only if there is a seat no one else wants

stand-in /ˈ· ·/ *n* person who takes the place or job of someone else for a time

stand·ing /ˈstændɪŋ/ *n* [U] **1** rank,

esp. based on experience or respect **2** continuance: *a friend of long standing* (= who has been a friend for a long time) ♦ *adj* continuing in use or force: *a standing invitation*

standing com·mit·tee /ˌ•• •ˌ••/ *n* permanent committee as of a LEGIS-LATURE

standing or·der /ˌ•• '••/ *n* order or instruction always in effect

stand·off·ish /ˌstænd'ɒfɪʃ/ *adj* rather unfriendly ~**ly** *adv* ~**ness** *n* [U]

stand·point /'stændpɔɪnt/ *n* POINT OF VIEW

stand·still /'stændˌstɪl/ *n* [S] condition of no movement; stop

stank /stæŋk/ *v past t.* of STINK

stan·za /'stænzə/ *n* division of a poem

sta·ple[1] /'steɪpəl/ *n* piece of wire put through sheets of paper and bent to fasten them together ♦ *vt* fasten with staples **stapler** *n*

staple[2] *adj* **1** used all the time; usual; ordinary **2** main product: *a staple among American products*

star /stɑr/ *n* **1** very large mass of burning gas in space, seen as a small bright spot in the night sky **2** figure with 5 or more points, used as a sign of something: *a five star hotel* (= a very good hotel) **3** heavenly body regarded as determining one's fate: *born under an unlucky star* **4** famous performer: *a movie star* **stars in one's eyes** an unthinking feeling that some wonderful thing is really possible **6 see stars** see flashes of light, esp. as a result of being hit on the head ♦ *v* -**rr**- **1** *vi/t* appear or have as a main character: *a film starring Charlie Chaplin* **2** *vt* mark with STARS (2) ~**ry** *adj* filled with stars

star·board /'stɑrbərd/ *n* [U] right side of a ship or aircraft for a person inside it facing the front

starch /stɑrtʃ/ *n* [U] **1** white tasteless substance that is an important part of foods such as grain and potatoes **2** substance for making cloth stiff *vt* stiffen with STARCH (2) ~**y** *adj* **1** full of, or like, STARCH **2** stiffly correct and formal –**ily** *adv*

star·dom /'stɑrdəm/ *n* [U] state of being a famous performer

stare /steər/ *vi* look for a long time with great attention ♦ *n* long steady look

stare down *vt* look at someone till they turn away

star·fish /'stɑrˌfɪʃ/ *n* flat sea animal with 5 arms forming a star shape

stark /stɑrk/ *adj* **1** hard, bare, or severe in appearance **2** complete: *stark terror* ♦ *adv* completely: *stark naked* | *stark raving mad* (= completely crazy)

star·let /'stɑrlɪt/ *n* young actress hoping to become famous

star·ling /'stɑrlɪŋ/ *n* common green-black European bird

starry-eyed /ˌ•• '•◂/ *adj* full of unreasonable hopes

Stars and Stripes /ˌ•• '•/ *n* [the+S] the flag of the US

star-stud·ded /ˌ• '••/ *adj* filled with famous performers

start[1] /stɑrt/ *v* **1** *vi/t* begin **2** *vi/t* (cause to) come into existence: *How did the trouble start?* **3** *vi/t* (cause to) begin operation: *The car won't start.* **4** *vi* begin a journey **5** *vi* make a sudden sharp movement, esp. from surprise **6 start something** cause trouble ~**er** *n* **1** person, etc., in a race or match at the start **2** person who gives the signal for a race to begin **3** instrument for starting a machine **4** first part of a meal **5 for starters** first of all

start[2] *n* **1** [C] beginning of activity **2** [*the*+S] first part or moments **3** [C] place of starting **4** [C;U] amount by which one is ahead of another **5** [C] sudden sharp movement – see also FLYING START, HEAD START

star·tle /'stɑrtl/ *vt* give a sudden slight shock to

starve /stɑrv/ *vi/t* **1** (cause to) suffer from great hunger **2** (cause to) not have enough: *starved of affection/ funds* **starvation** /stɑr'veɪʃən/ *n* [U]

star wars /'• ˌ•/ *n* [U] *infml* SDI

stash /stæʃ/ *vt infml* store secretly; hide ♦ **stash** *n*

state[1] /steɪt/ *n* **1** [C] particular way of being; condition: *the current state of our economy* **2** [C] *infml* a very nervous, anxious condition: *Don't get in(to) such a state.* **3** [C;U] government or political organization of a country: *industry controlled by the state* | *state secrets* **4** [C] nation; country **5** [C] area within a nation that governs itself: *the states of the US* **6** [U] official grandness and ceremony ~**less** *adj* belonging to no country ~**lessness** *n* [U] ~**ly** *adj* **1** formal; ceremonious **2** grand in style or size ~**liness** *n* [U]

state[2] *vt* say or mention, esp. formally or in advance

State De·part·ment /'• •ˌ••/ *n* [*the*] the American government department which deals with foreign affairs

state house /'• ˌ•/ *n* building for the state government

state·ment /'steɪtmənt/ *n* **1** (formal) written or spoken declaration **2** list showing money paid, received, etc.

state-of-the-art /ˌ•••• '•◂/ *adj* using the most modern methods or materials

state·room /ˈsteʸtruːm, -rʊm/ n passenger's private room on a ship

state's at·tor·ney /ˌ‧ ‧·‧/ n lawyer who represents the government in court

state's ev·i·dence /ˌ‧ ‧···/ n story of a crime told by one of the criminals against the other criminals

state·side /ˈsteʸtsaɪd/ adj in or toward the US

state troop·er /ˌ‧ ‧··/ n police for the state, usu. seen on HIGHWAYS

state u·ni·ver·si·ty /ˌ‧·‧‧·‧···/ n public university with money from the state

state·wide /ˈsteʸtwaɪd/ adj in all parts of a state: a statewide ban on the sale of alcohol

States /steʸts/ [the] infml the US

states·man /ˈsteʸtsmən/ n –men /-mən/ respected political or government leader – see also ELDER STATESMAN ~ship n [U]

stat·ic /ˈstætɪk/ adj 1 not moving or changing 2 of or being electricity that collects on the surface of objects ♦ n [U] electrical noise spoiling radio or television signals

sta·tion /ˈsteʸʃən/ n 1 (building at) a place where the stated public vehicles regularly stop: a bus station 2 building for the stated service or activity: a polling station (= where people vote) 3 broadcasting company or apparatus 4 fml one's position in life; social rank: She married beneath her station. – see also SPACE STATION ♦ vt put (esp. a person) into a certain place for esp. military duty

sta·tion·a·ry /ˈsteʸʃəˌneriʸ/ adj not moving

station break /ˈ·· ‧·/ n pause on the radio or television to give the station's name

sta·tion·er /ˈsteʸʃənər/ n seller of stationery

sta·tion·er·y /ˈsteʸʃəˌneriʸ/ n [U] paper, pens, pencils, envelopes, etc.

sta·tion·mas·ter /ˈsteʸʃənˌmæstər/ n person in charge of a train station

station wag·on /ˈ·· ‧··/ n car with a door at the back and folding back seats

sta·tis·tics /stəˈtɪstɪks/ n 1 [P] numbers which represent facts or measurements 2 [U] science that deals with and explains these –**tical** adj –**tically** /-kliʸ/ adv **statistician** /ˌstætəˈstɪʃən/ n person who works with statistics

stat·ue /ˈstætʃuʷ/ n (large) stone or metal likeness of a person, animal, etc.

stat·u·esque /ˌstætʃuʷˈɛsk/ adj like a statue in formal still beauty

stat·u·ette /ˌstætʃuʷˈɛt/ n small statue that goes on a table or shelf

stat·ure /ˈstætʃər/ n [C;U] fml 1 degree to which someone is regarded as important or worthy of admiration 2 person's height

sta·tus /ˈsteʸtəs, ˈstæ-/ n 1 [C;U] rank or condition in relation to others 2 [U] high social position 3 [C] state of affairs at a particular time

status quo /ˌsteʸtəs ˈkwoʷ, ˌstæ-/ n existing state of affairs

stat·ute /ˈstætʃuʷt/ n fml law

stat·u·to·ry /ˈstætʃəˌtoriʸ, -ˌtoʷriʸ/ adj fixed or controlled by law

staunch /stɔntʃ, stɑntʃ/ adj dependably loyal; firm ~**ly** adv ~**ness** n [U]

stave /steʸv/ v **stave off** phr vt keep away: just enough food to stave off hunger

stay /steʸ/ vi 1 remain in a place rather than leave 2 continue to be; remain: trying to stay healthy 3 live in a place for a while: staying at a hotel 4 **stay put** not move 5 **stay the course** last or continue for the whole length of ♦ n 1 period of living in a place 2 law stopping or delay: a stay of execution (= not carrying out a punishment)

stay on phr vt remain after the usual leaving time

staying pow·er /ˈ·· ‧··/ n [U] STAMINA

St Ber·nard /ˌseʸnt bərˈnɑrd/ n large strong Swiss dog used in mountain RESCUE

STD /ˌɛs tiʸ ˈdiʸ/ n sexually transmitted disease; a disease passed on by sexual activity: an STD clinic

stead /stɛd/ n **in someone's stead** fml instead of someone

stead·fast /ˈstɛdfæst/ adj fml or lit 1 firmly loyal 2 not moving or movable ~**ly** adv ~**ness** n [U]

stead·y /ˈstɛdiʸ/ adj 1 firm; not shaking: a steady hand 2 not varying wildly; regular: a steady speed 3 not likely to change: a steady job 4 dependable ♦ vi/t make or become steady –**ily** adv –**iness** n [U]

steak /steʸk/ n [C;U] flat piece of meat, esp. BEEF or FISH

steal /stiʸl/ v stole /stoʷl/, stolen /ˈstoʷlən/ 1 vi/t take (what belongs to someone else) without permission 2 vi move secretly or quietly 3 vt take secretly or improperly: stealing a look at someone 4 **steal the show** get all the attention and praise expected by someone else, at a show or other event ♦ n [S] infml something for sale very cheaply

stealth /stɛlθ/ n [U] acting quietly and secretly or unseen ~**y** adj

steam /stiʸm/ n [U] 1 water gas produced by boiling 2 power produced by steam under pressure:

The ship sailed full steam ahead. (= at its fastest speed) **3 let off steam** get rid of anger or unwanted ENERGY **4 under one's/its own steam** by one's/its own power or effort ♦ *v* **1** *vi* give off steam **2** *vi* travel by steam power **3** *vt* cook with steam **4** *vt* use steam on: *He steamed the letter open.* **~·er** *n* **1** ship driven by steam power **2** container for cooking food with steam **~·y** *adj* **1** of or containing steam **2** *infml* EROTIC

steam up *phr vi/t* **1** cover or become covered with a mist of cooling water **2** *infml* make angry or excited **steamed-up** *adj infml* excited and angry

steam·roll /ˈstiᵛmroˑⁱl/ *vt* force in spite of all opposition: *He was steamrollered into signing the agreement.*

steam·roll·er /ˈstiᵛmˌroˑlər/ *n* vehicle with heavy metal wheels for making new road surfaces flat

steam·ship /ˈstiᵛmˌʃɪp/ *n* a large non-naval ship driven by steam power

steed /stiᵛd/ *n lit* horse

steel /stiᵛl/ *n* [U] hard strong metal made from iron ♦ *vt* make (esp. oneself) unfeeling or determined **~·y** *adj* like steel in color or hardness

steel band /ˈ·ˌ·/ *n* West Indian band playing drums cut from metal oil BARRELS

steep¹ /stiᵛp/ *adj* **1** rising or falling at a large angle **2** (esp. of a price) too high **~·ly** *adv* **~·ness** *n* [U]

steep² *vt* **1** keep in liquid **2 steeped in** thoroughly filled or familiar with

stee·ple /ˈstiᵛpəl/ *n* high pointed church tower

stee·ple·chase /ˈstiᵛpəlˌtʃeᵛs/ *n* long race with fences to jump over

stee·ple·jack /ˈstiᵛpəlˌdʒæk/ *n* person who repairs towers, tall chimneys, etc.

steer¹ /stɪər/ *vt* **1** direct the course of (esp. a boat or road vehicle) **2 steer clear (of)** keep away (from); avoid

steer² *n* young male animal of the cattle family with its sex organs removed

steer·age /ˈstɪərɪdʒ/ *n* [U] part of a passenger ship for those with the cheapest tickets

steering wheel /ˈ··ˌ·/ *n* wheel turned to make a vehicle go left or right

stel·lar /ˈstɛlər/ *adj* of the stars

stem¹ /stɛm/ *n* **1** part of a plant on which leaves or smaller branches grow **2** narrow upright support: *the stem of a wineglass*

stem² *vt* **-mm-** stop (the flow of)

stem from *phr vt* result from

stench /stɛntʃ/ *n* very strong bad smell

sten·cil /ˈstɛnsəl/ *n* **1** card, etc., with patterns or letters cut in it **2** mark made by putting paint, etc., through the holes in this onto paper, etc. ♦ *vt* **-l-** make (a copy of) with a stencil

ste·nog·ra·phy /stəˈnɑgrəfiᵛ/ *n* [U] SHORTHAND **-pher** *n*

sten·to·ri·an /stɛnˈtɔriᵛən, -ˈtoᵛr-/ *adj fml* (of the voice) very loud

step¹ /stɛp/ *n* **1** act of moving by raising one foot and bringing it down somewhere else **2** the sound this makes **3** short distance: *It's just a step away from here.* **4** flat edge, esp. in a set one above the other, on which the foot is placed for going up or down **5** act, esp. in a set of actions, which should produce a certain result: *We must take steps* (= take action) *to improve matters.* **6** movement of the feet in dancing **7 in/out of step: a** moving/not moving the feet at the same time as others in marching **b** in/not in accordance or agreement with others **8 step by step** gradually **9 watch one's step** behave or act carefully

step² *vi* **-pp-** **1** go by putting one foot usu. in front of the other **2** bring the foot down **3 step on it!** go faster **4 step on someone's toes a** annoy someone by rudeness **b** cause someone to act by being pushy **5 step out of line** act differently from others or from what is expected

step down/aside *phr vi* leave one's job, position, etc.

step in *phr vi* INTERVENE

step up *phr vt* increase

step- see WORD BEGINNINGS, p. 498

step·lad·der /ˈstɛpˌlædər/ *n* folding ladder with 2 parts joined at the top

steppes /stɛps/ *n* [P] large treeless area in the former USSR and parts of Asia

stepping-stone /ˈ··ˌ·/ *n* **1** any of a row of large stones for walking across a stream on **2** way of improvement or getting ahead

ster·e·o /ˈstɛriᵛˌoᵛ, ˈstiᵛər-/ *adj* using a system of sound recording in which the sound comes from 2 different places ♦ *n* **-os 1** [C] stereo record player **2** [U] stereo sound – see also PERSONAL STEREO

ster·e·o·phon·ic /ˌstɛriᵛəˈfɑnɪk◂, ˌstiᵛər-/ *adj fml* stereo

ster·e·o·type /ˈstɛriᵛəˌtaɪp, ˈstiᵛər-/ *n usu. derog* fixed set of ideas about what a particular type of person or thing is like ♦ *vt derog* treat as an example of a fixed general type **-typical** /ˌstɛriᵛəˈtɪpɪkəl, ˌstiᵛər-/ *adj*

ster·ile /ˈstɛrəl/ *adj* **1** which cannot

produce young **2** free from all (harmful) bacteria, etc. **3** lacking new thought, imagination, etc. **4** (of land) not producing crops **–ility** /stə'rɪlət̬iʸ/ n [U] **–ilize** /'sterəlaɪz/ vt make STERILE (1,2) **–ilization** /ˌsterələ'zeʸʃən/ n [U]

ster·ling /'stɜrlɪŋ/ n [U] British money ♦ adj **1** (esp. of silver) of standard value **2** of the highest standard, esp. in being loyal and brave

stern¹ /stɜrn/ n severe and serious: *a stern look/reprimand* **~ly** adv **~ness** n [U]

stern² n back part of a ship

ste·roid /'stɪərɔɪd, 'ste–/ n chemical that has a strong effect on the workings of the body

steth·o·scope /'steθəˌskoʷp/ n tube with which doctors can listen to people's hearts beating

Stet·son /'stetsən/ n tdmk hat with a wide BRIM worn by COWBOYS

ste·ve·dore /'stiʸvəˌdɔr, -ˌdoʷr/ n person who loads and unloads ships

stew /stuʷ, styuʷ/ vi/t cook slowly and gently in liquid ♦ n **1** [C;U] dish of stewed meat and vegetables **2** [S] confused anxious state of mind

stew·ard /'stuʷərd, 'styuʷ–/ n **1 stewardess** /-dɪs/ fem. — n person who serves passengers on a ship, plane, etc. **2** person in charge of HOUSEHOLD duties – see also SHOP STEWARD

stick¹ /stɪk/ n **1** small thin piece of wood **2** thin wooden or metal rod used for support while walking, for hitting things, etc. **3** thin rod of any material: *a stick of chalk/celery* **4 get the wrong end of the stick** infml misunderstand – see also STICKS

stick² v stuck /stʌk/ **1** vt push: *She stuck her fork into the meat.* **2** vi/t fasten or be fastened with glue or a similar substance **3** vi/t (cause to) become fixed in position: *He got his finger stuck in the hole.* **4** vt infml put: *Stick your coat down over there.* **~er** n **1** LABEL with a message or picture, which can be stuck to things **2** infml determined person

stick around phr vi not go away

stick at phr vt continue to work hard at

stick by phr vt continue to support

stick out phr v **1** vi/t (cause to) come out beyond a surface: *His ears stick out.* **2** vt continue to the end of (something difficult) **3 stick one's neck out** infml take a risk

stick out for phr vt **1** refuse to accept less than

stick to phr vt **1** refuse to leave or change: *stick to one's decision* **2 stick to one's guns** infml continue to express one's beliefs or carry on

a course of action in spite of attacks

stick together phr vi (of 2 or more people) stay loyal to each other

stick up for phr vt defend (someone) by words or actions

stick with phr vt **1** stay close to **2 stick with it** infml continue in spite of difficulties

stick-in-the-mud /'· ··· ˌ·/ n person who will not change or accept new things

stick·ler /'stɪklər/ n person who demands the stated quality: *a stickler for punctuality*

sticks /stɪks/ n [the+P] infml a country area far from modern life

stick shift /'· ·/ n GEAR shift

stick-up /'· ·/ n infml robbery carried out by threatening with a gun

stick·y /'stɪkiʸ/ adj **1** like or covered with glue or a similar substance **2** difficult; awkward: *a sticky situation* **3 come to/meet a sticky end** (suffer) ruin, death, etc. **–iness** n [U]

stiff /stɪf/ adj **1** not easily bent or changed in shape **2** formal; not friendly **3** strong, esp. in alcohol **4** difficult; severe: *stiff competition* ♦ adv extremely: *I was scared stiff.* ♦ n sl **1** ordinary working person **2** dead body **~ly** adv **~en** vi/t make or become stiff **~ness** n [U]

stiff-necked /ˌ· '·◄/ adj proudly OBSTINATE

stiff upper lip /ˌ· ·· '·/ n [S] ability to accept bad luck or unpleasant events without appearing upset

sti·fle /'staɪfəl/ v **1** vi/t (cause to) be unable to breathe properly **2** vt keep from happening: *stifling a yawn*

stig·ma /'stɪgmə/ n feeling of shame **~tize** vt describe very disapprovingly

stig·ma·ta /'stɪgmətə, stɪg'mɑt̬ə/ n [P] (marks like) the nail marks on Christ's body

sti·let·to /stə'let̬oʷ/ n **-tos** small thin DAGGER

stiletto heel /·ˌ··· '·/ n high thin heel of a woman's shoe

still¹ /stɪl/ adv **1** (even) up to this/that moment: *He's still here.* **2** in spite of that: *It's raining. Still, we must go out.* **3** even: *a still greater problem* **4** yet: *He gave still another reason.*

still² adj **1** not moving **2** without wind **3** silent; calm **4** (of a drink) not containing gas **~ness** n [U]

still³ n photograph of a scene from a (cinema) film

still⁴ n apparatus for making alcohol

still·birth /'stɪlbɜrθ, ˌstɪl'bɜrθ/ n child born dead

still·born /'stɪlbɔrn, ˌstɪl'bɔrn◄/ adj born dead

still life /ˌ· ˈ·◂/ n **still lifes** [C;U] painting of objects, esp. flowers and fruit

stilt /stɪlt/ n either of a pair of poles for walking around on high above the ground

stilt·ed /ˈstɪltɪd/ adj very formal and unnatural

stim·u·late /ˈstɪmyəˌleʸt/ vt **1** cause to become more active, grow faster, etc. **2** fml excite (the body or mind) **–lant** n **1** drug which gives one more power to be active **2** stimulus **–lation** /ˌstɪmyəˈleʸʃən/ n [U]

stim·u·lus /ˈstɪmyələs/ n **–li** /-laɪ/ something that causes activity

sting /stɪŋ/ vi/t **stung** /stʌŋ/ **1** have, use, or prick with a STING (1) **2** (cause to) feel sharp pain: (fig.) stinging criticism ♦ n **1** organ used by certain insects and plants for attack or protection, producing pain **2** wound caused by this **3** sharp pain

stin·gy /ˈstɪndʒiʸ/ adj infml ungenerous; **–gily** adv

stink /stɪŋk/ vi **stank** /stæŋk/, **stunk** /stʌŋk/ **1** give off a strong bad smell **2** infml be very unpleasant or bad: Your plan stinks. ♦ n strong bad smell

stink out phr vt fill with a stink

stint /stɪnt/ n limited or fixed amount of time, shared work, etc. ♦ vt give too small an amount (of)

sti·pend /ˈstaɪpend/ n fixed or regular pay, esp. for a SCHOLARSHIP

sti·pen·di·a·ry /staɪˈpendiʸˌeriʸ/ adj receiving regular payment for professional services

stip·ple /ˈstɪpəl/ vt draw or paint (on) with dots instead of lines **–pling** n [U]

stip·u·late /ˈstɪpyəˌleʸt/ vt state as a necessary condition **–lation** /ˌstɪpyəˈleʸʃən/ n [C;U] statement of conditions

stir /stɜr/ v **–rr– 1** vt move around and mix (esp. liquid) with a spoon, etc. **2** vi/t make or cause a slight movement (in): She stirred in her sleep. **3** vt excite: a stirring tale of adventure **4** vi infml cause trouble between others ♦ n **1** [C] act of stirring **2** [S] (public) excitement

stir up phr vt **1** cause (trouble) **2** upset

stir·rup /ˈstɜrəp, ˈstɪrəp/ n metal piece shaped like a D, for a rider's foot to go in

stitch /stɪtʃ/ n **1** [C] amount of thread put with a needle through cloth or through skin to close a wound **2** [C] single turn of the yarn around the needle in knitting (KNIT) **3** [S] sharp pain in the side caused by running **4** [S] infml clothes: He didn't have a stitch on. (= was

completely NAKED) **5 in stitches** laughing helplessly ♦ vi/t sew

stock /stak/ n **1** [C] supply: a large stock of food **2** [C;U] (supply of) goods for sale: Do you have any blue shirts in stock? **3** [C;U] a money lent to a government or company **b** ownership of a company, divided into shares: stocks and bonds **4** [U] liquid made from meat, bones, etc., used in cooking **5** [U] farm animals, esp. cattle **6** [C;U] a family line, of the stated sort: She comes from farming/good stock. **7 take stock (of)** consider a situation carefully so as to make a decision ♦ vt keep supplies of ♦ adj commonly used, esp. without much meaning: stock excuses

stock up phr vi provide oneself with a full store of goods

stock·ade /staˈkeʸd/ n strong fence for defense

stock·brok·er /ˈstakˌbroʷkər/ n someone who buys and sells STOCKs (3) for others

stock ex·change /ˈ· ·ˌ·/ n place where STOCKs (3) are bought and sold

stock·hold·er /ˈstakˌhoʷldər/ n person who owns STOCK (3) in a company

stock·ing /ˈstakɪŋ/ n closely fitting garment for a woman's foot and leg

stock-in-trade /ˌ· · ˈ·/ n [U] things habitually used: A pleasant manner is part of a politician's stock-in-trade.

stock·man /ˈstakmən/ n **–men** /-mən/ man who looks after farm animals

stock mar·ket /ˈ· ˌ··/ n STOCK EXCHANGE

stock·pile /ˈstakpaɪl/ n large store for future use ♦ vt make a stockpile of

stock·tak·ing /ˈstakˌteʸkɪŋ/ n [U] examining a situation to understand it

stock·y /ˈstakiʸ/ adj thick, short, and strong **–ily** adv **–iness** n [U]

stodg·y /ˈstadʒiʸ/ adj uninteresting and difficult

sto·ic /ˈstoʷɪk/ n person who remains calm and uncomplaining **~al** adj patient when suffering, like a stoic **~ally** /-kliʸ/ adv **~ism** /-ˌsɪzəm/ n [U] stoical behavior

stoke /stoʷk/ vt fill (an enclosed fire) with FUEL **stoker** n

stole¹ /stoʷl/ v past t. of STEAL

stole² n long piece of material worn over the shoulders

sto·len /ˈstoʷlən/ v past p. of STEAL

stol·id /ˈstalɪd/ adj showing no excitement even when strong feelings might be expected

stom·ach /ˈstʌmək/ n **1** [C] baglike organ in the body where food is digested (DIGEST¹) **2** [C] front part of the body below the chest **3** [S;U] desire; liking: *He's got no stomach for a fight.* ◆ *vt* accept without displeasure; bear

stomach pump /'··· ·/ *n* apparatus for drawing the contents out of the stomach

stomp /stamp, stɔmp/ *vi* walk heavily

stone /stoʷn/ *n* **1** [C] fairly large piece of rock **2** [U] rock **3** [C] piece of hard material formed in an organ of the body ◆ *vt* throw stones at **stoned** *adj infml* under the influence of drugs **stony** *adj* **1** containing or covered with stones **2** cruel

stone- see WORD-BEGINNINGS p. 498

Stone Age /'· ·/ *n* earliest time in human history, when stone tools were used

stone broke /ˌ· '·/ *adj infml* having no money at all

stone·ma·son /'stoʷnˌmeʸsən/ *n* person who cuts stone for building

stone's throw /'· ·/ *n* [S] short distance

stone·wall /ˌstoʷn'wɔl/ *vi/t* refuse to obey

stone·work /'stoʷnwɜrk/ *n* [U] parts of a building made of stone

stood /stʊd/ *v past t. and p. of* STAND

stooge /stuʷdʒ/ *n* person who habitually does what another wants

stool /stuʷl/ *n* seat without back or arm supports

stool·pi·geon /'stuʷlˌpɪdʒɪn/ *n infml* person who helps the police to trap another

stoop /stuʷp/ *vt* **1** bend the upper body forwards and down **2** stand like this habitually ◆ *n* **1** [S] habitual stooping position **2** [C] PORCH

stoop to *phr vt* fall to a low standard of behavior by allowing oneself to do (something)

stop¹ /stɑp/ *v* –pp- **1** *vi/t* (cause to) no longer be moving or operating **2** *vi/t* (cause to) end: *The rain has stopped.* **3** *vt* prevent **4** *vi* pause **5** *vt* block: *The pipe's stopped up.* **6** *vt* stop from being given or paid: *stop a check* ~ **per** *n* object for closing a bottle

stop in *phr vi* visit

stop off *phr vi* make a short visit to a place while making a journey elsewhere

stop over *phr vi* make a short stay before continuing a journey

stop² *n* **1** act of stopping or the state of being stopped **2** BUS STOP **3** **pull all the stops out** do everything possible to complete an action

4 put a stop to stop (esp. an undesirable activity)

stop·cock /'stɑpkɑk/ *n* turnable apparatus for controlling the flow of water in a pipe

stop·gap /'stɑpgæp/ *n* something that fills a need for a time

stop·light /'stɑplaɪt/ *n* traffic light

stop·o·ver /'stɑpˌoʷvər/ *n* short stay between parts of a journey

stop·page /'stɑpɪdʒ/ *n* **1** [C] stopping, esp. of work **2** [C;U] blocked state

stop press /ˌ· '·◂/ *n* [the+S] late news put into a paper

stop·watch /'stɑpwɑtʃ/ *n* watch that can be started and stopped to measure periods exactly

stor·age /'stɔrɪdʒ, 'stoʷrɪdʒ/ *n* [U] (price and place for) storing

store /stɔr, stoʷr/ *vt* **1** make and keep a supply of for future use **2** keep in a special place while not in use ◆ *n* **1** building or room where goods are sold **2** supply for future use **3** place for keeping things **4 in store: a** being stored **b** about to happen: *There's trouble in store.* **6 set** ... **store by** feel to be of (the stated amount of) importance **stores** *n* [S;P] (building or room containing) military or naval goods and food

store·front /'stɔrfrʌnt, 'stoʷr-/ *n* building with a store facing the street at ground level

stork /stɔrk/ *n* large bird with a long beak, neck, and legs

storm /stɔrm/ *n* **1** rough weather condition with rain, strong wind, etc. **2** sudden violent show of feeling: *a storm of protest* **3 take by storm: a** conquer by a sudden violent attack **b** win great approval from (those who watch a performance) ◆ *v* **1** *vt* attack (a place) with sudden violence **2** *vi* go angrily ~ **y** *adj*

sto·ry¹ /'stɔriʸ, 'stoʷriʸ/ *n* **1** account of events, real or imagined **2** news article **3** lie: *Have you been telling stories again?* **4 the same old story** the usual excuse or difficulty

story² *n* floor or level in a building

sto·ry·book /'stɔriʸbʊk, 'stoʷr-/ *adj* as perfectly happy as in a fairy story for children

story line /'··· ·/ *n* events in a film, book, or play

stout /staʊt/ *adj* **1** rather fat **2** brave and determined **3** strong and thick ◆ *n* [U] strong dark beer ~ **ly** *adv* ~ **ness** *n* [U]

stout·heart·ed /ˌstaʊt'hɑrtɪd◂/ *adj lit* brave

stove /stoʷv/ *n* enclosed apparatus that can be heated for cooking or to provide warmth

stow /stoʷ/ vt put away or store, esp. on a ship

stow away phr vi hide on a ship or plane in order to make a free journey

stow·a·way /ˈstoʷəˌweʸ/ n person who stows away

strad·dle /ˈstrædl/ vt 1 have one's legs on either side of 2 be, land, etc., on either side of (something), rather than in the middle

strag·gle /ˈstrægəl/ vi move, grow, or spread untidily –**gler** n one who is behind a main group –**gly** adj growing or lying untidily

straight¹ /streʸt/ adj 1 not bent or curved 2 level or upright 3 neat; tidy 4 honest, open, and truthful 5 (of the face) with a serious expression 6 (of alcohol) without added water 7 correct: set the record straight 8 sl HETEROSEXUAL –**ness** n [U]

straight² adv 1 in a straight line 2 directly (and without delay): Get straight to the point. 3 clearly: I can't think straight. 4 **go straight** leave a life of crime

straight and nar·row /ˌ· · ˈ··/ n [U] honest life

straight·a·way /ˌstreʸtəˌweʸ/ adv at once ♦ n straight part, esp. on a race track

straight·en /ˈstreʸtn/ vt (cause to) become straight, level, or tidy

straighten out phr vt remove (the confusions or difficulties) in: straighten out one's business affairs

straighten up phr vi 1 get up from a bent position 2 improve one's bad behavior

straight·for·ward /ˌstreʸtˈfɔrwərd/ adj 1 honest and open, without hidden meanings 2 simple –**ly** adv –**ness** n [U]

strain¹ /streʸn/ v 1 vt damage (a body part) through too much effort or pressure 2 vi make (too) great efforts 3 vt separate (a liquid and solid) by pouring through esp. a strainer 4 vt force beyond acceptable or believable limits: straining the truth ♦ n [C;U] 1 (force causing) the condition of being tightly stretched 2 troubling influence 3 damage caused by straining a body part –**ed** adj 1 not natural in behavior; unfriendly 2 tired or nervous –**er** n instrument with a net for STRAINing (3) things

strain² n 1 breed or type of plant or animal 2 lit tune

strait /streʸt/ also **straits** pl. — n narrow water passage between 2 areas of land **straits** n [P] difficult situation: in dire straits

strait·ened /ˈstreʸtnd/ adj fml difficult because lacking money

strait·jack·et /ˈstreʸtˌdʒækɪt/ n 1 garment for a violently crazy person that prevents movement 2 something preventing free development

strait·laced /ˌstreʸtˈleʸstˈ/ adj having severe, old-fashioned ideas about morals

strand /strænd/ n single thin thread, wire, etc.

strand·ed /ˈstrændɪd/ adj in a helpless position, unable to get away

strange /streʸndʒ/ adj 1 unusual; surprising 2 unfamiliar ~**ly** adv ~**ness** n [U]

strang·er /ˈstreʸndʒər/ n 1 unfamiliar person 2 person in an unfamiliar place

stran·gle /ˈstræŋgəl/ vt 1 kill by pressing the throat to stop breathing 2 stop the proper development of –**gler** n –**gulation** /ˌstræŋgyəˈleʸʃən/ n [U]

stran·gle·hold /ˈstræŋgəlˌhoʷld/ n strong control which prevents action

strap /stræp/ n strong narrow band used as a fastening or support: a luggage strap ♦ vt –**pp**- fasten with straps

strap·ping /ˈstræpɪŋ/ adj big and strong

stra·ta /ˈstreʸtə, ˈstrætə, ˈstrɑtə/ n pl. of STRATUM

strat·a·gem /ˈstrætədʒəm/ n trick or plan for deceiving or gaining an advantage

stra·te·gic /strəˈtiʸdʒɪk/ adj 1 part of a plan, esp. in war 2 right for a purpose –**ally** /-kliʸ/ adv

strat·e·gist /ˈstrætədʒɪst/ n person skilled in (military) planning

strat·e·gy /ˈstrætədʒiʸ/ n 1 [U] skillful (military) planning 2 [C] particular plan for winning success

strat·i·fy /ˈstrætəˌfaɪ/ vt arrange in separate levels or STRATA –**fication** /ˌstrætəfəˈkeʸʃən/ n [C;U]

strat·os·phere /ˈstrætəˌsfɪər/ n outer air surrounding the Earth, starting at about 15 miles above the Earth

stra·tum /ˈstreʸtəm, ˈstræ-, ˈstrɑ-/ n –**ta** /-tə/ 1 band of a particular rock 2 part of something thought of as divided into different levels

straw /strɔ/ n 1 [U] dried stems of grain plants, such as wheat 2 [C] single such stem 3 [C] thin tube for sucking up liquid – see also LAST STRAW

straw·ber·ry /ˈstrɔˌberiʸ, -bəriʸ/ n (plant with) a small red juicy fruit

straw·boss /ˈstrɔbɔs/ n person whose job is the same as those of the people he or she manages

straw man /ˌ· ˈ·/ n 1 person of weak

character **2** imaginary opponent whose arguments can easily be defeated

straw vote /ˌ· ˈ·/ n unofficial examination of opinions before an election, to see what the result is likely to be

stray /streɪ/ vi wander away ♦ n animal lost from its home ♦ adj **1** wandering; lost **2** single; not in a group

streak /striːk/ n **1** thin line or band, different from what surrounds it **2** bad quality of character: a stubborn streak **3** period marked by a particular quality: a lucky streak **4** like a streak (of lightning) very quickly ♦ v **1** vi move very fast **2** vt cover with streaks ~**y** adj marked with streaks

stream /striːm/ n **1** small river **2** something flowing: a stream of traffic | (fig.) a stream of abuse **3** go with/against the stream agree/ not agree with a general way of thinking, etc., in society **4** on stream in(to) production ♦ v **1** vi flow strongly **2** vi move in a continuous flowing mass **3** vi float in the air ~**er** n long narrow piece of paper for throwing

stream·line /ˈstriːmlaɪn/ vt **1** give a smooth shape which moves easily through water or air **2** make more simple and effective –**lined** adj

street /striːt/ n **1** road in a town **2** up/down one's street one's area of interest

street·car /ˈstriːtkɑr/ n usu. electric bus that runs on metal tracks set in the road

street-cred·i·bil·i·ty /ˌ· ··ˈ···/ also **street-cred** /ˈstriːt kred/ infml n [U] popular acceptance among young people

street gang /ˈ· ˌ·/ n group of young men who steal, fight, and kill in big cities

street peo·ple /ˈ· ˌ··/ n homeless people who live in the streets

street·wise /ˈstriːtwaɪz/ adj infml clever enough to succeed and live well in the hard world of the city streets

strength /streŋkθ, streŋθ/ n **1** [U] (degree of) being strong **2** [C] way in which something is good or effective: the strengths and weaknesses of the plan **3** [U] force measured in numbers: The police are at full strength. **4** on the strength of persuaded or influenced by ~**en** vi/t become or make stronger or stronger

stren·u·ous /ˈstrenjuʷəs/ adj **1** needing great effort **2** showing great activity: a strenuous denial ~**ly** adv ~**ness** n [U]

stress /stres/ n [C;U] **1** (worry resulting from) pressure caused by difficulties **2** force of weight caused by pressure **3** sense of special importance **4** degree of force put on a part of a word when spoken, or on a note in music: In 'under' the main stress is on 'un'. ♦ vt **1** mention strongly **2** put STRESS (4) on

stretch /stretʃ/ v **1** vi/t (cause to) become wider or longer **2** vi spread out: The forest stretched for miles. **3** vi be elastic **4** vi straighten one's limbs to full length: stretch out your arms **5** vt allow to go beyond exact limits: stretch a rule **6** stretch one's legs have a walk esp. after sitting for a long time ♦ n **1** [C] act of stretching **2** [U] elasticity **3** [C] long area of land or water **4** [C] continuous period: 14 hours at a stretch (= without stopping) **5** at full stretch using all one's powers ~**y** adj elastic

stretch·er /ˈstretʃər/ n covered frame for carrying a sick person

strew /struː/ vt strewed, strewn /struːⁿn/ or strewed esp. lit **1** scatter **2** lie scattered over

strick·en /ˈstrɪkən/ adj showing the effect of trouble, illness, etc.: grief-stricken

strict /strɪkt/ adj **1** severe in making people behave properly **2 a** exact: strict instructions **b** complete: in strict secrecy ~**ly** adv ~**ness** n [U]

stric·ture /ˈstrɪktʃər/ n fml expression of blame

stride /straɪd/ vi strode /stroʷd/, stridden /ˈstrɪdn/ walk with long steps ♦ n **1** long step **2** make strides improve or do well **3** take something in one's stride deal with a difficult situation easily and without complaint

stri·dent /ˈstraɪdnt/ adj with a hard sharp sound or voice ~**ly** adv ~**dency** n [U]

strife /straɪf/ n [U] trouble and quarreling between people

strike¹ /straɪk/ v struck /strʌk/ **1** vt hit sharply **2** vt make a (sudden) attack **3** vt harm suddenly: They were struck down with illness. **4** vt light (a match) **5** vi/t a make known (the time), esp. by the hitting of a bell: The clock struck 3. (= rang 3 times, for 3 o'clock) **b** (of time) be made known in this way **6** vi stop working because of disagreement **7** vt find; meet: strike oil/difficulties **8** vt have a particular effect on: Her behavior struck me as odd. | struck down with fear **9** vt come suddenly to mind **10** vt produce (a coin or similar object) **11** vt make (an agreement): strike a bargain/balance **12** strike a chord remind someone of something **13** strike a note of express (a need for): *The book strikes a warning note.* **14 strike it rich** find sudden wealth

strike off *phr vt* remove (someone or their name) from (an official list)

strike out *phr vt* **1** go purposefully in the stated direction **2 strike out on one's own** take up an independent life **3** CROSS **out**

strike up *phr vt* **1** begin playing or singing **2** start to make (a friend-ship)

strike² *n* **1** act or time of striking (STRIKE¹ (6)): *The workers are on strike.* **2** attack, esp. by aircraft **3** success in finding esp. a mineral in the earth: *an oil strike* **4** point against the BATTER³ in baseball — see also FIRST STRIKE, GENERAL STRIKE

strik·er /ˈstraɪkər/ *n* person on STRIKE² (1)

strik·ing /ˈstraɪkɪŋ/ *adj* very noticeable, esp. because beautiful or unusual ~**ly** *adv*

striking dis·tance /ˈ··ˌ··/ *n* within striking distance very close (to)

string¹ /strɪŋ/ *n* **1** [C;U] thin cord **2** [C] thin cord or wire stretched across a musical instrument to give sound: *a string of pearls* **4** [C] set of things, events, etc., following each other closely: *a whole string of complaints* **5 no strings attached** (esp. of an agreement) with no limiting conditions **6 pull strings** use secret influence **strings** *n* [P] all the (players of) VIOLINS, CELLOS, etc., in an ORCHESTRA ~**y** *adj* **1** (of food) full of unwanted threadlike parts **2** unpleasantly thin, so that the muscles show

string² *vt* strung /strʌŋ/ **1** put STRINGS¹ (2) on (a musical instrument or RACKET¹) **2** put with others onto a thread **3 highly strung** (of a person) very sensitive and easily excited **4 strung up** very excited, nervous, or worried

string along *phr v* **1** *vt* encourage the hopes of deceitfully **2** *vi/t* go (with someone else) for a time, esp. for convenience

string out *phr vt* spread out in a line

string up *phr vt* **1** hang high **2** kill by hanging

string bean /ˈ· ·/ *n* bean with a long eatable seed container

strin·gent /ˈstrɪndʒənt/ *adj* (esp. of rules, limits, etc.) severe ~**ly** *adv*

string·er /ˈstrɪŋər/ *n* reporter who works part of the time in a distant place

strip /strɪp/ *v* -**pp**- **1** *vt* remove (the covering or parts of) **2** *vi/t* undress, usu. completely ♦ *n* **1** narrow piece: *a strip of paper/land* **2** street with

stores, gas stations, restaurants, etc. on both sides ~**per** *n* **1** [C] STRIPTEASE performer **2** [C;U] tool or liquid for removing things: *paint stripper*

strip down *phr vt* remove the parts of (esp. an engine)

strip of *phr vt* take away (something of value) from

stripe /straɪp/ *n* **1** band of a different color **2** sign usu. shaped like a V worn on a uniform to show rank ~**striped** *adj* stripy *adj*

strip light·ing /ˈ· ˌ··/ [U] long lamps shaped like tubes

strip·ling /ˈstrɪplɪŋ/ *n lit* young man

stripped-down /ˈ· ˈ·/ *adj* with all unnecessary parts removed

strip·tease /ˈstrɪptiˈz, ˌstrɪpˈtiz/ *n* [U] removal of clothes by a person, performed as a show

strive /straɪv/ *vi* strove /stroʊv/ or strived, striven /ˈstrɪvən/ or strived *fml* or *lit* make a great effort

strode /stroʊd/ *v past t. of* STRIDE

stroke¹ /stroʊk/ *vt* pass the hand over gently **2** treat in a kind way, esp. to gain favor

stroke² *n* **1** hit, esp. with a weapon **2** act of stroking **3** line made by a single movement of a pen or brush **4** act of hitting a ball **5** (single movement or set of movements that is repeated in) a method of swimming **6** sudden bursting of a blood tube in the brain **7** unexpected piece (of luck) **8** sound of a clock striking: *on the stroke of* (= exactly at) *6 o'clock* **9 at a stroke** with one direct action

stroll /stroʊl/ *vi, n* (take) a slow walk for pleasure ~**er** *n* **1** person who strolls or is strolling **2** small chair on wheels for a child

strong /strɔŋ/ *adj* **1** having great power **2** not easily becoming broken, changed, destroyed, or ill **3** having a powerful effect on the mind or senses: *a strong smell* **4** (of a drink, drug, etc.) having a lot of the substance which gives taste, produces effect, etc.: *This coffee's too strong.* **5** having the stated number of members: *a club 50 strong* **6 (still) going strong** continuing with ENERGY, good health, etc. **7 strong on: a** good at doing **b** eager and active in dealing with ~**ly** *adv*

strong·box /ˈstrɔŋbɑks/ *n* firm lockable box for keeping valuable things in

strong·hold /ˈstrɔŋhoʊld/ *n* **1** fort **2** place where a particular activity is common

strong lan·guage /ˌ· ˈ··/ *n* [U] swearing; curses

strong point /ˈ· ·/ also strong suit — *n* something one is good at

stron·ti·um /ˈstrɑntʃiˈəm, -tiˈəm/ *n*

[U] soft metal, of which a harmful form (**strontium 90**) is given off by atomic explosions

strove /strəʊv/ v past t. of STRIVE

struck /strʌk/ v past t. and p. of STRIKE

struc·ture /ˈstrʌktʃər/ n 1 [C;U] way in which parts are formed into a whole 2 [C] large thing built ♦ vt arrange so that each part is properly related to others –**tural** adj –**turally** adv

strug·gle /ˈstrʌgəl/ vi 1 make violent movements, esp. in fighting 2 make a great effort ♦ n hard fight or effort

strum /strʌm/ vi/t –mm– play carelessly or informally on (esp. a GUITAR, BANJO, or other instrument with strings)

strung /strʌŋ/ v past t. and p. of STRING

strut[1] /strʌt/ n supporting rod in a structure

strut[2] vi –tt– walk proudly

strych·nine /ˈstrɪknaɪn, -niˑn/ n [U] poisonous drug

stub /stʌb/ n 1 short remaining part of esp. a pencil 2 part of a ticket returned to the user to show he has paid ♦ vt –bb– hit (one's toe) against something ~**by** adj short and thick: stubby fingers

stub out phr vt put out (a cigarette) by pressing

stub·ble /ˈstʌbəl/ n [U] 1 short growth of beard 2 remains of cut wheat –**bly** adj

stub·born /ˈstʌbərn/ adj 1 having a strong will; (unreasonably) determined 2 difficult to use, move, change, etc. ~**ly** adv ~**ness** n [U]

stuc·co /ˈstʌkoʊ/ n [U] PLASTER stuck (as decoration) onto walls

stuck[1] /stʌk/ v past t. and p. of STICK

stuck[2] adj 1 unable to go further because of difficulties 2 **stuck with** having to do or have, esp. unwillingly

stuck-up /ˌ·ˈ·◄/ adj infml too proud in manner

stud[1] /stʌd/ n 1 button-like fastener that can be removed, esp. for collars 2 nail with a large head ♦ vt –dd– cover (as if) with STUDs[1] (2)

stud[2] n 1 number of horses kept for breeding 2 [U] kind of POKER GAME 3 taboo man who has sex a lot and thinks he is very good at it

stu·dent /ˈstuˑdnt, ˈstyuˑ-/ n 1 person studying esp. at a high school, college or university 2 person with a stated interest: a student of life

stu·di·o /ˈstuˑdiˑˌoʊ, ˈstyuˑ-/ n 1 place where films, recordings, or broadcasts are made 2 room for a painter, photographer, etc. to work in

studio a·part·ment /ˌ···ˈ·ˌ··/ n very small one room apartment with kitchen and bathroom

stu·di·ous /ˈstuˑdiˑəs, ˈstyuˑ-/ adj 1 fond of studying 2 careful ~**ly** adv ~**ness** n [U]

stud·y /ˈstʌdiˑ/ n 1 [U] also **studies** pl. —act of studying 2 [C] thorough enquiry into a particular subject, esp. including a piece of writing on it 3 [C] room for working in; office 4 [C] drawing or painting of a detail: a study of a flower 5 [C] piece of music for practice ♦ v 1 vi/t spend time in learning 2 vt examine carefully **studied** adj carefully thought about or considered, esp. before being expressed: a studied remark

stuff /stʌf/ n 1 matter; material 2 one's possessions or the things needed to do something 3 **do one's stuff** show one's ability as expected 4 **know one's stuff** be good at what one is concerned with 5 **That's the stuff!** infml That's the right thing to do/say

stuff[2] v 1 fill 2 push so as to be inside 3 put STUFFINg (2) inside 4 fill the skin of (a dead animal) to make it look real 5 cause (oneself) to eat as much as possible 6 **get stuffed!** sl (an expression of dislike, esp. for what someone has said) ~**ing** n [U] 1 filling material 2 food cut up and put inside a chicken, etc., before cooking

stuff up phr vt block

stuffed shirt /ˌ·ˈ·, ˈ·ˌ·/ n dull person who thinks himself important

stuff·y /ˈstʌfiˑ/ adj 1 (having air) that is not fresh 2 derog formal and old-fashioned –**ily** adv –**iness** n [U]

stul·ti·fy /ˈstʌltəˌfaɪ/ vt fml make (someone's) mind dull –**fication** /ˌstʌltəfəˈkeɪʃən/ n [U]

stum·ble /ˈstʌmbəl/ vi 1 catch one's foot on something and start to fall 2 stop and/or make mistakes in speaking

stumble across/on/upon phr vt meet or find by chance

stumbling block /ˈ·· ˌ·/ n something preventing action or development

stump[1] /stʌmp/ n 1 base of a tree that has been cut down 2 useless end of something long that has been worn down, cut off, etc. ~**y** adj short and thick in body

stump[2] v 1 vt leave (someone) unable to reply 2 vi walk heavily or awkwardly 3 vi/t make political speeches (in a place) in order to gain votes

stun /stʌn/ vt –nn– 1 make unconscious 2 shock greatly 3 delight ~**ning** adj very attractive

stung /stʌŋ/ v past t. and p. of STING

stunk /stʌŋk/ v past p. of STINK

stunt[1] /stʌnt/ n 1 dangerous act of skill 2 action intended to attract attention: *publicity stunts* 3 **pull a stunt** do a trick, sometimes silly

stunt[2] vt prevent full growth (of)

stunt man /ˈ· ·/ **stunt woman** /ˈ· ˌ··/ fem. — n person who does STUNTS[1] (1) in films, etc.

stu·pe·fy /ˈstuːpəˌfaɪ, ˈstjuː-/ vt fml 1 surprise (and annoy) extremely 2 make unable to think –**faction** /ˌstuːpəˈfækʃən, ˌstjuː-/ n [U]

stu·pen·dous /stuːˈpendəs, stjuː-/ adj surprisingly great or good

stu·pid /ˈstuːpɪd, ˈstjuː-/ adj foolish ~**ly** adv ~**ity** /stuːˈpɪdəti, stjuː-/ n [U]

stu·por /ˈstuːpər, ˈstjuː-/ n [C;U] nearly unconscious unthinking state

stur·dy /ˈstɜrdi/ adj 1 strong and firm 2 determined –**dily** adv –**diness** n [U]

stut·ter /ˈstʌtər/ vi/t speak or say with difficulty in pronouncing esp. the first consonant of words ♦ n habit of stuttering

sty[1], **stye** /staɪ/ n infected place on the eyelid

sty[2] n PIGSTY

style /staɪl/ n 1 [C;U] (typical) manner of doing something: *the modern style of architecture | written in a formal style* 2 [C] fashion, esp. in clothes 3 [U] high quality of social behavior or appearance 4 [C] type or sort 5 **in style** in a grand way ♦ vt 1 DESIGN 2 give (a title) to: *He styles himself 'Sir'.* **stylish** adj **stylishly** attractive **stylist** n 1 person who invents styles or fashions 2 person with a (good) style of writing **stylize** vt present in a simple style rather than naturally **stylistic** /staɪˈlɪstɪk/ adj of STYLE (1)

sty·lus /ˈstaɪləs/ n -**luses** or -**li** /-laɪ/ needle-like instrument in a RECORD PLAYER that picks up sound signals from a record

suave /swɑv/ adj with smooth (but perhaps insincere) good manners –**ly** adv ~**ness** n [U]

sub /sʌb/ n infml 1 SUBMARINE 2 SUBSTITUTE 3 long bread roll filled with meat, cheese, etc.

sub·con·scious /sʌbˈkɑnʃəs/ adj, n (present at) a hidden level of the mind, not consciously known about ~**ly** adv

sub·con·ti·nent /ˌsʌbˈkɑntənənt, ˈsʌbˌkɑn-/ n large mass of land smaller than a CONTINENT, esp. India ~**al** /ˌsʌbˌkɑntənˈentəl/ n, adj (person) of or from India or Pakistan

sub·con·tract /ˌsʌbˈkɑntrækt, ˌsʌbkənˈtrækt/ vt hire someone else to do (work which one has agreed to do) ~**or** n person or firm that has had work subcontracted to it

sub·cu·ta·ne·ous /ˌsʌbkjuːˈteɪniʸəs◂/ adj med beneath the skin

sub·di·vide /ˌsʌbdəˈvaɪd, ˈsʌbdəˌvaɪd/ vt divide into even smaller parts –**division** /ˌsʌbdəˈvɪʒən/ n [C;U] 1 act of doing this 2 land area divided into lots for building houses

sub·due /səbˈduː, -ˈdjuː/ vt 1 gain control of 2 make gentler –**dued** adj 1 of low brightness or sound 2 unusually quiet in behavior

sub·ed·it /ˌsʌbˈedɪt/ vt look at and put right (material to be printed in a newspaper, etc.) ~**or** n

sub·ject[1] /ˈsʌbdʒɪkt/ n 1 thing being dealt with, represented, or considered: *the subject of the painting/ of the conversation* 2 branch of knowledge being studied 3 word that comes before a main verb and represents the person or thing that performs the action of the verb or about which something is stated 4 member of a state: *British subjects* ♦ adj 1 tending; likely: *He's subject to ill health.* 2 not independent: *a subject race* 3 **subject to** depending on: *subject to your approval* (= if you approve)

sub·ject[2] /səbˈdʒekt/ vt fml defeat and control –**ion** /-ˈdʒekʃən/ n [U] 1 act of subjecting 2 state of being severely controlled by others

subject to phr vt cause to experience or suffer

sub·jec·tive /səbˈdʒektɪv/ adj 1 influenced by personal feelings (and perhaps unfair) 2 existing only inside the mind; not real ~**ly** adv –**tivity** /ˌsʌbdʒekˈtɪvəti/ n [U]

sub ju·di·ce /ˌsʌb ˈjuːdɪˌkeʸ/ adj now being considered in a court of law, and therefore not allowed to be publicly mentioned

sub·ju·gate /ˈsʌbdʒəˌgeʸt/ vt defeat and make obedient –**gation** /ˌsʌbdʒəˈgeʸʃən/ n [U]

sub·junc·tive /səbˈdʒʌŋktɪv/ adj, n (of) a verb form expressing doubt, wishes, unreality, etc.: *In 'if I were you' the verb 'were' is in the subjunctive.*

sub·let /sʌbˈlet/ vt -**let**, pres. p. -**tt**- rent (property rented from someone) to someone else

sub·li·mate /ˈsʌbləˌmeʸt/ vt fml replace (natural urges, esp. sexual) with socially acceptable activities –**mation** /ˌsʌbləˈmeʸʃən/ n [U]

sub·lime /səˈblaɪm/ adj 1 very noble or wonderful 2 infml complete and usu. careless or unknowing ~**ly** adv

sub·lim·i·nal /sʌbˈlɪmənəl/ adj at a level which the ordinary senses are not conscious of

sub·ma·chine gun /ˌsʌbməˈʃiːn gʌn/ n light MACHINEGUN

sub·ma·rine /ˌsʌbməˈriːn, ˌsʌbmə-ˈriːn/ n (war)ship which can stay under water ♦ adj /ˌsʌbməˈriːn◂/ adj under or in the sea

sub·merge /səbˈmɜːdʒ/ vi/t 1 (cause to) go under the surface of water 2 cover or competely hide –mersion /-ˈmɜːʒən/ n [U] act of submerging or state of being submerged

sub·mit /səbˈmɪt/ v –tt– 1 vi admit defeat 2 vt offer for consideration 3 vt esp. law suggest –mission /-ˈmɪʃən/ n 1 [C;U] submitting 2 [U] fml opinion 3 [U] fml obedience 4 [C] law request; suggestion 5 [C] something submitted (2) –missive /-ˈmɪsɪv/ adj too obedient

sub·or·di·nate¹ /səˈbɔːdn-ɪt/ adj less important ♦ n someone of lower rank

sub·or·di·nate² /səˈbɔːdnˌeɪt/ vt put in a subordinate position –ation /səˌbɔːdnˈeɪʃən/ n [U]

sub·orn /səˈbɔːn/ vt fml persuade to do wrong, esp. tell lies in court

sub·poe·na /səˈpiːnə/ n written order to attend a court of law **subpoena** vt

sub·scribe /səbˈskraɪb/ vi pay regularly, esp. to receive a magazine –scriber n

   subscribe to phr vt agree with; approve of

sub·scrip·tion /səbˈskrɪpʃən/ n 1 act of subscribing (to) 2 amount paid regularly, esp. to belong to a society, receive a magazine, etc.

sub·se·quent /ˈsʌbsəkwənt/ adj coming afterwards or next ~ly adv

sub·ser·vi·ent /səbˈsɜːviənt/ adj too willing to obey ~ly adv –ence n [U]

sub·side /səbˈsaɪd/ vi 1 return to its usual level; become less: The flood waters/The wind/His anger subsided. 2 (of land or a building) sink down **subsidence** /səbˈsaɪdns, ˈsʌbsədəns/ n [U]

sub·sid·i·a·ry /səbˈsɪdiˌeriʸ/ adj connected with but less important than the main one ♦ n subsidiary company

sub·si·dy /ˈsʌbsədiʸ/ n paid, esp. by government, to make prices lower, etc. –**dize** vt give a subsidy to (someone) for (something): subsidized crops

sub·sist /səbˈsɪst/ vi fml remain alive ~ence n [U] 1 ability to live, esp. on little money or food 2 state of living with little money or food

sub·stance /ˈsʌbstəns/ n 1 [C] material; type of matter: a sticky substance 2 [U] fml truth: There is no substance in these rumors. 3 [U] fml real meaning, without the unimportant details 4 [U] fml wealth 5 [U] importance, esp. in relation to real life: There was no real substance in the speech.

sub·stan·tial /səbˈstænʃəl, -tʃəl/ adj 1 solid; strongly made 2 satisfactorily large: a substantial meal 3 noticeably large (and important): substantial changes 4 concerning the main part 5 wealthy ~ly adv 1 in all important ways: They are substantially the same. 2 quite a lot

sub·stan·ti·ate /səbˈstænʃiʸˌeɪt, -tʃiʸ-/ vt fml prove the truth of –ation /səbˌstænʃiʸˈeɪʃən, -tʃiʸ-/ n [U]

sub·stan·tive /ˈsʌbstəntɪv/ adj fml having reality, actuality, or importance

sub·sti·tute /ˈsʌbstəˌtuːt, -ˌtjuːt/ n one taking the place of another ♦ v 1 vt put in place of another 2 vi act or be used instead –tution /ˌsʌbstəˈtuːʃən, -ˈtjuː-/ n [C;U]

sub·sume /səbˈsuːm, -ˈsjuːm/ vt fml include

sub·ter·fuge /ˈsʌbtərˌfjuːdʒ/ n [C;U] deceiving or slightly dishonest trick(s)

sub·ter·ra·ne·an /ˌsʌbtəˈreɪniʸən◂/ adj underground

sub·ti·tles /ˈsʌbˌtaɪtlz/ n [P] translation printed over a foreign film

sub·tle /ˈsʌtl/ adj 1 hardly noticeable: subtle differences 2 clever in arrangement: a subtle plan 3 very clever in noticing and understanding –tly adv –tlety n [C;U]

sub·tract /səbˈtrækt/ vt take (a number or amount) from a larger one –ion /-ˈtrækʃən/ n [C;U]

sub·urb /ˈsʌbɜːb/ n outer area of a town, where people live ~an /səˈbɜːbən/ adj

sub·ur·bi·a /səˈbɜːbiʸə/ n [U] (life and ways of people who live in) suburbs

sub·vert /səbˈvɜːt/ vt try to destroy the power and influence of –versive adj trying to destroy established ideas or defeat those in power –version /-ˈvɜːʒən/ n [U]

sub·way /ˈsʌbweɪ/ n underground electric railroad in a big city

suc·ceed /səkˈsiːd/ v 1 vi do what one has been trying to do 2 vi do well, esp. in gaining position or popularity 3 vt follow after 4 vi/t be the next to take a rank or position (after): Hammond succeeded Jones as champion.

suc·cess /səkˈses/ n 1 [U] degree of succeeding; good result 2 [C] person or thing that succeeds ~ful adj ~fully adv

suc·ces·sion /səkˈseʃən/ n 1 [U] following one after the other: in quick succession 2 [S] many following each other closely: *a succession of visitors* **3** [U] SUCCEEDing (4)

suc·ces·sive /sək'sesɪv/ *adj* following each other closely in time ~**ly** *adv*

suc·ces·sor /sək'sesər/ *n* person who takes an office or position formerly held by another

suc·cinct /sək'sɪŋkt/ *adj* clearly expressed in few words ~**ly** *adv*

suc·cor /'sʌkər/ *vt, n* [U] *lit* help

suc·cu·lent /'sʌkyələnt/ *adj* juicy and tasting good -**lence** *n* [U]

suc·cumb /sə'kʌm/ *vi fml* stop opposing

such /sʌtʃ/ *predeterminer, determiner* **1** of that kind: *I dislike such people.* | *some flowers, such as* (= for example) *roses* **2** to so great a degree: *He's such a kind man.* **3** so great; so good, bad or unusual: *He wrote to her every day, such was his love for her.* ♦ *pron* **1** (things) of that kind **2** **any/no/some such** any/no/some (person or thing) like that: *No such person exists.* **3** **as such** properly so named

such and such /'·· ₁·/ *predeterminer infml* a certain (time, amount, etc.) not named

suck /sʌk/ *v* **1** *vi/t* draw (liquid) in with the muscles of the mouth **2** *vt* hold (something) in one's mouth and move one's tongue against it: *sucking one's thumb* **3** *vt* draw powerfully: *The current sucked them under.* **4** *vi sl* be of poor quality: *this film sucks.* **suck** *n*

suck·er /'sʌkər/ *n* **1** person or thing that sucks **2** flat piece which sticks to a surface by suction **3** a easily cheated person **b** someone who likes the stated thing very much: *a sucker for ice cream* **4** *infml* LOLLIPOP

suck·le /'sʌkəl/ *vi/t* feed with milk from the breast

suc·tion /'sʌkʃən/ *n* [U] drawing away air or liquid, esp. to lower the air pressure between 2 objects and make them stick to each other

sud·den /'sʌdn/ *adj* happening unexpectedly and quickly ~**ly** *adv* ~**ness** *n* [U]

suds /sʌdz/ *n* [P] mass of soapy BUBBLES

sue /suʷ/ *vi/t* bring a legal claim (against)

suede /sweʸd/ *n* [U] soft leather with a rough surface

su·et /'suʷɪt/ *n* [U] hard fat used in cooking

suf·fer /'sʌfər/ *v* **1** *vi* experience pain or difficulty **2** *vt* experience (something unpleasant) **3** *vt* accept without dislike: *He doesn't suffer fools gladly.* **4** *vi* grow worse: *His work has suffered since his illness.* ~**ing** *n* [C;U]

suf·fer·ance /'sʌfərəns/ *n* **on sufferance** with permission, though not welcomed

suf·fice /sə'faɪs/ *vi/t fml* **1** be enough (for) **2** **suffice it to say that** ... I will say only that ...

suf·fi·cient /sə'fɪʃənt/ *adj* enough ~**ly** *adv* -**ciency** *n* [S;U] *fml*

suf·fix /'sʌfɪks/ *n* group of letters or sounds added at the end of a word (as in kind*ness*, quick*ly*)

suf·fo·cate /'sʌfə₁keʸt/ *vi/t* (cause to) die because of lack of air -**cation** /₁sʌfə'keʸʃən/ *n* [U]

suf·frage /'sʌfrɪdʒ/ *n* [U] right to vote in national elections

suf·fuse /sə'fyuʷz/ *vt* spread all through -**fusion** /-'fyuʷʒən/ *n* [U]

sug·ar /'ʃʊɡər/ *n* [U] sweet white or brown plant substance used in food and drinks ♦ *vt* put sugar in ~**y** *adj* **1** containing or tasting of sugar **2** too sweet, nice, kind, etc., in an insincere way

sug·ar·beet /'ʃʊɡər₁biʸt/ *n* root vegetable from which sugar is made

sug·ar·cane /'ʃʊɡər₁keʸn/ *n* [U] tall tropical plant from whose stems sugar is obtained

sugar dad·dy /'·· ₁··/ *n infml* older man who provides a young woman with money and presents in return for sex and companionship

sugar ma·ple /'·· ₁··/ *n* tree with very sticky substance that is used to make sugar and SYRUP

sug·gest /səɡ'dʒest, sə'dʒest/ *vt* **1** state as an idea for consideration: *I suggest we do it this way.* **2** give signs (of): *The latest figures suggest that business is improving.* ~**ive** *adj* **1** (perhaps) showing thoughts of sex **2** *fml* which leads the mind into a particular way of thinking ~**ion** /səɡ'dʒestʃən, sə'dʒes-/ *n* [C;U] act of suggesting or something suggested

su·i·cide /'suʷə₁saɪd/ *n* **1** [C;U] killing oneself **2** [C] person who does this **3** [U] action that destroys one's position -**cidal** /₁suʷə'saɪdl◂/ *adj* **1** likely or wishing to kill oneself **2** likely to lead to death or destruction

suit¹ /suʷt/ *n* **1** short coat with pants or skirt of the same material **2** garment for a special purpose: *a bathing suit* | *a suit of armor* **3** any of the 4 sets of playing cards **4** **follow suit** do the same as everyone else

suit² *vt* **1** be convenient for; satisfy **2** match or look good on (someone): *That hairstyle doesn't suit you.* **3** **be suited (to/for)** be suitable for **4** **suit oneself** do what one likes

sui·ta·ble /'suʷtəbəl/ *adj* fit or right for a purpose -**bly** *adv* -**bility** /₁suʷtə'bɪlətiʸ/ *n* [U]

suit·case /'suʷtkeʸs/ *n* case for

carrying clothes and possessions when traveling

suite /swiʲt/ n **1** set of matching furniture **2** set of hotel rooms **3** piece of music made up of several parts

sui·tor /'suʷtər/ n lit man wishing to marry a particular woman

sul·fur /'sʌlfər/ n [U] substance found esp. as a light yellow powder

sul·fu·ric ac·id /sʌlˌfyuərɪk ˈæsɪd/ n [U] powerful acid

sulk /sʌlk/ vi be silently bad-tempered ~**y** adj ~**ily** adv ~**iness** n [U]

sul·len /'sʌlən/ adj showing silent dislike, bad temper, lack of interest, etc. ~**ly** adv ~**ness** n [U]

sul·ly /'sʌliʲ/ vt lit spoil

sul·tan /'sʌltən/ n (often cap.) Muslim ruler

sul·ta·na /sʌlˈtænə/ n **1** (often cap.) wife, mother, or daughter of a sultan

sul·try /'sʌltriʲ/ adj **1** (of weather) hot, airless, and uncomfortable **2** causing or showing strong sexual desire

sum¹ /sʌm/ n **1** total produced when numbers are added together **2** amount (of money) **3** simple calculation

sum² v -mm- **sum up** phr v **1** vi/t summarize **2** vt consider and form a judgment of

sum·ma·ry /'sʌməriʲ/ n short account giving the main points ♦ adj **1** short **2** done at once without attention to formalities: *summary dismissal* -**rize** vt make a summary of

sum·mer /'sʌmər/ n [C;U] season between spring and autumn ~**y** adj like or suitable for summer

summer school /'·· ˌ·/ n program of study offered in the summer to high school and college students

sum·mit /'sʌmɪt/ n **1** highest point **2** top of a mountain **3** meeting between heads of government

sum·mon /'sʌmən/ vt order officially to come

summon up phr vt get (a quality in oneself) ready for use

sum·mons /'sʌmənz/ n, vt order to appear in a court of law

sump /sʌmp/ n part of an engine holding the oil supply

sump·tu·ous /'sʌmptʃuʷəs/ adj expensive and grand ~**ly** adv

sum to·tal /ˌ· ˈ··/ n [the+S] the whole, esp. when less than expected or needed

sun /sʌn/ n **1** [the+S] star around which the Earth moves **2** [the+S;U] sun's light and heat: *sitting in the sun* **3** [C] star around which PLANETS may turn **4** **under the sun** at all ♦ vt -nn- place (oneself) in

sunlight ~**ny** adj **1** having bright sunlight **2** cheerful

sun·bathe /'sʌnbeʲð/ vi sit or lie in strong sunlight -**bather** n

sun·beam /'sʌnbiʲm/ n a beam of sunlight

sun·belt /'sʌnbɛlt/ n [the+S] southern and SW parts of the US

sun·burn /'sʌnbɜrn/ n [U] sore skin caused by too much strong sunlight -**burnt**, ~**ed** adj

sun·dae /'sʌndiʲ, -deʲ/ n ice cream dish with fruit, nuts, etc.

Sun·day /'sʌndiʲ, -deʲ/ n the 7th day of the week, between Saturday and Monday

Sunday Sup·ple·ment /ˌ·· ˈ···/ n magazine printed in color and given free with a newspaper, esp. a Sunday one

sun·der /'sʌndər/ vt lit separate

sun·dial /'sʌnˌdaɪəl/ n apparatus producing a shadow which shows the time

sun·down /'sʌndaʊn/ n [U] sunset

sun·dry /'sʌndriʲ/ adj **1** various **2** **all and sundry** all types of people; everybody **sundries** n [P] various small articles, esp. for personal use

sung /sʌŋ/ v past p. of SING

sun·glass·es /'sʌnˌglæsɪz/ n [P] glasses with dark glass for protection from sunlight

sunk /sʌŋk/ v past p. of SINK

sunk·en /'sʌŋkən/ adj **1** that has (been) sunk **2** below the surrounding level: *sunken eyes* | *a sunken garden*

sun·lamp /'sʌnlæmp/ n ULTRAVIOLET lamp for turning the skin brown

sun·light /'sʌnlaɪt/ n [U] light from the sun

sun·lit /'sʌnˌlɪt/ adj brightly lit by the sun

sunny-side up /ˌ·· · ˈ·/ adj (of an egg) cooked in fat without being turned over

sun porch /'· ·/ n glass room that lets the sunlight into the house

sun·rise /'sʌnraɪz/ n [U] time when the sun appears after the night

sun roof /'· ·/ n window in the roof of a car

sun·set /'sʌnsɛt/ n [C;U] time when the sun disappears as night begins

sun·shade /'sʌnʃeʲd/ n sort of UMBRELLA for protection from the sun

sun·shine /'sʌnʃaɪn/ n [U] strong sunlight

sun·spot /'sʌnspɑt/ n dark cooler area on the sun's surface

sun·stroke /'sʌnstroʷk/ n [U] illness caused by too much strong sunlight

sun·tan /'sʌntæn/ n brownness of the skin caused by being in strong sunlight

su·per /ˈsuʷpər/ adj wonderful; extremely good ♦ n infml abbrev. for SUPERINTENDENT (2)

su·per·an·nu·at·ed /ˌsuʷpərˈænyuˌeʸtɪd/ adj fml **1** too old for work **2** old-fashioned –**ion** /ˌsuʷpərˌænyu-ˈeʸʃən/ n [U] fml for PENSION

su·perb /suʊˈpɜrb/ adj excellent; wonderful ~**ly** adv

Su·per·bowl /ˈsuʷpərˌboʷl/ n last game to decide the winning team in a football competition

su·per·cil·i·ous /ˌsuʷpərˈsɪliʸəs/ adj fml derog (as if) thinking that others are of little importance ~**ly** adv ~**ness** n [U]

su·per·con·duc·tor /ˌsuʷpərkənˈdʌktər/ n metal which at very low temperatures allows electricity to pass freely

su·per·fi·cial /ˌsuʷpərˈfɪʃəl◂/ adj **1** on the surface; not deep **2** not thorough or complete ~**ly** adv –**ity** /ˌsuʷpərˌfɪʃiʸˈælətiʸ/ n [U]

su·per·flu·ous /suʊˈpɜrfluʷəs/ adj more than is necessary; not needed ~**ly** adv

su·per·high·way /ˌsuʷpərˈhaɪˌweʸ/ n large road for fast travel over long distances

su·per·hu·man /ˌsuʷpərˈhyuʷmən◂/ adj (as if) beyond or better than human powers

su·per·im·pose /ˌsuʷpərɪmˈpoʷz/ vt put (something) over something else, esp. so that both can be (partly) seen

su·per·in·tend /ˌsuʷpərɪnˈtend/ vt be in charge of and direct ~**ent** n **1** person in charge **2** person in charge of keeping a building in good order

su·pe·ri·or /suʊˈpɪəriʸər, sə-/ adj **1** of higher rank **2** better **3** of high quality **4** derog (as if) thinking oneself better than others ♦ n person of higher rank –**ity** /səˌpɪəriʸˈɔrətiʸ, -ˈar-, suʊ-/ n [U]

su·per·la·tive /səˈpɜrlətɪv, suʊ-/ adj **1** gram expressing 'most' **2** extremely good ♦ n gram superlative form of an adjective or adverb

su·per·mar·ket /ˈsuʷpərˌmarkɪt/ n large food store where one serves oneself

su·per·nat·u·ral /ˌsuʷpərˈnætʃə-rəl◂/ adj of or caused by the power of spirits, gods, and magic ~**ly** adv

su·per·pow·er /ˈsuʷpərˌpaʊər/ n very powerful nation

su·per·sede /ˌsuʷpərˈsiʸd/ vt take the place of

su·per·son·ic /ˌsuʷpərˈsanɪk◂/ adj (flying) faster than the speed of sound

su·per·star /ˈsuʷpərˌstar/ n very famous performer

su·per·sti·tion /ˌsuʷpərˈstɪʃən/ n [C;U] (unreasonable) belief based on old ideas about luck, magic, etc. –**tious** adj

su·per·struc·ture /ˈsuʷpərˌstrʌk-tʃər/ n upper structure built on a base

su·per·vise /ˈsuʷpərˌvaɪz/ vt watch (people or work) to make sure things are done properly –**visor** n –**visory** /ˌsuʷpərˈvaɪzəriʸ◂/ adj –**vision** /ˌsuʷpərˈvɪʒən/ n [U]

sup·per /ˈsʌpər/ n [C;U] evening meal

sup·plant /səˈplænt/ vt take the place of

sup·ple /ˈsʌpəl/ adj bending easily and gracefully ~**ness** n [U]

sup·ple·ment /ˈsʌpləmənt/ n **1** additional amount to supply what is needed **2** additional separate part of a newspaper, magazine, etc. – see also SUNDAY SUPPLEMENT ♦ /ˈsʌplə-ˌment/ vt make additions to ~**ary** /ˌsʌpləˈmentəriʸ◂/ adj additional

sup·ply /səˈplaɪ/ vt **1** provide (something) **2** provide things to (someone) for use ♦ n **1** amount for use: a supply of food **2** (system for) supplying: the supply of electricity **3** in short supply scarce – see also MONEY SUPPLY –**plier** n supplies n [P] things necessary for daily life, esp. food

supply and de·mand /ˌ·····ˈ·/ n [U] balance between the amount of goods for sale and the amount that people actually want to buy

sup·port /səˈpɔrt, -ˈpoʷrt/ vt **1** bear the weight of, esp. so as to prevent from falling **2** approve of and encourage **3** be loyal to: supporting the local merchants **4** provide money for (someone) to live on **5** strengthen (an idea, opinion, etc.) ♦ n **1** [U] state of being supported **2** [C] something that supports **3** [U] active approval and encouragement **4** [U] money to live on ~**er** n person who supports a particular activity or team, defends a particular principle, etc. ~**ive** adj providing encouragement, help, etc.

supporting part /·ˌ··ˈ·/ also **supporting role** — n small part in a play or film

sup·pose /səˈpoʷz/ vt **1** consider to be probable: As she's not here, I suppose she must have gone home. **2** be **supposed to: a** ought to; should **b** be generally considered to be ♦ conj **1** (used for making a suggestion): Suppose we wait a while. **2** what would/will happen if? –**dly** /-zɪdliʸ/ adv as is believed; as it appears –**posing** conj suppose

sup·po·si·tion /ˌsʌpəˈzɪʃən/ n **1** [U] act of supposing or guessing **2** [C] guess

sup·pos·i·to·ry /səˈpazəˌtɔriʸ, -ˌtoʷriʸ/ n piece of meltable medicine placed in the RECTUM or VAGINA

sup·press /sə'prɛs/ vt 1 bring to an end by force 2 prevent from being shown or made public: *suppressing her anger/the truth* ~**ion** /-'prɛʃən/ n [U]

su·preme /sə'priːm, sʊ-/ adj 1 highest in degree: *supreme happiness | the supreme sacrifice* (= giving one's life) 2 most powerful ~**ly** adv extremely **supremacy** /sə'prɛməsi/ n [U]

Supreme Court /·,· '·/ n [the+S] highest court in the US

sur·charge /'sɜrtʃɑrdʒ/ n (demand for) an additional payment ♦ vt make (someone) pay a surcharge

sure /ʃʊər/ adj 1 having no doubt 2 certain (to happen): *You're sure to* (= certainly will) *like it.* 3 confident (of having): *I've never felt surer of success.* 4 **be sure to** don't forget to 5 **make sure a** find out (if something is really true) **b** take action (so that something will certainly happen) 6 **sure of oneself** certain that one's actions are right ♦ adv 1 certainly 2 **for sure** certainly so 3 **sure enough** as was expected ~**ly** adv 1 I believe, hope, or expect: *Surely you haven't forgotten?* 2 safely ~**ness** n [U]

sure·fire /'ʃʊərfaɪər/ adj certain to succeed

sure·foot·ed /ˌʃʊər'fʊtɪd◂/ adj able to walk, climb, etc., in difficult places without falling

sure thing /ˌ· '·/ n infml something that is expected to be a success: *The nightclub was a sure thing.*

sur·e·ty /'ʃʊərəṭi/ n [C;U] 1 person who takes responsibility for the behavior of another 2 money given to make sure that a person will appear in court

surf /sɜrf/ n [U] white waves filled with air breaking on a shore ♦ vi ride as a sport over breaking waves near the shore, on a SURFBOARD ~**ing** n [U] sport of surfing ~**er** n person who goes surfing

sur·face /'sɜrfɪs/ n 1 outer part of an object 2 top of liquid 3 what is easily seen, not the main (hidden) part ♦ adj 1 not deep; SUPERFICIAL: *surface friendliness* ♦ vi come up to the surface of water: (fig.) *He doesn't usually surface* (= get out of bed) *until noon.*

surface mail /'··· ·/ n [U] mail carried by land or sea

surface-to-air /ˌ··· · '·◂/ adj (of a weapon) fired from the earth towards aircraft

surf·board /'sɜrf,bɔrd, -ˌboʷrd/ n board for riding on surf

sur·feit /'sɜrfɪt/ n fml [S] too large an amount

surge /sɜrdʒ/ n 1 sudden powerful forward movement 2 sudden increase of strong feeling ♦ vi 1 move forwards like powerful waves 2 (of a feeling) arise powerfully

sur·geon /'sɜrdʒən/ n doctor who does SURGERY (1)

sur·ge·ry /'sɜrdʒəriʸ/ n 1 [U] (performing of) medical operations: *He was in surgery for 5 hours.* 2 branch of medicine concerned with such treatment

sur·gi·cal /'sɜrdʒɪkəl/ adj 1 of or used for surgery 2 (of a garment) worn as treatment for a particular physical condition ~**ly** /-kliʸ/ adv

sur·ly /'sɜrliʸ/ adj having a bad temper and manners **surliness** n [U]

sur·mise /sər'maɪz/ vt fml suppose; guess

sur·mount /sər'maʊnt/ vt 1 succeed in dealing with (a difficulty) 2 be on top of

sur·name /'sɜrneʸm/ n person's family name – see LAST NAME

sur·pass /sər'pæs/ vt fml go beyond, esp. be better than

sur·plus /'sɜrplʌs, -pləs/ n, adj (amount) additional to what is needed or used

sur·prise /sər'praɪz, sə'praɪz/ n [C;U] 1 (feeling caused by) an unexpected event 2 **take by surprise** come on (someone) unprepared ♦ vt 1 cause surprise to 2 find, catch, or attack when unprepared

sur·pris·ing /sər'praɪzɪŋ, sə'praɪ-/ adj unusual; causing surprise ~**ly** adv

sur·re·al /sə'rɪəl/ adj having a strange dreamlike unreal quality ~**ism** n [U] modern art or literature that treats subjects in a surreal way ~**ist** n, adj (artist or writer) concerned with surrealism

sur·ren·der /sə'rɛndər/ v 1 vi/t give up or give in to the power (esp. of an enemy); admit defeat 2 vt fml give up possession of ♦ n [C;U] act of surrendering

sur·rep·ti·tious /ˌsɜrəp'tɪʃəs◂, ˌsʌr-/ adj done secretly, esp. for dishonest reasons ~**ly** adv

sur·ro·gate /'sɜrəˌgeʸt, -gɪt, ˌsʌr-/ n, adj (person or thing) acting or used in place of another

sur·round /sə'raʊnd/ vt be or go all around on every side ♦ n (decorative) edge or border ~**ing** adj around and near ~**ings** n [P] place and conditions of life

sur·veil·lance /sər'veʸləns/ n [U] close watch kept on someone or something

sur·vey /sər'veʸ, 'sɜrveʸ/ vt 1 look at or examine as a whole 2 examine the condition of (a building) 3 measure (land) ~**or** /sər'veʲər/ *n* person whose job is to SURVEY¹ (2,3)

survey² /'sɜrveʲ/ *n* **1** act of surveying: *a survey of public opinion/of a house* **2** general description

sur·vive /sər'vaɪv/ *vi/t* continue to live or exist (after), esp. after coming close to death: *She survived the accident.* –**vival** *n* **1** [U] act of surviving **2** [C] something which has survived from an earlier time –**vivor** *n*

sus·cep·ti·ble /sə'septəbəl/ *adj* **1** easily influenced (by) **2** likely to suffer (from) –**bility** /sə,septə'bɪlə-tⁱʲ/ *n*

sus·pect /sə'spekt/ *vt* **1** believe to be so; think likely: *I suspected he was ill but didn't want to ask him.* **2** believe to be guilty ♦ *n* /'sʌspekt/ person suspected of guilt ♦ *adj* of uncertain truth, quality, legality, etc.

sus·pend /sə'spend/ *vt* **1** *fml* hang from above **2** hold still in liquid or air **3** make inactive for a time: *The meeting was suspended while the lights were repaired.* **4** prevent from taking part for a time, esp. for breaking rules ~**ers** *n* [P] bands over the shoulders to keep pants up

sus·pense /sə'spens/ *n* [U] state of unsureness causing anxiety or pleasant excitement

sus·pen·sion /sə'spenʃən, -tʃən/ *n* **1** [U] act of suspending or fact of being suspended **2** [C] apparatus fixed to a vehicle's wheels to lessen the effect of rough roads

suspension bridge /·'·· · ·/ *n* bridge hung from strong steel ropes fixed to towers

sus·pi·cion /sə'spɪʃən/ *n* **1** [U] **a** a case of suspecting or being suspected (SUSPECT (2)): *under suspicion of murder* **b** lack of trust: *treat someone with suspicion* **2 a** a feeling of SUSPECTing: *I have a suspicion you're right.* **b** belief about someone's guilt: *They have their suspicions.* **3** [S] slight amount –**cious** *adj* **1** suspecting guilt, bad or criminal behavior, etc. **2** making one suspicious: *suspicious behavior* –**ciously** *adv*

sus·tain /sə'steʲn/ *vt* **1** keep strong **2** keep in existence over a long period **3** *fml* suffer: *The car sustained severe damage.* **4** *fml* hold up (the weight of)

sus·te·nance /'sʌstənəns/ *n* [U] *fml* food or its ability to keep people strong and healthy

swab /swab/ *n* piece of material that can take up liquid, esp. used medically ♦ *vt* -**bb**- clean (a wound) with a swab

swag·ger /'swægər/ *vi* walk or behave (too) confidently or proudly **swagger** *n* [S;U]

swal·low¹ /'swaloʷ/ *v* **1** *vi/t* move (the contents of the mouth) down the throat **2** *vt* accept patiently or with too easy belief: *It was an obvious lie, but he swallowed it.* **3** *vt* hold back (uncomfortable feelings); not show or express: *swallow one's pride* ♦ *n* act of swallowing or amount swallowed

swallow up *phr vt* take in and cause to disappear

swallow² *n* small bird with a tail with 2 points

swam /swæm/ *v* past t. of SWIM

swamp /swamp, swɔmp/ *n* [C;U] (area of) soft wet land ♦ *vt* cause to have (too) much to deal with ~**y** *adj* wet like a swamp

swan /swan/ *n* large white water bird with a long neck

swank /swæŋk/ *vi, n* [U] *infml* (act or speak too proudly, making) false or too great claims ~**y** *adj infml* very fashionable or expensive

swan·song /'swansɔŋ/ *n* one's last performance or piece of artistic work

swap /swap/ *vi/t* -**pp**- exchange (goods or positions) so that each person gets what they want ♦ *n* **1** exchange **2** something (to be) exchanged

swarm /swɔrm/ *n* large moving mass of insects: (fig.) *swarms of tourists* ♦ *vi* move in a crowd or mass

swarm with *phr vt* be full of (a moving crowd)

swar·thy /'swɔrðiʲ, -θiʲ/ *adj* having fairly dark skin

swash·buck·ling /'swaʃ,bʌkəlɪŋ, 'swɔʃ-/ *adj* full of showy adventures, sword fighting, etc.

swat /swat/ *vt* -**tt**- hit (an insect), esp. so as to kill it

SWAT /swat/ *n* special police kept ready for special action

swathe /swað, swɔð, sweʲð/ *v lit* **swathe in** *phr vt* wrap round in (cloth): (fig.) *hills swathed in mist*

sway /sweʲ/ *v* **1** *vi/t* swing from side to side **2** *vt* influence, esp. so as to change opinion ♦ *n* [U] **1** swaying movement **2** *lit* influence

swear /sweər/ *v* **swore** /swɔr, swoʷr/, **sworn** /swɔrn, swoʷrn/ **1** *vi* curse **2** *vi/t* make a solemn promise or statement, esp. by taking an OATH (1): *She swore to tell the truth/swore that she had been there.* **3** cause to take an OATH

swear by *phr vt* have confidence in (something)

swear in *phr vt* **1** cause (a witness) to take the OATH (1) in court **2** cause to make a promise of responsible action, etc.: *The new President was sworn in.*

sweat /swɛt/ n **1** [U] body liquid that comes out through the skin **2** [S] anxious state **3** [S] *infml* hard work **4 no sweat** *infml* (used for saying that something will not cause any difficulty) ♦ vi **1** produce sweat **2** be very anxious or nervously impatient **3 sweat blood** *infml* work unusually hard ~**y** adj **1** covered in or smelly with sweat **2** unpleasantly hot

sweat band /'· ·/ n piece of cloth worn around the head to keep sweat out of the eyes

sweat·er /'swɛtər/ n (woolen) garment for the upper body

sweat pants /'· ·/ n pants worn esp. for running and other sports

sweat·shirt /'swɛt-ʃərt/ n loose cotton garment for the upper body

sweat shop /'· ·/ n business that pays its workers very little money

sweep[1] /swip/ v swept /swɛpt/ **1** vt clean or remove by brushing **2** vi/t move (over) or carry quickly and powerfully: *A wave of panic swept over her.* | *We were swept along by the crowd.* **3** vi lie in a curve across land **4** vt win completely and easily, as in elections **5** vi (of a person) move in a proud, firm manner **6 sweep someone off their feet** fill someone with sudden love or excitement **7 sweep something under the rug** keep (something bad or shocking) secret ~**er** n ~**ing** adj **1** including many or most things: *sweeping changes* **2** too general: *a sweeping statement*

sweep aside *phr vt* refuse to pay any attention to

sweep[2] n **1** act of sweeping **2** long curved line or area of country: (fig.) *the broad sweep of her narrative* (= covering all parts of the subject) **3** person who cleans chimneys **4** sweepstake

sweep·stake /'swipsteɪk/ n form of risking money in which the winner gets all the losers' money

sweet /swit/ adj **1** tasting like sugar **2** pleasing to the senses: *sweet music* **3** charming; lovable: *What a sweet little boy!* — see also **short and sweet** (SHORT[1]) ~**en** vt **1** make sweeter **2** *infml* give money or presents in order to persuade ~**ly** adv ~**ness** n [U]

sweet·bread /'switbrɛd/ n sheep's or cow's PANCREAS used as food

sweet corn /'· ·/ n CORN grown for people to eat, rather than for animals, etc.

sweet·en·er /'switn-ər, 'switnər/ n **1** substance used instead of sugar to make food or drink taste sweet **2** *infml* money, a present, etc., given in order to persuade someone

sweet·heart /'swithart/ n **1** person whom one loves **2** (used when speaking to someone you love): *Yes, sweetheart.*

sweet talk /'· ͵·/ n [U] *infml* insincere talk intended to please or persuade **sweet-talk** /'· ͵·/ vt

sweet tooth /͵· '·, '· ͵·/ n [S] liking for sweet and sugary things

swell /swɛl/ vi/t swelled, swollen /'swoʷlən/ or swelled **1** increase gradually to beyond the usual or original size: *a swollen finger.* **2** fill or be filled, giving a full round shape ♦ n **1** [S] rolling up and down movement of the surface of the sea **2** [C] *often derog* classy person ♦ adj excellent ~**ing** n **1** act of swelling **2** swollen place on the body

swel·ter /'swɛltər/ vi experience the effects of unpleasantly great heat

swept /swɛpt/ v past t. and p. of SWEEP

swept-back /͵· '·◄/ adj having the front edge pointing backwards at an angle from the main part

swerve /swɜrv/ vi, n (make) a sudden change of direction

swift[1] /swɪft/ adj quick ~**ly** adv ~**ness** n [U]

swift[2] n small brown bird like a SWALLOW[2], that flies quickly

swig /swɪg/ vt -gg- *infml* drink, esp. in large mouthfuls swig n

swill /swɪl/ vt **1** wash with large streams of water **2** *infml* drink, esp. in large amounts ♦ n [U] partly liquid pig food

swim /swɪm/ v swam /swæm/, swum /swʌm/; present p. -mm- **1** vi move through water using the limbs, FINS, etc. **2** vt cross by doing this: *swim the English Channel* **3** vi be full of or surrounded with liquid **4** vi seem to spin around and around: *My head was swimming.* **5 swim with the tide** follow the behavior of other people around one ♦ n **1** [S] act of swimming **2 in the swim (of things)** knowing about and concerned in what is going on in modern life ~**mer** n

swimming pool /'·· ͵·/ n large container filled with water and used for swimming

swin·dle /'swɪndl/ vt cheat, esp. so as to get money ♦ n act of swindling **swindler** n

swine /swaɪn/ n swine **1** *fml* or *lit* pig **2** *sl* unpleasant person

swing /swɪŋ/ v swung /swʌŋ/ **1** vi/t move backwards and forwards or around and around from a fixed point: *Soldiers swing their arms as they march.* **2** vi/t move in a smooth curve: *The door swung shut.* **3** vi turn quickly **4** vi start smoothly and rapidly: *We're ready to swing into* *action.* ♦ *n* **1** [C] act of swinging, esp. a BAT at a baseball **2** [C] children's swinging seat fixed from above by ropes or chains **3** [C] noticeable change: *a big swing in public opinion* **4** [S] JAZZ music of the 1930s and 1940s with a strong regular active beat **5 in full swing** having reached a very active stage

swipe /swaɪp/ *vt* **1** hit hard **2** *infml* steal ♦ *n* sweeping blow – see also SIDESWIPE

swirl /swɜrl/ *vi/t* move with twisting turns ♦ *n* twisting mass

swish¹ /swɪʃ/ *vi/t* **1** move through the air with a sharp whistling noise **2** (of a man) walk like a woman ♦ *n* act of swishing

swish² *adj infml* in an EFFEMINATE way fashionable and expensive

Swiss /swɪs/ *adj* of Switzerland

switch /swɪtʃ/ *n* **1** apparatus for stopping or starting an electric current **2** sudden complete change ♦ *vi/t* change or exchange: *They switched jobs.* | *The lights have switched to green.*

   switch off/on *phr vt* turn (an electric light or apparatus) off/on with a switch

   switch over *phr vi* change completely

switch·back /'swɪtʃbæk/ *n* road on a mountain with many sharp turns

switch·blade /'swɪtʃbleɪd/ *n* knife with a blade operated by a spring, used as a weapon

switch·board /'swɪtʃbɔrd, -boʳrd/ *n* place where telephone lines in a large building are connected

swiv·el /'swɪvəl/ *vi/t* –l– turn around (as if) on a central point

swiz·zle stick /'swɪzəl ˌstɪk/ *n* rod for mixing drinks

swol·len /'swoʷlən/ *v past p. of* SWELL

swoon /swuʷn/ *vi lit* **1** experience deep joy, desire, etc. **2** FAINT

swoop /swuʷp/ *vi* come down sharply, esp. to attack **swoop** *n* **1** swooping action **2 in one fell swoop** all at once

swop /swɑp/ *v, n* SWAP

sword /sɔrd, soʷrd/ *n* **1** weapon with a long sharp metal blade and a handle **2 cross swords (with)** be opposed (to), esp. in argument

swords·man /'sɔrdzmən, 'soʷrdz-/ *n* –men /-mən/ (skilled) fighter with a sword ~**ship** *n* [U]

swore /swɔr, swoʷr/ *v past t. of* SWEAR

sworn /swɔrn, swoʷrn/ *v past p. of* SWEAR

swum /swʌm/ *v past p. of* SWIM

swung /swʌŋ/ *v past t. and p. of* SWING

syb·a·rit·ic /ˌsɪbəˈrɪtɪk◂/ *adj fml* being or liking great and expensive comfort, physical pleasures, etc.

syc·a·more /'sɪkəˌmɔr, -ˌmoʷr/ *n* common tree with broad leaves

syc·o·phant /'sɪkəfənt/ *n* person who praises people insincerely to gain personal advantage ~**ic** /ˌsɪkəˈfæntɪk◂/ *adj* ~**ically** /-kliʸ/ *adv* –**phancy** *n* [U]

syl·la·ble /'sɪləbəl/ *n* part of a word containing a single vowel sound: *There are two syllables in 'window': 'win-' and '-dow'.* –**labic** /səˈlæbɪk/ *adj*

syl·la·bus /'sɪləbəs/ *n* arrangement of subjects for study over a period of time

syl·lo·gis·m /'sɪləˌdʒɪzəm/ *n* arrangement of 2 statements which must lead to a third

sylph·like /'sɪlf-laɪk/ *adj* (of a woman) gracefully thin

syl·van /'sɪlvən/ *adj lit* of or in the woods

sym·bi·o·sis /ˌsɪmbaɪˈoʷsɪs, -biʸ-/ *n* [U] condition in which one living thing depends on another for existence ~**otic** /-ˈɑtɪk/ *adj*

sym·bol /'sɪmbəl/ *n* something that represents something else: *The dove is the symbol of peace.* ~**ism** *n* [U] use of symbols ~**ize** *vt* represent by or as a symbol ~**ic** /sɪmˈbɑlɪk/ *adj* representing: *The snake is symbolic of evil.* ~**ically** /-kliʸ/ *adv*

sym·me·try /'sɪmətriʸ/ *n* [C] **1** exact likeness in size, shape, etc., between opposite sides **2** effect of pleasing balance **symmetrical** /sɪˈmetrɪkəl/ *adj*

sym·pa·thy /'sɪmpəθiʸ/ *n* [U] **1** sensitivity to and pity for others' suffering **2** agreement and/or understanding: *I am in sympathy with their aims.* –**thize** *vt* feel or show sympathy **sympathies** *n* [P] feelings of support or loyalty ~**thetic** /ˌsɪmpəˈθetɪk◂/ *adj* feeling or showing sympathy ~**thetically** /-kliʸ/ *adv*

sym·pho·ny /'sɪmfəniʸ/ *n* piece of music for an ORCHESTRA, usu. in 4 parts

sym·po·si·um /sɪmˈpoʷziʸəm/ *n* –**ums** *or* –**a** /-ziʸə/ meeting to talk about a subject of study

symp·tom /'sɪmptəm/ *n* **1** outward sign of a disease **2** outward sign of inner change, new feelings; etc. ~**atic** /ˌsɪmptəˈmætɪk◂/ *adj* being a symptom

syn·a·gogue /'sɪnəˌgɑg, -ˌgɔg/ *n* building where Jews worship

syn·chro·nize /'sɪŋkrəˌnaɪz/ *vt* **1** cause to happen at the same time or speed **2** cause (watches, etc.) to

show the same time **–nization**
/ˌsɪŋkrənəˈzeʸʃən/ *n* [U]

syn·co·pate /ˈsɪŋkəˌpeʸt/ *vt* change
(the beat of music) by giving force
to the beats that are usu. less forceful **–pation** /ˌsɪŋkəˈpeʸʃən/ *n* [U]

syn·di·cate¹ /ˈsɪndəkɪt/ *n* group of
people or companies combined for
usu. business purposes

syn·di·cate² /ˈsɪndəˌkeʸt/ *vt* sell
(written work, pictures, PROGRAMS
(3), etc.) to many different newspapers, stations or magazines

syn·drome /ˈsɪndroʷm/ *n* **1** set of
medical SYMPTOMS which represent
an illness **2** any pattern of qualities,
happenings, etc., typical of a general
condition

syn·o·nym /ˈsɪnəˌnɪm/ *n* word with
the same meaning as another **~ous**
/sɪˈnɑnəməs/ *adj*

sy·nop·sis /sɪˈnɑpsɪs/ *n* short
account of something longer

syn·tax /ˈsɪntæks/ *n* [U] way in
which words are ordered and connected in sentences **–tactic** /sɪn-
ˈtæktɪk/ *adj*

syn·the·sis /ˈsɪnθəsɪs/ *n* **–ses** /-siʸz/
1 [U] combining of separate things,
ideas, etc., into a complete whole **2**
[C] something made by synthesis
–size *vt* make by synthesis, esp.
make (something similar to a
natural product) by combining
chemicals **–sizer** *n* electrical instrument, like a piano, that can

produce many sorts of different
sounds, used esp. in popular music

syn·thet·ic /sɪnˈθeţɪk/ *adj* artificial
~ally /-kliʸ/ *adv*

syph·i·lis /ˈsɪfəlɪs/ *n* [U] very serious illness passed on through sex

sy·phon /ˈsaɪfən/ *n, v* SIPHON

sy·ringe /səˈrɪndʒ, ˈsɪrɪndʒ/ *n* (medical) instrument with a hollow tube
for sucking in and pushing out liquid, esp. through a needle ♦ *vt*
clean with a syringe

syr·up /ˈsɪrəp, ˈsɜrəp/ *n* [U] **1** sweet
liquid, esp. sugar and water **2** mixture of sugar, water and medicine:
cough syrup

sys·tem /ˈsɪstəm/ *n* **1** [C] group of
related parts which work together
forming a whole: *a computer
system | the digestive system* **2** [C] or-
dered set of ideas, methods, or ways
of working: *the American system of
government* **3** [C] the body, thought
of as a set of working parts: *Traveling always upsets my system.* **4** [U]
orderly methods **5** [*the*+S] society
seen as something which uses and
limits INDIVIDUALS: *to fight the system* – see also EXPERT SYSTEM, OPER-
ATING SYSTEM **–atic** /ˌsɪstəˈmæţɪk◄/
adj based on orderly methods and
careful organization; thorough
~atically /-kliʸ/ *adv*

systems an·a·lyst /ˈ·· ˌ···/ *n* someone who studies (esp. business) activities and uses computers to plan
ways of carrying them out, etc.

T

T, t /tiʸ/ the 20th letter of the English alphabet

tab /tæb/ n **1** small piece of paper, cloth, metal, etc., fixed to something to hold it by, open it with, etc. **2 keep tabs on** watch closely

tab·by /ˈtæbiʸ/ n cat with dark and light bands of fur

tab·er·nac·le /ˈtæbərˌnækəl/ n **1** container for religious objects **2** large church

ta·ble /ˈteʸbəl/ n **1** piece of furniture with a flat top on upright legs **2** set of figures arranged in rows across and down a page **3 turn the tables on** gain an advantage over (someone who had an advantage over you) see also WATER TABLE ♦ vt leave until a later date for consideration

tab·leau /ˈtæbloʷ, tæˈbloʷ/ n scene on stage shown by a group of people who do not move or speak

ta·ble·spoon /ˈteʸbəlˌspuʷn/ n spoon for serving and measuring food

tab·let /ˈtæblɪt/ n **1** small solid piece of medicine **2** many sheets of paper fastened together **3** flat piece of stone or metal with words on it

table ten·nis /ˈ·· ˌ··/ n [U] indoor game in which a small ball is hit across a net on a table

tab·loid /ˈtæblɔɪd/ n newspaper with small pages and many pictures

ta·boo /təˈbuʷ, tæ-/ n –boos [C;U] strong social or religious custom forbidding something ♦ adj strongly forbidden by social custom: taboo words

tab·u·late /ˈtæbyəˌleʸt/ vt arrange as a TABLE (2) –lar adj –lation /ˌtæbyəˈleʸʃən/ n [U]

ta·cit /ˈtæsɪt/ adj accepted or understood without being openly expressed: tacit approval –ly adv

ta·ci·turn /ˈtæsəˌtɜrn/ adj tending to speak very little

tack /tæk/ n **1** small nail **2** sailing ship's direction: (fig.) a new tack on the crime problem **3** long loose stitch ♦ v **1** vt fasten with tacks **2** vi change the course of a sailing ship

tack·le /ˈtækəl/ n **1** [C] act of stopping or taking the ball away from an opponent in sport **2** [U] apparatus used in certain sports: fishing tackle **3** [C;U] (system of) ropes and wheels for heavy pulling and lifting ♦ v **1** vt take action in order to deal with **2** vt speak to fearlessly so as to deal

with a problem **3** vi/t stop or rob with a tackle (1)

tack·y /ˈtækiʸ/ adj **1** sticky **2** of low quality: a tacky hotel/remark (= in bad TASTE (3)) –iness n [U]

tact /tækt/ n [U] skill of speaking or acting without offending people ~ful adj ~fully adv ~less adj ~lessly adv

tac·tic /ˈtæktɪk/ n plan or method for gaining a desired result **tactics** n [U] art of arranging and moving military forces in battle **tactical** adj **1** of tactics **2** done to get a desired result in the end: a tactical retreat **tactician** /tækˈtɪʃən/ n person skilled in tactics

tac·tile /ˈtæktəl, -taɪl/ adj of or able to be felt by the sense of touch

tad·pole /ˈtædpoʷl/ n small creature that grows into a FROG or TOAD

taf·fy /ˈtæfiʸ/ n [U] (piece of) sticky candy

tag /tæg/ n **1** [C] small piece of paper or material fixed to something to show who owns it, its cost, etc. **2** [U] game in which one child chases the others until he/she touches one of them ♦ vt –gg- **1** fasten a tag to **2** provide with a name or NICKNAME **3** put (a player) out in baseball by touching him with the ball

tag along phr vi go with someone by following closely behind or when not welcome

tag on phr vt add

tail¹ /teʸl/ n **1** long movable growth at the back of a creature's body **2** last or back part (of something long): the tail of an aircraft **3** person employed to follow someone **4 turn tail** turn around ready to run away **tails** n [P] **1** side of a coin without a head on it **2** tailcoat

tail² vt follow (someone) closely, esp. without their knowledge

tail away/off phr vi lessen gradually

tail·coat /ˈteʸlkoʷt/ n man's coat with a long back divided into 2 below the waist

tail·gate /ˈteʸlgeʸt/ vi t drive too close (to the car ahead) ~gater n

tai·lor /ˈteʸlər/ n person who makes garments ♦ vt fit to a particular need ~-made /ˌ·· ˈ·◂/ adj exactly right for a particular need, person, etc.

tail·wind /ˈteʸlˌwɪnd/ n wind coming from behind

taint /teʸnt/ vt, n [S] (spoil with) a small amount of decay, infection, or bad influence

take¹ /teʸk/ v took /tʊk/, taken /ˈteʸkən/ **1** vt move from one place to another: Take the chair into the garden. | Take the children with you. | I had a tooth taken out. **2** vt remove without permission: *Someone's taken my pen.* **3** *vt* subtract: *What do you get if you take 5 from 12?* **4** *vt* get possession of; seize: *Rebels have taken the airport.* **5** *vt* get by performing an action: *Take his temperature.* | *He took notes.* | *Take a seat.* **6** *vt* start to hold: *She took my arm.* **7** *vt* use for travel: *I take the train to work.* **8** *vt* be willing to accept: *Will you take a check?* **9** *vt* accept as true or worthy of attention: *Take my advice.* | *Will you take his suggestion seriously.* **10** *vt* be able to contain: *The bus takes 55 passengers.* **11** *vt* be able to accept; bear: *I can't take his rudeness.* **12** *vt* need: *The journey takes* (= lasts) *2 hours.* | *It took 10 men to pull down the wall.* **13** *vt* do; perform: *He took a walk/a bath.* **14** *vt* put into the body: *take some medicine/a deep breath* **15** *vt* make by photography **16** *vt* have (a feeling): *take offense/pity* **17** *vt* have the intended effect; work: *Did the vaccination take?* **18** *vt* understand: *I take it you know each other.* **20 take care of** look after **21 take it easy** RELAX **22 take one's time: a** use as much time as is necessary **b** use too much time **23 take part** join in with others **24 take place** happen **25 take the cake** win **26 take the floor** begin to speak in a group

take aback *phr vt* surprise and confuse

take after *phr vt* look or behave like (an older relative)

take apart *phr vt* **1** separate into pieces **2** *sl* harm a place or person

take back *phr vt* **1** admit that (what one said) was wrong **2** cause to remember a former period in one's life: *That takes me back!*

take in *phr vt* **1** reduce the size of (a garment) **2** provide a home for **3** include **4** understand fully **5** deceive

take off *phr v* **1** *vt* remove (a garment) **2** *vi* (of a plane, etc.) rise into the air to begin a flight **3** *vi infml* leave without warning: *One day he just took off.* **4** *vt* copy the speech or manners of, esp. for humor; MIMIC **5** *vt* have as a holiday from work: *I took Tuesday off.*

take on *phr vt* **1** begin to have (a quality or appearance) **2** start to quarrel or fight with **3** accept (work, responsibility, etc.) **4** start to employ

take out *phr vt* **1** go somewhere with (someone) as a social activity **2** obtain officially: *take out insurance* **3 take someone out of himself** amuse or interest someone so that their worries are forgotten **4 take it out of someone** use all the strength of someone

take out on *phr vt* express (one's feelings) by making (someone) suffer: *He tends to take things out on his wife.*

take over *phr vi/t* gain control of and responsibility for (something)

take to *phr vt* **1** like, esp. at once **2** begin as a practice or habit: *He took to drink.* **3** go to (one's bed, etc.) for rest, escape, etc.

take up *phr vt* **1** begin to interest oneself in: *I've taken up the guitar.* **2** complain, ask, or take further action about: *I'll take the matter up with my lawyer.* **3** fill or use (space or time), esp. undesirably **4** accept (someone's) offer: *I'll take you up on that.* **5** continue (a story, etc.) **6** shorten (a garment) by folding up the bottom

take up with *phr vt* **1** become friendly with **2** be very interested in: *She's very taken up with her work.*

take² *n* **1** filming of a scene **2** takings

take·off /ˈteⁱk-ˌɔf/ *n* **1** [C;U] rising of a plane, etc., from the ground **2** amusing copy of someone's typical behavior

take·out /ˈteⁱk-aʊt/ *n* (meal from) a restaurant that sells food to eat elsewhere

take·o·ver /ˈteⁱkˌoʷvər/ *n* act of gaining control of esp. a business company

ta·ker /ˈteⁱkər/ *n* [*usu. pl.*] *infml* person willing to accept an offer

tak·ings /ˈteⁱkɪŋz/ *n* [P] money received, esp. by a store

tal·cum pow·der /ˈtælkəm ˌpaʊdər/ also **talc** *infml—n* [U] crushed mineral put on the body to dry it or make it smell nice

tale /teⁱl/ *n* **1** story **2** false story; lie

tal·ent /ˈtælənt/ *n* [S;U] special natural ability or skill ~ed *adj*

tal·is·man /ˈtælɪsmən, -lɪz-/ *n* –s object with magic protective powers

talk /tɔk/ *v* **1** *vi* speak: *Can the baby talk yet?* | *Is there somewhere quiet where we can talk?* **2** *vi* give information by speaking, usu. unwillingly: *We have ways of making you talk.* **3** *vi* speak about others' affairs; GOSSIP **4** *vt* speak about: *It's time to talk business.* ♦ *n* **1** [S] conversation **2** [C] *infml* LECTURE **3** [U] way of talking: *baby talk* **4** [*the*+S] subject much talked about: *Her sudden marriage is the talk of the town.* **5** [U] empty or meaningless speech **6 talk turkey** speak openly (about difficult matters) – see also SMALL TALK, SWEET TALK **talks** *n* [P] formal exchange of opinions ~**er** *n*

talk back *phr vi* reply rudely

talk down to *phr vt* speak to

(someone) as if one were more important, clever, etc.

talk into/out of *phr vt* persuade (someone) to do/not to do (something)

talk over *phr vt* speak about thoroughly and seriously

talk up *phr vt* speak favorably about, esp. to win support

talk·a·tive /'tɔkətɪv/ *adj* liking to talk a lot

talking point /'·· ·/ *n* subject of conversation or argument

talking-to /'·· ,·/ *n* angry talk in order to blame or CRITICIze

tall /tɔl/ *adj* **1** of greater than average height **2** of the stated height from top to bottom: *He is 6 feet tall.*

tall or·der /,· '··/ *n* [S] something unreasonably difficult to do

tal·low /'tæloʷ/ *n* [U] hard animal fat used for candles

tall tale /,· '·/ *n* story that is difficult to believe

tal·ly /'tæliʸ/ *n* recorded total of money spent, points made in a game, etc. ♦ *vi* be exactly equal; match

tal·on /'tælən/ *n* sharp powerful curved nail on a hunting bird's foot

tam·bou·rine /,tæmbə'riʸn/ *n* drumlike musical instrument with small metal plates around the edge

tame /teʸm/ *adj* **1** not fierce or wild **2** dull; unexciting ♦ *vt* make (an animal) tame **~ly** *adv* **~ness** *n* [U] **tamer** *n*

tam·per /'tæmpər/ *v* **tamper with** *phr vt* touch or change without permission, esp. causing damage

tam·pon /'tæmpɑn/ *n* mass of cotton put into a woman's sex organ to take up the monthly bleeding

tan /tæn/ *v* **-nn- 1** *vt* change (animal skin) into leather by treating with TANNIN **2** *vi/t* turn brown, esp. by sunlight ♦ *n* **1** [C] brown skin color from sunlight **2** [U] yellowish brown color

tan·dem /'tændəm/ *n* **1** bicycle for 2 riders **2 in tandem** with both working closely together

tang /tæŋ/ *n* strong sharp taste or smell **~y** *adj*

tan·gent /'tændʒənt/ *n* **1** straight line touching the edge of a curve **2 go/fly off at a tangent** change suddenly to a different course of action or thought **~ial** /tæn'dʒenʃəl, -tʃəl/ *adj* not concerned with the main subject

tan·ge·rine /,tændʒə'riʸn, 'tændʒə-,riʸn/ *n* sort of small orange

tan·gi·ble /'tændʒəbəl/ *adj* **1** clear and certain; real: *tangible proof* **2** touchable **-bly** *adv*

tan·gle /'tæŋgəl/ *vi/t* (cause to) become a confused mass of twisted threads ♦ *n* confused mass or state

tan·go /'tæŋgoʷ/ *n* **-gos** Latin-American dance

tank /tæŋk/ *n* **1** large liquid or gas container **2** enclosed armored military vehicle

tan·kard /'tæŋkərd/ *n* large usu. metal cup for beer, etc.

tank·er /'tæŋkər/ *n* ship, road vehicle, etc., carrying large quantities of liquid or gas

tan·nin /'tænɪn/ *n* [U] reddish acid found in parts of certain plants

tan·ta·lize /'tæntl,aɪz/ *vt* cause to desire something even more strongly by keeping it just out of reach

tan·ta·mount /'tæntə,maʊnt/ *adj* having the same effect (as): *Her answer is tantamount to a refusal.*

tan·trum /'tæntrəm/ *n* sudden uncontrolled attack of angry bad temper

tap[1] /tæp/ *vt* **-pp- 1** use or draw from: *tapping our reserves of oil* **2** listen secretly by making an illegal connection to (a telephone)

tap[2] *vi/t*, *n* **-pp-** (strike with) a light short blow: *She tapped her fingers on the table/tapped me on the shoulder.*

tap dance /'· ,·/ *n* dance in which one makes loud sounds on the floor with special shoes

tape /teʸp/ *n* [C;U] **1** (long piece of) narrow material: *Stick it on with some tape.* **2** (long piece of) narrow plastic MAGNETIC material on which sounds or pictures are recorded ♦ *vt* **1** record on tape (2) **2** fasten or tie with tape (1)

tape deck /'· ·/ *n* tape recorder

tape mea·sure /'· ,··/ *n* narrow band of cloth or bendable metal used for measuring

ta·per /'teʸpər/ *vi/t* make or become gradually narrower towards one end ♦ *n* thin candle

tape re·cord·er /'· ·,··/ *n* electrical apparatus for recording and playing sound with TAPE (2)

tap·es·try /'tæpɪstriʸ/ *n* [C;U] (piece of) cloth with pictures or patterns woven into it

tar /tɑr/ *n* [U] black meltable substance used for making roads, preserving wood, etc. ♦ *vt* **-rr- 1** cover with tar **2 tarred with the same brush** having the same faults **3 beat the tar out of** beat badly

ta·ran·tu·la /tə'ræntʃələ/ *n* large hairy poisonous SPIDER

tar·dy /'tɑrdiʸ/ *adj fml or lit* **1** late, esp. at school **-dily** *adv* **-diness** *n* [U] **2** slow in arriving or happening

tar·get /'tɑrgɪt/ *n* **1** something aimed at in shooting practice **2**

place, thing, or person at which an attack is directed **3** total or object which one tries to reach: *a production target of 500 cars a week* ♦ *vt* cause to be a target

tar·iff /'tærɪf/ *n* **1** tax on goods coming into a country **2** *fml* list of prices in a hotel, restaurant, etc.

tar·mac /'tɑrmæk/ *n* [U] **1** tar and small stones for making road surfaces **2** area where aircraft take off and land

tar·nish /'tɑrnɪʃ/ *vi/t* make or become discolored or less bright: *tarnished silver*/(fig.) *reputations*

tar·ot /'tæroʊ/ *n* set of 22 special cards used for telling the future

tar·pau·lin /tɑr'pɔlɪn, 'tɑrpəlɪn/ *n* [C;U] (sheet or cover of) heavy WATERPROOF cloth

tar·ry /'tæriʸ/ *vi lit* stay in a place for a while

tart[1] /tɑrt/ *adj* bitter ♦ ~**ness** *n* [U]

tart[2] *n* sexually immoral woman

tart[3] *n* pastry container holding fruit or JAM

tar·tan /'tɑrtn/ *n* [C;U] (woolen cloth with) a pattern of bands crossing each other, esp. representing a particular Scottish CLAN

tar·tar[1] /'tɑrtər/ *n* [U] chalklike substance that forms on teeth

tartar[2] *n infml* fierce person with a violent temper

tartar sauce /'·· ,·/ *n* food made from MAYONNAISE and PICKLES, eaten with fish

task /tæsk/ *n* **1** piece of (hard) work (to be) done **2 take someone to task** speak severely to someone for a fault or failure

task force /'· ·/ *n* military or police group set up for a special purpose

task·mas·ter /'tæsk,mæstər/, **–mistress** /-,mɪstrɪs/ *fem.*—*n* someone who makes people work very hard

tas·sel /'tæsəl/ *n* tied bunch of threads hung in a decorative way

taste /teʸst/ *n* **1** [C;U] quality by which a food or drink is recognized in the mouth: *Sugar has a sweet taste.* **2** [U] sense which recognizes food or drink as sweet, salty, etc. **3** [U] ability to make (good) judgments about beauty, style, fashion, etc. **4** [C;U] personal liking: *She has expensive tastes in clothes.* ♦ *v* **1** *vt* experience or test the taste of **2** *vi* have a particular taste: *These oranges taste nice.* **3** *vt lit* experience: *having tasted freedom* ~**ful** *adj* showing good TASTE (3) ~**less** *adj* **1** not tasting of anything **2** showing bad TASTE (3) **tasty** *adj* tasting pleasant

taste bud /'· ·/ *n* group of cells on the tongue used in tasting

tat·ters /'tætərz/ *n* **in tatters: a** (of clothes) old and torn **b** ruined ~**tered** *adj* (dressed in clothes that are) in tatters

tat·tle /'tætl/ *vi/t* tell (a secret)

tat·tle·tale /'tætl,teʸl/ *n* person who tattles

tat·too /tæ'tuʷ/ *n* **–toos** pattern made by tattooing ♦ *vt* make (a pattern) on the skin (of) by pricking with a needle and then pouring colored DYES in ~**ist** *n*

tat·ty /'tætiʸ/ *adj sl* untidy or in bad condition

taught /tɔt/ *past t. & p. of* TEACH

taunt /tɔnt, tɑnt/ *vt* try to upset with unkind remarks or by laughing at faults or failures ♦ *n* taunting remark

taut /tɔt/ *adj* stretched tight ~**ly** *adv* ~**ness** *n* [U]

tau·tol·o·gy /tɔ'tɑlədʒiʸ/ *n* [C;U] unnecessary repeating of the same idea in different words **–gical** /,tɔtə'lɑdʒɪkəl/ *adj*

tav·ern /'tævərn/ *n* BAR (4)

taw·dry /'tɔdriʸ/ *adj* cheaply showy; showing bad TASTE (3) **–driness** *n* [U]

taw·ny /'tɔniʸ/ *adj* brownish yellow

tax /tæks/ *n* [C;U] money which must be paid to the government ♦ *vt* **1** make (someone) pay a tax **2** charge a tax on: *Cigarettes are heavily taxed.* **3** push to the limits of what one can bear: *Such stupid questions tax my patience.* ~**able** *adj* that can be TAXed (2) ~**ation** /tæk-'seʸʃən/ *n* [U] (money raised by) taxing ~**ing** /'tæksɪŋ/ *adj* needing great effort

tax-de·duct·i·ble /,· ·'··/ *adj* that may legally be subtracted from one's total income before it is taxed

tax·i[1] /'tæksiʸ/ *also* **tax·i·cab** /'tæksiʸkæb/ — *n* car with a driver which carries passengers for money

taxi[2] *vi* (of an aircraft) move along the ground before taking off or after landing

tax·i·der·my /'tæksə,dɜrmiʸ/ *n* [U] filling the skins of dead animals so that they look real **–mist** *n*

taxi stand /'·· ,·/ *n* place where taxis wait for riders

TB /,tiʸ 'biʸ/ *abbrev. for:* TUBERCULOSIS

tbs. *abbrev. for:* TABLESPOON

tea /tiʸ/ *n* [C;U] **1** (drink made by pouring boiling water onto) the dried leaves of an Asian bush cut into pieces **2** drink made like tea from the stated leaves: *mint tea* **3 one's cup of tea** the sort of thing one likes: *Running isn't really my cup of tea.*

tea·bag /'tiʸbæg/ *n* small paper bag full of tea leaves

teach /tiʸtʃ/ v **taught** /tɔt/ **1** vi/t give knowledge or skill of (something) to (someone): *He taught me French.* **2** vt show (someone) the bad results of doing something: *I'll teach you to be rude to me!* (= a threat) ~**er** n person who teaches, esp. as a job ~**ing** n [U] **1** job of a teacher **2** also **teachings** pl. — moral beliefs taught by someone of historical importance: *the teachings of Christ*

teach-in /'· ˌ·/ n formal exchange of opinions about a subject of interest

teak /tiʸk/ n [U] hard yellowish brown wood from Asia, used for furniture

team[1] /tiʸm/ n **1** group of people who work or esp. play together: *a football team* **2** 2 or more animals pulling the same vehicle

team[2] v **team up** phr vi work together for a shared purpose

team·ster /'tiʸmstər/ n TRUCK driver, esp. one belonging to a labor union

team·work /'tiʸmwɜrk/ n [U] (effective) combined effort

tea·pot /'tiʸpɑt/ n container in which tea is made and served

tear[1] /teər/ v **tore** /tɔr, toʷr/, **torn** /tɔrn, toʷrn/ **1** vt pull apart by force, esp. so as to leave irregular edges **2** vi become torn **3** vt remove with sudden force: *He tore off his clothes.* **4** vi rush excitedly **5** be **torn be·tween** be unable to decide between **6** tear one's hair (out) be very upset ♦ n hole made by tearing

tear down phr vt pull down; destroy

tear into phr vt attack violently

tear up phr vt destroy completely by tearing

tear[2] /tɪər/ n **1** drop of salty liquid that flows from the eye, esp. because of sadness **2** in tears crying ~**ful** adj ~**fully** adv

tear gas /'tɪər ˌgæs/ n [U] gas that stings the eyes

tear·jerk·er /'tɪərˌdʒɜrkər/ n very sad book, film, etc.

tease /tiʸz/ v **1** vi/t make jokes (about) or laugh (at) unkindly or playfully **2** vt annoy on purpose **3** vt separate the threads in (wool, etc.) ♦ n someone fond of teasing

tea·spoon /'tiʸspuʷn/ n small spoon used for eating and measuring

teat /tiʸt, tɪt/ n animal's NIPPLE

tea tow·el /'· ˌ·/ n cloth for drying washed cups, plates, etc.

tech·ni·cal /'tɛknɪkəl/ adj **1** concerned with scientific or industrial subjects or skills **2** needing special knowledge in order to be understood: *His arguments are too technical for me.* **3** according to an (unreasonably) exact acceptance of the

rules ~**ly** /-kliʸ/ adv see also HIGH TECHNICAL

tech·ni·cal·i·ty /ˌtɛknɪ'kæləțiʸ/ n small (esp. unimportant) detail or rule

tech·ni·cian /tɛk'nɪʃən/ n highly skilled scientific or industrial worker

tech·nique /tɛk'niʸk/ n method of doing an activity that needs skill

tech·no·crat /'tɛknəˌkræt/ n often derog scientist or technician in charge of an organization

tech·nol·o·gy /tɛk'nɑlədʒiʸ/ n practical science, esp. as used in industrial production ~**gist** n ~**gical** /ˌtɛknə'lɑdʒɪkəl/ adj

ted·dy bear /'tɛdiʸ ˌbeər/ also **teddy** infml — n toy bear

te·di·ous /'tiʸdiʸəs/ adj long and uninteresting ~**ly** adv ~**ness** n [U]

te·di·um /'tiʸdiʸəm/ n [U] state of being tedious

tee /tiʸ/ n small object on which a GOLF ball is placed to be hit ♦ v

tee off phr vi drive the ball from a tee

tee up phr vi/t place (the ball) on a tee

teem /tiʸm/ vi to be full of or to be present in large numbers

teem with phr vt have (a type of creature) present in great numbers

teen·ag·er /'tiʸnˌeʸdʒər/ n person of between 13 and 19 years old **teen·age** adj

teens /tiʸnz/ n [P] period of being a teenager

tee·ny-ween·y /ˌtiʸniʸ 'wiʸniʸ◂/ adj infml extremely small

tee·ter /'tiʸțər/ vi stand or move in an unsteady manner

teeter-tot·ter /'·· ˌ··/ n SEESAW (1)

teeth /tiʸθ/ pl. of TOOTH

teethe /tiʸð/ vi (of a baby) grow teeth

teething troub·les /'·· ˌ··/ n [P] problems in the early stages of using something

tee·to·tal /ˌtiʸ'toʷțl◂/ adj drinking no alcohol ~**ler** n

Tef·lon /'tɛflɑn/ n tdmk [U] artificial substance to which things will not stick, used on kitchen pans, etc.: (fig.) *the Teflon president*

tel·e·com·mu·ni·ca·tions /ˌtɛləkəˌmyuʷnə'keʸʃənz/ n also **tel·e·comms** /'tɛləˌkɑmz/ infml [P] sending and receiving of messages by means of radio, telephone, SATELLITE, etc.

tel·e·gram /'tɛləˌgræm/ n message sent by telegraph

tel·e·graph /'tɛləgræf/ n [U] method of sending messages along wire by electric signals ♦ vt send a telegraph ~**ic** /ˌtɛlə'græfɪk◂/ adj

te·lep·a·thy /tə'lepəθiʸ/ n [U] sending of messages directly from one mind to another –**thic** /ˌtelə'pæθɪk◂/ adj

tel·e·phone /'teləˌfoʷn/ n [C;U] (apparatus for) the sending and receiving of sounds over long distances by electric means ♦ vi/t (try to) speak (to) by telephone

telephone pole /'··· ·/ n pole for supporting telephone wires

te·le·pho·to lens /ˌtelə,foʷtoʷ 'lenz/ n special LENS used for photographing very distant objects

tel·e·scope /'teləˌskoʷp/ n tube with a special piece of glass in it for looking at very distant objects ♦ vi/t shorten, esp. a by one part sliding over another **b** by crushing –**scopic** /ˌtelə'skapɪk◂/ adj **1** of or related to a telescope **2** that telescopes

tel·e·text /'teli,tekst/ n [U] system of broadcasting written information (e.g. news) on television

tel·e·vise /'teləˌvaɪz/ vt broadcast on television

tel·e·vi·sion /'teləˌvɪʒən/ n [C;U] (apparatus for receiving) the broadcasting of pictures and sounds by electric waves

tel·ex /'teleks/ n **1** [U] method of sending written messages around the world by telephone wires, SATELLITEs, etc. **2** [C] message sent by telex ♦ vt send by telex

tell /tel/ v **told** /toʷld/ **1** vt make (something) known to (someone) in words: Are you telling me the truth? | Tell me how to do it. **2** vt warn; advise: I told you it wouldn't work. **3** vt order: I told him to do it. **4** vi/t find out; know: How can you tell which button to press? | It was so dark that I couldn't tell if it was you. **5** all told when all have been counted **6** tell the time read the time from a watch or clock **7** there's no telling it is impossible to know **8** you're telling me (used as a strong way of saying) I know this already

tell off phr vt speak severely to (someone who has done something wrong)

tell on phr vt **1** have a bad effect on **2** infml (used esp. by children) inform against (someone)

tell·er /'telər/ n **1** bank clerk **2** person who counts votes

tell·ing /'telɪŋ/ adj sharply effective: a telling argument

tell·tale /'telteʸl/ adj being a small sign that shows something: a few telltale hairs on the murderer's sleeve

te·me·ri·ty /tə'merətiʸ/ n [U] fml foolish confidence

temp /temp/ n infml secretary

employed for a short time ♦ vi infml, work as a temp

tem·per /'tempər/ n **1** [C] state of mind; MOOD: He's in a good/bad temper. **2** [C;U] angry or impatient state of mind **3** keep one's temper stay calm **4** lose one's temper become angry ♦ vt **1** harden (esp. metal) by special treatment **2** make less severe: justice tempered with mercy

tem·pe·ra·ment /'tempərəmənt/ n person's character with regard to being calm, easily excited, etc. ~**al** /ˌtempərə'mentl◂/ adj **1** having or showing frequent changes of temper **2** caused by temperament ~**ally** adv

tem·pe·rance /'tempərəns/ n [U] **1** fml being TEMPERATE (2) **2** complete avoiding of alcohol

tem·pe·rate /'tempərɪt/ adj **1** (of an area's weather) neither very hot nor very cold **2** fml avoiding too much of anything

tem·pe·ra·ture /'tempərətʃər/ n **1** [C;U] degree of heat or coldness: the average temperature **2** [S] body temperature higher than the correct one; fever

tem·pest /'tempɪst/ n lit violent storm

tem·pes·tu·ous /tem'pestʃuəs/ adj full of wildness or anger

tem·plate /'templɪt/ n **1** shape used as a guide for cutting metal, wood, etc. **2** computer FILE used to make others

tem·ple[1] /'tempəl/ n building where people worship a god or gods, esp. in the Jewish and Mormon religions

temple[2] n flattish area on each side of the forehead

tem·po /'tempoʷ/ n –**pos 1** rate of movement or activity **2** speed of music

tem·po·ral /'tempərəl/ adj fml **1** of practical rather than religious affairs **2** of time

tem·po·ra·ry /'tempə,reriʸ/ adj lasting for only a limited time –**rily** adv

tempt /tempt/ vt (try to) persuade (someone) to do something wrong ~**ation** /temp'teʸʃən/ n **1** [U] act of tempting **2** [C] something that tempts, esp. by being very attractive ~**ing** adj very attractive

ten /ten/ determiner, n, pron 10

ten·a·ble /'tenəbəl/ adj fml **1** (of a point of view, etc.) that can be reasonably supported or held **2** (of a job) that can be held for the stated period

te·na·cious /tə'neʸʃəs/ adj bravely firm ~**ly** adv –**city** /tə'næsətiʸ/ n [U]

ten·ant /'tenənt/ n person who pays rent for the use of a building, land, etc. –**ancy** n **1** [C] length of time a person is a tenant **2** [U] use of land, etc., as a tenant

tend[1] /tend/ vt be likely: She tends to lose (= often loses) her temper if you disagree with her.

tend[2] vt take care of

ten·den·cy /'tendənsi/ n **1** likelihood of often happening or behaving in a particular way **2** special liking and natural skill: She has artistic tendencies.

ten·den·tious /ten'denʃəs/ adj fml (in discussion, article, etc.) unfairly leaving out other points of view ~**ly** adv

ten·der[1] /'tendər/ adj **1** not difficult to bite through **2** needing careful handling; delicate **3** sore **4** gentle, kind, and loving ~**ly** adv ~**ness** n [U]

tender[2] v fml **1** vt present for acceptance: She tendered her resignation. **2** vt offer in payment of debt **3** vi make a statement ♦ a statement of the price one would charge see also LEGAL TENDER

ten·der·heart·ed /ˌtendər'hɑrtɪd◂/ adj easily made to feel love, pity, or sorrow

ten·don /'tendən/ n strong cord connecting a muscle to a bone

ten·dril /'tendrəl/ n thin curling stem by which a plant holds on to things

ten·e·ment /'tenəmənt/ n large building divided into APARTMENTS, esp. in a poor city area

ten·et /'tenɪt/ n fml principle; belief

ten·nis /'tenɪs/ n [U] game played by hitting a ball over a net with a RACKET

ten·or /'tenər/ n **1** (man with) the highest man's singing voice **2** instrument with the same range of notes as this: a tenor saxophone **3** fml general meaning (of something written or spoken)

tense[1] /tens/ adj **1** stretched tight **2** nervously anxious ♦ vi/t (cause to) become tense ~**ly** adv ~**ness** n [U]

tense[2] n form of a verb showing time and continuity of action: the future tense

ten·sile /'tensəl/ adj of TENSION (1)

ten·sion /'tenʃən/ n **1** [C;U] degree to which something is (able to be) stretched **2** [U] nervous anxiety caused by problems, uncertain waiting, etc. **3** [C;U] anxious, untrusting, and possibly dangerous relationship: racial tensions in the inner city **4** [U] tech electric power: high-tension cables

tent /tent/ n cloth shelter supported usu. by poles and ropes, used esp. by campers

ten·ta·cle /'tentəkəl/ n long snake-like boneless limb of certain creatures: the tentacles of an octopus

ten·ta·tive /'tentətɪv/ adj **1** not firmly arranged or fixed: a tentative agreement **2** not firm in making statements or decisions ~**ly** adv

ten·ter·hooks /'tentər,hʊks/ n **on tenterhooks** anxiously waiting

tenth /tenθ/ determiner, adv, n, pron 10th

ten·u·ous /'tenyuʷəs/ adj slight: a tenuous connection ~**ly** adv ~**ness** n [U]

ten·ure /'tenyər/ n [U] **1** act, right, or period of holding a job or land **2** right to keep one's job, esp. as a university teacher

te·pee /'tiʲpiʲ/ n round tent with a pointed top

tep·id /'tepɪd/ adj only slightly warm: tepid water / (fig.) enthusiasm

te·quil·a /tə'kiʲlə/ n strong alcoholic drink made in Mexico

term /tɜrm/ n **1** word or expression, esp. as used in a particular activity: 'Tort' is a legal term. **2** fixed period: a 4-year term as president **3** division of the school or university year: the summer term **4 in the long/short term** over a long/short period – see also TERMS ♦ vt name; call; describe as

ter·mi·nal /'tɜrmənəl/ adj of or being an illness that will cause death ♦ n **1** main building for passengers or goods at an airport, port, etc. **2** apparatus for giving instructions to and getting information from a computer **3** place for electrical connections: the terminals of a battery ~**ly** adv

ter·mi·nate /'tɜrmə,neʲt/ vi/t fml (cause to) come to an end –**nation** /ˌtɜrmə'neʲʃən/ n [U]: the termination of a pregnancy

ter·mi·nol·o·gy /ˌtɜrmə'nɑlədʒiʲ/ n [U] (use of) particular TERMS (3): legal terminology –**logical** /ˌtɜrmənl'ɑdʒɪkəl/ adj

ter·mi·nus /'tɜrmənəs/ n –**ni** or –**nuses** end of a railroad line

ter·mite /'tɜrmaɪt/ n antlike insect that eats wood

terms /tɜrmz/ n [P] **1** conditions of an agreement or contract **2** conditions of sale **3 come to terms** reach an agreement **4 come to terms with** accept (something unwelcome) **5 on good/bad/friendly terms** having a good, bad, etc., relationship

ter·race /'terɪs/ n **1** level area cut from a slope **2** flat area next to a building **3** flat roof of a house ♦ vt form into TERRACES (1)

ter·ra cot·ta /ˌterə 'kɑtə◂/ n [U] (articles of) reddish brown baked clay

ter·rain /təˈreɪn/ n [C;U] (area of) land of the stated sort: *rocky terrain*

ter·res·tri·al /təˈrestriəl/ adj fml of the Earth or land, as opposed to space or the sea

ter·ri·ble /ˈterəbəl/ adj 1 extremely severe: *a terrible accident* 2 extremely bad or unpleasant: *a terrible dinner* **-bly** adv 1 extremely severely or badly 2 extremely: *terribly sorry*

ter·ri·er /ˈteriər/ n type of small active dog

ter·rif·ic /təˈrɪfɪk/ adj 1 excellent 2 very great ~ **ally** /-kli/ adv extremely

ter·ri·fy /ˈterə,faɪ/ vt frighten extremely: *a terrified horse*

ter·ri·to·ry /ˈterə,tɔːri, -,toʷri/ n [C;U] 1 (area of) land, esp. as ruled by one government: *This island is French territory.* 2 area belonging to (and defended by) a particular person, animal, or group 3 area for which one person or group is responsible **-rial** /,terəˈtɔːriəl◂, -,toʷr-/ adj 1 of or being land or territory 2 (of animals, birds, etc.) showing a tendency to guard one's own TERRITORY (2)

ter·ror /ˈterər/ n [U] extreme fear

ter·ror·is·m /ˈterə,rɪzəm/ n [U] use of violence for political purposes **-ist** n

ter·ror·ize /ˈterə,raɪz/ vt fill with terror by threats or acts of violence

terse /tɜːrs/ adj using few words, often to show anger ~ **ly** adv ~ **ness** n [U]

ter·tia·ry /ˈtɜːrʃiˌeri, -ʃəri/ adj fml 3rd in order

TESOL /ˈtesəl/ n [U] teaching English to speakers of other languages

test /test/ n 1 set of questions or jobs to measure someone's knowledge or skill: *a history/driving test* 2 short medical examination: *an eye test* 3 use of something to see how well it works: *nuclear weapon tests* 4 **put to the test** find out the qualities of (something) by use ♦ vt 1 study or examine with a test 2 provide difficult conditions for: *a testing time* (= a difficult period) *for the country* 3 search by means of tests: *The company is testing for oil.*

tes·ta·ment /ˈtestəmənt/ n 1 fml for WILL² (5) 2 (cap.) either of the 2 main parts of the Bible: *the Old Testament*

test ban /ˈ··/ n agreement between countries not to do NUCLEAR tests

tes·ti·cle /ˈtestɪkəl/ n either of the 2 round organs that produce SPERM in male animals

tes·ti·fy /ˈtestə,faɪ/ vi/t 1 make a solemn statement of truth 2 show (something) clearly; prove

tes·ti·mo·ni·al /,testəˈmoʷniəl/ n 1 formal written statement of someone's character and ability 2 something given or done to show respect, thanks, etc.

tes·ti·mo·ny /ˈtestə,moʷni/ n formal statement of facts, esp. in a court of law

test tube /ˈ· ·/ n small glass tube, closed at one end, used in scientific tests adj made by man in a test tube: *a test tube baby*

tes·ty /ˈtesti/ adj fml bad-tempered **-tily** adv

tet·a·nus /ˈtetn-əs/ n [U] serious disease, caused by infection of a cut, which causes the muscles to stiffen

tetch·y /ˈtetʃi/ adj sensitive in a bad-tempered way **-ily** adv **-iness** n [U]

tête-à-tête /,teʸt ə ˈteʸt, ,tet ə ˈtet/ n private conversation between 2 people

teth·er /ˈteðər/ n 1 rope, etc., to which an animal is tied 2 **the end of one's tether** the condition of being unable to bear any more difficulties, annoyances, etc. ♦ vt fasten with a tether

text /tekst/ n 1 [C;U] main body of printed words in a book 2 [C;U] exact original words of a speech, etc. 3 [C] textbook 4 [C] sentence from the Bible used by a priest in a SERMON ~ **ual** adj

text·book /ˈtekstbʊk/ n standard book used for studying a particular subject, esp. in schools ♦ adj 1 as it ought to be; IDEAL: *textbook journalism* 2 typical

tex·tile /ˈtekstaɪl, ˈtekstəl/ n woven material

tex·ture /ˈtekstʃər/ n [C;U] quality of roughness, smoothness, or fineness of a surface or substance

TGIF /,ti· dʒiː aɪ ˈef/ humor Thank God It's Friday

tha·lid·o·mide /θəˈlɪdə,maɪd/ n [U] drug no longer used because it caused unborn babies to develop wrongly

than /ðən; *strong* ðæn/ conj, prep 1 (used in comparing things): *This is bigger than that.* 2 when; as soon as: *No sooner had we started to eat than the doorbell rang.*

thank /θæŋk/ vt express one's gratefulness to **thanks** n [P] 1 (words expressing) gratefulness 2 **thanks to** because of ~ **ful** adj 1 glad 2 grateful ~ **fully** adv ~ **less** adj not likely to be rewarded with thanks or success

thanks /θæŋks/ interj thank you

thanks·giv·ing /,θæŋksˈgɪvɪŋ/ n [C;U] (an) expression of gratefulness, esp. to God

Thanksgiving Day /·ˈ··· ,·/ n

national holiday on the fourth Thursday in November

thank you /ˈ·ˌ·/ interj **1** (used for politely expressing thanks or acceptance) **2 no, thank you** (used for politely refusing an offer)

that¹ /ðæt/ determiner, pron **those** /ðoᵘz/ **1** (being) the person, thing, or idea which is understood or has just been mentioned or shown: *Look at that man over there.* | *Who told you that?* | *I'd like these apples, not those.* **2 that's that** that is the end of the matter

that² /ðət; strong ðæt/ conj **1** (used for introducing CLAUSES): *She said that she couldn't come.* **2** (used as a RELATIVE PRONOUN) which/who(m): *This is the book that I bought.*

that³ /ðæt/ adv to such a degree; so: *It wasn't that difficult.*

thatch /θætʃ/ vt, n [U] (make or cover with) a roof covering of STRAW: *a thatched roof/cottage*

thaw /θɔ/ v **1** vi/t change from a solid frozen state to being liquid or soft **2** vi become friendlier, less formal, etc. ♦ n **1** period when ice and snow melt **2** increase in friendliness

the /ðə; before vowels ði; strong ði/ definite article, determiner **1** (used for speaking or writing of a particular thing): *the sky* | *Close the door.* **2** (used with some names of places etc.): *the Rhine* | *the Pacific* **3** (used before a singular noun to make it general): *The lion is a wild animal.* **4** (used for making an adjective into a noun): *I like the French.* (= French people) | *To do the impossible.* **5** (used with measures) each: *paid by the hour* | *sold by the yard* **6** (used before names of musical instruments): *She plays the piano.* **7** (used before the plural of 20, 30, etc., to show a period of 10 years): *music of the 60s* ♦ adv **1** (used in comparisons, to show that 2 things happen together): *The more he eats, the fatter he gets.* **2** (in comparisons to show that someone or something is better, worse, etc., than before): *She looks all the better for having quit her job.* **3** (to show that someone or something is more than any other): *She's the cleverest/the most sensible of them all.*

the·at·er /ˈθiᵊətər/ n **1** building where plays are performed **2** the work of people involved with plays: *He's in the theater.* **3** large room where public talks are given **4** area of activity in a war –atrical /θiˈætrɪkəl/ adj **1** of the theater **2** too showy; not natural

the·at·er·go·er /ˈðiᵊətərˌgoʷər/ n person who goes regularly to THEATERS (1)

thee /ði/ pron lit (object form of **thou**) you

theft /θɛft/ n [C;U] stealing

their /ðər; strong ðɛər/ determiner of them; *their house*

theirs /ðɛərz/ pron of them; their one(s): *It's theirs.*

them /ðəm, əm; strong ðɛm/ pron (object form of **they**): *I want those books; give them to me.*

theme /θim/ n **1** subject of a talk, piece of writing, etc. **2** repeated idea, image, or tune in writing, music, etc.

theme park /ˈ·ˌ·/ n enclosed outdoor area containing amusements which are all based on a single subject (e.g. space travel)

theme song /ˈ·ˌ·/ n short piece of music used regularly to introduce a famous person or television program

them·selves /ðəmˈsɛlvz, ðɛm-/ pron **1** (reflexive form of **they**): *They saw themselves on television.* **2** (strong form of **they**): *They built it themselves.* **3 (all) by themselves: a** alone **b** without help **4 to themselves** not shared

then /ðɛn/ adv **1** at that time: *I was happier then.* **2** next; afterwards:...*and then we went home.* **3** in that case; as a result: *Have you done your homework? Then you can watch television.* **4** besides; also

thence /ðɛns/ adv fml from that place

the·ol·o·gy /θiˈɑlədʒi/ n [U] study of religious ideas and beliefs –ologian /ˌθiᵊˈloʷdʒən/ n –ological /ˌθiᵊˈlɑdʒɪkəl/ adj

theo·rem /ˈθiᵊrəm, ˈθiᵊrəm/ n MATHEMATICAL statement that can be proved by reasoning

the·o·ry /ˈθiᵊəri, ˈθiᵊri/ n **1** [C] statement intended to explain a fact or event **2** [U] general principles and methods as opposed to practice –retical /ˌθiᵊˈrɛtɪkəl/ adj existing in or based on theory, not practice or fact –rize /ˈθiᵊˌraɪz/ vi form a theory

ther·a·peu·tic /ˌθɛrəˈpyuʷtɪk/ adj **1** for the treating or curing of disease **2** having a good effect on one's health or state of mind: *I find swimming/knitting very therapeutic.*

ther·a·py /ˈθɛrəpiˌ/ n [C;U] treatment of illnesses of the body or mind –pist n

there¹ /ðɛər/ adv **1** at or to that place: *He lives over there.* **2** (used for drawing attention to someone or something): *There goes John.* **3 all there** healthy in mind **4 there and then** at that exact place and time **5 there you are: a** here is what you wanted **b** I told you so ♦ interj (used for comforting someone or expressing victory, satisfaction, etc.): *There, there. Stop crying.* | *There, I knew I was right.*

there² /pron (used for showing that something or someone exists or happens, usu. as the subject of **be**, **seem**, or **appear**): *There's someone at the door to see you.*

there·a·bouts /ˌðɛərəˈbauts, ˈðɛərəˌbauts/ *adv* near that place, time, number, etc.

there·af·ter /ðɛərˈæftər/ *adv fml* after that

there·by /ðɛərˈbaɪ, ˈðɛərbaɪ/ *adv fml* by doing or saying that

there·fore /ˈðɛərfɔr, -fo°r/ *adv* for that reason; as a result

there·up·on /ˈðɛərəˌpɒn, -ˌpɒn, ˌðɛərəˈpɒn, -ˈpɒn/ *adv fml* **1** about that matter **2** without delay

ther·mal /ˈθɜrməl/ *adj* of, using, producing, caused by or keeping in heat: *thermal underwear* (= for use in cold weather) ◆ *n* rising current of warm air

ther·mo·dy·nam·ics /ˌθɜrmoʷdaɪˈnæmɪks/ *n* [U] scientific study of heat and its power in driving machines

ther·mom·e·ter /θərˈmɑmətər/ *n* instrument for measuring temperature

ther·mos /ˈθɜrməs/ *n tdmk* bottle with a VACUUM between its 2 walls, for keeping liquids hot or cold

ther·mo·stat /ˈθɜrməˌstæt/ *n* apparatus for keeping a machine, room, etc., at an even temperature

the·sau·rus /θɪˈsɔrəs/ *n* dictionary with words arranged in groups according to similarities in meaning

these /ðiʸz/ *pl. of* THIS

the·sis /ˈθiʸsɪs/ *n* **-ses** /-siʸz/ **1** long piece of writing on a particular subject, done to gain a higher university degree **2** opinion or statement supported by reasoned arguments

they /ðeʸ/ *pron* (used as the subject of a sentence) **1** those people, animals, or things **2** people in general: *They say prices are going to rise.* **3** (used to avoid saying **he** or **she**): *If anyone knows, they should tell me.*

they'd /ðeʸd/ *short for:* **1** they had **2** they would

they'll /ðeʸl, ðel/ *short for:* they will

they're /ðər; *strong* ðɛər, ðeʸər/ *short for:* they are

they've /ðeʸv/ *short for:* they have

thick /θɪk/ *adj* **1** having a large or the stated distance between opposite surfaces: *thick walls* | *walls 2 feet thick* **2** (of liquid) not flowing easily **3** difficult to see through: *thick mist* **4** full of; covered with: *furniture thick with dust* **5** with many objects set close together: *a thick forest* **6** *sl* stupid ◆ *adv* **1** thickly **2 thick and fast** quickly and in large numbers ◆ *n* **1** [*the+*S] part, place, etc., of greatest activity **2 through thick and thin** through both good and bad times **~ly** *adv* **~en** *vi/t* make or become thicker **~ness** *n* **1** [C;U] being thick **2** [C] LAYER

thick·et /ˈθɪkɪt/ *n* thick growth of bushes and small trees

thick·set /ˌθɪkˈsɛt◂/ *adj* having a broad strong body

thick-skinned /ˌ·ˈ·◂/ *adj* not easily offended

thief /θiʸf/ *n* **thieves** /θiʸvz/ person who steals

thieve /θiʸv/ *vi* steal

thigh /θaɪ/ *n* top part of the leg in humans and some animals

thim·ble /ˈθɪmbəl/ *n* small cap put over the end of the finger when sewing

thin /θɪn/ *adj* **-nn-** **1** having a small distance between opposite surfaces **2** not fat **3** (of a liquid) flowing (too) easily; weak **4** with few objects widely separated: *a thin audience* **5** easy to see through: *thin mist* **6** lacking force or strength: *a thin excuse* **7 thin end of the wedge** something which seems unimportant but will open the way for more serious things of a similar kind ◆ *adv* thinly ◆ *vi/t* make or become thinner **~ly** *adv* **~ness** *n* [U]

thin air /ˌ· ˈ·/ *n* [U] *infml* state of not being seen or not existing

thine /ðaɪn/ *determiner* THY ◆ *pron lit* (*possessive form of* **thou**) yours

thing /θɪŋ/ *n* **1** [C] unnamed or unnameable object: *What do you use this thing for?* **2** [C] remark, idea, or subject: *What a nasty thing to say!* **3** [C] act; activity: *the first thing we have to do* **4** [C] event: *A funny thing happened today.* **5** [S] that which is necessary or desirable: *Cold beer's just the thing on a hot day.* **6** [S] the fashion or custom: *the latest thing in shoes* **7** [S] *sl* activity satisfying to one personally: *Tennis isn't really my thing.* **8 first thing** early in the morning **9 for one thing** (used for introducing a reason) **10 have a thing about** have a strong like or dislike for **11 a good/bad thing** it's sensible/not sensible: *It's a good thing we found you.* (= it's lucky) **12 make a thing of** give too much importance to **13 the thing is** what we must consider is **things** *n* [P] **1** general state of affairs; situation **2** one's personal possessions: *Pack your things.*

thing·a·ma·jig /ˈθɪŋəməˌdʒɪg/ *n infml* thing (1)

think /θɪŋk/ v **thought** /θɔt/ **1** vi use the mind to make judgments **2** vt have as an opinion; believe: *Do you think it will rain?* **3** vt understand; imagine: *I can't think why you did it.* **4** vt have as a plan: *I think I'll come this swimming tomorrow.* **5** **think aloud** to speak one's thoughts as they come ~ **er** n

think about phr vt consider seriously before making a decision

think of phr vt **1** form a possible plan for **2** have as an opinion about: *What do you think of that?* **3** take into account: *But think of the cost!* **4** remember **5** **not think much of** have a low opinion of **6** **think better of** decide against **7** **think highly/well/little of** have a good/ bad, etc., opinion of someone or something **8** **think nothing of** regard as usual or easy

think out/through phr vt consider carefully and in detail

think over phr vt consider seriously

think up phr vt invent (esp. an idea)

think·ing /ˈθɪŋkɪŋ/ n [U] opinion: *What's the director's thinking on this?* ♦ adj thoughtful; able to think clearly

thin-skinned /ˌ· ˈ·◄/ adj easily offended

third /θɜrd/ determiner, adv, n, pron 3rd

third de·gree /ˌ· ·ˈ·◄/ n [the+S] hard questioning and rough treatment

third par·ty /ˌ· ˈ··◄/ n **1** person other than the 2 main people concerned **2** person other than the holder protected by an insurance agreement

third-rate /ˌ· ˈ·◄/ adj of very low quality

Third World /ˌ· ˈ·◄/ n [the] the countries of the world which are industrially less developed

thirst /θɜrst/ n **1** [S;U] desire for drink **2** [U] lack of drink: *I'm dying of thirst* **3** [S] strong desire: *the thirst for knowledge* ~ **y** adj feeling or causing thirst

thir·teen /ˌθɜrˈtiʸn◄/ determiner, n, pron 13 ~ **th** determiner, adv, n, pron 13th

thir·ty /ˈθɜrt̬iʸ/ determiner, n, pron 30 –**tieth** determiner, adv, n, pron 30th

this /ðɪs/ determiner, pron **these** /ðiʸz/ **1** (one) going to be mentioned, to happen: *I'll come this morning.* | *Do it like this.* (= in the way about to be shown) **2** (one) near or nearer in place, time, thought, etc.: *Give me these, not those.* **3** infml a certain: *There were these two men standing there...* ♦ adv to this degree: *It was this big.*

this·tle /ˈθɪsəl/ n plant with prickly leaves and usu. purple flowers

thong /θɔŋ, θɑŋ/ n narrow length of leather used esp. for fastening

thongs /θɔŋz, θɑŋz/ n [P] leather or rubber shoes held on the foot with a thong

tho·rax /ˈθɔræks, ˈθoʷr-/ n med part of the body between the neck and the ABDOMEN

thorn /θɔrn/ n **1** sharp growth on a plant **2** **thorn in one's flesh/side** continual cause of annoyance ~ **y** adj **1** prickly **2** difficult to deal with

thor·ough /ˈθɜroʷ, ˈθʌroʷ/ adj **1** complete in every way: *a thorough search* **2** careful about details ~ **ly** adv ~ **ness** n [U]

thor·ough·bred /ˈθɜrəˌbred, ˈθʌrə-/ n, adj (animal, esp. a horse) from parents of one very good breed

thor·ough·fare /ˈθɜrəˌfeər, ˈθʌrə-/ n fml large public road

thor·ough·go·ing /ˌθɜrəˈgoʷɪŋ◄ ˌθʌrə-/ adj very thorough; complete

those /ðoʷz/ pl. of THAT

thou /ðaʊ/ pron lit (used of a single person) you

though /ðoʷ/ conj, adv **1** in spite of the fact (that): *Though it's hard work, I enjoy it.* **2** but: *I'll try, though I don't think I can.* **3** **as though** as if

thought[1] /θɔt/ v past t. & p. of THINK

thought[2] n **1** [C] something thought; idea, etc. **2** [U] thinking **3** [U] serious consideration **4** [U] intention: *I had no thought of causing any trouble.* **5** [C;U] attention; regard: *acting with no thought to her own safety* – see also SECOND THOUGHT ~ **ful** adj **1** thinking deeply **2** paying attention to the wishes, needs, etc., of others ~ **fully** adv ~ **less** adj showing a selfish or careless lack of thought ~ **lessly** adv

thou·sand /ˈθaʊzənd/ determiner, n, pron **thousand** or **thousands** 1000 ~ **th** determiner, adv, n, pron 1000th

thrall /θrɔl/ n [U] lit state of being completely interested: *He held me in thrall.*

thrash /θræʃ/ v **1** vt beat (as if) with a whip or stick **2** vt defeat thoroughly **3** vi move wildly or violently

thrash out phr vt find an answer (to) by much talk and consideration

thread /θred/ n **1** [C;U] very fine cord made by spinning cotton, silk etc. **2** [C] line of reasoning connecting the parts of an argument or story **3** [C] raised line that winds around the outside of a screw **4** **hang by a thread** in a very dangerous position ♦ vt **1** put thread through the hole in (a needle) **2** put (a film or TAPE) in place on an apparatus **3** put (things) together on a thread **4 thread one's way through** go carefully through (crowds, etc.)

thread·bare /ˈθrɛdbeəʳ/ *adj* (of cloth) very worn: (fig.) *a threadbare* (= too often used) *excuse*

threat /θrɛt/ *n* **1** [C;U] expression of an intention to harm or punish someone **2** [C] something or someone regarded as a possible danger

threat·en /ˈθrɛtn/ *v* **1** *vt* make a threat (against): *They threatened to blow up the plane.* **2** *vt* give warning of (something bad): *The sky threatened rain.* **3** *vi* (of something bad) seem likely: *Danger threatens.*

three /θriː/ *determiner, n, pron* **3**

three-D /ˌθriː ˈdiː◂/ *n* [U] three-dimensional form or appearance

three-di·men·sion·al /ˌ· ·ˈ···◂/ *adj* having length, depth, and height

three R's /ˌθriː ˈɑːz/ *n* [the+P] reading, writing, and ARITHMETIC, considered as forming the base of children's education

thresh /θrɛʃ/ *vt* separate the grain from (corn, etc.) by beating

thresh·old /ˈθrɛʃhoʷld, -ʃoʷld/ *n* **1** point of beginning: *scientists on the threshold of* (= about to make) *a research breakthrough* **2** piece of stone or wood across the bottom of a doorway

threw /θruː/ *v past t. of* THROW

thrice /θraɪs/ *adv lit* 3 times

thrift /θrɪft/ *n* [U] not spending too much money **~y** *adj* ♦ *n* SAVINGS AND LOAN ASSOCIATION

thrift shop /ˈ· ·/ *n* store that sells used goods cheaply

thrill /θrɪl/ *n* (something producing) a sudden strong feeling of excitement, fear, etc. ♦ *vi/t* (cause to) feel a thrill **~er** *n* book, film, etc., telling a very exciting (crime) story

thrive /θraɪv/ *vi* develop well and be healthy, strong, or successful

throat /θroʷt/ *n* **1** passage from the mouth down inside the body **2** front of the neck

throb /θrɑb/ *vi* **-bb-** (of a machine, the action of the heart, etc.) beat heavily and regularly ♦ *n* throbbing

throes /θroʷz/ *n* [P] **1** *lit* sudden violent pains, esp. caused by dying **2 in the throes of** struggling with (some difficulty)

throm·bo·sis /θrɑmˈboʷsɪs/ *n* **-ses** /-siːz/ having a thickened mass of blood in a blood tube or the heart

throne /θroʷn/ *n* ceremonial seat of a king, queen, etc.: (fig.) *He ascended the throne.* (= became king)

throng /θrɔŋ/ *n* large crowd ♦ *vi/t* go as or fill with a throng

throt·tle /ˈθrɑtl/ *vt* seize (someone)

by the throat to stop them breathing ♦ *n* VALVE controlling the flow of gas, etc., into an engine

through /θruː/ *prep, adv* **1** in at one side (of) and out at the other: *Water flows through this pipe.* | *I opened the door and went through.* **2** from beginning to end (of): *I read through the letter.* **3** so as to finish successfully: *Did you get through your exam?* **4** *past: He drove through a red light.* ♦ *prep* **1** by means of; because of: *The war was lost through bad organization.* **2** up to and including: *Wednesday through Saturday* ♦ *adv* **1** so as to be connected by telephone **2 through and through** completely ♦ *adj* **1** finished; done: *Are you through yet?* **2** having no further relationship: *I'm through with him!* **3** allowing a continuous journey: *a through train*

through·out /θruːˈaʊt/ *prep, adv* in, to, through, or during every part (of)

through·put /ˈθruːpʊt/ *n* amount of work, materials, etc., dealt with in a particular time

throw /θroʷ/ *v* **threw** /θruː/, **thrown** /θroʷn/ **1** *vi/t* send (something) through the air with a sudden movement of the arm **2** *vt* move or put forcefully or quickly: *The two fighters threw themselves at each other.* | *I'll just throw on some clothes.* **3** *vt* cause to fall to the ground: *Her horse threw her.* **4** *vt* direct: *I think I can throw some light on the mystery.* **5** *vt* operate (a SWITCH) **6** *vt* shape from wet clay when making POTTERY **7** *vt* make one's voice appear to come from somewhere other than one's mouth **8** *vt infml* arrange (a party) **9** *vt* confuse; shock: *Her reply really threw me.* **10 throw a fit** have a sudden uncontrolled attack of anger **11 throw oneself into** to start to work very busily at **12 throw oneself on/upon** put complete trust in **13 throw one's weight around** give orders to others, because one thinks one is important **14 throw oneself at** *phr vt* **a** rush violently towards someone **b** attempt forcefully to win someone's love ♦ *n* **1** act of throwing **2** distance thrown **~er** *n*

throw away *phr vt* **1** get rid of **2** waste (an opportunity, chance, etc.)

throw in *phr vt* **1** supply additionally without increasing the price **2 throw in the towel** admit defeat

throw off *phr vt* **1** recover from **2** escape from **3** confuse

throw open *phr vt* allow people to enter

throw out *phr vt* **1** get rid of **2** refuse to accept

throw over *phr vt* end a relationship with

throw together *phr vt* build or make hastily

throw up *phr v* **1** *vi* VOMIT **2** *vt* bring to notice: *The investigation has thrown up some interesting facts.* **3** *vt* build hastily

throw·a·way /ˈθroʷəweʸ/ *adj* made to be used and then got rid of: *a throwaway camera*

throw·back /ˈθroʷbæk/ *n* something as if from an earlier period

thrush¹ /θrʌʃ/ *n* common singing bird with a spotted breast

thrush² *n* [U] infectious disease of the mouth, throat, and VAGINA

thrust /θrʌst/ *vi/t* **thrust** push forcefully and suddenly ♦ *n* **1** [C] act of thrusting **2** [U] engine's power of moving forwards **3** [U] (main) meaning

thud /θʌd/ *vi, n* **-dd-** (make) the dull sound of something heavy falling

thug /θʌg/ *n* violent criminal

thumb¹ /θʌm/ *n* **1** short thick finger set apart from the others **4 2 all thumbs** *infml* very awkward with the hands **3 stick out like a sore thumb** *infml* seem out of place **4 thumb one's nose at** *infml* make fun of **5 thumbs up/down** *infml* an expression of approval/disapproval **6 under someone's thumb** *infml* under the control of someone – see also RULE OF THUMB

thumb² *v* **thumb a ride** ask passing motorists for a ride by signaling with one's thumb – see HITCHHIKE

thumb through *phr vi/t* look through (a book) quickly

thumb·nail /ˈθʌmneʸl/ *n* nail of the thumb ♦ *adj* small or short: *a thumbnail description/sketch*

thumb·screw /ˈθʌmskruʷ/ *n* instrument for crushing the thumbs to cause great pain

thumb·tack /ˈθʌmtæk/ *n* small nail pushed in with the thumb

thump /θʌmp/ *v* **1** *vt* hit hard **2** *vi* make a repeated dull sound: *My heart thumped.* ♦ *n* (sound of a) heavy blow

thun·der /ˈθʌndər/ *n* [U] **1** loud explosive noise that follows lightning: (fig.) *the thunder of distant guns* **2 steal someone's thunder** spoil the effect of someone's action by doing it first ♦ *v* **1** *vi* produce thunder **2** *vi* produce or go with a loud noise **3** *vt* shout loudly **~ous** *adj* very loud: *thunderous applause*

thun·der·bolt /ˈθʌndərboʷlt/ *n* **1** thunder and lightning together **2** event causing great shock

thun·der·clap /ˈθʌndərklæp/ *n* a single loud crash of thunder

thun·der·head /ˈθʌndərhɛd/ *n* large dark cloud likely to bring rain

thun·der·struck /ˈθʌndərstrʌk/ *adj* shocked

Thurs·day /ˈθɜrzdiʸ, -deʸ/ *n* the 4th day of the week, between Wednesday and Friday

thus /ðʌs/ *adv fml* **1** in this way **2** with this result **3 thus far** up until now

thwart /θwɔrt/ *vt* prevent from happening or succeeding

thy /ðaɪ/ *determiner lit (possessive form of* **thou**) your

thy·roid /ˈθaɪrɔɪd/ *n* organ in the neck that controls growth and activity

ti·a·ra /tiʸˈærə, tiʸˈɛərə, tiʸˈɑrə/ *n* piece of jewelry like a small crown

tic /tɪk/ *n* sudden unconscious movement of the muscles

tick¹ /tɪk/ *n* **1** short repeated sound of a watch or clock **2** mark ✓ showing esp. wrongness

tick² *v* **1** *vi* make a TICK¹ (1) **2 make someone/something tick** *infml* provide a person/thing with reasons for behaving, working, etc., in a particular way

tick off *phr vt infml* **1** cause anger **2** speak sharply to, expressing disapproval or annoyance

tick over *phr vi* continue working at slow steady rate

tick³ *n* very small insect that sucks blood from whatever it bites

tick·er-tape pa·rade /ˈ··· ·,·/ *n* a PARADE celebrating someone when CONFETTI is thrown from tall buildings onto the street below

tick·et /ˈtɪkɪt/ *n* **1** piece of paper or card showing that payment for a service has been made: *a bus/movie ticket* **2** piece of card showing the price, size, etc., of goods **3** printed notice of an offense against traffic laws **4** *infml* exactly the thing needed: *This hammer is just the ticket.*

tick·le /ˈtɪkəl/ *v* **1** *vt* touch (someone's body) lightly to produce laughter, a feeling of nervous excitement, etc.: *Stop tickling my toes!* **2** *vi* give or feel a prickly sensation **3** *vt* delight or amuse ♦ *n* [C;U] (act or feel of) tickling **–lish** *adj* **1** sensitive to being tickled **2** (of a problem or situation) rather difficult

tid·al wave /ˈ·· ·,·/ *n* very large dangerous ocean wave: (fig.) *a tidal wave of public disapproval*

tid·bit /ˈtɪdˌbɪt/ *n* small piece of particularly nice food: (fig.) *a few tidbits of information*

tide¹ /taɪd/ *n* **1** regular rise and fall of the sea: *The tide's out.* (= has fallen to its lowest point) **2** current caused by this: *strong tides* **3** feeling or tendency that moves or changes like the tide: *the tide of public opinion* **tidal** *adj*

tide² *v* **tide over** *phr vt* help (someone) through (a difficult period)

tide-mark /ˈtaɪdmɑːk/ *infml* mark left after the tide goes out

tid-ings /ˈtaɪdɪŋz/ *n* [P] *lit* news

ti-dy /ˈtaɪdiʸ/ *adj* **1** neat **2** *infml* fairly large: *a tidy income* ♦ *vi/t* make (things) tidy **tidily** *adv* **tidiness** *n* [U]

tie¹ /taɪ/ *n* **1** band of cloth worn around the neck **2** a card, string, etc., used for fastening something **3** something that unites: *the ties of friendship* **4** something that limits one's freedom **5** result in which each competitor gains an equal number of points, votes, etc.

tie² *v* **tied; pres. p. tying** *vt* fasten by knotting: *tie a parcel/one's shoe laces* **2** *vt* make (a knot or BOW²) **3** *vi/t* finish (a game or competition) with a TIE¹ (5)

tie down *phr vt* **1** limit the freedom **2** force to be exact

tie in *phr vi* have a close connection

tie up *phr vt* **1** limit free use of (money, property, etc.) **2** connect **3** **tied up** very busy

tie-breaker /ˈtaɪ ˌbreɪkər/ *n* play to decide who wins a tennis SET³ (4) or other competition

tie-in /ˈ· ·/ *n* product that is connected in some way with a new film, television show, etc.

tier /tɪər/ *n* **1** any of a number of rising rows of esp. seats **2** level of organization

tie tack /ˈ· ·/ *n* decorative CLIP for holding a TIE¹ (1) in place

tiff /tɪf/ *n* slight quarrel

ti-ger /ˈtaɪɡər/ **tigress** /ˈtaɪɡrəs/ *fem.* — *n* **1** large Asian wild cat that has yellowish fur with black bands **2** fierce or brave person – see also PAPER TIGER

tight /taɪt/ *adj* **1** firmly fixed in place; closely fastened: *The cases were packed tight in the back.* | *Is the roof watertight?* **2** fully stretched **3** fitting (too) closely; leaving no free room or time: *tight shoes* | *a tight schedule* **4** difficult to obtain: *Money is tight just now.* **5** marked by close competition: *a tight game/finish* **6** *sl* ungenerous with money **7** *sl* drunk **8** in a close relationship **9** in a tight corner/spot in a difficult position ♦ *adv* tightly ~**ly** *adv* ~**en** *vi/t* make or become tighter ~**ness** *n* [U] **tights** *n* [P] very close fitting garment covering the legs and lower body

tight-fist·ed /ˌtaɪtˈfɪstɪd◀/ *adj infml*

very ungenerous, esp. with money ~**ness** *n* [U]

tight-lipped /ˌ·ˈ·◀/ *adj* **1** having the lips pressed together **2** not saying anything

tight-rope /ˈtaɪt-rəʊp/ *n* rope tightly stretched high above the ground, on which someone walks

tile /taɪl/ *n* thin shaped piece of baked clay, etc., used for covering roofs, walls, floors, etc. ♦ *vt* cover with tiles

till¹ /tɪl, tl/ *prep, conj* until

till² /tɪl/ *n* drawer where money is kept in a store

till³ *vt lit* cultivate (the ground)

til-ler /ˈtɪlər/ *n* long handle for turning a boat's RUDDER

tilt /tɪlt/ *vi/t* (cause to) slope (as if) by raising one end ♦ *n* [C;U] **1** slope **2** (at) full tilt at full speed

tim-ber /ˈtɪmbər/ *n* **1** [U] wood for building **2** [U] growing trees **3** [C] wooden beam, esp. in a ship

time /taɪm/ *n* **1** [U] continuous measurable quantity from the past, through the present, and into the future **2** [S;U] period: *It happened a long time ago.* | *I don't have (the) time to do it.* (= I am too busy doing other things) **3** period in which an action is completed, esp. in a race: *Her time was just under 4 minutes.* **4** [U] particular point stated in hours, minutes, seconds, etc.: *The time is 4 o'clock.* **5** [C] particular point in the year, day, etc.: *We both arrived at the same time.* | *in summertime* | *It's time we were leaving.* **6** [C] occasion: *I've been here several times.* **7** [C] experience connected with a period or occasion: *We had a great time at the party.* **8** [C] point in history: *in ancient times* **9** [U] point when something should happen: *The plane arrived on time.* (= not early or late) **10** [U] rate of speed of a piece of music **11** ahead of one's time with ideas not accepted in the period in which one lives **12** all the time continuously **13** at a time singly/in groups of 2/3, etc.: *We went into her office 2 at a time.* **14** at all times always **15** at one time formerly **16** at the same time: a together b however; NEVERTHELESS **17** at times sometimes **18** behind the times old-fashioned **19** buy time *infml* delay an action or decision in order to give oneself more time **20** *sl* do time go to prison **21** for a time for a short period **22** for the time being for a limited period at present **23** from time to time sometimes **24** have no time for someone dislike someone **25** in no time very quickly **26** in time: a after a certain amount of time has passed b early or soon enough **27**

take one's time not hurry **28 the time of one's life** have a very enjoyable experience **29 time and (time) again/time after time** repeatedly – see also TIMES ♦ *vt* **1** arrange the time at which (something) happens **2** measure the time taken by or for **3** (in sports) make (a shot) at exactly the right moment ~**less** *adj* **1** unending **2** not changed by time ~**ly** *adj fml* happening at just the right time: *a timely warning* **timer** *n* person or machine that measures or records time – see also OLD TIMER

time and a half /ˌ· · ˈ·/ *n* rate of payment equal to 1½ times the usual rate: *we get paid time and a half on weekends.*

time bomb /ˈ· ·/ *n* **1** bomb set to explode at a particular time **2** situation likely to become very dangerous

time frame /ˈ· ·/ *n* period of time in which something is expected to happen

time im·me·mo·ri·al /ˌ· ··· ···ˈ···/ *n* [U] *lit* long ago in the past

time lim·it /ˈ· ˌ·/ *n* period of time in which something must be done

times /taɪmz/ *n* (used to show an amount that is calculated by multiplying something the stated number of times): *Their house is at least 3 times the size of ours.* ♦ *prep* multiplied by: *3 times 3 is 9.*

time-serv·er /ˈtaɪmˌsɜrvər/ *n derog* person who acts so as to please those in power at the time the ~**ing** *adj*, *n* [U]

time-shar·ing /ˈ· ˌ··/ *n* **1** use of one main COMPUTER by many people in different places **2** several people buying or renting a house (esp. for vacations), each using it for short periods each year

time sig·na·ture /ˈ· ˌ···/ *n* mark, esp. 2 numbers, to show what speed music should be played at

time-ta·ble /ˈtaɪmˌteɪbəl/ *n* **1** list of the traveling times of buses, trains, etc. **2** (list of) the order of events in a program, etc.

time zone /ˈ· ·/ *n* area within which all clocks are set to the same time: *the mountain time zone*

tim·id /ˈtɪmɪd/ *adj* fearful; lacking courage ~**ly** *adv* ~**ity** /tɪˈmɪdətɪ/ *n* [U]

tim·o·rous /ˈtɪmərəs/ *adj fml* fearful ~**ly** *adv* ~**ness** *n* [U]

tin /tɪn/ *n* **1** [U] soft whitish metal ♦ ~**ny** *adj* **1** of or like tin **2** having a thin metallic sound

tin can /ˌ· ˈ·/ *n* small closed metal container in which food is sold

tinc·ture /ˈtɪŋktʃər/ *n* [C;U] medical substance mixed with alcohol

tin·der /ˈtɪndər/ *n* [U] material that burns easily, used esp. for lighting fires

tin·foil /ˈtɪnfɔɪl/ *n* [U] very thin bendable sheet of shiny metal

tinge /tɪndʒ/ *vt* give a small amount of color to: *black hair tinged with gray* | (fig.) *admiration tinged with jealousy* ♦ *n* [S] small amount

tin·gle /ˈtɪŋgəl/ *vi*, *n* [S] (feel) a slight, not unpleasant, stinging sensation

tin·ker /ˈtɪŋkər/ *vi* work without a definite plan or useful results, making small changes, esp. when trying to repair or improve something ♦ *n* **1** [S] act of tinkering **2** [C] traveling mender of pots and pans

tin·kle /ˈtɪŋkəl/ *vi* **1** make light metallic sounds **2** *infml* urinate (URINE) ♦ *n* **1** tinkling sound **2** act of tinkling (2)

tin pan al·ley /ˌ· · ˈ··/ *n* [U] (*often caps.*) writers, players, and producers of popular music

tin·sel /ˈtɪnsəl/ *n* [U] **1** threads of shiny material used for (Christmas) decorations **2** something showy that is really cheap and worthless

tint /tɪnt/ *n* pale or delicate shade of a color ♦ *vt* give a tint to

ti·ny /ˈtaɪnɪ/ *adj* extremely small

tip¹ /tɪp/ *n* **1** (pointed) end of something: *the tips of one's fingers* **2** part stuck on the end: *cigarettes with filter tips* **3 on the tip of one's tongue** not quite able to be remembered ♦ *vt* -**pp**- put a tip on

tip² *v* -**pp**- **1** *vi/t* (cause to) fall over **2** *vi/t* (cause to) lean at an angle

tip³ *n* small amount of money given to someone who does a service ♦ *vi/t* -**pp**- give a tip (to)

tip⁴ *n* helpful piece of advice ♦ *vt* -**pp**- suggest as likely to succeed

tip off *phr vt* give a warning or piece of secret information to **tip-off** /ˈ· ·/ *n* **1** piece of secret information **2** beginning of play in BASKETBALL

tip·ster /ˈtɪpstər/ *n* person who gives advice about which horse or dog is likely to win races

tip·sy /ˈtɪpsɪ/ *adj infml* slightly drunk

tip·toe /ˈtɪptoʊ/ *n* **on tiptoe** on one's toes with the rest of the foot raised ♦ *vi* walk on tiptoe

tip-top /ˌ· ˈ··/ *adj infml* excellent

ti·rade /ˈtaɪreɪd, taɪˈreɪd/ *n* long, angry speech

tire¹ /taɪr/ *vi/t* (cause to) become tired ~**less** *adj* never getting tired ~**some** *adj* **1** annoying **2** uninteresting

tire² *n* thick band of rubber around the outside edge of a wheel

tired /taɪrd/ *adj* **1** needing rest or

sleep **2** no longer interested: *I'm tired of doing this; let's go for a walk.* **3** showing lack of imagination or new thought: *tired ideas* ~**ness** n [U]

tis·sue /ˈtɪʃuʷ/ n **1** [C;U] the material animals and plants are made of; cells: *lung tissue* **2** [U] thin light paper, esp. for wrapping **3** [C] paper handkerchief **4** [C] *fml* something formed as if by weaving threads together: *a tissue of lies*

tit /tɪt/ n *sl, not polite* woman's breast

ti·tan·ic /taɪˈtænɪk/ adj very great in degree: *a titanic struggle*

ti·ta·ni·um /taɪˈteɪniʸəm/ n [U] light strong metal used in compounds

tit for tat /ˌtɪt fər ˈtæt/ n [U] something unpleasant given in return for something unpleasant one has suffered

tithe /taɪð/ n tax paid to the church in former times

tit·il·late /ˈtɪtl̩ˌeʸt/ vt excite, esp. sexually **–lation** /ˌtɪtl̩ˈeʸʃ ən/ n [U]

ti·tle /ˈtaɪtl̩/ n **1** [C] name of a book, play, painting, etc. **2** [C] word such as 'Lord', 'President', or 'Doctor' used before someone's name to show rank, office, or profession **3** [S;U] legal right to ownership **4** [C] position of a person who has won: *the world heavyweight boxing title* **titled** adj having a noble title, such as 'Lord'

title deed /ˈ·· ˌ·/ n document showing ownership of property

tit·ter /ˈtɪtər/ vi laugh quietly in a nervous or silly way **titter** n

tit·u·lar /ˈtɪtʃələr/ adj holding a title but not having any real power: *a titular head of state*

tiz·zy /ˈtɪziʸ/ n *sl infml* state of excited worried confusion

TLC /ˌtiʸ ɛl ˈsiʸ/ n tender loving care; very kind and special treatment

TNT /ˌtiʸ ɛn ˈtiʸ/ n [U] powerful explosive

to /tə; before vowels tʊ; strong tuʷ/ prep **1** in a direction towards: *the road to Fredonia* **2 a** (used before a verb to show it is the INFINITIVE): *I want to go.* **b** used in place of infinitive: *We didn't want to come but we had to.* **3** in order to: *I came by car to save time.* **4** so as to be in: *I was sent to prison.* **5** up to: *Stick the paper to the wall.* **6** as far as: *from beginning to end* **7** for the attention or possession of: *I told/gave it to her.* **8** in connection with: *the answer to a question* **9** in relation or comparison with: *That's nothing to what it could have been.* | *We won by 6 points to 3.* **10** (of time): *It's 10 to 4.* **11** per: *This car does 30 miles to the gallon.* ♦ /tuʷ/ adv **1** so as to be

shut: *Pull the door to.* **2** into consciousness: *She came to.*

toad /toʷd/ n animal like a large FROG

toad·stool /ˈtoʷdstuʷl/ n (uneatable) FUNGUS

toad·y /ˈtoʷdiʸ/ vi be too nice to someone of higher rank, esp. for personal advantage ♦ n person who toadies

to and fro /ˌtuʷ ənd ˈfroʷ/ adv forwards and backwards or from side to side: *The door swung to and fro in the breeze.*

toast /toʷst/ n **1** [U] bread made brown by heating **2** [C] act of ceremonial drinking to show respect or express good wishes: *They drank a toast to their guest.* ♦ vt **1** make brown by heating **2** warm thoroughly **3** drink a TOAST (2) to ~**er** n electrical apparatus for making TOAST (1)

toast·mas·ter /ˈtoʷstˌmæstər/ n person who introduces TOASTS (2) and speakers at a formal dinner

to·bac·co /təˈbækoʷ/ n [U] dried leaves of a certain plant prepared esp. for smoking in cigarettes, pipes, etc. ~**nist** /təˈbækənɪst/ n seller of tobacco, cigarettes, etc.

to·bog·gan /təˈbagən/ n long board for carrying people over snow **toboggan** vi

to·day /təˈdeʸ/ adv, n [U] **1** (on) this day **2** (at) this present time

tod·dle /ˈtadl̩/ vi **1** walk, esp. with short unsteady steps **2** *infml* walk; go **–dler** n child who has just learnt to walk

to-do /tə ˈduʷ/ n *infml* **to-dos** state of excited confusion or annoyance

toe¹ /toʷ/ n **1** any of the 5 small movable parts at the end of the foot **2** part of a shoe or sock covering these **3 on one's toes** fully ready for action

toe² v **toe the line** act obediently

toe·hold /ˈtoʷhoʷld/ n place for putting the end of the foot when climbing

tof·fee /ˈtɔfiʸ, ˈtafiʸ/ n [C;U] (piece of) a hard brown candy made from sugar and butter

to·fu /ˈtoʷfuʷ/ n white soft food made from SOYBEANS

to·ga /ˈtoʷgə/ n loose outer garment worn in ancient Rome

to·geth·er¹ /təˈgɛðər/ adv **1** in or into a single group, body, or place **2** with each other **3** at the same time **4** in agreement; combined **5** together with in addition to ~**ness** n [U] friendliness

together² adj *infml* **1** (of a person) very much in control of life, actions, etc. **2 get it together** have things under control

tog·gle /ˈtɑgəl/ n **1** wooden button in a bar or WEDGE shape **2** electrical apparatus with two positions

toil /tɔɪl/ n [U] *lit* hard work ♦ *vi lit* work or move with great effort

toi·let /ˈtɔɪlɪt/ n **1** [C] a seatlike apparatus for receiving and taking away the body's waste matter **2** [U] *fml* act of washing, dressing oneself, etc.

toilet pa·per /ˈ·· ˌ··/ n [U] paper for cleaning oneself after passing waste matter from the body

toi·let·ries /ˈtɔɪlətriʸz/ n [P] things used in washing, making oneself tidy, etc.

toilet wa·ter /ˈ·· ˌ··/ n [U] weak form of PERFUME

to·ken /ˈtoʷkən/ n **1** outward sign: *They wore black as a token of mourning.* **2** small part that represents something larger – see also **by the same token** (SAME[1]) ♦ *adj* **1** being a small part representing something greater **2** *derog* done so as to seem acceptable: *a token effort*

told /toʷld/ v past t. & p. of TELL

tol·er·ate /ˈtɑləˌreʸt/ vt **1** permit (something one disagrees with) **2** suffer (someone or something) without complaining **–rable** adj fairly good; not too bad **–rably** adv *fml* fairly **–rance** n **1** [C;U] ability to suffer pain, hardship, etc., without being harmed or damaged: *a low tolerance to cold* **2** [U] allowing people to behave in a way one disagrees with, without getting annoyed **3** [U] toleration (1) **–rant** adj showing or practicing tolerance (2) **–ration** /ˌtɑləˈreʸʃən/ n [U] **1** allowing opinions, customs, etc., different from one's own to be freely held or practiced **2** tolerance (2)

toll[1] /toʷl/ n **1** tax paid for using a road, bridge, etc. **2** bad effect of illness, misfortune, etc.: *The death toll in the accident was 9.*

toll[2] vi/t ring (a bell) or be rung slowly and repeatedly

tom·a·hawk /ˈtɑməˌhɔk/ n Native American ax

to·ma·to /təˈmeʸtoʷ/ n **–toes** soft red fruit eaten raw or cooked as a vegetable

tomb /tuʷm/ n (large decorative cover for) a grave

tom·boy /ˈtɑmbɔɪ/ n spirited young girl who enjoys rough and noisy activities

tom·cat /ˈtɑmkæt/ n male cat

tome /toʷm/ n *lit or humor* large heavy book

tom·fool·er·y /ˌtɑmˈfuʷləriʸ/ n [U] *fml* foolish behavior

to·mor·row /təˈmɔroʷ, -ˈmɑr-/ adv on the day following today ♦ n **1** [S;U] day after today **2** [S;U] future

tom-tom /ˈtɑm tɑm/ n long narrow drum played with the hands

ton /tʌn/ n **1** a measure of weight equal to 2000 pounds **2** also **tons** pl. — a very large amount **3 come down on someone like a ton of bricks** *infml* turn the full force of one's anger against someone, usu. as a punishment **tons** adv sl very much

tone[1] /toʷn/ n **1** [C] quality of sound, esp. of a musical instrument or the voice **2** [C] variety or shade of a color **3** [U] general quality or nature **4** [U] proper firmness of the body's organs and muscles **tonal** adj

tone[2] v

tone down phr vt reduce in force

tone up phr vt make stronger, brighter, more effective, or healthy, etc.

tone-deaf /ˈ· ·/ adj unable to tell the difference between musical notes

tongs /tɑŋz, tɔŋz/ n [P] movable arms joined at one end, for holding and lifting things

tongue /tʌŋ/ n **1** movable organ in the mouth used for talking, tasting, licking (LICK), etc.: (fig.) *She has a sharp tongue.* (= a severe or unkind way of speaking) **2** object like this in shape or purpose: *tongues of flame* **3** *lit* language **4 hold one's tongue** remain silent **5 (with) tongue in cheek** saying or doing something one does not seriously mean

tongue-tied /ˈ· ·/ adj unable to speak freely, esp. because of nervousness

tongue twist·er /ˈ· ˌ··/ n word or phrase difficult to say

ton·ic /ˈtɑnɪk/ n **1** [C] something, esp. a medicine, that increases health or strength **2** [U] tonic water: *a gin and tonic*

tonic wa·ter /ˈ·· ˌ··/ n [U] gassy water usu. mixed with alcoholic drink

to·night /təˈnaɪt/ adv, n (during) the night of today

ton·nage /ˈtʌnɪdʒ/ n [C;U] **1** amount of goods a ship can carry, expressed in TONS **2** of ships, esp. those that carry goods

tonne /tʌn/ n a measure of weight equal to 1000 kilograms

ton·sil /ˈtɑnsəl/ n either of 2 small organs at the back of the throat

ton·sil·li·tis /ˌtɑnsəˈlaɪtɪs/ n [U] painful soreness of the tonsils

too /tuʷ/ adv **1** to a greater degree than is necessary or good: *You're driving too fast.* **2** also: *I've been to Montreal, and to Quebec too.* **3** in fact **4 only too** very

took /tʊk/ v past t. of TAKE

tool /tuʷl/ n instrument held in the hand, such as an ax, hammer, etc.

toot /tuʷt/ vt make a short warning sound with (a horn) **toot** n

tooth /tuʷθ/ n teeth /tiʸθ/ **1** small bony object growing in the mouth, used for biting **2** any of the pointed parts standing out from a comb, SAW, COG, etc. **3** ability to produce an effect: *The present law has no teeth.* **4** armed to the teeth very heavily armed **5** fight tooth and nail fight very violently **6** get one's teeth into do a job very actively and purposefully **7** in the teeth of against and in spite of: *in the teeth of fierce opposition* **8** lie through one's teeth lie shamelessly **9** set someone's teeth on edge give someone an unpleasant sensation caused by certain acid tastes or high sounds — see also SWEET TOOTH ~ **less** adj ~ **y** adj

tooth·brush /ˈtuʷθbrʌʃ/ n small brush for cleaning one's teeth

tooth·paste /ˈtuʷθpeʸst/ n [U] paste for cleaning one's teeth

tooth·pick /ˈtuʷθˌpɪk/ n short thin pointed stick for removing food from the teeth

top[1] /tɑp/ n **1** the highest or upper part: *the top of a tree* **2** the best or most important part or place: *at the top of the class* **3** cover: *bottle tops* **4** at the top of (one's) voice as loudly as possible **5** from top to bottom all through; completely **6** from top to toe (of a person) completely **7** get on top of infml be too much for: *This work is getting on top of me.* **8** on top of: a able to deal with b in addition to **9** on top of the world infml very happy — see also blow one's top (BLOW[1]) ~ **less** adj leaving the breasts bare ♦ adj highest, best, etc.: *at top speed* (= very fast)

top[2] vt –pp- **1** be higher, better, or more than: *Our profits have topped $1 million.* **2** form a top for: *a cake topped with whipped cream* **3** top the bill be chief actor or actress in a play

top off phr vt complete successfully by a last action

top[3] n **1** child's toy that spins around **2** sleep like a top sleep deeply and well

to·paz /ˈtoʷpæz/ n [C;U] (precious stone cut from) a yellowish mineral

top brass /ˌ· ˈ·/ n [U;P] sl officers of high rank, esp. in the armed forces

top dog /ˌ· ˈ·/ n person in the most advantageous or powerful position

top drawer /ˌ· ˈ··◄/ n highest level of society, etc.

Top 40 /ˌtɑp ˈfɔrtiʸ/ n 40 most popular songs (at a given time or now)

top hat /ˌ· ˈˌ·/ n man's formal tall usu. black or grey hat

top-heav·y /ˌ· ˈ···/ adj too heavy at the top

top·ic /ˈtɑpɪk/ n subject for conversation, writing, etc.

top·ic·al /ˈtɑpɪkəl/ adj of or being a subject of present interest ~ **ly** /-kliʸ/ adv

top-notch /ˌ· ˈ·◄/ adj being one of the best

to·pog·ra·phy /təˈpɑgrəfiʸ/ n [U] (science of describing) the shape and height of land –**phical** /ˌtɑpə-ˈgræfɪkəl/ adj

top·ple /ˈtɑpəl/ vi/t (cause to) become unsteady and fall down: (fig.) *The scandal toppled the government.*

top-se·cret /ˌ· ˈ···◄/ adj that must be kept extremely secret

top·sy-tur·vy /ˌtɑpsiʸ ˈtɜrviʸ◄/ adj, adv in complete disorder and confusion

torch /tɔrtʃ/ n **1** mass of burning material carried by hand to give light **2** lamp that blows a flame (e.g. for burning off paint) ♦ vt sl set fire to

tore /tɔr, toʷr/ v past t. of TEAR[1]

tor·ment[1] /ˈtɔrment/ n [C;U] very great suffering

torment[2] /tɔrˈment/ vt cause torment to ~ **or** n

torn /tɔrn, toʷrn/ v past p. of TEAR[1]

tor·na·do /tɔrˈneʸdoʷ/ n –does or –dos very violent wind that spins at great speed

tor·pe·do /tɔrˈpiʸdoʷ/ n –does long narrow explosive apparatus driven by a motor, which is fired through the sea to destroy ships ♦ vt attack or destroy (as if) with a torpedo

tor·pid /ˈtɔrpɪd/ adj fml derog inactive; slow

tor·por /ˈtɔrpər/ n [U] fml derog inactivity

tor·rent /ˈtɔrənt, ˈtɑr-/ n violently rushing stream of water: (fig.) *torrents of abuse* –**rential** /təˈrenʃəl, -tʃəl, tə-/ adj: *torrential rain*

tor·rid /ˈtɔrɪd, ˈtɑr-/ adj **1** (esp. of weather) very hot **2** full of strong feelings and uncontrolled activity, esp. sexual: *a torrid love affair*

tor·so /ˈtɔrsoʷ/ n –sos human body without the head and limbs

tort /tɔrt/ n law wrongful but not criminal act

tor·til·la /tɔrˈtiʸə/ n flat bread eaten with Mexican food

tor·toise /ˈtɔrtəs/ n land animal with a hard shell, that moves slowly

tor·toise-shell /ˈtɔrtəˌʃel, ˈtɔrtəsˌʃel/ n [U] material from a tortoise's or TURTLE's shell, brown with yellowish marks

tor·tu·ous /ˈtɔrtʃuʷəs/ adj **1**

twisted; winding **2** not direct in speech, thought or action ~**ly** adv

tor·ture /ˈtɔrtʃər/ vt cause great pain or suffering to out of cruelty, as a punishment, etc. ♦ n **1** [U] act of torturing **2** [C;U] severe pain or suffering -**turer** n

toss /tɔs/ v **1** vt throw **2** vi/t (cause to) move about rapidly and pointlessly: *He tossed and turned all night, unable to sleep.* **3** vt move or lift (part of the body) rapidly: *She tossed her head.* **4** vt mix lightly: *toss a salad* **5** vi/t throw (a coin) to decide something according to which side lands upwards: *There's only one cake left — let's toss for it.* ♦ n [C] act of tossing

toss-up /ˈ· ·/ n [S] even chance; unsureness

tot[1] /tɑt/ n very small child

tot[2] v -**tt**- **tot up** phr vt add up

to·tal /ˈtoʊtl/ adj complete; whole ♦ n **1** complete — see also GRAND TOTAL, SUM TOTAL **2** in total when all have been added up ♦ vt -**ll**- -**l**- **1** be when added up: *His debts totaled $9000.* **2** destroy completely: *His car was totaled in the accident.* ~**ly** adv: *totally different* ~**ity** /toʊˈtælətiʲ/ n [U] fml completeness

to·tal·i·tar·i·an /toʊˌtæləˈteəriʲən/ adj of or based on a centrally controlled system of government that does not allow any political opposition ~**ism** n [U]

tote /toʊt/ vt infml carry, esp. with difficulty

to·tem /ˈtoʊtəm/ n person or thing used as sign or SYMBOL of an organization, society, etc.

totem pole /ˈ·· ·/ n **1** tall wooden pole with faces cut into it and painted **2** **low man on the totem pole** person in a low position who does the dull work

tot·ter /ˈtɑtər/ vi move or walk in an unsteady manner, as if about to fall: (fig.) *their tottering economy*

touch[1] /tʌtʃ/ v **1** vi/t be separated (from) by no space at all: *Their hands touched.* **2** vi/t feel or make connection (with), esp. with the hands: *The model is fragile, don't touch (it).* **3** vt eat or drink: *You haven't touched your food.* | *I never touch alcohol.* **4** vt compare with: *Nothing can touch a cold drink on a hot day!* **5** vt cause to feel pity, sympathy, etc.: *a touching story* **6** **touch base** see (someone) in order to keep in CONTACT ~**ed** adj **1** grateful **2** slightly crazy ~**y** adj easily offended or annoyed ~**ily** adv ~**iness** n [U]

touch down phr vi (of a plane or spacecraft) land

touch off phr vt cause (a violent event) to start

touch on/upon phr vt talk about shortly

touch up phr vt improve with small additions

touch[2] n **1** [U] sense of feeling **2** [C] way something feels: *the silky touch of her skin* **3** [C] act of touching **4** [U] connection, esp. so as to receive information: *He's gone to Paris, but we keep in touch by letter.* **5** [S] particular way of doing things: *a woman's touch* **6** [C] small details: *putting the finishing touches to the plan* **7** [S] special ability: *I'm losing my touch.* **8** [S] slight attack of an illness: *a touch of the flu* **9** [S] slight amount: *It needs a touch more salt.* **10** **keep in touch** continue CONTACT **11** **lose touch** lose contact — see also SOFT TOUCH

touch-and-go /ˌ· · ·ˈ·◂/ adj of uncertain result; risky

touch·down /ˈtʌtʃdaʊn/ n **1** act of gaining 6 points in football **2** landing of a plane or spacecraft

touch foot·ball /ˈ· ˌ··/ n football game where players touch rather than TACKLE

touch·line /ˈtʌtʃlaɪn/ n line along each of the longer sides of a soccer field

touch·stone /ˈtʌtʃstoʊn/ n lit something used as a test or standard

tough /tʌf/ adj **1** not easily weakened or broken **2** difficult to cut or eat: *tough meat* **3** difficult: *a tough job/problem* **4** not kind, severe: *a tough new law against drunken driving* **5** unfortunate: *tough luck* ♦ n [C] rude or troublesome young man ~**ly** adv ~**en** vi/t make or become tougher ~**ness** n [U]

tou·pee /tuˈpeʲ/ n small WIG worn by a man

tour /tʊər/ n **1** act of traveling around a country, walking around a building, etc., looking at interesting things **2** period of duty in a job, esp. in a foreign country **3** journey esp. in part in performances, sports matches, etc. ♦ vi/t visit as a tourist ~**ism** n [U] **1** traveling for pleasure, esp. during one's vacation **2** the business of providing vacations for tourists ~**ist** n person traveling for pleasure

tour de force /ˌtʊər də ˈfɔrs, -ˈfoʊrs/ n [S] show of great skill

tour·na·ment /ˈtʊərnəmənt, ˈtɜr-/ n **1** competition: *a chess/tennis tournament* **2** (in former times) competition of fighting skill

tour·ni·quet /ˈtʊərnɪkɪt, ˈtɜr-/ n something twisted tightly around a limb to stop bleeding

tou·sle /ˈtaʊzəl/ *vt* make (hair) untidy

tout /taʊt/ *vt derog* **1** publicize as being valuable: *touting his new ideas* **2** try to persuade people to buy (one's goods or services)

tow /toʷ/ *vt* pull (esp. a vehicle) with a rope or chain ♦ *n* **1** act of towing **2 in tow** following closely behind

to·ward /tɔrd, toʷrd, təˈwɔrd/ *prep* **1** in the direction of: *He walked toward me.* | *She had her back toward me.* **2** just before in time: *We arrived toward noon.* **3** in relation to: *What are their feelings toward us?* **4** for the purpose of: *Each week we save $5 toward our vacation.*

tow·a·way zone /ˈtoʷəweʸ ˌzoʷn/ *n* area where cars cannot be left or they will be removed

tow·el /ˈtaʊəl/ *n* piece of cloth or paper for drying things ♦ *vt* –l– rub or dry with a towel

tow·el·ing /ˈtaʊəlɪŋ/ *n* [U] thickish cloth, used for making esp. towels

tow·er /ˈtaʊər/ *n* **1** tall (part of a) building: *a church tower* **2** tall metal framework for signaling or broadcasting ♦ *vi* be very tall: (fig.) *Intellectually he towers above* (= is much better than) *them all.* ~**ing** *adj* very great: *a towering rage*

tower of strength /ˌ··· ˈ·| *n* person who can be depended on for help or support

tow·head /ˈtoʷhed/ *n* person with hair of a light color

town /taʊn/ *n* **1** [C] large group of houses and other buildings where people live and work **2** [C] all the people who live in such a place **3** [U] the business or shopping center of a town **4** [U] the chief city in an area **5** [S] (life in) towns and cities in general **6 go to town** act or behave freely or wildly **7 (out) on the town** enjoying oneself, esp. at night **8 paint the town red** have a very enjoyable time, esp. in wild or noisy manner

town hall /ˌ· ˈ·| *n* public building for a town's local government

tow·path /ˈtoʷpæθ/ *n* path along the bank of a CANAL or river

tox·ic /ˈtɑksɪk/ *adj* poisonous ~**ity** /tɑkˈsɪsətiʸ/ *n* [U]

tox·in /ˈtɑksɪn/ *n* poison produced in plants and animals

toy¹ /tɔɪ/ *n* **1** object for children to play with **2** small breed of dog

toy² *v* **toy with** *phr vt* **1** consider (an idea) not very seriously **2** play with or handle purposelessly

trace¹ /treʸs/ *vt* **1** find, esp. by following a course **2** copy lines or the shape of something using transparent paper ♦ *n* **1** [C;U] mark or sign showing the former presence of someone or something: *She had vanished without trace.* (=completely) **2** [C] small amount of something: *traces of poison in his blood*

trace² *n* rope, chain, etc., fastening a cart or carriage to the animal pulling it

trac·e·ry /ˈtreʸsəriʸ/ *n* patterns with decorative branching and crossing lines

track¹ /træk/ *n* **1** marks left by a person, animal, or vehicle that has passed before **2** narrow (rough) path or road **3** railroad line **4** course for racing **5** piece of music on a record or TAPE (2) **6** group of students of similar ability **7 cover one's tracks** keep one's movements, activities, etc., secret **8 in one's tracks** *infml* where one is; suddenly **9 keep/lose track of** keep/fail to keep oneself informed about a person, situation, etc. **10 make tracks** leave, esp. in a hurry **11 off the beaten track** not well known or often visited **12 on the right/wrong track** thinking or working correctly/incorrectly **13 a one-track mind** *infml* a tendency to think only of one thing or subject

track² *vt* **1** follow the TRACK¹ (1) of **2** sort (students) according to ability ~**er** *n*

track down *phr vt* find by hunting or searching

track rec·ord /ˈ· ˌ··| *n* degree to which someone or something has performed well or badly up to now

track·suit /ˈtræksuʷt/ *n* suit that fits loosely, worn by people when training for sports

tract¹ /trækt/ *n* **1** wide stretch of land **2** system of related organs in an animal: *the digestive tract*

tract² *n fml* short article on a religious or moral subject

trac·ta·ble /ˈtræktəbəl/ *adj fml* easily controlled or governed

trac·tion /ˈtrækʃən/ *n* [U] **1** type of pulling power: *steam traction* **2** force that prevents a wheel from slipping **3** medical treatment with a pulling apparatus used to cure a broken bone or similar injury (INJURE)

trac·tor /ˈtræktər/ *n* motor vehicle for pulling farm machinery

trade¹ /treʸd/ *n* **1** [U] business of buying, selling, or exchanging goods, esp. between countries **2** [C] particular business: *the wine trade* **3** [C] job, esp. needing skill with the hands: *the printer's trade* **4** [S] stated amount of business: *doing a good trade* – see also FREE TRADE

trade² *v* **1** buy and sell goods **2** *vt* exchange: *I traded my radio for a typewriter.* | (fig.) *trading insults*

trade in *phr vt* give in part payment for something new: *I traded my old car in.*

trade off *phr vt* balance (one situation or quality) against another, with the aim of producing an acceptable or desirable result

trade·mark /'tre⁹dmɑrk/ *n* **1** sign or word put on a product to show who made it **2** thing by which a person or thing may habitually be recognized

trade name /'· ·/ *n* name given by a producer to a particular product

trade-off /'· ·/ *n* balance between two (opposing) situations or qualities

trade se·cret /ˌ· '··/ *n* information about a product known only to its makers

trade wind /'· ·/ *n* wind blowing almost continually towards the EQUATOR

tra·di·tion /trə'dɪʃən/ *n* **1** [C] opinion, custom, principle, etc., passed down from the past to the present **2** [U] (passing down of) such customs, etc.: *By tradition, brides in the West wear white.* **~al** *adj* **~ally** *adv*

traf·fic /'træfɪk/ *n* [U] **1** (movement of) vehicles on the road, planes in the sky, etc. **2** trade, esp. in illegal things **3** business done in carrying passengers or goods ◆ *v* **-ck-** **traffic in** *phr vt* trade in (esp. illegal things) **~ker** *n*: *drug traffickers*

traffic cir·cle /'·· ˌ··/ *n* area of circular traffic flow where several roads meet

traffic cop /'· ˌ·/ *n infml* official who controls the parking of vehicles on streets

traffic lights /'·· ˌ·/ *n* [P] set of colored lights for controlling road traffic

tra·ge·dy /'trædʒədi/ *n* [C;U] **1** serious play that ends sadly **2** [U] these plays considered as a group **3** terrible, unhappy, or unfortunate event

tra·gic /'trædʒɪk/ *adj* **1** of or related to TRAGEDY (2) **2** very sad, unfortunate, etc. **~ally** /-kli⁹/ *adv*

trail /tre⁹l/ *n* **1** track or smell followed by a hunter: *We're on their trail.* (= following them closely) **2** path across rough country **3** stream of dust, smoke, people, etc., behind something moving ◆ *v* **1** *vi/t* drag or be dragged along behind **2** *vt* track **3** *vi* (of a plant) grow along a surface **~er** *n*: **1** vehicle pulled by another **2** vehicle fastened to a car and used as a traveling home **3** small pieces of a new film shown to advertise it

train¹ /tre⁹n/ *n* **1** line of railroad cars pulled by an engine **2** set of related things one after another: *It*

interrupted my train of thought. **3** part of a long garment that spreads over the ground behind the wearer **4** long line of moving people, animals or vehicles

train *v* **1** *vi/t* give or be given instruction, practice, or exercise: *training a dog to jump over a fence* **2** *vt* aim (a gun, etc.) **3** *vt* direct the growth of (a plant) **~ee** *n* person being trained **~er** *n* **~ing** *n* [S;U] **1** practical instruction **2 in/out of training** in/not in a healthy condition for a sport, test of skill, etc.

traipse /tre⁹ps/ *vi* walk without purpose or aim

trait /tre⁹t/ *n fml* particular quality of someone or something

trai·tor /'tre⁹tər/ *n* someone disloyal, esp. to their country

tra·jec·to·ry /trə'dʒektəri⁹/ *n fml* curved path of an object fired or thrown through the air

tramp /træmp/ *vi* **1** walk heavily **2** sound of heavy walking **3** walk steadily, esp. over a long distance ◆ *n* **1** wandering person with no home or job who begs for food or money **2** long walk

tram·ple /'træmpəl/ *vi/t* step (on) heavily; crush under the feet

tram·po·line /ˌtræmpə'li⁹n, 'træmpəˌli⁹n/ *n* frame with springy material on which people jump up and down

tramp steam·er /'· ˌ··/ *n* ship that takes goods irregularly to various ports

trance /træns/ *n* sleeplike condition of the mind

tran·quil /'træŋkwəl/ *adj* pleasantly calm, quiet, or free from worry **~ize** *vt* make calm (esp. with tranquillizers) **~izer** *n* drug for reducing anxiety and making people calm **~ity** /træŋ'kwɪləti⁹/ *n* [U] calmness

trans·act /træn'sækt, -'zækt/ *vt fml* do and complete (a piece of business) **~ion** *n* **1** [U] act of transacting **2** [C] piece of business **transactions** *n* [P] records of meetings of a society

trans·at·lan·tic /ˌtrænsət'læntɪk◄, ˌtrænz-/ *adj* connecting or concerning countries on both sides of the Atlantic ocean

tran·scend /træn'send/ *vt fml or lit* go beyond (a limit or something within limits) **~ent** *adj* going far beyond ordinary limits

tran·scribe /træn'skraɪb/ *vt* **1** write an exact copy of **2** write down (something said) **3** arrange (a piece of music) for instrument or voice other than the original

tran·script /'trænˌskrɪpt/ *n* exact written or printed copy **~ion**

/trænˈskrɪpʃən/ n 1 [U] act or process of transcribing 2 [C] transcript

trans·fer[1] /ˈtrænsfər, trænsˈfɜr/ v -rr- 1 vi/t move from one place, job, etc., to another 2 vt give ownership of property to another person 3 vi move from one vehicle to another ~**able** adj

trans·fer[2] /ˈtrænsfər/ n 1 [C;U] act or process of transferring 2 [C] something transferred ~**ence** n [U]

trans·fig·ure /trænsˈfɪgyər/ vt fml or lit change so as to be more glorious

trans·fix /trænsˈfɪks/ vt fml make unable to move or think because of terror, shock, etc.

trans·form /trænsˈform/ vt change completely ~**ation** /ˌtrænsfərˈmeɪʃən/ n [C;U]: the transformation of heat into power ~**er** /trænsˈformər/ n apparatus for changing electrical force, esp. to a different VOLTAGE

trans·fu·sion /trænsˈfyuˈʒən/ n [C;U] act of putting one person's blood into another's body

trans·gress /trænsˈgres, trænz-/ v fml 1 vt go beyond (a proper or legal limit) 2 vi do wrong ~**ion** /-ˈgreʃən/ n [C;U] ~**or** /-ˈgresər/ n

tran·si·ent /ˈtrænʃənt, -tʃənt, -ʒənt/ adj fml lasting or staying for only a short time ♦ n person staying in a place only a short time ~**ence** n [U]

tran·sis·tor /trænˈzɪstər, -ˈsɪs-/ n 1 small apparatus for controlling the flow of electric current 2 small radio with TRANSISTORS ~**ize** vt provide with transistors (1)

tran·sit /ˈtrænsɪt, -zɪt/ n [U] going or moving of people or goods from one place to another: The parcel was lost in transit.

tran·si·tion /trænˈzɪʃən, -ˈsɪ-/ n [C;U] (act of) changing from one state to another ~**al** adj

tran·si·tive /ˈtrænsəţɪv, -zə-/ adj (of a verb) that must have an object or a phrase acting like an object

tran·si·to·ry /ˈtrænzəˌtoriʸ, -ˌtoʷriʸ/ adj TRANSIENT

trans·late /ˌtrænsˈleɪt, trænz-, ˈtrænsleɪt, ˈtrænz-/ vi/t change (speech or writing) into another language ~**lation** /-ˈleɪʃən/ n [C;U] ~**lator** /ˌtrænsˈleɪtər, trænz-, ˈtrænsleɪtər, ˈtrænz-/ n

trans·lit·e·rate /trænsˈlɪtəreɪt, trænz-/ vt fml write in a different alphabet

trans·lu·cent /trænsˈluˈsənt, trænz-/ adj allowing light to pass through (although not transparent)

trans·mit /trænsˈmɪt, trænz-/ v -tt- 1 vi/t broadcast: transmit a radio distress signal 2 vt pass to another person: transmit a disease 3 vt allow to pass through itself: Water transmits sound. ~**mission** /-ˈmɪʃən/ n 1

[U] act of transmitting 2 [C] television or radio broadcast 3 [C] parts of a vehicle that carry power to the wheels ~**ter** /-ˈmɪţər/ n broadcasting apparatus

trans·mute /trænsˈmyuˈt, trænz-/ vt fml change into something completely different (and better) ~**mutation** /ˌtrænsmyuˈweɪʃən, ˌtrænz-/ n [C;U]

tran·som /ˈtrænsəm/ n window over a door

trans·par·ent /trænsˈpærənt, -ˈpeər-/ adj 1 that can be seen through 2 fml easily understood 3 fml clear and certain: a transparent lie ~**ency** n 1 [U] quality of being transparent 2 [C] SLIDE (4)

tran·spire /trænˈspaɪər/ vt fml 1 become known 2 happen

trans·plant /trænsˈplænt/ vt 1 move (a plant) from one place and plant it in another 2 move (an organ, piece of skin, hair, etc.) from one part of body to another, or one person to another ♦ /ˈtrænsplænt/ n 1 something transplanted 2 act or operation of transplanting an organ: a heart transplant

trans·port /trænsˈport, -ˈpoʷrt/ v carry (goods, people, etc.) from one place to another ♦ n [U] ~**ation** /ˌtrænspərˈteɪʃən/ n (means or system of) transporting: travel by public transportation ~**er** /trænˈsportər, -ˈpoʷr-/ n long vehicle on which several cars can be carried

trans·pose /trænsˈpoʷz/ vt fml 1 change the order or position of (2 or more things) 2 to change the KEY of a piece of music ~**position** /ˌtrænspəˈzɪʃən/ n [C;U]

trans·verse /ˌtrænsˈvɜrs◂, ˈtrænzvɜrs/ adj fml lying or placed across: a transverse beam ~**ly** adv

trans·ves·tite /trænsˈvestaɪt, trænz-/ n person who likes to wear the clothes of the opposite sex ~**tism** n [U]

trap /træp/ n 1 apparatus for catching and holding an animal: a mousetrap 2 plan for deceiving (and catching) a person: The police set a trap to catch the thief. 3 vehicle with 2 wheels, pulled by a horse 4 sl mouth: Keep your trap shut! 5 (in GOLF) sandy place from which it is difficult to hit the ball ♦ vt -pp- 1 place or hold firmly with no hope of escape: The miners were trapped underground. 2 trick; deceive 3 catch (an animal) in a trap ~**per** n

trap·door /ˌtræpˈdor, -ˈdoʷr/ n small door in a roof or floor

tra·peze /træˈpiʸz/ n short bar hung high above the ground used by ACROBATS to swing on

trap·pings /ˈtræpɪŋz/ n [P] articles

of dress or decoration, esp. as an outward sign of rank

trash /træʃ/ n [U] **1** something of extremely low quality or value **2** waste material to be thrown away ~**y** adj

trash·can /'træʃkæn/ n container for dry waste materials

trau·ma /'trɔmə, 'traumə/ n damage to the mind caused by a shock or terrible experience ~**tic** /trə'mæ-tɪk, trɔ-, trau-/ adj deeply and unforgettably shocking

trav·el /'trævəl/ v –l– **1** vi/t make a journey (through) **2** vt cover (the stated distance) on a journey **3** vi go, pass, move, etc.: At what speed does light travel? **4** travel light travel without many bags, etc. ♦ n [U] traveling: foreign travel ~**ed** adj experienced in travel: a much traveled writer ~**er** person on a journey – see also FELLOW TRAVELER **travels** n [P] journeys, esp. to foreign countries

travel a·gent /'·· ,··/ n someone who makes people's travel arrangements

traveler's check /'··· ,·/ n check that can be exchanged abroad for foreign money

traveling sales·man /,··· '··/ n person who travels from place to place trying to get orders for goods

trav·el·og, –ogue /'trævə,lɔg, -,lɑg/ n film or talk describing foreign travel

tra·verse /trə'vɜrs, 'trævərs/ vt fml pass across, over, or through

trav·es·ty /'trævəsti/ n something that completely misrepresents the nature of the real thing: The trial was a travesty of justice. (= was very unjust)

trawl /trɔl/ vi/t, n (fish with) a large net drawn along the sea bottom ~**er** n boat that uses a trawl

tray /treɪ/ n flat piece of plastic, metal, etc., for carrying things, esp. food

treach·e·ry /'tretʃəri/ n **1** [U] disloyalty or deceit **2** [C] disloyal or deceitful act ~**rous** adj **1** very disloyal or deceitful **2** full of hidden dangers: treacherous currents ~**rously** adv

tread /trɛd/ v **trod** /trɑd/, **trodden** /'trɑdn/ **1** vi fml put one's foot when walking; step **2** vt fml walk along: tread a path **3** vt press firmly with the feet **4** tread water keep upright in water by moving the legs ♦ n **1** [S] act, way, or sound of walking **2** [C;U] pattern of raised lines on a tire **3** [C] part of a stair on which the foot is placed

trea·dle /'trɛdl/ n apparatus worked by the feet to drive a machine

tread·mill /'trɛd,mɪl/ n something

providing repeated uninteresting work

trea·son /'triːzən/ n [U] disloyalty to one's country, esp. by helping its enemies ~**able** adj law of or being treason

trea·sure /'trɛʒər/ n **1** [U] wealth in gold, jewels, etc. **2** [C] very valuable object or person ♦ vt keep or regard as precious: treasured memories

trea·sur·er /'trɛʒərər/ n person in charge of an organization's money

treasure trove /'trɛʒər ,troʊv/ n [U] something valuable found in the ground and claimed by no one

trea·su·ry /'trɛʒəri/ n government department that controls and spends public money

treat /triːt/ vt **1** act or behave towards: He treated his horses very cruelly. **2** deal with or handle: Treat the glass carefully. | He treated my request as a joke. **3** try to cure medically **4** put through a chemical or industrial action: metal treated against rust **5** pay for (someone's) food, drink, amusement, etc. ♦ n **1** something that gives great pleasure, esp. when unexpected: What a treat to have real champagne! **2** act of treating (TREAT (5)) someone: The meal's my treat, so put away your money. ~**ment** n **1** [U] act or way of treating someone or something **2** [C] substance or method for treating someone or something

trea·tise /'triːtɪs/ n serious book on a particular subject

treat·y /'triːti/ n formally signed agreement between countries

treb·le¹ /'trɛbl/ predeterminer fml 3 times as much or as many as ♦ vi/t make or become 3 times as great

treble² n [U] upper half of the whole range of musical notes

tree /triː/ n **1** tall plant with a wooden trunk or stem, that lives for many years **2** treelike bush: a rose tree ~**less** adj

trek /trɛk/ vi, n –kk– (make) a long hard journey, esp. on foot

trel·lis /'trɛlɪs/ n light upright wooden framework on which plants are grown

trem·ble /'trɛmbəl/ vi **1** shake uncontrollably **2** be very worried: I tremble to think what may happen. **tremble** n [S]

tre·men·dous /trɪ'mɛndəs/ adj **1** very great in amount or degree **2** wonderful: What a tremendous party! ~**ly** adv

trem·or /'trɛmər/ n shaking movement: an earth tremor (= a small EARTHQUAKE) | a tremor in his voice

trem·u·lous /'trɛmyələs/ adj slightly shaking ~**ly** adv

trench /trɛntʃ/ n long narrow hole

cut in the ground, esp. as a protection for soldiers

tren·chant /ˈtrenʃənt, -tʃənt/ adj (of language) forceful and effective

trench coat /ˈ· ·/ n long coat that ties at the waist

trend /trend/ n 1 general direction or course of development: a rising trend of violent crime 2 set a/the trend start or popularize a fashion ~y adj infml very fashionable

trend·set·ter /ˈtrend,setər/ n person who starts or popularizes the latest fashion –ting adj

trep·i·da·tion /ˌtrepəˈdeʸʃən/ n [U] fml anxiety

tres·pass /ˈtrespəs, -pæs/ vi go onto privately owned land without permission ♦ n 1 [C] lit for SIN 2 [C;U] (act of) trespassing ~er n

tress·es /ˈtresɪz/ n [P] lit woman's long hair

tres·tle /ˈtresəl/ n wooden beam with a pair of spreading legs

tri·al /ˈtraɪəl/ n 1 [C;U] (act of) hearing and judging a person or case in a court of law: He's on trial for murder. 2 [C;U] (act of) testing to find out if something is good: We gave her the job for a trial period. 3 [C] cause of worry or trouble 4 stand trial be tried in court 5 trial and error trying several methods and learning from one's mistakes

trial run /ˌ· ·ˈ·/ n testing of something new to see if it works properly

tri·an·gle /ˈtraɪˌæŋgəl/ n figure or shape with 3 straight sides and 3 angles –gular /traɪˈæŋgyələr/ adj

tribe /traɪb/ n people of the same race, beliefs, language, etc., living together under the leadership of a chief: a tribe of Amazonian Indians tribal adj

trib·u·la·tion /ˌtrɪbyəˈleʸʃən/ n fml TRIAL (3)

tri·bu·nal /traɪˈbyuʷnl, trɪ-/ n sort of court that deals with particular matters

trib·u·ta·ry /ˈtrɪbyəˌteriʸ/ n river that flows into a larger river

trib·ute /ˈtrɪbyuʷt/ n [C;U] something said or given to show respect or admiration: The chairman paid tribute to (= praised) their hard work.

trick /trɪk/ n 1 clever act or plan to deceive or cheat someone 2 something done to make someone look stupid: children playing tricks on their teacher 3 amusing or confusing skillful act: magic/card tricks 4 quick or clever way to do something 5 cards played or won in a single part of a card game 6 do the trick fulfil one's purpose ♦ vt deceive ♦ adj full of hidden difficulties: a trick question ~ery n [U] use of deceiving

tricks ~y adj 1 difficult to deal with: a tricky problem 2 (of a person or actions) cunning and deceitful

trick·le /ˈtrɪkəl/ vi flow in drops or a thin stream ♦ n [S] thin slow flow: (fig.) a trickle of inquiries

trick-or-treat /ˌ· · ·ˈ·/ vi (of children) go to people's houses on HALLOWE'EN and ask for TREATS (1) under threat of playing tricks on people who refuse

trick·ster /ˈtrɪkstər/ n deceiver; cheater

tri·col·or /ˈtraɪˌkʌlər/ n flag of 3 colors, esp. the national flag of France

tri·cy·cle /ˈtraɪsɪkəl/ n bicycle with 3 wheels

tri·dent /ˈtraɪdnt/ n forklike weapon with 3 points

tried /traɪd/ v past t. & p. of TRY

tried-and-true /ˌ· · ·ˈ·◂/ adj known to be worthy

tri·er /ˈtraɪər/ n person who always tries hard

tri·fle¹ /ˈtraɪfəl/ n 1 [C] fml something of little value or importance 3 a trifle fml rather: You were a trifle rude. –fling adj fml of little value or importance

trifle² v trifle with phr vt treat without seriousness or respect

trig·ger /ˈtrɪgər/ n piece pulled with the finger to fire a gun ♦ vt start (esp. a number of things that happen one after the other)

trigger-hap·py /ˈ·· ˌ··/ adj too eager to use violent methods

trig·o·nom·e·try /ˌtrɪgəˈnɑmətriʸ/ n [U] MATHEMATICS dealing with the relationship between the sides and angles of TRIANGLES

trill /trɪl/ vi/t, n (sing, play, or pronounce with) a rapidly repeated sound

tril·o·gy /ˈtrɪlədʒiʸ/ n group of 3 related books, plays, etc.

trim /trɪm/ vt –mm– 1 make neat by cutting 2 decorate, esp. around the edges 3 move (sails) into the correct position for sailing well ♦ n 1 [S] act of cutting (esp. hair) 2 in (good) trim [U] proper condition ♦ adj –mm– pleasingly neat ~ming n decoration or useful addition: roast turkey with all the trimmings (= vegetables, potatoes, SAUCE, etc.)

Trin·i·ty /ˈtrɪnətiʸ/ n [the] (in the Christian religion) the union of the 3 forms of God (the Father, Son, and Holy Spirit) as one God

trin·ket /ˈtrɪŋkɪt/ n small decorative object of low value

tri·o /ˈtriʸoʷ/ n –os 1 group of 3 2 piece of music for 3 players or performers

trip /trɪp/ v –pp– 1 vi/t (cause to) catch the foot and lose balance: I *tripped over a stone and fell down.* **2** *vi/t* (cause to) make a mistake: *He tried to trip me up with awkward questions.* **3** *vi lit* move or dance with quick light steps ♦ *n* **1** short journey, esp. for pleasure **2** act of tripping (TRIP (1)) **3** period under the influence of a drug that changes one's mind

tripe /traɪp/ *n* [U] **1** wall of a cow's stomach used as food **2** *sl* worthless talk or writing

trip·le /ˈtrɪpəl/ *adj* having 3 parts or members ♦ *vi/t* increase to 3 times the amount or number

trip·let /ˈtrɪplɪt/ *n* any of 3 children born to the same mother at the same time

trip·li·cate /ˈtrɪplɪkət/ *n* **in triplicate** in 3 copies, one of which is the original

tri·pod /ˈtraɪpɒd/ *n* support with 3 legs, esp. for a camera

trip·tych /ˈtrɪptɪk/ *n* picture with 3 folding parts

trip·wire /ˈtrɪpˌwaɪər/ *n* stretched wire that sets off a trap, explosive, etc., if touched

trite /traɪt/ *adj* (of a remark) common and uninteresting

tri·umph /ˈtraɪəmf/ *n* [C;U] (joy or satisfaction caused by) a complete victory or success ♦ *vi* be victorious ~**al** /traɪˈʌmfəl/ *adj* of or marking a triumph ~**ant** *adj* (joyful because one is) victorious ~**antly** *adv*

tri·um·vir·ate /traɪˈʌmvərɪt/ *n* group of 3, esp. 3 people in power

triv·i·a /ˈtrɪviə/ *n* [P] **1** trivial things **2** facts of general knowledge: *a trivia quiz*

triv·i·al /ˈtrɪviəl/ *adj* **1** of little worth or importance **2** ordinary ~**ality** /ˌtrɪviˈæləti/ *n* [C;U] ~**ize** /ˈtrɪviəˌlaɪz/ *vt*

trod /trɒd/ *v past t. of* TREAD

trod·den /ˈtrɒdn/ *v past p. of* TREAD

trog·lo·dyte /ˈtrɒgləˌdaɪt/ *n* (in former times) person who lived in a CAVE

Tro·jan horse /ˌtroʊdʒən ˈhɔrs/ *n* something or someone that attacks or weakens something secretly from within

trol·ley /ˈtrɒli/ *n* **1** small cart, esp. pushed by hand **2** trolleybus

trol·ley·bus /ˈtrɒliˌbʌs/ *n* bus driven by electricity from wires above it

trom·bone /trɒmˈboʊn/ *n* brass musical instrument with a long sliding tube

troop /truːp/ *n* **1** (moving) group of people or animals **2** group of soldiers esp. on horses **3** -**er** member of state police ♦ *vi* move in a group **troops** *n* [P] soldiers

tro·phy /ˈtroʊfi/ *n* **1** prize for winning a competition or test of skill **2** something kept as a reminder of success

trop·ic /ˈtrɒpɪk/ *n* line around the world at 23½° north (**the tropic of Cancer**) and south (**the tropic of Capricorn**) of the EQUATOR **tropics** *n* [P] hot area between these lines ~**al** *adj* **1** of the tropics **2** very hot: *tropical weather*

trot[1] /trɒt/ *n* [S] **1** horse's movement, slower than a CANTER **2** slow run

trot[2] *vi* -**tt**- move at the speed of a trot

trot out *phr vt* repeat in an uninteresting unchanged way: *trotting out the same old excuses*

trots /trɒts/ *n infml* DIARRHEA

trou·ba·dour /ˈtruːbəˌdɔr, -ˌdoʊr/ *n* traveling singer and poet of former times

trou·ble /ˈtrʌbəl/ *n* **1** [C;U] (cause of) difficulty, worry, annoyance, etc.: *I didn't have any trouble doing it; it was easy.* **2** [U] state of being blamed: *He's always getting into trouble with the police.* **3** [S;U] inconvenience or more than usual work or effort: *I took a lot of trouble to get it right.* **4** [C;U] political or social disorder **5** [U] failure to work properly: *engine/heart trouble* **6 ask/look for trouble** behave so as to cause difficulty or danger for oneself **7 get a girl into trouble** *infml* make PREGNANT ♦ *v* **1** *vi/t* worry **2** *vt* cause inconvenience to **3** *vi* make an effort; BOTHER ~**some** *adj* annoying

trou·ble·shoot·er /ˈtrʌbəlˌʃuːtər/ *n* person who finds and removes causes of trouble in machines, organizations, etc.

trough /trɒf/ *n* **1** long container for animal's food **2** long hollow area between waves **3** area of low air pressure

trounce /traʊns/ *vt* defeat completely

troupe /truːp/ *n* company of entertainers

trou·sers /ˈtraʊzərz/ *n fml* [P] PANTS

trous·seau /ˈtruːsoʊ, truːˈsoʊ/ *n* -**seaux** /-soʊz/ *or* -**seaus** clothes and other personal articles of a woman getting married

trout /traʊt/ *n* **trout** river (or sea) fish used for food

trove /troʊv/ *n see* TREASURE TROVE

trow·el /ˈtraʊəl/ *n* **1** tool with a flat blade for spreading cement, etc. **2** garden tool like a small spade

tru·ant /ˈtruːənt/ *n* student who stays away from school without permission -**ancy** *n* [U]

truce /truːs/ n [C;U] agreement for the stopping of fighting

truck¹ /trʌk/ n large motor vehicle for carrying goods ♦ vt carry by truck ~**er** n truck driver

truck² n **have no truck with** fml avoid any connection with

truck farm /'· ·/ n area for growing vegetables and fruit for sale

truc·u·lent /'trʌkyələnt/ adj willing or eager to quarrel or fight ~**ly** adv -**lence** n [U]

trudge /trʌdʒ/ vi walk slowly and with effort ♦ n long tiring walk

true /truː/ adj **1** in accordance with fact or reality **2** real: *true love* **3** faithful; loyal **4** exact: *a true likeness* **5 come true** happen as was wished, expected, or dreamt **truly** adv **1** in accordance with the truth **2** really: *a truly wonderful experience* **3** sincerely: *truly sorry* ♦ n **out of true** not having correct shape or balance

true-blue /ˌ· '·◄/ adj completely loyal

truf·fle /'trʌfəl, 'truː-/ n underground FUNGUS highly regarded as food

tru·ism /'truːɪzəm/ n statement that is clearly true

trump¹ /trʌmp/ n **1** card of a sort (SUIT¹ (3)) chosen to be of higher rank than other suits in a game **2 turn/come up trumps** do the right or needed thing, esp. unexpectedly at the last moment

trump² vt beat by playing a trump
    trump up phr vt invent (a false charge or reason)

trump card /'· ·/ n something that gives a clear and unquestionable advantage

trum·pet /'trʌmpɪt/ n brass musical instrument producing high notes, consisting of a long usu. winding tube ♦ v **1** vi (of an elephant) make a loud sound **2** vt declare or shout loudly ~**er** n trumpet player

trun·cate /'trʌŋkeyt/ vt shorten (as if) by cutting off the top or end

trun·dle /'trʌndl/ vi/t move heavily or awkwardly on wheels

trundle bed /'·· ˌ·/ n bed on wheels that fits under another

trunk /trʌŋk/ n **1** main stem of a tree **2** large box in which things are packed for traveling **3** ELEPHANT's long nose **4** body without the head or limbs **5** space at the back of a car for boxes, etc. **trunks** n [P] men's SHORTS for swimming

trunk line /'· ·/ n main road, etc. for traveling long distances

truss /trʌs/ vt **1** tie up firmly and roughly **2** tie (a bird's) wings and legs in place for cooking ♦ n **1** medical supporting belt worn by someone with a HERNIA **2** framework of beams built to support a roof, bridge, etc.

trust¹ /trʌst/ n **1** [U] firm belief in the honesty, goodness, worth, etc., of someone or something **2** [C;U] (arrangement for) the holding and controlling of money for someone else: *a charitable trust* **3** [C] group of companies working together to limit competition **4** [U] fml responsibility: *employed in a position of trust* **5 take on trust** accept without proof

trust² vt **1** believe in the honesty and worth of, esp. without proof **2** allow someone to do or have something: *Can he be trusted with a gun?* **3** depend on **4** fml hope, esp. confidently: *I trust you enjoyed yourself.* ~**ful**; also ~**ing** adj (too) ready to trust others ~**fully**, ~**ingly** adv ~**y** adj lit dependable
    trust in phr vt fml have faith in

trust ac·count /'· ·ˌ·/ n bank account for saving money

trust-bust·er /'trʌstˌbʌstər/ n FEDERAL official who tries to stop business TRUSTS

trust com·pa·ny /'· ˌ····/ n company that acts like a trustee

trust·ee /trʌˈstiy/ n **1** person in charge of a TRUST¹ (2) **2** member of a group controlling the affairs of a company, college, etc.

trust·wor·thy /'trʌstˌwɜrðiy/ adj dependable

truth /truːθ/ n truths /truːðz, truːθs/ **1** [U] that which is true: *Are you telling the truth?* **2** [U] quality of being true: *I doubted the truth of what he said.* **3** [C] true fact – see also MOMENT OF TRUTH ~**ful** adj **1** (of a statement) true **2** habitually telling the truth ~**fully** adv ~**fulness** n [U]

try /traɪ/ v **1** vi/t make an attempt: *I tried to persuade him, but failed.* **2** vt test by use and experience: *Have you tried this new soap?* | *We need to try the idea out in practice.* **3** vt examine in a court of law: *He was tried for murder.* **4** vt cause to suffer, esp. with small annoyances: *Her constant questions try my patience.* | *I've had a very trying day.* **5** vt attempt to open (a door, window, etc.) ♦ n attempt adj known to be good from experience

try on phr vt put on (a garment, etc.) to see if it fits or looks well

try out phr vt **1** test by use or experience **2 try out for** compete for a position on a team, etc: *try out for football*

tsar /zar, tsar/ n CZAR

tset·se fly /'tsetsiy flaɪ, 'tsetsiy-, 'tetsiy-/ n African fly that causes SLEEPING SICKNESS

T-shirt /'tiy ʃɜrt/ n light informal

collarless garment for the upper body

tsp. *abbrev. for:* teaspoon

tub /tʌb/ n 1 round container for washing, packing, storing, etc. 2 BATHTUB

tu·ba /ˈtuʷbə, ˈtyuʷbə/ n large brass musical instrument that produces low notes

tub·by /ˈtʌbiʸ/ adj infml rather fat

tube /tuʷb, tyuʷb/ n 1 hollow round pipe 2 small soft metal or plastic container for paint, paste, etc., which you get out by pressing: a tube of toothpaste 3 pipe in the body: the bronchial tubes **tubing** n [U] tubes **tubular** /ˈtuʷbyələr, ˈtyuʷ-/ adj 1 in the form of tubes 2 sl especially good

tu·ber /ˈtuʷbər, ˈtyuʷ-/ n fleshy underground stem, such as a potato

tu·ber·cu·lo·sis /tʊ,bɜrkyəˈloʷsɪs, tyʊ-/ n [U] serious infectious disease that attacks esp. the lungs **tubercular** /tʊˈbɜrkyələr, tyʊ-/ adj

tuck /tʌk/ vt 1 put (the edge of) into a tight place for neatness, protection, etc.: Tuck your shirt in. | She tucked the newspaper under her arm. 2 put into a private or almost hidden place: a house tucked away among the trees ♦ n narrow flat fold of material sewn into a garment

tuck in phr vi 1 eat eagerly 2 make (esp. a child) comfortable in bed by pulling the sheets tight

Tues·day /ˈtuʷzdiʸ, -deʸ, ˈtyuʷz-/ n the 2nd day of the week, between Monday and Wednesday

tuft /tʌft/ n small bunch of (hair, grass, etc.)

tug /tʌg/ vi/t -gg- pull hard ♦ n 1 sudden strong pull 2 also **tugboat** /ˈtʌgboʷt/ — small boat used for pulling and guiding ships in narrow places

tug-of-war /ˌ·· ·ˈ·/ n [C;U] sport in which 2 teams pull against each other on a rope

tu·i·tion /tuʷˈɪʃən, tyuʷ-/ n [U] money paid for education esp. at a university

tu·lip /ˈtuʷlɪp, ˈtyuʷ-/ n garden plant with large colorful flowers shaped like cups

tum·ble /ˈtʌmbəl/ vi 1 fall suddenly and helplessly, esp. rolling over 2 infml understand 3 perform GYMNASTICS without special equipment ♦ n fall

tumble down phr vi fall to pieces; COLLAPSE

tum·ble-down /ˈtʌmbəldaʊn/ adj nearly in ruins

tumble weed /ˈ··· ·/ n plant that breaks off and is blown in the wind

tum·my /ˈtʌmiʸ/ n infml stomach

tu·mor /ˈtuʷmər, ˈtyuʷ-/ n mass of quickly growing diseased cells in the body

tu·mult /ˈtuʷmʌlt, ˈtyuʷ-/ n [S;U] confused noise and excitement ~**uous** /tuʷˈmʌltʃuʷəs, tyʊ-/ adj noisy

tu·na /ˈtuʷnə, ˈtyuʷnə/ n tuna or tunas [C;U] large sea fish used for food

tune /tuʷn, tyuʷn/ n 1 (pleasing) pattern of musical notes 2 **call the tune** be in a position to give orders 3 **change one's tune** change one's opinion, behavior, etc. 4 **in/out of tune: a** at/not at the correct musical level **b** in/not in agreement or sympathy 5 **to the tune of** to the amount of ♦ vt 1 set (a musical instrument) to the correct musical level 2 put (an engine) in good working order ~**ful** adj having a pleasant tune **tuner** n person who tunes musical instruments

tune in phr vi turn on a radio, esp. so as to listen to a particular radio station

tune out phr vt stop listening to

tung·sten /ˈtʌŋstən/ n hard metal used esp. in making steel

tu·nic /ˈtuʷnɪk, ˈtyuʷ-/ n 1 loose usu. belted garment which reaches to the knees 2 short coat forming part of a uniform

tun·nel /ˈtʌnl/ n usu. artificial underground passage for road, railway, etc. ♦ vi/t -l- make a tunnel (under or through)

tunnel vi·sion /ˈ·· ˌ··/ n [U] tendency to consider only one part of a question, without even trying to examine others

tur·ban /ˈtɜrbən/ n 1 Asian head covering made by winding cloth around the head 2 woman's small hat which fits high on the head

tur·bid /ˈtɜrbɪd/ adj 1 (of a liquid) not clear; muddy 2 confused

tur·bine /ˈtɜrbɪn, -baɪn/ n motor in which liquid or gas drives a wheel to produce circular movement

tur·bo·jet /ˈtɜrboʷˌdʒɛt/ n (aircraft) engine that forces out a stream of gases behind itself

tur·bu·lent /ˈtɜrbyələnt/ adj violent and disorderly or irregular ~**lence** n [U] 1 being turbulent 2 turbulent air movements

turd /tɜrd/ n taboo 1 piece of solid waste passed from the body 2 sl offensive person

tu·reen /tʊˈriʸn, tyʊ-/ n large deep dish for serving soup from

turf¹ /tɜrf/ n 1 [U] grass surface [C] piece of this 3 (the+S) horse r ing 4 area of a town where a str GANG holds authority

turf² vt cover with turf

tur·gid /ˈtɜːdʒɪd/ *adj fml* (of language or style) too solemn and SELF-IMPORTANT

tur·key /ˈtɜːkiʸ/ *n* **1** [C;U] bird rather like a large chicken, used for food **2** *sl* play in theater or a film which does not succeed **3** *sl* stupid person **4 talk turkey** *infml* speak seriously and plainly esp. about business – see also COLD TURKEY

Tur·kish bath /ˌtɜːkɪʃ ˈbæθ/ *n* health treatment in which one sits in a very hot steamy room

tur·moil /ˈtɜːmɔɪl/ *n* [S;U] state of confusion and trouble

turn¹ /tɜːn/ *v* **1** *vi/t* move around a central point: *The wheels turned.* **2** *vi/t* move so that a different side faces upwards or outwards: *She turned the pages.* **3** *vi* change direction: *Turn right at the end of the road.* | *He turned to crime.* (= became a criminal) **4** *vt* go around: *The car turned the corner.* **5** *vi* look around: *She turned to wave.* **6** *vt* aim; point: *They turned their hoses on the burning building.* | *I turned my thoughts to home.* **7** *vi/t* (cause to) become: *His hair has turned gray.* | *The witch turned the prince into a frog.* **8** *vi* go sour: *The milk's turned.* **9** *vt* pass: *It's just turned 3 o'clock.* | *She's turned 40.* **10 turn a phrase** *fml* say a clever thing neatly **11 turn one's hand to** begin to practice (a skill) **12 turn one's head** make one too proud **13 turn one's stomach** make one feel sick **14 turn tail** start to run away **15 turn the other cheek** react patiently to cruelty **16 turn the tables** bring about the opposite of a situation

turn against *phr vt* (cause to) become opposed to

turn away *phr vt* **1** refuse to let in **2** refuse to help

turn down *phr vt* **1** refuse **2** reduce the force, speed, loudness, etc., of (something) by using controls: *Can you turn that radio down?*

turn in *phr v* **1** *vt* no longer continue **2** *vi* go to bed **3** *vt* deliver to the police **4** *vt* give back; return **5** hand in; deliver: *He's turned in some very poor work lately.*

turn off *phr vt* **1** stop the flow or operation of: *turn off the tap/television* ... **2** *sl* cause to lose interest, often ...ually

...n on *phr vt* **1** cause to flow or ...te: *turn on the tap/television* **2** ...l on **3** attack suddenly and ... warning **4** *sl* excite or in...ongly, often sexually **5** *sl* ...take an illegal drug, esp. ...time **6** *vt* cause to know ...e: *He turned me on to*

turn out *phr v* **1** *vt* stop the operation of (a light) **2** *vt* drive out; send away **3** *vi* come out or gather (as if) for a meeting or public event **4** *vt* produce: *The factory turns out 100 cars a day.* **5** *vt* empty (a cupboard, pocket, etc.) **6** happen to be in the end: *The party turned out a success.* **7** *vt* dress: *an elegantly turned-out woman*

turn over *phr vt* **1** think about; consider **2** deliver to the place **3** (of an engine) to run at the lowest speed **4** do business

turn over to *phr vt* give control of (something) to

turn to *phr vt* go to for sympathy, help, advice, etc.

turn up *phr v* **1** *vi* be found **2** *vi* arrive **3** *vt* find **4** *vt* turn over (a playing card) so that the number is showing: *turn up a King* **5** *vi* happen **6 turn up one's nose (at something or someone)** suggest by one's behavior that (something or someone) is not good enough for one

turn² *n* **1** act of turning (something) **2** change of direction **3** rightful chance or duty to do something: *It's my turn to speak.* | *We took turns doing it.* (= did it one after the other) **4** development: *She's taken a turn for the worse.* (= has become more ill) **5** point of change in time: *at the turn of the century* **6** attack of illness: *He had one of his funny turns.* **7** shock: *You did give me a turn, appearing like that suddenly!* **8 a good turn** a useful or helpful action **9 at every turn** in every place; at every moment **10 in turn** in proper order **11 out of turn** unsuitably: *I hope I haven't spoken out of turn.* **12 take turns** succeed in order **13 to a turn** (of food) cooked perfectly **~ing** *n* place where one road branches off from another

turn·coat /ˈtɜːnkoʷt/ *n* disloyal person

turn·ing point /ˈ·· ˌ·/ *n* point at which a very important change happens

tur·nip /ˈtɜːnɪp/ *n* [C;U] plant with a large round whitish root used as a vegetable

turn-off /ˈ· ·/ *n* **1** smaller road branching off from a main road **2** *infml* something that causes one to feel dislike or lose interest, esp. sexually

turn-on /ˈ·· ·/ *n infml* something that excites or interests one strongly, esp. sexually

turn-out /ˈtɜːnaʊt/ *n* **1** number of people who attend **2** occasion on which one empties all unwanted things from drawers, rooms, etc. **3** wide place in a narrow road

turn·o·ver /'tɜrn₁oʷvər/ n [S] **1** rate at which a particular kind of goods is sold **2** amount of business done **3** number of workers hired to fill the places of those who leave **4** small pie: *apple turnover*

turn·pike /'tɜrnpaɪk/ n main road which drivers have to pay to use

turn·stile /'tɜrnstaɪl/ n small gate that turns around, set in an entrance to admit people one at a time

turn·ta·ble /'tɜrn₁teʸbəl/ n **1** round spinning surface on which a record is placed to be played **2** machine including such a round surface

tur·pen·tine /'tɜrpən₁taɪn/ n [U] thin oil used esp. for cleaning off unwanted paint

tur·pi·tude /'tɜrpə₁tuʷd, -₁tyuʷd/ n [U] *fml* shameful wickedness

tur·quoise /'tɜrkwɔɪz, -kɔɪz/ n [C;U] (piece of) a precious green-blue mineral ♦ *adj* turquoise in color

tur·ret /'tɜrɪt, 'tʌr-/ n **1** small tower at the corner of a building **2** turning structure on a fighting ship, plane, etc., that contains a gun

tur·tle /'tɜrtḷ/ n **1** (sea) animal with 4 legs and a hard horny shell **2 turn turtle** (of a ship) turn over

tur·tle·neck /'tɜrtḷ₁nɛk/ n (garment with) a high collar that fits closely

tusk /tʌsk/ n very long pointed tooth, usu. one of a pair: *an elephant's tusks*

tus·sle /'tʌsəl/ vi *infml* fight roughly without weapons ♦ n rough struggle or fight

tut /tʌt/ *interj* (shows annoyance or disapproval)

tu·tor /'tuʷtər, 'tyuʷ-/ n private teacher ♦ vt teach ~**ial** /tuʷ'tɔriʸəl, -'toʷr, tyuʷ-/ n short period of instruction given by a TUTOR (1)

tu·tu /'tuʷtuʷ/ n short stiff skirt worn by women BALLET dancers

tux·e·do /tʌk'siʸdoʷ/ also **tux** /tʌks/ *infml* — n –**dos** man's formal suit

TV /₁tiʸ 'viʸ◂/ n [C;U] television

TV din·ner /₁· · '··/ n prepared frozen meal

twad·dle /'twadḷ/ n [U] *infml* nonsense

twain /tweʸn/ n [U] *lit* (set of) 2

twang /twæŋ/ n **1** quick ringing sound **2** sound of human speech as if produced partly through the nose ♦ vi/t (cause to) make a TWANG (1)

tweak /twiʸk/ vt **1** seize, pull, and twist: *He tweaked her ear.* **2** make a small improvement to (a computer program, engine, etc.) **tweak** n

tweed /twiʸd/ n [U] coarse woollen cloth **tweeds** n [P] (suit of) tweed clothes

tweet /twiʸt/ vi, n (make) the short weak high noise of a small bird

tweet·er /'twiʸtər/ n a LOUDSPEAKER that gives out high sounds

twee·zers /'twiʸzərz/ n [P] small jointed tool with 2 parts for picking up and pulling out very small objects

twelfth /twɛlfθ/ determiner, adv, n, pron 12th

twelve /twɛlv/ determiner, n, pron 12

twen·ty /'twɛntiʸ, 'twɛniʸ/ determiner, n, pron 20 –**tieth** determiner, adv, n, pron 20th

twerp /twɜrp/ n *sl* fool

twice /twaɪs/ predeterminer, adv **1** 2 times **2 think twice (about something)** consider (something) carefully

twid·dle /'twɪdḷ/ vi/t turn (something) around with one's fingers, usu. purposelessly

twig /twɪg/ n small thin stem on a tree or bush

twi·light /'twaɪlaɪt/ n [U] (faint darkish light at) the time when day is about to become night –**lit** adj

twill /twɪl/ n [U] strong woven cotton cloth

twin /twɪn/ n either of 2 people born to the same mother at the same time – also SIAMESE TWIN

twin bed /₁· '·/ n either of 2 beds in a room for 2 people

twine /twaɪn/ n [U] strong string ♦ vi/t twist; wind

twinge /twɪndʒ/ n sudden sharp pain: (fig.) *a twinge of conscience*

twin·kle /'twɪŋkəl/ vi **1** shine with an unsteady light: *The stars twinkled.* **2** (of the eyes) be bright with cheerfulness, amusement, etc. ♦ n [S] **1** twinkling light **2** brightness in the eye

twirl /twɜrl/ vi/t **1** spin **2** curl ♦ n sudden quick spin or circular movement

twist /twɪst/ v **1** vi/t bend, turn, etc., so as to change shape: *She twisted the wire into the shape of a star.* **2** vt wind: *Twist the wires together.* **3** vi move windingly **4** vt turn: *She twisted her head around.* **5** vt hurt (a joint or limb) by turning it sharply **6** vt *derog* change the true meaning of **7 twist someone's arm** persuade someone forcefully or threateningly **8 twist someone round one's little finger** be able to get someone to do what one wants ♦ n **1** act of twisting **2** bend **3** unexpected development: *a strange twist of fate* **4** popular dance of the 1960s ~**er** n **1** dishonest cheating person **2** *infml* (small) TORNADO

twitch /twɪtʃ/ vi/t move with a twitch: *His eyelid twitched.* ♦ n repeated short sudden unconscious muscle movement ~**y** adj nervous; anxious

twit·ter /ˈtwɪʇər/ *vi, n* [U] **1** (of a bird) (make) short high rapid sounds **2** state of nervousness or excitement

two /tuʷ/ *determiner, n, pron* **1** (the number) 2 **2 in two** in two parts **3 one or two** a few **4 put two and two together** calculate the meaning of what one sees or hears **5 two can play at that game** (used as a threat to someone who has been unfair, unkind, etc., to oneself)

two-by-four, 2 X 4 /ˌˌˈˈ ˈˌ/ *n* piece of cut wood used in building

two cents /ˌˌ ˈˌ/ *n* **1** a very small amount of money **2 one's two cents' worth** one's opinion on a subject

two·faced /ˌtuʷˈfeʸstˌ/ *adj* deceitful; insincere

two·some /ˈtuʷsəm/ *n* 2 people or things

two-time /ˈˌ ˈˌ/ *vt* be unfaithful to (a girl or boy friend)

two-way /ˌˌ ˈˌˌ/ *adj* moving or allowing movement in both directions

ty·coon /taɪˈkuʷn/ *n* rich powerful business person

ty·ing /ˈtaɪ-ɪŋ/ *v pres. p. of* TIE

type /taɪp/ *n* **1** [C] sort; kind; example of a group or class: *She's just that type of person.* **2** [U] small blocks with raised letters on them, used in printing **3** [U] printed letters: *italic type* **4 true to type** behaving or acting (esp. badly) just as one would expect ♦ *vi/t* write with a TYPEWRITER or WORD PROCESSOR

type·cast /ˈtaɪpkæst/ *vt* –**cast** repeatedly give (an actor) the same kind of part

type·face /ˈtaɪpfeʸs/ *n* size and style of printed letters

type·script /ˈtaɪpˌskrɪpt/ *n* typed copy of something

type·writ·er /ˈtaɪpˌraɪʇər/ *n* machine that prints letters by means of keys operated by one's fingers

ty·phoid /ˈtaɪfɔɪd/ *n* [U] infectious disease causing fever and often death, produced by bacteria in food or drink

ty·phoon /ˌtaɪˈfuʷnˌ/ *n* very violent tropical storm

ty·phus /ˈtaɪfəs/ *n* [U] infectious disease that causes fever, severe headaches, and red spots on the body

typ·i·cal /ˈtɪpɪkəl/ *adj* showing the usual or main qualities of a particular sort of thing: *a typical American movie, with lots of sex and violence* ~**ly** /-kliʸ/ *adv*

typ·i·fy /ˈtɪpəˌfaɪ/ *vt* be a typical mark, sign, or example of

typ·ist /ˈtaɪpɪst/ *n* secretary employed mainly for typing (TYPE) letters

ty·po·graph·i·cal er·ror /ˌtaɪpəˌgræfɪkəl ˈerər/ also **ty·po** /ˈtaɪpoʷ/ *infml* — *n* mistake in printing or typing (TYPE)

ty·pog·ra·phy /taɪˈpɑgrəfiʸ/ *n* [U] **1** preparing matter for printing **2** arrangement and appearance of printed matter –**phic** /ˌtaɪpəˈgræfɪkˌ/ *adj*

tyr·an·nize /ˈtɪrəˌnaɪz/ *vt* use power over (a person, country, etc.) with unjust cruelty

tyr·an·ny /ˈtɪrəniʸ/ *n* [U] use of cruel or unjust ruling power –**ical** /tɪˈrænɪkəl, taɪ-/ *adj*

ty·rant /ˈtaɪrənt/ *n* cruel unjust ruler

tzar /zɑr, tsɑr/ *n* CZAR

U

U, u /yuʷ/ the 21st letter of the English alphabet

u·biq·ui·tous /yuʷˈbɪkwətəs/ *adj fml* happening or existing everywhere

U-boat /ˈyuʷ boʷt/ *n* German SUB-MARINE of the Second World War

ud·der /ˈʌdər/ *n* organ of a cow, female goat, etc. that produces milk

UFO /ˌyuʷ ef ˈoʷ, ˈyuʷfoʷ/ *n* UFO's or UFOs strange object in the sky, thought of as a spacecraft from other worlds

ugh /ʊx, ʌg/ *interj* (expresses extreme dislike)

ug·ly /ˈʌgliʸ/ *adj* 1 unpleasant to see 2 very unpleasant or threatening: *in an ugly mood* **ugliness** *n* [U]

ugly duck·ling /ˌ·· ˈ··/ *n* person less attractive than others in early life but becoming attractive later

uh-huh /ˈʌ hʌ/ *interj infml* yes

UK /ˌyuʷ ˈkeʸ/ *n* [the] the United Kingdom (of Great Britain and Northern Ireland)

u·ku·le·le /ˌyuʷkəˈleʸliʸ/ *n* sort of small GUITAR

ul·cer /ˈʌlsər/ *n* sore place where the skin is broken ~ **ate** *vi* turn into or become covered with ulcers ~ **ous** *adj*

ul·te·ri·or /ʌlˈtɪəriʸər/ *adj* kept secret, esp. because bad: *an ulterior motive*

ul·ti·mate /ˈʌltəmɪt/ *adj* being or happening after all others: *our ultimate destination* ~ **ly** *adv*

ul·ti·ma·tum /ˌʌltəˈmeʸtəm/ *n* -**tums** *or* -**ta** /-tə/ statement of conditions to be met, not open to argument

ul·tra·ma·rine /ˌʌltrəməˈriʸn/ *adj* very bright blue

ul·tra·son·ic /ˌʌltrəˈsɑnɪk/ *adj* (of a sound wave) beyond the range of human hearing

ul·tra·vi·o·let /ˌʌltrəˈvaɪəlɪt/ *adj* (of light) beyond the purple end of the range of colors that can be seen by humans

um·bil·i·cal cord /ʌmˈbɪlɪkəl ˌkɔrd/ *n* tube of flesh which joins an unborn creature to its mother

um·brage /ˈʌmbrɪdʒ/ *n fml* **take umbrage** be offended

um·brel·la /ʌmˈbrelə/ *n* 1 folding frame covered with cloth, for keeping rain off the head 2 protecting power or influence 3 anything which covers or includes a wide range of different parts

um·laut /ˈʊmlaʊt/ *n* sign (··) over a letter

um·pire /ˈʌmpaɪər/ also **ump** /ʌmp/ *infml* — *n* judge in charge of certain games, such as baseball and tennis ♦ *vi/t* act as an umpire (for)

ump·teen /ˌʌmpˈtiʸn◂/ *determiner, pron infml* a large number (of) ~ **th** *n, determiner*

un·a·ble /ʌnˈeʸbəl/ *adj* not able

un·ac·coun·ta·ble /ˌʌnəˈkaʊntəbəl/ *adj fml* hard to explain; surprising –**bly** *adv*

un·ac·cus·tomed /ˌʌnəˈkʌstəmd◂/ *adj* 1 not used (to) 2 unusual

un·ad·vised /ˌʌnədˈvaɪzd◂/ *adj fml* not sensible

un·am·big·u·ous /ˌʌnæmˈbɪgyuʷəs/ *adj* very clear; impossible to misunderstand

u·nan·i·mous /yuʷˈnænəməs/ *adj* with everyone agreeing: *a unanimous decision* ~ **ly** *adv* –**nimity** /ˌyuʷnəˈnɪməṭiʸ/ *n* [U]

un·an·swe·ra·ble /ʌnˈæsərəbəl/ *adj* that cannot be answered or argued against

un·as·sum·ing /ˌʌnəˈsuʷmɪŋ◂, -ˈsyuʷm-/ *adj* quiet and unwilling to make claims about one's good qualities

un·at·tached /ˌʌnəˈtætʃt◂/ *adj* 1 not connected 2 not married or ENGAGED (1)

un·at·tend·ed /ˌʌnəˈtendɪd◂/ *adj* alone, with no one present or in charge

un·a·vail·ing /ˌʌnəˈveʸlɪŋ◂/ *adj* having no effect ~ **ly** *adv*

un·a·wares /ˌʌnəˈweərz/ *adv* unexpectedly or without warning: *I took/ caught her unawares.* (= surprised her by my presence)

un·bal·ance /ʌnˈbæləns/ *vt* make slightly crazy: *an unbalanced mind*

un·be·knownst /ˌʌnbiˈnoʷnst/, also **un·be·known** /-ˈnoʷn/ *adv* without the stated person knowing: *Unbeknownst to me, he had left.*

un·bend /ʌnˈbend/ *v* –**bent** /-ˈbent/ 1 *vi/t* straighten 2 *vi* behave more informally

un·blink·ing /ʌnˈblɪŋkɪŋ/ *adj* showing no emotion or doubt

un·bos·om /ˌʌnˈbʊzəm/ *vt fml or lit* **unbosom oneself** tell one's secret troubles and worries

un·bowed /ˌʌnˈbaʊd◂/ *adj esp. lit* not defeated

un·bri·dled /ʌnˈbraɪdld/ *adj* not controlled, and esp. too active or violent

un·bur·den /ʌnˈbɜrdn/ *vt fml* free (oneself, one's mind, etc.) by talking about a secret trouble

un·called-for /ʌnˈkɔld ˌfɔr/ *adj* not deserved, necessary, or right: *uncalled-for rudeness*

un·can·ny /ʌnˈkæniʸ/ adj not natural or usual; mysterious ~**nily** adv

un·cer·e·mo·ni·ous /ˌʌnserəˈmoʷniʸəs/ adj 1 informal 2 rudely quick ~**ly** adv: He was thrown out unceremoniously into the street.

un·cer·tain /ʌnˈsɜrtn/ adj 1 doubtful 2 undecided or unable to decide 3 likely to change: uncertain weather ~**ly** adv ~**ty** n [C;U]

un·chart·ed /ˌʌnˈtʃɑrtɪd◂/ adj esp. lit (of a place) not well known enough for maps to be made

un·cle /ˈʌŋkəl/ n brother of one's father or mother, or husband of one's aunt

un·clean /ˌʌnˈkliʸn◂/ adj not (religiously) pure

Uncle Sam /ˌʌŋkəl ˈsæm/ n infml lit the US, its people or its government

Uncle Tom /ˌʌŋkəl ˈtɑm/ n derog black person who is very friendly or respectful to white people

un·com·for·ta·ble /ʌnˈkʌmftəbəl, ʌnˈkʌmfərtəbəl/ adj 1 not comfortable 2 embarrassed –**bly** adv

un·com·mon·ly /ʌnˈkɑmənliʸ/ adv fml very

un·com·pro·mis·ing /ʌnˈkɑmprəˌmaɪzɪŋ/ adj (bravely) unchangeable in one's opinions, actions, etc.

un·con·scio·na·ble /ʌnˈkɑnʃənəbəl/ adj fml unreasonable in degree or amount –**bly** adv

un·con·scious /ʌnˈkɑnʃəs/ adj 1 having lost consciousness 2 not intentional

un·con·sti·tu·tion·al /ˌʌnkɑnstəˈtuʷʃənəl, -ˈtyuʷ-/ adj against the principles of a constitution, and so not legal

un·count·a·ble /ʌnˈkaʊntəbəl/ adj that cannot be counted: 'Furniture' is an uncountable noun — you can't say 'two furnitures'.

un·couth /ʌnˈkuʷθ/ adj fml rough, with bad manners

un·cov·er /ʌnˈkʌvər/ vt 1 remove a covering from 2 find out (something unknown or kept secret)

un·cut /ˌʌnˈkʌt◂/ adj 1 (of a film, book, etc.) with nothing taken out 2 pure; with nothing added

unc·tu·ous /ˈʌŋktʃuʷəs/ adj fml full of unpleasantly insincere kindness, interest, etc.

un·daunt·ed /ʌnˈdɔntɪd◂, -ˈdɑn-/ adj not at all discouraged or frightened

un·de·ceive /ˌʌndɪˈsiʸv/ vt fml inform (a mistaken person) of the truth

un·de·cid·ed /ˌʌndɪˈsaɪdɪd◂/ adj not yet having (been) decided; in doubt

un·de·ni·a·ble /ˌʌndɪˈnaɪəbəl◂/ adj clear and certain –**bly** adv

un·der /ˈʌndər/ prep 1 below; covered by: The ball rolled under the table. | (fig.) She wrote under the name of George Eliot. 2 less than: under $5 3 working for; controlled by: She has 3 secretaries under her. | Spain under Franco. 4 (expresses various states or relationships): He was under threat of (= was threatened with) dismissal. | I was under the impression (= thought) that you'd gone. 5 in the state or act of: under discussion/contract 6 under age too young in law, esp. for drinking alcohol, driving a car, etc. 7 under cover (of) hidden (by): They escaped under cover of darkness. ♦ adv 1 in or to a lower place 2 less: children of 9 or under

un·der·a·chieve /ˌʌndərəˈtʃiʸv/ v perform below the level of ability or expectation –**chiever** n

un·der·bel·ly /ˈʌndərˌbeliʸ/ n esp. lit weak or undefended part of a place, plan, etc.

un·der·brush /ˈʌndərˌbrʌʃ/ n [U] bushes and low plants growing around trees

un·der·car·riage /ˈʌndərˌkærɪdʒ/ n aircraft's wheels and wheel supports

un·der·charge /ˌʌndərˈtʃɑrdʒ/ vi/t take too small an amount of money from (someone)

un·der·class·man /ˈʌndərˌklæsmən/ n -**men** /-mən, -mɛn/ college student in the beginning years

un·der·clothes /ˈʌndərˌkloʷz, -ˌkloʷðz/ n [P] UNDERWEAR

un·der·coat /ˈʌndərˌkoʷt/ n covering of paint that goes under the main covering

un·der·cov·er /ˌʌndərˈkʌvər◂/ adj acting or done secretly, esp. as a SPY

un·der·cur·rent /ˈʌndərˌkɜrənt, -ˌkʌr-/ n 1 hidden current of water beneath the surface 2 hidden tendency: an undercurrent of discontent

un·der·cut /ˈʌndərˌkʌt, ˌʌndərˈkʌt/ vt -**cut**; pres. p. -**tt**- sell things more cheaply than (a competitor)

un·der·de·vel·oped coun·try /ˌʌndərdɪˌveləpt ˈkʌntriʸ/ n country that needs to develop its industries and improve living conditions

un·der·dog /ˈʌndərˌdɔg/ n one always treated badly by others or expected to lose in a competition

un·der·done /ˌʌndərˈdʌn◂/ adj not completely cooked

un·der·es·ti·mate /ˌʌndərˈestəˌmeʸt/ v 1 vi/t guess, too low a value (for) 2 vt have too low an opinion of ♦ n /-stəmɪt/ ESTIMATE which is too small

un·der·fed /ˌʌndərˈfed◂/ adj having not enough food

un·der·foot /ˌʌndərˈfʊt/ adv

beneath the feet: *The path was stony underfoot.*

un·der·go /ˌʌndərˈgoʷ/ *vt* **-went** /-ˈwent/, **-gone** /-ˈgɔn/ experience (esp. something unpleasant or difficult)

un·der·grad·u·ate /ˌʌndərˈgrædʒuʷɪt/ *n* person attending university for a first degree

un·der·ground /ˈʌndərˌgraʊnd/ *adj* **1** below the Earth's surface **2** secret; representing a political view not acceptable to the government ♦ *n* secret group fighting or opposing the rulers of a country ♦ *adv* /ˌʌndərˈgraʊnd/ **go underground** hide from political view for a time

un·der·hand¹ /ˌʌndərˈhænd/ *also* **un·der·hand·ed** /-ˈhændɪd◄/ — *adj* (secretly) dishonest

underhand² *adj*, *adv* (in sports) with the hand below the shoulder

un·der·lie /ˌʌndərˈlaɪ/ *vt* **-lay** /-ˈleʸ/, **-lain** /-ˈleʸn/ be a hidden cause or meaning of

un·der·line /ˈʌndərˌlaɪn, ˌʌndərˈlaɪn/ *vt* **1** draw a line under **2** give additional force to, so as to show importance

un·der·ling /ˈʌndərlɪŋ/ *n* person of low rank

un·der·manned /ˌʌndərˈmænd◄/ *adj* (of a factory, etc.) having too few workers

un·der·mine /ˌʌndərˈmaɪn, ˈʌndərˌmaɪn/ *vt* **1** weaken or destroy gradually: *Criticism undermines his confidence.* **2** wear away the earth beneath

un·der·neath /ˌʌndərˈniʸθ/ *prep*, *adv* under; below

un·der·pants /ˈʌndərˌpænts/ *n* [P] underclothes for the lower part of the body

un·der·pass /ˈʌndərˌpæs/ *n* path or road under another road, railroad, etc.

un·der·pin /ˌʌndərˈpɪn/ *vt* **-nn-** strengthen or support (an argument)

un·der·priv·i·leged /ˌʌndərˈprɪvəlɪdʒd◄/ *adj* poor and living in bad social conditions

un·der·rate /ˌʌndərˈreʸt, ˌʌndəˈreʸt/ *vt* give too low an opinion of

un·der·score /ˌʌndərˈskɔr, -ˈskoʷr/ *vt* UNDERLINE

un·der·shirt /ˈʌndərˌʃɜrt/ *n* undergarment for the upper body

un·der·side /ˈʌndərˌsaɪd/ *n* lower side or surface

un·der·signed /ˈʌndərˌsaɪnd/ *n fml* whose signature is/are beneath the writing: *We, the undersigned...*

un·der·stand /ˌʌndərˈstænd/ *v* **-stood** /-ˈstʊd/ **1** *vi/t* know or find the meaning (of): *She spoke in*

Russian, and I didn't understand. **2** *vt* know or feel closely the nature of (a person, feelings, etc.) **3** *vt* take or judge (as the meaning) **4** *vt fml* have been informed: *I understand you wish to join.* **5** *vt* add (something unexpressed) in the mind to make a meaning complete **6 make oneself understood** make one's meaning clear to others, esp. in speech **~able** *adj* **1** that can be understood **2** reasonable **~ably** *adv* **~ing** *n* **1** [U] mental power; ability to understand **2** [C] private informal agreement **3** [U] sympathy ♦ *adj* sympathetic

un·der·state /ˌʌndərˈsteʸt, ˈʌndərˌsteʸt/ *vt* express less strongly than one could or should — **ment** *n* [C;U]

un·der·stud·y /ˈʌndərˌstʌdiʸ/ *n* actor able to take over from another in a particular part if necessary ♦ *vt* be an understudy for

un·der·take /ˌʌndərˈteʸk/ *vt* **-took** /-ˈtʊk/, **-taken** /-ˈteʸkən/ *fml* **1** take up or accept (a position, work, etc.) **2** promise **-taking** /ˈʌndərˌteʸkɪŋ, ˌʌndərˈteʸk-/ *n* **1** piece of work; job **2** *fml* promise

un·der·tak·er /ˈʌndərˌteʸkər/ *n* funeral arranger **-ing** *n* [U]

un·der·tone /ˈʌndərˌtoʷn/ *n* **1** low voice **2** hidden meaning or feeling

un·der·wear /ˈʌndərˌwɛər/ *n* [U] clothes worn next to the body under other clothes

un·der·went /ˌʌndərˈwent/ *v* past t. *of* UNDERGO

un·der·world /ˈʌndərˌwɜrld/ *n* **1** criminals considered as a social group **2** home of the dead in ancient Greek stories

un·der·write /ˌʌndəˈraɪt/ *vt* **-wrote** /-ˈroʷt/, **-written** /-ˈrɪtn/ *fml* support, esp. with money **-writer** /ˈʌndərˌraɪtər/ *n* person who makes insurance contracts

un·de·si·ra·ble /ˌʌndɪˈzaɪərəbəl/ *adj fml* not wanted; unpleasant ♦ *n* someone regarded as immoral, criminal, or socially unacceptable **-bility** *n* /ˌʌndɪˌzaɪərəˈbɪlətiʸ/ [U]

un·de·vel·oped /ˌʌndɪˈvɛləpt/ *adj* (usu. of a place) not having industry, building, etc.

un·dies /ˈʌndiʸz/ *n* [P] *infml* (women's) UNDERWEAR

un·di·vid·ed /ˌʌndɪˈvaɪdɪd◄/ *adj* complete

un·do /ʌnˈduʷ/ *vt* **-did** /-ˈdɪd/, **-done** /-ˈdʌn/ **1** unfasten (something tied or wrapped) **2** remove the effects of: *The fire undid months of hard work.* **~ing** *n* [S] cause of someone's ruin, failure, etc.

un·doubt·ed /ˌʌnˈdaʊtɪd◄/ *adj* known for certain to be (so) **~ly** *adv*

un·dress /ʌnˈdrɛs/ *v* **1** *vi* take one's clothes off **2** *vt* take (someone's) clothes off ♦ *n fml* lack of clothes ~ed *adj* wearing no clothes

un·due /ˌʌnˈduː◂, -ˈdjuːʷ◂/ *adj* too much; unsuitable –**unduly** *adv: not unduly worried*

un·du·late /ˈʌndʒəˌleʸt, -dyə-/ *vi* rise and fall like waves –**lation** /ˌʌndʒəˈleʸʃən, -dyə-/ *n* [C;U]

un·dy·ing /ʌnˈdaɪ-ɪŋ/ *adj lit* which will never end

un·earth /ʌnˈɜrθ/ *vt* 1 dig up 2 discover

un·earth·ly /ʌnˈɜrθliʸ/ *adj* 1 very strange and unnatural 2 *infml* (of time) very inconvenient

un·eas·y /ʌnˈiʸziʸ◂/ *adj* worried; anxious –**ily** *adv* –**iness** *n* [U]

un·ec·o·nom·ic /ˌʌnekəˈnɑmɪk, -iʸkə-/ *also* **uneconomical** /-mɪkəl/ —*adj* not producing profit; wasteful

un·ed·i·fy·ing /ʌnˈedɪˌfaɪ-ɪŋ/ *adj* unpleasant or offensive to the moral sense

un·em·ployed /ˌʌnɪmˈplɔɪd◂/ *adj* not having a job ♦ *n* [*the*+S] people without jobs

un·em·ploy·ment /ˌʌnɪmˈplɔɪmənt/ *n* [U] 1 condition of lacking a job 2 lack of jobs for numbers of people in society 3 *infml* government money paid to those without work: *collecting unemployment*

un·en·vi·a·ble /ʌnˈenviʸəbəl/ *adj* not to be wished for, esp. because of difficulty

un·e·qualed /ʌnˈiʸkwəld/ *adj* the greatest possible

un·e·quiv·o·cal /ˌʌnɪˈkwɪvəkəl/ *adj* totally clear in meaning

un·er·ring /ʌnˈɜrɪŋ, -ˈɛr-/ *adj* without making a mistake

un·e·ven /ʌnˈiʸvən/ *adj* 1 not smooth, straight, or regular 2 ODD (2) 3 varying in quality: *uneven work* (= often fairly bad) ~**ly** *adv* ~**ness** *n* [U]

un·ex·cep·tio·na·ble /ˌʌnɪkˈsepʃənəbəl/ *adj fml* satisfactory

un·ex·pur·gat·ed /ʌnˈekspərˌgeʸtɪd/ *adj* (of a book, play, etc.) with nothing that is considered improper taken out; complete

un·fail·ing /ʌnˈfeʸlɪŋ/ *adj* continuous ~**ly** *adv*

un·faith·ful /ʌnˈfeʸθfəl/ *adj* having sex with someone other than one's regular partner

un·fath·o·ma·ble /ʌnˈfæðəməbəl/ *adj* that one cannot understand; mysterious

un·flap·pa·ble /ʌnˈflæpəbəl/ *adj* always calm, esp. in difficult situations

un·fold /ʌnˈfoʷld/ *v* 1 *vt* open from a folded position 2 *vi/t* (cause to) become clear, more fully known, etc.: *as the story unfolded*

un·for·get·ta·ble /ˌʌnfərˈgetəbəl/ *adj* too strong in effect to be forgotten –**bly** *adv*

un·for·tu·nate /ʌnˈfɔrtʃənɪt/ *adj* 1 that makes one sorry 2 unlucky 3 slightly rude ~**ly** *adv*

un·found·ed /ʌnˈfaʊndɪd◂/ *adj* not supported by facts

un·frock /ʌnˈfrɑk/ *vt* dismiss (a priest)

un·furl /ʌnˈfɜrl/ *vt* unroll and open (a flag, sail, etc.)

un·gain·ly /ʌnˈgeʸnliʸ/ *adj* not graceful; awkward

un·god·ly /ʌnˈgɑdliʸ/ *adj* 1 not religious 2 *infml* UNEARTHLY (2)

un·glued /ʌnˈgluʷd/ *adj infml* emotionally upset

un·grate·ful /ʌnˈgreʸtfəl/ *adj* 1 not grateful 2 *lit* (of work) giving no reward or result

un·guard·ed /ʌnˈgɑrdɪd◂/ *adj* unwisely careless, esp. in speech

un·hand /ʌnˈhænd/ *vt lit* stop holding or touching: *Unhand me, sir!*

un·heard-of /ʌnˈhɜrd əv/ *adj* very unusual

un·hinge /ʌnˈhɪndʒ/ *vt* upset or confuse

un·ho·ly al·li·ance /ʌnˌhoʷliʸ əˈlaɪ-əns/ *n* group of people or esp. organizations that are usu. separate or opposed but have come together for a bad purpose

u·ni·corn /ˈyuʷnəˌkɔrn/ *n* imaginary horselike animal with a single horn

u·ni·form /ˈyuʷnəˌfɔrm/ *n* sort of clothes worn by all members of a group: *nurse's/army uniform* ♦ *adj* the same all over; regular ~**ly** *adv* ~**ed** *adj: uniformed soldiers* ~**ity** /ˌyuʷnəˈfɔrməṭiʸ/ *n* [U]

u·ni·fy /ˈyuʷnəˌfaɪ/ *vt* bring together so as to be a single whole or all the same –**fication** /ˌyuʷnəfəˈkeʸʃən/ *n* [U]

u·ni·lat·e·ral /ˌyuʷnəˈlæṭərəl◂/ *adj* done by only one group: *unilateral disarmament*

un·im·pea·cha·ble /ˌʌnɪmˈpiʸtʃəbəl◂/ *adj fml* that cannot be doubted or questioned

un·im·proved /ˌʌnɪmˈpruʷvd◂/ *adj* (of land) not built on or farmed

un·i·ni·ti·at·ed /ˌʌnɪˈnɪʃiʸˌeʸtɪd/ *n* [*the*+P] *fml* people who are not among those who have special knowledge or experience

un·in·ter·est·ed /ʌnˈɪntərɪstɪd, -ˌres-/ *adj* not interested

u·nion /ˈyuʷnyən/ *n* 1 [C] club or society, esp. a LABOR UNION 2 [C] group of states: *the Soviet Union* 3 [U] *fml* joining 4 [C;U] *lit* (unity in) marriage

Union Jack /ˈ·· ˌ·/ *n* [*the*] British flag

u·nique /yuˈniʸk/ adj **1** being the only one of its type **2** unusual **3** better than any other ~**ly** adv

u·ni·sex /ˈyuʷnəˌseks/ adj of one type for both male and female

u·ni·son /ˈyuʷnəsən, -zən/ n [U] **1** being together in taking action **2** everyone singing or playing the same note

u·nit /ˈyuʷnɪt/ n **1** group within a larger organization: the hospital's intensive care unit **2** amount forming a standard of measurement: The dollar is a unit of currency. **3** whole number less than 10 **4** piece of furniture, etc., which can be fitted with others of the same type

u·nite /yuʷˈnaɪt/ v **1** vt join **2** vi become one **3** vi act together for a purpose

United King·dom /ˌ·ˌ··· ˈ···/ n [the] England, Scotland, Wales, and Northern Ireland

United States of A·mer·i·ca /ˌ·ˌ··· ˌ· ··ˈ·ˌ···/ [the] also **US, USA** — republic in North America, made up of 50 states with their own governments

u·ni·ty /ˈyuʷnəṭiʸ/ n [U] being united or in agreement

u·ni·verse /ˈyuʷnəˌvɜrs/ n [the+S] everything which exists in all space —**versal** /ˌyuʷnəˈvɜrsəl◂/ adj among or for everyone or in every place: universal agreement —**versally** adv

u·ni·ver·si·ty /ˌyuʷnəˈvɜrsəṭiʸ/ n **1** place of education at the highest level, where degrees are given **2** members of this place

un·kempt /ˌʌnˈkempt◂/ adj (esp. of hair) untidy

un·kind /ˌʌnˈkaɪnd◂/ adj not kind; cruel or thoughtless

un·known quan·ti·ty /ˌ·· ˈ·ˌ···/ n **1** person or thing whose qualities and abilities are not yet known **2** (in MATHEMATICS) a number represented by the letter x

un·leash /ʌnˈliʸʃ/ vt allow (feelings, forces, etc.) to act with full force

un·less /ʌnˈlɛs, ən-/ conj except if: Don't come unless I ask you to.

un·like·ly /ˌʌnˈlaɪkliʸ◂/ adj **1** not expected; improbable **2** not likely to happen or be true

un·load /ʌnˈloʷd/ v **1** vt remove (a load) from (something) **2** vt remove bullets from (a gun) or film from (a camera) **3** vt get rid of

un·loose /ʌnˈluʷs/ vt lit set free

un·loos·en /ʌnˈluʷsən/ vt loosen

un·mask /ʌnˈmæsk/ vt show the hidden truth about

un·men·tio·na·ble /ʌnˈmɛnʃənəbəl/ adj too shocking to be spoken about

un·mit·i·gat·ed /ˌʌnˈmɪṭəˌgeʸṭɪd◂/ adj in every way (bad): an unmitigated disaster

un·nat·u·ral /ˌʌnˈnætʃərəl/ adj **1** unusual **2** against ordinary good ways of behaving: unnatural sexual practices

un·nerve /ʌnˈnɜrv/ vt take away (someone's) confidence or courage

un·ob·tru·sive /ˌʌnəbˈtruʷsɪv/ adj not (too) noticeable ~**ly** adv

un·pack /ʌnˈpæk/ vi/t remove (possessions) from (a container)

un·pal·at·a·ble /ʌnˈpælətəbəl/ adj fml unpleasant and difficult for the mind to accept

un·pleas·ant /ʌnˈplɛzənt/ adj **1** not enjoyable **2** unkind

un·pre·ce·dent·ed /ʌnˈprɛsəˌdɛntɪd/ adj never having happened before

un·pre·ten·tious /ˌʌnprɪˈtɛnʃəs◂, -tʃəs◂/ adj not showing too great signs of wealth, importance, etc.; simple

un·prin·ta·ble /ʌnˈprɪntəbəl/ adj too offensive to express

un·qual·i·fied /ʌnˈkwɑləˌfaɪd/ adj **1** not limited **2** not having suitable knowledge or experience

un·ques·tio·na·ble /ʌnˈkwestʃənəbəl/ adj which cannot be doubted; certain —**bly** adv

un·rav·el /ʌnˈrævəl/ vt – | – **1** vi/t become or cause (threads, cloth, etc.) to become separated or unwoven **2** vt make clear (a mystery)

un·real /ˌʌnˈriʸəl◂/ adj seeming imaginary or unlike reality ~**ity** /ˌʌnriʸˈæləṭiʸ/ n [U]

un·re·mit·ting /ˌʌnrɪˈmɪṭɪŋ◂/ adj fml (of something difficult) never stopping

un·re·quit·ed /ˌʌnrɪˈkwaɪṭɪd◂/ adj fml not given in return

un·rest /ʌnˈrest/ n [U] troubled or dissatisfied confusion, often with fighting

un·ri·valed /ʌnˈraɪvəld/ adj better than any other

un·roll /ʌnˈroʷl/ vi/t open from a rolled condition

un·ru·ly /ʌnˈruʷliʸ/ adj **1** behaving wildly: unruly children **2** hard to keep in place: unruly hair

un·sa·vor·y /ʌnˈseʸvəriʸ/ adj unpleasant or unacceptable in moral values

un·scathed /ʌnˈskeʸðd/ adj not harmed

un·screw /ʌnˈskruʷ/ vt **1** remove the screws from **2** take (a lid) off

un·scru·pu·lous /ʌnˈskruʷpyələs/ adj not caring about honesty and fairness

un·sea·so·na·ble /ʌnˈsiʸzənəbəl/ adj unusual for the time of year, esp. bad **-bly** adv

un·seat /ʌnˈsiʸt/ vt **1** remove from a position of power **2** (of a horse) throw off (a rider)

un·seem·ly /ʌnˈsiˀmliˀ/ adj not proper or suitable (in behavior)

un·set·tle /ʌnˈsɛtl/ vt make more anxious, dissatisfied, etc. –**tled** adj (of weather, a situation, etc.) likely to get worse

un·sight·ly /ʌnˈsaɪtliˀ/ adj ugly

un·so·cial /ʌnˈsoˀʃəl◂/ adj unsuitable for combining with family and social life: working unsocial hours

un·spea·ka·ble /ʌnˈspiˀkəbəl/ adj terrible –**bly** adv

un·stint·ing /ʌnˈstɪntɪŋ/ adj fml very generous

un·stuck /ʌnˈstʌk/ adj not fastened

un·sung /ˌʌnˈsʌŋ◂/ adj lit not famous (though deserving to be)

un·swerv·ing /ʌnˈswɜrvɪŋ/ adj firm: unswerving loyalty

un·think·a·ble /ʌnˈθɪŋkəbəl/ adj that cannot be considered or accepted; impossible

un·til /ʌnˈtɪl, ən-/ prep, conj **1** up to (the time that): Don't start until she arrives. **2** as far as: We stayed on the train until Pittsburgh.

un·to /ˈʌntuˀ/ prep lit to

un·told /ˌʌnˈtoˀld◂/ adj very great: untold damage

un·to·ward /ˌʌnˈtɔrd, -ˈtoˀrd/ adj fml unexpected and undesirable

un·tram·mel·ed /ʌnˈtræməld/ adj fml allowed to act or develop with complete freedom

un·truth /ʌnˈtruˀθ/ n fml -**truths** /-ˈtruˀðz, -ˈtruˀθs/ lie

un·u·su·al /ʌnˈyuˀʒuˀəl, -ʒəl/ adj fml **1** not common **2** interesting because different from others ~**ly** adv **1** very **2** in an unusual way

un·ut·te·ra·ble /ʌnˈʌtərəbəl/ adj fml **1** terrible **2** complete: an unutterable fool –**bly** adv

un·var·nished /ʌnˈvɑrnɪʃt/ adj without additional description

un·veil /ʌnˈveˀl/ vt **1** remove a covering from **2** show publicly for the first time

un·war·rant·ed /ʌnˈwɔrəntɪd, -ˈwɑr-/ adj (done) without good reason

un·well /ʌnˈwɛl/ adj (slightly) ill

un·wiel·dy /ʌnˈwiˀldiˀ/ adj awkward to move, handle, or use

un·wind /ʌnˈwaɪnd/ v -**wound** /-ˈwaʊnd/ **1** vi/t undo (something wound) or become undone: unwinding a ball of yarn **2** vi become calmer and free of care

un·wit·ting /ʌnˈwɪtɪŋ/ adj not knowing or intended: their unwitting accomplice

un·writ·ten rule /ˌʌnrɪtn ˈruˀl/ n usual custom (not officially stated)

up /ʌp/ adv **1** to or at a higher level: She climbed up onto the roof. | He turned up his collar. **2** (shows increase): Turn the radio up. (= louder) **3** to the north: driving up to Canada **4** out of bed: We stayed up late. **5** so as to be completely finished: Eat up your vegetables. **6** into small pieces: She tore it up. **7** firmly; tightly: He tied up the package. **8** together: Add up the figures. **9** more loudly: Speak up! **10** on top: right side up **11** up against having to face (something difficult) **12** up and down: **a** higher and lower: jumping up and down **b** backwards and forwards: walking up and down **13** up to: **a** towards and as far as: He walked up to me and asked my name. **b** until: up to now **c** good, well, or clever enough for: He's not up to the job. **d** the duty or responsibility of: I'll leave it up to you. (= you must decide) **e** doing (something bad): What are you up to? **14** Up with We want or approve of: Up with the workers! ♦ prep **1** to or at a higher level on: walking up the stairs **2** to or at the top or far end of: They live just up the road. ♦ adj **1** directed up: the up escalator **2** at a higher level: Profits are up. **3** be up be happening; be the matter **4** be well up in/on know a lot about **5** up and about out of bed (again) and able to walk **6** up for: **a** intended or being considered for **b** on trial for **c** up for wanting to do or experience: Are you up for a movie? ♦ vt -**pp**- increase

up-and-com·ing /ˌ· · ˈ· · ·◂/ adj new and likely to succeed

up-and-up /ˌ· · ˈ·/ n on the up-and-up honest

up·braid /ˌʌpˈbreˀd/ vt fml for SCOLD

up·bring·ing /ˈʌpˌbrɪŋɪŋ/ n [S] (way of) training and caring for a child

up·chuck /ˈʌptʃʌk/ vt VOMIT

up·com·ing /ˈʌpˌkʌmɪŋ/ adj about to happen

up·date /ˌʌpˈdeˀt, ˈʌpdeˀt/ vt **1** make more modern **2** supply with the latest information

up·end /ʌpˈɛnd/ vt stand on a part that does not usually stand on the floor

up·front /ˌʌpˈfrʌnt/ adj very direct and making no attempt to hide one's meaning

up·grade /ˌʌpˈgreˀd, ˈʌpgreˀd/ vt **1** give a more important position to **2** improve by modernizing: upgrade a computer system ♦ n: software upgrade

up·heav·al /ʌpˈhiˀvəl/ n [C;U] great change and confusion, with much activity

up·held /ˌʌpˈhɛld/ past t. and p. of UPHOLD

up·hill /ˌʌpˈhɪl◂/ adj, adv **1** up a slope **2** difficult: an uphill task

up·hold /ʌpˈhoʷld/ vt **-held** /-ˈhɛld/ **1** prevent from being weakened or taken away **2** declare (a decision) to be right ~**er** n

up·hol·ster /ʌpˈhoʷlstər, əˈpoʷl-/ vt cover and fill (furniture) ~**er** n ~**y** n [U] material covering and filling furniture

up·keep /ˈʌpkiʸp/ n [U] (cost of) keeping something repaired and in order

up·lift /ʌpˈlɪft/ vt fml encourage cheerful or holy feelings in

up·on /əˈpɑn, əˈpɔn/ prep fml for ON¹ (1,3,4,6,7)

up·per /ˈʌpər/ adj at or nearer the top: the upper arm ♦ n **1** top part of a shoe **2** sl drug that speeds you up

upper class /ˌ·· ˈ·◄/ n highest social class, **upper-class** adj

upper hand /ˌ·· ˈ·/ n [the+S] control

up·per·most /ˈʌpərˌmoʷst/ adv in the highest or strongest position

up·right /ˈʌp-raɪt/ adj **1** exactly straight up; not bent or leaning **2** completely honest ♦ n upright supporting beam

up·ris·ing /ˈʌpˌraɪzɪŋ/ n act of the ordinary people suddenly and violently opposing those in power

up·roar /ˈʌp-rɔr, -roʷr/ n [S;U] confused noisy activity, esp. shouting ~**ious** /ʌpˈrɔriʸəs, -ˈroʷr-/ adj very noisy, esp. with laughter

up·root /ʌpˈruʷt, -ˈrʊt/ vt **1** tear (a plant) from the earth **2** remove from a home, settled habits, etc.

ups and downs /ˌ· · ˈ·/ n [P] good and bad periods

up·scale /ˈʌpskeʸl/ adj being or using goods produced to meet the demand of the wealthier social groups

up·set /ʌpˈsɛt/ vt **-set-**; pres. p. **-tt-** **1** turn over, esp. accidentally, causing confusion or scattering **2** cause to be worried, sad, angry, etc. **3** make slightly ill ♦ n /ˈʌpsɛt/ **1** slight illness: a stomach upset **2** unexpected result

up·shot /ˈʌpʃɑt/ n result in the end

up·side down /ˌʌpsaɪd ˈdaʊn/ adj **1** with the top turned to the bottom **2** in disorder

up·stage /ʌpˈsteʸdʒ/ vt take attention away from (someone) for oneself

up·stairs /ˌʌpˈstɛərz◄/ adv, adj on or to a higher floor

up·stand·ing /ˌʌpˈstændɪŋ/ adj **1** tall and strong **2** honest

up·start /ˈʌpstɑrt/ n someone who has risen too suddenly or unexpectedly to a high position

up·state /ˈʌpsteʸt/ n, adj (esp. northern) part of a state away from cities

up·stream /ˌʌpˈstriʸm/ adv, adj moving against the current of a river

up·take /ˈʌpteʸk/ n [U] ability to understand: He's pretty slow on the uptake.

up·tight /ˌʌpˈtaɪt◄/ adj infml anxious and nervous

up-to-date /ˌ·· ˈ·◄/ adj **1** modern **2** including or having all the latest information

up·town /ˌʌpˈtaʊn◄/ adj, n (of the) northern part of a city: the uptown bus

up·turn /ˈʌptɜrn/ n a favorable change

up·ward /ˈʌpwərd/ adj going up **upwards** adv more than

upwardly-mo·bile /ˌ··· ˈ··/ adj able or wishing to move into a higher social class and become more wealthy **upward mobility** /ˌ··· ·ˈ···/ n

u·ra·ni·um /yuˈreʸniʸəm/ n [U] radioactive (RADIOACTIVITY) metal used in producing atomic power

U·ra·nus /yuˈreʸnəs, ˈyʊrənəs/ n the PLANET 7th in order from the sun

ur·ban /ˈɜrbən/ adj of towns

ur·bane /ɜrˈbeʸn/ adj smoothly polite ~**ly** adv **-banity** /-ˈbænəṭiʸ/ n [U]

ur·chin /ˈɜrtʃɪn/ n small dirty untidy child – see also SEA URCHIN

urge /ɜrdʒ/ vt **1** try strongly to persuade: He urged me to reconsider. **2** drive forwards: He urged the horses onward with a whip. ♦ n strong desire or need

ur·gent /ˈɜrdʒənt/ adj that must be dealt with at once ~**ly** adv **urgency** n [U]

u·ri·nal /ˈyʊrənəl/ n container or building for (men) urinating

u·rine /ˈyʊrɪn/ n [U] liquid waste passed from the body **urinary** adj **urinate** vi pass urine from the body **urination** /ˌyʊrəˈneʸʃən/ n [U]

urn /ɜrn/ n **1** large metal container for serving tea or coffee **2** container for the ashes of a burned dead body

us /əs; strong ʌs/ pron (object form of we)

US /ˌyuʷ ˈɛs◄/ also **USA** /ˌyuʷ ɛs ˈeʸ/ — abbrev. for **1** the United States (of America) **2** of the United States: the US Navy

us·age /ˈyuʷsɪdʒ, -zɪdʒ/ n **1** [C;U] way of using a language: a book on English usage **2** fml (type or degree of) use

use¹ /yuʷs/ n **1** [U] using or being used **2** [U] ability or right to use something: He lost the use of his legs. **3** [C;U] purpose: A machine with many uses. **4** [U] advantage; usefulness: It's no use complaining. (= complaining will have no effect) **5**

in use being used **6 make use of use 7 of use** useful ~**ful** adj that fulfils a need well ~**fully** adv ~**fulness** n [U] ~**less** adj **1** not useful **2** unable to do anything properly ~**lessly** adv

use² /yuᵂz/ vt **1** employ for a purpose; put to use: Oil can be used as a fuel. **2** finish; CONSUME (2) **3** take unfair advantage of; EXPLOIT **usable** adj **used** adj that has already had an owner: used cars **user** n

use up phr vt finish completely

use³ /yuᵂs/ vi (used in the past tense for showing what always or regularly happened): I used to go there every week, but I no longer do.

used to /ˈyuᵂst tʊ,-tə/ adj no longer finding (something) strange or annoying because it has become familiar: I'm used to the noise.

user-friend·ly /ˌ·· ˈ···◂/ adj easy to use or understand

ush·er /ˈʌʃər/ n someone who shows people to their seats in a public place ♦ vt fml bring by showing the way: (fig.) The bombing of Hiroshima ushered in the nuclear age.

ush·er·ette /ˌʌʃəˈrɛt/ n female usher in a theater or performance hall

USS /ˈyuᵂ ɛs ɛs/ n United States Ship; title for a ship in the US navy

USSR /ˌyuᵂ ɛs ɛs ˈɑr/ abbrev. for: Union of Soviet Socialist Republics; the former Soviet Union; Russia

u·su·al /ˈyuᵂʒuᵂəl, -ʒəl/ adj in accordance with what happens most of the time: He lacked his usual cheerfulness. ~**ly** adv in most cases; generally

u·surp /yuᵂˈsɜrp, yuᵂˈzɜrp/ vt fml steal (someone else's power or position) ~**er** n

u·su·ry /ˈyuᵂʒəriʸ/ n [U] fml lending money to be paid back at an unfairly high rate of interest –**rer** n

u·ten·sil /yuᵂˈtɛnsəl/ n fml object with a particular use, esp. a tool or container

u·te·rus /ˈyuᵂtərəs/ n med for WOMB

u·til·i·tar·i·an /yuᵂˌtɪləˈtɛəriʸən/ adj fml, sometimes derog made to be useful rather than decorative

u·til·i·ty /yuᵂˈtɪlətiʸ/ n **1** [U] fml degree of usefulness **2** [C] public service, such as water supplies, electricity, etc.

u·til·ize /ˈyuᵂtɫˌaɪz/ vt fml for USE² (1) –**ization** /ˌyuᵂtɫ-əˈzeʸʃən/ n [U]

ut·most /ˈʌtmoᵂst/ adj fml very great: done with (the) utmost care ♦ n [U] the most that can be done: I did my utmost to prevent it.

u·to·pi·a /yuᵂˈtoᵂpiʸə/ n [C;U] perfect society -**pian** adj impractically trying to bring social perfection

ut·ter¹ /ˈʌtər/ adj (esp. of something bad) complete: utter nonsense ~**ly** adv

utter² vt fml make (a sound) or produce (words) ~**ance** n fml **1** [U] speaking **2** [C] something said

U-turn /ˈyuᵂ tɜrn/ n **1** turning movement in a vehicle which takes one back in the direction one came from **2** complete change, resulting in the opposite of what has gone before

u·vu·la /ˈyuᵂvyələ/ n small piece of flesh hanging down at the top of the throat

V

V, v /viː/ the 22nd letter of the English alphabet

v *abbrev. for:* **1** verb **2** VERSUS **3** very

va·can·cy /ˈveɪkənsiː/ n unfilled place, such as a job or hotel room

va·cant /ˈveɪkənt/ adj **1** empty **2** (of a job) having no worker to do it **3** showing lack of interest or serious thought ~**ly** adv

va·cate /ˈveɪkeɪt/ vt fml cease to use or live in: *Kindly vacate your seats.*

va·ca·tion /veɪˈkeɪʃən, və-/ n **1** [C] time of rest from work, school, etc. **2** [U] fml vacating ♦ vi have a vacation

vac·cine /ˈvæksiːn/ n [C;U] substance put into the body to protect it against disease –**cinate** /ˈvæksəˌneɪt/ vt put vaccine into –**cination** /ˌvæksəˈneɪʃən/ n [C;U]

vac·il·late /ˈvæsəˌleɪt/ vi keep changing one's mind –**lation** /ˌvæsəˈleɪʃən/ n [C;U]

vac·u·ous /ˈvækjuːəs/ adj fml **1** showing foolishness: *a vacuous grin* **2** with no purpose or meaning ~**ly** adv –**uity** /væˈkjuːəti, və-/ n [C;U]

vac·u·um /ˈvækjuːm, -kjuːəm/ n space completely without air or other gas: (fig.) *Her death left a vacuum* (= emptiness) *in our lives.* ♦ vt clean with a vacuum cleaner

vacuum clean·er /ˈ··· ˌ··/ n electric apparatus for sucking up dirt from floors, etc.

vacuum-packed /ˌ·· ˈ·◂/ adj wrapped in plastic with all air removed

vag·a·bond /ˈvægəˌbɒnd/ n lit person who lives a wandering life

va·ga·ry /ˈveɪɡəriː, vəˈɡeəriː/ n chance event that has an effect on one

va·gi·na /vəˈdʒaɪnə/ n passage from the outer female sex organs to the WOMB

va·grant /ˈveɪɡrənt/ n fml or law person with no home who wanders around and usu. begs **vagrancy** n [U] being a vagrant

vague /veɪɡ/ adj **1** not clearly seen, described, understood, etc. **2** unable to express oneself clearly ~**ly** adv ~**ness** n [U]

vain /veɪn/ adj **1** admiring oneself too much **2** unsuccessful; unimportant: *a vain attempt* **3 in vain** unsuccessfully **4 take someone's name in vain** talk disrespectfully about someone ~**ly** adv

val·ance /ˈvæləns/ n piece above a window to hide curtain tops

vale /veɪl/ n (in poetry and names of places) broad low valley

val·e·dic·tion /ˌvæləˈdɪkʃən/ n [C;U] fml or lit (act of) saying goodbye –**tory** /-ˈdɪktəriː/ adj used in valediction

va·len·cy /ˈveɪlənsiː/ n measure of the power of atoms to form compounds

val·en·tine /ˈvælənˌtaɪn/ n (card sent to) a lover chosen on **St Valentine's Day** (February 14th)

val·et /ˈvælɪt, ˈvæleɪ, væˈleɪ/ n **1** man's personal male servant **2** hotel servant who cleans and presses clothes

val·iant /ˈvæljənt/ adj esp. fml or lit very brave ~**ly** adv **1** very bravely **2** very hard: *He tried valiantly (but without success) to pass the exam.*

val·id /ˈvælɪd/ adj **1** (of a reason, argument, etc.) firmly based and acceptable **2** that can legally be used: *a ticket valid for 3 months* ~**ly** adv ~**ate** vt fml make valid **validity** /vəˈlɪdəti/ n [U]

val·i·um /ˈvæliːəm/ n tdmk widely used calming drug

val·ley /ˈvæliː/ n land between 2 lines of hills or mountains

val·or /ˈvælər/ n [U] esp. fml or lit great bravery ~**orous** adj

val·u·a·ble /ˈvæljəbəl, ˈvæljuːəbəl/ adj **1** worth a lot of money **2** very useful ♦ n something VALUABLE (1)

val·u·a·tion /ˌvæljuːˈeɪʃən/ n **1** [C;U] calculating how much something is worth **2** [C] value decided on

val·ue /ˈvæljuː/ n **1** [S;U] usefulness or importance, esp. compared with other things: *The map was of great value in finding the way.* **2** [C;U] worth in esp. money: *goods to the value of $500* **3** [U] worth compared with the amount paid: *a restaurant offering the best value in town* ♦ vt **1** calculate the value of **2** consider to be of great worth **values** n [P] standards or principles; people's ideas about the worth of certain qualities: *moral values* ~**less** adj ~**uer** n

value judg·ment /ˈ·· ˌ··/ n judgment about the quality of something, based on opinion rather than facts

valve /vælv/ n **1** part inside a pipe which opens and shuts to control the flow of liquid or gas through it **2** closed airless glass tube for controlling a flow of electricity

va·moose /vəˈmuːs, væ-/ vi sl leave quickly

vam·pire /ˈvæmpaɪər/ n imaginary evil creature that sucks people's blood

van /væn/ n covered road vehicle or railroad car for carrying esp. goods

van·dal /'vændl/ n person who destroys beautiful or useful things ~**ism** n [U] needless damage to esp. public buildings ~**ize** vt destroy or damage intentionally

vane /veɪn/ n bladelike turning part of a machine – see also WEATHER VANE

van·guard /'væŋgɑrd/ n 1 leading part of some kind of advancement in human affairs: scientists in the vanguard of medical research 2 front of a marching army

va·nil·la /və'nɪlə/ n [U] plant substance with a strong smell, used in food ♦ adj usual; ordinary

van·ish /'vænɪʃ/ vi 1 disappear 2 cease to exist

van·i·ty /'vænəṭiʸ/ n [U] 1 being too proud of oneself 2 quality of being without lasting value

van·quish /'væŋkwɪʃ, 'væn-/ vt esp. lit defeat completely

van·tage·point /'væntɪdʒ₁pɔɪnt/ n 1 good position from which to see 2 point of view

vap·id /'væpɪd/ adj fml dull

va·por /'veɪʸpər/ n [U] gaslike form of a liquid, such as mist or steam **vaporize** vi/t change into vapor **vaporous** adj

var·i·a·ble /'veəriʸəbəl/ adj that changes or can be changed; not fixed or steady ♦ n variable amount ~**bly** adv

var·i·ance /'veəriʸəns/ n fml at variance (with) not in agreement (with)

var·i·ant /'veəriʸənt/ n, adj (form, etc.) that is different and can be used instead: variant spellings

var·i·a·tion /₁veəriʸ'eɪʸʃən/ n 1 [C;U] (example or degree of) varying: price variations 2 [C] any of a set of pieces of music based on a single tune

var·i·cose veins /₁værəkoʷs 'veɪ̯nz/ n [P] swollen blood tubes, esp. in the legs

var·ied /'veəriʸd/ adj 1 VARIOUS (1) 2 (always) changing: a varied life

var·i·e·gat·ed /'veəriʸə₁geɪ̯ṭɪd/ adj marked irregularly with different colors ~**gation** /₁veəriʸə'geɪ̯ʃən/ n [U]

va·ri·e·ty /və'raɪəṭiʸ/ n 1 [U] not being always the same: a job lacking variety 2 [S] group containing different sorts of the same thing: a wide variety of colors 3 [C] sort: a new variety of wheat 4 [U] entertainment with many short performances of singing, dancing, telling jokes, etc.

variety store /·'··· ₁·/ n store selling clothing and goods for the home but usu. not food

var·i·ous /'veəriʸəs/ adj 1 different from each other: There are various ways of doing it. 2 several ~**ly** adv

var·nish /'vɑrnɪʃ/ n [C;U] liquid that gives a hard shiny surface to esp. wooden articles ♦ vt cover with varnish

varnish over phr vt cover up (something unpleasant)

var·y /'veəriʸ/ v 1 vi be different (from each other): Houses vary in size. 2 vi/t change, esp. continually: varying one's work methods

vas·cu·lar /'væskyələr/ adj of or containing VEINS

vase /veɪs, veɪz, vɑz/ n deep decorative pot for esp. flowers

va·sec·to·my /və'sektəmiʸ/ n operation for cutting the tubes that carry SPERM in a man, to prevent him from becoming a father

vas·sal /'væsəl/ n person of low social rank in the Middle Ages

vast /væst/ adj extremely large: a vast desert/improvement ~**ly** adv

vat /væt/ n large liquid container for industrial use: a whiskey vat

Vat·i·can /'væṭɪkən/ n (palace in Rome which is) the center of government of the Roman Catholic Church

vau·de·ville /'vɔdə₁vɪl, 'vɑ-, 'voʷ-/ n [U] old-fashioned stage entertainment

vault¹ /vɔlt/ n 1 room with thick walls, for storing valuable things 2 underground room, esp. for storing things or for dead bodies 3 place where money is kept safe in a bank 4 arched roof

vault² vi jump using the hands or a pole to gain more height ♦ n act of vaulting ~**er** n

vaunt /vɔnt/ vt esp. lit BOAST about

VD /₁viʸ 'diʸ/ n [U] VENEREAL DISEASE

VDU /₁viʸ diʸ 'yuʷ/ n visual display unit; apparatus with a SCREEN which shows information, esp. from a computer or WORD PROCESSOR

veal /viʸl/ n [U] meat from a young cow

veer /vɪər/ vi change direction

ve·gan /'viʸdʒən, 'viʸgən/ n person who eats no food that comes from animals ♦ adj

vege·ta·ble /'vedʒtəbəl, 'vedʒəṭə-/ n 1 plant grown for food to be eaten with the main part of a meal, rather than with sweet things: Potatoes and carrots are vegetables. 2 human being who exists but has little or no power of thought

veg·e·tar·i·an /₁vedʒə'teəriʸən◂/ n person who eats no meat ♦ adj 1 of or related to vegetarians **2** made up only of vegetables

veg·e·tate /ˈvedʒəˌteʸt/ *vi* lead a dull inactive life

veg·e·ta·tion /ˌvedʒəˈteʸʃən/ *n* [U] plants

veg·gies /ˈvedʒiʸz/ *n infml* [P] vegetables

ve·he·ment /ˈviʸəmənt/ *adj fml* forceful ~**ly** *adv* ~**mence** *n* [U]

ve·hi·cle /ˈviʸɪkəl/ *n* **1** something in or on which people or goods are carried, such as a car, bicycle, etc. **2** means of expressing or showing something: *He bought the newspaper company as a vehicle for his own political views.*

veil /veʸl/ *n* **1** covering for a woman's face **2** something that covers and hides: *a veil of mist* **3** **take the veil** (of a woman) become a NUN ♦ *vt* cover (as if) with a veil: *veiled in secrecy* ~**ed** *adj* expressed indirectly: *veiled threats*

vein /veʸn/ *n* **1** tube carrying blood back to the heart **2** thin line running through a leaf or insect's wing **3** crack in rock, containing metal **4** small but noticeable amount: *a vein of cruelty* **5** state of mind: *in a sad vein*

vel·cro /ˈvelkroʷ/ *n tdmk* [U] cloth with special surfaces that fasten to each other

ve·loc·i·ty /vəˈlɑsəṭiʸ/ *n fml* speed

vel·vet /ˈvelvɪt/ *n* [U] cloth with a soft furry surface on one side only ~**y** *adj* soft like velvet

ve·nal /ˈviʸnl/ *adj fml* acting or done to gain unfair reward or personal advantage rather than for proper honest reasons

ven·det·ta /venˈdeṭə/ *n* situation that lasts for a long time, in which one person repeatedly tries to harm another

vend·ing ma·chine /ˈvendɪŋ məˌʃiʸn/ *n* machine into which one puts money to obtain small articles

vend·or /ˈvendər/ *n fml* seller

ve·neer /vəˈnɪər/ *n* **1** thin covering of wood on an article **2** false outer appearance: *a veneer of respectability* ♦ *vt* cover with a veneer

ven·er·a·ble /ˈvenərəbəl/ *adj fml* deserving respect or honor because of great age or wisdom

ven·er·ate /ˈvenəˌreʸt/ *vt fml* treat (someone or something old) with great respect or honor ~**ration** /ˌvenəˈreʸʃən/ *n* [U]

ve·ne·re·al dis·ease /vəˌnɪəriʸəl dɪˈziʸz/ *n* [C;U] disease passed on by sexual activity

ve·ne·tian blind /vəˌniʸʃən ˈblaɪnd/ *n* window covering with long flat bars that can be turned to let in or shut out light

ven·geance /ˈvendʒəns/ *n* **1** [U] harm done in return for harm done to oneself: *He took vengeance on his tormentors.* **2** **with a vengeance** *infml* very greatly

venge·ful /ˈvendʒfəl/ *adj esp. lit* fiercely wishing to take vengeance ~**ly** *adv*

ve·ni·al /ˈviʸniʸəl/ *adj fml* (of a mistake, fault, etc.) not very serious, and therefore forgivable

ven·i·son /ˈvenəsən/ *n* [U] deer meat

ven·om /ˈvenəm/ *n* **1** liquid poison produced by certain animals **2** great anger or hatred ~**ous** *adj*: *a venomous snake/look*

vent¹ /vent/ *n* **1** opening or pipe by which gas, smoke, etc., escape **2** **give vent to** express freely: *giving vent to his anger*

vent² *v* **vent on** *phr vt* express by making (someone or something) suffer: *venting her fury on the cat*

ven·ti·late /ˈventlˌeʸt/ *vt* let or bring fresh air into (a room, building, etc.) ~**lator** *n* **1** apparatus for ventilating **2** apparatus for pumping air into and out of the lungs of someone who cannot breathe properly ~**lation** /ˌventlˈeʸʃən/ *n* [U]

ven·tri·cle /ˈventrɪkəl/ *n* space in the bottom of the heart that pushes blood out into the body

ven·tril·o·quist /venˈtrɪləkwɪst/ *n* someone who can make their voice seem to come from someone or somewhere else ~**quism** *n* [U]

ven·ture /ˈventʃər/ *v* **1** *vi* risk going: *She ventured too near the cliff edge, and fell over.* **2** *vt fml* dare to say ♦ *n* (new and risky) course of action: *her commercial venture*

venture cap·i·tal /ˈ·· ˌ·····/ *n* [U] money lent to start up a new business company, esp. a risky one

ven·ture·some /ˈventʃərsəm/ *adj* ready to take risks

ven·ue /ˈvenyuʷ/ *n law* place where something happened or where a case is tried

Ve·nus /ˈviʸnəs/ *n* the PLANET 2nd in order from the sun

ve·rac·i·ty /vəˈræsəṭiʸ/ *n* [U] *fml* truthfulness

ve·ran·da, -dah /vəˈrændə/ *n* open area with a floor and roof beside a house

verb /vɜrb/ *n* word or group of words that is used in describing an action, experience, or state, such as *wrote* in *She wrote a letter*, or *put on* in *He put on his coat*

verb·al /ˈvɜrbəl/ *adj* **1** spoken, not written **2** of words and their use **3** of a verb ~**ly** *adv* in spoken words

verb·al·ize /ˈvɜrbəˌlaɪz/ express (something) in words

verbal noun /₁·· ¹·/ n noun describing an action, formed by adding -ing to the verb: In the sentence 'The building of the bridge was slow work,' 'building' is a verbal noun.

ver·ba·tim /₁vɜr¹beᵞtɪm/ adv, adj repeating the actual words exactly

ver·bi·age /¹vɜrbiᵞɪdʒ/ n [U] fml too many unnecessary words

ver·bose /vɜr¹boʷs/ adj fml using too many words –bosity /-¹bɑsəṭiᵞ/ n [U]

ver·dant /¹vɜrdənt/ adj lit green with growing plants

ver·dict /¹vɜrdɪkt/ n 1 decision made by a JURY at the end of a trial about whether the prisoner is guilty 2 judgment; opinion

ver·dure /¹vɜrdʒər/ n [U] lit (greenness of) growing plants

verge¹ /vɜrdʒ/ n 1 edge, esp. of a path or road 2 on the verge of nearly; about to

verge² v verge on phr vt be near to: dark grey, verging on black

ver·i·fy /¹verə₁faɪ/ vt make certain that (something) is true –fiable adj –fication /₁verəfə¹keʸʃən/ n [U]

ver·i·si·mil·i·tude /₁verəsə¹mɪlə₁tuʷd, -₁tyuʷd/ n [U] fml quality of seeming to be true

ver·i·ta·ble /¹verəṭəbəl/ adj fml (used to give force to an expression) real: a veritable feast –bly adv

ver·mil·ion /vər¹mɪlyən/ adj bright reddish orange

ver·min /¹vɜrmɪn/ n [P] 1 insects and small animals that do damage 2 people who are a trouble to society

ver·mouth /vər¹muʷθ/ n [U] drink made from wine with substances added that have a strong taste

ver·nac·u·lar /vər¹nækyələr/ adj, n (in or being) the language spoken in a particular place

ver·sa·tile /¹vɜrsəṭl, -₁taɪl/ adj that can do many different things or has many uses –tility /₁vɜrsə¹tɪləṭiᵞ/ n [U]

verse /vɜrs/ n 1 [U] writing in the form of poetry, esp. with RHYMES – see also BLANK VERSE, FREE VERSE 2 [C] single division of a poem 3 [C] short numbered group of sentences in the Bible or other holy book

versed /vɜrst/ adj fml experienced; skilled: thoroughly versed in the arts of diplomacy

ver·sion /¹vɜrʒən, -ʃən/ n 1 form of something that is slightly different from others of the same sort: This dress is a cheaper version of the one we saw in the other shop. 2 one person's account of an event: The 2 eyewitnesses gave different versions of the accident.

ver·sus /¹vɜrsəs/ prep in competition with; against

ver·te·bra /¹vɜrṭəbrə/ n –brae /-briᵞ/, -breᵞ/ small bone in the BACKBONE

ver·te·brate /¹vɜrṭəbrɪt, -₁breᵞt/ n animal with a BACKBONE

ver·ti·cal /¹vɜrṭɪkəl/ adj forming a 90° angle with the ground or bottom; upright ~ly /-kliᵞ/ adv

ver·ti·go /¹vɜrṭɪ₁goʷ/ n [U] unpleasant feeling of being unsteady at great heights

verve /vɜrv/ n [U] forcefulness and eager enjoyment

ve·ry /¹veriᵞ/ adv 1 to a great degree: a very exciting book 2 in the greatest possible degree: I did my very best to help. 3 very good (used as a respectful form of agreement) of course 4 very well fml (used as a form of agreement, often with some degree of unwillingness) ♦ adj 1 (used for giving force to an expression) actual: He died in that very bed. 2 the very idea! (used for expressing surprise at something said by someone else)

ves·pers /¹vespərz/ n [P;U] church service in the evening

ves·sel /¹vesəl/ n 1 ship or large boat 2 (round) container, esp. for liquids 3 tube that carries liquid through a body or plant

vest¹ /vest/ n garment without arms worn under a coat

vest² v vest in/with phr vt fml give the legal right to possess or use (power, property, etc.) to (someone)

ves·tal vir·gin /₁vestl ¹vɜrdʒɪn/ n unmarried female temple servant in ancient Rome

vested in·ter·est /₁·· ¹··/ n a personal reason for doing something, because one gains advantage from it

ves·ti·bule /¹vestə₁byuʷl/ n fml 1 room or passage through which larger rooms are reached 2 enclosed passage at each end of a railroad car which connects it with the next car

ves·tige /¹vestɪdʒ/ n 1 (small) remaining part: the last vestiges of imperial power 2 slightest bit: not a vestige of truth

vest·ment /¹vestmənt/ n (priest's) ceremonial garment

ves·try /¹vestriᵞ/ n room in a church for esp. changing into vestments

vet /vet/ n animal doctor

vet·er·an /¹veṭərən/ n, adj 1 (person) with long service or (former) experience, esp. as a soldier 2 (thing) that has grown old with long use

vet·er·i·na·ry /¹veṭərə₁neriᵞ, ¹vetrə/ adj of the medical care of animals ~rian /₁veṭərə¹neriᵞən, ₁vetrə-/ n fml vet

ve·to /¹viᵞṭoʷ/ vt –toed; pres. p.

-**toing** officially refuse to allow ♦ *n* **vetoes** [C;U] (act of) vetoing

vex /veks/ *vt fml* displease; trouble ~**ation** /vekˈseɪʃən/ *n* [C;U]

vi·a /ˈvaɪə, ˈviˠə/ *prep* traveling through

vi·a·ble /ˈvaɪəbəl/ *adj* able to succeed in actual use: *an economically viable plan* –**bility** /ˌvaɪəˈbɪlətiˠ/ *n* [U]

vi·a·duct /ˈvaɪəˌdʌkt/ *n* high bridge across a valley

vial /ˈvaɪəl/ *n* small glass container

vi·brant /ˈvaɪbrənt/ *adj* **1** powerful and exciting **2** (of color or light) bright and strong ~**ly** *adv* **vibrancy** *n* [U]

vi·brate /ˈvaɪbreˠt/ *vi/t* (cause to) move with a slight continuous shake **vibration** /vaɪˈbreˠʃən/ *n* [C;U]

vic·ar /ˈvɪkər/ *n* priest in charge of an area (PARISH)

vic·ar·age /ˈvɪkərɪdʒ/ *n* vicar's house

vi·car·i·ous /vaɪˈkeəriˠəs/ *adj* experienced indirectly, by watching, reading, etc.: *vicarious pleasure* ~**ly** *adv*

vice /vaɪs/ *n* [C;U] **1** (kind of) evil behavior or living: *She was arrested by the vice squad for prostitution.* **2 a** fault of character: *Laziness is his one vice.* **b** bad habit: *Smoking is my only vice.*

vice·roy /ˈvaɪsrɔɪ/ *n* person ruling as a representative of a king or queen

vice ver·sa /ˌvaɪsə ˈvɜrsə, ˌvaɪs-, ˌvaɪsiˠ-/ *adv* the opposite way around

vi·cin·i·ty /vəˈsɪnətiˠ/ *n* [U] area which is near: (fig.) *a price in the vicinity of $50,000.*

vi·cious /ˈvɪʃəs/ *adj* **1** showing an unpleasant desire to hurt: *a vicious kick* **2** dangerous: *a vicious-looking knife* ~**ly** *adv*

vicious cir·cle /ˌ·· ˈ··/ *n* situation in which unpleasant causes and effects lead back to the original starting point

vi·cis·si·tudes /vəˈsɪsətuˠdz, -tyuˠdz, vaɪ-/ *n* [P] *fml* changes, esp. from good to bad, that have an effect on one

vic·tim /ˈvɪktɪm/ *n* one who suffers as the result of something: *the murderer's victim* (=the person he killed) | *the victims of the plane crash* ~**ize** *vt* cause to suffer unfairly ~**ization** /ˌvɪktəməˈzeˠʃən/ *n* [U]

vic·tor /ˈvɪktər/ *n fml or lit* person who wins

Vic·to·ri·an /vɪkˈtɔriˠən, -ˈtoˠr-/ *adj* **1** of the time when Queen Victoria ruled Britain (1837-1901) *Victorian architecture*

vic·to·ry /ˈvɪktəriˠ/ *n* [C;U] winning: *her victory in the election/golf tournament* –**torious** /vɪkˈtɔriˠəs, -ˈtoˠr-/ *adj* **1** that has won: *the victorious team* **2** showing victory: *a victorious shout*

vict·uals /ˈvɪtlz/ *n humor* food

vid·e·o /ˈvɪdiˠoˠ/ *adj* for (recording and) showing pictures on television ♦ *n* –**os** [C;U] videotape recording **2** [C] machine for making and showing these ♦ *vt* –**oed**; *pres. p.* –**oing** videotape

vid·e·o·re·cord·er /ˈvɪdiˠoˠrɪˌkɔrdər/ *n* VIDEO (2)

vid·e·o·tape /ˈvɪdiˠoˠteˠp/ *n* [C;U] band of MAGNETic material on which moving pictures are recorded ♦ *vt* record on videotape

vie /vaɪ/ *vi* vied; *pres. p.* **vying** compete

view /vyuˠ/ *n* **1** [C;U] what one can see: *The train came into view around the corner.* | *You get a beautiful view of the sea from this window.* **2** [C] opinion: *In my view, he's a fool.* **3 in view of** taking into consideration: *In view of the unusual circumstances, we'll cancel it.* **4 on view** being shown to the public **5 with a view to** with the intention of ♦ *vt* **1** consider; regard: *I view the matter very seriously.* **2** examine by looking **3** watch television ~**er** *n* person watching television

view·find·er /ˈvyuˠˌfaɪndər/ *n* apparatus on a camera showing a small picture of what is to be photographed

view·point /ˈvyuˠpɔɪnt/ *n* POINT OF VIEW

vig·il /ˈvɪdʒəl/ *n* act of staying (awake and) watchful for some purpose

vig·i·lance /ˈvɪdʒələns/ *n* [U] watchful care -**lant** *adj fml* always prepared for possible danger -**lantly** *adv*

vigilance com·mit·tee /ˈ··· ·ˌ··/ *n fml* group of vigilantes

vig·i·lan·te /ˌvɪdʒəˈlæntiˠ/ *n sometimes derog* person who tries by unofficial means to punish crime: *vigilantes on the New York subway*

vi·gnette /vɪˈnyɛt/ *n* short effective written description

vig·or /ˈvɪgər/ *n* [U] active strength or force -**orous** *adj* -**orously** *adv*

Vi·king /ˈvaɪkɪŋ/ *n* Scandinavian attacker (and settler) in northern and western Europe from the 8th to the 10th centuries

vile /vaɪl/ *adj* **1** *fml* low, shameful, and worthless: *a vile slander* **2** extremely unpleasant: *vile food* ~**ly** /ˈvaɪl-liˠ/ *adv*

vil·i·fy /ˈvɪləˌfaɪ/ *vt fml* say unfairly

bad things about –**fication** /ˌvɪləfə-ˈkeɪʃən/ n [C;U]

vil·la /ˈvɪlə/ n 1 house in a tourist town, esp. which one can rent 2 large ancient Roman country house

vil·lage /ˈvɪlɪdʒ/ n collection of houses in a country area, smaller than a town –**lager** n person who lives in a village

vil·lain /ˈvɪlən/ n 1 (esp. in stories) bad person 2 *infml* criminal ~**ous** adj threatening great harm; evil

vin·ai·grette /ˌvɪnəˈgret/ n [U] mixture of oil, VINEGAR, etc., put on SALADS

vin·di·cate /ˈvɪndəˌkeɪt/ vt 1 free from blame 2 prove (something that was in doubt) to be right –**cation** /ˌvɪndəˈkeɪʃən/ n [S;U]

vin·dic·tive /vɪnˈdɪktɪv/ adj wishing to harm someone who has harmed you ~**ly** adv ~**ness** n [U]

vine /vaɪn/ n climbing plant, esp. one that produces GRAPEs

vin·e·gar /ˈvɪnɪgər/ n [U] liquid with an acid taste, used in preparing food ~**y** adj

vine·yard /ˈvɪnyərd/ n piece of land with vines for making wine

vin·tage /ˈvɪntɪdʒ/ n particular year in which a wine is made ♦ adj 1 of the best quality (of cars, clothing, etc.) old but well preserved 3 *vintage year* a very good year for the stated thing

vi·nyl /ˈvaɪnl/ n [U] firm bendable plastic

vi·o·la /viˈoʊˈlə/ n musical instrument like a large VIOLIN

vi·o·late /ˈvaɪəˌleɪt/ vt 1 act against (something solemnly promised or officially agreed): *violate a treaty* 2 *fml* come violently into (and spoil) 3 have sex (with a woman) by force –**lation** /ˌvaɪəˈleɪʃən/ n [C;U]

vi·o·lent /ˈvaɪələnt/ adj using, showing or produced by great damaging force: *He became violent and began to hit her.* | *a violent storm* | *a violent death* ~**ly** adv –**lence** n [U] 1 extreme (and damaging) force 2 use of force to hurt people

vi·o·let /ˈvaɪəlɪt/ n small plant with purple flowers that smell sweetly – see also SHRINKING VIOLET

vi·o·lin /ˌvaɪəˈlɪn/ n small wooden musical instrument with 4 strings played by drawing a BOW² (2) across the strings –**ist** n

VIP /ˌviˀ aɪ ˈpiˀ/ n person of great influence or fame

vi·per /ˈvaɪpər/ n small poisonous snake

vir·gin /ˈvɜrdʒɪn/ n person who has not had sex ♦ adj unused; unspoiled ~**ity** /vɜrˈdʒɪnətiˀ/ n [U] state of being a VIRGIN

vir·ile /ˈvɪrəl/ adj having the strong

and forceful qualities expected of a man, esp. in matters of sex –**ility** /vəˈrɪlətiˀ/ n [U]

vir·tu·al /ˈvɜrtʃuʷəl/ adj almost or unofficially the stated thing: *Though her husband was king, she was the virtual ruler of the country.* ~**ly** adv almost; very nearly

vir·tue /ˈvɜrtʃuʷ/ n 1 [U] *fml* condition of being morally good 2 [C] morally good quality, such as truthfulness or loyalty 3 [C;U] advantage: *The plan's great virtue is its simplicity.* 4 *by virtue of* as a result of; by means of –**tuous** adj morally good

vir·tu·o·so /ˌvɜrtʃuʷˈoʷsoʷ/ n –**si** extremely skilled (musical) performer –**osity** /-ˈɑsətiˀ/ n [U] virtuoso's skill

vir·u·lent /ˈvɪryələnt, ˈvɪrə-/ adj 1 (of a poison, disease, etc.) very powerful and dangerous 2 *fml* full of bitter hatred: *virulent abuse* –**ly** adv –**lence** n [U]

vi·rus /ˈvaɪrəs/ n extremely small living thing that causes infectious disease: *the flu virus* **viral** adj

vi·sa /ˈviˀzə/ n official mark put on a PASSPORT to allow someone to enter or leave a particular country

vis·age /ˈvɪzɪdʒ/ n *lit* face

vis-à-vis /ˌviˀz ə ˈviˀ/ prep *fml* with regard to

vis·cous /ˈvɪskəs/ adj (of a liquid) thick and sticky –**cosity** /vɪsˈkɑs-ətiˀ/ n [U]

vise /vaɪs/ n tool with metal jaws for holding things firmly

vis·i·ble /ˈvɪzəbəl/ adj 1 that can be seen 2 noticeable –**bly** adv noticeably: *He was visibly shaken by the unpleasant experience.* –**bility** /ˌvɪzəˈbɪlətiˀ/ n [U] 1 clearness with which things can be seen over a particular distance 2 ability to give a clear view

vi·sion /ˈvɪʒən/ n 1 [U] ability to see 2 [U] wise understanding of the future 3 [C] picture in the mind: *I had visions of missing* (= thought I might miss) *my plane.* 4. [C] something supposedly seen when in a sleeplike state or as a religious experience

vi·sion·a·ry /ˈvɪʒəˌneriˀ/ adj 1 having VISION (2) 2 grand but impractical ♦ n visionary person

vis·it /ˈvɪzɪt/ v 1 *vi/t* go to and spend time in (a place) or with (a person): *We visited my uncle in Detroit.* 2 *vt* go to (a place) to make an official examination 3 *vt* stay with ♦ n act or time of visiting: *We paid him a visit.* (= visited him) ~**or** n

visit on *phr vt* direct (anger, etc.) against

visit with *phr vt* talk socially with

vi·sor /ˈvaɪzər/ n face or eye protector on a hat or HELMET

vis·ta /ˈvɪstə/ n view stretching away into the distance

vi·su·al /ˈvɪʒʊəl/ adj 1 of or done by seeing 2 having an effect on the sense of sight: *the visual arts* ~**ly** adv ~**ize** vt imagine, esp. as if by seeing

vi·tal /ˈvaɪtl/ adj 1 extremely necessary or important 2 necessary to stay alive 3 full of life and force ~**ly** adv in the highest possible degree

vi·tal·i·ty /vaɪˈtæləti/ n [U] 1 cheerful quality 2 ability to remain alive or effective

vital sta·tis·tics /ˌ··ˈ··/ n [P] information kept by the state about births, deaths, marriages, etc.

vit·a·min /ˈvaɪtəmɪn/ n chemical substance found in certain foods and important for growth and good health: *Oranges contain vitamin C.*

vi·ti·ate /ˈvɪʃiˌeɪt/ vt fml weaken: *inaccuracies that vitiated her argument*

vit·ri·ol /ˈvɪtriəl/ n [U] 1 extremely powerful acid 2 cruel wounding quality of speech and writing ~**ic** /ˌvɪtriˈɒlɪk◂/ adj fml fiercely cruel in speech or judgment

vi·tro /ˈviːtroʊ/ see IN VITRO

vi·tu·per·a·tive /vaɪˈtuːpərətɪv, -ˈtjuːˈp-, -ˌreɪtɪv/ adj fml full of angry disapproval

vi·va·cious /vɪˈveɪʃəs, vaɪ-/ adj (esp. of a woman) full of life and fun ~**ly** adv ~**city** /vɪˈvæsəti, vaɪ-/ n [U]

viv·id /ˈvɪvɪd/ adj 1 (of light or color) bright and strong 2 producing sharp clear pictures in the mind: *a vivid description* ~**ly** adv

viv·i·sec·tion /ˌvɪvɪˈsekʃən/ n [U] performing of operations on animals to test medical treatments, new products, etc.

vix·en /ˈvɪksən/ n female fox

V-neck /ˈviː nek/ n neck opening of a dress, shirt, etc., shaped like a V

vo·cab·u·la·ry /vəˈkæbyəˌleri, voʊ-/ n 1 [C;U] words known, learned, used, etc.: *a child's limited vocabulary* 2 [C] short list of words with their meanings

vo·cal /ˈvoʊkəl/ adj 1 of or produced by the voice: *vocal music* 2 expressing one's opinion loudly ~**ly** adv ~**ist** n singer

vocal cords /ˈ·· ·/ n [P] muscles in the throat that produce sounds when air passes through them

vo·ca·tion /voʊˈkeɪʃən/ n 1 [S] particular fitness or ability for a certain worthy kind of work, such as being a nurse 2 [C] job, esp. one which you do because you have a vocation ~**al** adj of or for a job: *vocational training*

vo·cif·er·ous /voʊˈsɪfərəs/ adj fml expressing oneself forcefully or noisily ~**ly** adv

vod·ka /ˈvɒdkə/ n [U] strong colorless Russian alcoholic drink

vogue /voʊg/ n [C;U] popular fashion: *Short skirts were in vogue then.* ♦ adj popular at present: *vogue words*

voice /vɔɪs/ n 1 [C;U] sound(s) produced in speaking or singing: *a loud/kind voice* | *She shouted at the top of her voice.* (= very loudly) 2 [C] ability to produce such sounds: *She's lost her voice.* 3 [S;U] right to express oneself: *I have no voice in* (= influence over) *the decision.* ♦ vt express in words, esp. forcefully: *voicing their opinions*

voice-o·ver /ˈ· ··/ n voice of an unseen person on a film or television show

void /vɔɪd/ n empty space ♦ adj law having no value or effect ♦ vt make void

vol·a·tile /ˈvɒlətl, -ˌtaɪl/ adj 1 quickly changing, esp. easily becoming angry or dangerous 2 (of a liquid) easily changing into gas ~**tility** /ˌvɒləˈtɪləti/ n [U]

vol-au-vent /ˈvɒl oʊ ˌvɒn/ n small pastry case filled with meat, vegetables, etc.

vol·ca·no /vɒlˈkeɪnoʊ/ n –**noes** or –**nos** mountain which sometimes throws out hot gases and melted rock –**canic** /-ˈkænɪk/ adj 1 of a volcano 2 violently forceful

vo·li·tion /voʊˈlɪʃən, və-/ n 1 WILL² (1) and (2) 2 **of one's own volition** fml because one wishes, not because told to by someone else

vol·ley /ˈvɒli/ n 1 many shots fired together: (fig.) *a volley of blows/ curses* 2 kicking or hitting of a ball before it has hit the ground ♦ v 1 vi (of guns) be fired together 2 vi/t hit or kick (as) a VOLLEY (2)

vol·ley·ball /ˈvɒliˌbɔl/ n [U] team game played by hitting a large ball across a net with the hands

volt /voʊlt/ n unit of electrical force ~**age** n [C;U] electrical force measured in volts

vol·u·ble /ˈvɒlyəbəl/ adj fml talking a lot ~**bly** adv ~**bility** /ˌvɒlyəˈbɪləti/ n [U]

vol·ume /ˈvɒlyəm, -yuːm/ n 1 [U] (degree of) loudness of sound: *Turn down the volume on the TV.* 2 [U] size of something measured by multiplying its length by its height by its width 3 [C] any of a set of books: *volume 9 of the encyclopedia* 4 [C;U] amount: *the increasing volume of passenger traffic* 5 **speak volumes (for something)** show or express (something) very clearly or fully

vo·lu·mi·nous /vəˈluʷmənəs/ adj fml **1** filling or containing a lot of space: a voluminous skirt/suitcase **2** producing or containing (too much) writing

vol·un·ta·ry /ˈvɑlənˌteriʸ/ adj acting or done willingly, without being forced –**arily** /ˌvɑlənˈteərəliʸ, ˈvɑlənˌteər-/ adv

vol·un·teer /ˌvɑlənˈtɪər/ n person who has volunteered ♦ v **1** vi/t offer to do something without payment or reward, or without being forced: Jenny volunteered to clear up afterwards. **2** vt tell without being asked: He volunteered a statement to the police.

vo·lup·tu·ous /vəˈlʌptʃuʷəs/ adj **1** suggesting or expressing sexual pleasure **2** giving a fine delight to the senses

vom·it /ˈvɑmɪt/ vi throw up (the contents of the stomach) through the mouth ♦ n [U] swallowed food thrown back up through the mouth

voo·doo /ˈvuʷduʷ/ n [U] set of magical religious practices in esp. Haiti

vo·ra·cious /vɔˈreʸʃəs, və-, voʷ-/ adj eating or wanting a lot of food: (fig.) a voracious reader (= who reads a lot) ~**ly** adv –**city** /-ˈræs-əṭiʸ/ n [U]

vor·tex /ˈvɔrtɛks/ n –**texes** or –**tices** /-təˌsiʸz/ **1** powerful circular moving mass of water or wind **2** lit situation that makes one powerless: sucked into the vortex of war

vo·ta·ry /ˈvoʷṭəriʸ/ n fml regular worshipper, admirer, etc.

vote /voʷt/ v **1** vi express one's choice officially, esp. by marking a piece of paper or raising one's hand: Which candidate will you vote for in the election? | As we can't reach an agreement, let's vote on it. **2** vt agree, by a vote, to provide (something) **3** vt infml agree as the general opinion: I vote we leave now. ♦ n **1** [C;U] (choice or decision made by) voting:

I'll cast my vote for Tom Smith. | Let's put the matter to a vote. **2** [U] number of such choices made by or for a particular person or group: an increase in the Republican vote **3** [U] right to vote in political elections

voter n

vouch /vaʊtʃ/ v **vouch for** phr vt state one's firm belief in the good qualities of, based on experience

vouch·er /ˈvaʊtʃər/ n **1** ticket usable instead of money **2** official paper given to prove that money has been paid

vouch·safe /vaʊtʃˈseʸf/ vt lit give, say, or do as a favor

vow /vaʊ/ vt, n (make) a solemn promise or declaration of intention: He vowed he would never steal again.

vow·el /ˈvaʊəl/ n speech sound made without closing the air passage in the mouth or throat: In English, vowels are represented by the letters a, e, i, o, u.

voy·age /ˈvɔɪ-ɪdʒ/ n long journey by ship ♦ vi lit make a voyage –**ager** n

voy·eur /vwɑˈyɜr/ n person who gets sexual excitement by (secretly) watching others have sex ~**ism** n [U]

vs. abbrev. for: VERSUS

vul·can·ize /ˈvʌlkəˌnaɪz/ vt strengthen (rubber) by chemical treatment

vul·gar /ˈvʌlgər/ adj **1** very rude or having bad manners **2** showing bad judgment in matters of beauty, style, etc. ~**ly** adv –**ity** /vʌlˈgærəṭiʸ/ n [U]

vul·ne·ra·ble /ˈvʌlnərəbəl/ adj **1** easy to attack **2** (of a person) easily harmed; sensitive –**bility** /ˌvʌlnərəˈbɪləṭiʸ/ n [U]

vul·ture /ˈvʌltʃər/ n **1** large tropical bird which feeds on dead animals **2** person who has no mercy and who uses people

vy·ing /ˈvaɪ-ɪŋ/ v pres. p. of VIE

W

W, w /ˈdʌbəlyuʷ/ the 23rd letter of the English alphabet

W *written abbrev. for*: **1** west(ern) **2** WATT

wack·y /ˈwæki/ *adj esp.* silly -**iness** *n* [U]

wad /wɑd/ *n* **1** many thin things pressed or folded thickly together: *a wad of $10 bills* **2** small thick soft mass: *a wad of cotton* **3** **shoot one's wad** spend all of one's money at one time

wad·ding /ˈwɑdɪŋ/ *n* [U] soft material used esp. for packing or in medicine

wad·dle /ˈwɑdl/ *vi* walk like a duck

wade /weʸd/ *vi/t* walk through (water) **wader** *n* **1** bird that wades to find its food **2** either of a pair of high rubber boots to protect the legs while wading

wade into *phr vt* begin (to attack) forcefully and with determination

wade through *phr vt* do or complete (something long or dull) with an effort

wa·fer /ˈweʸfər/ *n* **1** thin COOKIE or CRACKER **2** thin round piece of special bread used in the Christian ceremony of COMMUNION

wafer-thin /ˌ·· ˈ·◂/ *adj* extremely thin

waf·fle /ˈwɑfəl/ *n* light sweet cake marked with raised squares

waft /wɑft, wæft/ *vi/t* move lightly (as if) on wind or waves

wag¹ /wæg/ *vi/t* -**gg**- shake (esp. a body part) or be shaken from side to side: *The dog wagged its tail.* **wag** *n*

wag² *n infml* amusing person

wage /weʸdʒ/ *vt* carry on (a war)

wage freeze /ˈ· ·/ *n* attempt to keep pay from rising

wa·ger /ˈweʸdʒər/ *n, vi fml for* BET

wag·es /ˈweʸdʒɪz/ also **wage** [S] — *n* [P] payment for work done: *He gets his wages every Friday.*

wag·gle /ˈwægəl/ *vi/t* move quickly from side to side

wag·on /ˈwægən/ *n* **1** strong goods vehicle usu. pulled by a horse or horses **2** small vehicle with a handle used by children **3** police vehicle for carrying CRIMINALS **4** **on the wagon** no longer willing to drink alcohol

waif /weʸf/ *n esp. lit* child or animal that is homeless or not cared for

wail /weʸl/ *vi, n* (make) a long cry (as if) in grief or pain

waist /weʸst/ *n* **1** narrow part of the human body below the chest **2** narrow part of a garment or apparatus

waist·band /ˈweʸstbænd/ *n* strengthened part of pants, a skirt, etc., that fastens around the waist

waist·line /ˈweʸstlaɪn/ *n* (length or height of) an imaginary line around the waist: (fig.) *No sugar for me — I'm watching my waistline.* (= trying not to become fatter)

wait /weʸt/ *v* **1** *vi* do nothing in the expectation of something happening: *I had to wait 2 hours for the bus!* | *Are you waiting to use the phone?* **2** *vt not act until: You'll have to wait your turn.* **3** *vi* remain unspoken, unheard, etc.: *My news can wait till later.* **4** **wait and see** delay an action or decision until the future becomes clearer **5** **wait tables** serve meals, esp. as a regular job ♦ *n* [S] act or period of waiting ~**er**, ~**ress** /-trɪs/ *fem.* — *n* someone who serves food to people

wait on *phr vt* **1** serve food to, esp. in a restaurant **2** **wait on someone hand and foot** serve someone very humbly

waiting game /ˈ·· ˌ·/ *n* situation in which waiting is necessary before action can be taken

waiting list /ˈ·· ˌ·/ *n* list of people who will be dealt with later

waiting room /ˈ·· ˌ·/ *n* room at a station, doctor's office, etc., where people wait

waive /weʸv/ *vt fml* state that (a rule, claim, etc.) is no longer in effect **waiver** *n* written statement waiving a right, etc.

wake¹ /weʸk/ *vi/t* **woke** /woʷk/ *or* **waked, woken** /ˈwoʷkən/ *or* **waked** (cause) to stop sleeping: *I woke up late.* ~**ful** *adj* sleepless **waking** *adj* of the time when one is awake: *all my waking hours*

wake² *n* **1** track left by a ship: (fig.) *The car left clouds of dust in its wake.* **2** **in the wake of** as a result of: *war, with hunger and disease in its wake*

wake³ *n* gathering to grieve over a dead person

wak·en /ˈweʸkən/ *vi/t fml* wake

walk /wɔk/ *v* **1** *vi* move slowly on foot so that at least one foot is always touching the ground **2** *vt* walk along: *He'd walked the streets looking for work.* **3** *vt* go with on foot: *I'll walk you to the bus stop.* **4** *vt* take (an animal) for a walk ♦ *n* **1** [C] (short) journey on foot: *Let's go for a walk.* | *The station's just a 5-minute walk from here.* **2** [S] way of walking **3** [C] place, path, or course for walking ~**er** *n*

walk all over *phr vt* treat badly

walk into *phr vt* **1** get caught by

walkie-talkie

474

(something) through carelessness **2**
walk off/away with *phr vt* **1** steal
and take away **2** win easily

walk out *phr vi* **1** leave suddenly
and disapprovingly **2** go on STRIKE²
(1)

walk out on *phr vt* leave suddenly
walk·ie-talk·ie /ˌwɔkiʸ ˈtɔkiʸ/ *n*
radio for talking as well as listening,
that can be carried

walking pa·pers /ˈ·· ˌ··/ *n* official
notice that one must leave

walking stick /ˈ·· ˌ·/ *n* stick for support while walking

walk·man /ˈwɔkmən/ *n tdmk for* PER-
SONAL STEREO

walk of life /ˌ· · ˈ·/ *n* position in society, esp. one's job

walk-on /ˈ· ·/ *n* small usu. non-
speaking part in a play

walk·out /ˈwɔk-aut/ *n* **1** action of disapprovingly leaving a meeting, organization, etc. **2** STRIKE² (1)

walk·o·ver /ˈwɔkˌoʷvər/ *n* easy
victory

wall /wɔl/ *n* **1** side of a room or building: *pictures hanging on the wall* **2**
upright surface of brick or stone, for
enclosing something: *the boundary
wall* | (fig.) *a wall of flames* **3** enclos-
ing or inside surface: *the walls of a
blood vessel* **4** bang one's head
against a (brick) wall *infml* try to
do the impossible **5 go up the wall**
infml get very angry **6 push to the
wall** force into a bad situation **~ed**
adj surrounded with a wall

wall off *phr vt* separate with a wall
wall up *phr vt* close or enclose
with a wall

wal·let /ˈwɔlɪt/ *n* small flat case for
papers and paper money

wall·flow·er /ˈwɔlˌflaʊər/ *n* **1** garden
plant with flowers that smell sweet
2 person who gets left out of social
activity

wal·lop /ˈwɔləp/ *vt, n infml* (hit
with) a powerful blow

wal·low /ˈwɔloʷ/ *vi* move, roll, or
lie around happily in deep mud,
water, etc.: *wallowing in a hot bath*
/(fig.) *in self-pity*

wall·pa·per /ˈwɔlˌpeʸpər/ *n* [U]
decorative paper (for) covering the
walls of a room ♦ *vt* cover the walls
of (a room) with wallpaper

Wall Street /ˈ· ·/ *n* center of the
American business and money
world, in New York

wall-to-wall /ˌ· · ˈ·◄/ *adj* covering
the whole floor: *wall-to-wall carpet*

wal·nut /ˈwɔlnʌt/ *n* **1** [C] eatable nut
shaped like a brain **2** [U] wood from
its tree, used for furniture

wal·rus /ˈwɔlrəs, ˈwɔl-/ *n* **-ruses** *or*
-rus large sea animal with 2 very
long teeth that point downwards

waltz /wɔlts/ *vi, n* (do) a slow dance
for a man and a woman

wan /wɑn/ *adj esp. lit* weak and tired

wand /wɑnd/ *n* stick used by someone doing magic tricks

wan·der /ˈwɑndər/ *v* **1** *vi/t* move
about without a fixed course or purpose: *the wandering tribes of the Sa-
hara.* | (fig.) *The discussion seems to
have wandered from its main point.*
2 *vi* be or become confused and unable to make or follow ordinary conversation **~er** *n* **~ings** *n* [P] long
travels

wan·der·lust /ˈwɑndərˌlʌst/ *n* [S;U]
strong desire to travel to places far
away

wane /weʸn/ *vi* get gradually
smaller ♦ *n* **on the wane** becoming
smaller or weaker

wan·gle /ˈwæŋɡəl/ *vt infml* get by
a trick

want /wɑnt, wɔnt/ *vi* **1** have a strong
desire for: *I don't want to go.* **2** wish
the presence of: *Your mother wants
you.* **3** wish to find; hunt: *He's
wanted by the police for murder.* **4**
need: *The house wants painting.* **5**
fml lack: *to be found wanting* (= not
considered good, strong, etc.,
enough) ♦ *n* **1** [C;U] lack: *The plants
died for/from want of water.* **2** [U] severe lack of things necessary for life
~ing *adj fml* **1** lacking **2** not good
enough

want for *phr vt fml* lack: *The children want for nothing.*

want ad /ˈ· ·/ *n* small newspaper advertisement for a thing or person
wanted

wan·ton /ˈwɑntən, ˈwɔn-/ *adj fml* **1**
(of something bad) having no just
cause: *wanton disregard of the rules*
2 (esp. of a woman) sexually improper

war /wɔr/ *n* (example or period
of) armed fighting between nations:
The 2 countries are at war. | *World
War II* | (fig.) *waging a war against
poverty and ignorance* **~ring** *adj*
fighting (each other)

war·ble /ˈwɔrbəl/ *vi* (esp. of a bird)
sing with a continuous varied note
~bler *n* any of various songbirds

war clouds /ˈ· ·/ *n* [P] signs that
a war is getting likelier

war crime /ˈ· ·/ *n* illegal act done
while fighting a war

ward¹ /wɔrd/ *n* **1** part of a hospital
for a particular group of sick people
2 political division of a city **3** person legally protected by another:
*The children were made wards of
court.*

ward² *v* **ward off** *phr vt* keep away
(something bad)

war·den /ˈwɔrdn/ *n* person in charge
of a place or people

war·drobe /'wɔrdroʷb/ n 1 large cupboard for clothes 2 person's collection of clothes

ward·room /'wɔrdruʷm, -rʊm/ n officers' room in a fighting ship

ware·house /'weərhaʊs/ n -houses /-,haʊzɪz/ large building for storing things or selling things in quantity

wares /weərz/ n [P] esp. lit things for sale

war·fare /'wɔrfeər/ n [U] war

war game /'· ,·/ n pretended battle to test military plans

war·head /'wɔrhed/ n explosive front end of a MISSILE

war·like /'wɔrlaɪk/ adj fierce; liking to fight

war·lock /'wɔrlɑk/ n male WITCH

warm[1] /wɔrm/ adj 1 having enough heat or pleasant heat: a warm bath 2 able to keep one warm: warm clothes 3 showing strong good feelings: a warm welcome 4 seeming cheerful or friendly: warm colors

warm[2] vi/t make or become warm ~ly adv

warm to phr vt 1 begin to like 2 become interested in

warm up phr vi/t prepare for action or performance by exercise or operation in advance

warmed·o·ver /'· ,··/ adj not fresh

war·mon·ger /'wɔr,mʌŋgər, -,mɑŋ-/ n derog person who wants war

warmth /wɔrmθ/ n [U] being warm

warn /wɔrn/ v 1 vi/t tell of something bad that may happen, or of how to prevent it 2 vt give knowledge of some future need or action: We warned them we'd be away. ~ing n [C;U] 1 telling in advance: They attacked without warning. 2 something that warns: That's the second warning we've had.

warp /wɔrp/ vi/t turn or twist out of shape: a warped plank/(fig.) mind ♦ n 1 warped place 2 threads running along the length of cloth

war paint /'· ·/ n infml [U] MAKE-UP (1)

war·path /'wɔrpæθ/ n on the war-path angry and looking for someone to fight or punish

war·rant /'wɔrənt, 'wɑr-/ n [C] official paper allowing something: The police have a warrant for her arrest. 2 [U] fml proper reason for action ♦ vt 1 cause to seem right or reasonable 2 promise (that something is so)

warrant of·fic·er /'·· ,···/ n one just below an officer in rank

war·ran·ty /'wɔrəntiʸ, 'wɑr-/ n written GUARANTEE

war·ren /'wɔrən, 'wɑr-/ n 1 area where rabbits live 2 place where one can easily get lost

war·ri·or /'wɔriʸər, 'wɑr-/ n lit soldier

war·ship /'wɔrʃɪp/ n naval ship used for war

wart /wɔrt/ n small hard swelling on the skin

war·time /'wɔrtaɪm/ n [U] period during which a war is going on

war·y /'weəriʸ/ adj careful; looking out for danger –ily adv

was /wəz; strong wʌz, wɑz/ v 1st and 3rd person sing. past t. of BE

wash /wɑʃ, wɔʃ/ v 1 vt clean with liquid 2 vi be able to be cleaned with liquid without damage: This shirt doesn't wash well. 3 vi wash oneself 4 vt carry by the force of moving water: crops washed away by the floods 5 vi/t esp. lit flow (against or over) continually 6 vi be (easily) believed: His story won't wash. 7 wash one's dirty linen (in public) make public unpleasant subjects which ought to be kept private 8 wash one's hands of refuse to have anything more to do with or to accept responsibility for ♦ n 1 [S] act of washing 2 [U] things to be washed 3 [S;U] movement of water caused by a passing boat 4 come out in the wash infml a (of something shameful) become known b turn out all right in the end 5 in the wash being washed ~able adj ~ing [U] clothes that are to be washed or have just been washed

wash down phr vt 1 clean with a lot of water 2 swallow with the help of liquid

wash out phr vt 1 cause to wash free of an unwanted substance 2 destroy or prevent by the action of water, esp. rain

wash up phr v 1 vi WASH (3) 2 vt (of the sea) bring in to the shore 3 vt wash (dishes, knives, etc.,) after a meal

wash·bowl /'wɑʃboʷl, 'wɔʃ-/ — n basin for washing hands and face

wash·cloth /'wɑʃklɔθ, 'wɔʃ-/ n -cloths /-klɔðz, -klɔθs/ small cloth for washing the face

washed-out /,· '·◂/ adj 1 faded 2 very tired 3 prevented because of rain: The game was washed-out.

washed-up /,· '·◂/ adj infml with no further possibilities of success

wash·er /'wɑʃər, 'wɔ-/ n 1 ring of metal, plastic, etc., for making a joint tight under a screw, between 2 pipes, etc. 2 person or machine that washes

wash·er·wom·an /'wɑʃər,wʊmən, 'wɔʃ-/ n -women /-,wɪmɪn/ (in former times) woman who washed other people's clothes

washing ma·chine /'·· ·,·/ n machine for washing clothes

wash·out /'wɑʃ-aʊt, 'wɔʃ-/ n failure

wash·room /ˈwɒʃruʷm, ˈwɔʃ-, -ˌrʊm/ n public TOILET (1)

was·n't /ˈwʌzənt, ˈwɑ-/ short for: was not

wasp /wɒsp/ n black and yellow bee-like insect ~**ish** adj sharply bad-tempered and cruel ~**ishness** n [U]

WASP, Wasp /wɒsp/ n often derog White Anglo-Saxon Protestant; an American whose family was originally from N. Europe, esp. considered as a member of the class which has power or influence in society ~**ish** adj

wast·age /ˈweʸstɪdʒ/ n [S;U] **1** wasteful loss **2** reduction in numbers

waste /weʸst/ n **1** [S;U] loss through wrong use or less than full use: a waste of time | Don't let it go to waste. (= be wasted) **2** [U] used or unwanted matter: industrial/bodily waste **3** [U] wide empty lonely stretch of water or land ♦ vt **1** use wrongly or not at all: wasting his money on silly things **2** fml make (the body) extremely thin ♦ adj **1** (of ground) empty and unused **2** got rid of as used or useless: waste paper/products ~**ful** adj tending to waste things ~**fully** adv

waste·bas·ket /ˈweʸstˌbæskɪt/ also **waste pa·per bas·ket** /ˈ· ··· ˌ··/— n small container for throwing away unwanted paper, etc.

watch /wɒtʃ, wɔtʃ/ v **1** vi/t look (at) attentively: Watch me and you'll see how it's done. **2** vt be careful about: Watch what you're doing with that knife! **3** watch it! be careful **4** watch one's step act with great care **5** watch the clock be waiting for one's working day to end rather than thinking about one's work ♦ n **1** [C] small clock worn esp. on the wrist **2** [S;U] act of watching: The police are keeping (a) watch on their activities. **3** [C;U] period of duty on a ship ~**er** n ~**ful** adj careful to notice things

watch for phr vt look for; expect and wait for

watch out phr vi take care

watch out for phr vt **1** keep looking for **2** be careful of

watch over phr vt guard and protect; take care of

watch·dog /ˈwɒtʃdɒg, ˈwɔtʃ-/ n **1** dog kept to guard property **2** person or group that tries to prevent loss, waste, or undesirable practices

watch·man /ˈwɒtʃmən, ˈwɔtʃ-/ n **-men** /-mən/ guard, esp. of a building

watch·word /ˈwɒtʃwɜrd, ˈwɔtʃ-/ n **1** PASSWORD **2** word or phrase expressing a guiding principle

wa·ter /ˈwɒtər, ˈwɑ-/ n [U] **1** liquid found as rain, in the sea, etc., and commonly drunk **2** a mass of this: She dived into the water. | After the flood the fields were under water. | The goods came by water. (= by boat) **3** above water out of difficulty: keep one's head above water (= keep oneself out of difficulty) **4** hold water be true or reasonable: Your story doesn't hold water. **5** like water in great quantity: The wine flowed like water **6** pass water urinate (URINE) **7** throw cold water on point out difficulties in (a plan, idea, etc.) – see also HOT WATER ♦ v **1** vt pour water on (a plant or area) **2** vt supply (esp. animals) with water **3** vi (of the mouth or eyes) form or let out watery liquid **waters** n [P] **1** sea near or around a country: in Icelandic waters **2** water of the stated river, lake, etc. ~**y** adj **1** containing too much water **2** very pale

water down phr vt **1** weaken by adding water **2** reduce the force of: a watered-down report

wa·ter·bed /ˈwɒtərˌbed, ˈwɑ-/ n bag filled with heated water for sleeping on

water can·non /ˈ·· ˌ··/ n apparatus for shooting out a powerful stream of water, esp. for controlling crowds

water clos·et /ˈ·· ˌ··/ n TOILET

wa·ter·col·or /ˈwɒtərˌkɑlər, ˈwɑ-/ n **1** [C;U] paint mixed with water rather than oil **2** [C] picture painted with this

wa·ter·cress /ˈwɒtərˌkres, ˈwɑ-/ n [U] water plant with leaves used as food

wa·ter·fall /ˈwɒtərˌfɔl, ˈwɑ-/ n very steep fall of water in a river, etc.

wa·ter·front /ˈwɒtərˌfrʌnt, ˈwɑ-/ n land along a stretch of water, esp. in a port

wa·ter·hole /ˈwɒtərˌhoʷl, ˈwɑ-/ n pool where animals come to drink

watering can /ˈ··· ˌ·/ n container for pouring water onto garden plants

watering hole /ˈ··· ˌ·/ also **watering place** — n place where people gather to drink

water lev·el /ˈ·· ˌ··/ n height to which a mass of water has risen or sunk

wa·ter·line /ˈwɒtərˌlaɪn/ n level reached by water up the side of a ship

wa·ter·logged /ˈwɒtərˌlɒgd, -ˌlɑgd, ˈwɑ-/ adj **1** (of ground) very wet **2** (of a boat) full of water

wa·ter·loo /ˌwɒtərˈluʷ, ˌwɑ-/ n (deserved) defeat after a time of unusual success

wa·ter·mark /ˈwɒtərˌmɑrk, ˈwɑ-/ n **1** partly transparent mark in paper **2** mark that shows a level reached: the high watermark of her success

wa·ter·mel·on /ˈwɔtərˌmɛlən, ˈwɑ-/ n large round green fruit with juicy red flesh

wa·ter·mill /ˈwɔtərˌmɪl, ˈwɑ-/ n MILL¹ (1) driven by moving water

water po·lo /ˈ·· ˌ··/ n [U] game played by 2 teams of swimmers with a ball

wa·ter·pow·er /ˈwɔtərˌpaʊər, ˈwɑ-/ n [U] power from moving water to drive machines

wa·ter·proof /ˈwɔtərˌpruʷf, ˈwɑ-/ adj, n (an outer garment) which does not allow water, esp. rain, through ♦ vt make waterproof

wa·ter·shed /ˈwɔtərˌʃɛd, ˈwɑ-/ n 1 direction towards which water flows 2 point of very important change

wa·ter·side /ˈwɔtərˌsaɪd, ˈwɑ-/ n [U] edge of a river, lake, etc.

water ski·ing /ˈ·· ˌ··/ n [U] sport of being pulled across water on SKIS –er n

water sup·ply /ˈ·· ·ˌ·/ n flow of water provided for a building or area, and system of lakes, pipes, etc., that provides it

water ta·ble /ˈ·· ˌ··/ n level below which water can be found in the ground

wa·ter·tight /ˈwɔtərˌtaɪt, ˈwɑ-/ adj 1 which water cannot pass through 2 allowing or having no mistakes or possibility of doubt: a watertight plan

wa·ter·way /ˈwɔtərˌweʸ, ˈwɑ-/ n stretch of water which ships travel along

wa·ter·wheel /ˈwɔtərˌhwiʸl, -ˌwiʸl, ˈwɑ-/ n wheel which is turned by moving water, esp. to give power to machines

wa·ter·works /ˈwɔtərˌwɜrks, ˈwɑ-/ 1 place from which a public water supply is provided 2 infml body's system for removing water from the body 3 turn on the waterworks start to cry, esp. to get attention, or what one wants

watt /wɑt/ n measure of electrical power

wave /weʸv/ v 1 vi move (one's hand or something in it) as a signal: We waved as the train pulled out. 2 vt direct with a movement of the hand: The policeman waved the traffic on. 3 vi move gently from side to side in the air: The flags waved. 4 vi/t (cause to) curve regularly: waved hair ♦ n 1 raised moving area of water, esp. on the sea 2 movement of the hand in waving 3 feeling, way of behaving, etc., that suddenly starts and increases: a wave of nausea | a crime wave 4 form in which light, sound, etc., move: radio waves 5 evenly curved

part of the hair **wavy** adj having regular curves

wave aside phr vt push aside without giving attention to (esp. ideas, etc.)

wave·length /ˈweʸvˌlɛŋkθ, -lɛŋθ/ n 1 distance between 2 WAVES (4) 2 radio signal sent out on radio WAVES that are a particular distance apart: (fig.) We're on completely different wavelengths. (= completely different, cannot understand each other, etc.)

wa·ver /ˈweʸvər/ vi be uncertain or unsteady in direction or decision: Her loyalty never wavered.

wax¹ /wæks/ n [U] solid meltable fatty or oily substance ♦ vt put wax on, esp. as a polish ~y adj

wax² vi 1 (esp. of the moon) get gradually larger 2 lit (of a person) become: He waxed eloquent as he described his plans.

wax·works /ˈwæksˌwɜrks/ n –works (place with) models of people made in wax

way /weʸ/ n 1 [C] road, path, etc., to follow in order to reach a place: She asked me the way to the station. | We lost our way. 2 [C] direction: He went that way. 3 [S] distance: We're a long way from home. 4 [C] method: Do it this way. 5 [C] manner: the cruel way in which he treats his animals 6 [C] single part of a whole; detail; point: In many ways I agree with you, but I don't think you're completely right. 7 by the way (used to introduce a new subject in speech) 8 by way of: a by going through b as a sort of: a few sandwiches by way of lunch 9 get one's own way do or get what one wants in spite of others 10 go one's own way do what one wants 11 go out of the/one's way (to do) take the trouble (to do); make a special effort: I went out of my way to pick her up and she didn't even thank me. 12 have a way with one have an attractive quality which persuades others 13 have it both ways gain advantage from 2 opposing opinions or actions 14 out of/in the way (of) (not) blocking space for forward movement: You're in the way; move! 15 make one's way go 16 make way for leave so as to allow to develop freely 17 no way infml no: 'Will you help me?' 'No way!' 18 out of the way unusual or not commonly known 19 see one's way (clear) to (doing) feel able to do 20 under way moving forwards – see also RIGHT OF WAY ♦ adv far: That's way outside my area. **ways** n [P] customs; habits: mend one's ways (= improve one's manners, etc.)

way·far·er /ˈweʸˌfɛərər/ n lit traveler

way·lay /'weɪˌleɪ, weɪˈleɪ/ vt **-laid** /-leɪd, -ˈleɪd/, **-laying -laid** 1 attack (a traveler) 2 find or stop (someone) to speak to them

way-out /ˌ· '·◄/ adj infml strange; unusual

way·side /'weɪsaɪd/ n lit side of the road or path

ways and means /ˌ· · '·/ n [P] 1 method of doing something 2 plans to raise money, esp. for the government

way·ward /'weɪwərd/ adj 1 difficult to guide or control 2 not well aimed

we /wiː/ pron (used as the subject of a sentence) the people speaking; oneself and one or more others

weak /wiːk/ adj 1 having little power: weak muscles/eyes 2 easily becoming broken, changed, destroyed, or ill: a weak heart 3 having little taste: weak coffee 4 unable to control people: a weak teacher 5 not reaching a good standard: His math is pretty weak. **~ly** adv **-en** vi/t (cause to) become weaker **~ness** n 1 [U] fact or state of being weak 2 [C] part that spoils the rest: The plan's only weakness is its cost. 3 [C] fault in character 4 [C] strong liking: a weakness for chocolate

weak-kneed /ˌ· '·◄/ adj cowardly

weak·ling /'wiːk-lɪŋ/ n derog weak person

wealth /welθ/ n 1 [U] (large amount of) money and possessions 2 [S] fml large number: a wealth of examples **~y** adj rich

wean /wiːn/ vt gradually give (a baby) solid food instead of milk

wean from phr vt gradually persuade to give up (something one disapproves of)

weap·on /'wepən/ n something to fight with, such as a gun or sword **~ry** n [U] weapons

wear /weər/ v **wore** /wɔr, wɔər/, **worn** /wɔrn, woʷrn/ 1 vt have (esp. clothes) on the body 2 vt have (a particular expression) on the face 3 vi/t (cause to) show the effects of continued use, rubbing, etc.: You've worn a hole in your sock. 1 (fig.) That excuse is wearing thin. (= becoming unbelievable) 4 vi last in this condition: an old person who has worn well 5 vt infml find acceptable 6 **wear the pants** have control or authority: She wears the pants in that family. ♦ n 1 [U] clothes: evening wear | men's wear 2 act of wearing esp. clothes 3 damage from use: signs of wear 4 quality of lasting in use: There's a lot of wear in these shoes.

wear down phr vt weaken

wear off phr vi (of a feeling, effect, etc.) become gradually less

wear on phr vi pass slowly in time

wear out phr v 1 vi/t (cause to) be reduced to nothing or a useless state by use 2 vt tire greatly

wear and tear /ˌ· · '·/ n [U] damage from use; WEAR

wear·i·some /'wɪərɪsəm/ adj tiring and boring or annoying

wear·y /'wɪəriː/ adj very tired ♦ vi/t (cause to) become weary **-ily** adv **-iness** n [U]

wea·sel[1] /'wiːzəl/ n small fierce furry animal

weasel[2] v **weasel out** phr vi infml escape a duty by clever dishonest means

weasel words /'·· ˌ·/ n [P] speech that is not direct or courageous, esp. in a difficult situation

weath·er /'weðər/ n [U] 1 particular condition of wind, sunshine, rain, snow, etc.: a day of fine weather **under the weather** slightly ill ♦ v 1 vt pass safely through (a storm or difficulty) 2 vi/t change from the effects of air, rain, etc.: weathered stone

weather-beat·en /'·· ˌ·/ adj marked or damaged by the wind, sun, etc.

weather fore·cast /'·· ˌ·/ n description of weather conditions as they are expected to be

weath·er·man /'weðərˌmæn/ n **-men** /-ˌmen/ person who describes likely future weather conditions, esp. on television or radio

weather sta·tion /'·· ˌ·/ n place for noting weather conditions

weather vane /'·· ˌ·/ n small apparatus that is blown around to show the direction of the wind

weave /wiːv/ v **wove** /woʷv/, **woven** /'woʷvən/ 1 vi/t form threads into (material) by drawing them singly under and over a set of longer threads 2 vt twist; wind: a bird's nest woven from straws 3 vt produce (a story) esp. from a suggestion 4 (past t. and p. **weaved**) vi move twistingly: The cyclist weaved through the traffic. ♦ n style or pattern of woven material: a loose weave **weaver** n

web /web/ n 1 net of thin threads made by a SPIDER: (fig.) a web of lies 2 skin between the toes of certain swimming birds and animals **~bed** /webd/ adj having a WEB (2) between the toes

web·bing /'webɪŋ/ n [U] strong woven bands used for belts, supports, etc.

wed /wed/ vi/t **wedded** or **wed** esp. lit marry

we'd /wiːd/ short for: 1 we had 2 we would

wed·ding /ˈwɛdɪŋ/ n marriage ceremony

wedding ring /ˈ·· ˌ·/ n ring worn to show that one is married

wedge /wɛdʒ/ n 1 piece of wood, etc. shaped like a V, for keeping something in place or splitting something 2 piece shaped like a V: *a wedge of glass* 3 something shaped like this: *shoes with wedge heels* – see also **thin end of the wedge** (THIN) ♦ vt fix firmly (as if) with a wedge: *Wedge the door open.* | *I got wedged between 2 people on the bus.*

Wedg·wood /ˈwɛdʒwʊd/ n [U] tdmk fine CHINA, esp. blue and white

wed·lock /ˈwɛdlɑk/ n [U] lit 1 being married 2 **out of wedlock** of unmarried parents

Wednes·day /ˈwɛnzdiⁱ, -deⁱ/ n the 3rd day of the week, between Tuesday and Thursday

wee /wiⁱ/ adj 1 very small 2 very early; *in the wee hours of the morning*

weed¹ /wiⁱd/ n 1 unwanted wild plant 2 physically weak person ~**y** adj 1 thin and weak 2 full of weeds

weed² vi/t remove weeds from (a garden)

weed out phr vt get rid of (less good ones)

week /wiⁱk/ n 1 period of 7 days, usu. thought of as starting on Monday and ending on Sunday, but sometimes measured from Sunday to Saturday 2 period worked during a week: *a 35-hour week* 3 **week after week** also **week in, week out** — continuously

week·day /ˈwiⁱkdeⁱ/ n day other than Saturday or Sunday

week·end /ˈwiⁱkɛnd/ n period between Friday evening and Monday morning: *We usually go away (on) weekends.*

week·ly /ˈwiⁱkliⁱ/ adj, adv (happening) every week or once a week ♦ n magazine or newspaper which appears once a week

weep /wiⁱp/ vi **wept** /wɛpt/, **weeping** fml or lit cry —**ing** adj (of a tree) with branches hanging down

wee·vil /ˈwiⁱvəl/ n small insect which eats (and spoils) grain, seeds, etc.

weft /wɛft/ n WOOF²

weigh /weⁱ/ v 1 vt find the weight of: *weigh oneself* 2 vi have the stated weight: *It weighs 6lbs.* 3 vt consider or compare carefully 4 vt raise (an ANCHOR)

weigh down phr vt make heavy with a load: (fig.) *weighed down with grief*

weigh in phr vi have weight measured officially esp. in sports

weigh on phr vt worry: *His responsibilities weighed on him.*

weigh up phr vt form an opinion about, esp. by balancing opposing arguments

weigh·sta·tion /ˈweⁱˌsteⁱʃən/ n place for weighing vehicles and their loads

weight /weⁱt/ n 1 [C;U] (measured) heaviness of something: *The weight of the sack is 2 lbs.* 2 [C] something heavy: *lifting weights* 3 [C] piece of metal of known heaviness, used for weighing things 4 [U] system of standard measures of heaviness: *metric weight* 5 [U] value; importance: *I don't attach much weight to these rumors.* 6 [C] (something that causes) a feeling of anxiety: *a great weight off my mind* 7 **pull one's weight** do one's full share of work 8 **put on/lose weight** (of a person) become heavier/lighter 9 **throw one's weight around** give orders to others ♦ vt 1 make heavy, esp. by fastening weights 2 include conditions in (something) that give a (dis)advantage: *a competition weighted against younger children* ~**less** adj: *a weightless flight in space* ~**y** adj 1 heavy 2 fml important and serious

weight lift·ing /ˈ· ˌ··/ also **weight training** — n [U] sport of lifting heavy weights –**er** n

weir /wɪər/ n wall-like structure across a river controlling its flow

weird /wɪərd/ adj 1 strange; unusual: *a weird shriek* 2 unusual and not sensible or acceptable: *weird ideas* ~**ly** adv ~**ness** n [U]

weird·o /ˈwɪərdoʳ/ n –**os** sl strange person

wel·come /ˈwɛlkəm/ interj (a greeting to someone who has arrived) ♦ vt 1 greet (someone newly arrived), esp. with friendliness 2 wish to have; like: *I'd welcome some help.* ♦ adj 1 acceptable and wanted: *A cool drink is always welcome on a hot day.* 2 allowed freely (to have): *I have plenty of paper; you're welcome to some.* 3 **You're welcome** (a polite expression when thanked for something) ♦ n greeting

weld /wɛld/ vt join (metal) by melting ~**er** n

wel·fare /ˈwɛlfɛər/ n [U] 1 comfort, health, and happiness: *I was concerned for her welfare.* (= thought she might be in trouble) 2 help with living conditions, social problems, etc. 3 **on welfare** receiving money from the government to live on

welfare state /ˈ·· ˌ·/ n (country with) a system of social help for poor, sick, etc., people

well¹ adv **better** /ˈbɛtəʳ/, **best** /bɛst/ 1 in a good way: *She sings well.* | *a* *well-dressed man* **2** thoroughly: *They were well beaten.* **3** much; quite: *She finished well within the time allowed.* **4** suitably; properly: *I couldn't very well refuse.* **5 as well: a** also: *She came as well.* **b** with as good a result: *We might just as well have stayed at home.* **6 as well as** in addition to **7 come off well** be lucky in the end **8 do well** succeed or improve **9 do well out of** gain profit from **10 do well to** act wisely to **11 just as well** it is fortunate (that); there's no harm done **12 may well** could suitably **13 pretty well** almost **14 well and truly** completely **15 well underway** off to a good start **16 Well done!** (said when someone has been successful) ♦ *adj* better, best **1** in good health **2** in an acceptable state **3 It's all very well** (an expression of dissatisfaction when comparing what is practical to what is suggested): *It's all very well for you to laugh but what am I supposed to do?* ♦ *interj* **1** (expresses surprise) **2** (introduces an expression of surprise, doubt, etc.)

well² *n* **1** place where water can be taken from underground **2** OIL WELL **3** deep narrow space inside a building, for stairs or an ELEVATOR (2) ♦ *vi* flow

we'll /wil; *strong* wiʲl/ *short for:* **1** we will **2** we shall

well-ad·jus·ted /ˌ·· ·'··◄/ *adj* (of a person) fitting in well with society

well-ad·vised /ˌ·· ·'··◄/ *adj* sensible

well-be·ing /ˌ·· '··/ *n* [U] personal and physical comfort, esp. good health and happiness

well-bred /ˌ·· '·◄/ *adj* having or showing high social rank, with good manners

well-con·nect·ed /ˌ·· ·'··◄/ *adj* knowing or esp. related to people of high social rank or influence

well-done /ˌ·· '·◄/ *adj* thoroughly cooked

well-groomed /ˌ·· '·◄/ *adj* neat and clean

well-heeled /ˌ·· '·◄/ *adj infml* rich

well-in·formed /ˌ·· ·'·◄/ *adj* knowing a lot about several subjects or parts of a particular subject

well-in·ten·tioned /ˌ·· ·'··◄/ *adj* acting in the hope of good results, though often failing

well-known /ˌ·· '·◄/ *adj* known by many people; famous

well-mean·ing /ˌ·· '··◄/ *adj* well-intentioned

well-nigh /ˌwel 'naɪ◄/ *adv* almost: *well-nigh impossible*

well-off /ˌ·· '·◄/ *adj* **1** rich **2** lucky

well-pre·served /ˌ·· ·'·◄/ *adj* (of

someone or something old) still in good condition

well-read /ˌwel 'red◄/ *adj* having read many books and got a lot of information

well-spok·en /ˌ·· '··◄/ *adj* having a socially acceptable way of speaking

well-timed /ˌ·· '·◄/ *adj* said or done at the most suitable time

well-to-do /ˌ·· · '·◄/ *adj* rich

well-wish·er /ˈ·· ,··, ˌ· '··/ *n* person who wishes another to succeed, have good luck, etc.

well-worn /ˌ·· '·◄/ *adj* (of a phrase) too much used

welsh /welʃ/ *vi derog* avoid payment

Welsh *adj* of Wales

welt /welt/ *n* mark on the skin where one has been hit

wel·ter /ˈweltər/ *n* [S] confused mixture: *a welter of statistics*

wel·ter·weight /ˈweltərˌweɪt/ *n* boxer (BOX²) of middle weight

wench /wentʃ/ *n lit* young woman

wend /wend/ *v* **wend one's way: a** travel (slowly) **b** leave

went /went/ *v past t. of* GO

wept /wept/ *v past t. and p. of* WEEP

were /wɜrnt, 'wɜrənt/ *v past t. of* BE

we're /wɪr; *strong* wɪər/ *short for:* we are

were·wolf /ˈwɛərwʊlf, ˈwɪər-/ *n* (in stories) person who sometimes turns into a WOLF (1)

west /west/ *n* **1** (*often cap.*) direction towards which the sun sets **2** [*the*+S] (*cap.*) western Europe and the US ♦ *adj* **1** in the west **2** (of wind) from the west ♦ *adv* towards the west ~ **ward** *adj, adv*

west·er·ly /ˈwestərli/ *adj* west

west·ern /ˈwestərn/ *adj* of the west part of the world or of a country ♦ *n* story or film about life in the middle of the US in the past, with COWBOYS and gun fights ~ **er** *n* someone who lives in or comes from the WEST (2)

west·ern·ize /ˈwestərˌnaɪz/ *vt* cause to have or copy the customs typical of America and Europe

wet /wet/ *adj* –tt– **1** covered with or being liquid: *wet grass/paint* **2** rainy: *a wet day* **3** weak in character and unable to get things done ♦ *n* [*the*+S] rainy weather ♦ *vt* **wet** or **wetted**; *pres. p.* –tt– make wet ~ **ness** *n* [U]

wet blan·ket /ˈ· ,··/ *n* person who discourages others or prevents them from enjoying themselves

wet dream /ˌ· '·/ *n* sexually exciting dream resulting in a male ORGASM

wet-nurse /ˈ· ·/ *vt* treat with too much care

wet suit /ˈ· ·/ *n* rubber garment for

keeping the body warm in sea sports

we've /wiˀv/ *short for*: we have

whack /wæk/ *vt* hit with a noisy blow ♦ *n* **1** (noise of) a hard blow **2** trial or attempt **3 out of whack** out of order; in poor condition

whale /hweˀl, weˀl/ *n* **1** extremely large fishlike animal **2 a whale of a time** a very enjoyable time **whaler** *n* **a** a person who hunts whales **b** ship from which whales are hunted **whaling** *n* [U] hunting whales

whale watch-ing /ˈ· ˌ··/ *n* [u] sport of watching whales from boats

wham /wæm/ *n* (sound of) a hard blow

wharf /hwɔrf, wɔrf/ *n* **wharfs** or **wharves** /hwɔrvz, wɔrvz/ place where ships are tied up to unload and load goods

what /hwɑt, hwɑt, wɑt, wɑt; *weak* hwət, wət/ *predeterminer, determiner, pron* **1** (used in questions about an unknown thing or person): *What are you doing?* | *What color is it?* **2** the thing(s) that: *He told me what to do.* **3** (shows surprise): *What a strange hat!* **4 what for?** why? **5 what if?** what will happen if? **6 what's more** and this is more important **7 what's what** the true state of things: *to know what's what* **8 what's up** Any news? what's happening? ♦ *adv* **1** (used esp. in questions when no answer is expected) in what way: *What do you care?* (= I don't think you care at all) **2 what with** (used for introducing the cause of something, esp. something bad)

what-ev-er /hwɑtˈɛvər, wɑt-/ *determiner, pron* **1** no matter what: *Whatever I said, he'd disagree.* **2** anything: *They eat whatever they can find.* **3** *fml* (shows surprise) what: *Whatever is that peculiar thing?* ♦ *adj* at all: *I have no money whatever.*

what-not /ˈhwɑtˌnɑt, ˈhwɑt-, ˈwɑt-, ˈwɑt-/ *n* [U] *infml* anything (else): *carrying his bags and whatnot*

wheat /hwiˀt, wiˀt/ *n* [U] (plant producing) grain from which flour is made

whee-dle /ˈhwiˀdl, ˈwiˀ-/ *vi/t* try to persuade (someone) by pleasant but insincere words

wheel /hwiˀl, wiˀl/ *n* **1** circular frame which turns to allow vehicles to move, to work machinery, etc. **2** movement by which a group of marching soldiers curve to the left or right **3** [*the*+S] the STEERING WHEEL of a car or ship **4 at the wheel: a** driving or guiding a car or ship **b** in control **5 wheels within wheels** hidden influences having

effects on surface behavior ♦ *v* **1** *vt* move (a wheeled object) with the hands **2** *vi* turn around suddenly **3** *vi* (of birds) fly around and around in circles **4 wheel and deal** *vi infml* make deals, esp. in business or politics, in a skillful and perhaps dishonest way ~ **ed** *adj* having wheels

wheel-bar-row /ˈhwiˀlˌbæroʷ, ˈwiˀl-/ *n* small 1-wheeled cart pushed by hand

wheel-chair /ˈhwiˀltʃɛər, ˈwiˀl-/ *n* wheeled chair for someone who cannot walk

wheeler-deal-er /ˌ··· ˈ···/ *n* someone skilled at doing clever (but perhaps not always honest) deals, esp. in business or politics

wheel-ie /ˈhwiˀliˀ, ˈwiˀ-/ *n* act of riding a bicycle on its back wheel

wheeze /hwiˀz, wiˀz/ *vi* make a noisy whistling sound in breathing ♦ *n* wheezing sound **wheezy** *adj*

whelk /hwɛlk, wɛlk/ *n* sea animal that lives in a shell

whelp /hwɛlp, wɛlp/ *n derog* young animal, esp. a dog

when /hwɛn, wɛn; *weak* hwən, wən/ *adv, conj* **1** at what time; at the time that: *When will they come?* | *He looked up when she came in.* **2** considering that; although: *Why did you do it when I told you not to?*

whence /hwɛns, wɛns/ *adv, conj lit* from where

when-ev-er /hwɛˈnɛvər, wɛ-, hwə-, wə-/ *adv, conj* **1** at whatever time **2** every time

where /hwɛər, wɛər/ *adv, conj* at or to what place; at or to the place that: *Where do you live?* | *Sit where you like.*

where-a-bouts /ˈhwɛərəˌbauts, ˈwɛər-, ˌhwɛərəˈbauts, ˌwɛər-/ *adv* where in general (not exactly): *Whereabouts did I leave my glasses?* ♦ /ˈhwɛərəˌbauts, ˈwɛər-/ *n* [U] place where a person or thing is

where-as /hwɛərˈæz, wɛər-/ *conj fml* (shows an opposite) but: *They live in a house, whereas we have an apartment.*

where-by /hwɛərˈbai, wɛər-/ *adj fml* by means of which

where-fore /ˈhwɛərfɔr, -foʷr, ˈwɛər-/ *adv, conj lit* why

where-u-pon /ˌhwɛərəˈpɑn, -ˈpɔn, ˌwɛər-, ˈhwɛərəˌpɑn, -ˌpɔn, ˈwɛər-/ *conj* without delay after and because of which: *He stood up to speak, whereupon everyone cheered.*

wher-ev-er /hwɛərˈɛvər, wɛər-, hwər-, wər-/ *adv* **1** to or at whatever place **2** (shows surprise) where

where-with-al /ˈhwɛərwɪˌðɔl, -ˌθɔl, ˈwɛər-/ *n* [U] enough supplies or money

whet /hwɛt, wɛt/ *vt* **-tt- 1** sharpen

(a knife, etc.) **2 whet someone's appetite** make someone wish for more

wheth·er /ˈhweðər, ˈwe-/ *conj* if ... or not: *I'm trying to decide whether to go.*

whey /hweʸ, weʸ/ *n* [U] watery part of milk

which /hwɪtʃ, wɪtʃ/ *determiner, pron* **1** (used in questions, when a choice is to be made): *Which shoes shall I wear, the red ones or the brown?* **2** (shows what thing is meant): *This is the book which I told you about.* **3** (used to add more information about something): *The train, which only takes an hour, is quicker than the bus.* – see also EVERY WHICH WAY

which·ev·er /hwɪˈtʃevər, wɪ-/ *determiner, pron* **1** any (one) of the set that: *Take whichever seat you like.* **2** no matter which: *It has the same result, whichever way you do it.*

whiff /hwɪf, wɪf/ *n* [S] **1** temporary smell of something **2** a breath in: *A few whiffs of gas and she'll fall asleep.*

while[1] /hwaɪl, waɪl/ *n* [S] **1** length of time: *He's been gone quite a while.* (= a fairly long time) **2 once in a while** sometimes, but not often **3 worth one's/someone's while** WORTHWHILE to one/someone: *We'll make it worth your while.* (= pay you) ♦ *conj* **1** during the time that: *They arrived while we were having dinner.* **2** although: *While I agree with your reasons, I can't allow it.* **3** WHEREAS **4** and what is more

while[2] *v* **while away** *phr vt* pass (time) in a pleasantly lazy way

whim /hwɪm, wɪm/ *n* sudden (often unreasonable) idea or wish

whim·per /ˈhwɪmpər, ˈwɪm-/ *vi* make small weak trembling cries **whimper** *n*

whim·sy /ˈhwɪmziʸ, ˈwɪm-/ *n* whim **–sical** *adj* fanciful; with strange ideas

whine /hwaɪn, waɪn/ *vi* **1** make a high sad sound **2** complain (too much) in an unnecessarily sad voice ♦ *n*: *the whine of the jet engines*

whin·ny /ˈhwɪniʸ, ˈwɪni/ *vi* make a gentle sound that horses make

whip[1] /hwɪp, wɪp/ *n* **1** long piece of esp. rope or leather on a handle, used for striking sharp blows **2** (person who gives) an order to a member of Congress to attend and vote

whip[2] *v* **-pp-** **1** *vt* hit with a whip **2** *vi/t* move quickly: *He whipped out his gun.* **3** *vt* beat (esp. cream or eggs) until stiff **4** *vt infml* defeat **~ping** *n* beating as a punishment

whip up *phr vt* **1** cause (feelings) to become stronger, etc. **2** make quickly

whip·lash /ˈhwɪp-læʃ, ˈwɪp-/ *n* **1** blow from a whip **2** harm done by sudden violent movement of the head and neck, as in a car accident: *a whiplash injury*

whip·ping boy /ˈ··· ·/ *n* person who (unfairly) gets the blame and/or punishment

whirl /hwɜrl, wɜrl/ *vi/t* move around and around very fast ♦ *n* **1** [S] act or sensation of whirling: (fig.) *My head's in a whirl.* (= confused) **2** [C] very fast (confused) movement or activity **3 give something a whirl** *infml* try something

whirl·pool /ˈhwɜrlpuʷl, ˈwɜrl-/ *n* fast circular current of water

whirl·wind /ˈhwɜrlˌwɪnd, ˈwɜrl-/ *n* tall tube of air moving dangerously at high speed: (fig.) *a whirlwind romance* (= happening very quickly)

whirr /hwɜr, wɜr/ *vi, n* (make) the regular sound of something turning and beating against the air

whisk /hwɪsk, wɪsk/ *vt* **1** remove, either by quick light brushing or by taking suddenly: *She whisked my cup away before I'd finished.* **2** beat (esp. eggs), esp. with a whisk ♦ *n* small apparatus held in the hands, for beating eggs, cream, etc.

whis·ker /ˈhwɪskər, ˈwɪ-/ *n* long stiff hair near an animal's mouth **whiskers** *n* [P] hair on the sides of a man's face

whis·key /ˈhwɪskiʸ, ˈwɪ-/ *n* [U] strong alcoholic drink made from grain, esp. (in Ireland or the US)

whis·ky /ˈhwɪskiʸ, ˈwɪ-/ *n* [U] strong alcoholic drink made from grain, esp. in Scotland and Canada

whis·per /ˈhwɪspər, ˈwɪ-// *v* **1** *vi/t* speak or say very quietly **2** *vt* suggest or pass (information) secretly: *It's whispered he may resign.* ♦ *n* **1** very quiet voice **2** RUMOR

whist /hwɪst, wɪst/ *n* [U] card game for 4 players

whis·tle /ˈhwɪsəl, ˈwɪ-/ *n* **1** simple (musical) instrument played by blowing **2** high sound made by air blowing through a narrow opening ♦ *v* **1** *vi* make a WHISTLE (2), esp. by blowing through the lips: (fig.) *The wind whistled around us.* **2** *vt* produce (a tune) by whistling

whis·tle-blow·er /ˈhwɪsəlˌbloʷər, ˈhwɪ-/ *n* person who calls attention to illegal or wrong activity

whistle stop /ˈ··· ·/ *n* small unimportant town along a railroad

whit /hwɪt, wɪt/ *n* [S] *fml* small amount: *not a whit less interesting*

white /hwaɪt, waɪt/ *adj* **1** of the color of snow and milk **2** pale **3** of a race with pale skin **4** (of coffee) without milk or cream ♦ *n* **1** [U] white color

2 [C] WHITE (3) person **3** [C] part of an egg surrounding the central yellow part –**whiten** *vi/t* (cause to) become white(r)

white-col·lar /ˌ· ˈ··/ *adj* of or being office workers, indoor workers, etc.

white el·e·phant /ˌ· ˈ····/ *n* useless article

white flag /ˌ· ˈ·/ *n* sign that one accepts defeat

white heat /ˌ· ˈ·/ *n* [U] temperature at which metal turns white

White House /ˈ· ·/ *n [the]* **1** official Washington home of the US president **2** EXECUTIVE branch of the U.S. government

white knight /ˌ· ˈ·/ *n* person or organization that RESCUES, esp. one that puts money into a business company to save it from being taken over by another company

white lie /ˌ· ˈ·/ *n* harmless lie

white pages /ˈ· ˌ··/ *n* [P] book with an alphabetical list of people's names, addresses, and telephone numbers

white-tie /ˌ· ˈ·◄/ *adj* (of parties and other social occasions) at which the men wear white BOW TIES and tails (TAIL²)

white·wash /ˈhwaɪtwɑʃ, -wɔʃ, ˈwaɪt-/ *n* **1** [U] white liquid for covering walls **2** [C;U] *derog* attempt to hide something wrong **3** [C] complete defeat ♦ *vt* **1** cover with WHITEWASH (1) **2** make (what is bad) seem good

with·er /ˈhwɪðər, ˈwɪ-/ *adv lit* to which place

whit·tle /ˈhwɪţl, ˈwɪţl/ *vt* cut thin pieces off (wood): (fig.) *We've whittled the list of candidates down* (= reduced it) *to* 5.

whizz, whiz /hwɪz, wɪz/ *vi* –zz– move very fast (and noisily) ♦ *n* **1** [S] whizzing sound **2** [C] *infml* someone who is very fast, clever, or skilled in the stated activity

whizz kid /ˈ· ·/ *n* person who makes quick successes in life

who /huʷ/ *pron* (used esp. as the subject of a sentence) **1** what person?: *Who said that?* **2** (shows what person is meant): *the people who live in that house* **3** (adds more information about a person): *This is my father, who lives in Lockport.*

whoa /woʷ, hwoʷ, hoʷ/ *interj* (call to a horse to stop)

who·dun·it, whodunnit /ˌhuʷˈdʌnɪt/ *n* story, film, etc., about a crime mystery

who·ev·er /huʷˈɛvər/ *pron* **1** anyone at all: *I'll take whoever wants to go.* **2** no matter who: *Whoever it is, I don't want to see them.* **3** (shows surprise) who: *Whoever can that be at the door?*

whole /hoʷl/ *adj* **1** all; complete: *I spent the whole day in bed.* | *She swallowed it whole.* (= not divided up) **2 swallow something whole** accept something without questioning it ♦ *n* **1** complete amount, thing, etc. **2 on the whole** generally; mostly **wholly** /ˈhoʷl-liʸ/ *adv: not wholly to blame*

whole·food /ˈhoʷlfuʷd/ *n* [C;U] food in a simple natural form

whole-heart·ed /ˌ· ˈ··◄/ *adj* with all one's ability, interest, etc.; full: *whole-hearted support*

whole num·ber /ˌ· ˈ··/ *n* INTEGER

whole·sale /ˈhoʷlseʸl/ *adj, adv* **1** sold in large quantities to stores (rather than directly to customers) **2** *usu. derog* very great or complete: *wholesale slaughter* –**saler** *n* seller of goods wholesale

whole·some /ˈhoʷlsəm/ *adj* **1** good for the body: *wholesome food* **2** having a good moral effect ~**ness** *n* [U]

whole-wheat /ˈhoʷl-hwiʸt, -wiʸt/ *adj* (made from flour) without the covering of the grain being removed

whom /huʷm/ *pron fml* (object form of **who**): *To whom do you speak?*

whoop /huʷp, hwuʷp, wuʷp/ *vi* **1** make a loud cry, as of joy **2 whoop it up** *infml* enjoy oneself a lot ♦ *n* a loud shout of joy

whoo·pee /ˈhwuʷpiʸ, ˈwu-, hwuʷˈpiʸ, wu-/ *interj* (cry of joy) ♦ *n* **make whoopee** enjoy oneself a lot

whoop·ing cough /ˈhuʷpɪŋ ˌkɔf, ˈhup-/ *n* [U] (children's) disease with attacks of serious coughing and difficult breathing

whoops /hwups, wups, wuʷps/ *interj* (said when one has made a mistake)

whoosh /hwuʷʃ, wuʷʃ, hwuʃ, wuʃ/ *vi, n* (move quickly with) a rushing sound

whop·per /ˈhwɑpər, ˈwɑ-/ *n infml* **1** big thing **2** big lie –**ping** *adj, adv* very (big): *a whopping (great) bonus*

whore /hɔr, hoʷr/ *n lit or derog* for PROSTITUTE

whorl /hwɔrl, hwɜrl, wɔrl, wɜrl/ *n* shape of a line curving outwards from a center

whose /huʷz/ *determiner, pron* of whom: *Whose car is that?* (= who does it belong to?) | *That's the man whose house burned down.*

why /hwaɪ, waɪ/ *adv, conj* **1** for what reason: *Why did you do it?* **2** the reason why: *Is that why you did it?* **3 why not** (used in suggestions): *Why not sell it?* (= I suggest you sell it) ♦ *n* **the whys and wherefores (of)** reasons and explanations (for)

wick /wɪk/ *n* burning thread in a candle or lamp

wick·ed /ˈwɪkɪd/ *adj* **1** morally bad; evil **2** playfully bad: *a wicked* *twinkle in his eye* **3** *sl* excellent ~**ly** *adv* ~**ness** *n* [U]

wick·er·work /ˈwɪkərˌwɜrk/ *n* [U] (objects made from) woven CANES, sticks, etc. *adj* also **wicker** /ˈwɪkər/ — made of wickerwork: *wicker baskets*

wick·et /ˈwɪkɪt/ *n* **1** small door or gate next to a larger one **2** a small window in a door

wide /waɪd/ *adj* **1** large from side to side: *The car's too wide to go through the gate.* **2** covering a large range: *wide experience* ♦ *adv* **1** completely (open or awake) **2** (in sports) away from the correct or central point **3 wide of the mark** not suitable, correct, etc., at all ~**ly** *adv* over a wide range: *It's widely believed* (= believed by many people) *that carrots are good for the eyes.* **widen** *vi/t* make or become wider

wide-eyed /ˌ·ˈ··◂/ *adj* **1** with eyes very fully open **2** accepting or admiring things too easily

wide·spread /ˌwaɪdˈsprɛd◂/ *adj* common

wid·ow /ˈwɪdoʷ/ *n* woman whose husband has died

wid·ow·er /ˈwɪdoʷər/ *n* man whose wife has died

width /wɪdθ, wɪtθ/ *n* [C;U] size from side to side

wield /wiʲld/ *vt* have and/or use (power, influence, etc.)

wie·ner /ˈwiʲnər/ *n* FRANKFURTER

wife /waɪf/ *n* **wives** /waɪvz/ woman to whom a man is married

wig /wɪg/ *n* covering of false hair for the head

wig·gle /ˈwɪgəl/ *vi/t* move with quick small movements: *He wiggled his toes.*

wig·wam /ˈwɪgwɑm, -wɔm/ *n* Native American tent

wild /waɪld/ *adj* **1 a** living in natural conditions, not changed by human beings: *wild animals* **b** (of people) not civilized **2** uncontrollably violent **3** showing very strong feelings, esp. of anger **4** showing lack of thought or control: *a wild guess/throw* **5** *infml* having a very eager liking: *He's wild about football.* **6** *infml* good ♦ *n* [U] natural areas full of animals and plants, with few people ♦ *adv* **1 go wild** be filled with feeling, esp. anger or joy **2 run wild** behave as one likes, without control ~**ly** *adv*: *wildly* (= too greatly) *optimistic*

wild·cat strike /ˈwaɪldkæt ˌstraɪk/ *n* sudden unofficial stopping of work

wil·der·ness /ˈwɪldərnɪs/ *n* unchanging stretch of land, etc., with no sign of human presence

wild·fire /ˈwaɪldfaɪər/ *n* **like wildfire** very quickly

wild·fowl /ˈwaɪldfaʊl/ *n* [P] (water) birds shot for sport

wild-goose chase /ˌ·ˈ·ˌ·/ *n* useless search for something that cannot be found

wild·life /ˈwaɪldlaɪf/ *n* [U] animals living in natural conditions

wild oats /ˌ·ˈ·/ *n* **sow one's wild oats** behave wildly, esp. having many sexual partners while young

wiles /waɪlz/ *n* [P] tricks; deceitful persuading

will·ful /ˈwɪlfəl/ *adj* **1** doing what one wants in spite of other people **2** (of something bad) done on purpose ~**ly** *adv* ~**ness** *n* [U]

will¹ /wɪl/ *v aux 3rd person sing.* **will**, *pres. t. negative short form* **won't 1** (expresses the future tense): *Will it rain tomorrow?* **2** be willing to: *I won't go!* **3** (used in requests): *Shut the door, will you?* **4** (shows what always happens): *Oil will float on water.* **5** (used like **can** to show what is possible): *This car will hold 5 people.* **6** (used like **must** to show what is likely): *That will be the mailman at the door now.*

will² *n* **1** [C;U] power of the mind to make decisions and act in accordance with them: *You need a strong will to give up smoking.* – see also FREE WILL **2** [U] what someone wishes or intends: *She was forced to sign a confession against her will.* **3** [U] stated feelings towards someone: *I bear you no ill will.* **4** [S] force and interest: *They set to work with a will.* **5** [C] official statement of the way someone wants their property to be shared out after they die **6 at will** as one wishes **7 of one's own free will** according to one's own will **8 -willed** having a certain kind of WILL² (1) ♦ *vt* **1** make or intend to happen, esp. by the power of the mind **2** leave to someone in a WILL² (5)

will·ing /ˈwɪlɪŋ/ *adj* **1** ready: not refusing: *Are you willing to help?* **2** done or given gladly: *willing help* **3** eager: *a willing helper* ~**ly** *adv* ~**ness** *n* [U]

wil·low /ˈwɪloʷ/ *n* tree which grows near water, with long thin branches ~**y** *adj* pleasantly thin and graceful

will·pow·er /ˈwɪlˌpaʊər/ *n* [U] strength of WILL² (1)

wil·ly-nil·ly /ˌwɪliʸ ˈnɪliʸ/ *adv* regardless of whether it is wanted, or not

wilt /wɪlt/ *v* **1** *vi/t* become or cause (a plant) to become less fresh and start to die **2** *vi* (of a person) become tired and weaker

wil·y /ˈwaɪliʸ/ *adj* clever, esp. at getting what one wants **wiliness** *n* [U]

wimp /wɪmp/ *n* weak or useless person, esp. a man ~**ish** *adj*

win /wɪn/ v **won** /wʌn/, pres. p. **-nn-** **1** vi/t be first or best (in) beating one's opponent(s): Who won the race? **2** vt be given as the result of success: I won $100 in the competition. **3** vt gain: trying to win his friendship **4** vi be right in a guess or argument **5 win hands down** win easily ♦ n (esp. in sports) victory; success **~ner** n **~ning** adj very pleasing or attractive: a winning smile **~nings** n [P] money won

win over phr vt gain the support of by persuading

wince /wɪns/ vi move back suddenly (as if) from something unpleasant, often twisting the face

winch /wɪntʃ/ n apparatus that turns to pull up heavy objects ♦ vt pull up with a winch

wind¹ /wɪnd/ n **1** [C;U] strongly moving air **2** [U] breath or breathing: – see also SECOND WIND **3 get wind of** hear about, esp. accidentally or unofficially **4 see/find out which way the wind blows** find out what the situation is before taking action **5 (something) in the wind** (something, esp. that is secret or not generally known) about to happen/being done **6 take the wind out of someone's sails** infml take away someone's confidence or advantage, esp. by saying or doing something unexpected ♦ vt make breathless **~y** adj with a lot of wind: a windy day

wind² /waɪnd/ v **wound** /waʊnd/ **1** vt turn around and around: wind a handle **2** vt make into a twisted round shape: winding yarn **3** vi go twistingly: The path winds through the woods. **4** vt tighten the working parts of by turning: I wound the clock (up). **5** vt move by turning a handle: Wind down the car window. **6** vt place around several times: She wound a bandage around his arm.

wind down phr vi **1** (of a clock or watch) work more slowly before at last stopping **2** (of a person) to rest until calmer, after work or excitement **3** cause to be no longer in operation, esp. gradually: They're winding down their business in Hong Kong.

wind up phr v **1** vt bring to an end **2** vi get into the stated unwanted situation in the end: I wound up having to pay for it myself.

wind·bag /'wɪndbæg/ n person who talks too much

wind·break·er /'wɪnd,breʸkər/ n light JACKET

wind·fall /'wɪndfɔl/ n **1** unexpected lucky gift **2** fruit blown from a tree

wind in·stru·ment /'wɪnd ,ɪnstrəmənt/ n musical instrument played by blowing air through it

wind·mill /'wɪnd,mɪl/ n apparatus used to pump water, make electricity, etc. driven by large sails turned by the wind

win·dow /'wɪndoʷ/ n opening (filled with glass) in the wall of a building, in a car, etc., to let in light and air – see also FRENCH DOORS

window box /'·· ·/ n box of earth for growing plants outside a window

window dress·ing /'·· ,··/ n [U] **1** art of arranging goods in store windows **2** usu. derog something additional intended to attract people but hiding the true purpose

win·dow·pane /'wɪndoʷ,peʸn/ n one whole piece of glass in a window

window-shop /'·· ·/ vi **-pp-** look at goods in store windows without necessarily intending to buy

wind·pipe /'wɪndpaɪp/ n air passage from the throat to the lungs

wind·shield /'wɪndʃiʸld/ n piece of transparent material across the front of a vehicle, for the driver to look through

windshield wip·er /'·· ,··/ also **wiper** /··/ — n one of 2 movable arms which clears rain from the windshield of a car

wind·surf·ing /'wɪnd,sɜrfɪŋ/ n [U] sport of riding on SAILBOARDs **-er** n

wind·swept /'wɪndswept/ adj **1** open to continual strong wind: a windswept beach **2** as if blown into an untidy state: a windswept appearance

wind tun·nel /'wɪnd ,tʌnl/ n enclosed place through which air is forced at fixed speeds to test aircraft

wind·ward /'wɪndwərd/ n, adj, adv [U] (direction) against or facing the wind

wine¹ /waɪn/ n [C;U] **1** alcoholic drink made from GRAPES **2 new wine in old bottles** something new added to an old system

wine² vt **wine and dine** (cause to) have a meal and wine

wing /wɪŋ/ n **1** limb used by a bird, insect, etc., for flying **2** part standing out from a plane which supports it in flight **3** part standing out from the side: the west wing of the palace **4** (in sports) far left or right of the field **5** group with different opinions or purposes from the main organization: the left wing of the Democratic Party **6 on the wing** (of a bird) flying **7 take wing** fly (away) **8 under someone's wing** being protected, helped, etc., by someone ♦ v **1** vi fly (as if) on wings **2** vt wound slightly **wings** n [P] **1** sides of a stage, where an actor is hidden from view **2 in the wings** hidden and waiting for action **~ed** adj having wings **~er** n **1** player on the WINGS (5) **2** person on the stated WING (5)

wing·ding /'wɪŋdɪŋ/ n big party

wing·span /'wɪŋspæn/ also **wing·spread** /-spred/ — n distance from the end of one wing to the end of the other when both are stretched out

wink /wɪŋk/ vi/t **1** close and open (an eye) quickly **2** flash or cause (a light) to flash on and off ♦ n **1** [C] winking of the eye [S] even a short period of sleep: I didn't get a wink all night. (= didn't sleep at all) – see also FORTY WINKS

wink at phr vt pretend not to notice (something bad)

win·some /'wɪnsəm/ adj lit attractive

win·ter /'wɪntər/ n cold season between autumn and spring ♦ vi spend the winter –try /'wɪntriʲ/ adj

winter sports /ˌ·· '·/ n [P] sports done on snow or ice

wipe /waɪp/ vt **1** rub (a surface or object) to remove (dirt, liquid, etc.): Wipe your shoes on the mat. | She wiped the tears away. **2** wipe the floor with someone make someone feel deeply ashamed by severe scolding or by defeat in an argument ♦ n act of wiping

wipe off phr vt get rid of on purpose: to wipe off a debt

wipe out phr vt **1** destroy or remove all of **2** sl make very tired

wipe up phr v vt remove with a cloth: Wipe up that mess!

wip·er /'waɪpər/ n WINDSHIELD WIPER

wire /waɪər/ n **1** [C;U] (piece of) thin threadlike metal: a wire fence | electric wires **2** [C] TELEGRAM ♦ vt **1** connect up wires in (esp. an electrical system) **2** fasten with wire(s) **3** send a TELEGRAM to –**wiring** n [U] system of (electric) wires **wiry** adj thin, but with strong muscles

wire·less /'waɪərlɪs/ n old-fash radio

wire-tap·ping /'·ˌ··/ n [U] listening secretly to other people's telephone conversations with an electrical connection

wis·dom /'wɪzdəm/ n [U] quality of being wise

wisdom tooth /'·· ˌ·/ n large back tooth that grows later than the others

wise¹ /waɪz/ adj **1** sensible **2** having long experience and much knowledge **3** none the wiser knowing no more, after being told **4** -**wise: a** in the manner of **b** in the direction of: clockwise **c** in connection with: taxwise ~**ly** adv

wise² v wise up phr vi/t (cause to) learn or become conscious of the true situation or true nature of someone or something

wise·crack /'waɪzkræk/ vi, n (make) a clever joke

wise guy /'· ·/ n annoying person who pretends to know everything

wish /wɪʃ/ **1** vt want (something impossible): I wish I hadn't agreed. | I wish I were a bird. **2** vi want and try to cause something (as if) by magic: If you wish hard enough you may get what you want. **3** vt hope that (someone) will have (something), esp. expressed as a greeting: We wished him a safe journey. **4** vt fml want ♦ n **1** feeling of wanting something: the wish for these peace talks to succeed **2** thing wished for **3** attempt to make a wanted thing happen (as if) by magic

wish·bone /'wɪʃboʷn/ n chicken bone shaped like a V pulled apart before making a wish

wishful think·ing /ˌwɪʃfəl 'θɪŋkɪŋ/ n false belief that something is true or will happen simply because one wishes it

wish·y-wash·y /'wɪʃiʲ ˌwɒʃiʲ, -ˌwɔʃiʲ/ adj without determination or clear aims and principles

wisp /wɪsp/ n small twisted bunch, piece (of something): a wisp of hair/steam ~**y** adj

wist·ful /'wɪstfəl/ adj sad because of unfulfilled hopes or thoughts of the past ~**ly** adv ~**ness** n [U]

wit¹ /wɪt/ n **1** [U] ability to say clever amusing things **2** [C] witty person **3** [U] also wits pl — power of thought; cleverness: He hadn't the wit to say no. | (fig.) It scared me out of my wits. (= very much) **4** at one's wits end too worried by difficulties to know what to do next **5** have/keep one's wits about one ready to act quickly and sensibly ~**ty** adj having or showing WIT¹ (1) ~**tily** adv

wit² v to wit lit or law that is (to say)

witch /wɪtʃ/ n woman with magic powers

witch·craft /'wɪtʃkræft/ n [U] performing of magic

witch-doc·tor /'wɪtʃˌdɑktər/ n man who cures people by magic

witch-hunt /'·· ·/ n search for people with disliked political views, in order to remove them from power

with /wɪð, wɪθ/ prep **1** in the presence or company of: I went to the movies with Jim. **2** having: a book with a green cover **3** by means of; using: Cut it with scissors. | Fill it with jam. **4** in support of: Are you with us or against us? **5** against: competing with foreign companies **6** with regard to; in the case of: Be careful with that glass. | He's in love with you. **7** at the same time and rate as: *This wine improves with age.* **8** (used in comparisons): *The window is level with the street.* **9** in spite of: *With all his faults, I still like him.* **10** because of: *trembling with fear* **11 in with** a friend of (a person or group) **12 with it** giving proper attention to what is going on **13 with me/you** following my/your argument: *I'm not with you, what do you mean?* **14 with that** at once after that; then

with·draw /wɪð'drɔ, wɪθ-/ *v* **-drew** /-'druʷ/, **-drawn** /-'drɔn/ **1** *vt* take away or back: *She withdrew $50 from her bank account.* | *I withdraw that remark.* **2** *vi/t* move away or back: *I withdrew from* (= left) *the room.* **3** *vi/t* (cause to) not take part: *She withdrew from the election.* **~al** *n* [C;U] (act of) withdrawing **-drawn** *adj* quiet and not interested in other people

with·draw·al symp·toms /·'·· ˌ·'·/ *n* [P] painful or unpleasant effects which are the result of breaking or stopping a habit, esp. the taking of a drug

with·er /'wɪðər/ *vi/t* (cause to) become dry, pale, and lifeless: *The heat had withered the plants.* **~ing** *adj* sharply severe: *withering scorn*

with·hold /wɪθ'hoʷld, wɪð-/ *vt* **-held** /-'held/ refuse to give: *withhold payment*

withholding tax /·'·· ˌ·/ *n* money taken from one's wages and used to pay income tax

with·in /wɪ'ðɪn, wɪ'θɪn/ *adv, prep* **1** not more than: *He'll arrive within an hour.* **2** inside: *within the city limits*

with·out /wɪ'ðaʊt, wɪ'θaʊt/ *prep, adv* **1** not having; lacking: *a jar without a lid* | *He went out without telling me.* **2 do/go without** continue as usual in spite of the lack (of)

with·stand /wɪθ'stænd, wɪð-/ *vt* **-stood** /-'stud/ bear or support

wit·ness /'wɪtnɪs/ *n* **1** person who saw something happen **2** person who gives information to a court of law **3** person who watches another sign an official paper, and then signs it as proof of having seen the first signer **4 bear witness to** show or prove (a quality) ♦ *vt* **1** be present at and see **2** watch or sign as a WITNESS (3) **3** be a sign or proof of

witness stand /'·· ˌ·/ *n* enclosed area where witnesses stand in a court

wit·ti·cis·m /'wɪtəˌsɪzəm/ *n* clever amusing remark

wives /waɪvz/ *pl. of* WIFE – see also OLD WIVES' TALE

wiz·ard /'wɪzərd/ *n* **1** (in stories) old man with magical powers **2** extremely skillful person: *a computer wizard* **~ry** *n* [U]

wiz·ened /'wɪzənd/ *adj* (as if) dried up, with lines on the skin

wob·ble /'wɑbəl/ *vi/t* move in an unsteady manner from side to side: *Don't wobble the table.* **wobble** *n* **-bly** *adj* wobbling: *wobbly legs*

woe /woʷ/ *n fml or lit* **1** [U] great sorrow **2** [C] trouble **~ful** *adj* **1** *esp. lit* very sad **2** (of something bad) very great: *woeful ignorance* **~fully** *adv*

wok /wɑk/ *n* deep round Chinese cooking pan

woke /woʷk/ *v past t. of* WAKE

wok·en /'woʷkən/ *v past p. of* WAKE

wolf /wʊlf/ *n* **wolves** /wʊlvz/ **1** fierce wild animal of the dog family **2** man who wants women for sex only **3 cry wolf** call for help unnecessarily **4 keep the wolf from the door** earn enough to eat and live **5 a wolf in sheep's clothing** person who seems harmless but is hiding evil intentions ♦ *vt* eat quickly in large amounts

wolf whis·tle /'· ˌ··/ *n* whistle of admiration for an attractive woman

wom·an /'wʊmən/ *n* **women** /'wɪmɪn/ **1** adult female person **2** women in general **3** female nature or qualities **4 woman of the world** an experienced woman who knows how people behave **~hood** *n* [U] quality or time of being a woman **~ly** *adj* having good qualities suitable to a woman

wom·an·ize /'wʊməˌnaɪz/ *vi* (of a man) habitually pay attention to many women for sexual purposes **-izer** *n*

womb /wuʷm/ *n* round organ inside female MAMMALS in which young develop

women's move·ment /'·· ˌ··/ *n* [*the*+S] (all the women who join in making) a united effort to improve the social and political position of women

won /wʌn/ *v past t. and p. of* WIN

won·der /'wʌndər/ *n* **1** [U] feeling of strangeness, surprise, and usu. admiration **2** [C] wonderful or surprising thing **3 do/work wonders** bring unexpectedly good results **4 (it's) no/little/small wonder** it is not surprising; naturally ♦ *vi/t* **1** express a wish to know, in words or silently: *I wonder how you work this machine.* **2** be surprised: *We wondered at the life she chose.* ♦ *adj* unusually good or effective: *a wonder drug* **~ful** *adj* unusually good; causing pleasure or admiration **~fully** *adv* **~ment** *n* [U] WONDER (1)

won·drous /ˈwʌndrəs/ adj lit wonderful

wont /woʊnt, wɒnt, wɑnt, wʌnt/ adj fml likely (to) ♦ n [S] fml what the stated person usually does ~ **ed** adj fml customary

won't /woʊnt/ short for: will not

woo /wuː/ vt 1 lit try to make (a woman) love and marry one 2 try to gain the support of

wood /wʊd/ n 1 [U] substance of which trees are made 2 [C] also **woods** pl. — trees where trees grow, smaller than a forest 3 [the+S] barrels 4 **out of the woods** free from danger, difficulty, etc. ~ **ed** adj covered with trees ~ **en** adj 1 made of wood 2 stiff; unbending ~ **y** adj of or like wood

wood·chuck /ˈwʊdtʃʌk/ also **groundhog** — n small furry animal that lives underground and sleeps all winter

wood·land /ˈwʊdlənd, -lænd/ **woodlands** pl. — n [U] wooded country

wood·peck·er /ˈwʊdˌpekər/ n bird with a long beak that makes holes in trees

wood·wind /ˈwʊdˌwɪnd/ n [U;P] (players of) WIND INSTRUMENTS made of wood

wood·work /ˈwʊdwɜrk/ n [U] 1 skill of making wooden objects 2 parts of a house that are made of wood

wood·worm /ˈwʊdwɜrm/ n [U] damaged condition of wood caused by the young of certain BEETLES, which make holes

woof¹ /wʊf/ n, interj sound made by a dog

woof² /wuf, wuːf/ n thread running across a cloth

woof·er /ˈwʊfər/ n LOUDSPEAKER that gives out deep sounds

wool /wʊl/ n [U] 1 soft thick hair of sheep 2 material made from this 3 **pull the wool over someone's eyes** trick someone by hiding the facts ~ **en** — adj made of wool ~ **ly** adj 1 of or like wool 2 (of thoughts) not clear in the mind

wool·gath·er·ing /ˈwʊlˌgæðərɪŋ/ n [U] thinking of other things instead of what one should be paying attention to

woo·zy /ˈwuːziʸ, ˈwʊziʸ/ adj infml having an unsteady feeling in the head –**iness** n [U]

word /wɜrd/ n 1 [C] (written representation of) one or more sounds which can be spoken to represent an idea, object, etc. 2 [S] shortest (type of) statement: Don't say a word (= anything) about it to anyone. 3 [S] short conversation: I'd like a word with you. 4 [U] message or piece of news: He sent word that he wanted

to see me. 5 [S] promise: I give you my word that I'll do it. 6 [C] suggestion or recommendation (RECOMMEND): Put in a good word for her 7 **by word of mouth** by speaking and not by writing 8 **eat one's words** admit to having said something wrong 9 **get a word in edgeways** infml get a chance to speak 10 **have a word with someone** (speak to someone) secretly, esp. giving advice or asking a question 11 **(have) the last word (on)** (make) the remark which finishes an argument, etc. 12 **have words (with)** argue angrily (with) 13 **in other words** expressing the same thing in different words 14 **(not) in so many words** (not) directly expressed in those words but only suggested 15 **put words in(to) someone's mouth: a** tell someone what to say **b** claim falsely that someone has said a particular thing 16 **take someone's word for it** accept what someone says as correct 17 **the last word in** the most recent development in 18 **word for word** in exactly the same words ♦ vt express in words ~ **ing** n [U] words in which something is expressed ~ **y** adj using or containing more words than necessary

word-per·fect /ˌ· ˈ···/ adj repeating or remembering every word correctly

word pro·cess·or /ˈ· ˌ···/ n small computer for esp. ordinary office work

wore /wɔr, woʷr/ v past t. of WEAR

work¹ /wɜrk/ n 1 [U] activity done to produce something or gain a result rather than for amusement 2 [U] job; business: I go to work by train. 3 [U] something produced by work, esp. of the hands: This mat is my own work. (= I made it) | (fig.) The murder was the work of a madman. 4 [C] object produced by painting, writing, etc.: a work of art | the works of Shakespeare 5 **all in a day's work** not unusual 6 **at work (on)** doing something, esp. work 7 **go/set to work (on)** start doing 8 **have one's work cut out** have something difficult to do, esp. in the time allowed 9 **in/out of work** having a job/unemployed 10 **make short work of** finish quickly and easily – see also WORKS

work² v 1 vi do an activity which uses effort, esp. as one's job: She works at the factory. 2 vi (of a machine, plan, etc.) operate (properly): It works by electricity. | Your plan will never work. 3 vt make (a person) do work: They work us too hard. 4 vt make (a machine) do work: How do you work this thing?

5 *vt* make (one's way) by work or effort **6** *vi/t* make or become by small movements: *This little screw has worked itself loose.* **7** *vt* produce (an effect): *This medicine works wonders.* **8** *vt* arrange, esp. unofficially: *We'll work it so that we can all go together.* **9** *vi* move or act for a certain result: *This will work against you in the future.* – **able** *adj* which can be put into effect; usable: *a workable plan* – **er** *n* **1** person who works: *an office worker* **2** member of the WORKING CLASS

work off *phr vt* get rid of by work or effort: *He worked off his anger by chopping wood.*

work out *phr v* **1** *vt* calculate (the answer to) **2** *vi* have a result; develop: *The plan worked out very well in practice.* **3** *vt* plan; decide: *We're trying to work out how to get there.* **4** *vi* reach the stated amount by being calculated: *The cost works out at $10 each.* **5** *vi* exercise

work up *phr vt* **1** excite the feelings of: *He gets very worked up* (= anxious and upset) *about exams.* **2** cause oneself to have: *I couldn't work up much enthusiasm for it.*

work·a·day /ˈwɜrkəˌdeⁱ/ *adj* ordinary and/or dull

work·a·hol·ic /ˌwɜrkəˈhɒlɪk, -ˈhɑ-/ *n* person who likes to work too hard

work·bench /ˈwɜrkbentʃ/ *n* (a table with) a hard surface for working on with tools

work·book /ˈwɜkbʊk/ *n* school book with questions and exercises

work·day /ˈwɜrkdeⁱ/ *n* day when one works at a regular job, esp. Monday through Friday

work·force /ˈ··ˌ·/ *n* all the workers in a factory or in industry generally

work·horse /ˈwɜrkhɔrs/ *n* person who does most of the (dull) work

work·house /ˈwɜrkhaʊs/ *n* -houses /ˌhaʊzɪz/ prison school for young offenders

work·ing /ˈwɜrkɪŋ/ *adj* **1** used for work: *working clothes* **2** (of time) spent in work **3** useful as a base for further development: *a working hypothesis*

working class /ˈ·· ˌ·/ *n* social class of people who work with their hands **working-class** *adj*

working knowl·edge /ˌ·· ˈ··/ *n* [S] enough practical knowledge to do something

working or·der /ˌ·· ˈ··/ *n* [U] state of working well, with no trouble

working pa·pers /ˈ·· ˌ·/ *n* legal papers giving the right to work, esp. as needed by foreigners

working par·ty /ˈ·· ˌ·/ *n* committee which examines and reports on a particular matter

work·ings /ˈwɜrkɪŋz/ *n* [P] **1** way something works or acts: *the workings of an engine / of his mind* **2** parts of a mine which have been dug out

work·load /ˈwɜrkloʷd/ *n* amount of work that a person or machine is expected to do in a particular period of time

work·man /ˈwɜrkmən/ *n* -men /-mən/ man who works with his hands, esp. in a particular skill or trade ~ **like** *adj* showing the qualities of a good workman ~ **ship** *n* [U] (signs of) skill in making things

work·out /ˈwɜrkaʊt/ *n* period of physical exercise

works /wɜrks/ *n* **works 1** [P] moving parts of a machine **2** [C] factory: *a dye works* **3** give someone the **works** *sl* **a** give someone everything: *They gave us supper, wine, chocolates, the works.* **b** attack violently

work·shop /ˈwɜrkʃɒp/ *n* **1** room where heavy repairs and jobs on machines are done **2** period of group activity and study: *a drama workshop*

work·top /ˈwɜrktɒp/ *n* flat surface in a kitchen for preparing food

world /wɜrld/ *n* **1** [the-S] **a** the Earth: *the richest man in the world* **b** particular part of it: *the Old World* **2** [the-S] the universe **3** [the-S] group of living things: *the animal world* **4** [the-S] particular area of human activity: *the world of football* **5** [the-S] people generally: *We don't want the whole world* (= everyone) *to know about it.* **6** [the-S] human life and its affairs: *the ways of the world* **7** [C] PLANET: *life on other worlds* **8** large number or amount: *This medicine did me a world of good.* **9** [the-S] *fml* material standards: *to give up the world to serve God* **10** all the world to very important to **11** for all the world like/as if exactly like/as if **12** (have) the best of both worlds (to have) the advantage which each choice offers, without having to choose between them **13** in the world (in a question expressing surprise): *Where in the world have you been?* **14** not for the world certainly not: *I wouldn't hurt her for the world.* **15** on top of the world very happy **16** out of this world unusually good; wonderful **17** worlds apart completely different ~ **ly** *adj* **1** material: *my worldly goods* (= everything I own) **2** too much concerned with human society, rather than religious things ~ **liness** *n* [U]

world-beat·er /ˈ· ˌ··/ *n* person or thing thought able to compete successfully with anyone/anything in the world

world-class /ˌ· ˈ·◁/ adj among the best in the world

world-fam·ous /ˌ· ˈ··◁/ adj known all over the world

world pow·er /ˌ· ˈ··/ n nation with very great power and influence

world-wear·y /ˌ· ˈ··◁/ adj tired of life

world·wide /ˌwɜrld'waid◁/ adj, adv in or over all the world

worm /wɜrm/ n 1 small thin creature with no bones or limbs, like a tube of flesh 2 worthless, cowardly, etc., person ♦ vt move by twisting or effort: We wormed our way through the crack in the wall. | (fig.) He wormed his way into her affections.

worn /wɔrn, woʷrn/ v past p. of WEAR

worn-out /ˌ· ˈ·◁/ adj 1 no longer usable 2 very tired

wor·ry /ˈwʌriʸ, ˈwʌriʸ/ v 1 vi/t (cause to) be anxious or uncomfortable: worrying about the exams | Heights don't worry me. 2 vt (esp. of a dog) chase and bite (an animal) ♦ n [C;U] 1 feeling of anxiety 2 (person or thing that causes) anxiety –ried adj anxious ~ing adj

wor·ry·wart /ˈwɜriʸˌwɔrt, ˈwʌ-/ n infml person who worries a lot about unimportant things

worse /wɜrs/ adj 1 (comparative of BAD) of lower quality; more bad 2 more ill (than before) 3 none the worse (for) not harmed (by) 4 the worse for wear harmed by use over a period ♦ adv in a worse way or to a worse degree ♦ n [U] something worse **worsen** vi/t (cause to) become worse

wor·ship /ˈwɜrʃɪp/ n [U] (showing of) strong (religious) feelings of love, respect, and admiration ♦ vi/t show worship (to): to worship God | She worships her brother. (= admires him (too) greatly) ~er n

worst /wɜrst/ adj (superlative of BAD) of lowest quality; most bad ♦ n 1 worst worst thing or part: These ones are the worst. 2 at (the) worst if the worst happens 3 get the worst of suffer most from 4 if worst comes to worst if there is no better way 5 (in) the worst way very much ♦ adv (superlative of BADly) most badly: the worst-dressed man in the office

wor·sted /ˈwʊstɪd, ˈwɜrstɪd/ n [U] wool cloth

worth /wɜrθ/ prep 1 of the stated value: a painting worth $5000 2 deserving: That film isn't worth seeing. 3 for all one is worth with all possible effort 4 for what it's worth though I'm not sure it's of any value 5 worth it useful; worth-

while 6 worth one's salt worthy of respect or of being so called 7 worth one's/someone's while worthwhile to one/someone ♦ n [U] value ~less adj 1 of no value 2 (of a person) of bad character

worth·while /ˌwɜrθ'hwail◁, -'wail◁/ adj with a good enough result to deserve the trouble taken

wor·thy /ˈwɜrðiʸ/ adj 1 deserving respect or serious attention 2 deserving: worthy of admiration 3 good but not very exciting or interesting –thily adv –thiness n [U]

would /d, əd, wəd; strong wʊd/ v aux 1 (past of will): They said they would meet us at 10:30. 2 (shows what is likely or possible): What would you do if you won a million dollars? 3 (shows what always happened): We would meet for a drink after work. 4 (shows choice): I'd rather have eggs. 5 (expressing a polite request): Would you lend me your pencil?

would-be /ˈ· ·/ adj which one wants or intends to be, but isn't: a would-be musician

wouldn't /ˈwʊdnt/ short for: would not

wound[1] /wuʷnd/ n damaged place on the body, esp. caused by a weapon: a bullet wound ♦ vt cause a wound to: a wounded leg | (fig.) wounded pride

wound[2] /waʊnd/ v past t. and p. of WIND[2]

wound-up /ˌwaʊnd 'ʌp◁/ adj anxiously excited

wove /woʷv/ v past t. of WEAVE

wov·en /ˈwoʷvən/ v past p. of WEAVE

wow /waʊ/ interj infml (expresses surprise and admiration) ♦ n [S] sl a great success ♦ vt sl cause surprise and admiration in someone

wraith /reʸθ/ n lit for GHOST

wran·gle /ˈræŋgəl/ v, n (take part in) an angry or noisy quarrel

wrap /ræp/ vt -pp- 1 cover in material folded over: I wrapped the box in brown paper. | She had a bandage wrapped around her finger. 2 wrap someone around one's little finger make someone do what one wants ♦ n 1 garment for covering a woman's shoulders 2 under wraps secret ~per n loose paper cover ~ping n [C;U] material for folding around and covering something

wrap up phr vt 1 wear warm clothes 2 complete (a business arrangement, meeting, etc.) 3 summarize (SUMMARY) 4 wrapped up in giving complete attention to

wrap-up /ˈ· ·/ n SUMMARY

wrath /ræθ/ n [U] fml or lit strong fierce anger ~ful adj

wreak /riʸk/ vt esp. lit perform or bring about (something violent or unpleasant)

wreath /riʸθ/ n usu. circular arrangement of flowers or leaves **a** given at a funeral **b** placed on the head as a sign of honor **c** used as Christmas decoration

wreathe /riʸð/ vt esp. lit circle around and cover completely: Mist wreathed the hilltops.

wreck /rek/ n **1** [C] sunken or destroyed ship **2** [C] something in a very bad condition: Have you seen the old wreck he drives around in! **3** [U] fml ruin; destruction: the wreck of our hopes **4** [C] person whose health is destroyed ♦ vt destroy: a ship wrecked on the rocks | The bad weather wrecked our plans. ~**age** n [U] broken parts of a destroyed thing

wren /ren/ n very small brown bird

wrench /rentʃ/ vt **1** pull hard with a twist **2** twist and damage (a joint of the body) ♦ n **1** act of or damage caused by wrenching **2** separation that causes suffering of the mind **3** metal tool with jaws or a hollow end, for twisting NUTS (2)

wrest /rest/ vt **1** pull (away) violently **2** esp. lit obtain with difficulty

wres·tle /ˈresəl/ vi/t fight by trying to hold or throw one's opponent: (fig.) wrestling with a difficult problem **–tler** n person who wrestles as a sport

wretch /retʃ/ n **1** unfortunate person **2** annoying person

wretch·ed /ˈretʃɪd/ adj **1** very unhappy **2** of a bad type which makes one unhappy: a wretched headache **3** annoying: Why can't that wretched child behave himself! ~**ly** adv ~**ness** n [U]

wrig·gle /ˈrɪɡəl/ vi/t move from side to side: He wriggled uncomfortably on the hard seat. ♦ n wriggling movement

wriggle out of phr vt escape (a difficulty) by clever tricks

wring /rɪŋ/ vt wrung /rʌŋ/, ringing **1** twist or press (wet clothes) to remove (water) **2** twist (the neck) hard, causing death **3** press hard on, esp. hands: wringing her hands in sorrow **4** obtain by severe or cruel methods: Her torturers wrung a confession out of her. **5** **wringing wet** very wet ~**er** n machine for wringing clothes

wrin·kle /ˈrɪŋkəl/ n **1** small line or fold, esp. on the skin owing to age **2** infml useful suggestion or trick ♦ vi/t (cause to) form wrinkles **–kly** adj

wrist /rɪst/ n joint between the hand and the arm

wrist·watch /ˈrɪst-wɑtʃ/ n watch with a band for fastening around the wrist

writ /rɪt/ n official legal paper telling someone (not) to do a particular thing

write /raɪt/ v wrote /roʷt/, written /ˈrɪtn/ **1** vi/t make (marks representing letters or words) with a tool, esp. a pen or pencil **2** vt think of and record, esp. on paper: He wrote a report on the match. **3** vt complete by writing words: write a check **4** vi/t produce and send (a letter): He writes to me every week. **5** vi be a writer (of books, plays, etc.): She writes for television. **6** **be written on/all over** clearly showing because of the expression on: Guilt was written all over his face. **7** **writ large** lit on a larger or grander scale **writer** n **writing** n [U] **1 a** anything written by hand **b** style of writing by hand **2** written work or form: Put it down in writing. **3** activity of writing books, etc. **writings** n [P] written works

write away phr vi write to a far-off place, esp. to buy something

write down phr vt record (esp. what has been said) in writing

write off phr vt **1** accept as lost or useless or as a failure **2** remove (esp. a debt) from the record **3** write away

write out phr vt write in full

write up phr vt write (again) in a complete and useful form **write-up** /ˈ· ·/ n written report giving a judgment

writhe /raɪð/ vi twist the body (as if) in great pain

writ·ten /ˈrɪtn/ v past p. of WRITE

wrong /rɒŋ/ adj **1** not correct: the wrong answer **2** morally bad **3** not in a proper or healthy state: There's something wrong with the engine. **4** not suitable: the wrong time to visit ♦ adv **1** wrongly **2** **go wrong: a** stop working properly **b** make a mistake **c** end badly ♦ n **1** [U] morally bad behavior **2** [C] fml unjust or bad action **3** **in the wrong** mistaken or deserving blame ♦ vt be unfair to or cause to suffer ~**ful** adj unjust or illegal: wrongful arrest ~**fully** adv

wrong·do·ing /ˌrɒŋˈduʷɪŋ, ˈrɒŋˌduʷɪŋ/ n [C;U] (example of) bad or illegal behavior **wrongdoer** n [C]

wrote /roʷt/ v past t. of WRITE

wrought /rɔt/ adj lit made: wrought of steel

wrought i·ron /ˌ· ˈ··◂/ n [U] iron shaped into a useful, pleasing form

wrung /rʌŋ/ v past t. and p. of WRING

wry /raɪ/ adj showing a mixture of amusement and dislike, disappointment, etc.: a wry smile ~**ly** adv

X, x¹ /ɛks/ the 24th letter of the English alphabet

X² *adj* (of a film) which is not suitable for persons under 18

xen·o·pho·bi·a /ˌzɛnəˈfoʷbiʸə/ *n* [U] unreasonable fear and dislike of foreigners —**bic** *adj*

Xe·rox /ˈzɪərɑks, ˈziʸrɑks/ *vt, n* *tdmk* (make) a photographic copy on an electric copying machine

X·mas /ˈkrɪsməs, ˈɛksməs/ *n infml* CHRISTMAS

X-ray /ˈɛks reʸ/ *n* **1** powerful unseen beam which can pass through solid things, used esp. for photographing conditions inside the body **2** photograph taken with this **3** medical examination with this **x-ray** *vt* photograph, examine, or treat with X-rays

xy·lo·phone /ˈzaɪləˌfoʷn/ *n* musical instrument with many small wooden bars hit with a hammer

Y

Y, y /waɪ/ the 25th letter of the English alphabet

yacht /jɒt/ n 1 light sailing boat used esp. for racing 2 large pleasure boat with a motor **–ing** n [U] sailing in a yacht

yachts·man /ˈjɒtsmən/ **yachts·woman** /-ˌwʊmən/ fem. — n -men /-mən/ sailor in a yacht

yak¹ /jæk/ n cow of central Asia with long hair

yak² vi **-kk-** derog talk continuously about unimportant things

yam /jæm/ n tropical plant with a root eaten as a vegetable

yank /jæŋk/ vi/t pull suddenly and sharply **yank** n

Yank also **Yan·kee** /ˈjæŋkiʸ/ n derog — American person esp. from the north

yap /jæp/ vi **-pp-** derog 1 (of a dog) BARK continuously 2 talk noisily about unimportant things

yard¹ /jɑrd/ n a measure of length equal to 3 feet or .9144 meters

yard² n 1 area around a house with grass, flowers and trees 2 area enclosed for the stated activity or business: a lumberyard

yard·arm /ˈjɑrd-ɑrm/ n either end of a long pole that supports a sail

yard sale /ˈ· ·/ n sale of used articles

yard·stick /ˈjɑrdˌstɪk/ n 1 measuring stick one yard long 2 standard of measurement or comparison

yar·mul·ke /ˈjɑrməlkə, ˈjɑməkə/ n special small hat worn by Jewish men

yarn /jɑrn/ n 1 [U] long continuous thread used esp. in making cloth [C] story

yaw /jɔ/ vi (of a ship, aircraft, etc.) turn to the side out of the proper course

yawn /jɔn/ vi 1 open the mouth wide and breathe deeply, esp. from tiredness 2 be(come) wide open: a yawning chasm ♦ n 1 act of yawning 2 infml something dull

yd written abbrev. for: YARD(s)¹

ye /jiʸ/ pron lit (used of more than 1 person) you

yea /jeʸ/ adv lit yes

yeah /jeə/ adv infml yes

year /jɪər/ n 1 period of 365 (or 366) days, or 12 months, esp. as measured from January 1st to December 31st 2 period of about a year in the life of an organization: the school year 3 all the year round during the whole year 4 year after year continuously for many years 5 year in, year out regularly each year **~ly** adj, adv (happening) every year or once a year

year·ling /ˈjɪərlɪŋ/ n animal between 1 and 2 years old

year·long /ˈjɪərlɒŋ/ adj lasting a whole year

yearn /jɜrn/ vi esp. lit have a strong (sad) desire: I yearn for your return. **~ing** n [C;U] esp. lit strong desire

yeast /jiʸst/ n [U] form of very small plant with a chemical action used for producing alcohol in making wine and beer and for making bread light and soft **–y** adj

yell /jɛl/ vi/t, n shout

yel·low /ˈjɛloʷ/ adj 1 of the color of gold 2 infml cowardly ♦ vi/t (cause to) become yellow **~ish** adj

yellow fe·ver /ˌ·· ˈ··/ n [U] serious tropical disease

yellow pag·es /ˈ·· ˌ··/ n [P] book with telephone numbers of businesses

yelp /jɛlp/ vi, n (make) a sharp high cry, esp. of pain

yen¹ /jɛn/ n yen unit of Japanese money

yen² n strong desire

yes /jɛs/ adv 1 (used for accepting or agreeing) 2 (used for replying to a call)

yes-man /ˈ· ·/ n derog someone who always agrees with their leader or employer

yes·ter·day /ˈjɛstərdiʸ, -ˌdeʸ/ adv, n (on) the day before today

yes·ter·year /ˈjɛstərˌyɪər/ n [U] esp. lit the recent past

yet /jɛt/ adv 1 up until this time: He hasn't arrived yet. 2 in the future, and in spite of how things seem now: We may yet win. 3 even: a yet bigger problem 4 still: I have yet to be told. (= I have still not been told) 5 as yet YET (1) ♦ conj but even so: strange yet true

yet·i /ˈjɛtiʸ/ n large hairy manlike animal said to live in the Himalaya mountains

yew /yuʷ/ n tree with small dark leaves and red berries

Yid·dish /ˈjɪdɪʃ/ adj, n (language) of European Jews

yield /jiʸld/ v 1 vt produce: a tree which yields a large crop 2 vt fml give up control of: yield a position of advantage 3 vi fml or lit admit defeat 4 vi allow other traffic to go first ♦ n amount produced: a high yield of fruit **–ing** adj 1 not stiff or fixed 2 (too) easily persuaded

yip·pee /ˈyɪpiʸ, yɪˈpiʸ/ interj (shout of delight or success)

yo·del /ˈyoʷdl/ vi/t **-l-** sing with many changes between the natural voice and a very high voice

yo·ga /ˈyoʷgə/ n [U] Hindu system of control of the mind and body, often including special exercises

yo·gurt, yoghurt /ˈyoʷgərt/ n [U] milk that has thickened and turned slightly acid through the action of certain bacteria

yo·gi /ˈyoʷgiʸ/ n person who practices (and teaches) yoga

yoke /yoʷk/ n **1** bar joining 2 animals for pulling a vehicle or heavy load **2** frame across someone's shoulders for carrying 2 equal loads **3** lit controlling power: *the hated yoke of their conquerors* **4** part of garment from which the rest hangs ♦ vt join (as if) with a yoke

yo·kel /ˈyoʷkəl/ n simple or foolish country person

yolk /yoʷk/ n [C;U] yellow part of an egg

yon·der /ˈyɑndər/ adj, adv that; over there

yore /yɔr/ n [U] lit very long time ago

you /yə, yu; strong yuʷ/ pron (used as subject or object) **1** person or people being spoken to: *I love you.* **2** anyone; one: *You can't trust such people.* **3** (used for addressing someone, esp. angrily): *You fool!*

you'd /yəd, yud; strong yuʷd/ short for: **1** you had **2** you would

you'll /yəl, yul; strong yuʷl/ short for: **1** you will **2** you shall

young /yʌŋ/ adj **younger** /ˈyʌŋgər/, **youngest** /ˈyʌŋgɪst/ in an early stage of life or development ♦ n [P] **1** young people generally **2** young animals

young·ster /ˈyʌŋstər/ n person

your /yər; strong yuər, yɔr, yoʷr/ determiner of you: *your house*

you're /yər; strong yuər, yɔr, yoʷr/ short for: you are

yours /yuərz, yɔrz, yoʷrz/ pron **1** of you; your one(s) **2** (used at the end of a letter): *Sincerely yours, Janet Smith.* **3 yours truly: a** (polite phrase written at the end of a letter) **b** infml I; me; myself

your·self /yərˈsɛlf/ pron −**selves** /-ˈsɛlvz/ **1** (reflexive form of **you**): *Don't hurt yourself.* **2** (strong form of **you**): *Did you make it yourself?* **3** (**all**) **by yourself: a** alone **b** without help **4 to yourself** not shared

youth /yuʷθ/ n **youths** /yuʷðz, yuʷθs/ **1** [U] period of being young **2** [C] often derog young person, esp. male **3** [U;P] young people as a group: *the youth of today* ~**ful** adj (seeming) young

you've /yəv, yuv; strong yuʷv/ short for: you have

yuck·y /ˈyʌkiʸ/ adj infml extremely unpleasant

yule /yuʷl/ n [U] lit for CHRISTMAS

yup·pie, yuppy /ˈyʌpiʸ/ n young person in a professional job with a high income, esp. one who enjoys spending money and having a fashionable way of life

Z

Z, z /ziʲ/ the 26th and last letter of the English alphabet

za·ny /ˈzeʲniʲ/ adj amusingly foolish

zap /zæp/ v **-pp-** infml **1** vt attack and/or destroy **2** vi/t move quickly and forcefully **-py** adj full of life and force

zeal /ziʲl/ n [U] fml eagerness ~**ous** /ˈzeləs/ adj eager; keen ~**ously** adv

zeal·ot /ˈzelət/ n someone who is (too) eager in their beliefs

ze·bra /ˈziʲbrə/ n **-bra** or **-bras** horselike African animal with broad black and white lines

zen·ith /ˈziʲniθ/ n highest or greatest point of development, success, etc.

ze·ro¹ /ˈziʲəroʷ, ˈziʲroʷ/ n **-ros** or **-roes 1** (sign representing) the number 0 **2** point between + and − on a scale: *The temperature was below zero.* **2** nothing: *zero growth*

zero² v zero in on phr vt **1** aim a weapon directly at **2** aim one's attention directly towards

zero hour /ˈ·· ·/ n [U] time at which something important is to begin

zest /zest/ n **1** [S;U] pleasantly exciting quality: *The danger adds zest to the affair.* **2** [S;U] eagerness: *a zest for life* **-ful** adj

zig·zag /ˈzɪgzæg/ vi n **-gg-** (go in) a line shaped like a row of z's: *The path zigzags up the hill.*

zil·lion /ˈzɪlyən/ also **zillions** pl. — determiner, n, pron infml extremely large number

zinc /zɪŋk/ n [U] blue-white metal

zing /zɪŋ/ n [U] exciting or spirited taste or quality

Zi·on·is·m /ˈzaɪəˌnɪzəm/ n [U] political movement to establish and develop a Jewish state in Israel **-ist** adj, n

zip¹ /zɪp/ vi **1** fasten with a ZIPPER **2** n vi/t move very quickly and forcefully

zip² n [U] exciting or spirited quality

zip·per /ˈzɪpər/ n fastener with 2 sets of teeth and a sliding piece that joins the edges of an opening by drawing the teeth together

zip code /ˈ· ·/ n numbers added to an address to make it more exact for delivering letters

zith·er /ˈzɪðər/ n flat musical instrument played by pulling sharply at its strings

zits /zɪts/ n [P] sl spots on the skin

zo·di·ac /ˈzoʷdiʲˌæk/ n [the+S] imaginary belt in space along which the sun, moon, and nearest PLANETS seem to travel, divided into 12 equal parts used in ASTROLOGY

zom·bie /ˈzɑmbiʲ/ n **1** derog someone who moves or acts very slowly or lifelessly **2** dead person made to move by magic

zone /zoʷn/ n area marked off from others by particular qualities or activities: *a war/danger zone* ♦ vt give a particular purpose to (an area): *a part of town zoned for industrial development* **zonal** adj

zonked /zɑŋkt/ adj infml extremely tired

zoo /zuʷ/ n zoos park where many types of wild animal are kept for show

zo·ol·o·gy /zoʷˈɑlədʒiʲ/ n [U] scientific study of animals adj **-gist** n **zoological** /ˌzoʷəˈlɑdʒɪkəl/ adj

zoom /zuʷm/ vi **1** go quickly with a loud noise **2** (of a cinema camera) move quickly between a distant and a close view **3** increase suddenly and greatly

zoom lens /ˈ· ˌ·/ n curved piece of glass by which a camera can zoom in and out while keeping the picture clear

zuc·chi·ni /zuʷˈkiʲniʲ/ n **-ni** or **-nis** green SQUASH

Word beginnings

Afro- /ˈæfrəʊ/ **1** of Africa: *an Afro-American* **2** African and: *Afro-Asian peoples*

Anglo- /ˈæŋɡləʊ/ **1** of England or Britain: *an Anglophile* (someone who loves Britain) **2** English or British and: *an Anglo-American treaty*

ante- /ˈænti/ before: *antediluvian* — compare POST-

anti- /ˈænti, ˈænti, ˈæntai/ against; not in favor of; trying to prevent or destroy: *an anticancer drug* | *an antitank gun* | *He's very anti-war* — compare PRO-

arch- /ɑːtʃ, ɑːk/ chief; main: *our archenemy*

astro- /ˈæstrəʊ, ˈæstrə/ of or about the stars and space: *astrophysics*

audio- /ˈɔːdiəʊ/ of, for, or using sound, esp. recorded sound: *audiovisual teaching aids* — compare VIDEO

Austro- /ˈɒstrəʊ, ə-/ **1** Australian and: *Austro-Malayan* **2** Austrian and: *the Austro-Italian border*

be- /bɪ/ (makes verbs and adjectives) cause to be or have: *bedecked with garlands* (=decorated) | *She befriended me.*

bi- /bai/ two; twice: *a biannual publication* (=coming out twice a year)

bio- /ˈbaiəʊ/ connected with the study of) living things: *biochemistry*

centi- /ˈsenti/ hundredth part: *a centimeter* (=a hundredth of a meter)

co- /kəʊ/ with; together: *my coauthor, who wrote the book with me*

counter- /ˈkaʊntər/ done in return or so as to have an opposite effect or make ineffective: *a counterattack* | *counterespionage operations*

cross- /krɒs/ going between the stated things: *cross-cultural influences*

de- /diː, di/ **1** (showing an opposite): *a depopulated area* (=which all or most of the population has left) **2** to remove: *to dethrone a king* | *to debug a computer program* **3** to make less: *devalue the currency*

deca- /ˈdekə/ ten: *a decaliter* (=ten liters)

deci- /ˈdesə/ tenth part: *a deciliter* (=a tenth of a liter)

dis- /dis/ **1** not; the opposite of: *I disagree.* | *He is dishonest.* **2** removal: *nuclear disarmament*

em- /im; em/ (before b, m or p) EN: *emboldened*

en- /in; en/ (makes verbs) cause to be (more): *Enlarge the hole.*

equi- /ˈiːkwi, ˈiːkwə/ equally: *two points equidistant from a third*

Euro- /ˈjʊərəʊ, ˈjʊərə/ of Europe, esp. the EEC: *the Europarliament*

ex- /eks/ former: *my ex-husband*

extra- /ˈekstrə/ not (usu.) included; beyond; outside: *extracurricular lessons* | *extravehicular activity by astronauts*

fore- /fɔː, fɔːr/ **1** before; in advance: *I was forewarned of their visit.* **2** in or at the front: *a boat's foresail*

foster- /ˈfɒstər, fə-/ giving or receiving parental care although not of the same family: *my fosterparents*

Franco- /ˈfræŋkəʊ/ **1** of France: *a Francophile* (=someone who loves France) **2** French and: *the Franco-Prussian war*

geo- /ˈdʒiːəʊ/ connected with the study of the Earth or its surface: *geophysics*

hecto- /ˈhektəʊ, -tə/ hundred: *a hectoliter* (=a hundred liters) — compare CENTI-

hydro- /ˈhaidrəʊ, -drə/ concerning or using water: *hydroelectricity*

hyper- /ˈhaipər/ very or too much: *hyperactive* | *hypercritical*

il- /i/ (before l) not: *illiberal*

im- /im/ (before b, m, or p) IN-: *impossible*

in- /in/ **1** not: *indecisive* | *insane* **2** inwards: *a sudden inrush of water*

inter- /ˈintər/ between or including both or all: *intercontinental travel* | *an interdominational marriage ceremony*

ir- /i/ (before r) not: *irrational*

kilo- /ˈkiːləʊ, -lə/ thousand: *a kilogram* (=a thousand grams) — compare MILLI-

mal- /mæl/ bad(ly); wrong(ly): *a malformed body* | *maladministration*

maxi- /ˈmæksi/ unusually large or long — compare MINI-

mega- /ˈmegə/ **1** million: *a ten-megaton nuclear bomb* **2** *sl* very great: *a movie megastar*

micro- /ˈmaikrəʊ, -krə/ **1** (esp. with scientific words) extremely small: *a microcomputer* **2** using a microscope: *microsurgery* **3** millionth part: *a microsecond* (=a millionth of a second)

mid- /mid/ middle; in the middle of: *midwinter* | *in the mid-Atlantic* | *She's in her mid-20s.* (=is about 25 years old)

milli- /ˈmilə/ thousandth part: *a milliliter* (=a thousandth of a liter) — compare KILO-

mini- /mɪniʸ/ unusually small or short: *a miniskirt* | *a TV miniseries*

mis- /mɪs/ **1** bad(ly); wrong(ly): *He mistreats his dog terribly.* | *I misheard what you said.* **2** lack of; opposite of: *mistrust* | *misfortune*

mono- /manoʷ, -nə/ one; single; UNI-: *monosyllabic* | *a monoplane* (with one wing on each side) — compare POLY-

multi- /mʌltiʸ, -tɪ, -tə/ many: *a multipurpose tool* | *a multistorey building*

non- /nɑn/ not: *nonaddictive* | *non-profitmaking*

over- /oʷvər/ **1** too much: *an overindulgent parent* | *an overcooked dish* — compare UNDER- **2** above; across: *We took the overland route.*

poly- /pɑliʸ/ many: *polysyllabic* — compare MONO-

post- /poʷst/ after; later than: *the postwar years* — compare PRE-

pre- /priʸ/ before; earlier than: *the prewar years* | *a prelunch drink* — compare POST-

pro- /proʷ/ in favor of; supporting: *a pro-democracy movement* — compare ANTI-

pseudo- /suʷdoʷ, -də/ only pretending to be; false: *pseudo-intellectuals*

psycho- /saɪkoʷ, -kə/ connected with (illness of) the mind: *psychotherapy* | *psychosexual disorders*

quasi- /kwɑziʸ, kweʸzaɪ/ seeming to be; almost like: *a quasijudicial function*

re- /riʸ, rɪ-/ again: *The body was dug up and then reburied*

self- /sɛlf/ or by oneself or itself: *a self-charging battery* | *self-deception* | *She's a completely self-taught musician.*

semi- /sɛmiʸ, sɛmaɪ/ **1** half: *a semicircle* **2** partly; incomplete(ly): *semipermanent* | *in the semidarkness*

step- /stɛp/ related through a parent who has remarried: *my stepfather*

sub- /sʌb/ **1** under, below: *subsoil* | *subzero temperatures* **2** smaller part of: *a subcategory* **3** less than; worse than: *subhuman intelligence* **4** next in rank below: *a sublieutenant* — compare SUPER-

super- /suʷpər/ greater or more than: *superhuman strength* | *supertankers* (=very large ships) *carrying oil* — compare SUB-

trans- /træns, trænz/ across; on or to the other side of: *a transatlantic flight*

tri- /traɪ/ three: *trilingual* (=speaking three languages)

ultra- /ʌltrə/ very, esp. too: *ultramodern* | *ultracautious*

un- /ʌn/ **1** (*makes adjectives and adverbs*) not: *uncomfortable* | *unfairly* | *unwashed* **2** (*makes verbs*) make or do the opposite of: *She tied a knot, and then untied it.*

under- /ʌndər/ **1** too little: *undercooked potatoes* | *underproduction* **2** below: *an underwater cable* — compare OVER-

uni- /yuʷnə/ one; single; MONO-: *unicellular*

vice- /vaɪs/ next in rank below: *the vice-chairman of the committee*

video- /vɪdiʸoʷ/ of, for, or using recorded pictures, esp. as produced by a VIDEO (2): *a videocassette*

Word endings

-able, ible /əbəl/ (*in adjectives*) that can have the stated thing done to it: *a washable fabric*

-age /ɪdʒ/ (*in nouns*) **1** the action or result of doing the stated thing: *to allow for shrinkage* (=getting smaller) | *several breakages* (=things broken) **2** the cost of doing the stated thing: *Postage is extra* **3** the state or rank of: *in his dotage*

-al /əl/ **1** (*in adjectives*) of; connected with: *autumnal mists* | *a musical performance* **2** (*in nouns*) (an) act of doing something: *the arrival of the bus* | *several rehearsals*

-an /ən/ -IAN: *the Republican candidate*

-ance /əns/ (*in nouns*) (an example of) the action, state or quality of doing or being the stated thing: *his sudden appearance* (=he appeared suddenly) | *her brilliance* (=she is BRILLIANT)

-ant /ənt/ (*in adjectives and nouns*) (person or thing) that does the stated thing: *in the resultant confusion* | *a bottle of disinfectant*

-ar /ər/ **1** (*in adjectives*) of; connected with; being: *the Polar regions* **2** (*in nouns*) -ER²: *a liar*

-arian /eəriʸən/ (*in nouns*) person who supports and believes in: *a libertarian* (=person who supports freedom)

-ary /eriʸ, əriʸ/ (*in adjectives*) being: *with his customary* (=usual) *caution* | *her legendary* (=very famous) *courage*

-ate /ɪt, eʸt/ **1** (*in verbs*) (cause to) become or have: *a hyphenated word* **2** (*in adjectives*) having: *a fortunate* (=lucky) *woman*

-ation /eʸʃən/ (*in nouns*) (an) act or result of doing the stated thing: *the continuation of the story*

-ative /ətɪv, eʸtɪv/ (*in adjectives*) **1** liking or tending to have or do: *argumentative* | *talkative* **2** for the purpose of doing the stated thing: *a consultative meeting*

-bound /baʊnd/ (*in adjectives*) limited, kept in, or controlled in the stated way: *a fog-bound aircraft*

-cy /siʸ/ (*makes nouns from adjectives ending in /t/ or /tɪk/*) -ITY: *several inaccuracies in the report*

-d /d, t/ (*after e*) -ED: *a wide-eyed stare*

-dom /dəm/ (*in nouns*) **1** the condition of being the stated thing: *freedom* | *boredom* **2** country or area ruled by: *a kingdom* **3** people of the stated sort: *despite the opposition of officialdom*

-ean /iʸən/ -IAN

-ed /d, ɪd, t/ **1** (*makes regular past t. and p. of verbs*): *We landed safely.* **2** (*in adjectives*) wearing or having the stated thing; with: *a long-tailed dog* | *a costumed actor*

-ee /iʸ/ (*in nouns*) **1** a person to whom the stated thing is done: *an employee* | *a trainee* **2** person who is or does the stated thing: *an absentee*

-eer /ɪər/ (*in nouns*) person who does or is connected with the stated thing: *a mountaineer* | *The auctioneer asked for bids.*

-en /ən/ **1** (*in adjectives*) made of: *a wooden box* **2** (*in verbs*) make or become (more): *unsweetened juice* | *The sky darkened.*

-ence /əns/ (*in nouns*) -ANCE: *its existence* | *reference* | *occurrence*

-ent /ənt/ -ANT: *nonexistent*

-er¹ /ər/ (*in comparative of short adjectives and adverbs*) more: *faster* | *colder*

-er² /ər/ (*in nouns*) **1** person or thing that does the stated thing: *a singer* | *a chess player* | *an electric water heater* **2** person who comes from or lives in the stated place: *a New Yorker*

-ery /əriʸ/ (*in nouns*) **1** the stated condition; -NESS: *bravery* **2** the stated art or practice; -ING (2): *millinery* **3** place where the stated thing is done: *a brewery*

-es /ɪz/ (*after* /s, z, ʃ, tʃ, dʒ/) *bosses* | *matches*

-ese /iʸz/ (*in nouns and adjectives*) (language) of the stated country: *Do you speak Japanese?* | *Portuguese food*

-esque /esk/ (*in adjectives*) in the manner or style of; like: *statuesque beauty* | *Kafkaesque*

-ess /ɪs/ (*in nouns*) female: *an actress* (=a female actor) | *a lioness*

-est /ɪst/ (*in superlative of short adjectives and adverbs*) most: *slowest* | *loveliest*

-eth /ɪθ/ -TH: *the twentieth time*

-ette /et/ (*in nouns*) small: *a kitchenette*

-ey /iʸ/ (*esp. after y*) -Y: *clayey soil*

-fold /foʷld/ (*in adjectives and adverbs*) multiplied by the stated number: *a fourfold increase*

-free /friʸ/ **1** (*in adjectives*) -LESS (1): *a carefree attitude*

-friendly /frendliʸ/ (*in adjectives*) not difficult for the stated people to use: *a user-friendly computer*

-ful /fəl/ **1** (*in adjectives*) having or giving: *a sinful man* | *a restful day* **2** /fʊl/ (*in nouns*) amount contained by: *a handful of coins* | *two spoonfuls of sugar*

-hood /hʊd/ (*in nouns*) condition or period of being the stated thing: *falsehood* | *during her childhood*

-ial /iʲəl, yəl, əl/ -AL (1): *a commercial transaction* | *the presidential car*

-ian /iʲən, yən, ən/ **1** (*in adjectives and nouns*) of or connected with the stated place or person: *Parisian restaurants* | *I speak Russian.* **2** (*in nouns*) person who studies the stated subject; EXPERT: *a historian* | *a theologian*

-ible /əbəl/ -ABLE: *deductible*

-ic /ɪk/ *also* **-ical** /ɪkəl/ (*in adjectives*) connected with; having or showing: *The design is completely symmetric/symmetrical* | *an historic occasion* | *a historical novel*

-icide /əsaɪd/ (*in nouns*) killing of: *infanticide*

-ics /ɪks/ (*in nouns*) science or skill: *linguistics* | *aeronautics*

-ie /iʲ/ -Y (2)

-ify /əfaɪ/ (*in verbs*) make or become: *purify* | *simplify*

-ine /aɪn/ **1** of or concerning: *equine* (=of horses) **2** made of; like: *crystalline*

-ing /ɪŋ/ **1** (*makes pres. p. of verbs*): *I'm coming.* | *a sleeping child* **2** (*makes nouns from verbs*): *Eating chocolate makes you fat.* | *a fine painting*

-ise /aɪz/ *esp. BrE for* -IZE

-ish /ɪʃ/ **1** (*in nouns and adjectives*) (language) of the stated country: *I speak Swedish* | *British customs* **2** (*in adjectives*) **a** typical of: *a foolish man* | *girlish giggles* **b** like the stated quality *a reddish glow* **c** about the stated number: *He's fortyish* | *Come at sixish*

-ism /ɪzəm/ (*in nouns*) **1** set of beliefs: *Buddhism* | *socialism* **2** quality or way of behaving: *heroism* | *male chauvinism* **3** way of speaking: *Americanisms*

-ist /ɪst/ **1** (*in nouns*) person who works with or does the stated thing: *A violinist plays the violin.* | *A machinist works machines.* **2** (*in adjectives and nouns*) (follower) of a set of beliefs: *a Buddhist* **3** making unfair differences between people because of the stated thing: *racist* | *agist*

-ite /aɪt/ -IST (2): *a Trotskyite*

-itude /ɪtuʷd/ (*in nouns*) the state or degree of being: *exactitude* | *certitude* (=being certain)

-ity /əti̇ʲ/ (*in nouns*) the stated condition or quality; -NESS: *stupidity* | *sublimity*

-ive /ɪv/ (*in adjectives*) tending to do the stated thing: *a creative child* | *a supportive partner*

-ize /aɪz/ (*in verbs*) make or become: *popularizing a new brand of soap* | *to modernize our procedures*

-less /lɪs/ (*in adjectives*) **1** without: *a windless day* | *We are powerless to act.* **2** that never does the stated thing: *a tireless worker*

-let /lɪt/ (*in nouns*) small: *a little piglet*

-like /laɪk/ (*in adjectives*) typical of: *childlike innocence*

-ly /liʲ/ **1** (*in adverbs*) in the stated way: *Drive carefully!* **2** (*in adjectives and adverbs*) every: *an hourly report* | *I see him daily* **3** (*in adjectives*) typical of: *brotherly love* **4** (*in adverbs*) from the stated point of view: *Musically she's very gifted*

-man /mən/ **1** man who comes from the stated place: *a Frenchman* **2** person with the stated job or skill: *a mailman*

-manship /mənʃɪp/ (*in [U] nouns*) the art or skill of a person of the stated type: *seamanship* | *horsemanship*

-ment /mənt/ (*in nouns*) act or result of doing the stated thing; -ING (2): *enjoyment* | *encouragement*

-most /moʷst/ -EST: *the northernmost parts of the country*

-ness /nɪs/ (*in nouns*) the stated condition or quality: *loudness* | *gentleness*

-nik /nɪk/ (*in nouns*) person who is connected with or enthusiastic about: *a peacenik*

-ology /ɑlədʒiʲ/ (*in nouns*) science or study of: *toxicology* (=the study of poisons) | *musicology*

-or /ər/ -ER²: *a sailor*

-ory¹ /ɔriʲ, oʷriʲ, əriʲ/ (*in nouns*) place or thing used for doing the stated thing: *an observatory*

-ory² (*in adjectives*) that does the stated thing: *a congratulatory telegram*

-ous /əs/ (*in adjectives*) having; full of: *a dangerous place* | *a spacious room*

-phile /faɪl/ (*in nouns*) person who likes the stated thing or place very much: *a bibliophile* (=who likes books)

-phobe /foʷb/ (*in nouns*) person who dislikes or fears the stated thing or person very much: *an Anglophobe* (=who dislikes England)

-phobia /foʷbiʲə/ (*in nouns*) great dislike: *hydrophobia* (=fear of water)

-proof /pruᵂf/ **1** (*in adjectives*) treated or made so as not to be harmed by the stated thing: *a bullet-proof car* | *an ovenproof dish* **2** (*in verbs*) to treat or make in this way: *to soundproof a room*

-r /ər/ (*after e*) -ER

-ridden /rɪdn/ (*in adjectives*) **1** suffering from the effects of: *guiltridden* **2** too full of: *mosquito-ridden*

-ry /riʸ/ (*in nouns*) -ERY: *sheer wizardry*

-s /z, s/ **1** (*makes the pl. of nouns*): *one cat and two dogs* **2** (*makes the 3rd person pres. sing of verbs*): *She laughs too much*

-'s 1 (*forms the possessive case of sing. nouns and of plural nouns that do not end in -s*): *my sister's husband* | *yesterday's lesson* | *the sheep's head* **2** the store or home of: *I met him at Mary's*

-s' (*forms the possessive case of plural nouns*): *the girls' dresses*

-scape /skeʸp/ (*in nouns*) a wide view of the stated area: *some old Dutch seascapes*

-ship /ʃɪp/ (*in nouns*) **1** condition of having or being the stated thing: *a business in partnership with his brother* | *citizenship* **2** the stated skill: *her masterly musicianship*

-some /səm/ **1** (*in adjectives*) causing; producing: *a troublesome problem* **2** (*in nouns*) group of the stated number of people or things: *a twosome*

-speak /spiʸk/ *often derog* (*in nouns*) the special language, esp. slang word, used in the stated business or activity: *computerspeak*

-st /st/ (*after e*) -EST

-style /staɪl/ (*in adverbs*) in the way of: *They ate Indian-style, using their fingers.*

-th /θ/ (*makes adjectives from numbers, except those ending in 1, 2 or 3*): *the seventh day*

-tion /ʃən/ (*in nouns*) -ION

-tude /tuᵂd/ -ITUDE: *disquietude*

-ty /tiʸ/ -ITY: *cruelty*

-ure /jər, ər/ (*in nouns*) act or result of doing the stated thing; -ING (2): *the closure of the factory*

-ward /wərd/ also **-wards** /wərdz/ (*in adjectives and adverbs*) in the stated direction: *the homeward journey* | *traveling northwards*

-ware /weər/ (*in nouns*) containers, tools, etc., made of the stated material or for the stated purpose: *pewterware* | *kitchenware* (=for cooking)

-ways /weʸz/ -WISE: *sideways*

-wise /waɪz/ (*in adverbs*) **1** in the stated way or direction: *walked crabwise* **2** with regard to: *very inexperienced businesswise*

-y /iʸ/ **1** (*in adjectives*) of; like; having: *a lemony smell* | *a noisy room* **2** (*makes nouns more informal; used esp. when speaking to children*): *my mommy* | *a nice little doggy* **3** (*in nouns*) -ITY: *jealousy*

Irregular verbs

verb	past tense	past participle
abide	abided, abode	abided
arise	arose	arisen
awake	awoke, awakened	awakened, awoken
baby-sit	baby-sat *see dictionary entry*	baby-sat
bear	bore	borne
beat	beat	beaten
become	became	become
befall	befell	befallen
beget	begot (*also* begat *bibl*)	begotten
begin	began	begun
behold	beheld	beheld
bend	bent	bent
beseech	besought, beseeched	besought, beseeched
beset	beset	beset
bet	bet, betted	bet, betted
bid	bade, bid	bid, bidden
bind	bound	bound
bite	bit	bitten
bleed	bled	bled
bless	blessed, blest	blessed, blest
blow	blew	blown
break	broke	broken
breed	bred	bred
bring	brought	brought
broadcast	broadcast	broadcast
build	built	built
burn	burned, burnt	burned, burnt
burst	burst	burst
buy	bought	bought
cast	cast	cast
catch	caught	caught
chide	chided, chid	chided, chid, chidden
choose	chose	chosen
cleave	cleaved, cleft, clove	cleaved, cleft, cloven
cling	clung	clung
come	came	come
cost	cost	cost
creep	crept	crept
cut	cut	cut
deal	dealt /delt/	dealt
dig	dug	dug
dive	dove	dived
do	did	done
draw	drew	drawn
dream	dreamed, dreamt	dreamed, dreamt
drink	drank	drunk
drive	drove	driven
dwell	dwelt, dwelled	dwelt, dwelled
eat	ate	eaten
fall	fell	fallen
feed	fed	fed
feel	felt	felt
fight	fought	fought

verb	past tense	past participle
find	found	found
flee	fled	fled
fling	flung	flung
fly	flew	flown
forbear	forbore	forborne
forbid	forbade, forbad	forbidden
forecast	forecast, forecasted	forecast, forecasted
foresee	foresaw	foreseen
foretell	foretold	foretold
forget	forgot	forgotten
forgive	forgave	forgiven
forgo	forwent	forgone
forsake	forsook	forsaken
freeze	froze	frozen
gainsay	gainsaid	gainsaid
get	got	got, gotten
gird	girded	girded
give	gave	given
go	went	gone
grind	ground	ground
grow	grew	grown
hamstring	hamstrung	hamstrung
hang	hung, hanged	hung, hanged
have	had	had
hear	heard	heard
heave	heaved, hove	heaved, hove
hew	hewed	hewn, hewed
hide	hid	hidden
hit	hit	hit
hold	held	held
hurt	hurt	hurt
keep	kept	kept
kneel	kneeled, knelt	kneeled, knelt
knit	knitted, knit	knitted, knit
know	knew	known
lay	laid	laid
lead	led	led
leap	leaped, leapt	leaped, leapt
leave	left	left
lend	lended, lent	lended, lent
let	let	let
lie	lay	lain
light	lit, lighted	lit, lighted
lose	lost	lost
make	made	made
mean	meant	meant
meet	met	met
miscast	miscast	miscast
mislay	mislaid	mislaid
mislead	misled	misled
misspell	misspelled	misspelled
misspend	misspent	misspent
mistake	mistook	mistaken
misunderstand	misunderstood	misunderstood
mow	mowed	mowed, mown
outdo	outdid	outdone

verb	past tense	past participle
outgrow	outgrew	outgrown
outshine	outshone	outshone
overcome	overcame	overcome
overdo	overdid	overdone
overhang	overhung	overhung
overrun	overran	overrun
oversee	oversaw	overseen
oversleep	overslept	overslept
overtake	overtook	overtaken
overthrow	overthrew	overthrown
partake	partook	partaken
pay	paid	paid
prove	proved	proved, (*also* proven)
put	put	put
read	read /red/	read /red/
rend	rent	rent
repay	repaid	repaid
rethink	rethought	rethought
rid	rid, ridded	rid, ridded
ride	rode	ridden
ring	rang	rung
rise	rose	risen
run	ran	run
saw	sawed	sawn, sawed
say	said	said
see	saw	seen
seek	sought	sought
sell	sold	sold
send	sent	sent
set	set	set
sew	sewed	sewed, sewn
shake	shook	shaken
shear	sheared	shorn, sheared
shed	shed	shed
shine	shone, shined	shone, shined
shoe	shod	shod
shoot	shot	shot
show	showed	shown, showed
shrink	shrank, shrunk	shrunk
shut	shut	shut
sing	sang	sung
sink	sank, sunk	sunk
sit	sat	sat
slay	slew	slain
sleep	slept	slept
slide	slid	slid
sling	slung	slung
slink	slunk	slunk
slit	slit	slit
smell	smelled	smelled
smite	smote	smitten
sow	sowed	sown, sowed
speak	spoke	spoken
speed	sped, speeded	sped, speeded
spell	spelled	spelled
spend	spent	spent

verb	past tense	past participle
spill	spilled, spilt	spilled, spilt
spin	spun, span	spun
spit	spat (*also* spit)	spat (*also* spit)
split	split	split
spoil	spoiled	spoiled
spread	spread	spread
spring	sprang, sprung	sprung
stand	stood	stood
steal	stole	stolen
stick	stuck	stuck
sting	stung	stung
stink	stank, stunk	stunk
strew	strewed	strewn, strewed
stride	strode	stridden
strike	struck	struck
string	strung	strung
strive	strove, strived	striven, strived
swear	swore	sworn
sweep	swept	swept
swell	swelled	swollen, swelled
swim	swam	swum
swing	swung	swung
take	took	taken
teach	taught	taught
tear	tore	torn
tell	told	told
think	thought	thought
thrive	thrived	thrived
throw	threw	thrown
thrust	thrust	thrust
tread	trod	trodden, trod
unbend	unbent	unbent
undergo	underwent	undergone
understand	understood	understood
undertake	undertook	undertaken
undo	undid	undone
unwind	unwound	unwound
uphold	upheld	upheld
upset	upset	upset
wake	woke, waked	woken, waked
wear	wore	worn
weave	wove	woven
wed	wedded, wed	wedded, wed
weep	wept	wept
wet	wetted, wet	wetted, wet
win	won	won
wind /waɪnd/	wound	wound
withdraw	withdrew	withdrawn
withhold	withheld	withheld
withstand	withstood	withstood
wring	wrung	wrung
write	wrote	written

Grammar codes

[C] countable: a noun that can be counted and has a plural form: *This is a* **dictionary**. | *There are many* **dictionaries** *in the library.*

[U] uncountable: a noun that cannot be counted, and has no plural form: *We drink* **milk** *with our dinner.* | *There isn't much* **milk** *left.* | *The book contained some interesting* **information** *about the town.*

[P] plural: a noun that is used only with a plural verb or pronoun, and that has no singular form: *These* **pants** *are too tight.*

[S] singular: a noun that is used only in the singular, and that has no plural form: *There was a* **babble** *of voices.* | *Let me have a* **look** *at it.*

[the] a noun that is the name of an actual place, organization, etc., and that is always used with the definite article: *The* **White House** | *the* **Senate**

vt a transitive verb: a verb that is followed by a direct object, which can be either a noun phrase or a clause: *She* **rides** *a bicycle to school.* | *He* **made up** *a good excuse.* | *We* **decided** *to leave.* | *I've* **given up** *eating meat.*

vi an intransitive verb: a verb that has no direct object: *They all* **came** *yesterday.* | *We* **set off** *at 7 o'clock.*